The Wales Yearbook 2013

Sponsored by

WLGA · CLILC

Cynulliad
Cenedlaethol
Cymru

National
Assembly for
Wales

Royal Mail

The Wales Yearbook 2013

---

fba

ABBREVIATIONS

AF	*Anglesey forward*	NG	*No Group*
Alln	*Alliance*	NLP	*Natural Law Party*
Alt LD	*Alternative Liberal Democrat*	NMBP	*New Milliennium Bean Party*
ATCG	*Access the Countryside Ind Group*	NPT Ind	*Neath Port Talbot Independent Party*
BNP	*British National Party*	Oth	*Others*
CCI	*Caerphilly Constituency Inds*	Loony	*Monster Raving Loony Party*
Celt All	*Celtic Alliance*	PBP	*People Before Politics*
CG	*Coalition Group*	PC	*Plaid Cymru The Party of Wales*
C of S	*Communities of Swansea*	PDV	*People's Democratic Voice*
Comm	*Communist Party of Great Britain*	PFC	*People First Carmarthenshire*
Con	*Conservative Party*	Peo R	*People's Representative*
CPA	*Christian People's Party Alliance*	PV	*People's Voice*
DCSP	*Direct Customer Service Party*	PLA	*Prolife Alliance*
Dem All	*Democratic Alliance Group*	Powys Ind	*Powys Independents Group*
Dem All W	*Democratic Alliance Wales*	PP	*Partners for Progress*
Ecol	*Ecology Party*	RA	*Ratepayers/Residents Association*
Eng Dem	*English Democrats*	Rad	*Radical*
FW	*Forward Wales/Cymru Ymlaen*	Ref	*Referendum Party*
Green	*Green Party*	RI	*Radical Independents*
Ind	*Independent*	SNP	*Scottish National Party*
Ind Lab	*Independent Labour*	SIA	*Swansea Independent Association*
ILDA	*Independent Liberal Democratic Alliance*	Soc Alt	*Socialist Alternative*
Ind / NA All	*Independent & Non-Aligned Alliance*	Soc D	*Social Democratic Party*
Ind Grp Mont	*Monmouthshire Independents Group*	SEP	*Socialist Equality Party*
Ind Nat	*Independent Nationalist*	SLDP	*Social and Liberal Democratic Party*
Ind RA	*Independent Ratepayers Association*	SLP	*Socialist Labour Party*
Ind-UG	*Independent Ungrouped*	Tinker ATA	*Tinker Against The Assembly Party*
Ind WP	*Independent Wales Party*	UKIP	*United Kingdom Independent Party*
JMIP	*John Marek Independent Party*	UM	*Unaffiliated Member*
Lab	*Labour Party*	Utd Soc	*United Socialists*
Lib	*Liberal Party*	V	*Vacancy*
Lib D	*Liberal Democratic Party*	VER	*Veritas*
Lib D All	*Liberal Democratic Alliance*	V2STW	*Vote 2 Stop The War Party*
LG	*Llais Gwynedd*	WCP	*Welsh Christian Party*
MI	*Merthyr Independents*	WSA	*Welsh Socialist Alliance*
MWWPP	*Mid & West Wales Pensioners Party*	W Soc	*Welsh Socialist*
NA	*Non-Aligned*	W Ind	*Wrexham Independent*
NA PC	*Non-Aligned Plaid Cymru*	WW Ind	*West Wrexham Independent*
Non-All	*Non-Allocated*	☎	Telephone number
NF	*National Front*	🖪	Fax number

OFFICIAL SOURCES

Census 2001; Digest of Welsh Local Area Statistics 2001
Electoral Commission - National Assembly For Wales Elections 2003 & General Election Results 2005
Electoral Commission / National Assembly For Wales - General Election Results 2010
Parliamentary Information Management Services; StatsWales
Members Research Service National Assembly for Wales - Assembly Election Results 2007
Welsh Assembly Government - Wales in Figures 2010

Printed in Wales by Cambrian Printers, Aberystwyth

Contents

AMs, MPs & MEPs

NATIONAL ASSEMBLY FOR WALES   237

WELSH GOVERNMENT   261

WALES in WESTMINSTER

WALES in EUROPE

BUSINESS & FINANCE in WALES

Business Organizations

Financial Institutions

MEDIA in WALES

NATIONAL ORGANIZATIONS in WALES 365

HIGHER & FURTHER EDUCATION in WALES 421

ARMED FORCES & EMERGENCY SERVICES in WALES 445

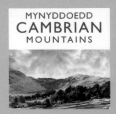

Preface

Since 1990, the Wales Yearbook has been published annually and each year has seen it grow proportionately to record and reflect the changing landscape of public and political life in Wales.

The new edition also marks something of a watershed in that the annual cycle for publication will now chime with the new pattern of all major elections taking place in May of relevant years.

As such, we hope it remains a valued reference source based on our values of accuracy, inclusivity and impartiality. *The Wales Yearbook 2013* has been compiled by a new team at FBA building on the trusted model of the past. To augment this, we are also planning a phased on-line service that will offer a wide range of new content and be an exciting, inter-active portal.

Meanwhile I must acknowledge and thank our principal sponsors, the National Assembly for Wales, the Welsh Local Government Association and Royal Mail as well as individual advertisers. Without their support the *Yearbook* would not appear. Similarly the continuing support of ITV Wales, particularly in respect of the annual Wales Yearbook Welsh Politician of the Year Awards, is greatly appreciated.

Previous editions of the Wales Yearbook were largely managed by myself and Julie Ebenezer, whose unstinting, sterling efforts were the mainstay of the book's success. We trust our legacy of databases, maps, content and contacts has served the new team well. Research for this edition has been undertaken firstly by Angharad Jones, but mainly by Rhys Flowers – no mean feat, not least in chasing and following up leads for information and checking accuracy. Typesetting and design has remained the responsibility of Charlotte Hughes-Evans, under the benign guidance of FBA's Studio Manager, Meirion Wyn Jones, whilst my colleague Delyth Davies has continued to recruit advertisers, chase contributors, charm customers and answer any queries as a formidable 'trouble-shooter'.

My greatest thanks however, must go to Meilyr Ceredig who as Managing Editor has assumed many of my previous responsibilities in respect of the Wales Yearbook. I wish him well for the future and look forward to continuing to enjoy the *Yearbook* in my retirement.

Diolch yn fawr iawn i bawb unwaith eto am eu cyfraniad gwerthfawr i lwyddiant *The Wales Yearbook*.

Aberystwyth
July 2012

Denis Balsom
Founding Editor

Cynulliad Cenedlaethol Cymru yw'r corff sy'n cael ei ethol yn ddemocrataidd i gynrychioli buddiannau Cymru a'i phobl, i ddeddfu ar gyfer Cymru ac i ddwyn Llywodraeth Cymru i gyfrif.

—

The National Assembly for Wales is the democratically elected body that represents the interests of Wales and its people, makes laws for Wales and holds the Welsh Government to account.

0845 010 5500
www.cynulliadcymru.org/www.assemblywales.org
neu dilynwch y Cynulliad ar/or follow the Assembly on:

Rosemary Butler
Presiding Officer

Cynulliad Cenedlaethol Cymru

National Assembly for Wales

FOREWORD

I am very pleased to be asked, as Presiding Officer of the National Assembly for Wales, to write the foreword for the Wales Yearbook. It is a very important publication that is a necessary resource for anyone involved in public and civic life in Wales, but also for citizens looking to access the correct organization to address your concerns.

It is a publication that has perhaps taken on even more significance since my predecessor wrote in the pages of the last edition. Since then, we have had a decisive "Yes" vote in a referendum on further law-making powers for the National Assembly and had an election that saw 23 new Members returned to the Senedd, bringing new experience and vigour to the Fourth Assembly.

I have made some fundamental changes to the way we do business at the National Assembly in order to ensure that the laws we make, and the issues we debate, are more reflective of the hopes and aspirations of all communities across Wales.

But my colleagues and I cannot do this work in isolation. So my challenge in these pages remains the same as the one I have been making to people the length and breadth of Wales since I was elected Presiding Officer. That is, for everyone in Wales to take an interest in, and get directly involved in, the work that we do. And I hope that this book will play a central role in opening up that access by providing all this valuable information about the people and organizations making the decisions in Wales.

RHAGAIR

Fel Llywydd Cynulliad Cenedlaethol Cymru, rwyf yn falch o gael fy ngwahodd i ysgrifennu'r rhagair ar gyfer y Wales Yearbook. Mae hwn yn gyhoeddiad pwysig sy'n adnodd angenrheidiol i unrhyw un sy'n cymryd rhan mewn bywyd cyhoeddus neu ddinesig yng Nghymru, yn ogystal â dinasyddion sydd am gael mynediad at y sefydliad addas ar gyfer mynd i'r afael â'u pryderon.

Mae'n bosibl bod y cyhoeddiad hwn wedi dod yn fwyfwy pwysig ar ôl i'm rhagflaenydd ysgrifennu darn yn y rhifyn diwethaf. Ers hynny, rydym wedi mwynhau pleidlais gadarnhaol bendant yn y refferendwm ar gael rhagor o bwerau deddfu i'r Cynulliad Cenedlaethol, ynghyd ag etholiad lle etholwyd 23 o Aelodau newydd i'r Senedd, gan ddod a phrofiadau a brwdfrydedd newydd i'r Pedwerydd Cynulliad.

Rwyf wedi gwneud rhai newidiadau sylfaenol i'r modd yr ydym yn cyflawni busnes yn y Cynulliad Cenedlaethol er mwyn sicrhau bod y deddfau yr ydym yn eu gwneud, a'r materion yr ydym yn eu trafod, yn adlewyrchu gobeithion a dyheadau'r holl gymunedau sy'n bodoli ledled Cymru.

Serch hynny, ni allwn fel Aelodau wneud y gwaith hwn ar ein pen ein hunain. Felly, yr her yr wyf yn ei gosod yn y tudalennau hyn yw'r un her a osodwyd gennyf i bobl ledled Cymru ers imi gael fy ethol yn Llywydd. Yr her hon yw i bawb yng Nghymru ymddiddori yn y gwaith yr ydym yn ei wneud ac i gymryd rhan yn uniongyrchol ynddo. Gobeithiaf y bydd y llyfr hwn yn chwarae rhan ganolog yn y broses o ehangu'r mynediad hwnnw drwy ddarparu'r wybodaeth bwysig hon am y bobl a'r sefydliadau sy'n gwneud penderfyniadau yng Nghymru.

Rosemary Butler

Darganfod
Discover Ceredigion

Cardigan Bay & the Cambrian Mountains

WALES · CYMRU · PAYS DE GALLES

Walk Ceredigion

www.tourism.ceredigion.gov.uk

Cllr Bob Wellington
WLGA Leader

WLGA·CLILC

FOREWORD

The WLGA is delighted to be working with the National Assembly for Wales to continue its support for the Wales Yearbook.

Local government is central to civic life in Wales, delivering front-line services that affect every citizen. Maintaining and constantly improving these services remains the central aim for every council in Wales. This applies equally to our members in the National Parks and the Fire and Rescue Services.

This is not without its challenges. The reality of delivering local services with reduced resources means councils are seeking to find innovative ways of protecting their communities from the negative impacts of cuts and mitigate where possible effects of key programmes such as Welfare Reforms.

Councils are working at the forefront of public service delivery as we develop new ways of doing business. This will entail increasing transformative change, collaborating with others, integrating services and basing our approach on tangible outcomes for communities. Equally, ensuring partnership across the wider public sector will be a key driver for change.

We start with a commitment to examine ways in a recession of using our resources to get people back into work through apprenticeships and training. The development of City Regions and Enterprise Zones all dramatically impact and Councils are looking to encourage new forms of businesses in their localities based on sustainable industries and innovative technologies.

Following the changes experienced during the 2012 local government elections, councillors in Wales now offer a real mix of experience and fresh ideas. The WLGA aims to harness this, and to work across all political party boundaries, in order to meet the challenges of service pressures, cuts and austerity head on.

RHAGAIR

Mae'n bleser gan CLILC fod yn gweithio gyda Chynulliad Cenedlaethol Cymru er mwyn parhau i gefnogi Blwyddlyfr Cymru.

Mae llywodraeth leol yn ganolog i fywyd dinesig yng Nghymru, yn cyflenwi gwasanaethau rheng flaen sy'n effeithio ar bob dinesydd. Mae cynnal a gwella'r gwasanaethau hyn yn barhaus yn dal yn brif nod i bob cyngor yng Nghymru. Mae hyn yr un mor berthnasol i'n haelodau yn y Parciau Cenedlaethol a'r Gwasanaethau Tân ac Achub.

Mae digon o heriau ynghlwm wrth hyn. Mae realaeth cyflenwi gwasanaethau lleol gyda llai o adnoddau yn golygu bod cynghorau yn ceisio dod o hyd i ffyrdd arloesol o ddiogelu eu cymunedau rhag effeithiau negyddol toriadau a, lle y bo'n bosibl, yn ceisio lliniaru effaith rhaglenni allweddol fel Diwygio Lles.

Mae cynghorau yn gweithio ar flaen y gad wrth gyflenwi gwasanaethau cyhoeddus, yn ogystal â datblygu ffyrdd newydd o wneud busnes. Bydd hyn yn golygu cynyddu newid trawsffurfiol, cydweithredu â gwasanaethau integreiddio eraill a seilio ein dull ar ganlyniadau gweladwy i'n cymunedau. Yn yr un modd, bydd sicrhau partneriaeth ar draws y sector cyhoeddus ehangach yn allweddol ar gyfer newid.

Rydym yn dechrau gydag ymrwymiad i archwilio ffyrdd mewn dirwasgiad anodd o ddefnyddio ein hadnoddau i gael pobl yn ôl i'r gwaith trwy brentisiaethau a hyfforddiant. Mae datblygiad Rhanbarthau Dinesig ac Ardaloedd Menter i gyd yn cael effaith ddramatig ac mae Cynghorau yn bwriadu annog mathau newydd o fusnesau yn eu lleoliadau yn seiliedig ar ddiwydiannau cynaliadwy a thechnolegau arloesol.

Yn dilyn y newidiadau a brofwyd yn ystod etholiadau llywodraeth leol 2012, mae cynghorwyr yng Nghymru bellach yn cynnig cymysgedd gwirioneddol o brofiad a syniadau newydd. Nod CLILC yw defnyddio hyn, a gweithio ar draws yr holl ffiniau gwleidyddol, er mwyn bodloni heriau'r pwysau ar wasanaethau, toriadau a chynilo yn uniongyrchol.

The Great ✷ Little Places Guide™

Part of the Welsh Rarebits Collection

| Gwestai Bach/Tafarndai/Ffermydd Tai Bwyta a Bythynnod. | Small Hotels/Inns/ Farms/ Guest Houses/ Cottages and Places to Eat. |

Os am gopi rhad o'n llyfryn neu os am brynu Tocyn Rhodd ewch i'n gwefan neu cysylltwch â ni dros y ffôn+44 (0) 1570 470785 /For a free copy of our brochure or to purchase a Gift Voucher, go to our website or call +44 (0) 1570 470785

Escape

Y Meirionnydd

Penmachno Hall

Venetia

Britannia Inn

Tal-y-Bryn

www.little-places.co.uk

WALES

Contemporary Wales

Wales is an integral part of the United Kingdom & Northern Ireland. The Acts of Union 1535 and 1542 integrated Wales with England, but the Welsh language and a strong sense of national identity persist. Wales has a population of just over 3m, approximately 5% of that of the UK. Two thirds of the population live along the coastal plain and in the Valleys of South Wales. There is a significant concentration of population in the north east, but the remainder of Wales is predominantly rural in character.

Economy: The Welsh economy, which traditionally relied on coal and steel, underwent major changes during the late 20th century. Wales attracted a range of manufacturing industries, with significant investment by overseas companies. More recently however, manufacturing too has declined leaving an economy increasingly dependent upon light industry and the service sector. Overall, unemployment has fallen from being significantly above the UK average to broad parity. Employment 'blackspots' persist and the impact of the current financial crisis suggests that unemployment will rise. Wales remains one of the more deprived areas of Britain and much of public policy is focussed upon regeneration, housing and social issues and economic development.

Language and Culture: At the 2001 census, the proportion of the population speaking Welsh was about 21per cent. In parts of the rural north and in west Wales, Welsh remains the first language of many people. The Welsh Language Act 1993 established the principle that, in public business and the administration of justice in Wales, Welsh and English should be treated on a basis of equality. Welsh is now more widely used for official purposes, in broadcasting and is taught - as a first or second language - to most pupils between the ages of 5 and 16. In 2012 a Welsh Language Commissioner was established for the first time.

Institutions: The United Kingdom has traditionally been a highly unitary state. In Wales, the thrust of much political activity and ambition, from the mid-nineteenth century onwards, has been to create institutions to govern Wales more directly without, necessarily, seceding from the Union. These demands were initially accommodated by minor adjustments to Parliamentary procedures, but, most significantly, by the creation of a multi-functional Welsh Office with a Secretary of State for Wales in the Cabinet in 1964.

Demands for further political devolution have persisted and a referendum on plans to create a Welsh Assembly was held, but defeated, in 1979. A further referendum for a similar proposal were accepted in 1997 however, and subsequently implemented in 1999. Prior to devolution, the Secretary of State had a wide range of executive responsibilities for implementing government policy in Wales. In 1999, most of these functions were transferred to the National Assembly for Wales which assumed responsibility across a wide range of domestic policy areas. Wales is now largely governed by a Welsh Government, under a First Minister and Cabinet. The Government of Wales Act 2006 granted the Welsh Assembly the right to pass primary legislation in a range of specific policy areas, but only following a complex Parliamentary procedure to establish 'Legislative Competence'. The Referendum in March 2011 granted the Welsh Assembly full competence to legislate in the subject areas defined in the GoWA 2006 where executive responsibility has been devolved. In all other respects, Wales remains subject to overall legislation from Westminster, especially in the major policy areas of tax, social security, defence, foreign affairs, etc.

Wales is currently represented in Parliament by 40 MPs and in the Assembly by 60 AMs. Legislation currently going through Parliament however, will reduce the number of MPs from Wales to 30, but it is expected that the number of AMs will remain constant. Wales retains a Secretary of State with a seat in the Cabinet whose primary function is to secure Government funding for public spending in Wales. The exact distribution of funds is the responsibility of the Assembly, but total expenditure is limited by a 'Block Grant'.

WALES

Wales Office

The Wales Office
Gwydyr House, Whitehall, London SW1A 2NP
Tel: (020) 7270 0534

1 Caspian Point, Caspian Way, Cardiff CF10 4DQ
Tel: (029) 2089 8758 Fax: (029) 2089 8138

Email: wales.office@walesoffice.gsi.gov.uk
Website: www.walesoffice.gov.uk

Ministers

Secretary of State for Wales: Rt Hon Cheryl Gillan MP

Overall strategic direction: Assembly liaison; Constitutional issues; major Acts of Parliament; elections; referendum; economy, finance & business; foreign affairs including interaction with the EU; public appointments; environment & energy; Royal matters; defence.

Special Adviser: Richard Hazlewood Tel: (020) 7270 0577 / (029) 2089 8549
Principal Private Secretary: Stephen Hillcoat Tel: (020) 7270 0550

Parliamentary Under-Secretary of State: David Jones MP

Regional development; welfare benefits & pensions; education & skills; transport; rural affairs; communication; television; local government & housing; law & order; fire & rescue; equality; immigration & borders; culture & tourism.

Assistant Government Whip: Stephen Crabb MP

Parliamentary Private Secretary: Glyn Davies MP

WALES

Welsh Government

Llywodraeth Cymru
Welsh Government

Welsh Government
Cathays Park, Cardiff CF10 3NQ
Tel: English (0300) 060 3300 or (0845) 010 3300
Welsh (0300) 060 4400 or (0845) 010 4400
Web: www.wales.gov.uk

The Welsh Government is the devolved Government for Wales. It consists of: The First Minister; Welsh Ministers; The Counsel General and Deputy Ministers.

The First Minister of Wales is the leader of the Welsh Government and is appointed by HM the Queen following nomination by Assembly Members. The First Minister's responsibilities include appointing the Cabinet of Welsh Ministers, Deputy Ministers and the Counsel General (with the approval of Her Majesty) who comprise the Welsh Government.

The Cabinet

First Minister
Rt Hon Carwyn Jones AM

Minister for
Education & Skills
Leighton Andrews AM

Minister for Environment
& Sustainable Development
John Griffiths AM

Minister for Health
& Social Services
Lesley Griffiths AM

Minister for Business, Enterprise,
Technology & Science
Edwina Hart MBE OStJ AM

Minister for Finance &
Leader of the House
Jane Hutt AM

Minister for Housing,
Regeneration & Heritage
Huw Lewis AM

Minister for Local
Government & Communities
Carl Sargeant AM

Counsel General
Theodore Huckle QC

WALES

National Assembly for Wales

Cynulliad
Cenedlaethol
Cymru

National
Assembly for
Wales

National Assembly for Wales
Cardiff Bay
Cardiff CF99 1NA
Tel: (0845) 010 5500

Website: www.assemblywales.org

The National Assembly for Wales is the democratically elected body that represents the interests of Wales and its people, makes laws for Wales, and holds the Welsh Government to account.

The Assembly is made up of 60 elected Assembly Members. Forty are chosen to represent individual constituencies, and 20 are chosen to represent the five regions of Wales.

Assembly Commission

Rosemary Butler AM
Presiding Officer of the Assembly &
Commission Chair

Private Secretary: Craig Stephenson *Tel (029) 2089 823*

Angela Burns AM   **Peter Black AM**   **Sandy Mewies AM**   **Rhodri Glyn Thomas AM**

National Assembly Commissioner for Standards   **Gerard Elias QC**

HRH THE PRINCE OF WALES

Clarence House
London SW1A 1BA
☎ (020) 7930 4832
Website:
www.princeofwales.gov.uk

HRH The Prince of Wales

In recognition of his special relationship with Wales, His Royal Highness pays regular visits as well as undertaking an annual week-long summer tour. The Prince of Wales and The Duchess of Cornwall own a home in Wales, Llwynywermod in Myddfai, Llandovery, which provides a base for their many Welsh activities.

The Prince's Charities are a group of not-for-profit organizations of which The Prince of Wales is President: the group is the largest multi-cause charitable enterprise in the United Kingdom, raising over £100 million annually. The organizations cover a broad range of issues, including opportunity and enterprise, education, health, the built environment, responsible business, the natural environment and the arts. All the charities are active and most have a base in Wales.

The Prince's Charities in Wales

Grahame Davies   Assistant Private Secretary to The Prince of Wales and Chairman of The Prince's Charities in Wales
Offices of TRH The Prince of Wales and The Duchess of Cornwall, University of Wales
King Edward VII Avenue, Cathays Park, Cardiff CF10 3NS
Charities in Wales: Tel: (029) 2037 5059 Email: grahame.davies@royal.gsx.gov.uk

The Prince's Trust Cymru – helps change young lives. Through a range of practical programmes it supports disadvantaged young people into jobs and training. Since it was founded in 1976, the Trust has supported around 80,000 young people in Wales. Tel: (029) 2043 7000 (www.princes-trust.org.uk/wales)

PRIME Cymru – provides support and advice to people over the age of 50 who wish to return to economic activity through business start-up, employment, training or volunteering as a stepping stone to more formal economic activity.
Tel: (01550) 721813 (www.primecymru.co.uk)

Business in the Community – a business led charity focused on promoting responsible business practice and working with the local community to tackle social and environmental issues. Tel: (029) 2078 0050 (www.bitc.org.uk)

The Prince's Foundation for Building Community – teaches and demonstrates sustainable development placing community engagement at the heart of its work. Tel: (020) 7613 8500 (www.princes-foundation.org)

The Prince's Regeneration Trust – focuses on heritage-led regeneration, rescuing buildings of architectural and heritage value and creating new uses that are of benefit to the community. Tel: (020) 3262 0560 (www.princes-regeneration.org)

Accounting for Sustainability – was set up in September 2010 as an umbrella under which to engage the accountancy community and business in Wales on issues surrounding sustainable development and sustainability reporting. (www.accountingforsustainability.org)

The Cambrian Mountains Initiative – is a wide-ranging project that aims to promote rural enterprise, protect the environment and add value to products and services in Mid Wales. Tel: (01970) 639 410 (www.cambrianmountains.co.uk)

Pub is the Hub – is an initiative inspired by HRH The Prince of Wales to bring and retain valuable local services to communities by using good licensees who run vibrant rural pubs to act as the focal point for provision and support. (www.pubisthehub.org.uk)

Young Dragons – is aimed at engaging with the young people of Wales and assisting them to contribute actively to their communities by joining a youth organization and to enhance their skills and experience. (www.youngdragons.org.uk)

WALES: NATION, STATE & SOCIETY

WELSH �֎ RAREBITS®
Hotels of Distinction

Gwestai gwlad unigryw a'r gorau yng Nghymru. Y llefydd delfrydol i ymlacio neu i ddathlu achlysur arbennig ac i gynnalcyfarfod neu gynhadledd ddethol.

Wales' best country house and resort hotels. Ideal venues for that special break or celebration and for important meeting, seminar or small conference.

Os am gopi rhad o'n llyfryn neu os am brynu Tocyn Rhodd ewch i'n gwefan neu cysylltwch â ni dros y ffôn +44 (0)1570 470785 /For a free copy of our brochure or to purchase a Gift Voucher, go to our website or call +44 (0)1570 470785

From left to right:
The Grove, Hotel Portmeirion,
Harbourmaster, Ye Olde Bull's Head,
St Tudno, Llansantffraed Court.

www.rarebits.co.uk

HIGH SHERIFFS, HM LORD-LIEUTENANTS & DEPUTY LIEUTENANTS

County Boundaries 1974-96

High Sheriffs in Wales

High Sheriff for Clwyd:
H M Dixon Esq

High Sheriff for Dyfed:
Emeritus Prof E C Stephens

High Sheriff for Mid Glamorgan:
Mrs C A Jenkins

High Sheriff for South Glamorgan:
Dr Arun Midha

High Sheriff for West Glamorgan:
W T Hopkins Esq

High Sheriff for Gwynedd:
E S Bailey Esq

High Sheriff for Gwent:
H Elizabeth Murray

High Sheriff for Powys:
Lady Large

HM Lord-Lieutenants & Deputy Lieutenants

Lord-Lieutenant for Powys:
The Hon Elizabeth Shân Legge-Bourke LVO
Vice Lord-Lieutenant: The Rt Hon Lord Davies
Deputy Lieutenants

Col Timothy John Van-Rees MBE	Robin Gibson-Watt
Major General The Rev'd Morgan Llewellyn, CB, OBE	Mrs Susanna Bowen
	William Lyon Corbett-Winder
Julian Salmon	John Vaughan
Nicholas Paravacini	Mrs Tia C Jones
David T Morgan	Trevor Trevor

Clerk to the Lieutenancy: Powys County Council,
County Hall Llandrindod Wells Tel: (01597) 826082

Lord-Lieutenant for West Glamorgan:
Mr D Byron Lewis, CStJ, FCA
Vice Lord-Lieutenant: Dr Edward Morgan Roberts
DL, MB, BCh, FRCGP
Deputy Lieutenants

Rt Hon Lord Anderson of Swansea	Lt Cmdr, Jill Ena Johnson QARNNS(R) RD
Lt Cmdr Bruce Charles Bagley	Lt Col Gwillym Lynn Martin
Mr Keith Broadbent MBE	Prof Prys Tomos Jon Morgan, MA, DPhil, FRHistS
Mr Thomas Philip Noel Crowley CBE, OStJ	Mr Michael Edward John Rush CBE
Mr David Peter Lloyd Davies	Mr Peter Douglas Scott
Mrs Elizabeth Anne Davis JP	Dr Patricia Ann Steane OBE
Squadron Leader Phillip Charles Flower MBE	Capt Brian John Thorne RD, RNR
Mrs Ann Marilyn Harries JP	Mr Huw Tregelles Williams OBE
Mr Edward Kynan Harris	

Clerk to the Lieutenancy: Mr Ken Sawyers OBE,
39 Southlands Drive, Swansea SA3 5RJ
Email: k.sawyers@ntlworld.com

Lord-Lieutenant for Clwyd:
Trefor Glyn Jones, Esq, CBE
Vice Lord-Lieutenant:
Edmund Francis Lloyd FitzHugh OBE, JP
Deputy Lieutenants

Prof Bimal Kanti Bhowmick OBE, MD, FRCP	The Lady Langford
Mrs Jean Marian Bryson, JP	Mrs Manikam Susheela Lourie, MBE, BA
David John Catherall, Esq	Roy Luff, Esq, OBE
His Honour Judge Roger Thomas Dutton, BA	James Peter O'Toole, Esq
Col Philip Eyton-Jones, TD, RIBA, FRSA	Mrs Cathleen Turnbull Owen, JP
	Michael Leslie Peters, Esq
Henry George Fetherstonhaugh, Esq, OBE	David Austin Savage, Esq, JP, BSc
Mrs Edith Frodsham MBE	Prof Michael Scott, BA(Hons) MA, Ph.D, FRSA
Rev Prebendary John Glover	Dr Ikram Ullah Shah
Mrs Ruth Griffith	Mrs Janie Wynne Smith
Brian John Howes, Esq, OBE	Roy Andrew Nicholas Whittington, Esq
Mrs Susan Gordon Hudson, JP	David Wyn Williams, Esq, ACIB
Christopher Robert Jackson, Esq, OBE	Col John Caledfryn Wynne Williams, MC
David Baden Jones, Esq	Capt William Reinallt Williams, JP
Lady Jones, JP	Sir David Watkin Williams-Wynn, Bt
Mrs Sarah Elizabeth Kearsley-Wooller MBE	Mrs Willow Williams MBE
The Lady Kenyon, JP	

Clerk to the Lieutenancy: Clwyd County Council,
County Hall, Mold CH7 6NB Tel: (01352) 702107

HM LORD-LIEUTENANTS & DEPUTY LIEUTENANTS (cont.)

Lord-Lieutenant for Mid Glamorgan:
Kathrin Thomas CVO JP

Vice Lord-Lieutenant: Roy Noble OBE OStJ

Deputy Lieutenants

Mrs C Eynon	Mr Mostyn James JP
Mr D S John	Mrs E Singer
Mr A R Lewis	Mr B F Butler JP
Mr T E Morgan MBE	Mrs A Y Morgan
Mr O A M Williams	Mr Gareth William Meredith
Col J Wrangham MBE	Col Philip James Hubbard
Major Dan Clayton-Jones	Miss Felicity Ladbrooke
TD OStJ KLJ	Mrs Bethan Guilfoyle
Ms Margaret M Jervis	Ms Christina Donnelly
The Hon Mr Justice	Mr Anthony Tal-Williams
Christopher Pitchford	Major John Charles
Mr Michael Eamonn McGrane	

Clerk to the Lieutenancy: Miss Mary Squire, 14 De Londres Close, Porthcawl CF36 3JE Tel: (01656) 789110

Lord-Lieutenant for Gwynedd: His Hon Huw Morgan Daniel, KStJ

Vice Lord-Lieutenant: Sir Richard Williams-Bulkeley Bt

Deputy Lieutenants

Major R C Williams-Ellis OBE	Mr Gerallt Wyn Hughes
Mr O G Thomas JP	Mrs Patricia J Hughes
Mr D Ll Carey-Evans OBE, JP, BSc	Dr David Jeffreys
Mr D E A Jones CBE	Mrs Jane Pullee
The Lord Stanley of Alderley	Mr David John Roberts
Mr R Hefin Davies MBE, JP	Mrs Victoria Primrose Gruffudd Jones
Mr Alun Evans CBE, FRAgS	
Mr John Anderson OBE, MA, FCA	Dr George Verghase Kurian
Mr William Wyn Roberts	Dr Dewi Wyn Roberts
Dr Elizabeth M N Andrews, MBE	Major Norman Trevor Corbett
Dr Gillian Davies	Cmdr David John Alexander RN
Mr Robin J Price	Mr Richard Andrew Meredyth Richards, JP
Mr Richard Cuthberston MBE, FRSA, BA(Hons)	Mr Jonathan Clough Williams-Ellis
Mrs Annwen Carey-Evans	Mrs Susan Wynn-Jones, JP
Mr Graham S Roy	Col Nick Beard, TD

Clerk to the Lieutenancy: Gwynedd County Council, Cyngor Gwynedd, Caernarfon LL55 1SH Tel: (01286) 679666

Lord-Lieutenant for South Glamorgan:
Dr Peter Beck

Vice Lord-Lieutenant: Sir Brooke Boothby

Deputy Lieutenants

Mr Raj Aggarwal OBE	Nicola Jane Gibson
Michael D Boyce	Col Michael Anthony Haley JP
Christopher Brain	Mrs Josephine Homfray
Mrs Margaret Anne Campbell JP	Isobel Jane Hughes
Major Duncan A Cantlay	Colin Jones QPM OStJ
Lt Col Gareth Wayne Chapman	Colonel Neil A Jones
David G Clarke TD	Rick Libbey
Mrs W L S Clay	Cmdr Peter Clive Machin
Cmdr J M D Curteis	Wing Comm Graeme Morgan
Ms Bet Davies	Lady Roisin Mary Pill
Byron Davies OBE	Margaret Pritchard
Geraint Talfan Davies	Lt Col Samuel Charles Smith
John Barrie Davies	Nigel Walker
Cllr Marion Drake	Lady Monjulee Webb
Mrs Elizabeth Elias JP	Paul Williams OBE
Mrs Lisa Gerson	

Clerk to the Lieutenancy: Jon House, Cardiff County Council, County Hall, Altlantic Wharf, Cardiff CF10 4UW Tel: 029 20 872401

Lord-Lieutenant for Gwent: Mr Simon Boyle

Vice Lord-Lieutenant: Commodore Toby Elliott OBE

Deputy Lieutenants

Brigadier Robert Hanbury Tenison Aitken CBE	Graham Alfred Hawker CBE
Samuel Anthony John Pierre Bosanquet	Lt General Sir Robert Hayman-Joyce KCB, CBE
	Murray Kerr
Mrs Helen Bosanquet	Roger Leadbeter OBE
Mrs Diana Bown MBE	Frederick David Morgan OBE
John Child	David Wyndham Morgan
Richard Cleeve	Michael Ross Murray
Priscilla Elizabeth Davies OBE	The Honourable Mrs Fiona Peel OBE
Thomas Gerald Reames Davies CBE	Lord David Rowe-Beddoe
Julian Fonseca	Jack Hanbury Tenison
Col Peter L Gooderson	Lt Col Andrew Tuggey
Mrs Joan Graham	William Neville Waters MBE, JP
Lt Col Michael John Howard Harry	Mrs Elizabeth Watkins

Clerk to the Lieutenancy: Mr Malgwyn Davies, 5 Hanfield Park, Croesyceiliog, Cwmbran NP44 2DT Tel: (01633) 874580

Lord-Lieutenant for Dyfed: The Hon R W Lewis OBE Vice Lord-Lieutenant: Miss Sara Edwards, DL

Deputy Lieutenants

Mr Jonathan Michael Griffith Andrews, BSc, FRICS	Mrs Rachel A Rowlands, MBE	Mrs Marilyn Ann Mason
Mr GL Wardell, M.Sc	Mrs Bethan Williams	Mr John S Allen-Mirehouse
Mr William Powell Wilkins CBE	Mr R Owen Watkin, OBE	Major George A S Hancock
Mrs Marylyn Haines-Evans	Mr J D Gwynne Hughes, MBE	Mr John M A Thomas-Ferrand
The Rt Hon The Lord Aberdare	David Lewis, Esq	Mr Stephen Watkins
Alderman Sir David Lewis	Mrs Beti Griffiths	Geoffrey Philipps, Esq
Lt Col D A Mathias, RLC(V)	Col D L Davies, TD, FRAgS	Mrs Sharron Kim Lusher, B Mus, MA, Dip ABRSM
Dr Medwin Hughes, DPhil, DPA, FRSA	Mr Thomas Owen Saunders Lloyd OBE, FSA	
Mr Patrick C A Mansel Lewis	Mr David Robert Smalley Clarke	Clerk to the Lieutenancy, Carmarthenshire County Council, County Hall, Carmarthen SA31 1JP Tel: (01267) 228609
Mr P A Loxdale	Mr D Fellows OBE	
	Mr Anthony Bowen, LVO	

BISHOPS & DIOCESES IN WALES

Bishop of Bangor
The Rt Rev A T G John
Tŷ'r Esgob, Upper Garth Rd,
Bangor LL57 2SS
Phone: (01248) 362895
Email: bishop.bangor@churchinwales.org.uk

Diocesan Bishop
The Rt Rev Tom Burns SM
Curial Office, 27 Convent St
Greenhill, Swansea SA1 2BX
Phone: (01792) 644017
Fax: (01792) 458641
Email: pa@menevia.org

Bishop of St. Davids
The Rt Rev J W Evans
Llys Esgob, Abergwili,
Carmarthen SA31 2JG
Phone: (01267) 236597
Fax: (01267) 243381
Email: bishop.stdavids@churchinwales.org.uk

Bishop of St. Asaph
The Rt Rev G K Cameron
Esgobty, St Asaph LL17 0TW
Phone: (01745) 583503
Email: bishop.stasaph@churchinwales.org.uk

Diocesan Bishop
Mgr Peter Brignall
Bishop's House, Sontley Rd
Wrexham LL13 7EW
Phone: (01978) 262726
Fax: (01978) 354257
Email: diowxm@globalnet.co.uk

Diocesan Archbishop
Archbishop'George Stack
Archbishop s House,
41-43 Catherdral Rd
Cardiff CF11 9HD
Phone: (029) 2022 0411
Fax: (029) 2037 9036
Email: arch@rcadc.org

BANGOR   ST. ASAPH

WREXHAM

MENEVIA

ST. DAVIDS

SWANSEA
& BRECON

CARDIFF

MONMOUTH

LLANDAFF

Bishop of Swansea & Brecon
The Rt Rev J D E Davies
Ely Tower, Castle Square,
Brecon, LD3 9DJ
Phone: (01874) 622008
Fax: (01874) 610927
Email: bishop.swanbrec@churchinwales.org.uk

Archbishop of Wales & Bishop of Llandaff
The Most Rev Dr B C Morgan
Llys Esgob, The Cathedral Green,
Llandaff, Cardiff CF5 2YE
Phone: (029) 2056 2400
Fax: (029) 2056 8410
Email: archbishop@churchinwales.org.uk

Bishop of Monmouth
The Rt Rev Dominic Walker OGS
Bishop's House, Bishopstow, Stow Hill
Newport NP20 4EA
Phone: (01633) 263510
Fax: (01633) 259946
Email: bishop.monmouth@churchinwales.org.uk

▬▬▬ Roman Catholic Church
▬▬▬ Church in Wales

THE WELSH CONSULAR CORPS

www.consularassociationinwales.org.uk

Belarus	Mr Michael A Rye	Tel: (029) 2061 1304
Brazil	Dr Lolita Tsanaclis, PhD*	Tel: 07900 931816
Canada	Mr Dan Clayton-Jones OBE, KStJ, TD, DL	Tel: (029) 2044 9635
Costa Rica	Tba	
Czech Republic	Tba	
Denmark	Dr Nicholas Wilson	Tel: (029) 2049 1474
Estonia	Sir Roger Jones	Tel: (01874) 611777
Finland	Mr Julian F Phillips, LLB	Tel: (01633) 416740
France	Mrs Claude A Rapport, MEd, MA, MIL	Tel: (029) 2075 3892
Germany	Mrs Helga Rother-Simmonds	Tel: 07967 442268
Hungary	Mr Alun Davies	Tel: (029) 2059 5585
Iceland	Mr Angus T H McFarlane	Tel: (029) 2047 5640
Israel	Mr Philip Kaye	
Italy	Mr Antonio Contino	Tel: (029) 2034 1757
Japan	Mr Hugh Thomas, CBE, GCStJ, DL, MA*	Tel: (01656) 657204
Jordan	Lt Col Rhodri Traherne	Tel: (01446) 760889
Kazakhstan	Mr Douglas Townsend	Tel: (01570) 423403
Latvia	Mr Andy Taurins	Tel: (01873) 857177
Lesotho	Dr Carl I Clowes, FFPHM	Tel: (01248) 450305
Lithuania	Mr Anthony Packer	Tel: (029) 2070 5356
Malta	Sir Brooke Boothby, DL*	Tel: (0871) 716 2357
Netherlands	Mr Sam C Smith, RD, DL*	Tel: (0871) 226 0180
Norway	Mr Sam C Smith, RD, DL*	Tel: (0871) 226 0180
Romania	Mr Clive Williams	Tel: (01685) 815200
Slovakia	Mr Nigel BH Payne	Tel: (029) 2034 3434
Sweden	Mrs Elisabeth Roth	Tel: (029) 2078 4225
Switzerland	Mrs Ruth Thomas-Lehmann BA CE	Tel: 07748 103142
Thailand	Mr John Iles	Tel: (029) 2046 5777
Tunisia	Mr Sam C Smith, RD, DL*	Tel: (0871) 226 0180
USA	Esther Pan Sloane	Tel: (029) 2002 6419

* Mr Anthony Packer - President of the Consular Association in Wales (anthony.packer@ntlworld.com)
* Mr Hugh Thomas - Vice-President of the Consular Association in Wales (dht7@sky.com)
* Mr Sam C Smith - Dean of the Consular Association in Wales (sam@samsmithtravel.com)
* Dr Lolita Tsanaclis - Secretary of the Consular Association in Wales (Tsanaclis@btinternet.com)
* Sir Brooke Boothby - Treasurer of the Consular Association in Wales (maltaconsul.wales@gov.mt)

PUBLIC HONOURS

Honours are awarded twice a year, in June on the Queen's official birthday and at New Year. They are awarded to people for all types of public service, including teachers, nurses, actors, scientists, diplomats and broadcasters. The following from Wales received Honours in 2012.

NEW YEAR HONOURS 2012

Commanders of the Order of the British Empire (CBE)

Dr Dannie Abse
Poet and Playwright. For services to Poetry and Literature. (London, NW11)

Meredydd John Hughes, QPM
Formerly chief Constable, South Yorkshire Police. For services to the Police. (Nottingham, Nottinghamshire)

Mark Vincent James
Chief executive, Carmarthenshire County Council For services to Local Government in Wales. (Carmarthen, Carmarthenshire)

Jonathan Jones
Director, Tourism and Marketing, Welsh Government. (Penarth, Vale of Glamorgan)

Andrew Marles, QFSM
Formerly chief Fire Officer, South Wales Fire and Rescue Service. For services to the Fire and Rescue Service. (Caldicot, Monmouthshire)

Peter Thomas
For services to Entrepreneurship, Sport and Charity in Wales. (Cardiff)

The Rt Hon Alexander Charles Lord Carlile Of Berriew, QC
Independent Reviewer of Terrorism Legislation, United Kingdom. For services to National Security. (London, N1).

Officers of the Order of the British Empire (OBE)

Mrs Mary Antoinette Campbell
Formerly Principal, Michaelston Community College. For services to Education. (Newport)

Dr Carl Iwan Clowes
For services to the community in Anglesey. (Anglesey)

Ms Joyce Cook
Chair, Level Playing Field (National Association of Disabled Supporters). For services to Disability Sports. (Carmel, Flintshire)

Councillor Hugh Hesketh Evans
Leader, Denbighshire County Council. For services to Local Government. (Ruthin, Denbighshire)

Dr Eleanor Anne Freeman
Consultant in Geriatric Medicine, Royal Gwent Hospital. For services to Stroke Medicine and Medical Education in Wales. (Cardiff)

Winston James Griffiths
Chair, Abertawe Bro Morgannwg University Health Board. For services to the NHS in Wales. (Bridgend)

Dr Christopher John Howard
Headteacher, Lewis School, Pengam, Caerphilly. For services to Education. (Cowbridge, Vale of Glamorgan)

Professor Robert Owen Jones
Monitor, Welsh Language Project in Patagonia. For services to safeguarding the Welsh language in Argentina. (Pontarddulais, Swansea)

Ms Catrin Myfanwy Maby
Chief executive Officer, Severn Wye Energy Agency. For services to the Environment and to Social Equity. (Highnam, Gloucestershire)

Ms Hayley Parsons
Founder and chief executive, GoCompare.com. For services to the Economy. (Newport)

Robert Parsons
Founder and lately Executive chairman of Care for the Family. For services to Family Support. (Cardiff)

Kefin Lloyd Wakefield
Head of Economic Development, Pembrokeshire County Council. For services to Local Government. (Pembrokeshire)

Members of the Order of the British Empire (MBE)

Mrs Susan Pippa Bonner
For voluntary service to the North Wales Wildlife Trust. (Benllech, Anglesey)

John Bonthron
Foster Carer. For services to Children in Caerphilly, South Wales. (Ynysddu, Caerphilly)

Mrs Patricia Bonthron
Foster Carer. For services to Children in Caerphilly, South Wales. (Ynysddu, Caerphilly)

Mrs Rowena Thomas-Breese
For services to Disabled Swimming and Charitable Fundraising. (Colwyn Bay, Conwy)

John Geraint Parcell Davies, JP
For services to the community in Swansea. (Swansea)

NEW YEAR HONOURS 2012 (cont.)

Members of the Order of the British Empire (MBE) (cont.)

Trevor George Evans
For services to Conservation and to Wildlife in Monmouthshire. (Chepstow, Monmouthshire)

Maj Martin James Everett, TD
For services to The Royal Welsh Regimental Museum. (Chepstow, Monmouthshire)

Terrance Michael Flynn
For services to the community in Cardiff and Crime Prevention in Wales. (Cardiff)

George Malcolm Green
For services to the community in Haverfordwest, Pembrokeshire. (Haverfordwest, Pembrokeshire)

Mrs Carol Greenstock
For services to Economic Development in Wales. (Llandeilo, Carmarthenshire)

David John Harris
Divisional managing director, Cowlin Construction. For services to Education and Training in the Construction Industry. (Chepstow, Monmouthshire)

Simon David Henry Holt
Chairman, South West Wales Breast Cancer Network. For services to Healthcare in Carmarthenshire and South West Wales. (Llanelli, Carmarthenshire)

Derek Holvey
Conductor, Four Counties Youth Orchestra. For services to Music in South East Wales. (Rhondda Cynon Taff)

Mrs Lynne Hughes
For services to the community in North Wales. (Flintshire)

Mrs Hilary Humphreys
For services to Education and Sport in North Wales. (Llanrwst, Conwy)

Walford John Hutchings
Musical director, Pontnewydd Male Voice Choir. For services to Music and to the Community in Torfaen. (Pontypool, Torfaen)

Meredydd Davies James
Formerly Headteacher, Rhymney Comprehensive School, Caerphilly. For services to Education. (Cathays, Cardiff)

Roy Lindsey Jones
Community Liaison manager, ScottishPower. For services to Young People in Wales. (Llay, Wrexham)

Dr Hasmukh Joshi
Formerly General Practitioner. For services to Medical Education and to the Royal College of General Practitioners. (Pontypool, Torfaen)

Mrs Mary Maunder
Coach, St. Joseph's Swimming Club. For voluntary service to the community in Cardiff. (Cardiff)

John Metcalf
Composer. For services to Music. (Lampeter, Ceredigion)

Mrs Alice Ellen Morgan
For services to the Girlguides in Pembrokeshire. (Haverfordwest, Pembrokeshire)

Peter Rice Muxworthy
For services to the community in Swansea. (Gower, Swansea)

Robert James Owen
Caretaker, Llanfawr Primary School. For services to the community in Holyhead, Anglesey. (Holyhead, Anglesey)

Alexander Glynn Francis Parry
Community Liaison Officer, Serious Organised Crime Agency. For services to Law Enforcement. (Ammanford, Dyfed)

Mrs Ann Picton
Formerly Headteacher, Clytha Primary School, Newport. For services to Education. (St Brides, Newport)

Christopher John Reed
For services to the Scouts and to the community in Llanelli, Carmarthenshire. (Llanelli, Carmarthenshire)

Mrs Beatrice June Rees
For charitable services in Pembrokeshire. (Milford Haven, Pembrokeshire)

Martin Lewis Rees
Formerly Higher Officer, Customer Operations, Cardiff, HM Revenue and Customs. (Treharris, Caerphilly)

Miss Deborah Laraine Roberts
Leader, 8th Llandudno (Gogarth) Rangers. For services to Young People in Conwy, North Wales. (Abergele, Conwy)

Mrs Eirwen Griffiths Roberts
For services to the community in Ynysddu, Newport. (Newport)

Neil Robinson
National Coach, Paralympics GB Table Tennis Team. For services to Disabled Sport. (Bridgend)

John Malcolm Thomas
Formerly D0irector, National Farmers' Union Cymru. For services to Agriculture in Wales. (Carmarthen, Carmarthenshire)

PUBLIC HONOURS

NEW YEAR HONOURS 2012 (cont.)

Julian John Wilding Thomas
Formerly National Library of Wales Conservation Treatment Unit manager. For services to Conservation Science and Bookbinding. (Borth, Ceredigion)

Mrs Margaret Thomas
For charitable services in Holyhead, North Wales. (Holyhead, Gwynedd)

Graham Douglas
Underdown. Charity Fundraiser. For services to Charitable Fundraising. (Barry, South Glamorgan)

Mrs Edwina Mary White
For services to Counselling in South East Wales. (Porthcawl, Bridgend)

Ms Elizabeth William
Formerly director, IT Wales, Swansea University. For services to Women in Science, Engineering and Technology. (Swansea)

John Williams
For services to the community in Foulden, Berwickshire. (Foulden, Berwickshire)

Martyn Elwyn Williams
For services to Rugby. (Llantrisant, Mid Glamorgan)

Thomas Michael Williams
Formerly Chair Betsi Cadwaladr University Health Board. For services to Healthcare in Wales. (Wrexham)

Queen's Police Medal (QPM)

Mark Lindsey Mathias
Chief Superintendent, South Wales Police.

QUEEN'S BIRTHDAY HONOURS 2012

Commanders of the Order of the British Empire (CBE)

Professor William Stuart COLE
For services to Transport. (Cardiff)

Professor Ian Richard HARGREAVES
Professor of Digital Economy, Cardiff University. For services to the Creative Economy & Higher Ed. (Cardiff)

Owen Griffith Ronald JONES
Executive Chairman, Tinopolis. For services to the Media Industry. (Carmarthenshire)

Professor Julie WILLIAMS
Professor, Cardiff University. For services to Alzheimer's Disease Research. (Cardiff)

Officers of the Order of the British Empire (OBE)

Adrian Paul CLARK
Lately Cardiff Location Director & Chief Operating Officer for Protection, Legal & General Assurance Society Ltd. For services to the Financial Services Sector. (Monmouthshire)

Dr Deborah COHEN
Senior Medical Research Fellow, Cardiff University. For services to Occupational Health. (South Glamorgan)

Professor Peter ELWOOD
Honorary Professor, Cardiff University. For services to Health. (Cardiff)

David GILBERT
Director of Regeneration, Carmarthenshire County Council. For services to Regeneration and Skills and to the community in West Wales. (Swansea)

David Michael GRIFFITHS
Lately Headteacher, Cardiff High School. For services to Education in Cardiff. (Cardiff)

Professor Sian HOPE
Executive Director of Innovation and Professor of Computer Science, Bangor University. For services to Innovation and Computing. (Anglesey)

Mrs Milica KITSON
Chief Executive, Constructing Excellence in Wales. For services to the Construction Industry in Wales. (Newport)

Stephen Lawton MARSHALL
Lately Headteacher, St Julian's School, Newport. For services to Education and to the community in South East Wales. (Newport)

Derrick Arthur Langley PRICE
Senior Investigating Officer, DEFRA Investigation Services and Counsellor, CRUSE Bereavement Care UK. (Gwent)

John Joseph William SPEIRS
Vice-President (Asia), Ensinger. For services to Advanced Material and Manufacturing in Wales. (Cardiff)

Richard Charles TURNER
Senior Inspector of Ancient Monuments, Welsh Government. (Vale of Glamorgan).

PUBLIC HONOURS

QUEEN'S BIRTHDAY HONOURS 2012 (cont.)

Members of the Order of the British Empire (MBE)

Mrs Rachel Mary AXFORD
Leader, Treborth Riding for the Disabled. For services to Disabled People in North Wales. (Anglesey)

Stephen John BAKER
Lately Head, Royal Society for the Prevention of Accidents, Wales. For services to Road Safety in Wales. (Torfaen)

Glyn CATLEY
Governor, Coleg Llandrillo, Colwyn Bay, Conwy. For services to Further Education in North Wales. (Conwy)

Paul Michael CHESHIRE
Bikesafe Co-ordinator, North Wales Police. For services to Policing. (Conwy)

Professor Kevin DAVIES
Chair of Nursing and Disaster Healthcare. For services to Healthcare Disaster Management. (Vale of Glam)

Mrs Susan Catherine DAVIS
For services to the Harriet Davis Seaside Holiday Trust and to Disabled People and their Families. (Pembs)

Michael David FREEMAN
Lately Curator, Ceredigion Museum. For services to Heritage in Ceredigion and to Museums in Wales. (Ceredigion)

Councillor John GIBBIN
For services to the community in West Wales. (Pembs)

Albert Ernest HARRIS
For services to the community in Swansea. (Swansea)

Dr Helen Margaret HERBERT
For services to the General Practice Profession in Wales. (Ceredigion)

Mrs Patricia Christine HILLMAN
For services to the Scout Movement in Monmouthshire. (Monmouthshire)

Robert James HOWELLS
Volunteer, British Trust for Ornithology.
For services to Ornithology in Swansea and West Glamorgan. (Swansea)

Mrs Agnes Rosemary JAMES
Lately Headteacher, St Mellons Church in Wales Primary School, Cardiff. For services to Primary Education. (Cardiff)

Mrs Ann JONES
For services to Occupational Health and Safety in Swansea and West Wales. (Swansea)

Mrs Joy JONES
Clinical Lead, Specialist Eating Disorders Service, Aneurin Bevan Health Board. For services to Healthcare. (Caerleon, Newport)

Lesley JONES
For charitable services to the Noah's Ark Appeal and the community in Powys. (Powys)

Mrs Janet KEAUFFLING
For services to Homeless and Vulnerable People in Swansea. (Swansea)

Steve KHAIREH
For services to Young People in Cardiff. (Cardiff)

Mrs Margaret MUNFORD
For charitable services to POD in Wales and the UK. (Powys)

Richard Trafford PHILLIPS
Executive Officer, Drivers Medical, Driver and Vehicle Licensing Agency. (West Glamorgan)

David William Spencer POWELL
Secretary, Cardiff Astronomical Society. For services to Science in the community. (Cardiff)

Colin PUGH
Lately Team Manager, Leaving Care Team, RCT. For services to Young People and their Families. (RCT)

Malcolm Ernest RIDGE
Chair, the Gower Society. For services to the community in Swansea. (Swansea)

Mrs Virginia SCOTT
Secretary, Hewell Grange Conservation and Advisory Group. For services to Conservation and to Heritage in Worcestershire. (Powys)

Brian Anthonie SPARKS
For services to Schools Basketball in Wales. (Bridgend)

Harry STEVENS
Head of Resuscitation Services, Prince Charles Hospital, Merthyr Tydfil. For services to Resuscitation Training. (Caerphilly)

Mrs Debbie Mees STONE
Specialist Osteoporosis Nurse, Bronglais Hospital, Hywel Dda Local Health Board. For services to Patients with Osteoporosis in Ceredigion. (Ceredigion)

Mrs Margaret Elizabeth SULLIVAN
Founder, In the Pink. For charitable services to Breast Cancer Research. (Blaenau Gwent)

Gavin THOMAS
For services to Post-16 Education and Training in Wales. (Cardiff)

Wayne Kendal THOMAS
President, Rhondda Boys' and Girls' Clubs. For services to Young People in Rhondda Cynon Taff. (RCT)

Councillor Jefferson Houseman TILDESLEY
For services to Local Government and to the community in Bridgend. (Bridgend)

Shane Mark WILLIAMS
For services to Rugby. (Carmarthenshire)

Mrs Joan WILSON
For charitable services in Cardiff. (Cardiff)

Councillor Ena Mary WYNNE
For services to Local Government and the community in Conwy. (Conwy)

SOCIO-ECONOMIC PROFILE

Key Indicators

Area (sq km)	**20,780**	Forecast capital expenditure (2011-12)	**£997m**
Population ('000s)	**3,006**	% dwellings in Band D (2012-13)	**16.1**
% able to speak Welsh	**24.8**	Band D council tax (2011-12)	**£1,162**
% born in Wales	**75.4**	% over retirement age (2010)	**18.6**
% non-white ethnic groups	**4.1**	% pupils 5+ GCSEs A*-C (2010-11)	**67.3**
Gross rev expenditure (2011-12)	**£6.7bn**	Unemployment (% claimant count 2011)	**3.9**

Health statistics

Life Expectancy	1999	2003	2008	2010
Males:	74.6	75.8	77.2	77.6
Females:	79.6	80.3	81.6	81.8

Directly employed NHS staff	2001	2009	2010	2011
Medical & dental	3,907	5,562	5,654	5,813
Nursing, midwifery & health visiting	24,751	28,199	28,168	27,999
Administration & estates	12,326	16,151	15,502	15,230
Of which: managers	1,339	2,763	2,343	2,092
Scientific, therapeutic and technical	7,605	11,202	11,483	11,450
Health care assistant & other support staff	7,781	9,920	10,049	9,711
Ambulance	1,103	1,403	1,429	1,458
Other	121	300	159	157

Ambulance response (%<8 mins)	1999-00	2004-05	2009-10	2011-12
	49.2	57.7	64.8	65.9

Referral to treatment times – patients waiting to start treatment, by Local Health Board of residence 2011

Local Health Board	Less than 26 weeks No.	%	26 to 36 weeks No.	%	Over 36 weeks No.	%	Total
Betsi Cadwaladr	63,188	94.7	2,522	3.8	989	1.5	66,699
Powys Teaching	8,342	97.2	208	2.4	30	0.3	8,580
Hywel Dda	41,727	94.5	1,983	4.5	457	1.0	44,167
ABM University	60,066	95.3	2,357	3.7	613	1.0	63,036
Cwm Taf	30,606	93.8	1,726	5.3	305	0.9	32,637
Aneurin Bevan	75,338	96.1	2,817	3.6	266	0.3	78,421
Cardiff & Vale Uni	54,755	89.4	3,945	6.4	2,526	4.1	61,226
Wales	334,022	94.2	15,558	4.4	5,186	1.5	354,766

Total NHS expenditure (£)	2006-07	2008-09	2009-10	2010-11
	4,577.9	5,059.0	5,230.8	5,355.0

SOCIO-ECONOMIC PROFILE

Economic output

Gross Value Added	1999	2007	2008	2010
Wales total (£bn)	30.9	44.3	45.6	45.5
Per head (Wales as % of UK)	77.4	74.4	74.3	74.0

Adult earnings	1999	2008	2009	2011
Full-time weekly earnings, men	£392	£545	£543	£553
Full-time weekly earnings, female	£301	£434	£456	£470

Labour market statistics

Employment	2001	2009	2011	2012
Employment rate (% of working age)	67.1	68.2	66.3	66.7
Annual economic inactivity rates	29.0	26.7	27.5	27.0

Young people not in education, employment or training (NEET) in Wales

	1999	2004	2007	2010
16-18 year olds	11.6	11.6	11.8	11.0
19-24 year olds	18.6	16.1	17.6	22.8

Employment in public and private sectors (2011)	Public	Private
Wales	30.4	69.6
United Kingdom	24.5	75.5

Workplace employment by industry (2010)	Wales	UK
Public admin, defence, education & health	32%	27%
Wholesale, retail, transport, hotels & food	26%	26%
Finance & business activities	16%	24%
Other industries	12%	12%
Production	11%	9%
Agriculture	3%	1%

Source: All statistics from Stats Wales / Welsh Government websites

SOCIO-ECONOMIC PROFILE

Overall Index of Multiple Deprivation 2011

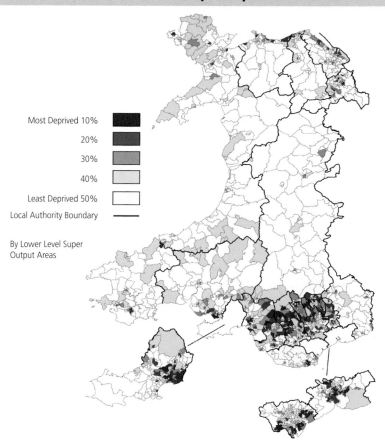

Most Deprived 10%
20%
30%
40%
Least Deprived 50%
Local Authority Boundary

By Lower Level Super
Output Areas

% of Local Authority wards below the 30% measure of deprivation

Rank			Rank		
1	Blaenau Gwent	66.0	12	Conwy	22.5
2	Merthyr Tydfil	61.1	13	Carmarthenshire	22.3
3	Rhondda Cynon Taf	50.7	14	Isle of Anglesey	20.5
4	Neath Port Talbot	44.0	15	Denbighshire	19.0
5	Newport	42.6	16	Vale of Glamorgan	17.9
6	Bridgend	40.0	17	Flintshire	17.4
7	Caerphilly	40.0	18	Pembrokeshire	14.1
8	Torfaen	35.0	19	Monmouthshire	8.6
9	Cardiff	34.5	20	Powys	7.5
10	Swansea	32.0	21	Gwynedd	6.7
11	Wrexham	29.4	22	Ceredigion	4.3

SOCIO-ECONOMIC PROFILE

% Born in Wales

Rank	Authority	%
1	Blaenau Gwent	92.1
2	Merthyr Tydfil	92.0
3	Caerphilly	89.9
4	Rhondda Cynon Taf	89.9
5	Neath Port Talbot	89.5
6	Torfaen	85.5
7	Bridgend	84.7
8	Swansea	82.1
9	Newport	81.1
10	Carmarthenshire	80.1
11	Vale of Glamorgan	75.7
12	Cardiff	74.9
13	Wrexham	71.9
14	Gwynedd	69.8
15	Pembrokeshire	68.7
16	Isle of Anglesey	67.6
17	Monmouthshire	61.3
18	Ceredigion	58.6
19	Denbighshire	57.9
20	Powys	55.6
21	Conwy	54.0
22	Flintshire	51.1
Wales		**75.4**

% Speaking Welsh

Rank	Authority	%
1	Gwynedd	70.5
2	Isle of Anglesey	60.9
3	Ceredigion	52.5
4	Carmarthenshire	46.5
5	Conwy	33.3
6	Denbighshire	30.4
7	Flintshire	25.3
8	Powys	23.9
9	Newport	18.9
10	Neath Port Talbot	18.8
11	Caerphilly	18.7
12	Torfaen	18.2
13	Rhondda Cynon Taf	18.0
14	Cardiff	17.8
15	Merthyr Tydfil	17.7
16	Vale of Glamorgan	17.0
17	Wrexham	17.0
18	Monmouthshire	16.7
19	Pembrokeshire	16.2
20	Swansea	16.2
21	Blaenau Gwent	15.5
22	Bridgend	15.5
Wales		**24.8**

Population

Rank	Authority	'000s
1	Cardiff	341.0
2	Rhondda Cynon Taf	234.3
3	Swansea	232.5
4	Carmarthenshire	180.7
5	Caerphilly	173.1
6	Flintshire	149.7
7	Newport	141.3
8	Neath Port Talbot	137.3
9	Bridgend	134.5
10	Wrexham	133.5
11	Powys	131.3
12	Vale of Glamorgan	124.9
13	Gwynedd	119.0
14	Pembrokeshire	117.0
15	Conwy	110.8
16	Denbighshire	96.7
17	Torfaen	90.5
18	Monmouthshire	88.0
19	Ceredigion	76.9
20	Isle of Anglesey	68.5
21	Blaenau Gwent	68.3
22	Merthyr Tydfil	55.6
Wales		**3,006**

Area

Rank	Authority	Sq. kms
1	Powys	5,196
2	Gwynedd	2,548
3	Carmarthenshire	2,372
4	Ceredigion	1,790
5	Pembrokeshire	1,619
6	Conwy	1,130
7	Monmouthshire	851
8	Denbighshire	838
9	Isle of Anglesey	714
10	Wrexham	504
11	Neath Port Talbot	442
12	Flintshire	438
13	Rhondda Cynon Taf	424
14	Swansea	378
15	Vale of Glamorgan	331
16	Caerphilly	277
17	Bridgend	251
18	Newport	190
19	Cardiff	140
20	Torfaen	126
21	Merthyr Tydfil	111
22	Blaenau Gwent	109
Wales		**20,780**

SOCIO-ECONOMIC PROFILE

Welsh Health Survey 2010

% Reporting Long-term limiting illness

Rank	Authority	%
1	Neath Port Talbot	33
2	Blaenau Gwent	31
3	Caerphilly	31
4	Merthyr Tydfil	31
5	Rhondda Cynon Taf	31
6	Torfaen	31
7	Carmarthenshire	30
8	Bridgend	29
9	Cardiff	28
10	Newport	28
11	Swansea	28
12	Pembrokeshire	26
13	Vale of Glamorgan	26
14	Gwynedd	25
15	Isle of Anglesey	25
16	Monmouthshire	25
17	Powys	25
18	Ceredigion	24
19	Denbighshire	24
20	Wrexham	24
21	Conwy	22
22	Flintshire	21
Wales		**27**

% Adults overweight or obese

Rank	Authority	%
1	Merthyr Tydfil	64
2	Torfaen	62
3	Blaenau Gwent	61
4	Carmarthenshire	61
5	Neath Port Talbot	61
6	Rhondda Cynon Taf	61
7	Bridgend	60
8	Caerphilly	60
9	Pembrokeshire	60
10	Powys	58
11	Newport	58
12	Flintshire	57
13	Gwynedd	57
14	Swansea	56
15	Denbighshire	55
16	Isle of Anglesey	55
17	Vale of Glamorgan	55
18	Monmouthshire	54
19	Wrexham	54
20	Conwy	52
21	Cardiff	51
22	Ceredigion	51
Wales		**57**

% adults reporting being a current smoker

Rank	Authority	%
1	Blaenau Gwent	28
2	Merthyr Tydfil	27
3	Rhondda Cynon Taf	27
4	Wrexham	27
5	Neath Port Talbot	26
6	Torfaen	26
7	Newport	25
8	Caerphilly	24
9	Cardiff	24
10	Carmarthenshire	23
11	Ceredigion	23
12	Gwynedd	23
13	Isle of Anglesey	23
14	Bridgend	22
15	Denbighshire	22
16	Pembrokeshire	22
17	Swansea	22
18	Conwy	21
19	Flintshire	21
20	Powys	21
21	Vale of Glamorgan	21
22	Monmouthshire	18
Wales		**23**

% adults consuming alcohol above guideline limits

Rank	Authority	%
1	Bridgend	48
2	Cardiff	48
3	Flintshire	47
4	Merthyr Tydfil	47
5	Neath Port Talbot	47
6	Caerphilly	46
7	Vale of Glamorgan	46
8	Newport	45
9	Rhondda Cynon Taf	45
10	Swansea	45
11	Denbighshire	44
12	Gwynedd	44
13	Wrexham	44
14	Blaenau Gwent	43
15	Isle of Anglesey	43
16	Monmouthshire	43
17	Ceredigion	42
18	Conwy	42
19	Torfaen	42
20	Carmarthenshire	40
21	Powys	39
22	Pembrokeshire	38
Wales		**44**

SOCIO-ECONOMIC PROFILE

Index of Income Domain 2011

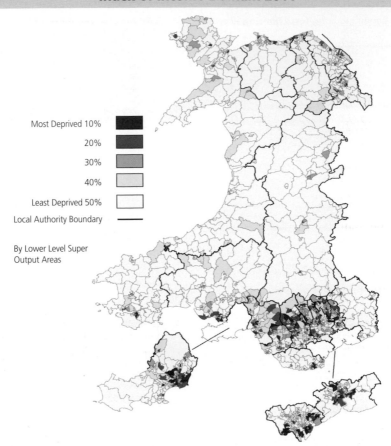

Most Deprived 10%
20%
30%
40%
Least Deprived 50%
Local Authority Boundary

By Lower Level Super
Output Areas

% of Local Authority wards in the most deprived 10% income domain

Rank			Rank		
1	Blaenau Gwent	21.3	12	Isle of Anglesey	6.8
2	Cardiff	21.2	13	Torfaen	6.7
3	Merthyr Tydfil	19.4	14	Wrexham	5.9
4	Newport	18.1	15	Flintshire	5.4
5	Neath Port Talbot	15.4	16	Conwy	4.2
6	Denbighshire	13.8	17	Pembrokeshire	4.2
7	Swansea	12.9	18	Gwynedd	4.0
8	Rhondda Cynon Taf	11.8	19	Carmarthenshire	3.6
9	Caerphilly	10.9	20	Powys	0
10	Vale of Glamorgan	7.7	21	Ceredigion	0
11	Bridgend	7.1	22	Monmouthshire	0

The**Wales**
Yearbook
13

POST-ELECTION
POLITICS

Post-Election Politics

a commentary

by
Denis Balsom

Single Party Government

The popular endorsement of greater powers for the National Assembly at the Referendum in March 2011 gave the Welsh General Election, held only a few weeks later in May, special significance. With the full acquisition of primary legislative powers, the ballot became truly the election of a Welsh Parliament. As such, the proposals put forward by each political party were, for the first time since devolution, policies that could be enacted by and for Wales. Such freedom however, would be dependent upon a Government being elected with a workable majority or creation of an effective Coalition, as pre-dated the election, with an agreed programme. Wales's hybrid electoral system demonstrated once again however, that such a majority was unobtainable. The Labour Party captured 28 of the 40 constituencies but, as a consequence of its dominance, secured only 2 further AMs. Carwyn Jones headed a party group of 30, *de facto* reduced to 29 by the accession of Rosemary Butler to the post of Presiding Officer. There was speculation concerning partnerships or coalitions but, in reality, Carwyn Jones chose to govern alone and defy the other parties to bring down his administration.

The election was also of note as two Members returned for the Liberal Democrats were found to have breached electoral regulations by standing as candidates whilst disbarred by their membership of proscribed public bodies. A full enquiry led to the disqualification of John Dixon from South Wales Central (replaced by Eluned Parrott), but Aled Roberts, a Liberal Democrat elected for North Wales, was re-instated on the grounds that the regulations published in Welsh, which he had consulted, were incorrect and appeared to validate his candidacy.

The Legislative Programme

The legislative programme announced by the incoming Welsh Government was not overly ambitious. This undoubtedly reflected the lack of an overall majority as well as a certain cautiousness on how to proceed in exercising the new powers and establishing new conventions and protocols with Westminster. Bills were promised requiring local authorities to further collaborate in the delivery of services; a new Food Hygiene Rating Scheme; a Schools and Standards Bill; measures on social services and homelessness and tenants' rights; an obligation on local authorities to provide and maintain walking and cycling paths. Most contentious was a proposed Organ Donation Bill to create an opt-out system for organ donation rather than the present opt-in convention. Irrespective of the moral and social issues implicit in the Organ Donation Bill, questions were raised whether such broad ranging legislation fell wholly within the powers devolved to the Assembly. Whilst this Bill has yet to be laid and these issues resolved, a much more modest proposal, the Local

Government (Byelaws) (Wales) Bill completed its passage through the Assembly in 2012 only for it to be referred to the Supreme Court by the Attorney General, Dominic Grieve, prior to receiving the Royal Assent, on the grounds that the range of its jurisdiction would encroach upon that of UK Ministers and in areas of policy not devolved to Wales.

Although currently unresolved, problems with the Byelaws legislation are indicative of the potential for on-going disagreement over the extent of Assembly powers. The specific definition of the 20 policy areas over which the Assembly now has legislative rights creates a legion of opportunities for legal challenge and is much more complex than the situation in Scotland where the Scottish Parliament's powers are presumed dominant unless specifically reserved to the United Kingdom Parliament. In Wales this problem will not go away. It will require much greater attention to the legal drafting of legislation and will inevitably inhibit proposed legislation that might be deemed 'political' rather than technical or bureaucratic. When the political complexion of Westminster Governments and Cardiff Bay administrations differ such tensions are bound to exist.

Conservative leadership

An unforeseen consequence of the Election was the loss of the Welsh Conservative leader, Nick Bourne. Since the creation of the Assembly in 1999, the Conservatives in Wales have generally fared well and the leadership of Nick Bourne has been central to that achievement. Often characterised as the 'English Party' and as the principal opponent to Devolution in both referendums, the Conservatives under Nick Bourne had evolved a position supportive of the new constitutional status of Wales and had increased their representation in Wales. Ironically, Nick Bourne became a victim of that success – and a perverse electoral system.

Had Nick Bourne been returned he may well have faced a leadership challenge, although his previous greatest rival, Glyn Davies, had been elected to Parliament in 2010. Paul Davies, AM

for Preseli, assumed temporary Group leadership whilst the full internal party election procedure was followed. Two candidates emerged; Andrew R T Davies, AM for South Wales Central and Nick Ramsay AM for Monmouth. In a one-member one-vote election Andrew R T Davies was elected with 53% of the vote and became Leader of the Opposition.

Plaid Cymru leadership

Following the Assembly election, Ieuan Wyn Jones, Leader of Plaid Cymru gave notice of his intention to stand down. A leadership election was put in place with the expectation that a new Leader would be in post for the Plaid Cymru Spring conference. The Party Constitution now requires that the Leader be an AM which, after a generally rather poor election, meant that only 11 AMs could be considered. A previous leadership candidate, Helen Mary Jones, would have almost certainly stood had she been returned at the election, as might have Nerys Evans. Eventually, the contest comprised Elin Jones, AM for Ceredigion and a former Minister in the One Wales Coalition Government; Simon Thomas, former MP for Ceredigion and now a newly elected list Member for Mid and West Wales, Leanne Wood, a list Member for South Wales Central and Dafydd Elis-Thomas, the former Presiding Officer of the Assembly who had led the Party 1984-91. The election was held on an alternative vote basis with all party members eligible to participate. The long lead time before nominations closed led to a considerable membership drive with both former members returning to the Party and other, generally younger, recruits being engaged via Facebook and other social media.

The premise for the leadership contest was complex. Plaid Cymru had, for the first time, participated in the Government of Wales through the One-Wales Coalition agreement. This was generally held to have been a success, but Plaid still lost seats at the subsequent election. The positive result of the further powers referendum held prior to the election was also deemed to be an achievement for Plaid Cymru as the Labour

Party might not have moved quite so quickly on this constitutional reform had it not been intrinsic to the Coalition Agreement. The dilemma for a new Plaid Cymru Leader however, was how to present a new agenda to the people of Wales with realisable goals that could follow the achievement of the *de facto* purpose of the Party since its conception – namely the creation of a Welsh Parliament. The campaign reflected this dilemma; Elin Jones became effectively the continuity candidate, building on her successful Ministerial record. Simon Thomas had served as Ieuan Wyn Jones's principal policy advisor throughout Plaid's time in Government and similarly appeared to offer more of the same. Before the election however, Simon Thomas withdrew and pledged his support to Elin Jones. Dafydd Elis-Thomas emphasised the importance of Plaid Cymru participating in the Government of Wales whilst seeking to define a more complex, modern, sustainable 'green' form of nationalism. Leanne Wood, by contrast, adopted a simple, almost single issue, campaign theme defining Plaid Cymru's future task to seek Independence for Wales. Independence remained a nebulous concept and all candidates had to address the 'I' word given the concurrent debate concerning the future status of Scotland following the SNP's spectacular majority victory in the Scottish Parliamentary elections. Youth and aspiration prevailed over experience; Leanne Wood won the first ballot, but did not achieve an overall majority; Dafydd Elis-Thomas was therefore eliminated and his supporters second preferences redistributed giving Leanne Wood the necessary majority to be elected. Subsequently, Leanne Wood has appointed Elin Jones as Deputy Leader of the Party.

Wales from Westminster

Whilst the position of the National Assembly had been greatly enhanced by the Government of Wales Act 2006 and further empowered by the subsequent Referendum on powers, the Westminster Government, the Wales Office and the Secretary of State continue to be major players in Welsh politics. Several proposals detailed in the Conservative – Liberal Democrat Coalition agreement concern Wales. Not least, arguably, Wales is especially vulnerable to the impact of the austerity measures being introduced by the Government to counter the financial crisis. In July 2011, the Secretary of State announced the creation of a Commission to assess, in the first instance, the financial accountability of the Welsh Government, especially in respect of the Assembly acquiring taxation powers, and secondly, to report subsequently on the Constitutional settlement in Wales in the light of the Devolution experience to date.

Silk Commission

A review panel has been appointed under the Chairmanship of Paul Silk, the former Clerk of the Assembly, initially to examine financial matters and, secondly, to assess current practice in respect of Assembly powers, procedures and electoral arrangements. The first Report of the Silk Commission is expected before the end of 2012. The Commission is made up of a nominee from each principal political party and two Independent members, Dyfrig John, a retired banker, and Professor Noel Lloyd, a former University Vice-Chancellor. The Commission is seeking submissions and has held public meetings around the country but interest appears to be slight. These matters are intensely political and it seems unlikely that a consensual report will be achieved. The parties will evolve their own positions on these matters, the substance of which will feature large in the next National Assembly elections in 2016, including the question of whether any change in taxation powers would require a further referendum to be held.

Police and Crime Commissioners

The Westminster Coalition Agreement also proposed the election of Police and Crime Commissioners to replace the current system of Police Authorities. This initiative stems from the Government's commitment to greater localism, an aspiration however, that received a considerable set back when a number of English cities rejected the opportunity to create elected Mayors when consulted by referendum in 2012. Policing is not a devolved matter and the election of Police Commissioners is to proceed for all of England and Wales. Candidates have been nominated by political parties and other interested groups, but it is likely that conventional party loyalties will prevail. In Wales the highest profile candidate to declare has been Alun Michael, MP for Cardiff South and Penarth and the former founding First Secretary of the National Assembly. To fight the election, Mr Michael will be standing down from Parliament and a by-election is expected to be held on the same day, as the ballots for the Commissioners, 15 November. Meanwhile, Alun Michael's son, Tal, is the Labour candidate for Police Commissioner in North Wales.

Parliamentary Boundary revisions

The Conservative Party fought the 2010 election on a commitment to reduce the size of the House of Commons and to adjust Parliamentary boundaries to ensure greater equality between constituencies. Following the election, this commitment was incorporated into the Coalition Agreement with the Liberal Democrats. The draft proposals set out a target membership of the House of Commons at 600 MPs with the number of electors per seat to vary by not more than 5% plus or minus the national average. Proportionately Wales has been over-represented in Parliament for many years. Successive Boundary Commissions have made allowances for sparsely populated areas, historical precedence and, perhaps, a sense that as a 'nation' within the United Kingdom Wales deserved a degree of over-representation. Given the predominance of Labour representation from Wales, this has not been without controversy, especially when the same argument has been made in respect of both Scotland and Northern Ireland and many majorities in the House of Commons have been relatively small. In recent years representation from both Scotland and Northern Ireland had been subject to extensive reapportionment leaving Wales in line to be most affected by the present proposals. Parliamentary representation for Wales at

Westminster is due to fall from 40 to 30 Members. This reduction is further exacerbated by the rules of variance in electorates resulting in urban areas being allocated proportionately more seats and sparsely populated rural areas fewer.

Although the passage of the Bill to effect these changes may fall victim to internal disagreements within the Coalition concerning Constitutional reform, the debate in Wales will continue under the aegis of the Green Paper published by the Secretary of State on the future electoral arrangements for the National Assembly of Wales. The public consultation now underway addresses issues such as the de-coupling of Westminster and Assembly seats, the balance between AMs elected in constituencies and those for political regions, as well as the length of National Assembly terms. Whenever implemented, it seems likely that any revision of seats will broadly follow the pattern suggested in the early draft proposals from the Boundary Commission and will thus be deemed to be disadvantageous for the Labour Party. The issue is further compounded by the on-going question of what the appropriate membership of the National Assembly for Wales should be, especially now that full law making powers were ratified in the 2011 referendum. In Scotland the advent of the Scottish Parliament accommodated such issues by adopting separate constituency boundaries for Westminster and Holyrood elections. There are now 59 Scottish seats in London and 73 Constituency seats (out of 129) in the Scottish Parliament. In Wales the Secretary of State has proposed that 60 seats be retained for the National Assembly with 30 Members being elected, first past the post for the new constituencies and 30 being elected, proportionately, from the political regions. Whilst the Conservatives see this as an elegant solution, the Labour Party has advocated 60 Members being elected on the basis of two per constituency on a simple plurality vote. As electoral matters are a non-devolved issue, the Wales Office (and therefore Westminster's) view might well be expected to prevail. The First

CAPITA SYMONDS

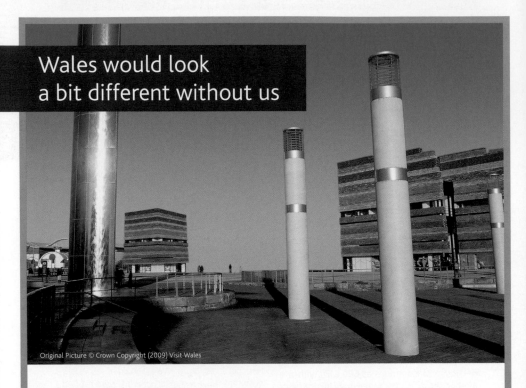

Wales would look
a bit different without us

Original Picture © Crown Copyright (2009) Visit Wales

As Wales's largest multidisciplinary consultancy, Capita Symonds has played a vital role in some of the country's largest and most iconic projects.

Our architects designed the Wales Millennium Centre (not pictured above), the Celtic Manor Hotel, the refurbishment of the Sherman Theatre and the OpTIC Technium in North Wales; our project managers delivered the Ebbw Valley Railway, the Bluestone Leisure Village and the Milford Haven Gas Pipeline; and our engineers planned the Llandysul Bypass, the Bargoed Regeneration Scheme and Newbridge's Calzaghe Bridge.

For further information visit **www.capitasymonds.co.uk**
or contact:

Cardiff
Stuart Creedon, Director   stuart.creedon@capita.co.uk   T: 029 2033 3777

Cwmbran / Treforest
Alun Parfitt, Director   alun.parfitt@capita.co.uk   T: 01633 463333 /01443 823200

North Wales
Paul Terry, Director   paul.terry@capita.co.uk   T: 01492 539200

successful people, projects and performance

Minister however, believes that he has received a commitment from the Prime Minister that the system for Assembly elections would not be changed without Wales's consent. In the interim, it seems most likely that if constituency boundaries change, these would be implemented for the next Westminster election, expected in 2015, but that the next Assembly election in 2016 would still be fought on existing rules and boundaries.

Wither Scotland?

Between now and the next Westminster General election in 2015, British politics will remain largely dominated by UK economic and financial matters, but domestic concerns will increasingly focus on Scotland and the fate of the Union. In 2011 Alex Salmon and the SNP achieved a stunning victory in the elections to the Scottish Parliament achieving an overall majority in place of the minority Government they had led for the previous four years. Foremost amongst their commitments was to bring forward a referendum on Independence for Scotland. Whilst the details and implications of such a fundamental constitutional debate will emerge in the coming months, certain issues are clear and will impact profoundly on the future of Welsh politics. There has always been, perhaps unfairly, a sense that the political debate in Wales advocating greater autonomy has been predicated on Scottish precedence. Wales today seems to be a good way behind Scotland on the road to self-government, but the nature of the Union embedded in the structure of the United Kingdom and Northern Ireland does need to evolve and adjust to the new pattern of devolved nations, as currently constituted, irrespective of further Scottish assertion. To this end, Carwyn Jones has set out a call for the creation of a Constitutional Convention to enable the four countries of the United Kingdom to consider the future ' ...ahead of the debate, not ...behind the tide of change.' Such an initiative would doubtless be helpful but is unlikely to be officially sanctioned, though it may emerge in the deliberations of some of the more objective and impartial 'think tanks'. Whilst the Scottish referendum is to be held in 2014, the issue of the future of Scotland is one for the United Kingdom as a whole and one on which all political parties, nations and regions have an essential interest in the outcome.

Looking Ahead...

The Local Government elections held in England and Wales in May 2012 were generally perceived to be good for the Labour Party. With the exception of the London Mayoralty, they were poor for the Conservatives and the Liberal Democrats who endeavoured to fight the elections independently. Since then, poll data suggests greater support for Labour and Ed Miliband and a fall of support for David Cameron and especially the Lib Dem leader Nick Clegg. Further Coalition tensions have also emerged such as over the reform of the House of Lords.

In Wales Labour recovered much of their former dominance in local government and now control 10 authorities, in contrast to before the election when they held only two Councils, Rhondda Cynon Taf and Neath Port Talbot. At a UK level, Carwyn Jones remains the only Labour politician to lead a major elected body. Whilst much of informed opinion in Britain is indifferent to Wales and the nuances of Welsh politics, the reverse however, is not the case. The Welsh Government appears to be presenting itself and its actions as an alternative to the Westminster Coalition rather than to the Opposition parties in the Assembly. It is perhaps difficult to see how this can be avoided at present but it remains the key challenge for all those involved in Welsh politics and public life, and for those who elect and appoint them, to create a vigorous and dynamic democracy in Cardiff which, in turn, will enshrine and ensure the place of Wales in Britain and Europe.

August 2012

GENERAL ELECTION 2010
Relative Majorites

Constituency	MP	Party	Majority	%	Swing required	Status
Cardiff North	Jonathan Evans	Con	194	0.4%	0.2%	Highly Marginal
Swansea West	Geraint Davies	Lab	504	1.4%	0.7%	Highly Marginal
Montgomeryshire	Glyn Davies	Con	1,184	3.5%	1.8%	Highly Marginal
Newport East	Jessica Morden	Lab	1,650	4.8%	2.4%	Highly Marginal
Arfon	Hywel Williams	PC	1,455	5.6%	2.8%	Highly Marginal
Bridgend	Madeleine Moon	Lab	2,263	5.9%	3.0%	Highly Marginal
Delyn	David Hanson	Lab	2,272	6.1%	3.1%	Marginal
Gower	Martin Caton	Lab	2,683	6.4%	3.2%	Marginal
Vale of Clwyd	Chris Ruane	Lab	2,509	7.1%	3.6%	Marginal
Ynys Môn	Albert Owen	Lab	2,461	7.1%	3.6%	Marginal
Alyn & Deeside	Mark Tami	Lab	2,919	7.3%	3.7%	Marginal
Pontypridd	Owen Smith	Lab	2,785	7.6%	3.8%	Marginal
Clwyd South	Susan Elan Jones	Lab	2,834	8.2%	4.1%	Marginal
Carms W & S Pembs	Simon Hart	Con	3,423	8.5%	4.3%	Marginal
Vale of Glamorgan	Alun Cairns	Con	4,307	8.8%	4.4%	Marginal
Newport West	Paul Flynn	Lab	3,544	8.9%	4.5%	Marginal
Carms E & Dinefwr	Jonathan Edwards	PC	3,481	9.2%	4.6%	Marginal
Brecon & Radnor	Roger Williams	Lib Dem	3,747	9.6%	4.8%	Marginal
Cardiff S & Penarth	Alun Michael	Lab	4,709	10.6%	5.3%	Marginal
Wrexham	Ian Lucas	Lab	3,658	11.1%	5.6%	Marginal
Aberconwy	Guto Bebb	Con	3,398	11.3%	5.7%	Marginal
Cardiff West	Kevin Brennan	Lab	4,750	11.6%	5.8%	Marginal
Preseli Pembs	Stephen Crabb	Con	4,605	11.6%	5.8%	Marginal
Llanelli	Nia Griffiths	Lab	4,701	12.5%	6.3%	Fairly Safe
Merthyr Tydfil	Dai Havard	Lab	4,056	12.6%	6.3%	Fairly Safe
Cardiff Central	Jenny Willott	Lib Dem	4,576	12.7%	6.4%	Fairly Safe
Clwyd West	David Jones	Con	6,419	16.8%	8.4%	Fairly Safe
Ceredigion	Mark Williams	Lib Dem	8,324	21.8%	10.9%	Fairly Safe
Dwyfor Meirionnydd	Elfyn Llwyd	PC	6,367	22.0%	11.0%	Fairly Safe
Monmouth	David Davies	Con	10,425	22.4%	11.2%	Fairly Safe
Torfaen	Paul Murphy	Lab	9,306	24.7%	12.4%	Safe
Neath	Peter Hain	Lab	9,775	26.3%	13.2%	Safe
Caerphilly	Wayne David	Lab	10,755	27.8%	13.9%	Safe
Cynon Valley	Ann Clwyd	Lab	9,617	32.2%	16.1%	Safe
Blaenau Gwent	Nick Smith	Lab	10,516	32.5%	16.3%	Safe
Swansea East	Sian James	Lab	10,838	33.2%	16.6%	Safe
Islwyn	Chris Evans	Lab	12,215	35.2%	17.6%	Safe
Aberavon	Hywel Francis	Lab	11,039	35.7%	17.9%	Safe
Rhondda	Chris Bryant	Lab	11,553	37.2%	18.6%	Solidly Safe
Ogmore	Huw Irranca-Davies	Lab	13,246	38.2%	19.1%	Solidly Safe

NATIONAL ASSEMBLY ELECTION 2011
Relative Majorites

Constituency	AM	Party	Majority	%	Swing required	Status
Cardiff Central	Jenny Rathbone	Lab	38	0.1%	0.1%	Higly Marginal
Llanelli	Keith Davies	Lab	80	0.3%	0.2%	Higly Marginal
Cardiff North	Julie Morgan	Lab	1,782	5.1%	2.6%	Higly Marginal
Carms W & S Pembs	Angela Burns	Con	1,504	5.3%	2.7%	Higly Marginal
Ceredigion	Elin Jones	PC	1,777	6.1%	3.1%	Marginal
Aberconwy	Janet Finch-Saunders	Con	1,567	7.7%	3.9%	Marginal
Preseli Pembs	Paul Davies	Con	2,175	7.9%	4.0%	Marginal
Brecon & Radnor	Kirsty Williams	Lib Dem	2,757	9.7%	4.9%	Marginal
Montgomery	Russell George	Con	2,324	10.1%	5.1%	Marginal
Vale of Glamorgan	Jane Hutt	Lab	3,775	11.3%	5.7%	Marginal
Ynys Môn	Ieuan Wyn Jones	PC	2,937	12.2%	6.1%	Fairly Safe
Delyn	Sandy Mewies	Lab	2,881	12.4%	6.2%	Fairly Safe
Clwyd South	Ken Skates	Lab	2,659	13.2%	6.6%	Fairly Safe
Carms E & Dinefwr	Rhodri Glyn Thomas	PC	4,148	14.9%	7.5%	Fairly Safe
Clwyd West	Darren Millar	Con	4,248	16.9%	8.4%	Fairly Safe
Vale of Clwyd	Ann Jones	Lab	4,011	17.3%	8.7%	Fairly Safe
Wrexham	Lesley Griffiths	Lab	3,337	17.8%	8.9%	Fairly Safe
Gower	Edwina Hart	Lab	4,864	18.2%	9.1%	Fairly Safe
Newport West	Rosemary Butler	Lab	4,220	18.3%	9.2%	Fairly Safe
Caerphilly	Jeff Cuthbert	Lab	4,924	19.2%	9.6%	Fairly Safe
Monmouth	Nick Ramsay	Con	6,117	20.4%	10.2%	Fairly Safe
Bridgend	Carwyn Jones	Lab	6,775	21.0%	10.5%	Safe
Swansea West	Julie James	Lab	4,654	21.3%	10.7%	Fairly Safe
Cardiff West	Mark Drakeford	Lab	5,901	22.2%	11.1%	Fairly Safe
Cardiff S & Penarth	Vaughan Gething	Lab	6,259	22.7%	11.4%	Fairly Safe
Alyn & Deeside	Carl Sargeant	Lab	5,581	24.5%	12.3%	Safe
Dwyfor Meironnydd	Dafydd Elis-Thomas	PC	5,417	26.1%	13.1%	Safe
Neath	Gwenda Thomas	Lab	6,390	26.8%	13.4%	Safe
Torfaen	Lynne Neagle	Lab	6,088	27.2%	13.6%	Safe
Newport East	John Griffiths	Lab	5,388	27.7%	13.8%	Safe
Arfon	Alun Ffred Jones	PC	5,394	30.5%	15.3%	Safe
Pontypridd	Mick Antoniw	Lab	7,694	32.9%	16.5%	Safe
Rhondda	Leighton Andrews	Lab	6,739	33.6%	16.8%	Safe
Cynon Valley	Christine Chapman	Lab	6,515	34.7%	17.4%	Safe
Islwyn	Gwyn R Price	Lab	7,589	36.3%	18.1%	Solidly Safe
Merthyr Tydfil	Huw Lewis	Lab	7,051	36.5%	18.2%	Solidly Safe
Swansea East	Mike Hedges	Lab	8,281	43.7%	21.9%	Solidly Safe
Blaenau Gwent	Alun Davies	Lab	9,120	45.1%	22.6%	Solidly Safe
Ogmore	Janice Gregory	Lab	9,576	47.2%	23.6%	Solidly Safe
Aberavon	David Rees	Lab	9,311	49.3%	24.7%	Solidly Safe

The**Wales** Yearbook

13

ELECTION STATISTICS

United Kingdom

Wales

General Election 1979 (3rd May)

Party	Total votes	%	Cands	MPs	Party	Total votes	%	Cands	MPs
Con	13,697,690	43.9	622	339	Con	526,254	32.2	35	11
Lab	11,532,148	36.9	623	269	Lab	768,458	47.0	35	21
Lib	4,313,811	13.8	577	11	Lib	173,525	10.6	28	1
PC	132,544	0.4	36	2	PC	132,544	8.1	36	2
SNP	504,259	1.6	71	2					
Others	1,039,563	3.3	647	13	Others	35,807	2.2	19	1*
Totals	31,222,279	76.0	2,576	635	Totals	1,636,588	79.4	153	36

* The Speaker

General Election 1983 (9th June)

Party	Total votes	%	Cands	MPs	Party	Total votes	%	Cands	MPs
Con	13,012,183	42.4	633	397	Con	499,310	31.0	38	14
Lab	8,456,934	27.6	633	209	Lab	603,858	37.5	38	20
Alln	7,781,082	25.4	633	23	Alln	373,358	23.2	38	2
PC	125,309	0.4	38	2	PC	125,309	7.8	38	2
SNP	331,975	1.1	72	2					
Others	963,654	3.1	569	17	Others	7,151	0.4	17	0
Totals	30,671,137	72.7	2,578	650	Totals	1,608,986	76.1	169	38

General Election 1987 (11th June)

Party	Total votes	%	Cands	MPs	Party	Total votes	%	Cands	MPs
Con	13,736,405	42.2	632	375	Con	501,316	29.5	38	8
Lab	10,029,797	30.8	633	229	Lab	765,199	45.1	38	24
Alln	7,341,623	22.6	633	22	Alln	304,230	17.9	38	3
PC	123,599	0.4	38	3	PC	123,599	7.3	38	3
SNP	416,473	1.3	71	3					
Others	881,671	2.7	318	18	Others	3,742	0.2	6	0
Totals	32,529,568	75.3	2,325	650	Totals	1,698,086	78.9	154	38

General Election 1992 (9th April)

Party	Total votes	%	Cands	MPs	Party	Total votes	%	Cands	MPs
Con	14,092,891	41.9	645	336	Con	499,677	28.6	38	6
Lab	11,559,735	34.2	634	271	Lab	865,633	49.5	38	27
Lib Dem	5,999,384	17.8	632	20	Lib Dem	217,457	12.4	38	1
PC	154,439	0.5	35	4	PC	154,439	8.8	35	4
SNP	629,552	1.9	72	3					
Others	1,176,692	3.5	930	17	Others	11,590	0.7	31	0
Totals	33,612,693	77.7	2,948	651	Totals	1,748,796	79.7	180	38

General Election 1997 (1st May)

Party	Total votes	%	Cands	MPs	Party	Total votes	%	Cands	MPs
Con	9,600,940	30.7	648	165	Con	317,127	19.6	40	0
Lab	13,517,911	43.2	639	418	Lab	886,935	54.7	40	34
Lib Dem	5,243,440	16.8	639	46	Lib Dem	200,020	12.4	40	2
PC	161,030	0.5	40	4	PC	161,030	9.9	40	4
SNP	622,260	2.0	72	6	Ref	39,098	2.4	36	0
Others	2,142,621	6.8	1,686	20	Others	15,834	1.0	27	0
Totals	31,287,702	71.5	3,724	659	Totals	1,620,044	73.6	223	40

Ceidwadwyr Cymreig | Welsh Conservatives

The Welsh Conservative Party

Ground Floor, Rhymney House
1-2 Copse Walk
Cardiff Gate Business Park
Pontprennau
Cardiff
CF23 8RB

Tel: 029 2073 6562
E-mail: info@welshconservatives.com

Y Blaid Geidwadol Gymreig

Llawr Gwaelod, Tŷ Rhymni
1-2 Copse Walk
Parc Busnes Porth Caerdydd
Pontprennau
Caerdydd
CF23 8RB

Ffôn: 029 2073 6562
E-bost: info@welshconservatives.com

Labour 🌹 Llafur

To join Welsh Labour call 029 2087 7700

Welsh Labour
1 Cathedral Rd
Cardiff CF11 9HA
Tel: 029 2087 7700
Fax: 029 2022 1153

E: wales@labour.org.uk
W: www.welshlabour.org.uk

Llafur Cymru
1 Ffordd yr Eglwys Gadeiriol
Caerdydd CF11 9HA
Ffôn: 029 2087 7700
Ffacs: 029 2022 1153

GENERAL ELECTION STATISTICS 2001-2010

United Kingdom

Wales

General Election 2001 (7th June)

Party	Total votes	%	Cands	MPs	Party	Total votes	%	Cands	MPs
Con	8,357,615	31.7	643	166	Con	288,665	21.0	40	0
Lab	10,724,953	40.7	640	412	Lab	666,956	48.6	40	34
Lib Dem	4,814,321	18.3	639	52	Lib Dem	189,434	13.8	40	2
PC	195,893	0.7	40	4	PC	195,893	14.3	40	4
SNP	464,314	1.8	72	5					
Others	1,810,287	6.9	1,285	20	Others	31,598	2.3	64	0
Totals	26,367,383	59.4	3,319	659	Totals	1,372,546	61.4	224	40

General Election 2005 (5th May)

Party	Total votes	%	Cands	MPs	Party	Total votes	%	Cands	MPs
Con	8,772,473	32.3	629	197	Con	297,830	21.4	40	3
Lab	9,547,944	35.2	626	355	Lab	594,821	42.7	40	29
Lib D	5,981,874	22.1	625	62	Lib Dem	256,249	18.4	40	4
PC	174,838	0.6	40	3	PC	174,838	12.6	40	3
SNP	412,267	1.5	59	6					
Others	2,234,256	8.2	1,567	22	Others	68,981	5.0	90	1
Totals	27,123,652	61.3	3,546	645	Totals	1,392,719	62.4	250	40

General Election 2010 (6th May)

Party	Total votes	%	Cands	MPs	Party	Total votes	%	Cands	MPs
Con	10,726,614	36.1	648	307	Con	382,730	26.1	40	8
Lab	8,609,527	29.0	631	258	Lab	531,602	36.2	40	26
Lib D	6,836,824	23.0	631	57	Lib Dem	295,164	20.1	40	3
PC	165,394	0.6	40	3	PC	165,394	11.3	40	3
SNP	491,386	1.7	59	6					
Others	2,861,635	9.7	2,245	19	Others	91,801	6.3	108	0
Totals	29,691,380	100.1	4,138	650	Totals	1,466,691	100.0	268	40

ELECTORAL TRENDS IN WALES 1979-2010

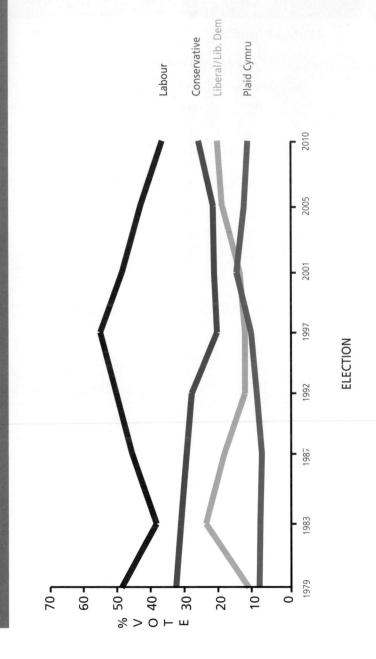

Labour Llafur
Wales / Cymru

Gen Election	Total Vote	%	MPs
1970	781,941	51.6	27
1974 Feb	745,547	46.8	24
1974 Oct	761,447	49.5	23
1979	768,458	48.6	22
1983	603,858	37.5	20
1987	765,199	45.1	24
1992	865,633	49.5	27
1997	886,935	54.7	34
2001	666,956	48.6	34
2005	594,821	42.7	29
2010	531,602	36.2	26

Welsh Liberal Democrats

Gen Election	Total Vote	%	MPs
1970	103,747	6.8	1
1974 Feb	255,423	16.0	2
1974 Oct	239,057	15.5	2
1979	173,525	10.6	1
1983	373,358	23.2	2
1987	304,230	17.9	3
1992	217,457	12.4	1
1997	200,020	12.4	2
2001	189,434	13.8	2
2005	256,249	18.4	4
2010	295,164	20.1	3

Ceidwadwyr Cymreig | Welsh Conservatives

Plaid
PLAID CYMRU

Gen Election	Total Vote	%	MPs
1970	419,884	27.7	7
1974 Feb	412,535	25.9	8
1974 Oct	367,230	23.9	8
1979	526,254	32.2	11
1983	499,310	31.0	14
1987	501,316	29.5	8
1992	499,677	28.6	6
1997	317,127	19.6	0
2001	288,665	21.0	0
2005	297,830	21.4	3
2010	382,730	26.1	8

Gen Election	Total Vote	%	MPs
1970	175,016	11.5	0
1974 Feb	171,374	10.7	2
1974 Oct	166,321	10.8	3
1979	132,544	8.1	2
1983	125,309	7.8	2
1987	123,599	7.3	3
1992	154,439	8.8	4
1997	161,030	9.9	4
2001	195,893	14.3	4
2005	174,838	12.6	3
2010	165,394	11.3	3

ELECTION STATISTICS

2011 ASSEMBLY ELECTION IN WALES

CONSTITUENCIES

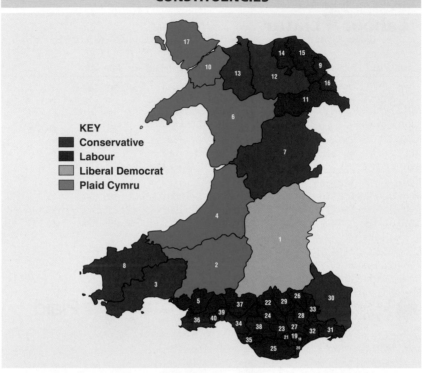

KEY
- Conservative
- Labour
- Liberal Democrat
- Plaid Cymru

REGIONAL LIST

Mid & West Wales

1 Brecon & Radnorshire
2 Carmarthen East & Dinefwr
3 Carms West & South Pembs
4 Ceredigion
5 Llanelli
6 Dwyfor
  Meirionnydd
7 Montgomery
8 Preseli Pembs

Regional AMs

North Wales

9 Alyn & Deeside
10 Arfon
11 Clwyd South
12 Clwyd West
13 Aberconwy
14 Vale of Clwyd
15 Delyn
16 Wrexham
17 Ynys Môn

Regional AMs

South Wales Central

18 Cardiff Central
19 Cardiff North
20 Cardiff South & Penarth
21 Cardiff West
22 Cynon Valley
23 Pontypridd
24 Rhondda
25 Vale of
   Glamorgan

Regional AMs

South Wales East

26 Blaenau Gwent
27 Caerphilly
28 Islwyn
29 Merthyr Tydfil
30 Monmouth
31 Newport East
32 Newport West
33 Torfaen

South Wales West

34 Aberavon
35 Bridgend
36 Gower
37 Neath
38 Ogmore
39 Swansea East
40 Swansea West

Party Balance in the Chamber

Labour	30
Conservative	14
Plaid Cymru	11
Liberal Democrat	5
Total	**60**

AMs	Party	Constituency	Year first elected
Leighton Andrews	Labour	Rhondda	2003
Mick Antoniw	Labour	Pontypridd	2011
Mohammad Asghar	Conservative	South Wales East	2007
Peter Black	Lib Dem	South Wales West	1999
Angela Burns	Conservative	Carmarthen W & S Pembs	2007
Rosemary Butler	Labour	Newport West	1999
Christine Chapman	Labour	Cynon Valley	1999
Jeff Cuthbert	Labour	Caerphilly	2003
Alun Davies	Labour	Blaenau Gwent	2011
(First elected as Regional Member for Mid & West Wales in 2007)			
Andrew R T Davies	Conservative	South Wales Central	2007
Byron Davies	Conservative	South Wales West	2011
Keith Davies	Labour	Llanelli	2011
Jocelyn Davies	Plaid Cymru	South Wales East	1999
Paul Davies	Conservative	Preseli Pembrokeshire	2007
Suzy Davies	Conservative	South Wales West	2011
Mark Drakeford	Labour	Cardiff West	2011
Rt Hon Dafydd Elis-Thomas	Plaid Cymru	Dwyfor Meirionnydd	1999
Rebecca Evans	Labour	Mid & West Wales	2011
Janet Finch-Saunders	Conservative	Aberconwy	2011
Russell George	Conservative	Montgomeryshire	2011
Vaughan Gething	Labour	Cardiff South & Penarth	2011
William Graham	Conservative	South Wales East	1999
Janice Gregory	Labour	Ogmore	1999
John Griffiths	Labour	Newport East	1999
Lesley Griffiths	Labour	Wrexham	2007
Llyr Huws Gruffydd	Plaid Cymru	North Wales	2011
Edwina Hart	Labour	Gower	1999
Mike Hedges	Labour	Swansea East	2011
Jane Hutt	Labour	Vale of Glamorgan	1999
Mark Isherwood	Conservative	North Wales	2003
Julie James	Labour	Swansea West	2011
Bethan Jenkins	Plaid Cymru	South Wales West	2007
Ann Jones	Labour	Vale of Clwyd	1999
Alun Ffred Jones	Plaid Cymru	Arfon	2003
Rt Hon Carwyn Jones	Labour	Bridgend	1999
Elin Jones	Plaid Cymru	Ceredigion	1999
Ieuan Wyn Jones	Plaid Cymru	Ynys Môn	1999
Huw Lewis	Labour	Merthyr Tydfil & Rhymney	1999
David Melding	Conservative	South Wales Central	1999
Sandy Mewies	Labour	Delyn	1999
Darren Millar	Conservative	Clwyd West	2007
Julie Morgan	Labour	Cardiff North	2011

CURRENT ASSEMBLY MEMBERS

AMs	Party	Constituency	Year first elected
Lynne Neagle	Labour	Torfaen	1999
Eluned Parrott	Lib Dem	South Wales Central	2011
William Powell	Lib Dem	Mid & West Wales	2011
Gwyn R Price	Labour	Islwyn	2011
Jenny Rathbone	Labour	Cardiff Central	2011
Nick Ramsay	Conservative	Monmouth	2007
David Rees	Labour	Aberavon	2011
Aled Roberts	Lib Dem	North Wales	2011
Antoinette Sandbach	Conservative	North Wales	2011
Carl Sargeant	Labour	Alyn & Deeside	2003
Ken Skates	Labour	Clwyd South	2011
Gwenda Thomas	Labour	Neath	1999
Rhodri Glyn Thomas	Plaid Cymru	Carmarthen East & Dinefwr	1999
Simon Thomas	Plaid Cymru	Mid & West Wales	2011
Joyce Watson	Labour	Mid & West Wales	2007
Lindsay Whittle	Plaid Cymru	South Wales East	2011
Kirsty Williams	Lib Dem	Brecon & Radnorshire	1999
Leanne Wood	Plaid Cymru	South Wales Central	2003

Party Composition of the National Assembly

Party	1999 AMs	2003 AMs	2007 AMs	2011 AMs
Labour	28	30	26	30
Conservative	9	11	12	14
Plaid Cymru	17	12	15	11
Liberal Democrat	6	6	6	5
Forward Wales	-	1	-	-
Independent	-	-	1	-
Total	60	60	60	60

ASSEMBLY ELECTION STATISTICS 1999-2011

Constituency Election   Regional Election

1999 Election (6th May)

Party	Total votes	%	Cands	AMs	Party	Total votes	%	Lists	AMs
Lab	384,671	37.6	40	27	Lab	361,657	35.5	5	1
PC	290,572	28.4	40	9	PC	312,048	30.6	5	8
Con	162,133	15.8	40	1	Con	168,206	16.5	5	8
Lib Dem	137,857	13.5	40	3	Lib Dem	128,008	12.5	5	3
Green	1,002	0.1	1	0	Green	25,858	2.5	5	0
Others	46,990	4.6	38	0	Others	26,080	2.4	19	0
Totals	1,023,225	100.0	199	40	Totals	1,021,857	100.0	44	20

2003 Election (1st May)

Party	Total votes	%	Cands	AMs	Party	Total votes	%	Lists	AMs
Lab	340,515	40.0	40	30	Lab	310,658	36.6	5	0
PC	180,185	21.2	40	5	PC	167,653	19.7	5	7
Con	169,432	19.9	40	1	Con	162,725	19.2	5	10
Lib Dem	120,220	14.1	40	3	Lib Dem	108,013	12.7	5	3
Others	40,053	4.8	40	1	Green	30,028	3.5	5	0
					Others	100,503	8.3	26	0
Totals	850,403	100.0	200	40	Totals	849,552	100.0	51	20

2007 Election (3rd May)

Party	Total votes	%	Cands	AMs	Party	Total votes	%	Lists	AMs
Lab	314,925	32.2	40	24	Lab	288,954	29.6	5	2
PC	219,121	22.4	40	7	PC	204,757	21.0	5	8
Con	218,730	22.4	40	5	Con	209,154	21.5	5	7
Lib Dem	144,410	14.8	40	3	Lib Dem	114,500	11.7	5	3
Others	80,906	8.3	37	1	Green	33,803	3.5	5	0
					Others	123,617	12.7	42	0
Totals	978,092	100.0	197	40	Totals	974,785	100.0	67	20

2011 Election (5th May)

Party	Total votes	%	Cands	AMs	Party	Total votes	%	Lists	AMs
Lab	401,677	42.3	40	28	Lab	349,935	36.9	5	2
Con	237,389	25.0	40	6	Con	213,773	22.5	5	8
PC	182,907	19.3	40	5	PC	169,799	17.9	5	6
Lib Dem	100,259	10.6	40	1	Lib Dem	76,349	8.0	5	4
Others	27,021	2.8	16	0	Green	32,649	3.4	5	0
					Others	106,386	11.2	35	0
Totals	949,253	100.0	176	40	Totals	948,891	100.0	60	20

	Total Vote	%	AMs
Assembly Constituency Election			
1999	384,671	37.6	27
2003	340,515	40.0	30
2007	314,925	32.2	24
2011	401,677	42.3	28

	Total Vote	%	AMs
Assembly Constituency Election			
1999	137,857	13.5	3
2003	120,220	14.1	3
2007	144,410	14.8	3
2011	100,259	10.6	1

Ceidwadwyr Cymreig | Welsh Conservatives

	Total Vote	%	AMs
Assembly Constituency Election			
1999	162,133	15.8	1
2003	169,432	19.9	1
2007	218,730	22.4	5
2011	237,389	25.0	6

Plaid PLAID CYMRU

	Total Vote	%	AMs
Assembly Constituency Election			
1999	290,572	28.4	9
2003	180,185	21.2	5
2007	219,121	22.4	7
2011	182,907	19.3	5

NATIONAL ASSEMBLY ELECTIONS 1999-2011

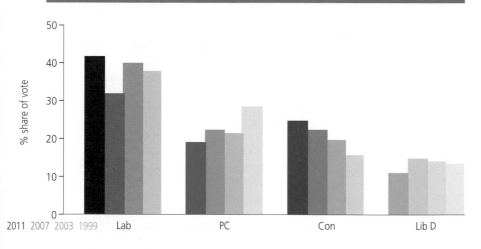

ELECTION STATISTICS

THE 2010 GENERAL ELECTION IN WALES

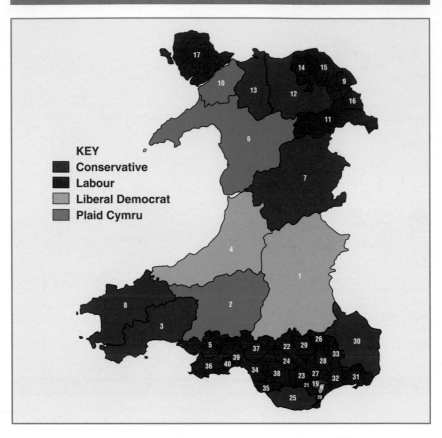

KEY
- Conservative
- Labour
- Liberal Democrat
- Plaid Cymru

Parliamentary Constituencies:

1 Brecon & Radnorshire
2 Carmarthen East & Dinefwr
3 Carmarthen West & S. Pembs
4 Ceredigion
5 Llanelli
6 Dwyfor Meirionnydd
7 Montgomeryshire
8 Preseli Pembrokeshire
9 Alyn & Deeside
10 Arfon
11 Clwyd South
12 Clwyd West
13 Aberconwy
14 Delyn
15 Vale of Clwyd
16 Wrexham
17 Ynys Môn
18 Cardiff Central
19 Cardiff North
20 Cardiff South & Penarth
21 Cardiff West
22 Cynon Valley
23 Pontypridd
24 Rhondda
25 Vale of Glamorgan
26 Blaenau Gwent
27 Caerphilly
28 Islwyn
29 Merthyr Tydfil & Rhymney
30 Monmouth
31 Newport East
32 Newport West
33 Torfaen
34 Aberavon
35 Bridgend
36 Gower
37 Neath
38 Ogmore
39 Swansea East
40 Swansea West

MPs	Party	Constituency	Year first elected
Guto Bebb	Con	Aberconwy	2010
Kevin Brennan	Lab	Cardiff West	2001
Chris Bryant	Lab	Rhondda	2001
Alun Cairns	Con	Vale of Glamorgan	2010
Martin Caton	Lab	Gower	1997
Rt Hon Ann Clwyd	Lab	Cynon Valley	1984
Stephen Crabb	Con	Preseli Pembrokeshire	2005
Wayne David	Lab	Caerphilly	2001
David Davies	Con	Monmouth	2005
Geraint Davies	Lab	Swansea West	2010
Glyn Davies	Con	Montgomeryshire	2010
Jonathan Edwards	PC	Carmarthen East & Dinefwr	2010
Chris Evans	Lab	Islwyn	2010
Jonathan Evans	Con	Cardiff North	2010
Paul Flynn	Lab	Newport West	1987
Dr Hywel Francis	Lab	Aberavon	2001
Nia Griffiths	Lab	Llanelli	2005
Rt Hon Peter Hain	Lab	Neath	1991
Rt Hon David Hanson	Lab	Delyn	1992
Simon Hart	Con	Carmarthen West & South Pembs	2010
Dai Harvard	Lab	Merthyr Tydfil & Rhymney	2001
Huw Irranca-Davies	Lab	Ogmore	2002
Elfyn Llwyd	PC	Dwyfor Meirionnydd	1992
Sian James	Lab	Swansea East	2005
David Jones	Con	Clwyd West	2005
Susan Elan Jones	Lab	Clwyd South	2010
Ian Lucas	Lab	Wrexham	2001
Rt Hon Alun Michael	Lab	Cardiff South & Penarth	1987
Madeleine Moon	Lab	Bridgend	2005
Jessica Morden	Lab	Newport East	2005
Rt Hon Paul Murphy	Lab	Torfaen	1987
Albert Owen	Lab	Ynys Môn	2001
Chris Ruane	Lab	Vale of Clwyd	1997
Nick Smith	Lab	Blaenau Gwent	2010
Owen Smith	Lab	Pontypridd	2010
Mark Tami	Lab	Alyn & Deeside	2001
Mark Williams	Lib D	Ceredigion	2005
Hywel Williams	PC	Arfon	2001
Roger Williams	Lib D	Brecon & Radnorshire	2001
Jenny Willott	Lib D	Cardiff Central	2005

REFERENDUMS IN WALES

The EEC Referendum 1975 (5th June)

County	Electorate	Turn-out	Yes Votes	% of Poll
Clwyd	272,798	65.8	123,980	69.1
Dyfed	241,415	67.5	109,184	67.6
Gwent	314,369	68.2	132,557	62.1
Gwynedd	167,706	64.3	76,421	70.6
Mid Glam	390,175	66.6	147,348	56.9
Powys	76,531	67.9	38,724	74.3
South Glam	275,324	66.7	127,932	69.5
West Glam	272,818	67.4	112,989	61.6
Wales		**66.7**	**869,135**	**64.8**
United Kingdom		64.0	17,378,581	67.2

The Devolution Referendum 1979 (1st March)

County	Electorate	Turn-out	Yes Votes	% of Poll	% of * Electorate
Clwyd	282,106	51.6	31,384	21.6	11.1
Dyfed	245,229	65.2	44,849	28.1	18.3
Gwent	316,545	55.8	21,369	12.1	6.8
Gwynedd	169,530	64.0	37,363	34.4	22.0
Mid Glam	390,755	59.1	46,747	20.2	12.0
Powys	80,097	66.6	9,843	18.4	12.3
South Glam	280,390	59.2	21,830	13.1	7.8
West Glam	273,398	58.0	29,663	18.7	10.8
Wales	**2,038,049**	**58.8**	**243,048**	**20.3**	**11.9**
Scotland	3,747,112	63.6	1,230,937	51.6	32.8

* The Wales Act 1978 made implementation of the Devolution proposals conditional upon the 40 percent rule. This clause mandated the Secretary of State to lay an order repealing the Devolution Acts if less than 40 percent of the eligible electorate voted in favour of the proposals.

Ceredigion Mayoral Referendum 2004 (20th May)

Do you support the proposal for a directly elected Mayor for Ceredigion County Council?

Votes for	5,308	27.5%
Votes against	14,013	72.5%
Total	19,321	
Turn out		36.3%

REFERENDUMS IN WALES

The Devolution Referendum 1997 (18th September)

County	Turn-out	Yes Votes	%	No votes	%
Blaenau Gwent	49.6%	15,237	55.8%	11,928	43.7%
Bridgend	50.8%	27,632	54.1%	23,172	45.4%
Caerphilly	49.5%	34,830	54.7%	28,841	45.3%
Cardiff	47.0%	47,527	44.2%	59,589	55.4%
Carmarthenshire	56.6%	49,115	65.3%	26,119	34.7%
Ceredigion	57.1%	18,304	58.8%	12,614	40.6%
Conwy	51.6%	18,369	40.9%	26,521	59.1%
Denbighshire	49.9%	14,271	40.8%	20,732	59.2%
Flintshire	41.1%	17,746	38.1%	28,707	61.6%
Gwynedd	60.0%	35,425	63.9%	19,859	35.8%
Isle of Anglesey	57.0%	15,649	50.7%	15,095	48.9%
Merthyr Tydfil	49.8%	12,707	57.9%	9,121	41.6%
Monmouthshire	50.7%	10,592	31.6%	22,403	66.9%
Neath Port Talbot	52.1%	36,730	66.3%	18,463	33.3%
Newport	46.1%	16,172	37.3%	27,017	62.3%
Pembrokeshire	52.8%	19,979	42.8%	26,712	57.2%
Powys	56.5%	23,038	42.7%	30,966	57.3%
Rhondda Cynon Taf	49.9%	51,201	58.5%	36,362	41.5%
Swansea	47.3%	42,789	52.0%	39,561	48.0%
Torfaen	45.6%	15,756	49.7%	15,854	50.0%
Vale of Glamorgan	54.5%	17,776	36.6%	30,613	63.1%
Wrexham	42.5%	18,574	45.2%	22,449	54.6%
Wales	**50.3%**	**559,419**	**50.3%**	**552,698**	**49.7%**
Scotland	61.5%	1,208,971	74.4%	440,623	25.6%

Assembly Powers Referendum 2011 (3rd March)

County	Turn-out	Yes Vote	%	No Vote	%	Total Votes Cast
Blaenau Gwent	32.4%	11,869	68.9%	5,366	31.1%	17,235
Bridgend	35.6%	25,063	68.1%	11,736	31.9%	36,799
Caerphilly	34.6%	28,431	64.4%	15,751	35.7%	44,182
Cardiff	35.2%	53,427	61.4%	33,606	38.6%	87,033
Carmarthenshire	44.4%	42,979	70.8%	17,712	29.2%	60,691
Ceredigion	44.1%	16,505	66.2%	8,412	33.8%	24,917
Conwy	33.8%	18,368	59.7%	12,390	40.3%	30,758
Denbighshire	34.5%	15,793	61.9%	9,742	38.2%	25,535
Flintshire	29.5%	21,119	62.1%	12,913	37.9%	34,032
Gwynedd	43.4%	28,200	76.0%	8,891	24.0%	37,091
Isle of Anglesey	43.8%	14,011	64.8%	7,620	35.2%	21,631
Merthyr Tydfil	30.1%	9,136	68.9%	4,132	31.1%	13,268
Monmouthshire	35.8%	12,381	49.4%	12,701	50.6%	25,082
Neath Port Talbot	38.0%	29,957	73.0%	11,079	27.0%	41,036
Newport	27.9%	15,983	54.8%	13,204	45.2%	29,187
Pembrokeshire	38.7%	19,600	55.0%	16,050	45.0%	35,650
Powys	39.7%	21,072	51.6%	19,730	48.4%	40,802
Rhondda Cynon Taf	34.6%	43,051	70.7%	17,834	29.3%	60,885
Swansea	32.9%	38,496	63.2%	22,409	36.8%	60,905
Torfaen	33.8%	14,655	62.8%	8,688	37.2%	23,343
Vale of Glamorgan	40.1%	19,430	52.5%	17,551	47.5%	36,981
Wrexham	27.0%	17,606	64.1%	9,863	35.9%	27,469
Wales	**35.4%**	**517,132**	**63.5**	**297,380**	**36.5**	**814,512**

LOCAL GOVERNMENT IN WALES

LOCAL ELECTION RESULTS 2012

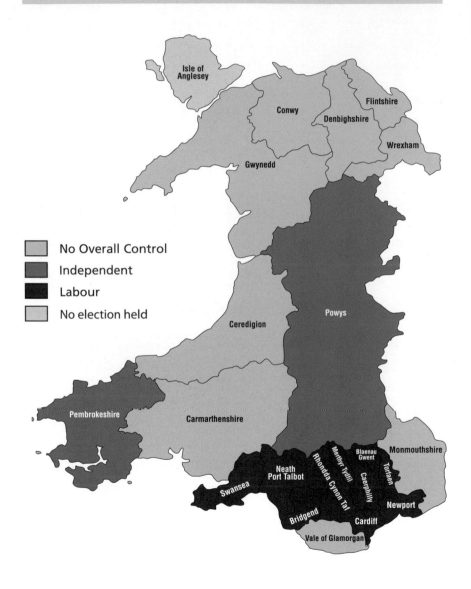

No Overall Control
Independent
Labour
No election held

Isle of Anglesey

Conwy

Flintshire

Denbighshire

Wrexham

Gwynedd

Powys

Ceredigion

Pembrokeshire

Carmarthenshire

Monmouthshire

Blaenau Gwent

Merthyr Tydfil

Neath Port Talbot

Rhondda Cynon Taf

Caerphilly

Torfaen

Swansea

Newport

Bridgend

Cardiff

Vale of Glamorgan

Local Elections Results 2012

County	Labour	Lib D	Con	PC	Ind	All Others	Votes Cast
Blaenau Gwent	**26,812**	**0**	**89**	**315**	**12,759**	**6,049**	**46,024**
2012	58.3%	0.0%	0.2%	0.7%	27.7%	13.1%	
2008	38.4%	5.9%	0.5%	1.1%	31.8%	22.3%	
Change	19.9%	-5.9%	-0.3%	-0.4%	-4.1%	-8.6%	
Bridgend	**28,989**	**4,130**	**5,824**	**3,444**	**10,156**	**912**	**53,455**
2012	54.2%	7.7%	10.9%	6.4%	19.0%	1.7%	
2008	44.0%	20.6%	18.2%	2.2%	14.9%	0.1%	
Change	10.2%	-12.9%	-7.3%	4.2%	4.1%	1.6%	
Caerphilly	**51,697**	**157**	**3,544**	**31,618**	**11,806**	**174**	**98,996**
2012	52.2%	0.2%	3.6%	31.9%	11.9%	0.2%	
2008	38.2%	1.5%	4.4%	41.2%	14.6%	0.1%	
Change	14.0%	-1.3%	-0.8%	-9.3%	-2.7%	0.1%	
Cardiff	**95,444**	**42,715**	**45,079**	**30,989**	**11,681**	**15,070**	**240,978**
2012	39.6%	17.7%	18.7%	12.9%	4.8%	6.3%	
2008	27.1%	26.2%	27.3%	12.5%	4.9%	2.0%	
Change	12.5%	-8.5%	-8.6%	0.4%	-0.1%	4.3%	
Carmarthenshire	**19,175**	**675**	**1,914**	**29,874**	**24,938**	**2,583**	**79,159**
2012	24.2%	0.9%	2.4%	37.7%	31.5%	3.3%	
2008	22.8%	1.1%	1.2%	38.0%	30.9%	5.9%	
Change	1.4%	-0.2%	1.2%	-0.3%	0.6%	-2.6%	
Ceredigion	**884**	**6,681**	**1,080**	**10,393**	**7,710**	**0**	**26,748**
2012	3.3%	25.0%	4.0%	38.9%	28.8%	0.0%	
2008	3.3%	23.4%	2.7%	43.3%	20.8%	6.4%	
Change	0.0%	1.6%	1.3%	-4.4%	8.0%	-6.4%	
Conwy	**7,000**	**5,356**	**16,641**	**6,690**	**14,235**	**1,312**	**51,234**
2012	13.7%	10.5%	32.5%	13.1%	27.8%	2.6%	
2008	11.0%	11.4%	37.8%	11.7%	25.6%	2.5%	
Change	2.7%	-0.9%	-5.3%	1.4%	2.2%	0.1%	
Denbighshire	**14,629**	**1,418**	**11,670**	**3,881**	**12,426**	**481**	**44,505**
2012	32.9%	3.2%	26.2%	8.7%	27.9%	1.1%	
2008	19.8%	4.3%	33.8%	11.3%	25.2%	5.6%	
Change	13.1%	-1.1%	-7.6%	-2.6%	2.7%	-4.5%	
Flintshire	**20,117**	**3,979**	**4,080**	**796**	**15,840**	**2,341**	**47,153**
2012	42.7%	8.4%	8.7%	1.7%	33.6%	5.0%	
2008	28.4%	16.6%	10.7%	0.9%	30.1%	13.2%	
Change	14.3%	-8.2%	2.0%	0.8%	3.5%	-8.2%	
Gwynedd	**2,891**	**701**	**405**	**12,797**	**7,594**	**7,314**	**31,702**
2012	9.1%	2.2%	1.3%	40.4%	24.0%	23.1%	
2008	10.6%	5.1%	1.4%	36.3%	23.8%	22.8%	
Change	-1.5%	-2.9%	-0.1%	4.1%	0.2%	0.3%	
Isle of Anglesey							
2012			No election held				
2008	12.7%	2.8%	5.0%	22.9%	47.4%	9.2%	
Merthyr Tydfil	**23,317**	**2,130**	**0**	**1,059**	**14,118**	**3,183**	**43,807**
2012	53.2%	4.9%	0.0%	2.4%	32.2%	7.3%	
2008	37.1%	17.7%	0.0%	2.3%	36.5%	6.5%	
Change	16.1%	-12.8%	0.0%	0.1%	-4.3%	0.7%	

Local Elections Results 2012

County	Labour	Lib D	Con	PC	Ind	All Others	Votes Cast
Monmouthshire	**7,241**	**1,785**	**8,572**	**567**	**5,971**	**221**	**24,357**
2012	29.7%	7.3%	35.2%	2.3%	24.5%	0.9%	
2008	15.1%	20.1%	46.1%	3.8%	12.7%	2.3%	
Change	14.0%	-12.8%	-10.9%	-1.5%	11.8%	-1.4%	
Neath Port Talbot	**38,596**	**1,057**	**669**	**11,575**	**4,628**	**11,035**	**67,560**
2012	57.1%	1.6%	1.0%	17.1%	6.9%	16.3%	
2008	49.0%	3.2%	0.8%	18.2%	10.8%	18.0%	
Change	8.1%	-1.6%	0.2%	-1.1%	-3.9%	-1.7%	
Newport	**47,083**	**9,569**	**25,116**	**1,749**	**3,245**	**844**	**87,606**
2012	53.7%	10.9%	28.7%	2.0%	3.7%	1.0%	
2008	35.9%	21.5%	37.6%	3.8%	1.2%	0.0%	
Change	17.8%	-10.6%	-8.9%	-1.8%	2.5%	1.0%	
Pembrokeshire	**3,780**	**238**	**5,499**	**2,621**	**13,351**	**7,434**	**32,923**
2012	11.5%	0.7%	16.7%	8.0%	40.6%	22.6%	
2008	14.3%	6.8%	17.2%	6.7%	36.0%	19.1%	
Change	-2.8%	-6.1%	-0.5%	1.3%	4.6%	3.5%	
Powys	**2,956**	**6,244**	**5,866**	**87**	**14,770**	**1,998**	**31,921**
2012	9.3%	19.6%	18.4%	0.3%	46.3%	6.3%	
2008	4.4%	21.9%	19.7%	0.4%	41.5%	12.3%	
Change	4.9%	-2.3%	-1.3%	-0.1%	4.8%	-6.0%	
RCT	**54,126**	**2,350**	**2,296**	**27,318**	**8,246**	**1,427**	**95,763**
2012	56.5%	2.5%	2.4%	28.5%	8.6%	1.5%	
2008	52.7%	3.6%	0.6%	36.9%	5.4%	0.8%	
Change	3.8%	-1.1%	1.8%	-8.4%	3.2%	0.7%	
Swansea	**79,341**	**25,967**	**15,961**	**7,363**	**9,455**	**10,394**	**148,481**
2012	53.4%	17.5%	10.7%	5.0%	6.4%	7.0%	
2008	31.0%	28.5%	16.8%	7.0%	6.2%	10.5%	
Change	22.4%	-11.0%	-6.0%	-2.0%	0.2%	-3.5%	
Torfaen	**23,471**	**533**	**5,781**	**3,608**	**15,516**	**909**	**49,818**
2012	47.1%	1.1%	11.6%	7.2%	31.1%	1.8%	
2008	43.7%	6.5%	11.0%	5.0%	25.5%	8.3%	
Change	3.4%	-5.4%	0.6%	2.2%	5.6%	-6.5%	
Vale of Glamorgan	**27,792**	**217**	**26,501**	**13,451**	**4,862**	**7,573**	**80,396**
2012	34.6%	0.3%	33.0%	16.7%	6.0%	9.4%	
2008	24.6%	1.4%	44.9%	20.6%	8.0%	0.5%	
Change	9.9%	-1.2%	-12.0%	-3.9%	-2.0%	9.1%	
Wrexham	**15,245**	**4,204**	**4,557**	**2,567**	**9,717**	**490**	**36,780**
2012	41.4%	11.4%	12.4%	7.0%	26.4%	1.3%	
2008	28.6%	20.1%	11.6%	3.3%	27.5%	9.0%	
Change	12.8%	-8.7%	0.8%	3.7%	-1.1%	-7.7%	
WALES	**590,586**	**120,106**	**191,144**	**202,762**	**233,024**	**81,744**	**1,419,366**
2012	**41.6%**	**8.5%**	**13.5%**	**14.3%**	**16.4%**	**5.8%**	
2008	**30.2%**	**14.2%**	**17.6%**	**15.7%**	**16.1%**	**6.2%**	
Change	**11.4%**	**-5.7%**	**-4.1%**	**-1.4%**	**0.3%**	**-0.4%**	

EUROPEAN PARLIAMENT ELECTIONS

The elections to the European Parliament on 4 June 2009 produced some remarkable results in Wales. For the first time in living memory, the Conservative Party topped the poll and, had this vote been based on Parliamentary constituencies, would have won 16 seats. The election was also notable in that the United Kingdom Independence Party (UKIP) polled 12.8% of the vote cast and were thus allocated one seat under the D'Hondt formula rules. The UKIP vote exceeded that of the Liberal Democrats. John Bufton, lead candidate on the UKIP list, was duly elected and joins a growing UKIP group of MEPs in the European Parliament.

Wales's other MEPs comprise one each for the Labour Party, the Conservative Party and Plaid Cymru. With the exception of Jill Evans (Plaid Cymru), all the MEPs are new Members. Overall Labour representation fell to one but, given the remarkable parity in vote for the first three parties, the proportional element of the electoral system accurately reflected public opinion as it is intended to do.

EUROPEAN ELECTION RESULT 2009

Party	Total Votes	%	MEPs elected
Conservatives	145,193	21.2	Dr Kay Swinburne
Labour	138,852	20.3	Derek Vaughan
Plaid Cymru	126,702	18.5	Jill Evans
UKIP	87,585	12.8	John Bufton
Liberal Democrats	73,082	10.7	-
Others	113,106	16.6	-
		Turnout	
Total	684,520	30.5%	

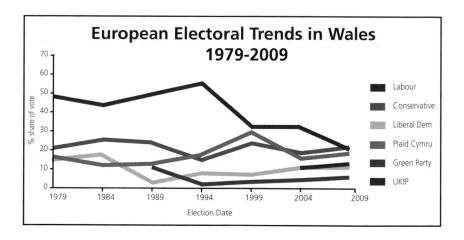

European Electoral Trends in Wales 1979-2009

EUROPEAN PARLIAMENT ELECTIONS

European Election 1979 (7th June)

Party	Total votes	%	MEPs
Con	259,729	36.6	1
Lab	294,978	41.5	3
Lib Dem	67,962	9.6	0
PC	83,399	11.7	0
Others	4,008	0.6	0
Total	710,076	36.0	4

European Election 1984 (14th June)

Party	Total votes	%	MEPs
Con	214,086	25.4	1
Lab	375,982	44.5	3
Lib Dem	146,947	17.4	0
PC	103,031	12.2	0
Others	4,266	0.5	0
Total	844,312	39.7	4

European Election 1989 (15th June)

Party	Total votes	%	MEPs
Con	209,313	23.5	0
Lab	436,730	48.9	4
Lib Dem	28,785	3.2	0
PC	115,062	12.9	0
Green	99,546	11.2	0
Others	3,153	0.4	0
Total	892,589	40.7	4

European Election 1994 (9th June)

Party	Total votes	%	MEPs
Con	138,323	14.6	0
Lab	530,749	55.9	5
Lib Dem	82,480	8.7	0
PC	162,478	17.1	0
Green	19,413	2.0	0
Others	16,689	1.8	0
Total	950,132	43.1	5

European Election 1999 (10th June)

Party	Total votes	%	MEPs
Con	142,631	22.8	1
Lab	199,690	31.9	2
Lib Dem	51,283	8.2	0
PC	185,235	29.6	2
Green	16,146	2.6	0
Others	31,440	5.0	0
Total	626,425	28.1	5

European Election 2004 (10th June)

Party	Total votes	%	MEPs
Con	177,771	19.4	1
Lab	297,810	32.5	2
Lib Dem	96,116	10.5	0
PC	159,888	17.4	1
UKIP	96,677	10.5	0
Green	32,761	3.6	0
Others	56,663	6.2	0
Total	917,686	41.9	4

EUROPEAN PARLIAMENT ELECTIONS

Elections to the European Parliament are held every five years. Between 1979 and 2004 Wales returned four MEPs elected from large regional seats made up of eight to ten Parliamentary constituencies. In 1994 these seats were reorganized slightly and five MEPs were returned. In 1999 the electoral system changed and Wales became a single electoral region, returning five members. Electors vote for a party list, electing the parties with the highest average number of votes per candidate elected. Following enlargement of the European Union, the number of MEPs returned from the United Kingdom was reduced from 87 to 79 and those from Wales from five to four. The method of election remained the same, based upon a simple, proportional, party list system.

MEPs from Wales 1979-2009

Mid & West Wales
Ann Clwyd	Labour	1979 - 1984
David Morris	Labour	1984 - 1989
Eluned Morgan	Labour	1989 - 1999

North Wales
Beata Brookes	Conservative	1979 - 1989
Joe Wilson	Labour	1989 - 1999

South Wales
Win Griffith	Labour	1979 - 1989
Wayne David	Labour	1989 - 1999

South East Wales
Allan Rogers	Labour	1979 - 1984
Llew Smith	Labour	1984 - 1994
Glenys Kinnock	Labour	1994 - 1999

South Wales Central
Wayne David	Labour	1994 - 1999

WALES
Eluned Morgan	Labour	1999 - 2009
Glenys Kinnock	Labour	1999 - 2009
Jill Evans	Plaid Cymru	1999 -
Eurig Wyn	Plaid Cymru	1999 - 2004
Jonathan Evans	Conservative	1999 - 2009
John Bufton	UKIP	2009 -
Kay Swinburne	Conservative	2009 -
Derek Vaughan	Labour	2009 -

WALES

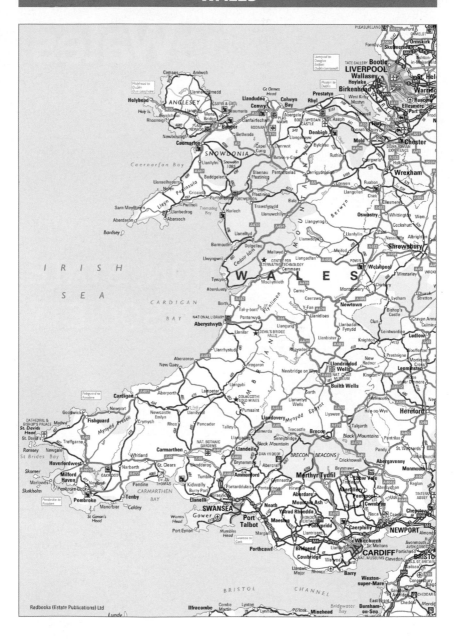

The Wales Yearbook

13

WALES: NATION, STATE & SOCIETY

The**Wales** Yearbook

13

WELSH POLITICIAN OF THE YEAR

The Wales Yearbook

Welsh Politician of the Year Awards

televised by **itv** Wales

The annual Wales Yearbook Welsh Political Awards were established to recognise the contribution made to Wales by MPs, AMs and MEPs. This contribution may comprise recognition for particular initiatives, committee work, persistent scrutiny, articulation of a constituency matter, or an amalgam of all these activities.

At a time of increasing disillusionment with politics and the political process, our purpose is to acknowledge and promote the outstanding Politicians of the Year.

Nominations for the awards are made on-line by viewers to ITV Wales and the general public. Further nominations are also proposed by members of the panel of judges.

2011 Awards

Lifetime Achievement	**Rt Hon Lord Morris of Aberavon**
Welsh Politician of the Year	**Leighton Andrews AM**
Local Politician of the Year	**Cllr Alun Thomas**
MP of the Year	**Rt Hon Cheryl Gillian MP**
AM of the Year	**Alun Ffred Jones AM**
Campaigner of the Year	**Chris Bryant MP**
Member to Watch	**Eluned Parrott AM**

Campaigner of the Year Chris Bryant MP
Labour, Rhondda

Since his election in 2001, Chris Bryant has had a highly successful Parliamentary career; rising from novice backbencher to senior Government Minister by 2010. In Opposition he has proved equally tenacious, becoming the scourge of the Murdoch empire. A victim of illegal intrusion of privacy himself, Chris Bryant has campaigned vigorously on the issue of phone hacking and other allegations against the News of the World and other newspapers. His leading role in pursuit of this wrongdoing was recognised by the Speaker of the House of Commons, who granted him the right to open an emergency debate on the phone hacking scandal. The campaign is ongoing, but his commitment to date easily warrants recognition as Campaigner of the Year.

Member to Watch Eluned Parrott AM
Liberal Democrat, South Wales Central

Eluned Parrott had not expected to join the Assembly following the election. As the second placed candidate on the Lib Dem list her chances seemed slight, but electoral swing and bureaucratic confusion combined to ensure her success. The Labour gain of Cardiff Central and the misfortune of her colleague, John Dixon, in being a member of a proscribed public body which led to his disqualification, secured her election. Despite this unorthodox arrival, Eluned Parrott soon established herself as an able and articulate Member, questioning and challenging Ministers and playing a full part in the much reduced Liberal Democrat Assembly group. Lib Dems in Wales can only ever aspire to Coalition Government but when future electoral circumstances create such an opportunity, Eluned Parrott is likely to have a significant role.

Welsh Politician of the Year Leighton Andrews AM
Labour, Rhondda

The restoration of single party government after the election gave the Labour Party full administrative authority for the Welsh Government, but, due to the lack of a clear majority, little opportunity for radical legislation. Individual Ministers however, have been able to take up their portfolios and confront current issues – none more so than Leighton Andrews, Minister for Education and Skills. He has made it abundantly clear that he thinks our schools can do better – and must do better. In higher education he has pressed for mergers and rationalisation and, in the face of major changes in student tuition fees in England, has determined that Wales should pursue its own agenda and priorities. His dynamism and persistence in this key policy field illustrates both the opportunities for Wales to take advantage of devolution and deliver the pledge to define its own future. His energy, commitment and determination to succeed have stood out clearly and warrant the award of Welsh Politician of the Year 2011.

Local Politician of the Year Cllr Alun Thomas
Labour, Neath Port Talbot County Borough Council

In the local elections of 2008 only Neath Port Talbot and Rhondda Cynon Taf retained Labour majorities. Labour had been reduced to its hard-core heartland. Appropriately enough, winner of the Local Politician of the Year is a former miner, the leader of Neath Port Talbot council, Councillor Alun Thomas. Under his leadership Neath Port Talbot has become an exemplar Council, called upon by the Minister for Local Government to take over some areas of local administration from other 'failing' Authorities. Alun – or Ali – Thomas also won great respect for the way he led the response to the tragedy at Gleision colliery. Proud of the fact that he's at his desk before eight o'clock every morning, this is no hardship at all, he insists, for someone who knows what it's like to dig coal underground for a living.

MP of the Year Rt Hon Cheryl Gillan MP
Conservative, Secretary of State for Wales

Perhaps it is becoming more difficult for our MPs to impact upon Welsh politics as the devolution settlement matures and the process continues. Many important decisions affecting Wales remain dependent on Westminster however, major infrastructure projects, for example, like the decision to electrify the mainline from Paddington to South Wales. The Secretary of State, Cheryl Gillan, has achieved this commitment from the Treasury at a time of general retrenchment and reductions in public expenditure. Add to this her facilitation of the referendum on further powers to the Assembly and the appointment of the Silk Commission to address further developments of devolution constitutes a record which has truly earned the title MP of the Year.

AM of the Year Alun Ffred Jones AM
Plaid Cymru, Arfon

Whilst the new Government of Wales Act 2006 gave the Assembly powers of primary legislation, the process was cumbersome and complex, however the issue is now resolved somewhat following the referendum in 2011. One of the achievements during this legislative interregnum was passage of the Welsh Language Measure. Not only was this one of the first pieces of Welsh legislation to be passed by the Assembly, but also a symbolic assertion of Welsh sovereignty over a uniquely Welsh issue. In the context of the One Wales Agreement, the Minister responsible for ensuring this measure becoming law was Alun Ffred Jones. Giving the Welsh language its rightful status was never going to be easy and the arguments raged from Cardiff Bay to Westminster and back during the then required procedures to establish Legislative Competence. The Minister for Heritage carries a wide and varied portfolio but enactment of this legislation will remain a lasting legacy.

Lifetime Achievement
Rt Hon Lord Morris of Aberavon QC, KG, Labour

John Morris recently published his autobiography 'Fifty Years in Politics and the Law' – few commentators can recall when he wasn't at the heart of Welsh politics. It's a decade since he moved from the Commons to the Lords, after 42 years as an MP. He was the only member of Tony Blair's first government to have any previous experience as Cabinet Minister, having previously served under both Harold Wilson and James Callaghan. Yet John Morris had an unlikely heritage for a Labour stalwart. A countryman, a farmers' son, a Welsh speaker from rural Wales, the formative Secretary of the Farmer's Union of Wales and a successful Barrister who still lists shooting and fishing amongst his recreations.

Yet he became MP for Aberavon, a constituency that's a centre of heavy industry. He joined Labour in Opposition in 1959, but was appointed to a succession of junior Ministerial posts in the early Governments' of Harold Wilson. After a further period of Opposition he was a surprise and relatively youthful choice when Harold Wilson made him Secretary of State for Wales in 1974. He held the office for more than five years, ending just after he sighted the elephant of devolution on his doorstep.

Further years in Opposition followed, but were doubtless tempered as his parallel career as a Barrister continued to flourish. He returned to office in 1997 as a Government Law Officer. Yet for all the glittering prizes, perhaps the greatest moments of satisfaction came when he buried that elephant, officiating as Attorney General at the Royal opening of the First Assembly, twenty years after his own devolution proposals were rejected and more like half a century since he had first supported the idea as an undergraduate at Aberystwyth. The achievement belonged not just to those who finally triumphed, but to those who had first argued for devolution when it seemed remote and unachievable.

Ennobled in 2001, admitted to the Order of the Garter in 2003, John Morris has indeed enjoyed a unique Lifetime of Achievement in Welsh politics.

PAC
Public Affairs Cymru
Promoting Professionalism with Integrity

Meithrin Proffesiynoldeb gydag Integriti

Public Affairs Cymru (PAC) is the national membership organisation for public affairs and government relations professionals in Wales. PAC members benefit from:

- Our Code of Conduct, which promotes and safeguards the reputation of the public affairs profession in Wales.

- Regular events and continuous professional development opportunities, including policy seminars, lectures and networking events such as the Annual Gala Dinner.

- A range of discounts for conferences, political events and publications.

Public Affairs Cymru (PAC) yw'r fudiad aelodaeth cenedlaethol ar gyfer gweithwyr materion cyhoeddus a chysylltiadau â'r llywodraeth proffesiynol yng Nghymru. Mae aelodau PAC yn elwa o:

- Ein Cod Ymddygiad, sy'n hyrwyddo a diogelu enw da'r proffesiwn materion cyhoeddus yng Nghymru.

- Digwyddiadau rheolaidd a chyfleon datblygiad proffesiynol parhaol, megis seminarau polisi, darlithoedd a digwyddiadau rhwydweithio fel y Cinio Mawreddog Blynyddol.

- Nifer o disgwontiau ar gyfer cynhadleddau, digwyddiadau gwleidyddol a cyhoeddiadau.

The Wales Yearbook

13

PARTIES & POLITICIANS

INDEX

ABERAVON

MP - Dr Hywel FRANCIS Labour
AM - David REES Labour

South Wales West Regional AMs

Peter Black (Lib D)   Suzy Davies (Con)

Byron Davies (Con)   Bethan Jenkins (PC)

Area:	176 sq km	% born in Wales:	90.7%
% speaking Welsh:	16%	% Unemployment *(Apr 2012)*	7%

The constituency comprises the following electoral wards:
Aberavon, Baglan, Briton Ferry East, Briton Ferry West, Bryn and Cwmavon, Coedffranc Central, Coedffranc North, Coedffranc West, Cymmer, Glyncorrwg, Gwynfi, Margam, Port Talbot, Sandfields East, Sandfields West, Tai-bach.

Aberavon is a Labour stronghold and following the 2010 General Election is Labour's third safest Parliamentary seat in Wales. This parallels the situation after the 2011 election where Aberavon is the second safest Assembly seat. Following an initial challenge in 1999 Assembly Election, Plaid Cymru went on to secure second place in the constituency, at both the 2001 General Election and the 2003 Assembly election, but in 2005 were displaced by a stronger Liberal Democrat performance. While the Liberal Democrats were again runners up at the 2010 General Election, Plaid Cymru displaced them at the 2011 National Assembly election, holding off a strong challenge from the Conservatives, pushing the Liberal Democrats into fourth place. Such competition for second place however is largely academic, as the Labour Party seem unlikely to ever lose control of this solidly safe seat.

Aberavon remains an industrial constituency, but one which has seen considerable economic change and renewal. The traditional industrial base of steel and petro-chemicals remain, but have been radically re-structured. Port Talbot appears to have fared better than Llanwern in the rationalisation of steelmaking in Wales and the decision by Tata to replace the blast furnace destroyed in a tragic explosion has been taken to demonstrate a long-term commitment to Port Talbot. To help counter the run-down in employment in traditional sectors, the Baglan Energy Park was established, bringing a gas-fired power station and a range of new industrial opportunities. Baglan is also the site of a new district hospital. In November 2007 it was announced that the largest biomass power station in the world, burning wood chips, was to be built in Port Talbot.

Electoral Trends 1979 - 2010

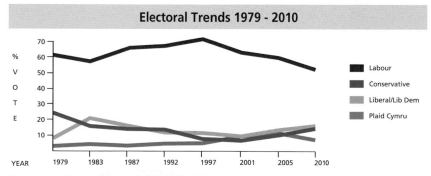

Previous MPs: **Sir John Morris QC (Lab) 1959-2001**
Previous AMs: **Dr Brian Gibbons (Lab) 1999-2011**

MP for Aberavon

Dr Hywel FRANCIS Labour
Majority: 11,039 (35.7%)

House of Commons, London SW1A 0AA
Tel: (020) 7219 8121
Email: francish@parliament.uk

Constituency Office:
Unit 7, Water Street Business Centre
Gwyn Terrace, Port Talbot SA12 6LG
Tel: (01639) 897660 Fax: (01639) 891725
Website: www.hywelfrancis.co.uk

Dr Hywel Francis was first elected MP in 2001. Born 6 June 1946 in Neath, he is the son of the former Welsh miners' leader, Dai Francis. Educated in Llangatwg and Whitchurch Secondary Schools before studying at Swansea University, he was Chair of the Welsh Congress in support of Mining Communities 1984-86 and is Vice-President of Carers UK. A founder and Trustee of the Bevan Foundation, he is also a Trustee of the Paul Robeson Wales Trust and Vice-President of Llafur, the Welsh People's History Society. Prior to entering politics he worked as a historian and was Professor of Continuing Education at Swansea University, being appointed Professor Emeritus in 2006. He is a former Chair of the Select Committee on Welsh Affairs 2005-10 and has previously served as special adviser to Paul Murphy MP, the then Secretary of State for Wales.

In Parliament, Hywel is currently Chair of the Joint Committee on Human Rights and the All Party Archives and History Group, as well as the Vice-Chair of the All Party Carers Group. He also sits on the Liaison Select Committee. A fluent Welsh speaker and married with two children, he is President of Port Talbot Town Cricket Club, the Briton Ferry Brunel Dock Project and the South Wales Miners Museum. He is an Honorary Parliamentary Patron of NIACE, the adult learners' body.

2010 General Election Result

	Party	Votes Cast	%	Change 05-10
Hywel Francis	Lab	16,073	51.9	-8.1%
Keith Davies	Lib D	5,034	16.3	+2.5%
Caroline Jones	Con	4,411	14.2	+4.1%
Paul Nicholls-Jones	PC	2,198	7.1	-4.7%
Kevin Edwards	BNP	1,276	4.1	+4.1%
Andrew Tutton	Ind	919	3.0	+3.0%
Captain Beany	NMBP	558	1.8	+1.8%
Joe Callan	UKIP	489	1.6	+1.6%

Electorate: 50,838 Turnout: 61.0%

AM for Aberavon

David REES Labour
Majority: 9,311 (49.3%)

National Assembly for Wales
Cardiff Bay, Cardiff CF99 1NA
Tel: (029) 2089 8751
Email: david.rees@wales.gov.uk

Constituency Office:
Water Street Business Centre,
Water Street, Port Talbot SA12 6LF
Tel: (01639) 870779
Website: www.david-rees.com

David Rees was first elected to the National Assembly in 2011 having been the Labour Party's candidate for Brecon and Radnorshire in 2003 and a list candidate for South Wales West in 2007. Born in 1957 and a native of Port Talbot, he received an engineering degree from Cardiff University before completing a post-graduate teaching degree and a masters degree in Computer Science. David started his career as a teacher of mathematics at Cynffig Comprehensive School and subsequently became a computing lecturer at Afan College. Prior to becoming an AM, David was an Assistant Dean of Faculty at Swansea Metropolitan University.

David has held a number of positions since joining the Labour Party in 1982, and is a member of Labour's Welsh Executive Committee and the Welsh Policy Forum. He is a member of Unite Union and acts as the convenor of the Unite Group of AMs. In the Assembly, David is currently Chair of both the Cross Party Group on Industrial Communities and the Cross Party Group on Science & Technology. He also sits on the Common Fisheries Policy Task and Finish Group, the Enterprise and Business Committee, the Environment and Sustainability Committee and the Procurement Task and Finish Group. David is married with two children.

2011 Assembly Election Result

	Party	Votes Cast	%	Change 07-11
David Rees	Lab	12,104	64.1	+14.8%
Paul Nicholls-Jones	PC	2,793	14.8	-2.5%
TJ Morgan	Con	2,704	14.3	+4.6%
Helen Ceri-Clarke	Lib D	1,278	6.8	-0.3%

Electorate: 50,754 Turnout: 37.2%

Electoral Trends 1999 - 2011

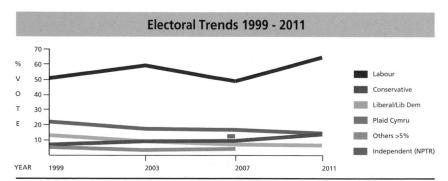

Legend:
- Labour
- Conservative
- Liberal/Lib Dem
- Plaid Cymru
- Others >5%
- Independent (NPTR)

ABERCONWY

MP - Guto BEBB Conservative

AM - Janet FINCH-SAUNDERS Conservative

North Wales Regional AMs

Llyr Huws Gruffydd (PC)   Aled Roberts (Lib D)

Mark Isherwood (Con)   Antoinette Sandbach (Con)

Area:	603 sq km	% born in Wales:	57.5%
% speaking Welsh: 37.5%		% Unemployment *(Apr 2012)*	4.7%

The constituency comprises the following electoral wards:
Betws y coed, Bryn, Caerhun, Capelulo, Conwy, Craig-y-Don, Crwst, Deganwy, Eglwys Bach, Gogarth, Gower, Llansanffraid, Marl, Mostyn, Pandy, Pant-yr-afon/Penmaenan, Penrhyn, Pensarn, Trefriw , Tudno, Uwch Conwy.

The new constituency of **Aberconwy** was created by the Boundary Commission in 2006 and fought for the first time at the 2007 Assembly election. Based primarily on the former Conwy constituency, it includes Llandudno, the coast west as far as Llanfairfechan and the Conwy valley downstream to Betws y Coed, which had previously fallen within Meirionnydd Nant Conwy. The new seat retains many of the characteristics of its predecessor, save the crucial difference of losing Bangor – home to a sizeable Labour vote. Having long been held by the Conservative Party, since the retirement of Sir Wyn Roberts the Tories have seen their majority erode and latterly, Conwy has become an extremely volatile seat. Initially the challenge was posed by the Liberal Democrats but this threat was displaced by Labour at Parliamentary level and Plaid Cymru at the first Assembly elections. At the Assembly election in 2003 Labour went even further and captured the seat from Plaid Cymru, if only by 72 votes.

At the Assembly election in 2007, the new seat of Aberconwy saw, effectively, a three party contest between the then AM, Denise Idris Jones for Labour, her predecessor, Gareth Jones for Plaid Cymru and the Conservatives. The outcome proved to be a fairly comfortable win for Plaid Cymru, but the complex politics of the new constituency were further confirmed when the Conservatives won the 2010 General Election. At the 2011 Assembly election, the Conservatives emerged victorious with an increased majority of 1,567. Meanwhile, Plaid Cymru were very nearly pushed into third place, narrowly beating Labour by 115 votes.

Electoral Trends 1979 - 2010

(Chart showing electoral trends 1979-2010 with % VOTE on the y-axis ranging from 0 to 70, and YEAR on the x-axis from 1979 to 2010)

Legend:
- Labour
- Conservative
- Liberal/Lib Dem
- Plaid Cymru

Previous MPs: Betty Williams (Lab) 1997-2010; Sir Wyn Roberts (Con) 1970-97
Previous AMs: Gareth Jones (PC) 1999-2003, 2007-2011; Denise Idris Jones (Lab) 2003-07

MP for Aberconwy

Guto BEBB Conservative
Majority: 3,398 (11.3%)

House of Commons, London SW1A 0AA
Tel: (020) 7219 7002
Email: guto.bebb.mp@parliament.uk

Constituency Office:
1 Ashdown House, Riverside Business Park
Benarth Road LL32 8UB
Tel: (01492) 583094
Website: www.gutobebb.co.uk

Guto Bebb was first elected MP in May 2010, when he became the first Member of Parliament for newly-formed Aberconwy constituency with a majority of 3,398. A former Plaid Cymru activist and Chair of the party in Caernarfon, Guto first entered the political scene for the Conservative Party as the Parliamentary candidate in the Ogmore by-election in 2002. He was subsequently adopted to fight the Assembly seat in the former Conwy constituency in 2003 where he increased the Conservative vote from 18% to 25%. He was adopted as the Parliamentary candidate for the General Election in 2005 and took the Welsh Conservative vote in Conwy to second place. Born and brought up in North Wales, he is a graduate of the University of Wales, Aberystwyth. In 1993 he founded Partneriaeth Egin Partnership, an economic development consultancy which has traded for sixteen years. He also founded and ran a bookshop in Caernarfon before selling the business in 2002.

In May 2012, Guto was elected to the executive of the influential Conservative 1922 Committee. He has been especially interested in European affairs for several years and is a member of the Welsh Affairs Select Committee and the Members' Expenses Committee. He was also previously a member of the Public Bill Committee on the Welfare Reform Bill. He is married with five children.

2010 General Election Result

	Party	Votes Cast	%	Change 05-10
Guto Bebb	Con	10,734	35.8	+6.8%
Ronald Hughes	Lab	7,336	24.5	-8.5%
Mike Priestley	Lib D	5,786	19.3	+0.2%
Phil Edwards	PC	5,341	17.8	+3.8%
Mike Wieteska	UKIP	632	2.1	+1.0%
Louise Wynne-Jones	WCP	137	0.5	+0.5%

Electorate: 44,593 Turnout: 67.4%

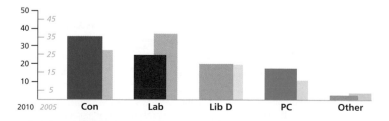

AM for Aberconwy

Janet FINCH-SAUNDERS Conservative
Majority: 1,567 (7.7%)

National Assembly for Wales
Cardiff Bay, Cardiff CF99 1NA
Tel: (029) 2089 8734
Email: janet.finchsaunders@wales.gov.uk

Constituency Office:
29 Madog Street, Llandudno LL30 2TL
Tel: (01492) 871198
Website: www.janetfinchsaunders.org.uk

Janet Finch-Saunders was elected to the Assembly in 2011 having previously contested Wrexham in 2003 and failing to get elected on the North Wales Regional List in 2003 and 2007. Originally from Lancashire, Janet moved to North Wales at the age of 11 and went on to study Business Management at Coleg Llandrillo Cymru. At the age of seventeen she opened her first retail venture, gradually expanding her business into other towns in North Wales. Since 1994 Janet has been a Llandudno Town Councillor and in 2004 she became a Conwy County Borough Councillor as well as being elected the Mayor of Llandudno. In 2008 Janet became the Welsh Conservative Group Leader and Leader of the Opposition on Conwy County Borough Council and former Welsh Conservative Leader Nick Bourne appointed her as a Policy Adviser for local government in January 2011.

In the Assembly Janet sits on the Communities, Equality and Local Government Committee as well as the Task and Finish Group on the outlook for the media in Wales. She is also Shadow Local Government Minister and is a long standing campaigner for increased direct funding for the local hospice movement. Janet is married with two children.

2011 Assembly Election Result

	Party	Votes Cast	%	Change 07-11
Janet Finch-Saunders	Con	6,888	34.0	3.6%
Iwan Huws	PC	5,321	26.2	-12.3%
Eifion Wyn Williams	Lab	5,206	25.7	+3.9%
Michael Priestley	Lid D	2,873	14.2	+4.9%

Electorate: 44,978 Turnout: 45.1%

Electoral Trends 1999 - 2011

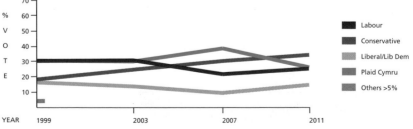

MP - Mark TAMI Labour

AM - Carl SARGEANT Labour

North Wales Regional AMs

Llyr Huws Gruffydd (PC)   Aled Roberts (Lib D)

Mark Isherwood (Con)   Antoinette Sandbach (Con)

Area:	155 sq km	% born in Wales:	43.1%
% speaking Welsh:	27.1%	% Unemployment *(Apr 2012)*	4.2%

The constituency comprises the following electoral wards:
Aston, Broughton North East, Broughton South, Buckley Bistre East, Buckley Bistre West, Buckley Mountain, Buckley Pentrobin, Caergwrle, Connah's Quay Central, Connah's Quay Golftyn, Connah's Quay South, Connah's Quay Wepre, Ewloe, Hawarden, Higher Kinnerton, Hope, Llanfynydd, Mancot, Penyffordd, Queensferry, Saltney Mold Junction, Saltney Stonebridge, Sealand, Shotton East, Shotton Higher, Shotton West, Treuddyn.

Alyn and Deeside is a heavily industrialised constituency with a rural hinterland. Historically Alyn and Deeside experienced severe unemployment following the cessation of steel-making at Shotton and further restructuring. The success of the European Airbus however, has brought new employment opportunities in the local aerospace industry. The BAE plant at Broughton has enjoyed significant support from the Welsh Government and is producing wings for the A380 'super-Jumbo'. It is hoped that such hi-tec employment will underpin long-term economic development and stability in the area. Toyota are also major employers and the level of unemployment remains below the national average.

Alyn and Deeside is a fairly safe Labour seat, an essentially two-party contest that has generally reflected national UK swings at General Elections. In 2010, the Conservatives enjoyed a positive swing without substantially altering the basic political complexion of the seat. The Assembly election in 2011 saw Labour increase their lead over the Conservatives with a majority of 5,581.

There persists however, an issue concerning the extent to which the people of Alyn and Deeside have embraced the significance of devolution, and de facto government from Cardiff, to the future well-being of their community. Local engagement with the new politics of Wales has been low. Flintshire voted heavily against devolution at the Referendum in 1997 and only 32% turned out in Alyn and Deeside at the first Assembly elections in 1999. In 2003, less than a quarter of the electorate bothered to vote - the lowest turnout in Wales; by comparison, the 35% who voted in May 2007 almost suggested a stampede to the polls. In 2011, 37% of the electorate turned out to vote.

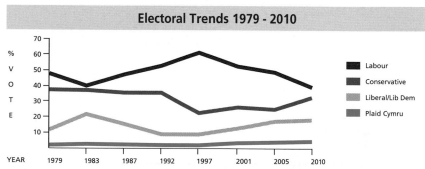

Electoral Trends 1979 - 2010

Previous MPs: **S. Barry Jones 1983-2001** (New seat 1983, formerly East Flint); **S. Barry Jones (Lab) 1970-83**
Previous AMs: **Tom Middlehurst (Lab) 1999-2003**

MP for Alyn & Deeside

Mark TAMI Labour
Majority: 2,919 (7.3%)

House of Commons, London SW1A 0AA
Tel: (020) 7219 8174
Email: tamim@parliament.uk

Constituency Office:
Unit 8, Deeside Enterprise Centre
Rowleys Drive, Shotton, Deeside CH5 1PP
Tel: (01244) 819854

Mark Tami was first elected to Parliament at the General election in 2001 having previously been Head of Policy at the Amalgamated Electrical Engineers Union and was closely involved with the negotiations to bring additional Airbus construction work to Broughton and to resist further redundancies at Shotton. Born in Enfield, 3 October 1962, Mark Tami was educated at Enfield Grammar School and is a History graduate from the University of Wales, Swansea.

Following his re-election in 2005, Mark Tami was appointed PPS to John Healey at HM Treasury, but, as a signatory to the backbench letter in September 2006 urging Tony Blair to retire from office, he resigned his post. Following Tony Blair's departure, he was appointed an Assistant Whip with special responsibility for Wales and Transport. He is now the Opposition Assistant Chief Whip and is Chair of the All Party Parliamentary Group on Stem Cell Transplantation. In Parliament he has championed the need for enhanced animal rights and is a member of the Labour Party's First Past the Post Campaign, which opposes proportional representation and is a strong supporter of compulsory voting. Since 2010 he has been a member of the Selection Committee and Administration Committee in Parliament. He is a former member of the TUC General Council and Treasurer of the Labour Friends of Australia. He is married with two children.

2010 General Election Result

	Party	Votes Cast	%	Change 05-10
Mark Tami	Lab	15,804	39.6	-9.2%
Will Gallagher	Con	12,885	32.3	+7.1%
Paul Brighton	Lib D	7,308	18.3	+0.9%
Maurice Jones	PC	1,549	3.9	+0.2%
John Walker	BNP	1,368	3.4	+3.4%
James Howson	UKIP	1,009	2.5	-0.1%

Electorate: 60,931 Turnout: 65.5%

```
70
60
50
40
30
20
10

2010  2005    Lab      Con      Lib D      PC       Other
```

Carl SARGEANT Labour
Majority: 5,581 (24.5%)

National Assembly for Wales
Cardiff Bay, Cardiff CF99 1NA
Tel: (029) 2089 8716
Email: carl.sargeant@wales.gov.uk

Constituency Office:
Unit 8, Deeside Enterprise Centre
Rowleys Drive, Shotton, Deeside CH5 1PP
Tel: (01244) 823547
Website: www.carlsargeant.org.uk

ALYN & DEESIDE

Carl Sargeant succeeded Tom Middlehurst as Labour AM for Alyn & Deeside in 2003. Born in 1968, he has lived and worked on Deeside throughout his life. He attended Connah's Quay High School and worked as a Process Operator at a chemical company and a Quality Environmental Auditor. A community worker for St. John's Ambulance for 10 years, an industrial fire-fighter and a member of the Salvation Army, he is also a school governor and a board member of Deeside College. He has also represented the Golftyn Ward on Connah's Quay Town Council.

Carl is currently the Minister for Local Government and Communities. He served on the Assembly committee producing the formal response to the Government's White Paper 'Better Governance for Wales' and was formerly Chief Whip and Deputy Business Manager for the Labour Group. His main political interests are skills training, the aerospace sector, the police and pensioners' rights. He enjoys reading, walking and the cinema and is a keen football fan, especially of Connah's Quay Tigers. He is married with two children.

2011 Assembly Election Result

	Party	Votes Cast	%	Change 07-11
Carl Sargeant	Lab	11,978	52.6	+13.8%
John Bell	Con	6,397	28.1	+5.2%
Peter Williams	Lib D	1,725	7.6	-2.3%
Shane Brennan	PC	1,710	7.5	+0.9%
Michael Whitby	BNP	959	4.2	-

Electorate: 61,751 Turnout: 36.9%

Electoral Trends 1999 - 2011

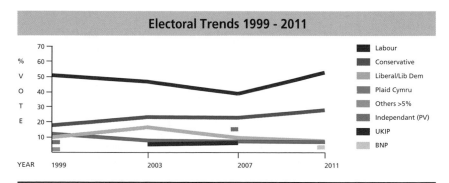

Labour
Conservative
Liberal/Lib Dem
Plaid Cymru
Others >5%
Independant (PV)
UKIP
BNP

ARFON

MP - Hywel WILLIAMS Plaid Cymru
AM - Alun Ffred JONES Plaid Cymru

North Wales Regional AMs

Llyr Huws Gruffydd (PC)   Aled Roberts (Lib D)

Mark Isherwood (Con)   Antoinette Sandbach (Con)

Area:	408 sq km	% born in Wales:	74.0%
% speaking Welsh:	75.2%	% Unemployment *(Apr 2012)*	5.3%

The constituency comprises the following electoral wards:
Allechwedd, Bethel, Bontnewydd, Cadnant, Cwm y Glo, Deiniol, Deiniolen, Dewi, Garth, Gerlan, Glyder, Groeslon, Hendre, Hirael, Llanberis, Llanllyfni, Llanrug, Llanwnda, Marchog, Menai (Bangor) Menai (Caernarfon), Ogwen, Peblig (Caernarfon), Penisarwaun, Petir, Penygroes, Seiont, Talysarn, Tregarth & Mynydd Llandygai, Waunfawr, Y Felinheli.

Caernarfon was the Parliamentary seat of the former Liberal Prime Minister, David Lloyd George, 1890-1945. LG was followed by Goronwy Roberts, who held Caernarfon for Labour for nearly thirty years, 1945-74. The election of Dafydd Wigley in 1974 swung the seat to Plaid Cymru and established the base for one of Wales' leading politicians of the last forty years. Dafydd Wigley was also elected to the Assembly in 1999 and on his retirement left both a formidable legacy and a daunting challenge for his successors. Elected in 2001, Hywel Williams became only the fourth MP to represent this strongly Welsh community in 111 years, a position he retained in 2005 and in 2010 was re-elected for the newly configured seat of Arfon.

The Boundary Commission abolished the old seat of Caernarfon prior to the 2007 Assembly elections. The new constituency of **Arfon**, is based primarily on the two centres of Caernarfon and Bangor. Much of the Llŷn peninsula, that was formerly part of Caernarfon, is now joined with Meirionnydd to form the new seat of Dwyfor Meirionnydd. Notwithstanding these changes, Arfon contains the highest proportion of Welsh speakers of any constituency in Wales. At the Assembly election in May 2003, the former Leader of Gwynedd County Council, Alun Ffred Jones, was comfortably elected confirming Plaid Cymru's total control of the constituency.

The General Election of 2010 and the Assembly election of 2011 were both fought on the new boundaries for Arfon, but the outcomes suggest that the new constituency remains a very safe seat for Plaid Cymru. The demise of the Caernarfon as a Parliamentary constituency however, meant the loss of an historic, iconic seat, one which has been at the forefront of Wales' political struggles from Cymry Fydd to devolution.

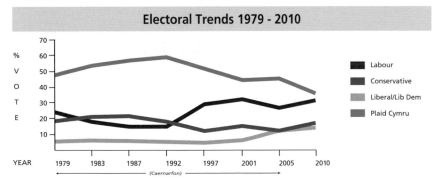

Electoral Trends 1979 - 2010

Legend: Labour, Conservative, Liberal/Lib Dem, Plaid Cymru

Previous MPs: (Caernarfon) Dafydd Wigley (PC) 1974-2001; Goronwy Roberts (Lab) 1945-74
Previous AMs: (Caernarfon) Dafydd Wigley (PC) 1999-2003

MP for Arfon

Hywel WILLIAMS Plaid Cymru
Majority: 1,455 (5.6%)

House of Commons
London SW1A 0AA
Tel: (020) 7219 8150
Email: hywel.williams.mp@parliament.uk

Constituency Office:
8 Stryd y Castell
Caernarfon, Gwynedd LL55 1SE
Tel: (01286) 672076
Website: www.hywelwilliams.plaidcymru.org

Hywel Williams was elected to Parliament for Caernarfon in June 2001, succeeding Dafydd Wigley who had represented the seat since 1974. Following boundary changes, Hywel Williams contested the new seat of Arfon in 2010. Born in Pwllheli in 1953, he was educated locally and at the University of Wales, Cardiff and University of Wales, Bangor. A psychology graduate, Hywel Williams made his career as a social worker, initially in Mid Glamorgan and thereafter with Gwynedd County Council Social Services Department. He joined the North and West Wales Practice Centre at Bangor University in 1985 and was Head of the Centre until he left to work freelance in his field between 1995 and his election in 2001. He was also responsible for many initiatives developing Welsh language services in social work.

In Parliament, he is Plaid Cymru Spokesperson for Work and Pensions, Health and International Development. Since 2010 he also speaks on Cabinet Office matters, Energy and Climate Change and Education. He is a member of the Speakers Panel of Chairmen and the Science & Technology Committee. His main political interests are social policy, health, culture, work and pensions, language and the arts. In Parliament, he voted against the war in Afghanistan and against a total ban on hunting. He is a fluent Welsh speaker whose recreations include walking, reading and films.

2010 General Election Result

	Party	Votes Cast	%	Change 05-10
Hywel Williams	PC	9,383	36.0	-9.6%
Alun Pugh	Lab	7,928	30.4	+3.4%
Robin Millar	Con	4,416	16.9	+4.5%
Sarah Green	Lib D	3,666	14.1	+1.5%
Elwyn Williams	UKIP	685	2.6	-

Electorate: 41,198 Turnout: 63.3%

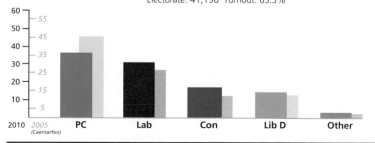

AM for Arfon

Alun Ffred JONES Plaid Cymru
Majority: 5,394 (30.5%)

National Assembly for Wales
Cardiff Bay, Cardiff CF99 1NA
Tel: (029) 2089 8414
Email: alunffred.jones@wales.gov.uk

Constituency Office:
8 Stryd y Castell, Caernarfon
Gwynedd LL55 1SE
Tel: (01286) 672076
Website: www.alunffredjones.plaidcymru.org

Alun Ffred Jones was first elected to the Assembly in 2003, when he succeeded Dafydd Wigley, the former Plaid Cymru President, as AM for Caernarfon. Following boundary changes, he fought and won the new seat of Arfon in May 2007 and again in 2011. Born in 1949 in Brynaman, he was educated at Ysgol y Berwyn, Bala and the University of Wales, Bangor. A former television director and producer at Ffilmiau'r Nant, Caernarfon, he is interested in broadcasting matters. He was previously a Welsh teacher and a journalist with HTV, working on the programmes 'Y Dydd' and 'Yr Wythnos'. Former Leader of Gwynedd County Council, he is Chairman of Antur Nantlle and Chairman of Nantlle Vale FC.

During the 'One Wales' Coalition, he was Heritage Minister in the Welsh Government, and was responsible for getting the new Welsh Language (Wales) Measure on the Statute Book. He is currently Plaid Cymru's Economic Spokesperson in the Assembly and sits on the Enterprise and Business Committee as well as the Procurement Task and Finish Group. In his spare time he enjoys a variety of sports, cinema, theatre, poetry, cycling and gardening.

2011 Assembly Election Result

	Party	Votes Cast	%	Change 07-11
Alun Ffred Jones	PC	10,024	56.8	+4.3%
Christina Rees	Lab	4,630	26.2	-0.6%
Aled Davies	Con	2,209	12.5	+3.0%
Rhys Jones	Lib D	801	4.5	-2.7%

Electorate: 41,093 Turnout: 43.0%

Electoral Trends 1999 - 2011

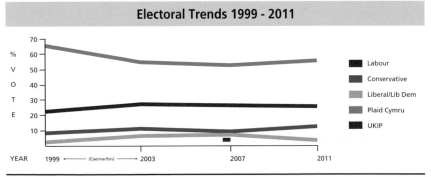

BLAENAU GWENT

MP - Nick SMITH Labour

AM - Alun DAVIES Labour

South Wales East Regional AMs

Mohammad Asghar (Con)   William Graham (Con)

Jocelyn Davies (PC)   Lindsay Whittle (PC)

Area:	109 sq km	% born in Wales:	92.1%
% speaking Welsh:	16.4%	% Unemployment *(Apr 2012)*	12.4%

The constituency comprises the following electoral wards:
Abertillery, Badminton, Beaufort, Blaina, Brynmawr, Cwm, Cwmtillery, Ebbw Vale North, Ebbw Vale South, Georgetown, Llanhilleth, Nantyglo, Rassau, Sirhowy, Six Bells, Tredegar Central and West.

Blaenau Gwent has become the most contentious seat in Wales. The successor in title to Ebbw Vale, the bastion of Aneurin Bevan and Michael Foot, became the home of a rebellion against the centralized over-control of New Labour. Formerly the safest Labour Parliamentary seat in Wales, and the fifth safest in Britain, in 2005, the sitting AM, Peter Law, defied his party and successfully stood for Parliament as an Independent candidate. His decision to stand was as a protest against an all-woman shortlist being imposed on Blaenau Gwent's nomination of a new Parliamentary candidate. Peter Law's subsequent expulsion from the Labour Party also deprived the Party of its majority in the Assembly. Peter Law's tragic death in April 2006 created therefore, two especially divisive by-elections. The Labour Party continued to be opposed by Peter Law's supporters, ensuring that his widow, Trish, and his former agent, Dai Davies, successfully retained both Parliamentary and Assembly seats. Trish Law became a pivotal Assembly Member, effectively exercising a casting vote for the remainder of the Assembly term. At the election in 2007, she retained her seat and increased her majority. Her colleague, Dai Davies stood for re-election to Westminster in 2010 but was defeated. In the face of a national, UK, swing to the Conservatives, old Labour loyalties re-asserted themselves in Blaenau Gwent and Labour won the 2011 Assembly election with a landslide majority of 9,120, making Blaenau Gwent the third safest seat in Wales.

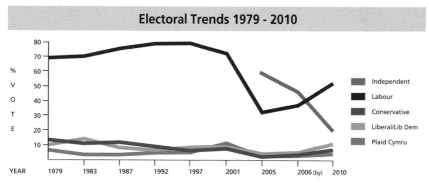

Electoral Trends 1979 - 2010

Legend:
- Independent
- Labour
- Conservative
- Liberal/Lib Dem
- Plaid Cymru

Previous MPs: **Dai Davies (Ind)** 2006(by)-2010; **Peter Law (Ind)** 2005-06; **Llew Smith (Lab)** 1992-2005; **Michael Foot (Lab)** 1983-92 (New seat 1983, formerly Ebbw Vale); **Michael Foot** 1960-83
Previous AMs: **Trish Law (Ind)** 2006-2011; **Peter Law (Lab/Ind)** 1999-2006

Nick SMITH Labour
Majority: 10,516 (32.5%)

House of Commons
London SW1A 0AA
Tel: (020) 7219 7018
Email: nick.smith.mp@parliament.uk

Constituency Office:
23 Beaufort Street, Brynmawr
Blaenau Gwent NP23 4AQ
Tel: (01495) 313167
Website: www.nicksmithmp.com

BLAENAU GWENT

Nick Smith was first elected to Westminster in May 2010. His election saw the highest swing to Labour in the UK of 29%, and the Labour majority in Blaenau Gwent is 10,516. Born in Cardiff, Nick was brought up in Blaenau Gwent, going to Tredegar Comprehensive School and gaining an MSc from Birkbeck College. Before entering Parliament he was the Director of Policy and Partnerships at the Royal College of Speech and Language Therapists. His previous roles also included Secretary General of the European Parliamentary Labour Party, Campaign Manager with the NSPCC and head of membership development with the Labour Party.

In Parliament Nick is Parliamentary Private Secretary to Douglas Alexander, the Shadow Foreign Secretary. He is also a member of the Public Accounts Committee, responsible for scrutinising government spending. His political interests include home affairs, justice and defence. Outside of politics, Nick lives in Nantyglo and enjoys hiking, rugby, reading and international politics.

2010 General Election Result

	Party	Votes Cast	%	Change 05-10
Nick Smith	Lab	16,974	52.4	+20.1%
Dai Davies	Ind (PV)	6,458	19.9	-38.2%
Matt Smith	Lib D	3,285	10.1	+5.9%
Liz Stevenson	Con	2,265	7.0	+4.7%
Rhodri Davies	PC	1,333	4.1	+1.7%
Anthony King	BNP	1,211	3.7	+3.7%
Mike Kocan	UKIP	488	1.5	+1.0%
Alyson O'Connell	SLP	381	1.2	+1.2%

Electorate: 52,442 Turnout: 61.8%

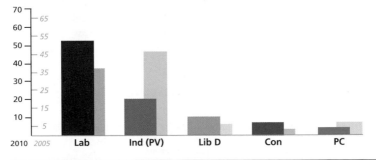

Alun DAVIES Labour
Majority: 9,120 (45.1%)

National Assembly for Wales
Cardiff Bay, Cardiff CF99 1NA
Tel: (029) 2089 8300
Email: alun.davies@wales.gov.uk

Constituency Office:
23 Beaufort Street, Brynmawr
Blaenau Gwent NP23 4AQ
Tel: (01495) 311160

Alun Davies was first elected to the Assembly in 2007 on the Mid & West Wales regional list. In 2011 however, he won the previously safe Labour seat of Blaenau Gwent back from the Independents with a landslide majority of 9,120 votes. He had previously been a Plaid Cymru Parliamentary candidate in South Wales before he contested Ceredigion for the Labour Party at the 2005 General Election. Born and brought up in Tredegar and he was educated at Tredegar Comprehensive School and University of Wales, Aberystwyth. He is a former President of the National Union of Students Wales. Prior to being elected to the Assembly, he enjoyed a public affairs career with the WWF, Oxfam, the UK Atomic Energy Authority, Hyder Plc and S4C. He later established his own public affairs company, Bute Communications, in Cardiff.

Since being elected to the Assembly he has been awarded the BBC Wales AM:PM award for "Newcomer of the Year" and has chaired the Rural Development Sub-Committee. He is currently Deputy Minister for Agriculture, Food, Fisheries and European Programmes.

2011 Assembly Election Result

	Party	Votes Cast	%	Change 07-11
Alun Davies	Lab/Co-op	12,926	64.0	+32.6%
Jayne Sullivan	Ind	3,806	18.8	-30.6%
Darren Jones	PC	1,098	5.4	+0.6%
Bob Hayward	Con	1,066	5.8	+1.2%
Brian Urch	BNP	948	4.7	-
Martin Blakebrough	Lib D	367	1.8	-3.9%

Electorate: 53,230 Turnout: 38.0%

Electoral Trends 1999 - 2011

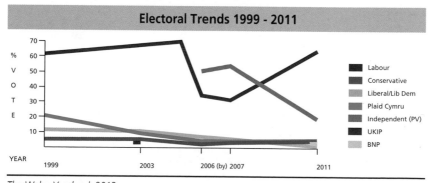

Labour
Conservative
Liberal/Lib Dem
Plaid Cymru
Independent (PV)
UKIP
BNP

BRECON & RADNORSHIRE

MP - Roger WILLIAMS Liberal Democrat

AM - Kirsty WILLIAMS Liberal Democrat

Mid & West Wales Regional AMs

Rebecca Evans (Lab)   Simon Thomas (PC)

William Powell (Lib D)   Joyce Watson (Lab)

Area:	3,007 sq km	% born in Wales:	60.2%
% speaking Welsh:	22.6%	% Unemployment *(Apr 2012)*	3.5%

The constituency comprises the following electoral wards:
Aber-craf, Beguildy, Bronllys, Builth, Bwlch, Crickhowell, Cwm-twrch, Disserth and Trecoed, Felin-fach, Glasbury, Gwernyfed, Hay, Knighton, Llanafanfawr, Llanbadarn Fawr, Llandrindod East/Llandrindod West, Llandrindod North, Llandrindod South, Llanelwedd, Llangattock, Llangors, Llangunllo, Llangynidr, Llanwrtyd Wells, Llanyre, Maescar/Llywel, Nantmel, Old Radnor, Presteigne, Rhayader, St.David Within, St.John, St.Mary, Talgarth, Talybont-on-Usk, Tawe Uchaf, Ynyscedwyn, Yscir, Ystradgynlais.

Brecon and Radnorshire is a border and largely rural seat extending from the Heads of the Valleys into the Cambrian Mountains - the largest constituency in Wales. Although largely rural and sparsely populated, a fringe of industrial villages and Ystradgynlais ensured the constituency was held by the Labour Party between 1945 and 1979. Captured by the Conservatives in 1979, Tom Hooson's sudden death in 1985 gave rise to a by-election and a famous victory for the late Richard Livsey, then a Liberal, fighting for the Alliance. Subsequently Brecon and Radnor became one of the most volatile seats in Britain, being characterised by bitter struggles between the Liberal Democrats and the Conservative Party. For Parliament this led to an alternation of MPs through the 1980s & 90s, but following their success in the Assembly elections, and latterly in General elections too, the Liberal Democrats now appear to have gained the upper hand in this rivalry. In 2011 Welsh Liberal Democrat Leader Kirsty Williams was returned with a reduced majority of 2,757. The constituency remains a two horse race between Liberal Democrats and the Conservatives.

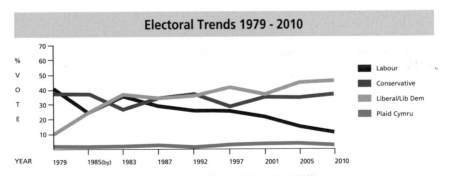

Electoral Trends 1979 - 2010

Legend: Labour, Conservative, Liberal/Lib Dem, Plaid Cymru

Previous MPs: Richard Livsey (Lib D) 1997-2001; Jonathan Evans (Con) 1992-97; Richard Livsey (Alln) 1985 – 1992; Tom Hooson (Con) 1979-85; Caerwyn Roderick (Lab) 1970-79

Roger WILLIAMS Liberal Democrat
Majority: 3,747 (9.6%)

House of Commons
London SW1A 0AA
Tel: (020) 7219 8145
Email: williamsr@parliament.uk

Constituency Office:
4 Watergate, Brecon LD3 9AN
Tel: (01874) 625739
Website: www.rogerwilliams.org.uk

BRECON & RADNOR

Roger Williams was elected to Parliament in June 2001, inheriting this volatile seat from the late Lord Livsey of Talgarth. In 2005, Roger enjoyed a positive swing from the Conservatives and now sits on a more comfortable, if not entirely safe, majority. A Powys County Councillor for 20 years, he fought Carmarthen West and South Pembrokeshire for the Liberal Democrats at the Assembly elections in May 1999. A livestock farmer, Roger Williams was born in Crickhowell in January 1948. He was educated at Christ College, Brecon and Selwyn College, Cambridge. He has previously served on the Development Board for Rural Wales, the Brecon Beacons National Park Authority and chaired the Mid-Wales Agri-Food Partnership.

In Parliament he has served on the Welsh Affairs Select Committee 2001-05 and the Environment, Food and Rural Affairs Committee 2005-10. He is currently a member of the Science and Technology Select Committee. A traditional, hard-working rural MP, Roger Williams is less prominent in the new Coalition politics in Westminster where he voted against Coalition policy on tuition fee rises for university students. Agriculture, small business and education are his chief political interests. He is currently Deputy Leader of the Welsh Liberal Democrats. Married with two children, he lists sport, walking and nature conservation amongst his personal interests and hobbies.

2010 General Election Result

	Party	Votes Cast	%	Change 05-10
Roger Williams	Lib D	17,929	46.2	+1.3%
Suzy Davies	Con	14,182	36.5	+1.9%
Christopher Lloyd	Lab	4,096	10.5	-4.5%
Janet Davies	PC	989	2.5	-1.1%
Clive Easton	UKIP	876	2.3	+0.4%
Dorienne Robinson	Green	341	0.9	+0.9%
Jeffrey Green	Christian Party	222	0.6	+0.6%
Lord Offa	Loony	210	0.5	+0.5%

Electorate: 54,177 Turnout: 72.5%

2010 _2005_ **Lib D**   **Con**   **Lab**   **PC**   **Other**

Kirsty WILLIAMS Liberal Democrat
Majority: 2,757 (9.7%)

National Assembly for Wales
Cardiff Bay, Cardiff CF99 1NA
Tel: (029) 2089 8743
Email: kirsty.williams@wales.gov.uk

Constituency Office:
4 Water Gate, Brecon, Powys LD3 9AN
Tel: (01874) 625739
Website: www.kirstywilliams.org.uk

BRECON & RADNOR

Kirsty Williams was first elected to the National Assembly in 1999, although she had previously contested Ogmore in the 1997 General Election. Born in 1971, she was educated at St Michael's School, Llanelli, and the universities of Manchester and Missouri. Before entering politics professionally, Kirsty worked as a Marketing & PR Executive and she served as a member of the National Assembly Advisory Group prior to its establishment.

When Kirsty was named Leader of the Welsh Liberal Democrats in 2008, she became the first female leader of any of the four main Welsh parties. In the Assembly, she currently sits on the Health and Social Care Committee, as well as the Standards of Conduct Committee. She is also the Chair of the Cross Party Group on Coeliac Disease and Dermatitis Herpetifomis. Her political interests include health, agriculture and young people. Married with three children, she lives on the family farm near Brecon, and in her spare time, enjoys helping on the farm, spending time with her family and shopping.

2011 Assembly Election Result

	Party	Votes Cast	%	Change 07-11
Kirsty Williams	Lib D	12,201	43.0	-9.2%
Chris Davies	Con	9,444	33.3	-0.3%
Christopher Lloyd	Lab	4,797	16.9	+8.2%
Gary Price	PC	1,906	6.7	+1.2%

Electorate: 53,546 Turnout: 52.9%

Electoral Trends 1999 - 2011

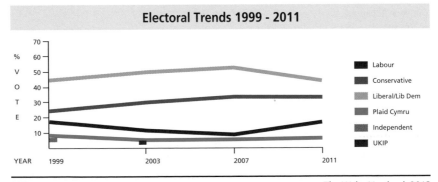

BRIDGEND

MP - Madeleine MOON Labour

AM - Rt Hon Carwyn JONES Labour

South Wales West Regional AMs

Peter Black (Lib D)   Suzy Davies (Con)

Byron Davies (Con)   Bethan Jenkins (PC)

Area:	85 sq km	% born in Wales:	80.7%
% speaking Welsh:	14.0%	% Unemployment *(Apr 2012)*	5.9%

The constituency comprises the following electoral wards:
Brackla, Bryntirion, Laleston and Merthyr Mawr, Cefn Glas, Coity, Cornelly, Coychurch Lower, Litchard, Llangewydd and Brynhyfryd, Morfa, Newcastle, Newton, Nottage, Oldcastle, Pendre, Pen-y-fai, Porthcawl East Central, Porthcawl West Central, Pyle, Rest Bay.

Bridgend is a mixed constituency, comprising urban, industrial and rural areas together with a long coastline. Manufacturing employment has prospered in the past 20 years, having attracted major inward investment projects, but is now vulnerable to the impact of globalization. Bridgend was created as a separate Parliamentary constituency in 1983 and was initially won by the Conservatives before being captured for Labour by Win Griffiths, the former MEP, in 1987. The Assembly elections in 1999 saw a substantial increase in local support for Plaid Cymru, but this has not been sustained. Win Griffiths stood down at the 2005 General Election, to be replaced by Madeleine Moon who has continued to be elected but with smaller majorities, as is often the case on the retirement of a long-standing member. The Assembly election of 2007 was fought on slightly revised boundaries, but the change in rules concerning candidature were of greater impact on the outcome. The choice of Alun Cairns to contest the regional election, left his successor as Tory candidate, Emma Greenow, to stand against a senior member of the Cabinet and latterly Leader of the Labour Party in Wales and First Minister, Carwyn Jones. In a climate of a Conservative renaissance, Bridgend proved more marginal at the 2010 General Election, but Carwyn Jones was not greatly threatened, and substantially increased his majority at the 2011 election.

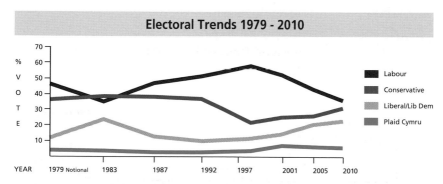

Previous MPs: **Win Griffiths 1987-2005; Peter Hubbard Miles (Con) 1983-87** (New seat 1983)

Madeleine MOON Labour
Majority: 2,263 (5.9%)

House of Commons
London SW1A 0AA
Tel: (020) 7219 4417
Email: moonm@parliament.uk

Constituency Office:
47 Nolton Street, Bridgend CF31 3AA
Tel: (01656) 750002
Website: www.madeleinemoonmp.com

Madeleine Moon was elected to Parliament in May 2005, the only female Labour candidate in Wales to have been selected from an open list. Born in Sunderland in 1950, she was educated at Whinney Hill School, Durham Girls School and the universities of Keele and Cardiff. She was a Councillor in Bridgend 1991-2004 and is former Mayor of Porthcawl. She represented the Borough Council on the Sports Council for Wales and on the Tourism Partnership South and West Wales and was previously a residential home care inspector for the Care Standards Inspectorate. She was also National Chairman of the British Resorts Association.

In Parliament she has worked as Parliamentary Private Secretary to Lord Hunt when he was Minister of State at the Department of Energy and Climate Change and to Jim Knight MP when he was Minister of State at the Department for Children, Schools and Families. Since 2009 she has been a member of the Defence Select Committee, while she is also a member of the UK Delegation to the NATO Parliamentary Assembly. Madeleine founded the All-Party Group on Suicide and Self Harm Prevention and supports several other groups including those on credit unions and China. She is Vice Chair of the All-Party Armed Forces Group, convening the RAF group. Her political interests include care for people with disabilities and older people, mental health, defence and the environment.

2010 General Election Result

	Party	Votes Cast	%	Change 05-10
Madeleine Moon	Lab	13,931	36.3	-6.6%
Helen Baker	Con	11,668	30.4	+5.4%
Wayne Morgan	Lib D	8,658	22.6	+0.5%
Nick Thomas	PC	2,269	5.9	-1.0%
Brian Urch	BNP	1,020	2.7	+2.7%
David Fulton	UKIP	801	2.1	+0.7%

Electorate: 58,700 Turnout: 65.3%

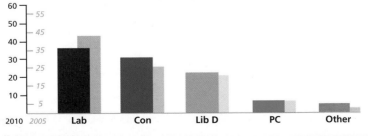

AM for Bridgend

Rt Hon Carwyn JONES Labour
Majority: 6,775 (28.1%)

National Assembly for Wales
Cardiff Bay, Cardiff CF99 1NA
Tel: (029) 2089 8468
Email: carwyn.jones@wales.gov.uk

Constituency Office:
Emlyn House, 36 Caroline Street
Bridgend CF31 1DQ
Tel: (01656) 664320

Carwyn Jones has been a member of the Assembly since 1999. Born in 1967, he was educated at Brynteg Comprehensive School, Bridgend, University of Wales, Aberystwyth and the Inns of Court School of Law, London. A barrister in chambers in Cardiff, Carwyn Jones was also a professional tutor at Cardiff University Law School. He served as a member of Bridgend County Borough Council for five years, chairing the Labour Group 1998-99. He was appointed to the Privy Council in June 2010 and is a member of Amnesty International, UNISON, TGWU, AMICUS and the Fabian Society. Carwyn became First Minister in December 2009 and following the defeat of Gordon Brown as Prime Minister in the 2010 General Election, he is now the most senior elected Labour representative and Minister in the UK. He has served as a Cabinet Minister since 2000 and was previously Minister for Rural Affairs; Minister for Environment, Planning & Countryside; Counsel General and Leader of the House.

Carwyn Jones is Welsh speaking, media-friendly and had long been thought a likely candidate for the leadership of the Labour Party in Wales. His non-political interests include sport, reading and travel and he is a patron of the Kenfig Hill Male Voice Choir.

2011 Assembly Election Result

	Party	Votes Cast	%	Change 07-11
Carwyn Jones	Lab	13,499	56.2	+15.9%
Alex Williams	Con	6,724	28.0	-1.9%
Tim Thomas	PC	2,076	8.6	-6.0%
Briony Davies	Lib D	1,736	7.2	-8.0%

Electorate: 59,104 Turnout: 40.7%

Electoral Trends 1999 - 2011

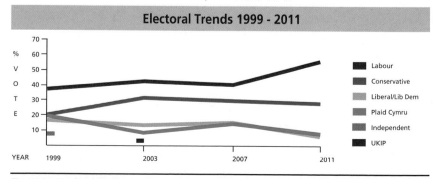

MP - Wayne DAVID Labour

AM - Jeff CUTHBERT Labour

South Wales East Regional AMs

Mohammad Asghar (Con)   William Graham (Con)

Jocelyn Davies (PC)   Lindsay Whittle (PC)

Area:	115 sq km	% born in Wales:	88.3%
% speaking Welsh:	21.6%	% Unemployment *(Apr 2012)*	7.8%

The constituency comprises the following electoral wards:
Aber Valley, Bargoed, Bedwas, Trethomas and Machen, Gilfach, Hengoed, Llanbradach, Morgan Jones, Nelson, Penyrheol, St.Cattwg, St.James, St.Martins, Ystrad Mynach.

Caerphilly might normally be thought to be a traditional, safe, South Wales, Labour seat. However, its political history shows periodic flirtations with Plaid Cymru, initially having almost succumbing at a by-election in 1968, and then losing control of the local authority on several occasions, including 1999 – 2004, Plaid Cymru's most recent electoral high-water mark. Plaid Cymru continues to enjoy a strong presence in the area and, following the departure from mainstream politics of the former Secretary of State, MP and AM Ron Davies, might have been expected to prosper. Labour loyalty prevailed however, with Wayne David winning the Parliamentary seat in 2001 and retaining it comfortably in 2005 and 2010. Jeff Cuthbert won the 2003 Assembly election, although Plaid Cymru continued to poll quite well. The Assembly election in 2007 introduced a further element into the contest however, with the re-emergence of Ron Davies to fight the seat as an Independent. Whilst having little chance of success, Ron Davies polled over 5,000 votes mostly, it appeared, at the expense of Labour. In 2011 he stood as a Plaid Cymru candidate but Jeff Cuthbert comfortably held on to the seat and increased his overall majority.

Caerphilly is a mixed constituency, with extensive rural areas. Manufacturing has replaced the former predominance of mining and steel, but, in turn, is now under threat. There has also been considerable residential 'overspill' from neighbouring Cardiff. Through all this however, Caerphilly retains a strong sense of Welsh identity which, in part, undoubtedly explains the resilience of the Plaid Cymru presence.

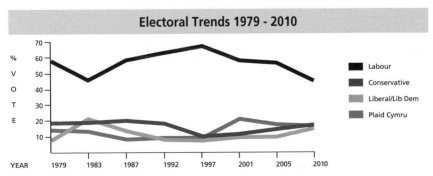

Electoral Trends 1979 - 2010

Previous MPs: Ron Davies 1983-2001; Ednyfed Hudson-Davies (Lab) 1979-83; Fred Evans (Lab) 1968 (by) -79
Previous AMs: Ron Davies 1999-2003

Wayne DAVID Labour
Majority: 10,755 (27.8%)

House of Commons, London SW1A 0AA
Tel: (020) 7219 8152
Email: wayne.david.mp@parliament.uk

Constituency Office:
The Community Council Offices, Newport Road
Bedwas, Caerphilly CF83 8YB
Tel: (029) 2088 1061
Website: www.waynedavid.labour.co.uk

CAERPHILLY

Wayne David, the former MEP for South Wales Central, was elected MP for Caerphilly in June 2001 following Ron Davies's election to the National Assembly for Wales. Born in Bridgend on 1 July 1957, he was educated at Cynffig Comprehensive School, University of Wales, Cardiff and University of Wales, Swansea. He qualified as a schoolteacher and later worked as a tutor-organizer for the Workers' Educational Association. He was first elected to the European Parliament in 1989 and went on to become Leader of the Labour Group. Wayne David stood down in 1999 to stand for Labour in Rhondda in the first Assembly election, only to become the most unlikely victim of Plaid Cymru's remarkable campaign.

A former Junior Minister in the Wales Office, in the House of Commons he has previously served on the European Scrutiny Select Committee and as Chair of the All-Party European Union Group. In 2005, when PPS to Adam Ingram, the Armed Forces Minister, he resigned in protest at Tony Blair's reluctance to announce a date for his departure. Following Gordon Brown's elevation to Prime Minister, he was promoted to an Assistant Whip, responsible for Wales. As Secretary of the Welsh group of the Parliamentary Labour Party, he was credited with helping secure support for the Government of Wales Bill amongst sceptical Labour backbenchers. He was Shadow Minister for Europe from 2010 to 2011 and is currently Shadow Minister for Political and Constitutional Reform.

2010 General Election Result

	Party	Votes Cast	%	Change 05-10
Wayne David	Lab	17,377	44.9	-10.5%
Maria Caulfield	Con	6,622	17.1	+2.4%
Lindsay Whittle	PC	6,460	16.7	-1.4%
Kay David	Lib D	5,688	14.7	+4.7%
Laurence Reid	BNP	1,635	4.2	+4.2%
Tony Jenkins	UKIP	910	2.4	+2.4%

Electorate: 62,731 Turnout: 62.0%

AM for Caerphilly

Jeff CUTHBERT Labour
Majority: 4,924 (19.2%)

National Assembly for Wales,
Cardiff Bay, Cardiff CF99 1NA
Tel: (029) 2089 8314
Email: jeff.cuthbert@wales.gov.uk

Constituency Office:
Bargoed YMCA, Aeron Place
Gilfach, Caerphilly CF81 8JA
Tel: (01443) 838542
Website: www.jeffcuthbert.com

Jeff Cuthbert was first elected to the Assembly in 2003, when he replaced Ron Davies as AM for Caerphilly. Born in Glasgow in June 1948 and educated at Whitchurch County Secondary School, he attended University College Cardiff where he did a degree in mining engineering and was President of the Students' Union from 1974-1975. Formerly a senior consultant with the Welsh Joint Education Committee, Jeff had also been a mining surveyor with the NCB at Markham and Oakdale collieries and later, part-time Principal of Aberbargoed Adult Education Centre. He is on the Board of Governors for Trinity Fields School, a member of the Court at Cardiff University and was formerly on the Board of Managers for the College at Ystrad Mynach. He is an active member of UNITE the Union and previously served as the Co-ordinator of the UNITE Group of Labour AMs.

In May 2011 Jeff was appointed Deputy Minister for Skills in the Welsh Government. He was previously a Labour spokesman for the economy and transport and has served as Chair of the All Wales Programme Monitoring Committee for EU Structural Funds, as well as the Cross-Party Built Environment Group, the Cross-Party Healthy Living Group and the Cross-Party Group on Diabetes.

2011 Assembly Election Result

	Party	Votes Cast	%	Change 07-11
Jeff Cuthbert	Lab	12,521	49.0	+14.4%
Ron Davies	PC	7,597	29.7	+3.9%
Owen Meredith	Con	3,368	13.2	+1.9%
Kay David	Lib D	1,062	4.2	-2.0%
Anthony King	BNP	1,022	4.0	-

Electorate: 62,049 Turnout: 41.2%

Electoral Trends 1999 - 2011

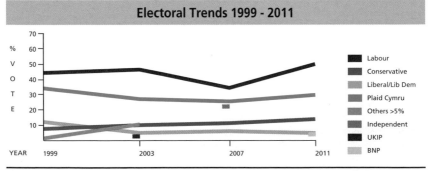

CARDIFF CENTRAL

MP - Jenny WILLOTT Liberal Democrat

AM - Jenny RATHBONE Labour

South Wales Central Regional AMs

Andrew R T Davies (Con)   Eluned Parrott (Lib D)

David Melding (Con)   Leanne Wood (PC)

Area:	17 sq km	% born in Wales:	63.0%
% speaking Welsh:	19.8%	% Unemployment *(Apr 2012)*	7.7%

The constituency comprises the following electoral wards:
Adamsdown, Cathays, Cyncoed, Pentwyn, Penylan, Plasnewydd.

The prosperous, commercial centre of Wales' capital city has, against all expectation, been through a period of an intense political struggle. Characterised by the municipal classicism of the Civic Centre, the Millennium Stadium and the bustle of the arcades and shopping malls, **Cardiff Central** was once a fairly comfortable Conservative seat. Aided by boundary changes in the Nineties, Labour emerged as the principal challenger and Jon Owen Jones captured the Parliamentary seat in 1992. By 1999 however, Cardiff Central provided one of the shock results of the Assembly elections, a feat repeated in 2003 when Jenny Randerson, of the Liberal Democrats, increased her vote to almost three times that of her Labour runner-up. Following the 2007 Assembly election, Cardiff Central was the third safest seat in Wales. At Parliamentary level, 2001 saw a tense Labour versus Liberal Democrat contest with Jon Owen Jones, the sitting Labour MP, hanging onto his seat by less than a thousand votes. By 2005, Jenny Willott and the Liberal Democrats enjoyed a remarkable swing of over 8% to, not only take the seat from Labour, but to do so with a comfortable majority. Following the retirement of Jenny Randerson however, Labour's Jenny Rathbone recaptured the Assembly seat in 2011. With a majority of only 38 she holds the most marginal seat in Wales. Despite Liberal Democrat support seemingly entrenched at local level at one stage, the pendulum seems to have swung once more with Labour gaining control of Cardiff Council at the 2012 Local Elections.

Cardiff Central is also home to the highest number of students in any Welsh constituency, a group which surely had an impact during the Assembly election.

Electoral Trends 1979 - 2010

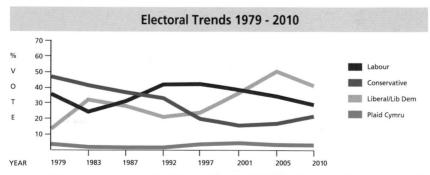

Previous MPs: Jon Owen Jones 1992-2005; Ian Grist (Con) 1983-92; (New seat 1974, formerly Cardiff North) Ian Grist 1974-83; Michael Roberts (Con) 1970-74
Previous AMs: Jenny Randerson (Lib Dem) 1999-2011

Jenny WILLOTT Liberal Democrat
Majority: 4,576 (12.7%)

House of Commons
London SW1A 0AA
Tel: (020) 7219 8418
Email: willottj@parliament.uk

Constituency Office:
99 Woodville Road, Cathays, Cardiff CF24 4DY
Tel: (029) 2046 2276
Website: www.jennywillott.com

Jenny Willott was elected to Parliament in May 2005, becoming the fourth youngest MP and the first woman to ever represent the seat. She had previously contested the seat in 2001. Born in London in 1974, Jenny Willott was educated at Wimbledon High School, Uppingham School and read Classics at Durham University before doing a post-graduate degree at the London School of Economics. Before becoming an MP Jenny worked for a number of charities, including the children's charity Barnardo's in their Welsh fostering and adoption project, and as Head of Advocacy for UNICEF UK.

In Parliament, Jenny has been a member of the Work and Pensions Select Committee and the Public Administration Select Committee, as well as being Opposition Deputy Chief Whip and Ministry of Justice Spokesperson. In June 2008 Jenny became Shadow Secretary of State for Work and Pensions before being appointed Shadow Chancellor of the Duchy of Lancaster. After the 2010 elections Jenny became co-Chair of the Liberal Democrat Parliamentary Party Committee on Work and Pensions. In the 2010 Coalition Government she was appointed PPS to Chris Huhne, Secretary of State for Energy and Climate Change but she resigned in protest against the Coalition Government's policy on university tuition fees. Jenny's particular interests include crime, human rights, social justice, and environmental issues. In February 2012 she returned to Government as an Assistant Whip.

2010 General Election Result

	Party	Votes Cast	%	Change 05-10
Jenny Willott	Lib D	14,976	41.4	-8.4%
Jenny Rathbone	Lab	10,400	28.8	-5.5%
Karen Robson	Con	7,799	21.6	+12.3%
Chris Williams	PC	1,246	3.4	-0.1%
Susan Davies	UKIP	765	2.1	+1.1%
Sam Coates	Green	575	1.6	+1.6%
Ross Saunders	Trade Unionist	162	0.4	+0.4%
Mark Beech	Loony	142	0.4	+0.4%
Alun Mathias	Ind	86	0.2	+0.2%

Electorate: 61,162 Turnout: 59.1%

| 2010 | 2005 | **Lib D** | **Lab** | **Con** | **PC** | **Other** |

Jenny RATHBONE Labour
Majority: 38 (0.1%)

National Assembly for Wales
Cardiff Bay, Cardiff CF99 1NA
Tel: (029) 2089 8286
Email: jenny.rathbone@wales.gov.uk

Constituency Office:
165 Albany Road, Cardiff CF24 3NT
Tel: (029) 2049 0352
Website: www.jennyrathbone.wordpress.com

CARDIFF CENTRAL

Jenny Rathbone entered the Assembly after defeating the Liberal Democrats' candidate by 38 votes in May 2011. Born in Liverpool, Jenny worked for 20 years in current affairs television, including roles as a researcher and reporter for Granada's World in Action, producer of the BBC's Money Programme, and some time working on Women's Hour on BBC Radio 4. Jenny chaired the Independent Review Panels of complaints for the NHS in London from 1996 to 2003. From 2002 to 2007, Jenny was programme manager of an award-winning Sure Start programme in north London and served as the lay representative on the Professional Executive Committee of Islington Primary Care Trust, working with doctors, nurses and allied health professionals to improve primary care. A former councillor in the London Borough of Islington, she is currently a school governor for Llanedeyrn High School and Ysgol y Berllan Deg.

In the Assembly she is a member of the Children and Young People Committee and the Public Accounts Committee. Her political interests include children, penal reform and social justice; and she is currently a member of Unite, the Co-operative Party and the Socialist Health Association and is on the National Executive of the Fabian Society.

2011 Assembly Election Result

	Party	Votes Cast	%	Change 07-11
Jenny Rathbone	Lab	8,954	37.9	+16.0%
Nigel Howells	Lib D	8,916	37.7	-13.4%
Matt Smith	Con	3,559	15.1	+1.1%
Chris Williams	PC	1,690	7.2	-1.1%
Mathab Khan	Ind	509	2.2	-

Electorate: 64,347 Turnout: 36.7%

Electoral Trends 1999 - 2011

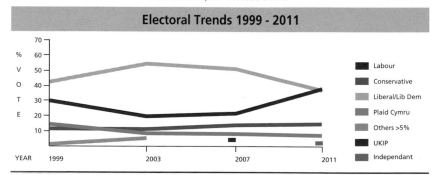

CARDIFF NORTH

MP - Jonathan EVANS Conservative

AM - Julie MORGAN Labour

South Wales Central Regional AMs

Andrew R T Davies (Con)

David Melding (Con)

Eluned Parrott (Lib D)

Leanne Wood (PC)

Area:	43 sq km	% born in Wales:	76.5%
% speaking Welsh: 19.2%		% Unemployment *(Apr 2012)* 3.8%	

The constituency comprises the following electoral wards:
Gabalfa, Heath, Lisvane, Llandaff North, Llanishen, Pontprennau/Old St. Mellons, Rhiwbina, Whitchurch & Tongwynlais.

Cardiff North takes in many of the more well-to-do Cardiff suburbs and contains one of the highest proportions of non-manual workers in Britain. The constituency had long been an established Conservative stronghold prior to the Labour landslide of 1997. The success of Julie Morgan raised the question of whether Cardiff North had fallen to Labour on the Blairite swing, or whether a more fundamental socio-economic shift had occurred. At the Assembly election in May 1999, Sue Essex took Cardiff North for Labour and withstood a further strong Conservative challenge in 2003. Julie Morgan retained the Parliamentary seat, despite negative swings, in both 2001 and 2005. When Sue Essex stood down in 2007, her Conservative challenger, Jonathan Morgan AM, was well known locally as a regional member and had previously contested the seat at both Assembly and Parliamentary levels. Together with a resurgence in the fortunes of the national Conservative Party, Jonathan Morgan successfully returned Cardiff North to the Tory fold. It was also expected that the Conservatives would comfortably recapture the seat at the 2010 General Election. The Conservative candidate, former Government Minister Jonathan Evans, seemed particularly appropriate for Cardiff North but his victory, against a clearly still popular Julie Morgan, was by less than 200 votes. However, Julie Morgan bounced back from the close defeat and recaptured the seat for Labour at the 2011 Assembly election. Had Jonathan Morgan been successful, it is quite likely that he would have been one of the favourites to become Leader of the Conservative Party in the Assembly.

Electoral Trends 1979 - 2010

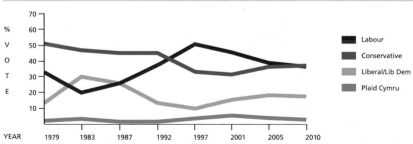

Previous MPs: **Julie Morgan (Lab) 1997-2010**; **Gwilym Jones (Con) 1983-97** (New seat 1983, formerly Cardiff North West); **Michael Roberts (Con) 1974-83** (New seat 1974, formerly Cardiff North); **Michael Roberts 1970-74**
Previous AMs: Jonathan Morgan (Con) 1999-2011

MP for Cardiff North

Jonathan EVANS Conservative
Majority: 194 (0.4%)

House of Commons, London SW1A 0AA
Tel: (020) 7219 7205
Email: jonathan.evans.mp@parliament.uk

Constituency Office:
54 Old Church Road, Whitchurch
Cardiff CF14 1AB
Tel: (029) 2061 3539
Website: www.jonathanevans.org.uk

Jonathan Evans returned to Westminster at the 2010 General election, winning Cardiff North with a majority of 194 from Labour's Julie Morgan. He was first elected to Parliament in 1992 when he succeeded in winning Brecon and Radnor from Liberal, Richard Livsey. His first Government appointment was as Parliamentary Private Secretary to the then Minister of State for Northern Ireland, Michael Mate. He was subsequently Corporate Affairs Minister at the DTI; Parliamentary Secretary to the Lord Chancellor – a role in which he was the first Roman Catholic to exercise Lord Chancellor's duties since the 1688 Act of Settlement; and Under Secretary of State for Wales 1996-1997.

Jonathan's Parliamentary career was interrupted in 1997 when he was one of the Conservative MPs who lost their seat at the General Election. He served the party from outside Parliament as its Chief Spokesman for Wales at the end of the 1990s and then as a Welsh Conservative MEP for a decade before standing down in 2009. Following his re-election in 2010, he became the Chairman of the All Party Parliamentary Group on Insurance and Financial Services. He is also the co-Chair of the All Party Parliamentary Group on Building Societies and Financial Mutuals and, as such, has led a short inquiry into corporate diversity in financial services. A solicitor by background, he has also served as the Deputy Chairman of Tai Cymru (the Welsh Housing Corporation) and the Welsh Sports Centre for the Disabled.

2010 General Election Result

	Party	Votes Cast	%	Change 05-10
Jonathan Evans	Con	17,860	37.5	+1.0%
Julie Morgan	Lab	17,666	37.1	-1.9%
John Dixon	Lib D	8,724	18.3	-0.4%
Llywelyn Rhys	PC	1,588	3.3	-0.9%
Lawrence Gwynn	UKIP	1,130	2.4	+1.2%
Christopher von Ruhland	Green	362	0.8	+0.8%
Derek Thomson	WCP	300	0.6	+0.6%

Electorate: 65,553 Turnout: 72.7%

| 2010 2005 | Con | Lab | Lib D | PC | Other |

Julie MORGAN Labour
Majority: 1,782 (5.1%)

National Assembly for Wales
Cardiff Bay, Cardiff CF99 1NA
Tel: (029) 2089 8297
Email: julie.morgan@wales.gov.uk

Constituency Office:
17 Plasnewydd, Whitchurch
Cardiff CF14 1NR
Tel: (029) 2061 4577 Fax: (029) 2061 6138
Website: www.juliemorgan.org

Julie Morgan was first elected to the Assembly at the 2011 election, having represented the same constituency as an MP since 1997 before losing her seat at the 2010 General Election. The wife of former First Minister Rhodri Morgan, Julie was born in Cardiff and educated at Howell's School, King's College London, the University of Manchester and Cardiff University. Prior to becoming an MP and then AM, Julie was a social worker in Cardiff and Barry, working in child protection and with disabled people. She served as a Councillor on both South Glamorgan and Cardiff Councils for more than a decade, and during her time in Parliament she presented three Private Member's Bills - one on banning smoking in public places, one on granting votes at 16, and most recently, one on preventing under-18s from using sunbeds. The latter became law in 2010.

In the Assembly she is currently a member of the Children and Young People Committee, the Finance Committee and the Public Accounts Committee. Julie is a member of the Unite union and a founder member of the Welsh Refugee Council. She is also a founder member of the Women's Arts Association, a patron of the Touch Trust and Advocacy Matters, a trustee of Life for African Mothers and Vice President of George Thomas Hospice.

2011 Assembly Election Result

	Party	Votes Cast	%	Change 07-11
Julie Morgan	Lab	16,384	47.6	+16.7%
Jonathan Morgan	Con	14,602	42.4	-2.8%
Ben Foday	PC	1,850	5.4	-2.0%
Matt Smith	Lib D	1,595	4.6	-8.1%

Electorate: 66,934 Turnout: 51.4%

Electoral Trends 1999 - 2011

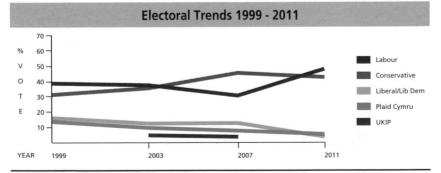

CARDIFF SOUTH & PENARTH

MP - Rt Hon Alun MICHAEL Labour
AM - Vaughan GETHING Labour

South Wales Central Regional AMs

Andrew R T Davies (Con)   Eluned Parrott (Lib D)

David Melding (Con)   Leanne Wood (PC)

| Area: | 46 sq km | % born in Wales: | 79.1% |
| % speaking Welsh: | 16.5% | % Unemployment *(Apr 2012)* | 8.1% |

The constituency comprises the following electoral wards:
Butetown, Cornerswell, Grangetown, Llandough, Llanrumney, Plymouth, Rumney, Splott, St. Augustine's, Stanwell, Sully, Trowbridge.

Cardiff South and Penarth combines middle-class, suburban Penarth with the traditionally poorer, ethnically diverse, Butetown area of Cardiff and the newly developed Cardiff Bay waterfront. Formerly the constituency of the Prime Minister, James Callaghan, who represented the docks and the southern parts of Cardiff from 1945 until 1987. James Callaghan was succeeded by Alun Michael, who went on to become Secretary of State for Wales before being elected as one of the new breed of Regional AMs and the founding First Secretary of the fledging Assembly in 1999. Barely a year into the post, Alun Michael resigned and retreated back to London and took up a succession of senior Government positions. Incorporating the former Cardiff Bay Development area, the constituency is now the home of the National Assembly for Wales and a rapidly growing commercial and residential district. The Wales Millennium Centre - the home for the Welsh National Opera, Urdd Gobaith Cymru and several other cultural organizations - opened in November 2004.

Although affected by minor boundary changes prior to the 2007 Assembly elections, Cardiff South and Penarth remains a fairly safe Labour seat and neither the Parliamentary, nor the Assembly, seat appear under any serious threat. With the retirement of sitting AM, Lorraine Barrett, Labour candidate Vaughan Gething almost tripled his party's majority in 2011 and dispelled any fears that a low turnout could impact on the result. However, whilst the creation of a permanent recreational waterfront has transformed the appearance of the former docklands, the traditionally diverse community of the area is changing more slowly. In time, 'gentrification' may well come to challenge Labour dominance and create a politically more competitive constituency, especially if the 'incomers' show a greater propensity to vote than the established population.

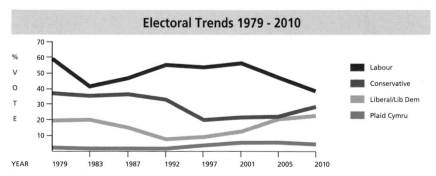

Electoral Trends 1979 - 2010

Previous MPs: **Sir James Callaghan (Lab) 1983-87;** (New seat 1983, formerly Cardiff South East); **James Callaghan 1950-83**
Previous AMs: **Lorraine Barrett (Lab) 1999-2011**

Rt Hon Alun MICHAEL Labour
Majority: 4,709 (10.6%)

House of Commons, London SW1A 0AA
Tel: (020) 7219 5980
Email: alun.michael.mp@parliament.uk

Constituency Office:
PO Box 453, Cardiff CF11 9YN
Tel: (029) 2022 3533
Website: www.alunmichael.com

CARDIFF S & PENARTH

Alun Michael has been adopted as the Labour candidate for the post of Police & Crime Commissioner (PCC) in South Wales at the upcoming election on 15th November 2012. MPs have to stand down to contest the position and it is therefore highly likely that a by-election will be held concurrently in late 2012.

Alun Michael was first elected to Parliament for Cardiff South and Penarth in 1987. Born at Bryngwran, Anglesey, on 22 August 1943, he was educated at Colwyn Bay Grammar School and Keele University. He became a magistrate in 1972 and was Chairman of the Cardiff Juvenile Bench. A Cardiff City Councillor 1973-89, he is a former Chief Whip of the Labour Group and Chair of the Economic Development Committee.

In 1999, he became the founding First Secretary of the National Assembly for Wales, but was forced to resign in February 2000 and subsequently stood down as a regional AM. Prior to devolution, he served as Minister of State in the Home Office, with special responsibility for Criminal Justice, the Police and the voluntary sector. He joined the Cabinet as Secretary of State for Wales in 1998. He is a member of the National Executive of the Co-operative Party, a Fellow of the RSA and sings in the Parliamentary choir. A fluent Welsh speaker, he is married with five children and six grandchildren.

2010 General Election Result

	Party	Votes Cast	%	Change 05-10
Alun Michael	Lab	17,262	38.9	-7.7%
Simon Hoare	Con	12,553	28.3	+4.4%
Dominic Hannigan	Lib D	9,875	22.3	+2.4%
Farida Aslam	PC	1,851	4.2	-1.1%
Simon Zeigler	UKIP	1,145	2.6	+1.2%
George Burke	Ind	648	1.5	+1.5%
Matt Townsend	Green	554	1.2	-0.6%
Clive Bate	WCP	285	0.6	+0.6%
Robert Griffiths	Comm	196	0.4	+0.4%

Electorate: 73,908 Turnout: 60.2%

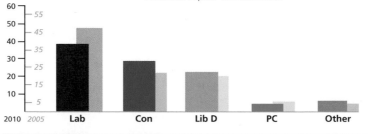

Vaughan GETHING Labour
Majority: 6,259 (22.7%)

National Assembly for Wales
Cardiff Bay, Cardiff CF99 1NA
Tel: (029) 2089 8276
Email: vaughan.gething@wales.gov.uk
Website: www.vaughangething.co.uk

CARDIFF S & PENARTH

Vaughan Gething was elected in 2011 after previously standing in the 1999 election on the Mid & West regional list. Vaughan was born in Zambia and brought up in Dorset. He was educated at Aberystwyth and Cardiff universities and now lives in Butetown with his wife Michelle. Prior to entering the Assembly, Vaughan was the first ever black President of the National Union of Students Wales. A solicitor by trade, he was a partner at law firm Thompsons and a member of the GMB and Unite unions. He became the youngest ever President of the TUC in Wales and also served as a Cardiff councillor 2004-8. Between 1999 and 2001, Vaughan worked as a researcher to former AMs Val Feld and Lorraine Barrett and was also the chair of Right to Vote – a cross-party project to encourage greater participation from black minority ethnic communities in public life.

In the Assembly Vaughan is Chair of the Common Agricultural Policy Task and Finish Group as well as sitting on the Environment and Sustainability Committee and the Health and Social Care Committee. He is also Chair of the Assembly's Cross Party Groups on Rail and Co-operatives and Mutuals.

2011 Assembly Election Result

	Party	Votes Cast	%	Change 07-11
Vaughan Gething	Lab	13,814	50.3	+12.5%
Ben Gray	Con	7,555	27.5	-0.0%
Liz Musa	PC	3,324	12.1	-2.2%
Sian Anne Cliff	Lib D	2,786	10.1	-10.2%

Electorate: 75,038 Turnout: 36.6%

Electoral Trends 1999 - 2011

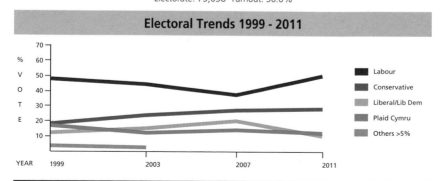

CARDIFF WEST

MP - Kevin BRENNAN Labour
AM - Mark DRAKEFORD Labour

South Wales Central Regional AMs

Andrew R T Davies (Con)   Eluned Parrott (Lib Dem)
David Melding (Con)   Leanne Wood (PC)

Area:	51 sq km	% born in Wales:	79.2%
% speaking Welsh:	20.3%	% Unemployment *(Apr 2012)*	4.4%

The constituency comprises the following electoral wards:
Caerau, Canton, Creigiau/St.Fagans, Ely, Fairwater, Llandaff, Pentyrch, Radyr, Riverside.

Cardiff West is a mixed constituency containing wealthy, middle-class suburbs, classic inner city wards, as well as a large public housing stock. Cardiff's 'Welsh Quarter', Pontcanna, home to media and creative folk, also lies within the seat. Llandaff, with its cathedral, is a 'city within a city' and St Fagans, with its world-famous National History Museum, are major tourist attractions. Cardiff West was formerly the seat of George Thomas, Speaker of the House of Commons 1976-83, and a Cardiff MP from 1945 to 1983. Following such a long Labour tenure, it was a major upset when, on George Thomas's retirement, Stefan Terlezki briefly won the seat for the Conservatives thanks to a strong intervention by the newly formed SDP. Recaptured by Labour in 1987, under Rhodri Morgan's control the Parliamentary, and later the Assembly, seat has become increasingly secure. That Kevin Brennan would succeed Rhodri Morgan as MP for Cardiff West was perhaps the safest bet of the 2001 General Election. Rhodri Morgan was the most popular politician in Wales and Kevin Brennan had been his long-term political lieutenant. Turnout at subsequent elections has fluctuated, whilst the Liberal Democrats, the Conservatives and Plaid Cymru have all seen an upturn in their fortunes, Cardiff West remains a fairly a safe Labour seat. Any fears that the retirement of Rhodri Morgan would have an impact on the result were disproved at the 2011 Assembly election, when Labour considerably increased their majority, and the Liberal Democrat vote all but collapsed.

Electoral Trends 1979 - 2010

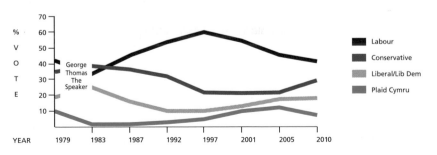

Previous MPs: Rhodri Morgan (Lab) 1987-2001; Stefan Terlezki (Con) 1983-87; George Thomas (Lab) 1950-83
Previous AMs: Rhodri Morgan (Lab) 1999-2011

MP for Cardiff West

Kevin BRENNAN Labour
Majority: 4,751 (11.6%)

House of Commons, London SW1A 0AA
Tel: (020) 7219 8156
Email: brennank@parliament.uk

Constituency Office:
Transport House, 1 Cathedral Road
Cardiff CF11 9SD
Tel: (029) 2022 3207
Website: www.kevinbrennan.co.uk

Kevin Brennan was elected to Parliament in June 2001 succeeding Rhodri Morgan who had represented Cardiff West since 1987. The son of a steel worker, Kevin Brennan was born in Cwmbran in 1959. He was educated at St Alban's Roman Catholic Comprehensive School; Pembroke College Oxford; University of Wales, Cardiff and the University of Glamorgan. At Oxford, in 1982, he was elected President of the Oxford Union in succession to William Hague. He was formerly Head of Economics at Radyr Comprehensive School in Cardiff. He was also a Cardiff City Councillor for Canton from 1991 until his election to Parliament.

Kevin was previously Rhodri Morgan's researcher from 1995 and was a Special Adviser in the National Assembly from October 2000. Kevin Brennan is currently a Shadow Minister for Education as well as being a member of UNITE, the Fabian Society, the Labour Campaign for Electoral Reform and the Canton Labour Club. Married with one child, he is a passionate supporter of Cardiff Blues and Wales and plays guitar in the Parliamentary rock group MP4.

2010 General Election Result

	Party	Votes Cast	%	Change 05-10
Kevin Brennan	Lab	16,893	41.2	-3.6%
Angela Jones-Evans	Con	12,143	29.6	+7.0%
Rachael Hitchinson	Lib D	7,186	17.5	+0.5%
Mohammed Sarul Islam	PC	2,868	7.0	-5.9%
Mike Henessey	UKIP	1,117	2.7	+0.6%
Jake Griffiths	Green	750	1.8	+1.8%

Electorate: 62,787 Turnout: 65.2%

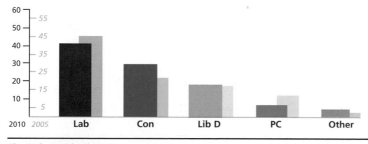

AM for Cardiff West

Mark DRAKEFORD Labour
Majority: 5,900 (21.2%)

National Assembly for Wales
Cardiff Bay, Cardiff CF99 1NA
Tel: (029) 2089 8724
Email: mark.drakeford@wales.gov.uk

Constituency Office:
33-35 Cathedral Road, Cardiff CF11 6LB
Tel: (029) 2022 3207
Website: www.markdrakeford.com

Mark Drakeford entered the National Assembly when he won the Cardiff West seat in May 2011, following in the footsteps of former First Minister Rhodri Morgan, who was the previous holder of the seat. Born and brought up in West Wales, Mark has lived in Cardiff for over thirty years with his wife and children. A former probation officer, youth justice worker and Barnardos project leader in Ely and Caerau, he is a Professor of Social Policy at Cardiff University. A member of the Labour Party since 1974, during the 1980s and 1990s he was a Labour Councillor on South Glamorgan County Council, specialising in education issues, including Welsh medium education. Between 2000 and 2010 he worked as the Cabinet's health and social policy adviser in the Welsh Government, and was latterly head of the First Minister's political office.

In the Assembly, Mark is currently the Chair of the Health and Social Care Committee as well as being a member of the Committee for the Scrutiny of the First Minister. Outside politics, he is a long-time member of Glamorgan County Cricket Club, has worked a Pontcanna allotment for more than quarter of a century and enjoys body boarding off the Pembrokeshire coast.

2011 Assembly Election Result

	Party	Votes Cast	%	Change 07-11
Mark Drakeford	Lab	13,067	47.1	+8.5%
Craig Williams	Con	7,167	25.9	+1.0%
Neil McEvoy	PC	5,551	20.0	-1.2%
David Morgan	Lib D	1,942	7.0	-8.2%

Electorate: 64,219 Turnout: 43.2%

Electoral Trends 1999 - 2011

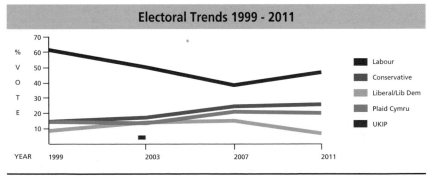

CARMARTHEN EAST & DINEFWR

MP - Jonathan EDWARDS Plaid Cymru

AM - Rhodri Glyn THOMAS Plaid Cymru

Mid & West Wales Regional AMs

Rebecca Evans (Lab)   Simon Thomas (PC)

William Powell (Lib D)   Joyce Watson (Lab)

Area:	1,555 sq km	% born in Wales:	75.7%
% speaking Welsh: 60.5%		% Unemployment *(Apr 2012)*	3.8%

The constituency comprises the following electoral wards:
Abergwili, Ammanford, Betws, Cenarth, Cilycwm, Cynwyl Gaeo, Garnant, Glanamman, Gorslas, Llanddarog, Llandeilo, Llandovery, Llandybie, Llanegwad, Llanfihangel Aberbythych, Llanfihangel-ar-Arth, Llangadog, Llangeler, Llangunnor, Llangyndeyrn, Llanybydder, Manordeilo & Salem, Penygroes, Pontamman, Quarter Bach, Saron, St.Ishmael.

The constituency of **Carmarthen East and Dinefwr** was formed with the division of the former county seat in 1997. Carmarthen has held a special place in the political history of Wales and its previous MPs have included Lady Megan Lloyd George and Gwynfor Evans, the first Welsh Nationalist MP. At the Devolution Referendum in 1997, Carmarthenshire also delivered the final crucial declaration to give the 'Yes' vote its narrow majority.

First fought in 1997, the new eastern division of the county has been a keen contest between Labour and Plaid Cymru. The constituency still has a large rural population, but the addition of part of the Amman Valley, the old anthracite coalfield, has intensified the political struggle. Rhodri Glyn Thomas of Plaid Cymru was elected the first AM for Carmarthen East in 1999. At the General Election of 2001, in a fierce contest, Adam Price, one of Plaid Cymru's brightest young candidates, prevailed against the sitting Labour MP, Dr Alan Williams. In 2003 Rhodri Glyn Thomas retained his Assembly seat, but again, the intensity of the contest gave Carmarthen East one of the highest turnouts of the election. Similarly at the General Election in 2005, a high profile, high turnout, contest saw Plaid Cymru increase its majority. By 2007, Rhodri Glyn Thomas, then Deputy Leader of the Plaid Cymru Group in the Assembly, had transformed the seat into one of the safest in Wales. Adam Price stood down from Parliament in 2010, but bequeathed his successor a secure constituency. Plaid Cymru comfortably held on to the seat at the 2011 Assembly election, but with half the majority enjoyed in 2007.

Electoral Trends 1979 - 2010

Legend:
- Labour
- Conservative
- Liberal/Lib Dem
- Plaid Cymru

%VOTE axis: 70, 60, 50, 40, 30, 20, 10

YEAR: 1979 1983 1987 1992 1997 2001 2005 2010

Previous MPs: **Adam Price (PC) 2001-2010; Alan Williams (Lab) 1997-2001;** (New seat 1997, formerly Carmarthen) Alan Williams 1987-97; Roger Thomas (Lab) 1979-87; Gwynfor Evans (PC) 1974-79; Gwynoro Jones (Lab) 1970-74

MP for Carmarthen East & Dinefwr

Jonathan EDWARDS Plaid Cymru
Majority: 3,481 (9.2%)

House of Commons, London SW1A 0AA
Tel: (020) 7219 5021
Email: jonathan.edwards.mp@parliament.uk

Constituency Office:
37 Wind Street, Ammanford
Carmarthenshire SA18 3DN
Tel: (01269) 597677
Website: www.jonathanedwards.org.uk

Jonathan Edwards was first elected in May 2010, succeeding the previous Plaid Cymru MP Adam Price, who stood down to pursue a research sabbatical in the United States. Born and rasied in the mining village of Capel Hendre near Ammanford, he attended Ysgol Gymraeg Rhydaman and Ysgol Gyfun Maes yr Yrfa before graduating in History and Politics at the University of Wales, Aberystwyth and gaining a postgraduate degree in International History specialising in the end of the Cold War. Jonathan previously worked as Chief of Staff for Rhodri Glyn Thomas AM and Adam Price MP for 7 years, where he led on political matters for both elected members. He is a former Carmarthen Councillor and was elected to the historical post of town Sheriff. In 2005 he was given responsibility for strategic matters within the party's new National Campaigns Directorate. He is considered one of Plaid's foremost strategic thinkers. After the 2007 Assembly election, Jonathan moved to work for Citizens Advice Cymru where he led on Public Affairs, Public Relations and Policy matters.

In Parliament he is currently the Plaid Cymru Spokesperson for Business, Innovation and Skills; Communities and Local Government; Culture, Olympics, Media and Sport; Transport and for the Treasury. He is also a member of the Welsh Affairs Select Committee and his main political interests include social justice and foreign affairs. His other interests include playing cricket for Penygroes and supporting Swansea City Football Club and the Scarlets.

2010 General Election Result

	Party	Votes Cast	%	Change 05-10
Jonathan Edwards	PC	13,546	35.6	-10.2%
Christine Gwyther	Lab	10,065	26.5	-1.8%
Andrew Morgan	Con	8,506	22.4	+8.7%
Willian Powell	Lib D	4,609	12.1	+2.4%
John Atkinson	UKIP	1,285	3.4	+1.7%

Electorate: 52,385 Turnout: 72.6%

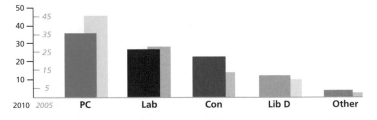

Rhodri Glyn THOMAS Plaid Cymru
Majority: 4,148 (14.9%)

National Assembly for Wales
Cardiff Bay, Cardiff CF99 1NA
Tel: (029) 2089 8055
Email: rhodri.thomas@wales.gov.uk

Constituency Office:
37 Stryd y Gwynt, Rhydaman SA18 3DN
Tel: (01269) 597677
Website: www.rhodriglynthomas.org

CARMARTHEN EAST

Rhodri Glyn Thomas was first elected to the Assembly in 1999. Born in Wrexham in 1953, he attended the universities of Aberystwyth, Bangor and Lampeter. He is a minister of religion and had previously contested Carmarthen in the 1992 General Election and Carmarthen East in 1997. A fluent Welsh speaker, he was Chair of CND Cymru, 1984-88 and also served as a Community Councillor. In the first Assembly he served as Chair of the Agriculture and Rural Development Committee and, later, Chair of the new Culture Committee. In 2003 he was appointed Deputy Leader of the Plaid Cymru Assembly group but later stood down. He unsuccessfully contested the leadership of the Plaid Cymru Assembly Group in 2003.

He was one of the Plaid Cymru Ministers in the 'One Wales' Coalition Government until his resignation of the Heritage brief in 2008. He currently sits on the Communities, Equality and Local Government Committee and The Assembly Commission. He is also his party's Spokesperson on Local Government, Communities and Europe. His political interests include agriculture and the rural economy, Europe, and transport issues. Rhodri is married with three children.

2011 Assembly Election Result

	Party	Votes Cast	%	Change 07-11
Rhodri Glyn Thomas	PC	12,501	44.9	-8.6%
Anthony Jones	Lab	8,353	30.0	+5.5%
Henrietta Hensher	Con	5,635	20.3	+4.3%
Will Griffiths	Lib D	1,339	4.8	-1.2%

Electorate: 54,243 Turnout: 51.3%

Electoral Trends 1999 - 2011

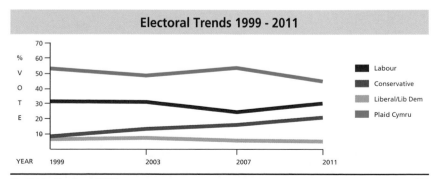

Labour
Conservative
Liberal/Lib Dem
Plaid Cymru

CARMARTHEN WEST & SOUTH PEMBS.

MP - Simon HART Conservative

AM - Angela BURNS Conservative

Mid & West Wales Regional AMs

Rebecca Evans (Lab)	Simon Thomas (PC)
William Powell (Lib D)	Joyce Watson (Lab)

Area:	1,018 sq km	% born in Wales:	69.3%
% speaking Welsh:	26.6%	% Unemployment *(Apr 2012)*	4.4%

The constituency comprises the following electoral wards:
Amroth, Carew, Carmarthen Town North, Carmarthen Town South, Carmarthen Town West, Cynwyl Elfed, East Williamston, Hundleton, Kilgetty/Begelly, Lampeter Velfrey, Lamphey, Laugharne Township, Llanboidy, Llansteffan, Manorbier, Martletwy, Narbeth, Narberth Rural, Pembroke Dock Central, Pembroke Dock Llanion, Pembroke Dock Market, Pembroke Dock Pennar, Pembroke Monkton, Pembroke St. Mary North, Pembroke St.Mary South, Pembroke St.Michael, Penally, Saundersfoot, St.Clears, Tenby North, Tenby South, Trelech, Whitland.

The seat of **Carmarthen West & South Pembrokeshire**, created in 1997, was an unlikely marriage of convenience between two disparate areas - the west of Carmarthenshire, still rural and agricultural, and the south coast of Pembrokeshire, the 'Welsh Riviera' and, for many, somewhere to retire. The former seats of Carmarthen and Pembroke have both, between them, returned MPs from all four main parties since the Second World War. Members of Lloyd George's family have represented both seats and Nicholas Edwards, Conservative Secretary of State for Wales 1979-87, and the late Gwynfor Evans, former President of Plaid Cymru, were two of the most influential Welsh MPs of their generation.

This division should have created a competitive party contest, but the seat proved to be fairly safe for the Labour Party up until the Assembly elections of 2003. Nick Ainger, Labour MP, had been returned fairly comfortably in the landslide elections of 1997 and 2001 and, although challenged further at the 2005 Election, held on with a reduced majority. Christine Gwyther was elected as the first AM in 1999 and, although re-elected in 2003, had been put under great pressure by Plaid Cymru. In 2007 however, Carmarthen West and South Pembs became a target seat for both Plaid Cymru and the Conservatives. To the surprise of most commentators, the Conservatives won by a margin of 98 votes. The overall result was an effective tie, with all three parties divided by less than 250 votes. The Conservatives captured the seat at the 2010 General Election and increased their majority at the 2011 Assembly election. However, on the basis of the 2011 figures, it remains one of the most marginal seats in Wales.

Electoral Trends 1979 - 2010

% V O T E

70
60
50
40
30
20
10

YEAR 1979 1983 1987 1992 1997 2001 2005 2010

■ Labour
■ Conservative
■ Liberal/Lib Dem
■ Plaid Cymru

Previous MPs: **Nick Ainger (Lab) 1997-2010;** (New seat 1997, formerly part of Pembroke) **Nick Ainger (Lab) 1992-97; Nicholas Bennett (Con) 1987-92; Nicholas Edwards (Con) 1970-87**
Previous AMs: **Christine Gwyther (Lab) 1999-2007**

MP for Carmarthen West & South Pembs.

Simon HART Conservative
Majority: 3,423 (8.5%)

House of Commons
London SW1A 0AA
Tel: (020) 7219 7228
Email: simon.hart.mp@parliament.uk

Constituency Office:
15 St John Street, Whitland SA34 0AN
Tel: (01994) 342002
Website: www.simon-hart.com

CARMARTHEN WEST

Simon Hart, who lives in Llanmill near Narberth, was elected the Conservative Member of Parliament for Carmarthen West and South Pembrokeshire in May 2010 with a majority of just over 3,400. Prior to being elected Simon Hart was, for seven years, Chief Executive of the Countryside Alliance, Europe's largest rural affairs lobby group. The campaign to oppose legislation against hunting was particularly active in Carmarthenshire and undoubtedly contributed to Simon Hart's adoption as Parliamentary candidate. He had previously worked as a chartered surveyor in Carmarthen and Haverfordwest and served with the Territorial Army for five years.

He is currently a member of the Commons Select Committee for Political and Constitutional Reform. He is also a member several All Party Parliamentary Groups, including being Vice-Chair of both the Electoral Reform Group and Rail in Wales Group. He is married with two children.

2010 General Election Result

	Party	Votes Cast	%	Change 05-10
Simon Hart	Con	16,649	41.1	+9.8%
Nick Ainger	Lab	13,226	32.7	-4.0%
John Gossage	Lib D	4,890	12.1	-2.1%
John Dixon	PC	4,232	10.4	-5.1%
Ray Clarke	UKIP	1,146	2.8	+1.4%
Henry Langen	Ind	364	0.9	+0.9%

Electorate: 58,108 Turnout: 70.4%

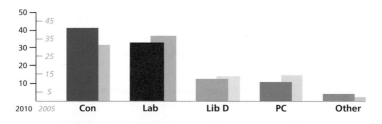

CARMARTHEN WEST

Angela BURNS Conservative
Majority: 1,504 (5.3%)

National Assembly for Wales
Cardiff Bay, Cardiff CF99 1NA
Tel: (029) 2089 8384
Email: angela.burns@wales.gov.uk

Constituency Office:
14 Market Square, Narbeth SA67 7AU
Tel: (01834) 862725
Website: www.angelaburns.org.uk

Angela Burns was elected to the Assembly in May 2007 in an extraordinary close contest which she won with a majority of only 98 votes. She was returned during the 2011 election with an increased majority of 1,504 votes. Angela was brought up in various countries around the world and when she left school moved into private business. She has subsequently worked for companies as diverse as Waitrose, Thorn Emi and Asda, as well as a number of smaller enterprises. In the Wales Yearbook Welsh Politician of the Year Awards 2007, she was recognised as the 'Member to Watch'.

In the Assembly she currently serves as the Conservative Shadow Minister for Education. She also sits on the Children and Young People Committee and The Assembly Commission. Furthermore, she also Chairs Cross Party Groups on Energy and also The Horse. Her political interests include the economy, health, schools and rural communities and aside from politics, Angela rides horses, shoots, dives, whilst also taking in the cinema and theatre. She is married with two children.

2011 Assembly Election Result

	Party	Votes Cast	%	Change 07-11
Angela Burns	Con	10,095	35.9	+5.8%
Christine Gwyther	Lab	8,591	30.5	+0.8%
Nerys Evans	PC	8,373	29.7	+0.5%
Selwyn Runnett	Lib D	1,097	3.9	-2.4%

Electorate: 58,435 Turnout: 48.2%

Electoral Trends 1999 - 2011

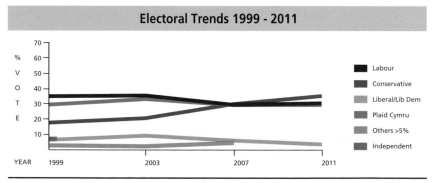

CEREDIGION

MP - Mark WILLIAMS Liberal Democrat
AM - Elin JONES Plaid Cymru

Mid & West Wales Regional AMs

Rebecca Evans (Lab)	Simon Thomas (PC)
William Powell (Lib D)	Joyce Watson (Lab)

Area:	1,794 sq km	% born in Wales:	58.6%
% speaking Welsh: 51.8%		% Unemployment *(Apr 2012)* 3.0%	

The constituency comprises the following electoral wards:
Aberaeron, Aberporth, Aberystwyth Bronglais, Aberystwyth Central, Aberystwyth North, Aberystwyth Penparcau, Aberystwyth Rheidol, Beulah, Borth, Capel Dewi, Cardigan-Mwldan, Cardigan-Rhyd-y-Fuwch, Cardigan-Teifi, Ceulanmaesmawr, Ciliau Aeron, Faenor, Lampeter, Llanarth, Llanbadarn Fawr-Padarn, Llanbadarn Fawr-Sulien, Llandyfriog, Llandysilio-gogo, Llandysul Town, Llanfarian, Llanfihangel Ystrad, Llangeitho, Llangybi, Llanrhystud, Llansantffraid, Llanwenog, Lledrod, Melindwr, New Quay, Penbryn, Pen-parc, Tirymynach, Trefeurig, Tregaron, Troedyraur, Ystwyth.

Ceredigion, formerly Cardiganshire, was a Liberal constituency for over a century, with the exception of a brief interlude, 1966-74, when Elystan Morgan held the seat for Labour. An informal alliance of Plaid Cymru and the Greens however, captured Ceredigion from Geraint Howells in 1992. Cynog Dafis further increased Plaid Cymru's majority in 1997, prior to being elected in 1999 as an AM via the regional list for Mid & West Wales. He subsequently resigned his Westminster seat and at the subsequent by-election in February 2000, Plaid Cymru easily retained the seat, but the Liberal Democrats, through Mark Williams, achieved a credible second place. Persistence prevailed and the Liberal Democrats further eroded Plaid Cymru's majority in 2001. In 2005 Mark Williams defeated Simon Thomas to restore Ceredigion to the Liberal Democrats. His miniscule majority appeared under threat in 2010 but, counter to all expectations Mark Williams achieved a positive swing of prodigious proportions and now enjoys a majority in excess of eight thousand.

In elections for the Assembly, Elin Jones was returned as Ceredigion's first AM in 1999 but following the loss of the seat to the Liberal Democrats at the Parliamentary election, Ceredigion became a key seat for Plaid Cymru. Subsequent campaigns saw Elin Jones retain the seat fairly comfortably in 2003 and 2007 and while she held on to the seat at the 2011 Assembly election, her majority was eroded still further to under 2,000. Ceredigion continues to have a large Welsh-speaking population, a high proportion of the workforce remains dependent upon agriculture and there are an unusually high number of students and the self-employed in the constituency.

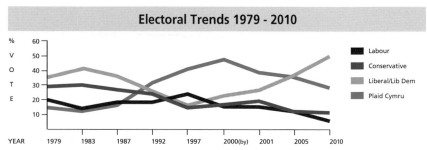

Electoral Trends 1979 - 2010

Legend: Labour, Conservative, Liberal/Lib Dem, Plaid Cymru

YEAR: 1979 1983 1987 1992 1997 2000(by) 2001 2005 2010

Previous MPs: **Simon Thomas 2000 (by)-05;** (New seat 1997, formerly part of Ceredigion and Pembroke North) **Cynog Dafis** (PC) 1992-2000; Geraint Howells (Alln/LD) 1983-92; (New seat 1983, formerly Cardigan) Geraint Howells (Lib) 1974-83; D Elystan Morgan (Lab) 1966-74

MP for Ceredigion

Mark WILLIAMS Liberal Democrat
Majority: 8,324 (21.8%)

House of Commons, London SW1A 0AA
Tel: (020) 7219 8469
Email: williamsmf@parliament.uk

Constituency Office:
32 North Parade, Aberystwyth
Ceredigion SY23 2NF
Tel: (01970) 627721
Website: www.markwilliams.org.uk

Mark Williams was elected for Ceredigion in May 2005, an election victory unexpected by all but the most ardent Liberal Democrats, and achieved with a tiny majority. In 2010 however he produced one of the UK's largest swings to the Liberal Democrats and increased his majority to over 8000. He previously fought Monmouth in 1997 and Ceredigion at the by-election in 2000. Born in Hertfordshire in 1966, he was educated at Richard Hale School and read Politics at the University of Wales, Aberystwyth. He worked as a Research Assistant for the Liberal Democrats in the House of Lords and as assistant to Geraint Howells, then MP for Ceredigion. He is a trained teacher and worked in Cornwall and Devon before becoming Deputy Head at Llangors Primary School in Powys.

Mark Williams's parliamentary career includes being appointed to the Welsh Affairs Select Committee in 2005, before becoming the Liberal Democrat spokesman for Wales, and at varying times a spokesman on schools and higher education. He is co-Chair of the Lib-Dem Backbench Group on Political and Constitutional Affairs, Secretary of the All-Party Group on Trains in Wales, and Chair of the APPG on Tourism in Wales. Married with four children, Mark lives in Borth, Ceredigion, and his interests include walking, political biographies and travelling.

2010 General Election Result

	Party	Votes Cast	%	Change 05-10
Mark Williams	Lib D	19,139	50.0	+13.5%
Penri James	PC	10,815	28.3	-7.6%
Luke Evetts	Con	4,421	11.6	-0.8%
Richard Boudier	Lab	2,210	5.8	-6.3%
Elwyn Williams	UKIP	977	2.6	+2.6%
Leila Kiersch	Green	696	1.8	-0.5%

Electorate: 58,464 Turnout: 64.8%

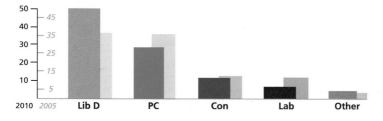

Elin JONES Plaid Cymru
Majority: 1,777 (6.1%)

National Assembly for Wales
Cardiff Bay, Cardiff CF99 1NA
Email: elin.jones@wales.gov.uk

Constituency Office:
Tŷ Goronwy, 32 Heol y Wig, Aberystwyth
Ceredigion SY23 2LN
Tel: (01970) 624516
Website: www.elinjones.plaidcymru.org

CEREDIGION

Elin Jones was first elected to the Assembly in 1999. Born in Carmarthen in 1966, Elin Jones grew up on a farm in Llanwnnen, near Lampeter. She graduated from University of Wales, Cardiff with a BSc in Economics and an MSc in Agricultural Economics at the University of Wales, Aberystwyth. Previously employed as a Regional Development Manager for the WDA, she was a Director of Radio Ceredigion and of Wes Glei Cyf, a television production company. Elin was the youngest-ever Mayor of Aberystwyth in 1997 and was Chair of Plaid Cymru 2000-02.

During the 'One Wales' Coalition Elin served as Minister for Rural Affairs and during that time she won the Farming Weekly's 'UK Farming Champion' award. She unsuccessfully contested the Plaid Cymru leadership in 2012. Elin is currently Plaid's Spokesperson for Health and she also sits on the Committee for the Scrutiny of First Minister and the Health and Social Care Committee. A fluent Welsh speaker, she is a member of Amnesty International and her political interests include rural economic development, the Welsh language, arts and culture and the European Union. She enjoys music, film and reading. She formerly sang with Cwlwm, but is now a member of a mixed choir in Aberystwyth, Côr ABC.

2011 Assembly Election Result

	Party	Votes Cast	%	Change 07-11
Elin Jones	PC	12,020	41.3	-7.9%
Elizabeth Evans	Lib D	10,243	35.2	-0.9%
Luke Evetts	Con	2,755	9.5	+1.6%
Richard Boudier	Lab	2,544	8.8	+3.7%
Chris Simpson	Green	1,514	5.2	-

Electorate: 56,983 Turnout: 51.0%

Electoral Trends 1999 - 2011

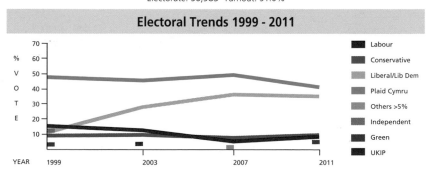

CLWYD SOUTH

MP - Susan Elan JONES Labour
AM - Ken SKATES Labour

North Wales Regional AMs

Llyr Huws Gruffydd (PC)   Aled Roberts (Lib D)

Mark Isherwood (Con)   Antoinette Sandbach (Con)

Area:	623 sq km	% born in Wales:	72.1%
% speaking Welsh: 25.2%		% Unemployment *(Apr 2012)*	5.1%

The constituency comprises the following electoral wards:
Bronington, Brymbo, Bryn Cefn, Cefn, Chirk North, Chirk South, Coedpoeth, Corwen, Dyffryn Ceiriog/Ceiriog Valley, Esclusham, Gwenfro, Johnstown, Llandrillo, Llangollen, Llangollen Rural, Marchwiel, Minera, New Broughton, Overton, Pant, Penycae, Penycae and Ruabon South, Plas Madoc, Ponciau, Ruabon.

Clwyd South combines the rural hinterland of Denbighshire, and its sizeable Welsh-speaking population, with the industrial fringes of Wrexham. The historic industries of this part of North-East Wales have now largely been replaced by modern assembly plants and light engineering. The remarkable International Eisteddfod at Llangollen continues to flourish, all giving Clwyd South a complex socio-economic makeup. Martyn Jones originally captured Clwyd South West, the forerunner of the present seat, from the Conservatives in 1987. He successfully defended Clwyd South West in 1992 and was re-elected for the new Clwyd South in 1997, 2001 and 2005. His successor, Susan Elan Jones, retained the seat for Labour at the 2010 election.

At the Assembly elections in May 1999, Karen Sinclair won the seat for Labour, but Plaid Cymru polled a surprising 25% of the votes cast. In 2003, Plaid Cymru retained second place, but, as elsewhere, their support slipped. Parliamentary politics in Clwyd South seems to be a two-party contest between Labour and Conservative. For Assembly elections however, the struggle has been between Labour and Plaid Cymru. In 2007 and 2011 however, a sizeable swing to the Conservatives restored the Tories to second place, but overall turnout remained poor. In this respect, Clwyd South illustrates particularly well the present political ambiguity of much of North-East Wales. The level of engagement with the new politics of Wales is low, yet there remains a residual Welsh and Welsh-speaking population that seeks to articulate its concerns in the more conducive political climate of a devolved Wales.

Electoral Trends 1979 - 2010

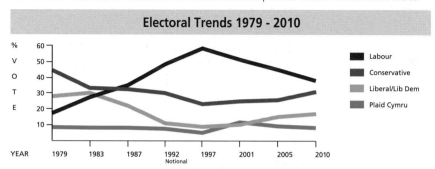

Previous MPs: **Martyn Jones (Lab) 1997-2010;** (New seat – 1997, formerly Clwyd South West) **Martyn Jones 1987-97; Robert Harvey (Con) 1983-87;** (New seat 1983, formerly Denbigh) **Geraint Morgan (Con) 1959-83**
Previous AMs: **Karen Sinclair (Lab) 1999-2011**

MP for Clwyd South

Susan Elan JONES Labour
Majority: 2,834 (8.2%)

House of Commons
London SW1A 0AA
Tel: (020) 7219 0920
Email: susan.jones.mp@parliament.uk

Constituency Office:
5 Enterprise Centre, Well Street
Cefn Mawr, Wrexham LL14 3AL
Tel: (01978) 824288
Website: www.susanelanjones.co.uk

Susan Elan Jones was first elected in May 2010, comes from Rhosllannerchrugog, and lives in Pentre Bychan. She went to Ponciau, Grango and Ruabon schools before going on to study at the universities of Bristol and Cardiff. After graduating, Susan taught English in Japan and speaks Japanese herself. Subsequently she spent 15 years working for charities before becoming an MP and is a former Councillor in the London Borough of Southwark, where she was Deputy Leader of the Opposition from 2007 to 2009. Fluent in Welsh, she took her Parliamentary Oath of Allegiance in the language and during her maiden speech in the House of Commons on 9 June 2010, spoke of the historic discrimination faced by speakers of the Welsh language.

Susan Elan Jones is currently a member of the Welsh Affairs Select Committee, and since October 2011 has been a front-bench member of Labour's Parliamentary team. She is also Vice Chair of the All Party Parliamentary Group on the Wood Panelling Industry, Vice Chair of the All Party Parliamentary Group on Heritage Railways and Secretary of the All Party Parliamentary Group on Waterways. Locally, she is a member of many different organizations – including the Friends of Llangollen International Eisteddfod; the Brymbo Heritage Group; St David's Church, Rhos and the Friends of the Stiwt (of which she is an Honorary Vice President).

2010 General Election Result

	Party	Votes Cast	%	Change 05-10
Susan Elan Jones	Lab	13,311	38.4	-6.8%
John Bell	Con	10,477	30.2	+4.8%
Bruce Roberts	Lib D	5,965	17.2	+1.7%
Janet Ryder	PC	3,009	8.7	-0.8%
Sarah Hynes	BNP	1,100	3.2	+3.2%
Nick Powell	UKIP	819	2.4	+0.4%

Electorate: 53,768 Turnout: 64.5%

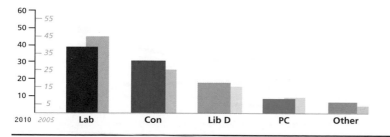

Ken SKATES Labour
Majority: 2,659 (13.2%)

National Assembly for Wales
Cardiff Bay, Cardiff CF99 1NA
Tel: (029) 2089 8136
Email: ken.skates@wales.gov.uk

Constituency Office:
Unit 19, The Malthouse Business Centre
Regent Street, Llangollen LL20 8RP
Tel: (01978) 869058
Website: www.kenskates.co.uk

Ken Skates became the Assembly Member for Clwyd South in May 2011, replacing previous Labour AM Karen Sinclair with 42.4 per cent of the vote. He had previously contested the 2007 election on the North Wales regional list. Born in 1976 in Wrexham, he was educated at Ysgol y Waun and Mold Alun comprehensive schools, before studying Social and Political Science at Cambridge University, specialising in European Regional Policy and Economics. Following university Ken spent time in America and worked as a journalist at the Wrexham Leader newspaper and studied for an NVQ in Journalism at Yale College. In 2008 he was elected as a community councillor for Pantymwyn and also worked as an assistant to Mark Tami MP.

Since being elected as an AM Ken has become a member of the Enterprise and Business Committee in the Assembly as well as the Communities, Equalities and Local Government Committee. He is currently Chair of the Cross Party Group on Mental Health. In January 2011 he proposed the first backbench Private Members Bill, since the Assembly took on new powers, to increase transition support for care leavers. In his free time, Ken enjoys running, swimming, hiking and curling as well as having an interest in art, historic trees and architectural design.

2011 Assembly Election Result

	Party	Votes Cast	%	Change 07-11
Ken Skates	Lab	8,500	42.4	+7.4%
Paul Rogers	Con	5,841	29.2	-0.2%
Mabon ap Gwynfor	PC	3,719	18.6	-1.4%
Bruce Roberts	Lib D	1,977	9.9	+0.4%

Electorate: 54,499 Turnout: 36.8%

Electoral Trends 1999 - 2011

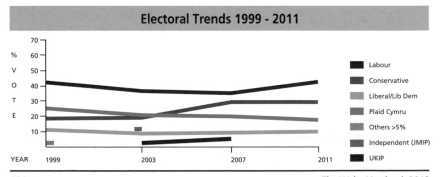

CLWYD WEST

MP - David JONES Conservative
AM - Darren MILLAR Conservative

North Wales Regional AMs

Llyr Huws Gruffydd (PC)   Aled Roberts (Lib D)

Mark Isherwood (Con)   Antoinette Sandbach (Con)

Area:	921 sq km	% born in Wales:	52.8%
% speaking Welsh: 35.9%		% Unemployment *(Apr 2012)*	5.2%

The constituency comprises the following electoral wards:
Abergele Pensarn, Betws yn Rhos, Colwyn, Efenechtyd, Eirias, Gele, Glyn, Kinmel Bay, Llanarmon-yn-Iâl/Llandegla, Llanbedr Dyffryn Clwyd/Llangynhafal, Llanddulas, Llandrillo yn Rhos, Llanfair Dyffryn Clwyd/Gwyddelwern, Llangernyw, Llanrhaeadr-yng-Nghinmeirch, Llansannan, Llysfaen, Mochdre, Pentre Mawr, Rhiw, Ruthin, Towyn, Uwchaled.

Clwyd West is a seat of great contrasts, from the coastal resort of Colwyn Bay to a large rural hinterland. It contains a diverse community with a high proportion of in-migrants on the coast and a sizeable Welsh-speaking population in the countryside.

Uniquely, the four main political party candidates fighting Clwyd West at the Assembly election in 2003 were all elected; Alun Pugh for Labour as the constituency AM, while those from Plaid Cymru, the Conservatives and the Liberal Democrats were returned as regional members for North Wales. This unusual electoral outcome provided the catalyst to the changes in electoral law that now require candidates to fight only one election or the other. Clwyd West has also enjoyed considerable prominence at recent elections as a highly marginal seat. Labour's Gareth Thomas won the new Parliamentary seat against a Tory challenge in 1997, defended it in 2001, but finally succumbed in 2005. The former MP, Rod Richards, defeated in 1997, was elected to the Assembly in 1999 as a Regional Member for North Wales. Following Rod Richards's resignation in 2002, David Jones served out the remaining term of the first Assembly until 2003. Switching to stand in the 2005 General Election, David Jones was elected Conservative MP for Clwyd West. Clwyd West was perceived to be a barometer seat at the last Assembly election. If Labour had retained the seat, the prospect of gaining a majority remained feasible; once lost to the Conservatives however, a Labour majority in the Assembly became almost inconceivable. In 2011 Darren Millar significantly increased his majority and as the Conservative Party in Wales becomes progressively more comfortable with its more explicit Welsh identity, so its ability to capture and hold seats such as Clwyd West, or Carmarthen West, becomes accepted, more established and more likely.

Electoral Trends 1979 - 2010

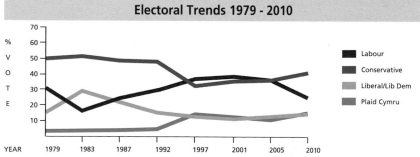

Previous MPs: **Gareth Thomas 1997-2005;** (New seat 1997, formerly Clwyd North West) **Rod Richards (Con) 1992-97;**
Sir Anthony Meyer (Con) 1983-92; (New seat 1983, formerly Flint West) **Sir Anthony Meyer (Con) 1970-83**
Previous AMs: **Alun Pugh (Lab) 1999-2007**

CLWYD WEST

David JONES Conservative
Majority: 6,419 (16.8%)

House of Commons, London SW1A 0AA
Tel: (020) 7219 8070 Fax: (020) 7219 0142
Email: jonesdi@parliament.uk

Constituency Office:
3 Llewelyn Road, Colwyn Bay LL29 7AP
Tel: (01492) 535845 Fax: (01492) 534157
Website: www.davidjonesmp.co.uk

David Jones was elected to Parliament for Clwyd West in May 2005, where he overturned the narrow majority of his Labour predecessor, Gareth Thomas. David had briefly served as a North Wales AM in 2002-03, following the resignation of Rod Richards. He previously contested Conwy at the 1997 General Election and the 1999 Assembly election before standing for Parliament in Chester in 2001. Born in London in 1952, he was educated at Ruabon Grammar School and went on to graduate in Law from University College, London. He qualified as a solicitor and later established his own practice in Llandudno. Whilst in the Assembly, he served as the Conservative Finance spokesman.

He is currently Parliamentary Under-Secretary of State at the Wales Office. He is also co-Chair of the All Party Group for Sustainable Resource and Patron of the Chinese Conservative Group. David is an Honorary Fellow of Cancer Research UK and has campaigned vigorously for the hospice movement. His political concerns include environment, law and order and constitutional affairs. Beyond politics, he is married with two sons, follows the fortunes of Liverpool FC and enjoys travel and motorcars.

2010 General Election Result

	Party	Votes Cast	%	Change 05-10
David Jones	Con	15,833	41.5	+5.4%
Donna Hutton	Lab	9,414	24.7	-11.3%
Llyr Huws Gruffydd	PC	5,864	15.4	+4.5%
Michele Jones	Lib D	5,801	15.2	+1.9%
Warwick Nicholson	UKIP	864	2.3	+0.8%
David Griffiths	WCP	239	0.6	+0.6%
Joe Blakesley	Ind	96	0.3	+0.3%

Electorate: 57,913 Turnout: 65.8%

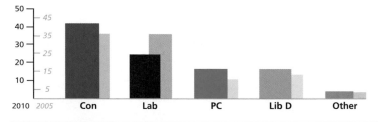

AM for Clwyd West

Darren MILLAR Conservative
Majority: 4,248 (16.9%)

National Assembly for Wales
Cardiff Bay, Cardiff CF99 1NA
Tel: (029) 2089 8731
Email: darren.millar@wales.gov.uk

Constituency Office:
55a Market St, Abergele LL22 7AF
Tel: (01745) 839117
Website: www.darrenmillaram.com

Darren Millar was elected to the National Assembly in May 2007, recapturing Clwyd West for the Conservative Party. He was re-elected with a significantly increased majority of 4,428 at the 2011 election. Before becoming an Assembly Member, Darren worked as a manager for an international charity. He has also been an accountant working in the construction, care home and telecommunications industries. Darren is a Fellow of the Chartered Management Institute, a Fellow of the Institute of Leadership and Management, and a Fellow of the Royal Society for the encouragement of Arts, Manufactures and Commerce. In 2000, Darren became the youngest serving Mayor in Wales when elected for the township of Towyn and Kinmel Bay. He has also served as a member of Conwy County Borough Council, the North Wales Police Authority and the North Wales Fire and Rescue Service.

Darren is currently Shadow Minister for Health. He is Chair of the Public Accounts Committee and sits as a member of the Health and Social Care Committee. He is also Chair of the Cross Party Group on Faith and the Cross Party Group on the Armed Forces and Cadets. Married with two children, he lives in Kinmel Bay and enjoys reading and history, and attends North Coast Church, Towyn.

2011 Assembly Election Result

	Party	Votes Cast	%	Change 07-11
Darren Millar	Con	10,890	43.3	+9.3%
Crispin Jones	Lab	6,642	26.4	-1.5%
Eifion Lloyd Jones	PC	5,775	23.0	-4.4%
Brian Cossey	Lib D	1,846	7.3	+0.8%

Electorate: 57,980 Turnout: 43.4%

Electoral Trends 1999 - 2011

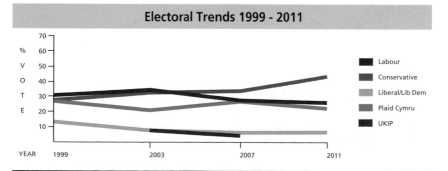

CYNON VALLEY

MP - Rt Hon Ann CLWYD Labour

AM - Christine CHAPMAN Labour

South Wales Central Regional AMs

Andrew R T Davies (Con)	Eluned Parrott (Lib D)
David Melding (Con)	Leanne Wood (PC)

Area:	182 sq km	% born in Wales:	91.1%
% speaking Welsh:	17.7%	% Unemployment *(Apr 2012)*	9.0%

The constituency comprises the following electoral wards:
Aberaman North, Aberaman South, Abercynon, Aberdare East, Aberdare West/Llwydcoed, Cilfynydd, Cwmbach, Glyncoch, Hirwaun, Mountain Ash East, Mountain Ash West, Penrhiwceiber, Pen-y-waun, Rhigos, Ynysybwl.

The seat of **Cynon Valley** is the successor in title to old constituency of Aberdare. The tradition of Labour Party dominance at Parliamentary elections, long associated with the Valleys, continues in Cwm Cynon as before. The death of Ioan Evans, MP 1974-1984, gave rise to the by-election that elected Ann Clwyd to Parliament. More than twenty five years on, Cynon Valley remains one of the safest Labour seats in Britain. It was a major shock therefore when, in 1999, at the National Assembly elections, Plaid Cymru came within a thousand votes of winning the seat. In the mid-1970s Aberdare had entertained a brief flirtation with Plaid Cymru, but the Nationalists' long search for a breakthrough at a General Election in an industrialized, largely English-speaking, constituency never materialised. At the second Assembly elections in 2003 however, Plaid Cymru failed to repeat their previous challenge, allowing the Labour Party to re-establish a large majority. In 2007, Plaid Cymru, and the Conservatives, made some progress but Cynon Valley remains defiantly safe for Labour. This was shown with the results of 2011, when Labour increased its majority. Cynon Valley is also the home of Tower Colliery, the last remaining deep mine in South Wales, where the miners successfully bought-out their own pit from British Coal rather than accept closure. Inevitably however, geology and market conditions now mean that Tower too, has closed. Notwithstanding the symbolic dignity and defiance of those at Tower, Cynon Valley remains one of Wales' most socially deprived areas and wedded to a fundamental Labour loyalty.

Electoral Trends 1979 - 2010

(chart showing % VOTE by YEAR from 1979 to 2010)

Legend:
- Labour
- Conservative
- Liberal/Lib Dem
- Plaid Cymru

YEAR: 1979 1983 1985(by) 1987 1992 1997 2001 2005 2010

Previous MPs: Ioan Evans 1983-84 (New seat 1983, formerly Aberdare) Ioan Evans (Lab) 1974-83; Arthur Probert (Lab) 1954 (by)-74

Rt Hon Ann CLWYD Labour
Majority: 9,617 (32.2%)

House of Commons
London SW1A 0AA
Tel: (020) 7219 6609
Email: ann.clwyd.mp@parliament.uk

Constituency Office:
4th Floor, Crown Buildings, Aberdare CF44 7HU
Tel: (01685) 871394

CYNON VALLEY

Ann Clwyd was first elected MP for Cynon Valley at a by-election in 1984. She previously contested Gloucester in 1974 and Denbigh in 1970. From 1979-84 she served as MEP for Mid and West Wales. She was a member of the Shadow Cabinet 1989-93, as Shadow Secretary of State for Overseas Development 1989-92, Shadow Welsh Secretary 1992, Shadow National Heritage Secretary 1992-93 and was Opposition Spokesperson for Employment 1993-94 and Foreign Affairs 1994-95. Overall Ann Clwyd was sacked from the Shadow Cabinet twice. Born on 21 March 1937, she was educated at Holywell Grammar School, Queen's School, Chester and Bangor University. Locally, she led the 'stay down' at Tower Colliery when the pit was threatened with closure

A former journalist, broadcaster and a fluent Welsh speaker, she is currently a member of the Foreign Affairs Committee. She is also Chair of the following: the All-Party Parliamentary Group on Human Rights; All-Party Parliamentary Iraq Group; All-Party Parliamentary Group on Cambodia and the All-Party Parliamentary Group on Social Work. Her political interests include human rights, overseas development, foreign affairs, women's issues, and the arts. She has been a consistent defender of the Kurds and was a long-standing, vociferous critic of Saddam Hussein's regime in Iraq. In 2004 she was appointed a Privy Counsellor and was Special Envoy to Iraq on Human Rights.

2010 General Election Result

	Party	Votes Cast	%	Change 05-10
Ann Clwyd	Lab	15,681	52.5	-10.5%
Dafydd Trystan Davies	PC	6,064	20.3	+6.8%
Lee Thacker	Lib D	4,120	13.8	+1.6%
Juliette Ash	Con	3,010	10.1	+1.5%
Frank Hughes	UKIP	1,001	3.4	+0.7%

Electorate: 50,650 Turnout: 59.0%

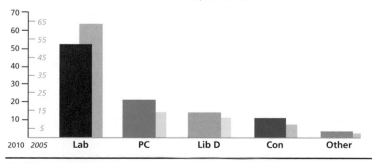

Christine CHAPMAN Labour
Majority: 6,515 (34.7%)

National Assembly for Wales
Cardiff Bay, Cardiff CF99 1NA
Tel: (029) 2089 8745
Email: christine.chapman@wales.gov.uk

Constituency Office:
Bank Chambers, 28a Oxford Street,
Mountain Ash CF45 3EU
Tel: (01443) 478098 Fax: (01443) 478311
Website: www.christinechapman4cynon.com

Christine Chapman was first elected as an Assembly Member for the Cynon Valley in 1999. Born in Porth in 1956, she was educated at Porth County School for Girls, the University of Wales, Aberystwyth, South Bank Polytechnic in London, the University of Wales, Cardiff and the University of Wales, Swansea. She was previously employed as an education and business partnership co-ordinator and as a director of Mid Glamorgan Careers Ltd. She is currently Secretary of the Labour UNISON Group in the Assembly and her political interests include social exclusion, education and training and women's issues.

In the Assembly, Christine briefly served as Deputy Secretary for Education and Economic Development in 2000 and was later appointed Chair of the Objective One Monitoring Group. She served as Deputy Minister for Education and Lifelong Learning and for Finance, Local Government and Public Services 2005-07. She is currently the Chair of Children and Young People Committee as well as sitting on the Finance Committee. She is also Chair of the Cross Party Women in Democracy Group. Christine is married with two children.

2011 Assembly Election Result

	Party	Votes Cast	%	Change 07-11
Christine Chapman	Lab	11,626	62.0	+5.3%
Dafydd Davies	PC	5,111	27.2	-0.6%
DanielSaxton	Con	1,531	8.1	-2.2%
Ian Walton	Lib D	492	2.6	-2.5%

Electorate: 52,133 Turnout: 36.0%

Electoral Trends 1999 - 2011

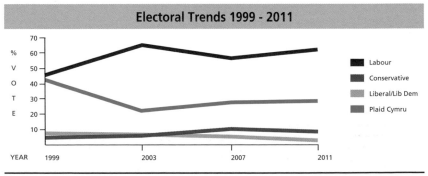

DELYN

MP - Rt Hon David HANSON Labour

AM - Sandy MEWIES Labour

North Wales Regional AMs

Llyr Huws Gruffydd (PC)   Aled Roberts (Lib D)

Mark Isherwood (Con)   Antoinette Sandbach (Con)

Area:	283 sq km	% born in Wales:	59.8%
% speaking Welsh: 35.1%		% Unemployment *(Apr 2012)* 4.5%	

The constituency comprises the following electoral wards:
Argoed, Bagillt East, Bagillt West, Brynford, Caerwys, Cilcain, Ffynnongroyw, Flint Castle, Flint Coleshill, Flint Oakenholt, Flint Trelawney, Greenfield, Gronant, Gwernaffield, Gwernymynydd, Halkyn, Holywell Central, Holywell East, Holywell West, Leeswood, Mold Broncoed, Mold East, Mold South, Mold West, Mostyn, New Brighton, Northop, Northop Hall, Trelawnyd and Gwaenysgor, Whitford.

When the seats of Clwyd were re-drawn in 1983, **Delyn** appeared a classic two-party, marginal constituency. Held by Keith Raffan for the Conservatives in 1983 and 1987, the national swing to the Labour Party in 1992 delivered Delyn to Labour. Keith Raffan subsequently went on to be elected a Liberal Democrat Member of the Scottish Parliament. Additional adjustments to the Parliamentary boundaries of Delyn in 1997 further altered the political complexion, removing Prestatyn to the new Vale of Clwyd constituency. Overall, these changes made Delyn a more secure seat for Labour, which, in the context of the 1997 landslide, gave David Hanson a substantial majority. This majority was reduced slightly in 2001, and again in 2005. In 2010 Conservatives support increased, as elsewhere on the North Wales coast, reducing the status of David Hanson's majority from 'fairly safe' to 'highly marginal'.

Delyn has a mixed economy and a rural hinterland. At the Assembly elections in May 1999, Labour retained its majority, notwithstanding substantial growth in support for Plaid Cymru in an area with no great tradition of nationalist voting. In 2003, following the retirement of Alison Halford, Delyn's first AM, Labour again took the Assembly seat, but with a reduced majority on a reduced turnout. Less than a third of voters engaged in the Assembly election, a level of detachment also found elsewhere in North-East Wales. At the 2007 Assembly election however, whilst Labour were returned again, a renewed Conservative challenge reduced Sandy Mewies's majority to a mere five hundred votes. Delyn has re-established itself as a classic two-party marginal where a national swing will always be reflected. This proved to be the case at the 2011 Assembly election, when Sandy Mewies significantly increased her majority to 2,881.

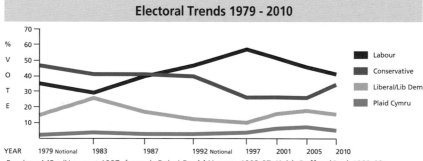

Electoral Trends 1979 - 2010

Legend: Labour, Conservative, Liberal/Lib Dem, Plaid Cymru

YEAR: 1979 Notional, 1983, 1987, 1992 Notional, 1997, 2001, 2005, 2010

Previous MPs: (New seat 1997, formerly Delyn) **David Hanson 1992-97; Keith Raffan (Con) 1983-92;** (New seat 1983)
Previous AMs: **Alison Halford 1999-2003**

DELYN

Rt Hon David HANSON Labour
Majority: 2,272 (6.1%)

House of Commons
London SW1A 0AA
Tel: (020) 7219 5064
Email: david.hanson.mp@parliament.uk

Constituency Office:
64 Chester Street, Flint
Flintshire CH6 5DH
Tel: (01352) 763159
Website: www.davidhanson.org.uk

David Hanson was first elected to Parliament in 1992, capturing Delyn at the second attempt having previously contested the seat in 1987. Born on 5 July 1957 in Liverpool, the son of a fork-lift truck driver and an office clerk, he was educated at Verdin Comprehensive School, Winsford and Hull University. A Regional Manager for SCOPE from 1982, he became the National Director of Re-Solv, the Society for the Prevention of Solvent Abuse in 1989. Previously a member of Vale Royal Borough Council, he became Leader of the Labour Group and led the Council 1989-91.

In Government he rose to Minister of State in the Home Office responsible for Policing, Crime and Security, having previously served in the Northern Ireland Office. He was appointed to the Privy Council in 2007. Parliamentary Private Secretary to the Prime Minister 2001-05, he had previously been a Junior Minister in the Wales Office, a Government Whip and earlier, PPS to the, then, Chief Secretary to the Treasury, Alistair Darling. He is currently Shadow Policing Minister and served as a Shadow Exchequer Secretary from 2010-11. Married with four children, he lists family life among his leisure activities, along with football, reading and the cinema.

2010 General Election Result

	Party	Votes Cast	%	Change 05-10
David Hanson	Lab	15,083	40.8	-4.9%
Antoinette Sandbach	Con	12,811	34.6	+8.5%
Bill Brereton	Lib D	5,747	15.5	-2.4%
Peter Ryder	PC	1,844	5.0	-2.4%
Jennifer Matthys	BNP	844	2.3	+2.3%
Andrew Haigh	UKIP	655	1.8	+0.2%

Electorate: 53,470 Turnout: 69.2%

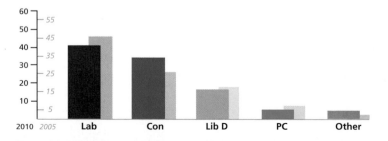

Sandy MEWIES Labour
Majority: 2,881 (12.4%)

National Assembly for Wales
Cardiff Bay, Cardiff CF99 1NA
Tel: (029) 2089 8736
Email: sandy.mewies@wales.gov.uk

Constituency Office:
Transport House, 64 Chester Street
Flint CH6 5DH
Tel: (01352) 763398
Website: www.sandymewies.org.uk

DELYN

Sandy Mewies was elected to the National Assembly in May 2003. Born in 1950 in Brymbo and educated at Grove Park Girls Grammar School, Sandy Mewies is a graduate of the Open University and an Honorary Fellow of Glyndwr University. A former Mayor of Wrexham, she was a County Councillor and served as Chair of Social Services, an Executive Board member and as Deputy Leader of the Authority. She was a Board member of the former Wales European Centre in Brussels and for ten years was a lay schools inspector. She has also worked as a journalist, becoming Deputy News Editor on the Evening Leader as well as being a former Director of the North Wales Probation Board. She has been a Board member of the Council of Museums in Wales and founded and ran an Agenda 21 group, supporting local community environmental projects.

In the Assembly, Sandy Mewies previously served for seven years as Chair of the Assembly's European and External Relations Committee, and was also Chair of the Communities and Culture Committee. She currently sits on the Assembly Commission and lists her main political interests as social justice, community inclusion, health and education. Married with one son, in her spare time she enjoys reading and cooking.

2011 Assembly Election Result

	Party	Votes Cast	%	Change 07-11
Sandy Mewies	Lab	10,695	46.11	+11.5%
Matt Wright	Con	7,814	33.69	+1.4%
Carrie Harper	PC	2,918	12.58	-2.1%
Michele Jones	Lib D	1,767	7.62	-4.7%

Electorate: 53,996 Turnout: 43.0%

Electoral Trends 1999 - 2011

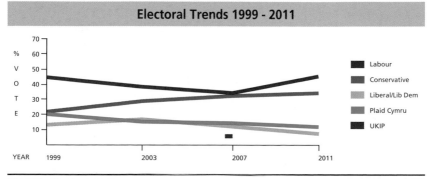

Labour
Conservative
Liberal/Lib Dem
Plaid Cymru
UKIP

DWYFOR MEIRIONNYDD

MP - Elfyn LLWYD Plaid Cymru

AM - Rt Hon Lord Dafydd ELIS-THOMAS Plaid Cymru

Mid & West Wales Regional AMs

Rebecca Evans (Lab)	Simon Thomas (PC)
William Powell (Lib D)	Joyce Watson (Lab)

Area:	2,127 sq km	% born in Wales:	65.9%
% speaking Welsh:	69.2%	% Unemployment *(Apr 2012)*	3.6%

The constituency comprises the following electoral wards:
Aberdaron, Aberdovey, Abererch, Abermaw, Abersoch, Bala, Botwnnog, Bowydd & Rhiw, Brithdir & Llanfachreth/Ganllwyd/Llanelltyd, Bryncrug/Llanfihangel, Clynnog, Corris/Mawddwy, Criccieth, Diffwys & Maenofferen, Dolbenmaen, Dolgellau North, Dolgellau South, Dyffryn Ardudwy, Efail-newydd/Buan, Harlech, Llanaelhaearn, Llanbedr, Llanbedrog, Llandderfel, Llanengan, Llangelynin, Llanuwchllyn, Llanystumdwy, Morfa Nefyn, Nefyn, Penrhyndeudraeth, Porthmadog East, Porthmadog West, Porthmadog-Tremadog, Pwllheli North, Pwllheli South, Teigl, Trawsfynydd, Tudweiliog, Tywyn.

The seat of Meirionnydd Nant Conwy had the smallest electorate in Wales and was thus ripe for re-apportionment by the Boundary Commission. At the 2007 Assembly elections the new constituency, **Dwyfor Meirionnydd**, was fought for the first time. The new division brings together much of the former Meirionnydd with Dwyfor from the former Caernarfon seat. The Nant Conwy portion of the former seat has now been detached to join the new Aberconwy constituency. Most of Dwyfor Meirionnydd still lies within the Snowdonia National Park and the principal industries are agriculture and tourism. Dwyfor Meirionnydd carried the scars of both its nineteenth and twentieth century industrial legacies. The oppressive waste of the slate quarrying industry still dominates the landscape of Blaenau Ffestiniog, whilst the now redundant nuclear power station at Trawsfynydd broods ominously over the upland moors. Attracting industry and jobs to these remote towns and villages remains highly problematic. Plaid Cymru had won Meirioneth from Labour in 1974 when, together with Caernarfon, the party returned its first MPs to be elected at a General Election. Despite considerable enlargement of the seat in 1983, Plaid Cymru has retained control. Notwithstanding the impact of now further Boundary Commission changes, the sitting MP, Elfyn Llwyd, appears well entrenched comfortably retaining the seat in May 2010. The former MP, Dafydd Elis Thomas, stood down in 1992 to go the House of Lords, but in 1999 returned to be elected to the Assembly and served as Presiding Officer until 2011. In 2007 Lord Elis-Thomas, contested the new constituency of Dwyfor Meirionnydd and created the safest seat in Wales. While an Independent candidate slightly eroded Plaid's hegemony in 2011, it remains a solidly safe seat for the party.

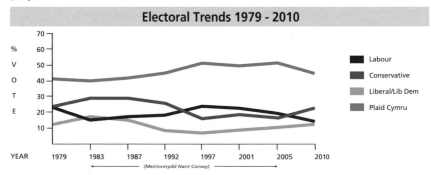

Electoral Trends 1979 - 2010

Previous MPs: **Dafydd Elis Thomas (PC) 1983-92;** (New seat 1983, formerly Meirioneth) **Dafydd Elis Thomas (PC) 1974-83; Will Edwards (Lab) 1966-74**

    The Wales Yearbook 2013

Rt Hon Elfyn LLWYD Plaid Cymru
Majority: 6,367 (22.0%)

House of Commons, London SW1A 0AA
Tel: (020) 7219 3555
Email: elfyn.llwyd.mp@parliament.uk

Constituency Office:
Angorfa, Heol Meurig, Dolgellau LL40 1LN
Tel: (01341) 422661
Email: jenkinssh@parliament.uk

DWYFOR MEIRIONNYDD

Elfyn Llwyd was elected to Westminster for Meirionnydd Nant Conwy in 1992, following the retirement from the House of Commons of Dafydd Elis-Thomas (now Lord Elis-Thomas). Following boundary changes he contested the new seat of Dwyfor Meirionnydd at the 2010 election and was returned with a comfortable majority. Born on 26 September 1951 in Betws-y-Coed, he was educated at Ysgol Dyffryn Conwy in Llanrwst, University College of Wales, Aberystwyth and the College of Law, Chester. He qualified as a solicitor in 1977 and was called to the Bar in 1997.

Elfyn Llwyd is currently Leader of the Plaid Cymru Group at Westminster. A member of the Justice Select Committee, he speaks for Plaid Cymru on the Constitution, Defence, Environment, Food & Rural Affairs, Foreign Affairs, Foreign and Commonwealth Affairs and Justice. He is also a member of the British-Irish Parliamentary Body and a Council member of the National Library of Wales. In 2006, he was shortlisted for Channel Four's Opposition Politician of the Year. A keen pigeon breeder, he also enjoys choral singing, rugby and fishing. His political interests include civil liberties, agriculture and tourism. A fluent Welsh speaker, in 1998 he was appointed to the highest order of the Gorsedd of the Bards. He is married with a son and a daughter.

2010 General Election Result

	Party	Votes Cast	%	Change 05-10
Elfyn Llwyd	PC	12,814	44.3	-6.4%
Simon Baynes	Con	6,447	22.3	+8.1%
Alwyn Humphreys	Lab	4,021	13.9	-7.8%
Steve Churchman	Lib D	3,538	12.2	+1.3%
Louise Hughes	Ind	1,310	4.5	+4.5%
Frank Wykes	UKIP	776	2.7	+0.3%

Electorate: 45,354 Turnout: 63.7%

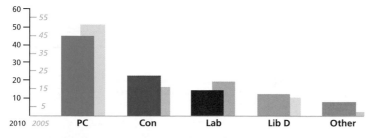

DWYFOR MEIRIONNYDD

Rt Hon Lord Dafydd ELIS-THOMAS Plaid Cymru
Majority: 5,417 (26.1%)

National Assembly for Wales
Cardiff Bay, Cardiff CF99 1NA
Tel: (029) 2089 8709
Email: dafydd.elis-thomas@wales.gov.uk

Constituency Office:
7 Bank Place, Porthmadog
Gwynedd LL49 9AA
Tel: (01766) 515028
Website: www.dafyddelisthomas.org

Dafydd Elis-Thomas was the first Assembly Member to represent Dwyfor Meirionnydd in May 2007, after representing Meirionnydd Nant Conwy from 1999 to 2007. He was Member of Parliament for Meirionnydd from 1974 to 1983 and Meirionnydd Nant Conwy from 1983 to 1992. On leaving the Commons he was nominated to the Lords in 1992 and served as Chair of the Welsh Language Board from 1993 to 1999. As a former researcher and teacher in adult and higher education, he maintains close links with Bangor University as President, and with Grŵp Llandrillo Menai as Honorary President. He is Vice-President of the National Trust Snowdonia Appeal which invests in sustainable farming and conservation in Snowdonia. He is also active in the Church in Wales.

From 1999-2011 he served as the Presiding Officer of the National Assembly and he is currently Plaid's Spokesperson for Rural Affairs, Fisheries and Food; Chair of the Environment and Sustainability Committee as well as sitting on the Enterprise and Business Committee. He was an unsuccessful candidate for the Plaid Cymru leadership in 2012. Dafydd Elis-Thomas has lived most of his life in the Snowdonia National Park, and enjoys the recreations of hill walking and jogging from the family cottage near Betws y Coed.

2011 Assembly Election Result

	Party	Votes Cast	%	Change 07-11
Dafydd Elis-Thomas	PC	9,656	46.6	-13.1%
Simon Baynes	Con	4,239	20.4	+0.8%
Louise Hughes	Llais Gwynedd	3,225	15.6	+15.5%
Martyn Singleton	Lab	2,623	12.7	+0.2%
Steve Churchman	Lib D	1,000	4.8	-3.5%

Electorate: 44,669 Turnout: 46.4%

Electoral Trends 1999 - 2011

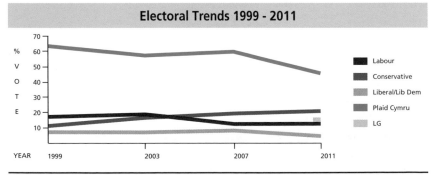

GOWER

MP - Martin CATON Labour
AM - Edwina HART MBE OStJ Labour

South Wales West Regional AMs

Peter Black (Lib D)   Suzy Davies (Con)

Byron Davies (Con)   Bethan Jenkins (PC)

Area:	297 sq km	% born in Wales:	82.0%
% speaking Welsh:	19.8%	% Unemployment *(Apr 2012)*	3.5%

The constituency comprises the following electoral wards:
Bishopston, Clydach, Fairwood, Gorseinon, Gower, Gowerton, Kingsbridge, Llangyfelach, Lower Loughor, Mawr, Newton, Oystermouth, Penclawdd, Penllergaer, Pennard, Penrheol, Pontardulais, Upper Loughor, West Cross.

Gower is a seat of 'two halves'. The famous peninsula, west of Swansea, is an area of outstanding natural beauty, has an agricultural heartland, but also contains some of Swansea's most prosperous suburbs. The inland and northerly section of the constituency, incorporating the industrial hinterland of the Lliw Valley, contains the majority of the population and gives Gower a strong Welsh identity.

Gareth Wardell was elected for the Labour Party at a by-election in 1982, notable as one of the first elections fought in Wales by the newly founded SDP. Gower became more marginal following the boundary revisions of 1983, but thereafter Labour has succeeded in increasing its majority at each subsequent General Election. In 1997 Gareth Wardell stood down leaving his successor, Martin Caton, to inherit a comfortably safe Labour seat. In the further Blair landslide of 2001, the Labour Party easily retained its hold, but saw a minor slippage in both 2005 and 2010. Plaid Cymru polled well in the 1999 Assembly elections, but were not to repeat such a strong performance in 2003, leaving the sitting Labour AM Edwina Hart with a comfortable majority. At the 2007 Assembly election there was little doubt that Edwina Hart would retain her seat, but a revival in the Conservative vote substantially reduced Labour's majority. This was reversed in 2011 when Labour once again increased its majority. A bedrock of support for Plaid Cymru will probably always prevent the Conservatives from displacing Labour, illustrating the complex political landscape created when a residual Welshness stands between more conventional two-party, still class dominated, politics.

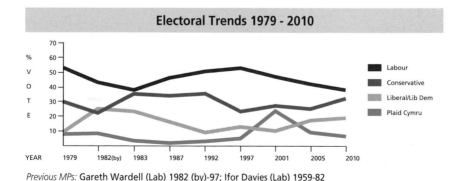

Electoral Trends 1979 - 2010

Previous MPs: **Gareth Wardell (Lab) 1982 (by)-97; Ifor Davies (Lab) 1959-82**

MP for Gower

**Martin CATON Labour
Majority: 2,683 (6.4%)**

House of Commons, London SW1A 0AA
Tel: (020) 7219 5111
Email: martin.caton.mp@parliament.uk

Constituency Office:
9 Pontardulais Road, Gorseinon
Swansea SA4 4FE
Tel: (01792) 892100
Email: daviesl@parliament.uk
Website: www.martin-caton.co.uk

Martin Caton was first elected MP for Gower in 1997 and was returned at the 2010 election with a majority of 2,683. Born in Bishop Stortford in 1951, he was educated at Newport Grammar School, Essex, Norfolk School of Agriculture and Aberystwyth College of Further Education. He was a Scientific Officer at the Institute of Grassland and Environmental Research in Aberystwyth 1974-84, before he became a full-time researcher and political assistant to David Morris, MEP for South West Wales. A member of the Labour Party since 1975, he served as a Swansea City Councillor 1988-95 and represented West Cross on the newly-formed City and County Council of Swansea 1995-97.

A former member of the Wales Labour Party Executive Committee, Martin is also a former Chair of the Welsh Grand Committee and member of the Welsh Affairs Select Committee. He is currently a member of the Environmental Audit Committee; the Panel of Chairs and the Joint Committee of Consolidation Bills. Married with two daughters, he is a member of the Socialist Health Association and the Socialist Environmental Resources Association. His political interests include environment, planning, education and the European Union.

2010 General Election Result

	Party	Votes Cast	%	Change 05-10
Martin Caton	Lab	16,016	38.4	-4.0%
Byron Davies	Con	13,333	32.0	+6.5%
Mike Day	Lib D	7,947	19.1	+0.6%
Darren Price	PC	2,760	6.6	-1.2%
Adrian Jones	BNP	963	2.3	+2.3%
Gordon Triggs	UKIP	652	1.6	-1.6%

Electorate: 61,696 Turnout: 67.5%

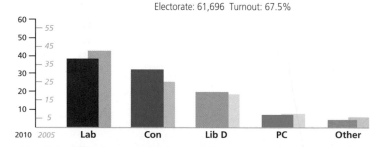

Edwina HART MBE OStJ Labour
Majority: 4,864 (18.2%)

National Assembly for Wales
Cardiff Bay, Cardiff CF99 1NA
Tel: (029) 2089 8562
Email: edwina.hart@wales.gov.uk

Constituency Office:
9 Pontardulais Road
Gorseinon, Swansea SA4 4FE
Tel: (01792) 895481
Website: www.edwinahart.com

GOWER

Edwina Hart was first elected to the Assembly in 1999. Born on 26 April 1957, she was previously employed in the banking industry, became President of BIFU, the banking staff trade union, and later Chair of the Wales TUC. Prior to being elected to the National Assembly, she also served on the BBC Broadcasting Council for Wales, the Board of the Wales Millennium Centre and had been a Director of Chwarae Teg. She was awarded the MBE in1998 for services to the trade union movement and remains a member of both Unite and Community.

Edwina unsuccessfully contested the Welsh Labour Party leadership in November 2009 and since 2011, has been a member of the Welsh Government as Minister for Business, Enterprise, Technology and Science. She has previously been the Minister for Health & Social Services; Social Justice and Regeneration; Finance and Communities and Finance Secretary. Generally perceived to be a strong Minister, Edwina Hart is deemed to have been one of the successes of successive Welsh Government Cabinets. Her main political interests are equal opportunities and economic development. Born and raised in Gowerton, Swansea, she still lives in the local community with her husband.

2011 Assembly Election Result

	Party	Votes Cast	%	Change 07-11
Edwina Hart	Lab	12,866	48.1	+13.9%
Caroline Jones	Con	8,002	29.9	+0.1%
Darren Price	PC	3,249	12.1	-6.4%
Peter May	Lib D	2,656	9.9	-0.7%

Electorate: 61,909 Turnout: 43.2%

Electoral Trends 1999 - 2011

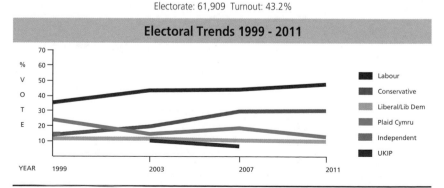

ISLWYN

MP - Chris EVANS Labour

AM - Gwyn R PRICE Labour

South Wales East Regional AMs

Mohammad Asghar (Con)   William Graham (Con)

Jocelyn Davies (PC)   Lindsay Whittle (PC)

Area:	112 sq km	% born in Wales:	90.8%
% speaking Welsh: 22.0%		% Unemployment *(Apr 2012)* 7.7%	

The constituency comprises the following electoral wards:
Aberbargoed, Abercarn, Argoed, Blackwood, Cefn Fforest, Crosskeys, Crumlin, Maesycwmmer, Newbridge, Pengam, Penmaen, Pontllanfraith, Risca East, Risca West, Ynysddu.

Islwyn is a classic working class Labour seat in the former Monmouthshire coalfield. Following Neil Kinnock's appointment to the European Commission, Don Touhig was elected for Labour at a by-election in 1995. In 1997, Labour was returned as usual, but experienced a calamitous result at the Assembly election in May 1999.

The capture of Islwyn by Plaid Cymru would have been the sensation of the day, had not Rhondda also fallen. The Labour Party were determined to avenge this loss and campaigned vigorously for the second Assembly elections in 2003. Islwyn was duly restored to Labour control with a comfortable majority, but not before a major re-evaluation of the threat posed by Plaid Cymru in the Valleys. Local government re-organization joined the former District Council of Islwyn with the neighbouring Rhymney Valley to form the new County Borough of Caerphilly. This too, went to Plaid Cymru in 1999, but returned to Labour control in 2004. At Parliamentary level, Labour's hegemony has never been seriously challenged and following the 2005 election Don Touhig held the second safest seat in Wales. His successor, Chris Smith, is slightly less well entrenched but it was only his first election.

The Assembly seat has also started to fully reinstate its Labour invulnerability of old. Despite a very strong challenge mounted by an Independent Councillor in 2007, inspired, in part, by the success of Trish Law and Dai Davies in neighbouring Blaenau Gwent, these 'rebels' have now come back into the fold. With Irene James retiring, her successor Gwyn Price increased the Labour majority to over 7,500 at the 2011 election.

Electoral Trends 1979 - 2010

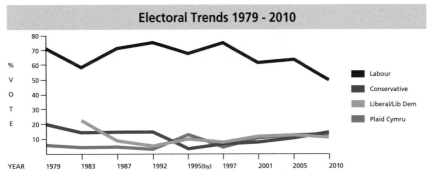

Previous MPs: Don Touhig (Lab) 1995-2010; Neil Kinnock (Lab) 1983-95 (New seat 1983, formerly Bedwellty) Neil Kinnock (Lab) 1970-83
Previous AMs: Irene James (Lab) 2003-2011; Brian Hancock (PC) 1999-2003

MP for Islwyn

Chris EVANS Labour
Majority: 12,215 (35.2%)

House of Commons
London SW1A 0AA
Tel: (020) 7219 7091
Email: chris.evans.mp@parliament.uk

Constituency Office:
6 Woodfieldside Business Park, Penmaen Road
Pontllanfraith, Blackwood NP12 2DG
Tel: (01495) 231990
Website: www.chrisevansmp.co.uk

Chris Evans was elected as MP for Islwyn in 2010, having unsuccessfully stood as the Labour candidate at the 2005 General Election in Cheltenham. Brought up in the Rhondda valleys, he was educated at Porth County Comprehensive, Pontypridd College and Trinity College, Carmarthen, where he graduated with a history degree. Upon leaving university, he worked in various roles as a bookmaker, in a bank and at the University of Glamorgan. In 2004 he was appointed as a full-time trade union official with the Union of Finance Staff. Prior to entering Parliament for Islwyn in 2010 he was the parliamentary researcher to Don Touhig.

Chris Evans has been a member of the Labour Party since he was 15 and held positions at every level of the party. He is a member of Unite, the Fabian Society and the Co-operative Party. In Parliament, he is a member of the Justice Committee, having previously sat on the Joint Committee on the Draft Defamation Bill. In March 2012 he tabled a 10 minute rule bill calling for the introduction of legislation to tackle the problem of financial exclusion. In his spare time Chris enjoys watching most sports, running and reading.

2010 General Election Result

	Party	Votes Cast	%	Change 05-10
Christopher Evans	Lab	17,069	49.2	-15.1%
Daniel Thomas	Con	4,854	14.0	+3.0%
Steffan Lewis	PC	4,518	13.0	+0.6%
Asghar Ali	Lib D	3,597	10.4	-1.8%
Dave Rees	Ind	1,495	4.3	+4.3%
John Voisey	BNP	1,320	3.8	+3.8%
Jason Crew	UKIP	936	2.7	+2.7%
Paul Taylor	Ind	901	2.6	+2.6%

Electorate: 55,292 Turnout: 63.3%

[Bar chart showing 2010 and 2005 results for Lab, Con, PC, Lib D, Other]

AM for Islwyn

Gwyn R PRICE Labour
Majority: 7,589 (36.3%)

National Assembly for Wales
Cardiff Bay, Cardiff CF99 1NA
Tel: (029) 2089 8309
Email: gwyn.price@wales.gov.uk

Constituency Office:
208 High Street, Blackwood NP12 1AJ
Tel: (01495) 225162
Website: www.gwynprice.co.uk

Gwyn Price entered the Assembly when he won the Islwyn seat in May 2011 with a majority of 7,589. Born in the South Wales valley town of Tirphil, he is a former Deputy Leader of Caerphilly County Borough Council, where he held the cabinet portfolio for Human Resources, Constitutional Affairs and Procurement. He was also Branch Chair of UCATT, Branch Treasurer of NUPE and executive member of Caerphilly UNISON. Gwyn is also a member of the Islwyn campaign team, was Chair of Governors for Penllwyn Primary School and Treasurer for Pontllanfraith BLP.

In the Assembly, Gwyn is currently a member of the Communities, Equality and Local Government Committee and the Public Accounts Committee. His political interests are listed as social policy, economic regeneration, health and safety, local government. In his spare time he enjoys DIY, reading and socialising with friends and family.

2011 Assembly Election Result

	Party	Votes Cast	%	Change 07-11
Gwyn Price	Lab	12,116	58.0	+20.3%
Steffan Lewis	PC	4,527	21.7	+0.1%
David Chipp	Con	2,497	11.9	+4.3%
Peter Whalley	BNP	1,115	5.3	-
Tom Sullivan	Lib D	653	3.1	-1.7%

Electorate: 54,893 Turnout: 38.1%

Electoral Trends 1999 - 2011

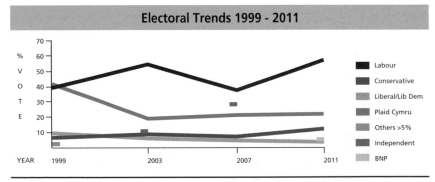

MP - Nia GRIFFITH Labour

AM - Keith DAVIES Labour

Mid & West Wales Regional AMs

Rebecca Evans (Lab)	Simon Thomas (PC)
William Powell (Lib D)	Joyce Watson (Lab)

Area:	235 sq km	% born in Wales:	86.1%
% speaking Welsh: 42.0%		% Unemployment *(Apr 2012)* 6.4%	

The constituency comprises the following electoral wards:
Bigyn, Burry Port, Bynea, Dafen, Elli, Felinfoel, Glanymor, Glyn, Hendy, Hengoed, Kidwelly, Llangennech, Llannon, Lliedi, Llwynhendy, Pembrey, Pontyberem, Swiss Valley, Trimsaran, Tŷcroes, Tŷisha.

Llanelli is an established Labour stronghold, but also an intensely Welsh constituency. These two traditions were well illustrated in the career of its former MP, James Griffiths, who served in Parliament 1935-70, was Charter Secretary of State for Wales 1964-66 and also Deputy Leader of the Labour Party. At the May 1999 Assembly elections however, Llanelli was unexpectedly captured by Helen Mary Jones, one of a handful of sensational results enjoyed by Plaid Cymru. Such success led to Plaid Cymru's high expectations at the General Election in 2001, but these were not to be fulfilled. The Labour Party fought the second Assembly election in 2003 much more assiduously and Catherine Thomas, the new Labour candidate, was successfully, if narrowly, returned. The energetic Helen Mary Jones was not lost to the Assembly however, being elected as a regional AM for Mid and West Wales. The previous MP, Denzil Davies, a senior Labour Member who no longer enjoyed office, stood down at the 2005 General Election and his successor, Nia Griffith, selected, from an all-women shortlist, was duly elected. In 2010 Nia Griffith was re-elected, but with a reduced majority. Recent Assembly elections have seen further head-to-head battles between Labour and Plaid Cymru. A fierce contest in 2007 resulted in victory for Plaid Cymru and Helen Mary Jones following a sizeable swing away from Labour. The 2011 Assembly contest lived up to its billing as one of the most anticipated of the campaign and did not disappoint with Labour's Keith Davies winning a dramatic victory by 80 votes, making it the second most marginal constituency in Wales. Llanelli is the last major urban area in Wales that is largely Welsh-speaking.

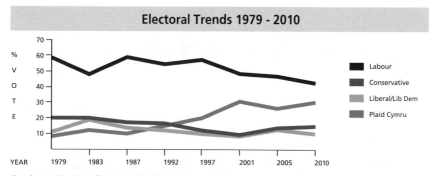

Electoral Trends 1979 - 2010

Previous MPs: **Denzil Davies 1970-2005**
Previous AMs: **Helen Mary Jones (PC) 2007-11, 1999-03; Catherine Thomas (Lab) 2003-07**

MP for Llanelli

Nia GRIFFITH Labour
Majority: 4,701 (12.5%)

House of Commons, London SW1A 0AA
Tel: (020) 7219 4903
Email: nia.griffith.mp@parliament.uk

Constituency Office:
6 Queen Victoria Road, Llanelli SA15 2TL
Tel: (01554) 756374
Website: www.niagriffith.org.uk

Nia Griffith entered Parliament in 2005, succeeding Denzil Davies as Labour MP for Llanelli having been selected as a candidate from an all-woman shortlist. She is only Llanelli's third MP since 1935. The two previous Members both served 35 year terms, setting a formidable precedent for a new MP. Nia was born in Dublin in 1956 and enjoyed a peripatetic childhood as her academic father moved between university posts. She is a Modern Languages graduate from Somerville College, Oxford and qualified as a teacher at the University of Wales, Bangor. Prior to her election, she was Head of Modern Languages at Morriston Comprehensive School in Swansea and had also worked as an education adviser and as a schools' inspector for Estyn.

An active member of the Labour Party since 1981, she is a former Councillor on Carmarthen Town Council and served as Sheriff of Carmarthen in 1997 and Deputy Mayor in 1998. In Parliament, Nia was previously a junior Shadow Minister for Business, Innovation and Skills and is currently Shadow Wales Minister. She is generally perceived to be of a left-wing disposition and voted against the whip on several key divisions during the Blair administration. She is a member of Amnesty International, USDAW and the NUT and outside of politics enjoys cycling and music. A fluent Welsh speaker, she also speaks French, Italian and Spanish.

2010 General Election Result

	Party	Votes Cast	%	Change 05-10
Nia Griffith	Lab	15,916	42.5	-4.5%
Myfanwy Davies	PC	11,215	29.9	+3.5%
Christopher Salmon	Con	5,381	14.4	+0.7%
Myrddin Edwards	Lib D	3,902	10.4	-2.5%
Andrew Marshall	UKIP	1,047	2.8	+2.8%

Electorate: 55,637 Turnout: 67.3%

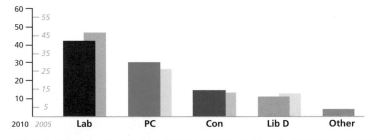

Keith DAVIES Labour
Majority: 80 (0.3%)

National Assembly for Wales
Cardiff Bay, Cardiff CF99 1NA
Tel: (029) 2082 1997
Email: keith.davies@Wales.gov.uk

Constituency Office:
6 Queen Victoria Road, Llanelli SA15 2TL
Tel: (01554) 774902
Website: www.keithdavies.org.uk

Keith Davies entered the Assembly at the 2011 election, having defeated Plaid's Helen Mary Jones by the slim margin of 80 votes. Born in 1940 in Gwaun-Cae-Gurwen in the Amman Valley, he was educated at Ystalyfera Grammar School before studying Mathematics and Physics at Swansea University. Keith qualified as a teacher and then took up senior positions in schools and colleges before entering local government, first as a schools inspector and eventually as Director of Education for Mid Glamorgan and Carmarthenshire. During his time as an inspector he represented South Wales and the West of England on the National Association of Inspectors and Educational Advisers. He also represented the Hengoed ward on Carmarthenshire County Council between 2004 and 2008 and currently represents Mid and West Wales on the Welsh Executive Committee.

In the Assembly Keith is currently a member of the Environment and Sustainability Committee and the Enterprise and Business Committee. In May 2012 he was censured by the Assembly and reprimanded by the Welsh Labour Party for drunken behaviour during a hotel stay on Assembly expenses. The married father-of-two accepted the Standards Committee report in its entirety.

2011 Assembly Election Result

	Party	Votes Cast	%	Change 07-11
Keith Davies	Lab	10,359	39.7	+3.7%
Helen Mary Jones	PC	10,279	39.4	-10.7%
Andrew Morgan	Con	2,880	11.1	+1.1%
Sian Caiach	Llanelli	2,004	7.7	-
Cheryl Philpott	Lib D	548	2.1	-1.7%

Electorate: 58,838 Turnout: 44.3%

Electoral Trends 1999 - 2011

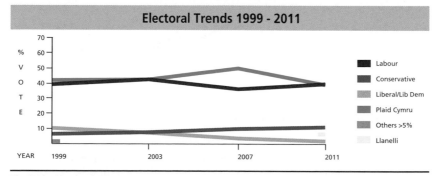

- Labour
- Conservative
- Liberal/Lib Dem
- Plaid Cymru
- Others >5%
- Llanelli

MERTHYR TYDFIL & RHYMNEY

MP - Dai HAVARD Labour

AM - Huw LEWIS Labour

South Wales East Regional AMs

Mohammad Asghar (Con)	William Graham (Con)
Jocelyn Davies (PC)	Lindsay Whittle (PC)

Area:	162 sq km	% born in Wales:	92.5%
% speaking Welsh:	15.9%	% Unemployment *(Apr 2012)*	11.7%

The constituency comprises the following electoral wards:
Bedlinog, Cyfartha, Darren Valley, Dowlais, Gurnos, Merthyr Vale, Moriah, New Tredegar, Park, Penydarren, Plymouth, Pontlottyn, Town, Treharris, Twyn Carno, Vaynor.

The leading Welsh historian, Professor K.O. Morgan, once described **Merthyr Tydfil** as 'the crucible of Welsh politics' with the founder of the Labour Party, Keir Hardie, having been elected here in 1900. S.O. Davies was MP from 1934 to 1972, finally being returned in 1970 as an Independent Labour MP. Ted Rowlands followed at the by-election following S.O.'s death, but against strong Plaid Cymru opposition. Plaid Cymru went on to enjoy some success in local government, but Merthyr soon reverted to overwhelming Labour hegemony. Ted Rowlands increased his majority at every General Election from the by-election in 1972 until 1992.

The Assembly elections in May 1999 showed that support for Plaid Cymru was still potentially strong, if normally dormant. Ted Rowlands retired prior to the 2001 General Election and, although Plaid Cymru achieved another positive swing, Labour's control of the seat has never been seriously threatened. Recent local elections have seen the emergence of community based parties, such as People before Politics, but Merthyr remains a safe Labour seat by any standard. Dai Havard was easily re-elected in 2005 and again in 2010, but this time with the Liberal Democrats running in second place. Dai Havard has a safe seat, even if he only enjoys a majority a fraction of that of his predecessor. In 2007, Huw Lewis, the sitting AM, faced an array of Independent and minority party candidates who, whilst not threatening his tenure of the seat, substantially reduced his majority. Merthyr however, remains a rock solid Labour seat, with Huw Lewis polling almost three times more votes in 2011 than his nearest Independent rival in second place.

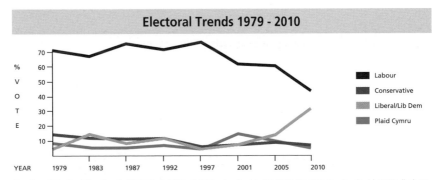

Previous MPs: **Ted Rowlands 1972 (by)-2001; S O Davies (Ind Lab) 1970-72, S O Davies (Lab) 1934 (by)-70**

Dai HAVARD Labour
Majority: 4,056 (12.6%)

House of Commons, London SW1A 0AA
Tel: (020) 7219 8255
Email: dai.havard.mp@parliament.uk

Constituency Office:
Unit 4, Triangle Industrial Estate, Pentrebach,
Merthyr Tydfil CF48 4TQ
Tel: (01685) 379247
Email: toomeyd@parliament.uk
Website: www.daihavardmp.co.uk

MERTHYR TYDFIL

Dai Havard was first elected to Parliament for Merthyr Tydfil & Rhymney in June 2001. Prior to the election he was Wales Secretary of AMICUS (MSF section), the 'white collar' union. Born 7 February 1950 in Graig, Quakers Yard, Dai was educated at Quakers Yard Grammar School and Afon Taf Comprehensive School before qualifying as a teacher at St Peter's College, Birmingham. He later took an MA in Industrial Relations at Warwick University. He was a tutor and trade union official for more than 25 years and has served as the Wales TUC representative on the Community Regeneration Forum and the Innovation and the Research and Development Forum. He is a member of the Co-operative Party.

In Parliament, he frequently proclaims his Socialist beliefs and aspirations and has proved an assertive backbencher, rebelling against the Whips on several critical divisions. He is a member of the Defence Select Committee and advocated that the Prime Minister should have supported an immediate ceasefire in the 2006 conflict between Israel and Lebanon. He is also a member of the Panel of Chairs. Aside from politics, he is a keen hill walker, horse rider and bird-watcher and 'came out of retirement' to play for the Commons and Lords Rugby team.

2010 General Election Result

	Party	Votes Cast	%	Change 05-10
Dai Havard	Lab	14,007	43.7	-16.8%
Amy Kitcher	Lib D	9,951	31.0	+17.0%
Maria Hill	Con	2,412	7.5	-1.4%
Clive Tovey	Ind	1,845	5.8	+5.8%
Glyndwr Cennydd Jones	PC	1,621	5.1	-4.9%
Richard Barnes	BNP	1,173	3.7	+3.7%
Adam Brown	UKIP	872	2.7	+0.4%
Alan Cowdell	SLP	195	0.6	-0.3%

Electorate: 54,715 Turnout: 58.6%

[Bar chart showing 2010 and 2005 results for Lab, Lib D, Con, PC, Other]

MERTHYR TYDFIL

Huw LEWIS Labour
Majority: 7,051 (36.5%)

National Assembly for Wales
Cardiff Bay, Cardiff CF99 1NA
Email: huw.lewis@wales.gov.uk

Constituency Office:
Venture Wales Building, Merthyr Industrial Park
Pentrebach, Merthyr Tydfil CF48 4DR
Tel: (01443) 692299

Huw Lewis has served as the Assembly Member for Merthyr Tydfil & Rhymney since 1999. Born in Merthyr Tydfil in 1964 and brought up in Aberfan, he was educated at Afon Taf High School and Edinburgh University. Prior to his election to the Assembly, he was Assistant General Secretary of the Labour Party in Wales. He is a member of Unite, the Co-op Party and the Fabian Society.

Huw is currently Minister for Housing, Regeneration and Heritage. Having unsuccessfully contested the leadership of the Welsh Labour Party in November 2009, he was appointed Deputy Minister for Children in Carwyn Jones's First Cabinet. He had previously resigned, in protest, from his position as party Whip following the resignation of Alun Michael in 2000. In the Partnership Government with the Liberal Democrats, he was appointed Deputy Minister for Education and Lifelong Learning, but later resigned in protest against the use of a landfill site in Merthyr for the disposal of foot and mouth carcasses without proper consultation. He was promoted again to be Deputy Minister with responsibility for Communities in May 2003 and briefly, following the 2007 election, was Deputy Minister with responsibility for regeneration. However he was relieved of this post due to his opposition to the 'One Wales' coalition with Plaid Cymru. He lives in Merthyr Tydfil with his wife Lynne Neagle (AM for Torfaen) and their two children.

2011 Assembly Election Result

	Party	Votes Cast	%	Change 07-11
Huw Lewis	Lab	10,483	54.3	+17.2%
Tony Rogers	Ind	3,432	17.8	-
Amy Kitcher	Lib D	2,480	12.8	-2.4%
Noel Turner	PC	1,701	8.8	-3.2%
Chris O'Brien	Con	1,224	6.3	+0.9%

Electorate: 55,031 Turnout: 35.1%

Electoral Trends 1999 - 2011

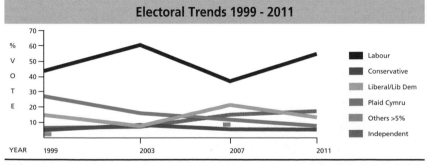

- Labour
- Conservative
- Liberal/Lib Dem
- Plaid Cymru
- Others >5%
- Independent

MONMOUTH

MP - David DAVIES Conservative

AM - Nick RAMSAY Conservative

South Wales East Regional AMs

Mohammad Asghar (Con)	William Graham (Con)
Jocelyn Davies (PC)	Lindsay Whittle (PC)

Area:	829 sq km	% born in Wales:	61.9%
% speaking Welsh: 16.7%		% Unemployment *(Apr 2012)* 3.8%	

The constituency comprises the following electoral wards:
Caerwent, Cantref, Castle, Croesonen, Croesyceiliog North, Croesyceiliog South, Crucorney, Devauden, Dixton with Osbaston, Drybridge, Goetre Fawr, Grofield, Lansdown, Larkfield, Llanbadoc, Llanelly Hill, Llanfoist Fawr, Llangybi Fawr, Llanover, Llantilio Crossenny, Llanwenarth Ultra, Llanyrafon North, Llanyrafon South, Mardy, Mitchel Troy, Overmonnow, Portskewett, Priory, Raglan, St Arfons, St Christopher's, St Kingsmark, St Mary's, Shirenewton, St.Mary's, Thornwell, Trellech United, Usk, Wyesham.

Monmouth is an English-speaking border constituency that has traditionally returned Conservative members to Parliament. It was previously the constituency of Peter Thorneycroft MP, 1945-66, a former Chancellor of the Exchequer and later Chairman of the Conservative Party. Labour won temporary control of the seat in Harold Wilson's landslide election of 1966, and, following the death of Sir John Stradling Thomas, secured a spectacular by-election victory in 1991. The Conservatives however, successfully re-captured the seat in 1992 confirming the rule that the Labour Party is generally unable to retain seats won in mid-term by-elections from the Tories. Further success for Labour at the 1995 local government elections and Huw Edwards's second victory at the 1997 General Election, suggested that Monmouth, rather than being a natural Tory constituency, was becoming a key 'swing' seat in Wales.

In May 1999, the alternation of party control continued with a Conservative victory at the Assembly election, a success that David Davies was to repeat in 2003. In between, the 2001 General Election saw the fourth Parliamentary contest between Roger Evans for the Conservatives and Huw Edwards for Labour. A second Labour landslide across the country retained the seat for Huw Edwards, but only after a recount. In 2005, the sitting AM, David Davies, contested the Parliamentary seat and, benefiting from the national swing to the Conservatives, successfully returned Monmouth to Tory control. David Davies retained a dual mandate for the two years between elections, but in 2007 gave way allowing his Assembly seat to pass to his Conservative successor, Nick Ramsay, which he went on to comfortably retain in 2011.

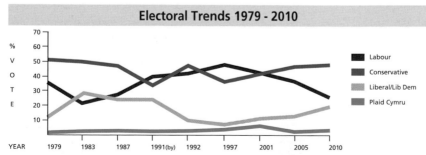

Electoral Trends 1979 - 2010

Previous MPs: Huw Edwards 1997-2005; Roger Evans (Con) 1992-97; Huw Edwards (Lab) 1991 (by)-92; Sir John Stradling Thomas (Con) 1970-91
Previous AMs: David Davies (Con) 1999-2007

David DAVIES Conservative
Majority: 10,425 (22.4%)

House of Commons
London SW1A 0AA
Tel: (020) 7219 8360
Email: david.davies.mp@parliament.uk

Constituency Office:
The Grange, 16 Maryport Street
Usk NP15 1AB
Tel: (01291) 672817 Fax: (01291) 672737
Website: www.david-daviesmp.co.uk

David Davies was already the Assembly Member for Monmouth when he was elected to Parliament in May 2005. Born in London in 1970 and educated at Bassaleg Comprehensive School, he travelled and worked in Australia and the USA before returning to join his family's tea importing business in Newport. Formerly Treasurer of the Wales Young Conservatives, he previously fought Bridgend at the 1997 General Election. He was a prominent 'No' campaigner during the Referendum campaign but went on to become a very effective Assembly Member. He is an accomplished Welsh learner and now regularly broadcasts in Welsh.

David stood down as AM prior to the 2007 Assembly elections, but was able to pass to his successor a relatively safe seat compared with the marginal he had inherited. In Parliament, David is Chair of the Welsh Affairs Committee and is a former member of the Home Affairs Committee. He is a member of the Liaison Select Committee; Vice-Chair of the All-Party Parliamentary China Group and a member of the All-Party Parliamentary British-German Group. In January 2012 the Prime Minister announced David's appointment as a member of the UK delegation to the Parliamentary Assembly of the Council of Europe. David Davies remains an articulate advocate on a range of issues particularly relevant to this English-speaking, border, constituency. Named MP of the Year in the 2010 Welsh Politician of the Year Awards, he has clearly managed the transition from Cardiff Bay to Westminster very successfully. He is married with a son and two daughters.

2010 General Election Result

	Party	Votes Cast	%	Change 05-10
David Davies	Con	22,466	48.3	+1.4%
Hamish Sandison	Lab	12,041	25.9	-11.1%
Martin Blakebrough	Lib D	9,026	19.4	+6.6%
Jonathan Clark	PC	1,273	2.7	+0.6%
Derek Rowe	UKIP	1,126	2.4	+1.2%
Steve Millson	Green	587	1.3	+1.3%

Electorate: 64,538 Turnout: 74.1%

2010 *2005*   **Con**   **Lab**   **Lib D**   **PC**   **Other**

Nick RAMSAY Conservative
Majority: 6,117 (20.4%)

National Assembly for Wales
Cardiff Bay, Cardiff CF99 1NA
Tel: (029) 2089 8735
Email: nicholas.ramsay@wales.gov.uk

Constituency Office:
The Grange, 16 Maryport Street
Usk NP15 1AB
Tel: (01291) 674898
Website: www.nickramsay.org.uk

MONMOUTH

Nick Ramsay was first elected to the National Assembly in 2007, having previously contested Torfaen during the 2003 election. Originally from Cwmbran, he was born in 1975 and was educated at Croesyceiliog Comprehensive School and Durham University, where he graduated in English and Philosophy. He later gained a Postgraduate Diploma in Applied Linguistics from Cardiff University. Before entering politics, Nick worked as a driving instructor in Monmouthshire and The Valleys from 1999 to 2001. He then served as County Councillor in Monmouthshire between 2004 and 2008, which had previously been in Labour hands for over 20 years. He has also previously worked for former Welsh Conservative party leader Nick Bourne and David Davies MP.

Nick is currently the Conservative Shadow Minister for Business, Enterprise and Technology, having been an unsuccessful candidate for Conservative leader in the National Assembly during 2011. Nick currently Chair's the Assembly's Enterprise and Business Committee. He is also Chairman of Cross-Party Groups on Biodiversity; Beer and Pubs and Waterways. Aside from politics, Nick is a keen follower of Welsh Rugby Union - his grandfather Jack Davies played for Pontypool Rugby Club in the 1950s.

2011 Assembly Election Result

	Party	Votes Cast	%	Change 07-11
Nick Ramsay	Con	15,087	50.3	-1.8%
Mark Whitcutt	Lab	8,970	29.9	+6.5%
Janet Ellard	Lib D	2,937	9.8	-5.0%
Fiona Cross	PC	2,263	7.5	+0.5%
Steve Uncles	Eng Dem	744	2.5	-0.2%

Electorate: 64,857 Turnout: 46.3%

Electoral Trends 1999 - 2011

% V O T E (y-axis: 10 to 70)

YEAR: 1999 2003 2007 2011

Legend:
■ Labour
■ Conservative
■ Liberal/Lib Dem
■ Plaid Cymru
■ Others >5%
■ Independent
□ Eng Dem

MONTGOMERYSHIRE

MP - Glyn DAVIES Conservative

AM - Russell GEORGE Conservative

Mid & West Wales Regional AMs

Rebecca Evans (Lab)	Simon Thomas (PC)
William Powell (Lib D)	Joyce Watson (Lab)

Area:	2,174 sq km	% born in Wales:	50.4%
% speaking Welsh:	28.6%	% Unemployment *(Apr 2012)*	3.0%

The constituency comprises the following electoral wards:
Banwy, Berriew, Blaen Hafren, Caersws, Churchstoke, Dolforwyn, Forden, Glantwymyn, Guilsfield, Kerry, Llanbrynmair, Llandinam, Llandrinio, Llandysilio, Llanfair Caereinion, Llanfihangel, Llanfyllin, Llanidloes, Llanrhaeadr-ym-Mochant, Llanrhaeadr-ym-Mochnant/Llansilin, Llansantffraid, Machynlleth, Meifod, Montgomery, Newtown Central, Newtown East, Newtown Llanllwchaiarn North, Newtown Llanllwchaiarn West, Newtown South, Rhiwcynon, Trewern, Welshpool Castle, Welshpool Gungrog, Welshpool Llanerchyddol.

Montgomeryshire is an agricultural, border constituency. The western part of the constituency extends into the Cambrian Mountains and is more traditionally Welsh and Welsh speaking.

Montgomeryshire has been a bastion of Liberalism in Wales for over a century, save a brief interlude when Delwyn Williams was returned to Parliament for the Conservatives, 1979-83. Montgomeryshire has a formidable Liberal heritage being the former seat of Clement Davies, Leader of the Liberal Party 1945-56, Emlyn Hooson (now Lord Hooson) 1962-79, and Alex Carlile (now Lord Carlile) 1983-97. In 1997, Lembit Öpik became MP for the Liberal Democrats, defeating a challenge from the Conservative, Glyn Davies. Mr Davies however, went on to become a Regional Member of the National Assembly for Wales, but not before losing to the Liberal Democrats again in the constituency election. The Liberal Democrats have continued to hold control in both Parliament and the Assembly and, until recently, seemed unlikely to be displaced. Whereas Lembit Öpik was returned to Parliament comfortably enough in 2005, Mick Bates, the Liberal Democrat Assembly Member, had a closer call in 2007 where the intervention of a UKIP candidate probably depressed the Conservative vote enough to safeguard the Liberal Democrats. The General Election in May 2010 however, saw a massive swing to the Conservatives and the election of Glyn Davies at the expense of Lembit Öpik. The trend continued in the 2011 Assembly election, when the Conservatives' Russell George won with a relatively comfortable majority, following the retirement of the incumbent member Mick Bates.

Electoral Trends 1979 - 2010

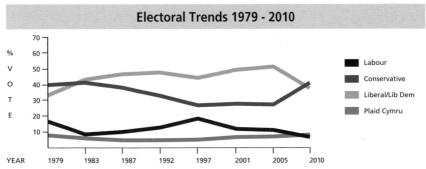

Previous MPs: Lembit Öpik (Lib D) 1997-2010; Alex Carlile (Lib D) 1983-97; Delwyn Williams (Con) 1979-83; Emlyn Hooson (Lib) 1962 (by) -79 // *Previous AMs:* Mick Bates 1999-2007 (Lib D)

MP for Montgomeryshire

Glyn DAVIES Conservative
Majority: 1,184 (3.5%)

House of Commons, London SW1A 0AA
Tel: (020) 7219 3806
Email: glyn.davies.mp@parliament.uk

Constituency Office:
20 High St., Welshpool, Powys SY21 7SP
Tel: (01938) 552315
Website: www.glyn-davies.co.uk

MONTGOMERYSHIRE

Glyn Davies was elected at the 2010 General Election, where he achieved the largest swing to the Conservatives to take the historically safe Liberal Democrat seat of Montgomeryshire. He had previously served as an Assembly Member for Mid & West Wales 1999-2007. During his time in the Assembly, he established himself as a front-rank politician and a leading Conservative in Wales. By consciously setting out to improve his Welsh, for example, he became a frequent broadcaster on S4C and Radio Wales and doubtless extended his political appeal across a wider electorate. Born in the village of Castle Caereinion, Montgomeryshire, he has farmed in Berriew for many years. He has previously been Chairman of Montgomeryshire District Council and the Development Board for Rural Wales. He also served as a member on the Wales Tourism Board and the board of the Welsh Development Agency. He is the current President of the Campaign for the Protection of Rural Wales and a trustee of the Montgomeryshire Wildlife Trust.

In Parliament, he is currently serving as Parliamentary Private Secretary to the Secretary of State for Wales and lists his political interests as energy policy, Welsh affairs and social care. Married with four children, outside of politics, Glyn likes to relax by playing golf.

2010 General Election Result

	Party	Votes Cast	%	Change 05-10
Glyn Davies	Con	13,976	41.3	+13.8%
Lembit Opik	Lib D	12,792	37.8	-12.5%
Heledd Fychan	PC	2,802	8.3	+1.3%
Nick Colbourne	Lab	2,407	7.1	-5.2%
David Rowlands	UKIP	1,128	3.3	+0.4%
Milton Ellis	NF	384	1.1	+1.1%
Bruce Lawson	Ind	324	1.0	+1.0%

Electorate: 46,766 Turnout: 69.4%

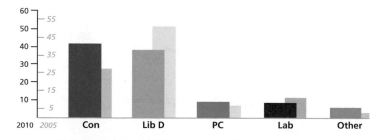

MONTGOMERYSHIRE

Russell GEORGE Conservative
Majority: 2,324 (10.1%)

National Assembly for Wales
Cardiff Bay, Cardiff CF99 1NA
Tel: (029) 2089 8733
Email: russell.george@wales.gov.uk

Constituency Office:
13 Parker's Lane, Newtown SY16 2LT
Tel: (01686) 610887
Website: www.russellgeorge.com

Russell George was elected in May 2011, winning the seat from the Liberal Democrats with a 5.1% swing of the vote and a majority of 2,324. Born in Welshpool in 1974, Russell has a degree in Information and Media Studies from the University of Central England. He was elected to Powys County Council in 2008 to represent the Newtown Central ward and also the County Councils' Welsh Conservative group to be one of its representatives on the Council's executive management board, where he held the portfolio for Customer Services and ICT.

Russell is currently the Welsh Conservatives Shadow Minister for Environment and Sustainable Development and in the Assembly he sits on the Petitions Committee and the Environment and Sustainability Committee. His political interests are transport, protection of the Welsh environment, local government and community regeneration. In his spare time, Russell's interests are keeping healthy and he is an active member of Hope Community Church in Newtown.

2011 Assembly Election Result

	Party	Votes Cast	%	Change 07-11
Russell George	Con	10,026	43.7	+13.6%
Wyn Williams	Lib D	7,702	33.6	-5.4%
Nick Colbourne	Lab	2,609	11.4	+4.5%
David Senior	PC	2,596	11.3	-2.5%

Electorate: 48,675 Turnout: 47.1%

Electoral Trends 1999 - 2011

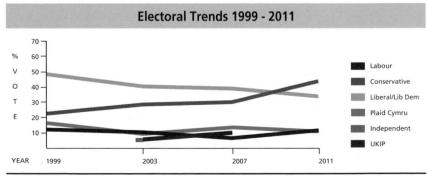

NEATH

MP - Rt Hon Peter HAIN Labour
AM - Gwenda THOMAS Labour

South Wales West Regional AMs

Peter Black (Lib D)	Suzy Davies (Con)
Byron Davies (Con)	Bethan Jenkins (PC)

Area:	265 sq km	% born in Wales:	88.4%
% speaking Welsh:	26.2%	% Unemployment *(Apr 2012)*	5.6%

The constituency comprises the following electoral wards:
Aberdulais, Allt-wen, Blaengwrach, Bryn-coch North, Bryn-coch South, Cadoxton, Cimla, Crynant, Cwmllynfell, Dyffryn, Glynneath, Godre'r graig, Gwaun-Cae-Gurwen, Lower Brynamman, Neath East, Neath North, Neath South, Onllwyn, Pelenna, Pontardawe, Resolven, Rhos, Seven Sisters, Tonna, Trebanos, Ystalyfera.

Neath is a classic South Wales industrial constituency. Solidly Labour, it covers the town of Neath and much of the upper Swansea Valley. Neath has the ninth highest proportion of Welsh speakers for a constituency in Wales. The residual strength of this cultural identity has been reflected in Plaid Cymru's strong presence in the seat , at the 1991 by-election in particular, but in successive elections to both Parliament and the Assembly.

Peter Hain played a major role in the Referendum campaign on devolution in September 1997 and was rewarded when the County Borough of Neath Port Talbot recorded the highest 'Yes' vote in Wales - 66.3%. Plaid Cymru enjoyed a further revival in support in 1999 at the Assembly elections, but Gwenda Thomas was still safely returned for Labour. Plaid Cymru went on to record a further positive swing of over 10% at the General Election of June 2001, but this did little to trouble Peter Hain's security of tenure. At the second Assembly elections in 2003, Plaid Cymru continued to run second, but Labour increased its majority. Labour saw some further slippage in its support at the General Election in 2005 and 2010, but this is of little consequence as Neath remains one of Labour's strongest constituencies in Wales. Labour have continued to control the seat in the National Assembly, but by a much smaller margin than at Westminster. Despite fears that Plaid Cymru could further erode Labour support at the 2011 Assembly elections, any fears proved unfounded as Gwenda Thomas significantly increased her majority to over 6,000.

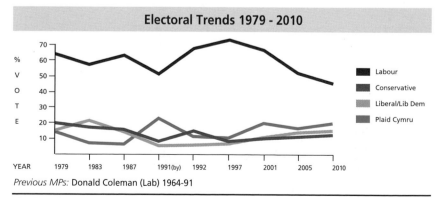

Electoral Trends 1979 - 2010

Previous MPs: **Donald Coleman (Lab) 1964-91**

Rt Hon Peter HAIN Labour
Majority: 9,775 (26.3%)

House of Commons
London SW1A 0AA
Tel: (020) 7219 3925
Email: hainp@parliament.uk

Constituency Office:
39 Windsor Road, Neath SA11 1NB
Tel: (01639) 630152
Website: www.peterhain.org

NEATH

Peter Hain was elected MP for Neath in 1991 at a by-election following the death of Donald Coleman. Born in Nairobi on 16 February 1950, he was educated at Pretoria Boys' High School and the Universities of London and Sussex. He was Chair of the Young Liberals 1971-73, but joined the Labour Party in 1977. He achieved international prominence in the anti-apartheid movement as leader of 'Stop the Seventy Tour', a campaign undertaken when he was only 19 and which led to him being branded by some as "public enemy number one" in his native South Africa. Prior to entering Parliament, he was head of research with the Union of Communication Workers.

In Parliament, he has previously served in Government as Secretary of State 2002-08, 2009-10; and also assumed the positions of Leader of the House and Lord Privy Seal. A candidate for the internal Labour Party election for the Deputy Leadership in 2007, he subsequently resigned following allegations of financial irregularities. Absolved of any wrongdoing, he rejoined the Government in 2009. Following the 2005 General Election, he had remained Secretary of State for Wales whilst simultaneously becoming Secretary of State for Northern Ireland, and in 2007 combined the post of Welsh Secretary with that of Secretary of State for Work and Pensions. He was appointed Shadow Secretary of State for Wales in the new Miliband Opposition Cabinet in September 2010 but stood down in May 2012 in order to concentrate on the project to create a Severn Barrage.

2010 General Election Result

	Party	Votes Cast	%	Change 05-10
Peter Hain	Lab	17,172	46.3	-6.3%
Alun Llewelyn	PC	7,397	19.9	+2.8%
Frank Little	Lib D	5,535	14.9	+0.6%
Emmeline Owens	Con	4,847	13.1	+1.5%
Michael Green	BNP	1,342	3.6	+3.6%
James Bevan	UKIP	829	2.2	+2.2%

Electorate: 57,295 Turnout: 64.9%

2010 _2005_   **Lab   PC   Lib D   Con   Other**

AM for Neath

Gwenda THOMAS Labour
Majority: 6,390 (26.8%)

National Assembly for Wales
Cardiff Bay, Cardiff CF99 1NA
Tel: (029) 2089 8750
Email: gwenda.thomas@wales.gov.uk

Constituency Office:
7 High Street, Pontardawe, Swansea SA8 4HU
Tel: (01792) 869993
Website: www.gwendathomas.com

Gwenda Thomas has been Labour Assembly Member for the Neath constituency since 1999. Born in Neath in 1942 and educated at Pontardawe Grammar School, Gwenda was previously a Civil Servant, having served in the County Courts branch of the then Lord Chancellor's Department as an Executive Officer, and then at the Benefits Agency. She represented her home village of Gwaun Cae Gurwen as both a Community and County Councillor for many years and was appointed Chair of the Social Services Committee of West Glamorgan County Council, becoming the first woman to chair a major committee. She later held the same post in Neath Port Talbot County Borough Council. Gwenda was also Chair of 'West Glamorgan Campaign for a Welsh Assembly' and Vice Chair of 'Yes for Wales', Neath. She is a member of the GMB Union.

Gwenda currently serves as Deputy Minister for Health and Social Services in the Welsh Governmnet and is a former Chair of the National Assembly Equality of Opportunity Committee and member of the Local Government and Housing Committee. She has previously served on the Local Government Partnership Council. A fluent Welsh speaker, her political interests include health and social services, childcare and the voluntary sector. Gwenda is married and has a son.

2011 Assembly Election Result

	Party	Votes Cast	%	Change 07-11
Gwenda Thomas	Lab	12,736	53.4	+10.0%
Alun Llewellyn	PC	6,346	26.61	-9.1%
Alex Powell	Con	2,780	11.66	-0.1%
Michael Green	BNP	1,004	4.21	-%
Matthew McCarthy	Lib D	983	4.12	-5.1%

Electorate: 57,533 Turnout: 41.5%

Electoral Trends 1999 - 2011

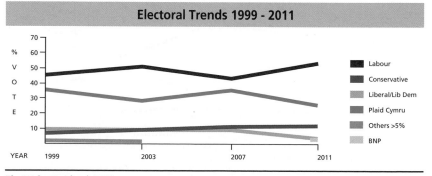

NEWPORT EAST

MP - Jessica MORDEN Labour

AM - John GRIFFITHS Labour

South Wales East Regional AMs

Mohammad Asghar (Con)   William Graham (Con)

Jocelyn Davies (PC)   Lindsay Whittle (PC)

Area:	122 sq km	% born in Wales:	80.1%
% speaking Welsh: 16.8%		% Unemployment *(Apr 2012)*	8.1%

The constituency comprises the following electoral wards:
Alway, Beechwood, Caldicot Castle, Dewstow, Green Lane, Langstone, Liswerry, Llanwern, Mill, Ringland, Rogiet, Severn, St.Julians, The Elms, Victoria, West End.

The seat of **Newport East** was created in 1983 when the former borough constituency of Newport was divided - East and West. Previous MPs have included former Home Secretary, Sir Frank Soskice, 1955-66, and the late Roy Hughes, 1966-97. In 1997, Newport East became the refuge of Alan Howarth, the former Conservative Member for Stratford-on-Avon, who defected from the Tories and went on to serve in Government for Labour. In 2005, following Alan Howarth's retirement, Jessica Morden, former General Secretary of Welsh Labour, secured selection as candidate from an all-women shortlist and was duly elected. Jessica Morden was re-elected in 2010 on a reduced majority following further gains in Liberal Democrat support. John Griffiths won the Assembly seat in 1999 and retained it comfortably in 2003. In 2007, Newport East threatened a shock result when it became clear during the election count that the Liberal Democrats had polled exceptionally well. John Griffiths was returned, but with the ignominy of seeing his majority reduced fivefold. However, the pendulum swung back in Labour's favour in 2011, when John Griffiths saw his large majority return as support for the Liberal Democrats dissipated.

Located on the Bristol Channel coast of Gwent, Newport East has enjoyed considerable inward investment and the development of high-technology industries. These enterprises have been attracted to Newport by good communications and ease of access to the wider British and European market. The progressive decline of steel-making and processing at Llanwern however, has created great uncertainty in the area and further new jobs remain at a premium.

Electoral Trends 1979 - 2010

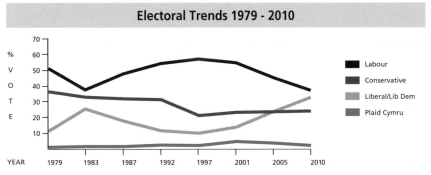

Previous MPs: **Alan Howarth 1997-2005; Roy Hughes (Lab) 1983-97;** (New seat 1983, formerly Newport) **Roy Hughes (Lab) 1966-83**

Jessica MORDEN Labour
Majority: 1,650 (4.8%)

House of Commons, London SW1A 0AA
Tel: (020) 7219 6213 Fax: (020) 7219 6196
Email: mordenj@parliament.uk

Constituency Office:
Suite 5, 1st Floor, Clarence House, Clarence Place
Newport NP19 7AA
Tel: (01633) 841726 Fax: (01633) 841727
Website: www.jessicamorden.com

Jessica Morden was elected to Parliament in May 2005 and in the process became the first ever female MP to represent a constituency in South East Wales. Born in 1968, brought up in Cwmbran, she attended Croesyceiliog Comprehensive School prior to reading History at Birmingham University. Formerly General Secretary to the Wales Labour Party, she joined the party headquarters in the aftermath of the 1999 Assembly elections and Labour's losses to Plaid Cymru. The vacancy at Newport East arose with the retirement and later elevation to the House of Lords of Alan Howarth, the former Conservative MP, who had been 'parachuted' into Newport prior to the 1997 General Election.

Jessica is a member of the GMB union and is considered a modernizer who had a considerable impact within the Labour Party in Wales during her tenure as General Secretary. Currently a member of the Welsh Affairs Select Committee, she has served as Parliamentary Private Secretary to Peter Hain on two separate occasions . Her other political interests include tackling anti-social behaviour, electoral issues, police, children and the steel industry.

2010 General Election Result

	Party	Votes Cast	%	Change 05-10
Jessica Morden	Lab	12,744	37.0	-8.2%
Ed Townsend	Lib D	11,094	32.2	+8.5%
Dawn Parry	Con	7,918	23.0	-0.5%
Keith Jones	BNP	1,168	3.4	+3.4%
Fiona Cross	PC	724	2.1	-1.7%
David Rowlands	UKIP	677	2.0	-1.0%
Liz Screen	SLP	123	0.4	-0.5%

Electorate: 54,305 Turnout: 63.6%

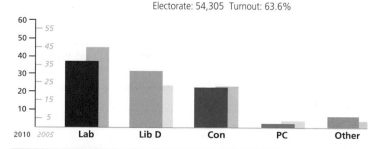

NEWPORT EAST

John GRIFFITHS Labour
Majority: 5,388 (27.7%)

National Assembly for Wales
Cardiff Bay, Cardiff CF99 1NA
Tel: (029) 2089 8315 Fax: (029) 2089 8308
Email: john.griffiths@wales.gov.uk

Constituency Office:
1st Floor, Clarence House, Clarence Place
Newport NP19 7AA
Tel: (01633) 222302
Website: www.johngriffithsam.com

John Griffiths was first elected to the Assembly in May 1999. Born in Newport in 1956, he is a Law graduate and has a Diploma in Psychology from University of Wales, Cardiff. He worked as an executive in market research and as a lecturer in further and higher education before becoming a solicitor. He is a former Gwent County Councillor and Newport County Borough Councillor. He is also a member of the Workers' Educational Association, UNITE and the Co-operative Party.

John currently serves as the Minister for Environment and Sustainable Development in the Welsh Government. He is a former Counsel General and Leader of the Legislative Programme during Carwyn Jones's first term in office. He has also previously served as Deputy Minister for Skills; Deputy Minister for Health and Social Services and as Deputy Economic Development Minister. His political interests include economic development, social inclusion, education, Europe, sport and sub-Saharan Africa. He is also Captain of the National Assembly Football and Cricket teams. Married with two sons, he has completed several London marathons for charity, is a keen swimmer, cyclist and walker.

2011 Assembly Election Result

	Party	Votes Cast	%	Change 07-11
John Griffiths	Lab	9,888	50.8	+18.7%
Nick Webb	Con	4,500	23.1	+0.5%
Ed Townsend	Lib D	3,703	19.0	-8.7%
Chris Paul	PC	1,369	7.0	-1.5%

Electorate: 55,120 Turnout: 35.3%

Electoral Trends 1999 - 2011

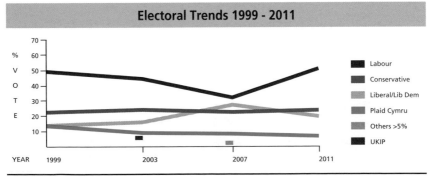

NEWPORT WEST

MP - Paul FLYNN Labour

AM - Rosemary BUTLER Labour

South Wales East Regional AMs

Mohammad Asghar (Con)   William Graham (Con)

Jocelyn Davies (PC)   Lindsay Whittle (PC)

Area:	96 sq km	% born in Wales:	79.6%
% speaking Welsh: 20.9%		% Unemployment *(Apr 2012)* 7.7%	

The constituency comprises the following electoral wards:
Allt-yr-Yn, Bettws, Caerleon, Gaer, Graig, Malpas, Marshfield, Pillgwenlly, Rogerstone, Shaftesbury, Stow Hill, Tredegar Park.

At the first General Election held following the division of the borough in 1983, **Newport West** was captured by the Conservatives. Mark Robinson MP went on to become a Junior Welsh Office Minister, but failed to defend his tiny majority in 1987, allowing Labour to re-gain control. At both the 1992 and 1997 General Elections the Labour Party substantially increased its majority. The National Assembly elections in 1999 also recorded a Labour victory in Newport West. As elsewhere, Plaid Cymru support increased dramatically, but from a minimal base, only achieving fourth place. The sitting MP, Paul Flynn, saw a similar surge by Plaid Cymru in June 2001, but was comfortably returned on a substantial, if slightly reduced, majority. Rosemary Butler was also safely re-elected to the Assembly in 2003 and Paul Flynn was comfortably returned to Parliament in both 2005 and 2010. A swing to the Conservatives at the 2007 Assembly election reduced Rosemary Butler's majority somewhat, but the threat of any repeat of the heady days of Tory success in Newport seems very remote as a large Labour majority was re-established during the 2011 election.

Newport has enjoyed major inward investment projects in electronics and other hi-tec industries. The Celtic Manor Resort Hotel, created by locally born multi-millionaire, Sir Terry Matthews, was the venue for the prestigious Ryder Cup. The tournament, despite being played in fearful weather conditions, was deemed a great success.

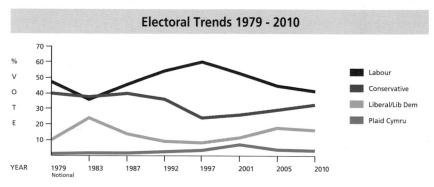

Electoral Trends 1979 - 2010

Previous MPs: **Mark Robinson (Con)** 1983-87; (New seat 1983, formerly part of Newport)

Paul FLYNN Labour
Majority: 3,544 (8.9%)

House of Commons
London SW1A 0AA
Tel: (020) 7219 3478
Email: paulflynnmp@talk21.com

Consituency Office:
Tel: (01633) 262348
Website: www.paulflynnmp.co.uk

Paul Flynn was elected to Parliament in 1987. Born 9 February 1935, he was educated at St. Illtyd's College, Cardiff and University of Wales, Cardiff. An industrial chemist in the Llanwern Steel Works from 1955 to 1982, he worked briefly as a local radio broadcaster before becoming, in 1984, a researcher for Llew Smith, then MEP for South East Wales. He served as a Gwent County Councillor 1974-83, having previously contested Denbigh for Labour at the October 1974 General Election.

Paul was briefly a frontbench Spokesperson on Welsh Affairs in 1988 and an Opposition Spokesperson on Social Security, 1988-90. Winner of the Campaign for Freedom of Information Award in 1991, he was also joint winner of The Spectator Backbencher of the Year award in 1996. In 2009 he was winner of the MP of the Year Welsh Political Award. During the last Government he was generally considered by the Labour Whips to be a paid-up member of the awkward squad. A fluent Welsh-speaker, he was elected to the Gorsedd of the Bards in 1991. His book, 'Commons Knowledge: How to be a Backbencher' was published in 1997 and in July 2000 published his account of the Welsh Labour Party's leadership elections - 'Dragons led by Poodles'. He is a member of the Public Administration Select Committee and the Political and Constitutional Reform Committee. His other political interests include legalisation of soft drugs, animal welfare, constitutional reform, pensions, social security, Welsh affairs and the modernisation of Parliament.

2010 General Election Result

	Party	Votes Cast	%	Change 05-10
Paul Flynn	Lab	16,389	41.3	-3.6%
Matthew Williams	Con	12,845	32.3	+2.8%
Veronica German	Lib D	6,587	16.6	-1.3%
Timothy Windsor	BNP	1,183	3.0	+3.0%
Hugh Moelwyn Hughes	UKIP	1,144	2.9	+0.5%
Jeff Rees	PC	1,122	2.8	-0.8%
Pippa Bartolotti	Green	450	1.1	-0.4%

Electorate: 62,111 Turnout: 64.8%

AM for Newport West

Rosemary BUTLER Labour
Majority: 4,220 (18.3%)

National Assembly for Wales
Cardiff Bay, Cardiff CF99 1NA
Tel: (029) 2089 8470
Email: rosemary.butler@wales.gov.uk

Constituency Office:
1 Transport House, Cardiff Road
Newport NP20 2EH
Tel: (01633) 222523
Website: www.rosemarybutleram.com

Rosemary Butler was first elected as Assembly Member in May 1999. Born in 1943, she has lived in Caerleon, part of the Newport West Constituency, for many years, and attended St Julian's High School. Rosemary joined the Labour party in 1971 and two years later she was elected Labour Councillor for Caerleon on Newport Borough Council, a position she held until 1999. While on the Council, she chaired the Leisure Services Committee for 12 years and served as Deputy Leader and Mayor of Newport. She is a former member of the BBC Broadcasting Council for Wales and the Sports Council for Wales. She has been a Museums and Galleries Commissioner and a Director of Tourism South & West Wales Ltd. She is also an Honorary Citizen of Kutaisi, Newport's twin city in Georgia and is a founder member of Newport Women's Aid.

Since 2011, Rosemary has been the Presiding Officer of the National Assembly, having previously served as Deputy Presiding Officer. She is also Chair of the Business Committee and the Assembly Commission. Appointed Secretary for Pre-16 Education in the first Assembly Cabinet in 1999, she was later Assembly representative on the European Union Committee of the Regions. Married with two daughters, apart from her family her interests range from museums, art galleries, concerts and opera, to foreign travel and family history.

2011 Assembly Election Result

	Party	Votes Cast	%	Change 07-11
Rosemary Butler	Lab	12,011	52.2	+11.7%
David Wiliams	Con	7,791	33.9	-0.7%
Lyndon Binding	PC	1,626	7.1	-3.3%
Liz Newton	Lib D	1,586	6.9	-5.0%

Electorate: 63,180 Turnout: 36.4%

Electoral Trends 1999 - 2011

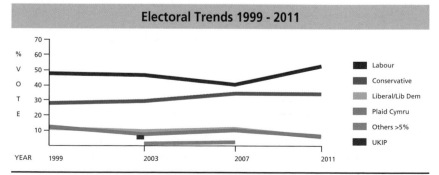

OGMORE

MP - Huw IRRANCA-DAVIES Labour

AM - Janice GREGORY Labour

South Wales West Regional AMs

Peter Black (Lib D)	Suzy Davies (Con)
Byron Davies (Con)	Bethan Jenkins (PC)

Area:	203 sq km	% born in Wales:	89.2%
% speaking Welsh:	18.9%	% Unemployment *(Apr 2012)*	6.6%

The constituency comprises the following electoral wards:
Aberkenfig, Bettws, Blackmill, Blaengarw, Bryncethin, Bryncoch, Brynna, Caerau, Cefn Cribwr, Felindre, Gilfach Goch, Hendre, Llangeinor, Llangynwyd, Llanharan, Llanharry, Maesteg East, Maesteg West, Nant-y-moel, Ogmore Vale, Penprysg, Pontycymmer, Sarn, Ynysawdre.

The historic constituency of **Ogmore** took in Ogmore Vale as well as Ogmore-by-Sea on the coast. Redefined by the Boundary Commission, since 1983 Ogmore has been a land-locked seat in the South Wales Valleys. Local government re-organization also saw the former Borough of Ogwr incorporated into the new County Borough of Bridgend.

A solidly industrial constituency, Ogmore has the second highest proportion of employees in the manufacturing sector in Wales. It has been a hugely 'safe' Labour seat historically and, for many years, the former MP, Sir Ray Powell, enjoyed one of the largest majorities in Parliament. At the by-election following Sir Ray's death, Labour were returned on a reduced mandate, but were never threatened with defeat. At the subsequent General Elections of 2005 and 2010, Huw Irranca-Davies, has restored Labour's majority to its former magnitude. In the election to the National Assembly in 1999, Sir Ray's daughter, Janice Gregory, won the seat, briefly giving the electors of Ogmore a unique, Labour Party, 'family' of elected representatives. The result of the Assembly election however, was a good deal closer than those normally seen in the constituency with Plaid Cymru doubling its previous vote to take second place. Janice Gregory's initial majority, of less than five thousand, improved significantly in 2003, restoring Ogmore to the exclusive group of Labour's safest seats. The 2011 Assembly election confirmed this when Janice Gregory was returned with a majority of 9,576, making Ogmore the safest seat in Wales.

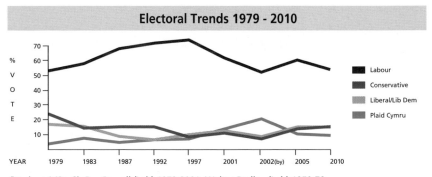

Electoral Trends 1979 - 2010

Previous MPs: Sir Ray Powell (Lab) 1979-2001; Walter Padley (Lab) 1950-79

Huw IRRANCA-DAVIES Labour
Majority: 13,246 (38.2%)

The House of Commons
London SW1A 0AA
Tel: (020) 7219 4027
Email: irrancadaviesh@parliament.uk

Constituency office:
Unit 2, 112-113 Commercial Street
Maesteg CF34 9DL
Tel: (01656) 737777
Website: www.huwirranca-davies.org.uk

OGMORE

Huw Irranca-Davies was first elected to Parliament in a February 2002 by-election, having unsuccessfully contested the Brecon and Radnorshire seat at the 2001 General Election. His nomination for the seat was not without controversy, having displaced several high-profile candidates in the struggle for selection. The Party hierarchy however, soon smoothed over this local difficulty and Huw was comfortably elected, seeing off a determined, but ultimately futile, challenge from Bleddyn Hancock, the Plaid Cymru candidate.

Huw was born in Gowerton in 1963 and educated at Gowerton Comprehensive School and at the Swansea Institute for Higher Education. He is married with three children, having retained his wife's Sardinian family name as part of his own. Prior to his election, he was a senior lecturer in the Business Faculty of the Swansea Institute for Higher Education. Following his re-election in 2005, Huw was appointed PPS to Tessa Jowell, Secretary of State for Culture, Media & Sport and promoted to become a junior Government Whip in 2006. Following the formation of the Gordon Brown Government, he was first appointed Parliamentary Under-Secretary in the Wales Office and later PUS in DEFRA. He is currently the Shadow Minister for DEFRA. A member of the GMB Trade Union, his other political interests include social justice and community regeneration.

2010 General Election Result

	Party	Votes Cast	%	Change 05-10
Huw Irranca-Davies	Lab	18,644	53.8	-7.1%
Emma Moore	Con	5,398	15.6	+1.4%
Jackie Radford	Lib D	5,260	15.2	+0.5%
Danny Clark	PC	3,326	9.6	-0.6%
Kay Thomas	BNP	1,242	3.6	+3.6%
Carolyn Passey	UKIP	780	2.3	+2.3%

Electorate: 55,527 Turnout: 62.4%

AM for Ogmore

Janice GREGORY Labour
Majority: 9,576 (47.2%)

National Assembly for Wales
Cardiff Bay, Cardiff CF99 1NA
Tel: (029) 2089 8748
Email: janice.gregory@wales.gov.uk

Constituency Office:
44a Penybont Road
Pencoed, Bridgend CF35 5RA
Tel: (01656) 860034
Website: www.janicegregoryam.co.uk

Janice Gregory was first elected as an Assembly Member for Ogmore in 1999. Born in Treorchy in 1955, she was educated at Bridgend Grammar School for Girls before becoming a PA to her father, the late Sir Raymond Powell, MP for Ogmore 1979-2001. She has been a member of the Labour Party for over 35 years and served as the Women's Officer of the Constituency Labour Party, 1987-2003. She is a member of UNITE, USDAW, T&GWU, the Co-operative Party and the Fabian Society.

Janice is currently the Government Chief Whip and the Labour Group's Business Manager and has served in these roles since December 2009. She is a former Chair of both the Social Justice & Regeneration Committee and the South Wales West Regional Committee 2006-07. She has been a member of one of the Permanent Legislative Committees, the Audit Committee, the Public Accounts Committee and Chair of the Communities & Culture Committee. Her political interests include community regeneration, tackling poverty and children. She is married with two daughters and outside of politics, enjoys family life, gardening and DIY.

2011 Assembly Election Result

	Party	Votes Cast	%	Change 07-11
Janice Gregory	Lab	12,955	63.9	+12.3%
Danny Clark	PC	3,379	16.7	-0.3%
Martyn Hughes	Con	2,945	14.5	+2.8%
Gerald Francis	Lib D	985	4.9	-4.6%

Electorate: 55,442 Turnout: 36.5%

Electoral Trends 1999 - 2011

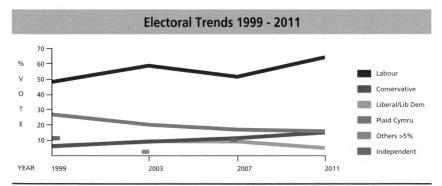

PONTYPRIDD

MP - Owen SMITH Labour
AM - Jane DAVIDSON Labour

South Wales Central Regional AMs

Andrew R T Davies (Con)

David Melding (Con)

Eluned Parrott (Lib D)

Leanne Wood (PC)

Area:	105 sq km	% born in Wales:	85.7%
% speaking Welsh:	20.3%	% Unemployment *(Apr 2012)*	5.4%

The constituency comprises the following electoral wards:
Beddau, Church Village, Graig, Hawthorn, Llantrisant Town, Llantwit Fardre, Pont-y-Clun, Pontypridd Town, Rhondda, Rhydfelen Central/Illan, Taffs Well, Talbot Green, Ton-teg, Tonyrefail East, Tonyrefail West, Trallwng, Treforest, Tyn-y-nant.

Pontypridd is a compact constituency, centred upon the towns of Pontypridd and Llantrisant.

A mixed industrial seat, though derived from a legacy of the mining industry, Pontypridd has a strong tradition of engineering and manufacturing. It also contains a sizeable commuter population for Cardiff and many new estates have been built in recent years, especially between Llantrisant, Beddau and Church Village. Pontypridd is the home of the University of Glamorgan, which has grown rapidly and is at the heart of the regeneration programme for the Valleys. The pioneering Welsh medium secondary school, Ysgol Rhydfelen, is also located in the constituency. At the 1989 by-election, following the death of Brynmor John, Plaid Cymru ran second to Kim Howells but have subsequently failed to seriously challenge Labour's dominance. The National Assembly elections in 1999 however, saw a revival of support for Plaid Cymru in Pontypridd and Jane Davidson, the new Labour AM, was initially returned with a majority of less than two thousand votes. No such threat troubled Dr Kim Howells at the 2001 General Election however and in 2003 Jane Davidson too, was able to restore Labour's majority to more traditional proportions. In 2005 Kim Howells, by now a fairly senior Government Minister, was again returned by a comfortable margin. Dr Howells retired in 2010 and whilst Labour retained the seat, there was a noticeable swing from Labour to the Liberal Democrats.

The third Assembly election in 2007 also saw some slippage in the Labour vote to the Liberal Democrats, but Labour hegemony returned in the 2011 election, when its majority more than doubled to over 7,500.

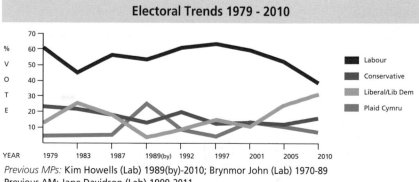

Electoral Trends 1979 - 2010

Previous MPs: Kim Howells (Lab) 1989(by)-2010; Brynmor John (Lab) 1970-89
Previous AM: Jane Davidson (Lab) 1999-2011

MP for Pontypridd

Owen SMITH Labour
Majority: 2,785 (7.6%)

The House of Commons
London SW1A 0AA
Tel: (020) 7219 7128
Email: owen.smith.mp@parliament.uk

Constituency Office:
Office of Owen Smith MP, GMB House
Morgan Street CF37 2DS
Tel: (01443) 401122
Website: www.owensmithmp.com

Owen Smith was first elected to Parliament in 2010, having previously fought a 2006 by-election in Blaenau Gwent. Brought up in Pontypridd and Barry, where he joined the Labour Party, aged 16, he studied History and French at the University of Sussex, before starting work at the BBC as a TV and Radio Producer. During his time at the BBC he produced Radio 4's 'Today' programme and BBC Wales' 'Dragon's Eye'.

Owen left the BBC in 2002, returning to live in Pontypridd, and working as Special Adviser to the Secretary of State for Wales, the Rt. Hon. Paul Murphy, MP. He worked as a Special Adviser for three years, first at the Wales Office then, for two years, in the Northern Ireland Office. In 2005 he left the Northern Ireland office when he moved from Pontypridd to Surrey to work as a policy and communications adviser in the pharmaceutical industry. Regarded as one of the Labour Party's rising stars, he had previously served as Shadow Exchequer Secretary before being appointed as Peter Hain's successor as Shadow Secretary of State for Wales in May 2012, where he vowed to build a "powerful partnership" with Labour First Minister Carwyn Jones. Owen is married with three children.

2010 General Election Result

	Party	Votes Cast	%	Change 05-10
Owen Smith	Lab	14,220	38.8	-15.4%
Michael Powell	Lib D	11,435	31.2	+11.2%
Lee Gonzalez	Con	5,932	16.2	+4.6%
Ioan Bellin	PC	2,673	7.3	-3.7%
David Bevan	UKIP	1,229	3.4	+0.8%
Simon Parsons	SLP	456	1.2	+1.2%
Donald Watson	WCP	365	1.0	+1.0%
John Matthews	Green	361	1.0	+1.0%

Electorate: 58,205 Turnout: 63.0%

2010 _2005_	**Lab**	**Lib D**	**Con**	**PC**	**Other**

AM for Pontypridd

Mick ANTONIW Labour
Majority: 7,694 (32.9%)

National Assembly for Wales
Cardiff Bay, Cardiff CF99 1NA
Tel: (029) 2089 8134
Email: mick.antoniw@wales.gov.uk

Constituency Office:
GMB House, Morgan Street
Pontypridd CF37 2DS
Tel: (01443) 406400
Website: mickantoniw.co.uk

Mick Antoniw was elected at the 2011 election where he increased Labour's majority to 7,694. Born in Reading, he came to Wales to study law at the Cardiff Law School in 1973. He was President of the National Union of Students Wales from 1977 to 1979 and from 1981 to 1989 was a member of South Glamorgan County Council. He is a trustee of the Bevan Foundation, a trustee of the Welsh Refugee Council, Vice President of the Brynsadler Community Trust in Pontyclun and honorary Vice President of the homeless charity Seren. A qualified solicitor, Mick is a member of Welsh Labour Grassroots, the Co-operative Party, GMB and the Musician's Union.

In the Assembly, Mick is the Chair of the Standards of Conduct Committee as well as being a member of the Health and Social Care and Environment and Sustainability Committees. A fluent Ukrainian speaker due to his father being a refugee after the war, he is married with three adopted children and is a former foster parent.

2011 Assembly Election Result

	Party	Votes Cast	%	Change 07-11
Mick Antoniw	Lab/Co-op	11,864	50.9	+9.1%
Michael Powell	Lib D	4,170	17.9	-9.7%
Joel James	Con	3,659	15.7	+2.8%
Ioan Bellin	PC	3,139	13.5	-4.3%
Ken Owen	Ind	501	2.2	-

Electorate: 60,028 Turnout: 38.9%

Electoral Trends 1999 - 2011

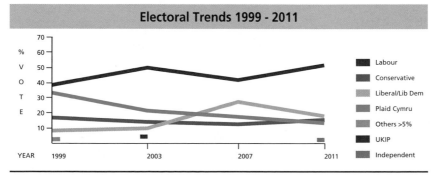

PRESELI PEMBROKESHIRE

MP - Stephen CRABB Conservative

AM - Paul DAVIES Conservative

Mid & West Wales Regional AMs

Rebecca Evans (Lab)　　　　　　Simon Thomas (PC)

William Powell (Lib D)　　　　　Joyce Watson (Lab)

Area:	1,180 sq km	% born in Wales:	70.6%
% speaking Welsh:	28.2%	% Unemployment *(Apr 2012)*	4.9%

The constituency comprises the following electoral wards:
Burton, Camrose, Cilgerran, Clydau, Crymych, Dinas Cross, Fishguard North East, Fishguard North West, Goodwick, Haverfordwest Castle, Haverfordwest Garth, Haverfordwest Portfield, Haverfordwest Prendergast, Haverfordwest Priory, Johnston, Letterston, Llangwm, Llanrhian, Maenclochog, Merlin's Bridge, Milford Central, Milford East, Milford Hakin, Milford Hubberston, Milford North, Milford West, Newport, Neyland East, Neyland West, Rudbaxton, Scleddau, Solva, St.David's, St.Dogmaels, St.Ishmael's, The Havens, Wiston.

The relatively new seat of **Preseli Pembrokeshire** was created in 1997, based on the former District Council area and extends from the northern shore of Milford Haven to the Preseli hills. A sizeable Welsh speaking population is largely concentrated in the north of the seat. This cultural diversity precludes an automatic attachment to a single political party and Preseli Pembrokeshire appears destined to remain a marginal seat. Labour captured Preseli in the landslide election of 1997, retained the seat at the 2001 General Election but succumbed to a strong Conservative challenge in 2005. The Conservatives retained the seat in 2010. Labour also won the Assembly elections in 1999 and 2003, but in 2007 Preseli followed the precedent of the Parliamentary contest and returned the Conservative candidate whom they re-elected in 2011, albeit on a slightly reduced majority.

Pembrokeshire as a whole has suffered considerable economic dislocation in recent years following the closure of major defence installations, the European fisheries dispute, the crisis in agricultural incomes and a reduction in oil refining capacity. Fishguard serves as a major transit link to Ireland and has attracted some corresponding European development funds, but much of the area as a whole is in need of major economic regeneration. Most of the constituency falls within the Pembrokeshire Coast National Park, which testifies to the beauty of the natural surroundings, but this sometimes creates competing priorities when trying to develop new economic opportunities.

Electoral Trends 1979 - 2010

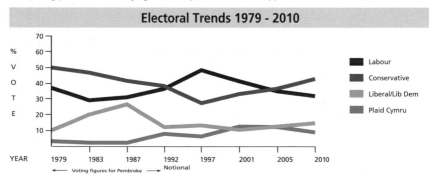

Previous MPs: Jackie Lawrence 1997-2005; (New seat 1997)
Previous AMs: Richard Edwards (Lab) 1999-2003; Tamsin Dunwoody (Lab) 2003-07

MP for Preseli Pembrokeshire

Stephen CRABB Conservative
Majority: 4,605 (11.6%)

The House of Commons, London SW1A 0AA
Tel: (020) 7219 0907
Email: stephen.crabb.mp@parliament.uk

Constituency Office:
Suite 1, 20 Upper Market St., Haverfordwest SA61 1QA
Tel: (01437) 767555
Email: jonesad@parliament.uk
Website: www.stephencrabb.com

Stephen Crabb was first elected to Parliament in May 2005 having previously contested Preseli in 2001. Born in Inverness in 1973, his family later moved to the area and he attended Tasker Milward School in Haverfordwest, before reading Politics and Economics at Bristol University and taking an MBA at the London Business School. He worked in and around politics as a researcher to a senior Tory MP, as Parliamentary Affairs Officer for the National Council for Voluntary Youth Services and as Campaigns Manager for the London Chamber of Commerce and Industry. He was Chair of the North Southwark and Bermondsey Conservative Association 1998-2000. Between 2001 and his election in 2005, Stephen established himself as an independent business consultant working for various clients including BAA and ZBD Displays Ltd.

In Parliament he has served on the Welsh Affairs, International Development and Treasury Select Committees. In January 2009 he was appointed to the frontbench as Opposition Whip. Following the formation of the Coalition Government in May 2011 Stephen was appointed as an Assistant Government Whip. Stephen is also the Leader of Project Umubano, the Conservative Party's social action project in Rwanda and Sierra Leone. Married with two children, outside of politics, he enjoys a wide range of sports including rugby, mountain biking, long-distance running, cooking and playing the guitar.

2010 General Election Result

	Party	Votes Cast	%	Change 05-10
Stephen Crabb	Con	16,944	42.8	+6.4%
Mari Rees	Lab	12,339	31.2	-3.7%
Nick Tregoning	Lib D	5,759	14.5	+1.5%
Henry Jones-Davies	PC	3,654	9.2	-3.3%
Richard Lawson	UKIP	906	2.3	+1.0%

Electorate: 57,400 Turnout: 69.0%

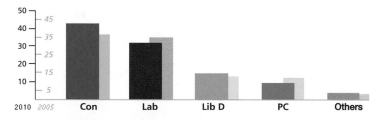

AM for Preseli Pembrokeshire

Paul DAVIES Conservative
Majority: 2,175 (7.9%)

National Assembly for Wales
Cardiff Bay, Cardiff CF99 1NA
Tel: (029) 2089 8725
Email: paul.davies@wales.gov.uk

Constituency Office:
20 Upper Market St, Haverfordwest
Pembrokeshire SA61 1QA
Tel: (01437) 766425
Website: www.pauldaviesam.co.uk

Paul Davies was first elected to the National Assembly at the 2007 election, having previously contested Preseli Pembrokeshire in 2003 and the Ceredigion Parliamentary by-election in 2000. Born in 1969, he grew up in Pontsian, just outside Llandysul, Ceredigion. He attended Tregroes Primary School, Llandysul Grammar School and Newcastle Emlyn Comprehensive School. Prior to being elected to the Assembly, he joined Lloyds Bank in 1987 where he worked as a Business Manager based in Haverfordwest encouraging and developing small businesses. He has also served as Chairman of the Ceredigion Conservative Association along with being Deputy Chairman of Mid and West Wales Conservatives.

Following the May 2011 National Assembly election, Paul was appointed as Interim Leader of the Welsh Conservative Assembly Group, a position he held until the election of Andrew RT Davies as Leader in July of that year. Paul was subsequently appointed Deputy Leader of the Welsh Conservative Assembly Group in addition to being named Shadow Minister for Finance. He currently sits on the Committee for the Scrutiny of the First Minister and the Finance Committee. Paul lives with his wife in Blaenffos, North Pembrokeshire, and his main interests outside politics are rugby, reading and visiting historical attractions.

2011 Assembly Election Result

	Party	Votes Cast	%	Change 07-11
Paul Davies	Con	11,541	42.4	+3.8%
Terry Mills	Lab	9,366	34.4	+7.0%
Rhys Sinnett	PC	4,226	15.5	-1.6%
Bob Kilminster	Lib D	2,085	7.7	-9.2%

Electorate: 57,758 Turnout: 47.1%

Electoral Trends 1999 - 2011

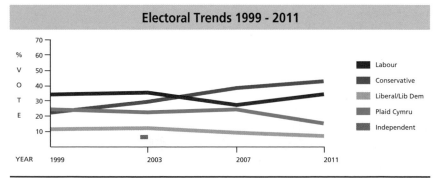

RHONDDA

MP - Chris BRYANT Labour

AM - Leighton ANDREWS Labour

South Wales Central Regional AMs

Andrew R T Davies (Con)   Eluned Parrott (Lib D)

David Melding (Con)   Leanne Wood (PC)

Area:	100 sq km	% born in Wales:	93.6%
% speaking Welsh: 14.5%		% Unemployment *(Apr 2012)*10.4%	

The constituency comprises the following electoral wards:
Cwm Clydach, Cymmer, Ferndale, Llwyn-y-pia, Maerdy, Pentre, Pen-y-graig, Porth, Tonypandy, Trealaw, Treherbert, Treorchy, Tylorstown, Ynyshir, Ystrad.

The **Rhondda** is an iconic place and community that epitomizes solidly Labour, working-class Wales and has done so for more than a century. Although coal is no longer deep-mined, culturally and emotionally this remains a mining community. It was thus a massive shock, both politically and psychologically, when Labour lost Rhondda to Plaid Cymru at the National Assembly elections in May 1999. Compounding this disaster, Labour also lost control of the County Borough Council to Plaid Cymru. Following these results, and the retirement of the former MP, Allan Rogers, the 2001 General Election attracted far greater attention from political observers. The Labour candidate, Chris Bryant, a somewhat contentious nominee, had anticipated a tough fight, but Labour's entrenched majority easily withstood a 7% swing to Plaid Cymru. At the second Assembly elections in 2003, the new Labour candidate, Leighton Andrews, reversed the Party's previous embarrassment and regained the seat from the Plaid Cymru AM, Geraint Davies. In June 2004 the Labour Party regained control of the County Borough Council and the historic staus quo ante had been restored. By 2005, Labour's Parliamentary majority was fully reclaimed and Rhondda was once again the safest seat in Wales. At the Assembly election in 2011 Leighton Andrews was returned comfortably, with both the Conservatives and Liberal Democrats polling less than 5% of the vote respectively.

Electoral Trends 1979 - 2010

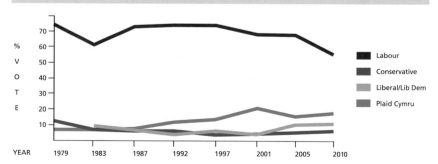

Previous MPs: **Allan Rogers (Lab) 1983-2001; Alec Jones (Lab) 1974-83** (New seat 1974, formerly Rhondda East and Rhondda West) **East – Elfed Davies 1959-74; West - Alec Jones (Lab) 1967 (by)-74**
Previous AMs: **Geraint Davies (PC) 1999-2003**

MP for Rhondda

Chris BRYANT Labour
Majority: 11,553 (37.2%)

The House of Commons, London SW1A 0AA
Tel: (020) 7219 8315
Email: bryantc@parliament.uk

Constituency Office:
Oxford House, Dunraven Street
Tonypandy CF40 1AU
Tel: (01443) 687697
Website: www.chris-bryant.co.uk

Chris Bryant was elected MP for the Rhondda in June 2001. Born in 1961 and brought up in Cardiff, he is a former Anglican vicar who resigned his curacy to stand for Parliament in Wycombe in 1997. Educated at Cheltenham College, Chris read English at Mansfield College, Oxford, before studying theology in Ripon. Prior to the 2001 election, he was Head of the European Affairs Unit for the BBC. From 1994-96 he ran Common Purpose, an educational charity. He was a Borough Councillor in Hackney 1993-98, serving as Chief Whip for the Labour Group 1994-95. Chris is a member of AMICUS, the Fabian Society and Amnesty International.

Following the election of 2005 he was appointed PPS to Lord Falconer, Secretary of State for Constitutional Affairs and Lord Chancellor. He resigned from this post in June 2006 in order to be able to make a greater contribution to the House of Lords reform debate. In the Brown Government he initially served as Deputy Leader of the House before moving to the Foreign Office. He exchanged posts with Baroness Kinnock and became Minister for Europe. In September 2006, Chris achieved widespread publicity as one of the originators of the letter to Tony Blair requesting that he set a date for his retirement. He is currently Shadow Minister for Immigration and Vice Chair of the Labour Movement for Europe, and among his political interests are European affairs, broadcasting and the information economy.

2010 General Election Result

	Party	Votes Cast	%	Change 05-10
Chris Bryant	Lab	17,183	55.3	-12.8%
Geraint Davies	PC	5,630	18.1	+2.2%
Paul Wasley	Lib D	3,309	10.6	+0.2%
Philip Howe	Ind	2,599	8.4	+8.4%
Juliet Henderson	Con	1,993	6.4	+0.9%
Taffy John	UKIP	358	1.2	+1.2%

Electorate: 51,554 Turnout: 60.3%

2010 2005   **Lab   PC   Lib D   Con   Other**

AM for Rhondda

Leighton ANDREWS Labour
Majority: 6,739 (33.6%)

National Assembly for Wales
Cardiff Bay, Cardiff CF99 1NA
Tel: (029) 2089 8784
Email: leighton.andrews@wales.gov.uk

Constituency Office:
Oxford House, Dunraven St
Tonypandy CF40 1AU
Tel: (01443) 685261
Website: www.leightonandrews.com

Leighton Andrews has been a member of the National Assembly since 2003, having won the Rhondda back from Plaid Cymru following their shock victory in 1999. Born in Cardiff and brought up in Barry and Dorset, Leighton Andrews holds a BA Honours from the University of Wales, Bangor, and an MA in History from the University of Sussex. He was head of public affairs for BBC Wales between 1993 and 1996 and was a visiting professor at the University of Westminster from 1997 to 2002. Immediately prior to his election, Leighton was a lecturer at Cardiff Journalism School and is an honorary professor at Cardiff University. In 1997 Leighton was co-founder of the 'Yes for Wales' campaign in the referendum on devolution and subsequently wrote the book Wales Says Yes which tells the story of the campaign. Leighton acted as convenor of the planning group for the cross-party Yes for Wales campaign in the March 2011 referendum and chaired Labour's election campaign strategy committee during the 2011 Assembly election campaign. In 2007, Leighton and Rhondda MP Chris Bryant campaigned with Burberry workers to protect jobs at the firm's Treorchy factory. Although the factory closed, both were jointly awarded Campaigner of the Year Award in the 2007 BBC Wales political awards.

Leighton is currently Minister for Education and Skills in the Welsh Government, with his ministerial responsibilities including the Welsh language. Away from politics, Leighton is a season ticket holder at Cardiff City FC and also watches local Rhondda sports teams. He is married with two children.

2011 Assembly Election Result

	Party	Votes Cast	%	Change 07-11
Leighton Andrews	Lab	12,650	63.2	+4.9%
Sera Evans-Fear	PC	5,911	29.5	-0.6%
George Summers	Lib D	969	4.8	-4.0%
James Jeffreys	Con	497	2.5	-2.6%

Electorate: 52,532 Turnout: 38.1%

Electoral Trends 1999 - 2011

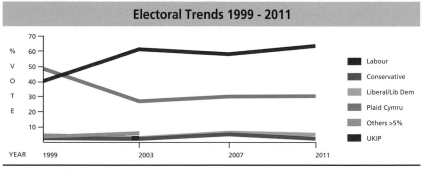

Legend: Labour, Conservative, Liberal/Lib Dem, Plaid Cymru, Others >5%, UKIP

SWANSEA EAST

MP - Siân JAMES Labour

AM - Mike HEDGES Labour

South Wales West Regional AMs

Peter Black (Lib D)	Suzy Davies (Con)
Byron Davies (Con)	Bethan Jenkins (PC)

Area:	49 sq km	% born in Wales:	89.1%
% speaking Welsh:	15.1%	% Unemployment *(Apr 2012)*	6.9%

The constituency comprises the following electoral wards:
Bonymaen, Cwmbwrla, Landore, Llansamlet, Morriston, Mynyddbach, Penderry, St. Thomas.

Swansea East has enjoyed considerable economic revitalisation over the last thirty years, having been one of the first industrial enterprise zones, and the transformation of the docks area into a marina and the prestigious SA1 development. Although Swansea East has recorded some of the lowest turnouts in Wales at the last three General Elections – only slightly over 50% - it remains a very safe Labour seat. This poor level of participation had also been evident at the first National Assembly election when only 36.1% of electors voted. Following the untimely death of Val Feld AM in 2001, a mere 22.6% voted in the subsequent by-election.

As Wales' second city, Swansea competes vigorously with Cardiff in all fields, be it in sport or for inward economic investment. Having voted 'Yes' in the Devolution referendum, unlike Cardiff, it appeared, for a brief few weeks in 1998, that the new National Assembly might find its home in Swansea. The final decision however, once again, favoured Cardiff. Whilst Donald Anderson's re-election in June 2001 was a formality, Plaid Cymru retained the second place that they had achieved at the National Assembly election. More recently however, the Liberal Democrats have emerged as the second party of the seat, but despite previously controlling Swansea Council (prior to the 2012 Local Government elections), they remain a long way short from challenging the Labour Party. Already enjoying a healthy lead, the 2011 Assembly election saw Labour double its majority.

Electoral Trends 1979 - 2010

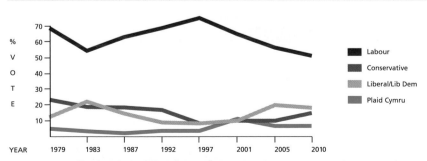

Previous MPs: Donald Anderson 1974-2005; Neil McBride (Lab) 1963 (by)-74
Previous AMs: Val Lloyd (Lab) 2001-11; Val Feld (Lab) 1999-2001

Siân JAMES Labour
Majority: 10,838 (33.2%)

The House of Commons, London SW1A 0AA
Tel: (020) 7219 6954
Email: sian.james.mp@parliament.uk

Constituency Office:
485 Llangyfelach Road, Brynhyfryd
Swansea SA5 9EA
Tel: (01792) 455089
Website: www.sianjamesmp.net\

SWANSEA EAST

Siân James was elected for Swansea East in May 2005, succeeding Donald Anderson upon his retirement and elevation to the House of Lords. Although the victim of a considerable swing to the Liberal Democrats in 2005 and some revival in Tory fortunes in 2010, such is the depth of Labour support in this part of Swansea that her majority remains almost impregnable. Born in Morriston in 1959, she worked in a variety of public affairs posts before becoming Communications Manager for the privately run Parc Prison in Bridgend. A well-known political activist, the antithesis of a 'Blair Babe', she has been involved in numerous local and national campaigns having first become politicised during the Miners' Strike of 1984-85. Prior to her election, Siân had been an active and innovative Director of Welsh Women's Aid. She contested Monmouth at the Assembly elections in 2003, was elected to Neath Town Council in 2004 and also made the ill-fated all-Women shortlist for Blaenau Gwent.

In Parliament she has previously served on the Justice Committee and Welsh Affairs Select Committee. Generally considered to be on the Left, she has been a 'rebel' on several key votes during the Labour Government. Among her many concerns are social inclusion and public transport and outside of politics she enjoys reading and antiques. She is married with two children.

2010 General Election Result

	Party	Votes Cast	%	Change 05-10
Siân James	Lab	16,819	51.5	-5.1%
Robert Speht	Lib D	5,981	18.3	-1.8%
Christian Holliday	Con	4,823	14.8	+4.7%
Dic Jones	PC	2,181	6.7	-0.2%
Clive Bennett	BNP	1,715	5.2	+2.8%
David Rogers	UKIP	839	2.6	+0.4%
Tony Young	Green	318	1.0	-0.6%

Electorate: 59,823 Turnout: 54.6%

[Bar chart comparing 2010 and 2005 results for Lab, Lib D, Con, PC, Other]

AM for Swansea East

Mike HEDGES Labour
Majority: 8,281 (43.7%)

National Assembly for Wales
Cardiff Bay, Cardiff CF99 1NA
Tel: (029) 2089 8317
Email: mike.hedges@wales.gov.uk

Constituency Office:
97 Pleasant Street, Morriston
Swansea SA6 6HJ
Tel: (01792) 790621
Website: www.mikehedges.org.uk

Mike Hedges entered the Assembly at the 2011 election, winning with a majority of 8,281. Born in Swansea in 1956, he attended Plasmarl, Parklands and Penlan Schools, and then went on into higher education at Swansea University where he studied Material Science & Economics, graduating with a BSc. Mike went onto take a PGCE in Further Education at Cardiff University. Originally a research scientist for British Steel at Port Talbot before entering the Assembly, Mike had spent the last 27 years as a senior lecturer in Pontypridd at Coleg Morgannwg, specialising in computing and information technology. He had represented Morriston on the City and County of Swansea Council since 1989 but stood down in May 2012. During his time as a Councillor, he held a number of senior posts on Swansea Council, including Council Leader, Business Manager, Cabinet Member for Technical Services and Chair of the Council's Finance Scrutiny Committee. During his time as Leader of Swansea Council, Mike was the Welsh Local Government Association Spokesperson for both social services and information.

Mike currently sits as a member on the Assembly's Finance Committee, Public Accounts Committee and on the Communities, Equality and Local Government Committee. He is also Chair of the Cross Party Group on Older People & Ageing. He is married with a daughter.

2011 Assembly Election Result

	Party	Votes Cast	%	Change 07-11
Mike Hedges	Lab	11,035	58.3	+16.9%
Dan Boucher	Con	2,754	14.6	+4.8%
Dic Jones	PC	2,346	12.4	-3.1%
Robert Samuel	Lib D	1,673	8.9	-8.7%
Joanne Shannon	BNP	1,102	5.8	-9.9%

Electorate: 60,246 Turnout: 31.4%

Electoral Trends 1999 - 2011

Labour
Conservative
Liberal/Lib Dem
Plaid Cymru
Others >5%
Independent
UKIP
BNP

MP - Geraint DAVIES Labour
AM - Julie JAMES Labour

South Wales West Regional AMs

Peter Black (Lib D)   Suzy Davies (Con)

Byron Davies (Con)   Bethan Jenkins (PC)

Area:	33 sq km	% born in Wales:	74.9%
% speaking Welsh: 13.0%		% Unemployment *(Apr 2012)*	6.8%

The constituency comprises the following electoral wards:
Castle, Cockett, Dunvant, Killay North, Killay South, Mayals, Sketty, Townhill, Uplands.

Alan Williams captured **Swansea West** from the Conservative Party at the 1964 election and went on to become 'Father' of the House of Commons before retiring in 2010. Swansea West was largely a marginal seat until boundary changes in 1983. Whilst the removal of Mumbles and areas of the Gower peninsula rendered the seat considerably less competitive, Swansea West still includes many of the more prestigious residential neighbourhoods of the city. In successive Parliamentary elections the Labour Party has consistently retained control with comfortable majorities.

At the National Assembly election in 1999 however, Labour's superiority was somewhat dented. Andrew Davies won the seat, but on a reduced share of the vote and a substantially smaller majority. Plaid Cymru polled more than a quarter of all votes and claimed second place, but were to slip back to fourth place at the 2001 General Election, restoring the Conservatives to runners-up. At the 2003 Assembly election Andrew Davies improved his position following further slippage in the Plaid Cymru vote. At the 2005 General Election, the Liberal Democrats enjoyed a positive swing of nearly 10%, to which the large student population in the constituency must have contributed, but Swansea West remained a fairly safe Labour seat. In 2010 however, the new Labour MP Geraint Davies, retained the seat but Labour's majority was virtually decimated by the Liberal Democrat challenge. Following this 'near miss', the retirement of Andrew Davies as AM led some to believe that victory could be within reach for the Liberal Democrats at the 2011 election. However, as was the case across much of Wales, the Liberal Democrat challenge failed to materialise, with Labour tripling its majority.

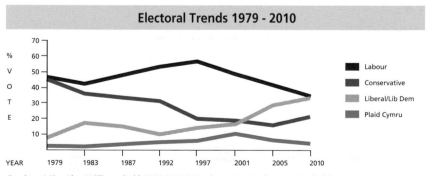

Electoral Trends 1979 - 2010

Previous MPs: **Alan Williams (Lab) 1964-2010 // Previous AMs: Andrew Davies (Lab) 1999-2011**

Geraint DAVIES Labour
Majority: 504 (1.4%)

The House of Commons
London SW1A 0AA
Tel: (020) 7219 7166
Email: geraint.davies.mp@parliament.uk

Constituency Office:
31 High Street, Swansea SA1 1LG
Tel: (01792) 475943
Email: info@geraintdavies.org
Website: www.geraintdavies.org.uk

Geraint Davies was elected MP for Swansea West in May 2010, succeeding Alan Williams, the outgoing 'Father of the House'. Born and brought up in Wales, he was first elected to Parliament as MP for Croydon Central in 1997, having previously been Labour Leader of Croydon Borough Council. Re-elected for Croydon Central in 2001, he was defeated in 2005 by 75 votes. On leaving Parliament, Geraint was recruited to head the Environment Agency Wales team to adapt Wales to climate change. He led an executive of Council Leaders, academics and environmentalists responsible for investing £30million in flood defences each year across Wales.

On his re-election for Swansea West in 2010 he became the first newly elected MP to present a Private Members Bill - The Credit Card Regulation (child pornography) Bill. The Bill penalises credit and debit card companies for facilitating the downloading of child abuse images. Geraint also serves on the Welsh Affairs Select Committee and is a Governor at Dylan Thomas Community School in Swansea. He is married with three children.

2010 General Election Result

	Party	Votes Cast	%	Change 05-10
Geraint Davies	Lab	12,335	34.7	-7.2%
Peter May	Lib D	11,831	33.2	+4.3%
Rene Kinzett	Con	7,407	20.8	+4.8%
Harri Roberts	PC	1,437	4.0	-2.5%
Alan Bateman	BNP	910	2.6	+2.6%
Tim Jenkins	UKIP	716	2.0	+0.2%
Keith Ross	Green	404	1.1	-1.1%
Ian McCloy	Ind	374	1.1	+1.1%
Rob Williams	Trade Unionist & Socialist Coalition	179	0.5	+0.5%

Electorate: 61,334 Turnout: 58.0%

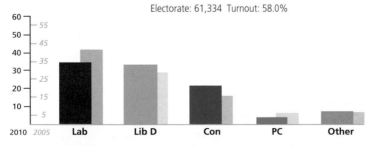

AM for Swansea West

Julie JAMES Labour
Majority: 4,654 (21.3%)

National Assembly for Wales
Cardiff Bay, Cardiff CF99 1NA
Tel: (029) 2089 8132
Email: julie.james@wales.gov.uk

Constituency Office:
30-31 High Street, Swansea SA1 1LG
Tel: (01792) 460836
www.juliejames4swanseawest.com

Julie James was elected at the 2011 election following the retirement of former Finance Minister Andrew Davies. Born in Swansea, she spent a significant amount of her early years living in various parts of the world with her family. Julie spent her early career in London and then moved back to Swansea with her husband to raise their three children and to be closer to her family. Prior to her election to the Assembly, Julie was a leading environmental and constitutional lawyer and an Assistant Chief Executive at Swansea Council. She has spent a large part of her legal career in local government, working as a policy lawyer with the London Borough of Camden before returning to Swansea to work for West Glamorgan County Council and then the City and County of Swansea. She left the Council in early 2006 for Clarkslegal LLP where she worked as a consultant (barrister) in environmental and public law.

Since her election in 2011 Julie has been a member of the Constitutional and Legislative Affairs Committee, the Environment and Sustainability Committee and the Enterprise and Business Committee. She has also chaired task and finish groups into the Common Fisheries Policy and Procurement in Wales. A member of Unison, Gray's Inn and ACSeS, she regards herself as a committed green campaigner, environmentalist and a keen swimmer and skier.

2011 Assembly Election Result

	Party	Votes Cast	%	Change 07-11
Julie James	Lab	9,885	45.3	+13.0%
Steve Jenkins	Con	5,231	24.0	+4.9%
Rob Speht	Lib D	3,654	16.8	-9.0%
Carl Harris	PC	3,035	13.9	-1.7%

Electorate: 62,345 Turnout: 35.0%

Electoral Trends 1999 - 2011

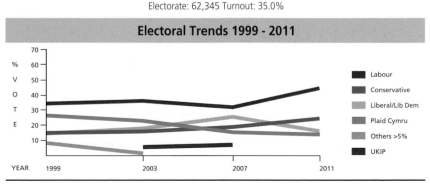

MP - Rt Hon Paul MURPHY Labour

AM - Lynne NEAGLE Labour

South Wales East Regional AMs

Mohammad Asghar (Con)	William Graham (Con)
Jocelyn Davies (PC)	Lindsay Whittle (PC)

Area:	117 sq km	% born in Wales:	86.1%
% speaking Welsh:	19.5%	% Unemployment *(Apr 2012)*	8.1%

The constituency comprises the following electoral wards:
Abersychan, Blaenavon, Brynwern, Coed Eva, Cwmyniscoy, Fairwater, Greenmeadow, Llantarnam, New Inn, Panteg, Pontnewydd, Pontnewynydd, Pontypool, St. Cadocs and Penygarn, St.Dials, Snatchwood, Trevethin, Two Locks, Upper Cwmbran, Wainfelin.

Torfaen is the successor constituency to Pontypool, whose famous former MP, Leo Abse, became one of the most distinguished backbenchers of his generation, introducing several major social reforms into Parliament. Based upon Cwmbran, Torfaen is a mixed industrial area where many manufacturing opportunities have been created and a range of light industries now provide a diverse employment base.

At the Assembly election in 1999, when many previously safe Labour seats faced a strong Plaid Cymru challenge and faltered, Torfaen saw a contest between the official Labour candidate and a number of maverick Labour Independents. Official Labour prevailed and secured a comfortable majority. In 2003, Lynne Neagle, unencumbered by such dissent, substantially increased her vote. In 2007 and 2011 however, dissent returned with a strong campaign mounted by Independent candidates. Lynne Neagle was not really threatened but her majority was reduced to that of a mixed seat rather than of a heartland constituency. The successor to Leo Abse in Parliament, Paul Murphy, has been able to pursue a distinguished political career confident in the Labour loyalty of Torfaen. Minor swings have occurred at recent Parliamentary elections, to both the Conservatives and Plaid Cymru, but this has never threatened the twice Secretary of State for Wales, Paul Murphy, whose majority remained solidly safe at the General Election in May 2010.

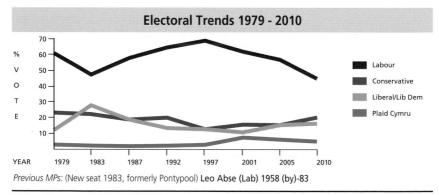

Electoral Trends 1979 - 2010

Previous MPs: (New seat 1983, formerly Pontypool) **Leo Abse (Lab)** 1958 (by)-83

Rt Hon Paul MURPHY Labour
Majority: 9,306 (24.7%)

The House of Commons, London SW1A 0AA
Tel: (020) 7219 3463
Email: paul.murphy.mp@parliament.uk

Constituency Office:
73 Upper Trosnant Street
Pontypool, Torfaen NP4 8AU
Tel: (01495) 750078
Website: www.paulmurphymp.co.uk

TORFAEN

Paul Murphy, was first elected for Parliament in 1987. Born in 1948, he was educated at St Francis Roman Catholic School, Abersychan, West Monmouth School, Pontypool and Oriel College, Oxford. He was a management trainee with the CWS 1970-71, before becoming a Lecturer in Government and History at Ebbw Vale College. Paul was Secretary of the constituency Labour Party 1971-87 and was a member of Torfaen Borough Council, 1973-87. He contested the seat of Wells in Somerset at the 1979 General Election. He was created a Knight of St Gregory in 1999 and an Honorary Fellow of the Oriel College, Oxford in 2001. He was Visiting Parliamentary Fellow of St. Anthony's College, Oxford from 2006 to 2007 and in 2009 was made a Fellow of Glyndŵr University, Wrexham.

Paul served as Secretary of State for Wales in 1999-02 and again, 2008-09. He also served as Secretary of State for Northern Ireland, 2002-05. His period in Northern Ireland was particularly challenging, overseeing the implementation of the 'Good Friday' Agreement' and resolving issues that forced the suspension of the Northern Ireland Assembly. In July 2005 he was appointed Chair of the Security and Intelligence Committee. Paul was appointed to the Privy Council in 1999. He currently resides on the Opposition backbenches as an 'Elder Statesman' and sits on the Joint Committee on National Security Strategy. He is also Vice Chair of the British-Irish Parliamentary Assembly.

2010 General Election Result

	Party	Votes Cast	%	Change 05-10
Paul Murphy	Lab	16,847	44.8	-12.1%
Jonathan Burns	Con	7,541	20.0	+4.2%
David Morgan	Lib D	6,264	16.6	+0.9%
Rhys ab Elis	PC	2,005	5.3	-0.9%
Jennifer Noble	BNP	1,657	4.4	+4.4%
Fred Wildgust	Ind	1,419	3.8	+3.8%
Gareth Dunn	UKIP	862	2.3	-0.9%
Richard Turner-Thomas	Ind	607	1.6	+1.6%
Owen Clarke	Green	438	1.2	+1.2%

Electorate: 61,183 Turnout: 61.5%

(Bar chart showing 2010 and 2005 results for Lab, Con, Lib D, PC, Other)

TORFAEN

Lynne NEAGLE Labour
Majority: 6,088 (27.2%)

National Assembly for Wales
Cardiff Bay, Cardiff CF99 1NA
Tel: (029) 2089 8151
Email: lynne.neagle@wales.gov.uk

Constituency Office:
73 Upper Trosnant St
Pontypool, Torfaen NP4 8AU
Tel: (01495) 740022 Fax: (01495) 755776

Lynne Neagle was first elected to the National Assembly in 1999, following a difficult local campaign. Born in 1968, she was educated at Cyfarthfa High School in Merthyr Tydfil and Reading University, where she studied French and Italian. She has held a number of posts in the voluntary sector with organizations such as Shelter Cymru, Mind and the CAB. She was Carers Development Officer with Voluntary Action Cardiff and was a Research Assistant to Glenys Kinnock MEP 1994 - 1997.

Lynne was a long-serving chair of the Labour Group in the Assembly until 2008 and she is currently a member of the Children and Young People Committee and the Health and Social Care Committee. Her political interests include health, housing, social services, Europe and the future of the valleys in South Wales. She has led high profile campaigns on issues like MMR uptake and disabled children's services. She is married to fellow AM Huw Lewis and they have two children.

2011 Assembly Election Result

	Party	Votes Cast	%	Change 07-11
Lynne Neagle	Lab/Co-op	10,318	46.2	+3.5%
Elizabeth Haynes	Ind	4,230	18.9	-
Natasha Asghar	Con	3,306	14.8	-4.7%
Jeff Rees	PC	2,716	12.2	+0.3%
Sue Harwood	BNP	906	4.1	-
Will Griffiths	Lib D	852	3.8	-7.6%

Electorate: 61,126 Turnout: 36.5%

Electoral Trends 1999 - 2011

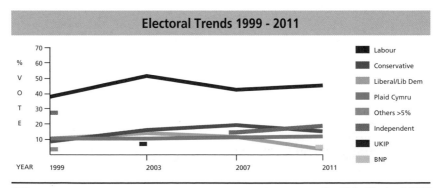

MP - Chris RUANE Labour
AM - Ann JONES Labour

North Wales Regional AMs

Llyr Huws Gruffydd (PC)   Aled Roberts (Lib D)

Mark Isherwood (Con)   Antoinette Sandbach (Con)

Area:	216 sq km	% born in Wales:	56.6%
% speaking Welsh: 24.2%		% Unemployment *(Apr 2012)* 6.1%	

VALE OF CLWYD

The constituency comprises the following electoral wards:
Bodelwyddan, Denbigh Central, Denbigh Lower, Denbigh Upper/Henllan, Dyserth, Llandyrnog, Prestatyn Central, Prestatyn East, Prestatyn Meliden, Prestatyn North, Prestatyn South West, Rhuddlan, Rhyl East, Rhyl South, Rhyl South East, Rhyl South West, Rhyl West, St. Asaph East, St. Asaph West, Trefnant, Tremeirchion.

The relatively new **Vale of Clwyd** constituency was created in 1997 from part of the old Clwyd North West, formerly the safest Conservative seat in Wales, and part of Delyn, a marginal seat captured by Labour in 1992. At the following General Election however, the national landslide to Labour ensured a comfortable success for Chris Ruane. Labour also won the subsequent National Assembly election from the Conservatives, but by a smaller margin of victory. Further Labour General Election victories in 2001 and 2005 have sustained Chris Ruane in Parliament, but small swings to the Conservatives, coupled with lower turnouts, has resulted in Vale of Clwyd proving to be a closer political contest than might have been expected. In 2010, Vale of Clwyd was the threshold seat which David Cameron and the Conservatives needed to capture to secure a majority - they failed and Britain has a coalition Government.

At the second Assembly election, Ann Jones maintained her position and the Conservatives remained runners-up. In 2007 however, doubtless buoyed up by their campaigning in neighbouring seats, a formidable Conservative challenge reduced Ann Jones's majority to less than a hundred. As across much of Wales, the 2011 Assembly election saw a large swing to Labour, with Ann Jones restoring a comfortable majority with over 4,000 votes separating her from her Conservative rival.

The Vale of Clwyd incorporates the resort towns of Rhyl and Prestatyn, as well as a rural hinterland. Alongside the gentility of the seaside promenades and guesthouses, are found some of Wales' most socially deprived wards.

Electoral Trends 1983 - 2010

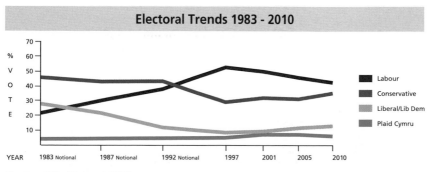

Previous MPs: (New seat 1997)

MP for Vale of Clwyd

Chris RUANE Labour
Majority: 2,509 (7.1%)

The House of Commons
London SW1A 0AA
Tel: (020) 7219 6378
Email: ruanec@parliament.uk

Constituency Office:
25 Kinmel Street, Rhyl
Denbighshire LL18 1AH
Tel: (01745) 354626 Fax: (01745) 334827
Website: www.chrisruane.org

Chris Ruane was elected to Parliament for the new constituency of Vale of Clwyd in 1997. Born on 18 July 1958 in St Asaph, he was educated in Rhyl before graduating in History and Politics from the University of Wales, Aberystwyth. He qualified as a teacher at Liverpool University and was Deputy Head of Ysgol Mair Primary School before entering Parliament. A member of the Labour Party since 1986, he was Chair of West Clwyd NUT in 1989 and 1990 and President of Vale of Clwyd NUT in 1998. He also served as a Rhyl Town Councillor between 1988 and 1997.

Chris Ruane has previously served on the House of Commons Select Committee on Welsh Affairs. He was appointed PPS to Peter Hain, the Secretary of State for Wales in 2002, a position he retained following the 2005 General Election but resigned in protest over the decision to renew the Trident nuclear deterrent. He was later PPS to David Miliband. He is Chair of the North Wales Group Labour MPs and a member of the Labour Group of Seaside MPs. He currently serves as an Opposition Whip and was previously Treasurer of the All-Party Group on Objective One funding. Married with two daughters, he lists cooking, walking and 'humour' among his interests.

2010 General Election Result

	Party	Votes Cast	%	Change 05-10
Chris Ruane	Lab	15,017	42.3	-3.6%
Matt Wright	Con	12,508	35.2	+3.5%
Paul Penlington	Lib D	4,472	12.6	+0.7%
Caryl Wyn Jones	PC	2,068	5.8	-1.4%
Ian Si'Ree	BNP	827	2.3	+2.3%
Tom Turner	UKIP	515	1.4	+0.3%
Mike Butler	Green Soc	127	0.4	+0.4%

Electorate: 55,781 Turnout: 63.7 %

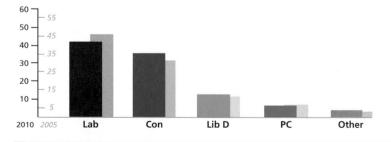

AM for Vale of Clwyd

Ann JONES Labour
Majority: 4,011 (17.3%)

National Assembly for Wales
Cardiff Bay, Cardiff CF99 1NA
Tel: (029) 2089 8753
Email: ann.jones@wales.gov.uk

Constituency Office:
25 Kinmel Street, Rhyl
Denbighshire LL18 1AH
Tel: (01745) 332813
Website: www.annjones.org.uk

Ann Jones has been Assembly Member for the Vale of Clwyd since 1999. Born in 1953 and educated in Rhyl High School, prior to entering politics she was a national official for the Fire Brigade Union, and had worked for Clwyd Fire Service and as a Fire Control Officer for Merseyside Fire Brigade. She is a former Rhyl Town Councillor, Denbighshire County Councillor and was Mayor of Rhyl 1996-97.

In the Assembly, Ann is currently Chair of the Communities, Equality, and Local Government Committee. She is also a member of the Finance Committee and Chair of the Cross Party Group on deaf issues. In 1999 she became the first Chair of the Assembly Labour Group and was a member of the Committee which drew up the new Standing Orders which were implemented for the Third National Assembly. In 2007 she also won the first ballot of AMs to introduce proposed orders of Legislative Competence (LCOs). Her proposal required all new build housing in Wales to be fitted with automatic fire sprinklers systems. Her political interests include education and community safety. She is a member of the Christian Socialist Movement and a season ticket holder of Rhyl Football Club.

2011 Assembly Election Result

	Party	Votes Cast	%	Change 07-11
Ann Jones	Lab	11,691	50.7	+14.3%
Ian Gunning	Con	7,680	33.3	-2.7%
Alun Lloyd Jones	PC	2,597	11.3	-6.2%
Heather Prydderch	Lib D	1,088	4.7	-5.5%

Electorate: 56,232 Turnout: 41.0%

Electoral Trends 1999 - 2011

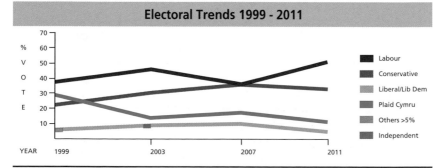

VALE OF GLAMORGAN

MP - Alun CAIRNS Conservative

AM - Jane HUTT Labour

South Wales Central Regional AMs

Andrew R T Davies (Con)

David Melding (Con)

Eluned Parrott (Lib D)

Leanne Wood (PC)

Area:	315 sq km	% born in Wales:	76.0%
% speaking Welsh:	18.4%	% Unemployment *(Apr 2012)*	5.5%

The constituency comprises the following electoral wards:
Baruc, Buttrills, Cadoc, Castleland, Court, Cowbridge, Dinas Powys, Dyfan, Gibbonsdown, Illtyd, Llandow/Ewenny, Llantwit Major, Peterston-super-Ely, Rhoose, St.Athan, St Bride's Major, Wenvoe.

The **Vale of Glamorgan** constituency succeeded the former Barry seat that had been represented by Sir Raymond Gower for the Conservatives since 1951. At the by-election following Sir Raymond's death in 1989, Labour achieved a major upset and captured the seat. Walter Sweeney re-gained Vale of Glamorgan for the Conservatives at the subsequent 1992 General Election, but by a margin of only nineteen votes, the smallest majority in Britain. By 1995 however, the overall national political climate had changed and even the Vale of Glamorgan elected a local Council with a Labour majority. At the General Election of 1997, Walter Sweeney's fragile Conservative lead could not withstand the Labour landslide and John Smith, the previous by-election victor, was once again returned to Parliament. Although the County Council reverted to the Conservatives in May 1999, Labour held on in the concurrent National Assembly election, returning Jane Hutt as the Vale's first AM.

At recent General Elections John Smith has suffered small negative swings, at the hands of Plaid Cymru, the Liberal Democrats and the Conservatives, but has retained the seat with a reduced majority. Following his retirement in 2010, the seat fell to Alun Cairns, one of the local Conservative regional AMs. The second Assembly elections in 2003 saw an extremely tense contest between Health Minister Jane Hutt and David Melding, her then Assembly 'Shadow'. Jane Hutt and Labour prevailed, against this strong challenge, but in 2007 the Conservatives went further and took Labour to the wire. Jane Hutt's majority collapsed, hanging on by a mere 83 votes. Despite hopes that the Tories could capture the seat in 2011, the Labour Party were returned with a substantially increased majority.

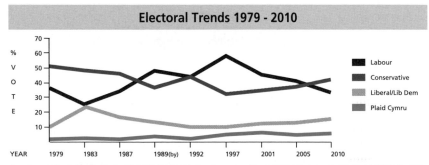

Electoral Trends 1979 - 2010

Previous MPs: John Smith (Lab) 1997-2010; Walter Sweeney (Con) 1992-97; John Smith (Lab) 1989 (by)-92; Sir Raymond Gower 1983-89; (New seat 1983, formerly Barry) Raymond Gower (Con) 1951-83

MP for Vale of Glamorgan

Alun Cairns Conservative
Majority: 4,307 (8.8%)

The House of Commons
London SW1A 0AA
Tel: (020) 7219 7175
Email: alun.cairns.mp@parliament.uk

Constituency Office:
29 High St, Barry, Vale of Glamorgan CF62 7EB
Tel: (01446) 403814
Website: www.aluncairns.co.uk

Alun Cairns was born in Clydach near Swansea in 1970 and was educated at Ysgol Gyfun Ystalyfera. Formerly a business development consultant for Lloyds TSB South Wales, he was Conservative Party policy co-ordinator for South Wales West and Deputy Chair of the Wales Young Conservatives. He contested Gower at the 1997 General election and Vale of Glamorgan in 2005. At both the 1999 and 2003 Assembly elections, Alun Cairns fought the Bridgend constituency for the Conservatives, but was elected to the Assembly via the regional list. Following the banning of dual candidacy in 2007 he again headed the Conservative list for South Wales West. Alun Cairns was adopted to fight the Vale of Glamorgan at the 2010 General Election, winning with a majority of 4,307. Although he chose not to immediately resign his Assembly seat, he did not seek re-election during the 2011 National Assembly election.

In Westminster, Alun Cairns currently serves on the Public Administration Select Committee, having previously sat on the Welsh Affairs Select Committee. A fluent Welsh speaker, he lives in the constituency with his wife Emma, who runs her own small business, and with their son Henri. In his spare time Alun also enjoys gardening, cycling and running.

2010 General Election Result

	Party	Votes Cast	%	Change 05-10
Alun Cairns	Con	20,341	41.8	+4.4%
Alana Davies	Lab	16,034	32.9	-7.8%
Eluned Parrott	Lib D	7,403	15.2	+2.0%
Ian Johnson	PC	2,667	5.5	+0.3%
Kevin Mahoney	UKIP	1,529	3.1	+1.4%
Rhodri Thomas	Green	457	0.9	+0.9%
John Harrold	WCP	236	0.5	+0.5%

Electorate: 70,262 Turnout: 69.3%

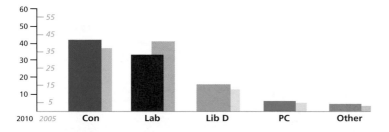

AM for Vale of Glamorgan

Jane HUTT Labour
Majority: 3,775 (11.3%)

National Assembly for Wales
Cardiff Bay, Cardiff CF99 1NA
Tel: (029) 2089 8469
Email: jane.hutt@wales.gov.uk

Constituency Office:
115 High Street, Barry CF62 7DT
Tel: (01446) 740981
Website: www.janehutt.co.uk

Jane Hutt was elected in May 1999 and has been a Cabinet Minister since the Assembly was first established. Born in 1949, she was brought up in England and East Africa. She studied at the University of Kent, the London School of Economics and Bristol University. She is a former Director of Chwarae Teg, a Director of Cardiff Community Healthcare Trust and the Welsh member of the New Opportunities Fund. Previously Vice-Chair of the Wales Council for Voluntary Action, she was a member of the Wales New Deal Taskforce and was also co-ordinator of Welsh Women's Aid 1978-88. She was a member of South Glamorgan County Council 1981-93 and at the 1983 General Election contested Cardiff North. Jane is an Honorary Fellow of the University of Wales Institute, Cardiff and a member of UNISON.

Jane is currently Minister for Finance and Leader of the House in the Welsh Government. Between 1999 and 2005 she served as Minister for Health and Social Services and from 2005 to 2007, she was Minister for Assembly Business and Chief Whip. In the first Cabinet of the Third Assembly she was appointed Minister for Budget and Assembly Business; while in the coalition Cabinet she became Minister for Children, Education, Lifelong Learning and Skills. In December 2009 she was appointed Minister for Business and Budget. Jane is married with two daughters.

2011 Assembly Election Result

	Party	Votes Cast	%	Change 07-11
Jane Hutt	Lab	15,746	47.4	+13.2%
Angela Jones-Evans	Con	11,971	36.0	+2.1%
Ian Johnson	PC	4,024	12.1	-1.8%
Damian Chick	Lib D	1,513	4.6	-6.6%

Electorate: 71,602 Turnout: 46.4%

Electoral Trends 1999 - 2011

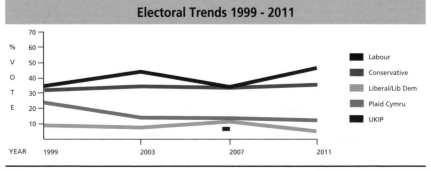

Legend:
- Labour
- Conservative
- Liberal/Lib Dem
- Plaid Cymru
- UKIP

MP - Ian LUCAS Labour

AM - Lesley GRIFFITHS Labour

North Wales Regional AMs

Llyr Huws Gruffydd (PC)   Aled Roberts (Lib D)

Mark Isherwood (Con)   Antoinette Sandbach (Con)

Area:	103 sq km	% born in Wales:	70.8%
% speaking Welsh:	19.4%	% Unemployment *(Apr 2012)*	5.3%

The constituency comprises the following electoral wards:
Acton, Borras Park, Brynyffynnon, Cartrefle, Erddig, Garden Village, Gresford East & West, Grosvenor, Gwersyllt East & South, Gwersyllt North, Gwersyllt West, Hermitage, Holt, Little Acton, Llay, Maesydre, Marford & Hoseley, Offa, Queensway, Rhosnesni, Rossett, Smithfield, Stansty, Whitegate, Wynnstay.

Wrexham prides itself on being the capital of North Wales but was denied city status again in 2012. Wrexham has a long industrial history of mining and metalwork, but is now largely dependent upon light manufacturing employment. The area has achieved considerable success in attracting inward investment from Japan and elsewhere.

Labour have represented Wrexham since 1935, though the former MP, Tom Ellis, had a flirtation with the SDP in the early 1980s. In 2001, the sitting MP, Dr John Marek, stood down to concentrate upon his duties as the Assembly Member for Wrexham. The new Labour candidate, Ian Lucas, retained Labour's majority, albeit based on a smaller turnout than at the previous election. Prior to the second Assembly election in 2003 however, and following a bitter internal party wrangle, Dr Marek was de-selected by the local Labour Party but was subsequently returned as an Independent Assembly Member.

Dr Marek remained Deputy Presiding Officer in the Assembly, but his expulsion compounded Labour's minority status for the latter part of the second Assembly. As ever, internal party disputes cut deep and campaigning can take on an aggressive tone. In 2007 however, Labour regained control, Lesley Griffiths becoming the new AM and in Wrexham it seems as if more normal party politics have re-asserted themselves. Ian Lucas was duly re-elected to Parliament in 2010 and in 2011 Lesley Griffiths saw off the challenge of Dr Marek – who was this time running as a Conservative candidate.

Electoral Trends 1979 - 2010

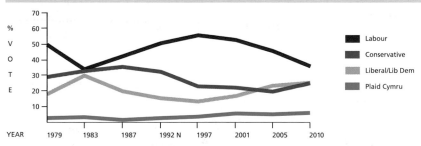

Previous MPs: **John Marek (Lab) 1983-2001; Tom Ellis (Lab) 1970-83**
Previous AMs: **John Marek (Lab) 1999-2007**

MP for Wrexham

Ian LUCAS Labour
Majority: 3,658 (11.1%)

The House of Commons, London SW1A 0AA
Tel: (020) 7219 8346 Fax: (020) 7219 1948
Email: ian.lucas.mp@parliament.uk

Constituency Office:
Vernon House, 41 Rhosddu Rd,
Wrexham LL11 2NS
Tel: (01978) 355743
Website: www.ianlucas.co.uk

Ian Lucas was first elected for Wrexham in June 2001. He was born in Gateshead in 1960, brought up on Tyneside and was educated at Newcastle Royal Grammar School, New College Oxford and the College of Law, Chester. He qualified as a solicitor and moved with his family to Wrexham in 1986, joining the Labour Party in the same year. In 1992 he established his own legal practice in Oswestry. He is a former Chair of the Wrexham Labour Party and a founder member of Gresford and Rossett Labour Party. He fought North Shropshire at the 1997 General Election and was previously a non-executive Director of the Robert Jones and Agnes Hunt Orthopaedic Hospital Trust in Gobowen.

In Westminster, Ian Lucas is currently a Shadow Minister for the Foreign and Commonwealth Office. Previously PPS to the Minister for Higher Education and Lifelong Learning, he resigned following his signature of the letter demanding a firm commitment from Tony Blair regarding his imminent retirement. He is also a former member of the Transport Committee and the Public Accounts Committee. His other political interests include home affairs, the environment and overseas development (especially the work of the UN). A member of AMICUS, the Society of Labour Lawyers and the Fabian Society, he is married with two children.

2010 General Election Result

	Party	Votes Cast	%	Change 05-10
Ian Lucas	Lab	12,161	36.9	-9.2%
Tom Rippeth	Lib D	8,503	25.8	+2.2%
Gareth Hughes	Con	8,375	25.4	+5.4%
Arfon Jones	PC	2,029	6.2	+0.4%
Melvin Roberts	BNP	1,134	3.4	+0.4%
John Humberstone	UKIP	774	2.3	+2.3%

Electorate: 50,872 Turnout: 64.8%

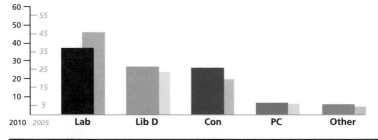

AM for Wrexham

Lesley GRIFFITHS Labour
Majority: 3,337 (17.8%)

National Assembly for Wales
Cardiff Bay, Cardiff CF99 1NA
Tel: (029) 2089 8536
Email: lesley.griffiths@wales.gov.uk

Constituency Office:
Vernon House, 41 Rhosddu Rd,
Wrexham LL11 2NS
Tel: (01978) 355743
Website: www.lesleygriffiths.org

Lesley Griffiths re-captured Wrexham for the Labour Party at the Assembly elections in 2007 when the former Labour MP and renegade Independent AM, John Marek, failed to maintain his majority. Born in Paisley in 1960, Lesley was educated at Ysgol Rhiwabon and Aston College and went on to work in the NHS for 20 years. She has previously served as a Community Councillor and school governor. Prior to her election she ran the constituency office of Ian Lucas, MP for Wrexham. A passionate follower of Wrexham Football Club, she was an elected Director of the Wrexham Supporters Trust until her election to the National Assembly for Wales. She is also a member of Unison, the Fabian Society and the Bevan Foundation.

In the Assembly, Lesley is currently Minister for Health and Social Services in the Welsh Government, having previously served as Deputy Minister for Skills, Innovation and Science. Her political interests include health, economic development, housing and children's issues. Lesley is married with two children.

2011 Assembly Election Result

	Party	Votes Cast	%	Change 07-11
Lesley Griffiths	Lab	8,368	44.8	+16.0%
John Marek	Con	5,031	26.9	+9.7%
Bill Brereton	Lib D	2,692	14.4	-2.3%
Marc Jones	PC	2,596	13.9	+4.3%

Electorate: 53,516 Turnout: 34.9%

Electoral Trends 1999 - 2011

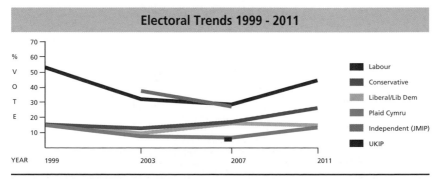

YNYS MÔN

MP - Albert OWEN Labour

AM - Ieuan Wyn JONES Plaid Cymru

North Wales Regional AMs

Llyr Huws Gruffydd (PC)   Aled Roberts (Lib D)

Mark Isherwood (Con)   Antoinette Sandbach (Con)

Area:	711 sq km	% born in Wales:	67.6%
% speaking Welsh:	63.1%	% Unemployment *(Apr 2012)*	6.4%

The constituency comprises the following electoral wards:
Aberffraw, Amlwch Port, Amlwch Rural, Beaumaris, Bodffordd, Bodorgan, Braint, Bryngwran, Brynteg, Cadnant, Cefni, Cwm Cadnant, Cyngar, Gwyngyll, Holyhead Town, Kingsland, Llanbadrig, Llanbedrgoch, Llanddyfnan, Llaneilian, Llanfaethlu, Llanfair-yn-Neubwll, Llanfihangel Ysgeifiog, Llangoed, Llanidan, Llannerch-y-medd, London Road, Maeshyfryd, Mechell, Moelfre, Morawelon, Parc a'r Mynydd, Pentraeth, Porthyfelin, Rhosneigr, Rhosyr, Trearddur, Tudur, Tysilio, Valley.

Ynys Môn is the true Welsh identity of the Isle of Anglesey. Former MPs include Lady Megan Lloyd George, as a Liberal 1929-51, and Cledwyn Hughes for Labour 1951-79. In 1979, following the retirement of Cledwyn Hughes (the late Lord Cledwyn), the Conservatives captured the seat in the shock result of the election. The new member, Keith Best, quickly established himself in the constituency, but was forced to stand down in 1987 following a personal financial scandal. In the highly politicised General Election that followed, Plaid Cymru emerged victorious. In 1992 Plaid Cymru's majority slipped, but Ieuan Wyn Jones retained the seat, as he did again at the 1997 election.

In 1999 Ieuan Wyn Jones was also successfully elected to the National Assembly and therefore retired from Parliament in 2001. Ynys Môn had always been the most marginal of the Plaid Cymru Parliamentary seats, but it constituted a major upset when the Labour Party won the subsequent General Election. This change gave rise to a closely fought second Assembly election in May 2003, where Plaid Cymru held on, but in the face of a revived Conservative challenge. The General Election of 2005 saw another tense struggle between Labour and Plaid Cymru with Labour victorious but only, according to some, as a consequence of a maverick campaign fought by the former Conservative AM, Peter Rogers. In 2007, Peter Rogers again fought an effective campaign as an Independent, but failed to prevent Ieuan Wyn Jones increasing his majority. A bi-focal politics may be emerging where Labour will represent Ynys Môn at Westminster, having been re-elected in 2010, whilst Plaid Cymru will remain the party of choice for representation in Cardiff Bay, with Ieuan Wyn Jones being returned in 2011 and a strong Conservative challenge having pushed Labour into third place.

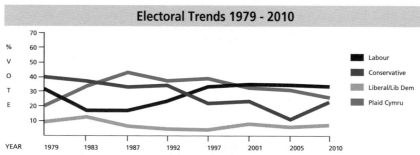

Electoral Trends 1979 - 2010

Previous MPs: **Ieuan Wyn Jones 1987-2001; Keith Best (Con) 1983-87;** (Seat renamed 1983, formerly Anglesey) **Keith Best (Con) 1979-83; Cledwyn Hughes (Lab) 1951-79**

Albert OWEN Labour
Majority: 2,461 (7.1%)

The House of Commons, London SW1A 0AA
Tel: (020) 7219 8415 Fax: (020) 7219 1951
Email: albert.owen.mp@parliament.uk

Constituency Office:
18a Thomas Street, Holyhead, Anglesey LL65 1RR
Tel: (01407) 769777 Fax: (01407) 765750
Email: albertowen.labour@gmail.com

YNYS MÔN

Albert Owen was elected to Parliament in June 2001 following a tense campaign against Plaid Cymru resulting in the Labour Party regaining the seat for the first time since the retirement of Cledwyn Hughes in 1979. Born in Bangor, 8 August 1959, he was brought up in Anglesey and attended Holyhead Comprehensive School. He served in the Merchant Navy, 1975-92, before returning to full-time education at Coleg Harlech. He went on to graduate from the University of York before becoming manager of an advice and training centre for the unemployed in Holyhead. He served as a town Councillor 1997-99. A keen devolutionist and 'Yes' campaigner, he was the Labour Party candidate for Ynys Môn in the National Assembly elections in May 1999.

Albert Owen currently serves on the Select Committee on Energy and Climate Change and is a member of the Panel of Chairs. He has generally been seen as a loyal backbencher but has occasionally voted against the Whip on issues such as tuition fees. He is a Director of a local homelessness project Digartref Ynys Môn. Married with two children, Albert Owen is a Welsh speaker whose non-political interests include gardening, cooking, walking, rail travel and family holidays.

2010 General Election Result

	Party	Votes Cast	%	Change 05-10
Albert Owen	Lab	11,490	33.4	-1.3%
Dylan Rees	PC	9,029	26.2	-4.9%
Anthony Ridge-Newman	Con	7,744	22.5	+11.4%
Matt Wood	Lib D	2,592	7.5	+0.7%
Peter Rogers	Ind	2,225	6.5	+6.5%
Elaine Gill	UKIP	1,201	3.5	+2.5%
David Owen	WCP	163	0.5	+0.5%

Electorate: 50,075 Turnout: 68.8%

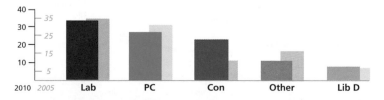

Ieuan WYN JONES Plaid Cymru
Majority: 2,937 (12.2%)

National Assembly for Wales
Cardiff Bay, Cardiff CF99 1NA
Tel: (029) 2089 8270
Email: ieuan.wynjones@wales.gov.uk

Constituency Office:
45 Bridge Street, Llangefni
Ynys Môn LL77 7PN
Tel: (01248) 723599
Website: www.ieuanwynjones.plaidcymru.org

Ieuan Wyn Jones was first elected as the Assembly Member for Ynys Môn in 1999, having served as MP for the constituency since 1987. He stepped down as MP in 2001. Born in 1949, he was educated at Pontardawe Grammar School, Ysgol y Berwyn, Bala, Liverpool Polytechnic and London University. A qualified solicitor, he was elected Leader of the Plaid Cymru Assembly Group in 2001, after Dafydd Wigley stood down for health reasons. Following a disappointing performance by Plaid at the 2003 election, discontent amongst the Party's Assembly ranks led to his resignation as Party President and Assembly Group Leader, only for him to be re-selected to the latter role following a leadership election three months later. In the aftermath of the 2007 Assembly election, he led his Party through intense negotiations to eventually secure the 'One Wales' coalition agreement, leading Plaid Cymru into government for the first time in its history. Following disappointing election results in 2011 he decided to stand down as Party Leader in March 2012. He has published two books, 'Europe: the challenge for Wales' in 1996 and in 1998 'Y Llinyn Arian', a biography of the Welsh nineteenth century publisher, Thomas Gee.

In the Assembly, Ieuan is currently Plaid Cymru's Spokesperson for Finance and Constitution. He is also a member of the Finance Committee. During the 'One Wales' coalition he served as both Deputy First Minister and the Minister for Economy & Transport. A fluent Welsh speaker, he is married with three children and is an elder in his local chapel. In his spare time he enjoys sport and local history and has been member of the National Eisteddfod Gorsedd since 2001.

2011 Assembly Election Result

	Party	Votes Cast	%	Change 07-11
Ieuan Wyn Jones	PC	9,969	41.4	+1.7%
Paul Williams	Con	7,032	29.2	+16.2%
Joe Lock	Lab	6,307	26.2	+8.8%
Rhys Taylor	Lib D	759	3.2	-0.2%

Electorate: 49,431 Turnout: 48.7%

Electoral Trends 1999 - 2011

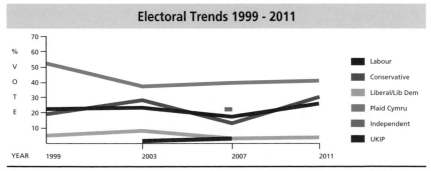

The Government of Wales Act 2006 made significant changes to the way in which regional contests, the PR element of the system adopted for elections to the National Assembly, operated. The five electoral regions, each returning four AMs were retained, but the rules governing candidacy were radically altered. Previously, many candidates contesting constituency seats were also included on their party's regional list. This is now forbidden, denying an 'insurance' candidacy to those defeated in a constituency. Regional members are elected on a proportional basis, using the d'Hondt formula. The votes cast in the regional election are divided by the number of AMs already elected for each party and an additional member is allocated to the party with the highest average of votes received per Member elected. This process is repeated four times in each region to elect a total of 20 regional AMs.

The particular pattern of partisanship in Wales has resulted in Members elected from the regional list being overwhelmingly drawn from the Opposition parties. Typically, senior party figures would fight a constituency, but also be highly ranked on their party's regional list. In 2003 this system produced the bizarre result whereby the four major party candidates who fought the Clwyd West election were all elected to the Assembly - Labour won the seat whilst the three other candidates topped their respective party lists. At the 2007 election, the new rules were applied, but to little overall effect as most existing Regional AMs remained list candidates, rather than fight largely unwinnable constituencies.

In 2011 however, a swing to the Conservatives in the constituencies of Mid & West Wales was to cost Nick Bourne, Leader of the Welsh Conservatives, his list seat.

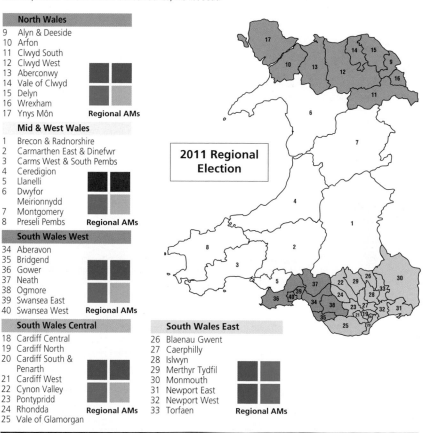

North Wales

9   Alyn & Deeside
10 Arfon
11 Clwyd South
12 Clwyd West
13 Aberconwy
14 Vale of Clwyd
15 Delyn
16 Wrexham
17 Ynys Môn   **Regional AMs**

Mid & West Wales

1   Brecon & Radnorshire
2   Carmarthen East & Dinefwr
3   Carms West & South Pembs
4   Ceredigion
5   Llanelli
6   Dwyfor
    Meirionnydd
7   Montgomery
8   Preseli Pembs   **Regional AMs**

South Wales West

34 Aberavon
35 Bridgend
36 Gower
37 Neath
38 Ogmore
39 Swansea East
40 Swansea West   **Regional AMs**

South Wales Central

18 Cardiff Central
19 Cardiff North
20 Cardiff South &
    Penarth
21 Cardiff West
22 Cynon Valley
23 Pontypridd
24 Rhondda   **Regional AMs**
25 Vale of Glamorgan

South Wales East

26 Blaenau Gwent
27 Caerphilly
28 Islwyn
29 Merthyr Tydfil
30 Monmouth
31 Newport East
32 Newport West
33 Torfaen   **Regional AMs**

MID & WEST WALES

Labour	**Plaid Cymru**	**Conservative**	**Liberal Democrat**	**UKIP**
Joyce Watson	Simon Thomas	Nick Bourne	William Powell	Christine Williams
Rebecca Evans	Rhys Davies	Lisa Francis	Mark Cole	Clive Easton
Matthew Dorrance	Llywelyn Rees	Ian Harrison	Edward Wilson	David W Rowlands
Iqbal Malik	Ellen ap Gwynn	Gareth Ratcliffe	Steffan John	Nick Powell
		Keith Evans	Gemma Bowker	
		Stephen Kaye		
		Dan Munford		
		Evan Price		

Mid & West Wales	Labour	Plaid Cymru	Conservative	Lib Dem	UKIP
Total	**47,348**	**56,384**	**52,905**	**26,847**	**9,211**
Share of Vote	22.5%	26.8%	25.2%	12.8%	4.4%
Electorate	433,147		Turnout	48.9%	

	Con	Lab	Lib D	PC
Constituency result	3	1	1	3
Additional Members:	0	2	1	1

Regional AMs: *Reserve*

Labour	Joyce Watson	Matthew Dorrance
Labour	Rebecca Evans	Iqbal Malik
Plaid Cymru	Simon Thomas	Rhys Davies
Liberal Democrats	William Powell	Mark Cole

Previous AMs: **Alun Michael** (Lab) 1999-2000; **Delyth Evans** (Lab) 2000-03; **Glyn Davies** (Con) 1999-2007; **Lisa Francis** (Con) 2003-07; **Cynog Dafis** (PC) 1999-2003; **Helen Mary Jones** (PC) 2003-07; **Nicholas Bourne** (Con) 1999-2011; **Alun Davies** (Lab) 2007-2011; **Nerys Evans** (PC) 2007-2011

MID & WEST WALES

Green Party	**WCP**	**BNP**	**Comm**	**SLP**
Leila Kiersch	Jeff Green	Kay Thomas	Catrin Ashton	Liz Screen
Marilyn Elson	Adam Bridgman	Watcyn Richards	Rick Newnham	Adam Kelsey
Pat McCarthy	Martin Wiltshire	Roger Phillips	Barbara Thomas	Barry Giddings
Neil Lewis	Sue Green	Gary Tumulty	Clive Eliassen	Robert Board
Ken Simpkin				
Rachael Sweeting				

Green	WCP	BNP	Comm	SLP	Total
8,660	**1,630**	**2,821**	**595**	**3,951**	**210,352**
4.1%	0.8%	1.3%	0.3%	1.9%	

Given the distribution of its support base in Wales, it is only in **Mid & West Wales** that the Labour Party are ever likely to be awarded additional Members. During the 2007 election, the loss by the Labour Party of the seats of Llanelli (which it regained in 2011), Carmarthen West & South Pembs and Preseli Pembs was in part compensated by gaining top-up seats from the regional ballot. Conversely, the Conservative victory in the last election in Montgomeryshire cost the party its only member, with the top-up seat being reallocated to the Liberal Democrats. Only Labour's Joyce Watson survives from the 2007 set of regional AMs, with her fellow party member Rebecca Evans joining her along with William Powell of the Liberal Democrats and former MP Simon Thomas for Plaid Cymru. Mid & West Wales is the only one out of the five regions where Labour is not the largest party, with Plaid Cymru being top, followed by the Conservatives.

Rebecca EVANS Labour

National Assembly for Wales
Cardiff Bay, Cardiff CF99 1NA
Tel: (029) 2089 8288
Email: rebecca.evans@wales.gov.uk

Constituency Office:
Ferry Lane Works, Ferry Lane
Pembroke Dock SA71 4RE
Tel: (01646) 622145
Website: www.rebeccaevansam.com

MID & WEST WALES

Rebecca Evans was first elected to the National Assembly for Wales in May 2011 to represent the region of Mid and West Wales. Rebecca studied History at the University of Leeds before moving to Sidney Sussex College, University of Cambridge, where she received a Master of Philosophy Degree for her thesis *'The Time for Waiting is Gone: Lyndon Johnson and the Voting Rights Act of 1965.'* Before being elected, Rebecca worked as Policy and Public Affairs Officer for a national charity representing people with a disability and their families. Rebecca is also a former Welsh Labour organiser for Mid and West Wales and a former Senior Researcher and Communications Officer for an Assembly Member.

In the Assembly, Rebecca has been appointed to the Assembly's Heath and Social Care Committee; Environment and Sustainable Development Committee as well as the Assembly's Common Agricultural Policy Task and Finish Group. In addition to these, she is also Chair of the Cross Party Group on Disability and the Cross Party Group on Nursing and Midwifery. Outside politics Rebecca enjoys travelling, reading and spending time with family and friends. She is a keen Welsh learner.

2011 Regional List Result

Parties	Total Vote	%	Constituency Result	Additional Members
Plaid Cymru	56,384	26.8	3	1
Conservative Party	52,905	25.2	3	0
Labour Party	**47,348**	**22.5**	**1**	**2**
Liberal Democrats	26,847	12.8	1	1
Others	26,868	12.8	0	0

Electorate: 433,147 Turnout: 48.6%

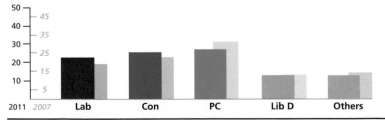

William POWELL Liberal Democrat

National Assembly for Wales
Cardiff Bay, Cardiff CF99 1NA
Tel: (029) 2089 8718
Email: william.powell@wales.gov.uk

Constituency Office:
3 Park Street, Newtown
Powys SY16 1EE
Tel: (01686) 625527
Website: www.williampowell.org.uk

William Powell was elected to the Assembly during the 2011 election, having previously stood in 2007. In 1999 he stood for the pro-European Conservatives in the European election in Wales, but joined the Liberal Democrats shortly afterwards. Born in 1966, he attended Talgarth School and Gwernyfed High School, gaining a scholarship to read Modern Languages at Pembroke College, Oxford. He graduated in 1986 and now lives with his family on their organic farm in the Black Mountains near Talgarth, Powys. A qualified teacher, he has taught French and German at a number of schools in Wales and the Marches. William has served as County Councillor for Talgarth since 2004 and has been active in rural regeneration projects. He is a former member and Audit Scrutiny Chair of the Brecon Beacons National Park Authority and was a founding board member of Wales in Europe and currently serves as Chair of the Wales Council European Movement. In addition, William is a Council Member of the European Liberal Democrats (ELDR) and works closely with Liberal sister-parties across the continent. He is a member of the FUW, a Governor of Talgarth CP School and Gwernyfed High School. William is a member of the Lloyd George Society, where he also serves on the committee.

He is presently the Welsh Liberal Democrats Spokesperson for Environment, Sustainability and Rural Affairs and also Chairs the Assembly's Petitions Committee and the Environment and Sustainability Committee.

2011 Regional List Result

Parties	Total Vote	%	Constituency Result	Additional Members
Plaid Cymru	56,384	26.8	3	1
Conservative Party	52,905	25.2	3	0
Labour Party	47,348	22.5	1	2
Liberal Democrats	**26,847**	**12.8**	**1**	**1**
Others	26,868	12.8	0	0

Electorate: 433,147 Turnout: 48.6%

| 2011 *2007* | **Lab** | **Con** | **PC** | **Lib D** | **Others** |

Simon THOMAS Plaid Cymru

National Assembly for Wales
Cardiff Bay, Cardiff CF99 1NA
Tel: (029) 2089 8476
Email: simon.thomas@Wales.gov.uk

Constituency Office:
Ty Bres, Heol Bres
Llanelli SA15 1UA
Tel: (01554) 774393
Website: simonthomas.plaidcymru.org

Simon Thomas was first elected to the Assembly at the 2011 election as a regional member for Mid and West Wales. He was the Plaid Cymru MP for Ceredigion from 2000 to 2005 before losing narrowly to the Liberal Democrats' Mark Williams by just 219 votes. Whilst in Parliament, he spoke for his party on Environment, Food and Rural Affairs, Transport, International Development, Energy, Culture, Media and Sport. He was also a member of the Environmental Audit Committee and became one of the longest-serving members of that body, being recognised as a constant Parliamentary advocate for the environment and sustainable development. After losing his seat he became a development manager for Technium in Pembrokeshire, before being appointed a senior special advisor to the Welsh Government, advising the Deputy First Minister and other Plaid Cymru Ministers.

Simon Thomas was an unsuccessful candidate for the leadership of Plaid Cymru in 2012 and is currently the party's Spokesperson for Education. He is a member of the Children and Young People Committee, along with the Constitutional and Legislative Affairs Committee. Simon is also the Director for Policy and Research of Plaid's National Executive and some of his political interests include the environment, food and rural affairs, transport, international development, energy and culture, media and sport. He lives in Aberystwyth with his wife and two children.

2011 Regional List Result

Parties	Total Vote	%	Constituency Result	Additional Members
Plaid Cymru	**56,384**	**26.8**	**3**	**1**
Conservative Party	52,905	25.2	3	0
Labour Party	47,348	22.5	1	2
Liberal Democrats	26,847	12.8	1	1
Others	26,868	12.8	0	0

Electorate: 433,147 Turnout: 48.6%

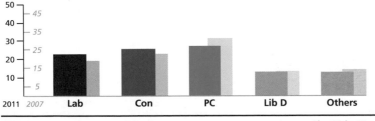

AM for Mid & West Wales

Joyce WATSON Labour

National Assembly for Wales
Cardiff Bay CF99 1NA
Tel: (029) 2089 8614
Email: joyce.watson@wales.gov.uk

Constituency Office:
3 Red Street, Carmarthen SA31 1QL
Tel: (01267) 233448
Website: www.joycewatson.org.uk

Joyce Watson was elected a regional AM for Mid and West Wales in May 2007 when, unexpectedly, the Labour Party secured two additional Members following losses in various constituencies in the region. Born in 1955, she was educated at Cardigan Comprehensive, Pembrokeshire College and Swansea University. Prior to entering the Assembly, Joyce was leader of the Labour group on Pembrokeshire Council. She was manager of Women's Voice, the Wales Women's National Coalition, and was a senior member of the Wales Gender Budget Group and the NHS Equality Reference Group. Joyce has worked with employers and trade bodies to get more young people and Welsh women into the construction industry and in 2009, she set up the Women in Construction network.

Joyce currently sits on the Assembly Committees for Enterprise and Business, Communities, Equality and Local Government and Petitions. Joyce also chairs the Assembly Cross Party Groups on Construction, Human Trafficking and Stroke. Joyce's political interests include promoting rural economic renewal – by working to raise workforce skills, reduce youth unemployment and invest in rural businesses. She is married with three children.

2011 Regional List Result

Parties	Total Vote	%	Constituency Result	Additional Members
Plaid Cymru	56,384	26.8	3	1
Conservative Party	52,905	25.2	3	0
Labour Party	**47,348**	**22.5**	**1**	**2**
Liberal Democrats	26,847	12.8	1	1
Others	26,868	12.8	0	0

Electorate: 433,147 Turnout: 48.6%

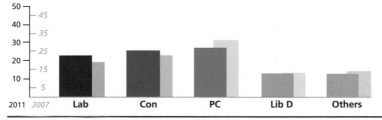

NORTH WALES

Labour	Plaid Cymru	Conservative	Liberal Democrat	BNP
Gwyneth Thomas	Llyr Huws Griffiths	Mark Isherwood	Aled Roberts	John Walker
David Phillips	Heledd Fychan	Antoinette Sandbach	Eleanor Burnham	Richard Barnes
Diane Green	Dyfed Edwards	Janet Howarth	Mark Young	Ian Si'Ree
Colin Hughes	Liz Saville Roberts	Julian Thompson-Hill	Anne Williams	Clive Jefferson
		Ranil Jayawardena	Victor Babu	
		Samantha Cotton		
		Martin Peet		
		Sam Rowlands		
		John Broughton		

North Wales	Labour	Plaid Cymru	Conservative	Lib Dem	BNP
Total	**62,677**	**41,701**	**52,201**	**11,507**	**4,785**
Share of Vote	32.2%	21.4%	26.8%	5.9%	2.5%
Electorate	473,476		Turnout	41.5%	

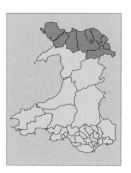

	Con	Lab	Lib D	PC
Constituency result	2	5	0	2
Additional Members:	2	0	1	1

Regional AMs: — *Reserve*

Conservative	Mark Isherwood	Janet Howarth
Conservative	Antoinette Sandbach	Julian Thompson-Hill
Plaid Cymru	Llyr Huws Griffiths	Heledd Fychan
Liberal Democrats	Aled Roberts	Eleanor Burnham

Previous AMs: **Christine Humphries** (Lib D) 1999-2001; **Rod Richards** (Con) 1999-2002; **David Jones** (Con) 2002-03; **Peter Rogers** (Con) 1999-2003; **Brynle Williams** (Con) 2003-2011; **Eleanor Burnham** (Lib D) 2001-2011; **Janet Ryder** (PC) 1999-2011

Green Party

SLP

UKIP

WCP

Comm

Green Party	SLP	UKIP	WCP	Comm
orienne Robinson	Kathrine Jones	Nathan Gill	Ralph Kinch	Glyn Davies
mothy Foster	David Jones	Warwick Nicholson	Louise Wynne-Jones	Trevor Jones
eter Haig	Robert English	Andrew Haigh	Lindsay Griffiths	Rhian Cartwright
nn Were	John Mcleod	Elwyn Williams	Neil Bastow	Graham Morgan

Ind

Jason Weyman

Green	SLP	UKIP	WCP	Comm	Ind	Total
4,406	4,895	9,608	1,401	523	1,094	194,798
2.3%	2.5%	4.9%	0.7%	0.3%	0.6	

Despite only one constituency seat changing hands in **North Wales** – Plaid's loss of Aberconwy – the only survivor from the 2007 set of regional AMs was the Conservatives' Mark Isherwood. The sad death in April 2011 of Brynle Williams saw Antoinette Sandbach replace him as second on the Conservatives' party list, while Plaid Cymru's Llyr Hughes Griffiths replaced the retiring Janet Ryder. As in South Wales Central, the election of the Liberal Democrat member was a controversial one. Having displaced incumbent Eleanor Burnham at the top of his party's list and won election, Aled Roberts was subsequently disqualified when it emerged that he was a member of the Valuation Tribunal for Wales – a public body which members seeking election are barred from. However, AMs voted to reinstate him after an investigation found he had been misled by out-of-date guidance for election candidates published in Welsh on the Electoral Commission website. Although the English-language guidance was correct, Aled Roberts had followed the Welsh-language guidance that listed previous regulations on proscribed organizations from 2006.

AM for North Wales

Llyr Huws GRUFFYDD Plaid Cymru

National Assembly for Wales
Cardiff Bay, Cardiff CF99 1NA
Tel: (029) 2089 8508
Email: llyr.gruffydd@wales.gov.uk

Constituency Office:
Plaid Cymru, Regent Street
Wrexham LL11 1RE
Tel: (01978) 365512
Website: www.llyrhuwsgruffydd.com

Llyr Huws Gruffudd was elected at the 2011 election having previously contested the Carmarthen West and South Pembrokeshire seat in 2003. He also stood for the Parliamentary seat in the 2001 General Election and contested Clwyd West at the 2010 General Election. Llyr lives on a family farm near Ruthin and before being elected as Plaid Cymru Assembly Member he worked as a consultancy manager for the National Trust in Wales. Prior to that he worked for an economic development company specialising in helping set up new businesses and assisting existing businesses to develop and grow. From 1999 to 2003 Llyr worked as a researcher and press officer for Plaid's Members of the European Parliament, Jill Evans and Eurig Wyn. He was also National Campaign Co-ordinator for the then Plaid Cymru President, Dafydd Wigley, in the run-up to the 1999 National Assembly elections. Raised and educated in Carmarthen, Llyr served as Mayor and Sheriff of the town.

He is Plaid Cymru Spokesperson for Environment, Housing and Regeneration and in the Assembly sits on the Environment and Sustainability Committee; Common Agricultural Policy Task and Finish Group; Common Fisheries Policy Task and Finish Group and the Standards Committee. He is also Chair of the Cross Party Group on Rural Affairs.

2011 Regional List Result

Parties	Total Vote	%	Constituency Result	Additional Members
Labour Party	62,677	32.2	5	0
Conservative Party	52,201	26.8	2	2
Plaid Cymru	**41,701**	**21.4**	**2**	**1**
Liberal Democrats	11,507	5.9	0	1
Others	26,712	13.7	0	0

Electorate: 473,476 Turnout: 41.1%

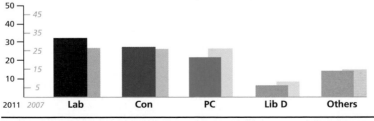

AM for North Wales

Mark ISHERWOOD Conservative

National Assembly for Wales
Cardiff Bay, Cardiff CF99 1NA
Tel: (029) 2089 8730
Email: mark.isherwood@wales.gov.uk

Constituency Office:
5 Halkyn St, Holywell, Flintshire CH8 7TX
Tel: (01352) 710232
Website: www.markisherwood.co.uk

NORTH WALES

Mark Isherwood was first elected to the National Assembly in 2003, having previously been Parliamentary candidate for Alyn & Deeside at the 2001 General Election. Though he unsuccessfully contested the Delyn seat in 2003, he was elected to the Assembly through the North Wales regional list. Born in 1959, he was educated at Stockport Grammar School and Newcastle University. He is an Associate of the Chartered Institute of Bankers and was North Wales Area Manager for the Cheshire Building Society. He has been a School Governor at Ysgol Parc y Llan, a former Community Councillor and Housing Association member. He is an Ambassador for Girl Guides Clwyd, a Vice President of the North Wales Play Association, Patron of the Tyddyn Bach HIV/AIDS Respite Centre in Penmaenmawr, member of Conwy CAB and was founder of CHANT (Community Hospitals Acting Nationally Together).

He is currently the Conservatives Shadow Minister for North Wales, Social Justice and Housing. He is a member of the Communities, Equality and Local Government Committee and Standards of Conduct Committee. He also Chairs the Cross Party Groups on Autism; Disability; Fuel Poverty; Funerals and Bereavement and Neurological Conditions. Married with six children his interests outside politics revolve around his family.

2011 Regional List Result

Parties	Total Vote	%	Constituency Result	Additional Members
Labour Party	62,677	32.2	5	0
Conservative Party	**52,201**	**26.8**	**2**	**2**
Plaid Cymru	41,701	21.4	2	1
Liberal Democrats	11,507	5.9	0	1
Others	26,712	13.7	0	0

Electorate: 473,476 Turnout: 41.1%

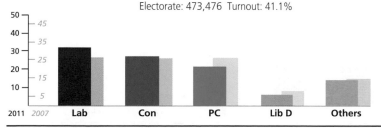

Aled ROBERTS Liberal Democrat

National Assembly for Wales
Cardiff Bay, Cardiff CF99 1NA
Tel: (029) 2089 8129
Email: aled.roberts@Wales.gov.uk

Constituency Office:
18 High Street, Johnstown
Wrexham LL14 2SN
Tel: (01978) 843300

Aled Roberts was elected to the Assembly in 2011, having displaced Eleanor Burnham at the top of the Liberal Democrats' North Wales regional list. Aled attended Ysgol y Ponciau, Ysgol y Grango and Ysgol Rhiwabon before going on to study Law at the University of Wales, Aberystwyth. After obtaining his solicitor's qualification, Aled practised in Wrexham. He is a former Chairman of Waste Awareness Wales and was also a member of the Wales Climate Change Commission. Aled was also Chair of the Wales Strategic Migration Partnership and served as the Welsh representative on the UK LGA's Asylum and Refugee Working Group. He was the Welsh Local Government Association Spokesperson for Housing from 2005 to 2011, and in 2008 was given additional responsibility when the portfolio was expanded to include Environment, Sustainability and Waste. He is a former Mayor of Wrexham and was Leader of Wrexham County Borough Council from March 2005 to May 2011. In November 2007, Aled was named "Local Politician of the Year" at the ITV Wales Politician of the Year Awards.

Aled is the Welsh Liberal Democrat Shadow Minister for Education; Spokesperson for Children and Young People; and Spokesperson for the Welsh Language. He also sits on the Public Accounts Committee and the Children and Young People Committee. He is married with two sons.

2011 Regional List Result

Parties	Total Vote	%	Constituency Result	Additional Members
Labour Party	62,677	32.2	5	0
Conservative Party	52,201	26.8	2	2
Plaid Cymru	41,701	21.4	2	1
Liberal Democrats	**11,507**	**5.9**	**0**	**1**
Others	26,712	13.7	0	0

Electorate: 473,476 Turnout: 41.1%

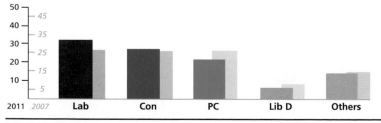

AM for North Wales

Antoinette SANDBACH Conservative

National Assembly for Wales
Cardiff Bay, Cardiff CF99 1NA
Tel: (029) 2089 8755
Email: antoinette.sandbach@wales.gov.uk

Constituency Office:
37 High Street, Denbigh LL16 3HY
Tel: (01745) 813345
Website: www.antoinettesandbach.org.uk

Antoinette Sandbach was elected to the Assembly in 2011, having previously contested Delyn at the 2007 Assembly election and the 2010 General Election. Born in 1969, she studied law before obtaining a Master degree in Environmental and Humanitarian Law at Nottingham University. Having qualified as a barrister in 1993, she practiced in London for twelve years before returning to Wales to live and work on the family farm. A former director at a local charity for a number of years, she has run two small businesses since 2005.

In the Assembly Antoinette is the Welsh Conservatives Shadow Minister for Rural Affairs. She also sits on the Environment and Sustainability Committee; Common Agricultural Policy Task and Finish Group and the Common Fisheries Policy Task and Finish Group. She has a young daughter and together they enjoy walking, cycling and art projects.

2011 Regional List Result

Parties	Total Vote	%	Constituency Result	Additional Members
Labour Party	62,677	32.2	5	0
Conservative Party	**52,201**	**26.8**	**2**	**2**
Plaid Cymru	41,701	21.4	2	1
Liberal Democrats	11,507	5.9	0	1
Others	26,712	13.7	0	0

Electorate: 473,476 Turnout: 41.1%

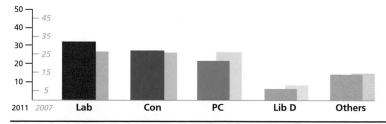

Labour	Plaid Cymru	Conservative	Liberal Democrat	BNP	
Jane Brencher	Leanne Wood	Andrew R T Davies	John Dixon	Gareth Connors	Kevin Philip
Craig Jones	Chris Franks	David Melding	Eluned Parrott	Mary John	Mahoney
Alex Thomas	Delme Bowen	Lyn Hudson	Rachael Hitchinson	Keith Fairhurst	Simon Christop
John David Drysdale	Richard Grigg	Richard Howard	Elgan Morgan	Edward O'Sullivan	David Zeigler
		Hopkins	Andrew Sherwood		Lawrence Doug
		Christopher Williams			Gwynn
		Kyle Robert Smith			Anthony John
		Axel Kaehne			Jenkins
		Helen Hancock			

S Wales Central	Labour	Plaid Cymru	Conservative	Lib Dem	BNP	UKIP
Total	**85,445**	**28,606**	**45,751**	**16,514**	**3,805**	**8,292**
Share of Vote	41.0%	13.7%	22%	7.9%	1.8%	4%
Electorate	506,293		Turnout	41.4%		

	Con	Lab	Lib D	PC
Constituency result	0	8	0	0
Additional Members:	2	0	1	1

Regional AMs:		*Reserve*
Conservative	Andrew R T Davies	Lyn Hudson
Conservative	David Melding	Richard Hopkins
Plaid Cymru	Leanne Wood	Chris Franks
Liberal Democrats	Eluned Parrott	Rachael Hitchinson

Previous AMs: **Owen John Thomas** (PC) 1999-2007; **Pauline Jarman** (PC) 1999-2003; **Jonathan Morgan** (Con) 1999-2007; **Chris Franks** (PC) 2007-2011

Green Party	Loony Party	SLP	TUSC	Comm	WCP
e Griffiths	Mark Beech	Andrew Jordan	Ross Saunders	Robert David	John Harrold
n Coates	Pinkandorevil	Adrian Dumphy	Sarah Mayo	Griffiths	Clive Bate
n Matthews	Gem	Diana Whitley-	Brian Lewis	Gwen Griffiths	Donald Watson
kt Townsend		Jones	Helen Jones	Fran Rawlings	Derek Thomson
ri Clark		Harry Parfitt	Andrew Price	Clive Griffiths	
			Filipa Machado		
			Leanne Francis		
			Rae Lewis-Ayling		
			Nagina Kabul		
			Glyn Matthews		
			Keiron Hopkins		
			Rowena Mason		

Green	Loony	SLP	TUSC	Comm	WCP	Total
10,774	1,237	4,690	830	516	1,873	208,333
5.2%	0.6%	2.3%	0.4%	0.3%	0.9%	

With twelve different parties listed on the ballot form, **South Wales Central** offered the largest choice of all the regional elections in Wales. The only change in membership from 2007 however saw Plaid Cymru's Chris Franks lose his seat at the expense of the Liberal Democrats' Eluned Parrott. This change came as a direct result of the Liberal Democrats losing Cardiff Central and despite the party seeing a drop of 6.1% in its share of the vote across the region. Andrew R T Davies and Leanne Wood - the respective leaders of the Conservatives and Plaid Cymru – both retained their seats along with the Conservatives' David Melding. The election of Eluned Parrott for the Liberal Democrats was not without its controversy. Having initially been selected in second position on the Liberal Democrats' list behind John Dixon, she was unexpectedly promoted after he was forced to stand down when it emerged that as a member of the Care Council for Wales he was ineligible to stand for election. In the regional election however, votes are for parties rather than individuals, so the Liberal Democrats' next ranked candidate - Eluned Parrott - was duly returned in his place.

Andrew R T DAVIES Conservative

National Assembly for Wales
Cardiff Bay, Cardiff CF99 1NA
Tel: (029) 2089 8747
Email: andrew.davies2@wales.gov.uk

Constituency Office:
Rhymney House, Copse Walk
Cardiff Gate Business Park, Cardiff CF23 8RB
Website: www.andrewrtdavies.com

SOUTH WALES CENTRAL

Andrew R T Davies was first elected to the National Assembly in 2007, having previously been a Parliamentary candidate in Cardiff West in 2001 and Brecon and Radnor in 2005. Born in Cowbridge in 1968 and educated at St Johns College, Porthcawl, he became a partner in the family farming business based near Cowbridge in the Vale of Glamorgan. Andrew is a former Welsh delegate on the Council of the National Farmers' Union and was the Royal Welsh Agricultural Society's Oxford Scholar in 2002. He is the Vice President of Llantrisant Young Farmers Club and former Chairman of Creative Communities, an organization which seeks to develop structural community development. Andrew is a life governor of the Royal Welsh Agricultural Society.

Having previously held Conservative Shadow Ministerial posts for Transport, Education, Health and Business, in July 2011 he was elected as Leader of the Welsh Conservative Group in the Assembly. His political interests are listed as health, education and rural affairs. Married with four children, outside of politics Andrew enjoys swimming, rugby, reading and spending time with his family.

2011 Regional List Result

Parties	Total Vote	%	Constituency Result	Additional Members
Labour Party	85,445	41.0	8	0
Conservative Party	**45,751**	**22.0**	**0**	**2**
Others	32,017	15.4	0	0
Plaid Cymru	28,606	13.7	0	1
Liberal Democrats	16,514	7.9	0	1

Electorate: 506,833 Turnout: 41.1%

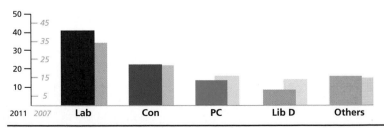

AM for South Wales Central

David MELDING Conservative

National Assembly for Wales
Cardiff Bay, Cardiff CF99 1NA
Tel: (029) 2089 8732
Email: david.melding@wales.gov.uk

Constituency Office:
29 High Street, Barry CF62 7EB
Tel: (01446) 744126

David Melding has been a member of the National Assembly for Wales since its creation in 1999. He was the Conservative Parliamentary candidate in Cardiff Central in 1997 and Blaenau Gwent in 1992 and stood for the Vale of Glamorgan at both the Assembly elections of 1999 and 2003, but was elected by virtue of being second on the Conservative regional list. In 2007 he headed the Conservative list. Born in Neath in 1962, he completed his undergraduate work in Cardiff University and received his Master's Degree in Government from the College of William and Mary in Virginia, USA. Before entering politics, David worked in the non-profit sector as the Welsh Director of a major UK campaigning charity. Although the Conservative Party initially opposed the establishment of the Welsh Assembly and Scottish Parliament, David has argued that a federal Britain is the best way forward and has published two books on the topic. As Director of Policy for the Welsh Conservative Group, he was responsible for producing the Assembly Manifestos in 2003, 2007 and 2011.

In the Assembly, David is the Deputy Presiding Officer and Chair of both the Committee for the Scrutiny of the First Minister and the Constitutional and Legislative Affairs Committee. He is also a member of the Business Committee. Some of David's policy interests are childrens issues (especially children in care), social enterprises, co-operatives and mental health. He currently chairs the All-Party Group on Children. Outside of politics, David enjoys walking, swimming and cycling.

2011 Regional List Result

Parties	Total Vote	%	Constituency Result	Additional Members
Labour Party	85,445	41.0	8	0
Conservative Party	**45,751**	**22.0**	**0**	**2**
Others	32,017	15.4	0	0
Plaid Cymru	28,606	13.7	0	1
Liberal Democrats	16,514	7.9	0	1

Electorate: 506,833 Turnout: 41.1%

	Lab	Con	PC	Lib D	Others
2011 2007					

Eluned PARROTT Liberal Democrat

National Assembly for Wales
Cardiff Bay, Cardiff CF99 1NA
Tel: (029) 2089 8343
Email: eluned.parrott@Wales.gov.uk

Constituency Office:
99 Woodville Road, Cathays
Cardiff CF24 4DY
Tel: (029) 2046 2326

Eluned Parrott has been an Assembly member since 6 July 2011, when she replaced John Dixon as a South Wales Central Regional AM following his disqualification. Eluned has a degree in Music from Cardiff University, and has a Postgraduate Diploma in Marketing from the Chartered Institute of Marketing. Before becoming an AM, she worked as a Community Engagement Manager for Cardiff University, leading a team that organises educational outreach and community events for the public. In December 2011 Eluned Parrott was the winner of the 'Member to Watch' award at the Wales Yearbook Welsh Politician of the Year awards ceremony.

At present, Eluned is the Welsh Liberal Democrats Shadow Minister for Enterprise, Transport, Europe and Business. She sits on Constitutional and Legislative Affairs Committee; Enterprise and Business Committee and the Procurement Task and Finish Group. She is also Chair to the Cross Party Groups on Community Transport and Dementia. She lives with her husband and two children in Rhoose, in the Vale of Glamorgan and enjoys walking, reading and sport, along with being a very poor cricket player.

2011 Regional List Result

Parties	Total Vote	%	Constituency Result	Additional Members
Labour Party	85,445	41.0	8	0
Conservative Party	45,751	22.0	0	2
Others	32,017	15.4	0	0
Plaid Cymru	28,606	13.7	0	1
Liberal Democrats	**16,514**	**7.9**	**0**	**1**

Electorate: 506,833 Turnout: 41.1%

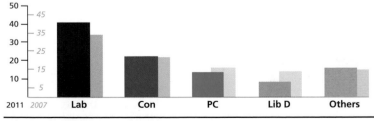

Leanne WOOD Plaid Cymru

National Assembly for Wales
Cardiff Bay, Cardiff CF99 1NA
Tel: (029) 2089 8285
Email: leanne.wood@wales.gov.uk

Constituency Office:
32 Gelliwastad Road, Pontypridd
Rhondda Cynon Taf CF37 2BN
Tel: (01443) 480291
Website: www.leannewood.com

Leanne Wood was first elected to the National Assembly in 2003 as the lead candidate on Plaid Cymru's South Wales Central regional list. Having joined Plaid Cymru in 1991, she became constituency secretary for the Rhondda and fought both the 1997 and 2001 General Elections as the Plaid Cymru candidate. A former member of Rhondda Cynon Taf Council, she was educated at Tonypandy Comprehensive School and the University of Glamorgan and later became a lecturer at University of Wales, Cardiff. Leanne is a qualified probation officer, active trade unionist and a former Chair of the South Wales Branch of the National Association of Probation Officers. She also worked as a political assistant to both Geraint Davies AM and Jill Evans MEP. A staunch left-winger and republican, she refused to attend the official opening of the Assembly by the Queen. She is also a member of the Plaid Cymru National Executive and has served as Co-chair of UNDEB, the Plaid Cymru trade union arm.

In March 2012, Leanne was elected as Ieuan Wyn Jones' successor as Plaid Cymru's Leader. In her acceptance speech she called for "real independence" for Wales and promised to be an "open, forward looking, positive and constructive leader". She currently Chairs the Cross Party Groups on Justice Unions and the Public and Commercial Services Union. Her political interests include international affairs, green issues, criminal justice and drugs, women and youth issues, mental health, poverty and social justice.

2011 Regional List Result

Parties	Total Vote	%	Constituency Result	Additional Members
Labour Party	85,445	41.0	8	0
Conservative Party	45,751	22.0	0	2
Others	32,017	15.4	0	0
Plaid Cymru	**28,606**	**13.7**	**0**	**1**
Liberal Democrats	16,514	7.9	0	1

Electorate: 506,833 Turnout: 41.1%

2011 *2007*   **Lab**   **Con**   **PC**   **Lib D**   **Others**

SOUTH WALES CENTRAL

Labour	Plaid Cymru	Conservative	Liberal Democrat	SLP
Debbie Wilcox	Jocelyn Davies	William Graham	Veronica German	Alyson O'Connell
Anthony Hunt	Lindsay Whittle	Mohammad Asghar	Phil Hobson	Susan Lesley Deare
Karen Wilkie	Bleddyn Hancock	Caroline Oag	Bob Griffin	Alan Brian Cowdel
Hefin David	Jonathan Clark	Benjamin Smith	Alison Willott	Joyce Irene Giblin
		Paul Pavia	Brendan D'Cruz	
		Susannah Beatson-Hird		
		Paul Williams		
		Paul Stafford		

S Wales East	Labour	Plaid Cymru	Conservative	Lib Dem
Total	**82,699**	**21,850**	**35,459**	**10,798**
Share of Vote	45.7%	12.1%	19.6%	6%
Electorate	469,486		Turnout	38.9%

	Con	Lab	Lib D	PC
Constituency result	1	7	0	0
Additional Members:	2	0	0	2

Regional AMs		*Reserve*
Conservative	William Graham	Caroline Oag
Plaid Cymru	Jocelyn Davies	Bleddyn Hancock
Conservative	Mohammad Asghar	Benjamin Smith
Plaid Cymru	Lindsay Whittle	Jonathan Clark

Previous AMs: **Phil Williams** (PC) 1999-2003; **Laura Anne Jones** (Con) 2003-07; **Mike German** (Lib D) 1999-2010; **Veronica German** (Lib D) 2010-2011

Green Party	English Democrat	UKIP	BNP	WCP
Christopher Were	Laurence Williams	David J Rowlands	Laurence Reid	Dave Owen
Pippa Bartolotti	Kim Burelli	Neil (Jock) Greer	Jennie Noble	Steve McCreery
Owen Clarke	Robin Tilbrook	Peter Osbourne	John Voisey	Raphael Martin
Alan Williams	Teresa Canon	Gareth Dunn	Jennifer Matthys	Tracey Martin
	Mike Tibby			

Comm

Tommy Roberts
Roy Evans
Julian Jones
Angharad Khan-Raja

SLP	Green	Eng Dem	UKIP	BNP	Comm	WCP	Total
4,427	4,857	1,904	9,526	6,485	578	2,441	181,024
2.5%	2.7%	1.1%	5.3%	3.6%	0.3%	1.4%	

The 2011 regional election in **South Wales East** returned one new member – making it the most settled region in Wales. The Conservatives' William Graham and Mohammed Asghar retained their seats, but with the latter being elected as a Conservative candidate for the first time, having initially been elected in 2007 as a Plaid Cymru member until his subsequent defection in 2009. Plaid Cymru's Jocelyn Davies was re-elected along with fellow party member Lindsay Whittle. The Liberal Democrats' Veronica German had joined the Assembly in 2010 when her husband, the former Party Leader Mike German, was elevated to the House of Lords. The Liberal Democrats however did not warrant an additional member in 2011 in light of the national swing towards the Conservatives. Labour dominance across the region remained high, and therefore the additional Member top-up seats will always favour the opposition parties, as the system is intended to do, reducing the degree of disproportionality in the first-past-the-post constituency election.

Mohammad ASGHAR Conservative

National Assembly for Wales
Cardiff Bay, Cardiff CF99 1NA
Tel: (029) 2089 8319
Email: mohammad.asghar@wales.gov.uk

Constituency Office:
Unit 1, Fairoak House, 15-17 Church Road
Newport NP19 7EJ
Tel: (01633) 220022
Website: www.mohammadasgharam.co.uk

Mohammad Asghar (known as 'Oscar') was first elected to the National Assembly as a Plaid Cymru Regional Member for South Wales East in 2007, having previously contested Newport East at the 2003 Assembly election and 2005 General Election. In December 2009 he defected to the Conservative Assembly Group and was returned as a Conservative nominee for South East Wales at the 2011 election. An accountant, Mohammed Asghar was born in Pashawar in 1945. Fluent in Urdu and Punjabi, he attended Pashawar University and later completed his accountancy training at Nash College, Newport. He had previously been a Plaid Cymru Councillor for the Victoria Ward of Newport County Council. When elected in 2007, he became the National Assembly for Wales' first ethnic minority AM.

In the Assembly, he is a member of the Public Accounts Committee. His political interests include economic development and combating social exclusion. His interests outside politics include cricket, athletics and badminton. He is also a qualified pilot.

2011 Regional List Result

Parties	Total Vote	%	Constituency Result	Additional Members
Labour Party	82,699	45.7	7	0
Conservative Party	**35,459**	**19.6**	**1**	**2**
Others	30,218	16.7	0	0
Plaid Cymru	21,850	12.1	0	2
Liberal Democrats	10,798	6.0	0	0

Electorate: 469,486 Turnout: 38.6%

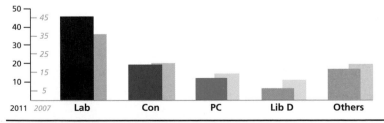

AM for South Wales East

Jocelyn DAVIES Plaid Cymru

National Assembly for Wales
Cardiff Bay, Cardiff CF99 1NA
Email: jocelyn.davies@wales.gov.uk

Constituency Office:
1 Griffiths Buildings, Victoria Terrace
Newbridge NP11 4ET
Tel: (01495) 241100
Website: www.jocelyndavies.plaidcymru.org

Jocelyn Davies was first elected to the National Assembly in 1999. Born in Usk in 1959, she was educated at Newbridge Grammar School, Gwent Tertiary College and later read Law at Oxford University. She previously worked in local government and was an Islwyn Borough Councillor 1987-91. In 1993 she became one of the first lay inspectors of schools in Wales. In 1995 she contested the Islwyn by-election for Plaid Cymru following the resignation of Neil Kinnock from Parliament and his appointment as a European Commissioner. In December 2010 Jocelyn Davies was named 'Welsh Politician of the Year' following the successful passage of the Housing LCO.

At present, Jocelyn serves as Plaid Cymru's Business Manager and Chief Whip. She Chairs the Finance Committee along with being a member of Business Committee and the Children and Young People Committee. She also Chairs the Cross Party Groups on Childhood Sexuality – Sexualisation and Equality and Violence Against Women and Children. Her political interests include constitutional affairs, special educational needs and housing. Jocelyn is married with three children.

2011 Regional List Result

Parties	Total Vote	%	Constituency Result	Additional Members
Labour Party	82,699	45.7	7	0
Conservative Party	35,459	19.6	1	2
Others	30,218	16.7	0	0
Plaid Cymru	**21,850**	**12.1**	**0**	**2**
Liberal Democrats	10,798	6.0	0	0

Electorate: 469,486 Turnout: 38.6%

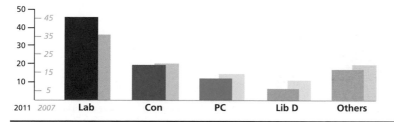

Lindsay WHITTLE Plaid Cymru

National Assembly for Wales
Cardiff Bay, Cardiff CF99 1NA
Tel: (029) 2089 8719
Email: lindsay.whittle@Wales.gov.uk

Constituency Office:
2 Portland Buildings, Commercial Street
Pontypool NP4 6JS
Tel: (01495) 763278
Website: www.lindsaywhittle.plaidcymru.org

Lindsay Whittle was elected to the Assembly in 2011, having previously contested the Caerphilly seat at the 2003 and 2007 elections, as well as the previous seven Westminster elections. Born in Caerphilly in 1953, prior to entering the Assembly Lindsay had a professional career of several decades as a Housing Manager in Cardiff. He has repeatedly won local council elections since he entered politics in 1976. He was first elected Leader of Caerphilly County Borough Council between 1999 and 2004 and for a second time from 2008 to 2011.

He is currently Plaid Cymru Spokesperson for Social Services, Children and Equal Opportunities and sits on the Health and Social Care Committee and the Public Accounts Committee. His political interests include housing and local government, as well as issues such as combating homelessness. Lindsay is a passionate Welsh Rugby fan, creating some controversy when he travelled to Australia to support Wales during the Assembly term in 2012.

2011 Regional List Result

Parties	Total Vote	%	Constituency Result	Additional Members
Labour Party	82,699	45.7	7	0
Conservative Party	35,459	19.6	1	2
Others	30,218	16.7	0	0
Plaid Cymru	**21,850**	**12.1**	**0**	**2**
Liberal Democrats	10,798	6.0	0	0

Electorate: 469,486 Turnout: 38.6%

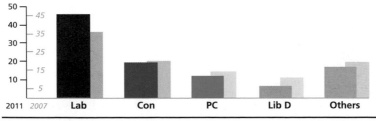

AM for South Wales East

William GRAHAM Conservative

National Assembly for Wales
Cardiff Bay, Cardiff CF99 1NA
Tel: (029) 2089 8348
Email: william.graham@wales.gov.uk

Constituency Office:
19a East Street, Baneswell
Newport NP20 4BR
Tel: (01633) 250455
Website: www.williamgrahamam.com

William Graham has been a regional member for South Wales East since 1999. He has contested Newport West in previous elections, but, due to the changes in electoral law, he has been a list candidate only since 2007. Born in 1949, he is the sixth generation principal of a family firm of surveyors established in Newport in 1844. He is a fellow of the Royal Institution of Chartered Surveyors, and has been Chairman of Newport Harbour Commission and Rougemont School Trust, Newport. A member of numerous organizations, he has been on the Listed Building Advisory Committee and the Rent Assessment Committee for Wales. He was Leader of the Conservative group on Newport County Borough Council until June 2004.

William is currently the Welsh Conservatives Shadow Minister for Social Services, Business Manager and Chief Whip. He is also a member of the Business Committee and the Health and Social Care Committee. He was an Assembly Commissioner from 2007 until 2011 and has previously held the Local Government, Social Justice and Education opposition portfolios. A married father of three, outside of politics, William is a breeder of pedigree Suffolk sheep.

2011 Regional List Result

Parties	Total Vote	%	Constituency Result	Additional Members
Labour Party	82,699	45.7	7	0
Conservative Party	**35,459**	**19.6**	**1**	**2**
Others	30,218	16.7	0	0
Plaid Cymru	21,850	12.1	0	2
Liberal Democrats	10,798	6.0	0	0

Electorate: 469,486 Turnout: 38.6%

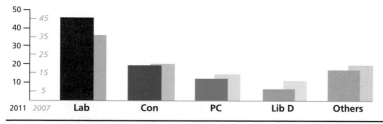

Labour	**Plaid Cymru**	**Conservative**	**Liberal Democrat**	**Comm**
Alana Davies	Bethan Jenkins	Suzy Davies	Peter Black	John Morrissey
Geraint Hopkins	David Lloyd	Byron Davies	Stuart Rice	Laura Picand
Marie John	Myfanwy Davies	Altaf Hussain	Cheryl Green	David Brown
Edward Jones	Linet Purcell	Helen Baker	Wayne Morgan	Dan Cole
		Matthew Voisey	Frank Little	
		Steve Gallagher		
		Dayne Powell		
		Gareth Williams		

S Wales West	Labour	Plaid Cymru	Conservative	Lib Dem	Comm	Green
Total	**71,766**	**21,258**	**27,457**	**10,683**	**464**	**3,952**
Share of Vote	46.5%	13.8%	17.8%	6.9%	0.3%	2.6%
Electorate	407,333			Turnout	38.2%	

	Con	Lab	Lib D	PC
Constituency result	0	7	0	0
Additional Members:	2	0	1	1

Regional AMs:		Reserve
Conservative	Suzy Davies	Altaf Hussain
Conservative	Byron Davies	Helen Baker
Plaid Cymru	Bethan Jenkins	Dai Lloyd
Liberal Democrats	Peter Black	Stuart Rice

Previous AMs: **Janet Davies** (PC) 1999-2007; **Dai Lloyd** (PC) 1999-2011; **Alun Cairns** (Con) 1999-2011

Green Party

WCP

UKIP

SLP

BNP

Green Party	WCP	UKIP	SLP	BNP
Keith Ross	David Griffths	David Bevan	David Leonard Davies	Clive Bennett
Huw Evans	Dick Van Steenis	John Atkinson	Derek Roy Isaacs	Adam Walker
Delyth Margaret Miller	Maggie Harrold	Tim Jenkins	Shangara Singh Bhatoe	Sion Owens
Andrew Paul Chyba	Ray Bridgman	David Rodgers	Ranjit Singh Bhatoe	Adam Lloyd

TUSC

Ronnie Job	Alec Thraves	Rob Williams	
Owen Herbert	Caroline Butchers	Rob Owen	
Mark Evans	Dave Phillips		
Les Woodward	Helen Stew		
Claire Job	Martin White		

WCP	UKIP	SLP	BNP	TUSC	Total
1,602	**6,619**	**5,057**	**4,714**	**809**	**154,381**
1.0%	4.3%	3.3%	3.1%	0.5%	

The regional election in **South Wales West** saw the Conservatives gain a seat at the expense of Plaid Cymru, who saw a 3.9% drop in their share of the vote. With Alun Cairns having been elected MP for the Vale of Glamorgan in 2010, two new faces were elected from the Conservative list in Suzy Davies and Byron Davies. Bethan Jenkins and Peter Black kept their seats for Plaid Cymru and the Liberal Democrats respectively while Dr Dai Lloyd was to lose out having first been elected during the first Assembly in 1999. Again, the overwhelming dominance of Labour - winning all seven constituency seats - left the other parties to claim the proportional list seats and yet again, the South Wales West region saw the lowest turnout in the whole of Wales.

Peter BLACK Liberal Democrat

National Assembly for Wales
Cardiff Bay, Cardiff CF99 1NA
Tel: (029) 2089 8744
Email: peter.black@wales.gov.uk
Website: www.southwaleslibdems.org.uk

Constituency Office:
1st Floor, 70 Mansel Street
Swansea SA1 5TN
Tel: (01792) 536353
Website: peterblack.blogspot.com

SOUTH WALES WEST

Peter Black has been a member for the Assembly's South Wales West region since 1999, although he did contest the Swansea East constituency in 1999 and 2003. Born in Bebington, Wirral in 1960, he was educated at Wirral Grammar School for Boys and Swansea University, graduating in English and History. A Councillor for the Cwmbwrla ward on Swansea City and County Council, he was Leader of the Liberal Democrat Group 1984-99. He previously worked as a research assistant for West Glamorgan Social Services and for the Land Registry for Wales, 1982-99. He is a past Chair of the Liberal Democrats Wales and of the Party's Finance and Administration Committee.

A former Deputy Minister in the 2000-03 coalition administration, he is currently his party's Business Manager and Spokesperson for Local Government, Heritage, Housing and Finance. Peter is currently a member of the Assembly Commission, Communities, Equality and Local Government Committee and the Finance Committee. His political interests include digital technologies, housing, local government and social justice and his personal interests include science fiction, film, theatre, and poetry.

2011 Regional List Result

Parties	Total Vote	%	Constituency Result	Additional Members
Labour Party	71,766	46.5	7	0
Conservative Party	27,457	17.8	0	2
Plaid Cymru	21,258	13.8	0	1
Others	23,217	15.0	0	0
Liberal Democrats	**10,683**	**6.9**	**0**	**1**

Electorate: 407,333 Turnout: 37.9%

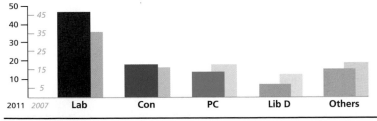

AM for South Wales West

Byron DAVIES Conservative

National Assembly for Wales
Cardiff Bay, Cardiff CF99 1NA
Tel: (029) 2089 8929
Email: Byron.Davies@Wales.gov.uk
Website: www.byrondavies.org.uk

Constituency Office:
Ground Floor, St James Gardens
Uplands, Swansea SA1 6DY
Tel: (01792) 654049
Website: www.byrondavies.org.uk

Byron Davies was elected in 2011, having previously contested the Gower constituency at the 2007 election. Born in 1952 in Gower, Byron was educated at Knelston County Primary School and Gowerton Boys' Grammar School and has an honours degree in law. He has spent his career in the Metropolitan Police service, where he served for a number of years at the UK National Crime Squad. During this time, he was seconded to the European Union as an advisor on combating organised crime. He also spent several years living and working in Eastern Europe, helping to prepare EU candidate countries for accession. He is the author of European Union Commission progress reports for several countries in the Balkan region and prior to election to the Assembly continued this work as an independent advisor.

He is currently the Welsh Conservatives Shadow Minister for Transport and Regeneration and also serves as the party's Whip. He sits on the Enterprise and Business Committee and the Procurement Task and Finish Group. He lists his political interests as home affairs, policing, foreign affairs, EU enlargement and transport.

2011 Regional List Result

Parties	Total Vote	%	Constituency Result	Additional Members
Labour Party	71,766	46.5	7	0
Conservative Party	**27,457**	**17.8**	**0**	**2**
Plaid Cymru	21,258	13.8	0	1
Others	23,217	15.0	0	0
Liberal Democrats	10,683	6.9	0	1

Electorate: 407,333 Turnout: 37.9%

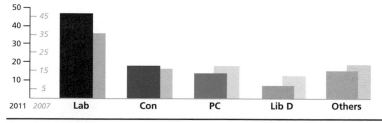

Bethan JENKINS Plaid Cymru

National Assembly for Wales
Cardiff Bay CF99 1NA
Tel: (029) 2089 8713
Email: bethan.jenkins@wales.gov.uk

Constituency Office:
75 Briton Ferry Rd, Melincryddan
Neath SA11 1AR
Tel: (01639) 643549
Website: www.bethanjenkinsblog.org.uk

SOUTH WALES WEST

Bethan Jenkins was first elected to the National Assembly in 2007, where, at the age of 25 she became the youngest Member of the institution. Born in 1981 in Aberdare, she is an Aberystwyth graduate in International Politics and International History. Whilst at University, she served as Women's Officer for the Aberystwyth Guild of Students, was Campaigns Officer in 2003 and President of the Students Union in 2004. During 2004-05 she established a new Plaid Cymru Youth Movement, Cymru X, and also worked as a research assistant for Jill Evans MEP. Bethan has also been a Senate member of Cymdeithas yr Iaith Gymraeg. During her time in office she has led a high-profile campaign to create a £1m framework to help those with eating disorders.

In the Assembly, Bethan is currently Plaid Cymru Spokesperson for Heritage, Welsh Language and Sport. She is a member of the Petitions Committee and the Communities, Equality and Local Government Committee. She is also Chair of the Cross Party Groups on Eating Disorders; Human Rights; Media and Broadcasting and Muscular Dystrophy. Bethan's political interests include economic development, international affairs, women's rights, asylum matters, the safeguarding of local services and eating disorder provision in Wales.

2011 Regional List Result

Parties	Total Vote	%	Constituency Result	Additional Members
Labour Party	71,766	46.5	7	0
Conservative Party	27,457	17.8	0	2
Plaid Cymru	**21,258**	**13.8**	**0**	**1**
Others	23,217	15.0	0	0
Liberal Democrats	10,683	6.9	0	1

Electorate: 407,333 Turnout: 37.9%

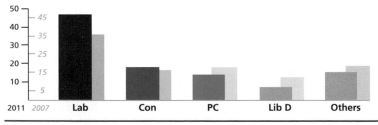

AM for South Wales West

Suzy DAVIES Conservative

National Assembly for Wales
Cardiff Bay, Cardiff CF99 1NA
Tel: (029) 2089 8883
Email: Suzy.Davies@wales.gov.uk
Website: www.suzydaviesam.com

Constituency Office:
Ground Floor, St James Gardens
Uplands, Swansea SA1 6DY

Suzy Davies was elected in 2011 having previously fought the Brecon & Radnor seat at the 2007 Assembly election and the 2010 General Election. Born in 1963, after a career in marketing and management which began at Swansea Grand Theatre, Suzy practised as a high street solicitor for many years. She has been a trustee of a number of children's projects and volunteered with community support groups. She has also been a member of two health focus groups and has served as a community councillor and a school governor. Suzy has written for various publications and was one of the founding board members of the Welsh International Film Festival.

Suzy was appointed Shadow Minister for Welsh Language and Culture in May 2011. She is also a member of the Assembly's Children and Young People Committee and the Constitutional and Legislative Affairs Committee. Suzy is married with two sons.

2011 Regional List Result

Parties	Total Vote	%	Constituency Result	Additional Members
Labour Party	71,766	46.5	7	0
Conservative Party	**27,457**	**17.8**	**0**	**2**
Plaid Cymru	21,258	13.8	0	1
Others	23,217	15.0	0	0
Liberal Democrats	10,683	6.9	0	1

Electorate: 407,333 Turnout: 37.9%

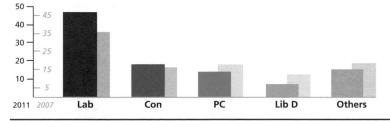

MEP for Wales

Jill EVANS Plaid Cymru

Office Address:
45 Gelligaled Rd
Ystrad, Rhondda CF41 7RQ
Tel: (01443) 441395
Fax: (01443) 441395

Email: jill.evans@europarl.europa.eu
Website: www.jillevans.net

Jill Evans was first elected to the European Parliament in 1999. In 2003 she was elected Vice President of Plaid Cymru. Born in the Rhondda in 1959, she is currently Plaid Cymru's sole representative in the European Parliament. She is a graduate of the University of Wales, Aberystwyth and the former Polytechnic of Wales. She worked for the National Federation of Women's Institutes in Wales, before taking up a post as Wales Regional Organiser for CHILD - the National Infertility Support Network. Jill Evans served as a Councillor for Ystrad for seven years. In the European Parliament she is a member of the Green / Europe Free Alliance (EFA) Group, serving as President of EFA and Vice-President of the Greens / EFA Group. She is also a member of the Committee on the Environment, Public Health and Food Safety and the Delegations for relations with Iraq. In 2007, Jill Evans stood for election to the Assembly as Plaid Cymru candidate for Rhondda. She was elected unopposed to the Presidency of Plaid Cymru in 2010.

MEP for Wales

Dr Kay SWINBURNE Conservative

Office Address:
Rhumney House, Copse Walk,
Cardiff Gate Business Park, Cardiff CF23 8RB
Tel: (029) 2054 0895

Email: kayswinburnemep@welshconservatives.com
Website: www.kayswinburne.co.uk

Dr Kay Swinburne was elected to the European Parliament in 2009, replacing Jonathan Evans who stood down to become the prospective Parliamentary candidate for Cardiff North. Born in Aberystwyth in 1967, and raised in Llandysul, she is a fluent Welsh speaker. She graduated in Biochemistry and Microbiology from King's College London, and gained a Ph.D from the University of Surrey. Previously, she worked as a city banker for Deutsche Bank before resigning following an employment tribunal which found in her favour. Later she became an adviser on Central and Eastern European healthcare issues and a government and corporate adviser on biotechnology and pharmaceutical privatisation. Kay Swinburne has also been a Community Councillor and a former town Mayor. She is currently the European Conservatives and Reformists Group's Co-ordinator on the Economics and Monetary Committee in the European Parliament; and the ECR Group's Co-ordinator on the Special Committee on the Financial, Economic and Social Crisis.

MEP for Wales

MEP for Wales

John BUFTON UKIP

Office Address:
1 Caspian Point
Pierhead Street, Cardiff Bay
Cardiff CF10 4DQ
Tel: (029) 2044 4060
Fax: (029) 2044 4061

Email: john.bufton@europarl.europa.eu
Website: www.johnbufton.eu

John Bufton was the first UKIP candidate to be elected in Wales, when his Party secured enough support at the European election in 2009 to return a member. Born in 1962 in Llanidloes, he was educated at Llandrindod Wells High School, before joining his family haulage business. He later pursued a career in the health and social care sector managing a Local Authority residential care home for the elderly. In 1987 he was elected to Rhayader Town Council before becoming an Independent Powys County Councillor for Rhayader in 1996. At the 1997 General Election, John Bufton was the Referendum Party candidate for Montgomeryshire before joining UKIP and fighting the Ceredigion by-election in 2000. He was the lead candidate on the North Wales regional list for UKIP at the National Assembly election in 2007. in 2009, John Bufton was appointed to serve on the Committee on Regional Development at the European Parliament. His social activities include rugby, swimming and music.

MEP for Wales

Derek VAUGHAN Labour

Office Address:
Labour European Office
4th Flr, Transport House, 1 Cathedral Road
Cardiff CF11 9SD
Tel: (029) 2022 7660
Fax: (029) 2022 4759

Email: contact@derekvaughanmep.org.uk
Website: www.derekvaughanmep.org.uk

Derek Vaughan was born in Merthyr Tydfil in 1961 and was educated at Afon Taf High School and Swansea University. He worked as an engineering apprentice at Hoover and the Valuation Office Agency before becoming a full time Trade Union official for the PCS union. From the mid-1980s he was a Community Councillor and Mayor, before being elected to the shadow Neath Port Talbot Council in 1995. He held a number of positions, including Cabinet Member for Economic Development, before becoming the Leader of the Council in 2004. He is also a former Leader of the Welsh Local Government Association. In the European Parliament, he is Vice-Chair of the Delegation to the ACP-EU Joint Parliamentary Assembly and a member of the Committee on Budgets. In his spare time, Derek enjoys playing and watching cricket and football.

grayling

We are Wales' longest standing public affairs and public relations agency, located in the heart of Cardiff Bay.

Grayling Wales provides the expertise and knowledge to help you get ahead and effectively engage with Welsh politics, media and society.

- Strategic political counsel and advice
- Political monitoring and analysis
- Influencing and engaging
- Event management
- Public relations
- Campaigns
- Public consultations

We benefit from being part of an integrated network of offices across Westminster, Edinburgh, Brussels and worldwide.

Ni yw'r asiantaeth materion cyhoeddus a chysylltiadau cyhoeddus hynaf yng Nghymru, yn gweithio o ganol Bae Caerdydd.

Mae Grayling Cymru yn cynnig yr arbenigedd a'r wybodaeth i'ch helpu i symud ymlaen a bod yn rhan effeithiol o wleidyddiaeth, y cyfryngau a chymdeithas yng Nghymru.

- Cyngor ac arweiniad gwleidyddol strategol
- Monitro a dadansoddi gwleidyddol
- Dylanwadu ac ymgysylltu
- Rheoli digwyddiadau
- Cysylltiadau cyhoeddus
- Ymgyrchoedd
- Ymgynghoriadau cyhoeddus

Rydym yn elwa o fod yn rhan o rwydwaith integredig o swyddfeydd yn San Steffan, Caeredin, Brwsel a ledled y byd.

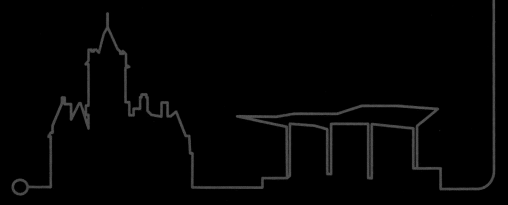

02920 462 507 | wales@grayling.com | www.grayling.co.uk/wales
2 Caspian Point | Caspian Way | Cardiff CF10 4DQ

The **Wales** Yearbook

13

NATIONAL ASSEMBLY

Cynulliad
Cenedlaethol
Cymru

National
Assembly for
Wales

National Assembly for Wales
Cardiff Bay
Cardiff CF99 1NA
Tel: (0845) 010 5500
Website: www.assemblywales.org

The National Assembly for Wales is the democratically elected body that represents the interests of Wales and its people, makes laws for Wales, and holds the Welsh Government to account. The Assembly is made up of 60 elected Assembly Members. Forty are chosen to represent individual constituencies, and 20 are chosen to represent the five regions of Wales (North Wales, Mid and West Wales, South Wales West, South Wales Central and South Wales East). Assembly Members represent their area as a member of a political party or as an independent candidate.

Presiding Officer

Rosemary Butler AM

The Assembly's Presiding Officer is Rosemary Butler AM. In addition to being the Chair of the Assembly Commission, one of the PO's key responsibilities is to chair the Assembly's Plenary meetings, ensuring that order is maintained at all times and that the rights of Members are protected. She is also responsible for the Assembly's Standing Orders and is the final authority on their interpretation.

The Presiding Officer chairs the Business Committee, which determines the business of Plenary meetings. It meets early in the Assembly week and its members are the Government's Minister with responsibility for business (the Leader of the House) and the Business Managers from each of the political parties. The Committee discusses and notes what business the Government has decided to schedule for the next few weeks, while it formally agrees how much time to allocate for Assembly business (such as opposition debates, committee debates and Individual Member debates). It also considers Assembly procedures and revisions to its Standing Orders as well as timetables for legislation and the committee structure and remits.

The Presiding Officer represents the Assembly at many events and hosts visits to the Senedd, including Royal visits and elected representatives from other parliaments and foreign dignitaries.

Deputy Presiding Officer

David Melding AM

The role of Deputy Presiding Officer, David Melding AM, is also set out in the Assembly's Standing Orders, and states "in the absence or at the request of the Presiding Officer, the Deputy must exercise the functions of the Presiding Officer..."

The main function of the Deputy Presiding Officer is to alternate with the Presiding Officer in chairing Assembly Plenary sessions. He also supports the Commission by leading on the Pierhead as a centre for Assembly development and debate, and its links with the Wales Governance Centre.

The Deputy Presiding Officer also attends meetings and functions in his own right as well as on behalf of the Presiding Officer in order to raise the profile of the National Assembly for Wales.

NATIONAL ASSEMBLY FOR WALES

The Assembly Commission

The Assembly Commission serves the National Assembly to help make it a strong, accessible and forward-looking democratic institution and legislature that delivers effectively for the people of Wales. Its role is to provide the National Assembly with the staff, property and services required to fulfil this role.

The Commission consists of the Presiding Officer and four Assembly Members, one nominated by each of the four party groups represented in the Assembly.

The portfolios of each Commissioner are detailed below:

Rosemary Butler AM (Welsh Labour)

Presiding Officer and Commission Chair, with lead responsibility for the Assembly's communications, and for the professional development of Assembly Members and their staff.

Angela Burns AM (Welsh Conservatives)

Commissioner with responsibility for budget, governance, including Audit Committee membership, and links with the Remuneration Board. Angela also has responsibility for the improvement of services to Assembly Members, as well as the Commission's role as the employer of Assembly staff.

Peter Black AM (Welsh Liberal Democrats)

Peter is the Commissioner with responsibility for ICT, broadcasting and e-democracy, the Assembly estate, facilities and the sustainability agenda.

Sandy Mewies AM (Welsh Labour)

Commissioner with responsibility for education services, the Assembly shop, front of house, catering and security. Sandy also has responsibility for the Commission's statutory equality functions.

Rhodri Glyn Thomas AM (Plaid Cymru)

Rhodri is the Commissioner with responsibility for the Commission's Welsh language functions and policy, legal services and Freedom of Information requests.

NATIONAL ASSEMBLY FOR WALES

Chief Executive and Clerk of the Assembly **Claire Clancy**

Claire Clancy took up post as Chief Executive and Clerk of the National Assembly in February 2007. She is responsible for ensuring that the Assembly, and the sixty Assembly Members, are provided with the property, staff and services necessary to help develop an Assembly that inspires confidence and has a reputation within Wales and beyond for accessible and efficient democracy.

Claire Clancy has spent many years working in organizations with a strong delivery culture, with a clear focus on serving customers. Before she joined the Assembly, she was Chief Executive of Companies House and Registrar of Companies, with a £70m turnover and 1,200 employees. Earlier she was Director of Corporate Services at the Patent Office. In the late 1990s, she spent two years on the island of St Helena while her husband was Chief Secretary and later Governor; here she did some teaching and other voluntary work such as preparing plans for a museum for the island. She joined the civil service in 1977 and has worked in the Manpower Services Commission, Department of Employment, Government Office for the South West and was Chief Executive of the private sector led Powys Training and Enterprise Council. She has a degree in psychology from the Open University.

The Fourth Assembly

In March 2011, the people of Wales voted 'yes' in a referendum that gave the National Assembly for Wales additional law-making powers. The result meant that the National Assembly is able to make laws on all matters in the 20 subject areas for which it has powers, without needing the UK Parliament's agreement.

The first year of the Fourth Assembly has also been a year in which the Assembly has significantly changed the way that business operates, through the work of Plenary and our Committee structures.

Making Plenary more responsive to the people of Wales

Plenary meetings are central to the Assembly's democratic role, where Members hold the Welsh Government's policies and actions to account, where they scrutinise and agree laws, and where Members raise issues of importance on behalf of the people they represent.

As part of the Presiding Officer's commitment to making the Assembly better reflect the needs of the people of Wales, there are new opportunities for Members to raise important issues that affect their constituents and to bring them to the attention of the Assembly and to seek a response from the Government.

Regular slots for **Individual Member Debates** have been introduced. These are motions that have the support of Members from at least three parties, and are selected by the Business Committee for debate once every half term.

The Presiding Officer has also introduced a specific slot during Questions to the First Minister for **Leaders' Questions**. Each of the leaders of the opposition groups (Welsh Conservatives, Plaid Cymru and the Welsh Liberal Democrats) are called in turn by the Presiding Officer to ask up to three questions without notice. This allows them the freedom to ask any question to the First Minister on matters within the Welsh Government's responsibilities.

Making the Assembly's committees more accessible

The National Assembly for Wales's committees are responsible for scrutinising legislation, policy, expenditure and the administration of the Welsh Government and associated public bodies. At the start of the Fourth Assembly, significant changes were also made to the structure of the Assembly's committee system.

Instead of having separate legislative and scrutiny committees, from the beginning of the Fourth Assembly, committees scrutinise both policy and legislation. As a result, Members with expertise in specific policy areas can apply that knowledge to legislation, and can understand the practical effects this legislation would have.

The change was also designed to make it easier for people to engage with the Assembly's scrutiny process. Under the new system, individuals or organizations are able to contact one committee that looks at both policy and legislation, rather than having to switch between separate committees and groups of Members.

An additional advantage of this approach is that it gives committees flexibility to deal with new parts of the legislative process such as White Papers, draft Bills, and Bills.

The streamlining of the committee system has resulted in a total of 11 committees, including five policy committees looking at legislation and policy areas.

These are the **Children and Young People Committee**, the **Communities, Equality and Local Government Committee**, the **Enterprise and Business Committee**, the **Environment and Sustainability Committee** and the **Health and Social Care Committee**.

The National Assembly's Committees have cross-cutting portfolios, and collectively, they can scrutinise any aspect of the Welsh Government's work. One of their primary methods for doing so is through an inquiry.

What is a committee inquiry?

The definition of a committee inquiry is quite broad. Depending on the issue under scrutiny, it can range from a committee taking evidence over several months, culminating in a report and recommendations to hearing oral evidence over the course of one day, which the committee publishes without writing a full report. (Instead, a review of the evidence could be sent directly to a Welsh Government Minister).

The inquiry can be undertaken either by the whole committee, or by a sub-group of some of its members (known as a rapporteur group or a task and finish group), who undertake the work on behalf of the committee.

Deciding which issue comes under a committee's scrutiny

There are a number of ways a committee can choose the subject of an inquiry. For example, it can result from Members' political and personal experiences and interests, or as a result of conversations Members may have had with representatives of organizations or individuals, either through contact with a committee as a whole, or with individual Members.

A committee can also look at issues that have come to the Assembly's notice as a result of a petition submitted to the Assembly's **Petitions Committee**. This Committee enables the people of Wales to raise issues and directly influence the work of the National Assembly. A petition is a way of asking the National Assembly to consider any issue, problem or proposal that it has the power to do something about.

Once a committee has decided on the subject of an inquiry, its work generally follows a set procedure, and offers a number of opportunities when individuals and organizations can influence the committee's work.

Call for evidence

After announcing the subject of its inquiry, a committee will typically issue a request for information (usually referred to by committees as a 'call for evidence'). This may be about the main themes of the inquiry, or specific questions might be asked. The call for evidence will normally be placed on the committee's pages on the Assembly website, on the Assembly's social network pages and through the media.

Anyone can respond to the committee's request for evidence. A committee will also generally contact any organizations it thinks will be interested in its work, or that it would specifically like to hear from.

Other ways of gathering information

As well as traditional written evidence, a committee may actively gather information in other ways, including **visits** to see people, organizations or places that will have a bearing on its work. Committees can also hold **informal meetings** in locations other than the Senedd, which are often less intimidating for people wanting to provide information to the committee. People are also able to submit **video-clips, images** and **multi-media presentations** for committees to use as evidence. The Assembly's clerking teams are always happy to discuss other ways of taking evidence that may be more appropriate for you or your organization.

The Assembly's new legislative competence

The Assembly is able to make laws on a number of different subjects, as set out in Schedule 7 of the Government of Wales Act 2006. A Bill is a draft law, and once it has been considered and passed by the Assembly, and given Royal Assent by the Monarch, it becomes an Act of the Assembly.

The Progress of an Assembly Bill

There are currently four different ways a Bill can be introduced in the Assembly. These are by means of a Government Bill; a Committee Bill; a Commission Bill; or a Member Bill. Following its introduction, there are four stages of scrutiny prior to receiving Royal Assent.

Further detail about a Bill's passage from Stage One onwards is set out below.

Stage 1

The role of the responsible Committee at Stage 1 is to consider and report on the general principles of the Bill (also referred to as Stage 1 Scrutiny). It is normal practice that the Committee will launch a general consultation, open to anyone, as well as invite stakeholders to provide written and oral evidence to inform its work. **It is at this point in the process where members of the public can get most involved with the scrutiny process by submitting their views on a Bill to the Committee**.

At the end of its Stage 1 scrutiny, the responsible Committee must publish a report, which may contain a recommendation that the Assembly either agrees or does not agree to the general principles of the Bill. The report may also contain recommendations for amendments to the Bill, based on the evidence the Committee has received during the course of its Stage 1 scrutiny.

Once the responsible Committee has reported on the Bill, the Assembly - in Plenary - will debate and decide whether to agree to the general principles of the Bill – the 'Stage 1 Debate'. If the Assembly has agreed to the general principles of a Bill at Stage 1, the Bill proceeds to Stage 2.

Stage 2

Stage 2 starts on the first working day after Stage 1 is completed. It is the first of two main amending stages in the Assembly's legislative process. Any Assembly Member may table an amendment for consideration at this stage, but only Committee members can vote on them. Time is built into the process to allow Assembly Members to receive representation from outside groups and to prepare and table amendments to the Bill.

For each Stage 2 Committee meeting, a Marshalled List and a Groupings List are prepared and published. These lists set out the order of proceedings. Voting on amendments in Committee is 'on the nod'. The Chair will put the question that an amendment be agreed and, unless there are any objections, that amendment is agreed. Where any Member objects, the Committee is asked to vote on the amendment in question, and a simple majority in favour of an amendment is required for that amendment to be agreed. Stage 2 is completed once the last amendment has been disposed of by the responsible Committee.

Stage 3

Stage 3 begins on the first working day after the completion of Stage 2. It is the second of the Assembly's main amending stages and takes place in Plenary. Again, any Assembly Member may table an amendment for consideration but at this stage, all Members are able to vote on them.

Unlike Stage 2 proceedings, where any admissible amendment is able to be moved and debated, the Presiding Officer may select those amendments which are to be taken at Stage 3 proceedings.

For each Stage 3 meeting, a Marshalled List and a Groupings List are prepared and published. Again, as with Stage 2 proceedings, a simple majority in favour of an amendment is required for that amendment to be agreed. Stage 3 is completed when the last amendment has been disposed of.

Standing Orders provide for a further, optional amendment stage, called the Report Stage. This Stage will only take place where the Member in charge of the Bill proposes it, and the Assembly agrees.

This Stage provides the last opportunity for Members to amend the Bill. The same procedures that apply for the purpose of Stage 3 also apply to Report Stage.

Stage 4

At Stage 4, the Assembly will vote on a motion to pass the final text of the Bill. A motion that a Bill be passed may not be moved unless the text of the Bill is available in both English and Welsh.

A simple majority in favour of the motion is required for the Bill to be passed.

Royal Assent

Once passed by the Assembly, a Bill must be submitted to the Queen for Royal Assent. Once a Bill has received Royal Assent, it becomes an Act of the Assembly.

The following pages set out, in diagram form, the process for introducing Assembly Bills through to them receiving Royal Assent:

GOVERNMENT BILLS*

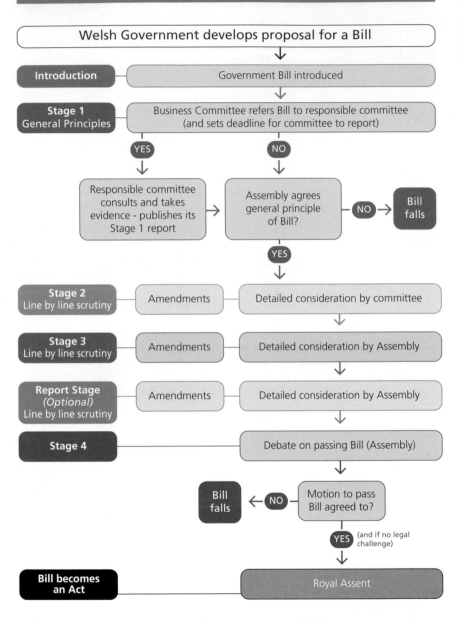

Welsh Government develops proposal for a Bill

Introduction — Government Bill introduced

Stage 1
General Principles — Business Committee refers Bill to responsible committee (and sets deadline for committee to report)

YES

NO

Responsible committee consults and takes evidence - publishes its Stage 1 report

Assembly agrees general principle of Bill?

NO → Bill falls

YES

Stage 2
Line by line scrutiny — Amendments — Detailed consideration by committee

Stage 3
Line by line scrutiny — Amendments — Detailed consideration by Assembly

Report Stage
(Optional)
Line by line scrutiny — Amendments — Detailed consideration by Assembly

Stage 4 — Debate on passing Bill (Assembly)

Bill falls ← NO — Motion to pass Bill agreed to?

YES (and if no legal challenge)

Bill becomes an Act — Royal Assent

* The process for the scrutiny of both **Committee** and **Commission Bills** follows the same procedure as for a Government Bill

MEMBER BILLS

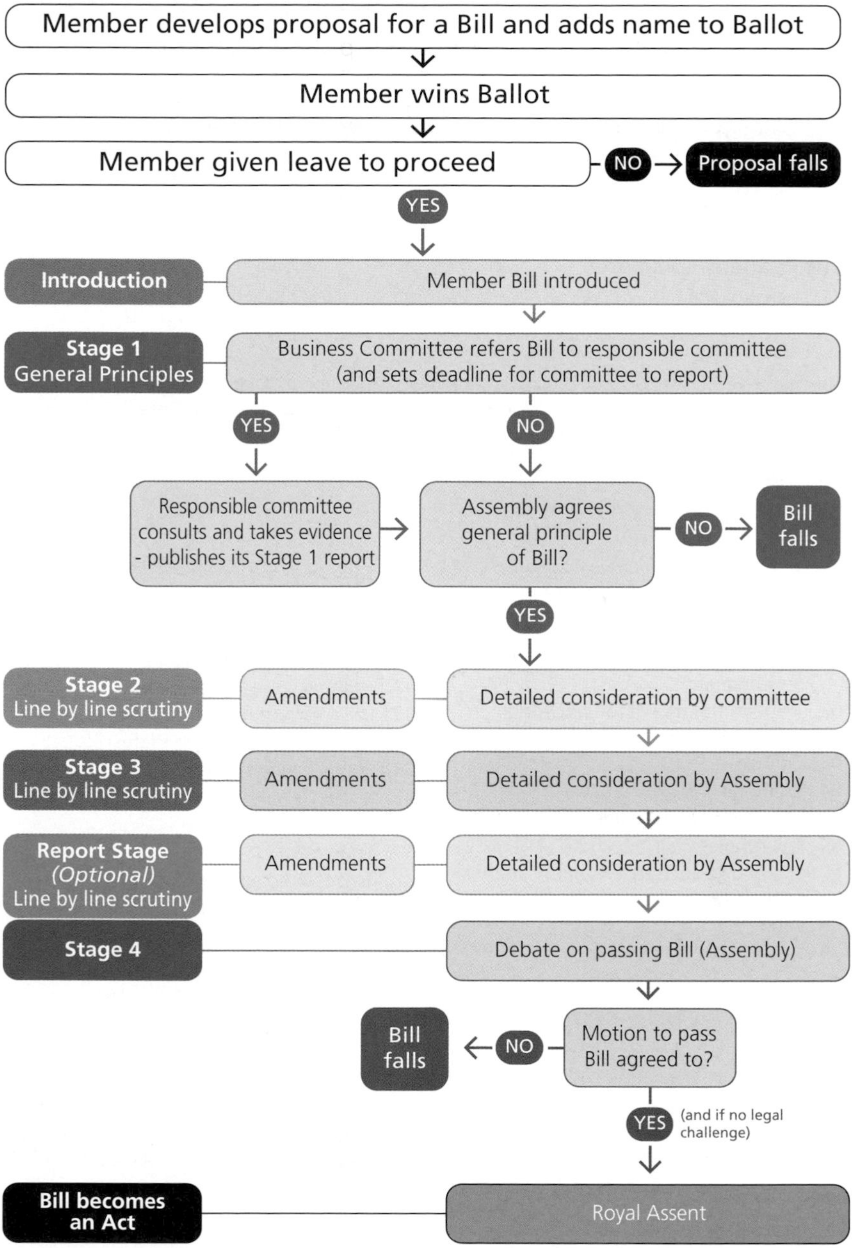

Member develops proposal for a Bill and adds name to Ballot

↓

Member wins Ballot

↓

Member given leave to proceed —**NO**→ **Proposal falls**

YES
↓

Introduction — Member Bill introduced

↓

Stage 1
General Principles — Business Committee refers Bill to responsible committee (and sets deadline for committee to report)

YES — **NO**

↓ ↓

Responsible committee consults and takes evidence - publishes its Stage 1 report → Assembly agrees general principle of Bill? —**NO**→ **Bill falls**

YES
↓

Stage 2
Line by line scrutiny — Amendments — Detailed consideration by committee

↓

Stage 3
Line by line scrutiny — Amendments — Detailed consideration by Assembly

↓

Report Stage
(Optional)
Line by line scrutiny — Amendments — Detailed consideration by Assembly

↓

Stage 4 — Debate on passing Bill (Assembly)

↓

Bill falls ←**NO**— Motion to pass Bill agreed to?

YES (and if no legal challenge)
↓

Bill becomes an Act — Royal Assent

NATIONAL ASSEMBLY

Petitioning the Assembly

The petitions process enables the people of Wales to raise issues and directly influence the work of the Assembly. A petition is a way of asking the National Assembly to consider any issue, problem or proposal that it has the power to do something about. Since launching its formal petitions system in 2007, the Assembly's Petitions Committee has, on average, considered 82 petitions a year on topics ranging from public toilets to pit ponies. The Assembly's system ensures that all admissible petitions are considered by a dedicated committee. The system was set up to enable members of the public who feel strongly about an issue to gather support and submit a petition to the Assembly in a way that is accessible and meaningful.

The Petitions Committee

The Assembly has set up a Petitions Committee to consider petitions and to decide what action should be taken. If there is something that you would like to change about life in Wales, you can start a petition to raise your concerns.

The Petitions Committee's role is to consider all admissible petitions that are submitted to the Assembly. The Petitions Committee is made up of four Assembly Members – **William Powell AM (Chair), Russell George AM, Bethan Jenkins AM and Joyce Watson AM**.

Your petition

Petitions must meet a small number of terms and conditions set by the Assembly for them to be considered by the Petitions Committee.

One of the main conditions is that your petition must be about one of the devolved subject areas in which the National Assembly for Wales can make laws for Wales.

The National Assembly can make laws for Wales in the following areas affecting your life:

01 Agriculture, fisheries, forestry and rural development
02 Ancient monuments and historic buildings
03 Culture
04 Economic development
05 Education and training
06 Environment
07 Fire and rescue services and promotion of fire safety
08 Food
09 Health and health services
10 Highways and transport
11 Housing
12 Local government
13 National Assembly for Wales
14 Public administration
15 Social welfare
16 Sport and recreation
17 Tourism
18 Town and country planning
19 Water and flood defence
20 Welsh language

As long as the issue you would like to raise falls in to one of these areas and meets the other terms and conditions, you can start a petition.

You can contact the Petitions team by emailing: **petition@wales.gov.uk** or calling: **(029) 2089 8998**.

Getting started

The easiest way to submit your proposal is through the Assembly website, **www.assemblywales.org**. We also welcome traditional paper petitions.

To help you get started, contact the Petitions team to discuss the wording of your petition. We'll work with you to help make sure that your petition can be considered by the National Assembly for Wales and we'll explain the types of issues that cannot be considered. We recommend you do this before you start collecting signatures.

Collecting signatures

As an individual, you will need to collect at least ten signatures for your petition to be considered. If you are an organization, or even an unincorporated association or group, you only need one signature.

See **www.assemblywales.org/e-petitions** for more details on collecting signatures online.

Submitting your petition

Petitions hosted on our website - Once the deadline for collecting signatures online has passed and as long as the petition has collected at least ten signatures, it will be placed on the next available Petitions Committee agenda for first consideration.

Paper petitions - You can also submit paper petitions to the Petitions team. We would always advise you to contact the Petitions team with your petition wording before collecting signatures. This is to make sure that the subject of your petition falls within the remit of the Welsh Government or the National Assembly for Wales. The Petitions Committee cannot consider petitions on subjects that do not fall within this remit. If the wording of your petition has not been discussed with the Petitions team beforehand, it will need to be assessed for admissibility before it goes any further.

If it is admissible, your petition will then be considered by the Petitions Committee. The Committee will consider your petition and will decide on the best course of action to take.

Presenting your petition - Once your petition has finished collecting signatures, you can formally present it to members of the Petitions Committee on the steps of the Senedd in Cardiff Bay. This provides you with an opportunity to meet committee members and chat to them about the issue, and also to gather some publicity for your petition.

What happens next?

The Committee can take a number of actions to progress your petition, including:

- writing to the Welsh Government or any other relevant organization for further information or clarification on an issue;
- inviting petitioners or any other body to present oral evidence. This usually does not happen until at least the second consideration of a petition. Not all petitioners will be invited to give evidence, and it is up to the Committee to decide who to invite;
- seeking further information from the Assembly's Research Service or Legal Service;
- conducting a short inquiry into the issue;
- asking another committee to consider the issue. Whether the issue is considered by that committee, and the form which that consideration takes, is up to the members of that committee.

When further information is received, the petition is considered again by the Petitions Committee. The Committee members decide what action to take in light of this new information. We'll get in touch with you before the Committee considers your petition to let you know when the meeting is taking place. We will also let you know the outcomes following the meeting. All committee meetings can be viewed online at: **www.senedd.tv**.

NATIONAL ASSEMBLY

Case studies

Since the petitions process was launched in 2007, the people of Wales have used petitions to make their voices heard in a number of ways.

Fishguard Trains

Two young people submitted a petition in 2009 calling for more train services to Fishguard. Their petition was part of a broader campaign, which included using Facebook to gather support and engaging with their local Assembly Member to raise the issue in the Assembly. The Petitions Committee wrote to the Minister with responsibility for this area and referred the issue to the Enterprise and Learning Committee who considered it as part of their inquiry into rail infrastructure in Wales. As a result of the combined representations and recommendations, the Minister funded five additional train services to and from Fishguard.

Ffynone and Cilgwyn Woodlands

In February 2011, the Public Accounts Committee reported on the Forestry Commission Wales and public funding of Ffynone and Cilgwyn woodlands.

The inquiry followed a petition received by the Assembly's Petitions Committee from people that were unhappy that half a million pounds was paid to a group for the purchase of woodland in north Pembrokeshire in 2006.

The inquiry that followed found that Forestry Commission Wales had, in this instance, failed in its duty to properly consult the local community and had not applied proper due process to ensure value for public money.

The Committee called on the Forestry Commission Wales to tighten up its processes for awarding grants.

Get in touch

Now the Assembly wants to hear from you. Whether it's something that affects your town or village, or an issue that is of concern to your interest group or society, petitions can help you make it known to the Assembly.

If you are interested in submitting a petition, please contact us on: **(029) 2089 8998** or email: **petition@wales.gov.uk**

We are also happy to meet you in person.

The Petitions team
National Assembly for Wales
Cardiff Bay CF99 1NA

www.assemblywales.org
www.assemblywales.org/e-petitions

NATIONAL ASSEMBLY COMMITTEES

National Assembly Committees

Committees in the Assembly carry out many functions, including scrutinising the expenditure and policies of the Welsh Government, holding Ministers to account, and examining proposed legislation.

Children & Young People Committee

The Committee was established on 22 June 2011 with a remit to examine legislation and hold the Welsh Government to account by scrutinising expenditure, administration and policy matters encompassing: the education, health and wellbeing of the children and young people of Wales, including their social care. Email: cypcommittee@wales.gov.uk

Chair: Christine Chapman (Lab) **Members:** Angela Burns (Con); Jocelyn Davies (PC); Rebecca Evans (Lab); Suzy Davies (Con); Julie Morgan (Lab); Lynne Neagle (Lab); Jenny Rathbone (Lab); Aled Roberts (Lib D); Simon Thomas (PC) **Clerk:** Claire Morris Tel: (029) 2089 8148

Committee for the Scrutiny of the First Minister

The Committee was established on 2 May 2012 with a remit to scrutinise the First Minister on any matter relevant to the exercise of the functions of the Welsh Government. Email: fm.scrutiny@wales.gov.uk

Chair: David Melding (Con) **Members:** Paul Davies (Con); Mark Drakeford (Lab); Elin Jones (PC); Eluned Parrott (Lib D)

Communities, Equality & Local Government Committee

The Committee was established on 22 June 2011 with a remit to examine legislation and hold the Welsh Government to account by scrutinising expenditure, administration and policy matters encompassing: Wales's culture; languages communities and heritage, including sport and the arts; local government in Wales, including all housing matters; and equality of opportunity for all. Email: celg.committee@wales.gov.uk

Chair: Ann Jones (Lab) **Members:** Peter Black (Lib D); Janet Finch-Saunders (Con); Mike Hedges (Lab); Mark Isherwood (Con); Bethan Jenkins (PC); Gwyn R Price (Lab); Ken Skates (Lab); Rhodri Glyn Thomas (PC); Joyce Watson (Lab) **Clerk:** Marc Wyn Jones Tel: (029) 2089 8120

Constitutional & Legislative Affairs Committee

The Committee was established on 15 June 2011 with a remit to carry out the functions of the responsible committee set out in Standing Orders 21.2 and 21.3 and to consider any other legislative matter, other than the functions required by Standing Order 26, referred to it by the Business Committee.
Email: cla.committee@wales.gov.uk

Chair: David Melding (Con) **Members:** Suzy Davies (Con); Julie James (Lab); Eluned Parrott (Lib D); Simon Thomas (PC) **Clerk:** Steve George Tel: (029) 2089 8242

Enterprise & Business Committee

The Committee was established on 22 June 2011 with a remit to examine legislation and hold the Welsh Government to account by scrutinising its expenditure, administration and policy, encompassing economic development; transport and infrastructure; employment; higher education and skills; and research and development, including technology and science. Email: enterprise.committee@wales.gov.uk

Chair: Nick Ramsay (Con) **Members:** Byron Davies (Con); Keith Davies (Lab); Julie James (Lab); Alun Ffred Jones (PC); Eluned Parrott (Lib D); David Rees (Lab); Ken Skates (Lab); Dafydd Elis-Thomas (PC); Joyce Watson (Lab) **Clerk:** Siân Phipps Tel: (029) 2089 8582

Environment & Sustainability Committee

The Committee was established on 22 June 2011 with a remit to examine legislation and hold the Welsh Government to account by scrutinising expenditure, administration and policy matters encompassing: the maintenance, development and planning of Wales's natural environment and energy resources.
Email: es.comm@wales.gov.uk

Chair: Dafydd Elis-Thomas (PC) **Members:** Mick Antoniw (Lab); Keith Davies (Lab); Russell George (Con); Vaughan Gething (Lab); Llyr Huws Gruffydd (PC); Julie James (Lab); William Powell (Lib D); David Rees (Lab); Antoinette Sandbach (Con) **Clerk:** Alun Davidson Tel: (029) 2089 8639

NATIONAL ASSEMBLY COMMITTEES

Finance Committee

The Committee was established on 22 June 2011. The Finance Committee's role is to carry out the functions set out in Standing Order 19. This includes consideration of the use of resources by the Assembly Commission or Welsh Ministers, and in particular reporting during the annual budget round. The Committee may also consider any other matter relating to expenditure from the Welsh Consolidated Fund. Email: financecommittee@wales.gov.uk

Chair: Jocelyn Davies (PC) **Members:** Peter Black (Lib D); Christine Chapman (Lab); Paul Davies (Con); Mike Hedges (Lab); Ann Jones (Lab); Julie Morgan (Lab); Ieuan Wyn Jones (PC) **Clerk:** Gareth Price Tel: (029) 2089 8409

Health & Social Care Committee

The Committee was established on 22 June 2011 with a remit to examine legislation and hold the Welsh Government to account by scrutinising expenditure, administration and policy matters encompassing: the physical, mental and public health of the people of Wales, including the social care system. Email: hsccommittee@wales.gov.uk

Chair: Mark Drakeford (Lab) **Members:** Mick Antoniw (Lab); Rebecca Evans (Lab); Vaughan Gething (Lab); William Graham (Con); Elin Jones (PC); Darren Millar (Con); Lynne Neagle (Lab); Lindsay Whittle (PC); Kirsty Williams (Lib D) **Clerk:** Llinos Dafydd Tel: (029) 2089 8403

Petitions Committee

The Petitions Committee was established on 15 June 2011. Its role is to consider all admissible petitions that are submitted by the public. Petitions must be about issues that the National Assembly has powers to take action on. The petitions process enables the public to highlight issues and directly influence the work of the National Assembly. Its specific functions are set out in Standing Order 23. Email: petition@wales.gov.uk

Chair: William Powell (Lib D) **Members:** Russell George (Con); Bethan Jenkins (PC); Joyce Watson (Lab) **Clerk:** Abigail Phillips Tel: (029) 2089 8421

Public Accounts Committee

The Committee was established on 22 June 2011. The role of the Public Accounts Committee is to ensure that proper and thorough scrutiny is given to Welsh Government expenditure. The specific functions of the Committee are set out in Standing Order 18. The Committee may consider reports prepared by the Auditor General for Wales on the accounts of the Welsh Government and other public bodies, and on the economy, efficiency and effectiveness with which resources were employed in the discharge of public functions. Their remit also includes specific statutory powers under the Government of Wales Act 2006 relating to the appointment of the Auditor General, his or her budget and the auditors of that office. Email: publicaccounts.comm@wales.gov.uk

Chair: Darren Millar (Con) **Members:** Mohammad Asghar (Con); Mike Hedges (Lab); Julie Morgan (Lab); Gwyn R Price (Lab); Jenny Rathbone (Lab); Aled Roberts (Lib D); Lindsay Whittle (PC) **Clerk:** Tom Jackson Tel: (029) 2089 8597

Standards of Conduct Committee

The Standards Committee was established on 22 June 2011. The Committee's role is to carry out the functions set out in Standing Order 22. These include: the investigation of complaints referred to it by the Standards Commissioner; consideration of any matters of principle relating to the conduct of Members; establishing procedures for the investigation of complaints, and arrangements for the Register of Members' interests and other relevant public records determined by Standing Orders. Email: standards@wales.gov.uk

Chair: Mick Antoniw (Lab) **Members:** Llyr Huws Gruffydd (PC); Mark Isherwood (Con); Kirsty Williams (Lib D) **Clerk:** Lara Date Tel: (029) 2082 1821

Business Committee

The Business Committee is responsible for the organization of Assembly Business. It is the only Committee whose functions and remit is set out in Standing Orders. Its role is to "facilitate the effective organization of Assembly proceedings" as stated in Standing Order 11.1. Email: business.committee@wales.gov.uk

Chair: Rosemary Butler (Lab) **Members:** Jocelyn Davies (PC); William Graham (Con); Jane Hutt (Lab); Aled Roberts (Lib D); David Melding (Con) **Clerk:** Anna Daniel Tel: (029) 2089 8144

AMs' Chamber Contributions

The following table provides information on the number of Written Questions, Oral Questions and Statements of Opinion tabled by each Assembly Member during the 4th Assembly up to 22 June 2012. The number of oral questions listed refers to those tabled by individual Members. Oral questions that are not answered by the Minister in the Chamber receive a written reply. Neither Ministers, nor the Presiding Officer, generally put down questions.

AMs	WQ	OQ	SO	AMs	WQ	OQ	SO
Antoniw, Mick	2	43	7	James, Julie	0	29	3
Andrews, Leighton (M)	0	0	0	Jenkins, Bethan	16	52	13
Asghar, Mohammed	62	29	2	Jones, Alun Ffred	8	43	2
Black, Peter	33	36	2	Jones, Ann	6	39	2
Burns, Angela	159	38	2	Jones, Carwyn (FM)	0	0	0
Butler, Rosemary (PO)	0	0	0	Jones, Elin	7	28	1
Chapman, Christine	0	38	1	Jones, Ieuan Wyn	10	13	0
Cuthbert, Jeff (DM)	0	0	0	Lewis, Huw (M)	0	0	0
Davies, Alun (DM)	0	1	0	Melding, David (DPO)	22	20	1
Davies, Andrew RT	439	52	7	Mewies, Sandy	0	29	2
Davies, Byron	42	10	0	Millar, Darren	266	29	4
Davies, Jocelyn	2	27	1	Morgan, Julie	5	52	4
Davies, Keith	0	53	1	Neagle, Lynne	14	45	3
Davies, Paul	87	45	0	Parrot, Eluned	38	33	2
Davies, Suzy	12	33	2	Powell, William	29	32	5
Drakeford, Mark	2	40	0	Price, Gwyn	0	28	1
Elis-Thomas, Dafydd	3	34	1	Ramsay, Nick	63	48	0
Evans, Rebecca Mary	145	32	10	Rathbone, Jenny	0	55	1
Finch-Saunders, Janet	73	28	0	Rees, David	14	33	1
George, Russell	51	28	3	Roberts, Aled	69	49	4
Gething, Vaughan	0	30	5	Sandbach, Antoinette	248	37	0
Graham, William	10	40	1	Sargeant, Carl (M)	0	0	0
Gregory, Janice (CW)	0	0	0	Skates, Ken	0	23	3
Griffiths, John (M)	0	0	0	Thomas, Gwenda (DM)	0	0	0
Griffiths, Lesley (M)	0	0	0	Thomas, Rhodri Glyn	25	33	8
Gruffydd, Llyr Huws	24	37	2	Thomas, Simon	46	70	6
Hart, Edwina (M)	0	0	0	Watson, Joyce	0	19	2
Hedges, Mike	10	44	12	Whittle, Lindsay	7	30	0
Hutt, Jane (M)	0	0	0	Williams, Kirsty	218	22	3
Isherwood, Mark	55	46	3	Wood, Leanne	40	32	1

Does not include data for Presiding Officer who does not normally table questions, make contributions to debates, or participate in divisions. Any records where Rosemary Butler (or any other AM temporarily in the Chair) is acting as Deputy Presiding Officer are counted as Presiding Officer records and do not appear in the AMs tally of contributions.

Key:

OQ - Oral Questions to Ministers
WQ - Written Questions to Ministers
SO - Statements of opinion

(M) - Minister
(DM) - Deputy Minister
(CW) - Chief Whip
(PO) - Presiding Officer
(DPO) - Deputy Presiding Officer

Register of AMs' Financial and Other Interests - April 2012

The form for National Assembly Members to register their interests is prescribed by the Presiding Officer and has the following ten categories:

Category 1: Directorships
Category 2: Remuneration Employment, Office, Profession, etc
Category 3: The Names of Clients
Category 4: Gifts, hospitality, material benefit or advantage
Category 5: Remuneration or other material benefit
Category 6: Financial sponsorships
Category 7: Overseas visits
Category 8: Land & Property
Category 9: Shareholdings
Category 10: Public bodies
Inspection of the Register

Leighton Andrews (Rhondda) – Labour

1. Directorship - Director of Powerhouse Building Trust (unremunerated) (SO 4.3 - Band 1 – Less than 5 hours per week). *2. Remunerated Employment* – Spouse: BTs Director for Wales; Commissioner for Wales – Equality and Human Rights commission; Executor of the Literary Estate of Gwenlyn Parry (unremunerated). *4. Gifts, hospitality, etc* – Ticket and hospitality for Wales v Scotland rugby match on 12 February 2012 from Scottish and Southern Electricity. *5. Remuneration or other material benefit* – Spouse is BTs Director for Wales. *6. Financial Sponsorship* – Expenses for 2011 Assembly Elections paid by Rhondda Constituency Labour Party. *8. Land and Property* – Owns a flat in London which is rented out. Spouse is co-owner of a property in Gwynedd which is rented out. *10. Membership/Chairmanship of bodies in receipt of Assembly funds* – Member: Author of a book published by Seren which may from time to time receive public funding. Honorary Professor - School of Journalism, Media and Cultural Studies, Cardiff University (unremunerated). Vice President - Rhondda Sea Cadets. Member - Rhondda Trust. Spouse: Member - All Wales Programme Monitoring Committee on behalf of Business Wales. Member - CBI Council for Wales.

Mick Antoniw (Pontypridd) – Labour

1. Directorships – Director – The Bevan Foundation (not for profit company/charity think tank on social justice issues) (SO 4.3 - Band 1 - Less than 5 hours per week). *2. Remunerated Employment, Office, Profession etc* – Management Committee member (unpaid) – people Press Printing Society Limited (SO 4.3 – Band 1 – Less than 5 hours a week). *6. Financial Sponsorship* – £5000 sponsorship for 2011 election from GMB Trade Union. *8. Land and Property* – Joint ownership with spouse of a flat in Bath. *10. Membership/Chairmanship of bodies in receipt of Assembly funds* – Member – Welsh Refugee Council; Member – Pen yr Enfys.

Mohammad Asghar (South Wales East) – Conservative

2. Remunerated Employment, Office, Profession etc – Proprietor in Accountancy firm. (SO 4.3 - Band 2 – between 5 and 20 hours per week). Spouse works as a part time assistant in Member's constituency office. *6. Financial Sponsorship* – All 2011 election expenses met by Conservative. Party. *8. Land and Property* – Member – owns a commercial property in Newport Spouse: Owns two properties, one in Newport and one in London. *10. Membership/Chairmanship of bodies in receipt of Assembly funds* – Patron - Life Map Planners. Employment of Family Members – Name of Employee: Mrs Firdaus Asghar ;Family Member of: Mohammad Asghar, AM Relationship of Employee to AM: Wife. Capacity in which employed: Case worker. Date employment commenced: 27 October 2008. Date employment ceased (if appropriate): N/A. Hours contracted to work: 22.2. Name of Employee: Natasha Asghar; Family Member of: Mohammad Asghar, AM; Relationship of Employee to AM: Daughter Capacity in which employed: Press Officer and Researcher; Date employment commenced: 3 January 2012 Date employment ceased (if appropriate): N/A; Hours contracted to work: 37.

Peter Black (South Wales West) – Liberal Democrat

2. Remunerated Employment, Office, Profession etc – Member: Councillor – City and County of Swansea (SO 4.3 - Band 2 – between 5 and 20 hours per week). Spouse: Employed as a translator by the City and County of Swansea. *4. Gifts, hospitality, etc* – Lunch provided by British Retail Consortium. Ticket and hospitality for Swansea v Wigan football game from City and County of Swansea. Ticket and hospitality for Wales v Switzerland football match (7 October 2011) from the Swiss Embassy. *5. Remuneration or other material benefit* – £12,858 pa as Councillor on Swansea Council. Rental income from Swansea and Gower Liberal Democrats – funds paid back to National Assembly for Wales. *6. Financial Sponsorship* – £21,000 sponsorship for 2011 elections from South Wales West Liberal Democrats. *10. Membership/Chairmanship of bodies in receipt of Assembly funds* – Member - City and County of Swansea. Member - Governing body of Pentrehafod Comprehensive School. Vice President - Heart of Wales Line Travellers Association. Vice President - West Glamorgan Ramblers Association. Member - Council and Court of Governors of Swansea University (ceased from 4/8/11). Governor – Cwmbwrla Manselton Primary School. Record of Membership of Societies – Bevan Foundation; Friends of Hay Festival; Institute of Welsh Affairs.

Angela Burns (Carmarthen West & South Pembrokeshire) – Conservative

1. Directorships – Spouse: Director of RHS.com Ltd – an Internet Shopping Service. *2. Remunerated Employment, Office, Profession etc* – Spouse: Director of RHS.com Ltd – an Internet Shopping Service. Employed part time by Angela Burns, AM as a senior researcher and case visitor. *6. Financial Sponsorship* – 2011 Election expenses met in part by Carmarthen West and South Pembrokeshire Conservative Association. *9. Shareholdings* – Member: Shareholder in RHS.com Ltd. Spouse: Shareholder in RHS.com Ltd. Employment of Family Members – Name of Employee: Andrew Burns; Family Member of: Angela Burns, AM; Relationship of Employee to AM: Husband; Capacity in which employed: Media/Press; Researcher; Constituency Surgeries and Visits Planning; Date employment commenced: 30 August 2007; Date employment ceased (if appropriate): N/A; Hours contracted to work: 18.5.

Rosemary Butler (Newport West) – Labour

4. Gifts, hospitality, etc – Two First Class Rail tickets from First Great Western – to be donated to local charity or other organization. *6. Financial Sponsorship* – 2011 Election expenses met by Newport West Constituency Labour Party and included a donation from UNITE (£1000).

Christine Chapman (Cynon Valley) – Labour

2. Remunerated Employment, Office, Profession etc – Spouse is a registered GP – Partner in a GP practice in Caerphilly. Payment received from the Committee of the Regions for rapporteur report. *6 Financial Sponsorship* – All 2011 election expenses paid through Cynon Valley Constituency Labour Party. *8. Land and Property* – Husband owns a share in Tonyfelin Medical Practice, Caerphilly. *10. Membership/Chairmanship of bodies in receipt of Assembly funds* – Member – South East Wales Construction Forum (unpaid); Member – Springboard Wales Advisory Board (unpaid) – Membership Ceased on 30 June 2011; Member of the Rathbone Cymru Advisory Council (unpaid).

Jeff Cuthbert (Caerphilly) – Labour

4. Gifts, hospitality, etc – Tickets to Wales v Australia rugby match as corporate guest of GE Aviation Tickets to Blues v Ospreys rugby match from GE Aviation. *6. Financial Sponsorship* – All 2011 election expenses met by Caerphilly Constituency Labour Party. Sponsorship for Christmas Card Competition totalling £320 from Nuaire Ltd and Thomas Carroll PLC. *8. Land and Property* – Owner of a flat in Llanishen (rented out). Owner of residential property in Rhiwbina. *10. Membership/Chairmanship of bodies in receipt of Assembly funds* – Chair – Caerphilly Miners' Centre for the Community; Member – Gelligaer Historical Society; Patron – Homestart Cwm Rhymni. Record of Membership of Societies – Corporate Member – Chartered Institute of Personnel and Development; Member – UNITE; Member – Co-Operative Party; Member – Bevan Foundation; Member – Diabetes UK; Member – Royal British Legion; President – Ystrad Mynach Boys and Girls Club; Vice President – Aber Valley YMCA; President – Caerphilly Parkinson's Society.

Alun Davies (Blaenau Gwent) – Labour

2. Remunerated Employment, Office, Profession etc – Partner: Member of Powys County Council; Employed by Alun Davies, AM as office manager on 6 month contract (30 hours per week). *6. Financial Sponsorship* – 2011 Election expenses met by the constituency Labour party, including contributions from UNISON (£500) and the Co-operative Party (£400). *8. Land and Property* – Member owns 50% of a property in Tredegar. Employment of Family Members – Name of Employee: Clair Powell; Family Member of: Alun Davies, AM; Relationship of Employee to AM: Partner; Capacity in which employed: Office Manager; Date employment commenced: 1 June 2011; Date employment ceased (if appropriate): (6 month contract); Hours contracted to work: 30.

Andrew R T Davies (South Wales Central) – Conservative

1. Directorships – T.J. Davies & Sons – Farming Business (SO 4.3 - Band 2 – between 5 and 20 hours per week). *2. Remunerated Employment, Office, Profession etc* – Partner in T.J. Davies & Sons – Farming Business (SO 4.3 Band 2 – between 5 and 20 hours per week). *4. Gifts, hospitality, etc* – 6 Nations rugby tickets and hospitality from WRU. *6. Financial Sponsorship* – 2011 Election expenses were met by the Welsh Conservative Party – South Wales Central. *8. Land and Property* – Farmland and Building in the Vale of Glamorgan. *10. Membership/Chairmanship of bodies in receipt of Assembly funds* – Member – National Farmers Union Fallen Stock Scheme; Life Governor – Royal Welsh Agricultural Society; 2 tickets and hospitality for Wales v Australia from the WRU. Employment of Family Members – Name of Employee: Julia Mary Davies; Family Member of: Andrew RT Davies, AM; Relationship of Employee to AM: Wife; Capacity in which employed: Research Analyst; Date employment commenced: 1 June 2007 (p/t –f/t from Sept 07); Date employment ceased (if appropriate): N/A; Hours contracted to work: 37.5.

Byron Davies (South Wales West) – Conservative

1. Directorships – Member and Spouse are Directors of Blueline Solutions Europe Ltd (training and investigations company) (SO 4.3 - Band 1 – less than 5 hours per week). *4. Gifts, hospitality, etc* – Train ticket to London from First Great Western to attend meeting of the Cross Party Group on Rail; Ticket and hospitality to Wales v France rugby match (6 Nations 2012) from Director BBC Cymru Wales. *6. Financial Sponsorship* – 2011 election expenses met by the Conservative Party. *8. Land and Property* – Own 1 residential rented property in Hertfordshire and 1 holiday cottage and 3 acres of land in Ceredigion.

Jocelyn Davies (South Wales East) – Plaid Cymru

2. Remunerated Employment, Office, Profession etc – Spouse: Councillor on Caerphilly CBC Employed part time by Jocelyn Davies, AM in her Constituency Office. *4. Gifts, hospitality, etc* – First Class train ticket to London from First Great Western to attend meeting of the Cross Party Group on Rail. *6. Financial Sponsorship* – £500 towards 2011 election expenses paid by Fire Brigades Union. Remainder paid by Plaid Cymru. *8. Land and Property* – Parental home in Gwent held in trust for siblings. *10. Membership/Chairmanship of bodies in receipt of Assembly funds* – Spouse: Chair - Pentwynmawr Community Centre; Chair of Governors at Pentwynmawr Primary School. Record of Membership of Societies – Member of Plaid Cymru Credit Union. Employment of Family Members – Name of Employee: Michael Davies; Family Member of: Jocelyn Davies, AM; Relationship of Employee to AM: Partner; Capacity in which employed: Constituency office administrative support; Date employment commenced: May 2007; Date employment ceased (if appropriate): N/A; Hours contracted to work: 24.

Keith Davies (Llanelli) – Labour

2. Remunerated Employment, Office, Profession etc – Spouse: Producer for Tinopolis (TV Company) Dependent Child: Part Time Bar person – Bucket and Spade Public House. *4. Gifts, hospitality, etc* – Two First Class Rail tickets from First Great Western – to be donated to local charity. *6. Financial Sponsorship* – 2011 Election expenses met by Constituency Labour Party. *8. Land and Property* – Spouse owns a residential rented property in Radyr. *10. Membership/Chairmanship of bodies in receipt of Assembly funds* – Governor – Strade School; Governor – Furnace Community Primary School.

Paul Davies (Preseli Pembrokeshire) – Conservative

2. Remunerated Employment, Office, Profession etc – Spouse: Financial administrator for Hywel Dda Local Health Board. *6. Financial Sponsorship* – All expenses for 2011 Assembly election paid by Welsh Conservative Party. *9. Shareholdings* – Member: Shares in Lloyds TSB; Spouse: Shares in Lloyds TSB. *10. Membership/Chairmanship of bodies in receipt of Assembly funds* – Member – North Pembrokeshire Transport Forum; President - Pembrokeshire Peoples First; Member - Clynderwen & District Young Farmers; Show Society; Member - Friends of Theatr Gwaun; Member – Pembrokeshire Agricultural Society; Spouse: Member - Clynderwen & District Young Farmers; Show Society Member – Pembrokeshire Agricultural Society; Member – Paul Sartori Foundation. Record of Membership of Societies – Patron – Cleddau Community Arts.

Suzy Davies (South Wales West) – Conservative

2. Remunerated Employment, Office, Profession etc – Spouse: Partner – H E Davies & Co (farming business); Partner – Bryn Uchel Caravan Park. 4. Gifts, hospitality, etc – Entry ticket to Urdd eisteddfod from the Urdd; Theatre ticket from WMC; Ticket to Wales v France (6 Nations 2012) from ITV Wales. *6. Financial Sponsorship* – 2011 Election expenses paid by South Wales West Conservatives. *8. Land and Property* – Spouse – owns a farm and caravan park in the Dyfi Valley, Powys. *10. Membership/Chairmanship of bodies in receipt of Assembly funds* – Member – Ystradgynlais Volunteer Centre; Governor – Ysgol Glantwymyn (Ceased).

Mark Drakeford (Cardiff West) – Labour

2. Remunerated Employment, Office, Profession etc – Professor: Research Supervision at Cardiff University. (SO 4.3 – Band 1 – less than 5 hours per week). *4. Gifts, hospitality, etc* – Ticket for Test Match at Cardiff from SWALEC (June 2011); Ticket for Cardiff Singer of the World from the BBC (June 2011); Guest at annual dinner – CBI Wales; Guest at annual political awards BMA Cymru; Two First Class rail tickets from Great Western to be donated to a local charity. *6 Financial Sponsorship* – All 2011 election expenses met by Cardiff West Labour Party. *7. Overseas Visits* – Cost of flights and accommodation for visit to Mondragon, Basque, Spain to research work of Mondragon Co-operative movement met by Co-Operative Group Ltd.

Dafydd Elis-Thomas (Dwyfor Meirionnydd) – Plaid Cymru

2. Remunerated Employment, Office, Profession etc – Member: Occasional Freelance contributor/presenter for: S4C; BBC Cymru; ITV Cymru and Literature Wales. (SO4.3 Band 1– less than 5 hours per week) Spouse: Head of the Parliamentary Translation and Reporting Service. *6. Financial Sponsorship* – All 2011 election expenses met by Plaid Cymru. *10. Membership/Chairmanship of bodies in receipt of Assembly funds* – President – University of Wales, Bangor; Honorary President of Coleg Llandrillo; Vice-President of the National Trust's Snowdonia Appeal. Record of Membership of Societies – Literature Wales.

Rebecca Evans (Mid & West Wales) – Labour

2. Remunerated Employment, Office, Profession etc – Member: Policy and Public Affairs Officer – National Autistic Society (employment ceased from 23-05-11); Spouse: Office Manager for John Griffiths, AM (from 2005). *6. Financial Sponsorship* – 2011 Election expenses met by Welsh Labour. Employment of Family Members – Name of Employee: Claire Elizabeth Stowell; Family Member of: Rebecca Evans, AM; Relationship of Employee to AM: Sister; Capacity in which employed: Office Assistant Date employment commenced: 11 May 2011 (6 month temporary contract permanent from 28 November 2011); Date employment ceased (if appropriate): N/A; Hours contracted to work: 14.48.

Janet Finch-Saunders (Aberconwy) – Conservative

2. Remunerated Employment, Office, Profession etc – Member: County Councillor – Conwy County Borough Council. (SO 4.3 - Band 2 – between 5 and 20 hours per week); Spouse: Proprietor – Pet Shop. *6. Financial Sponsorship* – 2011 Election expenses met by Aberconwy Conservative Association. *8. Land and Property* – Member and spouse joint owners of 4 retail properties and 2 residential properties (all rented out) in Aberconwy and Clwyd West areas. *10. Membership/Chairmanship of bodies in receipt of Assembly funds* – Member – "Friends of Queens Park" Craig-y-Don, Llandudno. Employment of Family Members; Name of Employee: Gareth Saunders; Family Member of: Janet Finch-Saunders, AM; Relationship of Employee to AM: Spouse Capacity in which employed: Office Manager; Date employment commenced: 15 March 2012; Date employment ceased (if appropriate): N/A; Hours contracted to work: 14.00.

Russell George (Montgomeryshire) – Conservative

1. Directorships – Director of Fuze Ltd – retail business. (SO 4.3 - Band 1 – less than 5 hours per week). 2. Remunerated Employment, Office, Profession etc – Fuze Ltd – Retail Business (SO 4.3 - Band 1 – less than 5 hours per week); County Councillor – Powys County Council (SO 4.3 - Band 2 – between 5 and 20 hours per week). *6. Financial Sponsorship* – Contribution to election expenses by Simon Baynes; Other election expenses met by Montgomeryshire Conservative Association. *10. Membership/Chairmanship of bodies in receipt of Assembly funds* – Member of Climate Change Commission for Wales.

Vaughan Gething (Cardiff South & Penarth) – Labour

2. Remunerated Employment, Office, Profession etc – Spouse – Solicitor with Thompsons Solicitors LLP. *4. Gifts, hospitality, etc* – Two First Class Rail tickets from First Great Western – to be donated to local charity/community group; Rail ticket to London from First Great Western for meeting of Cross Party Group on Rail. *6. Financial Sponsorship* – All 2011 Election expenses paid by Constituency Labour Party. *8. Land and Property* – Spouse – owns a residential property in Chester.

William Graham (South Wales East) – Liberal Democrat

2. Remunerated Employment, Office, Profession etc – Principal – Graham & Co, Chartered Surveyors. (SO4.3 - Band 2 – between 5 and 20 hours per week). *6. Financial Sponsorship* – All 2011 election expenses paid by Welsh Conservative Party. 8. Land and Property – Member and spouse own 5 commercial properties in Newport. Record of Membership of Societies – Member of Carlton Club, London SW1. Employment of Family Members; Name of Employee: William James Graham Family Member of: William Graham, AM; Relationship of Employee to AM: Son; Capacity in which employed: Researcher; Date employment commenced: May 2005; Date employment ceased (if appropriate): N/A; Hours contracted to work: 37.5.

Janice Gregory (Ogmore) – Labour

1. Directorships – Spouse – non-remunerated Director, Rockwool Woodland for Learning Centre. *2. Remunerated Employment, Office, Profession etc* – Member: Occasional fees (less than £100) from participating in research/surveys. Donated to Ogmore Constituency Labour Party. Spouse: Part time administrator for Janice Gregory, AM; Councillor – Bridgend County Borough Council; Member of Pencoed Town Council. *6. Financial Sponsorship* – 2011 Election expenses paid by Ogmore Constituency Labour Party including donations from UNITE (£1000) & USDAW (£2000). *8. Land and Property* – Joint ownership with spouse of a rental property abroad. *10. Membership/Chairmanship of bodies in receipt of Assembly funds* – Member: Patron – Brynawel House Alcohol Rehabilitation Centre (non-remunerated); Member – Maesteg Town Hall; Member – Bridgend Life Savers Credit Union; Vice President – Nantymoel Boys and Girls Club (unremunerated); Ambassador – Girl Guiding UK (Central Glamorgan Division), non–remunerated; Member – Gilfach Goch Communities First Partnership; Spouse: Governor – Croesty Primary School; Governor – Pencoed Primary School Member – Bridgend Life Savers Credit Union; Member – Pencoed Miners Welfare and Community Hall Management Committee. Employment of Family Members – Name of Employee: Kirsty Esther Twine; Family Member of: Janice Gregory, AM; Relationship of Employee to AM: Daughter; Capacity in which employed: Caseworker/Communications Officer; Date employment commenced: 23 June 2008; Date employment ceased (if appropriate): N/A; Hours contracted to work: 17.5. Name of Employee: Michael Gregory; Family Member of: Janice Gregory, AM; Relationship of Employee to AM: Husband; Capacity in which employed: Administrator / Researcher; Date employment commenced: 11 May 1999; Date employment ceased (if appropriate): N/A; Hours contracted to work: 18.

John Griffiths (Newport East) – Labour

2. Remunerated Employment, Office, Profession etc – Wife is employed by John Griffiths AM as an administrator. *4. Gifts, hospitality, etc* – Two First Class rail tickets from First Great Western – to be donated to local charity or other organization. *6. Financial Sponsorship* – Financial sponsorship for 2011 Assembly election from: UNITE (£1000); Community Trade Union (£1000); Co-operative Party (£400); UNISON (£250); Communications Workers Union (£110). Employment of Family Members – Name of Employee: Alison Kim Griffiths; Family Member of: John Griffiths, AM; Relationship of Employee to AM: Wife; Capacity in which employed: Administrator; Date employment commenced: 2 May 2003; Date employment ceased (if appropriate): N/A; Hours contracted to work: 37. Name of Employee: Paul Michael Evans; Family Member of: Rebecca Evans, AM; Relationship of Employee to AM: Spouse; Capacity in which employed: Office Administrator; Date employment commenced: 4 July 2005; Date employment ceased (if appropriate): N/A; Hours contracted to work: 37.5.

Lesley Griffiths (Wrexham) – Labour

2. Remunerated Employment, Office, Profession etc – Dependent Child – Catering Assistant, Grosvenor Garden Centre. Spouse (separated May 2008) – County Councillor Wrexham County Borough Council. *10. Membership/Chairmanship of bodies in receipt of Assembly funds* – Patron – The Venture, Wrexham; Vice President – North Wales Play and Playing Fields Association; Honorary President – National Eisteddfod, Wrexham 2011; Member – Wrexham Supporters Trust; Member – Bevan Foundation; Vice President – Llangollen International Musical Eisteddfod; Child (not dependent) Member of National Youth Choir for Wales. Record of Membership of Societies Honorary Member – Wrexham Rotary Club.

Llyr Huws Gruffydd (North Wales) – Plaid Cymru

2. Remunerated Employment, Office, Profession etc – Occasional broadcasting fees (SO 4.3 – Band 1 – Less than 5 hours a week). *6. Financial Sponsorship* – All costs for 2011 elections met by North Wales Region Committee, Plaid Cymru. *8. Land and Property* – Member and partner own a house in Rhuthun. *10. Membership/Chairmanship of bodies in receipt of Assembly funds* – Member - Royal Welsh Agricultural Society; Member – Barddas Member - Institute of Welsh Affairs; Chair - Llanfair DC, Pentrecelyn & Graigfechan Appeal Committee, Denbighshire National Eisteddfod 2013.

Edwina Hart (Gower) Labour

2. Remunerated Employment – Spouse is employed by Edwina Hart, AM as a part-time caseworker. *5. Remuneration or other material benefit* – Spouse is in receipt of a Civil Service pension; Spouse is an Employment Tribunal member. *6. Financial Sponsorship* – Expenses for 2011 Assembly Elections paid by Gower Constituency Labour Party and included donations from: Community Union (£1000); CWU, Valley Branch (£100); CWU, West Wales Branch (£300); UNITE (£1000) and ASLEF (£500). *8. Land and Property* – spouse owns a residential property in Swansea. *10. Membership/Chairmanship of bodies in receipt of Assembly funds* – Honorary Vice President - Heart of Wales Line; Travellers' Association Honorary Patron - Pontardulais Male Voice Choir; Honorary President - Ariosa Singers; Member of Women's Institute; Associate Member - RAFA – registered charity no. 226686; Honorary President (changed to Honorary Life Member with effect from 21/4/2012) - Gower Society; Honorary Patron - William King Educational Trust; Patron - Mumbles Symphony Orchestra; Honorary President - Forget-me-Not Dementia Day Clubs; Honorary President - Gorseinon Youth Choir; Honorary President - Voices in Harmony; Member - UNITE Union; Member - Community, the Union for Life. Employment of Family Members – Name of Employee: Robert Beveridge Hart; Family Member of: Edwina Hart, AM; Relationship of Employee to AM: Husband; Capacity in which employed: Caseworker (part time); Date employment commenced: 1/9/2000; Date employment ceased (if appropriate): N/A; Hours contracted to work: 30 hours per week reducing to 10 from 1 June 2011.

Mike Hedges (Swansea East) – Labour

2. Remunerated Employment, Office, Profession etc – Member: Councillor, Swansea Council (SO 4.3 - Band 2 –between 5 and 20 hours per week) Spouse: Community Care, Swansea Council. *4. Gifts, hospitality, etc* – Two First Class Rail tickets from First Great Western – to be donated to Ysgol Bryntawe for school raffle. *6. Financial Sponsorship* – 2011 Election expenses met by Swansea East Labour Party. *10. Membership/Chairmanship of bodies in receipt of Assembly funds* – Member of: UNITE; GMB; UNISON; Amnesty; OXFAM; Friends of the Earth; Socialist Health Association; Fabian Society; Governor – Ynystawe Primary; Governor – Glyncollen Primary.

Theodore Huckle (Counsel General)

2. Remunerated Employment, Office, Profession etc – Barrister – part time private practice (SO 4.3 -Band 2 – between 5 and 20 hours per week); Spouse: Solicitor – part time Associate with Morgan Cole, Cardiff. *5. Remuneration or other material benefit* – Spouse: - Morgan Cole, Solicitors Cardiff. *8. Land and Property* – Joint ownership with spouse of: Apartment – Les Arcs, France; Apartment – Cardiff Bay; House – Blaenavon.

Jane Hutt (Vale of Glamorgan) – Labour

2. Remunerated Employment, Office, Profession etc – Spouse is employed part time by the Joseph Rowntree Trust (Wales Advisor). *6. Financial Sponsorship* – Election 2011 expenses met by Vale of Glamorgan Labour Party. *10. Membership/Chairmanship of bodies in receipt of Assembly funds* – Member – SFUK (Shahjahan Foundation) (Resigned with effect from 30/7/11); Member - Gibbonsdown Communities First Partnership Board; Member - Vale Youth Forum; President - Vale Women's Network; Honorary President - Barry First Responders; Member - Vale People First; Patron - Thompson Street Estate Sensory Garden; Spouse: Trustee and Director - Vale of Glamorgan Music Festival; Chair, Trustee and Director - St Donats Arts Centre.

Mark Isherwood (North Wales) – Conservative

2. Remunerated Employment, Office, Profession etc – Spouse: Employed by Mark Isherwood, AM as a Constituency Assistant (5 hours per week); County Councillor for Llanfynydd on Flintshire County Council; Chair of Co-ordinating Scrutiny Committee (Flintshire County Council); Chair of Constitution Committee (Flintshire County Council); Member of Health and Social Care and Lifelong Learning Scrutiny Committees (Flintshire County Council); Dependent Child: Shop Assistant – New Look; Kitchen Porter – The Droid Inn; Assistant - McDonalds Restaurant. *6. Financial Sponsorship* – Election expenses met by the Member or the Welsh Conservative Party. *10. Membership/Chairmanship of bodies in receipt of Assembly funds* –

Patron - Tyddyn Bach Respite Centre; Vice President - North Wales Disability Resources Centre; Patron – British Association of Social Workers; Ambassador for Clwyd Girl Guides; Vice President – North Wales Play; Director – Wales Participatory Budgetary Unit; Vice Patron RORO sailing project; Patron – LGBT Foundation; Spouse: Chair of Governors – Abermorddu C.P School (Member from 1/3/12); Member – Dee Housing Shadow Board. Record of Membership of Societies – Member of Venture Housing Association; Former Member and Chairman – Mold Round Table; Shareholder Membership – Flintshire Care and Repair Ltd; Member – Vice President's Club, Boys and Girls Clubs of Wales; Member – North Wales Business Club; Spouse: Chair of Clwyd Theatre Cymru. Employment of Family Members – Name of Employee: Hilary Teresa Isherwood; Family Member of: Mark Isherwood, AM; Relationship of Employee to AM: Wife; Capacity in which employed: Constituency Caseworker; Date employment commenced: 2 May 2003; Date employment ceased (if appropriate): N/A; Hours contracted to work: 5.

Julie James (Swansea West) – Labour

1. Directorships – Director - Gower Research Consultancy Ltd (Consultancy services to Local Government and other public sector bodies) (SO 4.3 - Band 1 – less than 5 hours per week); Spouse: Director, Flattout Design Ltd (electronics consultancy). *2. Remunerated Employment, Office, profession etc* – Spouse: Consultant Engineer, Vivax-Metrotech Corporation. *6. Financial Sponsorship* – 2011 Election expenses were met by C.L.P.

Bethan Jenkins (South Wales West) – Plaid Cymru

10. Membership/Chairmanship of bodies in receipt of Assembly funds – Board Member – Wales Rugby League 2010; Member of Steering Group – Beat Cymru 2009 (Charity); Patron – British Association of Social Workers.

Alun Ffred Jones (Arfon) – Labour

6. Financial Sponsorship – All Election costs met by Plaid Cymru, Arfon Constituency. *8. Land and Property* – 2 rented properties – Caernarfon & Menai Bridge. *10 Membership/Chairmanship of bodies in receipt of Assembly funds* – Chair – Dyffryn Nantlle Football Club. Record of Membership of Societies – Honorary Member : Caernarfon Rotary Club.

Ann Jones (Vale of Clwyd) – Labour

2. Remunerated Employment, Office, Profession etc – Spouse employed by Ann Jones, AM as part time driver/general assistant. *6. Financial Sponsorship* – Election 2011 expenses paid by Vale of Clwyd Constituency Labour Party. *8. Land and Property* – Owner of a residential property in Rhyl. *10. Membership/Chairmanship of bodies in receipt of Assembly funds* – President - Radio Ysbyty Glan Clwyd; Vice President - North Wales Playing Fields Association; Patron - STARS in Denbighshire; Patron - Rhyl and District Junior Football League; President - Vale of Clwyd Scouts; Patron – Rhyl Swimming Club. Employment of Family Members – Name of Employee: John Adrian Jones; Family Member of: Ann Jones, AM; Relationship of Employee to AM: Husband; Capacity in which employed: Driver, General Assistant; Date employment commenced: 14 September 2002; Date employment ceased (if appropriate): N/A; Hours contracted to work: 12 hours per month.

Carwyn Jones (Bridgend) – Labour

2. Remunerated Employment, Office, Profession etc – Spouse is a project officer for Amnesty International – ceased in March 2012; Spouse works for Macmillan Cancer Charity (March 2012). *6. Financial Sponsorship* – £3000 sponsorship for 2011 Assembly elections from British Association of Physicians of Indian Origin (Wales). Remainder of election expenses met by Welsh Labour. Record of Membership of Societies – Honorary Member of Bridgend Rotary Club; Honorary Member of Southerndown Golf Club.

Elin Jones (Ceredigion) – Plaid Cymru

6. Financial Sponsorship – 100% of Election expenses met by Plaid Cymru. *9. Shareholdings Dyddiol Cyf* – Company to promote a Welsh newspaper. *10. Membership/Chairmanship of bodies in receipt of Assembly funds* – Member - Aberystwyth University Council.

Ieuan Wyn Jones (Ynys Môn) – Plaid Cymru

2. Remunerated Employment, Office, Profession etc – Wife is self-employed artist. *6. Financial Sponsorship* – Election expenses met by Plaid Cymru. *8. Land and Property* – Shared equity in a small flat in France.

Huw Lewis (Merthyr Tydfil & Rhymney) – Labour

2. Remunerated Employment, Office, Profession etc – Spouse is Assembly Member for Torfaen. *6. Financial Sponsorship* – Sponsorship for 2011 Assembly election: UNITE - £1000; Co-operative Party - £700; Merthyr Tydfil & Rhymney Constituency Labour Party - £4500 approximately; Sponsorship of 2011 Christmas card competition from: Wales & West Housing Association - £100; Tydfil Training Ltd - £100; Brecon Mountain Railway Company Ltd - £100; Stagecoach - £100. *10. Membership/Chairmanship of bodies in receipt of Assembly funds* – Member – Merthyr Tydfil Borough Credit Union; Member – Merthyr Alzheimer's Association; Member – Merthyr Tydfil Angling Association; Member – Osteoporosis Society, Merthyr Tydfil & District Support Group.

David Melding (South Wales Central) – Conservative

1. Directorships – Director - One Woodland Place Management Company (unremunerated) (SO4.3 - Band 1- less than 5 hours per week). *2. Remunerated Employment, Office, Profession etc* – Occasional fees for broadcasting and writing (less than £1000 per annum) (SO4.3 - Band 1- less than 5 hours per week); Occasional lecturing at the College of William and Mary, Virginia, USA – expenses covered by University (SO4.3 - Band 1- less than 5 hours per week). *7. Overseas Visits* – Visit to Williamsburg, Virginia. USA (30 March – 6 April 2012) to deliver a series of lectures on Welsh and British politics. Costs met by College of William and Mary. *10. Membership/Chairmanship of bodies in receipt of Assembly funds* – Governor - Meadowbank Special School, Cardiff; Governor – Headlands School, Penarth; Trustee – Welsh Centre for International Affairs; Member – Charity Bank Welsh Advisory Board; Member – Cardiff Astronomical Society; Member – Conservative History Group.

Sandy Mewies (Delyn) – Labour

2. Remunerated Employment, Office, Profession etc – Spouse: Employed by Sandy Mewies, AM as Communications and Research Manager. *6. Financial Sponsorship* – 2011 Election expenses paid by Delyn Labour Party and included donations from Unite (£2000) and the Co-op Party (£400). – Hon Fellow - Glyndŵr University (non- remunerated); Ordinary Member - Countess of Chester NHS Foundation Trust (non-remunerated); Honorary Vice President – Clwyd ME Group. Employment of Family Members – Name of Employee: Paul Albert Mewies; Family Member of: Sandy Mewies, AM; Relationship of Employee to AM: Spouse; Capacity in which employed: Communications/Research Manager; Date employment commenced: 19 January 2009; Date employment ceased (if appropriate): N/A; Hours contracted to work: 37.

Darren Millar (Clwyd West) – Conservative

2. Remunerated Employment, Office, Profession etc – Spouse is employed by Darren Millar, AM as an administrator and caseworker. *6. Financial Sponsorship* – 2011 Election expenses met by Conservative and Unionist Party (£11,077.27). *8. Land and Property* – Residential property in Cardiff jointly owned by Member and spouse; Residential property in Kinmel Bay jointly owned by Member and spouse; Property in Towyn, part owned by Member and spouse. *10. Membership/Chairmanship of bodies in receipt of Assembly funds* – Governor of St George Controlled School, Abergele; Member - Capel (Welsh Chapels Heritage Society); Vice Chair – North Wales Play Association; Patron – British Association of Social Workers (BASW) Cymru; Fellow – Chartered Institute of Management; Patron – Abergele Carnival; Fellow – Institute of Leadership and Management; Patron - Welsh Crown Green Bowling Association; Fellow - Royal Society for the encouragement of Arts, Manufacturers & Commerce; Family are members of North Coast Church; Member – Llanddulas and Rhyd-y-Foel Conservation Trust; Governor – St Brigid's School, Denbigh; Vice President – British Epilepsy Association (Epilepsy Action). Employment of Family Members – Name of Employee: Rebekah Ann Millar; Family Member of: Darren Millar, AM; Relationship of Employee to AM: Wife; Capacity in which employed: Administrator and Caseworker; Date employment commenced: 5/11/2007; Date employment ceased (if appropriate): N/A; Hours contracted to work: 22.2 hours per week.

Julie Morgan (Cardiff North) – Labour

4. Gifts, hospitality, etc – Two First Class Rail tickets from First Great Western – to be donated to local charity/community group. *6. Financial Sponsorship* – Election expenses met by Cardiff North Constituency Labour Party and included donations from: UNIT (£2000); Community Union (£1000) and USDAW (£2000); Individual donation from Unison (£500). *10. Membership/Chairmanship of bodies in receipt of Assembly funds* – Vice President – George Thomas Hospice Care (unpaid); Trustee – Life for African Mothers (unpaid); Patron – Touch Trust, Advocacy Matters (unpaid).

Lynne Neagle (Torfaen) – Labour

2. Remunerated Employment, Office, Profession etc – Spouse: Huw Lewis, Member for Merthyr Tydfil and Rhymney. *4. Gifts, hospitality, etc* – Two First Class rail tickets from First Great Western – donated to Gwent Cancer Support. *6. Financial Sponsorship* – 2011 Election expenses met by Torfaen Constituency Labour Party and included donations from: UNITE (£1000); FBU (£500); CWU (£100) and the Cooperative Party (£400). *10. Membership/Chairmanship of bodies in receipt of Assembly funds* – Patron – Torfaen Opportunity Group; Vice President – Torfaen Museum Trust; Patron – Tŷ Rosser Gwyn; Honorary Patron – Garnsychan Partnership; Patron – Gwent Cancer Support; Patron – Gwent Cancer Support Young Persons Project.

Eluned Parrott (South Wales Central) – Labour

2. Remunerated Employment, Office, Profession etc – Community Engagement Manager – Cardiff University (ceased 20/8/11); Spouse: Disability Assessment Centre Manager – Swansea University. *6. Financial Sponsorship* – 2011 Election expenses (£1922.60) met by South Wales Central Liberal Democrats.

William Powell (Mid & West Wales) – Liberal Democrat

1. Directorships – Director of EnergyseUK, a Carmarthenshire based renewable energy company, specialising in solar pv. (SO 4.3 - Band 1 – less than 5 hours per week); Director, Melin Talgarth Mill – community based mill, cafe and bakery enterprise. (SO 4.3 - Band 1 – less than 5 hours per week). *2. Remunerated Employment, Office, Profession etc* – Member:

Partner in a farming business – DJ & WD Powell; (SO 4.3 - Band 2 – between 5 and 20 hours per week); Member of Powys County Council; (SO 4.3 - Band 2 – between 5 and 20 hours per week); Occasional examiner for the OCR Examination Board at 'A' level (SO 4.3 - Band 1 – less than 5 hours per week); Spouse: Theatre nurse within the NHS. *4. Gifts, hospitality, etc* – Ticket and hospitality to 'Yes Prime Minister' at WMC on 28/06/11. *6. Financial Sponsorship* – Contribution to election expenses from Welsh Liberal Democrats. 8. Land and Property – 50% share in farm at Talgarth; Own a residential property in Ludlow; Jointly owner, with spouse, of a residential property in Cheltenham. *10. Membership/Chairmanship of bodies in receipt of Assembly funds* – Vice President – Talgarth YFC; Member - Talgarth Town Council; Committee Member - Talgarth Festival of the Black Mountains; Vice President – Cwmdu Eisteddfod; Governor - Talgarth CP School; Governor - Gwernyfed High School; Committee Member - Talgarth Town FC; Member – Brecon and District Credit Union. Record of Membership of Societies – Chair – Wales Council European Movement; Honorary Member – Black Mountains Lions Club; Life Member - Oxford Union Society; Member - Bronllys Hospital and Community League of Friends; Member - Lloyd George Society; Member - Friends of Hay Festival.

Gwyn R Price (Islwyn) – Labour

6. Financial Sponsorship – 2011 election expenses met by Islwyn C.L.P.

Nick Ramsay (Monmouth) – Conservative

1. Directorships – *Trustee (unpaid)* – Eleanor Rathbone Trust (Charity which makes grants to registered charities, mainly on Merseyside). (SO 4.3 - Band 1 – less than 5 hours per week). *2. Remunerated Employment, Office, Profession etc* – Partner – Self-employed management consultant. *6. Financial Sponsorship* – All 2011 election expenses met by Cardiff Central C.L.P. *8. Land and Property* – Own a restored barn in Conwy. *9. Shareholdings* – Halma Engineering; Albany Investment Trust; Pearson; Unilever; Henderson Smaller Companies; Standard Chartered; Reckitt Benckiser.

Jenny Rathbone (Cardiff Central) – Labour

1. Directorships – Trustee (unpaid) – Eleanor Rathbone Trust (Charity which makes grants to registered charities, mainly on Merseyside). (SO 4.3 - Band 1 – less than 5 hours per week). *2. Remunerated Employment, Office, Profession etc* – Partner – Self-employed management consultant. *6. Financial Sponsorship* – All 2011 election expenses met by Cardiff Central C.L.P. *8. Land and Property* – Own a restored barn in Conwy. *9. Shareholdings* – Halma Engineering; Albany Investment Trust; Pearson; Unilever; Henderson Smaller Companies; Standard Chartered; Reckitt Benckiser.

David Rees (Aberavon) – Labour

2. Remunerated Employment, Office, Profession etc – Spouse: Superintendent Radiographer, Abertawe Bro Morgannwg University Health Board; Member: Assistant Dean of Faculty at Swansea Metropolitan University (unremunerated from 9/5/11 and will cease from 31/8/11). *6. Financial Sponsorship* – All election 2011 expenses met by Aberavon Constituency Labour Party including donations from UCATT, UNITE, COMMUNITY and ASLEF Trade Unions.

Aled Roberts (North Wales) – Liberal Democrat

1. Directorships – Director and Company Secretary, STIWT Arts Trust Ltd (SO 4.3 – Band 1 – Less than 5 hours a week). *2. Remunerated Employment, Office, Profession etc* – Member: Local Councillor - Wrexham Borough Council (SO 4.3 – Band 2 – Between 5 and 20 hours per week); Solicitor - Geoffrey Morris & Ashton Solicitors, Wrexham (Partner between 1991 – 2007, now consultancy/relief cover with no regular remuneration) (SO 4.3 – Band 1 – Less than 5 hours a week); Irregular remuneration for broadcasting from various broadcasting companies. (SO 4.3 – Band 1 – Less than 5 hours a week); Renting part of the constituency office to the local Welsh Liberal Democrat Party. Any money received will be repaid to the National Assembly for Wales. Spouse: Management post – Yale College, Wrexham. *5. Remuneration or other material benefit* – Spouse – in receipt of a salary from Yale College, Wrexham. *6. Financial Sponsorship* – Contribution to 2011 election expenses from Welsh Liberal Democrats. *10. Membership/Chairmanship of bodies in receipt of Assembly funds* – Member: Chair – Wrexham and District National Eisteddfod 2011; Member – Finance Committee, Llangollen International Eisteddfod; Governor - Yale College, Wrexham; Company Secretary and Director – STIWT Arts Trust Ltd; Chair of Governors – Ysgol ID Hooson, Rhosllanerchrugog; Governor – Ysgol Maes y Mynydd, Rhosllanerchrugog; Member – Council and Management Board, National Eisteddfod; Member – Llangollen International Eisteddfod.

Antoinette Sandbach (North Wales) – Conservative

1. Directorships – Diligent Support Ltd (not remunerated and not currently trading) (SO 4.3 - Band 1 – less than 5 hours per week). *2. Remunerated Employment, Office, Profession etc* – Door Tenant (non-practicing), Legal Chambers, 9 Bedford Row, London. (SO 4.3 - Band 1 – less than 5 hours per week). *6. Financial Sponsorship* – 2011 Election expenses met by Welsh Conservatives. 8. Land and Property – Woodland, agricultural farmland and estate properties in Conwy; Residential property in London; Shares in Chambers Building (London). *9. Shareholdings* – Hafodunos Farms Ltd; Windpower Wales PLC. *10. Membership/Chairmanship of bodies in receipt of Assembly funds* – Member – Woodland Trust; Member – National Trust; Member – Bumblebee Conservation Trust; Member – William Mathias Music Centre; Patron – North Wales Chrysalis Trust; Vice President – Llangernyw Horticultural Society. Record of Membership of Societies – Member – Country Landowners Association; Member – Liveryman of Grocers Company; Member – Lincolns Inn; Member – Boodles.

Carl Sargeant (Alyn & Deeside) – Labour

2. Remunerated Employment, Office, Profession etc – Spouse employed by Carl Sargeant, AM as part time constituency support; Spouse employed as nursery nurse by Flintshire County Council. *6. Financial Sponsorship* – 2011 Election expenses met by Alyn and Deeside Labour Party. *10. Membership/Chairmanship of bodies in receipt of Assembly funds* – Non- remunerated ordinary member of Countess of Chester NHS Trust. Employment of Family Members – Name of Employee: Bernadette Sargeant; Family Member of: Carl Sargeant, AM; Relationship of Employee to AM: Spouse; Capacity in which employed: Constituency Assistant; Date employment commenced: 29 May 2003; Date employment ceased (if appropriate): N/A; Hours contracted to work: 12.

Ken Skates (Clwyd South) – Labour

6. Financial Sponsorship – All election expenses met by Clwyd South C.L.P. 10. Membership/Chairmanship of bodies in receipt of Assembly funds – Member of Gwernaffield Community Council (unremunerated).

Gwenda Thomas (Neath) – Labour

5. Remuneration or other material benefit – Member: Pension from Paymaster General; State Pension; Occasional Fees from Broadcasting; Spouse: Post Office Pension; Retirement Pension and Industrial Injuries Benefit. *6. Financial Sponsorship* – Sponsorship for 2011 elections from Neath Constituency Labour Party. *8. Land and Property* – Static caravan in Lydstep, Tenby. *10. Membership/Chairmanship of bodies in receipt of Assembly funds* – Vice President – Neath Port Talbot Alzheimer's Society; President – Cantorion Bro Nedd; Honorary President – It's Taster Bytes; Chair – Beyond Vision Steering Group; Member of Neath Port Talbot Credit Union; Spouse: Member – Gwaun Cae Gurwen Community Council; Member of Neath Port Talbot Credit Union. Record of Membership of Societies – Member – GMB Union.

Rhodri Glyn Thomas (Carmarthen East & Dinefwr) – Plaid Cymru

1. Directorships – Sgript Cyf (language consultancy) (SO 4.3 – No hours at all). *2. Remunerated Employment, Office, Profession etc* – Minister – St Clears Independent Churches (SO 4.3 –Band 1, Less than 5 hours); Spouse – Head of Education Department – University of Wales Trinity St David. *6. Financial Sponsorship* – Election 2011 expenses met by Plaid Cymru, Carmarthen East and Dinefwr.

Simon Thomas (Mid & West Wales) – Plaid Cymru

2. Remunerated Employment, Office, Profession etc – Spouse – Editor of New Welsh Review (Literature Magazine); Occasional fees for contributing to questionnaires and television and radio programmes – money paid to the party/charities. *5. Remuneration or other material benefit* – Ticket and hospitality for England v Sri Lanka cricket match (27-05-11) from SWALEC/SSE. *6. Financial Sponsorship* – All campaign expenses met by Plaid Cymru. *8. Land and Property* – Spouse: House, Llangwyrfon, Ceredigion (N/A from December 2011). *10. Membership/Chairmanship of bodies in receipt of Assembly funds* – Ordinary Member – Tai Cantref.

Joyce Watson (Mid & West Wales) – Labour

2. Remunerated Employment, Office, Profession etc – Spouse: Supervisor, T C Contractor. *6. Financial Sponsorship* – Election expenses met by the Labour Party. *10. Membership/Chairmanship of bodies in receipt of Assembly funds* – Member - Haven Credit Union; Member – Saveasy Credit Union; Member – National Trust; Member – RSPB; Member – Barnardos; Member – NSPCC; Member – Garth Youth and Community Project. Record of Membership of Societies – Member – Soroptomist International; Member – UNITE; Member – CO-OP Party; Member – Fawcett Society.

Lindsay Whittle (South Wales East) – Plaid Cymru

2. Remunerated Employment, Office, Profession etc – Caerphilly County Borough Council (Member does not claim any remuneration for this post) (SO 4.3 - Band 2 – between 5 and 20 hours per week); Leader of Caerphilly CBC until 14 June 2011. *6. Financial Sponsorship* – All expenses for 2011 election met by Plaid Cymru. *10. Membership/Chairmanship of bodies in receipt of Assembly funds* – Chair of Governors – Cwm Ifor Primary School.

Kirsty Williams (Brecon & Radnorshire) – Liberal Democrat

2. Remunerated Employment, Office, Profession etc – Spouse is a partner in a farming business - D.C. Rees & Son. *4. Gifts, hospitality, etc* – Tickets and hospitality to Test Match on 27/5/11 from Glamorgan CCC; Hospitality and tickets to 2 home rugby internationals from the WRU. *6. Financial Sponsorship* – Contribution to election expenses from Welsh Liberal Democrats. *8. Land and Property* – Spouse owns farm in Brecon. *10. Membership/Chairmanship of bodies in receipt of Assembly funds* – Vice President – Brecknock YFC; Honorary Associate – British Veterinary Association; Member – Royal British Legion; Honorary Member – Brecon Soroptimists; Vice President – Brecon Show; Vice President – Gwenddwr Show; Vice President – Pantydwr Show; Vice President – Cor Meibion Ystradgynlais; Honorary President – Brecknock Citizens Advocacy; Member – Brecon and District Credit Union. Record of Membership of Societies – Member – Pet Advisory Committee.

Leanne Wood (South Wales Central) – Plaid Cymru

6. Financial Sponsorship – All 2011 election expenses met by Plaid Cymru, including a donation of £500 from the Fire Brigades Union. *8. Land and Property* – 1 residential rented property in Cardiff; 1 residential rented property in Leeds. *10. Membership/Chairmanship of bodies in receipt of Assembly funds* – Chair – Cwm Cynon Women's Aid (Board of Trustees).

The**Wales** Yearbook **13**

WELSH GOVERNMENT

WELSH GOVERNMENT

Welsh Government
Cathays Park, Cardiff CF10 3NQ

Llywodraeth Cymru
Welsh Government

Tel: (0300) 060 3300
or (0845) 010 3300
Web: www.wales.gov.uk

The Welsh Government is elected by the people of Wales to carry out a programme of government. This involves making decisions and ensuring delivery on areas devolved on matters under 20 devolved areas and their exceptions, as set out under Schedule 7 of the Government of Wales Act 2006.

The First Minister of Wales is the leader of the Welsh Government and is appointed by HM the Queen following nomination by Assembly Members. The official office of the First Minister is in Tŷ Hywel and the Senedd in Cardiff Bay. An office is also kept at the Crown Buildings in Cathays Park.

The Cabinet

First Minister
Rt Hon Carwyn Jones AM

The First Minister is accountable/responsible for: Exercise of functions by the Welsh Government; Strategic and corporate planning in the Welsh Government; The legislative programme; The First Minister's Delivery Unit; Policy development and coordination of policy; Relationships with the rest of the United Kingdom, Europe, Internationally and Wales Abroad; All Welsh Government international offices and presence abroad; The strategic direction on European Union policy matters, including attendance at Joint Ministerial Council (Europe); Freedom of Information (including the access to Public Records and the National Archive for Wales); Overall responsibility for Openness in Government; Civil Contingencies; Oversight of Welsh Government relationships with the Wales Audit Office; The work of the Economic Research Advisory Panel; major energy facilities and infrastructure, devolution in energy matters, steel and coal; Major events; Overall strategic responsibility for communications; Staffing/Civil Service including the terms and conditions of Special Advisers and Welsh Government civil servants but not members of the Senior Civil Service; Overall responsibility for public appointments (i.e. ensuring that public appointments made by the Welsh Government are made in accordance with the Commissioner for Public Appointments' Code). Other Ministers will be responsible for public appointments issues within their portfolio area; The Ministerial Code.

Special Adviser: Jo Kiernan *Tel: (029) 2089 8690 Email: jo.kiernan@wales.gsi.gov.uk*
Principal Private Secretary: Des Clifford *Tel: (029) 2089 8765* / Elin Rowlands *Tel: (029) 2089 8792*
Senior Private Secretary: Rose Stewart *Tel: (029) 2089 8764 Email: ps.firstminister@wales.gsi.gov.uk*
Private Secretary: Rob Holmes *Tel: (029) 2089 8763*
Diary Secretary: Heulwen Jones *Tel: (029) 2089 8740*
Cabinet Secretary: Peter Greening *Tel: (029) 2089 8036 Email: peter.greening@wales.gsi.gov.uk*

The Minister for Education & Skills
Leighton Andrews AM

The Minister's portfolio includes the following: Welfare Reform; Control of fees charged to students by higher education institutions in Wales and associated bursary arrangements; Student and learner support, including policy on higher education tuition fees and bursaries; "For our Future" strategy and action plan for Higher Education in Wales; Widening participation in higher education; Higher education policy and funding, including sponsorship of the Higher Education Funding Council; GO Wales; Revenue funding of 6th forms, FE colleges, adult community learning and work based learning providers through the National Planning and Funding System; Capital funding for post-16 providers; Inclusion in schools with particular reference to looked after children, refugees and asylum seeker children, ethnic minorities, pupils who are carers, young parents, traveller children, gay/ bisexual/ transgender pupils; The School Effectiveness Framework; Standards of attainment by pupils in schools including Programme for International Student Assessment (PISA); Support for school improvement, in particular through the Better Schools Fund and Raising Attainment and Individual Standards in Education in Wales (RAISE) grant; Safeguarding children in education settings; Provision of food and drink in schools; School uniform; Early years education; Personal and social education including Education for Sustainable Development and Global Citizenship; School attendance, exclusions; Pupil behaviour, including bullying; Additional learning needs, including needs of pupils with severe, complex and/or specific learning difficulties, disabled pupils, able and talented pupils; Revenue funding of schools; School governance, organization, admissions; Complaints against Local Education Authorities and school governing bodies; Information Communications Technology in schools; Welsh immersion and linguistic continuity in schools; Commissioning Welsh-medium and bilingual classroom materials (print-based and electronic); Supporting the development of Welsh-medium qualification; Welsh medium and bilingual education; Welsh Medium Education Strategy; Welsh for Adults; Welsh language – including overseeing and co-ordinating general

The Cabinet

The Minister for Education & Skills (cont.)

Welsh language policy. (Other Ministers are responsible for Welsh language issues within their policy areas); Ministerial functions emanating from the Welsh Language Act 1993; Estyn work programme remit; Foundation Phase curriculum and assessment; 5-14 school curriculum and assessment arrangements; 14-19 curriculum and qualifications (including GCSE and GCE A/AS levels); The Welsh Baccalaureate Qualification; Statutory regulation of all qualifications (outside Higher Education), including the impact of the Disability Discrimination Act (DDA) on external qualifications; The statutory approval of qualifications used in Wales; Education and training research; The design and implementation of the National Planning and Funding System and the deployment of strategic investment in the post-16 sector; Development and implementation of 14–19 Learning Pathways; Extending Entitlement for people aged 11-25 years; Policy on youth work; The promotion of Wales as an excellent place in which to teach as well as to learn; Initial teacher training; Education workforce development, including leadership training and continuing professional development; Promoting teaching as a career; Teacher performance management; All-age, system-wide Transformation of the education and training system in Wales; 21st Century Schools programme; Medical Education (except for post graduate training).

The Minister for Education and Skills also has overall responsibility for those areas listed under the responsibilities allocated to the Deputy Minister for Skills. However, the Deputy Minister has for all practical purposes, day-to-day responsibility for these functions. In some cases Deputy Ministers will also have a relationship with other Ministers in respect of cross cutting issues.

Special Adviser: Matt Greenough *Tel: (029) 2089 8673 Email: matt.greenough@wales.gsi.gov.uk*

Senior Private Secretary: Helen Childs *Tel: (029) 2089 8783*
Email: correspondence.leighton.andrews@wales.gsi.gov.uk
Private Secretary: Matthew Mithan *Tel: (029) 2089 8771*
Diary Secretary: Mike Weatherhead *Tel: (029) 2089 8787*
Cabinet Secretary: Peter Greening *Tel: (029) 2089 8036 Email: peter.greening@wales.gsi.gov.uk*

The Minister for Housing, Regeneration & Heritage Huw Lewis AM

The Minister's portfolio includes the following: The housing and housing-related activities of local authorities and housing associations, including housing management and the allocation of social and affordable housing; Homelessness and housing advice; Regulation of registered social landlords; Matters relating to housing provided by the private rented sector; Support for private sector housing renewal; Aids and adaptations, including Disabled Facilities Grants and Physical Adaptation Grants; The provision of housing-related support (but not the payment of Housing Benefit); Matters relating to the supply of market and affordable housing to meet need (but not planning policy or Building Regulations); Quality of social and affordable housing; Strategic Regeneration Areas and legacy regeneration; Provision of sites and premises, derelict land and environmental improvements relating to regeneration; Physical Regeneration Fund; The regulation of commercial tenancies let by local authorities; Groundwork Wales; Coalfields' Regeneration Trust; Protection (including designation) of ancient monuments and historic buildings in Wales, and related matters, and their promotion as visitor attractions; Conserving and protecting the historic environment of Wales and promotion of heritage-led regeneration; Promoting access to and community engagement with Welsh heritage and the historic environment; Sponsorship of the Royal Commission on Ancient Monuments and support for the Welsh Archaeological Trusts; National strategy and policy for culture in Wales; Sponsorship of the Arts Council of Wales, including appointments of Chair and members; Sponsorship of the Sports Council for Wales, including appointments of the Chair and members; Sponsorship of Amgueddfa Cymru – National Museum Wales and the National Library of Wales, including appointments of the President and members; Lead responsibility for Welsh Government funding of the Wales Millennium Centre; National strategy and policy for sport, physical activity and active recreation in Wales; National Free Swimming initiative; Government Indemnity Scheme and the Acceptance in Lieu of Inheritance Tax Scheme; Non-national museums, public libraries and archives policy; Policy on broadcasting; Sponsorship of the Welsh Books Council; Issues surrounding the distribution of Lottery funding within Wales by the Big Lottery Fund, National Heritage Memorial Fund and Heritage Lottery Fund, Arts Council of Wales and Sports Council for Wales (allocation of funding between good causes and between countries remains the responsibility of the UK Government); National Botanic Garden of Wales.

Special Adviser: Tamsin Stirling *Tel: (029) 2089 8072 Email: tamsin.stirling@wales.gsi.gov.uk*

Senior Private Secretary: Tom Taylor *Tel: (029) 2089 8769*
Email: correspondence.huw.lewis@wales.gsi.gov.uk
Private Secretary: Sally Hunt *Tel: (029) 2089 8488*
Diary Secretary: Lyndon Evans *Tel: (029) 2089 8925*
Cabinet Secretary: Peter Greening *Tel: (029) 2089 8036 Email: peter.greening@wales.gsi.gov.uk*

WELSH GOVERNMENT

The Cabinet

The Minister for Health & Social Services
Lesley Griffiths AM

The Minister's portfolio includes the following: All aspects of the National Health Service (NHS) in Wales, including contracts with the primary care contractor professionals, other than (i) oversight of the medical professions; (ii) policy on surrogacy, xenotransplantation, embryology and human genetics; and (iii) licensing of medicines (these matters are not devolved); Charges for NHS services, including prescription, dental and ophthalmic and optical charges; The provision of services in Wales to the mentally ill; All aspects of public health and health protection in Wales, including food safety and the fluoridation of drinking water; The activities of the Food Standards Agency in Wales; The regulation of poisons; Genetically-modified food (but not the cultivation of genetically-modified crops - this is for the Minister for Environment and Sustainable Development); Receiving and responding to reports from, the Health Care Inspectorate for Wales; directing specific inspections when required; Oversight of the Wales Audit Office's activities so far as relating to the National Health Service in Wales; Research and Development in health and social care; Post-graduate medical education; The inspection and enforcement of the Medicine Act 1968 in Wales; Responsibility for the Prison Service health service, other than private contracts; Substance misuse (including delivery of the substance misuse strategy).

The Minister for Health and Social Services also has overall responsibility for those areas listed under the responsibilities allocated to the Deputy Minister for Children and Social Services. However, the Deputy Minister has for all practical purposes, day-to-day responsibility for these functions. In some cases Deputy Ministers will also have a relationship with other Ministers in respect of cross cutting issues.

Special Adviser: Jonathan Davies *Tel: (029) 2089 8965 Email: jonathan.davies@wales.gsi.gov.uk*

Senior Private Secretary: Chris Dawson *Tel: (029) 2089 8386*
Email: correspondence.lesley.griffiths@wales.gsi.gov.uk
Private Secretary: Margaret Powell *Tel: (029) 2089 8460*
Diary Secretary: Sarah Gwilliam *Tel: (029) 2089 8465*
Cabinet Secretary: Peter Greening *Tel: (029) 2089 8036 Email: peter.greening@wales.gsi.gov.uk*

The Minister for Finance & Leader of the House
Jane Hutt AM

The Minister's portfolio includes the following: Responsibility for managing the business of the Welsh Government in line with standing orders; Providing strategic financial direction and management of the resources of the Welsh Government; Putting in place sufficient and appropriate systems to allocate funding receipts between budgets for the next financial year in line with the requirements of the Government of Wales Act 2006 and Assembly Standing Orders; Publishing and consulting on the Welsh Government's budget proposals; General oversight of financial accounting and audit; Making most effective use of the Welsh Government's budget through rigorous in year budget monitoring and management; Operation of the devolved funding settlement and the Statement of Funding; Oversight of the Private Finance Initiative (PFI), but not priorities or policy decisions regarding PFI projects within another Minister's portfolio; Matters affecting Welsh Government Sponsored Bodies (WGSBs) collectively and in general, but not matters relating to specific WGSBs, which remain the responsibility of their respective Ministers; Ensuring value for money and effectiveness of spend across the Welsh Government's budget through continual challenge and development of underpinning systems on evidence and evaluation; The Location Strategy and the co-ordination of acquisition, maintenance and disposal of property and other assets used by the Welsh Government in the exercise of its functions; The co-ordination of National Statistics and the maintenance and development of the co-ordinating structure under the National Statistics Framework. (For other Welsh Ministers their role covers statistical activity in relation to their portfolio responsibilities); The content or conduct of the Census in Wales; Equality and equal opportunities (to include: gender issues, equal pay, race relations and equality, disability (including sensory deprivation), sexual orientation and the mainstreaming of equality, Digital Inclusion (including Communities 2.0), British Sign Language, Braille and all minority ethnic languages in Wales); Non devolved issues relating to asylum, immigration, migrant workers and community cohesion, except counter terrorism measures; Co-ordination of issues relating to gypsies and travellers, except where they relate specifically to other portfolios e.g. education policy.

Special Adviser: Jeff Andrews *Tel: (029) 2089 8193 Email: jeff.andrews@wales.gsi.gov.uk*

Senior Private Secretary: Emma Baff *Tel: (029) 2089 8770*
Email: correspondence.jane.hutt@wales.gsi.gov.uk
Private Secretary: Anna Whatley *Tel: (029) 2089 8790*
Diary Secretary: Chris Pascoe *Tel: (029) 2089 1814*
Cabinet Secretary: Peter Greening *Tel: (029) 2089 8036 Email: peter.greening@wales.gsi.gov.uk*

WELSH GOVERNMENT

The Cabinet

The Minister for Business, Enterprise, Technology & Science   Edwina Hart AM OStJ MBE

The Minister's portfolio includes the following: The provision of support and advice to assist the establishment, growth, modernisation or development of business in Wales; Finance Wales; The promotion of Wales as a location for business and investment; The promotion of Welsh exports; Property issues: provision of sites, premises, services and facilities for business; Bringing derelict land in Wales into use or improving its appearance; Environmental improvements in relation to industrial and commercial developments; Entrepreneurship, enterprise and business information; Economic sector panels; Social enterprise and the social economy; Tourism in and to Wales, including the marketing and promotion of Wales as a tourist destination and regulation of the tourism industry; Business rates policy; Science: development of science policy, including day to day liaison with the Chief Scientific Adviser; National Science Academy; Innovation: research & development, knowledge transfer and commercialisation; Maximising UK and European research and innovation income; Research Centres of Excellence; Technium network; Digital Wales: co-ordination of the cross-cutting Information Communication Technology (ICT) strategy; Broadband and ICT infrastructure; High Performance Computing for Wales project; A4B programme; Software Alliance.

The Minister for Business, Enterprise, Technology and Science also has overall responsibility for those areas listed under the responsibilities allocated to the Deputy Minister for Agriculture, Food, Fisheries and European Programmes. However, the Deputy Minister has for all practical purposes, day-to-day responsibility for these functions. In some cases Deputy Ministers will also have a relationship with other Ministers in respect of cross cutting issues.

Special Adviser: Andrew Bold *Tel: (029) 2089 8798 Email: andrew.bold@wales.gsi.gov.uk*
Senior Private Secretary: Richard Sewell *Tel: (029) 2089 8768*
Email: correspondence.edwina.hart@wales.gsi.gov.uk
Private Secretary: Cynthia Robins *Tel: (029) 2089 8451*
Diary Secretary: Hywel Williams *Tel: (029) 2089 8455*
Cabinet Secretary: Peter Greening *Tel: (029) 2089 8036 Email: peter.greening@wales.gsi.gov.uk*

The Minister for Environment & Sustainable Development   John Griffiths AM

The Minister's portfolio includes the following: Cross-cutting responsibility for sustainable development; Cross-cutting measures of mitigation and adaptation in relation to climate change; Land drainage, flood prevention and coastal protection; The control of air pollution in Wales (except vehicle emissions); Control of marine pollution in Welsh waters; Marine, terrestrial and freshwater biodiversity and nature conservation; The control of water quality and safeguarding of water resources in Wales, including regulation of drinking water quality, and the taking of special measures in time of drought; The oversight of the Dŵr Cymru and Dee Valley water companies, including their activities in those parts of their operational areas in England (ie parts of Herefordshire and Cheshire); The construction or enlargement of reservoirs, and the undertaking of ancillary works, in Wales by any person or corporation; Waste management in Wales including: implementation and review of the Wales waste strategy; regulation of local authority responsibilities for managing municipal waste; regulation of waste management, including European Union, UK and National Assembly for Wales legislation; support for sustainable resource management; contaminated land; Energy policy, small-medium scale energy production, domestic energy, energy efficiency including the provision of grants to aid energy efficiency and reduce fuel poverty; National Parks; All activities of the Countryside Council for Wales and the Environment Agency; Access to the countryside, including coastal access, rights of way and common land; Forestry and the activities of the Forestry Commission in Wales; Animal health and the welfare of livestock (including poultry, companion animals, equines, and bees); Responding to reports or outbreaks of notifiable animal diseases in Wales or elsewhere in Great Britain, which impacts on Wales (e.g. foot and mouth, avian influenza, Bovine Spongiform Encephalopathy (BSE), scrapie in sheep and bovine tuberculosis); The artificial insemination of livestock, including poultry, companion animals, equines, and bees; The importation of livestock, including poultry, and bees, and the importation of dangerous animals other than for agricultural purposes; The protection of wildlife in Wales, except the prescription of firearms to be used for the culling of certain wild animals (not devolved); The licensing of zoos by local authorities; The control of pests, weeds and vermin; The regulation of slaughterhouses in Wales; The regulation of plant health, seeds and pesticides in Wales, and the control of plant diseases; Assess with other UK competent authorities all Part C applications seeking approval for the uses of Genetically Modified (GM) crops in cultivation and importation in the European Union and the licensing of any GM crop trials in Wales; The power to require provision of information about crop prices; All aspects of planning policy, including the issue of statutory guidance to local authorities; Determination of planning disputes and appeals; Planning gain – Section 106 Agreements and Community Infrastructure Levy contained in the Town and Country Planning Act 1990 and Planning Act 2008 respectively; Building Regulations (The exemption of certain classes of building from Building Regulations, and the determination of appeals on matters relating to them); Strategic lead on allotments; The Wales Spatial Plan.

The Cabinet

The Minister for Environment & Sustainable Development (cont.)

For these purposes, "Welsh waters" means the sea around Wales within 12 nautical miles of the Welsh coast, except in the Bristol Channel and Dee Estuary, where Welsh waters are delimited by a line midway between the Welsh and English coasts. See Schedule 3 to the National Assembly for Wales (Transfer of Functions) Order 1999 (SI 1999/672).

Special Adviser: Anna McMorrin *Tel: (029) 2089 8592 Email: anna.mcmorrin@wales.gsi.gov.uk*
Senior Private Secretary: Peredur John *Tel: (029) 2089 8767*
Email: correspondence.john.griffiths@wales.gsi.gov.uk
Private Secretary: Shona O'Shea *Tel: (029) 2089 8479*
Diary Secretary: Nick Jones *Tel: (029) 2089 8428*
Cabinet Secretary: Peter Greening *Tel: (029) 2089 8036 Email: peter.greening@wales.gsi.gov.uk*

The Minister for Local Government & Communities   Carl Sargeant AM

The Minister's portfolio includes the following: The council tax rating system in Wales; Council Tax "capping" policy for local and police authorities; The unhypothecated funding of local authorities and police authorities in Wales through the local government revenue and capital settlements (although capital funding of police is a Home Office matter); Capital financing and accounting issues relating to local authorities including residual Private Finance Initiative approvals (responsibility for a police authority rests with the Home Office); Sponsorship of the Valuation Office Agency and the Valuation Tribunal Service; Local Government equal pay and Single Status Pay issues; Emergency financial assistance (formerly the "Bellwin" Scheme) to local authorities; The Local Government Partnership Council and relations between the Welsh Government and local government generally; The implementation of Wales Programme for Improvement (best value) by local authorities in Wales; Local authority performance and their accountability for it; Local strategic planning by local authorities and their local partners (NB not land use planning); Charging for, and trading in, non-statutory services by local government; The oversight and direction of local authorities in Wales and liaison with police authorities; The implementation of best value by local authorities in Wales; Councillors' allowances and standards of conduct; Public admission to local authority meetings; The regulation of burial grounds and crematoria by local authorities in Wales; Confirmation of byelaws made by local authorities in Wales; Timing of local elections;

NB for the purposes of the Minister's responsibilities above, the following are "local authorities": County councils and county borough councils; Fire and rescue authorities Community or town councils; Cross cutting responsibility for the strategic approach to the delivery of public services including performance, collaboration and citizen focus; Overall co-ordination of programmes of measures to improve the performance of public services; Oversight of regulation, audit and inspection as they relate to public service improvement; Taking forward the action to improve local service delivery; Communities First (including the Communities Facilities and Activities Programme); Cross cutting responsibility for Anti-Poverty initiatives; Financial inclusion, including credit unions; The Voluntary Sector and Volunteering; Community Safety, relations with the Police and other Criminal Justice Agencies, including counter-terrorism issues; Youth Justice; Domestic violence; The Fire and Rescue Services including community fire safety; Lead responsibility for monitoring Post Office and Royal Mail matters in Wales; Liaison point for the Armed Forces in Wales and Veterans (responsibility for the provision of services such as health and education etc rest with the relevant portfolio Minister); Transport policy, including the development of an integrated transport system in Wales; Road Safety including provision of safer routes to Schools and transport for children and young people; Regulation of pedestrian crossings in Wales; Regulation of on-street parking in Wales; Road transport, including construction, improvement and maintenance of trunk roads in Wales, except those parts of the Second Severn Crossing and the approaches thereto which are situated in Wales (not devolved) (NB roads other than trunk roads are the responsibility of local authorities); Delivery of passenger rail services through the Wales and Borders franchise; Funding and administration of programmes to local authorities and other bodies designed to deliver a range of transport schemes and services; Promotion and development of cycling.

Special Adviser: Sophie Howe *Tel: (029) 2089 8988 Email: sophie.howe@wales.gsi.gov.uk*
Senior Private Secretary: Glyn Stapleton *Tel: (029) 2089 8774*
Email: correspondence.carl.sargeant@wales.gsi.gov.uk
Private Secretary: Rhian Atkinson *Tel: (029) 2089 8517*
Diary Secretary: Kirsty Douglas *Tel: (029) 2089 8130*
Cabinet Secretary: Peter Greening *Tel: (029) 2089 8036 Email: peter.greening@wales.gsi.gov.uk*

WELSH GOVERNMENT

The Cabinet

Counsel General
Theodore Huckle QC

The main Counsel General's statutory responsibilities under Government of Wales Act 2006) are: Like the Welsh Ministers and the First Minister, the Counsel General may make appropriate representations about any matter affecting Wales. (s 62); If the Counsel General considers it appropriate to promote or protect the public interest, he may bring, defend or appear in legal proceedings, in the name of the Counsel General. However, the proceedings must relate to matters in respect of which Welsh Ministers or the Counsel General have functions (s 67); The Counsel General may refer to the Supreme Court a question of whether a provision of an Assembly Bill is within the Assembly's legislative competence (s 112); The Counsel General may bring legal proceedings to have a "devolution issue" decided, or may defend any such proceedings brought by other Law Officers in the UK. "Devolution issue" is defined in paragraph 1(1) of Schedule 9 to GOWA 2006. It includes (among other things) questions of whether an Assembly Act is within competence or whether the Welsh Ministers have particular functions. The Counsel General can also require devolution issues to be referred to the Supreme Court for a decision; Providing legal advice to, representing and overseeing the representation of the Welsh Government in legal proceedings; Holding meetings and discussions with other Law Officers; Holding meetings and discussions with the judiciary, members of the legal profession and others involved in the administration of justice; Improving the accessibility of devolved legislation in Wales for the legal profession and other members of the public, including considering the future consolidation of existing legislation; Responding to Law Commission and other (for example, UK Government) proposals or consultations where appropriate; Facilitating public debate on whether there should be a separate Welsh legal Jurisdiction.

Statutory Responsibilities - It should be noted that the Counsel General also has functions under other legislation.

Legal advice and representation to the Welsh Government, and Discussions with Law Officers; There are constraints on the Counsel General's ability to answer questions about these matters; Consultations about proposed changes to the law; In many cases these will be considered and responded to by the Minister with portfolio responsibility for the subject area to which the law relates.

Senior Private Secretary: David Rich *Tel: (029) 2082 3508 Email: pscounselgeneral@wales.gsi.gov.uk*
Cabinet Secretary: Peter Greening *Tel: (029) 2089 8036 Email: peter.greening@wales.gsi.gov.uk*

Janice Gregory AM is Chief Whip and attends Cabinet meetings.

Deputy Ministers

Lead Welsh Ministers retain responsibility for those functions allocated to Deputy Ministers for the purposes of representing those issues in Cabinet. For all other purposes, Deputy Ministers deliver those responsibilities on a day to day basis including answering Assembly Questions.

The Deputy Minister for Agriculture, Food, Fisheries & European Programmes   Alun Davies AM

The Deputy Minister's portfolio includes the following: Developing agri-food sector, associated supply chains and promotion of food from Wales; The provision of support to farmers in Wales, including the administration of the Common Agricultural Policy (CAP) and provision of assistance for conversion to organic production and for diversification of farm activities; The promotion of agri-environmental schemes in Wales and provision of associated support; The delivery via the Rural Development Plan of measures to support the competitiveness of agriculture and forestry, improve the environment and countryside, including agri-environment, organic and woodland activities and to enhance the social and economic well being of rural communities; The management of fishery harbours, but not harbours used for other purposes (in respect of which the Welsh Government has no devolved responsibility); Inland, coastal and sea fisheries: policy regulation and enforcement, including Common Fisheries Policy; Policy on and administration of European Union structural funds, related programmes and CAP.

For these purposes, "Welsh waters" means the sea around Wales within 12 nautical miles of the Welsh coast, except in the Bristol Channel and Dee Estuary, where Welsh waters are delimited by a line midway between the Welsh and English coasts. See Schedule 3 to the National Assembly for Wales (Transfer of Functions) Order 1999 (SI 1999/672).

Special Adviser: Andrew Bold *Tel: (029) 2089 8798 Email: andrew.bold@wales.gsi.gov.uk*

Private Secretary: Gemma Gittoes *Tel: (029) 2089 8458 Email: correspondence.alun.davies@wales.gsi.gov.uk*
Diary Secretary: Laura Osbourne *Tel: (029) 2089 8577*
Cabinet Secretary: Peter Greening *Tel: (029) 2089 8036 Email: peter.greening@wales.gsi.gov.uk*

WELSH GOVERNMENT

Deputy Ministers

The Deputy Minister for Skills
Jeff Cuthbert AM

The Deputy Minister's portfolio includes the following: Sector skills strategies; Sector Skills Councils' relicensing, performance and development; Sector skills development funds; Work with Sector Skills Councils and stakeholders on the development and piloting of Apprenticeship frameworks including Shared Apprenticeship model, Apprenticeship Clearing House, Young Recruits, Apprenticeship Unit, Apprenticeship pathways; Wales Employment and Skills Board and the Commission for Employment and Skills; Vocational qualifications for all ages; Key and Essential skills qualifications for all ages; Implementation of the Credit and Qualifications Framework for Wales; Wales Trades Union Congress (TUC) Learning Services and Wales Union Learning Fund; Chwarae Teg; European Structural Fund (ESF) priorities 2 and 3 relating to in- work skills development and higher level skills; Leadership and Management Skills development; Investors in People; Proact and its successor programme Skills Growth Wales; Simplification and integration of business skills and business development services; Development, retention and attraction of higher level research students for Wales; React and Adapt; Workforce Development Programme; Maximisation of economic benefits of higher education research and development; Programmes designed to support businesses to develop the skills of their workforce. This includes support for individuals and businesses and for strategic partnerships with key national and sectoral stakeholders; Workforce skills development, including support for individuals and businesses and for strategic partnerships with key stakeholders such as Sector Skills Councils and the Wales Employment and Skills Board in respect of assessing skills demand; Worldskills; Those not in education, employment or training (NEETS); Youth and Young Adult Employment; Prisoner learning; Apprenticeship and Skillbuild policy and delivery; 'Skills That Work For Wales' Strategy and Action Plan; Joint Employment Delivery Board for Wales including Labour Market Framework; ESF Priority 1 and for employability, Priority 2; Quality Effectiveness Framework in further education, work-based and lifelong learning; Work with stakeholders on the development and piloting of employability programmes, including Skillbuild; Young People's Guarantee; Jobs Growth Wales; Employability and careers advice, including sponsorship of Careers Wales; Further Education (other than Further Education Governance).

Special Adviser: Matt Greenough *Tel: (029) 2089 8673 Email: matt.greenough@wales.gsi.gov.uk*
Private Secretary: Helen March *Tel: (029) 2089 8717*
Email: correspondence.jeff.cuthbert@wales.gsi.gov.uk
Diary Secretary: Gareth Chard *Tel: (029) 2089 8545*
Cabinet Secretary: Peter Greening *Tel: (029) 2089 8036 Email: peter.greening@wales.gsi.gov.uk*

The Deputy Minister for Children & Social Services
Gwenda Thomas AM

The Deputy Minister's portfolio includes the following: Policy on care in the community; Policy on the provision of social services for children and its oversight; Adoption and fostering services in Wales, but not adoption of children by UK residents abroad; Oversight of all other social services activities of local authorities in Wales including the issuing of statutory guidance; Oversight of the Care Council for Wales (which is an Welsh Government Sponsored Body (WGSB); Regulation of residential, domiciliary, adult placements, foster care, under 8's care provision and private healthcare in Wales; Receiving and responding to reports from, the Care and Social Services Inspectorate for Wales; directing specific inspections when required; Inspection of, and reporting on, the provision of social services by local authorities in Wales (via the Care and Social Services Inspectorate for Wales), including joint reviews of social services; Cross cutting responsibility for health improvement and older people and carers; The Older People's Commissioner for Wales; Children's Commissioner for Wales; The Children and Family Court Advisory Support Service (CAFCASS); Parenting programmes; Play policy; Supervised Child Contact Centres; Child Poverty, including co-ordination of cross-government matters relating to Child Poverty; Families First; Cymorth funding; Children and Young People's Partnerships and Planning and information sharing under the Children Act 2004; Childcare; Flying Start Initiative for children 0-3; Child Trust Funds; Disabled Children Matter Wales campaign; Children's and young people's Rights and Entitlements; UN Convention on the Rights of the Child.

Special Adviser: Andy Pithouse *Tel: (029) 2089 8578 Email: andy.pithouse@wales.gsi.gov.uk*
Private Secretary: Ruth Parness *Tel: (029) 2089 8631*
Email: correspondence.gwenda.thomas@wales.gsi.gov.uk
Diary Secretary: Enfys Dixey *Tel: (029) 2089 8461*
Cabinet Secretary: Peter Greening *Tel: (029) 2089 8036 Email: peter.greening@wales.gsi.gov.uk*

WELSH GOVERNMENT COMMITTEES

PRIORITY SECTOR PANELS

The Welsh Government has outlined key priority sectors. Each of these sectors has their own panel in order to provide advice to Ministers on the opportunities and needs of the different sectors. Below sets out the membership of each priority sector panel:

Construction Sector Panel: David Joyce (Chair); David Harris; Ann-Marie Smale; Chris Jofeh; Danny Fellows OBE; Rhodri-Gwyn Jones.

Tourism Sector Panel: Dan Clayton Jones OBE, K.St J, TD, DL (Chair); Mike Morgan; Paul Lewin; Phillip Lay; Dr Manon Williams; Margaret Llewellyn OBE.

Creative Industries Sector Panel: Ron Jones (Chair); Fiona Stewart; Dai Davies; Jaynie Bye; Gwyn Roberts.

Energy & Environment Sector Panel: Kevin McCullough (Chair); David Williams; John Idris Jones; Garry Jewson; Alan Proctor; Nigel Annett (Co-opted member).

Food & Farming Sector Panel: Dr Haydn Edwards (Chair); Heather Jenkins; Professor Kevin Morgan; Sue Evans; Ieuan Edwards; Simon Wright; Melanie Leech; Dai Davies; Mary James; Nick Fenwick.

Life Sciences Sector Panel: Professor Sir Christopher Thomas Evans OBE (Chair); Professor Gareth Morgan; Dr Grahame Guilford; Gwyn Tudor; Penny Owen.

Information & Communication Sector Panel: Thomas Kelly (Chair): Andy Carr; Steve Dalton; Dr Mark Bentall; David Jones.

Financial & Professional Services Sector Panel: Christopher Nott (Chair); Allan Griffiths; Grant Hawkins; Vivienne Hole; Seth Thomas.

Advanced Materials & Manufacturing Sector Panel: Gareth Jenkins (Chair); Keith Baker; Dr Phil Clements; Dr Frank O'Connor; Deep Sagar; Roger Evans C.Eng. MIM MBE (Co-opted member).

PARTNERSHIP COUNCILS

The Partnership Council for Wales is intended to promote joint working and co-operation between Welsh Government and key groups. Listed below are some of the key Partnership Councils:

- Local Government Partnership Council
- Council for Economic Renewal
- Third Sector Partnership Council
- Welsh Language Partnership Council

PERMANENT SECRETARY

Dame Gillian Morgan*

Dame Gill Morgan became Permanent Secretary of the Welsh Government on 1st May 2008. Prior to this she was Chief Executive of the National Health Service (NHS) Confederation for 6 years after a career in both medicine and management. Gill is a Fellow of the Royal College of Physicians and the Faculty of Public Health and a member of the Royal College of General Practitioners. She holds an honorary doctorate from the City of London University. Gill was also the President of the Institute of Health Services Management in 1997-98.

She has served on a large number of national committees and working groups and is a past President of the International Hospital Federation. Dr Morgan was appointed Dame Commander of the Order of the British Empire (DBE) in June 2004.

In June 2012, Dame Gillian Morgan announced that she was to retire. Her successor has yet to be appointed.

WELSH GOVERNMENT

STRATEGIC DELIVERY & PERFORMANCE BOARD

The Board translates the strategic direction set by Welsh Cabinet Ministers and its committees into work that is joined-up across the Welsh Government's Departments and makes the best use of its resources. Board members also represent the Welsh Government externally, including Whitehall. The Strategic Delivery and Performance Board is made up of seven Directors General and three Non-executive Directors, and is chaired by the Permanent Secretary Gill Morgan.

The agendas, minutes and papers of the Board's monthly meetings are published online in accordance with Welsh Government Model Publication Scheme.

BOARD MEMBERSHIP

The current Board membership is as follows:

Dame Gillian Morgan	Permanent Secretary
Emyr Roberts	Education and Skills
James Price	Business, Enterprise, Technology and Science
David Sissling	Health, Social Services and Children and Chief Executive, NHS Wales
Michael Hearty	Strategic Planning, Finance and Performance
Bernard Galton	People, Places and Corporate Services
Gareth Jones	Sustainable Futures
June Milligan	Local Government and Communities
Elan Closs Stephens	Non-Executive Director
James Turner	Non-Executive Director
Sir Adrian Webb	Non-Executive Director

WELSH GOVERNMENT DIRECTORATES

Civil Service departments are grouped together into subject areas called Directorates. The seven Directorates are each headed by a Director General who leads cross-cutting programmes. These Directorates are:

- Business, Enterprise, Technology & Science
- Education and Skills (DfES)
- Health & Social Services
- Local Government and Communities
- People, Places & Corporate Services
- Strategic Planning, Finance & Performance
- Sustainable Futures

An eighth grouping also exists called Non-Directorate Services which falls outside of the Directorate structure and their lead civil servants report directly to the Permanent Secretary. This includes the Permanent Secretary's Division as well as Legal Services.

WELSH GOVERNMENT ORGANIZATION CHART

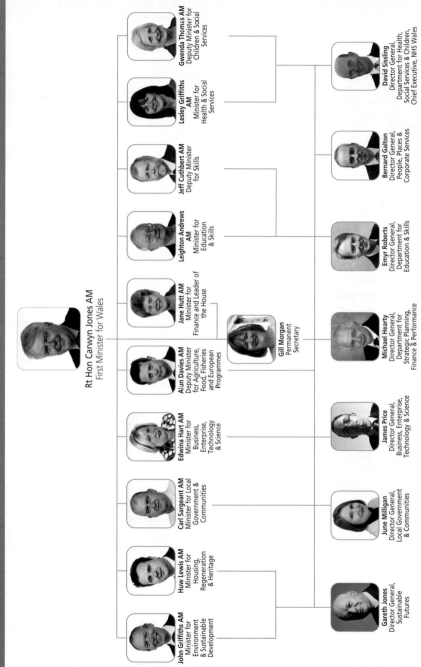

Rt Hon Carwyn Jones AM
First Minister for Wales

John Griffiths AM
Minister for Environment & Sustainable Development

Huw Lewis AM
Minister for Housing, Regeneration & Heritage

Carl Sargeant AM
Minister for Local Government & Communities

Edwina Hart AM
Minister for Business, Enterprise, Technology & Science

Alun Davies AM
Deputy Minister for Agriculture, Food, Fisheries and European Programmes

Jane Hutt AM
Minister for Finance and Leader of the House

Leighton Andrews AM
Minister for Education & Skills

Jeff Cuthbert AM
Deputy Minister for Skills

Lesley Griffiths AM
Minister for Health & Social Services

Gwenda Thomas AM
Deputy Minister for Children & Social Services

Gill Morgan
Permanent Secretary

Gareth Jones
Director General, Sustainable Futures

June Milligan
Director General, Local Government & Communities

James Price
Director General, Business, Enterprise, Technology & Science

Michael Hearty
Director General, Department for Strategic Planning, Finance & Performance

Emyr Roberts
Director General, Department for Education & Skills

Bernard Galton
Director General, People, Places & Corporate Services

David Sissling
Director General, Department for Health, Social Services & Children, Chief Executive, NHS Wales

WELSH GOVERNMENT

WELSH GOVERNMENT

Business, Enterprise, Technology & Science

Llywodraeth Cymru
Welsh Government

**Edwina Hart AM
MBE OStJ**

James Price

The Directorate for Business, Enterprise, Technology and Science delivers the economic agenda and promotes the sustainability of agriculture, fisheries and food and their associated supply chains across Wales.

The Director General for the Directorate is James Price.

The Directorate consists of:

Department for Business, Enterprise, Technology and Science

The department's aim is to work to encourage the best conditions and framework to enable the private sector to grow. Wanting a strong economy for businesses, people and communities in Wales, while at the same time placing sustainable development as a central organizing principle.

Department for Rural Affairs

The department aims to assist in providing a high quality of life for people who live and work in rural communities. It is responsible for delivering sustainable farming, forestry, food and fisheries industries; and for helping all departments across the Welsh Government to take account of the needs of rural areas in their work.

Department for Tourism and Marketing

The department is responsible for formulating tourism policy, encouraging investment in, and the development of the tourism industry. It is also responsible for marketing Wales both within the UK and overseas.

Welsh European Funding Office

The Welsh European Funding Office (WEFO) is part of the Welsh Government and manages the delivery of the European Union Structural Funds programme in Wales.

The Department for Education & Skills

Llywodraeth Cymru
Welsh Government

Leighton Andrews AM

Emyr Roberts

The Department for Education and Skills (DfES) provides leadership for education, skills and the Welsh language.

The Director General for the Directorate is Emyr Roberts.

Priorities

- Raising the standards of education and training provision, attainment and infrastructure across Wales so that everyone can reach their potential

- Deliver a suitably skilled workforce with high-quality opportunities for all learners

- Supporting individuals, families, communities and businesses in improving economic and social wellbeing and reducing inequality through education and training

- See the Welsh language thrive in Wales.

Structure

Education and Skills operates through three areas which are responsible for policy, planning, funding and monitoring services in their respective areas:

- Schools and Young People – Curriculum, Learning Improvement and Professional Development, Infrastructure Unit, Schools Management and Effectiveness, School Standards Unit, Support for Learners

- Skills, Higher Education and Lifelong Learning Group – Qualifications and Learning, Further Education, Higher Education, Transformation Programme Management, Business and Skills

- Welsh Language Unit – Strategy, Welsh Government Scheme, sponsorship of the Welsh Language Board, implementation of the Welsh Language Measure.

The department works in partnership with local authorities, schools, colleges, universities, training and skills providers and other public, private and voluntary sector organizations to deliver against our objectives.

WELSH GOVERNMENT

Health, Social Services & Children

Llywodraeth Cymru
Welsh Government

Lesley Griffiths AM

David Sissling

The Welsh Government notes that it is committed to supporting the people of Wales to live healthy and independent lives and to ensure that when they need health and social care services, they get the right care, in the right place, at the right time.

The Director General for Health and Social Services is David Sissling who is also Chief Executive of NHS Wales. The two departments which make Health, Social Services & Children are:

Department of Health, Social Services and Children

The Department for Health, Social Services and Children advises the Welsh Government on policies and strategies for health, social care and children's services in Wales. The department consists of the following units:

- Community, Primary Care and Health Service Policy Directorate
- Quality, Standards and Safety Improvement Directorate
- Resources Directorate
- Children's Health and Social Services Directorate
- Older People and Long-term Care Policy Directorate
- Corporate Management
- Service Delivery and Performance
- Strategy Unit
- Health and Social Services Human Resources
- Children and Family Court Advisory and Support Service in Wales (CAFCASS Cymru).

The department is subject to financial audit by the Wales Audit Office and liaises with the Wales Office in the processes of legislation.

Department of Public Health and Health Professions

The department leads on public health strategy and programmes, with the aim of protecting and improving health and reducing health inequalities.

The Director of DPHHP is the Chief Medical Officer for Wales, Dr Tony Jewell. The department consists of divisions with emphasis on Health Improvement and Health Protection. The lead health professionals in:

- Nursing
- Dentistry
- Environmental Health
- Pharmacy and
- Scientific and Therapy disciplines also report to the Chief Medical Officer.

Local Government & Communities

Llywodraeth Cymru
Welsh Government

Carl Sargeant AM

June Milligan

The Directorate for Local Government and Communities is seen by the Welsh Government as a pivotal vehicle for supporting and leading the agenda for change, integration, and performance development across the public services in Wales.

The Director General for the Directorate is June Milligan. The Directorate consists of three departments:

Department for Local Government and Public Services

The department is the Welsh Government's pivotal vehicle for supporting and leading the agenda for change, integration, and performance development across the public services in Wales. Priorities include:

- local government finance
- democracy, scrutiny and partnerships
- supporting better public service delivery.

Department for Communities and Social Justice

The department is working to regenerate communities, especially those suffering the greatest disadvantages, and to ensure people are safe and supported. The department also includes two Inspectorates. Priorities include:

- anti-poverty and community regeneration including Communities First
- community safety including provision for substance misuse, domestic abuse and youth justice
- supporting and enhancing the role of the Third Sector.

Department for Transport

The department's objective is to develop a world class transport system to provide safe, affordable and sustainable road, rail and air transport for all. Priorities include:

- managing, maintaining and improving the trunk road and motorway network in Wales
- delivering rail infrastructure projects and managing the Wales and Borders train franchise
- managing the Intra Wales Air Service and TrawsCymru bus and coach network across Wales
- working with local authorities on regional transport planning and to deliver local transport improvements, this includes road safety initiatives and walking and cycling schemes across Wales.

WELSH GOVERNMENT

Peoples, Places & Corporate Services

Llywodraeth Cymru
Welsh Government

Dame Gillian Morgan

Bernard Galton

The People, Places and Corporate Services Directorate's priority areas can be split between its internal and external facing role.

Responsible internally for the effective delivery of Human Resources; the Welsh Government estate and facilities; ICT services; security; resilience & business continuity, knowledge & information management and translation services.

Responsible externally for developing the Welsh Government's role across the Welsh public sector and within the wider UK Civil Service on shared people and places issues such as workforce; skills; estates; engagement; mobility and shared services.

The Director General for the Directorate is Bernard Galton.

Aims

The People, Places and Corporate Services Directorate aims to:

- assist Ministers and departments in the practical delivery of the Government's programme of work
- support the organization to become smaller, leaner and operating from the optimal number of locations
- provide expert professional advice across the portfolio of services above
- develop the Welsh Government's role externally on shared people and places issues and establish a collaborative approach to workforce and organizational development across the Welsh Public Service.

Strategic Planning, Finance & Performance

Llywodraeth Cymru
Welsh Government

Jane Hutt AM

Michael Hearty

Strategic Planning, Finance and Performance focuses on improving the Welsh Government's planning and use of money to deliver better outcomes for the people of Wales.

The Director General for the Directorate is Michael Hearty.

The aims of the Strategic Planning, Finance and Performance department are to:

- advise the Minister for Finance and Leader of the House, the Cabinet and senior Welsh Government officials on financial matters
- develop a business plan for the Welsh Government
- report on the financial position of the Welsh Government to further improve performance
- operate and develop the financial and performance systems required to support the Welsh Government's activities
- control and protect public money and resources
- provide statistics and evidence to support decision-making, research and debate
- provide effective internal scrutiny of finance and counter fraud services
- advise on the effectiveness of key business activities and performance
- improve purchasing across the Welsh public sector to secure best value for money.

Priorities

The Directorate aims to:

- ensure value for money by providing a good evidence base that informs policies and decision making
- provide the products and services that other departments in the Welsh Government need to deliver and monitor their key priorities
- be clear and open on how the Welsh Government uses its money
- provide advice and guidance across the Welsh public sector.

Sustainable Futures

Llywodraeth Cymru
Welsh Government

John Griffiths AM

Gareth Jones

Sustainable Futures is dedicated to securing the highest levels and fairest distribution of economic, social and environmental wellbeing for the people of Wales.

In the Welsh Government's sustainable development scheme, One Wales, One Planet, sustainable development is set out as the 'central organizing principle' for the Welsh Government.

The Director General for the Directorate is Gareth Jones. The Directorate consists of two departments:

Environment and Sustainable Development

- The Department for Environment and Sustainable Development has responsibility over making sustainable development central to everything the Welsh Government does
- It works to tackle climate change so Wales can become energy efficient, low carbon and a low waste society
- The department also works to ensure that the natural and historic environment is protected and land used sustainably.

Housing, Regeneration and Heritage

- The Department for Housing, Regeneration and Heritage works to create and sustain strong, prosperous communities, where people enjoy a good quality of life and creative ideas thrive
- The department is responsible for developing and delivering policies on housing, regeneration, the arts, culture, sport and active recreation, museums, archives and libraries, and the historic environment.

The Wales Yearbook

13

WALES in WESTMINSTER

The Wales Office
Gwydyr House, Whitehall, London SW1A 2NP
Tel: (020) 7270 0534

1 Caspian Point, Caspian Way, Cardiff CF10 4DQ
Tel: (029) 2089 8758 Fax: (029) 2089 8138

Email: wales.office@walesoffice.gsi.gov.uk
Website: www.walesoffice.gov.uk

The Wales Office

Secretary of State for Wales: Rt Hon Cheryl Gillan MP

Overall strategic direction: Assembly liaison; Constitutional issues; major Acts of Parliament; elections; referendum; economy, finance & business; foreign affairs including interaction with the EU; public appointments; environment & energy; Royal matters; defence.

Special Adviser: Richard Hazlewood Tel: (020) 7270 0577 / (029) 2089 8549
Principal Private Secretary: Stephen Hillcoat Tel: (020) 7270 0550

Parliamentary Under-Secretary of State: David Jones MP

Regional development; welfare benefits & pensions; education & skills; transport; rural affairs; communication; television; local government & housing; law & order; fire & rescue; equality; immigration & borders; culture & tourism.

Assistant Government Whip:
Stephen Crabb MP

Parliamentary Private Secretary:
Glyn Davies MP

Senior Personnel

Fiona Adams-Jones
Director

Glynne Jones
Deputy Director & Deputy Head of Policy

Stephen Hillcoat
Principal Private Secretary & Deputy Director
of Ministers, Accountability & Communications

Tricia Quiller-Croasdell
Head of Communications

Geth Williams Head of Constitution
Elizabeth Allen Head of Social Affairs
Jason Lintern Head of Strategy
Jodye Crabbe Head of Economy & Sustainability
Kim Tester Head of Human Resources
Amanda Latham Head of Finance
Stephen Knight Head of Corporate Services
Sue Olley Legal Adviser

WALES IN WESTMINSTER

Secretaries of State for Wales 1979-2010

Rt Hon Cheryl Gillan, Conservative (2010-)
Born 1952 in Llandaff, Cardiff, educated Cheltenham Ladies College and the College of Law. Previously worked as Senior Marketing Consultant, Ernst and Young 1986-91 and Marketing Director, Kidsons Impey 1991-1993. MP for Chesham and Amersham since 1992. PPS to Viscount Cranborne as Leader of the House of Lords and Lord Privy Seal 1994-95; Parliamentary Under-Secretary of State, Department of Education and Employment 1995-97; Shadow Minister for: Trade and Industry 1997-98, Foreign and Commonwealth Affairs 1998-2001, International Development 1998-2001; Opposition Whip 2001-03; Shadow: Minister for Home Affairs 2003-05, Shadow Secretary of State for Wales 2005-10.
Junior Minister: David Jones 2010-

Rt Hon Peter Hain, Labour (2002-2008; 2009-2010)
Born 1950, educated at Pretoria Boys' High School, University of London & Sussex University. MP for Neath since 1991. Junior Minister, former Welsh Office 1997-1999. Minister of State at the Foreign and Commonwealth Office 1999-2001. Minister of State at the Department of Trade & Industry in 2001-02, Minister for Europe at the FCO in 2001-02. Secretary of State for Wales, 2002- ; Leader of the House of Commons 2003-05; Lord Privy Seal 2003-05; Secretary of State for Northern Ireland 2005-07; Secretary of State for Work & Pensions 2007-08.
Junior Minister: Nick Ainger 2005-07; Huw Irranca-Davies 2007-08; Wayne David 2009-10

Rt Hon Paul Murphy, Labour (1999-2002; 2008-2009)
Born 1948, educated at St Francis Roman Catholic School, Abersychan, West Monmouth School, Pontypool, and Oriel College, Oxford. Previously a college lecturer. A member of Torfaen Borough Council from 1973-87. MP for Torfaen 1987- , a front bench spokesman on Wales in 1988. Spokesman on Northern Ireland in 1994, spokesman on Foreign Affairs in 1995 and shadow Defence Minister in 1997. Appointed Minister for Political Development in the Northern Ireland Office 1997-99, Secretary of State for Wales, 1999-2002, Secretary of State for Northern Ireland 2002-05.
Junior Minister: Don Touhig 2001-05; Wayne David 2008-09

Rt Hon Alun Michael, Labour (1998-99)
Born 1943, educated at Colwyn Bay Grammar School and Keele University. Previously a journalist and youth worker. A member of Cardiff City Council 1973 -89. Elected MP for Cardiff South and Penarth in 1987, AM for Mid & West Wales 1999-00, served as an Opposition front bench spokesman for Wales 1988-92 and Home Affairs 1992-97. Appointed Minister of State in the Home Office 1997 and Secretary of State for Wales in 1998-99, First Secretary of the National Assembly 1999-2000, Minister for Rural Affairs 2001-05; Minister for Industry & the Regions 2005-06.
Junior Minister: David Hanson 1999-2001

Rt Hon Ron Davies, Labour (1997-98)
Born 1946, educated at Bassaleg Grammar School, Portsmouth University and University of Wales, Cardiff. Previously a teacher and WEA tutor 1968-74, Further Education adviser, Mid Glamorgan 1974-83. MP for Caerphilly 1983-01, AM for Caerphilly 1999-2002, an Opposition Whip 1985-87, Opposition Spokesman for Agriculture, Fisheries and Food 1987-92, Shadow Secretary of State for Wales 1992-97, Secretary of State for Wales 1997-98.
Junior Ministers: Win Griffiths 1997-98; Peter Hain 1997-99; Jon Owen Jones 1998-99

Rt Hon William Hague, Conservative (1995-97)
Rt Hon John Redwood, Conservative (1993-95)
Rt Hon David Hunt, MBE, Conservative (1990-93)
Rt Hon Peter Walker, MBE, Conservative (1987-90)
Rt Hon Nicholas Edwards, Conservative (1979-87)

MPs' Register of Interests (cont.)

Geraint Davies (Swansea West) – Labour
8. Land and Property – Flat in London from which rental income is received. *9. Shareholdings* – (a) Pure Crete Ltd, tour operator to Crete.

Glyn Davies (Montgomeryshire) – Conservative
2. Remunerated employment, office, profession etc - Self-employed farmer. Payments for interviews for BBC News 24. Address: BBC Contributor Payments, PO Box 480, Manchester M14 0EL: 5 March 2012, received £150 for interview on 14 December 2011. Hours: 1 hr 45 mins. (Registered 19 April 2012). 5 March 2012, received £150 for interview on 11 January 2012. Hours: 1 hr 45 mins. (Registered 19 April 2012). 4 April 2012, received £150 for interview on 8 February 2012. Hours: 1 hr 45 mins. (Registered 19 April 2012). 27 March 2012, received £150 plus travel expenses for interview for BBC Welsh Language programme 'Pawb a'i Farn' on 15 March 2012. Address: BBC Wales, Llandaff, Cardiff, CF5 2YQ. Hours: 1 hr (Registered 19 April 2012). Payment of £500 from ComRes for seven opinion surveys undertaken in May 2011, June 2011, July 2011, September 2011, November 2011, January 2012 and February 2012. Address: Four Millbank, London SW1P 3JA. Hours: 30-45 minutes for each survey. Payment made direct to charity. (Registered 23 April 2012). *8. Land and Property* – Two-bedroom flat at Century Wharf, Cardiff Bay. Farmland, house and buildings near Castle Caereinion, Montgomeryshire. Farmland, house and buildings near Llanefydd, Montgomeryshire. I receive rental income from all the above properties. (Updated 20 April 2012).

Jonathan Edwards (Carmarthen East & Dinefwr) – Plaid Cymru
Nil.

Chris Evans (Islwyn) – Labour
2. Remunerated employment, office, profession etc – IPSOS Mori, 79-81 Borough Road, London SE1 1FY, for completing opinion survey: Received payment of £150 for taking part in survey on 15 June 2011. Hours: 1 hr. Payment donated to charity. (Registered 10 August 2011). Received payment of £150 for taking part in survey on 1 December 2011. Hours: 1 hr. Payment donated to charity. (Registered 26 January 2012). ComRes, 4 Millbank, London, SW1P 3JA, for completing opinion survey: Received payment of £75 for a survey in April 2011. Hours: 45 mins. Payment donated to local organization. (Registered 18 May 2011). Received payment of £75 for a survey in March 2011. Hours: 45 mins. Payment donated to local organization. (Registered 8 June 2011). Received payment of £75 for a survey in May 2011. Hours: 45 mins. Payment donated to local charity. (Registered 8 June 2011). Received payment of £75 for a survey in June 2011. Hours: 45 mins. Payment donated to local charity. (Registered 7 July 2011). Received payment of £75 for a survey in December 2011. Hours: 45 mins. Payment donated to local charity. (Registered 11 January 2012). Received payment of £75 for a survey in February 2012. Hours: 45 mins. Payment donated to local charity. (Registered 28 February 2012). Received payment of £75 for a survey in March 2012. Hours: 45 mins. Payment donated to local charity. (Registered 16 April 2012). Populus, 10 Northburgh Street, London EC1V 0AT, for opinion survey: Received 17 August 2011, payment of £75 for opinion survey in July 2011. Hours: 25 mins. Payment donated to local organization. (Registered 1 September 2011).

Jonathan Evans (Cardiff North) – Conservative
1. Directorships – I am Non-executive Chairman of the UK subsidiary companies of Phoenix Life Holdings Limited and Pearl Group Holdings (No.2) Limited: London Life Limited, Pearl Assurance Plc, National Provident Life Limited, NPI Limited, Phoenix and London Assurance Limited (until 22 March 2011), Phoenix Life Limited and Phoenix Pensions Limited, all of Juxon House, 100 St Paul's Churchyard, London EC4M 8BU. These companies are long-established life assurance and pensions companies, closed to new business and now owned by Phoenix Group (formerly Pearl Group) of which I was Group Chairman from 2005 to 2009. These companies are regulated by the UK Financial Services Authority. I am an FSA approved person in respect of this appointment. I attend and chair monthly consolidated Board meetings in London as well as regularly advising the executive officers. Received £9,167 gross on 20 May 2011 in respect of Board fees. Hours: 14 hrs. (Registered 24 May 2011). Received £9,167 gross on 22 June 2011 in respect of Board fees. Hours 14 hrs. (Registered 23 June 2011). Received £9,167 gross on 22 July 2011 in respect of Board fees. Hours 14 hrs. (Registered 10 August 2011). Received £9,167 gross on 22 August 2011 in respect of Board fees. Hours 14 hrs. (Registered 7 September 2011).Received £9,167 gross on 22 September 2011 in respect of Board fees. Hours 14 hrs. (Registered 11 October 2011). Received £9,167 gross on 21 October 2011 in respect of Board fees. Hours 14 hrs. (Registered 25 October 2011). Received £9,167 gross on 23 November 2011 in respect of Board fees. Hours 14 hrs. (Registered 8 December 2011). Received £9,167 gross on 22 December 2011 in respect of Board fees. Hours: 14 hrs. (Registered 12 January 2012). Received £9,167 gross on 20 January 2012 in respect of Board fees. Hours: 14 hrs. (Registered 23 January 2012). Received £9,167 gross on 22 February 2012 in respect of Board fees. Hours: 14 hrs. (Registered 29 February 2012). Received £9,167 gross on 23 March 2012 in respect of Board fees: Hours: 14 hrs. (Registered 18 April 2012). Received £9,167 gross on 21 April 2012 in respect of Board fees. Hours: 14 hrs. (Registered 9 May 2012). *11. Miscellaneous* – Solicitor of the Supreme Court (non-practising).

Paul Flynn (Newport West) – Labour
Nil.

MPs' Register of Interests (cont.)

Hywel Francis (Aberavon) – Labour
Nil.

Nia Griffith (Llanelli) – Labour
8. Land and Property – Smallholding in Carmarthenshire..

Rt Hon Peter Hain (Neath) – Labour
2. Remunerated employment, office, profession etc – Payments from Biteback Publishing Ltd, 375 Kennington Lane, London SE11 5QY: Fee of £4,100 received as advance for writing a book. Hours unknown. (Registered 25 May 2011). £1,785 received as additional payment following publication of memoirs. No additional hours worked. (Registered 30 April 2012). Payment of £275 from The Guardian, Kings Place, 90 York Way, London N1 9GU, for an article. Hours: 5 hrs. (Registered 12 March 2012) *5. Gifts, benefits and hospitality (UK)* – Name of donor: Motor Sports Association; Address of donor: Motor Sports House 1 Riverside Park Colnbrook SLG 0HK; Amount of donation or nature and value if donation in kind: two tickets for British Grand Prix 9-10 July 2011, value £782; Date of receipt of donation: 9 July 2011; Date of acceptance of donation: 9 July 2011; Donor status:. Company No 1344829 (Registered 18 July 2011). *6. Overseas visits* – Name of donor: ResultsUK Address of donor: 13 Maddox Street, London W1S 2QG; Amount of donation (or estimate of the probable value): flights, in-country transport and accommodation; cost £2,600; Destination of visit: South Africa; Date of visit: 11-17 February 2012; Purpose of visit: participation in delegation to South Africa to study the impact of TB and TV/HIV co-infection (Registered 7 March 2012). *8. Land and Property* – Share in small family property near Malaga, Spain.

Rt Hon David Hanson (Delyn) – Labour
2. Remunerated employment, office, profession etc – Payments from ComRes, Four Millbank, London SW1P 3JA, for opinion surveys: March /April 2011, payment of £75. Hours: 45 mins. (Registered 5 May 2011). May 2011, payment of £75. Hours: 45 mins. (Registered 6 June 2011). June 2011, payment of £75. Hours: 45 mins. (Registered 1 July 2011). July 2011, payment of £75. Hours: 45 mins. (Registered 15 August 2011). October-November 2011, payment of £75. Hours: 45 mins. (Registered 14 December 2011). November-December 2011, payment of £75. Hours: 45 mins. (Registered 3 January 2012). January-February 2012, payment of £75. Hours: 45 mins. (Registered 21 February 2012). February-March 2012, payment of £75. Hours: 45 mins. (Registered 26 April 2012). Payments from Ipsos MORI, 79-81Borough Road, London SE1 1FY, for survey of MPs: Payment of £150. Hours: 1.5 hrs. (Registered 3 August 2011). Payment of £150. Hrs; 1.5 hrs. (Registered 14 February 2012). Payments from Dod's Parliamentary Communications, 21 Dartmouth St, London SW1H 9BP, for Criminal Justice Sector Knowledge Seminars: Payment of £150 Hours: 1.5 hrs. (Registered 14 February 2012). Payment of £100 from Dod's Parliamentary Communications, 21 Dartmouth St, London SW1H 9BP, for four surveys. Hours: 1.25 hrs. Payment donated to charity. (Registered 3 August 2011). *4. Sponsorships* – (b) Support in the capacity as an MP: Name of donor: PriceWaterhouseCoopers; Address of donor: 1 Embankment Place, London WC1N 6RH; Amount of donation or nature and value if donation in kind: ad hoc advice provided to the frontbench Treasury team during the passage of the Finance (No.3) Bill to the value of £55,800; Date of receipt: 4 April – 31 July 2011; Date of acceptance: 31 July 2011; Donor status: limited liability partnership (Registered 23 August 2011).

Simon Hart (Carmarthen West & South Pembs.) – Conservative
2. Remunerated employment, office, profession etc - Payments received as Trustee of the Sundorne Estate. Payments for administration and attending meetings made by Balfours, Windsor House, Windsor Place, Shrewsbury SY1 2BY: Payment of £850. Hours: 5 hrs. (Registered 23 January 2012). Payments from IPC Media, Blue Fin Building, 110 Southwark Street, London SE1 0SU: Payment of £300 for Country Life magazine article. Hours: 2 hrs. (Registered 13 May 2011). Payments from ComRes, Four Millbank, London SW1P 3JA, for completing Parliamentary Panel Surveys: £75 received in March 2011. Hours: 15 mins. (Registered 30 June 2011). £75 received in April 2011. Hours: 15 mins. (Registered 30 June 2011). £75 received in May 2011. Hours: 15 mins. (Registered 30 June 2011). £75 received in June 2011. Hours: 15 mins. (Registered 25 August 2011). £75 received in July 2011. Hours: 15 mins. (Registered 25 August 2011). £75 received in September 2011. Hours: 15 mins. (Registered 7 November 2011). £75 received in October 2011. Hours: 15 mins. (Registered 7 November 2011). £75 received in November 2011. Hours: 15 mins. (Registered 19 December 2011). £75 received in January 2012. Hours: 15 mins. (Registered 10 January 2012). £75 received in February 2012. Hours: 15 mins. (Registered 20 February 2012). £75 received in April 2012. Hours: 15 mins. (Registered 26 April 2012). *5. Gifts, benefits and hospitality (UK)* – Name of donor: Mr M A R Galadari; Address of donor: private; Amount of donation or nature and value if donation in kind: entry and hospitality to cricket at The Oval for two people; total value £1,190 plus VAT; Date of receipt of donation: 20 August 2011; Date of acceptance of donation: 20 August 2011; Donor status: individual (Registered 6 September 2011)..

Dai Havard (Merthyr Tydfil & Rhymney) – Labour
Nil.

MPs' Register of Interests (cont.)

Nick Smith (Blaenau Gwent) – Labour
6. *Overseas visits* – Name of donor: 9.All Party Parliamentary China Group, sponsored by GKN plc, City of London, London Export Corporation (LEC), John Swire & Sons, GlaxoSmithKline, Astra Zeneca, Arup, University of Cambridge Local Examinations Syndicate, HSBC. 10.Virgin Atlantic Address of donor: 9.c/o Great Britain China Centre, 15 Belgrave Square, London SW1X 8PS 10.Customer Relations, PO Box 747, Dunstable LU6 9AH; Amount of donation (or estimate of the probable value): 9. £2,654.48, return flights to China, internal travel in China, accommodation and meals. I also received some meals and hospitality provided locally. 10.£1,500, flight upgrade on outward journey; Destination of visit: China; Shanghai, Beijing and Chengdu; Date of visit: 16-23 December 2011; Purpose of visit: to maintain and strengthen relations between Parliament and the National People's Congress of China; to learn about and support British businesses operating in China; and to deepen the knowledge and understanding of parliamentarians of China. (Registered 20 January 2012).

Mark Tami (Alyn & Deeside) – Labour
5. *Gifts, benefits and hospitality (UK)* – Name of donor: Heineken UK Limited; Address of donor: 2-4 Broadway Park, South Gyle Broadway, Edinburgh EH12 9JZ; Amount of donation or nature and value if donation in kind: my wife and I were guests at the Grand National Race Meeting on 14 April 2012, including overnight accommodation; value approx £1,000 Date of receipt of donation: 14 April 2012; Date of acceptance of donation: 14 April 2012; Donor status: company, registration no SCO65527 (Registered 12 May 2012). 8. *Land and Property* – Apartment in Portugal.

Hywel Williams (Arfon) – Plaid Cymru
Nil.

Mark Williams (Ceredigion) – Liberal Democrat
Nil.

Roger Williams (Brecon and Radnorshire) – Liberal Democrat
2. *Remunerated employment, office, profession etc* – Partner in R. H. Williams; a farming partnership. I provide administrative support for the partnership, amounting to less than 3 hours a week. 8. *Land and Property* – Half share in farmland at Tredomen Court, Wales. Half share in three houses in Tredomen, Brecon, from which rental income is received. Half share in a house in Exmouth, Devon, from which rental income is received

Jenny Willott (Cardiff Central) – Liberal Democrat
2. *Remunerated employment, office, profession etc* – Associate Editor of The House Magazine. (Up to £5,000) August 2011, received £4,458.34 for the period March 2009 to August 2011. Hours: 100 hrs approx, plus additional time writing articles (Registered 27 March 2012).

WALES IN WESTMINSTER

The House of Lords

Wales has no special place in the procedures and conventions of the House of Lords. Rt. Hon. Lord Wallace of Tankerness QC (Lib Dem) speaks for the Government on Welsh Affairs. Rt Hon Lord Davies of Oldham is the Opposition spokesman.

The House of Lords Act 1999 excluded hereditary peers from sitting in the House of Lords. During its consideration by the Lords, the Bill was amended to allow 92 hereditary peers to continue as Members of the House until a final reform of the House is enacted. In 2012 proposals were made for further reforms but were subsequently withdrawn following a backbench Conservative rebellion.

The following members of the House of Lords have varying connections with Wales:

Life Peers

Conservative

Lord Crickhowell 1987
Rt Hon Nicholas Edwards, Secretary of State for Wales 1979-87.

Lord Griffiths of Fforestfach 1991
Professor Brian Griffiths, Head of the Prime Minister's Policy Unit 1985-90.

Lord Howe of Aberavon 1992
Rt Hon Geoffrey Howe, Chancellor of the Exchequer 1979-83, Foreign Secretary 1983-89 and Deputy Prime Minister and Leader of the House of Commons 1989-90.

Lord Garel-Jones 1997
Rt Hon Tristan Garel-Jones, Minister of State, Foreign and Commonwealth Office 1990-93.

Lord Roberts of Conwy 1997
Rt Hon Sir Wyn Roberts, MP for Conwy 1970-97, Minister in the Welsh Office 1979-94.

Lord Heseltine 2001
Rt Hon Michael Heseltine, Various Cabinet posts 1979-1986, 1990-1995. Deputy Prime Minister and First Secretary of State 1995-97.

Lord Temple-Morris 2001
Peter Temple-Morris, Conservative MP for Leominster 1974-97, Independent MP 1997-98, Labour MP 1998-99. Raised to the peerage as Baron Temple-Morris, of Llandaff in the County of South Glamorgan and of Leominster in the County of Herefordshire.

Labour

Lord Brooks of Tremorfa 1979
Jack Brooks DL, former Leader of South Glamorgan County Council.

Lord Prys-Davies 1982
Gwilym Prys-Davies, Special Adviser to the Secretary of State for Wales 1974-78.

Lord Williams of Elvel 1985
Charles Williams CBE, Director of Mirror Group newspapers 1989-92.

Lord Richard 1990
Rt Hon Ivor Richard QC, UK Permanent Representative at the UN 1974-79, EEC Commissioner 1981-85.

Lord Davies of Coity 1997
Garfield Davies CBE, General Secretary of USDAW 1986-97.

Lord Brookman 1998
David Keith Brookman, General Secretary Iron & Steel Trades Confederation 1993-99.

Baroness Gale 1999
Anita Gale, Women's Officer and Assistant Organizer Wales Labour Party 1976-84, General Secretary 1984-99.

Baroness Andrews 2000
Elizabeth Kay Andrews OBE, Director of Education Extra.

Lord Evans of Temple Guiting 2000
Matthew Evans CBE, Chair, EFG Private Bank.

Lord Morgan 2000
Kenneth Owen Morgan FBA, FRHistS, Vice-Chancellor, University of Wales, Aberystwyth 1989-95.

Lord Morris of Aberavon 2001
Rt Hon John Morris KG QC, Secretary of State for Wales 1974-79, Attorney General 1997-99, Chancellor, University of Glamorgan, 2002-.

Baroness Golding 2001
Lin Golding, MP for Newcastle-under-Lyme 1986-2001, daughter of late Ness Edwards MP.

Lord Jones 2001
Rt Hon Barry Jones, MP for East Flint 1970-83, Alyn and Deeside 1983-2001, Parliamentary Under-Secretary of State for Wales 1974-79.

Lord Griffiths of Burry Port 2004
Leslie Griffiths, Superintendent Minister at Wesley's Chapel, London, since 1996.

Baroness Morgan of Drefelin 2004
Delyth Morgan, Chief Executive, Breakthrough Breast Cancer. Parliamentary Under Secretary for Children, Young People and Families.

Lord Rowlands 2004
Ted Rowlands CBE, MP for Merthyr Tydfil & Rhymney 1972-83, Cardiff North 1966-70, Minister of State, Foreign & Commonwealth 1976-79.

Baroness Royall of Blaisdon 2004
Janet Royall, Head of the European Commission Office in Wales (2003-4).

Lord Kinnock 2004
Rt Hon Neil Kinnock, former MP for Bedwellty 1970-83, Islwyn 1983-95, Leader of the Labour Party 1983-92, European Commissioner 1995-2004.

Lord Anderson of Swansea 2005
Rt Hon Donald Anderson, MP for Monmouth 1966-70, Swansea East 1974-2005.

Lord Howarth of Newport 2005
Rt Hon Alan Thomas Howarth CBE, MP for Newport East 1997-2005.

Baroness Jones of Whitchurch 2006
Margaret Jones, Former UNISON Official and member of the Labour Party NEC.

Baroness Kinnock of Holyhead 2009
Glenys Kinnock, Minister of State, Foreign and Commonwealth Office 2009-10; MEP 1994-2009.

Lord Davies of Abersoch 2009
Evan Mervyn Davies CBE, Former Banker and Minister of State for UK Trade, Investment and Business.

Lord Williams of Baglan 2010
Dr Michael Williams United Nations diplomat. Neath Port Talbot.

Lord Touhig 2010
Rt Hon Don Touhig MP for Islwyn 1995(by)-2010. Parliamentary Under-Secretary of State, Wales Office 2001-05.

Lord Prescott 2010
Rt Hon John Prescott MP for Kingston-upon-Hull East 1970-2010; Deputy Prime Minister 1997–2007.

Baroness Morgan of Ely 2010
Eluned Morgan, Low Carbon Development Wales, SSE; MEP Wales 1994-2009.

Liberal Democrats

Lord Thomas of Gresford 1996
Martin Thomas OBE, QC, a Deputy High Court Judge, former Liberal Democrat parliamentary candidate.

Lord Carlile of Berriew 1999
Alex Carlile QC, MP for Montgomery 1983-97.

Lord Roberts of Llandudno 2004
Roger Roberts, Superintendent Methodist Minister at Llandudno, President of the Welsh Liberal Democrats.

Lord German 2010
Michael German AM for South Wales East 1999-2010 Leader, Welsh Liberal Democrats in the Assembly 1999-2008.

Baroness Randerson 2010
Jenny Randerson, AM for Cardiff Central 1999-2011.

Crossbenchers

Lord Chalfont 1964
Rt Hon Alun Gwynne Jones OBE, MC, Minister of State for Foreign Affairs 1964-70.

Lord Elystan-Morgan 1981
Elystan Morgan, MP for Cardigan 1966-74, Under-Secretary of State at the Home Office 1968-70. A Crown Court Judge since 1987.

Lord Griffiths 1985
Rt Hon William Hugh Griffiths MC, Lord Justice of Appeal 1980-85 and a Lord Appeal in Ordinary 1985-93.

Lord Elis-Thomas 1992
Rt Hon Dafydd Elis-Thomas, MP for Meirioneth 1974-83, Meirionnydd Nant Conwy 1983-92.

Lord Snowdon (1961) 1999
Antony Armstrong-Jones was created the first Earl of Snowdon in 1961 following his marriage to Princess Margaret. He was given the life peerage, Lord Armstrong-Jones, in 1999.

Baroness Finlay of Llandaff 2001
Ilora Finlay, Vice-Dean School of Medicine, University of Wales College of Medicine 2000-. Appointed by the House of Lords Commission in 2001.

Lord Harries of Pentregarth 2006
Prof Richard Harries, Former Bishop of Oxford 1987-2006

Lord Rowe-Beddoe 2006
David Rowe-Beddoe, Former Chairman, Welsh Development Agency 1993-2001.

Baroness Grey-Thompson 2010
Tanni Grey-Thompson DBE CB, Para-Olympian and TV presenter.

Baron Wigley of Caernarfon 2010
Dafydd Wigley, MP for Caernarfon 1974-2001.

Hereditary Peers in the Lords

Lord Aberdare 1873
Alastair John Lyndhurst Bruce, the fifth Baron Aberdare acceded to the title in 2005. Trustee, National Botanic Garden of Wales 1994-2006.

Lord Colwyn 1917
Ian (Anthony) Hamilton-Smith CBE, the third Baron Colwyn acceded to the title in 1966.

Lord Moran 1943
Richard John McMoran Wilson KCMG, the second Baron Moran acceded to the title in 1977.

Lord Trefgarne 1947
Rt Hon David Trefgarne, the second Baron Trefgarne acceded to the title in 1960.

Viscount Tenby 1957
William Lloyd George, the third Viscount Tenby acceded to the title in 1983.

Bishops

Archbishop of Canterbury 2002
Most Rev. & Rt Hon Rowan Williams, former Archbishop of Wales.

Other Welsh Hereditary Peers

Lord Boston 1761
George Willaim Eustace Boteler Irby, the eleventh Baron Boston acceded to the title in 2007.

Earl Radnor 1765
William Pleydell-Bouverie, the ninth Earl Radnor acceded to the title in 2008.

Lord Dynevor 1780
Hugo Griffith Uryan Rhys, the tenth Baron Dynevor acceded to the title in 2008.

Lord Kenyon 1788
Lloyd Tyrell-Kenyon, the sixth Baron Kenyon acceded to the title in 1993.

Earl Powis 1804
John George Herbert, the eighth Earl Powis acceded to the title in 1993.

Marquess of Anglesey 1815
George Charles Henry Victor Paget, the seventh Marquess of Anglesey acceded to the title in 1947.

Lord Mostyn 1831
Llewellyn Roger Lloyd Lloyd-Mostyn, the sixth Baron Mostyn acceded to the title in 2000.

Lord Stanley of Alderley 1839
Thomas Henry Oliver Stanley, the eighth Baron Stanley acceded to the title in 1971.

Lord Penrhyn 1866
Simon Douglas-Pennant, the seventh Baron Penrhyn acceded to the title in 2003.

Lord Harlech 1876
Francis David Ormsby-Gore, the sixth Baron Harlech acceded to the title in 1985.

Lord Swansea 1893
Richard Anthony Hussey Vivian, the fifth Baron Swansea acceded to the title in 2005.

Lord Glanusk 1899
Christopher Russell Bailey, the fifth Baron Glanusk acceded to the title in 1997.

Lord Aberconway 1911
Henry Charles McLaren, the fourth Baron Aberconway acceded to the title in 2003.

Viscount St Davids 1918
Rhodri Phillips, the fourth Viscount St Davids acceded to the title in 2009.

Lord Clwyd 1919
John Murray Roberts, the fourth Baron Clwyd acceded to the title in 2006.

Lord Davies 1932
David Davies of Llandinam, the third Baron Davies acceded to the title in 1944.

Earl Lloyd George of Dwyfor 1945
David, Viscount Gwynedd, 4th Earl Lloyd George, acceeded to the title in 2010.

Lord Ogmore 1950
Morgan Rees Rees-Williams, the third Baron Ogmore acceded to the title in 2004.

The**Wales** Yearbook

13

EUROPE

EUROPEAN OFFICES

European Commission Office in Wales

Head of Office
David Hughes

European Commission Office in Wales,
2 Caspian Point, Caspian Way, Cardiff CF10 4QQ
Tel: (029) 2089 5020 Fax: (029) 2089 5035
Website: www.ec.europa.eu/wales

The European Commission Office in Wales was opened in 1976 as a key link between Wales and Brussels for every European issue on the Welsh agenda. It is one of four EC offices in the United Kingdom. Its chief responsibilities are:

• Representing the European Commission, and speaking as its voice, in Wales.

• Reporting back to the European Commission on political, economic and social developments in Wales.

• Maintaining relations with the National Assembly, the Welsh Government, Welsh political parties and other Welsh organizations.

• Providing EU information to the general public through a range of outlets, in particular the Europe Direct Centres in Carmarthen, Llangollen and Wrexham.

Through its activities in Wales, the EC Office tries to ensure that people, organizations and authorities understand the issues and work of the EU.

Press Enquiries: **Rachael Langlands-Brown**
Information Enquiries: **Leri Davies; Siân Stoodley**
PA to Head of Office: **Christine McGrath**

Committee of the Regions

The Committee of the Regions was established in 1993, under the Maastricht Treaty, in response to local and regional authorities' demand for greater representation within the European Union. It was designed to complement the three major Community institutions: Council, Commission and Parliament. The Committee sets out to be the guardian of the principle of subsidiarity, which advocates that decisions should be taken at the level of government closest to the citizen concerned. The CoR's areas of responsibility were further expanded by the Amsterdam Treaty in 1997 and the 2002 Nice Treaty, whilst the 2009 Lisbon Treaty strengthened recognition of the COR's role.

The Committee comprises 344 members and an equal number of alternates, who are appointed for five years by the Council of the European Union following nomination by member states. There are 18 full and 20 alternate nominees from the UK, who together form the UK Delegation, four of whom represent Wales (two full and two alternate).

Members:

Cllr Bob Bright
(Labour Party of European Socialists)

Newport City Council, Civic Centre, Newport NP20 4UR
Tel: (01633) 254315 Fax: (01633) 254315
Email: bob.bright@newport.gov.uk
On the CoR, Bob Bright is a member of the Education & Culture Commission (EDUC) and a member of the Commission for Territorial Cohesion Policy (COTER)

EUROPEAN OFFICES

**Christine Chapman, Assembly Member
(Labour/Party of European Socialists)**

National Assembly for Wales, Cardiff Bay, Cardiff CF99 1NA
Tel: (029) 2089 8745 Fax: (029) 2089 8366
Email: christine.chapman@wales.gov.uk
On the CoR, Christine Chapman is a member of the Commission for Economic & Social Policy (ECOS) and a member of the Commission for Natural Resources (NAT)

Alternate members:

Cllr Chris Holley (Liberal Democrats/Alliance of Liberals and Democrats for Europe)
Swansea City Council, Civic Centre, County Hall, Swansea SA1 3SN
Tel: (01792) 636923 Fax: (01792) 636196
Email: chris.holley@swansea.gov.uk

Rhodri Glyn Thomas, Assembly Member (Plaid Cymru/European Alliance)
National Assembly for Wales, Cardiff Bay, Cardiff CF99 1NA
Tel: (01269) 597677
Email: rhodri.thomas@wales.gov.uk

European Economic & Social Committee

The European Economic and Social Committee (EESC) is a consultative body that gives representatives of Europe's socio-occupational interest groups, and others, a formal platform to express their points of view on EU issues. Its opinions are forwarded to the larger institutions: the Council, the Commission and the European Parliament. It thus has a key role to play in the Union's decision-making process.

The 344 members of the EESC are drawn from economic and social interest groups in Europe. Members are nominated by national governments and appointed by the Council of the European Union for a renewable 5-year term of office. The next renewal will be in September 2015.

Members from Wales:

Brian Curtis
Regional Organiser, Wales and the West of England, National Union of Rail, Maritime and Transport Workers (RMT)

Dr Rose D'Sa
Consultant in EU, Commonwealth and International Law - Consultant in Legal Education/Distance Learning

Tom Jones
Legal Services Commissioner - Vice-President of the Wales Council for Voluntary Action (WCVA) - farmer

EUROPE

EUROPEAN OFFICES

Welsh Government EU Office

Tŷ Cymru/Wales House, Rond-Point Schuman 11, B-1040 Brussels, Belgium
Tel: 00 32 (0)2 506 4487 Fax: 00 32 (0)2 223 2482
Email: steven.mcgregor@wales.gsi.gov.uk
Website: www.wales.gov.uk
Acting Head of Office **Steven McGregor**

The Welsh Government's European Union interests are represented by its office in Brussels. It is staffed by Welsh Government officials who have diplomatic status accredited by the UK Permanent Representation to the EU. The Welsh Government aims to reflect, through Ministerial and official level participation, Welsh interests in the EU decision making process.

The EU is a major source of funding for Welsh economic development and other areas of policy. The Welsh Government has particular interest in the European policy areas for which it and the National Assembly have devolved responsibility. WG also takes an active lobbying interest in broader EU issues likely to affect Wales.

The Welsh Government's EU Office is also an important platform for developing relationships with other nations and regions across Europe.

National Assembly for Wales EU Office

Tŷ Cymru/Wales House, 6th Floor, Rond-Point Schuman 11, B-1040 Brussels, Belgium
Tel: 00 32 (0)2 226 6692 Fax: 00 32 (0)2 226 6694
Mob: 0044 781 616 4455
Email: Gregg.Jones@wales.gov.uk
Website: www.assemblywales.org

Head of Office **Gregg Jones**

The National Assembly for Wales Parliamentary Service established a presence in Brussels at the end of 2004. The drive to establish an independent office came from the Assembly Members themselves, as a means of providing them directly with early intelligence on key EU issues for Wales. Without this opportunity for early scrutiny, by the time EU legislation reaches the implementation stage at the Assembly there is normally very little opportunity to influence the policy options made.

Head of Office
Gregg Jones

The Office, which is located in Wales House alongside the Welsh Government and other Welsh representations, works closely with the Assembly's Committees to provide briefings and advice to support Members' scrutiny of the Welsh Government in relation to EU matters. It aims to ensure that links are made between what's going on in the EU's Institutions and the Assembly Committees to support their direct engagement with the EU. It also organises high level meetings in Brussels for delegations of Assembly Members. With an increasing recognition of the role of regional assemblies and parliaments in helping to bridge the gap between Brussels and the citizen, the Office helps raise awareness of the work of the National Assembly for Wales on EU issues.

EUROPE

EUROPEAN OFFICES

Welsh Local Government Association European Office

Tŷ Cymru/Wales House, Rond-Point Schuman 11, B-1040 Brussels, Belgium
Tel: 00 32 (0)2 506 4477 Fax: 00 32 (0)2 502 8360
UK Local Rate Tel: 020 3328 0961
Email: brussels.office@wlga-brussels.org.uk
Website: www.wlga.gov.uk/europe
European Affairs Manager **Iwan Williams**

The Welsh Local Government Association (WLGA) European Office was established in April 2003 and shares accommodation in Brussels with the National Assembly for Wales and the Welsh Higher Education Office. It has two members of staff working on European policy developments with implications for its thirty two members drawn from Local Government, the National Parks and the Fire and Police Authorities.

Working closely with both the Welsh Government and other representatives of local and regional government, the Office seeks to influence Commission proposals at an early stage, providing a warning service of forthcoming issues and developing lobbying strategies for Local Government. The Office also works closely with the Welsh Members of the European Parliament and has two members on the Committee of Regions.

Welsh Higher Education Brussels
Addysg Uwch Cymru Brwsel

Tŷ Cymru/Wales House, Rond-Point Schuman 11, B-1040 Brussels, Belgium
Tel: 00 32 (0)2 226 6698 Fax: 00 32 (0)2 502 8360
Email: berwyn@wheb.ac.uk info@wheb.ac.uk
Website: www.wheb.ac.uk
Head of Office **Berwyn Davies**

Located within Wales House in the heart of the EU district of Brussels, WHEB aims to build closer links with a wide range of other stakeholders, promoting Welsh excellence in pursuit of Europe-wide goals.

Welsh Higher Education Brussels (WHEB) has been established to:

* Promote the interests of the Welsh Higher Education sector in Europe
* Enable the sector to engage more fully with European priorities such as the Lisbon Strategy and the Bologna Process
* Facilitate stronger relationships between Welsh Higher Education Institutions, European Institutions and Regional Partners from the EU and beyond.

WHEB is a partnership established with the support of:

* 11 of the Higher Education Institutions in Wales
* Higher Education Wales
* Higher Education Funding Council for Wales
* Welsh Government.

EUROPE

EUROPEAN OFFICES

EURES

Set up in 1993, Eures is a co-operation network between the EC and the Public Employment Services of the EEA Member States (the EU countries plus Ireland, Norway and Lichtenstein) and other partner organizations. The purpose of Eures is to provide information, advice and recruitment/placement (job matching) services for the benefit of workers and employers as well as anyone wishing to benefit from the principle of free movement of persons.

EURES offers a network of advisers to provide the information required by jobseekers and employers through personal contacts. There are more than 850 EURES advisers across Europe and the number is growing.

EURES advisers are trained specialists who provide the three basic EURES services of information, guidance and placement, to both jobseekers and employers interested in the European job market. They have developed specialised expertise in the practical, legal and administrative matters relating to mobility at national and cross-border levels. They work within the Public Employment Service of each member country, or within other partner organizations in the EURES network.

Europe Direct Centres

Part of a network of over 400 centres across Europe, the role of the Europe Direct Centres is to provide an information service for citizens and businesses which answers questions about subjects related to the EU.

West Wales European Centre,
Dewi Building, 2nd Floor,
Trinity College,
Carmarthen SA31 3EP
Tel: (01267) 242360
Fax: (01267) 234279
Email:
wwec@carmarthenshire.gov.uk
Website: www.wwec.org.uk
Lorena Prist, European
Information Officer

ECTARC,
Parade Street, Llangollen,
Denbighshire,
North Wales LL20 8RB
Tel: (01978) 861514
Fax: (01978) 861804
Email:
europedirect@denbighshire.gov.uk
Vanessa Baldry, European
Information Officer

Europe Direct, Wrexham Library,
Rhosddu Road,
Wrexham LL11 1AU
Tel: (01978) 292090
Fax: (01978) 292611
Email:
europedirect@wrexham.gov.uk
Eleanor Staple, European
Information Officer

European Documentation Centres

European Documentation Centres, located in Aberystwyth and Cardiff, receive the complete range of official EU documentation and have privileged access to EU databases.

Aberystwyth University,
Hugh Owen Library, University of Wales, Aberystwyth,
Penglais Campus, Aberystwyth SY23 3DZ
Tel: 01970 622401 Fax: (01970) 622404

Cardiff University,
The Guest Building, PO Box 430,
Colum Drive, Cardiff CF10 3EU
Tel: (029) 2087 4262 Fax: (029) 2087 4717
Email: edc@cardiff.ac.uk

Enterprise Europe Network Wales

A one-stop shop for Welsh businesses, Enterprise Europe Network Wales combines and builds on the former Innovation Relay Centres and Euro Info Centres. It is funded by the European Commission and the Welsh Government, and has offices in Cardiff and Mold.

As part of the wider Enterprise Europe Network which consists of over 250 centres across Europe and beyond, it can offer effective solutions to entrepreneurs and companies from over 40 countries.

Enterprise Europe Network forms part of a unique network, both in terms of its wide geographic reach and of the wide range of integrated services it provides to SMEs and other business actors. This is made possible due to the coordinated action of nearly 600 local partner organizations, employing around 4,000 experienced staff working to support the competitiveness of EU businesses. More information can be obtained on: Tel (029) 2087 9192 or visit: www.enterpriseeuropewales.org.uk

European Public Information Centres

European Public Information Centres are a partnership between Library Authorities and the Commission Representation in Wales to afford citizens access to information in their area.

Brecon Library
Rebecca Pugh, Branch Librarian
Tel: (01874) 623346 Fax: (01874) 622818
Email: chrispr@ntmail.powys.gov.uk

Bridgend County Library
Kath Ewins, Information Services Manager
Tel: (01656) 767451 Fax: (01656) 645719
Email: blis@bridgend.gov.uk

Mark Halliwell, Corporate Policy Co-ordinator
Tel: (01656) 643346 Fax: (01656) 768098
Email: hallim@bridgend.gov.uk

Caerphilly County Borough Council
Lisa Thomas, Information & Computer
Services Manager,
Email: thomal4@caerphilly.gov.uk

Cardiff County Council
Rob Davis, Information Librarian
Tel: (029) 2038 2116 Fax: (029) 2087 1588
Email: rdavis@cardiff.gov.uk
Website: www.cardiff.gov.uk/libraries

Ceredigion County Council
William H Howells, County Libraries Officer
Tel: (01970) 633703 Fax: (01970) 625059
Email: Williamh@ceredigion.gov.uk
Website: www.ceredigion.gov.uk/libraries

Chepstow Library
Sally Bradford, Information & Learning Manager
Tel: (01291) 635730 Fax: (01291) 635736
Email: sallybradford@monmouthshire.gov.uk

City & County of Swansea
Claire Tranter, Information Services Librarian
Tel: (01792) 636464 Fax: (01792) 636235
Email: Claire.Tranter@swansea.gov.uk
Website: www.swansea.gov.uk/libraries

Conwy County Borough Council
Sheila Evans, Assistant Librarian
Tel: (01492) 532358
Email: sheila.evans@conwy.gov.uk
Website: www.conwy.gov.uk/library

County Borough of Blaenau Gwent
Julie Davies, Librarian
Tel: (01495) 303069 Fax: (01495) 350547
Email: julie.davies@blaenau-gwent.gov.uk

Denbighshire County Council
Lucy Williams, Reference & Information
Services Librarian
Tel: (01824) 708087 Fax: (01824) 708202
Email: lucy.williams@denbighshire.gov.uk

Gwynedd Council
Alun Williams, Information Services Manager
Tel: (01286) 679465 Fax: (01286) 671137
Email: AlunHughesWilliams@gwynedd.gov.uk

Isle of Anglesey County Council
John Thomas, Assistant Director -
Libraries, Information Services
Fax: (01248) 750365 Email: jrtlh@ynysmon.gov.uk

Merthyr Tydfil Central Library
Geraint James, Information Librarian
Education - Central Library
Tel: (01685) 723057 Fax: (01685) 370690
Email: library.services@merthyr.gov.uk

Neath Port Talbot County Borough Council
Stephen Morris, Librarian
Tel: (01792) 862261 Fax: (01792) 869688
Email: pontardawe.library@neath-porttalbot.gov.uk

Hilary Smith, Port Talbot Library
Tel 1: (01639) 763490 Tel 2: (01639) 763431
Email: port.ref.library@npt.gov.uk

Claire Smith, Neath Reference Library
Tel: (01639) 764230
Email: neath.library@npt.gov.uk

Newport Central Library
Rhodri Matthews, Library Manager
Tel: (01633) 656656 Fax: (01633) 222615
Email: reference.library@newport.gov.uk

Newtown Library
Mair Dafydd, Branch Librarian
Tel: (01686) 626934 Fax: (01686) 624935
Email: mair.dafydd@powys.gov.uk

Pembrokeshire County Council
Sandra Matthews, Group Librarian Central Services
Tel 1: (01437) 775242 Tel 2: (01437) 775248
Fax: (01437) 767092
Email: sandra.matthews@pembrokeshire.gov.uk

EUROPE

EUROPEAN OFFICES

European Public Information Centres (cont.)

Rhondda Cynon Taf County Borough Council
Nick Kelland, Information Services Librarian
Tel: (01685) 885318 Fax: (01685) 881181
Email: nick.e.kelland@rhondda-cynon-taff.gov.uk

Vale of Glamorgan Council
Katherine Owen, Information Services Librarian,
Vale of Glamorgan Libraries
Tel: (01446) 735722 Fax: (01446) 709377
Email: KOwen@valeofglamorgan.gov.uk

Wrexham County Borough Council
Hedd ap Emlyn, Community Librarian
Tel: (01978) 292620 Fax: (01978) 292611
Email: hedd.apemlyn@wrexham.gov.uk
Website: www.wrexham.gov.uk

Eurodesk

Eurodesk provides an internet enquiry service for young people and those who work with them.
www.eurodesk.org

Basement Information Services
Blackwood Library, 192 High Street,
Blackwood, South Wales NP12 1AJ
Tel: (01495) 233007
Email: thebasement@caerphilly.gov.uk
Website: www.caerphilly.org.uk

Basement Youth Information Network
Crumlin 'Stute, Hillside Road, Crumlin,
Newport NP11 4QB Tel: (01495) 244064
Fax: (01495) 249881 Email: vennk@caerphilly.gov.uk /
markg@caerphilly.gov.uk

Bridgend Youth Services
Bridgend County Borough Council, The Old Church
School, Maesteg Road, Tondu, Bridgend CF32 9BT
Tel: (01656) 724057 Fax: (01656) 728587
Email: jeannette.Renley@bridgend.gov.uk

Cwmbran Centre for Young People
Glyndwr Road, Cwmbran Town Centre,
Torfaen, South Wales NP44 1QS
Tel: (01633) 875851 Fax: (01633) 489755
Email: ccyp@ccyp.org.uk Web: www.ccyp.org.uk

Flintshire Youth & Community Service
Flintshire Youth & Community Service, Bagillt Youth
Centre, Sunnyside, Holywell Road CH6 6LW
Tel: (01352) 710390 Fax: (01352) 710390
Email: katie.connolly@flintshire.gov.uk

INFO for Young People (Wrexham)
2 North Arcade, Chester Street, Wrexham LL13 8BB
Tel: (01978) 358900 Fax: (01978) 265261
Email: infoshop@wrexham.gov.uk

Merthyr Tydfil Youth Service
Merthyr Tydfil County Borough Council,
Ty Keir Hardie, Riverside Court, Avenue de Clichy,
Merthyr Tydfil CF47 8XD
Tel: (01685) 721965
Website: www.merthyr.gov.uk

Penarth Youth Project
West House Cottage, Stanwell Road,
Penarth, Vale of Glamorgan CF64 2ZA
Tel: (029) 2040 5305 Fax: (029) 2040 5305
Email: penarthyouthproject@hotmail.com

The Doorway (BLAENAFON)
Youth Information Centre, 69-70 Broad Street,
Blaenafon, Torfaen NP4 9NH
Tel: (01495) 793109 Fax: (01495) 793109
Email: sianne.morgan@blaenavon.fsnet.co.uk

Torfaen Youth Service
Pontypool Community Education Centre,
The Settlement, Trosnant Street,
Pontypool, Torfaen NP4 8AU
Tel: (01495) 758868 Fax: (01495) 758868
Email: margaret.biggs@torfaen.gov.uk
Website: www.torfaen.plus.com

West Wales European Centre
Dewi Building, Trinity College,
Carmarthen SA31 3EP
Tel: (01267) 242369 Fax: (01267) 234279
Email: wwec@carmarthenshire.gov.uk
Website: www.wwec.org.uk/english/eu

The Wales Yearbook

13

BUSINESS & FINANCE

CLEC
Creative Leadership & Enterprise Centre

Cardiff Metropolitan University
Prifysgol Fetropolitan Caerdydd
———— UWIC ————

The Creative Leadership and Enterprise Centre (CLEC) is based at UWIC's new Cardiff School of Management. We have an experienced academic team and have forged partnerships with specialist consultancies to provide an excellent learning experience.

CLEC has quickly carved out a niche as the leading centre of excellence for the design and delivery of leadership development programmes for the public and private sectors. We are also engaged in a range of research programmes on entrepreneurship and regional development.

Our current flagship project is the *20 Twenty Leadership* Programme for SMEs which has created a consortium of small businesses working together to grow their businesses along side a leadership programme tailor-made for the sector.

CLEC is also delivering the *Leadership for Collaboration* programme (L4C), to public sector participants across Wales and a Leadership for Social Enterprise programme (L4SE) - a series of development workshops for social entrepreneurs.

For more details on these programmes please contact:
Professor Brian Morgan
Cardiff School of Management, (UWIC)
Llandaff, Cardiff CF5 2YB
Tel: +44 (0)29 2041 6358 Email: brianmorgan@uwic.ac.uk

TOP 100 WELSH BUSINESSES

CLEC has compiled a list of the top 100 Companies in Wales as an indicator of the strength of the economy as a whole and also of some crucial sub-sectors of the manufacturing and service sectors. A number of factors should be taken into account when reading this list. Firstly, the list is based on recent trading figures for private and publicly quoted companies and provides a ranking of the Top Welsh companies based on a number of key economic and financial factors that have been reported to Companies House. To be included in the Top 100, the company must be registered and trading in Wales. For these reasons there will undoubtedly be some well-known names missing from the list mainly due to the fact that their head office is not registered in Wales - even though they may undertake important activities in Wales.

ALPHABETICAL INDEX

BUSINESS & FINANCE

TOP 100 WELSH BUSINESSES

1 CISCO INTERNATIONAL LTD
Selling internet protocol based networking and other products and services.
1 Callaghan Square, Cardiff, CF10 5BT ☎ (01244) 830100
Turnover (£m): 4,504.67   **Number of Employees:** 233

▲ NEW ▼

2 ICELAND FOODS GROUP LTD
A group engaged as retail grocers.
Second Avenue, Deeside Industrial Park, Deeside CH5 2NW ☎ (01244) 830100
Turnover (£m): 2,388.38   **Number of Employees:** 22953

△ -1 ▼

3 GE AIRCRAFT ENGINE SERVICES LTD
The overhaul and repair of aircraft engines and modules; company also performs repairs to aircraft engine components.
Caerphilly Road, Nantgarw, Cardiff CF15 7YJ ☎ (01443) 841041
Turnover (£m): 1,208.40   **Number of Employees:** 1091

△ -1 ▼

4 GLAS CYMRU CYF
A group engaged in the provision of water and sewerage services.
Pentwyn Road, Nelson, Treharris, Mid Glamorgan, CF46 6LY ☎ (08000) 520130
Turnover (£m): 676.70   **Number of Employees:** 1727

△ -1 ▼

5 CELSA (UK) HOLDINGS LTD
A group engaged in the manufacture and sale of steel products.
Building 58, East Moors Road, Cardiff, CF24 5NN ☎ (02920) 351800
Turnover (£m): 590.48   **Number of Employees:** 1196

△ -1 ▼

6 ADMIRAL GROUP PLC
Group's principal activities are the selling and administration of private motor, travel and home insurance and related products.
Capital Tower, Greyfriars Road, Cardiff, CF10 3AZ ☎ (08718) 828282
Turnover (£m): 574.60   **Number of Employees:** 4252

▲ +13 ▽

7 CALSONIC KANSEI EUROPE PLC
Manufacture of automotive components.
Calsonic Kansei Europe Plc, Llethri Road, Llanelli, Carmarthenshire, SA14 8HU
☎ (01554) 747000
Turnover (£m): 566.20   **Number of Employees:** 1637

▲ +1 ▽

8 REDROW PLC
Residential development which includes mixed use development.
Redrow House, St. Davids Park, Ewloe, Deeside, Clwyd, CH5 3RX
☎ (01454) 625000
Turnover (£m): 452.70   **Number of Employees:** 933

△ -2 ▼

9

DOW CORNING LTD
A group engaged in the manufacture and marketing of silicone products.
Barry Plant, Cardiff Road, Barry, Glamorgan, CF63 2YL ☎ (01676) 528000
Turnover (£m): 440.43   **Number of Employees:** 581

△ -2 ▽

10

PHS GROUP PLC
A group engaged in the provision of workplace services in the fields of
hygiene and waste management.
Western Industrial Estate, Lon-Y-Llyn, Caerphilly, CF83 1XH
☎ (02920) 851000
Turnover (£m): 394.59   **Number of Employees:** 4940

△ -1 ▽

11

WYNNSTAY GROUP PLC
Supply of agricultural farm inputs to both livestock and arable farm enterprises and
retailing of specialist merchandise through country stores and pet product shops.
Eagle House, Llansantffraid Ym Mechain, Powys, SY21 7AD ☎ (01691) 828512
Turnover (£m): 346.18   **Number of Employees:** 783

▲ +7 ▽

12

WALES & WEST UTILITIES LTD
A group engaged in the management of gas transportation assets.
Wales & West House, Spooner Close, Coedkernew, Newport, South Wales, NP10 8FZ
☎ (08701) 650597
Turnover (£m): 312.80   **Number of Employees:** 1449

△ -1 ▽

13

KRONOSPAN HOLDINGS LTD
A group engaged in the manufacture and sale of chipboard, medium density
fibreboard, oriented strand board, sawn timber and related products.
Maesgwyn Farm Holyhead Road, Chirk, Wrexham, LL14 5NT ☎ (01691) 773361
Turnover (£m): 292.19   **Number of Employees:** 919

▲ +2 ▽

14

ARRIVA TRAINS WALES/TRENAU ARRIVA CYMRU LTD
The operation of passenger railway services.
St Mary's House, 47 Penarth Road, Cardiff, CF10 5DJ ☎ (02920) 720500
Turnover (£m): 272.40   **Number of Employees:** 1998

▲ +2 ▽

15

PRINCIPALITY BUILDING SOCIETY
The provision of mortgage finance and other financial products
PO Box 89, Principality Buildings, Queen Street, Cardiff, CF10 1UA ☎ (02920) 382000
Turnover (£m): 257.40   **Number of Employees:** 1173

▲ NEW ▼

16

CAPPER & CO. LTD
Retail distribution and subsidiary operates retail stores within the Spar group.
Lanelay Road, Talbot Green, Pontyclun, Mid Glamorgan, CF72 8XX
☎ (01443) 225500
Turnover (£m): 235.00   **Number of Employees:** 645

△ -3 ▼

BUSINESS & FINANCE

17

MC 478 LTD
A group engaged in trading as motor dealers.
Avondale Road, Pontrhydyrun, Cwmbran, Gwent, NP44 1TT
Turnover (£m): 229.77   ***Number of Employees:*** 536

NEW

18

MON MOTORS LTD
The operation of car dealerships and in the provision of coach services.
Cwmbran Ford, Avondale Road, Pontrhydyrun, Cwmbran, Gwent, NP44 1TT
☎ (01633) 485255
Turnover (£m): 229.63   ***Number of Employees:*** 536

-1

19

KINGSPAN LTD
Manufacture of cold rolled sections and architectural wall panels,
and the distribution of insulated panels.
2-4 Greenfield Business Park, Bagillt Road, Greenfield, Holywell, Clwyd, CH8 7GJ
☎ (01352) 716100
Turnover (£m): 227.07   ***Number of Employees:*** 632

NEW

20

SINCLAIR MOTOR HOLDINGS LTD
Purchase, sale and repair of motor vehicles and the sale of vehicle parts and fuel.
C/O Sinclair Garages Port Talbot, Dan-Y-Bryn Road, Port Talbot, SA13 1AL
☎ (01792) 894949
Turnover (£m): 219.22   ***Number of Employees:*** 598

+1

21

HOOVER LTD
A group engaged in the manufacture, marketing and servicing of domestic appliances.
Pentrebach, Merthyr Tydfil, Mid Glamorgan, CF48 4YA   ☎ (01685) 721222
Turnover (£m): 215.18   ***Number of Employees:*** 471

+2

22

ROYAL MINT
Manufacture and supply of circulating coins and blanks for overseas central
banks, issuing authorities and mints.
The Royal Mint, Llantrisant, Pontyclun, Mid Glamorgan, CF72 8YT
☎ (01443) 222111
Turnover (£m): 215.15   ***Number of Employees:*** 892

NEW

23

CONVATEC
Manufacture and marketing of ostomy, incontinence and other skin care products.
20 First Avenue, Deeside Industrial Park, Deeside, Clwyd, CH5 2NU   ☎ (0800) 282254
Turnover (£m): 201.02   ***Number of Employees:*** 900

NEW

24

THE FIRST MILK CHEESE COMPANY LTD
The manufacture and sale of cheese and other dairy products.
Pickhill Lane, Cross Lanes, Wrexham, LL13 0UE   ☎ (01437) 761505
Turnover (£m): 194.09   ***Number of Employees:*** 408

NEW

BUSINESS & FINANCE

25

FINSBURY FOOD GROUP PLC
Group producing premium and speciality breads and cakes.
Maes Y Coed Road, Cardiff, CF14 4XR ☎ (02920) 357500
Turnover (£m): 189.58   ***Number of Employees:*** 2576

-3

26

MONEYSUPERMARKET.COM GROUP PLC
The group introduces business to the financial, insurance, travel and home services and other product or service providers through it's websites.
Moneysupermarket House, St David's Park, Ewloe, Chester, Cheshire, CH4 0AE
☎ (01244) 665700
Turnover (£m): 181.05   ***Number of Employees:*** 430

NEW

27

C E M DAY LTD
Retail distribution of new and used vehicles.
Llanelli Road, Garngoch, Swansea, SA4 4LL ☎ (01792) 222111
Turnover (£m): 178.86   ***Number of Employees:*** 525

-2

28

ARTENIUS PET PACKAGING UK LTD
The manufacture of PET bottles and preforms for the beverage market.
Gresford Industrial Park, Gresford, Wrexham, Clwyd, LL12 8LX ☎ (01978) 856111
Turnover (£m): 170.79   ***Number of Employees:*** 290

=

29

PANASONIC MANUFACTURING UK LTD
The manufacture of television sets and microwave ovens for sale in UK and Europe.
Wyncliffe Road, Pentwyn Industrial Estate, Cardiff, CF23 7XB ☎ (02920) 540011
Turnover (£m): 168.60   ***Number of Employees:*** 518

-9

30

CORBETT GROUP LIMITED
A group engaged as turf accountants, on course bookmakers and operators of a bingo hall, members social club, hotel, public house and a sports stadium.
74-78 Welsh Road, Garden City, Deeside, Clwyd, CH5 2HU
Turnover (£m): 162.07   ***Number of Employees:*** 160

NEW

31

YUASA BATTERY SALES (UK) LTD
A group engaged in the manufacture and sale of automotive and special industrial batteries and associated equipment.
Unit 22, Rassau Industrial Estate, Ebbw Vale, Gwent, NP23 5SD
☎ (08708) 500312
Turnover (£m): 155.31   ***Number of Employees:*** 461

+32

32

DAWNUS HOLDINGS LTD
A group engaged as civil engineers.
7 Dyffryn Court, Riverside Business Park, Swansea, SA7 0AP
☎ (01792) 781870
Turnover (£m): 136.62   ***Number of Employees:*** 1524

+30

BUSINESS & FINANCE

33

EURO ALLOYS LTD
Traders in aluminium products. Accounts data expressed in US Dollars.
Alder House, 5 Cedar Court, Hazell Drive, Newport, Gwent, NP10 8FY
☎ (02086) 531703
Turnover (£m): 134.85   *Number of Employees:* 12

▲ ▽ **+13**

34

BRO-TECH LTD
Manufacture and sale of ion exchange resins.
Unit D, Llantrisant Business Park, Llantrisant, Pontyclun, CF72 8LF
☎ (01443) 229334
Turnover (£m): 133.43   *Number of Employees:* 748

▲ ▽ **+15**

35

SPTS TECHNOLOGIES UK LTD
Design, manufacture and distribution of a range of highly specialised machines.
Ringland Way, Newport, Gwent, NP18 2TA
☎ (01633) 414000
Turnover (£m): 131.51   *Number of Employees:* 405

▲ **NEW** ▼

36

INTERTISSUE LTD
Manufacture and sale of soft tissue products.
Brunel Way, Baglan Energy Park, Briton Ferry, Neath, SA11 2GA
☎ (01639) 825380
Turnover (£m): 126.68   *Number of Employees:* 300

▲ ▽ **+11**

37

CONTROL TECHNIQUES DRIVES LTD
The manufacture and sale of electronic variable speed drives.
The Gro, Newtown, Powys, SY16 3BE   ☎ (01686) 612000
Turnover (£m): 125.91   *Number of Employees:* 384

▲ ▽ **+29**

38

BRC LTD
Reinforcement solutions for the construction industry.
Corporation Road, Newport, Gwent, NP19 4RD   ☎ (01633) 280816
Turnover (£m): 123.56   *Number of Employees:* 295

▲ **NEW** ▼

39

TETRA PAK LTD
*The sale and lease of machines for liquid food packaging and the supply of
related packaging materials.*
Bedwell Road, Cross Lanes, Wrexham, Clwyd, LL13 0UT   ☎ (08704) 426000
Turnover (£m): 122.38   *Number of Employees:* 128

△ ▼ **-9**

40

GMAC UK PLC
*Financing the distribution of new products to dealers for resale
and financing the dealers' retail instalment sales of new and used vehicles.*
Heol Ygamlas Parc Nantgarw, Treforest, Cardiff, South Glamorgan, CF15 7QU
☎ (0844) 871 2222
Turnover (£m): 122.02   *Number of Employees:* 325

▲ **NEW** ▼

41

SPEAR GROUP HOLDINGS LTD
Provides innovative and value added film pressure-sensitive labelling technology.
Christopher Grey Court, Lakeside, Llantarnam Industrial Park, Cwmbran NP44 3SE
☎ (01633) 627600
Turnover (£m): 127.71   **Number of Employees:** 661

-9

42

GLOBAL FOODS LTD
Suppliers to the catering industry.
1-3 Stadium Close, Off Penarth Road, Cardiff, CF11 8TS   ☎ (02920) 384835
Turnover (£m): 118.62   **Number of Employees:** 124

+2

43

SOLUTIA UK LTD
Manufacture, marketing and sale of speciality chemicals, window films and specialist industrial components.
Corporation Road, Newport, South Wales, NP19 4XF   ☎ (01633) 278221
Turnover (£m): 115.85   **Number of Employees:** 230

-7

44

STS UK HOLDCO II
Travel agent, tour operator and travel wholesaler.
Glendale House, Glendale Business Park, Deeside, Clwyd, CH5 2DL
☎ (0844) 826 2600
Turnover (£m): 114.77   **Number of Employees:** 368

NEW

45

THE NUMBER (UK) LTD
The provision of directory assistance.
Sterling House, Malthouse Avenue, Cardiff Gate Business Park, Cardiff, CF23 8RA
☎ (08702) 331000
Turnover (£m): 112.91   **Number of Employees:** 180

-14

46

WATKIN JONES & SON LTD
Building contractors.
Llandegai Industrial Estate, Bangor, Gwynedd, LL57 4YH   ☎ (01248) 362516
Turnover (£m): 112.71   **Number of Employees:** 243

-19

47

OLAER GROUP LTD
Design, manufacture and marketing of processing and packaging of fluid components in complex hydraulic systems.
Glendale Avenue, Sandycroft Industrial Estate, Deeside, Clwyd, CH5 2QP
☎ (01244) 526211
Turnover (£m): 112.18   **Number of Employees:** 474

-12

48

QIOPTIQ LTD
Design, development, manufacture and assembly of specialised optical modules, sub-assemblies and components for use in both military and commercial markets.
Glascoed Road, St Asaph, Denbighshire, LL17 0LL
☎ (01745) 588000
Turnover (£m): 110.11   **Number of Employees:** 520

-15

BUSINESS & FINANCE

BUSINESS & FINANCE

49 ALCOA MANUFACTURING (G.B.) LTD
Aluminium Production.
Princess House, Princess Way, Swansea, SA1 3LW ☎ (01792) 873301
Turnover (£m): 106.38   *Number of Employees:* 436

NEW

50 MITEL NETWORKS LTD
The research and development, sales and marketing of communications software, solutions and applications and the provision of professional services.
Castlegate Business Park, Portskewett, Monmouthshire, NP26 5YR
☎ (01291) 430000
Turnover (£m): 104.85   *Number of Employees:* 431

-10

51 IPSEN BIOPHARM LTD
The manufacture and sale of pharmaceutical products.
Ash Road, Wrexham Industrial Estate, Wrexham, LL13 9UF ☎ (01753) 627700
Turnover (£m): 104.48   *Number of Employees:* 379

NEW

52 GOCOMPARE.COM LTD
Provision of web based insurance, marketing and intermediary services.
Unit 6 Imperial Courtyard, Newport, Gwent, NP10 8UL
☎ (01633) 654060
Turnover (£m): 101.49   *Number of Employees:* 84

+3

53 BIOMET UK LTD
The manufacture and sale of reconstructive devices, internal fixation devices, orthopaedic support devices and operating room supplies.
Waterton Industrial Estate, Bridgend, South Wales, CF31 3XA
☎ (01656) 655221
Turnover (£m): 101.07   *Number of Employees:* 548

-27

54 S A BRAIN & COMPANY LTD
A group engaged as brewers, bottlers, wine and spirit merchants and licensed property owners and managers.
The Cardiff Brewery, Crawshay Street, Cardiff, CF10 5DS ☎ (02920) 402060
Turnover (£m): 99.28   *Number of Employees:* 1907

-16

55 EXPRESS REINFORCEMENTS LTD
Wholesale of metals and metal ores
Eaglesbush Works, Milland Road, Neath, SA11 1NJ ☎ (01639) 645555
Turnover (£m): 98.82   *Number of Employees:* 174

-10

56 ALCONTROL UK LTD
A laboratory Services company providing investigation, compliance and assurance testing services for environmental, food and fuel sectors.
Unit 7-8 Manor Lane, Hawarden, Deeside, Clwyd, CH5 3US ☎ (01244) 528700
Turnover (£m): 97.00   *Number of Employees:* 1660

+33

57 **B A CASH & CARRY (CARDIFF) LTD**
Wholesale and retail distribution of food, wine, spirits and cigarettes.
Hadfield Ind Est, Hadfield Rd, Leckwith, Cardiff, CF11 8AQ
☎ (02920) 229962
Turnover (£m): 96.91   *Number of Employees:* 170

-16

58 **IR NEWPORT LTD**
Development, manufacture, marketing and sale of semiconductor devices for assembly.
Cardiff Road, Newport, NP10 8YJ
☎ (01633) 810121
Turnover (£m): 95.27   *Number of Employees:* 523

+39

59 **MERITOR HEAVY VEHICLE BRAKING SYSTEMS (UK) LTD**
The design, manufacture and sale of braking equipment for heavy road and off-road vehicles.
Arvinmeritor Grange Road, Cwmbran, Gwent, NP44 3XU
☎ (01633) 834040
Turnover (£m): 93.92   *Number of Employees:* 390

=

60 **ACORN (SYNERGIE) UK LTD**
Recruitment agents and suppliers of temporary labour and training services.
Somerton House, Hazell Drive, Newport, Gwent, NP10 8FY
☎ (01633) 222258
Turnover (£m): 93.51   *Number of Employees:* 243

+7

61 **NICE-PAK INTERNATIONAL**
Manufacture and wholesale of disposable premoistened wipes.
Aber Park, Aber Road, Flint, Clwyd, CH6 5EX   ☎ (01352) 736700
Turnover (£m): 90.96   *Number of Employees:* 915

NEW

62 **MOMENTIVE SPECIALTY CHEMICALS UK LTD**
Manufacture and sale of adhesives and resins for use in a wide variety of applications.
Sully Moors Road, Penarth, South Glamorgan, CF64 5YU   ☎ (01446) 725500
Turnover (£m): 88.76   *Number of Employees:* 149

NEW

63 **DUNBIA (WALES)**
Wholesale of Meat and Meat Products
Dunbia Wales Teify Park, Lampeter Road, Llanybydder, Carmarthenshire, SA40 9QE
☎ (01570) 480284
Turnover (£m): 86.69   *Number of Employees:* 440

-15

64 **CATALENT CTS (WALES)** (PREV. APTUIT)
A group engaged in the management of pre-clinical activities, pharmaceutical development and sterile manufacturing.
Unit 107, Tenth Avenue, Deeside Industrial Park, Deeside, Clwyd, CH5 2UA
☎ (01244) 845700
Turnover (£m): 85.06   *Number of Employees:* 876

-21

BUSINESS & FINANCE

65

CASSIDIAN LTD (PREV EADS DEFENSE AND SECURITY SYSTEMS LTD)
The provision of secure communications solutions that address the demands of the defence market, homeland security and other government departments.
Quadrant House, Celtic Springs, Coedkernew, Newport, NP10 8FZ
☎ (01633) 713000
Turnover (£m): 84.26   **Number of Employees:** 832

-31

66

SHAW HEALTHCARE (GROUP) LTD
Provision of care services, including the operation of nursing and residential homes.
1 Links Court, Links Business, Park Fortran Road, St. Mellons, Cardiff, CF3 0LT
☎ (02920) 364411
Turnover (£m): 80.92   **Number of Employees:** 3371

+4

67

EURO FOODS GROUP LTD
Distribution of frozen meats and vegetables to the catering industry and wholesale businesses.
Churchgate House, 3 Church Road, Whitchurch, Cardiff, CF14 2DX
☎ (01633) 636000
Turnover (£m): 80.62   **Number of Employees:** 762

+1

68

WARWICK INTERNATIONAL GROUP LTD
A group engaged in the manufacture and marketing of performance chemicals.
Coast Road, Mostyn, Holywell, Clwyd, CH8 9HE   ☎ (01745) 560651
Turnover (£m): 78.82   **Number of Employees:** 225

NEW

69

MAINUNIT LTD
Development and Selling of Real Estate.
21 Nevill Street, Abergavenny, Monmouthshire, NP7 5AA   ☎ (01873) 857211
Turnover (£m): 78.75   **Number of Employees:** 528

NEW

70

ROCKWOOL LTD
Manufacture and distribution of thermal, acoustic and fire-safe insulation materials.
Pencoed, Bridgend, Mid Glamorgan, CF35 6NY
☎ (08452) 412586
Turnover (£m): 78.68   **Number of Employees:** 427

-6

71

ALUN GRIFFITHS (CONTRACTORS) LTD
Building and civil engineering contractors.
Waterways House, Merthyr Road, Llanfoist, Abergavenny, NP7 9LN
☎ (01873) 857211
Turnover (£m): 78.52   **Number of Employees:** 504

-19

72

J H LEEKE & SONS LTD
Operation of out of town department stores.
Mwyndy Business Park, Mwyndy, Pontyclun, Mid Glamorgan, CF72 8PN   ☎ (01443) 667600
Turnover (£m): 73.94   **Number of Employees:** 791

+7

73

NORGINE LTD
The manufacture and distribution of pharmaceutical products.
New Rd Tiryberth, Hengoed, Mid-Glam, South Wales, CF82 8SJ ☎ (01443) 812183
Turnover (£m): 73.41   **Number of Employees:** 585

NEW

74

WOCKHARDT UK LTD
Sale and distribution of pharmaceutical products and the provision of related services.
Ash Road North, Wrexham Industrial Estate, Wrexham, LL13 9UF
☎ (01978) 661261
Turnover (£m): 72.97   **Number of Employees:** 58

-21

75

HYDRO ALUMINIUM EXTRUSION LTD
Aluminium production
Pantglas Industrial Estate, Bedwas, Caerphilly, CF83 8DR
☎ (02920) 854600
Turnover (£m): 72.78   **Number of Employees:** 302

-24

76

IQE PLC
Group are engaged in the manufacture of advanced semiconductor materials.
Pascal Close, St Mellons, Cardiff, South Glamorgan, CF3 0LW ☎ (02920) 839400
Turnover (£m): 72.65   **Number of Employees:** 352

+11

77

BROTHER INDUSTRIES (UK) LTD
The manufacture of electronic typewriters, fax machines and dot matrix printers.
Vauxhall Industrial Estate, Ruabon, Wrexham, LL14 6HA
☎ (01978) 813400
Turnover (£m): 72.11   **Number of Employees:** 199

+3

78

BAYV INVESTMENTS LTD
The manufacture and sale of automotive filtration equipment.
Kingsway Buildings, Bridgend Industrial Estate, Bridgend, CF31 3RY ☎ (01443) 445000
Turnover (£m): 71.87   **Number of Employees:** 649

-18

79

SOGEFI FILTRATION LTD
Manufacture of parts and accessories for motor vehicles and their engines
Llantrisant Ind Est, Llantrisant, Pontyclun CF72 8YU ☎ (01443) 223000
Ultimate Holding Company: De Benedetti Carlo
Turnover (£m): 71.79   **Number of Employees:** 715

-25

80

TINOPOLIS LTD
Making of television, film, online and other audio-visual productions.
Tinopolis Centre, Park Street, Llanelli, Carmarthenshire, SA15 3YE
☎ (01554) 880880
Turnover (£m): 71.34   **Number of Employees:** 386

-7

81

W R DAVIES (MOTORS) LTD
Sale of new and used vehicles and the provision of other garage services.
Waterloo Place, Salop Road, Welshpool, Powys, SY21 7HE
☎ (01686) 625514
Turnover (£m): 71.03   **Number of Employees:** 254

-10

BUSINESS & FINANCE

82

CELTIC ENERGY LTD
Opencast coal mining and associated activities.
9 Beddau Way, Castlegate Business Park, Cardiff, CF83 2AX ☎ (02920) 760990
Turnover (£m): 68.45   ***Number of Employees:*** 317

-17

83

SOFA BRANDS INTERNATIONAL LTD
Manufacture, sale and distribution of furniture and associated furnishings
Wilson House, Ashtree Court, Woodsy Close, Cardiff, CF23 8RW ☎ (02920) 730840
Turnover (£m): 67.89   ***Number of Employees:*** 870

-6

84

G WALTERS (HOLDINGS) LTD
Groups main activities include the provision of plant hire & maintenance services, civil engineering & opencast mining & demolition & salvage contracting.
Hirwaun Industrial Estate, Hirwaun, Aberdare, Mid Glamorgan, CF44 9UL
☎ (01685) 815100
Turnover (£m): 67.86   ***Number of Employees:*** 289

NEW

85

ABINGDON FLOORING LTD
A group engaged in the manufacture of tufted and other major types of carpets.
Parkway, Pen Y Fan Industrial Estate, Croespenmaen Crumlin, Newport, NP11 3XG
☎ (01495) 246220
Turnover (£m): 66.88   ***Number of Employees:*** 464

-9

86

SEDA UK LTD
The manufacture, import and distribution of packaging materials.
10 Salvatore D'amato Court, Hawtin Park, Gellihaf, Blackwood, Gwent, NP12 2EU
☎ (01443) 811888
Turnover (£m): 66.71   ***Number of Employees:*** 223

-5

87

HARRIS PYE GROUP LTD
Marine engineering including offshore oil and gas projects and land-based boiler contracts.
David Davies Road, No.2 Barry Dock, Barry, South Glamorgan, CF63 4AB ☎ (01446) 720066
Turnover (£m): 66.55   ***Number of Employees:*** 560

-15

88

HUWS GRAY LTD
Builders merchants.
Head Office, Industrial Estate, Llangefni, Anglesey, LL77 7HL ☎ (01248) 724750
Turnover (£m): 66.45   ***Number of Employees:*** 336

-6

89

CASTELL HOWELL FOODS LTD
The wholesale distribution of food products, predominantly frozen foods.
Cross Hands Food Park, Cross Hands, Llanelli, SA14 6SX ☎ (01267) 222000
Turnover (£m): 65.44   ***Number of Employees:*** 353

-6

90

S DUDLEY & SONS LTD
Building, shop fitting and supply of architectural aluminium.
Tydu Works, Tregwilym Road, Rogerstone, Nr. Newport, Gwent, NP1 9EQ
☎ (01633) 892244
Turnover (£m): 65.30   ***Number of Employees:*** 129

NEW

BUSINESS & FINANCE

91

PETER'S HOLDINGS LTD (PREV PETER'S FOOD SERVICE LTD)
A group engaged in the manufacture and distribution of food products.
Unit 1, Greenway, Caerphilly CF83 8XP ☎ (02920) 853200
Turnover (£m): 64.62   **Number of Employees:** 746

-17

92

ROWECORD HOLDINGS LTD
Supply and erection of fluid storage systems, distribution of industrial valves, civil engineering, structural steel fabrication and erection.
Neptune Works, Usk Way, Newport, Gwent, NP9 2SS ☎ (01633) 256433
Turnover (£m): 64.34   **Number of Employees:** 903

-55

93

THE GLOBAL TRAVEL GROUP LTD
Management of independent travel agencies and travel agency retailers.
Glendale House, Glendale Business Park, Sandycroft CH5 2DL ☎ (08707) 350736
Turnover (£m): 63.52   **Number of Employees:** 230

-24

94

CABOT CARBON LTD
The manufacture and marketing of performance chemicals.
Finance Dept. Sully Moors Road, Sully, Penarth, Vale Of Glamorgan, CF64 5RP
☎ (01446) 736999
Turnover (£m): 63.26   **Number of Employees:** 113

NEW

95

INEXUS GROUP LTD
Ownership and operation of gas and electric infrastructure.
Driscoll 2, Ellen Street, Cardiff, CF10 4BP ☎ (02920) 908550
Turnover (£m): 62.82   **Number of Employees:** 215

+4

96

HYDRO ALUMINIUM DEESIDE LTD
Toll conversion and the manufacture of aluminium extrusion billet, rolling slab and remelt ingot from scrap and virgin metal.
Bridge Road, Wrexham Industrial Estate, Wrexham, Clwyd, LL13 9PS ☎ (01978) 660231
Turnover (£m): 60.85   **Number of Employees:** 44

NEW

97

NU-OVAL ACQUISITIONS 1 LTD
Manufacture of non-domestic cooling and ventilation equipment, solar equipment and related ancillaries
Western Industrial Estate, Caerphilly, Mid Glamorgan, CF83 1XH ☎ (08705) 121400
Turnover (£m): 60.54   **Number of Employees:** 422

-13

98

DRAGON LNG GROUP LTD
Operation of liquid natural gas ('lng') import and storage terminal in Milford Haven.
Main Road, Waterston, Milford Haven, Pembrokeshire, SA73 1DR ☎ (01646) 691730
Turnover (£m): 58.30   **Number of Employees:** 56

NEW

99

BASF COATINGS LTD
The manufacture and sale of industrial coatings
10th Avenue, Deeside Industrial Park, Deeside, CH5 2UA
☎ (01244) 281315
Turnover (£m): 57.76   **Number of Employees:** 112

-3

100

DR J D HULL & ASSOCIATES LTD
Dentist.
Building 1, Eastern Building Park, St. Mellons, Cardiff, CF3 5EA
Turnover (£m): 56.85   **Number of Employees:** 454

NEW

BUSINESS & FINANCE

ACAS WALES

Third Floor
Fusion Point 2, Dumballs Road
Cardiff CF10 5BF

☎ (08457) 38 37 36
Helpline: (08457) 47 47 47
Fax: (029) 2076 8107

Email: gpetty@acas.org.uk
Website: www.acas.org.uk

ACAS Chair
Ed Sweeney

Regional Director - Wales
Robert Johnson

The Acas ambition is to improve organizations and working life through better employment relations. Acas has 11 main regional centres throughout England, Scotland and Wales and advisers based in the Acas Wales regional office (Cardiff) together with the North Wales area office (Wrexham) deliver the full range of Acas services throughout Wales.

Although publicly funded, sponsored by the Department for Business Innovation & Skills (BIS), Acas is statutorily independent of government. With over 30 years experience of working with people in businesses and organizations of every size and sector Acas advisers do not just help resolve differences between parties - they are very much involved in preventing disputes. Services include: providing up-to-date information and advice, high quality training and working with employers and employees to solve problems and improve performance.

PRINCIPAL OFFICERS

Robert Johnson	Regional Director - Wales & Southern England	d/t 01179 065279
Gareth Petty	Area Director - Wales	d/t 029 2076 8114
David Jones	Senior Adviser - North Wales	d/t 029 2076 8144
Gill Mason	Senior Adviser - West Wales	d/t 029 2076 8131
Hywel Hopkin	Senior Adviser - South/Mid Wales	d/t 029 2076 8106
Lorna Wilson	Senior Adviser - South East Wales	d/t 029 2076 8104

Total no. permanent staff: 50

ACCA CYMRU/WALES

Head of ACCA Wales
Ben Cottam

ACCA Cymru/Wales
PO Box 2520
Cardiff
CF23 0GN

☎ (029) 2026 3657
Fax: (029) 2026 3700

Website:
www.wales.accaglobal.com

Email: wales@accaglobal.com

Wales Committee Chair
John Cullen

ACCA has 154,000 members and 432,000 students globally. ACCA aims to provide quality professional opportunities to people of ability and application throughout their working careers. It's five-year growth illustrates that it is the fastest-growing body overall among all international professional accountancy bodies. ACCA Cymru/Wales opened its Wales office in 2001 and there are now more than 4,300 members and students in Wales, in every sector of the economy.

REGIONAL MEMBERS' NETWORK

North Wales	President: Alison Rennison FCCA	Panel Members: Andrew Kane FCCA; Andrew Stevens FCCA Simon Moulton FCCA; Victoria Davies FCCA Colin Bell FCCA; High Prys Jones FCCA
Swansea & West Wales	President: Jane Heard FCCA	Panel Members: Sandra McAlister FCCA; Garry Astley FCCA Rhidian Davies FCCA; Don Thomas FCCA Claire Wilcock ACCA; Steven Flather FCCA Sian Way FCCA; Nicola Owen FCCA
South Wales	President: Richard Lewis FCCA	Panel Members: Lindsay Hogg FCCA; Rhian Staples ACCA Holly Edwards-Davies FCCA; James Slatter ACCA Kathryn Bates ACCA; Trisha Evans FCCA Bethan Walker ACCA; Natalie Forde FCCA

STAFF

Ben Cottam - *Head of ACCA Wales;* Ceri Maund - *Services & Communications Manager Wales;* Stacey Aggrey - *Business Development Manager;* Maria Hampson-Jones - *Administrative Assistant;* Tori Booth - *Student Business Relationship Manager*

Join us for a season of talks and dinners

Cardiff Business Club
Celebrating the first 100 years
1912–2012

www.cardiffbusinessclub.org

Cardiff Business Club
PO Box 1073
Cardiff CF11 1SD
☎ (029) 2066 6555

Email: office@cardiffbusinessclub.org
Website: www.cardiffbusinessclub.org

President
Lord Rowe-Beddoe DL

Chair
Gerald Davies CBE DL

Cardiff Business Club

FLOREAT CARDIFF

Patron HRH The Prince of Wales

Founded in 1912, Cardiff Business Club is the leading organization of its kind outside of London and looks forward to its centenary celebrations in the autumn of 2012. The Club is fortunate to have HRH The Prince of Wales as Patron. The Club's principal activity is the organization of high profile dinners with guest speakers of international standing to address the members. These events are usually held in Cardiff between October and April.

The lectures are inclusive events and open to all. Dinners and other social activities are primarily for Members of the Club but, subject to availability, may be open to a wider audience. Full details about membership of this historic Club, and the future events are available on the Club website www.cardiffbusinessclub.org

DIRECTORS & ADVISERS

Gerald Davies CBE DL (Chair)
Alun Davies (Honorary Secretary)
Jonathon Poyner (Honorary Membership Secretary)
Peter Umbleja (Honorary Treasurer)
Raj Aggarwal OBE
Alan Edmunds
Chris Haines

Melanie Hamer
Alison Hoy
Laurence James
David Lermon
Harry Lewis
David Myrddin-Evans

Robert Shepherd
Jonathan Smith
David Stevens
Jemma Terry
Roy J Thomas

Club Coordinator - Liz Brookes, Grapevine Events
Club Photographer - Richard Bosworth
Auditors: PwC

Season Sponsors for 2012/13 are:  ODGERS BERNDTSON ADMIRAL

BUSINESS & FINANCE

CBI CYMRU WALES

2 Caspian Point, Caspian Way,
Cardiff Bay, Cardiff CF10 4DQ
☎ (029) 2097 7600
Fax: (029) 2097 7619

Email: emma.georgiades@cbi.org.uk
Website: www.cbi.org.uk/wales

LLAIS BUSNESAU
THE VOICE OF BUSINESS
CYMRU/WALES

Chair
Graham Edwards

Director
Emma Watkins

The CBI's mission is to promote the conditions in which businesses of all sizes and sectors in Wales can compete and prosper for the benefit of all. The CBI represents companies of every size, including FTSE 100, FTSE 350, mid – caps, SMEs and microbusinesses drawn from every sector including automotive, aerospace & defence, construction, creative industries, IT, professional services, retail, transport and utilities.

COUNCIL MEMBERS   ♂ 44 ♀ 13

Chair: Graham Edwards - *Chief Executive, Wales & West Utilities Ltd*

Scott Waddington, (Vice Chair) - *Chief Executive, S A Brain & Co Ltd;* Nigel Annett - *Managing Director, Dŵr Cymru Welsh Water;* Neil Ashbridge - *Agent for Wales, Bank of England Agency for Wales;* Ann Beynon OBE - *Director, Wales, BT;* Andy Billcliff - *Head of Hydro Operations & Maintenance (UK), RWE npower Renewables plc;* Robert Bizzell - *Director Finance, TATA Steel Strip Products UK;* Mark Bulanda - *President, Control Techniques Ltd;* Lynda Campbell -*General Manager Wales, British Gas Centrica;* Nick Canning - *Executive Director, People & Customers, Iceland Foods Ltd;* Louise Casella - *Director of Strategic Development, Cardiff University;* Tony Chapman - *Vice-Chancellor, Cardiff Metropolitan University;* Mike Cox - *General Manager, VALE Europe Ltd;* Michael Cuddy - *Joint Managing Director, Cuddy Group;* Owain Davies - *Managing Director, Amacanu Ltd;* Patrick Edwards - *Director of Commercial, Tarmac Ltd;* Peter Griffiths - *Chief Executive, Principality Building Society;* Robert Haase - *Technical Director, International Rectifier;* Wayne Harvey - *Senior Partner, Deloitte LLP;* Jeremy Haskey - *Vice President Systems Engineering, Alcatel-Lucent;* Mary James - *Director, National Farmers' Union Wales;* David Jones - *Principal/Chief Executive, Deeside College;* Huw Glyn Jones - *Managing Director, Jones Brothers Ruthin (Civil Engineering) Co Ltd;* Kathryn Jones - *Organizational Development Director, Buy As You View Ltd;* Pamela Joseph - *Commercial Director, Bluestone Resorts Ltd;* Arnold H C Kammerling MBE - *Director, Carl Kammerling International Ltd;* Saleem Kidwai OBE - *Chief Executive, EBSP Ltd;* Rob Lewis - *Regional Chairman, PriceWaterhouseCoopers LLP;* Warren Lewis - *Head of Corporate Banking, HSBC Bank PLC;* Julie Lydon - *Vice-Chancellor, University of Glamorgan;* Nicholas Main - *Operations Materials Leader, GE Aviation;* Andy Mallett - *Chief Executive, Ludlow Street Healthcare Group Ltd;* Marcella Maxwell - *Director, Working Links Wales;* Bill Mayne - *Chief Executive, MSS Group;* Ian Menzies - *Senior Programmes Director UK & International;* Matthew Morgan - *Chief Operating Officer, Cassidian;* Stuart Morgan - *Head of Claims, Admiral Group PLC;* Eoghan Mortell - *Managing Director, Working Word Public Relations Ltd;* Robert Mudie - *Finance Director/Company Secretary, Hoover Candy Group;* Dave Ott - *Site Manager/Director Barry Plant, Dow Corning;* Hayley Joanne Parsons - *Chief Executive Officer, Gocompare.com;* Jackie Pearson - *European Publishers Business Controller, UPM-Kymmene (UPM Shotton);* Karen Phillips - *Deputy Principal, Coleg Morgannwg;* Michael Plaut - *Managing Director, Northmace & Hendon Ltd;* Gareth Powell - *Chief Operating Officer, BBC Wales;* Michael Prior - *Partner, Morgan Cole;* Mark Rees - *Finance Director, Qioptic Ltd;* Stuart Rowlands - *Managing Director, Redrow Homes (South Wales) Ltd;* Jeremy Salisbury - *Director, Salisbury & Co;* Robert Salisbury - *Senior Partner, Gamlins;* Mike Scott - *Vice-Chancellor & CEO, Glyndŵr University;* Sajid Shah - *Supply Chain Manager, Advanced Elastomer Systems Ltd;* Victoria Stuart - *UK HR Manager, Ball Packaging Europe UK Ltd;* Chris Sutton - *Lead Director, Jones Lang LaSalle;* Steve Thomas - *Government Affairs Executive, Airbus UK;* Ceri Vaughan - *Call Centre Manager, Everything Everywhere Ltd;* Rhys Wynne - *Managing Director, UPL-Utility Partnership Ltd*

PRINCIPAL OFFICERS

Emma Watkins - *Director;* Ian Price - *Assistant Director;* Leighton Jenkins - *Assistant Director, Policy*   **Total no. staff: 6**

ICAEW

PO Box 4274
Cardiff CF14 8GA
☎ 029 2002 1481

Email: wales@icaew.com
Website: icaew.com/wales

Chair
Jeremy Salisbury

Director for Wales
David Lermon

ICAEW opened its office in Wales in 2001 as part of its commitment to Wales and Welsh affairs post devolution. ICAEW is the largest professional accountancy body in Europe, with more the 138,000 members, some 3,000 of whom work in and with business in Wales. ICAEW operates under a Royal Charter, working in the public interest. Its primary objectives are to educate and train Chartered Accountants, to maintain high standards of professional conduct among members, to provide services to members and students, and to advance the theory and practice of accountancy.

PRINCIPAL COMMITTEE MEMBERS   ♂ 13 ♀ 2

Strategy Board for Wales

Chair	**Background**
Jeremy Salisbury	*Salisbury & Company, St Asaph*
Other Members	
Stuart Castledine	*Non-Executive Director, Cardiff*
Katy Chamberlain	*Chwarae Teg, Cardiff*
Prof Roy Chandler	*Cardiff Business School*
Chris Davies	*Graig Shipping, Cardiff*
Carla Edgley	*Cardiff Business School*
Philip Hunkin	*WBV Limited, Neath*
John Jenkins	*Xodus Group, Aberystwyth*
Mererid Jones	*Mudiad Ysgolion Meithrin, Aberystwyth*
Murray MacFarlane	*Monmouth*
Laurie Pavelin	*Penarth*

South Wales Society of Chartered Accountants

President - Brenig Preest   *Excalibur, London & Cardiff*
Deputy President - Glyn Davies   *Charity Trustee, Bridgend*
Vice President - Andrew Williams   *Haraled Consultancy, Cardiff*

Chester & North Wales Society of Chartered Accountants
Chair - Robin Dillamore   *Dillamore & Co, Wrexham*

Council Members
Frank Edwards   *Frank Edwards & Co, Cardiff*
John Tiernay   *TiernayFedrick, Llandudno*

PRINCIPAL STAFF

David Lermon - *Director for Wales;* Andrew Garvey - *Business Development Manager;* Emma Friedl - *Regional Executive;* Phil Nifield - *Media & Public Affairs Consultant*

Total no. permanent staff: 4

BUSINESS & FINANCE

Wales Co-operative Centre

Canolfan Cydweithredol Cymru

Byddwn yn dathlu deng mlynedd ar hugain o Ganolfan Cydweithredol Cymru yn 2012. Sefydlodd TUC Cymru'r Ganolfan i achub swyddi yn ystod y dirwasgiad yn y 1980au ac rydym wedi bod yn creu gwaith ac yn helpu i wella bywydau ers hynny.

Mae ein cylch gwaith nawr yn cynnwys cyfiawnder cymdeithasol a datblygu economaidd, drwy brosiectau a gwaith ymgynghori ar ddatblygu mentrau cymdeithasol a chydweithredol, cynhwysiant digidol a chynhwysiant ariannol.

Rydym yn fudiad sy'n cael ei arwain gan werthoedd ac yn credu'n gryf mewn defnyddio atebion cydweithredol i ddatblygu busnesau cynaliadwy a chymunedau cynhwysol, cryf.

I gael rhagor o wybodaeth am ein gwaith, ewch i
www.walescooperative.org

In 2012 we will be celebrating thirty years of the Wales Co-operative Centre. The Wales TUC set up the Centre to save jobs during the 1980s recession and we have been creating employment and helping improve lives ever since.

Our remit now encompasses social justice and economic development, through projects and consultancy work on co-operative and social enterprise development, digital inclusion and financial inclusion.

We are a values led organisation with a firm belief in using co-operative solutions to develop sustainable businesses and strong, inclusive communities.

To find out more about our work, visit
www.walescooperative.org

Wales Co-operative Centre
Canolfan Cydweithredol Cymru
CYLCHWYL **30** ANNIVERSARY

CENHEDLOEDD UNEDIG **20** UNITED NATIONS
BLWYDDYN RYNGWLADOL Y **INTERNATIONAL YEAR**
MENTRAU CYDWEITHREDOL **OF CO-OPERATIVES**
Rydym yn creu byd gwell **12** We build a better world

WALES CO-OPERATIVE CENTRE

Wales Co-operative Centre
Llandaff Court, Fairwater Road
Cardiff CF5 2XP

☎ (0300) 111 5050
Fax (0300) 111 5051

Email: info@walescooperative.org
Website: www.walescooperative.org

Chair
David Jenkins

Chief Executive
Derek Walker

 Wales Co-operative Centre
Canolfan Cydweithredol Cymru

The Wales Co-operative Centre delivers a range of projects to promote economic development and social justice. Its team of advisors work with co-operatives, social enterprises, community groups and voluntary organizations across Wales. For thirty years, it has helped emerging and established organizations by providing expert, reliable and flexible support.

COMMITTEE MEMBERS   ♂ 14 ♀ 5

Chair
David Jenkins

Background
Founding Member

Vice-Chair
David White

Member

Members
Jeff Andrews	Welsh Government
Mike Ash-Edwards	The Co-operative Wales
Cllr Paul Cannon	Rhondda Cynon Taff Council
John Chown	Chartered Accountant
Julie Cook	Wales TUC
Keith Edwards	Chartered Institute of Housing
Cllr Wynne Evans	Pembrokeshire County Council
John Hughes	Chartered Accountant
Nigel Keane	Chartered Accountant
Amy Sanders	Director, Dynamix
Anne Stephenson	Welsh Government (retired)
Ian Taylor	Co-operative & Community Finance
Susan Thomas	Health Librarian

CO-OPTED MEMBERS

Mike Williams - *Centre Staff;* Christobel Tweedie - *Centre's Bankers;* Robin Williams - *Centre's legal advisors;* Martin Mansfield - *Wales TUC*

BUSINESS & FINANCE

CHARTERED INSTITUTE OF MARKETING

The Chartered Institute of
Marketing, PO Box 4217
Cardiff, CF14 8DF

☎ 075 0008 5468

Email: wales@cim.co.uk
Website: www.cim.co.uk/wales

Chair, Wales Board
Dr Jonathan Deacon

Director for Wales
Richard Houdmont

 The Chartered
Institute of Marketing

The Chartered Institute of Marketing is the leading international professional marketing and sales body with members worldwide. First established in 1911 it has for almost a century defined the marketing standards that operate in the UK and is the global champion of best marketing practice. The Institute exists to develop the marketing profession, maintain professional standards and improve the skills of marketing practitioners, enabling them to deliver exceptional results for their organizations. It does this by providing membership, qualifications and training to marketing professionals around the world. The Wales office was established in 2006.

BOARD MEMBERS ♂5 ♀4

Chair
Jonathan Deacon

Background
University of Wales, Newport

Members
Andrew Barker
Jade Bourke
Lisa Marie Brown
Anne Marie Doherty
James Horsham
Carol Jones
Carl Mather
Roger Pride

Mangar Ltd
D S Smith Recycling
Pinkspiration
University of Glamorgan
Brand/68
Chapter Arts Centre
Grŵp Llandrillo Menai
Cardiff & Co

PRINCIPAL STAFF

Richard Houdmont FCIM - *Director for Wales*

CO-OPERATIVES AND MUTUALS WALES

15 Samuels Crescent
Whitchurch, Cardiff, CF14 2TH

☎ 07914 762 546

Email:
alex@cooperatives-wales.coop
Website:
www.cooperatives-wales.coop

Executive Chair
Alex Bird

Treasurer
Paul Mallett

CO-OPERATIVES
and Mutuals Wales

Co-operatives and Mutuals Wales is the representative body for the wider Co operative movement in Wales, and the National/Regional arm of Co operativesUK, the apex body for all kinds of co-operatives in the UK.

Co operativesUK was established in 1869, it represents a movement across the UK which has created and sustains 236,000 jobs, turns over £33 billion per annum and is owned and controlled by over 13 million members. In Wales 386 co-operatives turn over £1.3billion and provide over 7,000 jobs.

Co-operatives and Mutuals Wales campaigns for and represents the entire movement in Wales, from Retail Co-operatives, Financial Co operatives (including local Credit Unions, Building Societies and the Co-operative Bank), Community Co operatives, Farmers Co operatives, Secondary Co operatives, Mutuals, Employee Owned Businesses and Worker Co operatives of all sizes.

EXECUTIVE BOARD MEMBERS ♂6 ♀3

Member	Background
Alex Bird (Chair)	UK Co-operative Forum
Paul Mallett (Treasurer)	Co-operative Banking Group
Nick Bennett	Community Housing Cymru
Mike Ash-Edwards	Co-operative Group Regional Secretary
Julie-Ann Haines	Principality Building Society
Liz Moyle (or Martin Morris)*	Co-operative Group Regional Committee
Alun Taylor	Cardiff Credit Union
Derek Walker	Wales Co-operative Centre
Karen Wilkie	Co-operative Party

* Martin Morris to be a substitute for Liz Moyle if required

PRINCIPAL OFFICERS

Alex Bird - *Executive Chair (07914 762 546)*; Paul Mallett - *Treasurer*; Jackie Aplin - *Development Officer (07768 770 165)*

BUSINESS & FINANCE

FEDERATION OF SMALL BUSINESSES IN WALES

1 Cleeve House
Lambourne Crescent
Cardiff CF14 5GP

☎ (029) 2074 7406
Fax: (029) 2074 7595

Email: wales.policy@fsb.org.uk
Website: www.fsb.org.uk/wales

Chair
Janet Jones

Head of External Affairs
Iestyn Davies

Formed in 1974, the FSB is a non party-political campaigning group that exists to promote and protect the interests of all who manage or own small businesses. With 10,000 members in Wales, a Welsh Policy Unit, two regional committees and twelve branch committees throughout the country, it maintains constant contact with small firms at grass roots level.

WELSH POLICY UNIT ♂ 5 ♀ 3

Chair
Janet Jones

Background
Great Porthamel Farm, Talgarth, Powys

Members
Gwyn Evans - *Gwyn Evans Recovery, Ruthin;* Mike Jones - *Whitethorn Place, Swansea;* Jennifer Langley - *Fron Farm, Llanfynydd;* Julie Williamson - *First Call Coffee, Swansea;* Raymond Evans - *William Evans & Sons Ltd, Pentreberw;* Sue Morris - *Merrymoon, Llandudno;* Philip Stapleton - *Aelybryn, Swansea;* Tony Baron - *Llantegols House, Pembrokeshire*

Regional Committees
South Wales: Janet Jones - *Regional Chairman;* Julie Williamson - *Regional Vice Chairman, National Councillor;* Philip Stapleton - *Regional Vice Chairman, Deputy National Councillor;* Mike Jones - *Regional Secretary;* Lesley Walton - *Regional Treasurer;* Dai Davies - *South Wales Development Manager*
North Wales: Gwyn Evans - *Regional Chairman;* Tony Feliciello - *Regional Vice Chairman;* Raymond Evans - *Regional Vice Chairman;* Jennifer Langley - *Regional Secretary;* Tom Brown - *Regional Treasurer;* Susan Morris - *National Councillor;* Mike Scott - *Deputy National Councillor;* Mike Learmond - *North Wales Development Manager*

Chairs of Branch Committees
North Wales & Chester: Raymond Evans - *Anglesey;* James Dick - *Chester & Wrexham;* Dr Katherine Bean - *Conwy County;* Gwyn Evans - *Denbighshire;* Ron Dunn - *Flintshire;* Ian Nellist - *Gwynedd*
South Wales: Chris Olchawski - *Carmarthenshire;* Sheryl Gellatly - *Ceredigion;* Julie Williamson - *Swansea Bay;* Stephen Cole - *Pembrokeshire;* Edward Talbot - *South East Wales;* Steve Kaye - *Powys*

PRINCIPAL OFFICERS

Iestyn Davies - *Head of External Affairs;* Dai Davies - *South Wales Development Manager;* Mike Learmond - *Development Manager for North Wales*

Total no. staff: 7

BUSINESS & FINANCE

THE FINANCE WALES GROUP

Oakleigh House, Park Place
Cardiff CF10 3DQ
☎ 0800 587 4140
Fax: (029) 2033 8101

Email: info@financewales.co.uk
Website: www.financewales.co.uk

**FINANCE WALES
CYLLID CYMRU**

Chair
Ian Johnson

Chief Executive
Sian Lloyd Jones

The Finance Wales Group is a leading UK investor in SMEs. The Group comprises Finance Wales, FW Capital and xénos, the Wales Business Angel Network.

Finance Wales invests in the growth of SMEs throughout Wales and makes commercial debt and equity investments ranging from £5,000 to £2 million in a single round. Finance Wales specialises in early stage, development capital, succession and acquisition deals. It also co-invests with banks, business angels, venture capital funds and others.

Finance Wales has more than £387 million of funds under management including its £150 million fund as well as the new £40 million Wales SME Investment Fund backed by the Welsh Government and Barclays.

Since it was established in 2000 Finance Wales has invested over £230 million through 2700 investments. These investments have leveraged an additional £400 million in private sector investment.

MEMBERS ♂ 7 ♀ 1

Chair
Ian Johnson

Members
Ivar Grey

Clive John
Mike Killick
Chris Rowlands

Sian Lloyd Jones

Kevin O'Leary

Background
Former CEO, Biotrace International plc; Former Chair & Deputy Chair, AIM listed Evans Analytical Group & AOI Medical Inc; Chair, Celsis Group Ltd; non-executive director, MyCelx Technologies Corporation, Lumora Ltd & Ruskinn Life Sciences Ltd

Chartered Accountant; Member, Competition Commission; School Governor; Business Adviser
Former Senior Director, LDC; Chartered Accountant
Chief Financial Officer, Thorntons
Non-executive Chair & Director, MSS Group; adviser, Hermes Private Equity; Former Director, 3i Investments plc; author & chair, UK Government's Rowlands Growth Capital Review
Chief Executive, Finance Wales plc; former Chief Executive, Development Board for Rural Wales; Executive Director, Welsh Development Agency

Finance & Administration Director, Finance Wales plc

Welsh Government representative
Rob Hunter

Director of Finance & Performance Division, Department of Business, Enterprise, Technology & Science

PRINCIPAL OFFICERS

Sian Lloyd Jones - *Chief Executive;* Kevin O'Leary - *Finance & Administration Director*

GLAS CYMRU

Dŵr Cymru Welsh Water
PO Box 690
Cardiff CF3 5WL
☎ (0800) 052 0145

Website: www.dwrcymru.com

Dŵr Cymru
Welsh Water

Chair
Bob Ayling

Managing Director
Nigel Annett

Glas Cymru is a single purpose company formed to own, finance and manage Welsh Water. It is a 'company limited by guarantee' and because it has no shareholders, any financial surpluses are retained for the benefit of Welsh Water's customers. Under Glas Cymru's ownership, Welsh Water's assets and capital investment are financed by bonds and retained financial surpluses. The Glas Cymru business model aims to reduce Welsh Water's asset financing cost, the water industry's single biggest cost. Financing efficiency savings to date have largely been used to build up reserves to insulate Welsh Water and its customers from any unexpected costs and also to improve credit quality so that Welsh Water's cost finance can be kept as low as possible in the years ahead.

Although Glas Cymru has no shareholders it does have a group of 72 Members who perform some of the same vital roles. Members are appointed for terms of three years and have a key role in corporate governance of Glas Cymru. They are responsible for appointing the company's directors, approving the annual report and accounts, and ensuring that the company continues to deliver high quality, good value services. They also play an important part in making sure that the company continues to focus on its sole purpose of providing the best quality water and sewerage services at an affordable price. The names of individuals appointed as members are published on the company's website www.dwrcymru.com.

DIRECTORS   ♂8 ♀2

Bob Ayling	Chair
Nigel Annett	Managing Director
Chris Jones	Finance Director
Peter Perry	Operations Director
John Bryant	Non-Executive Director
Prof Stephen Palmer	Non-Executive Director
Menna Richards	Non-Executive Director
James Strachan	Non-Executive Director
Anna Walker	Non-Executive Director
John Warren	Non-Executive Director

GROUNDWORK WALES

Unit G5, Main Avenue
Treforest Industrial Estate
Pontypridd CF37 5YL

☎ (01443) 844866
Fax: (01443) 844822

Email: info@groundworkwales.org.uk
Website: www.groundworkwales.org.uk

Board Chair
Gareth John

Executive Director
Ian McIntosh

**WALES
CYMRU**

Groundwork in Wales is a leading local, regional and national environmental regeneration network building sustainable communities across Wales.

With more than 20 years successful track record working in urban and rural areas right across Wales, Groundwork in Wales assists the Welsh Government, local authorities and other national bodies as well as major corporates like Marks and Spencer and Cadbury to achieve their aims. Its programmes meet a range of Government objectives, with a particular focus on supporting Training & Employment, addressing the Low Carbon agenda, improving Health and Well being and empowering local people & communities.

There are five Groundwork Trusts (collectively known as 'Groundwork in Wales') operating nationally and across the South East, South West and North Wales regions. The national organization is Groundwork Wales which supports the local Trusts, provides a national voice, delivers national programmes, explores new funding opportunities and develops new partnerships across Wales. Groundwork Wales is also the only body in Wales able to certify the Green Dragon Environmental Standard.

During 2010/2011 Groundwork in Wales saved almost 6,000 tonnes of CO_2, diverted more than 1,400 tonnes from landfill, created and safeguarded 1155 jobs, worked with more than 660 businesses and over 280 schools, provided over 10,000 weeks' worth of training, supported nearly 135,000 days volunteering by young people, planted more than 7,900 trees, improved and maintained over 3,877,000 sqm of land.

BOARD MEMBERS ♂6 ♀2

Chair	Background
Gareth John	Director, Gareth John Consulting
Members	
Bryn Davies	Principal, The College Ystrad Mynach
Geoff Hunt	Director, Arup
Marianne Jones	Consultant
Saleem Kidwai	Chief Executive, Ethnic Business Support Programme
Helen Northmore	Director, National & EU Programme Development, Energy Saving Trust Wales
Brian Rees	Consultant
John Troth OBE	Chair, Careers Wales North East

MANAGEMENT TEAM

Ian McIntosh	Executive Director
Ian Colbourne	Director of Finance
Van Griffiths	Business Development Director

Total no. permanent staff: 12

HYBU CIG CYMRU
MEAT PROMOTION WALES

Tŷ Rheidol, Parc Merlin
Llanbadarn Fawr, Aberystwyth
SY23 3FF

☎ (01970) 625050
Fax: (01970) 615148

Email: info@hccmpw.org.uk
Website: www.hccmpw.org.uk

Chair
Dai Davies

Chief Executive
Gwyn Howells

Hybu Cig Cymru - Meat Promotion Wales is the organization responsible for the development, promotion and marketing of Welsh red meat. HCC implements, on behalf of all Welsh farmers and other key industry participants, a strategic plan to develop profitable and sustainable markets for Welsh red meat to derive benefit for all in the supply chain.

BOARD MEMBERS   ♂ 12 ♀ 0

Chair	**Background**
Dai Davies	Primary Producer
Board	
John Brereton	Independent
John Collins	Independent
Prof Will Haresign	Independent
Gwyn Angell Jones	Independent
Prys Morgan	Processor
Graham Probert	Primary Producer
Glyn Roberts	Primary Producer
Richard Rogers	Primary Producer
Richard Tudor	Primary Producer
Wyn Williams	Processor
John Yeomans	Primary Producer

PRINCIPAL OFFICERS

Gwyn Howells	Chief Executive
Sion Aron Jones	Industry Development Manager
Bryan Regan	Corporate Services Manager
Alan Morris	Communications Manager
Laura Dodds	Market Development Manager

INSTITUTE OF DIRECTORS WALES

IoD Wales, The Park House Club
20 Park Place
Cardiff CF10 3DQ

☎ (029) 2038 9990
Fax: (029) 2038 9989

Email: iod.wales@iod.com
Website: www.iod.com/wales

Chair
Huw Roberts

Director, Wales
Robert Lloyd Griffiths

The Institute of Directors is the professional body for company directors in Wales. Its objectives are to further the interests of its members and to improve their professional skill by providing training and seminars. The IoD also encourages it's members to use their skills in public life for common good.

IoD Wales   ♂2 ♀2

Chair
Huw Roberts

Director
Robert Lloyd Griffiths

Branch Chairs
Jacquie Williams

Helen Watson

Background
Chair, IoD Wales, Chair, Arts & Business Cymru; Governor, Barry Island School; Deputy Chair, National Energy Action; Deputy Chair, Artes Mundi

IoD Director, Wales, Fellow of Chartered Institute of Marketing, Committee; member, Wales Festival of Remembrance, Business Mentor, Arts & Business Cymru, Member, Arts & Business Cymru Investment panel, Wales Autism Employment Ambassador; Ambassador, Duke of Edinburgh Awards - Wales

Chair, IoD South & West Wales Branch, Managing Director, SCS Aftercare; Founder, Welsh Women Walking
Chair, IoD North Wales Branch, Partner, Aaron & Partners

Total no. staff: 2

Tyfwch eich busnes gyda gwarant dosbarthu mewn pryd

Os yw'n hanfodol i'ch busnes eich bod yn cynnig gwasanaeth sy'n dosbarthu y diwrnod canlynol am bris cystadleuol, defnyddiwch Special Delivery® y Post Brenhinol Mae'n gwarantu dosbarthu erbyn 9am neu 1pm y diwrnod canlynol neu fe gewch eich arian yn ôl
Am fwy o wybodaeth ewch i royalmail.com/specialdelivery, ffoniwch 08457 950 950 neu ewch i Swyddfa'r Post® yn lleol

Grow your business with guaranteed on time delivery

When it's critical to your business that you offer a service that gives you next day delivery at a competitive price use Royal Mail Special Delivery®
It guarantees delivery by 9am or 1pm the next day or your money back
To find out more visit royalmail.com/specialdelivery, call 08457 950 950 or visit your local Post Office®

Royal Mail®

ROYAL MAIL GROUP & POST OFFICE LIMITED

Royal Mail Group
External Relations
Cardiff Mail Centre
3rd Floor, 220 Penarth Rd
Cardiff, CF11 8TA

☎ (020) 2039 2500
Fax: (020) 2039 2505
Email:
external.relations.wales@royalmail.com
pressofficewales@postoffice.co.uk
Website: www.royalmailgroup.com

Head of External Relations,
Royal Mail Group
Heulyn Gwyn Davies

Head of External Relations,
Post Office Ltd, Wales
Stuart Taylor

Royal Mail®

As of 1 April 2012, Royal Mail and Post Office Ltd became sister companies as result of the Postal Services Act 2011. Royal Mail Group is unique in reaching everyone in the UK through its mails, Post Office and parcels businesses – which directly employ over 151,000 people in the UK. Every working day Royal Mail processes and delivers over 59 million items to 29 million addresses for prices that are amongst the lowest in Europe. Each week we serve over 20 million customers through our network of over 11,500 Post Office branches and each year our domestic and European parcels businesses – General Logistics Systems and Parcelforce Worldwide – handle some 404 million parcels.

MANAGEMENT TEAM

Heulyn Gwyn Davies	Head of External Relations, Royal Mail Group
Val Bodden	External Relations Manager, Royal Mail Group
Mike Norman	External Relations Manager, Royal Mail Group
Stuart Taylor	Head of External Relations, Post Office Ltd, Wales

Public Services Contacts

Royal Mail Group - External Relations	02920 392500
Post Office Ltd - External Relations	02920 392213
Royal Mail Customer Services	08457 740740
Royal Mail Business Customer Services	08457 950950
Parcelforce Worldwide Customer Services	08448 004466
Post Office Branches Helpline	08457 223344
Welsh Language Customer helpline	08457 468469
Textphone (for hard of hearing)	0845 600 0606
Postcode Inquiry Line	0906 302 1222

PROFESSIONS GROUP WALES
GRŴP CYRFF PROFFESIYNOL CYMRU

Head, ACCA
Wales
Ben Cottam

CIM Director,
Wales
Richard Houdmont

ICAEW Director,
Wales
David Lermon

Manager-Wales,
The Law Society
Lowri Morgan

An all-Wales grouping of professional organizations established in 2001 to enable the professions in Wales to work in partnership and establish stronger links with the National Assembly for Wales, the Welsh Government and other institutions operating in Wales.

There are over 13,000 members and students of the organizations comprising Professions Group Wales.

Primary aims and objectives:

- *To represent and develop the professions and their practitioners in Wales, including the provision of a programme of compulsory Continuing Professional Development programmes for members*
- *To promote and develop the professions in Wales*
- *To work in collaboration with further and higher education authorities in Wales*
- *To promote the principle of open access to the professions*

REPRESENTATIVES OF PROFESSIONS GROUP WALES

ACCA Wales
Ben Cottam, Head of ACCA Cymru/Wales, Regus House,
Malthouse Avenue, Cardiff Gate Business Park, Cardiff CF23 8RU
Tel: 029 2026 3657 Email: ben.cottam@uk.accaglobal.com
Website: www.accaglobal.com/wales

 The Chartered
Institute of Marketing

The Chartered Institute of Marketing
Richard Houdmont, Director for Wales, The Chartered Institute of Marketing, PO Box 4217, Cardiff CF14 8DF
Tel: 075 0008 5468 Email: richardhoudmont@cim.co.uk
Website: www.cim.co.uk/wales

ICAEW
David Lermon, Director for Wales, ICAEW Wales, PO Box 4274,
Cardiff CF14 8GA
Tel: 029 2002 1481 Email david.lermon@icaew.com
Website: icaew.com/wales

Cymdeithas y Cyfreithwyr
The Law Society

The Law Society
Lowri Morgan, Manager-Wales, The Law Society, Capital Tower,
Greyfriars Road, Cardiff CF10 3AG
Tel: 029 2064 5254 Email: lowri.morgan@lawsociety.org.uk
Website: www.lawsociety.org.uk

RICS WALES

Royal Institution of Chartered Surveyors
7 St Andrews Place
Cardiff CF10 3BE
☎ (029) 2022 4414
Fax: (029) 2022 4416

Email: ljenkins@rics.org
Website: www.rics.org/wales

Chair
Neil Brierley

Director, Wales & Northern Ireland
Ben Collins

RICS is the world's leading qualification when it comes to professional standards in land, property and construction. In a world where more and more people, governments, banks and commercial organizations demand greater certainty of professional standards and ethics, attaining RICS status is the recognised mark of property professionalism.

Over 100,000 property professionals working in the major established and emerging economies of the world have already recognised the importance of securing RICS status by becoming members.

RICS is an independent professional body originally established in the UK by Royal Charter. Since 1868, RICS has been committed to setting and upholding the highest standards of excellence and integrity – providing impartial, authoritative advice on key issues affecting businesses and society. RICS is a regulator of both its individual members and firms enabling it to maintain the highest standards and providing the basis for unparalleled client confidence in the sector.

RICS Wales was set up in 2000 on the devolution of secondary legislation powers to the Welsh Government, many of which affect the prime markets of land, property and construction in which chartered surveyors operate. RICS Wales has a thriving local member group network and actively works to raise the profile of chartered surveyors in the business life and in the society of Wales.

BOARD MEMBERS ♂ 11 ♀ 2

Chair
Neil Brierley

Members
Edward Bampton
Owain Llywelyn
Karen Thomas
Trefor Williams
Wyn Walters
Mike Bird (Chair, North Wales Local Association)
Chris Clarke (Chair, South East Wales Local Association)
Francis Chester Master (Chair, Mid Wales Local Association)
Andrew Davies (Chair, Swansea Bay Local Association)
Ben Collins
Anna Roberts (Chair, RICS Matrics North Wales)
Jonathan Davies (Chair, RICS Matrics South Wales)

Background
Davis Langdon, Cardiff

(former) Welsh Government, Pontypridd
University of Glamorgan, Pontypridd
Independent chartered surveyor, Cardiff
University of Glamorgan, Pontypridd
WRW Construction, Llanelli
Mostyn Estates, Llandudno
Chris Clarke Surveyors, Cardiff
Chester Master Ltd, Powys
Hurley & Davies, Swansea
RICS Director Wales
Flintshire County Council, Flint
Davis Langdon, Cardiff

PRINCIPAL STAFF

Ben Collins - *Director, Wales & Northern Ireland;* Elinor Weekley - *Membership Business Development Manager;* David Morgan - *Policy Manager;* Lois Jenkins - *PR & Communications Officer;* Elizabeth Ross - *Conference Logistics Coordinator;* Rebecca Heeley - *Member Services Administrator;* Christina Hirst - *Training Advisor*

BUSINESS & FINANCE

WALES AUDIT OFFICE

Auditor General for Wales
Huw Vaughan Thomas

Wales Audit Office
Swyddfa Archwilio Cymru
24 Cathedral Road, Cardiff CF11 9LJ

☎ (029) 2032 0500 Fax: (029) 2032 0600
Email: info@wao.gov.uk website: www.wao.gov.uk

WALES AUDIT OFFICE
SWYDDFA ARCHWILIO CYMRU

The Auditor General and the auditors he appoints in local government are the independent statutory external auditors of most of the Welsh public sector. They are responsible for the annual audit of most of the public money spent in Wales, including the £14 billion of funds that are voted to Wales annually by the Westminster Parliament.

Elements of this funding are passed by the Welsh Government to the NHS in Wales (over £5 billion) and to local government (nearly £4 billion).

AUDITOR GENERAL FOR WALES, ASSISTANT AUDITORS GENERAL, GROUP DIRECTORS & DIRECTORS

Auditor General for Wales: Huw Vaughan Thomas
Assistant Auditors General: Anthony Barrett, Gillian Body, Kevin Thomas
Group Directors: Paul Dimblebee, Simon Edge (Auditor General for Wales' Private Secretary),
John Herniman, Jane Holownia, Ann-Marie Harkin, Alan Morris, Mike Usher
Directors: Richard Harries, Derwyn Owen, Dave Thomas

Recently published Reports

February 2012:	Public participation in Waste Recycling
February 2012:	Local Authority Accounts 2010-11
January 2012:	Progress in delivering the Welsh Housing Quality Standard
December 2011:	Report in the Public interest, Mawr Community Council - Audits of Accounts 2005-06 to 2009-10
December 2011:	Report in the Public Interest, Clydach Community Council - Audits of Accounts 2004-05 to 2009-10
November 2011:	Grants Management in Wales
October 2011:	A Picture of Public Services 2011
August 2011:	The delivery of ICT services and ICT projects under the Merlin contract
July 2011:	Adult Mental Health Services - Follow up Report
May 2011:	Business Improvement Approaches in the Public Sector in Wales
March 2011:	Hospital Catering and Patient Nutrition
January 2011:	Major Transport Projects
December 2010:	Cost of Producing School Meals - Wales
November 2010:	Councils' response to the financial challenges: Key messages from the Wales Audit Office preliminary corporate assessments

Total no. staff: approx 250

WALES INTERNATIONAL BUSINESS COUNCIL

Chair
Byron Davies OBE

WIBC, Kiln Suite
The Maltings, East Tyndall Street
Cardiff CF24 5EA

☎ (029) 2009 0041

Email: enquiries@walesibc.com
Website: www.walesibc.com

Paul Hopkins

Andrew Walker

Business Development
Directors

Wales International Business Council was formed in November 2010, identifying the need to extend international business links to a wider global network. It aims to position Wales as a country that recognises the importance of international business and create a network for international companies and indigenous business in Wales, particularly small and medium enterprise companies, who wish to explore international business opportunities.

As a private sector initiative, it draws on the existing talent of business, academia and governmental bodies across Wales to develop and support organizations wishing to connect with the global economy. It acts as a sounding board for International companies wishing to do business in Wales and uses its extensive global networks on a reciprocal basis for enterprises in Wales. Through its partnerships it is developing a creative and innovative private/public network approach that will position and benefit Wales plc internationally.

BOARD DIRECTORS   ♂ 7 ♀ 1

Chair	**Background**
Byron Davies	Managing Director BD Consulting UK
Members	
Andrew Walker	Director of Development Cardiff Metropolitan University; Trustee, Fairwood Trust
Paul Hopkins	Member Geldards LLP, Head of Dispute Resolution Services, International Partner, CEDR accredited mediator
Caroline Rowlands	Management Training & Marketing Consultant, Total Training Wales
Andrew Reid-Jones	Partner, Quantum Advisory
Mike Tan	Founder of Career Change Wales; part-time lecturer, University of Glamorgan
Raj Aggarwal	Board Member, National Pharmacy Association; Chair, (SE) Community Pharmacy Wales; Chair, Kidney Wales Foundation; Board Member, Millennium Stadium; on the council of "The Russell Group" Cardiff University
Russell Lawson	Managing Director, The Ideas Distillery

BUSINESS & FINANCE

WALES TUC CYMRU

President
Amarjite Singh

Transport House,
1 Cathedral Road
Cardiff CF11 9SD

☎ (029) 2034 7010
Fax: (029) 2022 1940

Email: wtuc@tuc.org.uk
Website: www.wtuc.org.uk

General Secretary
Martin Mansfield

With member unions representing nearly half a million working people, the Wales TUC is the voice of Wales at work. The declared objective of the Wales TUC is to be a high-profile organization which campaigns successfully for trade union aims and values, assists trade unions to increase membership and effectiveness, and promotes trade union solidarity. A major role of the Wales TUC is to co-ordinate the trade union approach to the National Assembly of Wales and ensure that the interests of Wales's half a million trade unionists are properly represented in the whole range of Assembly decision making.

EXECUTIVE COMMITTEE ♂ 11 ♀ 4

Members	Background
Amarjite Singh - President	CWU
David Evans - Vice President	NUT
Andy Richards - Past President	Unite
John Burgham	Unite
Nick Ireland	Usdaw
Nicholas Blundell	Ucatt
Margaret Thomas	Unison
Peter Crews	Unison
Win Wearmouth	Unison
Mick Moore	Unite
Sheila Bearcroft	GMB
Pam Drake	GMB
Sian Gale	Bectu
John Howells	GMB
Gareth Howells	Prospect

PRINCIPAL OFFICERS

Martin Mansfield - *General Secretary*; Julie Cook - *Head of TUC Education*; Siân Cartwright - *Head of Learning Services*

Total no. staff: 18

FINANCIAL & LEGAL PRACTITIONERS

Bank of England Agency for Wales
4 Village Way, Greenmeadow Springs,
Tongwynlais, Cardiff CF15 7NE
Tel: (029) 2061 4678 Fax: (029) 2046 3605
Email: wales@bankofengland.co.uk
Website: www.bankofengland.co.uk
Agent for Wales: Neil Ashbridge
Deputy Agent: Ian Derrick

London Stock Exchange plc
10 Paternoster Square, London EC4M 7LS
Tel: (020) 7797 1000
Email: mrusson@londonstockexchange.com
Website: www.londonstockexchange.com
Key Personnel: Mark Russon

ACCOUNTANTS

Broomfield & Alexander
Pendragon House, Caxton Place,
Pentwyn, Cardiff CF23 8XE
Tel: (029) 2054 9939 Fax: (029) 2073 9430
Email: cardiffenquiry@broomfield.co.uk
Managing Director: Robert Preece

Deloitte
5 Callaghan Square, Cardiff CF10 5BT
Tel: (029) 2046 0000 Fax: (029) 2046 4444
Website: www.deloitte.co.uk
Office Senior Partner: John Foster Thomas

Grant Thornton
11-13 Penhill Road, Cardiff CF11 9UP
Tel: (029) 2046 5591 Fax: (029) 2038 3803
Partners & Directors: Geraint Davies,
Louise Evans, John Golding, Trefor Griffith,
Geoff Mesher, Mark Naughton,
Rebecca L Pritchard, David Thomas,
Alistair Wardell

KPMG
3 Assembly Square, Britannia Quay,
Cardiff Bay CF10 4AX
Tel: (029) 2046 8000 Fax: (029) 2046 8200
Website: www.kpmg.co.uk
Office Senior Partner: Simon Jones

PricewaterhouseCoopers
1 Kingsway, Cardiff CF10 3PW
Tel: (029) 2023 7000 Fax: (029) 2080 2400
Website: www.pwc.com
Regional Chair: Rob Lewis

BANKS

Allied Irish Bank (GB)
2 Callaghan Square, Cardiff CF10 5AZ
Tel: (029) 2049 3757 Fax: (029) 2049 2642
Email: cardiff@aib.ie
Website: www.aibgb.co.uk

Barclays Bank plc
121 Queen Street, Cardiff CF10 2BJ
Tel: (08457) 555 555
Website: www.barclays.co.uk
Regional Liaison Manager for Wales: Jonathon
Brenchley
Email: jonathan.brenchley@barclays.com
Regional Corporate Banking Director:
Simon Moore

BANKS (cont.)

Co-operative Bank
South Wales Business Centre, 16-17 High St,
Cardiff CF10 1Ax
Tel: (029) 2064 4265 Fax: (029) 2022 4743
Email: swales.corpcentre@co-operativebank.co.uk
Website: www.co-operativebank.co.uk
Senior Corporate Manager: John Williams
Business Development Manager: Andrew
Hannah

Coutts & Co
3rd Floor, 1 Kingsway, Cardiff CF10 3AQ
Tel: (029) 2050 1038 Fax: (029) 2050 1051
Website: www.coutts.com
Senior Manager: Paul Kirk

Lloyds TSB Bank plc
Wales & West Director's Office,
Carlyle House, 5 Cathedral Road,
Cardiff CF11 9RH
Tel: (029) 2072 8846 Fax: (029) 2072 8040
Website: www.lloydstsb.com
Regional Director: Richie Coulson
Regional Director, South & West Wales:
Allan Griffiths
Area Director (Corporate Banking): Jason Evans

HSBC Bank plc
Divisional Management Centre,
97 Bute Street, Cardiff CF10 5XH
Tel: (029) 2035 1136 Fax: (029) 2035 1194
Email: westandwalescbc@hsbc.com
Website: www.hsbc.co.uk
Head of Corporate Banking: Mark Bennett

Natwest plc
96 Queen Street, Cardiff CF10 2GR
Tel: (0845) 301 7545
Website: www.natwest.com
Regional Managing Director: John Fox

BUILDING SOCIETIES

Monmouthshire Building Society
Monmouthshire House, John Frost Square,
Newport NP20 1PX
Email: webenquiry@monbsoc.co.uk
Tel: (01633) 844400 Fax: (01633) 844445
Website: www.monbsoc.co.uk
Managing Director: Andrew Lewis

Principality Building Society
Customer Contact Centre, PO Box 89,
Principality Buildings, Queen Street,
Cardiff CF10 1UA
Tel: (0845) 045 0006 Fax: (0845) 371 5313
Email: enquiries@principality.co.uk
Website: www.principality.co.uk
Chair: Dyfrig John
Deputy Chair: Christopher Rowlands
Group Chief Executive: Peter L Griffiths

Swansea Building Society
11-12 Cradock Street, Swansea SA1 3EW
Email: info@swansea-bs.co.uk
Website: www.swansea-bs.co.uk
Tel: (01792) 483700 Fax: (01792) 483718
DX 39595 Swansea 1
Chief Executive: Alun Williams

CREDIT UNIONS IN WALES

Credit unions are financial co-operatives, owned and controlled by their members. They offer a friendly, convenient and easy place to save with access to low cost loans. Credit Unions are one aspect of the Wales Co-operative Centre's work. The Wales Co-operative Centre was established in 1982 as part of a Wales TUC initiative to combat unemployment. The Centre promotes, supports and develops co-operatives, community businesses and credit unions and is able to provide a full advice and consultancy service to anyone wishing to establish any form of co-operative business. Existing co-operatives can also access advice, support services and training programmes.

WALES CO-OPERATIVE CENTRE LIMITED
Llandaff Court, Fairwater Road, Cardiff CF5 2XP Tel: (0300) 111 5050 Fax: (0300) 111 5051
Email: info@walescooperative.org Website: www.walescooperative.org

All Flintshire Credit Union Ltd
27 High Street, Holywell, Flintshire CH8 7TE
Tel: (01352) 715555 Fax: (01352) 715555
Email: tecwyn@flintshire-creditunion.co.uk
Treasurer: Tecwyn Jones

Bargoed, Aberbargoed & Gilfach (BAG) Credit Union
47 Commercial Street, Aberbargoed,
Caerphilly CF81 9BT
Tel: (01443) 838605 Fax: (01443) 833533
Email: bagcredunion@aol.com
Treasurer: Pam Farrant

Brecon and District Credit Union Ltd
12 Steeple House, Steeple Lane, Brecon LD3 7DJ
Tel: (01874) 620104 Fax: (01874) 620104
Email: breconcu@btconnect.com
Credit Committee Chairman: Ms Sally Moore

Bridgend Lifesavers Credit Union Ltd
The Lifelong Learning Centre, Murfield Close,
Sarn, Bridgend CF32 9SW Tel: (01656) 729912
Fax: (01656) 724895 Email: nicola@blscu.co.uk
Manager: Ms Nicola Field

Cardiff & The Vale Credit Union Ltd
Room 267, County Hall, Atlantic Wharf,
Cardiff CF10 4UW Tel: (029) 2087 2373
Fax: (029) 2087 2642 Email: ccu@cardiffcu.com
Manager: Mrs Glenda Porter

CredCer Credit Union
46 St Mary Street, Cardigan, Ceredigion SA43 1HA
Tel: (01239) 621408 Fax: (01239) 621408
Email: info@credcer.co.uk
Contact: Carol Morgan

Dragon Savers Credit Union Ltd
107 Bute Street, Treorchy CF42 6AU
Tel: (01443) 777043 Fax: (01443) 777043
Email: stonemanc@dragonsavers.org
General Manager: Mrs Christina Stoneman

Gateway Credit Union Ltd
21 Commercial St, Pontypool NP4 6JQ
Tel: (01495) 750020 Fax: (01495) 740011
Email: info@gatewaycu.co.uk
Manager: Mr John Richards

Haven Credit Union Ltd
19 Charles Street, Milford Haven SA73 2AA
Tel: (01646) 694080
Email: admin@mhcu.freeserve.co.uk
Office Administrator: Mrs Debra Smith

Islwyn Community Credit Union Ltd
Wesley Road, Blackwood NP12 1PP
Tel: (01495) 222832 Fax: (01495) 220400
Email: info@islwyncu.co.uk
Contact: Ms Helen Thomas

L.A.S.A. Credit Union Ltd
1st Floor Offices, 10 Calvert Terrace, Swansea SA1 6AR
Tel: (01792) 643632 Fax: (01792) 643634
Email: query@lasacreditunion.org.uk
Manager: Mrs Claire Smith

Llynfi Valley Credit Union Ltd
15a Talbot Street, Maesteg, Bridgend CF34 9BW
Tel: (01656) 731392 Fax: (01656) 731392
Email: llynficredit@tiscali.co.uk
Manager: Mrs Mandy Evans

Marches Credit Union Ltd
The Old Police Station, 1 Market Hall Street,
Kington, Herefordshire HR5 3D
Tel: (01544) 231926 Fax: (01544) 231926
Email: mcukington@kc3.co.uk
Secretary: Mr Mick Rand

Merthyr Tydfil Borough Credit Union Ltd
19 Park Place, Merthyr Tydfil, CF47 0DJ
Tel: (01685) 377888
Email: info@mtbcu.org.uk
Business Services Officer: Mrs Delyth Shearing

Neath Port Talbot Credit Union
41-43 Windsor Road, Neath SA11 1NH
Tel: (01639) 632100
Email: b.warlow@nptcu.co.uk
Development Officer: Brian Warlow

Newport Credit Union Ltd
5 Market Arcade, Newport NP20 1FS
Tel: (01633) 214913 Fax: (01633) 214912
Email: newportcreditunion@hotmail.co.uk

CREDIT UNIONS IN WALES

North Wales Credit Union Ltd
144 Conwy Road, Llandudno Junction,
Conwy LL31 9NP
Tel: (01492) 580028 Fax: (01492) 585162
Email: info@llandudnocu.co.uk
Credit Union Manager: Barry Roberts

Red Kite Credit Union
(Undeb Credyd y Barcud Coch Cyfyngedig)
20 Market Street, Builth Wells LD2 4EA
Tel: (01982) 551000/(01597) 824000
Email: enquiry@redkitecreditunion.co.uk
Chair: Mr Richard Bramhall

Robert Owen (Montgomeryshire)
Credit Union Ltd
26 Market Street, Newtown SY16 2PD
Tel: (01686) 623741 Fax: (01686) 623741
Email: rina@romcul.co.uk
Manager & Community Bank Co-ordinator:
Ms Rina Clarke

Save-Easy Llanelli and District Credit Union Ltd
6-8 Bridge St, Llanelli SA15 3UF
Tel: (01554) 770867 Fax: (01554) 770876
Email: saveeasy@btopenworld.com
Manager: Halina Ashley

Smart Money Credit Union Ltd
Abacus House, 44 Windsor Street, Caerphilly CF83 1FW
Tel: (029) 2088 3751 Fax: (029) 2088 3785
Email: info@smartmoneycreditunion.co.uk
Manager: Ms Andrina Davies

St Therese (Port Talbot) Credit Union Ltd
40 Victoria Road, Port Talbot SA12 6AD
Tel: (01639) 892124
Email: peter.reynolds21@btopenworld.com
Contact: Mr Peter Reynolds

Undeb Credyd Plaid Cymru Credit Union Ltd
Ty'r Cymry, 11 Gordon Road, Cathays,
Cardiff CF24 3AJ
Tel: (029) 2049 1888
Email: post@ucpccu.org
Secretary: Mr Stuart Fisher

LEADING COMMERCIAL LAWYERS

Eversheds
1 Callaghan Square, Cardiff CF10 5BT
Tel: (0845) 497 9797 Fax: (0845) 498 7333
Website: www.eversheds.com
Senior Office Partner: Alan Meredith

Edward Geldard
Dumfries House, Dumfries Place,
Cardiff CF10 3ZF
Tel: (029) 2023 8239
Fax: (029) 2023 7268
Website: www.geldards.com
Chief Exec: Jeff Pearson

Hek Jones
2nd Floor, The Wharf,
Schooner Way, Cardiff CF10 4EU
Tel: (029) 2044 0070 Fax: (029) 2045 5874
Website: www.hekjones.com
Partners:
Dispute Resolution: Andrew Jones
Commercial Property: Paul Jones
Residential Conveyancing: Darren Hek

Hugh James
Hodge House,114-116 St Mary Street,
Cardiff, CF10 1DY
Tel: (029) 20224871
Fax: (029) 2038 8222
Email: GeneralOfficeEmail@hughjames.com
Website: www.hughjames.com
Managing Partner: Matthew Tossell
Senior Partner: Gareth Williams

Morgan Cole
Bradley Court, Park Place, Cardiff CF10 3DP
Tel: (029) 2038 5385 Fax: (029) 2038 5300
DX 33014
Email: cardiff@morgan-cole.com
Chair: Robin Havard

13

TheWales
Yearbook

THE MEDIA in WALES

BBC CYMRU WALES

Broadcasting House
Llandaff
Cardiff
CF5 2YQ

☎ (029) 2032 2000
Fax: (029) 2032 2280

Email: feedback.wales@bbc.co.uk
Website: bbc.co.uk/wales

National Trustee for Wales
Prof Elan Closs Stephens CBE

Director
Rhodri Talfan Davies

The BBC's Royal Charter confirms the Corporation's commitment to broadcasting in Wales. BBC Cymru Wales provides services in Welsh and English on radio, television and online. The Audience Council Wales advises the BBC Trust on the performance of the BBC in Wales. The National Trustee for Wales is appointed by HM the Queen on the recommendation of the Secretary of State for Culture, Media and Sport.

AUDIENCE COUNCIL WALES   ♂6 ♀5

	In office until	Background
Chair		
Prof Elan Closs Stephens CBE	10/14	Emeritus Professor of Communication & Creative Industries, Aberystwyth University
BBC National Trustee for Wales: (Remuneration £37,600 - 2½ days per week)		
Members (No remuneration)		
Andrew Carter	03/13	Senior Winners Advisor, Camelot
Rhian Connick	03/15	Head of the National Federation of Women's Institutes, Wales Office
Bethan Darwin	03/13	Solicitor & published novelist
Robert Humphreys	03/13	Head, Open University, Wales
Pamela Hunt	03/13	Founder, Raw Charm
Aled Jones-Griffith	03/13	Faculty Director, Coleg Menai FE college
Ruth Marks	03/14	Public & third sector professional
Ian Stevens	03/15	Chartered Town Planner
Ceri Stradling	03/14	Chartered Accountant
Alun Williams	03/15	Cardiff & Vale University Health Board Welsh language officer

PRINCIPAL OFFICERS

Rhodri Talfan Davies - *Director, BBC Cymru Wales;* Adrian Davies - *Head of English Language Programmes & Services;* Sian Gwynedd - *Head of Welsh Language Programmes & Services;* Clare Hudson - *Head of BBC Wales Productions;* Mark O'Callaghan - *Head of News & Current Affairs;* Gareth Powell - *Chief Operating Officer;* Jude Gray - *Head of HR & Development;* Richard Thomas - *Head of Marketing, Communications & Audiences*

Total no. staff: 1,250

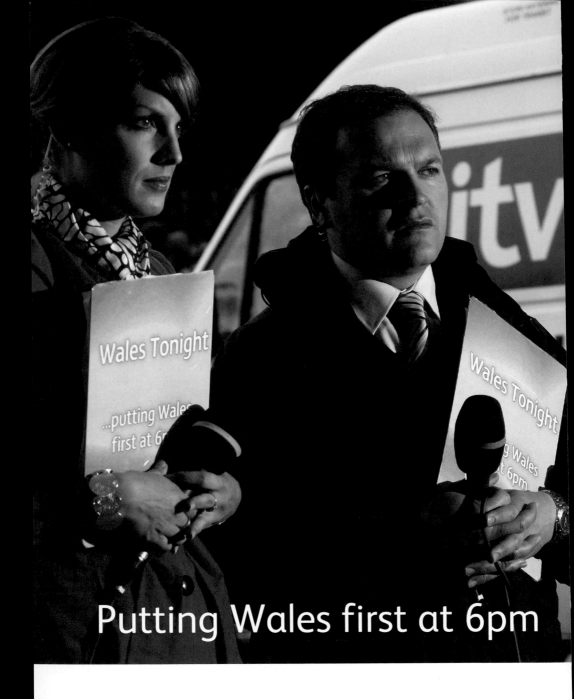
Putting Wales first at 6pm

ITV WALES

The Television Centre
Culverhouse Cross
Cardiff CF5 6XJ

☎ 0844 881 0100

Email: wales@itv.com
Website: www.itv.com/wales

Head of News
& Programmes
Phil Henfrey

As an arm of ITV plc, ITV Wales is part of the UK's most popular commercial broadcaster. We deliver four hours of news and 90 minutes of current affairs, politics and factual programming each week on ITV1 Wales. ITV also produces an innovative rolling digital news service for Wales that is available online at itv.com/wales.

Our flagship news programme WALES TONIGHT, presented by Jonathan Hill and Andrea Byrne, was voted News Programme of the Year in the ITV Regions & Nations Awards 2012. The programme also won gold in the Live Presentation category.

The ITV Wales news team operates from our digital newsroom at Culverhouse Cross, Cardiff. Multi-skilled reporters also work out of bureaux at the National Assembly for Wales and Colwyn Bay. We also have reporters based in Merthyr Tydfil, Swansea and Aberystwyth.

Welsh politics is comprehensively covered in WALES TONIGHT, in the weekly programme SHARP END with Political Editor Adrian Masters and in our coverage of the annual WALES YEARBOOK POLITICAL AWARDS.

We also have a strong commercial relationship with S4C, providing some of the channel's most successful current affairs, factual and factual entertainment programming.

ITV WALES MANAGEMENT TEAM

Phil Henfrey - *Head of News & Programmes;* Huw Rossiter - *Public Affairs Manager;* Jonathan Hill - *News Presenter & Editor, English Language Programmes;* Andy Collinson - *Programme & Digital Editor;* Geraint Evans - *Editor Welsh Language Programmes;* Nia Britton - *Operations Manager;* Zoe Thomas - *News Editor;* Sarah Drew - *Planning Editor;* Mike McCullagh - *Finance Manager;* Sue Williams - *Assistant to the Management Team*

**MEDIA
ITV WALES**

Total no. staff: 105

S4/C

Calon Cenedl
Heart of the Nation

**Yng nghanol bywyd Cymru,
yr iaith a diwylliant ein cenedl.**

At the heart of Welsh life, language
and the culture of our nation.

Y Clwb Rygbi   Gwaith Cartref   Cyw   Hwb

s4c.co.uk
facebook.com/s4c.co.uk
twitter.com/s4carlein

S4C

The Welsh Fourth Channel Authority

Parc Tŷ Glas, Llanishen
Cardiff CF14 5DU

Doc Fictoria, Caernarfon
Gwynedd LL55 1TH

☎ (029) 2074 7444
Fax: (029) 2075 4444

Email: s4c@s4c.co.uk
Website: s4c.co.uk

Chair
Huw Jones

Chief Executive
Ian Jones

S4/C Calon Cenedl
Heart of the Nation

S4C is a public service broadcaster providing a range of high quality Welsh language programmes on television and online. S4C was established by the 1981 Broadcasting Act. The S4C Authority is accountable to the Department for Culture, Media and Sport. Authority Members are appointed by the Secretary of State for Culture, Media and Sport following consultation with the Welsh Government. S4C is a wholly Welsh language channel.

Mae S4C yn ddarlledwr gwasanaeth cyhoeddus sy'n darparu ystod o raglenni Cymraeg o ansawdd uchel ar deledu ac ar-lein. Cafodd S4C ei sefydlu gan Ddeddf Darlledu 1981. Mae Awdurdod S4C yn atebol i'r Adran dros Ddiwylliant, Cyfryngau a Chwaraeon. Mae aelodau'r Awdurdod yn cael eu penodi gan yr Ysgrifennydd Gwladol dros Ddiwylliant, Cyfryngau a Chwaraeon, ar ôl ymgynghori â Llywodraeth Cymru. Mae S4C yn sianel gwbl Gymraeg.

AUTHORITY MEMBERS ♂7 ♀1

	In office until	Background
Chair		
Huw Jones	06/15	Media
Members (Remuneration £9,650 pa - 1 day per week)		
Bill Davies	07/12	Personnel
John Davies	03/14	Agriculture & Local Government
Cenwyn Edwards	07/12	Media
Dyfrig Jones	04/13	Media
Dr Glenda Jones	03/14	Broadcasting & Training
Winson Roddick, CB, QC	08/12	Legal
Rheon Tomos	11/14	Finance

MANAGEMENT TEAM

Chief Executive: Ian Jones
Members: Elin Morris - *Director of Commercial & Corporate Policy;* Kathryn Morris - *Director of Finance & Human Resources;* Dafydd Rhys - *Director of Content;* Garffild Lloyd Lewis - *Director of Communications, Marketing & Partnerships*

Total no. staff: 132 FTE

MEDIA
S4C

OFCOM

Chair of Advisory
Committee, Wales
Ian Clarke

2 Caspian Point, Caspian Way
Cardiff CF10 4DQ
☎ (029) 2046 7200
Fax: (029) 2046 7233
Email: wales@ofcom.org.uk
Website: www.ofcom.org.uk

Director Wales
Elinor Williams

Ofcom is the independent regulator and competition authority for the UK communications industries with responsibilities across television, radio, telecommunications, wireless communications and postal services. Ofcom's office in Wales is responsible for communicating regulatory policy and reflecting the concerns of citizens and consumers in Wales to Ofcom.

Wales is represented by the Member for Wales on Ofcom's Content Board, which is a committee of the main Ofcom Board. The Content Board's key statutory functions are the regulation of broadcast content, media literacy and to champion the broadcast interests of citizens across the UK.

Wales is also represented by the Member for Wales on Ofcom's Communications Consumer Panel, the independent policy advisory body on consumer interests in telecommunications, broadcasting and spectrum markets.

Ofcom's Advisory Committee for Wales provides guidance on those aspects of Ofcom's work which are of particular importance to Wales. The Committee also responds to relevant Ofcom consultations.

The Ofcom Nations' Committee is also a committee of the main Ofcom Board. The Chairman of the Ofcom Advisory Committee for Wales and Director Wales represent Wales on this Committee.

CONTENT BOARD MEMBER FOR WALES

Glyn Mathias

COMMUNICATIONS CONSUMER PANEL MEMBER FOR WALES

Kim Brook

MEMBERS OF ADVISORY COMMITTEE WALES

Chair
Ian Clarke - *Radio Telecommunications Consultant*
Members
Julie Barton - *Media Consultant;* John Davies - *Telecommunications Consultant;* Simon Gibson OBE - *Chief Executive, Wesley Clover Corp;* Glyn Mathias - *Former Electoral Commissioner Wales*

PRINCIPAL OFFICERS

Elinor Williams - *Director Wales*

Commercial Radio

Station	Area served	Frequency	Audience	Ownership
Bridge FM	Bridgend & Vale of Glamorgan	106.3FM	37,000	Town & Country Broadcasting
Calon FM	Wrexham/Flintshire	105.0FM	n/a	Glyndŵr University
Capital FM South Wales	South East Wales	97.4 & 103.2FM	207,000	Global Radio
Radio Carmarthenshire	Carmarthenshire	97.1FM	38,000	Town & Country Broadcasting
Radio Ceredigion	Ceredigion & Cardigan Bay	96.6, 97.4 & 103.3FM	10,000	Town & Country Broadcasting
Gold North Wales & Cheshire	North East Wales	1260 AM	30,000	Global Radio
Gold South Wales	South East Wales	1359AM	54,000	Global Radio
GTFM	Pontypridd	107.9FM	n/a	Community Radio
Radio Hafren	Mid Wales & The Borders	756MW	n/a	Radio Hafren
Heart Cymru	Anglesey & Gwynedd	103.0FM	34,000	Global Radio
Heart North West & Wales	North East Wales	96.3, 97.1 & 103.4FM	72,000	Global Radio
Kiss 101	South Wales & South West England	101FM	263,000	Bauer Radio
Nation 80s (Formerly Swansea Bay Radio)	South West Wales	102.1FM	n/a	Town & Country Broadcasting
Nation Radio	South Wales	106.8 & 107.3FM	100,000	Town & Country Broadcasting
Radio Pembrokeshire	Pembs. & West Carms.	102.5FM	47,000	Town & Country Broadcasting
Real Radio Wales	Wales	105-106FM	467,000	Guardian Media Group
Scarlet FM	Llanelli & Carms. Coast	97.5FM	n/a	Town & Country Broadcasting
Sunshine Radio	Monmouthshire & Herefordshire	107.8FM	n/a	Murfin Music International
Swansea Sound	South West Wales	1170AM	62,000	UTV Radio
The Wave	Swansea, Llanelli, Neath Port Talbot	96.4FM	141,000	UTV Radio

Total known Welsh audience **1,562,000**

NATIONAL & REGIONAL PRESS

National All-Wales

Daily	Circulation	Ownership
Western Mail	25,898	Trinity Mirror Plc
Daily Post	30,606	Trinity Mirror Plc
Sunday		
Wales on Sunday	28,662	Trinity Mirror Plc
Weekly		
Y Cymro	5,000	Tindle Newspapers Ltd
Golwg	12,000	Golwg Cyf
Total National Circulation	**102,166**	

Regional - North East Wales

Daily	Circulation	Ownership
The Leader	15,497	North Wales Newspapers Ltd
(Wrexham, Flintshire & Chester)		
Weekly		
Flintshire Chronicle	18,027	Trinity Mirror Plc
(Buckley, Deeside, Flint, Holywell, Mold)		
Denbighshire Free Press Series	6,581	North Wales Newspapers Ltd
(Bala, Corwen, Denbigh, Ruthin, St Asaph)		
Flintshire Standard	21,878	North Wales Newspapers Ltd
(Flintshire)		
The Rhyl, Prestatyn & Abergele Journal	28,229	North Wales Newspapers Ltd
(Abergele, Prestatyn, Rhuddlan, Rhyl, St Asaph)		
North Wales Pioneer	25,142	North Wales Newspapers Ltd
(Colwyn Bay, Conwy, Deganwy, Llandudno, Penrhyn Bay, Rhos-on-Sea)		
Wrexham Leader	32,384	North Wales Newspapers Ltd
(Brymbo, Cefn Mawr, Chirk, Gresford, Hope, Llay, Rhosllanerchrugog, Rossett, Wrexham)		
Total NE Wales Circulation	**147,738**	

NATIONAL & REGIONAL PRESS

Regional - North West Wales

Weekly	Circulation	Ownership
Caernarfon & Denbigh Herald	10,962	Trinity Mirror Plc
(Gwynedd, Isle of Anglesey)		
Holyhead & Bangor Mail	9,655	Trinity Mirror Plc
North Wales Chronicle	30,010	North Wales Newspapers Ltd
(Amlwch, Bangor, Bethesda, Blaenau Ffestiniog, Caernarfon, Harlech, Holyhead, Llangefni, Menai Bridge, Porthmadog, Pwllheli)		
Y Dydd	n/a	Tindle Newspapers Ltd
(Dolgellau)		
North Wales Weekly News	12,816	Trinity Mirror Plc
(Betws-y-Coed, Colwyn Bay, Conwy, Deganwy, Llandudno, Llanrwst, Penrhyn Bay)		
Total NW Wales Circulation	**63,443**	

Regional - South East Wales

Daily	Circulation	Ownership
Metro (South Wales)	25,531	Associated Press Ltd
South Wales Argus	22,314	Newsquest Media Group
(Abercarn, Abergavenny, Blackwood, Caerleon, Chepstow, Cwmbran, Monmouth, Newport, Risca, Tutshill)		
South Wales Echo	31,009	Media Wales Ltd
(Abercarn, Abercarniad, Aberdare, Bargoed, Barry, Bedwas, Bridgend, Bryncoch, Cardiff, Ferndale, Llantrisant, Merthyr Tydfil, Newport, Rhondda, Taff's-Well)		

Weekly		
Abergavenny Chronicle	8,794	Tindle Newspapers Ltd
(Abergavenny, Blaenavon, Brynmawr, Crickhowell, Monmouth)		
Barry & District News	5,227	Newsquest Media Group
(Barry, Dinas-Powis, Llantwit-Major, Penarth, Rhoose, St Athan)		
Campaign	28,566	Newsquest Media Group
(Caerphilly, Ystrad Mynach & Bargoed)		
Cardiff & South Wales Advertiser	30,000	Hot Press Publications
(South Wales)		
Cynon Valley Leader	5,540	Trinity Mirror Plc
(Abercynon, Aberdare, Cwmbach, Mountain Ash)		
Free Press - Monmouth	6,115	Newsquest Media Group
(Monmouth)		
Glamorgan Gem Series	30,288	Tindle Newspapers Ltd
(Glamorgan)		
Gwent Gazette	5,373	Trinity Mirror Plc
(Abergavenny, Abertillery, Brynmawr, Cwm, Ebbw-Vale, Tredegar)		

Regional - South East Wales (cont.)

Weekly	Circulation	Ownership
Merthyr Express *(Abercarniad, Merthyr Tydfil, Merthyr Vale, Troedyrhiw)*	10,727	Trinity Mirror Plc
Monmouthshire Beacon *(Monmouth)*	5,286	Tindle Newspapers Ltd
Penarth Times *(Penarth)*	4,979	Newsquest Media Group
Pontypridd & Llantrisant Observer *(Beddau, Croeserw, Glyncoch, Llanharan, Llantrisant, Pontypridd, Tonyrefail)*	6,067	Trinity Mirror Plc
Rhondda Leader *(Rhondda)*	9,944	Trinity Mirror Plc
Rhymney Valley Express *(Rhymney Valley)*	10,727	Trinity Mirror Plc
Weekly Argus *(Newport & District)*	19,814	Newsquest Media Group
Total SE Wales Circulation	**266,301**	

Regional - South West Wales

Daily	Circulation	Ownership
South Wales Evening Post *(Ammanford, Carmarthen, Clydach, Llanelli, Neath, Port Talbot, Swansea, Ystradgynlais)*	38,364	Northcliffe Newspapers Group Ltd

Weekly	Circulation	Ownership
South Wales Guardian *(Ammanford, Brynamman, Carmarthen, Clydach, Cross Hands, Llandovery, Llanelli, Pontardulais, Pontyberem, Swansea)*	5,837	Newsquest Media Group
Glamorgan Gazette *(Aberkenfig, Bridgend, Bryncoch, Llanharry, Pencoed, Porthcawl, Pyle)*	13,677	Trinity Mirror Plc
Llanelli Star *(Burry Port, Carmarthen, Cross Hands, Llanelli, Pembrey, Pontyberem, Trimsaran)*	12,996	Northcliffe Newspapers Group Ltd
Total SW Wales Circulation	**70,874**	

MEDIA PRESS

Regional - Mid & West Wales

Daily	Circulation	Ownership
Shropshire Star	51,240	Midland News Association
(Albrighton, Bridgnorth, Chirk, Ellesmere, Knighton, Llanfyllin, Llangollen, Llanidloes, Machynlleth, Rhayader, Telford, Wrexham)		

Weekly		
Hereford Times	32,654	Newsquest Media Group
(Abergavenny, Brecon, Hay-on-Wye, Hereford, Knighton, Leominster, Monmouth, Presteigne, Tenbury-Wells)		
Oswestry & Border Counties Advertiser	8,749	North Wales Newspapers Ltd
(Chirk, Ellesmere, Gobowen, Oswestry, Whittington)		
Cambrian News	24,258	Tindle Newspapers Ltd
(Aberaeron, Aberystwyth, Bala, Barmouth, Cardigan, Lampeter, Llanidloes, Machynlleth, Porthmadog, Rhayader, Tywyn)		
Brecon & Radnor Express	12,000	Tindle Newspapers Ltd
(Brecon, Builth Wells, Crickhowell, Hay-on-Wye, Knighton, Llandovery, Llandrindod Wells, Presteigne, Rhayader, Ystradgynlais)		
Hereford Journal	39,071	Shropshire Newspapers Ltd
(Hereford & Borders)		
Powys County Times & Express	15,081	North Wales Newspapers Ltd
(Aberdovey, Barmouth, Builth Wells, Dolgellau, Knighton, Llanidloes, Machynlleth, Newtown, Rhayader, Tywyn, Welshpool)		
County Echo & St Davids City Chronicle	2,738	Cambrian News Ltd
(Cardigan, Fishguard, Haverfordwest, Milford Haven, Newport, St David's)		
Carmarthen Journal	16,408	Northcliffe Newspapers Group Ltd
(Ammanford, Cardigan, Carmarthen, Llandovery, Newcastle Emlyn, Whitland)		
Mid Wales Journal	5,100	Shropshire Newspapers Ltd
(Mid Wales & Borders)		
Milford & West Wales Mercury	3,515	Newsquest Media Group
(Haverfordwest, Milford Haven, Neyland, Pembroke, Pembroke Dock)		
Tenby Observer	6,935	Tindle Newspapers Ltd
(Narberth, Pembroke, Pembroke Dock, Tenby, Whitland)		
Cardigan & Tivy-Side Advertiser	6,719	Newsquest Media Group
(Aberaeron, Cardigan, Fishguard, New Quay, Newcastle Emlyn, Newport)		
Western Telegraph	19,582	Newsquest Media Group
(Cardigan, Carmarthen, Fishguard, Milford Haven, Narberth, Neyland, Pembroke, St David's, Tenby, Whitland)		
Total M & W Wales Circulation	**244,050**	

MEDIA PRESS

Papurau Bro

Title *(First Published)*	Distribution
Yr Angor (1977)	Aberystwyth, Comins Coch, Llanbadarn Fawr, Penparcau and Waunfawr
Yr Angor (1979)	Merseyside
Yr Arwydd (1983)	Eastern Anglesey
Y Barcud (1976)	Tregaron and District
Y Bedol (1977)	Ruthin and District
Y Bigwn (1988)	Denbigh
Blewyn Glas (1978)	Machynlleth
Y Cardi Bach (1979)	Taf Valley
Y Clawdd (1987)	Wrexham and District
Clonc (1982)	Lampeter and District
Cwlwm (1978)	Carmarthen
Dail Dysynni (1979)	Dysynni Valley
Dan y Landsker (2007)	Pembroke Dock and District
Y Dinesydd (1973)	City of Cardiff and District
Y Ddolen (1978)	Llanfarian and Llanrhystud
Eco'r Wyddfa (1976)	Llanrug and Llanberis
Y Fan a'r Lle (1996)	Brecon and District
Y Ffynnon (1976)	Eifionydd
Y Gadlas (1976)	Conwy and Clwyd
Y Gambo (1982)	South East Ceredigion
Y Garthen (1981)	Teifi Valley
Y Glannau (1982)	Clwyd Valley
Glo-Man (1977)	Amman Valley
Y Gloran (1977)	Rhondda Fawr
Y Glorian (1977)	Llangefni and District
Goriad (1980)	Bangor and Felinheli
Yr Hogwr (1987)	Ogmore and District
Llafar Bro (1975)	Blaenau Ffestiniog
Llais (1979)	Tawe Valley
Llais Aeron (1976)	Aeron Valley
Llais Ardudwy (1975)	Ardudwy
Llais Ogwan (1974)	Ogwen Valley
Llanw Llŷn (1975)	Llŷn Peninsula
Lleu (1975)	Nantlle Valley

MEDIA PRESS

NATIONAL & REGIONAL PRESS

Papurau Bro

Y Llien Gwyn (1979)	Fishguard and District
Y Lloffwr (1978)	Dinefwr and District
Nene (1978)	Penycae, Johnstown and Rhosllannerchrugog
Newyddion Mynwy (2004)	Monmouthshire
Yr Odyn (1975)	Nant Conwy
Papur Dre (2002)	Caernarfon and District
Papur Fama (1979)	Mold and District
Papur Menai (1976)	Glan Menai, Landdona and Brynsiencyn
Papur Pawb (1974)	Talybont, Taliesin and Tre'r ddôl
Papur y Cwm (1981)	Gwendraeth Valley
Y Pentan (1979)	Conwy Valley
Pethe Penllyn (1974)	Parish of Penllyn
Plu'r Gweunydd (1978)	Llanfair Caereinion, Montgomery, Welshpool and District
Y Rhwyd (1979)	Anglesey
Seren Hafren (1983)	Dyffryn Hafren
Sosbanelli (2002)	Llanelli
Tafod-Élai (1985)	Taff-Ely District and Ynys-y-Bwl
Y Tincer (1977)	Bow Street and Borth
Tua'r Goleuni (1997)	Rhymney Valley
Wilia (1977)	Swansea and District
Yr Wylan (1977)	Penrhyndeudraeth and Porthmadog
Yr Ysgub (1980)	Ceiriog Valley and Oswestry

MEDIA
PRESS

The**Wales** Yearbook **13**

NATIONAL ORGANIZATIONS

artes **mundi**

Wales International Visual Art Exhibition and Prize
06 October 2012 – 13 January 2013
National Museum of Art, Cardiff

Gwobr ac Arddangosfa Gelf Weledol Ryngwladol Cymru
06 Hydref 2012 – 13 Ionawr 2013
Amgueddfa Gelf Genedlaethol, Caerdydd

Shortlist
Miriam Bäckström, Sweden
Tania Bruguera, Cuba
Phil Collins, England
Sheela Gowda, India
Teresa Margolles, Mexico
Darius Mikšys, Lithuania
Apolonija Šušteršič, Slovenia

www.artesmundi.org

Artes Mundi is publicly funded by the Arts Council of Wales, the Welsh Government and the City and County of Cardiff. Bank of America Merrill Lynch is the principal sponsor of Artes Mundi 5.

ARTES MUNDI

St John's Chambers
High Street Arcade
Cardiff CF10 1BD

☎ (029) 2055 5300
Fax: (029) 2023 3182

Email: info@artesmundi.org
Website: www.artesmundi.org

Chair
William Wilkins

Artistic Director
Ben Borthwick

Wales International Visual Art
Exhibition and Prize

Gwobr ac Arddangosfa Gelf
Weledol Ryngwladol Cymru

Artes Mundi aims to present a landmark programme of international, contemporary visual art that will enrich the cultural and educational life of Wales and its people, develop and inspire new audiences and become an important voice in cultural debate and discourse worldwide.

TRUSTEES ♂8 ♀4

William Wilkins CBE DL	Rev Robin Morrison
Sue Balsom	Huw Roberts
Tim Davies	Adam Salkeld
Jeremy Lancaster	Jon Sheppard
Christine Lewis OBE	David Thorp
Julie Lomax	Sian Williams

PRINCIPAL STAFF

Ben Borthwick	*Artistic Director*
Carl Grainger	*Head of Finance & Operations*
Caron Thomas	*Head of Development*
Ffion Rhys	*Project Co-ordinator*
Catriona Wright	*Communications & Marketing Manager*

ARTS & BUSINESS CYMRU

South Wales Office
16 Museum Place
Cardiff CF10 3BH
☎ (029) 2030 3023

North Wales Office
Room 40, The Town Hall
Llandudno LL30 2UP
☎ (01492) 574003

Email: contactus@aandbcymru.org.uk
Website: www.aandbcymru.org.uk

Chair
Huw Roberts

Chief Executive
Rachel Jones

Arts &Business
Cymru

A membership organization and charity, A&B Cymru is the specialist in assisting business and the arts to work together in partnerships of mutual benefit. From offices in Cardiff and Llandudno, the team delivers tailored programmes and services to a wide range of individuals and organizations across the country. A&B Cymru knows that when the two sectors work in truly mutual partnership, the results benefit society in far reaching and tangible ways. Its work has proven value in the current economic climate of Wales. The impact it has can be felt on children, people in the workplace, communities large and small. A&B Cymru is funded by the Welsh Government and Arts Council of Wales.

BOARD MEMBERS   ♂3 ♀3

Chair
Huw Roberts   Retired Director, Welsh Affairs; Royal Mail Group
Members
Samantha Maskrey   Vice Chair, Director, Present Choices
Jon Field   Relationship Manager, Unity Trust Bank
Simon King   Managing Director, Core Matters Consultancy
Alison Love   Managing Director, Alison Love Ltd
Lynne Sheehy   CSR Manager, Legal & General

PRINCIPAL OFFICERS

Rachel Jones - *Chief Executive*

ARTS COUNCIL OF WALES

Chair
Prof Dai Smith

Bute Place
Cardiff
CF10 5AL
with offices at
Cardiff, Carmarthen
and Colwyn Bay

☎ (0845) 8734900
Fax: (029) 2044 1400

Minicom: ☎ (029) 2045 1023
Email: info@artswales.org.uk
Website: www.artswales.org.uk

Chief Executive
Nick Capaldi

Cyngor Celfyddydau Cymru
Arts Council of Wales

Noddir gan
Lywodraeth Cymru
Sponsored by
Welsh Government

Arts Council of Wales is accountable to the Welsh Government for administering government funding of the arts in Wales, and to Parliament through the Secretary of State for Culture, Media and Sport for the distribution of National Lottery funds to the arts in Wales. In 2012/13 the Council's total budget is £52.1m. Council Members are appointed by the Welsh Government.

COUNCIL MEMBERS   ♂9 ♀6

	In office until	Background
Chair (2 days per week)		
Prof Dai Smith	3/13	Research Professor, Swansea University; Historian; Writer; Broadcaster
Members (No remuneration - 10 days per year)		
Dr Emma Evans	3/14	Creative Manager & Producer
John Geraint	3/13	Creative Director, Green Bay Media
Michael Griffiths	3/15	Educational consultant & former Headteacher.
Melanie Hawthorn	3/15	Creative Industries Development Officer, University of Glamorgan
Dr Lesley Hodgson	3/15	co-founder of Glamorgan GATES, a Community Arts Project, Merthyr Tydfil; Vice Chair, Merthyr Tydfil Global Village Festival
Margaret Jervis MBE DL	3/11	Operational Director, Valleys Kids
Marian Wyn Jones	3/15	Former Head of Centre, BBC in North Wales; journalistic career; Media Consultant; Member of public bodies & charitable trusts
Andrew Miller	3/15	Head of Creative Programming, Royal Welsh College of Music; previous career in television as a presenter, producer & director
Osi Rhys Osmond	3/13	Lecturer, Swansea Metropolitan University School of Art & Design
Richard Turner	3/13	Deputy Director, Global Innovation Academy, University of Wales
Alan Watkin	3/13	Cultural Advisor, WLGA; Member, Legacy Trust Advisory Board, Cultural Olympiad in Wales; Member, Welsh books Council
Prof Gerwyn Wiliams	3/13	Professor, School of Welsh, Bangor University
John Carey Williams	3/13	Director, Theatr Iolo
Dr Kate Woodward	3/14	Lecturer, Theatre, Film & Television Studies, Aberystwyth University

SENIOR STAFF

Nick Capaldi - *Chief Executive*; Hywel Tudor - *Finance & Central Services Director;* David Alston - *Arts Director*

Total no. staff: 98

Plas Crug
Aberystwyth
Ceredigion SY23 1NJ

☎ (01970) 621200
Fax: (01970) 627701

Email: nmr.wales@rcahmw.gov.uk
Website: www.rcahmw.gov.uk

Chair
Eurwyn Wiliam

Secretary
Peter Wakelin

Established in 1908, the Royal Commission is the investigation body and national archive for the historic environment of Wales. It has the lead role in ensuring that Wales's archaeological, built and maritime heritage is authoritatively recorded and seeks to promote the understanding and appreciation of this heritage nationally and internationally. The Commission's strategic plan is available on its website. It also publishes an Annual Review.

BOARD OF COMMISSIONERS   ♂ 6 ♀ 2

Chair	In Office Until	Background
Eurwyn Wiliam	2013	Former Deputy Director General, Amgueddfa Cymru - National Museum Wales
Commissioners		
Anne Eastham	2014	Archaeozoologist, specialising in bird & micro-faunas
Catherine Hardman	2015	Collections Development Manager, Archaeology Data Service
Jonathan Hudson	2016	Independent Consultant
Thomas Lloyd	2015	Independent Architectural Historian & Author
Henry Owen-John	2016	Planning & Development Director, North-West Region, English Heritage
Mark Redknap	2013	Curator of Medieval and Later Archaeology, Amgueddfa Cymru - National Museum Wales
Christopher Williams	2013	Director of Swansea University's Centre for the History of Wales and its Borderlands

Secretary: Dr Peter Wakelin

PRINCIPAL OFFICERS

Stephen Hughes - *Projects Director;* Hilary Malaws - *Services Director*

Total no. staff: 35

THE BEVAN FOUNDATION

The Innovation Centre
Festival Drive
Victoria Business Park
Ebbw Vale
NP23 8XA

☎ (01495) 356702
Fax: (01495) 356703

Email: info@bevanfoundation.org
Website: www.bevanfoundation.org

Chair
Paul O'Shea

Director
Victoria Winckler

The Bevan Foundation is an independent 'think tank' which promotes social justice in Wales. We develop new ideas about poverty, social inclusion, equality and empowerment through research, discussion and debate, and articles and pamphlets. Our work is highly regarded and often informs public policy. The Foundation is funded by its membership, which is open to anyone who supports its aims, and by grants and commissions.

President: Lord Kinnock   **Hon Patron:** Dr Rowan Williams, Archbishop of Canterbury

TRUSTEES   ♂ 11 ♀ 3

BRITISH COUNCIL WALES

2nd Floor, 1 Kingsway,
Cardiff CF10 3AQ

☎ (029) 2092 4300
☎ (029) 2092 4310 (Welsh Language)
Fax (029) 2092 4301

Email: wales.enquiries@britishcouncil.org
Website: www.britishcouncil.org/wales
Twitter: http://twitter.com/bcwales

Chair
Aled Eirug

Director
Simon Dancey

The British Council creates international opportunities for the people of the UK and other countries and builds trust between them worldwide. We are a Royal Charter charity, established as the UK's international organization for educational opportunities and cultural relations.

Our 7000 staff in over 100 countries work with thousands of professionals and policy makers and millions of young people every year through English, arts, education and society programmes.

We earn over 75% of our annual turnover of nearly £700 million from services which customers pay for, education and development contracts we bid for and from partnerships. A UK Government grant provides the remaining 25%. We match every £1 of core public funding with over £3 earned in pursuit of our charitable purpose.

It has been active in Wales since its establishment in 1934, opening its first office in Cardiff in 1944. The Committee structure that supports these activities brings together experts from across Wales in all of the fields it works in.

COMMITTEE MEMBERS   ♂ 10 ♀ 1

Chair
Aled Eirug

Members
Gary Davies
Richard Davies
John Howells
Euryn Ogwen Williams
Berwyn Rowlands
Nicholas Bourne

Laura McAllister
Ashok Ahir
Colm McGivern
Simon Dancey

Background
Policy Consultant & Media Advisor

Director of European & External Affairs, Welsh Government
Registered Commissioner, Infrastructure Planning Commission
Director of Culture, Welsh Government
Consultant in Electronic Media, Digital Media
Managing Director, The Festivals Company Ltd
Former Assembly Member & Leader, Welsh Conservative Party
Member, Silk Commission
Professor of Governance, University of Liverpool's School of Management
Executive Editor, Politics, BBC Cymru Wales
Regional Director - UK, British Council
Director, British Council Wales

PRINCIPAL OFFICER

Simon Dancey - *Director Wales*

BUSINESS IN THE COMMUNITY CYMRU / WALES

2nd Floor, Riverside House,
Cathedral Road
Cardiff CF11 9HB
☎ (029) 2078 0050
Fax: (029) 2023 5116

Additional office in
Mold ☎ (01352) 706213

Email: wales@bitc.org.uk
Website: www.bitc.org.uk/wales

Chair
John Union

Wales Director
Simon Harris

Business in the Community (BITC) is a business-led charity that promotes responsible business.

It has a growing membership of over 850 companies and a further 10,700 companies engaged in campaigns.

BITC asks its members to work together to transform communities by tackling social and environmental issues where business can make a real difference.

It also offers its members practical support to help them to integrate responsible business practices wherever they operate.

One of The Prince's Charities, BITC has 30 years experience of working with communities in greatest need.

WALES EXECUTIVE BOARD ♂8 ♀4

Nigel Annett	Dŵr Cymru Welsh Water	Vanessa Griffiths	Groundwork North Wales
Noreen Bray OBE	Good Relations	Katharine Finn	PwC
Sandra Busby	Welsh Contact Centre Forum	Jeffrey Harris	Castle Leisure
Graham Edwards	Wales & West Utilities	Andrew Padmore	Egnida
Ifan Evans	Welsh Government	John Union	Barclays Corporate
Simon Farrington	Media Wales	Graeme Yorston	Principality Building Society

MEMBER COMPANIES IN WALES

AB Glass	Dŵr Cymru Welsh Water	Office for National Statistics	SERS Ltd
Avox	Egnida	Orchard Media & Events	St David's Hotel, Ewloe
Bluestone	Finance Wales	P&A Group	Stradform (Vinci PLC)
Brother Industries	Golley Slater	Partners IT	The Open University
Buy As You View	Hafod Housing Association	PHS Group	Total Flood Solutions
Cardiff Bus	HLN Architects	Principality Building Society	UES Energy
Castell Howell Foods	Holder Mathias Architects	RCT Homes	UK Intellectual Property
Castle Leisure Ltd	International Rectifier	Real Radio	Office
Castleoak Care Partnerships	Kaplan Altior	Rhondda Housing	University of Glamorgan
Costain	Kingspan	Association	University of Wales
Crystal Collections	Mabey Bridge	Rockwool	Newport
Dolmans Solicitors	Media Wales	Santia	Wales & West Utilities
Dow Corning	Network Rail Wales	S A Brain & Co Ltd	Yuasa Battery

Cefnogi Dyfodol Pobl Cymru
Supporting Welsh Futures

 gyrfacymru.com | careerswales.com

Llywodraeth Cymru
Welsh Government

CAREERS WALES

Careers Wales, Head Office
Ty Glyn, Unit 1, Brecon Court
William Browne Close
Llantarnam Park, Cwmbran

☎ (01633) 487600
Fax: (01633) 487601

Email:
headoffice@careerswalesgyrfacymru.com
Website: www.careerswales.com

Chair
Phillip Westwood

Chief Executive
Trina Neilson

From 1st April 2012 the six former Careers Wales Companies have re-structured to form a single organization Career Choices Dewis Gyrfa.

Contracted to deliver services by the Welsh Government, Career Choices Dewis Gyrfa provides a full range of free, bilingual careers information, advice and guidance services for all age groups under the familiar Careers Wales brand.

Careers Wales services can be accessed via a network of careers centres across Wales, online via careerswales.com and through the free helpline on 0800 100 900.

BOARD OF DIRECTORS ♂ 10 ♀ 3

Chair: Phillip Westwood
Vice-Chair: David Roberts
Members
Ruth Brooks; Phil Davy; Geraint Evans; Neil Frow; Hywel Jones; Karen Lennox; Ivan Maund; Trina Neilson; William Norris; Iwan Prys Jones; Annesley Wright

PRINCIPAL OFFICERS

Trina Neilson - *Chief Executive*

CARE COUNCIL FOR WALES

Chair
Arwel Ellis Owen

Southgate House
Wood Street
Cardiff CF10 1EW

☎ (029) 2022 6257
Minicom: (029) 2078 0680
Fax: (029) 2038 4764

Email: info@ccwales.org.uk
Website: www.ccwales.org.uk

 Cyngor Gofal Cymru
Care Council for Wales

Hyder mewn Gofal - Confidence in Care

Chief Executive
Rhian Huws Williams

The Care Council for Wales was set up under the Care Standards Act 2000 as the first regulatory organization for the social care profession, to ensure that the social care workforce in Wales is safe to practice; has the appropriate skills and qualifications to perform to a high professional standard and is attracting enough of the right people into its ranks to deliver quality social care now and in the future.

It has a duty to set high standards for skills, training and behaviour for those working in the sector and to make sure that everyone employed as a social worker, or social care worker, is acting in a safe way, a way that makes the most of their training.

The Care Council is the Sector Skills Council for the social care, early years, children and young people's workforce in Wales. This means having an understanding of the numbers of people in the workforce, their age and qualifications, as well as the skills needed for social care in the future. In its role as an SSC the Council works with colleges across Wales to make sure the qualifications, infrastructure, and funding is in place to better match the learning needs of employers. This happens following consultation with carers, employers and service users so as to help modernise social care and ensure qualifications and standards are continually adapted to meet the changing needs of people who use social care services.

MEMBERS ♂ 11 ♀ 4

Chair	In Office Until	Background
Arwel Ellis Owen	07/13	Media & Communications
Members		**Sector**
Philip Champness	09/12	General Public
Peter Crews	02/13	Trade Union
Ian Davies	02/13	Service Users
Stephen Elliott	02/15	Professional Organizations
Roger Gant	07/13	Representing the Voluntary Sector
Penny Gripper	05/13	Service Users
Kate Hawkins	02/15	Education & Training
Martin Lewis	02/13	Carers
Pauline Jones	05/14	Carers
Kenneth Jones	02/13	Carers
Martyn Pengilley	02/13	General Public
Barbara Roberts	05/14	General Public
Brian West	02/13	Private Sector Employers
Ellis Williams	03/12	Public Sector Employers

PRINCIPAL OFFICERS

Rhian Huws Williams - *Chief Executive;* Joanne Oak - *Director of Corporate Services & Resources;* Gerry Evans - *Director of Regulation & Professional Standards;* Roberta Hayes - *Director of Learning & Development*

Total no. staff: 86

CHILDREN'S COMMISSIONER FOR WALES
COMISIYNYDD PLANT CYMRU

Penrhos Manor, Oak Drive, Colwyn Bay, Conwy LL29 7YW
☎ (01492) 523333 Fax: (01492) 523336
Oystermouth House, Charter Court, Phoenix Way,
Llansamlet, Swansea SA7 9FS
☎ (01792) 765600 Fax: (01792) 765601
Email: post@childcomwales.org.uk
Website: www.childcomwales.org.uk
Twitter: @childcomwales / @complantcymru

Children's
Commissioner for Wales
Keith Towler

The Children's Commissioner for Wales is an independent children's rights institution established in 2001. His principal aim is to safeguard and promote the rights and welfare of children and young people. The Commissioner and his team are there for children and young people aged under 18, living in Wales or who are normally resident in Wales. Also included within his powers is the ability to help older young people who have been in care and the ability to act in relation to past circumstances that affected children who are now adults, if there are implications for today's children and young people.

Working across two offices – in Swansea and Colwyn Bay – the Commissioner's team:

- support children and young people to find out about children's rights
- listen to children and young people to find out what's important to them
- advise children, young people and those who care for them if they feel they've got nowhere else to go with their problems
- influence government and other organizations who say they're going to make a difference to children's lives, making sure they keep their promises to children and young people
- speak up for children and young people nationally on important issues – being the children's champion in Wales.

In exercising his functions, the Commissioner must have regard to the United Nations Convention on the Rights of the Child (UNCRC). This is the most widely ratified international human rights instrument and gives children and young people a wide range of civil, political, economic, social and cultural rights. In 2005, the Welsh Government adopted the UNCRC as the basis of all policy making for children and young people.

The Commissioner's remit covers all areas of the devolved powers of the National Assembly for Wales insofar as they affect children and young people's rights and welfare and he may also make representations to the National Assembly for Wales about any matter affecting the rights and welfare of children and young people in Wales.

Legislation also enables the Commissioner to give advice and information to children and young people – via his advice and support service – and the power to review the effect on children on any function of the Welsh Government, local authorities, health authorities and Assembly-sponsored public bodies. The Children's Commissioner for Wales is also a prescribed regulator for whistleblowers.

CHILDREN'S COMMISSIONER

COMMUNITY HOUSING CYMRU GROUP

2 Ocean Way
Cardiff CF24 5TG

☎ (029) 2067 4800
Fax: (029) 2067 4801

Email: enquiries@chcymru.org.uk
Website: www.chcymru.org.uk

Chair
Peter Cahill

 Grŵp
Cartrefi
Cymunedol
Cymru

Community
Housing
Cymru
Group

Group Chief Executive
Nick Bennett

Community Housing Cymru Group is the membership body for housing associations, community mutuals and associated support providers in Wales. Through providing a range of conferences, training sessions, information programmes, forums and networks, they ensure that the social housing movement in Wales is properly informed on key issues. They have formed a group structure with Care & Repair Cymru and the Centre for Regeneration Excellence Wales (CREW) which encourages collaborative working across housing, care and regeneration.

NATIONAL COUNCIL   ♂16 ♀6

Chair
Peter Cahill
Representative Members
Andrew Lycett - *RCT Homes;* Peter Maggs - *Pembrokeshire Housing;* Amanda Davies - *Seren Group;* Kevin Protheroe - *Cardiff Community HA;* Tim Blanch - *Coastal Housing;* Peter Cahill - *Newport City Homes*

Voluntary Committee Members
Roger Waters - *Pennaf Group;* Jasper Roberts - *Cadwyn HA;* Doiran Jones - *Melin Homes;* Amanda Protheroe - *Newydd HA;* Stephen Cripps - *Tai Ceredigion;* Elgar Lewis - *Hafod HA*

South East Regional Council
John Keegan - *Monmouthshire Housing;* Christine Rutson - *United Welsh*

South West Regional Council
Shayne Hembrow - *Wales & West HA;* Steve Jones - *Tai Ceredigion*

North & Central Regional Council
Shane Perkins - *Mid Wales HA;* Anne Hinchey - *Wales & West HA*

Co-opted Members
Mark Sheridan, Taff Housing - *Chair, Supported Housing Services Forum;* Steve Higginson, Monmouthshire Housing - *Chair, Financial Services Forum;* Helen Armstrong, Cadwyn HA - *Chair, Housing Services Forum;* Andrew Bateson, Cadwyn HA - *Chair, Technical Services Forum;* Dave Lewis, Care & Repair Cymru - *Chair*

PRINCIPAL OFFICERS

Nick Bennett - *Group Chief Executive;* Sioned Hughes - *Director of Policy & Social Enterprise;* Phillipa Knowles - *Director of Central Services;* Amanda Oliver - *Head of Policy & Research;* Steve Evans - *Head of Finance & ICT;* Edwina O'Hart - *Head of Communications;* Chris Jones - *Managing Director of Care & Repair Cymru;* Prof Dave Adamson - *Chief Executive of CREW*

COUNTRYSIDE COUNCIL FOR WALES

Maes y Ffynnon
Penrhosgarnedd
Bangor
Gwynedd
LL57 2DW

☎ (0845) 1306229
Fax: (01248) 385505

Email: enquiries@ccw.gov.uk
Website: www.ccw.gov.uk

Chair
Morgan Parry

Chief Executive
Roger Thomas

Cyngor Cefn Gwlad Cymru
Countryside Council for Wales

The Countryside Council for Wales champions the environment and landscapes of Wales and its coastal waters as sources of natural and cultural riches, as a foundation for economic and social activity, and as a place for leisure and learning opportunities. We aim to make the environment a valued part of everyone's life in Wales. Council Members are appointed by the National Assembly for Wales, to which the CCW is accountable. The budget for 2011/12 for CCW is £40.6m.

Noddir gan
Lywodraeth Cymru
Sponsored by
Welsh Government

COUNCIL MEMBERS   ♂6 ♀2

In office until   Background

Chair (Remuneration £43,810 - 2.5 days per week)
Morgan Parry   02/13   Member of JNCC

Members (Remuneration £8,460 - 2.5 days per month or £11,844 - 3.5 days per month or £14,100 - 4.2 days per month)

	In office until	Background
Dr Susan Gubbay	01/14	Freelance Marine Consultant
Dr Ieuan Joyce	03/13	Farmer; Member of WAG's Upland Forum; Member of JNCC
W Pat O'Reilly	03/13	Self-employed Broadcaster; Former Chair, Fisheries, Ecology & Recreation Advisory Committee (FERAC), to the Environment Agency for Wales
Andy Middleton	01/14	Founder & CEO, Tŵr y Felin Group
Lynnette Thomas	01/14	Director of Operations DECIPHer, Cardiff Institute for Society, Health & Ethics
Alan Underwood	03/13	Director, Wastesavers Ltd; Chair, WCVA's 'Environment Wales' Grants Advisory Panel
Rod Williams	03/13	Former Regional Agricultural Manager for HSBC, North Wales; Chair, Heather & Hillforts Project

PRINCIPAL OFFICERS

Roger Thomas - *Chief Executive;* David M Parker - *Director Evidence & Advice;* Adrian Williams - *Director Planning & Resources*

Total no. staff: 512

---

* Under current plans by the Welsh Government, on the 1st April 2013, a new single body will bring together the functions of the Countryside Council for Wales, the Environment Agency Wales, and the Forestry Commission Wales.

CONSUMER FOCUS WALES
LLAIS DEFNYDDWYR CYMRU

Ground Floor, Portcullis House
21 Cowbridge Road East
Cardiff CF11 9AD
☎ (029) 2078 7100
Fax: (029) 2078 7101
Email:
contactwales@consumerfocus.org.uk
Website: www.consumerfocus.org.uk/wales

Llais Defnyddwyr Cymru
Gwarchod Buddiannau Defnyddwyr

Consumer Focus Wales
Wales' Consumer Champion

Chair
Vivienne Sugar

Senior Director
Rhys Evans

Consumer Focus Wales' goal is to make the consumer voice heard and make it count. We seek to represent, empower and engage with consumers over 5 major work areas; energy, post, financial services, public services & rights, redress & regulation and we have a particular commitment to working on behalf of vulnerable or disadvantaged consumers.

Consumer Focus Wales was formed by the merger of the Welsh Consumer Council, Energywatch, and Postwatch in 2008.

BOARD MEMBERS ♂6 ♀1

Background

Chair (Remuneration £28,000 pa)
Vivienne Sugar — Snr Associate, Solace Enterprises Ltd; Pro Chancellor, Swansea Univ; Fellow, Chartered Institute of Housing; Former Chief Exec, City & County of Swansea & Wales Adviser, Joseph Rowntree Foundation

Members (Meetings allowance £5,280 pa)
Dr Kevin Fitzpatrick — Disability Rights Commissioner for Wales (2000-07); Director, Inclusion21; Non-exec Member, Welsh Ambulance Services Trust; Associate, Welsh Inst of Health & Social Care, Univ of Glamorgan; Chairs, Boards of Trustees, St David's Children Soc & Arts Care/Gofal Celf

Dr Malcolm Smith — Freelance writer; Board Member, Environment Agency; former Chief Scientist & Deputy Chief Exec, Countryside Council for Wales

Bob Chapman — Management Consultant, legal & advice sector; Member, Welsh Committee, Administrative Justice & Tribunals Council; Fellow, Chartered Institute of Management; Trustee, Bevan Foundation; Chair, Neath Port Talbot CAB

Eifion Pritchard QPM — Former Deputy Chief Constable, Dyfed Powys Police; former Chair, Wales Ambulance Service & Postwatch Wales; Committee Member, CAB Cymru; Audit Committee, Older People's Commissioner for Wales

Prof Marcus Longley — Professor of Applied Health Policy & Director, Welsh Institute for Health & Social Care, Univ of Glamorgan; Member, WAG's Self Care Board; Fellow, Faculty of Public Health, Royal Colleges of Physicians

Prof John Williams — Professor of Law, Aberystwyth University; Member, Standing Committee Legal Wales & CAFCASS Cymru Advisory Committee; Trustee, Age UK & Age Scotland; Trustee, Aberystwyth CAB

PRINCIPAL OFFICERS

Rhys Evans - *Senior Director;* Liz Withers - *Head of Policy*

DESIGN COMMISSION FOR WALES

Design Commission for Wales
4th Floor, Building Two
Caspian Point, Caspian Way
Cardiff Bay CF10 4DQ

☎ (029) 2045 1964
Fax (029) 2045 1958

Email: info@dcfw.org
Website: www.dcfw.org

Chair
Alan Francis

Chief Executive
Carole-Anne Davies

The Design Commission for Wales (DCFW) is a national organization established by the Welsh Assembly Government to champion better buildings, spaces and places.

DCFW's mission is to champion high standards of architecture, landscape and urban design in Wales, promoting wider understanding of the importance of good quality in the built environment, supporting skill building, encouraging social inclusion and sustainable development. We believe that the quality of our built environment has a direct impact on the quality of all our lives.

MEMBERS ♂6 ♀2

Chair	Background
Alan Francis	Founding Partner, Gaunt Francis Architects
Commissioners	
Eileen Adams	Educationalist & Author
Mark Hallett	Director, Igloo Regeneration
Phil Jardine	Partner, Morgan Cole
Ewan Jones	Architect, Grimshaws
Gayna Jones	Consultant
Gerard F Ryan	Architect, Nicholas Hare Associates
Trevor Skempton	Architect & Urban Designer

PRINCIPAL OFFICERS

Carole-Anne Davies	Chief Executive

DESIGN REVIEW PANEL MEMBERS 2012-13

Toby Adam	Simon Hartley	Simon Power
Jonathan Adams	David Harvey	Prof John Punter (Co-Chair)
Roger Ayton	Jonathan Hines	Wendy Richards (Co-Chair)
Ashley Bateson	Christopher Jones	Elfed Roberts
Simon Carne	Ewan Jones (Co-Chair)	Phil Roberts
Kedrick Davies	Richard Keogh	Gerard Ryan
Glen Dyke	Martin Knight	Ben Sibert
Alan W Francis (Co-Chair)	Andrew Linfoot	Steve Smith
Michael Griffiths	Kieren Morgan	Lynne Sullivan
Mark Hallett	Prof Richard Parnaby	Angela Williams

EISTEDDFOD GENEDLAETHOL CYMRU
NATIONAL EISTEDDFOD OF WALES

40 Parc Tŷ Glas, Llanisien
Caerdydd CF14 5DU

☎ (0845) 4090 300
(0845) 4090 400
Fax: (029) 2076 3737

E-bost/Email: gwyb@eisteddfod.org.uk
Safle We/Website:
www.eisteddfod.org.uk

Llywydd / President
Prydwen Elfed-Owens

Prif Weithredwr /
Chief Executive
Elfed Roberts

Un o wyliau mawr y byd sy'n denu dros 160,000 o ymwelwyr bob blwyddyn. Dyma'r prif lwyfan i ddiwylliant a'r celfyddydau yng Nghymru, gyda gweithgareddau sy'n apelio at bobl o bob oed. Mae'r Eisteddfod Genedlaethol yn ŵyl deithiol sy'n ymweld ag ardaloedd yng ngogledd a de Cymru bob yn ail.

One of the world's great festivals, attracting over 160,000 visitors every year. This is the main stage for culture and the arts in Wales, with activities for people for all ages. The National Eisteddfod travels around the country visiting north and south Wales alternately.

SWYDDOGION CENEDLAETHOL / NATIONAL OFFICERS ♂9♀1

Prydwen Elfed-Owens	Llywydd y Llys / Court President
Garry Nicholas	Is-Gadeirydd y Cyngor / Council Vice-Chair
Geraint R Jones	Ysgrifennydd y Llys / Eisteddfod Court Secretary
Eric Davies	Trysorydd / Treasurer
Aled Lloyd Davies	Cymrodwr / Fellow
R Alun Evans	Cymrodwr / Fellow
Emyr Byron Hughes	Ysgrifennydd y Cwmni / Company Secretary
John Gwilym Jones	Cymrodwr / Fellow
James Nicholas	Cymrodwr / Fellow
Alwyn Roberts	Cymrodwr / Fellow

PRIF SWYDDOGION / PRINCIPAL OFFICERS

Elfed Roberts - *Prif Weithredwr / Chief Executive;* Hywel Wyn Edwards - *Trefnydd / Organizer;* Peter R Davies - *Cyllid / Finance;* Alan Gwynant - *Technegol / Technical;* Gwenllian Carr - Pennaeth *Cyfathrebu / Head of Communications;* Alwyn M Roberts - *Dirprwy Drefnydd / Deputy Organizer*

EISTEDDFOD

Y Comisiwn Etholiadol

Rydym yn gorff annibynnol a sefydlwyd gan Senedd y Deyrnas Unedig.

Ein nod yw sicrhau uniondeb ac ennyn ffydd y cyhoedd yn y broses ddemocrataidd yng Nghymru.

Rydym yn:
* cofrestru pleidau gweidyddol
* gofalu bod pobl yn deall ac yn dilyn y rheolau sy'n ymwneud â chyllid pleidiau ac etholiadau
* cyhoeddi manylion yn dweud o ble y mae pleidiau ac ymgeiswyr yn cael arian a sut y maent yn ei wario
* pennu'r safonau ar gyfer rhedeg etholiadau a chy hoeddi i ba raddau y cedwir at y safonau hynny
* gofalu bod pobl yn deall ei bod yn bwysig cofrestru i bleidleisio a'u bod yn gwybod sut i bleidleisio
* rhedeg unrhyw refferenda yn unol â'r Ddeddf Pleidau Gwleidyddol, Etholiadau a Refferenda 2000

Cysylltwch â ni
Y Comisiwn Etholiadol
Tŷ Caradog
1-6 Plas Sant Andreas
Caerdydd CF10 3BE

Ffôn   029 2034 6800
Ffacs   029 2034 6805
Ebost   gwybodaeth@comisiwnetholiadol.org.uk
Gwefan   www.comisiwnetholiadol.org.uk

The Electoral Commission

We are an independent body set up by the UK parliament.

Our aim is integrity and public confidence in the democratic process in Wales.

We:
* register political parties
* make sure people understand and follow the rules on party and election finance
* publish details of where parties and candidates money from and how they spend it
* set the standards for running elections and repc on how well this is done
* make sure people understand it us important to register to vote, and know how to vote
* run any referendums held in accordance with th Political Parties, Elections and Referendums Ac 2000

Contact us
The Electoral Commission
Caradog House
1-6 St Andrews Place
Cardiff CF10 3BE

Tel   029 2034 6800
Fax   029 2034 6805
Email   infowales@electoralcommission.org.uk
Web   www.electoralcommission.org.uk

THE ELECTORAL COMMISSION

Commissioner Wales
Ian Kelsall OBE

Wales Office, Caradog House
1-6 St Andrews Place
Cardiff CF10 3BE

☎ (029) 2034 6800
Fax: (029) 2034 6805

Website:
www.electoralcommission.org.uk
Safle gwe:
www.comisiwnetholiadol.org.uk
Email:
infowales@electoralcommission.org.uk
Ebost:
gwybodaeth@comisiwnetholiadol.org.uk

Head of Office
Kay Jenkins

The Electoral Commission is an independent body set up by the UK Parliament. Its aim is integrity and public confidence in the democratic process. Our role is to:

- *register political parties*
- *make sure people understand and follow the rules on party and election finance*
- *publish details of where parties and candidates get money from and how they spend it*
- *set the standards for electoral registration and running elections and report on how well this is done*
- *make sure people understand it is important to register to vote, and know how to vote*
- *run any referendums held in accordance with the Political Parties, Elections and Referendums Act 2000*

The Electoral Commission provides guidance and instructions to those electoral officials who are involved with running elections and referendums. We also provide advice and tailored resources to political parties, candidates and agents on how to contest elections and conform with the regulatory requirements in place.

COMMISSIONER FOR WALES

Appointed by Royal Warrant

Ian Kelsall OBE   Former Director, CBI Wales
Remuneration £359 per day, in office until 31 December 2012

MANAGEMENT TEAM WALES

Kay Jenkins   Head of Office
Rhydian Huw Thomas   Deputy Head of Office

Total no. Wales Office staff: 6

THE ELECTORAL COMMISSION

The Royal International Pavilion
Abbey Road, Llangollen
Denbighshire LL20 8SW

☎ (01978) 862000
Fax: (01978) 862002

Email:
info@international-eisteddfod.co.uk
Website:
www.international-eisteddfod.co.uk

President
Terry Waite CBE

Chair
J Philip Davies

EISTEDDFOD
GERDDOROL
RYNGWLADOL
LLANGOLLEN

LLANGOLLEN
INTERNATIONAL
MUSICAL
EISTEDDFOD

The Llangollen International Musical Eisteddfod provides a platform for people of all nations to meet and communicate through the international languages of music and dance, thereby promoting peace, harmony and a greater understanding of world culture.

The festival has very strong links to the United Nations and was nominated for a Nobel Peace Prize in 2004. The International Eisteddfod's Patron is the Prince of Wales and Terry Waite CBE is the current President.

NATIONAL OFFICERS ♂ 5 ♀ 0

J Philip Davies	Chair
Ian Lebbon	Vice-Chair
H Gethin Davies	Company Secretary
Brian Evans	Competitors' Liaison Officer
Eilir Owen Griffiths	Music Director

Standing Board
21 Elected Members, 1 Co-opted member & Life Vice Presidents

Committee Chairs
Enid Law - *Music & Staging;* Sandra Roberts - *Hospitality;* Ian Lebbon - *Marketing;* Keith Potts - *Tickets;* Jill Sanders - *Finance;* Peter Adair - *Grounds;* Sandie Attenburrow - *Floral;* Barrie Potter - *Archive*

ENVIRONMENT AGENCY WALES

Tŷ Cambria
29 Newport Road
Cardiff CF24 0TP

☎ (0870) 850 6506
Fax: (029) 2046 6411

Email:
enquiries@environment-agency.wales.gov.uk
Website:
www.environment-agency.wales.gov.uk

Board Member for Wales
Dr Madeleine Havard

Director Wales
Chris Mills

Noddir gan
Lywodraeth Cymru
Sponsored by
Welsh Government

Asiantaeth yr
Amgylchedd Cymru
Environment
Agency Wales

Environment Agency Wales was set up under the Environment Act 1995 and became an Assembly Sponsored Public Body in 1999. Its role includes: reducing the harm caused by flooding and pollution incidents, reducing industry's impacts on the environment and enforcing pollution legislation. It also oversees the management of waste, water resources and freshwater fisheries; cleaning up rivers, coastal waters and contaminated land and improving wildlife habitats. By influencing others to change attitudes and behaviour, it aims to make the environment cleaner and healthier.

NATIONAL BOARD MEMBER

Dr Madeleine Havard
Member for Wales

Appointed by the Welsh Government to serve on the Agency's Board for England and Wales
In office until 10/13
Remuneration: £21,001 pa - 5 days per month

PRINCIPAL COMMITTEE CHAIRS

Prof Thomas Pritchard OBE, JP
Dr Graeme Harris
Deep Sagar

Environment Protection Advisory Committee
Fisheries, Ecology, Recreation Advisory Committee
Flood Risk Management Wales

LEADERSHIP TEAM WALES

Chris Mills
Steve Brown
Ceri Davies
David Edwell
Gareth O'Shea
Andrew Jervis
Helen Davies
Graham Hillier
Joanne Sherwood

Director Wales
Area Manager, South West
Strategic Unit Manager
Area Manager, North
Area Manager, South East
Finance Manager
Human Resources Manager
Flood & Coastal Risk Management Manager
Corporate Services Manager

Total no. permanent staff: 1,010

* Under current plans by the Welsh Government, on the 1st April 2013, a new single body will bring together the functions of the Countryside Council for Wales, the Environment Agency Wales, and the Forestry Commission Wales.

EQUALITY & HUMAN RIGHTS COMMISSION

3rd Floor, 3 Callaghan Square,
Cardiff, CF10 5BT

☎ (029) 2044 7710
Fax: (029) 2044 7712
Minicom: (029) 2044 7713
Helpline
☎ (0845) 604 8810
Textphone: (0845) 604 8820

Email: wales@equalityhumanrights.com
Website: www.equalityhumanrights.com

Commissioner for Wales
Ann Beynon OBE

National Director, Wales
Kate Bennett

**Equality and
Human Rights**
Commission

Comisiwn
**Cydraddoldeb a
Hawliau Dynol**

The Equality and Human Rights Commission in Wales aims to reduce inequality, eliminate discrimination, strengthen good relations between people and promote and protect human rights.

The Equality and Human Rights Commission was established under the Equality Act 2006 and launched on 1 October 2007 when it took over the responsibilities of the Commission for Racial Equality, Disability Rights Commission and Equal Opportunities Commission. Its remit covers age, disability, gender, race, religion and belief, pregnancy and maternity, marriage and civil partnership, sexual orientation and gender reassignment – as well as human rights. The Commission has extensive powers to enforce equality legislation.

The Commission is a non-departmental public body (NDPB) – accountable for its public funds, but independent of government.

The Commission in Wales works to ensure that GB policy-making reflects the needs of Wales and to deliver a programme of work specific to Wales. A Wales Commissioner and Committee direct its work.

MEMBERS OF THE WALES COMMITTEE ♂2 ♀6

Ann Beynon OBE	Commissioner for Wales; Director, BT in Wales
Anne Crowley	Policy & Research Consultant
Rhian Davies	Chief Executive, Disability Wales
Karen Dusgate	Chief Executive, Merthyr Tydfil Housing Association
Rev Aled Edwards OBE	Chief Executive, Churches Together in Wales (CYTUN)
Siân Gale	Director, Pawb Ltd
Clifton Robinson	Chief Executive, Housing Diversity Network
Olwen Williams	Chief of Staff for Primary Community & Specialist Medicine, Betsi Cadwaladr UHB

PRINCIPAL OFFICERS

Kate Bennett	National Director Wales

Total no. permanent staff: 23

EQUALITY COMMISSION

FORESTRY COMMISSION WALES

Forestry Commission Wales
Welsh Government
Rhodfa Padarn, Llanbadarn Fawr
Aberystwyth, Ceredigion SY23 3UR

☎ (0300) 068 0300
Fax: (0300) 068 0301

Email: fcwenquiries@forestry.gsi.gov.uk
Website: www.forestry.gov.uk

Comisiwn Coedwigaeth Cymru
Forestry Commission Wales

Jon Owen Jones

Judith Webb

Forestry Commissioners
for Wales

Director
Forestry Commission Wales
Trefor Owen

NATIONAL COMMITTEE   ♂7 ♀1

*The **National Committee** provides strategic direction to all Forestry Commission Wales activities, including approving corporate plans and annual reports on behalf of Welsh Ministers. It sets targets and monitors the performance of Forestry Commission Wales and ensures the safeguarding of resources through internal control systems. It is also responsible for grant-aiding and regulating woodland owners.*
Chair
Jon Owen Jones - *Forestry Commissioner for Wales; was a Member of Parliament 1992-05, and a former Minister 1998-99*
Members
Judith Webb - *Forestry Commissioner for Wales;* Roger Cooper - *Chair, Woodland Strategy Advisory Panel;* John Lloyd Jones OBE - *Member, National Committee Forestry Commission Wales;* Trefor Owen - *Director, Forestry Commission Wales;* Peter Garson - *Head of Estate Management, Forestry Commission Wales;* Richard Siddons - *Head of Forest Services, Forestry Commission Wales*

WOODLAND STRATEGY ADVISORY PANEL

The Woodland Strategy Advisory Panel (WSAP) is appointed by the National Committee for Wales. Its primary function is 'To act as an Advisory Panel to both Ministers and Forestry Commissioners on the implementation of the Wales Woodland Strategy and its periodic reviews'. A sub-committee of this Panel can be formed under the Forestry Act 1967 to adjudicate on disputed applications for grant aid or for felling licences and in disputes arising from Forestry Commission Wales forest design plans.
Chair
Roger Cooper MBE - *Senior Lecturer in Forest Products, Marketing & Economics, Bangor University (Retired)*
Members
Nigel Ajax-Lewis MBE - *Senior Conservation Officer - Wildlife Trust for South & West Wales;* Dr John Edington - *Part-time tutor on environmental issues, Cardiff University Centre for Lifelong Learning;* David Edwards - *District Manager, UPM Tilhill;* Helena Fox - *Consultant, Education for Sustainable Development;* Dr Alun Gee - *Former Strategy Manager, Environment Agency Wales;* Sue Gittins - *Past Deputy Director for Wales, Ramblers' Association;* Rory Francis - *Public Affairs Officer, Coed Cadw (The Woodland Trust in Wales);* David Jenkins MBE - *Director, Coed Cymru;* Tim Kirk - *Woodland Investment Adviser, Tilhill Forestry (retired);* Bernard Llewellyn - *Chair, NFU Cymru's Welsh Rural Affairs Committee;* John Lloyd Jones OBE - *Member, National Committee Forestry Commission Wales;* Fiona McFarlane - *(Observer), Senior Rural Development Advisor, Sustainable Futures - SEED, Welsh Government;* Kath McNulty - *National Manager for Wales, ConFor;* Hilary Miller - *Senior Land Use Policy Officer, Countryside Council for Wales;* Philippe Morgan - *SME with a trading co-operative, Sustainable Forest Management & SelectFor;* Prof Colin Price - *Prof, Environmental & Forestry Economics, Bangor University;* Celia Thomas - *Woodland Officer, Pembrokeshire Coast National Park;* Bob Vaughan - *Environment Agency Wales;* Dr Jenny Wong - *Director, Wild Resources LTD*

Total no. staff: 406

* Under current plans by the Welsh Government, on the 1st April 2013, a new single body will bring together the functions of the Countryside Council for Wales, the Environment Agency Wales, and the Forestry Commission Wales.

FORESTRY COMMISSION

BOOST YOUR BOTTOM-LINE PERFORMANCE
WITH EEF

Join the hundreds of manufacturers in Wales that benefit from our unique combination of business services, intelligence and manufacturing insight. **Not to mention:**

- **policy representation that gets results**
  - at regional, national and European level
- **commercial advantages for you and your people**
  - leveraging our buying power to save you money
- **networking events to help you learn from the best**
  - spot new business opportunities and collaborate with your professional and industry peers
- **services that make a real difference**
  - from HR and employment law to health and safety, occupational health to environment; our consultancy, advice and training services are designed to improve your business performance

No other organisation can bring together such a breadth of service and combine it with a deep understanding of modern manufacturing.

www.eef.org.uk

FOOD STANDARDS AGENCY – WALES

11th Floor
Southgate House
Wood Street
Cardiff CF10 1EW

☎ (029) 2067 8999

Email: wales@foodstandards.gsi.gov.uk
Website: www.food.gov.uk

Board member for Wales
John Spence

Director Wales
Steve Wearne

Asiantaeth
Safonau
Bwyd
food.gov.uk
Food
Standards
Agency

The Food Standards Agency is an independent government department set up by an Act of Parliament in 2000 to protect the public's health and consumer interests in relation to food. The commitment is to improve food safety and standards in Wales and protect the health of the population of Wales in relation to food.

NATIONAL BOARD MEMBER

John Spence
Member for Wales

Appointed by Welsh Government
In office until 03/13
Remuneration: £25,000-£30,000

WELSH FOOD ADVISORY COMMITTEE MEMBERS ♂4 ♀4

As specified in the Food Standards Act 1999, the role of the Food Advisory Committee is to give advice or information to the Agency about matters connected with its functions including in particular matters affecting or otherwise relating to Wales.

As part of this function, the Committee offers advice to the Food Standards Agency which, in turn, advises the appropriate authorities.

The scope of the Food Advisory Committee's remit includes, in particular, but is not limited to, matters that affect or otherwise relate to the relevant part of the United Kingdom.

The Food Advisory Committee sets its own work programme, collecting information, consulting with stakeholders and conducting such other work as is needed to support it in discharging its statutory function.

Members of the Food Advisory Committee are appointed to act collectively in the public interest, and not to represent specific sectors or other interests. The membership of the Committee reflects the range of interests in food safety and standards issues in Wales.

Chair
John Spence

Members
Steve Bolchover; Louise Fielding; Kate Hovers; Hugh Jones; Sue Jones; Katie Palmer; Derek Morgan

Total no. staff: 33

NASUWT CYMRU

The Teachers' Union

Undeb yr Athrawon

- **Centres in Cardiff and St Asaph –** with professional staff to provide legal advice and representation.

- **Canolfannau yng Nghaerdydd a Llanelwy –** gyda staff proffesiynol i ddarparu cyngor cyfreithiol a chynrychiolaeth.

- **Local networks of serving teachers –** only a phone call away, providing advice and support.

- **Rhwydweithiau lleol o athrawon –** o fewn galwad ffon, yn darparu cyngor a chefnogaeth.

- **First class advice and information –** to your home, online and in your workplace.

- **Cyngor heb ei ail a gwybodaeth –** i'ch cartref, ar-lein ac yn eich gweithle.

The largest teachers' union in Wales and the UK.
Yr undeb athrawon fwyaf yng Nghymru a'r DU.

NASUWT Cymru
Greenwood Close/Clos Greenwood
Cardiff Gate Business Park/Parc Busnes Porth Caerdydd
Cardiff/Caerdydd CF23 8RD
Tel/Ffôn: 029 2054 6080
Fax/Ffacs: 029 2054 6089
E-mail/E-bost: rc-wales cymru@mail.nasuwt.org.uk

GENERAL TEACHING COUNCIL FOR WALES

9th Floor, Eastgate House
35-43 Newport Road
Cardiff CF24 0AB

☎ (029) 2046 0099
Fax: (029) 2047 5850

Email: information@gtcw.org.uk
Website: www.gtcw.org.uk

Chair
Angela Jardine

Cyngor Addysgu Cyffredinol Cymru
General Teaching Council for Wales

Chief Executive
Gary Brace

COUNCIL MEMBERS ♂ 10 ♀ 14

Chair
Angela Jardine - *Teacher, Gabalfa Primary School, Cardiff*

Deputy Chair
Elwyn Davies - *Former Headteacher, Pencoed Comprehensive School, Bridgend*

Members
Philip Bassett - *Lecturer, Dean of Teaching & Learning, Glyndŵr University, Wrexham;* Celia Blomeley - *Assistant Headteacher, Holywell High School;* Frank Bonello - *Tutor & Area Development Officer, Welsh Language Teaching Centre, Cardiff University;* Irene Cameron - *Vice Chair, Newport School Forum;* Tim Cox - *Teacher, Bryn Hafren Comprehensive School, Vale of Glamorgan;* Beth Davies - *Headteacher, Alltwen Primary School, Pontardawe;* Mal Davies - *Headteacher, Willows High School, Cardiff;* Roberto De Benedictis - *Teacher, Llangatwg Comprehensive School, Neath;* David Healey - *Deputy Headteacher, Ysgol Friars, Bangor;* Gareth Jones - *Former Headteacher, Derwen Primary School, Flintshire;* Margaret Morris - *Retired Headteacher, Rhosgoch School, Powys;* Suzanne Nantcurvis - *Teacher, Ysgol Dinas Brân, Denbighshire;* Sue O'Halloran - *Headteacher, Nottage Primary School, Porthcawl;* Hugh Pattrick - *Vice-Chair of Governors Wales;* Susan Rivers - *Deputy Headteacher, Bedwas High School, Caerphilly;* Jane Setchfield - *Teacher, Llanedeyrn High School, Cardiff;* Cleo Wilson-Sollars - *Teacher, St Therese's Primary School, Port Talbot;* Anna Spokes - *Teacher, Archbishop Rowan Williams Primary School, Caldicot;* Sarah Stockford - *Teacher, Ysgol y Foryd, Conwy;* Adrian Williams - *Retired Headteacher, Penybryn & Maytree Residential Special School, Swansea;* Jetsun Williams - *Bar Vocational Course Leader, External Relations, Cardiff University*

SENIOR STAFF

Gary Brace - *Chief Executive;* Hayden Llewellyn - *Deputy Chief Executive (Teachers' Qualifications, Registration & Professional Standards);* Julia Evans - *Deputy Chief Executive (Finance, Personnel & Corporate Services);* Karen Evans - *Policy & Planning Manager*

Total no. staff: 27

GEN TEACH COUNCIL WALES

25 years
thinking Wales forward

This year marks the IWA's first quarter of a century, an era that has seen a transformation in the political, economic and cultural fortunes of Wales. Twenty-five years ago the Welsh economy was still dominated by heavy industry coming apart in the wake of the miners' strike. Welsh politics were in thrall to a Quango-driven state. Meanwhile a little-noticed cultural revival was gathering pace.

Today that era looks altogether like sepia-veiled history. In its place Welsh democracy has been born with the creation of the National Assembly that was granted primary legislative powers in last year's referendum. While still struggling with the downturn, the Welsh economy has broken free of what 25 years ago was a third-world structure and developed a more balanced profile. Meanwhile, Welsh culture has flourished with sport, the arts and the media all gaining recognition on the world stage. Throughout these 25 years these changes have been closely followed, analysed and promoted by the activities of the Institute. In this period our size and influence has grown in response to the emergence of Wales's civic culture. We now have a staff of six, a high-powered Board of Trustees reflecting every aspect of Welsh life, over 1,000 individual members, more than 100 Fellows, and 150 corporate members. We have developed a branch network that covers the whole of Wales, produced a raft of publications including our journal *Agenda*, and launched a daily online news magazine ClickonWales.

To celebrate our 25th anniversary we will be publishing *25/25 Vision: Welsh Horizons across 50 years*, a collection of essays in which 25 writers cast their minds back over their experience of the past quarter-of-a-century in Wales and reflect on what this inspires them to hope for in the next 25 years. It will be an opportunity for us to look forward to what we can hope our country will achieve in the next few decades and plan for the continuing contribution that will be made by the Institute. It will be a moment to reflect that all our achievements and our continuing contribution depends on the vital support of our members. As a charitable trust we rely on our membership to sustain us and to guarantee our independence. Without the membership the IWA would not exist and Wales would lose part of the intelligence that is so vital in steering its course.

Join the iwaˢ today.
www.iwa.org.uk

INSTITUTE OF WELSH AFFAIRS

Second Floor, 4 Cathedral Road
Cardiff
CF11 9LJ

☎ (029) 2066 0820

Email: wales@iwa.org.uk
Website: www.iwa.org.uk

Chair
Geraint Talfan Davies

Director
John Osmond

Sefydliad Materion Cymreig
Institute of Welsh Affairs

The Institute of Welsh Affairs is an independent, membership-based think tank, dedicated to promoting the economic, social, environmental and cultural well-being of Wales. It owes no allegiance to any political or economic interest group. Its only interest is in seeing Wales flourish as a country in which to work and live. It believes that can be done only by the effective mobilisation of all Wales's intellectual resources.

DIRECTORS
♂ 14 ♀ 5

Geraint Talfan Davies	Director, Glas Cymru; Chair, Welsh National Opera
Guy Clarke	Senior Partner, Morgan Cole, Solicitors
Rhys David	Consultant
Peter Davies	Consultant & Sustainable Development Commissioner for Wales
Nigel Griffiths	Company Director
Dr Eurfyl ap Gwilym	Company Director
Gerald Holtham	Managing Partner, Cadwyn Capital
Rob Humphreys	Director, Open University in Wales
Robert Jolliffe	Investment Banker
Prof Merfyn Jones	Specialist Adviser, Welsh Assembly Government
Ruth Marks	Former Older People's Commissioner For Wales
Megan Mathias	Director and co-founder of Kafka Brigade UK
Prof Laura McAllister	Chair, Sport Wales
Chris O'Malley	Pro Vice-Chancellor, University of Wales, Newport
Wendy Sadler	Director, Science Made Simple Ltd
Prof John Tucker	Chair, Swansea Bay Branch
Paul Valerio	Consultant, Leisure Industry
Sir Adrian Webb	Education Consultant
Dr Ruth Williams	Welsh Affairs Manager, The National Trust Wales; Director, Sustainable Development Forum Wales

PRINCIPAL OFFICERS

John Osmond - Director; *Kirsty Davies* - Deputy Director & Company Secretary; *Emma Brennan* - Events Manager; *Dr Helen Sims-Coomber* - Finance & I.T. Officer; *Dr Stevie Upton* - Research Officer

INSTITUTE OF WELSH AFFAIRS

CRONFA LOTERI FAWR
BIG LOTTERY FUND

Wales Offices:
10th Floor, Helmont House
Churchill Way, Cardiff CF10 2NB
2nd Flr, Ladywell House,
Newtown, Powys SY16 1JB

☎ (029) 2067 8200/
(01686) 611700
Fax: (029) 2066 7275/
(01686) 622458

Email: enquiries.wales@biglotteryfund.org.uk
Website: www.biglotteryfund.org.uk

Chair
Sir Adrian Webb

Director
John Rose

The Big Lottery Fund is the largest of the Lottery distributors responsible for awarding money raised for good causes by the National Lottery. It has grant programmes available for the community, voluntary, public and private sector. Following legislation the Fund can now also distribute non-lottery money.

The Big Lottery Fund is committed to bringing real improvements to communities, and to the lives of people most in need.

More information on the work of the Fund can be found on the website or by calling the office.

WALES COMMITTEE ♂ 4 ♀ 3

Chair
Sir Adrian Webb

Background
Previously Vice-Chancellor, Glamorgan University; experience of leading at executive management level in public, not for profit and education sectors; involved in many UK and Welsh Government initiatives, including chairing the independent review into further education in Wales (the Webb Review) and Wales Employment & Skills Board; member of the Beecham Review of Public Services in Wales; part of HM Treasury Public Service Productivity Panel

Members
Graham Benfield OBE	Chief Executive, Wales Council Voluntary Action
Gareth Newton	Former Director of Lifelong Learning, Rhondda Cynon Taf
Janet Reed OBE	Retired National Manager Wales, British Gas
Fran Targett	Director, Citizens Advice Cymru
Mike Theodoulou	Founder Chair & current Director, Chamber Wales
Barbara Wilding CBE, QPM	Retired Chief Constable, South Wales Police

PRINCIPAL OFFICERS

John Rose	Director
Mike Walsh	Senior Head of Corporate Management
Lara Ramsay	Head of Funding
Adele Davies	Head of Corporate Management
Fflur Lawton	Head of Communications

Total no. staff: 54

HERITAGE LOTTERY FUND COMMITTEE FOR WALES

☎ (029) 2034 3413
Fax: (029) 2034 3427

Email: wales@hlf.org.uk
Website: www.hlf.org.uk

Chair
Dr Manon Williams

cronfa
dreftadaeth y loteri
heritage lottery fund

Head of HLF, Wales
Jennifer Stewart

Valuing our heritage - Investing in our future

Using money raised through the National Lottery, the Heritage Lottery Fund sustains and transforms our heritage. From museums, parks and historic places to archaeology, natural environment and cultural traditions we invest in every part of our diverse heritage.

Since 1994, Heritage Lottery Fund has invested over £224 million in Wales. During 2012, a new strategic framework will be launched which will inform grant giving from April 2013 onwards. Further details available on the Heritage Lottery Fund website www.hlf.org.uk

COMMITTEE FOR WALES   ♂2 ♀5

Background

Chair
Dr Manon Williams   Public Affairs & Management Consultant
Members
Madeleine Havard   Environmental scientist
Natasha Hirst   Photographer & Equality Consultant
Carys Howell   Marketing & Communications Consultant
Ted Sangster   Retired Chief Executive, Milford Haven Port Authority
Dei Tomos   Broadcaster
Rhian Thomas   Freshwater Ecologist, Countryside Council for Wales

PRINCIPAL OFFICERS

Jennifer Stewart   Head of HLF, Wales
Martin Buckridge   Casework Manager
Liz Girling   Development Manager
Robert Vokes   Senior Grants Officer

Total no. staff: 14

THE NATIONAL BOTANIC GARDEN OF WALES

Llanarthne
Carmarthenshire
SA32 8HG

☎ (01558) 668768
Fax: (01558) 668933

Email: info@gardenofwales.org.uk
Website: www.gardenofwales.org.uk

National Botanic
Garden of Wales
Gardd Fotaneg
Genedlaethol Cymru

Chair
Robert Jolliffe

Director
Dr Rosetta Plummer

The National Botanic Garden of Wales is a limited company and a registered charity. It is the first national botanic garden of the new millennium worldwide, and opened to the public in 2000. It is now a recognised national icon and has established itself as a major centre for tourism, environmental education and plant conservation.

LLYFRGELL GENEDLAETHOL CYMRU
THE NATIONAL LIBRARY OF WALES

Aberystwyth SY23 3BU
☎ (01970) 632800
Fax: (01970) 615709
Website: www.llgc.org.uk

President
Sir Deian Hopkin

Librarian
Andrew Green

The National Library of Wales was established in 1907 and celebrated its centenary year in 2007. It was granted a supplemental Royal Charter in 2006. It is a Registered Charity, Number 525775. It is the nation's largest library and is a legal deposit library. It houses a vast collection of books, manuscripts, maps, photographs, and archive audio/visual material. It has a programme of art and photographic exhibitions and often hosts travelling exhibitions. Admission is free. The National Library received Grant in Aid from the National Assembly for Wales of £11.7m in 2011/2012.

BOARD MEMBERS   ♂ 11 ♀ 3

President	In office until	Background
Sir Deian Hopkin	11/15	Former Vice-Chancellor & Chief Executive, London South Bank University; Emeritus Professor, London South Bank University & University of East London
Vice President		
Aled Gruffydd Jones	04/16	Senior Pro Vice-Chancellor, Aberystwyth University
Treasurer		
Colin John	07/13	Senior Partner, Llewelyn Davies Chartered Accountants
Members		
David Barker	12/14	Library Services Manager
Tricia Carter	12/14	Commercial Business
Roy Evans CBE	11/12	Former Vice-Chancellor, Bangor University
John Gittins	09/15	Executive Director (retired), Cheshire Landscape Trust
Wyn Penri Jones	02/14	Chartered Banker
Elspeth Mitcheson	12/14	Former Director of Leisure & Heritage
Enid Morgan	09/15	Retired Parish Priest
Roy Roberts	11/12	Former Deputy Manager, regional broadcasting, BBC
Michael Trickey	12/15	Wales adviser, Joseph Rowntree Foundation
Gareth Haulfryn Williams	11/15	Heritage & archives consultant
Huw Williams	03/14	Vice-Chair, Geldards LLP

PRINCIPAL OFFICERS

Andrew Green - *Librarian;* Avril Jones - *Director of Collection Services;* David Michael - *Director of Corporate Services;* R Arwel Jones - *Director of Public Services;* Pedr ap Llwyd - *Head of Administration, Clerk to the Board & Advisory Body*

Total no. staff: 315

OLDER PEOPLE'S COMMISSIONER FOR WALES

Cambrian Buildings,
Mount Stuart Square,
Cardiff CF10 5FL
☎ (08442) 640670
Fax: (08442) 640680

Email: ask@olderpeoplewales.com
Website: www.olderpeoplewales.com
Twitter: @talkolderpeople

Older People's
Commissioner for Wales
Sarah Rochira

Deputy
Commissioner
Sarah Stone

Older People's Commissioner for Wales
Comisiynydd Pobl Hŷn Cymru

The Office of the Commissioner for Older People in Wales was established under Section 1 of the Commissioner for Older People (Wales) Act 2006 and came into existence with the appointment of the first Commissioner on 21 April 2008.

The role of the Older People's Commissioner for Wales is to be an independent champion for older people across Wales, to make sure that all older people have a voice that is heard, that they have choice and control, that they don't feel isolated or discriminated against and that Wales is a good place to grow older.

The Older People's Commission:

* *Promotes awareness of the rights and interests of older people in Wales*
* *Challenges discrimination against older people in Wales.*
* *Encourages best practice in the treatment of older people in Wales*
* *Reviews the law affecting the interests of older people in Wales.*
* *Holds to account those that fail to deliver for older people in Wales.*

OLDER PEOPLE'S COMMISSIONER

PRIME CYMRU

Mile End, 9 Broad Street,
Llandovery, Carmarthenshire
SA20 0AR

☎ (0800) 587 4085
☎ (01550) 721813
Fax: (01550) 721291

Email: enquiries@prime-cymru.co.uk
Website: www.prime-cymru.co.uk

Chair
Stephen Pegge

Chief Executive
David Pugh

President: HRH The Prince of Wales

Founded by HRH The Prince of Wales in 2001, PRIME Cymru is a registered charity dedicated to providing practical support to people aged 50 and over who want to become and remain economically active. Through our staff, trained mentors and associates we provide clients throughout Wales with tailored one to one support whether they wish to start their own business, return to the workforce or volunteer to develop skills and confidence. To date we have engaged with over 20,000 individuals in Wales who are economically inactive and seeking dedicated tailored support and advice. This has enabled us to help over 1,600 individuals to start their own business, helped create in excess of 2,700 jobs and supported nearly 1,500 individuals to take-up volunteering opportunities which have enabled them to develop skills and confidence to move closer to the labour market.

TRUSTEES   ♂5 ♀2

Chair
Stephen Pegge   Director of SMEs, Lloyds Banking Group; Chairman Small Firms, British Bankers' Association

Deputy Chair
Catherine Eva   Former European Commission Representative in Wales
Members
Hugh Child   Retired Accountant/Managing Director
Peter Davies OBE   Sustainable Futures Commissioner for Wales; Chair, Climate change Commission for Wales; Coordinator, Prince's Charities in Wales
Huw Evans   Private Banker, Coutts & Co
Elinor Jones   TV Broadcaster & Presenter
Dylan Jones-Evans   Professor & Director, Enterprise & Innovation, University of Wales; Director, Wales Fast Growth 50

PRINCIPAL OFFICERS

David Pugh   Chief Executive
Oenwen Jones   Finance Officer
Sharon Richards   HR & Administration Manager
Hayley Ridge-Evans   Director of Operations

BRECON BEACONS NATIONAL PARK AUTHORITY

Chair
Julie James

Plas y Ffynnon
Cambrian Way, Brecon
Powys LD3 7HP
☎ (01874) 624437
Fax: (01874) 622574
Email: enquiries@breconbeacons.org
Website: www.breconbeacons.org

BRECON BEACONS
NATIONAL PARK

Chief Executive
John Cook

Designated in 1957, the Brecon Beacons National Park has a total area of 519 sq miles (1,344 sq kilometres). The approved spend for BBNPA for 2009/10 was £6,717,360 of which 75% was directly funded by the Welsh Government and the other 25% was levied from 7 of the 9 constituent local authorities found within the Park's boundaries.

AUTHORITY MEMBERS   ♂ 18 ♀ 6

	In office until	Background
Chair (Remuneration - £8,875pa inclusive of Basic Salary plus mileage allowance)		
Julie James*	3/13	Former Director of Personnel Aviation Industry
Deputy Chair (Remuneration - £5,920 pa inclusive of Basic Salary plus mileage allowance)		
Cllr Geraint Hopkins	5/17	Former portfolio holder for Environment, Highways & Transport; Powys County Council
Members (Remuneration - £3,550pa plus mileage allowance)		
Cllr E T Morgan	5/17	Magistrate, farms in Sennybridge
Cllr M J Jones	5/17	Farmer, Churchstoke
Cllr P Ashton	5/17	Former Building Services Engineer, Mayor of Brecon
Martin Buckle*	3/13	Planning, Transport & Regeneration consultant; Member, RTPI; Institutes Wales Executive; Urban Design Group
Cllr C Davies	5/17	Manager, Hay Veterinary Practice
Melanie Doel*	3/14	Former BBC Presenter & Journalist
Cllr J Holmes	5/17	Former career in Fire Service
Carys Howell*	5/14	Comms & Marketing Consultant; Member, HLFC Wales
Prof Alan Lovell*	3/14	Member, RSPB; Member, Brecknock Wildlife Trust
Edward John Evans*	12/16	Director, Exemplar & Demonstration Programmes, Construction Excellence Wales
Cllr D Meredith	5/17	Former Education Officer, retail experience
Cllr P Pritchard	5/17	Business & Sports management, currently Chair, FAW
Cllr M Hickman	5/17	Former financier
Ian Rowat*	12/16	Executive Director, Malvern Hill Conservators, Worcestershire
Cllr Mrs A Webb	5/17	Family farm near Trellech
Cllr A James	5/17	Former CEO of Welsh Black Cattle Society, Tourism Operator
Cllr G Davies	5/17	TV Producer
Cllr R Thomas	5/17	Retired plumbing supervisor, former Leader, Merthyr Tydfil CBC
Cllr A Furzer	5/17	Lecturer in Maths & Science
Cllr B Pagett	5/17	Former town councillor
Margaret Underwood*	3/14	Third Sector Development & Training Consultancy
Cllr Mrs J Ward	5/17	Former Mayor of RCT, career in the voluntary sector

* denotes appointments by the Welsh Government

PRINCIPAL OFFICERS

John Cook - *Chief Executive;* Chris Morgan - *Director of Planning;* Julian Atkins - *Director of Countryside & Land Management*

Total no. staff: 130

PEMBROKESHIRE COAST NATIONAL PARK AUTHORITY

Llanion Park, Pembroke Dock
Pembrokeshire SA72 6DY
☎ (0845) 345 7275
Fax: (01646) 689076

Email: info@pembrokeshirecoast.org.uk
Website: www.pembrokeshirecoast.org.uk

Chair
Cllr J A (Tony) Brinsden

Chief Executive
Tegryn Jones

Established in 1952, the purposes of the National Park under the Environment Act of 1995 are to conserve the natural and built environment of the Park and its cultural heritage and to promote enjoyment and understanding. It works through these purposes to foster the social and economic well-being of the local community. From a net total of £4,737,872, 75% of the Authority's net expenditure is directly funded by the Welsh Government. The other 25% comes from Pembrokeshire County Council in the form of a levy.

AUTHORITY MEMBERS ♂ 13 ♀ 5

	In office until	Background
Chair (Remuneration - Senior Salary of £8,875 pa as Chair inclusive of Basic Salary)		
Cllr J A (Tony) Brinsden	5/17	Appointed by Pembrokeshire County Council
Vice-Chair (Remuneration - Senior Salary of £5,920 pa as Deputy Chair inclusive of Basic Salary)		
Cllr Mike James	5/17	Appointed by Pembrokeshire County Council
Members (Remuneration - Basic Salary of £3,550 pa)		
Cllr Paul Harries	5/17	Appointed by Pembrokeshire County Council
Cllr Lyn Jenkins	5/17	Appointed by Pembrokeshire County Council
Cllr Bob Kilmister	5/17	Appointed by Pembrokeshire County Council
Cllr Alison Lee	5/17	Appointed by Pembrokeshire County Council
Gwyneth Hayward^	1/14	Appointed by Welsh Government
Allan G Archer	11/15	Appointed by Welsh Government
Cllr Reg Owen	5/17	Appointed by Pembrokeshire County Council
David Ellis	1/14	Appointed by Welsh Government
Melinda Thomas	11/15	Appointed by Welsh Government
Cllr Rob M Lewis	5/17	Appointed by Pembrokeshire County Council
Cllr Peter J Morgan	5/17	Appointed by Pembrokeshire County Council
Cllr Michael Williams	5/17	Appointed by Pembrokeshire County Council
Cllr David WM Rees	5/17	Appointed by Pembrokeshire County Council
Cllr AW (Tony) Wilcox	5/17	Appointed by Pembrokeshire County Council
Ted Sangster	3/14	Appointed by Welsh Government
Christine Gwyther	1/16	Appointed by Welsh Government

^ denotes Chair of Development Management Committee, which receives a Senior Salary of £5,920 pa (inclusive of Basic Salary)
Authority Members can only receive one Special Salary

PRINCIPAL OFFICERS

Tegryn Jones - *Chief Executive (National Park Officer)*; Jane Gibson - *Director of Park Direction & Planning*; James Parkin - *Director of Park Delivery & Discovery*

Total no. staff: 132 (plus seasonal & casual workers)

SNOWDONIA NATIONAL PARK AUTHORITY

Penrhyndeudraeth
Gwynedd LL48 6LF

☎ (01766) 770274
Fax: (01766) 771211

Email:
[first name].[surname]@eryri-npa.gov.uk
Website: www.eryri-npa.gov.uk

Chair
Cllr E C Roberts OBE JP

Chief Executive
Aneurin Phillips

Established in 1951, Snowdonia National Park covers an area of 2141 square kilometers from the mountains to the sea. Its statutory purposes are (i) to conserve and enhance the natural beauty, wildlife and cultural heritage of the area (ii) promote opportunities for the understanding and enjoyment of the special qualities of the area by the public. It has a duty to seek to foster the economic and social well-being of local communities. From a net budget of £6,004,204, 75% is funded by WAG grant and 25% is funded by levies on constituent authorities. In addition the Welsh Government has allocated a capital grant of £116,666 for 2012/13.

AUTHORITY MEMBERS ♂ 14 ♀ 4

	In office until	Background
Chair (Remuneration - £5,326 pa plus basic allowance)		
Cllr E Caerwyn Roberts OBE JP	5/16	Farmer; Member, Gwynedd Council
Vice-Chair (Remuneration - £2,370 pa plus basic allowance)		
Dr Iolo ap Gwynn*	3/13	Part Time Lecturer, Aberystwyth University
Members (Remuneration - Basic allowance of £3,550 pa from 13 June)		
Cllr Elwyn Edwards	5/16	Businessman; Member, Gwynedd Council
Cllr Thomas Griffith Ellis	5/16	Farmer; Member, Gwynedd Council
Cllr Alwyn Gruffydd	5/16	Public Relations Consultant; Member, Gwynedd Council
Cllr Aeron Maldwyn Jones	5/16	Member, Gwynedd Council
Cllr Sion Wyn Jones	5/16	Housing Agent & builder; Member, Gwynedd Council
M June Jones*	2/14	Regional Food Development Officer
Marian W Jones*	6/14	Media Consultant
Cllr I Dilwyn Lloyd	5/16	Retired Healthcare worker; Member, Gwynedd Council
Denis P McAteer*	3/13	Management Consultant
John Lewis Morgan*	2/14	NW Area Manager, National Trust
David Leonard Roberts*	5/16	Organic Farmer
Cllr Elizabeth Roberts	5/16	Retired Health visitor; Member, Conwy CBC
Cllr Paul Gareth Roberts	5/16	Self employed Entrepreneur; Member, Conwy CBC
Cllr Dyfrig Siencyn	5/16	Surveyor & Valuer; Member, Gwynedd Council
Cllr Joan Vaughan	5/16	Retired Education professional
Cllr Eurig Wyn	5/16	Retired MEP; Member, Gwynedd Council

* denotes appointment by the Welsh Government

PRINCIPAL OFFICERS

Aneurin Phillips - *Chief Executive;* Dafydd Edwards - *Chief Finance Officer;* Iwan Jones - *Director of Corporate Services;* Emyr Williams - *Director of Land Management;* Aled Sturkey - *Director of Planning & Cultural Heritage*

Total no. staff: 146

NATIONAL PARK
SNOWDONIA

PRINCE'S TRUST CYMRU

Head Office:
Prince's Trust Cymru
Head Office, Baltic House
Mount Stuart Square
Cardiff CF10 5FH

☎ (029) 2043 7000
Fax: (029) 2043 7001

Email: webinfo@princes-trust.org.uk
Website: www.princes-trust.org.uk

Chair
Steve Thomas

Director
Rick Libbey

Prince's Trust
Cymru

The Prince of Wales established The Prince's Trust in 1976 to help young people overcome barriers and get their lives working through training, mentoring and financial assistance. It targets 13-30 year olds who may have struggled at school, been in care, been in trouble with the law, or are long-term unemployed. During 2011, the Prince's Trust Cymru assisted more than 3,000 of the hardest to reach young people throughout Wales, particularly in areas where our help is most needed. Our programmes provide young people in Wales with the necessary stepping stones to success.

President: HRH The Prince of Wales

COUNCIL MEMBERS   ♂4 ♀3

Chair
Steve Thomas

Background
Chief Executive, Welsh Local Government Association

Members
Chris Jones
Victoria Provis
David Rosser
Nonna Woodward
Peter Vaughan
Alison Ward

Finance Director, Dŵr Cymru
Partner, Odgers Ray & Berndtson
Director, CBI Wales
Vice-Chair, North Wales Newspapers
Chief Constable South Wales Police
Chief Executive, Torfaen CBC

PRINCIPAL OFFICERS

Rick Libbey - *Director*

NATIONAL TRUST
YMDDIRIEDOLAETH GENEDLAETHOL

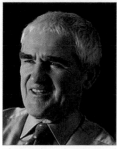

The National Trust
Office for Wales, Trinity Square,
Llandudno LL30 2DE
☎ (01492) 860123
Fax: (01492) 860233

Email:
wa.customerenquiries@nationaltrust.org.uk
Website:
www.nationaltrust.org.uk/wales

Chair Wales Advisory Board
Keith James OBE

**Ymddiriedolaeth Genedlaethol
National Trust**

Director for Wales
Justin Albert

The National Trust looks after one fifth of the Welsh coast, 45,000 hectares of land and ten of the fourteen peaks over 3000 ft. It is the guardian of 18 of Wales's finest castles, houses, gardens and industrial sites.

A charity supported by over 100,000 members in Wales and 4 million in the UK, it is not dependent on Government funding. It is the largest tourism business in Wales welcoming nearly 1 million visitors to its pay-for-entry properties and at least 4 million people enjoy free access to the coast and countryside cared for by the Trust. It runs the biggest holiday cottage business in Europe. The National Trust is committed to lifelong learning and every year 50,000 children, young people and community groups enjoy visits to National Trust properties making it the biggest non-government provider of educational visits in Wales. It is the largest social enterprise in Wales and over 5,000 volunteers donate almost 200,000 volunteer hours to the charity. The National Trust is a major landowner working hard to show leadership in the countryside by innovative demonstration farming, the development of micro-renewables and sustainable agriculture. The charity promotes the understanding of the natural and cultural heritage of Wales.

President: HRH The Prince of Wales

WALES ADVISORY BOARD MEMBERS   ♂7 ♀2

Chair

Keith James OBE	Former Chair, Eversheds LLP & Former Chair, Institute of Welsh Affairs

Members

Mark Baker	Author & Academic, expert on the Welsh County House
Derek Barker	Former Chief Executive, Conwy County Borough Council
Prof Hazel Walford Davies	Visiting Professor, the University of Glamorgan
Geraint Edwards	Former Managing Director, Isle of Anglesey County Council
Bettina Harden MBE	Gardens expert
Jane Bridget Haworth	Music co-ordinator
Prof Gareth Wyn Jones	Professor, Bangor University
D Gwyn Griffiths OBE	Civil Egineer & expert in regeneration & land reclamation

SENIOR OFFICERS *(as at Sept 2012)*

Justin Albert - *Director for Wales;* Adam Ellis-Jones & Vanessa Griffiths - *Assistant Directors, Operations;* Emma Plunkett-Dillon - *Head of Conservation;* Jane Richardson - *Head of Marketing & Supporter Development*

Ombudsman
Peter Tyndall

1 Ffordd yr Hen Gae,
Pencoed, Bridgend CF35 5LJ

☎ (01656) 641150
Fax: (01656) 641199

Email:
ask@ombudsman-wales.org.uk

Website:
www.ombudsman-wales.org.uk

Twitter:
@OmbudsmanWales

Director of Investigations
& Legal Adviser
Elizabeth Thomas

Ombudsman
Ombwdsmon
PUBLIC SERVICES OMBUDSMAN FOR WALES
OMBWDSMON GWASANAETHAU CYHOEDDUS CYMRU

The office of Public Services Ombudsman for Wales was established by the Public Services Ombudsman (Wales) Act 2005, which came into force on 1 April 2006.

The Ombudsman's role is to look into complaints about public services in Wales. He is independent and impartial, and his service is free of charge. He expects public bodies to treat people fairly, considerately and efficiently.

The bodies he can look into include local government (county/county borough councils and community councils); National Health Service organizations, including GPs; housing associations; the Welsh Government and many of the public bodies which it funds.

The Ombudsman also investigates complaints that local authority councillors (including community councillors) have broken their authority's code of conduct.

The Ombudsman's vision is to contribute to the development of excellent public services in Wales by ensuring that service providers continue to value and learn from complaints.

The Ombudsman's service seeks to:

1. put things right - aiming to put people back in the position they would have been in if they had not suffered an injustice, and working to secure the best possible outcome where injustice has occurred

2. recognise and share good practice

3. work with public bodies so that lessons from investigations are learnt

4. ensure continued improvement in the standards of public services in Wales by helping bodies to get it right first time and work to reduce complaints by helping service providers to improve their initial decision making.

PUBLIC SERVICE MANAGEMENT WALES (PSMW) / ACADEMI WALES

Welsh Government
Second Floor, Cathays Park
Cardiff CF10 3NQ

☎ (029) 2082 6687

Email: psmw@wales.gsi.gov.uk
Website: www.wales.gov.uk/psmw

Director
Dr Neil Wooding

Llywodraeth Cymru
Welsh Government

Head of PSMW
Jo Carruthers

Public Service Management Wales
Rheoli yng Ngwasanaeth Cyhoeddus Cymru

Public Service Management Wales (PSMW) was set up by the Welsh Government to develop the potential of those who work for the Welsh public service using world class and leading edge learning and development interventions designed to improve the skills, knowledge and understanding of managers and leaders. PSMW will this year be developing a new strategic centre for leadership excellence, to be known as 'Academi Wales'. The Academi will build on the foundation of PSMW's stakeholder relationships and will be launched in September 2012. The current offerings from PSMW/Academi include:

- Summer School – an annual intensive five day residential learning experience addressing key leadership issues.
- Welsh Government Programme of Learning – a comprehensive range of programmes and interventions designed and developed specifically to equip managers with the skills to deliver the best public services for the people of Wales.
- Talent Management & Succession – developing a pan-Wales talent strategy and supporting conference.
- International Learning Opportunities – eight week placements to work on strategic development projects in sub-Saharan Africa.
- Insight Seminars & Tours – exploring the practicalities of different approaches across the public and private sectors through formal presentations and informal conversations.
- Coaching & Mentoring – support for public service coaches through the Programme of Learning and Welsh Government coaches through WG's Talent Management and Succession strategy, and annual conference, and support for senior officials through the Chief Executive Coaching Programme.
- New Academi Wales products including, 'Arwain Cymru' the first pan-sector public service senior leaders programme; support for newly Elected Members and a new Bursary programme.
- Learning Hub via the Academi website, incorporating research and development, online tools and e-based learning.

KEY PARTNERS

Local Authorities & Health Boards pan-Wales, National Leadership & Innovation Agency for Healthcare (NLIAH), Wales Audit Office (WAO), Welsh Local Government Association (WLGA), Welsh Council for Voluntary Action (WCVA), Cardiff University, Newport University, University of Glamorgan, Bangor Business School, South & North Wales Police

MANAGEMENT TEAM

Dr Neil Wooding - *Director;* Jo Carruthers - *Head of PSMW/Academi Wales;* Zoe Sweet - *Organizational Development;* Christine Jones - *Talent Management & Succession;* Tony Mizen - *LEAN Operations;* Mark Hodder - *Learning Design & Delivery;* Paula James & Jayne Beeslee - *Strategy;* Ian Williams - *Special Projects;* Andrew Pryse - *Business Support*

SPORT WALES

Sophia Gardens
Cardiff
CF11 9SW

☎ (0845) 045 0904
Fax: (0845) 846 0014

Email: info@sportwales.org.uk
Website: www.sportwales.org.uk

Chair
Prof Laura McAllister

sport wales
chwaraeon cymru

Chief Executive
Dr Huw G Jones

The Sports Council for Wales was established in 1972 and is the main advisory body to the Welsh Assembly Government on sporting matters. Responsible for the development and promotion of sport and physical recreation, the Council also distributes funds from the National Lottery to sport in Wales. Council members are appointed by the Welsh Assembly Government. Sport Wales became the trading name for the Sports Council for Wales on April 1st 2010.

COUNCIL MEMBERS ♂8 ♀1

	In office until	Background
Chair		
Prof Laura McAllister	03/13	Prof of Governance, University of Liverpool
Members		
Prof John Baylis	03/14	Retired Prof of Politics & International Relations
Richard Cuthbertson	03/14	Businessman & Treasurer, Black Environment Network
Andrew Morgan	03/14	Dental Surgeon & Chair, Golf Development Wales
Simon Pirotte	03/14	Principal & Chief Executive, Coleg Powys
David Ll Roberts	03/14	Solicitor & former athlete
Paul Thorburn	03/14	Businessman & former Wales rugby international
Martin Warren	03/14	Chartered Accountant & Director of Finance UWIC
Alan Watkin	03/14	Retired Chief Libraries, Leisure & Culture Officer
Vacancies x4		

PRINCIPAL OFFICERS

Dr Huw G Jones - *Chief Executive;* Chris James - *Corporate Director;* Mark Frost - *Corporate Director;* Sarah Powell - *Corporate Director;* Sian Thomas - *Corporate Director*

Total no. staff: 161

SUSTRANS CYMRU

123 Bute Street,
Cardiff Bay CF10 5AE

☎ (029) 2065 0602

Email:
sustranscymru@sustrans.org.uk
Website:
www.sustrans.org.uk/wales

Chair
Lawrence Conway

Director
Lee Waters

Sustrans Cymru is part of the UK's leading sustainable transport charity. Our vision is a world in which people choose to travel in ways that benefit their health and the environment. Our mission is to work everyday on practical and imaginative solutions to enable people to walk, cycle and use public transport more.

ADVISORY BOARD ♂9 ♀3

Background

Chair
Lawrence Conway — Former Director, First Minister's Office, Welsh Government
Members
John Fox — Head of Built Environment, Capita Symonds
Alan Kreppel — Chair, Traveline Cymru
Brett Kibble — Sustrans Volunteer Ranger and former Arriva Executive
Delyth Lloyd — Public Affairs Manager, British Heart Foundation Cymru
Dr Wyn Morgan — Retired GP; Director, Menter Môn
Anna Nicholl — Independent Policy & Research Consultant
John Palmer — Sustrans Volunteer Ranger
Gareth Price — Clerk, National Assembly for Wales
Elizabeth Randall — Communities First Development Officer, Cwmafan
Colin Stevens — Publisher EU Reporter
Dr Dafydd Trystan — Development Manager, Centre for Welsh Medium Higher Education

PRINCIPAL STAFF

Lee Waters — National Director
Jane Lorimer — Deputy Director (Smarter Choices)
Ryland Jones — Deputy Director (National Cycle Network)

President
Rt Hon Carwyn Jones AM

Chair
Robert Ll John

President
Rt Hon Cheryl Gillan MP

Wales in London
15 Richmond Crescent
London N1 0LZ

Email: Robert.john@rllj.com
Website: www.walesinlondon.com

Wales in London is a forum to enable those based outside of Wales to contribute to the national discussion on social, economic, sporting, creative and business issues. Most of our wide range of activities take place in London though both as an organization and as members of Wales in London we continue to build linkages with organizations and politicians in Wales. Although the bedrock of our activities focus around politics, business and sport we reflect our cultural heritage by organising events to respond to and celebrate that aspect of our national life. With over 1800 members and an "active" (and well visited) webpage we are increasingly acting as a conduit for news of Wales and from Wales to a wider readership.

We hope through our activities to provoke debate, stimulate thinking or even involvement with Wales and its businesses. There are opportunities at our events to get together to relax, compare notes and share confidences with other members. There is no fee for membership - visit our webpage www.walesinlondon.com to join.

Presidents

Rt Hon Cheryl Gillan MP
Rt Hon Carwyn Jones AM

Secretary of State for Wales
First Minister, Welsh Government

Vice Presidents

Rt Hon Lord Crickhowell
Rt Hon Lord Morris of Aberavon KG, QC
Rt Hon Lord Elis-Thomas
Rt Hon Lord Roberts of Conwy

H Hugh Thomas
David Waterstone CBE
Rt Hon Lord Hunt of Wirral MBE

BOARD OF DIRECTORS

Chair: Robert Ll John - *Directorships include: Wales Millennium Centre; London Legacy Development Corporation*

Madoc Batcup - *Independent Financial Consultant;* Carol Bell - *Non-Executive Board Member, Consultant to the Oil & Gas, Financial Services & Media Industries & Archaeologist;* Jonathan Haydn Williams - *Goodman Derrick;* Gaenor Howells - *BBC World Services;* Dan Langford - *Group Marketing & Communications Director, Acorn Group;* Rhian Medi Roberts - *Working for Plaid Cymru in London;* Stephen Owen - *Director, Property;* John Parker - *Director, Zeno Agency;* Nicola Richards - *Partner, Macfarlanes;* Tim Sadler - *Sadler Associates;* Seth Thomas - *Oxford University;* W (Bill) Tudor John - *Senior Adviser to Nomura International Plc;* Peter L Walker - *Chair, Pielle Consulting Group;* Brian Williams - *Partner, SRLV Accountants*

WALES MILLENNIUM CENTRE

Wales Millennium Centre
Bute Place, Cardiff CF10 5AL
☎ (029) 2063 6400
Fax: (029) 2063 6401
Box Office: (029) 2063 6464

Email: info@wmc.org.uk
Website: www.wmc.org.uk

 CANOLFAN
MILENIWM
CYMRU
WALES
MILLENNIUM
CENTRE

Chair
Sir Emyr Jones Parry

General Manager
Mathew Milsom

The award-winning Wales Millennium Centre is a vibrant, stunning and internationally recognised arts and culture venue. Since opening in 2004 the Centre has attracted over 10 million visitors, making it Wales' No.1 visitor attraction. Wales Millennium Centre provides a world-class stage for a broad range of performances from major hit musicals to ballet, opera to contemporary dance. The Centre's cultural ambition from the outset has been to bring the best of the world to Wales and to present the best of Wales to the world. Having staged many UK and European premières and hosted the Mariinsky Theatre's opera and ballet companies, Cape Town Opera, and several international dance companies of world renown, the Centre has now earned an international reputation for its artistic programming as well as its architecture. The Centre has signed strategic partnership agreements with The Mariinsky Theatre, Cape Town Opera and Galeri in Caernarfon.

There are regular free foyer performances, tours, exhibitions, business and private function facilities, a choice of bars, restaurants and spectacular views of Cardiff's bay area. It is also home to some of Wales leading cultural organizations including WNO, BBC National Orchestra of Wales, National Dance Company Wales, Touch Trust, Tŷ Cerdd, Urdd, Hijinx and Literature Wales.

BOARD MEMBERS ♂9 ♀3

Chair
Sir Emyr Jones Parry

Background
President, Aberystwyth University; Former Chair, All Wales Convention; Permanent UK Representative, UN (2003-07); Permanent UK Representative to NATO (2001-03);

Life President
Lord Rowe-Beddoe DL

President & Former Chair, Royal Welsh College of Music & Drama (1993-04); Former President, Llangollen International Music Eisteddfod (2001-05); President, Cardiff Business Club; Former Chair, WDA (1993-01); Pro Chancellor, University of Glamorgan; Chair of the Representative Body of the Church in Wales; Deputy Chair, Statistics Board

Members
Raj Aggarwal OBE — MD Aggarwal Group & Community Pharmacist
Hugh Child — Leading Businessman; Former Finance Director, The Peacock Group
Janet Davies — Founder, Prysg Translation Services
Henry Engelhardt CBE — CEO Admiral Insurance
Luke Fletcher — Solicitor, Bates Wells & Braithwate London LLP
David Jackson — Former Head of Music BBC Wales
Dyfrig John CBE — Chair, Principality Building Society; Former Chief Exec & Deputy Chair, HSBC Bank plc
Robert John — Chair, Wales in London; Director of several private sector companies
Eirlys Pritchard Jones — Former Chair, Menter a Busnes & former Headteacher
Dr Steven Luke — Director, Ove Arup & Partners Ltd, Cardiff Office
Anna Southall — Vice Chair UK Board Big Lottery Fund; Former Director National Museum of Wales

Company Secretary
Huw Williams

Partner, Geldard LLP; Trustee, Amgueddfa Cymru - National Museum Wales

PRINCIPAL OFFICERS

Mathew Milsom - *General Manager & Finance Director;* Conrad Lynch - *Artistic Director;* David Pearce - *Director Commercial & Visitor Services;* Jonathon Poyner - *Venue Operations Director;* Marie Wood - *Development Director;* Jonathan Harper - *Director Marketing & Communications*

Total no. staff: 210 FTE

WALES MILLENNIUM CENTRE

THE FOOTBALL ASSOCIATION OF WALES

The Football Association of
Wales Ltd, 11/12 Neptune Court,
Vanguard Way, Cardiff CF24 5PJ
☎ (029) 2043 5830
Fax: (029) 2049 6953

Email: info@faw.co.uk
Website: www.faw.org.uk

President
Philip C Pritchard

Chief Executive
Jonathan Ford

The Football Association of Wales is the third oldest association in the world, having been founded in 1876. The Association has governed football in Wales continuously since that date. The FAW is a member of FIFA and UEFA and is one of the five associations that make up the International Football Association Board, guardians of the "Laws of the Game".

The FAW also has responsibility for running the eight international teams of Wales: the A team, U21s, U19s, U17s, Semi-Professional, the Women's team, Women's U19s and Women's U17s. The administration of football in Wales is governed by the FAW Council comprising: a President, two Vice-Presidents, Treasurer and nineteen elected / nominated members. In addition, there are five Life Vice-Presidents and two Life Members. Her Majesty The Queen is patron of the FAW.

The FAW Council is responsible for the overall direction of Welsh football, whilst the day to day management of the affairs of the FAW are directed by the Chief Executive and staff.

MEMBERS   ♂ 32 ♀ 0

President	In Office From	
P C Pritchard	08/09	Member of Council 1992-
Vice-Presidents		
T Lloyd Hughes	08/09	Member of Council 1989-
K Tucker	08/09	Member of Council 1989-
Honorary Treasurer		
D Griffiths	08/09	Member of Council 1992-

Life Vice-President
T R Forse; J O Hughes; T M Evans MBE; B Fear; D W Shanklin; P Rees

Members
R Bridges; M Casey; K Davies; A. Edwards; C Evans; R Fry; A W Griffiths; J Harris; T V Harris; R K Hughes; D.A. Jones; P A Jones; K O'Connor; J Phillips; R Smiles; A Watkins; R M Waygood; C Whitley; I Williams; G Williams; S Williams; P Woosnam

Welsh Premier League
P Rees

PRINCIPAL OFFICERS

Jonathan Ford - *Chief Executive;* Mark Evans - *Head of International Department;* Andrew Howard - *Head of Competitions Department;* Leighton Norris - *Head of Finance Department;* Paul Evans - *Head of Compliance Department*

Total no. staff: 26

WELSH RUGBY UNION

Westgate Terrace
Millennium Stadium
Westgate Street
Cardiff CF10 1NS

☎ (0870) 013 8600

Email: info@wru.co.uk
Website: www.wru.co.uk

Chair
David Pickering

Group Chief Executive
Roger Lewis

The Welsh Rugby Union's principal activity is to promote, foster, encourage, control and improve the game of rugby football throughout Wales. The WRU also wholly owns and operates the Millennium Stadium and together, the two companies form the WRU Group.

The Group's vision is to take Wales to the world with our rugby, to welcome the world to Wales in our stadium and to define Wales as a nation. The Group's mission evolves around three pillars:

- *Elite rugby – leading Welsh rugby back to the forefront of the global game in performance and reputation*
- *Community rugby – developing grassroots rugby, increasing participation, supporting clubs and bringing communities together*
- *Stadium – promoting the Millennium Stadium as a unique, must-play, must-visit venue.*

A priority for the WRU is to continue to build the systems and pathways to create a winning Wales team which in turn will drive Welsh rugby forward by increasing participation, building support and attracting more volunteers to help maintain the game at the heart of all our communities throughout the nation.

Patron Her Majesty Queen Elizabeth II
Vice Patron Duke of Cambridge
President Dennis Gethin

BOARD MEMBERS ♂ 18 ♀ 0

Non-Executive Chair
David Pickering

Executive
Roger Lewis (Group Chief Executive)

Non-Executive
Gerald Davies; Martin Davies; Ken Hewitt; Mal Beynon; Geraint Edwards; Humphrey Evans; Gordon Eynon; Brian Fowler; Richard Gwynn; Russell Howell; Roy Giddings; Peredur Jenkins; Alan Jones; Aurwel Morgan; Steve Pike; Ray Wilton

EXECUTIVE BOARD

Roger Lewis - *WRU Group Chief Executive;* Rhodri Lewis - *Head of Legal Affairs;* Joe Lydon - *Head of Rugby;* Craig Maxwell - *Head of Group Sales & Marketing;* Julie Paterson - *Head of Group Compliance;* Steve Phillips - *Group Finance Director;* Gerry Toms - *Stadium Manager;* John Williams - *Head of Communications*

Total no. staff: 205 (WRU Group)

WELSH BOOKS COUNCIL
CYNGOR LLYFRAU CYMRU

Castell Brychan
Aberystwyth
Ceredigion
SY23 2JB

☎ (01970) 624151
Fax: (01970) 625385

Email: castellbrychan@cllc.org.uk
Website: www.cllc.org.uk

Chair
Prof M Wynn Thomas OBE

Chief Executive
Elwyn Jones

The Welsh Books Council is a national organization with charitable status funded by the Welsh Assembly Government. The grant-in-aid received for 2011/12 was £4.06 million.

Established in 1961, the Welsh Books Council is responsible for promoting all sectors of the publishing industry in Wales, in both languages, in conjunction with publishers, booksellers, libraries and schools. The Council is also responsible for distributing publishing grants towards Welsh and English language publications. The Council's wholesale Distribution Centre had a turnover in 2011/12 of over £4.38 million gross.

COUNCIL MEMBERS ♂ 37 ♀ 10

Chair
Prof M Wynn Thomas OBE

Vice-Chair
Gareth Davies Jones
Hon Secretary - D Geraint Lewis

Hon Treasurer - W Gwyn Jones
Hon Counsel - Gwydion Hughes
Hon Solicitor - Alun P Thomas

Background
Professor of English & Director of CREW (Centre for Research into the English Literature & Language of Wales), Swansea University

Former HM Inspector of Schools (Wales)
Former Assistant Director, Cultural Services, Ceredigion County Council
Director of Finance, Ceredigion County Council
Barrister
Solicitor

Also up to 22 members representing Local Authorities and circa 25 representatives of literary, educational and cultural bodies in Wales.

STAFF

Elwyn Jones - *Chief Executive;* Arwyn Roderick - *Finance & Business;* Moelwen Gwyndaf - *Administration;* D Philip Davies - *Information Services;* Delyth Humphreys - *Children's Books;* Richard Owen - *Publishing Grants;* Neville Evans - *Distribution Centre Manager;* Tom Ferris - *Sales & Marketing;* Sion Ilar - *Design;* Marian Beech Hughes - *Editorial*

Total no. staff: 50

Comisiynydd y Gymraeg
Siambrau'r Farchnad
5–7 Heol Eglwys Fair
Caerdydd CF10 1AT

☎ (0845) 6033 221

Ebost: post@comisiynyddygymraeg.org
Gwefan: comisiynyddygymraeg.org

Comisiynydd y Gymraeg
Welsh Language Commissioner

Meri Huws
Comisiynydd
y Gymraeg

Mae Comisiynydd y Gymraeg yn gorff annibynnol a grëwyd gan Fesur y Gymraeg (Cymru) 2011. Prif nod y Comisiynydd yw hybu a hwyluso defnyddio'r Gymraeg. Gwneir hyn drwy ddwyn sylw i'r ffaith bod statws swyddogol i'r Gymraeg yng Nghymru a thrwy osod Safonau ar sefydliadau. Bydd Safonau'n nodi sut mae disgwyl i sefydliadau ddefnyddio'r Gymraeg mewn gwahanol gyd-destunau.

Mae'r Comisiynydd yn gweithredu ar sail yr egwyddor na ddylid trin y Gymraeg yn llai ffafriol na'r Saesneg yng Nghymru ac y dylai pobl yng Nghymru allu byw eu bywydau drwy gyfrwng y Gymraeg os ydynt yn dymuno gwneud hynny.

Blaenoriaethau'r Comisiynydd ar gyfer 2012-13 yw:

- Paratoi i osod dyletswydd ar sefydliadau i ddefnyddio'r Gymraeg trwy gyfundrefn Safonau a gorfodi cydymffurfiaeth â hwy
- Parhau i weithredu cyfundrefn cynlluniau iaith hyd nes daw Safonau i rym cyfreithiol
- Gwrando ar farn a phryderon unrhyw berson trwy weithredu system gwynion
- Craffu ar ddatblygiadau polisi o ran y Gymraeg
- Cynnal ymholiadau (o dan Fesur y Gymraeg (Cymru) 2011)
- Hwyluso isadeiledd i gefnogi'r Gymraeg.

TÎM RHEOLI

Cyfarwyddwyr	Swydd
Meri Huws	Comisiynydd y Gymraeg
Gwenith Price	Cyfarwyddwr Strategol: Polisi a Chydymffurfiaeth
Gwyn Williams	Cyfarwyddwr Strategol: Polisi a Chyfarthrebu
Enid Lewis	Cyfarwyddwr Strategol: Gwasanaethau Corfforaethol

WELSH LANGUAGE COMMISSIONER

Meri Huws
Welsh Language
Commissioner

Welsh Language Commissioner
Market Chambers
5–7 St Mary Street
Cardiff CF10 1AT

☎ (0845) 6033 221

Email: post@welshlanguagecommissioner.org
Website: welshlanguagecommissioner.org

**Comisiynydd y
Gymraeg
Welsh Language
Commissioner**

The Welsh Language Commissioner is an independent body established by the Welsh Language (Wales) Measure 2011. The principal aim of the Commissioner is to promote and facilitate use of the Welsh language. This entails raising awareness of the official status of the Welsh language in Wales and by imposing Standards in relation to the Welsh language on organizations. Statutory Standards will specify how organizations are required to use the Welsh language in different contexts.

The Commissioner operates on the basis of the principals that the Welsh language should be treated no less favourably than the English language in Wales and that people in Wales should be able to live their lives through the medium of the Welsh language if they choose to do so.

The Commissioner's priorities in 2012-13 are to:

- *Prepare to impose a duty on organizations to use the Welsh language by complying with Standards*
- *Continue to implement the system of language schemes until Standards come into legal force*
- *Listen and respond to the views and concerns of any persons through implementing a complaints procedure*
- *Scrutinize policy for Welsh language considerations*
- *Instigate inquiries (under the Welsh Language (Wales) Measure 2011)*
- *Facilitate a supportive infrastructure for the Welsh language.*

MANAGEMENT TEAM

Directors	Title
Meri Huws	Welsh Language Commissioner
Gwenith Price	Strategic Director: Policy & Compliance
Gwyn Williams	Strategic Director: Policy & Communications
Enid Lewis	Strategic Director: Corporate Services

WELSH LANGUAGE COMMISSIONER

13

The**Wales** Yearbook

HIGHER & FURTHER EDUCATION

HIGHER EDUCATION WALES
THE VOICE OF HIGHER EDUCATION IN WALES

The sector in 2012-13 continues to:

Innovate - leading the way with innovative projects in science and research

Collaborate - year on year increases in the capture of research income through collaboration

Provide employability - work with employers to provide some of the most innovative graduates in any part of the UK

Accessibility - widening access to universities to those that traditionally may not have had the chance to access higher education at all

Ensuring language of choice - supporting a flourishing higher education sector through the medium of both Welsh and English

ADDYSG UWCH CYMRU
LLAIS ADDYSG UWCH YNG NGHYMRU

Yn 2012-13 mae'r sector yn parhau i:

Arloesi - arwain y ffordd gyda phrosiectau arloesol mewn gwyddoniaeth ac ymchwil

Cydweithio - incwm ymchwil yn cynyddu o flwyddyn i flwyddyn trwy gydweithio

Creu cyflogadwyedd - gweithio gyda chyflogwyr i ddarparu rhai o'r graddedigion mwyaf blaengar mewn unrhyw ran o wledydd Prydain

Hygyrchedd - ehangu mynediad i brifysgolion i'r sawl na fyddent yn draddodiadol efallai wedi cael y cyfle i fanteisio ar addysg uwch o gwbl

Sicrhau dewis iaith - cefnogi sector addysg uwch ffyniannus trwy gyfrwng y Gymraeg a'r Saesneg

Higher
Education
Wales Cymru
Addysg
Uwch

www.hew.ac.uk

HIGHER EDUCATION WALES

2 Caspian Point, Caspian Way,
Cardiff Bay, Cardiff CF10 4DQ
☎ (029) 2044 8020
Fax: (029) 2048 9531

Email: hew@hew.ac.uk
Website: www.hew.ac.uk

**Higher
Education
Wales Cymru
Addysg
Uwch**

Chair
Prof John Hughes

Director
Amanda Wilkinson

Higher Education Wales (HEW) was established in 1996 to represent the higher education sector in Wales. HEW is the national council in Wales of Universities UK (formerly the Committee of Vice-Chancellors and Principals of the United Kingdom). HEW's mission is to be the voice of higher education in Wales. HEW aims to deliver its mission by:

- *providing an expert resource on all aspects of Welsh higher education*
- *promoting and supporting higher education in Wales*
- *representing the interests of its members*
- *negotiating on behalf of Welsh higher education*

COMMITTEE MEMBERS   ♂ 10 ♀ 2

Prof Antony J Chapman	Cardiff Metropolitan University
Prof Richard B Davies	Swansea University
Prof Stephen Hagen	University of Wales, Newport
Prof John Hughes	Bangor University
Prof Medwin Hughes	University of Wales*
Prof Medwin Hughes	University of Wales: Trinity Saint David*
Rob Humphreys	The Open University in Wales
Prof Julie Lydon	University of Glamorgan
Prof April McMahon	Aberystwyth University
Prof Colin Riordan	Cardiff University
Prof Michael Scott	Glyndŵr University
Prof David Warner	Swansea Metropolitan University*

*It is anticipated that during the Academic Year 2012-13, these three universities will come together to form one institution.

PRINCIPAL OFFICERS

Amanda Wilkinson - *Director;* Lisa Newberry - *Assistant Director;* Ben Arnold - *Policy Adviser;* Tamsin Evans - *Officer Manager;* Kerry Howe - *Events & Administration Coordinator*

HEW

Linden Court, The Orchards
Ilex Close, Llanishen
Cardiff CF14 5DZ
☎ (029) 2076 1861
Fax: (029) 2076 3163

Email: info@hefcw.ac.uk
Website: www.hefcw.ac.uk

Chair
Roger Thomas OBE

Cyngor Cyllido Addysg
Uwch Cymru
**Higher Education Funding
Council for Wales**

Chief Executive
Dr David Blaney

The Higher Education Funding Council for Wales (HEFCW) is a Welsh Government Sponsored Body, established in May 1992. Under the Further and Higher Education Act 1992, HEFCW administers funds made available by the Welsh Government to support education, research and related activities at higher education institutions, and certain higher education courses at further education colleges. HEFCW's responsibilities for initial teacher training are covered under the Education (School Teachers' Qualifications) (Wales) Regulations 2004 and the Education Act 2005.

HEFCW's vision is to develop and sustain internationally excellent higher education in Wales, for the benefit of individuals, society and the economy, in Wales and more widely. HEFCW's funding commitments are £384.69 million (recurrent, 2011/12 academic year funding) and £10.41 million (2011/12 financial year funding for, eg, reconfiguration and UHOVI).

MEMBERS ♂ 5 ♀ 5

Chair	In Office until	Background
Roger Thomas OBE	05/14	Former Chair of Governors, University of Glamorgan
Members		
Dr David Blaney *(Term of office begins Oct 2012)*		Chief Executive
David Allen	11/14	Registrar & Deputy Chief Executive, University of Exeter
Dame Alexandra Burslem	11/14	Former Vice-Chancellor, Manchester Metropolitan University
Prof Mari Lloyd-Williams	12/12	Director of Community Studies, University of Liverpool
Prof Katherine (Leni) Oglesby	11/14	Former Senior Deputy Vice-Chancellor, University of Teesside
Prof Robin Williams	07/15	Former Vice-Chancellor, Swansea University
Bethan Guilfoyle	03/13	Headteacher of Treorchy Comprehensive School
David Mason	03/13	Former Principal/Chief Executive, Coleg Gwent
Nina Park	03/13	Vice President for Control Techniques

PRINCIPAL OFFICERS

Dr David Blaney - *Chief Executive;* Roger Carter; Richard Hirst; Celia Hunt; Bethan Owen; Nick Williams

Total no. staff: 56

PRIFYSGOL ABERYSTWYTH UNIVERSITY

Old College
King Street, Aberystwyth
Ceredigion SY23 2AX
☎ (01970) 623111
Fax: (01970) 628548

Email: vice-chancellor@aber.ac.uk
Website: www.aber.ac.uk

President
Sir Emyr Jones Parry

Vice-Chancellor
Prof April McMahon

Aberystwyth University was established in 1872, and funded by pennies given by coal miners who recognised the benefits that a university, and a university education, could bring. The University still shares a strong bond with the community, and there is a friendly and mutually beneficial relationship between the University and the town. Today, the University community is a global one, with students and staff from over 120 countries.

With a student population of over 11,000 and a team of staff totalling just over 2,200 – in a town of 21,000 people – the University makes a significant contribution to the local community. Applications to the University have shown a year on year increase with 2011/12 being the most popular ever. On a global stage, the University contributes world-leading research across a variety of subject areas including International Politics; Biology; Computer Science; Theatre Film and Television Studies and has vibrant new departments of Psychology and Sport and Exercise Science.

League tables consistently place Aberystwyth as the leader of Welsh universities and amongst the frontrunners for UK publicly-funded residential UK higher education institutions in terms of the student experience. It enjoys an exceptionally high student satisfaction rating according to the 2011 National Student Survey and The Times Good University Guide 2012. According to the 2012 International Student Barometer, Aberystwyth University ranked amongst the top three universities in the world for student satisfaction. Prifysgol Aberystwyth University has an annual budget (2012-13) of £113.7m.

COUNCIL MEMBERS ♂ 17 ♀ 7

President
Sir Emyr Jones Parry GCMG PhD FInstP
Vice-Presidents
Elizabeth France CBE BSc Econ Hon DSc Hon DLitt
Gwerfyl Pierce Jones MA
Dr Glyn Rowlands
Treasurer
Dr Timothy Brain QPM BA PhD FRSA

Vice-Chancellor
Prof April McMahon MA PhD FBA FRSE FLSW
Pro-Vice-Chancellors
Rebecca Davies BLib
Prof Martin Jones BA PhD
Prof Aled Jones BA MA PhD FRHistS
Prof John Grattan BA MSc PhD FRGS FHEA

Representative Members
Organization of Students - Ben Meakin, Student Union President; Carys Thomas, UMCA President
Appointed Members
Roger Banner BSc FCA; Mick Buckley BSc FRSA; Janet Davies BA; Keith Evans; Ian MacEachern BSc BA MSc MBA OBE; Prof Wynne Jones OBE; Prof Gareth Roberts; Sir John Skehel FRS
Elected Members
Elected by the Senate - Prof Mike Foley BA MA PhD; Prof Tim Woods BA MA PhD; Vacancy
Elected by Non-academic staff - Rachel Hubbard *Co-opted* - Andrew Green MA ALA; Vacancy

PRINCIPAL OFFICERS

Prof April McMahon - *Vice-Chancellor;* Rebecca Davies, Prof John Grattan, Prof Martin Jones, Prof Aled Jones - *Pro Vice-Chancellors;* Susan Chambers - *Director of Human Resources;* Dr Catrin Hughes - *Registrar & Secretary;* Tba - *Director of Finance;* Tba - *Director of Planning*

Total no. staff: 2,108

UNIVERSITIES

BANGOR UNIVERSITY

Bangor, Gwynedd LL57 2DG
☎ (01248) 351151
Fax: (01248) 370451

Email: d.m.roberts@bangor.ac.uk
Website: www.bangor.ac.uk

PRIFYSGOL
BANGOR
UNIVERSITY

Chair of Council
Lord Davies of Abersoch

Vice-Chancellor
Prof John Hughes

Our mission is to be a world-class research-led university, to provide teaching and learning of the highest quality, and to contribute to the development of the economy, health and culture of a sustainable Wales and a sustainable world. Bangor University has 11,440 students, 2,169 staff, and the annual budget (2011-12) is £130,555,000.

MEMBERS OF COUNCIL   ♂ 16 ♀ 10

President
Rt Hon Lord Elis-Thomas

Vice-President
Sir Peter Davis

Chair
Lord Davies of Abersoch

Treasurer & Deputy Chair
David Williams

Vice-Chancellor
Prof John Hughes

Deputy Vice-Chancellor
Prof David Shepherd

Pro Vice-Chancellors
Prof Colin R Baker; Mr Wyn Thomas
Prof Carol Tully

Representative of Bangor University Court: Geraint Jones

Representative of the Court of the University of Wales: Elinor Bennett

Representatives of the Senate: Prof Paul Spencer; Prof Helen Wilcox

Representative of the Academic Staff: Dr Andrew Edwards

Representative of the Old Students' Association: Alwyn Roberts

Representatives of Public Bodies in North Wales: Elfed Wynn Roberts, Marian Wyn Jones

Representative of the Support Staff: Laura Pritchard-Jones

Representatives of the Students' Union: Jo Caulfield; Danielle Buckley

Co-opted Members: Dr Dewi Wyn Roberts, Richard Parry-Jones, Mary Burrows, Dr Malcolm Jones, Dr Gwyneth Roberts, Betty Williams

PRINCIPAL OFFICERS

Dr David Roberts - *Secretary & Registrar;* David Fordham - *Deputy Registrar;* Dewi Hughes - *Director of Programme Management;* Kevin Mundy - *Director of Planning;* Dylan Roberts - *Acting Director of Estates;* Alan Parry - *Director of Corporate Communications & Marketing;* Lyn Meadows - *Director of HR;* Mike Davies - *Director of Finance;* David Learmont - *Director of Business Improvement*

Total no. staff: 2,169

CARDIFF UNIVERSITY

Cardiff CF10 3XQ
☎ (029) 2087 4000

Website: www.cardiff.ac.uk
Twitter: @cardiffuni

President
**Prof Sir Martin Evans
FRS**

Vice-Chancellor
Prof Colin Riordan

Cardiff University has 28,842 students, 6,154 staff, and an annual turnover of £411.5 million. The University is a dynamic and successful centre of higher education with an international reputation for high quality teaching and research. Three major new Research Institutes, offering radical new approaches to neurosciences and mental health, cancer stem cells, and sustainable places have been established by the University. Cardiff is a member of the Russell Group of the UK's leading research universities.

MEMBERSHIP OF COUNCIL ♂ 23 ♀ 7

Chair
John Jeans CBE
Honorary Treasurer
Philippa Herbert

Members
Guy Clarke; Alex Embiricos; Prof Roy Evans; David Francis; Simon Gibson OBE; Dr Grahame Guilford; Gethin Lewis; Fiona Peel OBE; Revd Gareth Powell; Dr Gabe Treharne; Glenys Williams; Susan Gwyer-Roberts; Richard Roberts CBE; Raj Aggarwal OBE

Staff Members
Prof Elizabeth Treasure - *Deputy Vice-Chancellor;* Prof Jonathan Osmond - *Pro Vice-Chancellor for Education & Students;* Prof Graham Hutchings - *Pro Vice-Chancellor for Research;* Prof Terry Threadgold - *Pro Vice-Chancellor for Staff & Diversity;* Prof Hywel Thomas - *Pro Vice-Chancellor for Engagement & International;* Prof Walter Gear - *Cardiff School of Physics & Astronomy;* Prof Tim Wess - *Pro Vice-Chancellor for Estates;* Prof Keith Meek - *Cardiff School of Optometry & Vision Sciences;* Prof Dylan Jones - *Cardiff School of Psychology;* Prof Greg Maio - *Cardiff School of Psychology;* Patrizia Donovan - *Planning Division;* Ricardo Calil - *Information Services;* Daniel Hodgson - *School of Medicine;* Marcus Coates-Walker - *President of Cardiff Students' Union;* Samantha Reid - *Academic & University Affairs Officer, Cardiff Students' Union*

PRINCIPAL OFFICERS

Hugh Jones - *Chief Operating Officer;* Jayne Dowden - *Director of Human Resources, Safety, Health & Environment;* Mike Davies - *Director of Physical & Financial Resources;* Dr Chris Turner - *Director of Registry, Governance & Students;* Louise Casella - *Director of Strategic Development;* Prof Peter Halligan - *Dean of Strategic Futures & Interdisciplinary Studies*

Total no. staff: 6,154

UNIVERSITIES

Coleg
Cymraeg
Cenedlaethol

Mae'r Coleg Cymraeg Cenedlaethol yn gyfrifol am gynllunio, datblygu ac hyrwyddo addysg prifysgol drwy'r Gymraeg. Mae'n cynllunio'r ddarpariaeth yn genedlaethol ac yn cyllido darlithyddiaethau, prosiectau strategol ac ysgoloriaethau.

The Coleg Cymraeg Cenedlaethol supports, develops and promotes higher education through the medium of Welsh. We are working to expand study opportunities, in partnership with Welsh universities, by funding lectureships, strategic projects and scholarships.

Y Coleg Cymraeg Cenedlaethol
Y Llwyfan
Heol y Coleg/College Road
Caerfyrddin/Carmarthen
SA31 3EQ

Ebost/Email:
gwybodaeth@colegcymraeg.ac.uk
www.colegcymraeg.ac.uk

Y COLEG CYMRAEG CENEDLAETHOL

Y Coleg Cymraeg Cenedlaethol
Y Llwyfan, College Road
Carmarthen SA31 3EQ
☎ (0844) 800 7375

Email:
gwybodaeth@colegcymraeg.ac.uk
Website:
www.colegcymraeg.ac.uk

Chair
Prof R Merfyn Jones

Chief Executive
Dr Ioan Matthews

Mae'r Coleg Cymraeg Cenedlaethol yn gyfrifol am gynllunio, datblygu ac hyrwyddo addysg prifysgol drwy'r Gymraeg. Mae'n cynllunio'r ddarpariaeth yn genedlaethol ac yn cyllido darlithyddiaethau, prosiectau strategol ac ysgoloriaethau.

The Coleg Cymraeg Cenedlaethol supports, develops and promotes higher education through the medium of Welsh. We are working to expand study opportunities, in partnership with Welsh universities, by funding lectureships, strategic projects and scholarships.

BOARD OF DIRECTORS - MEMBERSHIP

Chair
Prof R Merfyn Jones

Directors from Higher Education Institutions
Jacqui Hare; Prof Medwin Hughes; Prof Aled Jones; Prof Iwan Davies; Prof Hywel Thomas; Wyn Thomas

Student Representative Director
Luke Young, President NUS Wales

Staff Representative Director
Dr Hefin Jones

Independent Directors
Geraint James; Gareth Pierce; Ieuan Wyn; Linda Wyn

UNIVERSITIES

SWANSEA UNIVERSITY

Singleton Park
Swansea SA2 8PP

☎ (01792) 205678
Fax: (01792) 295157

Email: info@swansea.ac.uk
Website: www.swansea.ac.uk

Chair of Council
Sir Roger Jones OBE

**Swansea University
Prifysgol Abertawe**

Vice-Chancellor
Prof Richard B Davies

Founded in 1920, Swansea University has over 15,000 students, 2,704 staff and offers over 400 undergraduate and 185 taught masters postgraduate courses. Set in parkland overlooking Swansea Bay, on the edge of the breathtaking Gower Peninsula, the University enjoys an outstanding location. The annual budget (2010/11) was £173 million.

MEMBERS OF COUNCIL ♂21 ♀9

Chancellor
Rt Hon Rhodri Morgan

Pro-Chancellor & Chair of Council
Sir Roger Jones

Pro-Chancellor
Vivienne Sugar

Treasurer
Carl Hadley

Vice-Chancellor
Prof Richard B Davies

Pro-Vice-Chancellors
Prof Ian Cluckie; Prof Iwan Davies; Prof Alan Speight (in attendance); Prof Noel Thompson; Prof Hilary Lappin Scott (in attendance)

Appointed by Court: Jill Burgess; Prof Dame June Clark; Prof Julian Hopkin; Ralph Miller; Howard Morgan; Brian Thompson

Academic Staff appointed by the Senate: Prof David Blackaby; Dr Katharina Hall; Prof Gareth Morgan; Chris Whyley

Co-opted Members: Sir Roderick Evans; Huw Jones; John Mahoney; Jeannette McLellan; Rosemary Morgan; Ann Owen

Student Members: Tom Upton - *President of Students' Union;* Imogen Stanley - *Students' Union Sports Officer*

Employees nominated by the university's recognised Trade unions: Dr Simon Hoffman; John Tregembo

PRINCIPAL OFFICERS

Raymond Ciborowski - *Registrar & Head of Administration;* Kevin Daniel - *Director of Information Services & Systems;* Phillip Gough - *Director, Finance;* Dr Martin Lewis - *Administrative Secretary;* Huw Morris - *Academic Registrar;* Catherine Mullin - *Director, Marketing;* Jan Nielson - *Director, Research & Innovation;* Craig Nowell - *Director, Estates & Facilities Management;* Pat Price - *Director, Planning & Strategic Projects Unit;* David Williams - *Director, Human Resources;* Sarah Huws-Davies - *Director, Student Services*

Total no. staff: 2,704

UNIVERSITIES

UNIVERSITY OF GLAMORGAN

Pontypridd CF37 1DL

☎ (01443) 480480

Fax: (01443) 654050

Email: press@glam.ac.uk
Website: www.glam.ac.uk

Admissions Enquiries ☎ (0845) 6434 030

Chancellor
**The Rt Hon Lord Morris
of Aberavon KG QC**

UNIVERSITY OF • PRIFYSGOL

Glamorgan
Morgannwg

CARDIFF • PONTYPRIDD • CAERDYDD

Vice-Chancellor
Prof Julie Lydon

The University of Glamorgan has expanded enormously in recent years as its popularity has grown. It now has more than 23,000 students, taught at three campuses in Treforest, Glyntaff and at the Cardiff-based School of Creative and Cultural Industries, as well a sustainable energy research base at Baglan. A £130m investment programme in the University's infrastructure has produced state-of-the-art science laboratories, an iconic new students' union and superb sports facilities used by the touring South Africa and Australia rugby teams.

A member of the St David's Day Group of leading Welsh Universities, Glamorgan has a strong emphasis on applied research across the University, and has pioneered cross-disciplinary research units in Enterprise and Entrepreneurship; Regeneration and Sustainable Communities, and Disaster Management and Emergency Response.

Glamorgan is a partner in UHOVI, the innovative new Universities Heads of the Valleys Institute. Together with the University, the Royal Welsh College of Music and Drama and Merthyr Tydfil College are part of the University of Glamorgan Group, which offers educational provision from FE through to advanced doctoral and conservatoire study.

BOARD OF GOVERNORS ♂ 16 ♀ 6

Chair
Prof John Andrews CBE

Deputy Chair
Michael Lawley

Independent Governors
Stephen Best OBE; Hélène Mansfield OBE
Tony Morgan; David Lewis; Sandra Spray
Haydn Warman; Gareth Williams
Prof Mo Wahab

Vice-Chancellor
Prof Julie Lydon

Co-opted members
Judith Evans; Helen Marshall; Huw Williams
Terry Driscoll; Prof Teresa Rees CBE
Vincent McNabb; Prof David Baker

Academic Board nominees
Dr Andrew Rogers
Prof Danny Saunders OBE

Student Governor
Ashley Price

Clerk to Board of Governors
William Callaway

PRINCIPAL OFFICERS

Huw Williams - *Deputy Vice-Chancellor (Strategic Resource Development);* Helen Marshall - *Deputy Vice-Chancellor for Academic & Business Development;* Prof Clive Mulholland - *Deputy Vice-Chancellor (Research & Student Experience)*

Total no. staff: 2,865

ROYAL WELSH COLLEGE OF MUSIC & DRAMA

Principal
Hilary Boulding

ROYAL WELSH COLLEGE OF MUSIC & DRAMA
COLEG BRENHINOL
CERDD A DRAMA CYMRU

Castle Grounds, Cathays Park, Cardiff CF10 3ER
☎ (029) 2034 2854 Fax: (029) 2039 1304
Email: info@rwcmd.ac.uk Website: www.rwcmd.ac.uk

Part of the University of Glamorgan Group

Annual Budget (2011-12)	No. of Students (Full time)	Total no. Staff (FTE)
£10.845m	691	102

UNIVERSITY OF WALES

Vice-Chancellor
Prof Medwin Hughes DL

University Registry
King Edward VII Avenue
Cardiff CF10 3NS
☎ (029) 2037 6999
Fax: (029) 2037 6980

Email: uniwales@wales.ac.uk
Website: www.wales.ac.uk

**Prifysgol Cymru
University of Wales**

Chair of Council
Alun Thomas

The University has decided to merge with the University of Wales: Trinity Saint David and Swansea Metropolitan University. The unified institution will be merged under the 1828 Royal Charter of the University of Wales: Trinity Saint David. This is a historic decision and offers the transformed University the opportunity to continue to serve higher education both within a Welsh and international context.

OFFICERS OF THE UNIVERSITY

Chancellor - HRH The Prince of Wales; **Pro-Chancellor -** The Most Revd Barry Morgan, Archbishop of Wales; **Vice-Chancellor -** Prof Medwin Hughes; **Chair of the University Council -** Alun Thomas; **Deputy Chair of the University Council -** Margaret Evans

UNIVERSITIES

UNIVERSITY OF WALES TRINITY SAINT DAVID*

Carmarthen Campus:
☎ (01267) 676767
Lampeter Campus:
☎ (01570) 422351

Website: www.trinitysaintdavid.ac.uk

Chair of Council
Dr Geoffrey P Thomas

PRIFYSGOL CYMRU
Y Drindod Dewi Sant
UNIVERSITY OF WALES
Trinity Saint David

Vice-Chancellor
Prof Medwin Hughes DL

The University of Wales Trinity Saint David came into existence through the merger of Trinity University College, Carmarthen and the University of Wales Lampeter. The University was formed to serve the needs of communities in South West Wales within an international context. The University has 5,500 students. Its annual budget is £32 million.

COUNCIL BOARD

President: Dr R Brinley Jones CBE; **Members:** Dr Geoffrey Thomas *(Vice President, Chair of Council, Chair of Corporate Governance & Nominations Committee);* The Venerable Randolph Thomas *(Vice President, Deputy Chair of Council, Chair of Senior Remuneration Committee);* Prof Medwin Hughes *(Vice Chancellor);* Dr John Walters; Eifion Griffiths *(Treasurer & Chair of Finance & Strategic Planning Committee);* Prof Cecilia Crighton; Andrew Curl; Gordon Llewellyn *(Chair of Human Resources Committee);* Lewis Evans; Maria Jones *(Chair of Audit & Risk Committee);* Anthony Jenkins; Conny Matera-Rogers; Ceredig Emanuel; Cennydd Powell; Sian Wyn Siencyn; Peter Bosley; Mattias Eken *(Student President);* Gwyndaf Tobias; Michael McGrane *(Chair of Estates & Network Services Committee);* Revd Dr William Strange

SENIOR MANAGEMENT

Prof Medwin Hughes - *Vice-Chancellor;* Dr Catrin Thomas - *Pro-Vice Chancellor, Academic;* Gwyndaf Tobias - *Pro-Vice Chancellor, Finance & Resources;* Roger Maidment - *Dean, Faculty of Arts & Social Studies;* Gwilym Dyfri Jones - *Dean, Faculty of Education & Training;* Dr Mirjam Plantinga - *Dean, Faculty of Humanities;* Annette Gravell - *Director of Human Resources;* Wendy Xerri - *Director of Knowledge & Information;* Ray Selby - *Director of Planning/Clerk to Council;* David Rogers - *Director of Student Services*

*It has been announced that University of Wales Trinity Saint David and Swansea Metropolitan University have agreed in principle to merge.

UNIVERSITIES

SWANSEA METROPOLITAN UNIVERSITY*

Mount Pleasant
Swansea SA1 6ED
☎ (01792) 481000
Email: enquiry@smu.ac.uk
Website: www.smu.ac.uk

Chair
Dr Gerald Lewis

Vice-Chancellor
Prof David Warner CBE

Swansea Metropolitan University is a comprehensive, vocational, student-centred institution of higher education committed to widening participation, lifelong learning and the enhancement of employment opportunities. The University encourages regional, national and international access. The University is determined to provide a stimulating, progressive and sustainable environment for learning through excellence in teaching, applied research and consultancy. Swansea Metropolitan University has 4,500 full time students and the annual budget (2010-11) is £38 million. The total number of staff is 600.

BOARD OF GOVERNORS

Chair: Dr Gerald Lewis; **Vice-Chair:** Mr Phil Owen; **Members:** Pam Berry; Lewis J Evans; Jill Burgess; Sybil Crouch; Kathryn David; Eifion Griffiths; Jack Girvin; Gareth Harries; Kelvin Hughes; Abul Hussain; Olive Hopker; Prof Gareth E Jones; Prof Andrea Liggins; John St.C. Williams; Rosemond Nelson; Prof Keith Robbins; George Sambrook; Prof David Warner; Beth Winkley

PRINCIPAL OFFICERS

Dr Brian Lewis - *Director of Finance & Resources;* Dr Nick Potter - *Head of Academic Services;* David Overment - *Director of Estates;* Thomas Cadwalladr - *Head of Marketing & Communications;* Olive Hopker - *Head of Planning & Development*

UNIVERSITIES

It has been announced that University of Wales Trinity Saint David and Swansea Metropolitan University have agreed in principle to merge.

CARDIFF METROPOLITAN UNIVERSITY

Chair
Barbara Wilding
CBE, QPM

Western Avenue
Cardiff
CF5 2YB
☎ (029) 2041 6070
Fax: (029) 2041 6286

Email: info@cardiffmet.ac.uk
Website: www.cardiffmet.ac.uk
Twitter: www.twitter.com/cardiffmet

Cardiff Metropolitan University
Prifysgol Fetropolitan Caerdydd
———————— UWIC ————————

Vice-Chancellor
Prof Antony J Chapman

Cardiff Met is made up of five Academic Schools: the renowned Cardiff School of Art & Design; the Cardiff School of Education – one of the leading providers of teacher training in the UK; the Cardiff School of Health Sciences – with its state-of-the-art research centre; the Cardiff School of Management – which offers the largest on-campus MBA in the UK; and its famous Cardiff School of Sport. The University has 13,485 students and 1,116 (FTE) staff. The annual turnover in 2010/11 was £83.2 million.

BOARD OF GOVERNORS ♂ 14 ♀ 9

Chair: Barbara Wilding CBE, QPM
Vice-Chair: Lord Boswell of Aynho

Members
Zoe Harcombe; Monazza Hassan; Satish Mathur; Revd Canon Robin Morrison; Adrian Piper; Dr Jim Port OBE; Baroness Jenny Randerson; Elfyn Thomas; John Foster Thomas; Peter Williams CBE

Academic Board Nominee
Dr Russell Smith

Student Governor
Nichola James

Co-opted Governors
Dr Peter Easy; Baroness Ilora Finlay of Llandaff; Anna Hayes; Steven Jones; Dr Matthew Waring

Vice-Chancellor & Principal
Prof Antony J Chapman

External Co-opted Members of the Audit Committee
Jackie Royall; Helen Cunningham

Clerk to the Board of Governors
Richard Walters

PRINCIPAL OFFICERS

Jacqui Hare - *Deputy Vice-Chancellor;* Pam Ackroyd - *Pro-Vice-Chancellor (Operations);* Prof David Brooksbank - *Pro-Vice-Chancellor (Enterprise);* Prof Sheldon Hanton - *Pro-Vice-Chancellor (Research);* Richard Moremon - *Director of Marketing & Communications;* Martin J Warren - *Director of Finance;* David Price - *Director of Strategy Development*

UNIVERSITIES

UNIVERSITY OF WALES, NEWPORT

Caerleon Campus, Lodge Road,
Caerleon, Newport NP18 3QT
☎ (01633) 432432
Fax: (01633) 432046

Email: uic@newport.ac.uk
Website: www.newport.ac.uk

Chair
Andrew Wilkinson

Vice-Chancellor (Acting)
Prof Stephen Hagen

| **University of Wales, Newport** | **Prifysgol Cymru, Casnewydd** |

The University of Wales, Newport traces its roots back to 1841. It has a long tradition of providing high quality undergraduate, postgraduate and professional courses. Widely regarded as one of the best University's in Britain for widening participation and its community links, it has areas of genuine international excellence including film and photography.

With a traditional campus in Caerleon and a brand new campus in the centre of Newport, the University continues to provide excellent facilities including some of the best equipped workshops and studios in Europe.

The University has 10,041 students, many of whom are part time and from the local area and employs 704 (FTE).

BOARD OF GOVERNORS ♂ 12 ♀ 8

Chair: Andrew Wilkinson
Deputy Chair: Chris Freegard
Vice-Chancellor (Acting): Prof Stephen Hagen
Students' Union President: Pablo Riesco
Members:
Nicola Channon; Huw Edwards; Richard Flatman; Gerry Keighley; Mel Knight; Robert Lawson; Nicky Lewis; Angela Lloyd; Graham Moore; Helen Mortlock; Deborah Perkin; Kevin Perkins; Hazel Taylor; David Topping; Alison Ward; Tim Wess

UNIVERSITY EXECUTIVE

Prof Stephen Hagen - Acting Vice-Chancellor; Graham Rogers - Deputy Vice-Chancellor; Denis Jones - Pro Vice-Chancellor (Resource Planning) & Director of Finance; Dr Chris O'Malley - Pro Vice-Chancellor (Regional & International Development); Bethan Edwards - Pro Vice-Chancellor (Human Resources); Mike Hill - Director of Commercial & External Services; Dr Carl Peters - Executive Dean, Faculty of Education & Social Sciences; Prof Paul Coyle - Executive Dean, Faculty of Arts & Business; Karen Jones - University Registrar & Clerk to the Board of Governors

UNIVERSITIES

Total no. staff: 704

GLYNDŴR UNIVERSITY WREXHAM

Plas Coch, Mold Road,
Wrexham LL11 2AW

☎ (01978) 290666
Fax: (01978) 290008

Email: g.beer@glyndwr.ac.uk
Website: www.glyndwr.ac.uk

Chancellor
Sir Jon Shortridge

Vice-Chancellor & Chief Executive
Prof Michael Scott DL

PRIFYSGOL

Glyndŵr University strives to be a market led, student centred university of international significance open to all. It has approximately 8,000 students and 612 full-time equivalent staff, including subsidiary companies. Its annual budget is £42 million.

MEMBERSHIP OF GOVERNING BODY ♂ 12 ♀ 4

Chair: Michael Cant
Vice-Chair: Derek Griffin
Vice-Chancellor & Chief Executive: Prof Michael Scott DL

Members:
Colette Bleakley; Mervyn Cousins; Adam Fuller; Julia Grime; Brian Heath; David Howard; Pam Hope; John Kenworthy; Karen Lennox; Bruce Roberts; Vincent Ryan; Prof Peter Toyne DL; Ian Williams

President Students' Guild:
Adam Fuller

PRINCIPAL OFFICERS

Dr Allan Howells - *Pro Vice-Chancellor, Operations;* Prof Graeme Wilkinson - *Pro Vice-Chancellor Academic Affairs;* Prof Helen James - *Pro Vice-Chancellor;* Paul Whiting - *Executive Director of Finance & Estates;* Prof Peter Heard - *Executive Director Graduate School;* Lynda Powell - *Executive Director of Campus Management & Commercial Services;* Prof Colyn Gardner - *Executive Director of Corporate Development;* Prof Chris Lewis - *Dean of University Institute for Health, Medical Sciences & Society;* Prof Peter Excell - *Dean of University Institute for Arts, Science & Technology;* Gillian Bridgett - *Academic Registrar*

Total no. staff: 612

THE OPEN UNIVERSITY IN WALES

18 Custom House Street
Cardiff CF10 1AP
☎ (029) 2047 1019
Fax: (029) 2038 8132

Email: wales@open.ac.uk
Website: www.open.ac.uk/wales

Vice Chancellor
Martin Bean

Director
Rob Humphreys

The Open University
Y Brifysgol Agored

Wales Cymru

The Open University is open to people, places, methods and ideas. It is the world leader in modern distance learning, the pioneer of teaching and learning methods which enable people to achieve their career and life goals studying at times and in places to suit them. The Open University in Wales is the nation's leading provider of part-time undergraduate study, with over 9,000 students. It is the only university to be a member of all 3 HEFCW regional strategies; was the first University to receive a 'Quality Award' from the Wales TUC; and has been top for student satisfaction in Wales for seven successive years.

STAFF TUTORS ♂ 7 ♀ 6

Jane Butler	Staff Tutor, Health & Social Care
Rosemary Dale	Staff Tutor, Maths, Technology & Computing
Judith Davies	Staff Tutor, Health & Social Care
Dr Anthony Howell	Staff Tutor, Faculty of Arts
Dr Rob Janes	Staff Tutor, Faculty of Science
Dr Tim Jilg	Lecturer in Welsh
Dr Hugh Mackay	Staff Tutor, Social Sciences
Dr Dave Middleton	Staff Tutor, Social Science
Lorraine Morgan	Staff Tutor, Health & Social Care
Dr Ian Oldham	Staff Tutor, Maths, Technology & Computing
Dr Martin Rhys	Staff Tutor, Education
Margaret Southgate	Staff Tutor, Languages
Jane Williams	Staff Tutor, Maths, Computing & Technology

PRINCIPAL OFFICERS

Rob Humphreys - *Director;* Michele Looker - *Assistant Director (Planning & Resources);* Cerys Furlong - *Assistant Director (External Strategy);* Simon Horrocks - *Assistant Director (Development, Learning & Teaching);* Bea Bown, Ruth Brooks, Ceri Wilcock, Dr Ella Tarnowska, Ceri Phillips - *Student Services Managers;* Victoria Jones - *Marketing Planning Manager;* Tracey Marenghi - *Marketing Manager;* Dewi Knight - *Policy & Public Affairs Manager;* Kevin Pascoe - *Employer Engagement Development Officer;* Gayle Hudson, Eleri Chilcott - *Widening Access Development Officers;* Dr Jessica Davies, Dr Helen Barlow - *Arts Faculty Managers;* Lisa Green - *Associate Lecturer Services;* Cath Collins - *Office & IT Services Manager*

Total no. staff: 58

Am y newyddion diweddaraf am golegau addysg bellach ewch i

For the latest news on further education colleges visit

www.colegaucymru.ac.uk
www.collegeswales.ac.uk

E-bost: **helo@colegaucymru.ac.uk**
E-mail: **hello@collegeswales.ac.uk**

Ffôn Tel: **029 2052 2500**

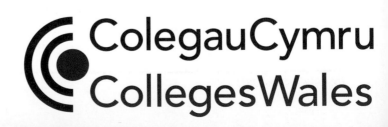

COLEGAUCYMRU
COLLEGESWALES

Unit 7 Cae Gwyrdd,
Greenmeadow Springs Business Park,
Tongwynlais, Cardiff
CF15 7AB

☎ (029) 2052 2500
Fax: (029) 2052 8372
Email:
helo@colegaucymru.ac.uk
hello@collegeswales.ac.uk
Website:
www.colegaucymru.ac.uk
www.collegeswales.ac.uk

Chair
David Jones

Chief Executive
Dr John Graystone

ColegauCymru / CollegesWales is the national educational charity that represents all 19 further education (FE) colleges and institutions in Wales. Its mission is to raise the profile of further education with key decision-makers to improve opportunities for learners in Wales.

BOARD MEMBERS   ♂9 ♀1

Chair	**Background**
David Jones	Principal, Deeside College
Members	
Jim Bennett	Principal, Coleg Gwent
Nick Bennett (Vice-Chair)	Principal, Gower College Swansea
Judith Evans	Principal, Coleg Morgannwg
Glyn Jones OBE	Chief Executive, Grŵp Llandrillo Menai
Mark Jones (Senior Vice-Chair)	Principal, Bridgend College
Derek Lloyd	Corporation Chair, Pembrokeshire College
David Mason	Chair of Directors, Merthyr Tydfil College Ltd
Jon Parry	Chair of Governors, Coleg Harlech WEA N
Simon Pirotte	Principal, Coleg Powys

PRINCIPAL STAFF

Dr John Graystone - *Chief Executive;* Greg Walker - *Deputy Chief Executive;* Julie Lewis - *Company Secretary;* Carolyn Thomas - *Director of Finance;* Cheryl Brown - *WFEPC Manager;* Sylvia Davies - *Head of Public Affairs & PR;* Sian Holleran - *International Coordinator;* Catrin Stephens - *Director of Bilingualism*

COLEGAUCYMRU

NORTH & MID WALES

Coleg Ceredigion
Jacqui Weatherburn, Principal
Llanbadarn Fawr
Aberystwyth
Ceredigion SY23 3BP
T: 01970 639700
W: www.ceredigion.ac.uk

Yale College
Coleg Iâl
Jasbir Dhesi, Principal
Grove Park Road
Wrexham LL11 7AA
T: 01978 311794
W: www.yale-wrexham.ac.uk

Coleg Harlech/WEA (N)
Trefor Fon Owen, Principal
Harlech, Gwynedd LL46 2PU
T: 01766 780363
W: www.harlech.ac.uk

Coleg Powys
Simon Pirotte, Principal
Llanidloes Road, Newtown
Powys SY16 4HU
T: 0845 4086 200
W: www.coleg-powys.ac.uk

Grŵp Llandrillo Menai
(including Coleg Llandrillo,
Coleg Menai and Coleg
Meirion Dwyfor)

Glyn Jones OBE, Chief Executive
Llandudno Road
Rhos-on-Sea, Colwyn Bay
Conwy LL28 4HZ
T: 01492 546666
W: www.gllm.ac.uk

Deeside College
Coleg Glannau Dyfrdwy
David Jones, Principal
Deeside College, Kelsterton Road
Connah's Quay, Deeside
Flintshire CH5 4BR
T: 01244 831531
W: www.deeside.ac.uk

SOUTH WEST WALES

Coleg Sir Gâr
Barry Liles, Principal
Graig Campus
Sandy Road, Llanelli
Carmarthenshire SA15 4DN
T: 01554 748000
W: www.colegsirgar.ac.uk

Neath Port Talbot College
Coleg Castell Nedd Port Talbot
Mark Dacey, Principal
Dŵr y Felin Road
Neath SA10 7RF
T: 01639 648000
W: www.nptc.ac.uk

Gower College Swansea
Coleg Gŵyr Abertawe
Nick Bennett, Principal
Tycoch Road
Swansea SA2 9EB
T: 01792 284000
W: www.gowercollegeswansea.ac.uk

Pembrokeshire College
Coleg Sir Benfro
Sharron Lusher, Acting Principal
Merlins Bridge, Haverfordwest
Pembrokeshire, SA61 1SZ
T: 01437 753000
W: www.pembrokeshire.ac.uk

COLEGAUCYMRU
COLLEGESWALES

SOUTH EAST WALES

Cardiff and Vale College
Coleg Caerdydd a'r Fro
Mike James, Principal
Trowbridge Road,
Rumney
Cardiff CF3 1XZ
T: 030 3030 1010
W: www.cardiffandvalecollege.ac.uk

Bridgend College
Coleg Penybont
Mark Jones, Principal
Cowbridge Road
Bridgend CF31 3DF
T: 01656 302302
W: www.bridgend.ac.uk

Coleg Gwent
Jim Bennett, Principal
The Rhadyr, Usk,
Monmouthshire NP15 1XJ
T: 01495 333333
W: www.coleggwent.ac.uk

Coleg Morgannwg
Judith Evans, Principal
Heol yr Odyn
Parc Nantgarw
Cardiff CF15 7QX
T: 01443 662800
W: www.morgannwg.ac.uk

Merthyr Tydfil College,
University of Glamorgan
Coleg Merthyr Tudful,
Prifysgol Morgannwg
John O'Shea, Principal, Merthyr Tydfil College
Ynysfach, Merthyr Tydfil CF48 1AR
T: 01685 726000
W: www.merthyr.ac.uk

St David's Catholic College
Coleg Catholig Dewi Sant
Mark Leighfield, Principal
Tŷ Gwyn Road, Penylan
Cardiff CF2 5YD
T: 029 2049 8555
W: www.st-davids-coll.ac.uk

The College Ystrad Mynach
Y Coleg Ystrad Mynach
Brynley Davies, Principal
Twyn Rd, Ystrad Mynach
Hengoed, Caerphilly CF82 7XR
T: 01443 816888
W: www.ystrad-mynach.ac.uk

YMCA Wales Community College
Coleg Cymunedol YMCA
Mark Isherwood, Head of College
Unit 6 Cleeve House
Lambourne Crescent
Cardiff Business Park
Llanishen, Cardiff CF14 5GP
T: 029 2075 5444
W: www.ymca-wales.ac.uk/

WEA South
Cymdeithas Addysg y Gweithwyr (de)
Maggi Dawson MBE,
General Secretary/Chief Executive
Unit 7 Coopers Yard
Curran Rd, Cardiff CF10 5NB
T: 029 2023 5277
W: www.swales.wea.org.uk

COLEGAUCYMRU

ColegauCymru
CollegesWales

Universities Heads of the Valleys Institute is a ground breaking education initiative for the Heads of the Valleys. Backed by the Welsh Government, UHOVI is a strategic partnership between the University of Glamorgan and University of Wales, Newport. Working closely with further education colleges and training providers, local authorities, businesses, schools and the voluntary sector, UHOVI is developing industry-specific learning tailored to the needs of the region.

By providing access locally to a range of courses and higher education qualifications, UHOVI is helping improve the skills of the local workforce, contributing to the longer term regeneration of the region.

By 2015 UHOVI is expected to attract over 4000 students from the region, and is a key part of the Welsh Government's aim of increasing level 4 qualifications in the Heads of the Valleys.

UHOVI offers a wide range of learning opportunities across a number of key sectors including science and technology, community development, creative industries and business. Courses are developed in consultation with employers in the area and sector experts, to ensure they meet the needs of existing and developing industries as well as learners.

As well as full and part time foundation degrees, UHOVI also delivers bite-sized courses, certificates of higher education, top-up degrees, postgraduate study and work-based learning courses. Anyone over school age living or working in Blaenau Gwent, Caerphilly, Merthyr Tydfil, Rhondda Cynon Taf or Torfaen can study with UHOVI.

Tel: 0800 1223 220 Email: enquiries@uhovi.ac.uk Web: www.uhovi.ac.uk

Delivery partners include:

Coleg Gwent
Tel: (01495) 333000 Email: info@coleggwent.ac.uk Web: www.coleggwent.ac.uk

Coleg Morgannwg
Tel: (01685) 887500 Email: college@morgannwg.ac.uk Web: www.morgannwg.ac.uk

The College Merthyr Tydfil
Tel: (0800) 169 3825 Email: college@merthyr.ac.uk Web: www.merthyr.ac.uk

The College Ystrad Mynach
Tel: (01443) 816888 Email: enquiries@ystrad-mynach.ac.uk Web: www.ystrad-mynach.ac.uk

University of Wales, Newport (Centre for Community & Lifelong Learning)
Tel: (01495) 722973 Email: uic@newport.ac.uk Web: www.newport.ac.uk

The**Wales** Yearbook **13**

ARMED FORCES & EMERGENCY SERVICES

ROYAL NAVY

University of Wales RN Unit
c/o HMS Cambria, Hayes Lane, Sully
Vale of Glamorgan CF64 5XU
Tel: (01446) 744044
Officer Commanding:
Lt B Power RN

Naval Regional Command HQ
(Wales & Western England)
Naval Regional Management Centre, HMS Flying
Fox, Winterstoke Rd, Bristol BS3 2NS
Tel: (01179) 786010
Officer Commanding: Naval Regional
Commander Commodore Jamie Miller CBE RN

RMR Cardiff
c/o Tŷ Llewellyn TA Centre, Morgan Street,
Cardiff, South Glamorgan CF10 4FG
Tel: (01179) 733523
Officer Commanding:
Lt Col R J W Bucknall RM

RNR Training Centre
HMS Cambria, Hayes Lane, Sully
Vale of Glamorgan CF64 5XU
Tel: (01446) 744044
Officer Commanding:
Commander Neil Pugh RN

RMR Cardiff (Headquarters)
Dorset House, Litchfield Place,
Clifton, Bristol BS8 3NA
Tel: (01179) 733523
Officer Commanding:
Lt Col R J W Bucknall RM

RNR Centre Swansea
c/o TS Ajax, Pilot Wharf House
Maritime Quarter, Swansea SA11 4HO
Tel: (01792) 477100
Officer Commanding:
Lt R Humphreys RNR

South West & Wales Sea Cadet Headquarters
HMS Flying Fox,
Winsterstoke Road, Bristol BS3 2NS
Tel: (01179) 531991
Officer Commanding:
Lt Col John Davies RM

ARMY

160 (Wales) Brigade
The Barracks, Brecon, Powys LD3 7EA
Tel: (01874) 613242
Commander: Brigadier P M L Napier OBE
Late R WELSH

14th Signal Regiment (EW)
Cawdor Barracks, Haverfordwest,
Pembrokeshire SA62 6NN
Tel: (01437) 725716
Commanding Officer: Lt Col J P Townsend R
Signals

1st Battalion The Rifles
Beachley Barracks, Chepstow
Monmouthshire NP16 7YG
Tel: (01291) 645377
Commanding Officer:
Lt Col J De La Billiere

Infantry Battle School
Dering Lines, Brecon LD3 7RA
Tel: (01874) 613662
Commanding Officer:
Lt Col A H Ward

HQ Defence Training Estate Wales & West
Sennybridge, Brecon LD3 8PN
Tel: (01874) 635461
Commandant:
Col (Retd) Howard-Gash

HQ Defence Training Estate
Pembrokeshire SA71 5EB
Tel: (01646) 662340
Commandant:
Major B Inglis MBE

University of Wales Officer Training Corps
Ty Richard Wain VC, Maindy Barracks,
Cardiff CF14 3YE
Tel: (029) 2072 6183
Commanding Officer:
Lt Col H M Evans TD BSc RA (V)

Home HQ 1st The Queen's Dragoon Guards
Maindy Barracks, Cardiff CF14 3YE
Tel: (029) 2078 1227
Regimental Secretary:
Lt Col W R Brace MBE

The Welsh Guards Liaison Office
Maindy Barracks, Cardiff CF14 3YE
Tel: (029) 2078 1209
NCO in charge: CSgt Griffiths

RHQ The Royal Welsh
Maindy Barracks, Cardiff CF14 3YE
Tel: (029) 2078 1202
Regimental Secretary:
Col P L Gooderson TD JP DL

RHQ The Royal Welsh (Outstation)
Hightown Barracks, Wrexham LL13 8RD
Tel: (01978) 264521
Regimental Secretary:
Capt E D Williams DCM DES

Royal Monmouthshire Royal Engineers (Militia)
The Castle, Monmouth NP25 3BS
Tel: (01600) 712935
Commanding Officer:
Lt Col P Fisk RE (V)

104 Regiment Royal Artillery (V)
Raglan Barracks, Newport NP20 5XE
Tel: (01633) 242613
Commanding Officer:
Lt Col P Shepherd-Walwyn MBE RA

3rd Bn The Royal Welsh
Maindy Barracks, Cardiff CF14 3YE
Tel: (029) 2078 1243
Commanding Officer:
Lt Col J W Cleverly R Welsh

Welsh Transport Regiment RLC (V)
Maindy Barracks,
Cardiff CF14 3YE
Tel: (029) 2078 1251
Commanding Officer:
Lt Col D Allen MBE RLC

203 (Welsh) Field Hospital (V)
Gabalfa Avenue, Llandaff North,
Cardiff CF14 2HX
Tel: (029) 2056 2291
Commanding Officer:
Colonel WCJ Donnelly TD DL CCMI QARANC
Late QA

101 Battalion REME (V)
Hightown Barracks, Wrexham LL13 8RD
Tel: (01978) 316125
Commanding Officer:
Lt Col J Heardman

Clwyd & Gwynedd Army Cadet Force
Kinmel Park Camp, Nr Rhyl LL18 5UU
Tel: (01745) 583794
Commandant: Col A V Jones

ARMED FORCES

ARMY (cont.)

Dyfed & Glamorgan Army Cadet Force
Heol West Plas, Litchard, Bridgend CF31 1PA
Tel: (01656) 657593
Commandant: Col J B Davies OBE DL

Gwent & Powys Army Cadet Force
HQ & Cadet Training Centre
Cwrt-y-Gollen, Crickhowell,
Powys NP8 1TH
Tel: (01873) 813756
Commandant: Col R E Stafford-Tolley

ROYAL AIR FORCE

Air Officer for Wales
Air Commodore R A Williams
OBE ADC MA BA FCILT RAFR

RAF Community Relations Officer for Wales
Squadron Leader A M Fox
Email: air-xo-mccrowalesso2@mod.uk

Office Manager to Air Officer & Community
Relations Officer for Wales
Mr D Hodges, The Barracks, Brecon LD3 7EA
Tel: (01874) 613889
Website: www.facebook.com/pages/RAF-
Community-Relations-Officer-for-Wales
www.twitter.com/RAFCROWales

RAF Valley
Holyhead, Gwynedd LL65 3NY
Station Commander:
Group Captain Adrian Hill ADC RAF

No.4 School of Technical Training (RAF)
MOD St Athan
Barry, Vale of Glamorgan CF62 4WA
Tel: (01446) 798798

DTE Pembrey Sands (RAF)
Burry Port,
Carmarthenshire SA16 0HZ
Tel: (01554) 890261

MISCELLANEOUS

Reserve Forces & Cadets Association
RFCA for Wales, Maindy Barracks,
Cardiff CF14 3YE
Tel: (029) 2022 0251
Chief Executive: Col N R Beard TD DL

Armed Forces Careers Office - Swansea
Llanfair Buildings, 19 Castle Street
Swansea SA1 1JF
Tel: (01792) 653362
ACO2: Major M John

Armed Forces Careers Office - Cardiff
8th Floor, Southgate House, 84 Wood Street
Cardiff CF10 1GR
Tel: (029) 2072 6828
ACO2: Major P Dickson

Armed Forces Careers Office
Halkyn House, 21 Rhosddu Road,
Wrexham LL11 1NF
Tel: (01978) 263635
ACO2: Major N L Hill RMLY

Qinetiq
MOD Aberporth Range, Parcllyn,
Cardigan SA43 2BU
Tel: (08700) 100942 Central Switchboard

Qinetiq
Llanmiloe, Carmarthen SA33 4UA
Tel: (01994) 452200

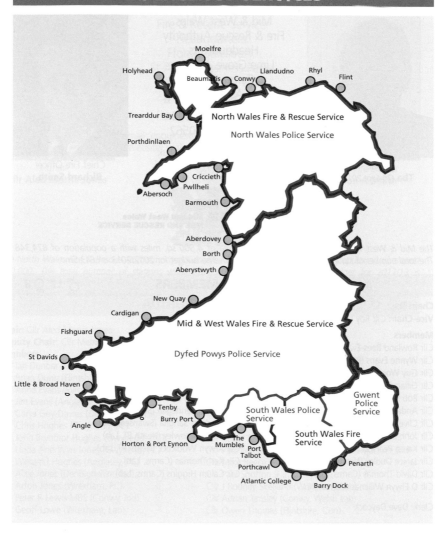

Moelfre
Holyhead
Beaumaris Conwy Llandudno Rhyl Flint
Trearddur Bay

North Wales Fire & Rescue Service

Porthdinllaen

North Wales Police Service

Criccieth
Pwllheli
Abersoch
Barmouth

Aberdovey
Borth
Aberystwyth

New Quay
Cardigan

Mid & West Wales Fire & Rescue Service

Fishguard
St Davids

Dyfed Powys Police Service

Little & Broad Haven

Tenby
Angle Burry Port

Horton & Port Eynon The Mumbles Port Talbot

Porthcawl

Atlantic College Barry Dock

South Wales Police Service

Gwent Police Service

South Wales Fire Service

Penarth

Lifeboats
Royal National Lifeboat Institution

━━━ Fire & Rescue Service
━━━ Police Service

EMERGENCY SERVICES

SOUTH WALES POLICE AUTHORITY*

Tŷ Morgannwg
Police Headquarters
Bridgend CF31 3SU
☎ (01656) 869366
Fax: (01656) 869407

Email:
police.authority@south-wales.pnn.police.uk
Website: www.southwalespoliceauthority.org.uk

Interim Chair
John Littlechild MBE JP

Chief Constable
Peter Vaughan

The South Wales Police Authority comprises representatives from constituent Local Authorities and independent members. The revenue budget for 2012/13 is £249.3 million.

AUTHORITY MEMBERS ♂11 ♀7

Members	Background
Anne Abel	Independent Member, Rhondda Cynon Taf Area
Arjan Ali	Independent Member, Swansea Area
Graham Bingham	Independent Member, Swansea Area
Cllr Ernie Goldsworthy	Member, Merthyr Tydfil County Borough Council
Cllr Pauline Jarman	Member, Rhondda Cynon Taf County Borough Council
Michael Lewis	Independent Member, Swansea Area
John Littlechild MBE JP	Independent Member, Cardiff Area
Robert J Lloyd	Independent Member, Swansea Area
Cllr Kate Lloyd	Member, Cardiff County Council
Cllr Gretta Marshall	Member, Cardiff County Council
Cllr Neil Moore	Member, Vale of Glamorgan Council
Cllr Mel Nott	Member, Bridgend County Borough Council
Helen Roberts	Independent Member, Rhondda Cynon Taf Area
Cllr Pearleen Sangha	Member, City & County of Swansea
Cllr Bob Smith	Member, Rhondda Cynon Taf County Borough Council
Cllr Gareth Sullivan	Member, City & County of Swansea
Cllr Alun Thomas	Member, Neath Port Talbot County Borough Council
Joy Whinney	Independent Member, Vale of Glamorgan Area

Authority Chief Officers: Chief Executive (Interim), Monitoring Officer: Cerith Thomas, Treasurer: Umar Hussain

PRINCIPAL OFFICERS

Peter Vaughan - *Chief Constable;* Colette Paul - *Deputy Chief Constable;* Matt Jukes - *ACC Specialist Crime;* Julian Kirby - *ACC Territorial Policing;* Nicholas Croft - *ACC Human Resources;* Umar Hussain - *Director of Finance;* Gareth Madge - *Director of Legal Services*

Total no. Police Officers: 2,915
Total no. of Civilian Staff: 1,926

* Under the Police Reform and Social Responsibility Act 2011 provision is made for elected police and crime commissioners in Wales and England. The first elections will take place on 15 November 2012.

RNLI LIFEBOATS

Regional Head Office:

RNLI Divisional Base West
Unit 9, Ffordd Richard Davies,
St Asaph Business Park South,
St Asaph, Denbighshire LL17 0LJ

Tel: (01745) 585162
Email: wales@rnli.org.uk

Royal National Lifeboat Institution

The Royal National Lifeboat Institution is a registered charity that saves lives at sea. It provides, on call, the 24-hour lifeboat search and rescue service to 100 miles out from the coast of the United Kingdom and the Republic of Ireland. The RNLI continues to rely on voluntary contributions and legacies for its income.

There are 31 lifeboat stations strategically placed around the coast of Wales (see Pg 449).

Divisional Media Relations Manager: Danielle Rush
Tel: (01745) 585162 Mob: 07786 668829
Email: danielle_rush@rnli.org.uk

HM COASTGUARD

The Maritime and Coastguard Agency implements the government's maritime safety policy in the UK and works to prevent the loss of life on the coast and at sea.

It provides a 24-hour maritime search and rescue service around the UK coast and in the international search and rescue region through HM Coastguard and inspects and surveys ships to ensure that they are meeting UK and international safety rules. It also provides certification to seafarers, registers vessels and responds to pollution from shipping and offshore installations.

Maritime and Coastguard Agency

In Wales, there are three Maritime Rescue Co-ordination Centres and two Marine Offices.

Swansea	**Milford Haven**	**Holyhead**
HM Coastguard	HM Coastguard	HM Coastguard
Tutt Head, Mumbles,	Gorsewood Drive, Hakin, Milford	Prince of Wales Road, Holyhead,
Swansea SA3 4EX	Haven, Pemrokeshire SA73 3HB	Anglesey, North Wales LL26 1ET
Tel: (01792) 366534	Tel: (01646) 690909	Tel: (01407) 762051 / 763911
Fax: (01792) 369005	Fax: (01646) 692176	Fax: (01407) 764373
RCC Manager: Julie-Anne Wood	RCC Manager: Carl Evans	RCC Manager: Jim Paton
Tel: (01792) 365313	Tel: (01646) 699601	Tel: (01407) 767951
Operational Area: Marsland Mouth, North Devon/Cornwall Border to River Towy, Camarthen	Operational Area: River Towy, Camarthen to near Froig	Operational Area: From Near Froig to Queensferry on the River Dee North Wales

Milford Haven Marine Office	**Cardiff Marine Office**
Gorsewood Drive, Hakin,	Anchor Court, Keen Road,
Milford Haven SA73 3HB	Cardiff, CF24 5JW
Tel: (01646) 699604	Tel: (029) 2044 8822
Fax: (01646) 699606	Fax: (029) 2044 8810

EMERGENCY SERVICES

13

The**Wales** Yearbook

OTHER PUBLIC APPOINTMENTS in WALES

Adjudication Panel for Wales

Adjudication Panel for Wales Support Unit, First Floor, North Wing (N04), Cathays Park, Cardiff CF10 3NQ
Tel: (029) 2082 6705 / 6414 Fax: (029) 2082 3442 Email: adjudication.panel@wales.gsi.gov.uk
Website: www.adjudicationpanelwales.org.uk
Total 13. President, 6 legal members and 6 lay members appointed by Welsh Ministers.

President	Occupation	Remuneration	Commitment	Term of Office
J Peter Davies	Solicitor	£474 per day	occasionally	10
Legal Members				
Helen Cole	Solicitor	£398 per day	occasionally	10
Hywel James	District Judge	£398 per day	occasionally	10
Stewert Sandbrook-Hughes	Barrister	£398 per day	occasionally	10
Kate Berry	Solicitor	£398 per day	occasionally	5-10
Emma Boothroyd	Solicitor	£398 per day	occasionally	5-10
Gwyn Davies	Solicitor	£398 per day	occasionally	5-10
Lay Members				
Ian Blair	Civil Engineering Consultant	£244 per day	occasionally	10-20
Colin Evans	Councillor	£244 per day	occasionally	10-20
Christine Jones		£244 per day	occasionally	10-20
Juliet Morris	Organic Farmer	£244 per day	occasionally	10-20
Susan Hurds		£244 per day	occasionally	5-10
Andrew Bellamy		£244 per day	occasionally	5-10

Advisory Committee on Pesticides

Mallard House, Kings Pool, 3 Peasholme Green, York YO1 7PX Tel: (01904) 455702
Fax: (01904) 455711 Email: acp@hse.gsi.gov.uk Website: www.pesticides.gov.uk/acp_home.asp
Total 20. Chair, Deputy Chair and 18 members.
Although there is currently no Member of the ACP living in Wales, the Welsh Government does provide an Assessor to the Committee.

Advisory Panel on Substance Misuse (APoSM)

Substance Misuse Branch, Department for Health and Social Services, Welsh Government, Merthyr Tydfil Office, Rhydycar, Merthyr Tydfil CF48 1UZ Tel: (0300) 062 8096 Fax: (0300) 062 8547
Email: aposm@wales.gsi.gov.uk Website: www.wales.gov.uk/substancemisuse
Members of the Panel are appointed by the Minister for Health and Social Services

Chair	Occupation	Remuneration	Commitment	Term of Office
Vacant		Nil	Minimum of 6 days pa	-
Members Wales				
Vacant	Health / Primary Care	Nil	Minimum of 3 days pa	-
Vacant	Youth Services	Nil	Minimum of 3 days pa	-
Zoe Lancelott	Education	Nil	Minimum of 3 days pa	10-13
Rossana Oretti	Health / Secondary Care	Nil	Minimum of 3 days pa	10-13
Owain Aneurin Owen	Alcohol Services	Nil	Minimum of 3 days pa	12-12
Vacant	Social Services	Nil	Minimum of 3 days pa	-
Ifor Glyn	Voluntary Sector	Nil	Minimum of 3 days pa	12-14
Josephine Smith	Public Health Wales	Nil	Minimum of 3 days pa	12-14
Vacant	Nursing	Nil	Minimum of 3 days pa	-
Rosemary Allgeier		Nil	Minimum of 3 days pa	10-13
Nominated Representatives				
ACC Julian Kirby	Police Service	Nil	Minimum of 3 days pa	11-14
Eryl Drew	Prison Service	Nil	Minimum of 3 days pa	11-14
Nicola Davies	Probation Service	Nil	Minimum of 3 days pa	11-14

Advisory Panel to the Welsh Language Commissioner

Welsh Language Commissioner, Market Chambers, 5-7 St Mary Street, Cardiff CF10 1AT
Tel: (0845) 6033 221 Email: post@welshlanguagecommissioner.org
The Advisory Panel was appointed under the Welsh Language (Wales) Measure 2011.
The Commissioner may consult the Advisory Panel in connection with the exercise of his or her functions.

Members
Dr Ian Rees – Chair   Virgina Isaac
Gareth Jones   Prof Gwynedd Parry

Agricultural Wages Board for England & Wales

Area 8E, DEFRA, 9 Millbank, c/o 17 Smith Square, London SW1P 3JR
Tel: (020) 7238 6523 Email: Dermot.McInerney@defra.gov.uk Total 21. Chair and 20 members.
Joint appointments DEFRA, Welsh Government plus 8 employers and 8 workers representatives.

Member Wales	Occupation	Remuneration	Commitment	Term of Office
Dr Lionel Walford	Retired Civil Servant	£174 per meeting	Approx 4 days pa	07-10 (Cardiff)

Arts Strategy Board

Allyn Davies, Arts strategy Board Secretatriat, Welsh Government, Cathays Park, Cardiff CF10 3NQ
Email: allyn.davies@wales.gsi.gov.uk
The Arts Strategy Board is a Ministerial advisory group with a remit to challenge, inform and help shape future arts policy and strategies of the Welsh Government. The status of the Board is advisory; it has no decision making powers and there are no formal voting procedures.

Members
Minister for Housing, Regeneration & Heritage (Chair)   Chair ACW
Chief Executive ACW   Director of Arts ACW
Director Lifelong Learning, Leisure & Information WLGA   Spokesperson for Culture WLGA
Director Arts & Business   Director Wales Arts International
Wales Co-ordinator Voluntary Arts Wales   Head of Culture, Welsh Language & Sport WAG
Head of Arts Welsh Government

British Pharmacopoeia Commission

Medicines and Healthcare products Regulatory Agency, 151 Buckingham Palace Road, London SW1W 9SZ
Email: bpcom@mhra.gsi.gov.uk Total 19. Chair and 18 members appointed by the Appointments Commission on behalf of Secretary of State. The British Pharmacopoeia Commission is responsible for the publication of annual editions of the British Pharmacopoeia and British Pharmacopoeia (Veterinary) and for the establishment and publication of British Approved Names.

Member Wales	Occupation	Remuneration	Commitment	Term of Office
Mr V Fenton-May	Specialist quality controller	£975 pa	3 meetings pa	11-13

British Wool Marketing Board

British Wool Marketing Board, Wool House, Roysdale Way, Euroway Trading Estate, Bradford BD4 6SE
Tel: (01274) 688666 Fax: (01274) 652233 Email: mail@britishwool.org.uk Website: www.britishwool.org.uk
Total 11. To give a farming perspective. Appointed by wool producers.

Member Wales	Occupation	Remuneration	Commitment	Term of Office
Bedwyr Jones (Nant Gwynant)	Farmer	£8,450 pa	Approx 20 days pa	11-14
Gethin Hayard (Brecon)	Farmer	£8,450 pa	Approx 20 days pa	10-13

Building Regulations Advisory Committee for Wales

Construction Unit, Environmental and Sustainable Development Directorate, Welsh Government, Rhydycar, Merthyr Tydfil, CF48 1UZ. Email: enquiries.brconstruction@wales.gsi.gov.uk
Under section 14(5) of the Act (as amended by the TFO) the Welsh Ministers have a duty to appoint a Building Regulations Advisory Committee for Wales (BRACW) for the purpose of advising the Welsh Ministers on the exercise of their power to make building regulations and on other subjects connected with building regulations.

Members   *Sector*
Prof Phil Jones Chair   Cardiff University
James Chambers   Architecture

Building Regulations Advisory Committee for Wales (cont.)

Andrew Sutton	Sustainability
James Player	Builder
Nigel Smith	House Builder
Christopher Jones	Local Authority Building Control
Christopher Lynn	Mechanical & Electrical Services
Andrew Thomas	Private Sector Building Control
Alan Hunt	Needs of the Disabled

Climate Change Commission

Peter Davies, c/o Cynnal Cymru - Sustain Wales, Ground Floor, Cambrian Buildings, Mount Stuart Square, Cardiff Bay Cardiff CF10 5FL E-mail peter@pdpartnership.co.uk
The Climate Change Commission brings together key sectors and organizations across Wales to build agreement on the action needed to tackle climate change in Wales.

Member	Occupation
Peter Davies	Chair
Paul Allen	Centre for Alternative Technology
David Proctor	Confederation of British Industry
Clive Walmsley	Countryside Council for Wales
Helen Northmore	Energy Saving Trust
Chris Mills	Environment Agency Wales
Non Rhys	Federation of Small Businesses
Lewis Harding	Funky Dragon
Bethan Adshead	Funky Dragon
Prof Hywel Thomas	Higher Education Sector
Prof Gareth Wyn Jones	Land Use & Climate Change Group
Simon Dean	NHS Wales
Mike Batt	The Carbon Trust
Prof Kevin Anderson	The Tyndall Centre
Dr Lorraine Whitmarsh	Transport
Garry Metcalf	UK Climate Impacts Programme
Peter Jones	Wales Environment Link
Graham Benfield	Wales Council for Voluntary Action
Janet Davies	Plaid Cymru
Russell George AM	Welsh Conservatives
John Griffiths AM	Welsh Labour Party
Peter Randerson	Welsh Liberal Democrats
Specialist Advisor:	UK Committee on Climate Change
Specialist Advisor:	Met Office

Commission on Human Medicines - Neurology, Pain & Psychiatry EAG

Department of Health, 151 Buckingham Palace Road, Victoria, London SW1W 9SZ
Total 16. Appointed jointly by UK Health Ministers and Welsh Assembly Government/Sec State Wales.

Members	Occupation	Remuneration	Commitment	Term of Office
Prof Kenneth	Emeritus of Geriatric	£200 per day	1 day per mth	09-13
Walter Woodhouse	Medicine	(plus expenses)		
(Penarth, Vale of Glam) Cardiff University School of Medicine				

Commission on Human Medicines - Pharmacovigilance EAG

Department of Health, 151 Buckingham Palace Road, Victoria, London SW1W 9SZ
Total 14. Appointed jointly by UK Health Ministers and Welsh Government/Sec State Wales.

Members	Occupation	Remuneration	Commitment	Term of Office
Prof Kenneth	Emeritus of Geriatric	£200 per day	1 day per mth	09-13
Walter Woodhouse	Medicine	(plus expenses)		
(Penarth, Vale of Glam) Cardiff University School of Medicine				

Distribution Sub Group

Robery Hay, Welsh Government, Cathays Park, Cardiff CF10 3NQ
E-mail localgovernmentsettlement@wales.gsi.gov.uk
The role of the Distribution Sub-Group (DSG) is to advise the Partnership Council for Wales (PCfW) on the Local Government Settlement formula to calculate standard spending assessments (SSAs) for local authorities in Wales.

Members

Robert Hay – Chair	Debra Carter
Emma Cane	Wesley Harris
Gareth Furminger	Jon Rae
Geoff Petty	Steve Greenslade
Andrew Stephens	Derek Davies
Chris Barton	Dilwyn Owen Williams
David McAuliffe	Hugh Coombs
Mike Piggott	Ness Young
Paul McGrady	Mark Lewis
Rhys Andrews	

Environment Protection Advisory Committee Wales (EPAC)

Environment Agency Wales, Cambria House, 29 Newport Rd, Cardiff CF24 OTP Tel: (0870) 850 6506
Total 21. Chair appointed by Welsh Assembly Government, 15 members appointed by Environment Agency Wales, 5 members appointed by WLGA.

Chair	Occupation	Remuneration	Commitment	Term of Office
Prof Thomas Pritchard OBE, JP	Retired	£17,641	5 days per mth	08-13 (March 31st 2013)

Farm Animal Welfare Council

Farm Animal Welfare Committee, Area 8B, 9 Millbank, c/o Nobel House, 17 Smith Square, London SW1P 3JR Tel: (020) 7238 4926 / 6340 / 5016 Email: fawcsecretariat@defra.gsi.gov.uk
Website: www.defra.gov.uk/fawc
Total 18. Chair and 17 members appointed jointly by Government Departments in Wales, England and Scotland.

Member Wales	Occupation	Remuneration	Commitment	Term of Office
Huw Davies	Sheep Farmer	£148 per day	15-20 days pa	06-14

Fire & Rescue Consultative Forum

Contact: Kingsley Rees Tel: (0300) 062 8219
The remit of the Forum is to provide a forum for senior officials to discuss issues of mutual concern and interest in advance of the Minister's meetings with FRA Chiefs and Chairs. The Forum will continue to have an important role in taking forward the current and future iterations of the National Framework for Wales. It will provide advice to the Minister for Local Government and communities on any aspect which it feels affects the effectiveness of FRAs and the safety of Welsh communities. The Forum may establish specific Task and Finish Groups to take activity forward or look to use existing bodies where these already exist.

Members

Deputy Director – Community Safety Division
Fire and Rescue Service Advisor to the Welsh Government
Chief Fire Officer, South Wales FRA
Chief Fire Officer, Mid & West Wales FRA
Chief Fire Officer, North Wales FRA
Welsh Local Government Association Official
Fire Brigades Union (Wales Executive Member)

Other representative bodies and Departments within Welsh Assembly Government who the Forum feel will add to policy deliberations will contribute on an ad hoc basis and may be co-opted with the Chair's agreement to facilitate the deliberation of specific agenda items.

OTHER PUBLIC APPOINTMENTS

Flood Risk Management Wales (FRMW)

Environment Agency Wales, Cambria House, 29 Newport Rd, Cardiff CF24 0TP Tel: (0870) 850 6506
Total 18. Chair appointed by Welsh Government. 8 members appointed by WLGA, 9 members appointed by Environment Agency Wales. Statutory regional flood and coastal committee of Environment Agency.

Chair	Occupation	Remuneration	Commitment	Term of Office
Deep Sagar	Non-executive Director	£17,503	5 days a month	10-14

Historic Environment Group

Alyson Evans, Historic Advisory Panel Secretariat, Plas Carew, Unit 5/7 Cefn Coed Parc, Nanygarw Rhondda Cynon Taf Email: alyson.evans@wales.gsi.gov.uk
The Historic Environment Group will advise the Welsh Government on action to benefit and promote the historic environment of Wales.

Members

Cadw – Chair (when Minister is unavailable) and Secretariat
CyMAL
Visit Wales
Royal Commission on the Ancient & Historical Monuments of Wales
The Architectural Heritage Fund
The National Trust Wales
The Civic Trust for Wales
Council for British Archaeology Wales
National Library of Wales
Welsh Archaeological Trusts (one representative)
The Heritage Lottery Fund
Welsh Local Government Association/WLGA Advisers
Countryside Council for Wales
Amgueddfa Cymru-National Museum Wales
Institute for Historic Buildings Conservation
Forestry Commission Wales
The Wales Council for Voluntary Action
Historic Houses Association/Country Land & Business Association (combined representation)
British Waterways
National Parks/Areas of Outstanding Natural Beauty (combined)
History Research Wales
Observers (and receiving papers)
Arts Council for Wales

Independent Adjudicator for Local Authorities in Wales

Welsh Government, Cathays Park, Cardiff CF10 3NQ Tel: (029) 2082 3413 Fax: (020) 2082 5346
Total 1. Appointed by NAfW.

Member	Occupation	Remuneration	Commitment	Term of office
Peter Davies	Solicitor	-	Case by case basis	Until 4/13

Independent Appeals Panel for Farmers in Wales

c/o Independent Appeals Panel Secretariat, Government Buildings, Spa Rd East, Llandrindod Wells, Powys LD1 5HA Tel: (01597) 828226 Fax: (01597) 828304.
Total 20. Appointed by Welsh Government's Minister for Rural Affairs. To hear Stage 2 Appeals under the two-stage Independent Appeals Process for Farmers and Foresters in Wales and to make a recommendation to the Deputy Minister for Agriculture, Food, Fisheries and European Programmes based on their findings.

Members Wales	Occupation	Remuneration	Commitment	Term of Office
Elenor Bonner-Evans	Farmer & Lawyer	£250 per day	As required	Until 31/03/2014
W Roy Davies	Retired agri advisor	£250 per day	As required	Until 20/11/2014
D Rhodri W Evans	Farmer & Councilor	£250 per day	As required	Until 31/03/2014
Peter W Francis	Farmer	£250 per day	As required	Until 20/11/2014
David F R George	Farmer	£250 per day	As required	Until 20/11/2014
Fiona M Hillman	Farmer	£250 per day	As required	Until 31/03/2014
T Christopher B Horne	Retired agri advisor	£250 per day	As required	Until 20/11/2014
William J P Jenkins	Farmer	£250 per day	As required	Until 20/11/2014
Aled R Jones	Chartered Surveyor	£250 per day	As required	Until 31/03/2014
E Alice Jones	Councillor	£250 per day	As required	Until 20/11/2014

Independent Appeals Panel for Farmers in Wales (cont.)

David J Jones	Farmer	£250 per day	As required	Until 20/11/2014
G Emyr Jones	Farmer	£250 per day	As required	Until 31/03/2014
W J Gareth Jones	Farmer	£250 per day	As required	Until 20/11/2014
Judith M Jones	Farmer	£250 per day	As required	Until 31/03/2014
Gareth J Lloyd	Chartered Surveyor	£250 per day	As required	Until 20/11/2014
David O J S Lort-Phillips	Farmer	£250 per day	As required	Until 20/11/2014
Dafydd O Owen	Farmer & Better Organic Business Links Project Manager	£250 per day	As required	Until 31/03/2014
Robert G Parry	Farmer & Councilor	£250 per day	As required	Until 20/11/2014
David F C Peace	Independent Business Consultant	£250 per day	As required	Until 31/03/2014
Gillian Preece	Farmer & Independent Agricultural Consultant	£250 per day	As required	Until 31/03/2014
Gwyn O Thomas	Farmer	£250 per day	As required	Until 20/11/2014
Margaret A Watson	Farmer & retired Civil Servant	£250 per day	As required	Until 31/03/2014
Roderick A Williams	Farmer & retired Agri advisor	£250 per day	As required	Until 20/11/2014

Independent Groundwater Complaints Administrator for the Cardiff Bay Barrage Groundwater Protection Scheme

"Greenbower", Dukestown Road, Tredegar, Gwent Tel: (01495) 711161
Total 1. Appointed by Welsh Ministers. To consider and determine any complaints made in relation to the way Cardiff City Council operates the Groundwater Protection Scheme.

Member	Occupation	Remuneration	Commitment	Term of office
Ralph James	Complaints Administrator	Fixed allowance of £2,000 pa	As required	Until 2019

Independent Remuneration Panel for Wales

Secretariat, Independent Remuneration Panel for Wales, 1st Floor,North Wing M05, Crown Buildings, Cathays Park, Cardiff CF10 3NQ Tel: (029) 2080 1047 Fax: (029) 2082 5346
Email: irpmailbox@wales.gsi.gov.uk Website: www.remunerationpanelwales.org.uk

Established in 2008 by the then Welsh Government Minister for Social Justice and Local Government following a public appointments exercise. In 2012,the following were reappointed by the Welsh Government Minister for Local Government and Communities for a term of one year.

To make determinations on the range level of allowances to be paid to Councillors and certain co-opted members of County and County Borough Councils, National Park Authorities, Fire and Rescue Authorities and Community & Town Councils in Wales each year.

Chair	Occupation	Remuneration	Commitment	Term of Office
Richard Penn	Former NAfW Commissioner for Standards & Former Local Authority Chief Exec	£256 per day	2 days per mth	08-12
Members				
John Bader	Retired Civil Servant	£198 per day	2 days per mth	08-12
Dr Declan Hall	Former Academic; Currently Independent Consultant specialising in Member roles, development, support & remuneration.	£198 per day	2 days per mth	08-12
Gareth Newton	Retired Local Govt Officer	£198 per day	2 days per mth	08-12

Joint Nature Conservation Committee

Joint Nature Conservation Committee, Monkstone House, City Rd, Peterborough PE1 1JY
Tel: (01733) 562626 Fax: (01733) 555948 Website: www.jncc.gov.uk Email: reception@jncc.gov.uk
Total 14. Chair and 5 members appointed jointly by Welsh Government / Sec State Wales, Sec State Scotland, Sec State Environment, Transport & Regions and 7 ex-officio and 2 non-voting members.

Chair	Occupation	Remuneration	Commitment	Term of office
Prof Michael Kaiser	Law Zoology	£9,836 pa	2.5 days per month	09-11
David Pritchard	International Conservationist	£13,771 pa	3.5 days per month	11-12
Judith Webb	Conservationist	£9,836 pa	2.5 days per month	12-12
Dr Bob Brown	Conservationist	£9,836 pa	2.5 days per month	12-12
Guy Duke	Conservationist	£9,836 pa	2.5 days per month	12-12

OTHER PUBLIC APPOINTMENTS

Local Government Boundary Commission for Wales

1st Floor, Caradog House, 1-6 St. Andrews Place, Cardiff CF10 3BE Tel: (029) 2039 5031
Fax: (029) 2039 5250 Email: lgbc.wales@wales.gsi.gov.uk Website: www.lgbc-wales.gov.uk
Established in 1974 under the Local Government Act 1972. To keep under review all local government areas in Wales and their electoral arrangements and to make proposals to the Welsh Government as necessary.

Chair	Occupation	Remuneration	Commitment	Term of office
Owen Watkin	Former Local Authority Chief Executive	£269 per day	Up to 4 days per month	12-15
Member				
Ceri Stradling	Retired Auditor	£198 per day	Up to 4 days per month	12-15
David Powell		£198 per day	Up to 4 days per month	12-15

National Assembly Remuneration Board

Clerk of the Remuneration Board, National Assembly for Wales, Cardiff Bay CF99 1NA
Email: Remuneration@wales.gov.uk
A statutory independent body with responsibility for deciding and monitoring the level of salaries and other financial support for Assembly Members, including allowances for travel, pensions and office support. The Board will ensure that Assembly Members receive a level of remuneration which fairly reflects the complexity and importance of their duties and provides them with adequate resources to exercise their functions as Assembly Members. The Board will also ensure and be able to demonstrate probity, accountability, value for money and transparency in the expenditure of public funds.

Chair	Occupation	Remuneration	Term of office
Rt Hon George Reid	Scottish politician, journalist & academic	£243	Until 2015
Member			
Prof Monojit Chatterj	Chair, National Joint Council of UK Fire & Emergency Services	£185	Until 2015
Stuart Castledine	Chartered Accountant	£185	Until 2015
Mary Carter	Member Armed Forces Pay Review Body	£185	Until 2015
Sandy Blair CBE	Former Director WLGA	£185	Until 2015

National Partnership Forum for Older People in Wales

Welsh Government, OPLTCP4, Cathay's Park, Cardiff CF10 3NQ Tel: (029) 2082 3454
Fax: (029) 2082 3924 Email: christopher.pickett@wales.gsi.gov.uk Website: www.npfforolderpeople.net
To provide independent expert and informed advice to the Welsh Government on the development of its policies for older people. Total 18. Appointed by the Welsh Government.

Chair	Occupation	Remuneration	Commitment
Wendy Bourton OBE	Former CEO Care & Repair Cymru	£249 per day	2 days per month
Vice Chair			
Annie Williams	Principal Coleg Harlech	expenses	Min 6 days pa
Lay Members			
Clive Owen	Former County Councillor, Older People's Champion, NPT CBC	expenses	Min 6 days pa
Members Wales			
Gaynor Davies	COPA		Min 6 days pa
Pat Charles	COPA		Min 6 days pa
William Ellis Jones	COPA		Min 6 days pa
Barry Jones	COPA		Min 6 days pa
Nominated Members			
Older People's Organizations Sector			
Nancy Davies	Retired Teacher	expenses	Min 6 days pa
Judith Phillips	OPAN		
Margaret Morgan	Welsh Senate of Older People		
Phyllis Preece	Pensioner Forum South Wales		
Norma Glass	OMEN		
John Davies	National OAP Association		
Andrew Jacobs	Digital Inclusion		

National Partnership Forum for Older People in Wales (cont.)

Local Government
Beverlea Frowen   WLGA

Care Sector
Mario Kreft MBE   Care Home Proprietor & Chief Exec, Care Forum Wales   expenses   Min 6 days pa

Education Sector
Lorraine Morgan   Academic Manager (Health & Nursing) OU   expenses   Mid 6 days pa

Mental Health
Andrea Matthews   Community Health Wales

Housing Sector
John Puzey   Housing Alliance

Voluntary Organsiations Sector
Alan Hatton Yeo   Beth Johnson Foundation
Rob Taylor   Age Cymru
Andrew Hinchcliff   LGBT
Jim Crowe   LDW
Rhian Davies   Disability Wales
Rachel Penman   Funky Dragon
Matthew Walker   Funky Dragon
Angela Roberts   Carers Alliance Wales & Acting Chair for Age Alliance Wales

Transport Sector
Alan Kreppel   Sustrans

Employment Sector
Terry Mills   Former Chief Executive, PRIME Cymru   expenses   Min 6 days pa

Research
Prof Vanessa Burholt   Prof Gerontology & Director, Centre of   expenses   Min 6 days pa
      Innovative Ageing, Swansea University
Hilda Smith   Until October 2012
Tom Moran   Until October 2012
Royston Orringe   Until October 2012
Pradeep Khanna   Until October 2012
Brian Bigwood   Until October 2012

NHS National Delivery Group

Repa Antonio, Deputy Head of the Department of Health and Social Services, Government Business Team
E-mail DHSSCBriefingsandMeeting@wales.gsi.gov.uk
The National Delivery Group, forming part of the Welsh Government's Health and Social Services
Directorate General (HSSDG), is responsible for providing strategic leadership and management of the NHS.
Chaired by the Chief Executive, NHS Wales, it provides policy advice to the Minister and oversees the
development and delivery of NHS services across Wales, in accordance with the direction set by the
Minister. The Group is also responsible for planning and performance management of the NHS on behalf
of Welsh Ministers.

Members	*Occupation*
David Sissling	Chair- Director General/ Chief Executive NHS Wales
Internal WG members	
Tony Jewell	Chief Medical Officer
Robert Pickford	Director of Social Services
Gwyn Thomas	Chief Information Officer
Jean White	Chief Nursing Officer
Chris Jones	Medical Director
Jo Jordan	Director of Corporate Services & Partnerships
Neil Wooding	Director of Workforce & OD
Alan Brace	Finance Director
Richard Bowen	Director of Operations
Abigail Harris	Director of Strategy & Policy
External/Independent Members	
John Collins	Independent
Peter Marx	Independent
Zoe Harcombe	Independent

Passenger Focus

7th Floor, Piccadilly Gate, Manchester M1 2WD Tel: (0300) 123 2140
Email: info@passengerfocus.org.uk Website: www.passengerfocus.org.uk
Total 9. Chair and 8 members including 1 member appointed by National Assembly for Wales, 1 member by Scottish Executive, and 1 member by London Assembly. Up to 14 members may be appointed by Sec State for Transport. An independent public body tasked with protecting the interests of Britain's rail passengers. The board is responsible for setting the strategic direction and main policies of the organization, and providing corporate governance and oversight of the finances and operations.

Members Wales	Occupation	Remuneration	Commitment	Term of office
Stella Mair Thomas	Media, Communication, Transport & Consumer Affairs Consultant	£16,494 pa	Up to 6 days per month	06-13

Public Transport Users' Committee

Public Transport Users' Committee for Wales Secretariat, Welsh Government, Cathays Park, Cardiff CF10 3NQ
Email: ptucwales@wales.gsi.gov.uk
The Public Transport Users Committee for Wales is an advisory committee responsible for providing advice to Welsh Ministers about strategic issues relating to public transport services in Wales.

Members

Adele Baumgardt – Chair	Christine Court
Graham Walter	Dan Butler
Elly Foster	Greg Pycroft
Steve Hale	Ted Sangster
Chris Yewlett	John Ablitt
Stella Mair Thomas	David Groves

Public Service Leadership Group

Contact: Bethan Boyd Tel: (029) 2082 3366
The key responsibilities of the PSLG are ensuring coherence in the implementation of overall public service reform agenda in Wales, including oversight of the implementation of the Compact and building coherence with the reforms in education, social services, health and other areas; sponsorship and mandating of national action to improve the effectiveness and efficiency of public services; and the development of effective regional leadership for collaboration, building on existing regional leadership structures and the Welsh Government's geographical footprint for regional collaboration.

Chair	Occupation
Carl Sargeant AM	Minister for Local Government & Communities

Member	
June Milligan	Director General, Local Government & Communities
Emyr Roberts	Director General, Education and Skills
David Sissling	Director General, Health, Social Services & Children
Michael Hearty	Director General, Strategic Planning, Finance & Performance
Jack Straw	Swansea City Council
Tracey Lee	Newport City Council
Andrew Goodall	Aneurin Bevan Health Board
Mary Burrows	Betsi Cadwaladr Health Board
Mark James	Carmarthenshire County Council
Steve Phillips	Neath Port Talbot Council

Qualifications Review Project Board

Kate Crabtree / Tamlyn Rabey, Welsh Government, Qualifications & Learning Division,
Department for Education and Skills (DfES), Ty'r Afon, Bedwas Road, Bedwas CF83 8WT
E-mail: ReviewofQuals@wales.gsi.gov.uk Contact number: (01443) 663968
The role of the Board will be to provide advice to Ministers on how to ensure Wales has qualifications that are valued and understood and meet the needs of our young people and the Welsh economy.

Chair	Occupation
Huw Evans	Principal of Coleg Llandrillo

Member	
John Hughes	Vice-Chancellor of Bangor University & Chair of Higher Education Wales
Nick Bennett	Principal of Gower College, Swansea
Jackie Pearson	Mill Controller at UPM Shotton

Qualifications Review Project Board (cont.)

Roger Evans	Plant Director at Schaeffler (UK) Ltd
Ann Evans	Chief Executive of Careers Wales Mid Glamorgan & Powys
Katherine Davies	Headteacher of Ysgol Gyfun Gwyr, Swansea
Arwyn Watkins	Chair of National Training Federation for Wales (NTfW) and Managing Director of Cambrian Training Company
Michael Griffiths	Former Headteacher of Cardiff High School
Kate Crabtree	Deputy Director, Further Education Division, Welsh Government
Jo-Anne Daniels	Deputy Director, Curriculum Division, Welsh Government
Andrew Clark	Deputy Director, Further Education Division, Welsh Government
Cassy Taylor	Head of General Qualifications Monitoring, Qualifications & Learning Division, Welsh Government

Residential Property Tribunal

Residential Property Tribunal, First Floor, West Wing, Southgate House, Wood St, Cardiff CF10 1EW

Tel: (029) 2092 2777 Fax: (029) 2023 6146 Email: rpt@wales.gsi.gov.uk Total 37. 15 professional and 11 lay members appointed by WAG. President, Vice-President and 9 Chairs appointed by Lord Chancellor.

President	Occupation	Remuneration	Commitment	Term of office
Andrew D Morris	Solicitor	£38,410 pa	2 days per week	09-13
Vice President				
David R Davies FRICS	Surveyor	£18,162 pa	1 day per week	09-13
Chairpersons				
D J Evans (Dinas Powys)	Solicitor	£405 per day	As required	09-14
J D M Jones (Mold)	Solicitor	£405 per day	As required	09-13
Mrs A V S Lobley (Gloucester)	Solicitor	£405 per day	As required	08-13
E W Paton (Bridgend)	Barrister	£405 per day	As required	08-13
R J Payne (Bristol)	Solicitor	£405 per day	As required	08-13
S A Povey (Carmarthen)	Solicitor	£405 per day	As required	08-13
Jack Rostron (Southport, Merseyside)	Lawyer	£405 per day	As required	09-14
R S Taylor (Penarth)	Barrister	£405 per day	As required	08-13
P H Williams (Llansov, Usk)	Solicitor	£405 per day	As required	09-13
Professional Members Wales				
Thomas A Daulby (Abergele, Clwyd Denbighshire)	Chartered Surveyor	£288 per day	As required	09-13
B G R Davies (Cowbridge, Vale of Glamorgan)	Chartered Surveyor	£288 per day	As required	09-13
Roger B Griffiths (Mold, Flintshire)	Chartered Surveyor	£288 per day	As required	04-13
N F G Hill (Chepstow, Monmouthshire)	Chartered Surveyor	£288 per day	As required	09-13
Harold Michael Abraham (Neath, Port Talbot)	Surveyor	£288 per day	As required	12-17
Roger William Baynham (Barry)	Surveyor	£288 per day	As required	12-13
David Oliver Evans (Aberystwyth)	Surveyor	£288 per day	As required	12-17
Paul Knight Lucas (Haverfordwest, Pembrokeshire)	Chartered Surveyor	£288 per day	As required	09-13
J Singleton (Fordingbridge)	Chartered Surveyor	£288 per day	As required	09-13
David Allan Tillman (Llanelli)	Surveyor	£288 per day	As required	12-17
Ruth E Thomas (Swansea)3	Chartered Surveyor	£288 per day	As required	09-13
Ceri Trotman-Jones (Bonvilston)	Surveyor	£288 per day	As required	09-13
Colin Hanson Williams (Colwyn Bay)	Surveyor	£288 per day	As required	12-17

Residential Property Tribunal (cont.)

Elfed R Williams (Holyhead, Ynys Môn)	Chartered Surveyor	£288 per day	As required	09-13
Lay Members Wales				
Angie Ash (Usk)	Consultant	£187 per day	As required	12-17
Christine EM Borland (Swansea)	Housewife	£187 per day	As required	09-13
Bill Brereton (Nercwys)	Retired	£187 per day	As required	12-17
Carole Calvin-Thomas (Cardiff)	Housewife	£187 per day	As required	09-13
David James Francis (Cardiff)	Retired	£187 per day	As required	12-17
Wilma Hainsworth (Swansea)	Retired	£187 per day	As required	12-17
H E Jones (Ynys Môn)	Retired	£187 per day	As required	12-17
Marilyn A Mason (Haverfordwest, Pembrokeshire)	Retired	£187 per day	As required	09-13
Juliet Playfair (Maesteg, Mid Glamorgan)	Housewife	£187 per day	As required	09-13
G E Pritchard (Carmarthen)	Retired	£187 per day	As required	12-17
K D E Watkins (Newport)	Retired	£187 per day	As required	09-13

Science Advisory Council for Wales

To report and provide advice to the Chief Scientific Adviser for Wales on a full range of science, technology, engineering and mathematics issues. Appointed by the Chief Scientific Adviser for Wales.

Chair	Occupation	Remuneration	Commitment	Term of Office
Prof John Harries	Chief Scientific Advisor for Wales	Nil	4 days pa	10-
Independent Co Chair				
Prof Chris Pollock	Honorary Research Professor, Aberystywth University	Nil	4 days pa	10-
Members				
Prof Huw Beynon	Cardiff University (retired)	Nil	4 days pa	10-
Prof Simon Bradley	Head of Global Innovation Network, Office of CTO,EADS	Nil	4 days pa	10-
Kevin Bygate	Director Business Development Tata Steel UK Ltd	Nil	4 days pa	10-
Prof Bridget Emmett	Centre for Ecology & Hydrology, Bangor	Nil	4 days pa	10-
Prof Sir Martin Evans	Nobel Laureate President, Cardiff University	Nil	4 days pa	10-
Prof Chris Gaskell	Principal, Royal Agricultural College, Cirencester	Nil	4 days pa	10-
Prof Sian Hope	Director, RIVIC, Bangor University	Nil	4 days pa	10-
Rebecca Villis	Head, Innovation Policy, Intellectual Property Office, Newport	Nil	4 days pa	10-
D John Jeans	Dep Chief Exec & Chief Operating Officer-Medical Research Council	Nil	4 days pa	10-
Prof Tavi Murray	Head, Glaciology Group, Swansea University	Nil	4 days pa	10-
Prof Ole H Petersen CBE	Director, School of Bioscience, Cardiff University	Nil	4 days pa	10-
Wendy Sadler	Director, Science Made Simple c/o Cardiff University	Nil	4 days pa	10-
Prof John Meurig Thomas	Cambridge University	Nil	4 days pa	10-
Prof Ken Walters	Distinguished Research Professor, Aberystwyth University	Nil	4 days pa	10-
Prof Robin Williams CBE	Emeritus Professor, Swansea University	Nil	4 days pa	10-

Sea Fish Industry Authority

Sea Fish Industry Authority, 18 Logie Mill, Logie Green Rd, Edinburgh EH7 4HS
Tel: (0131) 558 3331 Fax: (0131) 558 1442 Website: www.seafish.org
Sea Fish Industry Authority, Origin Way, Europarc, Grimsby DN37 9TZ Tel: (01472) 252300
Total 12. Chair, Deputy Chair. 4 independent members appointed jointly by Fisheries Minister
Wales/Scotland/Northern Ireland/England, and 8 members nominated by industry.

Member	Occupation	Remuneration	Commitment	Term of office
Prof M Kaiser	Academic	£5,670	1.5 days per month	11-14
James Wilson	Aquaculture	£5,670	1.5 days per month	11-14

Special Educational Needs Tribunal for Wales

Unit 32, Ddole Rd Enterprise Park, Llandrindod Wells, Powys LD1 6DF Tel: (01597) 829800
Fax: (01597) 829801 Email: tribunalenquiries@wales.gsi.gov.uk Website: www.sentw.gov.uk
Legal Members Appointed by Lord Chancellor. Lay Members Appointed by Welsh Ministers.

President	Occupation	Remuneration	Commitment	Term of Office
Rhiannon Ellis Walker	Deputy District Judge	£560 per day	50 days pa	5yrs (renewable)
Chairperson				
Mark Allen	Barrister	£459.00 per day	15 days pa	5yrs (renewable)
Jacqueline Blackmore	Solicitor	£459.00 per day	15 days pa	5yrs (renewable)
Gwyn Davies	Solicitor	£459.00 per day	15 days pa	5yrs (renewable)
Meleri Tudur	Tribunal Judge	Travel and Subsistence only	15 days pa	5yrs (renewable)
Lay Members				
Richard Elis Owen	Educational psychologist	£233.50 per day	15 days pa	5yrs (renewable)
Catrin Mair Lewis	Educational psychologist	£233.50 per day	15 days pa	5yrs (renewable)
Dr Hilary Hayward	Educational psychologist	£233.50 per day	15 days pa	5yrs (renewable)
Sandra Boyle	Retired	£233.50 per day	15 days pa	5yrs (renewable)
Norman Donovan	Retired	£233.50 per day	15 days pa	5yrs (renewable)
Gwyn Griffiths	Retired	£233.50 per day	15 days pa	5yrs (renewable)
Dr Gareth Roberts	Deputy Headteacher	£233.50 per day	15 days pa	5yrs (renewable)
Dr Sian Wyn Siencyn	Head of the School of Early Childhood Trinity University College	£233.50 per day	15 days pa	5yrs (renewable)
Susan Taylor	Retired	£233.50 per day	15 days pa	5yrs (renewable)
Andrew Wilson	Senior Local Authority Officer Additional Learning Needs	£233.50 per day	15 days pa	5yrs (renewable)

Tackling Poverty External Advisory Group

Welsh Government, Rhyd y Car, Merthyr Tydfil CF48 1UZ Tel: (0300) 062 8097
Members Current Total: 6 - All appointed by Welsh Government.

Member	Occupation	Area of Expertise	Term of Appointment	Remuneration	Commitment
Fran Targett	Director	Welfare Rights & Advice	01/05/12 - 01/05/16	Travel Expenses	4 days pa
Stephen Doughty	Head of Oxfam Cymru	Generic Poverty	01/05/12 - 01/05/16	Travel Expenses	4 days pa
Sean O'Neill	Policy Director	Child Poverty	01/05/12 - 01/05/16	Travel Expenses	4 days pa
John Puzey	Director	Housing	01/05/12 - 01/05/16	Travel Expenses	4 days pa
Malcolm Fisk	Co-Director	Older People	01/05/12 - 01/05/16	Travel Expenses	4 days pa
David Egan	Senior Policy Adviser	Education	01/05/12 - 01/05/16	Travel Expenses	4 days pa

Tenant Advisory Panel

Email: tapwales@welshtenantsfed.org.uk Tel: (01685) 723922
The Tenant Advisory Panel consists of housing association tenants from around Wales who all have
knowledge in the housing sector and are able to represent other tenants. They are working to develop
networks; find more ways to engage with all tenants and to provide a voice for those who find it difficult
to be heard. TAP members will then discuss all tenant views and consider the key issues before presenting
them to the Regulatory Board Wales for assessment.

Members

Christine Kemp-Philp
Doug Illing
Gail McFee
Steve Thrupp
James Rides

Lynn Wilkinson-Owen
Lyn Bond
Mike Wiseman
Pip Williams

Upland Forum

Upland Forum Secretariat, Agriculture, Fisheries and Rural Strategy Division, Welsh Government, Rhodfa Padarn, Llanbadarn Fawr, Aberystwyth, Ceredigion SY23 3UR Tel: (0300) 062 2161 Total 13. Appointed by Deputy Minister for Agriculture, Food, Fisheries and European Programmes.

Associate Chair	Occupation	Remuneration	Commitment	Term of office
Derek Morgan	Farmer	Nil	5/6 days pa	11-13
Members Wales				
Edmund Bailey	Farmer	Nil	5/6 days pa	11-13
Lorraine Howells	Farmer	Nil	5/6 days pa	11-13
William Jenkins	Farmer	Nil	5/6 days pa	11-13
Dr Ieuan Joyce	Farmer	Nil	5/6 days pa	11-13
Aled Rees	Farmer, Hotelier	Nil	5/6 days pa	11-13
Dr Liz Bickerton	Rural Consultant	Nil	5/6 days pa	11-13

Violence Against Women & Domestic Abuse Implementation Board

Contact: Sarah King; Tel: 0300 062 8053
The primary purpose of the Violence against Women and Domestic Abuse Implementation Board is to assist the Welsh Government to implement their six year integrated strategy for tackling all forms of violence against women.

Members
Deputy Director – Community Safety Division
Head of the Violence Against Women & Domestic Abuse team
Dept for Health, Social Services & Children
National Offender Management Service
Society of Local Authority Chief Executives & Senior Managers (SOLACE)
Association of Chief Police Officers in Wales
Victim Support Service
Association of Directors of Social Services
National Society for the Protection of Cruelty to Children (NSPCC)
Welsh Women's Aid
Hafan Cymru
Wales Probation Trust
Welsh Local Government Association
Ministry of Justice
Home Office Wales
Black Association of Women Step Out (BAWSO)
CAFCASS Cymru
Gwent Police
Professor Jonathan Shepherd, Cardiff University (advisory member)

Wales Resilience Forum

Wyn Price Tel: (029) 2082 3872
Aims to promote good communication and the enhancement of resilience across agencies and services in Wales by providing a forum for Chief Officers to discuss with Welsh Ministers strategic issues of emergency preparedness.

Members
First Minister for Wales
Minister for Local Government & Communities
Chief Executive, Welsh Local Government Association
Council Leader, Welsh Local Government Association
Society of Local Authority Chief Executives and Senior Managers (SOLACE)
Chief Fire Officer (representing the three Fire Brigades)
Chief Constable (representing the four Police Forces & the four LRF Chairs)
Chief Executive, Wales Ambulance Services Trust
Director-General, Local Government & Communities, Welsh Government
Chief Medical Officer, Welsh Government
Public Health Wales
Chief Scientific Adviser, Welsh Government
Chief Veterinary Officer, Welsh Government
Commander 160 (Wales) Brigade
Naval Regional Commander (Wales & Western England)

Wales Resilience Forum (cont.)

Air Officer Wales
Director, Environment Agency Wales
Civil Contingencies Co-ordinator, Maritime and Coastguard Agency
Cabinet Office, Civil Contingencies Secretariat
Regional Manager, HSE
Director of Communications, Welsh Government
Deputy Head, Community Safety Division, Welsh Government

Wales Youth Justice Advisory Panel

Sarah Cooper Tel: (0300) 062 8629. To assist the Welsh Government and the Youth Justice Board in the implement of policy that prevents offending and reoffending by children and young people in Wales.

Members

Deputy Director – Community Safety Division

Representatives from the Youth Justice Board (YJB) including:
  Head of YJB Wales
  YJB Board member for Wales

Chief Executive – YJB for England & Wales
Head of Youth Justice Policy Branch, Welsh Government

Representatives of the following areas:
  Association of Chief Police Officers in Wales

National Offender Management Service
Welsh Local Government Association
Society of Local Authority Chief Executives & Senior Managers (SOLACE)
Health
Association of Directors of Education Wales
Association of Directors of Social Services
National Association for the Care & Resettlement of Offenders (NACRO)
Wales probation trust
YOT Managers Cymru
Youth Magistrates in Wales
Her Majesty's Courts & Tribunals Service
Welsh Centre for Crime & Social Justice
Prosecution Service

Welsh Committee of the Administrative Justice & Tribunals Council

Administrative Justice & Tribunals Council, 1st Floor, 81 Chancery Lane, London WC2A 1BQ
Tel: (020) 7855 5200 Fax: (020) 7855 5201 Email: enquiries@ajtc.gsi.gov.uk Website: www.ajtc.gov.uk
1 member appointed by Welsh Ministers with the concurrence of the Lord Chancellor and Scottish Ministers plus a further 3 members appointed solely by Welsh Members.
The Welsh Committee takes the lead in overseeing administrative justice, tribunals and inquiries in Wales, including the working in Wales of tribunals which also sit in other parts of the UK, as well as tribunals which operate only in Wales.

Chair	Occupation	Remuneration	Commitment	Term of office
Sir Adrian Webb	Former Vice-Chancellor	£28,025	65 days pa	5 years
Members				
Bob Chapman	Management Consultant	£6,408	22 days pa	5 years
Gareth Lewis	Director	£6,408	22 days pa	5 years
Rhian Williams-Flew	Mental Health Nurse	£6,408	22 days pa	5 years

Welsh Dental Committee

HPG, Welsh Government, Cathays Park, Cardiff, CF10 3NQ
Tel: (029) 2082 3446 Website: cmo.wales.gov.uk
To advise the Welsh Government on the provision of dental services in Wales and to consider and comment or advise on any matter referred to it by Welsh Government. Committee meets three times a year. Members are not appointed by Welsh Government.

Chair	Occupation	Remuneration	Commitment
Karl Bishop	Consultant in Restorative Dentistry & Oral Rehabilitation	Nil	3 days pa
Members			
Warren Tolley	Powys Dental Services Advisory Group	Nil	3 days pa

Welsh Dental Committee (cont.)

Hugh Bennett	Public Health Wales	Nil	3 days pa
Mark Robotham	Gwent Local Dental Committee	Nil	3 days pa
Paul Bartley	Bro Taf Local Dental Committee	Nil	3 days pa
David Westcott	Morgannwg Local Dental Committee	Nil	3 days pa
Mick Horton	North Wales Local Dental Committee	Nil	3 days pa
Dr Ian Jones	Dyfed Powys Local Dental Committee	Nil	3 days pa
Dr Robert Shaw	North Wales Dental Advisory Forum	Nil	3 days pa
Dr Will McLaughlin	Cardiff & Vale Oral Health Advisory Group	Nil	3 days pa
Prof Nick Moran	Cwm Taf Oral Health Strategy Group	Nil	3 days pa
Mary Dodd	Hywel Dda Dental Services Group	Nil	3 days pa
Simon Hodder	ABMU Dental Strategy Group	Nil	3 days pa
Anup Karki	Aneurin Bevan Oral Health Advisory Group	Nil	3 days pa
Prof Jonathan Cowpe	Director of Postgraduate Education	Nil	3 days pa
Prof Mike Lewis	Dental School, UWCM	Nil	3 days pa
Gareth Lloyd	Wales General Dental Practitioner Committee	Nil	3 days pa
Ken Hughes	Wales Committee for Community Dentistry	Nil	3 days pa
Sue Greening	British Dental Association (Wales)	Nil	3 days pa
Kirstie Moons	Dental Care Professionals	Nil	3 days pa
Stuart Geddes	Director British Dental Association (Wales)	Nil	3 days pa
Dr Ann Rockey	Dental School	Nil	3 days pa

Welsh Industrial Development Advisory Board

Invest Wales, Department for the Economy & Transport, QED Centre, Main Avenue, Treforest, Pontypridd CF37 5YR Tel: (01443) 845729 Fax: (01443) 845869 Email: lisa.roberts-clarke@wales.gsi.gov.uk
Website: www.wales.gov.uk

Total 5. Appointed by Welsh Ministers. The Welsh Industrial Development Advisory Board is a Welsh Government sponsored body established under section 13 of the Welsh Development Agency Act 1975. Since April 2006, the board has also provided advice through section 41 of the Government of Wales Act 1998 on applications of £500,000 and over.

Chair	Occupation	Remuneration	Commitment	Term of office
Valerie Barrett	Controller Management Reporting Rockwool Ltd	£256 per day	24 days pa (approx)	05-14
Members				
Kerry Diamond	Chief Financial Officer, Zytek Group Ltd	£198 per day	24 days pa (approx)	03-15
Daniel Fellows OBE DL	Retired Regional Industrial Organizer T&GWU	£198 per day	24 days pa (approx)	10-12
David Williams	Retired Bank Director	£198 per day	24 days pa (approx)	03-15
Alan Proctor	Non-executive Director, National Metrology Office	£198 per day	24 days pa (approx)	10-19

Welsh Marine Fisheries Advisory Group

Secratariat, Fisheries Unit, Agriculture, Fisheries and Rural Strategy (AFRS) Llywodraeth Cymru - Welsh Government, Rhoddfa Padarn, Aberystwyth, SY23 3UR Tel: (0300) 062 2204

Appointed by Welsh Government Minister for Rural Affairs, following a public appointments exercise. Directly advise the Welsh Government Fisheries Unit and Welsh Ministers on national policy, strategic direction and the development of action plans and legislation

Chair	Occupation	Period	Remuneration
Nicholas O'Sullivan	Charter Boats UK	1 year	£6144 pa plus (travel and subsistence) expenses based on a commitment of 2 days work per month.

Welsh Medical Committee

Health Protection Group - Committee secretariat, Welsh Government, Cathays Park
Cardiff CF10 3NQ Tel: (029) 2082 3121 Fax: (029) 2082 3430

To advise the Welsh Government on the provision of Medical Services in Wales and to consider and comment or advise on any matter referred to it by the Assembly.

Chair	Occupation	Remuneration	Commitment	Term of office
Dr Akram Baig	General Practitioner	Nil	4 days pa	06-
Vice Chair				
Dr David Leopold	Abertawe Bro Morgannwg Medical Advisory Group	Nil	4 days pa	10-

Welsh Medical Committee (cont.)

Members

Dr Ian Millington	General Practitioner	Nil	4 days pa	10-
Dr Tom Williams	Aneurin Bevan Medical Advisory Group	Nil	4 days pa	11-
Dr Susan Fairweather	General Practitioner	Nil	4 days pa	10-
Dr Sam Abraham	North Wales Medical Advisory Group	Nil	4 days pa	07-
Dr Richard Penketh	Cardiff & Vale Medical Advisory Group	Nil	4 days pa	10-
Dr Keith Myers	Cwm Taf Medical Advisory Group	Nil	4 days pa	10-
Dr Bill Harris	Cwm Taf Medical Advisory Group	Nil	4 days pa	10-
Dr Asheesh Vaishnavi	Hywel Dda Medical Advisory Group	Nil	4 days pa	12-
Dr Dylan Williams	Hywel Dda Medical Advisory Group	Nil	4 days pa	12-
Dr Alisa Dunn	Mid Wales Medical Advisory Group	Nil	4 days pa	10-
Dr Paul Metcalfe	General Practitioner	Nil	4 days pa	10-
Dr Michael Thomas	Consultant, Public Health Medicine	Nil	4 days pa	10-
Dr Maryisa Hamilton-Kirkwood	Consultant, Public Health Medicine	Nil	4 days pa	10-
Prof Peter Stevenson	Public Health North Wales	Nil	4 days pa	10-

Welsh Nursing & Midwifery Committee

Health Professionals Group, Cathays Park, Cardiff CF10 3NQ
Tel: (029) 2082 3446 Website: www.cmo.wales.gov.uk
To advise the Welsh Government on the provision of Nursing and Midwifery services in Wales and to consider and comment or advise on any matter referred to it by WG. Committee meets three times a year. Members are not appointed by Welsh Government.

Chair	Occupation	Remuneration	Commitment	Term of Office
Jill Patterson	Hywel Dda LHB Professional Forum	Nil	3 days pa	06-
Chair since 09				
Members				
Lesley Jenkins	Hywel Dda LH Professional Forum	Nil	3 days pa	11-
Lesley Lewis	Cwm Taf LH Professional Forum	Nil	3 days pa	09-
Amanda Cassidy	Cwm Taf LHB Professional Forum	Nil	3 days pa	11-
Alex Scott	Cardiff & Vale LH Professional Forum	Nil	3 days pa	11-
Mary Coakley	Cardiff & Vale LH Professional Forum	Nil	3 days pa	11-
Lorna Burdge	Betsi Cadwaladr LH Professional Forum	Nil	3 days pa	06-
Lynne Grundy	Betsi Cadwaladr LH Professional Forum	Nil	3 days pa	08-
Tanya Spriggs	Aneurin Bevan LH Professional Forum	Nil	3 days pa	11-
Louise Taylor	Aneurin Bevan LH Professional Forum	Nil	3 days pa	11-
Cathy Dowling	Abertawe Bro Morgannwyg LH Professional Forum	Nil	3 days pa	11-
Cheryl Evans	Abertawe Bro Morgannwyg LH Professional Forum	Nil	3 days pa	11-
Prof Donna Mead	CYNGOR	Nil	3 days pa	11-
Denise Shanahan	All Wales Consultant Nursing & Midwifery Group	Nil	3 days pa	11-
Bev Thomas	NHS Wales Informatics Service	Nil	3 days pa	08-
Tba	Powys LH Professional Forum	Nil	3 days pa	
Tba	Powys LH Professional Forum	Nil	3 days pa	

Welsh Optometric Committee

Welsh Government, Cathays Park, Cardiff CF10 3NQ Tel: (029) 2080 1453   Fax: (029) 2082 3430
To advise the Welsh Assembly Government on the provision of Optical Services in Wales and to consider and comment or advise on any matter referred to it by the Assembly.

Chair	Occupation	Remuneration	Commitment	Term of office
Ian Jones	Optometrist	Nil	3 days pa	03-
Vice Chair				
Alton Murphy	Practising Optician	Nil	3 days pa	03-
Members				
Brian Allport	Practising Optician	Nil	3 days pa	03-
Ben Cope	Practising Optician	Nil	3 days pa	00-
Huw Davies	Hospital Optometrist	Nil	3 days pa	Continuous
Fred Giltrow-Taylor	Dept of Optometry, Bristol Eye Hospital	Nil	3 days pa	03-

Welsh Optometric Committee (cont)

Paul Harries	Practising Optician	Nil	3 days pa	03-
Dick Roberts	Optometric Adviser, WG	Nil	3 days pa	02-
Prof John Wild	Dept of Optometry & Vision Sciences, Univ of Wales, Cardiff	Nil	3 days pa	03-
Kevin Milsom	Association of Dispensing Opticians in Wales	Nil	3 days pa	10-
Robin Baker	Optometrist	Nil	3 days pa	10-
Annette Dobbs	Optometrist	Nil	3 days pa	10-

Welsh Pharmaceutical Committee

Health Professionals Group, Welsh Government, Cathays Park, Cardiff CF10 3NQ
Tel: (029) 2082 3446 Website: www.cmo.wales.gov.uk
To advise the Welsh Government on the provision of dental services in Wales and to consider and comment or advise on any matter referred to it by the Welsh Government. Committee meets three times a year. Members are not appointed by Welsh Government.

Chair	Occupation	Remuneration	Commitment	Term of office
David Thomas	Community Pharmacy, Aneurin Bevan Health Board	Nil	3 days pa	07-
Members				
Brian Hawkins	Head of Pharmacy & Medicines Management, Cwm Taf Health Board	Nil	3 days pa	07-
Dr Berwyn Owen	Head of Pharmacy & Medicines Management, Betsi Cadwaladr Health Board	Nil	3 days pa	08-
Kevin Smith	Heads of Pharmacy Medicines Management, Powys Health Board	Nil	3 days pa	10-
Mari Treharne	Head of Pharmacy & Medicines Management, Hywel Dda Health Board	Nil	3 days pa	11-
Anne Sprackling	Head of Pharmacy & Medicines Management, Aneurin Bevan Health Board	Nil	3 days pa	07-
Judith Vincent	Head of Pharmacy & Medicines Management, Abertawe Bro Morgannwg Health Board	Nil	3 days pa	10-
Mr Darrell Baker	Head of Pharmacy & Medicines Management, Cardiff & Vale Health Board	Nil	3 days pa	11-
Ian Cowan	Community Pharmacy - Betsi Cadwaladr Health Board	Nil	3 days pa	10-
Sam Fisher	Community Pharmacy - Powys Health Board	Nil	3 days pa	10-
Marc Donovan	Community Pharmacy - Cwm Taf Health Board	Nil	3 days pa	10-
Peter John Jones	Community Pharmacy	Nil	3 days pa	10-
Paul Mayberry	Community Pharmacy - Cardiff & Vale Health Board	Nil	3 days pa	06-
Phil Parry	Community Pharmacy - Hywel Dda Health Board	Nil	3 days pa	05-
Nuala Brennan	Pharmaceutical Public Health - Public Health Wales	Nil	3 days pa	10-
Bethan Tranter	Chief Pharmacist - Velindre NHS Trust	Nil	3 days pa	10-
Russell Goodway	Chief Executive, Community Pharmacy Wales	Nil	3 days pa	10-
Paul Gimson	Director, Welsh Board, Royal Pharmaceutical Society	Nil	3 days pa	08-
Janet Gilbertson	Welsh Committee for Professional Development of Pharmacy	Nil	3 days pa	10-
Prof Gary Baxter	Head of Welsh School of Pharmacy at Cardiff University	Nil	3 days pa	05-
Jeremy Felvus	Wales Industry Group of the Association of British Pharmaceutical Industry	Nil	3 days pa	07-
Carol Lamyman-Davies	All Wales Grouping of the Community Health Councils	Nil	3 days pa	08-
Lesley Morgan	Association of Pharmacy Technicians/ General Pharmaceutical Council	Nil	3 days pa	08-

Welsh Scientific Advisory Committee

PHPD3, Welsh Government, Cathays Park, Cardiff CF10 3NQ Tel: (029) 2082 5201 Fax: (029) 2082 3430.
To advise the Welsh Government on the provision of Scientific Services in Wales and to consider and
comment or advise on any matter referred to it by the Assembly. Members are not appointed by the
Welsh Government.

Chair	Occupation	Remuneration	Commitment	Term of office
Dr Huw Griffiths	Consultant Clinical Scientist	Nil	3 days pa	97-
Vice Chair				
Clive Sparkes	Clinical Psychology	Nil	3 days pa	10-
Members				
Dr Bernadette McCarthy	Clinical Oncology	Nil	3 days pa	00-
Prof Roger Taylor	Clinical Oncology	Nil	3 days pa	08-
Dr Maire Doran	Clinical Physiology	Nil	3 days pa	08-
Shane Exton	Clinical Physiology	Nil	3 days pa	11-
Dr Sharon Evans	Medical Imaging	Nil	3 days pa	10-
Marilyn Williams	Medical Imaging	Nil	3 days pa	10-
Dr Dave Hullian	Laboratory Services	Nil	3 days pa	09-
Dr Mike Simmons	Laboratory Services	Nil	3 days pa	08-
Mike Poole	Laboratory Services	Nil	3 days pa	00-
Dr Will Evans	Medical Physics & Clinical Engineering	Nil	3 days pa	02-
Patrick Hill	Medical Physics & Clinical Engineering	Nil	3 days pa	09-
Dr Nigel Shapcott	Medical Physics & Clinical Engineering	Nil	3 days pa	10-
Prof John Watkins	Public Health Wales	Nil	3 days pa	10-
Stephen Griffiths	NLIAH	Nil	3 days pa	08-
Prof Michael Rees	Welsh Medical Committee	Nil	3 days pa	04-
Prof Julian Sampson	Medical Genetics	Nil	3 days pa	04-
Dr Has Shah	General Practitioner	Nil	3 days pa	09-
Dr Rhonwen Parry	Applied Psychology	Nil	3 days pa	11-
Dr Chris White	Director of Therapies & Science	Nil	3 days pa	11-
Dr Owen Crawley	Chief Scientific Adviser	Nil	3 days pa	00-
Christine Morrell	Deputy Chief Scientific Adviser	Nil	3 days pa	11-
Jane Fitzpatrick	Modernisation Diagnostic Services	Nil	3 days pa	10-

Welsh Statistical Liaison Committee

Sue Leake, Head of Sustainable Futures Analytical team, Knowledge and Analytical Services, Welsh Government
Tel: (029) 2080 1341 Email: sue.leake@wales.gsi.gov.uk
The Welsh Statistical Liaison Committee promotes liaison and consultation between public sector organizations in
Wales concerning data and statistical issues. The committee meets four times a year and includes members from
across the public sector.

Member	Occupation	Member	Occupation
Karen Armstrong	Flintshire County Council	Chris Ashford	ONS
Chris Batsford	Cardiff County Council	Mark Bowler	Conwy County Council
Hywel Butts	Welsh Government	Kate Chamberlain	Welsh Government
Ian Clark	South Wales Police	Lee Clarke	Cardiff County Council
Jamie Clegg	North Wales Police	Hugo Cosh	National Public Health Service
Sally Cox	Health Solutions Wales	Chris Davies	Rhondda Cynon Taf County Council
Brett Davis	South Wales Police	John Dickers	NHS Wales Business Service Centre
CeriDowsett	Newport County Council	Vicki Doyle	Caerphilly County Council
Jill Edge	Monmouthshire County Council	Janine Edwards	Conwy County Council
Rhian Edwards	North Wales Police	Carol Evans	Conwy County Council
Rhys Fidler	Local Government Data Unit	Erin Fôn Jones	Gwynedd County Council
Helen Fry	Brecon Beacons National Park Authority	Andrea Gartner	Public Health Wales
Diana Greaves	Powys County Council	Lucie Griffiths	Welsh Government
Darren Hatton	Welsh Government	Karen Hawkes	Denbighshire County Council
Robert Hay	Welsh Government	Richard Hayward	Bridgend County Council
Mike Hemming	NHS Wales Business Service Centre	Neil Hemmington	Welsh Government
Victoria Hill	North Wales Fire Service	Stephanie Howarth	Welsh Government
Neil Jackson	Office for National Statistics	Martin Jennings	Assembly Commission
Gareth John	Health Solutions Wales	Susan Jones	Bridgend County Council
Glyn Jones	Welsh Government	Nia Jones	Welsh Government
Hywel Jones	Welsh Government	Steve King	Swansea County Council
Sue Leake	Welsh Government	Nathan Lester	Public Health Wales

Welsh Statistical Liaison Committee (cont)

Chris Lewis	Bridgend County Council	**Chris Llewelyn**	Welsh Local Government Association
Duncan Mackenzie	Merthyr Tydfil County Borough Council	**Louise Mackie**	Flintshire County Council
Steven Marshall	Welsh Government	**Jacqueline Maunder**	Mid & West Wales Fire & Rescue Service
Sioned Moffett	Estyn	**David Morgan**	Pembrokeshire County Council
Geraint Morgan	Powys County Council	**James Morris**	Cardiff County Council
Shan Morris	North Wales Fire Service	**Jenny Murphy**	Local Government Data Unit
Rachel Owen	Bridgend County Council	**Elliw Owen**	Snowdonia National Park Authority
Andrew Parker	Blaenau Gwent County Council	**Jeff Phillips**	Welsh Government
David Powell	Wrexham County Council	**Lesley Rees**	Carmarthenshire County Council
Eifion Rees	Mid & West Wales Fire & Rescue Service	**Roberta Roberts**	WCVA
Sara Roberts	Snowdonia National Park Authority	**Stephen Routledge**	South Wales Police
Beverly Searle	Vale of Glamorgan Council	**Jamie Smith**	Welsh Government
Andrew Stephens	Local Government Data Unit	**Aled Sturkey**	Snowdonia National Park Authority
Tim Thomas	Neath Port Talbot County Council	**Jamie Thorburn**	Ceredigion County Council
YvonneTonks	Flintshire County Council	**Alison Vaughan**	Ceredigion County Council
James Walford	Dyfed Powys Police	**Sion Ward**	Cardiff County Council
Russell Watts	Vale of Glamorgan Council	**Emma White**	ONS
Alexandra Williams	Rhondda Cynon Taf County Council	**Rachel Willis**	Brecon Beacons National Park Authority
Andy Wilson	Torfaen County Council	**Iwan Wyn Jones**	Gwynedd County Council
Tba	Pembrokeshire Coast National Park		

Welsh Therapies Advisory Committee

PHPD3, Welsh Government, Cathays Park, Cardiff CF10 3NQ Tel: (029) 2082 5417 Fax: (029) 2082 3430
Website: www.wales.gov.uk/topics/health/ocmo/professionals/committees/therapies/?lang=en
To provide expert professional advice to the Welsh Government on Therapy Services in Wales, and to advise on matters relating to the training and education of therapists. Members are not appointed by the Welsh Government.

Chair	Occupation	Remuneration	Commitment	Term of office
Julie Wilkins	Physiotherapist	Nil	4 days pa	11-
Vice Chair				
Christine Griffiths	Speech & Language Therapy	Nil	4 days pa	07-
Members				
Liz Coombes	Art Therapist	Nil	4 days pa	09-
Denise Jenkins	Orthotics & podiatry	Nil	4 days pa	11-
Debbie Davies	Physiotherapy	Nil	4 days pa	07-
Paul Dunning	Occupational Therapy	Nil	4 days pa	11-
Martin Cope	Art Therapist	Nil	4 days pa	08-
Eve Parkinson	Occupational Therapy	Nil	4 days pa	11-
Judyth Jenkins	Dietetics	Nil	4 days pa	08-
Adam Fox	Chiropody & Podiatry	Nil	4 days pa	11-
Sue Dimmick	Speech & Language Therapy	Nil	4 days pa	11-
Alison Hooper	Orthoptist	Nil	4 days pa	07-
Zoe Paul-Gough	Dietetics	Nil	4 days pa	11-
Gwilym Roberts	CYNGOR	Nil	4 days pa	09-
Kathryn Davies	Director of Therapies & Science	Nil	4 days pa	07-
Carys Norgain	Physiotherapy	Nil	4 days pa	11-
Elspeth Lynburn	Orthoptics	Nil	4 days pa	11-
Alison Strode	Therapies Adviser	Nil	4 days pa	11-
Lance Reed	Aneurin Bevan Local Healthcare Professional Forum	Nil	4 days pa	11-
Sally Bloomfield	Abertawe Bro Morgannwg Local Healthcare Professional Forum	Nil	4 days pa	11-
Sian Williamson	Cwm Taf Local Healthcare Professional Forum	Nil	4 days pa	11-
Sandra Morgan	Hywel Dda Local Healthcare Professional Forum	Nil	4 days pa	11-
Iain Mitchell	Betsi Cadwaladr Local Healthcare Professional Forum	Nil	4 days pa	11-
Rose Whittle	Cardiff & Vale Local Healthcare Professional Forum	Nil	4 days pa	11-

The Wales Yearbook

13

THE HEALTH SERVICE

THE HEALTH SERVICE IN WALES

Director General of Health & Social Care
Welsh Government
Paul Williams OBE

Chief Medical Officer
Welsh Government
Dr Ruth Hussey

Following devolution, management of the NHS in Wales forms one of the major functions of the Welsh Government. In July 2001 the Welsh Government published its proposals for structural change titled *The NHS in Wales,* and implementation of this programme has formed a major strand of its reform of the NHS. Some changes required primary legislation and this was achieved through specific clauses in a related bill for England and in the Health (Wales) Act 2003.

The resultant NHS Wales differs in several significant respects from the reforms enacted for England. In Wales the five regional health authorities ceased to function in April 2003 and were replaced by three regional offices of the new NHS in Wales. The Regional Offices are responsible for performance, managing and developing the NHS Trusts and the Local Health Boards within the regions.

In September 2008, the then Minister for Health and Social Services announced further reforms to the NHS in Wales. Commencing in April 2009, the 22 Local Health Boards were replaced by seven new NHS local bodies.

Further reorganization of NHS Wales, which came into effect on October 1st 2009, has created single local health organizations that are responsible for delivering all healthcare services within a geographical area, rather than the Trust and Local Health Board system that existed previously. The NHS now delivers services through seven Health Boards and three NHS Trusts in Wales.

A new Delivery Group is responsible for the day to day operational work of these seven organizations, and is chaired by the Chief Executive of the NHS in Wales. The role of the current Community Health Councils has also been reformed to ensure a greater public health presence within Local Government. The NHS in Wales, as a whole, is overseen by the National Advisory Board, comprised of independent appointees and chaired by the Minister of Health and Social Services.

HEALTH

Members of the National Advisory Board

Chair Lesley Griffiths AM, Minister for Health & Social Services

Vice-Chair Gwenda Thomas AM, Deputy Minister for Health & Social Services

Members

David Sissling; Dr Ruth Hussey; Dr Gwyn Thomas; Dr Chris Jones; Rob Pickford; Jonathan Davies; Prof Sir Mansel Aylward; Catriona Williams; Tina Donnelly; Dr Arun Midha; Dr John Bullivant; Repa Antonio; Prof Jean White; Meryl Gravell

Board members are appointed for up to four years for a commitment of twenty days per year including approximately ten meetings per year. Board Members will receive a remuneration of £332 per day plus expenses.

National Delivery Group

The Chief Executive, NHS Wales, is responsible for providing the Minister with policy advice and for exercising strategic leadership and management of the NHS. To support this role, the Chief Executive chairs a National Delivery Group which forms part of the Health and Social Services Directorate General.

This Group is responsible for overseeing the development and delivery of NHS services across Wales, in accordance with the direction set by the Minister, and for planning and performance management of the NHS on behalf of Welsh Ministers.

Role of the National Delivery Group

The National Delivery Group, forming part of the Welsh Government's Department for Health and Social Services (DHSS), is responsible for providing strategic leadership and management of the NHS. Chaired by the Chief Executive, NHS Wales, it provides policy advice to the Minister and oversees the development and delivery of NHS services across Wales, in accordance with the direction set by the Minister. The Group is also responsible for planning and performance management of the NHS on behalf of Welsh Ministers.

Membership of the National Delivery Group

Chief Executive, NHS Wales

Department for Health and Social Services Senior Directors Team

Welsh Government Medical Director

Welsh Government Nurse Director

Welsh Government Director of Public Health

Three Independent Members, who together hold key specialist skills in Finance, Human Resources and Legal issues.

.

THE HEALTH SERVICE IN WALES

Healthcare Inspectorate Wales

Bevan House, Caerphilly Business Park
Van Rd, Caerphilly CF83 3ED
☎ (029) 2092 8850
Email: hiw@wales.gsi.gov.uk
Web: www.hiw.org.uk

Healthcare Inspectorate Wales (HIW) is the independent inspectorate and regulator of all health care in Wales. HIW's primary focus is on:

- Making a significant contribution to improving the safety and quality of healthcare services in Wales
- Improving citizens' experience of healthcare in Wales whether as a patient, service user, carer, relative or employee
- Strengthening the voice of patients and the public in the way health services are reviewed
- Ensuring that timely, useful, accessible and relevant information about the safety and quality of healthcare in Wales is made available to all

Chief Executive: Dr Peter Higson
Deputy Chief Executive & Director, Inspections & Regulation: Mandy Collins
Director, Service Review & Organization Development: Alyson Thomas

Welsh NHS Confederation

Welsh NHS Confederation
Unit 3, Waterton Park
Bridgend CF31 3PH
☎ (01656) 643800
Web: www.welshconfed.org

Chair
Win Griffiths

Director
Helen Birtwhistle

The Welsh NHS Confederation brings together the full range of organizations that make up the modern NHS in Wales. They act as an independent voice in the drive for better health and healthcare through their policy and influencing work and by supporting members with events, information and training.

Vice-Chair: Trevor Purt
Management Board: Comprises Chairs and Chief Executive Officers of the seven Health Boards and three NHS Trusts Boards in Wales, plus Director of Welsh NHS Confederation

HEALTH BOARDS

Abertawe Bro Morgannwg University Health Board

Headquarters, One Talbot Gateway, Baglan Energy Park, Baglan, Port Talbot SA12 7BR
☎ (01656) 752752 Fax: (01639) 687675/687676
Web: www.abm.wales.nhs.uk Twitter: http://twitter.com/ABMhealth

Abertawe Bro Morgannwg Health Board provides primary and secondary health care services mainly for the 600,000 residents of Bridgend, Neath Port Talbot and Swansea. The Health Board has four acute hospitals providing a range of services; these are Singleton and Morriston Hospitals in Swansea, Neath Port Talbot Hospital in Port Talbot and the Princess of Wales Hospital in Bridgend and is responsible for providing a number of specialist regional services including cardiac, burns and plastic surgery and neonatal.

Forensic Mental Health services are provided for the whole of South Wales, while Learning Disability services are provided from Swansea to Cardiff. A range of community based services are also delivered in patients' homes, via community hospitals, health centres and clinics.

The Health Board contracts with independent practitioners in respect of primary care services which are delivered by GPs, Opticians, Pharmacists and Dentists.

Chair: Win Griffiths **Vice Chair:** Ed Roberts **Chief Executive:** Paul Roberts
Director of Finance: Eifion Williams **Medical Director:** Bruce Ferguson **Director of Nursing:** Victoria Franklin **Director of Planning:** Paul Stauber **Director of Workforce & Organizational Development:** Debbie Morgan **Chief Operating Officer & Director of Primary, Community & Mental Health Services:** Alexandra Howells **Director of Public Health:** Sara Hayes **Director of Therapies & Health Science:** Andrew Phillips **Board Secretary:** Steve Combe **Director of Clinical Strategy:** Hamish Laing
Locality Directors: Jan Worthing (Swansea), Dorothy Edwards (Bridgend), Hilary Dover (NPT); *Local Authority:* Cllr Mel Nott; *Third Sector:* Gaynor Richards; *Community:* Chantal Patel; *Finance:* Charles Janczewski; *ICT:* Barry Goldberg; *Capital Estates:* Prof Michael Williams; *Legal:* Paul Newman; *Swansea University:* Prof Ceri Phillips; *Trade Union:* Sandra Miller

Aneurin Bevan Health Board

Headquarters, Mamhilad House, Mamhilad Park Estate, Pontypool, Torfaen NP4 0YP
☎ (01873) 732732 Email: abhb.enquiries@wales.nhs.uk Web: www.aneurinbevanlhb.wales.nhs.uk

Aneurin Bevan Health Board plans and delivers services for the populations of Blaenau Gwent, Caerphilly, Monmouthshire, Newport , Torfaen and South Powys. There are two major acute hospitals in the area and also a network of other hospitals providing a range of services. There are also local clinics and primary care facilities providing medical, dental, pharmacy and optometric services. Local facilities and community based teams also provide mental health and learning disability services and support.

Chair: David Jenkins OBE **Vice Chair:** Susan Kent MBE **Chief Executive:** Dr Andrew Goodall
Executive Directors: Director of Planning, Operations & Deputy Chief Executive: Judith Paget **Director of Primary, Community & Mental Health:** Joanne Absalom **Director of Workforce & Organizational Development:** Anne Phillimore **Nurse Director:** Denise Llewellyn **Medical Director:** Dr Grant Robinson **Director of Finance:** Alan Brace **Director of Therapies & Health Science:** Jan Smith **Board Secretary:** Richard Bevan **Director of Public Health:** Dr Gill Richardson **Director of Performance Improvement:** Allan Davies

Independent Members: *Third Sector:* Wendy Bourton OBE; *University:* Prof Helen Houston; *Finance:* Christopher Koehli; *Local Authority:* Cllr Brian Mawby; *Community:* Joanne Smith; *Community:* Peter Sampson; *ICT:* Prof Janet Wademan; *Community:* Philip Robson; *Trade Union:* Jane Carroll; *Associate Independent Member - Chair of the Stakeholder reference Group:* Mark Gardner; *Associate Independent Member - Chair of the Health Professionals' Forum:* Dr Sue Greening; *Associate Independent Member – Director of Social Services:* Stewart Greenwell

HEALTH

HEALTH BOARDS

Betsi Cadwaladr Health Board

Headquarters, Ysbyty Gwynedd, Penrhosgarnedd, Bangor, Gwynedd LL57 2PW
☎ (01248) 384384 Web: www.bcu.wales.nhs.uk

Betsi Cadwaladr University Health Board provides a full range of primary, community, mental health and acute hospital services for 676,000 people across the six counties of North Wales as well as some parts of mid Wales, Cheshire and Shropshire. It is responsible for the operation of three district general hospitals (Ysbyty Gwynedd in Bangor, Ysbyty Glan Clwyd near Rhyl, and Wrexham Maelor Hospital).

Chair: Prof Merfyn Jones **Chief Executive:** Mary Burrows **Vice Chair:** Dr Lyndon Miles **Medical Director & Director of Clinical Services:** Mr Mark Scriven
Director of Nursing, Midwifery & Patient Services: Jill Galvani **Director of Therapies & Health Sciences:** Dr Keith Griffiths **Director of Finance:** Helen Simpson **Director of Workforce & Organizational Development:** Martin Jones **Director of Primary, Community & Mental Health Services:** Geoff Lang **Director of Planning:** Neil Bradshaw **Director of Public Health:** Andrew Jones **Director of Improvement & Business Support:** Mark Common **Director of Governance & Communications:** Grace Lewis-Parry

Members: Reverend Hywel Davies; Jenie Dean; Keith McDonogh; Harri Owen Jones; Hilary Stevens; Dr Chris Tillson; Liz Roberts; Marian Wyn Jones

Cardiff & Vale University Health Board

Executive Headquarters, Whitchurch Hospital, Park Road Cardiff CF14 7XB
☎ 029) 2074 5895 (HQ switchboard)
Email: enquiries@cardiffandvale.wales.nhs.uk Web: www.cardiffandvaleulhb.wales.nhs.uk

Cardiff and Vale University Health Board provides a wide and unique range of services to the local population and wider-Wales. As a teaching Health Board and a centre of excellence for many areas, it employs some of the best clinicians in their field. It provides routine services as well as numerous specialist services. eg. IVF Wales and Vascular Surgery.

Chair: Maria Battle **Vice Chair:** Mutale Merrill **Chief Executive:** Adam Cairns
Executive Director of Planning / Deputy Chief Executive: Paul Hollard **Executive Director of Public Health:** Dr Sharon Hopkins **Executive Director of Therapies & Health Science:** Fiona Jenkins **Executive Director of Finance:** Alun Lloyd **Executive Director of Workforce & Organizational Development:** Tracy Myhill **Executive Medical Director:** Dr Graham Shortland **Executive Director of Nursing:** Ruth Walker **Director of Innovation & Improvement:** Andrew Lewis **Director of Governance (Board Secretary):** Alison Gerrard **Chief Operating Officer:** Vacant

Third (Voluntary) Sector: Morgan Fackrell; *Finance:* Ivar Grey; *Information Communication & Technology:* David Jones; *University:* Prof Malcolm Jones; *Third (Voluntary) Sector:* Margaret McLaughlin; *Local Government:* Vacant; *Legal:* Martyn Waygood; *Community:* Prof Howard Young; *Trade Union:* Stuart Egan

Cwm Taf Health Board

Headquarters, Ynysmeurig House, Navigation Park, Abercynon CF45 4SN
☎ (01443) 744800 Web: www.cwmtafhb.wales.nhs.uk

Cwm Taf Health Board was established on 1 October 2009 and is responsible for the provision of health care services to over 325,000 people principally covering the Merthyr Tydfil and Rhondda Cynon Taf Local Authority areas. These include general medical, surgical, maternity, rehabilitation care, accident and emergency services, and some specialist services.

Chair: Chris Jones **Vice-Chair:** Prof Vivienne Harpwood **Chief Executive:** Allison Williams
Director of Strategic & Operational Planning: Alison Lagier **Director of Finance & Procurement:** David Lewis **Medical Director:** Mr Kamal Asaad **Executive Nurse Director:** Angela Hopkins

Cwm Taf Health Board (cont.)

Director of Primary, Community & Mental Health: Bernardine Rees   **Director of Workforce & Organizational Development:** Ian Stead   **Director of Public Health:** Nicola John   **Director of Therapies & Health Science:** Chris White   **Board Secretary/Corporate Director:** Stephen Harrhy **Turnaround Director:** John Palmer

Assistant Medical Directors: Dr David Cassidy; Dr John Geen; Dr Mike Page; Dr Richard Quirke; Mr Kevin Conway

Independent Board Members: Cllr Clive Jones, Geoffrey Bell, Prof Donna Mead; John Hill - Tout; Anthony Seculer; Gaynor Jones; 3 vacancies. Associate Board Members ; Ellis Williams; Selwyn Williams; 1 vacancy

Hywel Dda Health Board

Hywel Dda Health Board Headquarters, Merlin's Court, Winch Lane,
Haverfordwest, Pembrokeshire SA61 1SB
☎ (01437) 771220 Web: www.hywelddahb.wales.nhs.uk

Hywel Dda Local Health Board provides healthcare services to a total population of around 372,320 throughout Carmarthenshire, Ceredigion and Pembrokeshire. It provides Acute, Primary, Community, Mental Health and Learning Disabilities services via General and Community Hospitals, Health Centres, GP's, Dentists, Pharmacists and Optometrists and other sites.

Chair: Chris Martin   **Vice Chair:** Sian-Marie James   **Chief Executive:** Trevor Purt **Director of Planning, Performance & Delivery:** Tony Chambers; **Director of Nursing & Midwifery:** Caroline Oakley; **Medical Director:** Dr Sue Fish; **Medical Director:** Dr Simon Mahon; **Director of Primary, Community & Mental Health Services:** Karen Howell; **Director of Therapies & Health Science:** Kathryn Davies; **Director of Finance & Economic Reform:** Karen Miles; **Director of Workforce & Organizational Development:** Janet Wilkinson; **Director of Corporate Services:** Chris Wright; **Director of Strategic Partnerships:** Sarah Veck; **Director of Clinical Services:** Dr Phil Kloer

Community: Margaret Rees-Hughes; *Finance Specialist:* Don Thomas; *Capital Estates:* Eifion Griffiths; *Swansea University:* Prof Melanie Jasper; *Local Authority:* Cllr David Wildman; *Voluntary Sector:* Julie James; *Trade Union:* Neil Sandford; *Information Management & Technology:* David Powell

Powys Teaching Health Board

Headquarters, Mansion House, Bronllys, Brecon, Powys LD3 0LS
☎ (01874) 711661
Email: geninfo@powyslhb.wales.nhs.uk
Web: www.powysthb.wales.nhs.uk

Powys Teaching Health Board provides a range of hospital, community, mental health and learning disability services. It is also responsible for arranging secondary health care and hospital services and co-ordinating the delivery of primary care services for the people of Powys.

Chair: Mel Evans   **Vice Chair:** Jo Mussen   **Chief Executive:** Andrew Cottom **Medical Director:** Brendan Lloyd   **Finance Director:** Rebecca Richards   **Nursing Director:** Carol Shillabeer   **Director of Planning:** Chrissie Hayes   **Workforce & Organizational Director:** Julie Rowles **Public Health Director:** Christopher Potter   **Therapies & Health Science:** Amanda Smith; **Strategic Planning & Public Health:** Vacant

Local Authority: Cllr Rosemarie Harris; *Third Sector organization:* Gloria Jones-Powell; *Trade Union:* Jackie Walters; *University:* Prof Paul Dummer; *Legal:* Roger Eagle; *Voluntary/Community:* Andrew Leonard; *ICT:* Mark Baird; *Capital Estates:* Gyles Palmer; *Finance specialist:* Gareth Jones; *Associated Members:* Chief Executive, Powys County Council: Jeremy Patterson; Chair, Stakeholder Reference Group: Alan Austin; Chair, Professional Forum

HEALTH

HEALTH BOARDS

Public Health Wales NHS Trust

14 Cathedral Rd, Cardiff, CF11 9LJ
☎ (029) 2082 7621 Fax: (029) 2082 7622
Email: general.enquiries@wales.nhs.uk
Web: www.publichealthwales.org
www.iechydcyhoedduscymru.wales.nhs.uk

Public Health Wales provides an expert public health resource. Its purpose is to give people power to protect and improve health and wellbeing and reduce inequities by informing, advising and speaking up for them. It works locally and nationally and, in particular, supports the Directors of Public Health as part of an integrated public health system in Wales. Together, it supports the NHS, local government and others. Public Health Wales has a budget of £81 million and employs 1,300 staff.

Chair: Prof Sir Mansel Aylward **Chief Executive:** Bob Hudson **Executive Director of Finance:** Huw George **Executive Director of Public Health Services:** Dr Hilary Fielder **Executive Director of Public Health Development:** Dr Peter Bradley **Executive Director of Planning & Performance:** Mark Dickinson **Board Secretary:** Keith Cox **Director of Communications:** Chris Lines **Director of Workforce and Organizational Development:** Ruth Davies
Members
Third Sector Representative: Dr Carl Clowes **Local Government Representative:** Vacant **Independent Members:** John Spence; Terry Rose; Prof Simon Smail **University Representative:** Prof Gareth Williams

Velindre NHS Trust

Velindre NHS Trust Corporate Headquarters, Unit 2 Charnwood Court,
Parc Nantgarw, Nantgarw, Cardiff, CF15 7QZ
☎ (029) 2019 6161 Fax: (01443) 841 878
Email: corporate.services2@wales.nhs.uk
Web: www.velindre-tr.wales.nhs.uk

Velindre NHS Trust provides a range of specialist services at local, regional and all Wales levels. Areas of the Trust include Velindre Cancer Centre and the Welsh Blood Service. Units hosted by the Trust include Cancer Services Coordinating Group, Cardiac Networks Coordinating Group of Wales, NCC-C, South East Wales Cancer Network, NHS Wales Informatics Service (NHSWIS) and Shared Services.

Chair: Rosemary Kennedy **Chief Executive:** Simon Dean **Director of Nursing & Quality:** Dr Sue Morgan **Executive Director of Human Resources:** Ian Sharp **Executive Director of Finance:** Steve Ham **Medical Director:** Prof Peter Barratt-Lee **Independent Members:** June Smail; Paul Griffiths; Harry Ludgate, Ray Singh, Phil Roberts

In addition to the above members, the following people are also regular attendees of the Trust Board meetings: **Director of Velindre Cancer Centre:** Mrs A Hague **Director of the Welsh Blood Service:** Mr G Poole **Board Secretary:** Mrs G Galletly; Miss J Sinnott (Secretary)

HEALTH

HEALTH TRUSTS

Welsh Ambulance Services NHS Trust

Trust Headquarters, HM Stanley Hospital, St Asaph, Denbighshire LL17 0RS
☎ (01745) 532900 Fax: (01745) 532901
Email: caroline.jones13@wales.nhs.uk
Web: www.ambulance.wales.nhs.uk

Providing ambulance services across Wales

Chair: Stuart Fletcher **Chief Executive:** Elwyn Price- Morris **Director of Medical & Clinical Services:** Dr Paul Hughes **Director of Workforce & OD:** Judith Hardisty **Director of Strategy, Planning & Performance:** Carl James **Director of Service Delivery:** Sue Jenkins **Nurse Director:** Sara Jones **Interim Director of Finance:** John Jones **Non Executive Director:** Peter Price **Non Executive Director:** Nina Park **Non Executive Director:** Dr Kevin Fitzpatrick OBE **Non Executive Director:** Philip James **Non Executive Director/Vice-Chair:** Dilwyn Evans **Non Executive Director:** Stuart Castledine **Non Executive Director:** John Morgan

Corporate Secretary: Dawn Sharp

REGIONAL HEADQUARTERS

Central & West Region	Trust Headquarters	South East Region
Tŷ Maes y Gruffudd, Cefn Coed Hospital, Cockett, Swansea SA2 0GP	H M Stanley Hospital Site St Asaph, Denbighshire LL17 0RS	Vantage Point House, Tŷ Coch Way, Cwmbran NP44 7HF
☎ (01792) 562900	☎ (01745) 532900	☎ (01633) 626262
Fax: (01792) 281184	Fax: (01745) 532924	Fax: (01633) 626299

HEADS OF SERVICE

Betsi Cadwaladr University Health Board: Gordon Roberts

Cardiff & Vale Health Board: Robert Toby

Cwm Taf Health Board: Judith White

Abertawe Bro Morgannwg University Health Board: Mike Collins

Hywel Dda Health Board: Rob Jeffrey

Powys Health Board: Tba

Aneurin Bevan Health Board: Tba

HEALTH

COMMUNITY HEALTH COUNCILS

Community Health Councils (CHC) were formed in 1974 and are statutory lay bodies that represent the interests of the public in the health service in their district. They give people an independent voice in their local NHS and the services it provides. The number of CHCs has now been reduced to 7 contiguous with the new Local Heath Boards. The 7 new CHCs will be underpinned by 23 area associations with strong local links.

Board of Community Health Councils in Wales

2nd Floor, 33-35 Cathedral Rd, Cardiff CF11 9HB
☎ (0845) 6447 814 Fax: (029) 2023 5574
Email: enquiries@waleschc.org.uk Web: www.communityhealthcouncils.org.uk

Chair: Peter Dolan **Vice-Chair:** April Harper
Director: Carol Lamyman-Davies **Business Manager:** Jenna Trotman

Abertawe Bro Morgannwg Community Health Council

Water Street Business Centre, Water Street, Aberafan, Neath Port Talbot SA12 6LF
☎ (01639) 892271 Email: office@abmchc.org.uk
Web: www.communityhealthcouncils.org.uk/abm/

Chair: Emrys Davies **Vice-Chair:** Clive Owen **Chief Officer:** Phillip Williams

Local Authority: Cllr Edith Hughes (Bridgend), Cllr Pam Davies (Bridgend), Cllr Marlene Thomas (Bridgend), Cllr Marian Lewis (Neath Port Talbot), Cllr Audrey N Chaves (Neath Port Talbot), Cllr Sheila M Penry (Neath Port Talbot), Cllr Uta Clay (Swansea), Cllr John Davies (Swansea), Cllr Jane E C Harris (Swansea)

Voluntary Organizations: Alan Phillips (Bridgend), Diana Griffith (Bridgend), Lindsay Morgan (Bridgend), Byron Adams (Neath Port Talbot), Lee Ellery (Swansea), Jennifer Gomes (Swansea), Carol Ross (Swansea)

Welsh Government: Kerry Davies (Bridgend), Owen Davies (Bridgend), Phillip Fairclough (Bridgend), Sheila Rano (Neath Port Talbot), Jacqueline McCarthy (Neath Port Talbot), Susan Evans (Neath Port Talbot), Neil Thomas (Swansea), Joan A Henry (Swansea), J Margaret Buckley (Swansea)

Co-opted Members: Stephen Colinese, Elizabeth Davies, Julie King, Beryl Tyler, Gillian Davies, Redvers Davies

Aneurin Bevan Community Health Council

Raglan House, 6-8 William Brown Close, Llantarnam Business Park, Cwmbran NP44 3AB
☎ (01633) 838516 Fax: (01633) 484623
Email: abchc@abchc.org.uk Web: www.communityhealthcouncils.org.uk/aneurinbevan

Chair: Byron Grubb **Chief Officer:** Catherine O'Sullivan

Local Authority Members: Blaenau Gwent: Cllr Shirley Ford, Cllr Clive Meredith; Caerphilly: Cllr Judith Pritchard, Cllr Summers; Monmouthshire: Cllr Valerie Smith, Cllr John Prosser, Cllr Penny Jones; Newport: Cllr Christine Jenkins, Cllr Debbie Harvey; Torfaen: Cllr Peter Cathcart

Third Sector Appointment: Blaenau Gwent: Byron Grubb; Caerphilly: Ann Darlington, Robert Dutt; Newport: Joyce Steven, Edward Watts, Naseem Babur; Torfaen: Stuart Evans

Public Appointments: Blaenau Gwent: Richard Essery, Brian Potts, Anne Thomas, Sonia Stainer, Brian Kember, David Evans. Caerphilly: Bryan Lloyd, Steven Connolly, Michael Williams. Monmouthshire: Rev Nigel Burge, Susan Campbell, Elvin Hart, Anna Smith, Joy Perrott, Gary Jones. Newport: Peter Dolan, John Hopkins, John Pearce, Kate Thomas, John Thompson, Wendy Thomas. Torfaen: Helen Ford, John McGeehan, Lynne Tanner, Jane Morris, Peter Davies, Helen Binnie

Co-opted Members: Blaenau Gwent: Mr Barry Davies. Caerphilly; Elsie Ball, Laurence Clay, Barbara Evans, Gwyneth Jones, Alun Jones, Joyce Morgan. Monmouthshire: George Clemow, Susan Sandham. Newport: Lyndon Curnock, Adrian Gillard, Jan Atkinson, Valerie Cheeseman, Margaret Went, Pamela Jones. Torfaen: Carole Lynch

COMMUNITY HEALTH COUNCILS

Betsi Cadwaladr Community Health Council

Denbighshire/Flintshire/Wrexham Locality Office:
Cartrefle, Cefn Road, Wrexham LL13 9NH
☎ (01978) 356178 Fax: (01978) 346870
Email: admin@bcchc.org.uk
Web: www.communityhealthcouncils.org.uk/betsicadwaladr

Conwy/Gwynedd/Ynys Môn Locality Office:
Arran House, Arran Road, Dolgellau LL40 1HW
☎ (01341) 422236 Fax: (01341) 422897
Email: meirchc@nwwaleschc.org.uk

Chair: Christine Evans **Vice-Chair:** April Harper **Chief Officer:** Pat Billingham

Welsh Government: Geoffrey Richardson (Llandudno), Kevin Sibbons (Abergele), Carole Lapham, Rhyl, Eirlys Pritchard (Denbigh), Dr Ahmed Valijan (Colwyn Bay), Dr Sibani Roy (Colwyn Bay), Vacancy (Denbighshire), Russell Jones (Ewloe), Vacancy (x3), Mair Jones (Bangor), Jean Preston (Dinas Mawddwy), Hilary Scott (Penygroes), Vera Wilson (Bangor), David Cooper (Llangollen), Jan Greasley (Chirk), Patricia Rannard (Caergeliog), Elizabeth Hayworth (Llangollen), Brace Griffiths (Llangefni), Mark Thornton (Amlwch)

Local Authority: Cllr Abdul Khan (Colwn Bay), Cllr Ronald Peacock (Abergele), Cllr John Pitt (Abergele), Cllr John Raymond Bartley (Denbigh), Cllr J Ann Davies (Rhuddlan), Cllr Christine Evans (Denbighshire), Cllr Hilary June McGuill (Mold), Cllr Huw Edwards (Arfon), Cllr Eryl Jones-Williams (Meirionnydd), Cllr Peter Read (Dwyfor), Cllr Judith C Connolly (Pandy), Cllr Hugh Jones (Rossett), Cllr Joan Lowe (Penycae), Cllr Eric Jones (Gaerwen), Cllr Raymond Jones (Holyhead), Cllr Lewis Davies (Beaumaris)

Voluntary Sector: Nerys Cossey (Colwyn Bay), April Harper (Old Colwyn), Pearl Roberts (Abergele), Roma Goffett (Rhyl), Gordon Donaldson (Mold), Colin Herbert (Hawarden), Frances Parry (Buckley), Neil Taylor (Rhyl), Edward Llewelyn Evans (Arthritis Care), Melanie Jones (Barnardos), Vacancy (Gwynedd), Elizabeth Mary Williams (Acton Park), Sylvia Margaret Prankard (Bradley), Valerie Ann Morris (Penley), Denise Harris-Edwards (Ynys Môn), Patricia Jones (Soroptimist International of Great Britain & Ireland-Anglesey Club), Delyth Wilson (Scouting Wales, Eryri & Anglesey Area)

Co-opted: Cllr Peter Jones (Mochdre), Robin Holden (Llandudno), Mrs M Hughes (Rhyl), Dr Jeffrey Evans (Corwen), Jennifer M Harley (Flintshire), Dr Cheryl Jones (Flintshire), Jacqueline Jones (Flintshire), Margaret Kewley (Flintshire), Karen Shepherd (Flintshire), Margaret Baker (Tywyn), Mrs M Carol Davies (Caernarfon), Martha Hughes (Criccieth), Arwel Pierce (Tywyn), Emlyn Phennah (Wrexham), Jean Williams (Wrexham), Margaret Williams (Wrexham), Andy Burgen (Beaumaris)

Brecknock & Radnor Community Health Council

Neuadd Brycheiniog, Cambrian Way, Brecon, Powys LD3 7HR
☎ (01874) 624206 Fax: (01874) 611602
Email: breconchc@breconchc.org.uk
Web: www.communityhealthcouncils.org.uk/brecknockradnor

Chair: Krishn Pathak **Vice Chair:** Carolyn Flynn **Chief Officer:** David Adams
Local Authority: Cllr Kelvyn Curry, Cllr Krish Pathak, Cllr D Gillian Thomas
Voluntary Organization: Carolyn Flynn
Welsh Government: Heather Barrow, Ann Mathias, Ieuan Williams

HEALTH

COMMUNITY HEALTH COUNCILS

Cardiff & Vale of Glamorgan Community Health Council

3rd Floor, Park House, Greyfriars Rd, Cardiff CF10 3AF
☎ (029) 2037 7407 Fax: (029) 2066 5470
Email: chief.officer@cavogchc.org.uk
Web: www.communityhealthcouncils.org.uk/cardiffandvale

Chair: Robert Woodward OBE **Vice Chair:** Lesley Jones
Chief Officer: Stephen Allen **Deputy Chief Officer:** Desmond Kitto MBE

Welsh Government (Public Appointments Branch): Sybil Arthur (Vale of Glamorgan), Dr Stephen Barasi (Vale of Glamorgan), Jason Bartlett (Cardiff), Clare Clements (Cardiff), Eleri Jones (Cardiff), Lesley Jones (Cardiff), Jennifer Robbins (Vale of Glamorgan), Phillip Thomas (Cardiff), John Viney (Vale of Glamorgan), Julie Williams (Vale of Glamorgan), Robert Woodward (Cardiff), Vacancy (Vale of Glamorgan)

Local Authority: Cllr Janice Birch (Vale of Glamorgan), Cllr Ed Bridges (Cardiff), Cllr Lyn Hudson (Cardiff), Cllr Jim Murphy (Cardiff), Cllr Gwyn Roberts (Vale of Glamorgan), Cllr Mark Wilson (Vale of Glamorgan)

Voluntary Organization: Alan Brown (Cardiff), Annie Duddridge (Vale of Glamorgan), Jill Shelton (Cardiff), Patricia Matthews (Vale of Glamorgan), Vacancy (Cardiff), Vacancy (Vale of Glamorgan)

Co-Opted: Margaret Davies (Cardiff), Dr Cathy Kerby (Cardiff), Anita Morgan (Vale of Glamorgan), Freda Webster (Cardiff), Dr Ron Walton (Vale of Glamorgan)

Cwm Taf Community Health Council

Unit 10, Maritime Offices, Woodland Terrace, Maesycoed
Pontypridd CF37 1DZ
☎ (01443) 405830
Email: enquiries@cwmtafchc.org.uk
Web: www.communityhealthcouncils.org.uk/cwmtaf

Chair: Mel Jehu **Vice Chair:** Jeff Morgan **Chief Officer:** Dr Paul Worthington

Co-opted Members: Jacqueline Jones, Elfed Lewis, Ann Morgan, Angela Drake Fyler

Merthyr Local Committee members

Welsh Government: Sandra Scott Jones (Chair), Dora Powell, Jeff Moore, Merryl Kay Jones, Laura Guard, Mel Jehu

Merthyr County Borough Council Appointments: Cllr Alan Jones, Tony Chaplin, Cllr Graham Davies

Voluntary Organization: Yvonne Wood, Helen Thomas (Vice Chair), Shelagh McCarthy

Rhondda Cynon Taf Local Committee members

Welsh Government: Mary Williams, Jeffrey Morgan, Dr Andrea Thomas, Rowena Myles, Carole Withey, Lynne Southway

Rhondda Cynon Taf County Borough Council: Cllr Teressa Bates, Cllr Dennis Weeks, Cllr Sharon Rees

Voluntary Sector: Ann Williams, Jimmy Browne, Myra Davies

COMMUNITY HEALTH COUNCILS

Hywel Dda Community Health Council

Pembrokeshire Office (Head Office):
Suite 1, Cedar Court, Haven's Head, Milford Haven
Pembrokeshire SA73 3LS
☎ (01646) 697610 Fax: (01646) 697256
Email: pembrokeshire@chcwales.org.uk

Carmarthenshire Office:
Suite 5, 1st Floor, Ty Myrddin, Old Station Road, Carmarthen
Carmarthenshire SA31 1BT
☎ (01267) 231384
Email: carmarthen@chcwales.org.uk

Ceredigion Office:
Merlin House, Merlin Park Aberystwyth
Ceredigion SY23 3FF
☎ (01970) 613086
Email: ceredigion@chcwales.org.uk
Web: www.communityhealthcouncils.org.uk/hyweldda

Chair: Tony Wales **Vice-Chair:** Gabrielle Heathcote **Chief Officer:** Ashley Warlow

Executive Committee: Tony Wales (Chair), Prof Gabrielle Heathcote (Vice-Chair), Dr Chris Slader, Glennis Gratwick, Paul Hinge, Janet Waymont, Raymond Hine, Jane Tremlett, Ashley Warlow (Chief Officer)

Carmarthenshire Local Committee: Jane Tremlett (Chair), Dr Chris Slader (Vice Chair); Keith Skivington, Dorothy McDonald, Barbara Hartley, Keith Skivington, Dr Peter Hogg, Christopher Downward, Robert Hacon Williams, Shirley Matthews, Andrew James, Emlyn Dole, Kate Waldron, John Phillips

Ceredigion Local Committee: Paul Hinge (Chair) Glennis Gratwick (Vice Chair), Alvin Jones (Vice-Chair), Prof Gabrielle Heathcote, Colin Sanders, Eirlys Davies, Ann Winfield, Bill Messer, David Thomson, Paul Hinge, Gareth Lloyd, Eirlys Davies, Patricia Challis, Shirley Oliver, Jeean Harrison, Lisa Francis

Pembrokeshire Local Committee: Janet Waymont (Chair), Ray Hine (Vice Chair) Elizabeth Griffiths, Simon Hancock, Wynne Evans, Lyn Jenkins, Dr Elisabeth David, Islwyn Howells, Peter Milewski, Alun Jones, Susan Jones, Mollie Roach, Pamela Parsons, Jim Codd, Tony Wales

Montgomeryshire Community Health Council

Room 20, Ladywell House, Newtown, Powys SY16 1JB
☎ (01686) 627632
Fax: (01686) 629091
Email: info@montchc.org.uk
Web: www.communityhealthcouncils.org.uk/montgomery

Chair: Tba **Vice-Chairs:** Tba **Interim Chief Officer:** J David Adams

Powys County Council: Cllr Kath Roberts-Jones, Cllr Peter Harris, 1 vacancy

Welsh Government: Maria Emptage, Margaret Evitts, Dr John Morgan, Roy Norris, Maxine Roberts, 1 vacancy

Voluntary Organization: 3 vacancies

HEALTH

Leap into Action with Wales Air Ambulance as we campaign to raise the funds needed to upgrade Wales' third lifesaving helicopter.

LEAP INTO ACTION • GWEITHREDWCH NAWR
www.walesairambulance.com

nationalchildrens
airambulance.com

AMBIWLANS AWYR CYMRU
WALES AIR AMBULANCE

Arbed amser - Arbed bywydau
Saving time - Saving lives

For more information visit
leap.walesairambulance.com
0844 85 84 999

FRSB
give with confidence

RCN 1083645

PRIVATE HEALTHCARE IN WALES

BMI Werndale Hospital

Bancyfelin, Carmarthen, Carmarthenshire SA33 5NE
☎ (01267) 225652
Web: www.bmihealthcare.co.uk

Spire Abergele Consulting Rooms

Ground Floor, Priory House, North Wales Business Park, Abergele, Conwy LL22 8LJ
☎ (01745) 828900 Fax: (01745) 828908
Web: www.spirehealthcare.com/yale/abergele-consulting-rooms/

Spire Cardiff Hospital

Croescadarn Rd, Pentwyn, Cardiff CF23 8XL
☎ (0845) 600 1654 Fax: (029) 2073 5821
Web: www.spirehealthcare.com/cardiff

Spire Yale Hospital

Wrexham Technology Park, Croesnewydd Rd, Wrexham LL13 7YP
☎ (01978) 291306 Fax: (01978) 291397
Web: www.spirehealthcare.com/yale

Sancta Maria Hospital

Ffynone Rd, Swansea SA1 6DF ☎ (01792) 479040 Fax: (01792) 641452
Email: admin@sanctamaria.co.uk
Web: www.sanctamaria.co.uk

St. Joseph's Hospital

Harding Avenue, Malpas, Newport NP20 6ZE ☎ (01633) 820300 Fax: (01633) 858164
Email: mail@stjosephshospital.org.uk
Web: www.stjosephshospital.org.uk

Vale Healthcare

Hensol Castle Park, Hensol, nr. Cardiff, Vale of Glamorgan, South Wales, CF72 8JX
☎ (029) 2083 6700 Fax (01443) 449222
Web: www.vale-healthcare.com

HEALTH

HWB CYMRU

Non Rhys

Nia Davies

HWB Cymru specialises in economic development through bringing government, organisations and businesses closer.

HWB means to 'Boost' in Welsh. Let's see if we can give you a HWB with business.

Mae HWB Cymru yn arbenigo mewn datblygiad economaidd trwy ddod a llywodraeth, mudiadau a busnesau'n agosach.

Cysylltwch i weld sut gallwn roi HWB i chi.

HWB i Fusnes | Helping With Business

 /nonrhys
/niadavieshwb

 /hwb.cymru

53 Ffordd Ty Unnos
Caerdydd CF14 4NJ

 /hwbcymru

 029 2052 9158

 www.hwbcymru.com

 hwbcymru

 info@hwbcymru.com

www.hwbcymru.com | 029 20529158 | gwybodaeth@hwbcymru.com

The**Wales**
Yearbook

13

THE LEGAL SYSTEM

THE LAW SOCIETY WALES

Capital Tower,
Greyfriars Road
Cardiff CF10 3AG

☎ (029) 2064 5254
Fax: (029) 2022 5944

Email: wales@lawsociety.org.uk
Website: www.lawsociety.org.uk

Chair
David Dixon

Manager
Lowri Morgan

Cymdeithas y Cyfreithwyr
The Law Society

The Law Society represents over 150,000 solicitors in England and Wales. It strives to guarantee:
- *to the public - access to high quality legal services*
- *to solicitors - vigorous promotion of their interests*
- *to society - a leading voice on law reform*

The legal profession in Wales makes a significant contribution to the vibrancy of the Welsh economy.

THE LAW SOCIETY WALES COMMITTEE

Chair
David Dixon

Members

Robin ap Cynan	Dylan Lloyd Jones
Mair Hickman	John Pickup
Michael Imperato	Mandy Rowsell
Carolyn Kirby	Jonathan Stephens
Jane Lang	Clive Thomas
Peter Jones	

STAFF

Lowri Morgan	Manager
Kay Powell	Policy Adviser
Rhys Jones	Development Executive

LEGAL

THE LEGAL SYSTEM IN WALES

Wales, unlike Scotland, does not have its own legal system. The administration of justice in Wales, as in England, now falls within the jurisdiction of the new Ministry of Justice.

The Crown Prosecution Service maintains a major office in Cardiff. The principal Crown Courts of Mold, Carmarthen and Cardiff are equipped with simultaneous translation facilities enabling trials to be conducted through the medium of Welsh.

Since April 2007, the Welsh Legal Circuit has stood alone and is known as HMCTS Wales.

However, laws made in Wales, for Wales, still form part of the law of England and Wales. This is because England and Wales share a single legal jurisdiction. This is not the case in Scotland and Northern Ireland who have separate legal jurisdictions.

There has been much discussion about whether or not Wales should also be a separate legal jurisdiction. In 2011, the First Minister of Wales, Rt Hon Carwyn Jones AM made a speech to the Legal Wales Conference announcing the need for a public debate on the issue of a Separate Legal Jurisdiction for Wales. The Welsh Government ran a consultation over March – June 2012 in order to garner views on this subject.

The purpose of the consultation was to seek views on the specific aspects of a potential Welsh jurisdiction and the underlying issues beneath the broader questions raised. The consultation's findings are set to be published in mid-2012.

HER MAJESTY'S COURTS & TRIBUNALS SERVICE WALES

Senior Presiding Judge England & Wales:
Rt Hon Lord Justice Goldring
Presiding Judges, HMCTS Wales:
Mr Justice John Griffith Williams & Mr Justice Wyn Williams

HMCTS Wales Delivery Director

Mark Swales, 3rd Floor, Churchill House, Churchill Way, Cardiff CF10 2HH
DX: 121723 Cardiff 9
☎ (029) 2067 8311 Fax: (029) 2067 8406

Head of Crime HMCTS Wales

Luigi Strinati, 3rd Floor, Churchill House, Churchill Way, Cardiff CF10 2HH
☎ (029) 2067 8300 Fax: (029) 2067 8406

Head of Civil Family and Tribunals HMCTS Wales

Hugh Simkiss, 3rd Floor, Churchill House, Churchill Way, Cardiff CF10 2HH
☎ (029) 2067 8300 Fax: (029) 2067 8406

Cluster Manager Crime HMCTS Wales

Lynne Mills, 3rd Floor, Churchill House, Churchill Way, Cardiff CF10 2HH
☎ (029) 2067 8300 Fax: (029) 2067 8406

Cluster Manager Civil Family & Tribunals HMCTS Wales

Tim Luke, 3rd Floor, Churchill House, Churchill Way, Cardiff CF10 2HH
☎ (029) 2067 8300 Fax: (029) 2067 8406

LEGAL

HER MAJESTY'S COURTS & TRIBUNALS SERVICE WALES

HMCTS Wales Enforcement

Enforcement Director: Lyn Harding
HMCTS, 4th Floor, Gwent House, Gwent Square, Cwmbran NP44 1PL ☎ (01633) 645039

Assistant to Enforcement Director: Jan Quinn
HMCTS, 4th Floor, Gwent House, Gwent Square, Cwmbran NP44 1PL ☎ (01633) 645015

Senior Enforcement Manager: Kay Bird
Port Talbot Magistrates' Courts, Cramic Way, Port Talbot SA13 1RU ☎ (01639) 889492

Enforcement Manager: Debbie Tossell
Port Talbot Magistrates' Courts, Cramic Way, Port Talbot SA13 1RU ☎ (01639) 889508

Accounts Office Manager: Bridgett Burke
Port Talbot Magistrates' Courts, Cramic Way, Port Talbot SA13 1RU ☎ (01639) 889465

Fixed Penalty Manager: Lisa McCall
The Court House, Grove Road, Denbigh LL16 3UU ☎ (01745) 812683

Contact/Compliance Centre Manager: Sharon Holder
HMCTS, 4th Floor, Gwent House, Gwent Square, Cwmbran NP44 1PL ☎ (01633) 645125

South East Wales

David Richmond, Clerk to the Justices, The Courthouse, Fitzalan Place, Cardiff CF24 0RZ
☎ (029) 2046 3040

Judges

3rd Floor, Churchill House, Churchill Way, Cardiff CF10 2HH
☎ (029) 2067 8300 Fax: (029) 2067 8406

Judge Neil Bidder QC	Cardiff Crown Court
Judge Nicholas M Chambers QC	Cardiff Civil Justice Centre
Judge John Curran	Merthyr Crown Court
Judge Patrick Curran QC	Cardiff Crown Court
Judge Mark Furness	Newport County Court
Judge William Gaskell	Cardiff Crown Court/Cardiff Civil Justice Centre
Judge Stephen Hopkins QC	Cardiff Crown Court
Judge Milwyn Jarman QC	Cardiff Civil Justice Centre
Judge Terry John	Cardiff Civil Justice Centre
Judge Crispin Masterman	Cardiff Civil Justice Centre
Judge D Wynn Morgan	Cardiff Crown Court
Judge E M Rees (Recorder of Cardiff)	Cardiff Crown Court
Judge Philip Richards	Cardiff Crown Court
Judge Wyn Rees	Pontypridd County Court
Judge Seys Llewellyn QC	Cardiff Civil Justice Centre
Judge Richard Twomlow	Merthyr Crown Court

LEGAL

South East Wales (cont.)

Crown Courts

Cardiff
Court House: The Law Courts, Cathays Park, Cardiff CF10 3PG
☎ (029) 2067 8730 Fax: (029) 2067 8732 DX: 99450 Cardiff 5
Email: cardiff.crn.cm2@hmcts.gsi.gov.uk
Court Manager: Mike Bevan

Merthyr Tydfil (Combined Crown & County Court)
Court House: The Law Court, Glebeland Place, Merthyr Tydfil, Mid Glamorgan CF47 8BH
☎ (01685) 727600 Fax: (01685) 727703 DX: 99582 Merthyr Tydfil 2
Email: merthyrtydfil.enquiries@merthyrtydfil.crowncourt.gsi.gov.uk
Court Manager: Huw Evans

Newport
Court House: Crown Court, Faulkner Rd, Newport NP20 4PR
☎ (01633) 266211 Fax: (01633) 216824 DX: 99460 Newport 1/2
Email: newport.crn.cm@hmcts.gsi.gov.uk
Court Manager: Mike Bevan
Divisional Manager: Margaret Lewis

County Courts

Blackwood Civil & Family Court
Court House: 8 Hall Street, Blackwood South Wales, NP12 1NY
☎ (01495) 238200 Fax: (01495) 238203 DX: 99470 Blackwood 2
Email: blackwood.enquiries@hmcts.gsi.gov.uk
Court Manager: Nicola Roberts

Bridgend (Combined County & Magistrates' Court)
Court House: The Law Courts, Sunnyside, Bridgend CF31 4AJ
☎ (01656) 673833 Fax: (01656) 647124
Email: enquiriesbridgendlawcourts@hmcts.gsi.gov.uk

Cardiff Civil Justice Centre
Court House: 2 Park St, Cardiff CF10 1ET
☎ (029) 2037 6400 Fax: (029) 2037 6475 DX: 99500 Cardiff 6
Email: enquiries@cardiff.countycourt.gsi.gov.uk
Court Manager: Neil Pring

Merthyr Tydfil (Combined Crown & County Court)
Court House: The Law Court, Glebeland Place, Merthyr Tydfil CF47 8BH
☎ (01685) 727600 Fax: (01685) 727702
Email: enquiries@merthyrtydfil.countycourt.gsi.gov.uk
Court Manager: Huw Evans

Newport Civil & Family Court
Court House: 5th Floor Clarence House, Clarence Place, Newport, Gwent NP19 7AA
☎ (01633) 245040 Fax: (01633) 245041 DX: 99480 Newport South Wales 4
Email: enquiries@newportgwent.countycourt.gsi.gov.uk
Court Manager: Diana Edwards

Pontypridd
Court House: Court House St, Pontypridd CF37 1JR
☎ (01443) 490800 Fax: (01443) 480305 DX: 99620 Pontypridd 2
Email: enquiries@pontypridd.countycourt.gsi.gov.uk
Court Manager: Sue Cumpston

LEGAL

HER MAJESTY'S COURTS & TRIBUNALS SERVICE WALES

South East Wales (cont.)

Magistrates' Courts

Abergavenny
Court House: Magistrates' Court, Tudor St, Abergavenny, Gwent NP7 5DL
☎ (01633) 645000 Fax: (01633) 645177
Email: gw-adminenq@hmcts.gsi.gov.uk
Admin address: HMCTS Gwent, PO Box 83, Cwmbran NP44 1ZW

Bridgend (Combined County & Magistrates' Court)
Court House: The Law Courts, Sunnyside, Bridgend CF31 4AJ
☎ (01656) 673800 Fax: (01656) 668981 DX: 99751

Caerphilly
Court House: Magistrates' Court, Mountain Rd, Caerphilly CF83 1HG
☎ (01633) 645000 Fax: (01633) 645177
Email: gw-adminenq@hmcts.gsi.gov.uk
Admin address HMCTS Gwent, PO Box 83, Cwmbran NP44 1ZW
Acting Court Manager: Sue Sullivan

Cardiff
Court House: Fitzalan Place, Cardiff CF24 0RZ
☎ (029) 2046 3040 Fax: (029) 2046 0264
Email: sw-cardiffmcenq@hmcts.gsi.gov.uk
Court Manager: Tania Pendlington

Cwmbran
Court House: Magistrates' Court, Tudor Rd, Cwmbran, Gwent NP44 3YA
☎ (01633) 645000 Fax: (01633) 645177
Email: gw-adminenq@hmcts.gsi.gov.uk
Admin address: HMCTS Gwent, PO Box 83, Cwmbran, NP44 1ZW
Acting Court Manager: Sue Sullivan

Merthyr Tydfil
Court House: The Law Courts, Glebeland Place, Merthyr Tydfil CF47 8BU
☎ (01685) 727600 Fax: (01685) 723919
Email: sw-merthyrmcenq@hmcts.gsi.gov.uk
Court Manager: Huw Evans

Newport
Court House: Civic Centre, Newport, Gwent NP20 4UR
☎ (01633) 645000 Fax: (01633) 645177
Email: gw-adminenq@hmcts.gsi.gov.uk
Admin address: HMCTS Gwent, PO Box 83, Cwmbran NP44 1ZW
Acting Court Manager: Sue Sullivan

Pontypridd
Court House: Union St, Pontypridd CF37 1SD
☎ (01443) 480750 Fax: (01443) 485472
Email: sw-pontypriddmcenq@hmcts.gsi.gov.uk
Court Manager: Huw Evans

LEGAL

HER MAJESTY'S COURTS & TRIBUNALS SERVICE WALES

North Wales

Iolo W Thomas, Clerk to the Justices, The Courthouse, Conwy Road, Llandudno LL30 1GA
☎ (01492) 863868

Judges

Judge Gareth Jones	Rhyl County Court
Judge Dafydd Hughes	Caernarfon County Court
Judge R Philip Hughes	Wrexham County Court
Judge Merfyn Hughes QC	Mold & Caernarfon Crown Court
Judge Niclas Parry	Mold & Caernarfon Crown Court

Crown Courts

Caernarfon
Court House: Criminal Justice Centre, Llanberis Rd, Caernarfon, Gwynedd LL55 2DF
☎ (01352) 707340 Fax: (01352) 753874 DX: 774382 Caernarfon 6
Email: enquiries@mold.crowncourt.gsi.gov.uk
Admin address: The Law Courts, Mold, CH7 1AE
Court Manager: Mike Higgins ☎ (01352) 707344 Fax: (01352) 753874

Mold
Court House: The Law Courts, Civic Centre, Mold, Flintshire CH7 1AE
☎ (01352) 707340 Fax: (01352) 753874 DX: 702521 Mold 2
Court Manager: Mike Higgins

County Courts

Caernarfon
Court House: The Court House, Llanberis Rd, Caernarfon LL55 2DF
☎ (01286) 684600 Fax: (01286) 678965 DX: 702483 Caernarfon 2
Email: enquiries@caernarfon.countycourt.gsi.gov.uk
Admin address: The Law Courts, Mold, CH7 1AE
Court Manager: Llinos Roberts

Conwy & Colwyn
Court House: Conwy Road, Llandudno, Conwy LL30 1GA
☎ (01745) 352940 Fax: (01745) 336726 DX: 702489 Rhyl 2
Email: N/A
Admin address: The Courthouse, Clwyd Street, Rhyl, Denbighshire, LL18 3LA

Llangefni
Court House: County Court Buildings, Glanhwfa Rd, Llangefni, Anglesey LL77 7EN
☎ (01248) 750225 Fax: (01248) 750778 DX: 702480 Llangefni 2
Email: enquiries@llangefni.countycourt.gsi.gov.uk
Court Manager: Llinos Roberts

LEGAL

North Wales (cont.)

County Courts (cont.)

Mold
Court House:	Law Courts, County Civic Centre, Mold CH7 1AE
	☎ (01978) 317400 Fax: (01978) 358213 DX: 702521 Mold 2
	Email: enquires@wrexham.countycourt.gsi.gov.uk
Admin address:	Wrexham Law Courts, Bodhyfryd, Wrexham, LL12 7BP
Court Manager:	Cheryl Chesters

Rhyl
Court House:	Court House, Clwyd St, Rhyl LL18 3LA
	☎ (01745) 352940 Fax: (01745) 336726 DX: 702489 Rhyl 2
	Email: enquiries@rhyl.countycourt.gsi.gov.uk
Court Manager:	Llinos Roberts

Wrexham
Court House:	Wrexham Law Courts, Bodhyfryd, Wrexham, Denbighshire LL12 7BP
	☎ (01978) 317400 Fax: (01978) 358213 DX: 745320 Wrexham 9
	Email: enquiries@wrexham.countycourt.gsi.gov.uk
Court Manager:	Cheryl Chesters

Magistrates' Courts

Caernarfon
Court Houses:	The Court House, Llanberis Road, Caernarfon, LL55 2DF
	☎ (01286) 669700 Fax: (01286) 669798 DX 744382 Caernarfon 6
Clerk to the Justices:	Iolo W Thomas
Court Manager:	Ffion Williams

Denbigh
Court Houses:	The Court House, Grove Rd, Denbigh LL16 3UU;
	The Court House, Victoria Rd, Prestatyn
	☎ (01492) 871333 Fax: (01492) 872321
	Email: nw-llandudnoenq@hmcts.gsi.gov.uk
Admin address:	The Court House, Conwy Road, Llandudno LL30 1GA
Court Manager:	Mike Higgins

Holyhead
Court Houses:	The Law Courts, Stanley Street, Holyhead, Anglesey LL65 1HG
	☎ (01286) 669700 Fax: (01286) 669798 DX: 774382 Caernarfon 6
	Email: nw-caernarfonmcenq@hmcts.gsi.gov.uk
Court Manager:	Ffion Williams
Admin address:	The Court House, Llanberis Road, Caernarfon LL55 2DF

Llandudno
Court Houses:	The Court House, Conwy Road, Llandudno, Conwy LL30 1GA
	☎ (01492) 871333 Fax: (01492) 872321 DX 11635 Llandudno
	Email: nw-llandudnomcenq@hmcts.gsi.gov.uk
Court Manager:	Ffion Williams

LEGAL

HER MAJESTY'S COURTS & TRIBUNALS SERVICE WALES

North Wales (cont.)

Magistrates' Courts (cont.)

Mold
Court House: Law Courts, County Civic Centre, Mold CH7 1AE
    ☎ (01352) 707330 Fax: (01352) 707333 DX: 702521 Mold 2
    Email: nw-wrexhammcenq@hmcts.gsi.gov.uk.cjsm.net
Admin address: Wrexham Law Courts, Bodhyfryd, Wrexham, LL12 7BP
Court Manager: Cheryl Chesters

Prestatyn
Court House: Law Courts, Victoria Road, Prestatyn, Denbighshire LL19 7TE
    ☎ (01745) 851916 Fax: (01745) 887046
    Email: nw-llandudnomcenq@hmcts.gsi.gov.uk

Wrexham
Court House: The Law Courts, Bodhyfryd, Wrexham LL12 7BP
    ☎ (01372) 707330 Fax: (01372) 707333 DX: 745320 Wrexham
    Email: N/A
Admin address   The Law Courts, Mold, CH7 1AE
Court Manager: Cheryl Chesters

LEGAL

Mid & West Wales

Stephen Whale, Clerk to the Justices (Dyfed Powys)
Magistrates' Clerk's Office, 21 Alban Street, Aberaeron, Ceredigion SA46 0DB
☎ (01545) 573057 Fax: (01545) 570295, DX 92405 Aberaeron

James P F Hehir, Clerk to the Justices (Swansea, Neath & Port Talbot)
Magistrates' Court, Grove Place, Swansea SA1 5DB
☎ (01792) 478300 Fax: (01792) 651066

Judges

Judge H Davies QC	Swansea Crown Court
Judge P Heywood	Swansea Crown Court
Judge H Mifflin	Swansea Civil Justice Centre
Judge I C Parry	Swansea Civil Justice Centre
Judge Rowlands	Swansea Crown Court
Judge Paul Thomas QC	Swansea Crown Court
Judge Keith G Thomas (Recorder of Swansea)	Swansea Crown Court
Judge C J Vosper QC	Swansea Civil Justice Centre

Crown Courts

Carmarthen

Court Houses: The Guildhall, Guildhall Square, Carmarthen SA31 1PR

☎ (01792) 637000 Fax: (01792) 637049
Email: contacts@swansea.crowncourt.gsi.gov.uk
Admin address   The Law Courts, St Helen's Road, Swansea SA1 4PF
Court Manager: Caroline Bevan

Swansea
Court Houses: The Law Courts, St Helens Rd, Swansea SA1 4PF
☎ (01792) 637000 Fax: (01792) 637049 DX: 99540 Swansea 4
Email: contacts@swansea.crowncourt.gsi.gov.uk
Court Manager: Caroline Bevan

County Courts

Aberystwyth
Court House: Y Lanfa, Aberystwyth, Ceredigion SY23 1AS
☎ (01970) 636370 Fax: (01970) 625985 DX: 99560 Aberystwyth 2
Email: enquiries@aberystwyth.countycourt.gsi.gov.uk
Court Manager: Gwen Botting

Brecon Law Courts
Court House: Brecon Law Court, Cambrian Way, Brecon, Powys LD3 7HR
☎ (01874) 622993 Fax: (01685) 727703 DX: 124340 Brecon 2
Email: breconmagscrt@hmcts.gsi.gov.uk
Admin address: Merthyr Tydfil Combined Courts, The Law Courts, Glebeland Place,
Merthyr Tydfil, CF47 8BH
Court Manager: Huw Evans

LEGAL

Mid & West Wales (cont.)

County Courts (cont.)

Carmarthen
Court House: The Hearing Centre, Hill House, Picton Terrace, Carmarthen SA31 3BS
☎ (01267) 245060 Fax: (01267) 225047 DX: 99570 Carmarthen 2
Email: enquiries@carmarthen.countycourt.gsi.gov.uk
Court Manager: Elin Lloyd

Haverfordwest
Court House: The Law Courts, Penffynnon, Hawthorn Rise, Haverfordwest SA61 2AX
☎ (01437) 772060 Fax: (01437) 769222 DX: 99610 Haverfordwest 2
Email: enquiries@haverfordwest.countycourt.gsi.gov.uk
Court Manager: Susan James

Llanelli
Court House: 2nd Floor, Court Buildings, Town Hall Square, Llanelli SA15 3AL
☎ (01554) 757171 Fax: (01554) 758079 DX: 99510 Llanelli 2
Email: enquiries@llanelli.countycourt.gsi.gov.uk
Court Manager: Meurig Thomas

Neath & Port Talbot
Court House: Forster Road, Neath SA11 3BN
☎ (01639) 642267 Fax: (01639) 633505 DX: 99550 Neath 2
Email: enquiries@neath.countycourt.gsi.gov.uk
Court Manager: Lyn Pardoe

Swansea Civil Justice Centre
Court House: Caravella House, Quay West, Quay Parade, Swansea SA1 1SP
☎ (01792) 485800 Fax: (01792) 485810 DX: 99740 Swansea 5
Email: enquiries@swansea.countycourt.gsi.gov.uk
Court Manager: Marilyn Jeffreys

Welshpool & Newtown
Court House: Welshpool Law Courts, The Mansion House, 24 Severn St, Welshpool, Powys SY21 7UX
☎ (01978) 317400 Fax: (01978) 358213 DX: 702524 Welshpool 2
Email: enquiries@wrexham.countycourt.gsi.gov.uk

Admin address: Wreham Law Courts, Bodhyfryd, Wrexham, Denbighshire LL12 7BP
Court Manager: Lesley Hyde

Magistrates' Courts

Aberystwyth
Court Houses: Magistrates' Court, Y Lanfa, Aberystwyth, Ceredigion SY23 1AS
☎ (01545) 570886 Fax: (01545) 570295
Email: aberaeronmagscrt@hmcts.gsi.gov.uk
Admin address: 21 Alban Street, Aberaeron, Ceredigion, SA46 0DB
Court Manager: Ann Beaumont

LEGAL

Mid & West Wales (cont.)

Magistrates' Courts (cont.)

Brecon Law Courts
Court House: Brecon Law Court, Cambrian Way, Brecon, Powys LD3 7HR
☎ (01874) 622993 Fax: (01685) 727703 DX: 124340 Brecon 2
Email: breconmagscrt@hmcts.gsi.gov.uk
Admin address: Merthyr Tydfil Combined Courts, The Law Courts, Glebeland Place, Merthyr Tydfil, CF47 8BH
Court Manager: Huw Evans

Carmarthen
Court House: Magistrates' Court, The Guildhall, Carmarthen SA31 1PR
Admin Court Office: ☎ (01554) 757201 Fax: (01554) 759669 DX 99512, Llanelli 2
Email: llanellimagscrt@hmcts.gsi.gov.uk
Admin address: Magistrates' Court, Town Hall Square, Llanelli SA15 3AW
Court Manager: Paul Grove

Haverfordwest
Court House: Magistrates' Court, Penffynnon, Hawthorn Rise, Haverfordwest SA61 2AX
☎ (01437) 772090 Fax: (01437) 771399 DX: 99610, Haverfordwest 2
Email: dy-pembsmcinfo@hmcts.gsi.gov.uk
Court Manager: David Williams

Llanelli
Court House: Magistrates' Court, Town Hall Square, Llanelli SA15 3AW
☎ (01554) 757201 Fax: (01554) 779986 DX: 99512, Llanelli 2
Email: llanellimagscrt@hmcts.gsi.gov.uk
Court Manager: Paul Grove

Neath
Court Houses: Neath Magistrates' Court, Fairfield Way, Neath SA11 1RF
☎ (01639) 765900 Fax: (01639) 765954
Court Manager: Kim Lewis

Swansea
Court House: Swansea Magistrates' Court, Grove Place, Swansea SA1 5DB
☎ (01792) 478300 Fax: (01792) 478352
Email: sw-swanseamagscrt@hmcts.gsi.gov.uk
Court Manager: John Harris

Welshpool
Court House: Welshpool Law Courts, 24 Severn St, Welshpool, Powys SY21 7UX
☎ (01938) 555968 Fax: (01938) 554593 DX: 702535, Welshpool 2
Email: dy-powysmcinfo@hmcts.gsi.gov.uk
Court Manager: Sandra Jones

LEGAL

CROWN PROSECUTION SERVICE WALES

Cymru Wales Area

20th Floor, Capital Tower, Greyfriars Rd, Cardiff CF10 3PL
☎ (029) 2080 3902 Fax: (029) 2080 3840
DX: 33056 Cardiff 1
Email: wales.communications@cps.gsi.gov.uk

Chief Crown Prosecutor: Jim Brisbane
Deputy Chief Crown Prosecutor: Ed Beltrami
Area Business Manager: Mike Grist
Area Communications Manager: Anthony Hobbs

LOCAL OFFICES

Cardiff
Capital Tower, Greyfriars Rd
Cardiff, CF10 3PL
☎ (029) 2080 3800
Fax: (029) 2080 3906
DX: 33056 Cardiff 1

Carmarthen
Cae Banc, Heol Penlanffos, Tanerdy
Carmarthen, SA31 2EZ
☎ (01267) 242 100
Fax: (01267) 242 111
DX: 51411 Carmarthen

Colwyn Bay
Llys Eirias, Heritage Gate, Abergele Rd
Colwyn Bay, LL29 8AW
☎ (01492) 806 800
Fax: (01492) 806 859
DX: 718060 Colwyn Bay 3

Cwmbran
Vantage Point, 1st Floor, Tŷ Coch Way
Cwmbran, NP44 7XX
☎ (01633) 261 100
Fax: (01633) 261 106
DX: 743270 Cwmbran 4

Merthyr Tydfil
Cambria House, Merthyr Tydfil, Industrial Park
Pentrebach, Merthyr Tydfil, CF48 4XA
☎ (01443) 694 800
Fax: (01443) 694 804
DX: 744250 Merthyr Tydfil 5

Newtown
Afon House, The Park
Newtown, SY16 2PQ
☎ (01686) 616 700
Fax: (01686) 616 709
DX: 29233 Newtown (Powys)

Swansea
Princess House, Princess Way
Swansea, SA1 3LY
☎ (01792) 452 900
Fax: (01792) 452 930
DX: 92056 Swansea 3

Grove Place
Swansea Police Station, Grove Place
Swansea SA1 5AE
☎ (01792) 555 600
Fax: (01792) 476 588
DX: 92076 Swansea

Wrexham
Bromfield House, Ellice Way
Wrexham, LL13 7YW
☎ (01978) 346 000
Fax: (01978) 346 001
DX: 26684 Wrexham

LEGAL

WALES PROBATION TRUST

Wales Probation Trust
33 Westgate Street
Cardiff CF10 1JE
☎ (029) 2023 2999
Fax: (029) 2023 0384

The 1st April 2010, marked a new era for probation services with the creation of Wales Probation Trust (WPT). The Offender Management Act 2007 enabled the four former Probation Areas/Trusts in Wales the opportunity to form the Wales Probation Trust. There has been a logical progression toward forming a unified Probation organization in Wales over the years and the decision to apply for Wales Probation Trust Status was based on a clear business case and on the experience of the two First Wave Trusts in Wales since April 2008.

Chief Executive: Sarah Payne
Chair: Sue Fox

PRISON ESTABLISHMENTS IN WALES

National Offender Management Service Cymru (NOMS)
Welsh Government,
Cathays Park, Ground Floor East,
CP2, Cardiff CF10 3NQ
☎ (02920) 826684

HMP Cardiff
No 1 Knox Rd,
Cardiff CF24 0UG
☎ (029) 2092 3100
Fax: (029) 2092 3318
Governor: Richard Booty

HMP Swansea
200 Oystermouth Rd,
Swansea SA1 3SR
☎ (01792) 485300
Fax: (01792) 485430
Governor: Neil Lavis

HMP & YOI Parc
Heol Hopcyn John,
Bridgend CF35 6AP
☎ (01656) 300200
Fax: (01656) 300316
Director: Janet Wallsgrove

HMP Prescoed (Prescoed)
Coed y Paen, Pontypool,
Monmouthshire NP4 0TB
☎ (01291) 675000
Fax: (01291) 675158
Governor: Steve Cross

HMP Usk/Prescoed (Usk)
47 Maryport St,
Usk NP15 1XP
☎ (01291) 671600
Fax: (01291) 671752
Governor: Steve Cross

LEGAL

The Wales Yearbook

13

LOCAL GOVERNMENT

LOCAL ELECTION RESULTS 2012

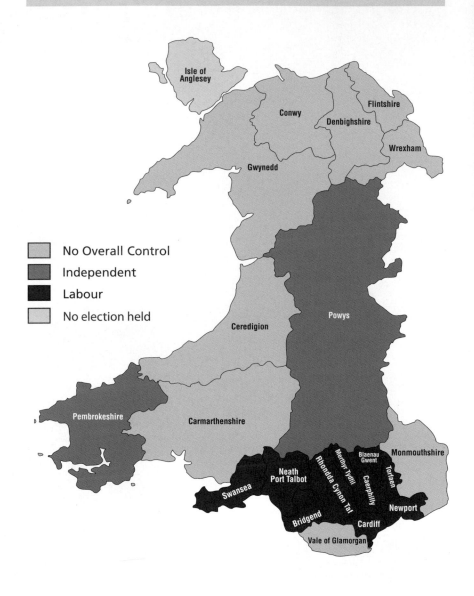

Legend:
- No Overall Control
- Independent
- Labour
- No election held

Map labels: Isle of Anglesey, Conwy, Flintshire, Denbighshire, Wrexham, Gwynedd, Powys, Ceredigion, Pembrokeshire, Carmarthenshire, Neath Port Talbot, Merthyr Tydfil, Blaenau Gwent, Monmouthshire, Rhondda Cynon Taf, Caerphilly, Torfaen, Swansea, Bridgend, Cardiff, Newport, Vale of Glamorgan

WELSH LOCAL GOVERNMENT ASSOCIATION

Leader
Cllr Bob Wellington

WLGA · CLILC

Local Government House
Drake Walk, Cardiff CF10 4LG
Tel: (029) 2046 8600
Fax: (029) 2046 8601
Email: wlga@wlga.gov.uk
Website: www.wlga.gov.uk

Chief Executive
Steve Thomas CBE

Leader

Cllr Bob Wellington
Leader
(Torfaen)

Cllr Ali Thomas
Deputy Leader
(Neath Port Talbot)

Cllr Aaron Shotton
Deputy Leader
(Flintshire)

Presiding Officer

Cllr Mel Nott
Presiding Officer
(Bridgend)

Cllr Dyfed Edwards
Deputy Presiding Officer
(Gwynedd)

Cllr David Jones
Deputy Presiding Officer
(Powys)

Cllr Bob Greenland
Deputy Presiding Officer
(Monmouthshire)

Cllr Kevin Madge
Deputy Presiding Officer
(Carmarthenshire)

Group Leaders

Cllr Bob Wellington
Labour Group Leader
(Torfaen)

Cllr Dyfed Edwards
Plaid Cymru Group Leader
(Gwynedd)

Cllr Hugh Evans
Independent Group Leader
(Denbighshire)

Cllr Peter Fox
Conservative Group Leader
(Monmouthshire)

WELSH LOCAL GOVERNMENT ASSOCIATION

Spokespersons

Cllr David Phillips
Anti Poverty,
Welfare Reform
& Heritage
(Swansea)

Cllr Brendan Toomey
Community Safety,
Policing & Fire
(Merthyr Tydfil)

Cllr Ali Thomas
Education /
Workforce
(Neath Port
Talbot)

Cllr Heather Joyce
Employment,
Training & Skills
(Cardiff)

Cllr Bryan Owen
Energy & Power
(Isle of Anglesey)

Cllr Neil Rogers
Environment, Sustainable
Development & Waste
(Wrexham)

Cllr Ellen ap Gwynn
Equalities & Active Ageing
(Ceredigion)

Cllr Bob Bright
European Affairs
(Newport)

Cllr Aaron Shotton
Finance & Resources
(Flintshire)

Cllr Mel Nott
Health & Social Care
(Bridgend)

Cllr Dyfed Edwards
Housing & Welsh
Language
(Gwynedd)

Cllr Peter Fox
ICT & Digital Inclusion
(Monmouthshire)

Cllr Hugh Evans
Improvement & Performance
(Denbighshire)

Cllr Hedley McCarthy
Leisure, Tourism &
Major Events
(Blaenau Gwent)

Cllr Harry Andrews
Regeneration & Economic
Development
(Caerphilly)

Cllr Neil Moore
Regulatory & Frontline Services
(Vale of Glamorgan)

Cllr Anthony Christopher
Roads, Infrastructure & Transport
(Rhondda Cynon Taf)

Cllr Jamie Adams
Rural Affairs
(Pembrokeshire)

Directorate

Steve Thomas CBE
Chief Executive

Jon Rae
Director of Resources

Chris Llewelyn
Director of Lifelong Learning,
Leisure & Information

Anna Freeman
Director of
Employment

Tim Peppin
Director of Regeneration &
Sustainable Development

Naomi Alleyne
Director of Equalities
& Social Justice

LOCAL GOVERNMENT

Welsh Local Government Association (WLGA): *The WLGA represents the interests of local government and promotes local democracy in Wales. Its membership includes the 22 local authorities in Wales, the 4 police authorities (shortly to be replaced by Police Commissioners), 3 fire and rescue authorities and 3 national park authorities as associate members. The WLGA's primary purpose is to promote better local government and enhance its reputation. The WLGA aims to support local authorities in the development of policies and priorities which improve public services and democracy. All councils play a full and active role within the WLGA and the organization derives its mandate from the WLGA Council which is made up of all the 22 Welsh Council Leaders and 79 of the most senior councillors in Wales.*

Democratic & Political Mandate: *The WLGA is an essential part of wider Welsh governance. The organization is responsible for negotiating the £5bn finance settlement for local government and for promoting the 700 plus function delivered by local government in Wales. The main representational and lobbying activities are carried out by the council leaders in their role as WLGA Spokespeople and by Deputy Spokespeople drawn from the wider WLGA Council. They are mandated to perform these roles by the WLGA Council, which also performs a fundamental role in terms of shaping policy and direction. WLGA Spokespeople regularly liaise with Welsh Government and UK Ministers over policy development, emerging strategies and finance issues.*

Inclusive Politics: *The WLGA is a political organization representing all authorities across the political spectrum. Its membership reflects the varied political local leadership across Wales. The WLGA also works with a range of partners throughout the public, private and voluntary sector. Crucial to WLGA business is its effective working relationship with the Welsh Government, Ministers and National Assembly officials. Central to this relationship is the statutory Partnership Council, the vehicle by which Welsh Ministers liaise with senior leaders from local government to discuss policies and strategic WLGA issues.*

Professional Support & Engagement: *The WLGA also relies on the professional support and expertise of officials throughout the 22 local authorities, not only through policy or professional networks, but through advice of the professional associations. It has a network of formally nominated professional advisors within specific service and policy fields across the 22 authorities and wider associate members.*

Collaboration & Regionalism: *Wales' 22 councils are leading the way in terms of public sector innovation and collaboration and through the WLGA and SOLACE Cymru. Wales' councils have established 4 regional boards:*

- *North Wales*
- *South East Wales*
- *South West*
- *Central Wales*

Through these Boards, councils are pooling expertise, sharing best practice and will increasingly plan and deliver joint services. This will not only lead to improved public services but should also see substantial efficiency savings. The Boards are supported by WLGA Regional Coordinators and aim to develop multi authority collaborative projects in service areas such as education, social care and waste management.

WLGA Directorate: *Originally established in 1996 primarily as a policy development and representative body, the WLGA has since developed into an organization that also leads on improvement and development, equalities, procurement, employment issues and hosts a range of partner bodies supporting local government, including:*

- *Waste Awareness Wales*
- *Social Services Improvement Agency*
- *Association of Directors of Education in Wales*
- *National Exercise Referral Scheme*
- *Food in Schools*

WLGA

WELSH LOCAL GOVERNMENT ASSOCIATION

Policy and Representation: *The WLGA delivers a range of support services for local authorities aimed at improving performance across key service areas and achieving high standards for the benefit of service users and communities. Its core strategic priorities reflect the political, financial and service challenges facing local government. These include:*

- *Finance and corporate governance*
- *Waste Management, Sustainability and Climate Change*
- *Lifelong Learning*
- *Social Care*
- *Improvement and Development*
- *Strategic Housing*
- *Transport and Highways*
- *Employer support*
- *Equalities and Social Justice*

The WLGA's Directorate is based in offices in Cardiff Bay, in 'Wales House' in Brussels and has a number of regional officers based in local authorities around Wales.

Local Government Data Unit: *The Local Government Data Unit-Wales is a partnership venture, funded by the Welsh Government and local government in Wales. The Data Unit provides support and guidance on a range of data and statistical issues including collecting data, commissioning surveys and identifying and exploiting existing data sources.*

WLGA

LOCAL GOVERNMENT DATA UNIT ~ WALES

3-7 Columbus Walk
Cardiff
CF10 4SD
Tel: (029) 2090 9500
Fax: (029) 2090 9510
Email: enquiries@dataunitwales.gov.uk
Website: www.dataunitwales.gov.uk
www.unedddatacymru.gov.uk
Twitter:
www.twitter.com/DataUnitWales

Chair
Cllr Jeffrey James

Executive Director
Andrew Stephens

UNED DDATA LLYWODRAETH LEOL ~ CYMRU
LOCAL GOVERNMENT DATA UNIT ~ WALES

The Data Unit is an independent company housed within the local government family in Wales. We exist to help local government and other organizations use data effectively to improve the services they provide to their customers.

The main objectives of the Data Unit are to:
* *Improve the quality and availability of local government data;*
* *Facilitate meaningful access to a broad range of other relevant data;*
* *Provide contextual information to facilitate effective use of data; and*
* *Improve the way in which data is used to drive improvement.*

BOARD MEMBERS*

Appointed by the Welsh Local Government Association (WLGA):
Cllr Colin Mann - Caerphilly
Cllr Mary Jones - Swansea
Cllr Kevin Madge - Carmarthenshire
Cllr David Wildman - Pembrokeshire
Cllr Julian Thompson Hill - Denbighshire
Cllr David Sage - Bridgend
Cllr Des Hillman OStJ - Blaenau Gwent
Cllr Leslie G Davies - Powys

Advisers:
Graham Jones - Neath Port Talbot
Dr Paul Williams - Cardiff Metropolitan University
Huw Rees - Wales Audit Office
Dr Dawn S Jones - Glyndŵr University
Dr Rhys Andrews - Cardiff Business School
Jonathan Rae - WLGA

Co-opted Directors:
Steve Thomas CBE - Chief Executive, WLGA
John Maitland Evans - Chief Executive, Vale of Glamorgan
Cllr Jeffrey James OStJ - Vale of Glamorgan

*At the time of going to print the new Board membership has yet to be confirmed following the 2012 Local Government election.

MANAGEMENT TEAM

Andrew Stephens
Richard Palmer
Philip Franklin

Total no. permanent staff: 25

LOCAL GOVERNMENT

BLAENAU GWENT COUNTY BOROUGH COUNCIL
CYNGOR BWRDEISDREF SIROL BLAENAU GWENT

Municipal Offices, Civic Centre,
Ebbw Vale NP23 6XB
Tel: (01495) 311556
Fax: (01495) 315265

Website:
www.blaenau-gwent.gov.uk

Leader
Hedley McCarthy

Chief Executive
David Waggett

Cyngor Bwrdeisdref Sirol
Blaenau Gwent
County Borough Council

LABOUR CONTROL	Lab **33** Ind **9**	TOTAL 42

ELECTION RESULT 2012

	Seats	Change	Votes	Share
Labour	33	16	26,812	58.3%
Independent	9	-7	12,759	27.7%
Others	0	-9	6,049	13.1%
Plaid Cymru	0	-	315	0.7%
Conservative	0	-	89	0.2%

Socio-economic Profile

		Rank 1<22
Area (sq km)	109	22
Population ('000s)	68.4	21
% able to speak Welsh	15.5	21
% born in Wales	92.1	1
% non-white ethnic groups	2.0	21
Gross rev expenditure (2011-12)	£173.0m	19
Forecast capital expenditure (2011-12)	£45.3m	11
% dwellings in Band D (2012-13)	4.7	22
Band D council tax (2011-12)	£1,426.29	1
% over retirement age	18.4	12
% pupils 5+ GCSEs A*-C (2010-11)	54.0	22
Unemployment (% claimant count)	7.1	1
Index of Deprivation (2011)	66	1
(% of Authority in most deprived 30%)		

Road ——

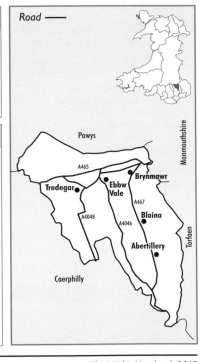

LOCAL GOVERNMENT

BLAENAU GWENT

Principal Officers

Chief Executive:	**David Waggett**
Director of Environment & Regeneration:	**John Parsons**
Director of Education & Leisure Services:	**Sylvia Lindoe**
Director of Social Services:	**Liz Major**
Chief Finance Officer:	**David McAuliffe**

Executive Members 2012-2013

Leader:	**Hedley McCarthy** (Lab)
Deputy Leader/Executive Business Manager:	**Stephen Thomas** (Lab)
Environment & Community Safety:	**Keith Hayden** (Lab)
Governance:	**Jim McIlwee** (Lab)
Highways & Transportation:	**David White** (Lab)
Leisure & Young People:	**David Wilkshire** (Lab)
Regeneration:	**Brian Scully** (Lab)
Resources:	**Barrie Sutton** (Lab)
Work Transformation & Partnership:	**Haydn Trollope** (Lab)
Social Services:	**Anita Hobbs** (Lab)

Committees & Chairs 2012-2013

Corporate Overview Committee:	**Malcolm Dally** (Lab)
Education & Leisure Committee:	**Brian Clements** (Lab)
Social Services Committee:	**John Mason** (Ind)
Regeneration & Environment Committee:	**Jennifer Morgan** (Lab)
Planning Committee:	**Dennis Owens** (Lab)
Licensing Committee:	**Diane Rowberry** (Lab)

Salary

Basic Salary: £12,175 per annum
Senior Salaries: Leader: £42,300; Deputy Leader: £29,820
Executive Member: £25,660; Chairs of Scrutiny Committees: £21,910
Chairs of Other Committees: £21,910
Mayor: £19,035; Deputy Mayor: £14,805

Councillors ♂ 35 ♀ 7

Mayor: Cllr Graham Bartlett Deputy Mayor: Cllr Mostyn Lewis

Peter Baldwin *(Lab: Nantyglo)*,
82a King Street, Nantyglo,
NP23 4LG ☎ (01495) 313817
Peter.Baldwin@blaenau-gwent.gov.uk

Graham Bartlett *(Lab: Cwmtillery)*,
95 Gwern Berthi Road, Cwmtillery,
NP13 1QZ ☎ (01495) 212126
Graham.Bartlett@blaenau-gwent.gov.uk

Mike Bartlett *(Lab: Llanhilleth)*,
48 Hafodarthen Estate, Brynithel,
Abertillery, NP13 2HY
☎ (01495) 214203
Mike.Bartlett@blaenau-gwent.gov.uk

Keren Bender *(Lab: Cwm)*,
Falcon House, Falcon Terrace, Cwm,
NP23 7SA ☎ (01495) 370375
Keren.Bender@blaenau-gwent.gov.uk

Derrick Bevan *(Lab: Cwm)*,
19 Brynhyfryd Terrace, Waunlwyd,
Ebbw Vale, NP23 6TW
☎ (01495) 370668 / 07881 365586
Derrick.Bevan@blaenau-gwent.gov.uk

Kevin Brown *(Ind: Brynmawr)*,
1 George Street, Brynmawr,
NP23 4TW ☎ (01495) 310238 /
07970993911
Kevin.Brown@blaenau-gwent.gov.uk

Keith Chaplin *(Lab: Abertillery)*,
53 Newall Street, Abertillery,
NP13 1EJ ☎ (01495) 211771
Keith.Chaplin@blaenau-gwent.gov.uk

Brian Clements *(Lab: Ebbw Vale
South)*, 6 Bryn Deri, Ebbw Vale,
NP23 6NU ☎ (01495) 307216 /
07952 516203
Brian.Clements@blaenau-gwent.gov.uk

Garth Collier *(Ind: Blaina)*, Camrose
Bungalow, Cwm Cottage Road,
Abertillery, NP13 1AT
☎ (01495) 290225
Garth.Collier@blaenau-gwent.gov.uk

Derek John Coughlin *(Lab: Ebbw
Vale North)*, 16 Blaen Wern, Ebbw
Vale, NP23 6WG ☎ 07971 780441
Derek.Coughlin@blaenau-gwent.gov.uk

Malcolm Cross *(Lab: Sirhowy)*,
4 Willow Court, Nantybwch,
NP22 4ST ☎ (01495) 723316 /
07971 624414
Malcolm.Cross@blaenau-gwent.gov.uk

Malcolm Dally *(Lab: Nantyglo)*,
29 King Street, Nantyglo, NP23 4JN
☎ (01495) 310301
Malcolm.Dally@blaenau-gwent.gov.uk

Nigel Daniels *(Ind: Abertillery)*,
5 Roch Street, Abertillery, NP13 1HF
☎ (01495) 215157
Nigel.Daniels@blaenau-gwent.gov.uk

Denzil Hancock *(Ind: Six Bells)*,
29 High Street, Six Bells, Abertillery,
NP13 2QD ☎ (01495) 214628
Denzil.Hancock@blaenau-gwent.gov.uk

Keith Hayden *(Lab: Georgetown)*,
5 Woodfield Road, Tredegar,
NP22 4RP ☎ (01495) 711997 /
07800 930448
Keith.Hayden@blaenau-gwent.gov.uk

Anita Hobbs *(Lab: Tredegar Central
& West)*, 7 Bedwellty Pits, Tredegar,
NP22 4BW ☎ (01495) 717916 /
07808 401855
Anita.Hobbs@blaenau-gwent.gov.uk

Mark Holland *(Lab: Six Bells)*, 60
Bryngwyn Road, Six Bells, Abertillery,
NP13 2PD ☎ (01495) 212266
Mark.Holland@blaenau-gwent.gov.uk

John Hopkins *(Ind: Brynmawr)*,
Green Gables, Rhyd Clydach,
Brynmawr, NP23 4SJ
☎ (01495) 310457 / 07791 184627
John.Hopkins@blaenau-gwent.gov.uk

Richard (Dickie) Jones *(Lab:
Abertillery)*, 15 Cromwell Street,
Abertillery, NP13 1QG
☎ (01495) 217662
Richard.Jones@blaenau-gwent.gov.uk

Ann Lewis *(Lab: Ebbw Vale North)*,
35 Alfred Street, Ebbw Vale,
NP23 6NQ ☎ (01495) 305203
Ann.Lewis@blaenau-gwent.gov.uk

Mostyn Lewis *(Lab: Ebbw Vale
South)*, 35 Alfred Street, Ebbw Vale,
NP23 6NQ ☎ (01495) 305203 /
07746 093012
Mostyn.Lewis@blaenau-gwent.gov.uk

John Mason *(Ind: Nantyglo)*, 34
Waun Fawr Winchestown, Nantyglo,
NP23 4QP ☎ (01495) 311455 /
07791 059824
John.Mason@blaenau-gwent.gov.uk

Hedley McCarthy *(Lab: Llanhilleth)*,
29 Old Woodland Terrace,
Aberbeeg, Abertillery, NP13 2EW
☎ (01495) 214371
Hedley.McCarthy@blaenau-gwent.gov.uk

Jim McIlwee *(Lab: Llanhilleth)*,
1 Baillie Smith Avenue, Swffryd,
NP11 5HR ☎ (01495) 244600
Jim.McIlwee@blaenau-gwent.gov.uk

Clive Meredith *(Ind: Badminton)*,
15 Fitzroy Avenue, Ebbw Vale,
NP23 5NL ☎ (01495) 309487 /
07837 021490
Clive.Meredith@blaenau-gwent.gov.uk

Mrs Jennifer Morgan, JP *(Lab:
Ebbw Vale North)*, 12 Princes Court,
Newtown, Ebbw Vale, NP23 5PL
☎ (01495) 304806
Jennifer.Morgan@blaenau-gwent.gov.uk

John Morgan *(Lab: Georgetown)*,
19 St James Park, Tredegar,
NP22 4NH ☎ (01495) 726682 /
07939 241486
John.Morgan@blaenau-gwent.gov.uk

Dennis Owens *(Lab: Sirhowy)*,
19 Lindsay Gardens, Tredegar,
NP22 4RP ☎ (01495) 722276 /
07977 984275
Dennis.Owens@blaenau-gwent.gov.uk

Bob Pagett *(Lab: Blaina)*, 39 East
Pentwyn, Blaina, Abertillery,
NP13 3JE ☎ (01495) 291305
Bob.Pagett@blaenau-gwent.gov.uk

BLAENAU GWENT

Diane Rowberry *(Lab: Sirhowy)*,
30 Tynewydd, Nantybwch, Tredegar,
NP23 3SQ ☎ (01495) 723455 /
07929513081
Diane.Rowberry@blaenau-gwent.gov.uk

Brian Scully *(Lab: Badminton)*,
40 Cwm Hir, Ebbw Vale, NP23 5LW
☎ (01495) 302468 / 07576 396049
Brian.Scully@blaenau-gwent.gov.uk

Tim Sharrem *(Lab: Cwmtillery)*,
16 Blaenau Gwent Rows, Abertillery,
NP13 1 PE ☎ (01495) 321202
Tim.Sharrem@blaenau-gwent.gov.uk

Barrie Morgan Sutton *(Lab:*
Brynmawr), 28 Brynawel, Brynmawr,
NP23 4RY ☎ (01495) 618796
Barrie.Sutton@blaenau-gwent.gov.uk

Godfrey Thomas *(Ind: Beaufort)*,
Allt-Mawr, 31 Beaufort Hill,
Ebbw Vale, NP23 5QN
☎ (01495) 308324 / 07768 347691
Godfrey.Thomas@blaenau-gwent.gov.uk

Stephen Thomas *(Lab: Tredegar*
Central & West), 26 Pembroke
Street, Tredegar, NP22 3HD
☎ (01495) 726220 / 07850 074276
Stephen.Thomas@blaenau-gwent.gov.uk

Christine Ann Tidey *(Lab:*
Cwmtillery), 25 Oxford Street,
Cwmtillery, Abertillery, NP13 1QQ
☎ (01495) 215003
Christine.Tidey@blaenau-gwent.gov.uk

Haydn Trollope *(Lab: Tredegar*
Central & West), 71 Gainsborough
Rd, Tredegar, NP22 3TQ
☎ (01495) 718276 / 07974 073170
Haydn.Trollope@blaenau-gwent.gov.uk

David William White *(Lab:*
Beaufort), 1 Llandaff Road, Beaufort,
Ebbw Vale, NP23 5RL
☎ (01495) 309780
David.White@blaenau-gwent.gov.uk

David Wilkshire *(Lab: Rassau)*,
2 Pant-y-Poplar, Rassau, Ebbw Vale,
NP23 5BX ☎ (01495) 307538 /
07973 407420
David.Wilkshire@blaenau-gwent.gov.uk

John Williams, MBE, JP *(Ind:*
Rassau), Ty-Ffynon Union St,
Tredegar, NP22 3QQ
☎ (01495) 711329 / 07773 316160
John.Williams@blaenau-gwent.gov.uk

Bernard Willis *(Lab: Tredegar*
Central & West), 70 Charles Street,
Tredegar, NP22 4AF
☎ (01495) 725619 / 07977 772981
Bernard.Willis@blaenau-gwent.gov.uk

Lisa Catherine Winnett *(Lab:*
Blaina), Llanwenfan, Surgery Road,
Blaina, NP13 3AZ
☎ (01495) 290012
Lisa.Winnett@blaenau-gwent.gov.uk

Clerks to the Community Councils

Abertillery & Llanhilleth
Community Council, *Graham*
Bartlett, Council Offices,
Mitre Street, Abertillery
☎ (01495) 217323

Brynmawr Town Council,
Angela Davies, Town Council Office,
Orchard Street, Brynmawr,
NP23 4ET ☎ (01495) 312205

Nantyglo & Blaina Town Council,
Steve Bartlett, New Town Council
Offices, High Street, Blaina
☎ (01495) 292817

Tredegar Town Council,
Christine Keane, Bedwellty House,
Tredegar ☎ (01495) 722352

BRIDGEND COUNTY BOROUGH COUNCIL
CYNGOR BWRDEISTREF SIROL PEN-Y-BONT AR OGWR

Civic Offices, Angel Street,
Bridgend CF31 4WB
Tel: (01656) 643643
Fax: (01656) 668126
Email: talktous@bridgend.gov.uk
Website: www.bridgend.gov.uk

Cyngor Bwrdeistref Sirol

BRIDGEND
County Borough Council

Leader
Mel Nott

Chief Executive
Darren Mepham

LABOUR CONTROL	Lab **39** Ind **10** Lib D **3** Con **1** PC **1**	TOTAL 54

ELECTION RESULT 2012

	Seats	Change	Votes	Share
Labour	39	12	28,989	54.2%
Independent	10	1	10,156	19.0%
Lib D	3	-8	4,130	7.7%
Conservative	1	-5	5,824	10.9%
Plaid Cymru	1	-	3,444	6.4%
Others	0	-	912	1.7%

Socio-economic Profile

		Rank 1<22
Area (sq km)	251	17
Population ('000s)	134.5	9
% able to speak Welsh	15.5	21
% born in Wales	84.7	7
% non-white ethnic groups	3.1	9
Gross rev expenditure (2011-12)	£311.6m	9
Forecast capital expenditure (2011-12)	£34.3m	14
% dwellings in Band D (2012-13)	15.5	15
Band D council tax (2011-12)	£1,288.04	5
% over retirement age	18.2	15
% pupils 5+ GCSEs A*-C (2010-11)	63.2	17
Unemployment (% claimant count 2011)	4.1	9
Index of Deprivation (2011)	40	6
(% of Authority in most deprived 30%)		

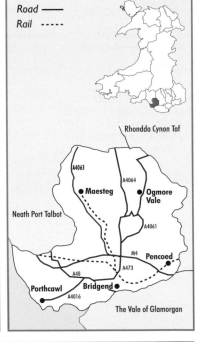

Road ——
Rail -----

Rhondda Cynon Taf

A4063

A4064

● Maesteg

● Ogmore Vale

Neath Port Talbot

A4061

M4 Pencoed ●

A48

A473

Porthcawl

Bridgend ●

A4016

The Vale of Glamorgan

LOCAL GOVERNMENT

BRIDGEND

Principal Officers

Chief Executive:	**Darren Mepham**
Assistant Chief Executive - Legal & Regulatory Services:	**Andrew Jolley**
Assistant Chief Executive - Performance:	**Ness Young**
Corporate Director Communities:	**Louise Fradd**
Corporate Director Children:	**Hilary Anthony**
Corporate Director Well-being:	**Simon Brindle**

Cabinet Members 2012-2013

Leader:	**Mel Nott** (Lab)
Deputy Leader:	**David Sage** (Lab)
Children:	**Huw David** (Lab)
Communities:	**Phil White** (Lab)
Resources:	**Mike Gregory** (Lab)
Well-being:	**Lyn Morgan** (Lab)

Committee Chairs 2012-2013

Appeals Panel:	**Reg Jenkins** (Lab)
Licensing Committee:	**Richard Williams** (Lab)
Development Control Committee:	**Hywel Williams** (Lab)
Town & Community Council Forum Committee:	**Mel Nott** (Lab)
Democratic Services Committee:	**Jeff Tildesley** (Ind)
Community Safety & Governance Overview & Scrutiny Committee:	**Nora Clarke** (Lib D)
Corporate Resources & Improvement Overview & Scrutiny Committee:	**Mal Reeves** (Lab)
Children & Young People's Overview & Scrutiny Committee:	**Peter Foley** (Ind)
Community Renewal & Environment Overview & Scrutiny Comm.:	**John Spanswick** (Lab)
Health and Well-being Overview & Scrutiny Committee:	**Malcolm Francis** (Lab)
Audit Committee:	**Tba**
Standards Committee:	**J Irvine**

Salaries

Basic Salary: £13,175
Senior Salaries: Leader: £47,500; Deputy Leader: £33,460
Cabinet Members: £28,780; Chairs of Scrutiny Committees: £21,910; Chairs of Other
Committees: £21,910; Chair of Standards Committee £256 daily fee or £128 1/2 day fee
Mayor: £21,375; Deputy Mayor: £16,625

LOCAL GOVERNMENT

Councillors ♂ 38 ♀ 16

Mayor: Cllr Marlene Thomas
Deputy Mayor: Cllr Clive James

Sean Aspey *(Ind: Porthcawl West Central)*, 14 Forge Way, Nottage, Porthcawl, CF36 3RP
☎ (01656) 772988
Cllr.Sean.Aspey@bridgend.gov.uk

Megan Butcher *(Ind: Cornelly)*, 5 Ffordd-Yr-Eglwys, North Cornelly, Bridgend, CF33 4HW
☎ (01656) 740451
Cllr.Megan.Butcher@bridgend.gov.uk

Norah Clarke *(Lib D: Nottage)*, 16 Kittiwake Close, Porthcawl, Bridgend, CF36 3UU
☎ (01656) 786018
Cllr.Norah.Clarke@bridgend.gov.uk

Huw David *(Lab: Cefn Cribwr)* , Edendale Court, Cefn Road, Cefn Cribwr, Bridgend, CF32 0AH ☎ (01656) 742116
Cllr.Huw.David@bridgend.gov.uk

Gerald Davies *(Lib D: Rest Bay)*, 12 Kittiwake Close, Porthcawl, Bridgend, CF36 3UU
☎ (01656) 786580
Cllr.Gerald.Davies@bridgend.gov.uk

Pamela Davies *(Lab: Bryntirion Laleston and Merthyr Mawr)*, 1 Maes Eirlys, Broadlands, Bridgend, CF31 5DG ☎ (01656) 658490
Cllr.Pam.Davies@bridgend.gov.uk

Wyn Davies *(Lab: Caerau)*, 12 Glan-Yr-Afon, Cwmfelin, Maesteg, CF34 9HU ☎ (01656) 736751
Cllr.Wyn.Davies@bridgend.gov.uk

Ella Dodd *(Ind: Coity)*, 8 Pwll Evan Ddu, Coity, Bridgend, CF35 6AY
☎ (01656) 650954
Cllr.Ella.Dodd@bridgend.gov.uk

Keith Edwards *(Lab: Maesteg East)*, 140 Mill View, Garth, Maesteg, CF34 0DD ☎ (01656) 734379
Cllr.Keith.Edwards@bridgend.gov.uk

Luke Ellis *(Lab: Pyle)*, 29 Trederwen, Kenfig Hill, Bridgend, CF33 6FB
☎ (01656) 741093
Cllr.Luke.Ellis@bridgend.gov.uk

Peter Foley *(Ind: Ann: Morfa)*, 5 Caeffatri Close, Bridgend, CF31 1LZ ☎ (01656) 645243
Cllr.Peter.Foley@bridgend.gov.uk

Malcolm Francis *(Lab: Llangewydd and Brynhyfryd)*, 6 Chiswick Close, Bridgend, CF31 4RA
☎ (01656) 657660
Cllr.Malcolm.Francis@bridgend.gov.uk

Cheryl Green *(Lib D: Bryntirion Laleston and Merthyr Mawr)*, Bryn Y fro, 55 High Street, Laleston, CF32 0HL ☎ (01656) 659288
Cllr.Cheryl.Green@bridgend.gov.uk

Mike Gregory *(Lab: Felindre)*, 1 Hafod Las, Pencoed, Bridgend, CF35 5NB ☎ (01656) 861307
Cllr.Mike.Gregory@bridgend.gov.uk

Della Hughes *(Ind: Ogmore Vale)*, 9 Waun Wen, Nantymoel, Bridgend, CF32 7NB ☎ (01656) 841000
Cllr.Della.Hughes@bridgend.gov.uk

Edith Hughes *(Lab: Oldcastle)*, 9 The Retreat, Bridgend, CF31 3NU
☎ (01656) 654528
Cllr.Edith.M.Hughes@bridgend.gov.uk

Clive James *(Lab: Pyle)*, 30 South View, Waunbant Road, Kenfig Hill, Bridgend, CF33 6DG
☎ (01656) 741160
Cllr.Clive.James@bridgend.gov.uk

Malcolm James *(PC: Llangynwyd)*, 156 Mill View, Garth, Maesteg, CF34 0DP ☎ (01656) 734732
Cllr.Malcolm.James@bridgend.gov.uk

Pauline James *(Lab: Pyle)*, 30 South View, Waunbant Road, Kenfig Hill, Bridgend, CF33 6DG
☎ (01656) 741160
Cllr.Pauline.James@bridgend.gov.uk

Reg Jenkins *(Lab: Pontycymmer)*, 168 Oxford Street, Pontycymmer, Bridgend, CF32 8DG
☎ (01656) 871540
Cllr.Reg.Jenkins@bridgend.gov.uk

Phil John *(Lab: Caerau)*, 85 Victoria Street, Caerau, Maesteg, CF34 0YP
☎ (01656) 730280
Cllr.Phil.John@bridgend.gov.uk

Brian Jones *(Ind: Porthcawl East Central)*, 23 Heol Y Goedwig, Porthcawl, CF36 5DU
☎ (01656) 788562
Cllr.Brian.Jones@bridgend.gov.uk

Cherie Jones *(Lab: Litchard)*, 106 Heol Castell Coety, Litchard, Bridgend, CF31 1PX
☎ (07874) 241810
Cllr.Cherie.Jones@bridgend.gov.uk

Craig Jones *(Lab: Brackla)*, 16 Nant-Y-Ffynnon, Brackla, Bridgend, CF31 2HT
☎ (01656) 656652
Cllr.Craig.L.Jones@bridgend.gov.uk

David Lewis *(Lab: Pen-Y-Fai)*, 30 Park Place, Sarn, Bridgend, CF32 9UA ☎ (01656) 723085
Cllr.David.Lewis@bridgend.gov.uk

John McCarthy *(Lab: Hendre)*, 25 Cae Talcen, Pencoed, Bridgend, CF35 6RP ☎ (01656) 861984
Cllr.John.McCarthy@bridgend.gov.uk

Christopher Michaelides *(Lab: Bettws)*, Mole End, Bettws Road, Bettws, Bridgend, CF32 8UR
☎ (01656) 720356
Cllr.Christopher.Michaelides@bridgend.gov.uk

Haydn Morgan *(Lab: Morfa)*, 7 Herbert Street, Bridgend, CF31 1TJ ☎ (01656) 655465
Cllr.Haydn.Morgan@bridgend.gov.uk

Lyn Morgan (*Lab: Ynysawdre*), 12 Llangeinor Road, Brynmenyn, Bridgend, CF32 9LY
☎ (01656) 721123
Cllr.Lyn.Morgan@bridgend.gov.uk

Mel Nott (*Lab: Sarn*), 49 Woodland Way, Sarn, Bridgend, CF32 9QA
☎ (01656) 721452
Cllr.MEJ.Nott@bridgend.gov.uk

Alexander Owen (*Lab: Penprysg*), Rowan House, High Street, Heol Y Cyw, Bridgend, CF35 6HY
☎ (01656) 864033
Cllr.Alex.Owen@bridgend.gov.uk

David Owen (*Ind: Nantymoel*), 3 Llewellyn Street, Nantymoel, Bridgend, CF32 7RF
☎ (01656) 840010
Cllr.David.Owen@bridgend.gov.uk

Pat Penpraze (*Lab: Bryncoch*), 3 Adams Avenue, Tyn-Y-Coed, Bryncethin, Bridgend, CF32 9RX,
☎ (01656) 720177
Cllr.Pat.Penpraze@bridgend.gov.uk

Gareth Phillips (*Lab: Oldcastle*), Rockfields, Nottage, Porthcawl, CF36 3NS ☎ (01656) 782525
Cllr.Gareth.Phillips@bridgend.gov.uk

David Pugh (*Lab: Blaengarw*), 9 David Street, Blaengarw, Bridgend, CF32 8AD ☎ (01656) 870565
Cllr.David.Pugh@bridgend.gov.uk

Christina Rees (*Lab: Newcastle*), 14 Manor Grove, Danygraig, Porthcawl, CF36 5HD
☎ (01656) 789441
Cllr.Christina.Rees@bridgend.gov.uk

Ceri Reeves (*Lab: Maesteg West*), 16 Aneurin Bevan's Way, Maesteg, CF34 0SX ☎ (01656) 731100
Cllr.Ceri.Reeves@bridgend.gov.uk

Mal Reeves (*Lab: Maesteg East*), 16 Aneurin Bevan's Way, Maesteg, CF34 0SX ☎ (01656) 731100
Cllr.Mal.Reeves@bridgend.gov.uk

David Sage (*Lab: Brackla*), 35 The Spinney, Brackla, Bridgend, CF31 2JD ☎ (01656) 662871
Cllr.David.Sage@bridgend.gov.uk

John Spanswick (*Lab: Brackla*), 5 Min-Y-Coed, Brackla, Bridgend, CF31 2AF ☎ (01656) 646534
Cllr.John.Spanswick@bridgend.gov.uk

Gary Thomas (*Lab: Bryncethin*), 1 Broad Oak Way, Bryntirion, Bridgend, CF31 4EQ
☎ (01656) 657317
Cllr.Gary.Thomas@bridgend.gov.uk

Marlene Thomas (*Lab: Llangeinor*) 1 Railway Terrace, Blaengarw, Bridgend, CF32 8AT
☎ (01656) 871439
Cllr.Marlene.Thomas@bridgend.gov.uk

Ross Thomas (*Lab: Maesteg West*), 6 Brick Row, Maesteg, CF34 9HD
☎ (01656) 734462
Cllr.Ross.Thomas@bridgend.gov.uk

Jeff Tildesley (*Ind: Cornelly*), Llanberis House, 23 Heol Fach, North Cornelly, Bridgend, CF33 4LB
☎ (01656) 740320
Cllr.Jeff.Tildesley@bridgend.gov.uk

Hailey Townsend (*Lab: Brackla*), 84 Erw Hir, Brackla, Bridgend, CF31 2DE ☎ (01656) 667163
Cllr.Hailey.J.Townsend@bridgend.gov.uk

Elaine Venables (*Ind: Coychurch Lower*), 2 Well Cottages, Coychurch, Bridgend, CF35 5HD
☎ (01656) 869044
Cllr.Elaine.Venables@bridgend.gov.uk

Ken Watts (*Con: Newton*), Seagulls, Bryneglwys Avenue, Newton, Porthcawl, CF36 5NN
☎ (01656) 788131
Cllr.Ken.Watts@bridgend.gov.uk

Cleone Westwood (*Lab: Cefn Glas*) 23 Burns Crescent, Cefn Glas, Bridgend, CF31 4PY
☎ (01656) 657707
Cllr.Cleone.Westwood@bridgend.gov.uk

David White (*Lab: Newcastle*), 64 Priory Avenue, Bridgend, CF31 3LR ☎ (01656) 648191
Cllr.David.White@bridgend.gov.uk

Phil White (*Lab: Caerau*), 28 Duffryn Madog, Nantyffyllon, Maesteg, CF34 0BE
☎ (01656) 731217
Cllr.Phil.White@bridgend.gov.uk

Hywel Williams (*Lab: Blackmill*), Dolau Ifan Ddu Farm, Blackmill, Bridgend, CF35 6DT
☎ (01656) 840465
Cllr.Hywel.Williams@bridgend.gov.uk

Richard Williams (*Lab: Hendre*), 15 Deri Close, Pencoed, Bridgend, CF35 6UA ☎ (01656) 862264
Cllr.Richard.Williams@bridgend.gov.uk

Mel Winter (*Ind: Aberkenfig*), 3 Laurel Close, Bryncoch, Bridgend, CF32 9TJ ☎ (01656) 721234
Cllr.Mel.Winter@bridgend.gov.uk

Richard Young (*Lab: Pendre*), 44 Wyndham Crescent, Bridgend, CF31 3DN ☎ (01656) 669527
Cllr.Richard.Young@bridgend.gov.uk

Clerks to the Community Councils

Brackla, *Anne Wilkes, c/o Oak Tree Surgery*, Whitethorn Drive, Brackla, Bridgend, CF31 2PQ
☎ (01656) 767072
clerk@bracklacommunitycouncil.gov.uk

Bridgend Town, *Deborah Rees*, Town Clerk, Council Offices, Glanogwr, Bridgend, CF31 3PF
☎ (01656) 659943
Bridgend.tc@btconnect.com

Cefn Cribwr, *Mr D L Jones*, 47 Cefn Road, Cefn Cribwr, Bridgend, CF32 0BA ☎ (01656) 741354
davidlloyd.jones@btinternet.com

Coity Higher, *Ann Harris, 66,* Priory Oak, Brackla, Bridgend CF31 2HZ
☎ (07532) 223474
clerkcoityhighercc@hotmail.co.uk

Cornelly, *Mrs D Evans,* 20 Moriah Place, Kenfig Hill, Bridgend, CF33 6DW ☎ (07882) 044798
Cornellyclerk@dawn5.orangehome.co.uk

Coychurch Higher, *Ms K Carter,* Strawberry Fields, Off High Street, Heol-y-Cyw, Bridgend CF35 6HY
☎ (01656) 863418
clerk2chcc@live.co.uk

Coychurch Lower, *Mr P A Smith,* Council Offices, Main Road, Coychurch, Bridgend, CF35 5HB
☎ (01656) 647216
clerkcoychurch@gmail.com

Garw Valley, *Nicola Eyre,* 72 Morfa Street, Bridgend CF31 1HD
☎ (07765) 414448
garwclerk@talktalk.net

Laleston, *Mr T Lardeau-Randall,* 19 Austin Avenue, Porthcawl, CF36 5RS ☎ (01656) 771880
glardeau@talktalk.net

Llangynwyd Lower, *Iris Hill, (Temp Clerk)* St. Arvans, Nicholls Road, Coytrahen, Bridgend, CF32 0EP
☎ (01656) 720840
isa70@talktalk.net

Llangynwyd Middle, *Mrs A Wilkes,* Cwmfelin Community Centre, Jenkins Terrace, Cwmfelin, Maesteg, CF34 9LA ☎ (01656) 738804
annewilkes.clerk@hotmail.com

Maesteg, *Mrs J Fielding,* Council Offices, Talbot St., Maesteg, CF34 9BY ☎ (01656) 732631
clerk@maestegcouncil.org

Merthyr Mawr, *Glyn Bryan,* 6 Eurgan Close, Llantwit Major, Glamorgan, CF61 1QY
☎ (07799) 116180
Merthyrmawr.clerk@hotmail.co.uk

Newcastle Higher, *Mr J Richfield,* Rock Farm, Rock Road, St Athan, Vale of Glamorgan CF62 4PG
☎ (01446) 750663
clerknhcc@btinternet.com

Ogmore Valley, *Louvain Lake,* Ty Heddwyn, Vale View Villas, Ogmore Vale CF32 7DP
☎ (01656) 849402
louvain.lake@aol.com

Pencoed Town, *David Prosser,* The Miners' Welfare Hall, Heol-y-Groes, Pencoed, Bridgend, CF35 5PE
☎ (01656) 869031
pencoedtownclerk@btconnect.com

Porthcawl Town, *Miss A Leyshon,* Council Offices, Tŷ Draw, 24 Victoria Avenue, Porthcawl, CF36 3HG
☎ (01656) 782215
Alison.leyshon@bridgend.gov.uk

Pyle, *Harold J Phillips,* The Talbot Community Centre, 9 Prince Road, Kenfig Hill, Bridgend, CF33 6ED
☎ (07792) 010043,
Clerk.pylecc@yahoo.co.uk

St. Brides Minor, *Mr B G Rees,* Council Office, The Life Long Learning Centre, Merfield Close, Sarn, Bridgend, CF32 9SW
☎ (01656) 651500
BReesConsultants@aol.com

Ynysawdre, *Mr G W Davies,* 12 Glan Yr Afon, Cwmfelin, Maesteg, CF34 9HU
☎ (01656) 736751
g.davies192@btinternet.com

CAERPHILLY COUNTY BOROUGH COUNCIL
CYNGOR BWRDEISTREF SIROL CAERFFILI

Penallta House,
Tredomen Park, Ystrad Mynach,
Hengoed CF82 7PG
Tel: (01443) 815588
Fax: (01443) 864240

Email: info@caerphilly.gov.uk
Website: www.caerphilly.gov.uk

Leader
Harry Andrews

Chief Executive
Anthony O'Sullivan

LABOUR CONTROL	Lab **50** PC **20** Ind **3**	TOTAL 73

ELECTION RESULT 2012

	Seats	Change	Votes	Share
Labour	50	18	51,697	52.2%
Plaid Cymru	20	-12	31,618	31.9%
Independent	3	-6	11,806	11.9%
Conservative	0	-	3,544	3.6%
Lib D	0	-	157	0.2%
Others	0	-	174	0.2%

Socio-economic Profile

		Rank 1<22
Area (sq km)	277	16
Population ('000s)	171.1	5
% able to speak Welsh	18.7	11
% born in Wales	89.9	3
% non-white ethnic groups	2.4	18
Gross rev expenditure (2011-12)	£402.8m	4
Forecast capital expenditure (2011-12)	£30.2m	16
% dwellings in Band D (2012-13)	11.7	17
Band D council tax (2011-12)	£1,095.42	17
% over retirement age	16.8	20
% pupils 5+ GCSEs A*-C (2010-11)	62.5	18
Unemployment (% claimant count 2011)	5	4
Index of Deprivation (2011)	40	7
(% of Authority in most deprived 30%)		

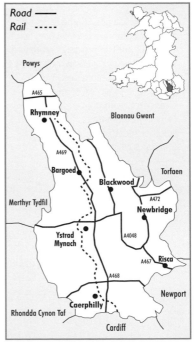

Road ——
Rail - - - - -

LOCAL GOVERNMENT

CAERPHILLY

Principal Officers

Chief Executive:	**Anthony O'Sullivan**
Deputy Chief Executive:	**Nigel Barnett**
Corporate Director Education, Lifelong Learning & Leisure:	**Sandra Aspinall**
Corporate Director, Social Services:	**Albert Heaney**

Cabinet Members 2012-2013

Leader:	**Harry Andrews** (Lab)
Deputy Leader & Cabinet Member for Corporate Services:	**Keith Reynolds** (Lab)
Deputy Leader & Cabinet Member for Housing:	**Gerald Jones** (Lab)
Performance & Asset Management:	**David Hardacre** (Lab)
Education & Lifelong Learning:	**Rhianon Passmore** (Lab)
Human Resources & Governance/Business Manager:	**Christine Forehead** (Lab)
Community & Leisure Services:	**David Poole** (Lab)
Social Services:	**Robin Woodyatt** (Lab)
Regeneration, Planning & Sustainable Development:	**Ken James** (Lab)
Highways, Transportation & Engineering:	**Tom Williams** (Lab)

Committee Chairs 2012-2013

Policy & Resources / Crime & Disorder Scrutiny Committee:	**Hefin David** (Lab)
Health, Social Care & Well-being Scrutiny Committee:	**Lyn Ackerman** (PC)
Education for Life Scrutiny Committee:	**Wynne David** (Lab)
Regeneration & Environment Scrutiny Committee:	**D Tudor Davies** (Lab)
Appointments Committee:	**Christine Forehead** (Lab)
Democratic Services Committee:	**Colin Mann** (PC)
Licensing Committee:	**John Bevan** (Lab)
Planning Committee:	**Stan Jenkins** (Lab)
Audit Committee:	**Tba**
Standards Committee:	**Len Davies**

Salaries

Basic Salary: £13,175 per annum;
Senior Salaries:
Leader: £47,500; Deputy Leaders: £31,120
Cabinet Member: £28,780; Chairs of Scrutiny Committees: £21,910
Chairs of Other Committees: £21, 910
Mayor: £21,375; Deputy Mayor: £16,625

Councillors ♂ 38 ♀ 16

Mayor: Cllr Marlene Thomas
Deputy Mayor: Cllr Michael Gray

Lyn Ackerman *(PC: Newbridge)*, 37 Blaen Blodau Street, Newbridge, NP11 4GG
☎ (01495) 245214
lynackerman@caerphilly.gov.uk

Mike Adams *(Lab: Pontllanfraith)*, 3 Brynteg Avenue, Pontllanfraith, Blackwood, NP12 2BY
☎ (01495) 225511
michaeladams@caerphilly.gov.uk

Elizabeth Aldworth *(Lab: Bedwas Trethomas & Machen)*, Cartref Fach, 20 Navigation Street, Trethomas, Caerphilly, CF83 8FR
☎ (029) 2086 6929
lizaldworth@caerphilly.gov.uk

Harry Andrews *(Lab: Gilfach)*, 14 Victoria Place, Gilfach, Bargoed, CF81 8JB ☎ (01443) 830942
harryandrews@caerphilly.gov.uk

Alan Angel *(PC: Ystrad Mynach)*, 27 Heol Brynteg, Ystrad Mynach, Hengoed, CF82 7EY
☎ 07935 272163
alanangel@caerphilly.gov.uk

Katherine Baker *(PC: Newbridge)*, 36 North Road, Newbridge, NP11 4AE ☎ (01495) 244573
kathbaker@caerphilly.gov.uk

Gina Bevan *(Lab: Moriah)*, 5 Arthur Street, Abertysswg, Rhymney, Tredegar, NP22 5AN
☎ (01685) 843578
ginabevan@caerphilly.gov.uk

John Bevan *(Lab: Moriah)*, 5 Arthur Street, Abertysswg, Rhymney, Tredegar, NP22 5AN
☎ (01685) 843578,
johnbevan@caerphilly.gov.uk

Phil Bevan *(PC: Morgan Jones)*, 75 Pontygwindy Road, Caerffili, CF83 3HG ☎ (029) 2086 6185
philbevan@caerphilly.gov.uk

Lyndon Binding *(PC: Aber Valley)*, 5 Church Road, Abertridwr, Caerffili, CF83 4DL
☎ (029) 2083 0826
lyndonbinding@caerphilly.gov.uk

Anne Blackman *(Ind: Nelson)*, 127 Shingrig Road, Nelson, Treharris, CF46 6DU
☎ (01443) 451834
anneblackman@caerphilly.gov.uk

Dennis Bolter *(PC: Hengoed)*, 12 Heol Y Felin, Cefn Hengoed, Hengoed, CF82 8FL
☎ (01443) 262676
dennisbolter@caerphilly.gov.uk

David Carter *(Lab: Bargoed)*, 49 John Street, Bargoed, CF81 8PH
☎ (01443) 839744
davidcarter@caerphilly.gov.uk

Anne Collins *(PC: Penyrheol)*, 1 Cefn-Y-Lon, Penyrheol, Caerffili, CF83 2JS ☎ (029) 2088 4696,
annecollins@caerphilly.gov.uk

Patricia Cook *(Lab: Blackwood)*, 13 Sycamore Court, Woodfield Park Estate, Blackwood, Gwent, NP12 0DA ☎ 07811 135454
patriciacook@caerphilly.gov.uk

Carl J Cuss *(Lab: Twyn Carno)*, 22 Tŷ Coch, Rhymney, Tredegar, NP22 5DG ☎ (01685) 844860
carlcuss@caerphilly.gov.uk

Hefin David *(Lab: St Cattwg)*, 2 Bryncoed Terrace, Penpedairheol, Hengoed, CF82 8DE
☎ 07902 287 223,
hefindavid@caerphilly.gov.uk

Wynne David *(Lab: St Cattwg)*, Hafren, 9 Tairheol, Penpedairheol, Hengoed, CF82 8DL ☎ (01443) 832278
wynnedavid@caerphilly.gov.uk

D Tudor Davies *(Lab: Bargoed)*, 26 East View, Bargoed,CF81 8LU
☎ (01443) 832169
tudordavies@caerphilly.gov.uk

Huw Davies *(Lab: Penyrheol)*, 14 Chepstow Court, Hendredenny, Caerphilly, CF83 2TH
☎ (029) 2086 7169
huwdavies@caerphilly.gov.uk

Ray Davies *(Lab: Bedwas Trethomas & Machen)*, 172 Pandy Road, Bedwas, Caerphilly, CF83 8EP
☎ (029) 2088 9514
raydavies@caerphilly.gov.uk

Kevin Dawson *(Lab: Pengam)*, 57 Fair View, Blackwood, NP12 3NR
☎ (01443) 821492
kevindawson@caerphilly.gov.uk

Nigel Dix *(Lab: Blackwood)*, 15 Montclaire Avenue, Blackwood, NP12 1EE ☎ (01495) 227908
nigeldix@caerphilly.gov.uk

Colin Durham *(Lab: Ynysddu)*, 4 Caerllwyn Terrace, Ynysddu, Crosskeys, Newport, NP11 7LE
☎ (01495) 358562
colindurham@caerphilly.gov.uk

Diana Ellis *(Lab: Blackwood)*, 11 St Tudors View, Blackwood, Caerphilly, NP12 1AQ
☎ 07530 083344
dianaellis@caerphilly.gov.uk

Colin Elsbury *(PC: St Martins)*, 13 Bryn Gwyn, Caerphilly, CF83 1ES ☎ 07891 925578
colinelsbury@caerphilly.gov.uk

Christine Forehead *(Lab: St James)*, 10 Heol Maerdy, Mornington Meadows, Caerphilly, CF83 3PZ ☎ (029) 2086 8941,
christineforehead@caerphilly.gov.uk

Elaine Forehead *(Lab: St James)*, 36 The Crescent, Trecenydd, Caerphilly, CF83 2SW
☎ (029) 2088 8894
elaineforehead@caerphilly.gov.uk

LOCAL GOVERNMENT

James Fussell *(PC: St Martins)*, 10 Clos Enfys, Castle View, Caerffili, CF83 1SB
☎ (029) 2086 2968
jamesfussell@caerphilly.gov.uk

June Gale *(Lab: Bedwas Trethomas & Machen)*, 2 Tyn-Y-Waun Road, Machen, Caerphilly, CF83 8LA ☎ (01633) 441409, junegale@caerphilly.gov.uk

Leon Gardiner *(Lab: Argoed)*, Islwyn View, 69 Penylan Road, Argoed, Blackwood, NP12 0AZ
☎ (01495) 225943, leongardiner@caerphilly.gov.uk

Nigel George *(Lab: Risca East)*, 7 Rosemont Avenue, Gelli Park, Risca, NP11 6HT ☎ 07816 980093
nigelgeorge@caerphilly.gov.uk

Colin J Gordon *(Lab: Pontllanfraith)*, 28 Cherry Tree Road, Pontllanfraith, Blackwood, NP12 2PY ☎ 07854 410 137
colingordon@caerphilly.gov.uk

Rob Gough *(PC: Llanbradach)*, 1 James Street, Llanbradach, Caerffili, CF83 3LJ ☎ (029) 2086 7982
robgough@caerphilly.gov.uk

Michael Gray *(Lab: Crosskeys)*, 19 Fields Park Terrace, Crosskeys, NP11 7DA ☎ (01495) 270253
michaelgray@caerphilly.gov.uk

Phyllis Ann Griffiths *(Ind: Risca West)*, 15 Cromwell Road, Risca, NP11 7AF ☎ (01495) 270210
phyllisgriffiths@caerphilly.gov.uk

David Hardacre *(Lab: Darren Valley)*, 10 Ogilvie Terrace, Deri, Bargoed, CF81 9JB ☎ (01443) 831202
davidhardacre@caerphilly.gov.uk

Derek Havard *(Lab: Bedwas Trethomas & Machen)*, 75 Ridgeway, Machen, Caerphilly, CF83 8RD ☎ (029) 2086 6079
derekhavard@caerphilly.gov.uk

Chris Hawker *(Lab: Cefn Fforest)*, 3 St Anne's Road, Bonnie View, Blackwood, Gwent, NP12 3PG
☎ (01443) 833246
christopherhawker@caerphilly.gov.uk

Alan Higgs *(Lab: Aberbargoed)*, 29 Duffryn Street, Aberbargoed, Bargoed, CF81 9ET ☎ 07950 956 550
alanhiggs@caerphilly.gov.uk

Graham John Hughes *(Lab: St Cattwg)*, 11 Hengoed Road, Penpedairheol, Hengoed, CF82 8BQ ☎ (01443) 820791
grahamhughes@caerphilly.gov.uk

Ken James *(Lab: Abercarn)*, Glenview, The Graig, Cwmcarn, Newport, NP11 7FA
☎ (01495) 270537
kenjames@caerphilly.gov.uk

Martyn James *(PC: Ystrad Mynach)*, 2 Hill Street, Ystrad Mynach, Hengoed, CF82 7AU
☎ (01443) 813694
martynjames@caerphilly.gov.uk

Stan Jenkins *(Lab: Risca East)*, 172 Manor Way, Tŷ Sign, Risca, NP11 6AD ☎ (01633) 614963
stanjenkins@caerphilly.gov.uk

Gary Johnston *(Lab: Newbridge)*, 2 West View, Newbridge, Gwent, NP11 4FL ☎ (01495) 240711
garyjohnston@caerphilly.gov.uk

Barbara Jones *(Lab: St James)*, 5 Edward Thomas Close, Rudry, Caerphilly, CF83 3EP
☎ (029) 2088 3740
barbarajones@caerphilly.gov.uk

Gerald Jones *(Lab: New Tredegar)*, 71 Derlwyn Street, Phillipstown, New Tredegar, NP24 6AZ ☎ (01443) 834354
geraldjones@caerphilly.gov.uk

Jan Jones *(Lab: Ynysddu)*, 16 The Avenue, Wyllie, Blackwood, NP12 2HJ ☎ (01495) 201171
janetjones@caerphilly.gov.uk

Steve Kent *(PC: St Martins)*, 29 St. David's Way, Watford Farm, Caerffili, CF83 1EY
☎ (029) 2088 6362
stephenkent@caerphilly.gov.uk

Gez Kirby *(Lab: Pontllanfraith)*, 15 St Andrews Drive, Pontllanfraith, NP12 2ET ☎ (01495) 228987
gezkirby@caerphilly.gov.uk

Andrew Lewis *(Lab: Crumlin)*, Morningside, Hafodyrynys, Crumlin, Newport, NP11 5BE
☎ (01495) 244698
andrewlewis@caerphilly.gov.uk

Keith Lloyd *(PC: Crumlin)*, 9 Windsor Terrace, Cwmnantgwynt, Aberbeeg, Abertillery, NP13 2DE,
☎ (01495) 214733
keithlloyd@caerphilly.gov.uk

Colin Mann *(PC: Llanbradach)*, 2 Coed-Y-Pia, Llanbradach, Caerffili, CF83 3PT ☎ (029) 2086 2460
colinmann@caerphilly.gov.uk

Sean Morgan *(Lab: Nelson)*, 15 Llanfabon Road, Nelson, CF46 6PF ☎ 07973 989721
seanmorgan@caerphilly.gov.uk

Gaynor D Oliver *(Lab: Pontlottyn)*, Cloverdale, Farm Road, Pontlottyn, Bargoed, CF81 9QG ☎ (01685) 844615
gaynoroliver@caerphilly.gov.uk

Rhianon Passmore *(Lab: Risca East)*, Tallis House, 42 Sycamore Crescent, Tŷ Sign, Risca, NP11 6AF
☎ (01633) 619080
rhianonpassmore@caerphilly.gov.uk

David Poole *(Lab: Pengam)*, 4 Britannia Walk, Pengam, Blackwood, NP12 3TQ
☎ (01443) 832545
davidpoole@caerphilly.gov.uk

Denver Preece *(Lab: Abercarn)*, Ger-Y-Coed, Rhyswg Road, Abercarn, NP11 5HB ☎ (01495) 247584
denverpreece@caerphilly.gov.uk

Mike Prew *(PC: Morgan Jones)*, 9 Dol-y-felin Street, Caerffili, CF83 3AF ☎ (029) 2086 0648
michaelprew@caerphilly.gov.uk

Dianne Price *(Lab: Bargoed)*, 12 Llancayo Park, Bargoed, CF81 8TS ☎ (01443) 836679
dianneprice@caerphilly.gov.uk

James Pritchard *(Lab: Morgan Jones)*, 36 Celyn Avenue, Caerphilly, CF83 3FL
☎ (029) 2088 3257
jamespritchard@caerphilly.gov.uk

Judith Pritchard *(PC: Hengoed)*, 14 Barry Close, Penpedairheol, Hengoed, CF82 8HJ
☎ (01443) 832785
judithpritchard@caerphilly.gov.uk

Dave Rees *(Ind: Risca West)*, 1 Old School Court, Pandy View, Crosskeys, NP11 7DL
☎ (01495) 273255
daverees@caerphilly.gov.uk

Keith Reynolds *(Lab: Aberbargoed)*, 4 School Street, Aberbargoed, Bargoed, CF81 9DA, ☎ (01443) 822140
keithreynolds@caerphilly.gov.uk

John Roberts *(PC: Aber Valley)*, 15 Graig-Y-Fedw, Abertridwr, Caerffili, CF83 4AQ
☎ (029) 2083 1668,
johnroberts@caerphilly.gov.uk

Roy Saralis *(Lab: Penmaen)*, 13 Yew Grove, Woodfieldside, Blackwood, Gwent, NP12 0DD
☎ (01495) 225738,
roystonsaralis@caerphilly.gov.uk

Margaret Sargent *(PC: Penyrheol)*, 10 Heol Glyn, Energlyn, Caerffili, CF83 2LZ
☎ (029) 2088 2910
margaretsargent@caerphilly.gov.uk

Jean Summers *(Lab: Penmaen)*, 3 New Road, Woodfieldside, Blackwood, Gwent, NP12 0BU
☎ (01495) 227549
jeansummers@caerphilly.gov.uk

John Taylor *(PC: Aber Valley)*, 7 Danygraig, Abertridwr, Caerffili, CF83 4BJ ☎ (029) 2083 1972
johntaylor@caerphilly.gov.uk

Lindsay Whittle *(PC: Penyrheol)*, Tŷ Watkyn, 4a Church Road, Abertridwr, Caerffili, CF83 4DL
☎ (029) 2083 1076
lindsaywhittle@caerphilly.gov.uk

Tom J Williams *(Lab: Cefn Fforest)*, 14 Craiglas Crescent, Cefn Fforest, Blackwood, NP12 3JY ☎ (01443) 830731
tomwilliams@caerphilly.gov.uk

Robin Woodyatt *(Lab: Maesycwmmer)*, 27 Park Road, Maesycwmmer, Hengoed, CF82 7PZ ☎ (01443) 815259
robinwoodyatt@caerphilly.gov.uk

Vacancy *(New Tredegar)*

Clerks to the Community Councils

Aber Valley Community Council, *Mrs S Hughes,* Abertridwr Library, Aberfawr Road, Abertridwr, CF83 4EJ
☎ (029) 2083 2061
abervalleycc@caerphilly.gov.uk

Argoed Community Council, *Mr G James,* 13 Cherry Tree Road, Pontllanfraith, Blackwwod, NP12 2PY ☎ 07855 556483

Bargoed Community Council, *Mrs L Tams,* The Settlement', 35 Cardiff Road, Bargoed, CF81 8NZ ☎ (01443) 830184

Bedwas, Trethomas & Machen Community Council, *Mrs S Chick,* Council Offices, Newport Road, Bedwas, Caerphilly, CF83 8YB
☎ (029) 2088 5734

Blackwood Community Council, *Mr J Hold Heddfan,* 12 Aspen Way, Blackwood, NP12 1WW
☎ (01495) 224636

Caerphilly Community Council, *Mr K Williams,* Twyn Community Centre, The Twyn, Caerphilly, CF83 1JL ☎ (029) 2088 8777

Darren Valley Community Council, *Mr G Williams,* 29 Bishops Grove, Merthyr Tydfil, CF47 9LJ
☎ (01685) 382553

Draethen, Waterloo & Rudry Community Council, *Sally Chick,* Tŷ Cyw, Starbuck Street, Rhydri, Caerphilly, CF83 3DP
☎ (029) 2086 0067
tycyw@hotmail.co.uk

Gelligaer Community Council, *Mrs C Mortimer,* Council Offices, Llwyn Onn, Penpedairheol, Hengoed, CF82 8BB
☎ (01443) 821322

Llanbradach & Pwllypant Community Council, *Mr W M Thompson,* 12 Mountain View, Machen, CF83 8QA
☎ (01633) 440492

Maesycwmmer Community Council, *Mrs G Thomas,* 33 Bryn Lane, Pontllanfraith, Blackwood, NP12 2PG ☎ (01495) 221070

Nelson Community Council, *Mr A Hoskins,* Ty'r Ffynon', 40 High Street, Nelson, Treharris, CF46 6EU ☎ (01443) 450047

New Tredegar Community Council, *Mrs D Gronow,* 7 Clyde Close, Pontllanfraith, NP12 2FY
☎ (01495) 226809

Penyrheol, Trecenydd & Energlyn Community Council, *Mrs H Treherne,* Golwg-y-cwm, Lower Brynhyfryd Terrace, Senghenydd, CF83 4GR
☎ (029) 2083 0666

Rhymney Community Council, *Mr G Williams,* 29 Bishops Grove, Merthyr Tydfil, CF47 9LJ
☎ (01685) 382553
Geraint235@btinternet.com

Van Community Council, *Mr J Dilworth,* 3 School Street, Pont-y-Clun, CF72 9AA
☎ (01443) 228535
john@jdilworth49.plus.com

CARDIFF COUNTY COUNCIL
CYNGOR SIR CAERDYDD

County Hall, Atlantic Wharf,
Cardiff CF10 4UW
Tel: (029) 2087 2087
Fax: (029) 2087 2086
Website: www.cardiff.gov.uk

CARDIFF
CAERDYDD

Leader
Heather Joyce

Chief Executive
Jon House

LABOUR CONTROL
Lab **46** Lib D **16** Con **7** Ind **4** PC **2**
TOTAL 75

ELECTION RESULT 2012

	Seats	Change	Votes	Share
Lab	46	33	95,444	39.6%
Lib D	16	-19	42,715	17.7%
Con	7	-10	45,079	18.7%
Ind	4	1	11,681	4.8%
PC	2	-5	30,989	12.9%
Others	0	-	15,070	6.3%

Socio-economic Profile

		Rank 1<22
Area (sq km)	140	19
Population ('000s)	341.0	1
% able to speak Welsh	17.8	14
% born in Wales	74.9	12
% non-ethnic groups	11.2	1
Gross rev expenditure (2011-12)	£737.6m	1
Forecast capital expenditure (2011-12)	£109.7m	1
% dwellings in Band D (2012-13)	23.5	1
Band D council tax (2011-12)	£1,086.23	20
% over retirement age	13.1	22
% pupils 5+ GCSEs A*-C (2010-11)	63.9	16
Unemployment (% claimant count 2011)	4.3	7
Index of Deprivation (2011)	35	8
(% of Authority in most deprived 30%)		

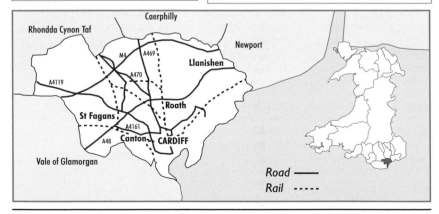

Road ——
Rail -----

CARDIFF

Corporate Directors

Chief Executive:	**Jon House**
Chief Operating Officer:	**Andrew Kerr**
Chief Corporate Services & Section 151 Officer:	**Christine Salter**
Corporate Chief Officer (Shared):	**Phillip Lenz**
Corporate Chief Officer (Communities):	**Sarah McGill**
Chief Officer Legal & Democratic Services (Monitoring Officer):	**Melanie Clay**

Executive Portfolios 2012-2013

Leader:	**Heather Joyce** (Lab)
Deputy Leader / Strategic Planning, Highways, Traffic & Transportation:	**Ralph Cook** (Lab)
Communities, Housing & Social Justice:	**Lynda Thorne** (Lab)
Education & Lifelong Learning:	**Julia Magill** (Lab)
Environment:	**Ashley Govier** (Lab)
Finance, Business & Local Economy:	**Russell Goodway** (Lab)
Social Care, Health & Well-being - Childrens Services:	**Richard Cook** (Lab)
Social Care, Health & Well-being - Adult Services:	**Luke Holland** (Lab)
Sport, Leisure & Culture:	**Huw Thomas** (Lab)

Committees & Chairs 2012-2013

Chair of the Council:	**Cerys Furlong** (Lab)
Vice-Chair of the Council:	**Keith Jones** (Lab)
Children & Young People Scrutiny Committee:	**Siobhan Corria** (Lab)
Community & Adult Services Scrutiny Committee:	**Ramesh Patel** (Lab)
Economy & Culture Scrutiny Committee:	**Craig Williams** (Con)
Environmental Scrutiny Committee:	**Bob Derbyshire** (Lab)
Policy Review & Performance Scrutiny Committee:	**Elizabeth Clark** (Lib D)
Planning Committee:	**Michael Michael** (Lab)
Licensing Committee:	**Derrick Morgan** (Lab)
Democratic Services Committee:	**Jayne Cowan** (Ind)
Constitution Committee:	**Cerys Furlong** (Lab)
Public Protection Committee:	**Derrick Morgan** (Lab)
Employment Conditions Committee:	**Cerys Furlong** (Lab)
Council Appeals Committee:	**Ralph Cook** (Lab)
Audit Committee:	**Tba**
Corporate Parenting Committee:	**Tba**
Standards & Ethics Committee:	**Akmal Hanuk**

Salaries

Basic Salary £13,175 per annum; Senior Salaries: Leader: £52,700; Deputy Leader: £37,100
Cabinet Members: £31,900; Chairs of Scrutiny Committees: £21,910; Chairs of Other Committees: £21,910
Leader of Main Opposition Group: £21,910; Chair of Council: £23,715; Vice-Chair of Council £18,445

Councillors   ♂ 47 ♀ 28

Lord Mayor of Cardiff: Tba
Chair of Council: Cerys Furlong Vice Chair: Keith Jones

Manzoor Ahmed (Lab: Adamsdown),
55 Woodvale Avenue, Cyncoed,
Cardiff, CF23 6SP ☎ 07595 353589
Manzoor.Ahmed@cardiff.gov.uk

Ali Ahmed (Lab: Butetown),
86 Torrens Drive, Cardiff, CF23 6DR
Ali.Ahmed@cardiff.gov.uk

Dilwar Ali (Lab: Llandaff North),
64 College Road, Llandaff North,
Cardiff, CF14 2JZ ☎ (029) 2062 4134
Dilwar.Ali@cardiff.gov.uk

CARDIFF

Gareth Aubrey (*Lib D: Llandaff*),
14 Burne Jones Close, Danescourt,
Cardiff, CF5 2RY ☎ (029) 2055 2600
/ 07557769791
gaubrey@cardiff.gov.uk

Phil Bale (*Lab: Llanishen*),
13 Llangranog Road, Llanishen,
Cardiff, CF14 5BL ☎ 07581 421282
Phil.Bale@cardiff.gov.uk

Fenella Bowden (*Ind: Heath*),
5 Welwyn Road, Heath, Cardiff,
CF14 1TG ☎ (029) 2069 2435
fbowden@cardiff.gov.uk

Joe Boyle (*Lib D: Penylan*), 15 Deri
Road, Penylan, Cardiff, CF23 5AH
☎ (029) 2046 2187
Joe.Boyle@cardiff.gov.uk

Peter Bradbury (*Lab: Caerau*),
10 Yarrow Close, Westfield Park,
Cardiff, CF5 4QS ☎ (029) 2059 1735
Peter.Bradbury@cardiff.gov.uk

Ed Bridges (*Lib D: Gabalfa*),
15 Quentin Street, Gabalfa, Cardiff,
CF14 3JW ☎ (029) 2061 4925
ebridges@cardiff.gov.uk

Patricia Burfoot (*Lib D: Penylan*),
12 Barons Court Road, Penylan,
Cardiff, CF23 9DF ☎ (029) 2087 2020
PBurfoot@cardiff.gov.uk

Joseph Carter (*Lib D: Pentwyn*),
45 Ael Y Bryn, Llanedeyrn, Cardiff,
CF23 9LG ☎ (029) 2073 4659
JCarter@cardiff.gov.uk

Paul Chaundy (*Lib D: Pentwyn*),
87 Bryn Pinwydden, Pentwyn,
Cardiff, CF23 7DF ☎ (029) 2073 4313
pchaundy@cardiff.gov.uk

Elizabeth Clark (*Lib D: Cathays*),
4 Denbigh Street, Cardiff, CF11 9JQ
☎ (029) 2063 0311
eclark@cardiff.gov.uk

Richard Cook (*Lab: Canton*),
17 Pencisely Crescent, Canton,
Cardiff, CF5 1DS ☎ (029) 2056 7428
riCook@cardiff.gov.uk

Ralph Cook (*Lab: Trowbridge*),
1 Cemaes Crescent, Trowbridge,
Cardiff, CF3 1TA ☎ (029) 2079 3809
/ 07966522149
ralphcook@cardiff.gov.uk

Siobhan Corria (*Lab: Llandaff
North*), 28 Station Road, Llandaff
North, Cardiff, CF14 2FF
Siobhan.Corria@cardiff.gov.uk

Jayne Cowan (*Ind: Rhiwbina*),
Brynlake, 174 Manor Way, Rhiwbina,
Cardiff, CF14 1RN
☎ (029) 2062 7757 / 07970013332
JCowan@cardiff.gov.uk

Kirsty Davies (*Lib D: Llandaff*),
16 Radyr Court Rise, Llandaff,
Cardiff, CF5 2QH ☎ (029) 2056 2979
kirstydavies@cardiff.gov.uk

Chris Davies (*Lab: Whitchurch &
Tongwynlais*), 25 Hanover Street,
Cardiff, CF5 1LS
Chris.Davis@cardiff.gov.uk

Daniel De'Ath (*Lab: Plasnewydd*),
133 Cyfarthfa Street, Roath,
Cardiff, CF24 3HH
Daniel.De'Ath@cardiff.gov.uk

Bob Derbyshire (*Lab: Rumney*),
876 Newport Road, Rumney, Cardiff,
CF3 4LJ ☎ (029) 2036 3748
Bob.Derbyshire@cardiff.gov.uk

Jonathan Evans (*Lab: Whitchurch &
Tongwynlais*), 52 Marguerites Way,
St Fagans, Cardiff, CF5 4QW
☎ (029) 2059 7084
Jonathan.Evans@cardiff.gov.uk

Lisa Ford (*PC: Fairwater*), 31 Hirst
Crescent, Fairwater, Cardiff,
CF5 3LG ☎ (029) 2055 1516
lisaford@cardiff.gov.uk

Cerys Furlong (*Lab: Canton*),
8 Egham Street, Canton, Cardiff,
CF5 1FQ ☎ (029) 2023 3510
cfurlong@cardiff.gov.uk

Susan Goddard (*Lab: Ely*), 2 Elford
Road, Ely, Cardiff, CF5 4HZ
☎ (029) 2065 9330 / 07963634116
sgoddard@cardiff.gov.uk

Russell Goodway (*Lab: Ely*), c/o
Members Services, CY7, County Hall,
Cardiff, CF10 4UW
☎ (029) 2087 2020 / 07962251439
r.v.goodway@cardiff.gov.uk

Iona Gordon (*Lab: Riverside*),
73 Conway Road, Riverside, Cardiff,
CF11 9NW ☎ (029) 2034 5213
Iona.Gordon@cardiff.gov.uk

Ashley Govier (*Lab: Grangetown*),
34 Jones Point House, Ferry Court,
Grangetown, Cardiff, CF11 0JF
Ashley.Govier@cardiff.gov.uk

Andrew Graham (*Con: Llanishen*),
163 Heol Hir, Thornhill, Cardiff,
CF14 9LB ☎ (029) 2075 1364
Andrew.Graham@cardiff.gov.uk

David Groves (*Lab: Whitchurch &
Tongwynlais*), 140 Llanrumney
Avenue, Llanrumney, Cardiff, CF3 4EA
David.Groves@cardiff.gov.uk

Phil Hawkins (*Lab: Riverside*),
9 Fields Park Road, Cardiff, CF11 9JP
☎ (029) 2037 2994
Phil.Hawkins@cardiff.gov.uk

Graham Hinchey (*Lab: Heath*), 30 St
Edwen Gardens, Heath, Cardiff, CF14
4LA Graham.Hinchey@cardiff.gov.uk

Gareth Holden (*Lib D: Gabalfa*),
2 Pen-y-Bryn Road, Gabalfa, Cardiff,
CF14 3LG Gareth.Holden@cardiff.gov.uk

Luke Holland (*Lab: Splott*),
76C Ninian Road, Roath, Cardiff,
CF23 5EN ☎ (029) 2091 0035
Luke.Holland@cardiff.gov.uk

Nigel Howells (*Lib D: Adamsdown*),
59 Cecil Street, Adamsdown, Cardiff,
CF24 1NW ☎ (029) 2046 5233
nhowells@cardiff.gov.uk

Lyn Hudson (*Con: Heath*),
19 Heathwood Road, Heath, Cardiff,
CF14 4JL ☎ (029) 2052 2654
lhudson@cardiff.gov.uk

Garry Hunt (*Lab: Llanishen*), 35
Woodside Court, Llanishen, Cardiff,
CF14 0RY Garry.Hunt@cardiff.gov.uk

Keith Hyde (*Lib D: Pentwyn*),
227 Hillrise, Llanedeyrn, Cardiff,
CF23 6UQ ☎ (029) 2073 2807
KHyde@cardiff.gov.uk

Mohammad Javed (*Lab:
Plasnewydd*), 84 Celyn Avenue,
Lakeside, Cardiff, CF23 6EQ
☎ (029) 2068 9440
Mohammad.Javed@cardiff.gov.uk

Margaret Jones (*Lib D: Cyncoed*),
22 Cefn Coed Avenue, Cyncoed,
Cardiff, CF23 6HG ☎ (029)2075 8175
mjones@cardiff.gov.uk

Keith Jones (*Lab: Llanrumney*),
5 Parracombe Crescent, Llanrumney,
Cardiff, CF3 5LS ☎ (029) 2036 4151
Keith.Jones@cardiff.gov.uk

Heather Joyce (*Lab: Llanrumney*),
32 Okehampton Avenue, Llanrumney,
Cardiff, CF3 5QZ ☎ (029) 2087 2500
HJoyce@cardiff.gov.uk

Bill Kelloway (*Lib D: Penylan*),
40 Dan-y-Coed Road, Cyncoed,
Cardiff, CF23 6NB ☎ (029) 2075 6886
BKelloway@cardiff.gov.uk

Sam Knight (Lab: Cathays), 68 Cyfarthfa Street, Cardiff, CF24 3HF
Sam.Knight@cardiff.gov.uk

Sue Lent (Lab: Plasnewydd), 7 Pen-y-Wain Place, Roath, Cardiff, CF24 4GA
Sue.Lent@cardiff.gov.uk

Kate Lloyd (Lib D: Cyncoed), 48 Duffryn Avenue, Cyncoed, Cardiff, CF23 6JL ☎ (029) 2075 3710
klloyd@cardiff.gov.uk

Chris Lomax (Lab: Grangetown), Flat 27 Worcester Court, Holmesdale Street, Grangetown, Cardiff, CF11 7HA ☎ (029) 2037 2853
Chris.Lomax@cardiff.gov.uk

Cecilia Love (Lab: Riverside), First Floor Flat, 99 Cathedral Road, Riverside, Cardiff, CF11 9PG
Cecilia.Love@cardiff.gov.uk

Julia Magill (Lab: Llanishen), Bridge Cottage, Lisvane Road, Llanishen, Cardiff, CF14 0SE ☎ (029) 2087 2396
Julia.Magill@cardiff.gov.uk

Gretta Marshall (Lab: Splott), 51 Tŷ Glas Avenue, Llanishen, Cardiff, CF14 5DX ☎ (029) 2075 9241
Gretta.Marshall@cardiff.gov.uk

Neil McEvoy (PC: Fairwater), c/o Members Services, CY7, County Hall, Cardiff, CF10 4UW ☎ (029) 2087 3348
nmcevoy@cardiff.gov.uk

Mary McGarry (Lab: Plasnewydd), 17 Pen-y-Wain Road, Roath, Cardiff, CF24 4GD Mary.McGarry@cardiff.gov.uk

Roderick McKerlich (Con: Radyr & Morganstown), St Elmo, 36 Heol Isaf, Radyr, Cardiff, CF15 8DY
☎ (029) 2084 3106
RMckerlich@cardiff.gov.uk

Sarah Merry (Lab: Cathays), 235 Albany Road, Cardiff, CF24 3NW ☎ (029) 2037 2301
Sarah.Merry@cardiff.gov.uk

Michael Michael (Lab: Trowbridge), 123 Fairwater Road, Fairwater, Cardiff, CF5 3JR ☎ (029) 2056 7068
Michael.Michael@cardiff.gov.uk

Paul Mitchell (Lab: Fairwater), 68 St Fagans Road, Fairwater, Cardiff, CF5 3AL ☎ (029) 2056 4637
Paul.Mitchell@cardiff.gov.uk

Derrick Morgan (Lab: Llanrumney), 5 Exford Crescent, Llanrumney, Cardiff, CF3 4JQ ☎ (029) 2077 9183
DerrickMorgan@cardiff.gov.uk

Jim Murphy (Lab: Ely), 32 Marloes Road, Ely, Cardiff, CF5 4JR
☎ (029) 2059 2441
Jim.Murphy@cardiff.gov.uk

Jacqueline Parry (Lab: Rumney), 24 Claremont Avenue, Rumney, Cardiff, CF3 4LR ☎ (029) 2077 9760
JackieParry@cardiff.gov.uk

Ramesh Patel (Lab: Canton), 3 Wembley Road, Canton, Cardiff, CF5 1NG ☎ (029) 2037 2035
rapatel@cardiff.gov.uk

Georgina Phillips (Lab: Pontprennau / Old St. Mellons), Hill House, Druidstone Road, Old St Mellons, Cardiff, CF3 6XE
☎ (029) 2036 0692
Georgina.Phillips@cardiff.gov.uk

David Rees (Lib D: Cyncoed), 236 Cyncoed Road, Cyncoed, Cardiff, CF23 6RT ☎ (029) 2075 0310
davrees@cardiff.gov.uk

Dianne Rees (Con: Pontprennau / Old St. Mellons), Marleigh Lodge, Druidstone Road, Old St Mellons, Cardiff, CF3 6XD ☎ (029) 2079 4918
DiRees@cardiff.gov.uk

Adrian Robson (Ind: Rhiwbina), Brynlake, 174 Manor Way, Rhiwbina, Cardiff, CF14 1RN ☎ (029) 2062 7757
ARobson@cardiff.gov.uk

Eleanor Sanders (Ind: Rhiwbina), 3 Cefn Craig, Rhiwbina, Cardiff, CF14 6SW ☎ (029) 2062 8587
Eleanor.Sanders@cardiff.gov.uk

Elaine Simmons (Lab: Caerau), 1 Reardon Smith Court, Cardiff, CF5 3JD ☎ (029) 2056 9349
Elaine.Simmons@cardiff.gov.uk

Graham Thomas (Con: Creigiau & St Fagans), 18 Parc-y-Fro, Creigiau, Cardiff, CF15 9SA
Graham.Thomas@cardiff.gov.uk

Huw Thomas (Lab: Splott), 19 Wilson Street, Splott, Cardiff, CF24 2NZ
Huw.Thomas@cardiff.gov.uk

Ben Thomas (Lab: Whitchurch & Tongwynlais), 9 Brynadar, Pantmawr, Cardiff, CF14 7HH ☎ (029) 2062 8773
Ben.Thomas@cardiff.gov.uk

Lynda Thorne (Lab: Grangetown), 51 Bessborough Drive, Grangetown, Cardiff, CF11 8NE
Lynda.Thorne@cardiff.gov.uk

David Walker (Con: Lisvane), 19 Clos Llysfaen, Lisvane, Cardiff, CF14 0UP ☎ (029) 2076 5836
dwalker@cardiff.gov.uk

Monica Walsh (Lab: Trowbridge), 2 Manorbier Crescent, Rumney, Cardiff, CF3 3NB ☎ (029) 2077 9541
MoWalsh@cardiff.gov.uk

Christopher Weaver (Lab: Cathays), 49 Cwmdare Street, Cardiff, CF24 4JZ
Christopher.Weaver@cardiff.gov.uk

Craig Williams (Con: Pentyrch), 15 Heol Gam, Pentyrch, Cardiff, CF15 9QA ☎ (029) 2089 2457
CrWilliams@cardiff.gov.uk

Judith Woodman (Lib D: Pentwyn), 42 Bryn Cyn, Pentwyn, Cardiff, CF23 7BJ ☎ (029) 2054 1534
JWoodman@cardiff.gov.uk

Clerks to the Community Councils

Lisvane Community Council, Mrs G Lawson, 45 Ridgeway, Lisvane, Cardiff, CF14 0RS
☎ (029) 2075 3868

Pentyrch Community Council, Mr A Davies, Police Station, 1 Penuel Road, Pentyrch, Cardiff, CF15 9LJ
☎ (029) 2089 1417

Radyr & Morganstown Community Council, Mrs H Fox, Old Church Rooms, Park Road, Radyr, Cardiff, CF15 8DF
☎ (029) 2084 2213

St Fagans Community Council, Mr D Barnard, 4 Leamington Road, Rhiwbina, Cardiff, CF14 6BX
☎ (029) 2061 0861

Tongwynlais Community Council, Mrs C Lane, 24 Queen Street, Tongwynlais, Cardiff, CF15 7NL ☎ (029) 2081 1422

Old St Mellons Community Council, Vacancy

LOCAL GOVERNMENT

CYNGOR SIR GÂR
CARMARTHENSHIRE COUNTY COUNCIL

County Hall,
Carmarthen SA31 1JP
Tel: (01267) 234567
Fax: (01267) 230848
Email:
information@carmarthenshire.gov.uk
Website:
www.carmarthenshire.gov.uk

Leader
Kevin Madge

Chief Executive
Mark James

NO OVERALL CONTROL

PC **28** Lab **23** Ind **22** Others **1**

TOTAL 74

ELECTION RESULT 2012

	Seats	Change	Votes	Share
PC	28	-2	29,874	37.7%
Lab	23	12	19,175	24.2%
Ind	22	-10	24,938	31.5%
Others	1	1	2,583	3.3%
Con	0	-	1,914	2.4%
Lib D	0	-1	675	0.9%

Socio-economic Profile

		Rank 1<22
Area (sq km)	2,371	3
Population ('000s)	180.7	4
% able to speak Welsh	46.5	4
% born in Wales	80.1	10
% non-white ethnic groups	2.8	13
Gross rev expenditure (2011-12)	£396.3m	5
Forecast capital expenditure (2011-12)	£71.4m	3
% dwellings in Band D (2012-13)	16.0	13
Average band D council tax (2011-12)	£1,187.59	9
% over retirement age	21.0	8
% pupils GCSEs A*-C (2010-11)	67.1	12
Unemployment (% claimant count 2011)	3.2	18
Index of Deprivation (2011)	22	13
(% of Authority in most deprived 30%)		

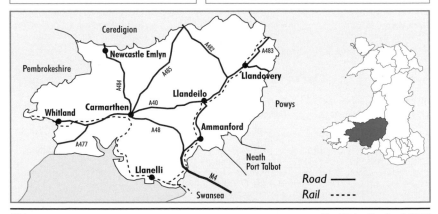

CARMARTHENSHIRE

Principal Officers

Chief Executive:	**Mark James**
Director of Regeneration & Leisure:	**Dave Gilbert**
Director of Resources:	**Roger Jones**
Director of Education & Children's Services:	**Robert Sully**
Director of Social Care, Health & Housing:	**Bruce McLernon**
Director of Technical Services:	**Richard Workman**

Executive Board Members 2012-2013

Leader:	**Kevin Madge** (Lab)
Deputy Leader of the Council / Housing:	**Tegwen Devichand** (Lab)
Deputy Leader of the Council / Community & Rural Affairs:	**Pam Palmer** (Ind)
Education & Children:	**Keith Davies** (Lab)
Health & Social Care:	**Jane Tremlett** (Ind)
Resources:	**Jeff Edmunds** (Lab)
Human Resources, Efficiencies & Collaboration:	**Mair Stephens** (Ind)
Regeneration & Leisure:	**Meryl Gravell** (Ind)
Environmental & Public Protection:	**Jim Jones** (Ind)
Street Scene:	**Colin Evans** (Lab)

Committee Chairs 2012-2013

Policy & Resources Scrutiny Committee:	**Hugh Richards** (Ind)
Environment & Pubic Protection Scrutiny Committee:	**Peter Cooper** (Lab)
Community Scrutiny Committee:	**Derek Cundy** (Lab)
Education & Children Scrutiny Committee:	**Eirwyn Williams** (PC)
Social Care & Health Scrutiny Committee:	**Emlyn Dole** (PC)
Appeals Committee:	**Hugh Richards** (Ind)
Appointments Committee A - Directors:	**Kevin Madge** (Lab)
Appointments Committee B - Heads of Service:	**Pam Palmer** (Ind)
Audit Committee:	**Tba**
Democractic Services Committee:	**Wyn Evans** (Ind)
Housing Review Committee:	**Jack James** (Lab)
Investment Panel Committee:	**Wyn Evans** (Ind)
Licensing Committee:	**Tom Theophilus** (Ind)
Member Appointments Committee:	**Janice Williams** (Lab)
Planning Committee:	**Anthony Jones** (Lab)
Standards Committee:	**Paul Stait**

Salaries

Basic Salary: £13,175 per annum
Senior Salaries: Leader: £47,500; Deputy Leader: £31,120
Executive Board Members: £28,780; Chairs of Scrutiny Committees: £21,910
Chairs of Other Committees: £21,910; Leader of Main Opposition Group: £21,910
Chair of Council: £21, 375; Vice-Chair of Council: £16,625

LOCAL GOVERNMENT

Councillors ♂ 54 ♀ 20

Chair: Cllr Ivor Jackson

Sue Allen *(Ind: Hendy Gwyn / Whitland)*, Penycoed Farm, Whitland, Carmarthenshire, SA34 0LR ☎ (01994) 240036
SMAllen@carmarthenshire.gov.uk

Ryan Bartlett *(Lab: Betws)*, Swn-y-Llan, 55 Betws Road, Betws, Ammanford, SA18 2HE
☎ (01269) 593108
RBartlett@carmarthenshire.gov.uk

Theressa Bowen *(Lab: Llwynhendy)*, 1 Lewis Crescent, Bryn, Llanelli, SA14 9EW ☎ (01554) 779190
ThBowen@carmarthenshire.gov.uk

Sian Caiach *(PF: Hengoed)*, Park Farm, Trimsaran Rd, Llanelli, SA15 4RD ☎ (01554) 741461
SMCaiach@sirgar.gov.uk

Cefin Campbell *(PC: Llanfihangel Aberbythych)*, Ty'r Gat, Gelli Aur, Carmarthen, SA32 8NG
☎ (01558) 668663
CACampbell@carmarthenshire.gov.uk

Mansel Charles *(PC: Llanegwad)*, Sarn Gelli, Llanegwad, Nantgaredig, Caerfyrddin, SA32 7NL
☎ (01558) 668823
Mcharles@sirgar.gov.uk

Peter Cooper *(Lab: Saron)*, 107 Saron Road, Saron, Ammanford, SA18 3LH ☎ (01269) 596843
APCooper@carmarthenshire.gov.uk

Deryk Cundy *(Lab: Bynea)*, 38 Berwick Road, Bynea, Llanelli, SA14 9SS ☎ 07850 153837
DCundy@carmarthenshire.gov.uk

Alun Davies *(PC: Saron)*, 81 Parklands Road, Penybanc, Ammanford, SA18 3TD
☎ (01269) 597060
AlunDavies@carmarthenshire.gov.uk

Daff Davies *(Ind: Llansteffan)*, Maesgwynne Mansion, Llangain, Carmarthen, SA33 5AL
☎ (01267) 241494
DBDavies@carmarthenshire.gov.uk

Glynog Davies *(PC: Quarter Bach)*, Gwynfryn, 47 Hall Street, Brynamman, Ammanford, SA18 1SG ☎ (01269) 823240
GlDavies@carmarthenshire.gov.uk

Ieuan Davies *(Ind: Llanybydder)*, 277 Clasemont Road, Morriston, Swansea, SA6 6BT ☎ 07817 617957
IWDavies@carmarthenshire.gov.uk

Joseph Davies *(Ind: Manordeilo & Salem)*, Cwmifor Farm, Cwmifor, Llandeilo, SA19 7AW
☎ (01558) 823284
JosDavies@carmarthenshire.gov.uk

Sharen Davies *(Lab: Llwynhendy)*, 1 Llys Bryngwyn, Dafen, Llanelli, SA14 8WG ☎ (01554) 757101
SDavies@carmarthenshire.gov.uk

Terry Davies *(Lab: Gorslas)*, 5 Heol Cross Hands, Gorslas, Llanelli, SA14 6RR ☎ (01269) 842784
TeDavies@carmarthenshire.gov.uk

Keith Davies *(Lab: Kidwelly)*, 52 Morfa Maen, Kidwelly, Carms, SA17 4UF ☎ (01554) 890867
WKDavies@carmarthenshire.gov.uk

Anthony Davies *(Ind: Llandybie)*, 116 Ammanford Road, Llandybie, Carmarthenshire, SA18 2JY
☎ (01269) 850282
AntDavies@sirgar.gov.uk

Tom Defis *(PC: Camarthen Town West)*, Brodirion, Ffynnonddrain, Caerfyrddin, SA31 1TY
☎ (01267) 236411
TDefis@carmarthenshire.gov.uk

Tegwen Devichand *(Lab: Dafen)*, 3 Dafen Road, Dafen, Llanelli, SA14 8LY ☎ (01554) 228599
TDevichand@carmarthenshire.gov.uk

Emlyn Dole *(PC: Llannon)*, Fferm Capel Ifan, Pontyberem, Llanelli, Sir Gaerfyrddin, SA15 5HF
☎ (01269) 870239
EDole@sirgar.gov.uk

Jeff Edmunds *(Lab: Bigyn)*, Mascolee, 13A Capel Terrace, Llanelli, SA15 1QA ☎ (01554) 755853
JEdmunds@carmarthenshire.gov.uk

George Edwards *(Lab: Hengoed)*, 41 Maes yr Haf, Pwll, Llanelli, SA15 4AT ☎ (01554) 780163
GeEdwards@carmarthenshire.gov.uk

Colin Evans *(Lab: Pontamman)*, 41 Pontamman Road, Ammanford, SA18 2HX ☎ (01269) 592582
CoEvans@carmarthenshire.gov.uk

Hazel Evans *(PC: Cenarth)*, Glynderw, Heol Ebenezer, Castell Newydd Emlyn, SA38 9BS
☎ (01239) 710452
HazelEvans@sirgar.gov.uk

Linda Evans *(PC: Llanfihangel-Ar-Arth)*, Ceu-Nant, Llanllwni, Llanybydder,Sir Gaerfyrddin, SA40 9SQ ☎ (01570) 481098
LDaviesEvans@sirgar.gov.uk

Wyn Evans *(Ind: Llanddarog)*, Tyrynys, Llanddarog, Carmarthen, SA32 8BL ☎ (01267) 275384
WJWEvans@carmarthenshire.gov.uk

Tyssul Evans *(PC: Llangyndeyrn)*, Cysgod-y-Glyn, Pontnewydd, Pontiets, Llanelli, SA15 5TL
☎ (01554) 810396
WTEvans@sirgar.gov.uk

Meryl Gravell *(Ind: Trimsaran)*, Hen-Blas, 31 Heol Waun-y-Clun, Trimsaran, Cydweli, SA17 4BL
☎ (01554) 810634
MGravell@carmarthenshire.gov.uk

Deian Harries *(PC: Ammanford)*, 18 Talbot Road, Ammanford, SA18 3BA ☎ (01269) 596361
DeHarries@carmarthenshire.gov.uk

Calum Higgins *(Lab: Tycroes)*, 116 Penygarn Road, Tycroes, Ammanford, SA18 3PF
☎ (01269) 591913
CHiggins@carmarthenshire.gov.uk

Gwyn Hopkins *(PC: Llangennech)*, 46 Parc Cleviston, Llangennech, Llanelli, SA14 9UP ☎ (01554) 820249
WGHopkins@sirgar.gov.uk

Ken Howell *(PC: Llangeler)*, Penlan Fawr, Penboyr, Felindre, Llandysul, SA44 5JF ☎ (01559) 370555
KenHowell@carmarthenshire.gov.uk

Peter Hughes Griffiths *(PC: Carmarthen Town North)*, 20 Waundew, Caerfyrddin, SA31 1HE
☎ (01267) 232240
PHughes-Griffiths@sirgar.gov.uk

Philip Hughes *(Ind: St Clears)*, The Old Board School, High Street, St Clears, Carmarthen, SA33 4DY
☎ (01994) 231572
PMHughes@carmarthenshire.gov.uk

Ivor Jackson *(Ind: Llandovery)*, 118 Maesglas, Llandovery, SA20 0DW ☎ (01550) 720056 IJJackson@carmarthenshire.gov.uk

Andrew James *(Ind: Llangadog)*, Barons Court, Llangadog, Carms, SA19 9HR ☎ 07532 247170 AndJames@carmarthenshire.gov.uk

Jack James *(Lab: Burry Port)*, 18 Parc y Minos Street, Burry Port, Carmarthenshire, SA16 0BN ☎ 07949 967496 JohnJames@carmarthenshire.gov.uk

David Jenkins *(PC: Glanamman)*, 12 High Street, Glanamman, Carms, SA18 1DX ☎ (01269) 822598 DMJenkins@sirgar.gov.uk

John Jenkins *(NA: Elli)*, 22 Brettenham Street, Llanelli, SA15 3ED ☎ (01554) 749649 JPJenkins@carmarthenshire.gov.uk

Anthony Jones *(Lab: Llandybie)*, 15 Maesllwyn, Bonllwyn, Ammanford, SA18 2EG ☎ (01269) 595465 AWJones@carmarthenshire.gov.uk

Gareth Jones *(PC: Carmarthen Town North)*, 3 Meysydd y Coleg, Caerfyrddin, SA31 3GR ☎ (01267) 231497 GOJones@sirgar.gov.uk

Irfon Jones *(Ind: Cynwyl Elfed)*, Man-Del, Bronwydd, Carmarthen, SA33 6BE ☎ (01267) 234868 HIJones@carmarthenshire.gov.uk

Patricia Jones *(Lab: Burry Port)*, Rosedale, 18 Dolau Fan, Burry Port, SA16 0RD ☎ (01554) 832132 PEMJones@carmarthenshire.gov.uk

Jim Jones *(Ind: Y Glyn)*, Tir Gof, 9 Heol Hen, Five Roads, Llanelli, SA15 5HJ ☎ (01269) 860138 TJJones@carmarthenshire.gov.uk

Winston Lemon *(PC: Glanymor)*, 25 Cambrian Street, Seaside, Llanelli, SA15 2PN ☎ 07791 118229 WJLemon@sirgar.gov.uk

Alun Lenny *(PC: Carmarthen Town South)*, Porth Angel, 26 Teras Picton, Caerfyrddin, SA31 3BX ☎ (01267) 232577 AlunLenny@carmarthenshire.gov.uk

Roy Llewellyn *(PC: Llanboidy)*, Bro Gronw, Cwmfelin Mynach, Hendygwyn-ar-Daf, SA34 0DH ☎ (01994) 448283 DJRLlewellyn@sirgar.gov.uk

Kevin Madge *(Lab: Garnant)*, 19 Highfield Road, Twyn, Garnant, Ammanford, SA18 1JL ☎ (01269) 825438 KMadge@carmarthenshire.gov.uk

Shirley Matthews *(Lab: Pembrey)*, 29 Tŷ Tan-y-Bryn, Burry Port, Carms, SA16 0HP ☎ (01554) 830975 SMatthews@carmarthenshire.gov.uk

Giles Morgan *(Ind: Swiss Valley)*, 61 Oaklands, Swiss Valley, Llanelli, SA14 8DH ☎ (01554) 754442 AGMorgan@carmarthenshire.gov.uk

Eryl Morgan *(Lab: Bigyn)*, Berso, 29 Capel Isaf Road, Llanelli, SA15 1QD ☎ (01554) 759115 EMorgan@carmarthenshire.gov.uk

Jeff Owen *(PC: Tyisha)*, 7 Charles Terrace, Llanelli, SA15 2UD ☎ (01554) 778280 JeffOwen@carmarthenshire.gov.uk

Pam Palmer *(Ind: Abergwili)*, Ffynnoniago, Rhydargaeau, Carmarthen, SA32 7JL ☎ (01267) 253429 PAPalmer@carmarthenshire.gov.uk

Darren Price *(PC: Gorslas)*, 11 Heol Rhosybonwen, Cefneithin, Llanelli, SA14 7DJ ☎ (01269) 842645 DaPrice@carmarthenshire.gov.uk

Hugh Richards *(Ind: Felinfoel)*, Hengoed Fawr Farm, Felinfoel, Llanelli, SA15 4PB ☎ (01554) 774810 DWHRichards@carmarthenshire.gov.uk

Louvain Roberts *(Lab: Glanymor)*, 24 George Street, Llanelli, SA15 2NB ☎ (01554) 773791 LoRoberts@carmarthenshire.gov.uk

Hugh Barrie *(Ind: Pembrey)*, 12 Elkington Park, Burry Port, Carms, SA16 0AU ☎ (01554) 834377 HBShepardson@carmarthenshire.gov.uk

Alan Speake *(PC: Camarthen Town West)*, 8 Pen y Cae, Johnstown, Carmarthen, SA31 3SD ☎ (01267) 234377 ADTSpeake@sirgar.gov.uk

Mair Stephens *(Ind: St Ishmael)*, The Coach House, Glanmorlais, Kidwelly, SA17 5AW ☎ (01267) 267428 LMStephens@carmarthenshire.gov.uk

Tom Theophilus *(Ind: Cilycwm)*, Ty Cornel, Cilycwm, Llandovery, SA20 0ST ☎ (01550) 720086 TTheophilus@carmarthenshire.gov.uk

Edward Thomas *(Ind: Llandeilo)*, Golwg yr Crug, 31 Parc Pencrug, Llandeilo, SA19 6RZ ☎ 07842 649261 EGThomas@carmarthenshire.gov.uk

Gareth Thomas *(PC: Hendy)*, Goitre Fach, Hendy, Pontarddulais, Swansea, SA4 0YA ☎ (01792) 882569 GBThomas@carmarthenshire.gov.uk

Gwyneth Thomas *(PC: Llangennech)*, 14 Llys y Felin, Llangennech, Llanelli, SA14 8BA ☎ (01554) 821637 GwyThomas@sirgar.gov.uk

Jeff Thomas *(PC: Carmarthen Town South)*, 55 Heol Bronwydd, Carmarthen, SA31 2AP ☎ (01267) 236227 JeffThomas@carmarthenshire.gov.uk

Keri Thomas *(Lab: Tyisha)*, 105B Dillwyn Street, Tyisha, Llanelli, SA15 1BT ☎ (01554) 784821 KPThomas@carmarthenshire.gov.uk

Kim Thomas *(Lab: Llanon)*, 71 Cae Glas, Cross Hands, Llanelli, SA14 6NH ☎ (01269) 842794 MKThomas@carmarthenshire.gov.uk

Sian Thomas *(PC: Penygroes)*, Brynteg, Heol Maes-Y-Bont, Castell-Y-Rhingyll, Llanelli, SA14 7NA ☎ (01269) 842151 SEThomas@sirgar.gov.uk

Dai Thomas *(Ind: Trelech)*, Treparcau, Penybont, Carmarthen, SA33 6QJ ☎ (01994) 484220 WDThomas@carmarthenshire.gov.uk

Bill Thomas *(Lab: Lliedi)*, 114 Old Castle Road, Llanelli, SA15 2SN ☎ (01554) 752600 BThomas@carmarthenshire.gov.uk

Jane Tremlett *(Ind: Laugharne Township)*, The Ship & Castle, King Street, Laugharne, Carmarthenshire, SA33 4RY ☎ (01994) 427709 JTremlett@carmarthenshire.gov.uk

Elwyn Williams *(PC: Llangunnor)*, Cystanog, Capel Dewi Road, Carmarthen, SA32 8AY ☎ (01267) 290247 DEWilliams@carmarthenshire.gov.uk

Eirwyn Williams *(PC: Cynwyl Gaeo)*, Cilgell Uchaf, Parc-y-Rhos, Cwm-Ann, Lampeter, SA48 8DY ☎ (01570) 423542 JEWilliams@sirgar.gov.uk

Janice Williams *(Lab: Lliedi)*, 42 Tyrfran Avenue, Llanelli, SA15 3LP ☎ (01554) 756351 JanWilliams@carmarthenshire.gov.uk

Joy Williams *(PC: Pontyberem)*, Amgoed, Heol Mynachlog, Pontyberem, Llanelli, SA15 5EY ☎ (01269) 870368 JSWilliams@sirgar.gov.uk

LOCAL GOVERNMENT

Clerks to the Community Councils

Abergwili Community Council, *Judith Kemp-Smith,* Maenllwyd, Llangynog, Carmarthen, SA33 5JA ☎ (01267) 211342 / 07966905544

Abernant Community Council, *Rhiannon Mathias,* Aelybryn, Bryn Iwan, Cynwyl Elfed, Caerfyrddin, SA33 6TE ☎ (01994) 484396

Ammanford Town Community Council, *Miriam Phillips,* Tŷ Tadcu, 4 Llys y Nant, off Kings Road, Llandybie, Ammanford, SA18 2TL ☎ (01269) 850870 miriam.phillips@btinternet.com

Betws Community Council, *Cerith Griffiths,* Glan yr Afon, Llwynteg, Llannon, Llanelli, Carmarthenshire, SA14 8JS ☎ (01269) 842961 Betwscommunitycouncil@hotmail.co.uk

Bronwydd Community Council, *Neil John,* 19 Bronwydd Road, Carmarthen, SA31 2AJ ☎ (01267) 243272 / (01267) 224478 clercbcc@ymail.com

Carmarthen Town Community Council, *Selwyn Thomas,* St Peter's Civic Hall, Nott Square, Carmarthen, SA31 3PG ☎ (01267) 235199

Cenarth Community Council, *Mr K Davies,* Arwelfa, Capel Iwan, Newcastle Emlyn, SA38 9LS ☎ (01559) 370539

Cil-y-cwm Community Council, *Mrs P A Jones,* Maes yr Haul, Cil-y-Cwm, Llandovery, Carmarthenshire, SA20 0ST ☎ (01550) 720454

Cilymaenllwyd Community Council, *Anwen Phillips,* 9 Brodeirian, Glandy Cross, Clunderwen, SA66 7XF

Cwmamman Town Community Council, *Mr D Davies,* Cwmffrwd Farm, Llandeilo Road, Glanaman, Ammanford, SA18 2DZ

Cynwyl Elfed Community Council, *Gwyn Jones,* Brynteg, Hermon, Cynwyl Elfed, Carmarthen, SA33 6SR ☎ (01267) 281439

Cynwyl Gaeo Community Council, *Mrs M Jones,* Tremafon, Pumsaint, Llanwrda, SA19 8BQ ☎ (01558) 650351

Dyffryn Cennen Community Council, *Eleri Griffiths,* Cysgod y Berllan, Trap, Llandeilo, Carmarthenshire, SA19 6TR ☎ (01558) 824 363

Eglwys Gymyn Community Council, *Mrs M Bowen,* Llwynbedw, Bethlehem Road, Pwlltrap, St Clears, SA32 4JZ ☎ (01994) 230607

Gors-las Community Council, *Elfryn Williams,* Talar Deg, Llanddarog, Carmarthen, SA32 8BJ ☎ (01267) 275562

Henllan Fallteg Community Council, *Ella Beattie,* Bwthyn yr Afon, Llanfallteg, Whitland, SA34 0UN ☎ (01437) 563149

Kidwelly Town Community Council, *Geraint Thomas,* The Town Clerk, The Council Offices, Gwenllian Centre, Kidwelly, SA17 4UL ☎ (01554) 890203 towncouncil@kidwelly.gov.uk

Laugharne Rural Community Council, *Chris Delaney,* The Farmhouse, Sir Johns Hill Farm, Gosport Street, Laugharne, Carmarthenshire, SA33 4TD ☎ (01994) 427019 cdelaneyheritage@btinternet.com

Llanarthne Community Council, *Gethin James,* Troed y Bryn, Llanarthne, Carmarthen, SA32 8JE ☎ (01558) 668143 gethinjames@btinternet.com

Llanboidy Community Council, *Kate Richards,* Glasnant, Llanboidy, Whitland, SA34 0EH

Llanddarog Community Council, *Elfryn Williams* Talar Deg, Llanddarog, Carmarthen, SA32 8BJ ☎ (01267) 275562

Llanddeusant Community Council, *Mrs I Jones,* 6 New Road, Llandovery, SA20 0ED ☎ (01550) 721134

Llanddowror Community Council, *Ms M J Cory,* Talfan Farm, St Clears, Carms, SA33 4HJ ☎ (01994) 231505 mjcory@aol.com

Llandeilo Town Community Council, *Roger Phillips,* Shire Hall, Carmarthen Street, Llandeilo, SA19 6AF ☎ (01558) 823850 clerk@llandeilo.gov.uk

Llandovery Town Community Council, *Henry Caldecote,* Crud Yr Awel, Llanwrda, Carmarthenshire, SA19 8HD ☎ (01550) 779226 hcaldecote@googlemail.com

Llandybie Community Council, *Dilys Griffiths,* 57 Wernddu Road, Ammanford, SA18 2NE ☎ (01269) 597124 cc@llandybie.org.uk

Llandyfaelog Community Council, *Arfon Davies,* No 2 Brynedda, Llansaint, Kidwelly, SA17 5JL ☎ (01267) 267647

Llanedi Community Council, *Owen Jones,* 60 Parc Howard Avenue, Llanelli, SA15 3JY ☎ (01554) 751059 owenjjones@hotmail.co.uk

Llanegwad Community Council, *Gaynor Davies Glynteg,* Felindre, Dryslwyn, Carmarthen, SA32 8RJ ☎ (01558) 669099, gaynor.d.davies@postoffice.co.uk

Llanelli Rural Community Council, *Mark Galbraith,* Vauxhall Buildings, Vauxhall, Llanelli, SA15 3BD ☎ (01554) 774103

Llanelli Town Community Council, *Mel Edwards,* Town Clerk, Old Vicarage, Town Hall Square, Llanelli, SA15 3DD ☎ (01554) 774352 meledwards@llanellitowncouncil.gov.uk

Llanfair-ar-y-Bryn Community Council, *Heulwen Jones,* Clynmawr, Rhandirmwyn, Llandovery, SA20 0NG ☎ (01550) 720462

Llanfihangel Aberbythych Community Council, *Eleri Jones,* Maespant, 24 Heol Caerfyrddin, Llandeilo, SA19 6RS

Llanfihangel ar Arth Community Council, Sarah Anita Evans, Frongelli, New Inn, Pencader, SA39 9AZ ☎ (01559) 384266

Llanfihangel Rhos y Corn Community Council, *Linda Davies,* Esgair Gynddu, Abergorlech, Carmarthen, SA32 ☎ (01558) 685046

Llanfynydd Community Council, *Lucy Wigley,* Fronhaul, Heol Groes, Dryslwyn, Carmarthen, SA32 8SA ☎ (01558) 668398

Llangadog Community Council, *June Madeira-Cole,* Ysgubor-lan, Capel Gwynfe, Llangadog, SA19 9RD ☎ (01550) 740602 j.madeiracole@btinternet.com

Llangain Community Council, *Iwan Griffiths,* Cysgod-y-Dderwen, Alltyferin Road, Pontargothi, Carmarthen, SA32 7NE ☎ (01267) 290199 iwangriffiths12@yahoo.co.uk

Llangathen Community Council, *Meirwen Rees,* Crachdy Isaf, Capel Isaac, Llandeilo, SA32 8LP ☎ (01558) 668349

Llangeler Community Council, *Stella Jones,* Awelon, Penboyr, Velindre, Llandysul, SA44 5JF ☎ (01559) 370773 ccllangeler@awelon.plus.com

Llangennech Community Council, *Mr E W Evans,* 45 Pendderi Road, Bryn, Llanelli, SA14 9PL ☎ (01554) 820181

Llangyndeyrn Community Council, *Julia Jones,* Morawel, 14 Heol Bancyroffis, Pontiets, Llanelli, SA15 5SA ☎ (01269) 860648

Llangunnor Community Council, *Clive Thomas,* 59 Nantyrarian, Carmarthen, SA31 3JQ ☎ (01267) 232665 clerk@llangunnor-cc.org.uk

Llangynin Community Council, *Lynn Bowen,* Carreg Wen, Salem Road, St Clears, Carmarthen, SA33 4DH ☎ (01994) 230994 hl.bowen@virgin.net

Llangynog Community Council, *Karen Guy,* Moelfre Uchaf, Llangynog, Carmarthen, SA33 5BS ☎ (01267) 211802 karen@chrisguy.plus.com

Llanllawddog Community Council, *Elfyn Williams,* 7 Maesdolau, Idole, Carmarthen, SA32 3DQ ☎ (01267) 230418

Llanllwni Community Council, *Eirlys Davies,* Cwmderi, Abergiar, Llanllwni, Llanybydder, SA40 9SQ ☎ (01570) 481041 eirlyscwmderi@btinternet.com

Llannon Community Council, *David Davies,* Cwmffrwd Farm, Llandeilo Road, Glanamman Carmarthenshire, SA18 2DZ ☎ 07971 026493 daidoc@yahoo.co.uk

Llanpumsaint Community Council, *One Voice Wales,* 24 College Street, Ammanford, SA18 3AF ☎ (01269) 595400

Llansadwrn Community Council, *Joy Waters,* 56 Heol Rhydaman, Tycroes, Ammanford, SA18 3QN ☎ (01269) 594157

Llansawel Community Council, *Janet Phillips,* Derwen Deg, Llansawel, Llandeilo, Carmarthenshire, SA19 7PE ☎ (01558) 685446

Llansteffan & Llanybri Community Council, *Liz Dutch,* Brig Y Don, The Green, Llanstephan, Carmarthen, SA33 5LW ☎ (01267) 241585 liz.dutch@googlemail.com

Llanwinio Community Council, *Geraint Evans,* Fronfelin, Cwmbach, Whitland, SA34 0DR ☎ (01994) 484211

Llanwrda Community Council, *Joy Waters,* 56 Heol Rhydaman, Tycroes, Ammanford, SA18 3QN ☎ (01269) 594157

Llanybydder Community Council, *Mrs M Y Beynon,* Castle Green, Bryn Road, Lampeter, SA48 7EF ☎ (01570) 422348

Llanycrwys Community Council, *Mrs J E Stacey,* Ty'n Waun, Ffaldybrenin, Llanwrda, SA19 8QA ☎ (01558) 650238

Manordeilo & Salem Community Council, *Jane Davies,* Stoneyford, Manordeilo, Llandeilo, SA19 7BP ☎ (01550) 777527 dav.stoneyford@tiscali.co.uk

Meidrim Community Council, *Joy Waters,* 56 Heol Rhydaman, Tycroes, Ammanford, SA18 3QN ☎ (01269) 594 157

Myddfai Community Council, *Mrs S A Beard,* Prestbury Lodge, Llandovery, SA20 0JT

Newcastle Emlyn Town Community Council, *Stella Jones,* Awelon, Penboyr, Velindre, Llandysul, SA44 5JF ☎ (01559) 370773 clerk@newcastleemlyntowncouncil.gov.uk

Newchurch & Merthyr Community Council, *Mr B A Davies,* 14 Ystrad Drive, Johnstown, Carmarthen, SA31 3PG ☎ (01267) 237555

Pembrey & Burry Port Town Community Council, *Diane Probert,* Council Offices, Memorial Hall, Parc y Minos Street, Burry Port, Carmarthenshire, SA16 0BN ☎ (01554) 834346

Pencarreg Community Council, *Mr E Williams,* Y Fedw, Cwmann, Lampeter, SA48 8DT ☎ (01570) 422425 ericfedw@onetel.com

Pendine Community Council, *Chris Delaney,* The Farmhouse, Sir Johns Hill Farm, Gosport Street, Laugharne, Carmarthenshire, SA33 4TD ☎ (01994) 427019 cdelaneyheritage@btinternet.com

Pontyberem Community Council, *Owen Jones,* 60 Parc Howard Avenue, Llanelli, SA15 3JY ☎ (01554) 751059 owenjjones@hotmail.co.uk

Quarter Bach Community Council, *Mr A Pedrick,* Erw'r Delyn, Brynceunant, Brynamman, Ammanford, SA18 1AH ☎ (01269) 822287

St Clears Town Community Council, *Lynn Bowen,* Carreg Wen, Salem Road, St Clears, SA33 4DH ☎ (01994) 230994 hl.bowen@virgin.net

St Ishmael Community Council, *Iris Williams,* Highbury, 2 Park View Drive, Kidwelly, SA17 5UP ☎ (01554) 890599 clerk@stishmaels.org

Talley Community Council, *Mrs J Morgan,* Maes y Wawr, Talley, Llandeilo, SA19 7YP ☎ (01558) 685737

Trelech a'r Betws Community Council, *Tom Howells,* Eithinduon-Isaf, Meidrim, Carmarthen, SA33 5PU ☎ (01994) 230332

Trimsaran Community Council, *Hugh Harries,* Plas y Sarn Leisure Centre, Trimsaran, Llanelli, SA17 4AA ☎ (01554) 810155

Whitland Town Community Council, *Suzanne Davies,* 41 Maes Abaty, Spring Gardens, Whitland, Carmarthenshire, SA34 0HQ shmaes41@hotmail.co.uk

LOCAL GOVERNMENT

CYNGOR SIR CEREDIGION
CEREDIGION COUNTY COUNCIL

Neuadd Cyngor Ceredigion,
Penmorfa, Aberaeron,
Ceredigion SA46 0PA

Tel: (01545) 570881 Fax: (01545) 572009

Email: info@ceredigion.gov.uk
Website: www.ceredigion.gov.uk

Leader
Cllr Ellen ap Gwynn

Chief Executive
Bronwen Morgan

NO OVERALL CONTROL

PC **19** Ind **15** Lib D **7** Lab **1**

TOTAL 42

ELECTION RESULT 2012

	Seats	Change	Votes	Share
PC	19	-	10,393	38.9%
Ind	15	3	7,710	28.8%
Lib D	7	-3	6,681	25.0%
Lab	1	-	884	3.3%
Con	0	-	1,080	4.0%

Socio-economic Profile

		Rank 1<22
Area (sq km)	1,794	4
Population ('000s)	76.9	19
% able to speak Welsh	52.5	3
% born in Wales	58.6	18
% non-white ethnic groups	4.1	5
Gross rev expenditure (2011-12)	£168.8m	20
Forecast capital expenditure (2011-12)	£28.5m	17
% dwellings in Band D (2012-13)	21.1	3
Band D council tax (2011-12)	£1,132.55	15
% over retirement age	21.3	6
% pupils 5+ GCSEs A*-C (2010-11)	71.4	6
Unemployment (% claimant count 2011)	1.9	22
Index of Deprivation (2011)	4	22
(% of Authority in most deprived 30%)		

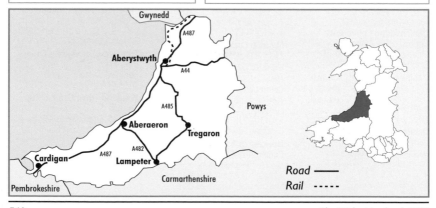

CEREDIGION

Principal Officers

Chief Executive:	**Bronwen Morgan**
Director of Environmental Services & Housing:	**Bryan Thomas**
Director of Highways, Property & Works:	**Huw Morgan**
Director of Social Services:	**Parry Davies**
Director of Finance:	**Gwyn Jones**
Director of Education & Community Services:	**Eifion Evans**

Cabinet Member Portfolios 2012-2013

Leader:	**Ellen ap Gwynn** (PC)
Transformation & Performance Management:	**Ray Quant** (Ind)
Education & Lifelong Learning:	**Hag Harris** (Lab)
Social Services & Housing:	**Catherine Hughes** (PC)
Corporate Resources:	**Peter Davies** (Ind)
Economic Development, Community Development, Leisure & Culture:	**Gareth Lloyd** (Ind)
Environment, Regulation & Planning:	**Dafydd Edwards** (Ind)
Transport, Waste & Carbon Management:	**Alun Williams** (PC)

Committee Chairs 2012-2013

Development Control Committee:	**Odwyn Davies** (Ind)
Licensing Committee:	**Paul James** (PC)
Democratic Services:	**Ceredig Davies** (Lib D)
Shortlisting:	**Tba**
Thriving Communities Scrutiny:	**Gethin James** (Ind)
Healthier Communties Scrutiny:	**Alun-Lloyd Jones** (PC)
Learning Communities Scrutiny:	**Paul Hinge** (Lib D)
Corporate Resources Scrutiny:	**Gill Hopley** (Ind)
Overview & Scrutiny Committees Co-ordinating Committee:	**Gareth Davies** (PC)
Audit Committee:	**Tba**
Ethics & Standards:	**R D Pritchard**

Salaries

Basic Salary: £13,175 per annum
Special Salaries: Leader: £42,300; Deputy Leader: £29,820
Cabinet Members: £25,660; Chairs of Scrutiny Committees: £21,910
Chairs of Other Committees: £21,910; Leader of Main Opposition Group £21,910
Chair of the Council: £19,035; Deputy Chair of the Council: £14,805

LOCAL GOVERNMENT

CEREDIGION

Councillors ♂ 37 ♀ 5

Chair: Cllr Mark Cole Vice-Chair: Cllr John Adams-Lewis

John Adams-Lewis *(PC: Aberteifi/Cardigan (Mwldan)*, Grove House, Feidrhenffordd Aberteifi/Cardigan, SA43 1NL
☎ (01239) 613341
john.adams-lewis@ceredigion.gov.uk

Ellen ap Gwynn *(PC: Ceulanamaesmawr)*, Garreg Wen, Talybont, SY24 5HJ
☎ (01970) 832551
ellen.apgwynn@ceredigion.gov.uk

Mark Cole *(Lib D: Aberteifi/Cardigan (Rhydyfuwch)*, Aneddfa, 2 Rhydyfelin, Aberteifi/Cardigan, SA43 1AU
☎ 07817 865712
mark.cole@ceredigion.gov.uk

Bryan Davies *(PC: Llanarth)*, Synod Uchaf, Synod Inn, Llandysul, SA44 6JD ☎ (01545) 580422
bryan.davies@ceredigion.gov.uk

Ceredig Davies *(Lib D: Aberystwyth Canol/Central)*, 9 Padarn Crescent, Llanbadarn Fawr, Aberystwyth, SY23 3QW ☎ (01970) 626552
ceredig.davies@ceredigion.gov.uk

Rhodri Davies *(PC: Melindwr)*, Gwalia, Llywernog, Ponterwyd, Aberystwyth, SY23 3AB
☎ (01970) 890437
rhodri.davies@ceredigion.gov.uk

Euros Davies *(Ind: Llanwenog)*, Y Cartws, Rhydowen, Llandysul, SA44 4QE ☎ (01545) 590280
euros.davies@ceredigion.gov.uk

Gareth Davies *(PC: Llanbadarn Fawr (Padarn))*, 6 Dol yr Odyn, Llanbadarn Fawr, Aberystwyth, SY23 3SS ☎ (01970) 624929
gareth.davies@ceredigion.gov.uk

Ifan Davies *(Ind: Lledrod)*, Dolyrychain, Pontrhydfendigaid, Ystrad Meurig, SY25 6EL
☎ (01974) 831241
ifan.davies@ceredigion.gov.uk

Aled Davies *(Ind: Aberystwyth Rheidol)*, Craig y Mor, 31 Queens Road, Aberystwyth, SY23 2HN
☎ (01970) 611402
aled.davies@ceredigion.gov.uk

Odwyn Davies *(PC: Llangybi)*, Olmarch Fawr, Llangybi, Llanbedr Pont Steffan/Lampeter, SA48 8NL
☎ (01570) 493303
odwyn.davies@ceredigion.gov.uk

Steve Davies *(PC: Aberystwyth Penparcau)*, 26 Heol Tynyfron, Penparcau, Aberystwyth, SY23 3RW ☎ (01970) 626087
steve.davies2@ceredigion.gov.uk

Peter Davies MBE *(Ind: Capel Dewi)*, Hafan Hedd, Aberbanc, Penrhiwllan, Llandysul, SA44 5NP
☎ (01559) 371281
peter.davies@ceredigion.gov.uk

Dafydd Edwards *(Ind: Llansantffraed)*, Lledal, Bethania, Llanon, Aberystwyth, SY23 5NJ
☎ (01974) 272528
dafydd.edwards@ceredigion.gov.uk

Elizabeth Evans *(Lib D: Aberaeron)*, Ynys Hir, Ffosyffin, Aberaeron, SA46 OHB ☎ (01545) 570622
elizabeth.evans@ceredigion.gov.uk

Towyn Evans *(PC: Llandyfriog)*, Afallon, Adpar, Castell Newydd Emlyn, SA38 9PX ☎ (01239) 710684
towyn.evans@ceredigion.gov.uk

Rhodri Evans *(Ind: Llangeitho)*, Ysgoldy, Llanio Road, Tregaron, SY25 6UW ☎ (01974) 298076
rhodri.evans2@ceredigion.gov.uk

Peter Evans *(PC: Tref Llandysul Town)*, Awel Dyfi, Parc yr Ynn, Llandysul, SA44 4JU
☎ (01559) 362196
peter.evans3@ceredigion.gov.uk

Hag Harris *(Lab: Llanbedr Pont Steffan/Lampeter)*, 1 Tŷ Hen Uchaf, Llanbedr Pont Steffan/Lampeter, SA48 7RZ ☎ (01570) 423402
hag.harries@ceredigion.gov.uk

Paul Hinge *(Lib D: Tirymynach)*, 10 Tregerddan, Bow Street, SY24 5AU ☎ (01970) 822092
paul.hinge@ceredigion.gov.uk

Gill Hopley *(Ind: Cei Newydd/New Quay)*, Gwalia, Uplands Square, Cei Newydd/New Quay, SA45 9QH
☎ (01545) 560085
gill.hopley@ceredigion.gov.uk

Catherine Hughes *(PC:Tregaron)*, Y Fron, Heol Dewi, Tregaron, SY25 6JW ☎ (01974) 298700
catherine.hughes@ceredigion.gov.uk

Gethin James *(Ind: Aberporth)*, Golwgfor, Aberporth, Aberteifi/Cardigan, SA43 2EX
☎ (01239) 811650
gethin.james@ceredigion.gov.uk

Gwyn James *(Ind: Penbryn)*, Bron-y-glyn, Glynarthen, Llandysul, SA44 6PS ☎ (01239) 858808
gwyn.james@ceredigion.gov.uk

Paul James *(PC: Llanbadarn Fawr (Sulien)*, Glascoed, 4 Primrose Hill, Llanbadarn Fawr, Aberystwyth, SY23 3SF ☎ (01970) 617870
paul.james@ceredigion.gov.uk

Alun Lloyd Jones *(PC: Llanfarian)*, Murmur yr Ystwyth, 14 Maes Isfryn, Llanfarian, Aberystwyth, SY23 4UG
☎ (01970) 623661
alun.lloydjones@ceredigion.gov.uk

Lorrae Jones-Southgate *(PC: Aberystwyth Penparcau)*, 30 Cefn Esgair, Llanbadarn Fawr, Aberystwyth, SY23 3JG
☎ (01970) 626665
lorrae.jones-southgate@ceredigion.gov.uk

Rowland Jones MBE *(Lib D: Ystwyth)*, Afallon, 5 Dolfelen, Llanilar, Aberystwyth, SY23 4PW
☎ (01974) 241328
rowland.jones@ceredigion.gov.uk

Thomas Lewis *(Ind: Penparc)*, Mount Pleasant, Y Ferwig, Aberteifi/Cardigan, SA43 1QJ ☎ (01239) 612015
thomaslewis34@mypostoffice.co.uk

Maldwyn Lewis *(Ind: Troedyraur)*, Y Mans, Glynarthen, Llandysul, SA44 5NT ☎ (01239) 851005
maldwyn.lewis@ceredigion.gov.uk

Gareth Lloyd *(Ind: Llandysiliogogo)*, Hafanclettwr, Talgarreg, Llandysul, SA44 4XD
☎ (01545) 590298 / 590772
gareth.lloyd@ceredigion.gov.uk

William David Lyndon Lloyd *(PC: Beulah)*, Penglais, Beulah, Castell Newydd Emlyn, SA38 9QE
☎ (01239) 811092

John Lumley *(PC: Ciliau Aeron)*, Cilcennin, Hafan, Llanbedr Pont Steffan/Lampeter, SA48 8RH
☎ (01570) 470934
john.lumley@ceredigion.gov.uk

Dai Mason *(Ind: Trefeurig)*, Cwmisaf, Cwmsymlog, Aberystwyth, SY23 3EZ
☎ (01970) 828128
dai.mason@ceredigion.gov.uk

Catrin Miles *(PC: Aberteifi/Cardigan (Teifi)*, Ardwyn, Spring Gardens, Heol Llandudoch, SA43 3AU
☎ (01239) 613637
catrin.miles@ceredigion.gov.uk

Ray Quant MBE *(Ind: Borth)*, Pinecroft, Llandre, Bow Street, Aberystwyth, SY24 5BS
☎ (01970) 820603
ray.quant@ceredigion.gov.uk

Rowland Rees-Evans *(Lib D: Llanrhystud)*, Ystrad Teilo, Llanrhystud, SY23 5AY
☎ (01974) 202238
rowland.rees-evans@ceredigion.gov.uk

John Roberts *(Lib D: Faenor)*, Erwír Delyn, 9 Maeshendre, Waunfawr, Aberystwyth, SY23 3PR ☎ (01970) 617733
john.roberts@ceredigion.gov.uk

Mark Strong *(PC: Aberystwyth Gogledd/North)*, Tŷ Blodwen, Ffordd Bryn y MÙr, Aberystwyth, SY23 2HX ☎ (01970) 636578
mark.strong@ceredigion.gov.uk

Alun Williams *(PC: Aberystwyth Bronglais*, Y Gelli, Llwyn Afallon, Aberystwyth, SY23 2HA
☎ (01970) 617544
alun.williams@ceredigion.gov.uk

Ivor Williams *(Ind: Llanbedr Pont Steffan/Lampeter)*, 10 Ffynnonbedr, Llanbedr Pont Steffan/Lampeter, SA48 7EH
☎ (01570) 422441
ivor.williams@ceredigion.gov.uk

Lynford Thomas *(PC: Llanfihangel Ystrad)*, Talfryn, Felinfach, Llanbadr Pont Steffan/Lampeter, SA48 7PG
☎ (01570) 470102
lynford.thomas@ceredigion.gov.uk

Clerks to the Community Councils

Aberaeron Town Council, *Mr J D Gwynne*, 26 Alban Square, Aberaeron, SA46 0AL ☎ (01545) 570861

Aberporth Community Council, *Mrs S V Owens*, Llanina, Aberporth, Aberteifi/Cardigan, SA43 2EY
☎ (01239) 814992
AberporthCC@aol.com

Aberteifi/Cardigan Town Council, *Mr W Jones*, Cardigan Town Council, Cardigan Town Council Office, 36 Pendre, Cardigan, SA43 1JS ☎ (01239) 621527
caernant@yahoo.co.uk

Aberystwyth Town Council, *Mr J O Griffiths*, 11 Baker Street, Aberystwyth, SY23 2BJ
☎ (01970) 624761
council@aberystwyth.gov.uk
www.aberystwyth.gov.uk

Beulah Community Council, *Mrs C A Harries*, 5 Heol Gollen, North Park, Cardigan, SA43 1NF
☎ (01239) 614074

Blaenrheidol Community Council, *Elaine Lewis*, Erwbarfe, Ponterwyd, Aberystwyth, SY23 3JR
☎ (01970) 890251

Borth Community Council, *Margaret Walker*, Mirella, Borth, SY24 5JF ☎ (01970) 871932

Cei Newydd/New Quay Town Council, *Mrs D Jones*, Pencnwc Bach, Cross Inn, Llandysul, SA44 6NL ☎ (01545) 561017
danajones3@hotmail.co.uk

Ceulanamaesmawr Community Council, *Mr G Huws*, Pengwern, Talybont, SY24 5EN
☎ (01970) 832231

Ciliau Aeron Community Council, *Mrs D Jones*, Hen Tŷ'r Ysgol, Cilcennin, Llanbedr Pont Steffan/Lampeter, SA48 8RH
☎ (01570) 471212 / 07974 109402

Dyffryn Arth Community Council, *Mr E D Ellis*, Nantgwynfynydd, Bethania, Llanon, SY23 5NJ ☎ (01974) 272369

Faenor Community Council, *Mrs M A Jenkins*, Dolwerdd, Lon Rhydgwin, Llanfarian, Aberystwyth, SY23 4DD
☎ (01970) 617101 / 07531972045
mj328@hotmail.co.uk

Geneu'r Glyn Community Council, *Mrs D Harvey*, Abel-gur, Lôn Glanfred, Llandre, Aberystwyth, SY24 5BY
☎ (01970) 820418

Henfynyw Community Council, *Mrs E E Jones*, Erwau Glas, Ffosyffin, Aberaeron SA46 0HA ☎ (01545) 571065

Llanarth Community Council, *Mrs M Lewis*, Blodfa, Mydroilyn, Llanbedr Pont Steffan/Lampeter, SA48 7QY ☎ (01545) 580391

Llanbadarn Fawr Community Council, *Peter Rees*, Llygad y Fro, Rhydyfelin, Aberystwyth, SY23 4QD
☎ (01970) 617966

Llanbedr Pont Steffan/Lampeter Town Council, *Miss M E Thomas*, 38 Penbryn, Llanbedr Pont Steffan/Lampeter, SA48 7EU
☎ (01570) 421496
clerc@lampeter-tc.gov.uk

Llancynfelin Community Council, *Gillian Jones*, Blaenddol, Tre'r Ddol, Machynlleth, SY20 8PL
☎ (01654) 781226

Llandyfriog Community Council, *Anwen Evans,* Swn Yr Awel, Penlon Road, Newcastle Emlyn, Carmarthenshire, SA38 9HR ☎ (01239) 711084

Llandysiliogogo Community Council, *Shân Gwyn* Haulfan, Llanarth, SA47 0NH ☎ (01545) 580818

Llandysul Community Council, *Mrs H M Davies,* Awel Gerdd, Llanfihangel-Ar-Arth, Pencader, Carmarthenshire, SA39 9HX ☎ (01559) 389001

Llanddewibreffi Community Council, *Mrs M Davies,* Brynderwen, Llanddewi Brefi, Tregaron, SY25 6UU ☎ (01974) 298636

Llanfair Clydogau Community Council, *Mrs E H Mercer,* Gelli Ddyfod, Llanfair Clydogau, Llanbedr Pont Steffan/Lampeter, SA48 8LG ☎ (01570) 493393

Llanfarian Community Council, *Mrs M A Jenkins,* Dolwerdd, Lon Rhydgwin, Llanfarian, Aberystwyth, SY23 4DD ☎ (01970) 617101 / 07531972045 mj328@hotmail.co.uk

Llanfihangel Ystrad Community Council, *Mr J B Hughes,* Cwmere, Felinfach, Llanbedr Pont Steffan /Lampeter, Ceredigion, SA48 8BG ☎ (01570) 470401

Llangeitho Community Council, *Mrs H Bulman,* Delfryn, Llwynpiod, Llangeitho, Tregaron, SY25 6TA ☎ (01974) 298367 / 07929 970 547 heulwenbulman@freeuk.com

Llangoedmor Community Council, *Diane Quinnell,* 58 Parc y Plas, Aberporth, SA43 2BZ ☎ (01239) 811432 dquinnelle@tiscali.co.uk

Llangrannog Community Council, *Shân Gwyn,* Haulfan, Llanarth, SA47 0NH ☎ (01545) 580818

Llangwyryfon Community Council, *Mrs M Williams,* Tynant, Llangwyryfon, Aberystwyth, SY23 4SR ☎ (01974) 272684

Llangybi Community Council, *Mrs M E Spate,* Maesffynnon, Llangybi, Llanbedr Pont Steffan/Lampeter, SA48 8LY ☎ (01570) 493325

Llanilar Community Council, *Ms M E Davies,* 20 Talardeg, Llanilar, Aberystwyth, SY23 4NL ☎ (01974) 241311

Llanllwchaearn Community Council, *Shân Gwyn,* Haulfan, Llanarth, SA47 0NH ☎ (01545) 580818

Llanrhystud Community Council, *Christine Evans,* Diddanle, 5 Heol Isfoel, Llanrhystud, SY23 5BJ ☎ (01974) 202048

Llansantffraed Community Council, *Alison Lovatt,* Llainlwyd, Llanon, SY23 5HH ☎ (01974) 202719

Llanwenog Community Council, *Gwennan Davies,* Blaenderi, 13 Penbryn, Llanbedr Pont Steffan/Lampeter, SA48 7EU ☎ 07852 264336

Llanwnnen Community Council, *Mrs E Williams,* Cwmawel, Llanllwni, Sir Gaerfyrddin, SA39 9DR ☎ (01559) 395802

Lledrod Community Council, *Mrs T Jones,* Blaenresgair Uchaf, Tynreithin, Tregaron, SY25 6LS ☎ (01974) 251269

Melindwr Community Council, *Miss M Evans,* 22 Heol Isfoel, Llanrhystud, SY23 5BJ ☎ 07725 501617

Nantcwnlle Community Council, *Mrs D Morgan,* Rhen Ysgol, Bwlchllan, Llanbedr Pont Steffan/Lampeter, SA48 8QQ ☎ (01570) 470742

Penbryn Community Council, *Mr G Harries,* Bromyrnnach, Heol Gollen, Aberteifi/Cardigan, SA43 1NF ☎ (01239) 614074

Pontarfynach Community Council, *Mrs M E Williams,* Ty Capel, Rhydyfagwyr, Cnwch Coch, Aberystwyth, SY23 4LQ ☎ (01974) 261483 william@mynach371.fsnet.co.uk

Tirymynach Community Council, *Parch/Rev Richard Lewis,* 40 Maes Ceiro, Bow Street, Aberystwyth, SY24 5BG ☎ (01970) 828102 maesceiro@fsmail.net

Trawsgoed Community Council, *Mr D J Baskerville,* Penygeulan, Abermagwr, Trawsgoed, Aberystwyth, SY23 4AR ☎ (01974) 261222 derekbaskerville@btinternet.com

Trefeurig Community Council, *Mrs M A Jenkins,* Dôl Werdd, Lon Rhydgwin, Llanfarian, Aberystwyth, SY23 4DD ☎ (01970) 617414 mj328@hotmail.co.uk

Tregaron Town Council, *Mrs H Bulman,* Delfryn, Llwynpiod, Llangeitho, Tregaron, SY25 6TA ☎ (01974) 298367 / 07929970547 heulwenbulman@freeuk.com

Troedyraur Community Council, *Eleanor Colbourne,* Anor, Ffostrasol, Llandysul, SA44 4DT ☎ (01239) 858930

Y Ferwig Community Council, *Mrs H Owen,* Caernant, Gwbert Road, Cardigan, SA43 1PH ☎ (01239) 612932 caernant@yahoo.co.uk

Ysbyty Ystwyth Community Council, *Ian Williams,* 6 Maesyderi, Pontrhydygroes, Ystrad Meurig, SY25 6DL ☎ (01974) 282387

Ysgubor y Coed Community Council, *Dr Tamsin Davies,* Flat Llawr Gwaelod, Glendower, Y Borth, SY24 5JP ☎ (01970) 871573 ted@aber.ac.uk

Ystrad Fflur Community Council, *Miss M E Thomas,* 38 Penbryn, Llanbedr Pont Steffan/Lampeter, SA48 7EU ☎ (01570) 422103

Ystrad Meurig Community Council, *Miss A Isaac,* Gwylfa, Ystrad Meurig, SY25 6AD ☎ (01974) 831668

Leader
Cllr Dilwyn Roberts

Bodlondeb, Conwy LL32 8DU
Tel: (01492) 574000
Fax: (01492) 592114

Website: www.conwy.gov.uk

CONWY
CYNGOR BWRDEISTREF SIROL
COUNTY BOROUGH COUNCIL

Chief Executive
Iwan Davies

NO OVERALL CONTROL	Ind **18** Con **13** PC **12** Lab **10** Lib Dem **5** Oth **1**	TOTAL 59

ELECTION RESULT 2012

	Seats	Change	Votes	Share
Independent	18	4	14,235	27.8%
Conservative	13	-9	16,641	32.5%
Plaid Cymru	12	-	6,690	13.1%
Labour	10	3	7,000	13.7%
Lib Dem	5	1	5,356	10.5%
Others	1	1	1,312	2.6%

Socio-economic Profile

		Rank 1<22
Area (sq km)	1,126	6
Population ('000s)	110.8	15
% able to speak Welsh	33.3	5
% born in Wales	54.0	21
% non-white ethnic groups	3.1	10
Gross rev expenditure (2011-12)	£248.8m	15
Forecast capital expenditure (2011-12)	£44.1m	12
% dwellings in Band D (2012-13)	20.8	4
Band D council tax (2011-12)	£1,088.63	19
% over retirement age	24.5	1
% pupils 5+ GCSEs A*-C (2010-11)	72.7	4
Unemployment (% claimant count 2011)	3.9	10
Index of Deprivation (2011)	23	12
(% of Authority in most deprived 30%)		

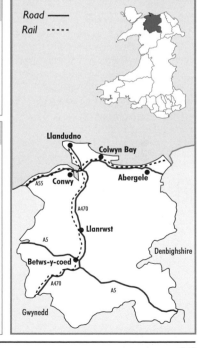

Road ——
Rail - - - - -

LOCAL GOVERNMENT

CONWY

Principal Officers

Chief Executive:	**Iwan Davies**
Strategic Director Economy and Place:	**Sasha Davies**
Strategic Director Democracy, Regulation & Support:	**Ken Finch**
Strategic Director Finance & Efficiencies:	**Andrew Kirkham**

Cabinet Members 2012-2013

Leader:	**Dilwyn Roberts** (PC)
Deputy Leader:	**Ronnie Hughes** (Lab)
Finance & Resources:	**Jason Weyman** (Ind)
Communication, Marketing & Leisure:	**Graham Rees** (Ind)
Social Care & Health:	**Chris Hughes** (Lab)
Skills & Lifelong Learning:	**Wyn Ellis Jones** (PC)
Environment:	**Dave Cowans** (Ind)
Communities:	**Phil Edwards** (PC)
Governance & Regulation:	**Philip Evans** (Ind)
Highways & Property:	**Mike Priestley** (Lib D)

Committee Chairs 2012-2013

Principal Overview & Scrutiny Committee:	**William Knightly** (Con)
Communities Overview & Scrutiny Committee:	**Linda Groom** (Ind)
Customers Overview & Scrutiny Committee:	**Adrian Tansley** (Lab)
Partnerships Overview & Scrutiny Committee:	**Sue Lloyd-Williams** (PC)
Audit Committee:	**Tba**
Democratic Services Committee:	**Cheryl Carlisle** (Con)
Licensing & Regulation Committee:	**Ken Stevens** (Lab)
Planning Committee:	**Trevor Stott** (Lib D)

Salaries

Basic Salary: £13,175
Senior Salaries:
Leader: £47,500; Cabinet Members: £28,780
Chairs of Scrutiny Committees: £21,910; Chairs of Other Committees: £21,910
Leader of Main Opposition Group: £21,910

CONWY

Councillors   ♂ 44 ♀ 15

Chair: Cllr Dr Stuart Anderson   Vice-Chair: Cllr Elizabeth Roberts

Sara Allardice *(Lab: Conwy)*, Dolwar, 9 Cadnant Park, Conwy, LL32 8PR ☎ 07557 480337 cllr.sara.allardice@conwy.gov.uk

Dr Stuart Anderson *(Ind: Kinmel Bay)*, The Gables, 50 Denbigh Circle, Kinmel Bay, LL18 5HW ☎ (01745) 332172 / 07557323416 cllr.dr.stuart.anderson@conwy.gov.uk

Frank Bradfield *(Con: Craig y Don)*, 14 Amalfi Court, Craig y Don, Llandudno, LL30 1BH ☎ (01492) 874395 / 07557480287 cllr.frank.bradfield@conwy.gov.uk

Cheryl Carlisle *(Con: Colwyn)*, 432 Abergele Road, Old Colwyn, Colwyn Bay, LL29 9AH ☎ (01492) 514755 / 07741181794 cllr.cheryl.carlisle@conwy.gov.uk

Chris Cater *(Ind: Penrhyn)*, 96 Llandudno Road, Penrhyn Bay, Llandudno, LL30 3HL ☎ (01492) 548106 / 07733012900 cllr.christopher.cater@conwy.gov.uk

Brian Cossey *(Lib D: Colwyn)*, 7 Brooklands, Dolwen Road, Old Colwyn, Colwyn Bay, LL29 8EN ☎ (01492) 518908 / 07733013383 cllr.brian.cossey@conwy.gov.uk

Samantha Cotton *(Con: Deganwy)*, 9 Sefton Terrace, Deganwy, LL31 9BU ☎ (01492) 573964 / 07557480299 cllr.samantha.cotton@conwy.gov.uk

Dave Cowans *(Ind: Eirias)*, 230D Abergele Road, Old Colwyn, Colwyn Bay, LL29 8AS ☎ 07733 013381 cllr.dave.cowans@conwy.gov.uk

Bill Darwin *(Ind: Kinmel Bay)*, 50 Roseview Crescent, Kinmel Bay, LL18 5BY ☎ (01745) 344904 / 07557480298 cllr.bill.darwin@conwy.gov.uk

Mary Doyle *(Con: Rhiw)*, 46 Cherry Tree Lane, Upper Colwyn Bay, LL28 5YH ☎ (01492) 535955 cllr.mary.doyle@conwy.gov.uk

Phil Edwards *(PC: Llandrillo yn Rhos)*, 6 Whitehall Road, Rhos on Sea, LL28 4HW ☎ (01492) 548741 / 07557 323415 cllr.phil.edwards@conwy.gov.uk

Keith Eeles *(Ind: Llanddulas)*, Bryn Awelon, Abergele Road, Llanddulas, Abergele, LL22 8EN ☎ (01492) 515957 / 07557480297 cllr.keith.eeles@conwy.gov.uk

Philip Evans JP *(Ind: Tudno)*, Lygan y Wern, 9 Gwydyr Road, Llandudno, LL30 1HQ ☎ (01492) 877696 / 07733013382 cllr.philip.evans@conwy.gov.uk

Linda Groom *(Ind: Penrhyn)*, Penffordd Farm, Bodafon Road, Llandudno, LL30 3DU ☎ (01492) 540301 / 07733012742 cllr.linda.groom@conwy.gov.uk

Janet Haworth *(Con: Gogarth)*, Abbey Lodge, 14 Abbey Road, Llandudno, LL30 2EA ☎ (01492) 878042 / 07733012914 cllr.janet.haworth@conwy.gov.uk

Andrew Hinchliff *(Lab: Bryn)*, Strathmore, Shore Road West, Llanfairfechan, LL33 0BP ☎ (01248) 681274 / 07738129874 cllr.andrew.hinchliff@conwy.gov.uk

Jobi Hold *(Lab: Mostyn)*, 36 Mowbray Road, Llandudno, LL30 2DJ ☎ 07775 030240 cllr.jobi.hold@conwy.gov.uk

Chris Hughes *(Lab: Glyn)*, Braeside, 3 Seafield Road, Colwyn Bay, LL29 7HB ☎ 07733 012901 / 07960 014931 cllr.chris.hughes@conwy.gov.uk

Ronnie Hughes *(Lab: Tudno)*, 32 Norman Road, Llandudno, LL30 1DU ☎ (01492) 879806 / 07733012621 cllr.ronnie.hughes@conwy.gov.uk

R Meirion Hughes *(PC: Pensarn)*, 50 Ronald Avenue, Llandudno Junction, LL31 9EY ☎ (01492) 585109 / 07717543499 cllr.meirion.hughes@conwy.gov.uk

Dr Ahmed Jamil JP *(Ind: Betws yn Rhos)*, Glasfryn, Llanfairtalhaiarn, Abergele, LL22 8SN ☎ 07557 480296 / 07778 367089 cllr.dr.ahmed.jamil@conwy.gov.uk

Ian Jenkins *(PC: Gower)*, 1 Maes Tawel, Llanrwst, LL26 0TS ☎ (01492) 641168 / 07900063935 cllr.ian.jenkins@conwy.gov.uk

Gareth Jones OBE *(PC: Craig y Don)*, Dolarfon, 21 Roumania Drive, Craig-y-Don, Llandudno, LL30 1UY ☎ (01492) 879534 / 07557480295 cllr.gareth.jones@conwy.gov.uk

Ray Jones *(Lab: Pandy)*, Blaenau Cottage, Llanfairfechan, LL33 0EY ☎ (01248) 680883 / 07557480294 cllr.ray.jones@conwy.gov.uk

Wyn Ellis Jones *(PC: Uwch Conwy)*, Hafod Geunan, Nebo, Llanrwst, LL26 0TD ☎ (01690) 710326 / 07717543691 cyng.wyn.ellis.jones@conwy.gov.uk

Abdul Khan *(PC: Glyn)*, 3 Trevor Road, Colwyn Bay, LL29 8ED ☎ (01492) 533066 / 07883073647 cllr.abdul.khan@conwy.gov.uk

William Knightly *(Con:Tywyn/Towyn)*, Franklin, Sandbank Road, Towyn, Abergele, LL22 9LD ☎ 07831 139149 cllr.william.knightly@conwy.gov.uk

Peter Lewis MBE *(Ind: Uwchaled)*, Groudd Hall, Cerrigydrudion, Corwen, LL21 9TA ☎ (01490) 420353 / 07733013358 cllr.peter.lewis@conwy.gov.uk

Sue Lloyd-Williams *(PC: Llansannan)*, Hwlffrordd, Llansannan, Denbigh, Ll16 5NN ☎ (01745) 870678 / 07775030228 cllr.sue.lloyd-williams@conwy.gov.uk

Margaret Lyon *(Ind: Gogarth)*, 124 Glan y Mor Road, Penrhyn Bay, Llandudno, LL30 3PR ☎ (01492) 545681 / 07774221957 cllr.margaret.lyon@conwy.gov.uk

LOCAL GOVERNMENT

Delyth MacRae *(PC: Gele)*, Coedwig, 21 Compton Way, Abergele, LL22 7BL
☎ 07557 480293
cllr.delyth.macrae@conwy.gov.uk

John Maclennan *(Con: Pentremawr)*, 19 Lon Garnedd, Abergele, LL22 7EW ☎ (01745) 826901 / 07557480292 / 07850407996
cllr.john.maclennan@conwy.gov.uk

Anne McCaffrey *(Ind: Capelulo)*, Bodnant, Old Mill Road, Dwygyfylchi, LL34 6TG
☎ (01492) 623373
cllr.anne.mccaffrey@conwy.gov.uk

Dewi Miles *(Ind: Mostyn)*, Penmorfa, 2 Church Crescent, West Shore, Llandudno, LL30 2EQ
☎ 07748 803156
cllr.dewi.miles@conwy.gov.uk

Donald Milne *(Con: Llandrillo-yn-Rhos)*, 11 Malvern Rise, Rhos on Sea, Colwyn Bay, LL28 4RX
☎ (01492) 547772 / 07557480291
cllr.donald.milne@conwy.gov.uk

Edgar Parry *(Ind: Crwst)*, Fron View, 30 Watling Street, Llanrwst, Conwy, LL26 0LS ☎ (01492) 640305 / 07557480289 / 07919095092
cllr.edgar.parry@conwy.gov.uk

Roger Parry *(Con: Llandrillo-yn-Rhos)*, 220 Dinerth Road, Rhos on Sea, Colwyn Bay, LL28 4UH,
☎ (01492) 545242 / 07795300316
cllr.roger.parry@conwy.gov.uk

Mike Priestley *(Lib D: Marl)*, 60 Pendyffryn, Llandudno Junction, LL31 9AS
☎ (01492) 582581 / 07733013317
cllr.michael.priestley@conwy.gov.uk

Mike Rayner *(PC: Eglwysbach)*, Dryll Heulyn, Ffordd Trwyn, Swch, Llanddoged, Llanrwst, LL26 0DZ ☎ (01492) 640936 / 07775030251
cllr.mike.rayner@conwy.gov.uk

Graham Rees JP *(Ind: Llansanffraid)*, Bryn Ydlan, 1 Tan-y-Maes, Glan Conwy, Colwyn Bay, LL28 5LQ
☎ (01492) 573243 / 07733013380
cllr.graham.rees@conwy.gov.uk

Dave Roberts *(Con: Llandrilloyn Rhos)*, 9 Allanson Road, Rhos on Sea, Colwyn Bay, LL28 4HN
☎ (01492) 540926
cllr.david.m.roberts@conwy.gov.uk

Dilwyn Roberts *(PC: Llangernyw)*, Plas yn Trofarth, Llangernyw, Abergele, LL22 8RD
☎ (01745) 860246 / 07717543690
cyng.dilwyn.roberts@conwy.gov.uk

Elizabeth Roberts *(PC: Betws y Coed)*, Fron Cottage, Dolwyddelan, LL25 0NQ ☎ (01690) 750246 / 07717543690
cllr.liz.roberts@conwy.gov.uk

John Roberts *(Lib D: Rhiw)*, 28 Marston Road, Rhos-on-Sea, Colwyn Bay, LL28 4SG ☎ (01492) 546691
cllr.john.roberts@conwy.gov.uk

Paul Roberts *(Con: Caerhun)*, Richmond House, Iolyn Park, Llanrwst Road, Conwy, LL32 8UX
☎ 07557 480288 / 07801 863581
cllr.paul.roberts@conwy.gov.uk

Hilary Rogers-Jones *(PC:Trefriw)*, Treflys, Church Square, Trefriw, LL27 0UQ ☎ (01492) 641213
cllr.hilary.rogers-jones@conwy.gov.uk

Sam Rowlands *(Con: Pentremawr)*, Llais Afon, High Street, Abergele, LL22 7AR
☎ 07733 012884 / 07825 588621
cllr.sam.rowlands@conwy.gov.uk

Tim Rowlands *(Con: Gele)*, The Warren Cottage, Tan y Fron Road, Abergele, LL22 9BB
☎ (01745) 833820 / 07733013122
cllr.tim.rowlands@conwy.gov.uk

Susan Shotter *(Lib D: Marl)*, 29 Overlea Avenue, Deganwy, LL31 9TA
☎ (01492) 582652 / 07775030227
cllr.susan.shotter@conwy.gov.uk

Deion Smith *(Lab: Llysfaen)*, 72 Alltwen, Llysfaen, Colwyn Bay, LL29 8PG ☎ (01492) 517590 / 07976722095
cllr.deion.smith@conwy.gov.uk

Nigel Smith *(Ind: Kinmel Bay)*, Abbeydale, 57 Clwyd Park, Kinmel Bay, LL18 5EJ ☎ (01745) 339793 / 07557480290
cllr.nigel.smith@conwy.gov.uk

Bob Squire *(Ind: Eirias)*, 27 Holyrood Avenue, Colwyn Bay, LL29 8BA ☎ (01492) 512862
cllr.bob.squire@conwy.gov.uk

Ken Stevens *(Lab: Pant yr Afon/Penmaenan)*, "Tyddyn Pen", 6 Victoria Terrace, High Street, Panmaenmawr, LL34 6NN
☎ 07974 659311
cllr.ken.stevens@conwy.gov.uk

Trevor Stott *(Lib D: Rhiw)*, 29 Troon Way, Colwyn Bay, LL29 6AP ☎ (01492) 531783
cllr.trevor.stott@conwy.gov.uk

Jean Stubbs *(Lab: Abergele/Pensarn)*, 9 Lon Kinmel, Pensarn, Abergele, LL22 7SG ☎ (01745) 822465
cllr.jean.stubbs@conwy.gov.uk

Adrian Tansley *(Lab: Mochdre)*, 14 Ffordd y Mynach, Mochdre, LL28 5DL ☎ (01492) 545559 / 07934394013
cllr.adrian.tansley@conwy.gov.uk

Joan Vaughan *(Ind: Conwy)*, 48 Maes Gweryl, Conwy, LL32 8RU
☎ (01492) 592735 / 07733013315
cllr.joan.vaughan@conwy.gov.uk

Jason Weyman *(Ind: Deganwy)*, 3 Lon Pedr, Llanrhos, Llandudno, Conwy, LL30 1SS
☎ (01492) 592843 / 07717543289
cllr.jason.weyman@conwy.gov.uk

Andrew Wood *(Ind: Gele)*, 18 Llwyn Onn, Abergele, LL22 7EG ☎ (01745) 822579
cllr.andrew.wood@conwy.gov.uk

Clerks to the Community Councils

Abergele Town Council, *Mandy Evans*, Town Hall & Council Offices, Llanddulas Road, Abergele, LL22 7BT
☎ (01745) 833242
info@abergele-towncouncil.co.uk

Bay of Colwyn Town Council, *Tina Earley*, Town Hall, 7 Rhiw Road, Colwyn Bay, LL29 7TG
☎ (01492) 532248
colwyncouncil@freenetname.co.uk

Betws y Coed Community Council, *Mr E C Roberts*, Rhoslan, Cerrig-y-Drudion, Conwy, LL21 9UA ☎ (01490) 420486
ecrhoslan@yahoo.com

Betws yn Rhos Community Council, *Gwyndaf Morris,* Wenallt, 34 Heol Conwy, Abergele, Conwy, LL22 7UT
gwyndaf@morrisg43.wanadoo.co.uk

Bro Garmon Community Councnl, *Eirian Roberts,* Gwern Hywel Ucha, Ysbyty Ifan, Betws y Coed, LL24 0PD ☎ (01690) 770249
eirian@eirianroberts.wanadoo.co.uk

Bro Machno Community Council, *Elfed Williams,* Plas Padog, Betws-Y-Coed, LL24 0HN
☎ (01690) 770205
elfed.williams@yahoo.co.uk

Caerhun Community Council, *Sian Griffiths,* 26 Glan y Wern, Tyn y Groes, LL32 8TW
☎ 07884 135672
sianwyngirffiths_caerhuncc@yahoo.co.uk

Capel Curig Community Council, *Mrs A Cousins,* Llugwy, Capel Curig, LL24 0ES
☎ (01690) 720218

Cerrigydrudion Community Council, *Mr E C Roberts,* Rhoslan, Cerrig-y-Drudion, Conwy, LL21 9UA ☎ (01490) 420486
ecrhoslan@yahoo.com

Conwy Town Council, *Helen Armitage,* Guildhall, Conwy, LL32 8LD ☎ (01492) 596254
conwy.towncouncil@btinternet.com

Dolgarrog Community Council, *David Williams,* 2 Tayler Avenue, Dolgarrog, Conwy, LL32 8JN
☎ (01492) 660632
dafydd41williams@btinternet.com

Dolwyddelan Community Council, *Mr G Roberts,* Alltrem, 2 Pentrefelin, Dolwyddelan, LL25 0DZ ☎ (01690) 750331
roberts565@btinternet.com

Eglwysbach Community Council, *Einir Jones,* Tu Hwnt iir Afon, Ffordd Pennant, Eglwysbach, LL28 5UN ☎ (01492) 650565
clerceglwysbach@hotmail.co.uk

Henryd Community Council, *Mrs N Jones, Llechen Uchaf, Llechwedd, Conwy, LL32 8LY*
☎ (01492) 592451

Llanddoged & Maenan Community Council, *Delyth Algieri,* Bryn Dedwydd, Penrhiw, Llanddoged, LL26 0BZ
☎ 01492 642183
clerk@llanddoged-maenan.org.uk

Llanddulas & Rhyd-y-Foel Community Council, *Gwyndaf Morris,* 34 Heol Conwy, Abergele, Conwy, LL22 7UT
gwyndaf@morrisg43.wanadoo.co.uk

Llandudno Town Council, *Tessa Wildermoth,* Town Council Office, Town Hall, Lloyd Street, Lllandudno, LL30 2UP
☎ (01492) 879130
towncouncil@llandudno.gov.uk

Llanfairfechan Town Council, *Mrs Shephard,* The Clerk, Town Hall, Llanfairfechan, LL33 0AA ☎ (01248) 681697
llanfairfechantc@ukgateway.net

Llanfair Talhaiarn Community Council, *John MacLennan,* 19 Lôn Garnedd, Abergele, LL22 7EW
☎ (01745) 826901 / 07850 407996
llanfair-th-council@mail.co.uk

Llanfihangel Glyn Myfyr Community Council, *Carol Humphreys,* Tai Draw, Cerrigydrudion, Corwen, LL21 9UF
☎ (01490) 420270
carol-humphreys@hotmail.co.uk

Llangernyw Community Council, *Elwen Owen,* Arfryn, Pandy Tudur, Abergele, LL22 8UL
☎ (01745) 860333
elwenowen@yahoo.co.uk

Llangwm Community Council, *Gwenan Haf Jones,* Bryn Clochydd, Llangwm, Corwen, LL21 0RA
☎ (01490) 420087
cbllangwm@hotmail.co.uk

Llannefydd Community Council, *Dewi Jones,* 5 Aled Terrace, Llansannan, Denbigh, Conwy, LL16 5HP ☎ 07920 025919
dewijones50@yahoo.co.uk

Llanrwst Town Council, *Gwenda Jones,* Sycharth, Tan y Graig, Llanrwst, LL26 0NA
☎ (01492) 643221 / 640746
gwendamai@yahoo.co.uk

Llandanffraid Glan Conwy Comnmunity Council, *Mr J Hughes-Jones,* 32 Ffordd Naddyn, Glan Conwy, Colwyn Bay, LL28 5NH ☎ (01492) 580445
jd.gc@talktalk.net

Llansannan Community Council, *Ifan Gwyn Davies,* 11 Maes Caenog, Clocaenog, Ruthin, LL15 2AE
☎ (01824) 750283 / 07887955613
daviesg@denbighshire.gov.uk

Llysfaen Community Council, *Gwyndaf Morris,* Wenallt, 34 Heol Conwy, Abergele, Conwy, LL22 7UT
gwyndaf@morrisg43.wanadoo.co.uk

Mochdre Community Council, *Dave Cowans, 230D Abergele Road, Colwyn Bay, LL29 8AS*
☎ 07733 013381
dave.cowans@towynand
kinmelbaytowncouncil.gov.uk

Penmaenmawr Town Council, *Cllr Vivienne Mooney,* 3 Conwy Road, Penmaenmawr, LL34 6AB
☎ (01492) 623221 / 621443 /
07952 008694
viv.mooney@hotmail.co.uk /
clerk@penmaenmawr.org

Pentrefoelas Community Council, *Gwyn H Roberts,* The Cottage, Pentrefoelas, Betws y Coed, Conwy, LL24 0LR
☎ (01690) 770 223
julieagwyn@hotmail.co.uk

Towyn & Kinmel Bay Town Council, *Mr D Cowans,* The Community Resource Centre, Foryd Road, Kinmel Bay, LL18 5BT
☎ (01745) 355899
dave.cowans@towynandkinmelbay
towncouncil.gov.uk

Trefriw Community Council, *Valerie Hannah, Pen y Bryn,* Trefriw, Llanrwst, LL27 0JU
☎ (01492) 640245
v.hannah@tiscali.co.uk

Ysbyty Ifan Community Council, *Eirian Roberts,* Gwernhywel Ucha, Ysbyty Ifan, Betws y Coed LL24 0PD ☎ (01690) 770249
eirian@eirianroberts.wanadoo.co.uk

CYNGOR SIR DDINBYCH
DENBIGHSHIRE COUNTY COUNCIL

County Hall, Wynnstay Road,
Ruthin LL15 1YN
Tel: (01824) 706000
Fax: (01824) 707446
Email:
customerservice@denbighshire.gov.uk **or**
gwasanaethcwsmer@sirddinbych.gov.uk
Website:
www.denbighshire.gov.uk **or**
www.sirddinbych.gov.uk

Leader
Cllr Hugh H Evans

Chief Executive
Dr Mohammed Mehmet

CYNGOR
Sir Ddinbych
Denbighshire
COUNTY COUNCIL

NO OVERALL CONTROL	Lab **18** Ind **12** Con **9** PC **7** Lib D **1**	TOTAL 47

ELECTION RESULT 2012

	Seats	Change	Votes	Share
Labour	18	11	14,629	32.9%
Independent	12	-1	12,426	27.9%
Conservative	9	-9	11,670	26.2%
Plaid Cymru	7	-1	3,881	8.7%
Lib Dem	1	-	1,418	3.2%
Others	0	-	481	1.1%

Socio-economic Profile

		Rank 1<22
Area (sq km)	**847**	8
Population ('000s)	**96.7**	16
% able to speak Welsh	**30.4**	6
% born in Wales	**57.9**	19
% non-white ethnic groups	**3.7**	6
Gross rev expenditure (2011-12)	**£221.6m**	16
Forecast capital expenditure (2011-12)	**£47.0m**	9
% dwellings in Band D (2012-13)	**17.4**	10
Band D council tax	**£1,270.03**	6
% over retirement age	**21.7**	5
% pupils 5+ GCSEs A*-C (2010-11)	**71.4**	5
Unemployment (% claimant count 2011)	**3.8**	12
Index of Deprivation (2011)	**19**	15
(% of Authority in most deprived 30%)		

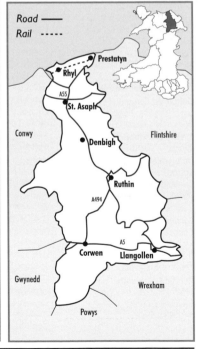

Road ——
Rail -----

LOCAL GOVERNMENT

DENBIGHSHIRE

Principal Officers

Chief Executive:	**Dr Mohammed Mehmet**
Corporate Director - Economic & Community Ambition:	**Tba**
Corporate Director - Modernisation & Well-being:	**Sally Ellis**
Corporate Director - Customers:	**Hywyn Williams**

Cabinet Members 2012-2013

Leader:	**Hugh H Evans** (Ind)
Deputy Leader / Education:	**Eryl Williams** (PC)
Social Care & Children's Services:	**Bobby Feeley** (Ind)
Customers & Communities:	**Hugh Irving** (Con)
Tourism, Leisure & Youth:	**Huw Ll. Jones** (PC)
Modernising & Performance:	**Barbara Smith** (Ind)
Public Realm:	**David Smith** (Ind)
Finance & Assets:	**Julian Thompson-Hill** (Con)

Committee Chairs 2012-2013

Partnerships Scrutiny Committee:	**Brian Blakeley** (Lab)
Communities Scrutiny Committee:	**Huw Hilditch-Roberts** (Ind)
Performance Scrutiny Committee:	**Colin Hughes** (Lab)
Planning Committee:	**Dewi Owens** (Con)
Corporate Governance Committee:	**Jason McClellan** (Lab)

Salaries

Basic Salary: £13,030 per annum;
Senior Salaries: Leader: £29,125; Deputy Leader: £16,645
Cabinet Members: £12,485; Chairs of Scrutiny Committees: £8,735; Chairs of Other
Committees: £8,785; Leader of Main Opposition Group: £8,735; Group Leaders (of political
parties not less than 10% of all council members): £3,745

Councillors ♂ 35 ♀ 12

Chair: Cllr Jeanette Chamberlain-Jones Vice-Chair: Cllr Raymond Bartley

Ian William Armstrong *(Lab: Rhyl West)*, 1 Emlyn Grove, Rhyl, LL18 1PS ☎ (01745) 336629
ian.armstrong@denbighshire.gov.uk

Raymond Bartley *(Ind: Denbigh Lower)*, Bodnant, 32 Trewen, Denbigh, LL16 3HF
☎ (01745) 812623
ray.bartley@denbighshire.gov.uk

Brian Blakeley *(Lab: Rhyl South East)*, 12 Cambrian Walk, Rhyl, Denbighshire, LL18 4UR
☎ (01745) 342550 / 07544 941959
brian.blakeley@denbighshire.gov.uk

Joan Butterfield MBE JP *(Lab: Rhyl West)*, 20 Tynewydd Road, Rhyl, LL18 3BB ☎ (01745) 332015
joan.butterfield@denbighshire.gov.uk

Jeanette Chamberlain Jones *(Lab: Rhyl South)*, 36 North Drive, Rhyl, LL18 4SP ☎ (01745) 331082 / 07713 244510
jeanette.c.jones@denbighshire.gov.uk

Bill Cowie *(Ind: St Asaph West)*, Ty'n Ddol, Lower Denbigh Road, St Asaph, LL17 0EL
☎ (01745) 584522 / 07747 152791
bill.cowie@denbighshire.gov.uk

Ann Davies *(Con: Rhuddlan)*, c/o County Hall, Wynnstay Road, Ruthin, LL15 1YN ☎ (01745) 591247
j.ann.davies@denbighshire.gov.uk

James Davies *(Con: Prestatyn East)*, Mayfield, 8 Gronant Road, Prestatyn, LL19 9DS
☎ 07940 282545
james.davies@denbighshire.gov.uk

Richard Davies *(Ind: Denbigh Lower)*, 7 Lon Caerau, Colomendy, Denbigh, LL16 3DX
☎ (01745) 813930
richard.lulu.davies@denbighshire.gov.uk

LOCAL GOVERNMENT

DENBIGHSHIRE

Stuart Davies *(Ind: Llangollen)*, Tyn-y-Ffridd, Fron Bache, Llangollen, LL20 7BP
☎ (01978) 869384 / 07967 313792
stuart.a.davies@denbighshire.gov.uk

Peter Duffy *(Lab: Prestatyn Central)*, 42 Grosvenor Road, Prestatyn, LL19 7NP
☎ (01745) 855038 / 857513
peter.duffy@denbighshire.gov.uk

Hugh Evans OBE *(Ind: Llanfair DC / Gwyddelwern)*, Bryndy, Llanelidan, LL15 2HY
☎ (01824) 750635 / 706003
hugh.evans@denbighshire.gov.uk

Peter Evans *(Ind: Prestatyn Meliden)*, 32 Brynllys, Meliden, LL19 8PP ☎ (01745) 887645
peter.evans@denbighshire.gov.uk

Bobby Feeley *(Ind: Ruthin)*, Branas, Llanfair D C, Ruthin, LL15 2SH
☎ (01824) 705040 / 07770 891193
bobby.feeley@denbighshire.gov.uk

Carys Guy-Davies *(Lab: Prestatyn North)*, Heskett House, 117 Victoria Road, Prestatyn, LL19 7SR
☎ (01745) 284078,
carys.guy-davies@denbighshire.gov.uk

Huw Hilditch-Roberts *(Ind: Ruthin)*, Berth, Pentrecelyn, Ruthin, LL15 2HH ☎ 07772 305877
huw.hilditch-roberts@denbighshire.gov.uk

Martyn Holland *(Con: Llanarmon / Llandegla)*, 19 Maes Ial, Llanarmon yn Ial, Nr Mold, CH7 4PZ ☎ (01824) 780703
martyn.holland@denbighshire.gov.uk

Colin Hughes *(Lab: Denbigh Upper Henllan)*, 10 Castle View, Denbigh, LL16 3EG ☎ (01745) 798611
colin.hughes@denbighshire.gov.uk

Trefor Rhys Hughes *(PC: Llangollen)*, Tan Y Fron Farm, Eglwyseg, Llangollen, LL20 8EL
☎ (01978) 860335
rhys.hughes@denbighshire.gov.uk

Hugh Irving *(Con: Prestatyn Central)*, 45 Plas Uchaf Ave, Prestatyn, LL19 9NR ☎ (01745) 854132
hugh.irving@denbighshire.gov.uk

Alice Jones *(Ind: Bodelwyddan)*, Llys Menyn, Nant-y-Faenol Road, Bodelwyddan, LL18 5UL
☎ (01745) 590286
alice.jones@denbighshire.gov.uk

Huw Jones *(PC: Corwen)*, 2 Vale View, Penybryn, Corwen, LL21 0BA ☎ (01490) 412933 / 07881 482800
huw.jones@denbighshire.gov.uk

Pat Jones *(Lab: Rhyl South West)*, 8 Fforddlas, Rhyl, LL18 2DY
☎ (01745) 330589
pat.jones@denbighshire.gov.uk

Gwyneth Kensler *(PC: Denbigh Central)*, 44 Stryd y Dyffryn, Dinbych, LL16 3BW
☎ (01745) 814323
gwyneth.kensler@denbighshire.gov.uk

Meirick Lloyd Davies *(PC:Trefnant)*, Gwelfryn, 1 Ffordd Glascoed, Cefn Meiriadog, Abergele, Sir Conwy, LL22 9DW
☎ (01745) 582740
meirick.davies@denbighshire.gov.uk

Geraint Lloyd-Williams *(Lab: Denbigh Upper Henllan)*, 44 Love Lane, Denbigh, LL16 3LU
☎ 07778 270141
geraint.lloyd-williams@denbighshire.gov.uk

Barry Mellor *(Lab: Rhyl East)*, 32 Hardy Avenue, Rhyl, LL18 3BG
☎ (01745) 350067
barry.mellor@denbighshire.gov.uk

Margaret McCarroll *(Lab: Rhyl South West)*, 12 Weston Road, Rhyl, LL18 2AW ☎ (01745) 342769
margaret.mccarroll@denbighshire.gov.uk

Jason McLellan *(Lab: Prestatyn North)*, 8 The Avenue, Woodland Park, Prestatyn, LL19 9RD
☎ (01745) 859137 / 07917 446201
jason.mcclellan@denbighshire.gov.uk

Win Mullen-James *(Lab: Rhyl South East)*, 13 Weaver Avenue, Rhyl, LL18 4HL ☎ 07963 293032
win.mullen-james@denbighshire.gov.uk

Bob Murray *(Lab: Prestatyn South West)*, 8 Lon Gwyn Daf, Prestatyn, LL19 8YG ☎ (01745) 854106
bob.murray@denbighshire.gov.uk

Dewi Owens *(Con: St Asaph East)*, Bryn Eglwys, Mount Road, St. Asaph, LL17 ODB
☎ (01745) 584825
dewi.owens@denbighshire.gov.uk

Merfyn Parry *(Ind: Llandyrnog)*, Craiglea, Llandyrnog, Denbigh, LL16 4EY ☎ (01824) 790338 / 07793 560351
merfyn.parry@denbighshire.gov.uk

Allan Pennington *(Con: Prestatyn North)*, 87 Seabank Drive, Prestatyn, LL19 7PS ☎ (01745) 859403
allan.pennington@denbighshire.gov.uk

Arwel Roberts *(PC: Rhuddlan)*, Fachwen, Ffordd Rhyl, Rhuddlan, LL18 2TP ☎ (01745) 590869
arwel.roberts@denbighshire.gov.uk

Gareth Sandilands *(Lab: Prestatyn South West)*, 16 Llandaff Drive, Prestatyn, LL19 8AS ☎ (01745) 859365
gareth.sandilands@denbighshire.gov.uk

David Simmons *(Lab: Rhyl East)*, 1 Highlands Road, Rhuddlan, Rhyl, LL18 2SA ☎ (01745) 592626
david.simmons@denbighshire.gov.uk

Barbara Smith MBE *(Ind: Tremeirchion)*, Graig Las, Cwm, LL18 5SG ☎ (01745) 571794
barbara.smith@denbighshire.gov.uk

David Smith *(Ind: Ruthin)*, Rugog, Llanfair Road, Ruthin, LL15 1BY
☎ (01824) 702935
david.smith@denbighshire.gov.uk

Bill Tasker *(Lab: Rhyl South East)*, 21 Trellewelyn Road, Rhyl, LL18 4ES ☎ (01745) 336152
bill.tasker@denbighshire.gov.uk

Julian Thompson-Hill *(Con: Prestatyn East)*, 87 Gronant Road, Prestatyn, LL19 9NA
☎ (01745) 854059
julian.thompson-hill@denbighshire.gov.uk

Joe Welch *(Ind: Llanrhaeadr yng Nghinmeirch)*, Plas Farm, Nantglyn, Denbigh, LL16 5RB
☎ (01745) 550680
joseph.welch@denbighshire.gov.uk

Cefyn Williams *(PC: Llandrillo)*, Tyn y Wern, Llangar, Cynwyd, Corwen, LL21 OHW
☎ (01490) 412784
cefyn.williams@denbighshire.gov.uk

Cheryl Williams *(Lab: Rhyl South)*, 59 Meredith Crescent, Rhyl, LL18 2HP ☎ (01745) 369299 / 07845 256711
cheryl.williams@denbighshire.gov.uk

Huw Owen Williams *(Con: Llanbedr DC Llangynhafal)*, Rhesgoed Farm, Llanbedr DC, Ruthin, LL15 1YE
☎ (01824) 709750
huw.o.williams@denbighshire.gov.uk

Clerks to the Community Councils

Aberwheeler Community Council, *Helen Williams,* Candy Mill, Bodfari, LL16 4DR
☎ (01745) 710535
aberchwiler@yahoo.co.uk

Betws Gwerfil Goch Community Council, *Elin Roberts,* Fferm Tŷ Cerrig, Melin-Y-Wig, Corwen, LL21 9RH ☎ (01824) 750570

Bodelwyddan Community Council, *Mrs J Prendergast,* 53 Ffordd Parc Bodnant, Prestatyn, LL19 9LJ ☎ (01745) 854926

Bodfari Community Council, *Helen Howard,* 42 Regent Road, Rhyl, LL18 4BA ☎ (01745) 334334
helen.howard@denbighshire.gov.uk

Bryneglwys Community Council, *Nia Roberts,* Bryn-Llan, Bryneglwys, Corwen, LL21 9LL ☎ (01490) 450258

Cefn Meiriadog Community Council, *Ann Jones,* Cae Cogau, Groesffordd Marli, Abergele, LL22 9DR ☎ (01745) 582441

Clocaenog Community Council, *Gwyn Davies,* 11 Maes Caenog, Clocaenog, Ruthin, LL15 2AU
☎ (01824) 750283
daviesg@denbighshire.gov.uk

Corwen Community Council, *Pamela Williams,* 5 Cefn Rhug, Corwen, LL21 0EH ☎ (01490) 413400
cyngorbro.corwen@denbighshire.gov.uk

Cyffylliog Community Council, *Gwyn Davies,* 11 Maes Caenog, Clocaenog, Ruthin, LL15 2AU
☎ (01824) 750283
daviesg@denbighshire.gov.uk

Cynwyd Community Council, *Alwyn Jones,* Parry Nythni - Tawelfan', Llandrillo, Corwen, LL21 0TH ☎ (01490) 440203

Denbigh Town Council, *Medwyn Jones,* Town Hall, Crown Lane, Denbigh, LL16 3TB ☎ (01745) 815984
townclerk@denbightowncouncil.gov.uk

Derwen Community Council, *Gwyn Davies,* 11 Maes Caenog, Clocaenog, Ruthin, LL15 1AU
☎ (01824) 750283
daviesg@denbighshire.gov.uk

Dyserth Community Council, *Mr A D B Pirie,* 25 South Drive, Rhyl, LL18 ☎ (01745) 360641
dyserthcommunitycouncil@denbighshire.gov.uk

Efenechtyd Community Council, *Peter G Palmer,* Bodafon, 3 Glaslyn, Pwllglas, Ruthin, LL15 2PF ☎ (01824) 704873

Gwyddelwern Community Council, *Carys Williams,* Is Awel, Bryn Saith Marchog, Corwen, LL21 9SB ☎ (01824) 750262

Henllan Community Council, *Gwyn Davies,* 11 Maes Caenog, Clocaenog, Ruthin, LL15 2AU
☎ (01824) 750283
daviesg@denbighshire.gov.uk

Llanarmon yn Iâl Community Council, *Mrs N Wright,* Bryn Llyn, Black Mountain, Treuddyn, Mold, CH7 4BW ☎ (01824) 780358
norma_helen_wright@yahoo.co.uk

Llanbedr Dyffryn Clwyd Community Council, *Jackie Ditchburn,* The Tithe Barn, Llangynhafal, Ruthin, LL15 1RT
☎ (01824) 702512
admin@tech8.co.uk

Llandegla Community Council, *Mrs G A Dillon,* Rhos Ddigre, Llandegla, Wrexham, LL11 3AU
☎ (01978) 790269
gwyneth.dillon@denbighshire.gov.uk

Llandrillo Community Council, *Hefina Roberts,* Glascoed, Cynwyd, Corwen, LL21 0NA ☎ (01490) 412476
robert.roberts171@btinternet.com

Llandyrnog Community Council, *R Bryn Davies,* Bryn Ffolt, Llandyrnog, Denbigh, LL16 4HN
☎ (01824) 790542
brynd@fsmail.net

Llanelidan Community Council, *Gwyn Davies,* 11 Maes Caenog, Clocaenog, Ruthin, LL15 2AU
☎ (01824) 750283
daviesg@denbighshire.gov.uk

Llanfair Dyffryn Clwyd Community Council, *Michael Shorter,* 35 Haulfryn, Ruthin, LL15 1HD ☎ (01824) 704012

Llanferres Community Council, *Gwyneth A Dillon,* Rhos Ddigre, Llandegla, Wrexham, LL11 3AU
☎ (01978) 790269
gwyneth.dillon@denbighshire.gov.uk

Llangollen Town Council, *Ian F Parry,* Town Hall, Parade Street, Llangollen, LL20 8PH
☎ (01978) 861345
iparry@btconnect.com

Llangynhafal Community Council, *John L Roberts,* Rhos Newydd, Gellifor, Ruthin, LL15 1RY ☎ (01824) 704776

Llanrhaeadr Yng Nghinmeirch Community Council, *Gwyn Davies,* 11 Maes Caenog, Clocaenog, Ruthin, LL15 2AU ☎ (01824) 750283
daviesg@denbighshire.gov.uk

Llantysilio Community Council, *Sandra Baker,* Rockliffe, Abbey Road, Llangollen, LL20 8EF
☎ (01978) 861451
llantysiliocommunitycouncil@denbighshire.gov.uk

Llanynys Community Council, *Gwyn Davies,* 11 Maes Caenog, Clocaenog, Ruthin, LL15 2AU
☎ (01824) 750283
daviesg@denbighshire.gov.uk

Nantglyn Community Council, *Non Roberts,* Ty'n y Ffrith, Nantglyn, Denbigh, LL16 5RG
☎ (01745) 550594
non.roberts@catsystems.co.uk

Prestatyn Town Council, *Nigel Acott,* 7/9 Nant Hall Road, Prestatyn, LL19 9LN ☎ (01745) 857185
nigel.acott@prestatyntc.co.uk

Rhuddlan Town Council, *Terry Pemberton,* 1 The Avenue, Woodland Park, Prestatyn, LL19 9RD ☎ (01745) 855730
rhuddlantownclerk@hotmail.com

Rhyl Town Council, *Gareth Nickels,* Civic Offices, Wellington Centre, Wellington Road, Rhyl, LL18 1LE ☎ (01745) 331114
enquiries@rhyltowncouncil.gov.uk

Ruthin Town Council, *Dafydd Williams,* Town Hall, Wynnstay Road, Ruthin, LL15 1AS
☎ (01824) 703797
ruthintowncouncil@denbighshire.gov.uk

St Asaph Community Council, *Andrew Pirie,* 25 South Drive, Rhyl, LL18 4SU ☎ (01745) 360641
stasaphtowncouncil@denbighshire.gov.uk

Trefnant Community Council, *Mrs A R Alexander,* Arfon Cottage, 19 Roe Parc, St Asaph, LL17 0LD
☎ (01745) 583798
alison.alexander@btinternet.com

Tremeirchion Cwm & Waen Community Council, *Ann Davies,* Trelogan Isaf, Trelogan, Holywell, Flintshire, CH8 9BE ☎ (01745) 560327
ann.davies@denbighshire.gov.uk

CYNGOR SIR Y FFLINT
FLINTSHIRE COUNTY COUNCIL

County Hall, Mold CH7 6NB
Tel: (01352) 752121
Email:
info@flintshire.gov.uk
Website:
www.flintshire.gov.uk

CYNGOR
Sir y Fflint
Flintshire
COUNTY COUNCIL

Leader
Cllr Aaron Shotton

Chief Executive
Colin Everett

NO OVERALL CONTROL	Lab **31** Ind **19** Con **8** Lib D **7** Others **4** PC **1**	TOTAL 70

ELECTION RESULT 2012

	Seats	Change	Votes	Share
Labour	31	9	20,117	42.7%
Independent	19	-7	15,840	33.6%
Conservative	8	-1	4,080	8.7%
Lib Dem	7	-4	3,979	8.4%
Others	4	4	2,341	5.0%
Plaid Cymru	1	-	796	1.7%

Socio-economic Profile

		Rank 1<22
Area (sq km)	438	12
Population ('000s)	149.7	6
% able to speak Welsh	25.3	7
% born in Wales	51.1	22
% non-white ethnic groups	2.1	20
Gross rev expenditure (2011-12)	£312.4m	8
Forecast capital expenditure (2011-12)	£31.4m	15
% dwellings in Band D (2012-13)	18.6	7
Average band D council tax (2011-12)	£1,150.68	12
% over retirement age	17.6	16
% pupils 5+ GCSEs A*-C (2010-11)	69.8	10
Unemployment (% claimant count 2011)	3.3	17
Index of Deprivation (2011)	17	17
(% of Authority in most deprived 30%)		

Road ——
Rail -----

FLINTSHIRE

Principal Officers

Chief Executive:	**Colin Everett**
Director of Community Services:	**Neil Ayling**
Director of Environment:	**Carl Longland**
Director of Lifelong Learning:	**Ian Budd**

Executive 2012-2013

Leader & Finance	**Aaron Shotton** (Lab)
Deputy Leader & Environment:	**Bernie Attridge** (Lab)
Corporate Management:	**Billy Mullin** (Lab)
Social Services:	**Christine Jones** (Lab)
Housing:	**Helen Brown** (Ind)
Education:	**Chris Bithell** (Lab)
Regeneration, Enterprise & Leisure:	**Peter Macfarlane** (Lab)
Public Protection, Waste & Recycling:	**Kevin Jones** (Lab)

Committee Chairs 2012-2013

Planning & Development Control Committee:	**David Wisinger** (Lab)
Community Profile & Partnerships Overview & Scrutiny Committee:	**Brian Dunn** (Ind)
Corporate Resources Overview & Scrutiny Committee:	**Richard Jones** (Lib D)
Environment Overview & Scrutiny Committee:	**Matt Wright** (Con)
Housing Overview & Scrutiny Committee:	**Ron Hampsom** (Lab)
Lifelong Learning Overview & Scrutiny Committee:	**Ian Roberts** (Lab)
Social & Healthcare Overview & Scrutiny Committee:	**Carol Ellis** (Ind)
Audit Committee:	**Alison Halford** (Con)
Licensing Committee:	**Tony Sharps** (Ind)
Constitution Committee:	**Robin Guest** (Lib D)
Democratic Services Committee:	**Robin Guest** (Lib D)

Salaries

Basic Salary: £13,715
Senior Salaries: Leader: £47,500; Deputy Leader: £33,460
Executive Members: £28,780; Chairs of Scrutiny Committees: £21,910
Chairs of Other Committees: £21,910; Clwyd Pensions Panel: £16,920
Chair of Council: £21,375; Vice-Chair of Council: £16,625

Councillors ♂ 52 ♀ 18

Chair: Cllr Ann Minshull

Alex Aldridge OBE (*Lab: Flint Coleshill*), 12 Third Avenue, Flint, Flintshire, CH6 5LT
☎ (01352) 761809

Bernie Attridge (*Lab: Connah's Quay Central*), 95 Fron Road, Connahís Quay, CH5 4PJ
☎ (01244) 812440
bernie.attridge@flintshire.gov.uk

Glyn Banks (*Lab: Ffynnongroyw*), Bodwyn, Tanlan, Holywell, Flintshire, CH8 9JH
☎ 01745 561641,
pbanks101@btinternet.com

Haydn Bateman (*Ind: Mold Broncoed*), Cortonwood, Blackbrook Road, Sychdyn, Mold, CH7 6LT
☎ (01352) 754510 / 07714 155446
haydn.bateman@flintshire.gov.uk /
haydn.bateman@yahoo.co.uk

Marion Bateman (*Ind: Northop*), Cortonwood, Blackbrook Road, Sychdyn, Mold, CH7 6LT
☎ (01352) 754510
marion.bateman@flintshire.gov.uk

Chris Bithell (*Lab: Mold East*), The Coppins, 88 Hendy Road, Mold, CH7 1QR ☎ (01352) 754578
robert.c.bithell@talk21.com /
christopher.bithell@flintshire.gov.uk

Amanda Bragg (*Lib D: New Brighton*), 20 Uwch-Y-Nant, Myndd Isa, Mold, CH7 6YP
☎ (01352) 755261,
amanda.bragg@flintshire.gov.uk

Helen Brown (*Ind: Aston*), 15 Wirral View, Hawarden, CH5 3ET
☎ (01244) 528907 / 07990 780856
helenbrown@flintshire.gov.uk

Derek Butler (*Lab: Broughton South*), 19 Hawker Close, Broughton, Flintshire, CH4 0SQ
☎ (01244) 536760
derek.butler@flintshire.gov.uk

Clive Carter (*Con: Hawarden*), Carelia, 8 Overlea Drive, Hawarden, Deeside, CH5 3HS
☎ (01244) 458102
clive.carver@flintshire.gov.uk

David Cox (*Lab: Flint Coleshill*), 3 Beech Grove, Manor Estate, Flint, CH6 5RY ☎ (01352) 735333 / 07933 256989
davidcox3b@gmail.com

Peter Curtis (*Lab: Holywell Central*), 48 Pen-y-Maes Gardens, Holywell, CH8 7BN ☎ (01352) 711738
peter.curtis@flintshire.gov.uk /
snowy.curtis@virgin.net

Ron Davies (*Lab: Shotton Higher*), 32 Dale Road, Aston Park, Queensferry, CH5 1XE
☎ (01244) 811828 / 07786 570591
rsdavi3s@aol.com

Adele Davies-Cooke (*Con: Gwernaffield*), Gerddi-Duon Farm, Gwysaney, Denbigh Road, Mold, CH7 5HE ☎ (01352) 759034
adeledaviescooke@btinternet.com

Alan Diskin (*Lab: Mancott*), Ambleside, Duckers Lane, Mancot, CH5 2ED ☎ (01244) 531557
adiskin@sky.com /
alan.diskin@flintshire.gov.uk

Glenys Diskin (*Lab: Mancott*), Ambleside, Duckers Lane, Mancot, CH5 2ED ☎ (01244) 531557
adiskin@tsky.com /
glenys.diskin@flintshire.gov.uk

Chris Dolphin (*Lib D: Whitford*), 11 Ffordd Aelwyd, Carmel, Holywell, CH8 8SH
☎ (01352) 713415 / 0784 9459 568
chris_dolphin@hotmail.co.uk

Rosetta Dolphin (*Lib D: Greenfield*), 11 Ffordd Aelwyd, Carmel, Holywell, CH8 8SH
☎ (01352) 713415
rosetta.dolphin@hotmail.co.uk

Ian Dunbar (*Lab: Connah's Quay South*), 1 Wepre Hall Crescent, Connahís Quay, CH5 4HZ
☎ (01244) 813920 / 07790192924
iandunbar57@aol.com

Brian Dunn (*Ind: Connah's Quay Wepre*), 92 High Street, Connahís Quay, CH5 4DD ☎ (01244) 812078
briandunn92@hotmail.com /
brian.dunn@flintshire.gov.uk

Carol Ellis (*Ind: Buckley Mountain*), 96 Liverpool Road, Buckley, CH7 3LJ ☎ (01244) 544906
carol.ellis@flintshire.gov.uk

David Evans (*Lab: Shotton East*), 57a Nelson Street, Shotton, CH5 1DH
☎ (01244) 822402 / 07758 321333
det2dee@aol.com

Ted Evans (*Lab: Flint Trelawny*), 3 Third Avenue, Flint, CH6 5LT
☎ (01352) 734255
ted.evans@flintshire.gov.uk

Jim Falshaw (*Con: Caerwys*), Bell House, High Street, Caerwys, Mold, CH7 5AN
☎ (01352) 720476
jamesfalshaw@aol.com /
jim.falshaw@flintshire.gov.uk

Veronica Gay (*Ind: Saltney Stonebridge*), 39 Sandy Lane, Saltney, Chester, CH4 8UB
☎ (01244) 671360 / 07790 751690
saltneystonebridge@hotmail.com /
veronica.gay@flintshire.gov.uk

Robin Guest (*Lib D: Mold South*), 36 Ffordd Pentre, Mold, CH7 1UY
☎ (01352) 757408
tobyreggie@hotmail.com /
robin.guest@flintshire.gov.uk

Alison Halford (*Con: Ewloe*), 2 Prospect Close, Ewloe, Deeside, CH5 3RL ☎ (01244) 534281
councillor@alisonhalford.co.uk /
alison.halford@flintshire.gov.uk

Ron Hampson (*Lab: Buckley Bistre West*), 10 Melbourne Road, Buckley, CH7 2LH ☎ (01244) 547056
ronald.hampson@flintshire.gov.uk

George Hardcastle (*Ind: Aston*), 16 Rowan Road, Aston Park, Deeside, CH5 1XR
☎ (01244) 814572
george.hardcastle@flintshire.gov.uk

Patrick Heesom (*Ind: Mostyn*), Pentre Ucha, Gwespyr, CH8 9LW
☎ 07990 774374
patrick.heesom@flintshire.gov.uk

Cindy Hinds (*Lab: Penyffordd*), 38 Berwyn Avenue, Penyffordd, Nr. Chester, CH4 0HS
☎ (01978) 761354
hdencin@aol.com

Trefor Howorth (*Lab: Flint Trelawny*), 2 Coed y Bryn, Pentre Hill, Flint Mountain, CH6 5QP
☎ (01352) 761096
margaret@howorth2.wanadoo.co.uk

Raymond Hughes (*Ind: Leeswood*), 3 Erith Street, Leeswood, CH7 4SE
☎ (01352)771372 / 07794 208550
raymond.hughes@flintshire.gov.uk

Dennis Hutchinson *(Ind: Buckley Pentrobin)*, Newlyn, Padeswood Road, Buckley, CH7 2JW
☎ (01244) 543907 / 07966 405212
dennis.hutchinson@flintshire.gov.uk

Hilary Isherwood *(Con: Llanfynydd)*, 'Fernleigh', Ffordd-y-Bont, Pontybodkin, CH7 4TS
☎ (01352) 771379
hilaryisherwood@googlemail.com

Joe Johnson *(Lab: Holywell East)*, Kasara, 168 Pen-Y-Maes Road, Holywell, CH8 7HH
☎ (01352) 713763
joe.johnson@flintshire.gov.uk

Rita Johnson *(Ind: Flint Oakenholt)*, 4 Atis Cross, Oakenholt, Flintshire, CH6 5HA
☎ (01352) 734729
rita.johnson@flintshire.gov.uk

Christine Jones *(Lab: Sealand)*, 31 Welsh Road, Garden City, Deeside, CH5 2HU
☎ (01244) 811556
jonahmikejp@yahoo.co.uk / christine.m.jones@flintshire.gov.uk

Kevin Jones *(Lab: Bagillt East)*, 12 Roman's Way, Bagillt, CH6 6DL
☎ (01352) 733191
jones.kevin89@yahoo.co.uk

Richard Jones *(Lib D: Buckley Bistre East)*, Tŷ Gwyn Farm, Well Street, Buckley, CH7 2PQ
☎ (01244) 546982 / 07762 820350
richie.jones@yahoo.com / richard.jones@flintshire.gov.uk

Stella Jones *(Lab: Caergwrle)*, Tegfan, 25 Pen-y-Bryn, Hope, Nr. Wrexham, LL12 9NQ
☎ (01978) 761602
stella.jones@flintshire.gov.uk

Colin Legg *(Ind: Halkyn)*, 'Minffordd', Rhesycae, Holywell, CH8 8JQ ☎ (01352) 780707
colin.legg@flintshire.gov.uk

Phil Lightfoot *(Ind: Higher Kinnerton)*, 57 Kirkett Avenue, Higher Kinnerton, CH4 9BN
☎ (01244) 660884
phil.lightfoot@aol.com

Brian Lloyd *(Ind: Old West)*, Pwll Glas Farm Cottage, Gwernaffield Road, Mold, CH7 1RQ
☎ (01352) 753107
brian.lloyd@flintshire.gov.uk

Richard Lloyd *(Ind: Saltney Mold Junction)*, 'Cornerways', 2 Saltney Ferry Road, Saltney Ferry, CH5 0BN
☎ (01244) 682480
t.r.lloyd@hotmail.co.uk

Mike Lowe *(Lab: Broughton South)*, 61 Forest Drive, Broughton, CH4 0QJ ☎ (01244) 534961
mike.lowe@flintshire.gov.uk

Peter Macfarlane *(Lab: Connah's Quay)*, Golftyn, 59 Dee View Road, Connah's Quay, Flintshire, CH5 4AY
☎ (01244) 813909 / 07900 053584
peter.macfarlane@flintshire.gov.uk

David Mackie *(Ind: Ewloe)*, Parmelea, Old Aston Hill, Ewloe, Flintshire, CH5 3AH
☎ (01244) 538643
david.mackie@flintshire.gov.uk

Nancy Matthews *(Lib D: Gwernymynydd)*, The Croft, Ffordd Bryn Gwyn, Gwernymynydd, CH7 5JW ☎ (01352) 757328
sendittonancy@googlemail.com / nancy.matthews@flintshire.gov.uk

Hilary McGuill *(Lib D: Argoed)*, Wylfa House, Wylfa Hill, Mold Road, Mynydd Isa, CH7 6TG
☎ (01352) 757350
hilary.mcguill@flintshire.gov.uk

Ann Minshull JP *(Lab: Shotton West)*, 69 Taliesin Avenue, Shotton, Deeside, CH5 1HX
☎ (01244) 819041
ann.minshull@flintshire.gov.uk

Billy Mullin *(Lab: Broughton North East)*, 11 Little Roodee, Manor Lane, Hawarden, CH5 3PU
☎ (01244) 531413
billy.mullin@flintshire.gov.uk

Tim Newhouse *(Lib D: Hope)*, Shordley Hall Annexe, Shordley Road, Hope LL12 9RT
☎ (01978) 761914
tim@hopetimes.co.uk / tim.newhouse@flintshire.gov.uk

Mike Peers *(Ind: Buckley Pentrobin)*, 7 Pinewood Road, Drury, Buckley, CH7 3JZ
☎ (01244) 546115 / 07751 627657
mike.peers@tiscali.co.uk / mike.peers@flintshire.gov.uk

Neville Phillips OBE *(Lib D: Buckley Bistre West)*, Highfield, Tabernacle Street, Buckley, CH7 2JT
☎ (01244) 543188 / 07792 375851
neville.phillips@flintshire.gov.uk

Mike Reece *(Lab: Bagillt West)*, Holly Hill House, Top Hill, Bagillt, CH6 6HU ☎ (01352) 712983
mike.reece@talktalk.net

Gareth Roberts *(PC: Holywell West)*, 6 Pistyll, Treffynnon, CH8 7SH ☎ (01352) 710826
h.gareth.roberts@flintshire.gov.uk

Ian Roberts *(Lab: Flint Castle)*, 12 Maes Teg, Flint, CH6 5TQ

Tony Sharps *(Ind: Northop Hall)*, Gentone, Village Road, Northop Hall, Nr. Mold, CH7 6HS
☎ (01244) 830109 / 07788 184446
tony.sharps@flintshire.gov.uk

Aaron Shotton *(Lab: Connah's Quay Central)*, 48 Pinewood Avenue, Connah's Quay, Deeside, CH5 4SJ
☎ (01244) 810467 / 07979 923069
aaron.shotton@flintshire.gov.uk

Paul Shotton *(Lab: Connah's Quay Golftyn)*, 48 Pinewood Avenue, Connah's Quay, Deeside CH8 9NA ☎ (01244) 810467
paul.shotton@flintshire.gov.uk

Ian Smith *(Lab: Connah's Quay South)*, 27 Normanby Drive, Connah's Quay
ian.smith@flintshire.gov.uk

Nigel Steele-Mortimer *(Con: Trelawnyd & Gwaenysgor)*, Golden Grove, Llanasa, Holywell, CH8 9NA ☎ (01745) 854452
nigel.ann.mortimer@lineone.net

Carolyn Thomas *(Ind: Treuddyn)*, Cartrefle, Corwen Road, Pontybodkin, Nr. Mold, CH7 4TG
☎ (01352) 770946
carolyn.thomas@flintshire.gov.uk

Owen Thomas *(Con: Cilcain)*, Bryn Gwawr, Ffordd-y-Berth, Cilcain, Nr. Mold, CH7 5NE
☎ (01352) 740056
owen.thomas@flintshire.gov.uk / thomasowen@aol.com

David Williams *(Ind: Penyffordd)*, Cae Derw, Wrexham Road, Penyffordd, CH4 0HT
☎ (01978) 762486
david.m.williams@flintshire.gov.uk

Sharon Williams *(Lab: Gronant)*, 3 Dee View, Llanasa Road, Gronant, LL19 9TL
☎ (01745) 284104
david.wisinger@flintshire.gov.uk

David Wisinger (*Lab: Queensferry*), 7 Church Cottages, Sealand Road, Sealand, CH1 6BR ☎ (01244) 881680 jonahmikejp@yahoo.co.uk / david.wisinger@flintshire.gov.uk

Arnold Woolley (*Ind: Buckley Bistre East*), 75 Bryn Awelon, Bistre Heights, Buckley, CH7 2QF ☎ (01244) 549421 arnold.woolley@flintshire.gov.uk

Matt Wright (*Con: Brynford*), Bryn Tirion, Denbigh Road, Nannerch, CH7 5QU ☎ (01352) 741835 matt@valeofclwyd.orangehome.co.uk

Clerks to the Community Councils

Argoed Community Council, *Rhodri Hampson-Jones*, Council Office, Mynydd Isa Community Square, Mercia Drive, Mynydd Isa, CH7 6UH ☎ (01352) 751490 argoedcc@btconnect.com

Bagillt Community Council, *Gareth Roberts*, 5 Ffordd Owain, Acton, Wrexham, LL12 8JL ☎ (01978) 354617 gareth@garethroberts62.entadsl.com

Broughton & Bretton Community Council, *Mr N Barnes*, 113 The Highway, Hawarden, Deeside, CH5 3DL ☎ (01244) 533692 mail@broughtonandbrettoncommunitycouncil.gov.uk

Brynford Community Council, *Mr A Roberts*, Crecas Cottage, Carmel Hill, Pantasaph, Holywell, CH8 8NZ ☎ (01352) 710335

Buckley Town Council, *Mr M Wright*, Council Offices, Buckley, Flintshire, CH7 2JB ☎ (01244) 544540 mbw@buckleytc.org.uk

Caerwys Town Council, *Mrs E Snowden*, 10 Llys y Fron, Mold, Flintshire, CH7 1QZ ☎ (01352) 757288 elizabeth.snowden1@btinternet.com

Cilcain Community Council, *Mr A Evans*, Gwel Hyfryd, Pentre Hill, Flint Mountain, CH6 5QN ☎ (01352) 761241

Connah's Quay Town Council, *Ian Jones*, Town Council Offices, Fron Road, Connah's Quay, CH5 4PJ ☎ (01244) 819420 info@connahs-quay.co.uk

Flint Town Council, *Mr G N I Jones*, Town Hall, Market Square, Flint, CH6 5NW ☎ (01352) 734414 townclerk@flinttowncouncil.co.uk

Gwernaffield Community Council, *Mr N Roberts*, Xoanon, Argoed Avenue, New Brighton, Mold, CH7 6QL ☎ (01352) 753261

Gwernymynydd Community Council, *Mr T M Richardson*, 2 Church Close, Northop Hall, Mold, CH7 6HY ☎ (01244) 815083 t1967mr@hotmail.com

Halkyn Community Council, *R Phillip Parry*, Tŷ Cornel, 51 St Michael's Drive, Caerwys, CH7 5BS ☎ (01352) 720547 halkyn.council@btinternet.com

Hawarden Community Council, *Mr N Barnes*, 113 The Highway, Hawarden, Deeside, CH5 3DL ☎ (01244) 533692 mail@hawardencommunitycouncil.gov.uk

Higher Kinnerton Community Council, *Elizabeth Corner*, 13 Deans Way, Higher Kinnerton, CH4 9DZ ☎ (01244) 660277 liz.corner@vodafoneemail.co.uk

Holywell Town Council, *Mr D C Pierce*, Bank Place Offices, Holywell, CH8 7TJ ☎ (01352) 711757 holyewelltown@btconnect.com

Hope Community Council, *Mr A Rushton*, 5 Ainsdale Close, Buckley, CH7 2NE ☎ (01244) 546966 hope.community@tiscali.co.uk

Leeswood Community Council, *Mr G N I Jones*, 4 Howards Close, Penyffordd, Chester, CH4 0GG ☎ (01244) 547440

Llanasa Community Council, *Mr A Williams*, Plas Iolyn, Picton, Holywell, CH8 9JG ☎ (01745) 560699

Llanfynydd Community Council, *Carolyn Thomas*, Droed y Mynydd, Corwen Road, Pontybodkin, CH7 4TG ☎ (01352) 771102 carolyn_fg@hotmail.com

Mold Town Council, *Mr F Boneham*, Town Hall, Earl Road, Mold, CH7 1AB ☎ (01352) 758532 townclerk@moldtowncouncil.org.uk

Mostyn Community Council, *Mr M R Thomas*, 23 Julius Close, Oakenholt, Flint, CH5 5EN ☎ (01352) 733070

Nannerch Community Council, *Arwel Owen*, 2 West View, Mold, CH7 1DW ☎ (01352) 750921, arwelwynowen@hotmail.com

Nercwys Community Council, *Susan Lyth*, Ffynnonfa, Wern Road, Rhosesmor, Mold, CH7 6P ☎ (01352) 780270 slyth.nccclerk@gmail.com

Northop Community Council, *Mr G Connah*, Ffordd Las, Sychdyn, Mold, CH7 6DU ☎ (01352) 757188 grahamconnah@btinternet.com

Northop Hall Community Council, *Bridget Thomas*, Sans Souci, 77 Northop Road, Flint, CH6 5LG ☎ (01352) 733667 northophallcc@mail.com

Penyffordd Community Council, *Mr G N I Jones*, 4 Howards Close, Penyffordd, Chester, CH4 0GG ☎ (01244) 547440

Queensferry Community Council, *Janet Jones*, The Orchard, 39 Wood Street, Sandycroft, Deeside, CH5 2PL ☎ (01244) 520642 janetjones@queensferrycc.co.uk

Saltney Town Council, *Mr A Thorniley*, The Arches, 49 Meadowsway, Upton by Chester, CH2 1HZ ☎ (01244) 398829 athorniley@aol.com

Sealand Community Council, *Peter Richmond*, 3 Blakeley Court, Raby Mere, Wirral, CH63 0ND, ☎ (0151) 334 2247 / 07932 925958 sealandcc@googlemail.com

Shotton Town Council, *Mrs S L Cartwright*, Town Council Offices, Alexandra Street, Shotton, Deeside, CH5 1DL ☎ (01244) 822119 shottontowncouncil@btconnect.com

Trelawnyd & Gwaenysgor Community Council, *Mr R D Owens*, 11 Fford Talargoch, Meliden, Prestatyn, Denbighshire, LL19 8LA ☎ (01745) 856950 david.owens@vto.gsx.gov.uk

Treuddyn Community Council, *Carolyn Thomas*, Droed y Mynydd, Corwen Road, Pontybodkin, Nr Mold, CH7 4TG ☎ (01352) 771102 carolyn_fg@hotmail.com

Whitford Community Council, *Arwel Owen*, 2 West View, Mold, CH7 1DW ☎ (01352) 750921

Ysceifiog Community Council, *Mr A Roberts*, Crecas Cottage, Carmel Hill, Pantasaph, Holywell, CH8 8NZ ☎ (01352) 710335

CYNGOR GWYNEDD
GWYNEDD COUNCIL

Swyddfa'r Cyngor, Stryd y Jêl
Caernarfon LL55 1SH
Tel: (01766) 771000
Fax: (01286) 678962
Email: enquiries@gwynedd.gov.uk
Website: www.gwynedd.gov.uk

Leader
Cllr Dyfed Edwards

Chief Executive
Harry Thomas

NO OVERALL CONTROL	PC **37** Ind **18** Llais Gwynedd **13** Lab **4** Lib D **2**	TOTAL 74

ELECTION RESULT 2012

	Seats	Change	Votes	Share
Plaid Cymru	37	2	12,797	40.4%
Independent	18	-	7,594	24.0%
Llais Gwynedd	13	1	7,139	22.5%
Labour	4	-	2,891	9.1%
Lib Dem	2	-3	701	2.2%
Con	0	-	405	1.3%
Others	0	-	175	0.6%

Socio-economic Profile

		Rank 1<22
Area (sq km)	2,548	2
Population ('000s)	119.0	13
% able to speak Welsh	70.5	1
% born in Wales	69.8	14
% non-white ethnic groups	3.0	11
Gross rev expenditure (2011-12)	£283.3m	11
Forecast capital expenditure (2011-12)	£52.7m	7
% dwellings in Band D (2012-13)	17.3	11
Band D council tax (2011-12)	£1,236.66	7
% over retirement age	20.3	9
% pupils 5+ GCSEs A*-C (2010-11)	70.7	8
Unemployment (% claimant count 2011)	3.0	19
Index of Deprivation (2011)	7	21
(% of Authority in most deprived 30%)		

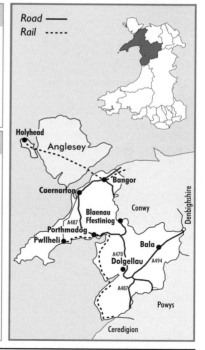

Road ——
Rail - - - - -

LOCAL GOVERNMENT

GWYNEDD

Principal Officers

Chief Executive:	**Harry Thomas**
Corporate Director:	**Iwan Trefor Jones**
Corporate Director:	**Dafydd P Lewis**
Corporate Director:	**Dilwyn Owen Williams**

Cabinet Members 2012-2013

Leader:	**Dyfed Edwards** (PC)
Deputy Leader / Education:	**Sian Gwenllian** (PC)
Care:	**R H Wyn Williams** (PC)
Environment:	**Gareth Roberts** (PC)
Deprivation:	**Brian Jones** (Lab)
Economy:	**John Wynn Jones** (PC)
Planning:	**John Wyn Williams** (PC)
Resources:	**Peredur Jenkins** (PC)
Customer Care:	**Ioan Thomas** (PC)
Healthy Gwynedd:	**Paul Thomas** (PC)

Committe Chairs 2012-2013

The Council:	**Selwyn Griffiths** (PC)
Corporate Scrutiny Committee:	**Simon Glyn** (LG)
Communities Scrutiny Committee:	**Eric M Jones** (Ind)
Services Scrutiny Committee:	**Dyfrig Siencyn** (PC)
Audit Committee:	**Tba**
Democratic Services Committee:	**Dewi Owen** (Ind)
Planning Committee:	**Gwen Griffith** (Lab)
Central Licensing Committee:	**Tudor Owen** (PC)
Pensions Committee:	**Tba**
Employment Appeals Committee:	**Jean Forsyth** (Ind)
Language Committee:	**Liz Saville Roberts** (PC)

Salaries

Basic Salary: £13,175; Senior Salaries:
Leader: £47,500; Deputy Leader: £33,460
Cabinet Members: £28,780; Chairs of Scrutiny Committees: £21,910
Chairs of Other Committees: £21,910
Chair of Council: £21,375; Vice-Chair of Council: £16,625

GWYNEDD

Councillors   ♂ 55 ♀ 19

Chair: Cllr Evan Selwyn Griffiths   Vice-Chair: Cllr Huw Edwards

Craig ab Iago *(PC: Llanllyfni)*, Arthog, 59 Ffordd Rhedyw, Llanllyfni, Gwynedd, LL54 6SN
☎ (01286) 479093 / 07825661721
Cynghorydd.Craigablago@gwynedd.gov.uk

Llywarch Bowen Jones *(LG: Llanaelhaearn)*, Gwydir Bach, Trefor, Caernarfon, Gwynedd, LL54 5LB
☎ (01286) 660481 / 07549014089
Cynghorydd.LlywarchBowenJones@gwynedd.gov.uk

Stephen Churchman *(Lib D: Dolbenmaen)*, Minffordd House, Garndolbenmaen, Gwynedd, LL51 9TX
☎ (01766) 530661 / 07917301858
Cynghorydd.StephenChurchman@gwynedd.gov.uk

Endaf Cooke *(LG: Seiont)*, 21 Stryd Llyn, Caernarfon, Gwynedd, LL55 2AD
☎ (01286) 678605 / 07747405562
Cynghorydd.EndafCooke@gwynedd.gov.uk

Anwen Jane Davies *(LG: Efailnewydd / Buan)*, Plasyng Ngheidio, Boduan, Pwllheli, Gwynedd, LL53 8YL
☎ (01758) 720327 / 07526121313
Cynghorydd.AnwenJaneDavies@gwynedd.gov.uk

Lesley Day *(Ind: Garth)*, Tyddyn Sydney, Treborth, Bangor, Gwynedd, LL57 2NJ ☎ (01248) 355180
Cynghorydd.LesleyDay@gwynedd.gov.uk

Edward Dogan *(PC: Dewi)*, 5 Four Crosses, Treborth, Bangor, Gwynedd, LL57 2NZ ☎ (01248) 364096

Dyfed Edwards *(PC: Penygroes)*, Swyddfa'r Arweinydd, Cyngor Gwynedd, Swyddfair Cyngor, Caernarfon, Gwynedd, LL55 1SH
☎ (01286) 679298 / (01286) 880954 / 07824415345
Cynghorydd.DyfedWynEdwards@gwynedd.gov.uk

Elwyn Edwards *(PC: Llandderfel)*, Bodaeron, Heol Pensarn, Y Bala, Gwynedd, LL23 7SR
☎ (01678) 520378 / 07879337371
Cynghorydd.ElwynEdwards@gwynedd.gov.uk

Gwynfor Edwards *(Lab: Deinol)*, 4 Nant Cottages, Minffordd, Bangor, Gwynedd, LL57 4DR
☎ (01248) 352794 / 07703824182
Cynghorydd.GwynforEdwards@gwynedd.gov.uk

Huw Edwards *(PC: Cadnant)*, 23 Rhes yr Hafod, Caernarfon, Gwynedd, LL55 2AR
☎ (01286) 675607 / 07818651752

Trevor Edwards (Ind: Llanberis), 17 Stryd Fawr, Llanberis, Gwynedd, LL55 4EN ☎ (01286) 872319
Cynghorydd.TrevorEdwards@gwynedd.gov.uk

Thomas Ellis *(Ind: Trawsfynydd)*, Tyddyn Du, Trawsfynydd, Gwynedd, LL41 4YE ☎ (01766) 540227 / 07867982584
Cynghorydd.TomEllis@gwynedd.gov.uk

Aled Evans *(PC: Llanystumdwy)*, Bryn Llwyn, Chwilog, Pwllheli, Gwynedd, LL53 6NX ☎ (01766) 810703
Cynghorydd.AledLloydEvans@gwynedd.gov.uk

Jean Forsyth *(Ind: Hirael)*, 23 Maes y Dref, Bangor, Gwynedd, LL57 1YL
☎ (01248) 355798
Cynghorydd.JeanForsyth@gwynedd.gov.uk

Gweno Glyn *(LG: Botwnnog)*, Bwlch Groes, Llaniestyn, Pwllheli, Gwynedd, LL53 8SD
☎ (01758) 730872 / 07811441326
Cynghorydd.GwenoGlyn@gwynedd.gov.uk

Simon Glyn *(LG: Tudweiliog)*, Coed Anna, Nanhoron, Pwllheli, Gwynedd, LL53 8PR
☎ (01758) 730326 / 07929348432
Cynghorydd.SimonGlyn@gwynedd.gov.uk

Gwen Griffith *(Lab: Tregarth & Mynydd Llandgai)*, 19 Llwybr Main, Mynydd Llandygai, Bangor, Gwynedd, LL57 4LJ
☎ (01248) 601081 / 07941736483
Cynghorydd.GwenGriffith@gwynedd.gov.uk

Selwyn Griffiths *(PC: Porthmadog West)*, 5 Cefn y Gader, Morfa Bychan, Porthmadog, Gwynedd, LL49 9JA ☎ (01766) 513142 / 07789035084
Cynghorydd.SelwynGriffiths@gwynedd.gov.uk

Alwyn Gruffydd *(LG: Porthmadog / Tremadog)*, Llidiart Ysbyty, Tremadog, Gwynedd, LL49 9RN
☎ (01766) 513025 / 07836366899
Cynghorydd.AlwynGruffydd@gwynedd.gov.uk

Sian Gwenllian *(PC: Y Felinheli)*, Awelfryn, Pen y Bryn, Y Felinheli, Gwynedd, LL56 4YQ
☎ (01248) 670866 / 07775642202
Cynghorydd.SianGwenllian@gwynedd.gov.uk

Annwen Hughes *(PC: Llanbedr)*, Plas Uchaf, Talsarnau, Gwynedd, LL47 6YA ☎ (01766) 780971 / 07919582741
Cynghorydd.AnnwenHughes@gwynedd.gov.uk

Christopher Hughes *(PC: Bontnewydd)*, 4 Cae'r Eglwys, Rhostryfan, Caernarfon, Gwynedd, LL54 7LQ ☎ (01286) 831553 / 07530164624
Cynghorydd.ChristopherHughes@gwynedd.gov.uk

John Brynmor Hughes *(LG: Llanengan)*, The Sun Inn, Llanengan, Pwllheli, Gwynedd, LL53 7LG
☎ (01758) 712660 / 07909922571
Cynghorydd.JohnBrynmorHughes@gwynedd.gov.uk

Louise Hughes *(LG: Llangelynnin)*, 20 Maesegryn, Llanegryn, Gwynedd, LL36 9SH ☎ (01654) 711051
Cynghorydd.LouiseHughes@gwynedd.gov.uk

Jason Humphreys *(LG: Porthmadog East)*, 29 Heol Newydd, Porthmadog, Gwynedd, LL49 9ED
☎ 07788425716
Cynghorydd.JasonHumphreys@gwynedd.gov.uk

Peredur Jenkins *(PC: Brithdir & Llanfachreth / Y Ganllwyd / Llanelltyd)*, Cae Glas, Llanfachreth, Dolgellau, Gwynedd, LL40 2EH
☎ (01341) 423693 / 07799761735
Cynghorydd.PeredurJenkins@gwynedd.gov.uk

Aeron Jones *(LG: Llanwnda)*, Pant y Rhedyn, Llanwnda, Caernarfon, Gwynedd, LL54 5TL
☎ (01286) 832425 / 07882847043
Cynghorydd.AeronMaldwynJones@gwynedd.gov.uk

Brian Jones *(Lab: Cwm y Glo)*, Cefn y Bwlch, Lon y Bwlch, Cwm y Glo, Caernarfon, Gwynedd, LL55 4ED
☎ (01286) 870831 / 07964 286372
Cynghorydd.BrianJones@gwynedd.gov.uk

Dyfrig Jones *(PC: Gerlan)*, Yr Hen Fecws, Carneddi, Bethesda, Gwynedd, LL57 3SF
☎ (01248) 605468 / 07810 874882
Cynghorydd.DyfrigJones@gwynedd.gov.uk

Eric Jones *(Ind: Y Groeslon)*, Afallon, Y Groeslon, Caernarfon, Gwynedd, LL54 7TU
☎ (01286) 830626 / 07780 923375
Cynghorydd.EricMerfynJones@gwynedd.gov.uk

Sion Jones *(Lab: Bethel)*, 10 Cremlyn, Bethel, Caernarfon, Gwynedd, LL55 1AJ
☎ (01248) 671755 / 07940 281735
Cynghorydd.SionJones@gwynedd.gov.uk

Alan Jones Evans *(PC: Llanuwchllyn)*, Cefn Isaf, Rhyduchaf, Y Bala, Gwynedd, LL23 7SD
☎ 07879 227819
Cynghorydd.AlanJonesEvans@gwynedd.gov.uk

Eryl Jones-Williams *(Ind: Dyffryn Ardudwy)*, 22 Pentre Uchaf, Dyffryn Ardudwy, Gwynedd, LL44 2HF
☎ (01341) 242758 / 07796833767
Cynghorydd.ErylJones-Williams@gwynedd.gov.uk

LOCAL GOVERNMENT

Beth Lawton *(Ind: Bryncrug / Llanfihangel)*, 22 Maeshyfryd, Bryncrug, Gwynedd, LL36 9PS
☎ (01654) 711851

Dilwyn Lloyd *(Ind: Talysarn)*, Eryri House, Carmel, Caernarfon, Gwynedd, LL54 7AB
☎ (01286) 882149
Cynghorydd.DilwynLloyd@gwynedd.gov.uk

Anne Lloyd Jones *(Ind: Tywyn)*, Hendy, Tywyn, Gwynedd, LL36 9RU
☎ (01654) 710457
Cynghorydd.AnneLloyd-Jones@gwynedd.gov.uk

June Marshall *(Lib D: Menai - Bangor)*, 30 Maes Berea, Bangor, Gwynedd, LL57 4TQ
☎ (01248) 370955 / 07788134010
Cynghorydd.JuneMarshall@gwynedd.gov.uk

Dafydd Meurig *(PC: Arllechwedd)*, Isfryn, Llanllechid, Bethesda, Gwynedd, LL57 3LB
☎ (01248) 369602 / 07765400140
Cynghorydd.DafyddMeurig@gwynedd.gov.uk

Dilwyn Morgan *(PC: Y Bala)*, Ger y Llŷn, 41 Heol Tegid, Y Bala, Gwynedd, LL23 7EH
☎ (01678) 520685 / 07824983305
Cynghorydd.DilwynMorgan@gwynedd.gov.uk

Linda Morgan *(PC: Dolgellau South)*, Meusydd, 5 Blaen Ddôl, Dolgellau, Gwynedd, LL40 1SE
☎ (01341) 421355 / 07551301187
Cynghorydd.LindaMorgan@gwynedd.gov.uk

Christopher James O'Neal *(Ind: Marchog)*, Tan-y-Bryn YHA, Llandygai Road, Bangor, Gwynedd, LL57 1PZ ☎ 07879 333087
Cynghorydd.ChristopherJamesO'Neal@gwynedd.gov.uk

Dewi Owen *(Ind: Aberdyfi)*, Esgairgyfela, Aberdyfi, Gwynedd, LL35 0SP ☎ (01654) 767267 / 07866201803
Cynghorydd.DewiOwen@gwynedd.gov.uk

Ioan Thomas *(PC: Menai - Caernarfon)*, Strade, 65 Cae Gwyn, Caernarfon, Gwynedd, LL55 1LL
☎ (01286) 673828 / 07810648647
Cynghorydd.IoanCeredigThomas@gwynedd.gov.uk

Michael Sol Owen *(PC: Pwllheli North)*, Plas y Coed, Lôn Caernarfon, Pwllheli, Gwynedd, LL53 5LG
☎ (01758) 612132 / 07786 500420
Cynghorydd.MichaelSolOwen@gwynedd.gov.uk

Roy Owen *(Ind: Seiont)*, 39 Maes Meddyg, Llanbeblig Road, Caernarfon, Gwynedd, LL55 2SF
☎ (01286) 672618 / 07522 611591
Cynghorydd.WilliamRoyOwen@gwynedd.gov.uk

Nigel Pickavance *(Ind: Marchog)*, 30 Kingsley Avenue, Maesgeirchen, Bangor, Gwynedd, LL57 1TA
☎ (01248) 370166 / 07944694801
Cynghorydd.NigelPickavance@gwynedd.gov.uk

John Pughe Roberts *(Ind: Corris / Mawddwy)*, Cerddin, Llanymawddwy, Machynlleth, Powys, SY20 9AJ ☎ (01650) 531234 / 07713165941
Cynghorydd.JohnPugheRoberts@gwynedd.gov.uk

Peter Read *(LG: Abererch)*, Parc Glas, Pentreuchaf, Pwllheli, Gwynedd, LL53 8DX
☎ (01758) 750196 / 07876725730
Cynghorydd.PeterRead@gwynedd.gov.uk

William Gareth Roberts *(PC: Aberdaron)*, Cwrt, Aberdaron, Pwllheli, Gwynedd, LL53 8DA
☎ (01758) 760478 / 07967467379
Cynghorydd.WilliamGarethRoberts@gwynedd.gov.uk

Mair Rowlands *(PC: Menai - Bangor)*, 16 Albert Street, Bangor, Gwynedd, LL57 2EY
☎ (01248) 388006 / 07912433202
Cynghorydd.MairRowlands@gwynedd.gov.uk

Angela Ann Russell *(Ind: Llanbedrog)*, Brig-y-Don, Llanbedrog, Pwllheli, Gwynedd, LL53 7NU ☎ (01758) 740555 / 07789554507
Cynghorydd.AngelaAnnRussell@gwynedd.gov.uk

Liz Saville Roberts *(PC: Morfa Nefyn)*, Tan yr Onnen, Lôn Isaf, Morfa Nefyn, Pwllheli, Gwynedd, LL53 6BW ☎ (01758) 720646 / 07900577599
Cynghorydd.LizSavilleRoberts@gwynedd.gov.uk

Dyfrig Siencyn, *(PC: Dolgellau (North)*, Plas y Bryn, Ffordd y Gader, Dolgellau, Gwynedd, LL40 1RS
☎ (01341) 422243 / 07712199541
Cynghorydd.DyfrigLewisSiencyn@gwynedd.gov.uk

Mike Stevens, *(Ind: Tywyn)*, Verano, Pier Road, Tywyn, Gwynedd, LL36 9LW
☎ (01654) 712225 / 07778564755
Cynghorydd.MichaelStevens@gwynedd.gov.uk

Gareth Thomas, *(PC: Penrhyndeudraeth)*, Alaw Cynfal, Penrhyndeudraeth, Gwynedd, LL48 6PR ☎ (01766) 770015 / 07855441206
Cynghorydd.GarethThomas@gwynedd.gov.uk

Paul Thomas, *(PC: Bowydd & Rhiw)*, 9 Penlan, Tanygrisiau, Blaenau Ffestiniog, Gwynedd, LL41 3SF ☎ (01766) 830072 / 07780618755
Cynghorydd.PaulThomas@gwynedd.gov.uk

William Tudor Owen, *(PC: Peblig)*, Langdale, 2 Uxbridge Square, Caernarfon, Gwynedd, LL55 2RE
☎ (01286) 672441 / 07774628909
Cynghorydd.WilliamTudorOwen@gwynedd.gov.uk

Elin Walker Jones, *(PC: Glyder)*, 8 LÙn y Bryn, Eithinog, Bangor, Gwynedd, LL57 2LH
☎ (01248) 364234 / 07808472204
Cynghorydd.ElinWJones@gwynedd.gov.uk

Ann Williams, *(PC: Ogwen)*, 14/4 Stryd y Ffynnon, Gerlan, Bethesda, Gwynedd, LL57 3TR
☎ (01248) 601583 / 07778552247
Cynghorydd.AnnWilliams@gwynedd.gov.uk

Eirwyn Williams, *(Ind: Cricieth)*, 20 Mîn y Môr, Criccieth, Gwynedd, LL52 0EF ☎ (01766) 522802
Cynghorydd.EirwynWilliams@gwynedd.gov.uk

Gethin Glyn Williams, *(PC: Abermaw)*, Cae Hir, Bontddu, Dolgellau, Gwynedd, LL40 2UR
☎ (01341) 430683 / 07890705180
Cynghorydd.GethinGlynWilliams@gwynedd.gov.uk

Gruffydd Williams, *(LG: Nefyn)*, 3 Llys Llywelyn, Nefyn, Pwllheli, Gwynedd, LL53 6JF ☎ 07810481949
Cynghorydd.GruffyddWilliams@gwynedd.gov.uk

Hefin Williams, *(PC: Penisarwaun)*, Ffiolau'r Grug, Rhiwlas, Bangor, Gwynedd, LL57 4GA
☎ (01248) 352890 / 07922997592
Cynghorydd.R.HefinWilliams@gwynedd.gov.uk

Owain Williams, *(LG: Clynnog)*, Yr Erw Wen, Llanllyfni, Caernarfon, Gwynedd, LL54 6SY
☎ (01286) 660440 / 07768960695
Cynghorydd.OwainWilliams@gwynedd.gov.uk

Mandy Williams-Davies, *(PC: Diffwys & Maenofferen)*, 19 Y Sgwâr, Blaenau Ffestiniog, Gwynedd, LL41 3UL
☎ (01766) 830652 / 07787934308
Cynghorydd.MandyWDavies@gwynedd.gov.uk

Robert Wright, *(LG: Pwllheli (South)*, 3A Bro Cymerau, Pwllheli, Gwynedd, LL53 5PY
☎ (01758) 701103 / (01758) 612368
Cynghorydd.RobertWright@gwynedd.gov.uk

Eurig Wyn, *(PC: Waunfawr)*, Y Frenni, Waunfawr, Caernarfon, Gwynedd, LL55 4YY
☎ (01286) 650512 / 07880717523
Cynghorydd.EurigWyn@gwynedd.gov.uk

Elfed Wyn Williams, *(Ind: Deiniolen)*, 12 Ffordd Deiniol, Deiniolen, Caernarfon, Gwynedd, LL55 3LL ☎ (01286) 871406 / 07729394230
Cynghorydd.ElfedWynWilliams@gwynedd.gov.uk

GWYNEDD

R Hywel Wyn Williams, *(PC: Abersoch)*, Llwyn, Lôn Rhoslyn, Abersoch, Pwllheli, Gwynedd, LL53 7BE ☎ (01758) 712779 / 07855000167
Cynghorydd.RHywelWynWilliams@gwynedd.gov.uk

Charles Wynn Jones, *(PC: Llanrug)*, Dwyros, Ffordd Glanffynnon, Llanrug, Caernarfon, Gwynedd, LL55 4PP ☎ (01286) 676733
Cynghorydd.CharlesWynJones@gwynedd.gov.uk

John Wynn Jones, *(PC: Hendre)*, 131 Ffordd Penchwintan, Bangor, Gwynedd, LL57 2YG
☎ (01248) 352670 / 07734173407
Cynghorydd.JohnWynnJones@gwynedd.gov.uk

Linda Ann Wynn Jones, *(PC: Teigl)*, Llys Gwilym, Llan Ffestiniog, Blaenau Ffestiniog, Gwynedd, LL41 4NY ☎ (01766) 762775 / (01766) 832378
Cynghorydd.LindaAnnWynnJones@gwynedd.gov.uk

John Wynn Williams, *(PC: Pentir)*, 1 Blaen y Wawr, Bangor, Gwynedd, LL57 4TR ☎ (01248) 370737 / 07989134456
Cynghorydd.JohnWynnWilliams@gwynedd.gov.uk

E Caerwyn Roberts, *(PC: Harlech / Talsarnau)*, Ysgubor, Llandanwg, Harlech, Gwynedd, LL46 2SB
☎ (01766) 780344 / 07704805767
Cynghorydd.E.CaerwynRoberts@gwynedd.gov.uk

Clerks to the Community Councils

Abergwyngregyn Community Council, *Eirlys Mai Williams*, 1 Tanaber, Abergwyngregyn, Llanfairfechan, Gwynedd, LL33 0LB ☎ (01248) 681145

Bangor (City) Council, *Gwyn Hughes*, Council Offices, Ffordd Gwynedd, Bangor, Gwynedd, LL57 1DT ☎ (01248) 352421
council@bangorcc.plus.com

Bethesda Community Council, *Aled Parry*, 15 Bryn Caseg, Ffordd Abercaseg, Bethesda, Gwynedd, LL57 3RW ☎ (01248) 601732
cyngorbethesda@btinternet.com

Betws Garmon Community Council, *Menna Ellis*, Gelli Ffrydiau, Nantlle, Caernarfon, Gwynedd, LL54 6BT ☎ (01286) 880030
mennaellis@btconnect.com

Bontnewydd Community Council, *Bryn Hughes*, 11 Bro Wyled, Rhostryfan, Caernarfon, Gwynedd, LL54 7LP ☎ (01286) 831861
hughesbryn@yahoo.co.uk

Caernarfon (Royal Town) Council, *Katherine Owen*, Institute Buildings, Allt Pafiliwn, Caernarfon, Gwynedd, LL55 1AT ☎ (01286) 672943
clercydref@caernarfontowncouncil.gov.uk / townclerk@caernarfontowncouncil.gov.uk

Llanberis Community Council, *Dei Tomos*, Ty'n Twll, Nantperis, Caernarfon, Gwynedd, LL55 4UL ☎ (01286) 871250 / 07831426649
deitomos@btopenworld.com

Llandygai Community Council, *Gwilym Evans*, Heddfan, Niwbwrch, Ynys Môn, LL61 6TN
☎ (01248) 440611

Llandwrog Community Council, *David Roberts*, Bryn Meurig, Carmel, Caernarfon, Gwynedd, LL54 7DS ☎ (01286) 881920
david.carmel@tiscali.co.uk

Llanddeiniolen Community Council, *John B Jones*, Ceris, Deiniolen, Caernarfon, Gwynedd, LL55 3LU ☎ (01286) 871416
benmar402@btinternet.com

Llanllechid Community Council, *Morfudd Wyn Roberts*, Llwyn Meurig, 1 Rhos y Nant, Bethesda, Gwynedd, LL57 3PP
☎ (01248) 600501
cyngorllanllechid@gmail.com

Llanllyfni Community Council, *Alwen Johnson*, 1 Rhos y Nant, Bethesda, Gwynedd, LL57 3PP
☎ (01248) 600501

Llanrug Community Council, *Emma Williams*, Llyfni, 22 Nant y Glyn, Llanrug, Gwynedd, LL55 4AH ☎ (01286) 673344 / 07734462460
deianllyfni@aol.com

Llanwnda Community Council, *Bethan Williams*, Pencaenewydd, Rhos Isaf, Caernarfon, Gwynedd, LL54 7NG ☎ (01286) 831443
bethancwilliams@tiscali.co.uk

Pentir Community Council, *June Jones*, 2 Constantine Terrace, Caernarfon, Gwynedd, LL55 2HL
☎ (01286) 669180
jiwnjones@gmail.com

Waunfawr Community Council, *Shoned Griffith*, Tŷ Awelog, Waunfawr, Caernarfon, LL55 4AZ ☎ (01286) 650136
griffith.tyawelog@btinternet.com

Y Felinheli Community Council, *Heather Lynne Jones*, 3 Maes Padarn, Llanberis, Gwynedd, LL55 4TE ☎ (01286) 872655 / 07867982518
clercfelinheli@aol.com

Aberdaron Community Council, *Iwan Hughes*, Derlwyn, Llanbedrog, Pwllheli, Gwynedd, LL53 7NU ☎ (01758) 740196
iwan.hughes2@btinternet.com

Beddgelert Community Council, *Kenneth Williams*, 18 Stryd Glaslyn, Porthmadog, Gwynedd, LL49 9EG ☎ (01766) 513633

Botwnnog Community Council, *Gwenda Roberts*, Gwyndy, Bryncroes, Pwllheli, Gwynedd, LL53 8ET ☎ (01758) 730357

Buan Community Council, *Rhian Holt*, Cil Llidiart, Lon Cefn Morfa, Morfa Nefyn, Pwllheli, LL53 8UW
☎ (01758) 721033
Rhian@nefyn.eclipse.co.uk

Clynnog Community Council, *Ken Williams*, Bodwyn, Pontllyfni, Caernarfon, Gwynedd, LL54 5EG ☎ (01286) 660141,
ccclynnogfawr@hotmail.co.uk

Criccieth Community Council, *Robin Hughes*, 5 Stryd Fawr, Criccieth, Gwynedd, LL52 0RN ☎ (01766) 522641
robinyclerc@btinternet.com

Dolbenmaen Community Council, *Bethan Griffith*, 24 Lôn Ceredigion, Pwllheli, Gwynedd, LL53 5PP
☎ (01758) 613027 / 07917612819
bethg@talk21.com

Llanaelhaearn Community Council, *Mary Jones*, Merbwll, Penlon Trefor, Clynnog Road, Caernarfon, Gwynedd, LL54 5AB ☎ (01286) 660768 / 07879825459
mary.jones17@btinternet.com

Llanbedrog Community Council, *John Harris*, Henllys Isaf, Llanbedrog, Pwllheli, Gwynedd, LL53 7PG ☎ (01758) 740061
johnharris.henllys@gmail.com

Lanengan Community Council, *Einir Wyn*, Fferm Cae Du, Abersoch, Pwllheli, Gwynedd, LL53 7HT ☎ (01758) 712707
caedu@dialstart.net

Llannor Community Council, *Haydn Jones*, Bryn y Felin, Penrallt, Pwllheli, Gwynedd, LL53 5UE ☎ (01758) 614291 haydn.brynyfelin@tiscali.co.uk

Llanystumdwy Community Council, *Richard Roberts*, Aelybryn, Llanystumdwy, Cricieth, Gwynedd, LL52 0SS ☎ (01766) 522258 richardaelybryn@yahoo.co.uk

Nefyn Town Council, *John Griffiths*, Graig Las, Stryd Fawr, Nefyn, Pwllheli, Gwynedd, LL53 6HD ☎ (01758) 720507

Pistyll Community Council, *Elin Tudur*, 1 Fron Oleu, Ffordd Caernarfon, Pwllheli, Gwynedd, LL53 5LN ☎ (01758) 701698 elin@llynjoinery.com

Porthmadog Town Council, *Alaw Medi Roberts*, 24 East Avenue, Porthmadog, Gwynedd, LL49 9EN ☎ 07786 323243 robertsalawm@hotmail.co.uk

Pwllheli Town Council, *Robin W Hughes*, Siambr y Cyngor, 9 Stryd Penlan, Pwllheli, Gwynedd, LL53 5DH ☎ (01758) 701454 cyngortrefpwllheli@btconnect.com

Tudweiliog Community Council, *Glenys Peters*, Llwyn Helyg, Llangwnnadl, Pwllheli, Gwynedd, LL53 8NS ☎ (01758) 770252

Aberdyfi Community Council, *Neil Storkey*, Council Office, Literary Institute, Aberdyfi, Gwynedd, LL35 0LN ☎ (01654) 767816 aberdyficouncil@btconnect.com

Barmouth Town Council, *Jacqueline Hughes*, Clerk to the Council, 33 Bro Enddwyn, Dyffryn Ardudwy, Gwynedd, LL44 2BG ☎ (01341) 247998 jacqueline.hughes1984@btinternet.com

Arthog Community Council, *Susan Jones*, 1 St. Mary's Terrace, Arthog, Gwynedd, LL39 1BQ ☎ (01341) 250406 / 07557640740 suejones.arthog@virgin.net

Y Bala Town Council, *Iona Roberts*, Swyddfa'r Cyngor, Henblas, Stryd Fawr, Y Bala, Gwynedd, LL23 7AE ☎ 07786 662905 cyngor.bala@tiscali.co.uk

Brithdir, Llanfachreth & Rhydymain Community Council, *Henry Edwards*, Arfryn, 16 Cae'r Dderwen, Dolgellau, Gwynedd, LL40 1GE ☎ (01341) 422232

Bryncrug Community Council, *Eileen Jones*, Hafan Deg, Abertrinant, Bryncrug, Tywyn, Gwynedd, LL36 9RG ☎ (01654) 782281 / (01654) 711181

Corris Community Council, *Christina Miller*, Suite 1, Fronfelen Hall, Corris, Machynlleth, Powys, SY20 9TF ☎ (01654) 761307

Dolgellau Town Council, *Rhys Williams*, 12 Nantygader, Dolgellau, Gwynedd, LL40 1LB ☎ (01341) 421071

Dyffryn Ardudwy & Thalybont Community Council, *Annwen Hughes*, Plas Uchaf, Talsarnau, Gwynedd, LL47 6YA ☎ (01766) 780971 annwen@btconnect.com

Ffestiniog Town Council, *Ann Coxon*, Council Office,5 Stryd Fawr, Blaenau Ffestiniog, Gwynedd, LL41 3ES ☎ (01766) 832398 cyngortrefffestiniog@yahoo.co.uk

Ganllwyd Community Council, *Sarah Roberts*, Beudy Hendre, Abergeirw, Dolgellau, Gwynedd, LL40 2PF ☎ (01341) 440248 sarahthomas972@aol.com

Harlech Town Council, *Annwen Hughes*, Plas Uchaf, Talsarnau, Gwynedd, LL47 6YA ☎ (01766) 780971 annwen@btconnect.com

Llanbedr Community Council, *Morfudd Lloyd*, Tyddyn Hendre, Cwm Nantol, Llanbedr, Gwynedd, LL45 2PL ☎ (01341) 241645 tyddynhendre@tiscali.co.uk

Llandderfel Community Council, *Bethan Jones*, Hafod y Bryn, Cwmtirmynach, Y Bala, Gwynedd, LL23 7ED ☎ (01678) 520632 bethanj632@btinternet.com

Llanegryn Community Council, *Llywela Carol Hughes*, Ty'r Ysgol, Llanegryn, Tywyn, Gwynedd, LL36 9SS ☎ (01654) 710613 c.hughes74@btinternet.com

Llanelltyd Community Council, *Henry Edwards*, Arfryn, 16 Cae'r Dderwen, Dolgellau, Gwynedd, LL40 1GE ☎ (01341) 422232

Llanfair Community Council, *Annwen Hughes*, Plas Uchaf, Talsarnau, Gwynedd, LL47 6YA ☎ (01766) 780971 annwen@btconnect.com

Llanfihangel-y-Pennant Community Council, *Eileen Jones*, Hafan Deg, Abertrinant, Bryncrug, Tywyn, Gwynedd, LL36 9RG ☎ (01654) 782281

Llanfrothen Community Council, *Kenneth Williams*, 18 Stryd Glaslyn, Porthmadog, Gwynedd, LL49 9EG, (01766) 513633

Llangelynnin Community Council, *Mrs G Edwards*, Elfan, Llwyngwril, Gwynedd, LL37 2JJ ☎ (01341) 250291

Llangywer Community Council, *Lis Puw*, Bedw Gwynion, Llanuwchllyn, Y Bala, Gwynedd, LL23 7TW ☎ (01678) 540654 / 07896964120 lis_puw@hotmail.co.uk

Llanuwchllyn Community Council, *Lis Puw*, Bedw Gwynion, Llanuwchllyn, Y Bala, Gwynedd, LL23 7TW ☎ (01678) 540654 / 07896964120 lis_puw@hotmail.co.uk

Llanycil Community Council, *Bethan Jones*, Hafod y Bryn, Cwmtirmynach, Y Bala, Gwynedd, LL23 7ED, (01678) 520632, bethanj632@btinternet.com

Maentwrog Community Council, *Carys Haf Jones*, 4 Heol Bowydd, Blaenau Ffestiniog, Gwynedd, LL41 3HL, (01766) 832442, carys_haf@yahoo.co.uk

Mawddwy Community Council, *Huw Thomas Jones*, Henllys, Mallwyd, Machynlleth, Powys, SY20 9HS ☎ (01650) 531405 huwjones792@btinternet.com

Pennal Community Council, *Deilwen Breese*, Gogarth, Pennal, Machynlleth, Powys, SY20 9LB ☎ (01654) 791235 brees2000@aol.com

Penrhyndeudraeth Town Council, *Glyn Roberts*, Ysw 3 Tai Meirion, Beddgelert, Gwynedd, LL55 4NB ☎ (01766) 890483 glynctp@btinternet.com

Talsarnau Community Council, *Annwen Hughes*, Plas Uchaf, Talsarnau, Gwynedd, LL47 6YA ☎ (01766) 780971 annwen@btconnect.com

Trawsfynydd Community Council, *Ellan ap Dafydd*, Adminstrative Officer, Traws - Newid, Llys Ednowain, Trawsfynydd, Gwynedd, LL41 4UB ☎ (01766) 770324 Trawsnewid@btconnect.com

Tywyn Town Council, *Elwyn Evans*, Swyddfa'r Cyngor, Stryd Fawr, Tywyn, Gwynedd, LL36 9AD ☎ (01654) 712411 tywyntowncouncil@btconnect.com

ISLE OF ANGLESEY COUNTY COUNCIL
CYNGOR SIR YNYS MÔN

County Offices, Llangefni,
Anglesey LL77 7TW
Tel: (01248) 750057
Fax: (01248) 750839
Email:
communications@anglesey.gov.uk
Website: www.anglesey.gov.uk

CYNGOR SIR
YNYS MÔN
ISLE OF ANGLESEY
COUNTY COUNCIL

Leader
Cllr Bryan Owen

Chief Executive
Richard Parry Jones

INDEPENDENT CONTROL

Ind **18** PC **7** Lab **5** Lib D **2** Con **2**
U **4** V **2** (Current political composition)

TOTAL 40

ELECTION RESULT 2008*

	Seats	Change	Votes	Share
Ind	23	-5	11,124	47.4%
PC	8	-	5,358	22.9%
Lab	5	4	2,978	12.7%
Lib D	2	1	662	2.8%
Con	2	-	1,168	5.0%
Oth	0	-	2,157	9.2%

*No election held in 2012

Socio-economic Profile

		Rank 1<22
Area (sq km)	714	9
Population ('000s)	68.5	20
% able to speak Welsh	60.9	2
% born in Wales	67.6	16
% non-white ethnic groups	2.0	22
Gross rev expenditure (2011-12)	£152.5m	21
Forecast capital expenditure (2011-12)	£23.7m	19
% dwellings in Band D (2012-13)	21.2	2
Band D council tax (2011-12)	£1,094.41	18
% over retirement age	21.9	3
% pupils 5+ GCSEs A*-C (2010-11)	65.8	14
Unemployment (% claimant count 2011)	4.3	7
Index of Deprivation (2011)	21	14
(% of Authority in most deprived 30%)		

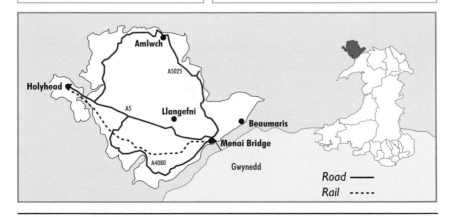

Road ———
Rail - - - - -

LOCAL GOVERNMENT

ISLE OF ANGLESEY

Principal Officers

Chief Executive:	**Richard Parry Jones**
Deputy Chief Executive:	**Bethan Jones**
Director of Social Services (Community):	**Gwen Carrington**
Director of Education (Lifelong Learning):	**Gwynne Jones**
Director of Sustainable Development:	**Arthur W Owen**

Cabinet Members 2012-2013

Leader / Economic Development & Tourism:	**Bryan Owen** (Ind)
Deputy Leader / Social Services:	**Kenneth Hughes** (Ind)
Education, Children & Young People:	**Goronwy Parry** (Ind)
Housing, Building Maintenance Unit & Fleet Management:	**O Glyn Jones** (Ind)
Finance, Information Technology & Human Resources:	**John Chorlton** (Lab)
Planning:	**Robert Lloyd Hughes** (Ind)
Highways & Maritime:	**Bob Parry** (PC)
Leisure & Environment	**Trefor Lloyd Hughes** (PC)

Committee Chairs 2012-2013

Corporate Scrutiny Committee:	**Selwyn Williams** (Ind)
Environment & Technical Services Scrutiny Committee:	**Keith Evans** (Ind)
Education & Leisure Scrutiny Committee:	**Derlwyn Hughes** (Ind)
Housing & Social Services Scrutiny Committee:	**Lewis Davies** (PC)
Economic Development, Tourism & Property Scrutiny Committee:	**John Owen**(Ind)
Planning & Orders Committee:	**J Arwel Roberts** (Lab)
Appointments Committee:	**Tba**
Licensing Committee:	**J Arwel Roberts** (Lab)
Audit Committee:	**Tba**
Democratic Services Committee:	**H Eifion Jones**

Salaries

Basic Salary: £11,664 per annum
Senior Salaries:
Leader: 0; Deputy Leader: £0
Other Executive Committee Members: £0
Chairs of Scrutiny Committees: £7,473; Chairs of Other Committees: £7,473
Care Allowance (if payable): £4,353
Chair of Council: £6,453; Vice-Chair of Council: £4,608

Councillors ♂ 38 ♀ 2

Chair: Cllr Robert Llewelyn Jones Vice-Chair: Cllr Eurfryn Davies

W John Chorlton *(Lab: Kingsland)*, 80 Penrhyn Geiriol, Trearddur Bay, Holyhead, LL65 2YW ☎ (01407) 860216 JohnChorlton@anglesey.gov.uk

Lewis Davies *(PC: Llangoed)*, Pentrafalyn, Llangoed, Beaumaris, LL58 8SA ☎ (01248) 490248 LewisDavies@anglesey.gov.uk

Richard Dew *(Ind: Rhosneigr)*, Glan Gors, Llanfaelog, Tŷ Croes, LL63 5SR ☎ (01407) 810825 RichardDew@anglesey.gov.uk

Jim Evans *(Ind: Braint)*, Penyffordd, Holyhead Road, Llanfairpwllgwyngyll, LL61 5TX ☎ (01248) 714246 JimEvans@anglesey.gov.uk

Keith Evans *(Ind: Cadnant)*, Straits Gaze, Holyhead Road, Menai Bridge, LL59 5RH ☎ (01248) 712464

Clifford Lloyd Everett *(Lab: Holyhead Town)*, 23 Nant y Felin, Kingsland, Holyhead, LL65 2TQ ☎ (01407) 760167 CliffordEverett@anglesey.gov.uk

Eurfryn Griffith-Davies *(PC: Cwm Cadnant)*, Gwel y Don, Lôn Brynteg, Glyngarth, Llandegfan, LL59 5UA ☎ (01248) 713464 EurfrynDavies@anglesey.gov.uk

Derlwyn Rees Hughes *(Ind: Moelfre)*, Gwelfor, Moelfre, LL78 8LH ☎ (01248) 410816

Fflur Mai Hughes *(PC: Cefni)*, Rhandir Mwyn, 2 Brig Y Nant, Llangefni, LL77 7QD ☎ (01248) 724992 FflurHughes@anglesey.gov.uk

Kenneth P Hughes *(Ind: Llanfaethlu)*, Garn-For, 4 Tan y Felin, Rhydwyn, Holyhead, LL65 4EJ ☎ (01407) 730269 KennethHughes@anglesey.gov.uk

Robert Lloyd Hughes *(Ind: Bodorgan)*, Cefn Canol, Llangristiolus, Bodorgan, LL62 5PW ☎ 07771 801 554 RobertHughes@anglesey.gov.uk

Trefor Ll Hughes *(PC: Maeshyfryd)*, 8 Bryngwyn Road, Holyhead, LL72 8LH ☎ (01407) 764801 / 07889 652068 TreforLloydHughes@anglesey.gov.uk

Vaughan Hughes *(PC: Gwyngyll)*, 21 Lôn Twrcelyn, Benllech LL74 8RN ☎ (01248) 852 873

William I Hughes *(PC: Bodffordd)*, Cefn Gwyn, Bodedern, Holyhead, LL65 3UN ☎ (01407) 720307 WilliamIHughes@anglesey.gov.uk

William Thomas Hughes *(Ind: Llanbadrig)*, Betws, Cemaes Bay, LL67 ONA ☎ (01407) 710007 WilliamTHughes@anglesey.gov.uk

Aled Morris Jones *(Lib D: Llaneilian)*, Seibiant, Rhosybol, Amlwch, LL68 9TR ☎ (01407) 832640 AledMorrisJones@anglesey.gov.uk

Dylan Jones *(Lab: Amlwch Port)*, Tŷ Nesa, Madyn Farm, Amlwch, LL68 9DA ☎ (01407) 830886 RDylanJones@anglesey.gov.uk

Eric Jones *(Ind: Llanfihangel Esceifiog)*, Rhoswen, 14 Bronllys, Gaerwen, LL60 6JN ☎ (01248) 421667 EricJones@anglesey.gov.uk

Gwilym O Jones *(Ind: Llanfair yn Neubwll)*, 6 Tre Ifan, Caergeiliog, Holyhead, LL65 3YB ☎ (01407) 740105 GwilymJones@anglesey.gov.uk

Hywel Eifion Jones *(Ind: Llanidan)*, Tanpencefn Bach, Brynsiencyn, LL61 6TJ ☎ (01248) 430145 HywelEifionJones@anglesey.gov.uk

Owen Glyn Jones *(Ind: Aberffraw)*, Maerdy, Stryd Llewelyn, Aberffraw, LL63 5AZ ☎ (01407) 842200 GlynJones@anglesey.gov.uk

Raymond Jones *(Lab: London Road)*, 1 Bryn y Môr, Turkeyshore Road, Holyhead, LL65 2HN ☎ (01407) 760796 RaymondJones@anglesey.gov.uk

Robert Ll Jones *(Unaffil: Porthyfelin)*, Namor, 19 Tan Y Bryn Road, Holyhead, LL65 1AR ☎ (01407) 763718 RobertLlJones@anglesey.gov.uk

Thomas H Jones *(Llais i Fôn: Llanfechell)*, Maes Mawr, Llanfechell, Amlwch, LL68 OSE ☎ (01407) 710888 ThomasJones@anglesey.gov.uk

Rhian Medi *(PC: Cyngar)*, Rhosgerdd, 14 Maes y Coed, Talwrn, Llangefni, LL77 7UA ☎ (01248) 722184 RhianMedi@anglesey.gov.uk

Clive McGregor *(Ind: Llanddyfnan)*, 11 Maes y Coed, Talwrn, Llangefni, LL77 7UA ☎ (01248) 724568 CliveMcGregor@anglesey.gov.uk

Alun Wyn Mummery *(Unaffil: Gwyngyll)*, 39, Trem Eryri, Llanfairpwll, LL61 5JF ☎ (01248) 714 938

Bryan Owen *(Ind: Tudur)*, Adlais yr Engan, Capel Mawr, Bodorgan, LL62 5NT ☎ (01407) 842114 BryanOwen@anglesey.gov.uk

John Owen (*Ind: Parc a'r Mynydd*), Llys y Foel, South Stack, Holyhead, LL65 1YH ☎ (01407) 762695
JohnVOwen@anglesey.gov.uk

Richard L Owen (*Ind: Beaumarris*), Tunnel Lodge, Wexham Street, Beaumaris, LL58 8ES ☎ (01248) 811370 / 07750 590742
RichardLOwen@anglesey.gov.uk

Goronwy O Parry MBE (*Ind: Valley*), Hafod yr Ynys, Valley, Holyhead, LL65 3HB, ☎ (01407) 741092
GoronwyOParry@anglesey.gov.uk

Robert G Parry OBE (*PC: Trewalchmai*), Treban Meurig, Bryngwran, Holyhead, LL65 3YN ☎ (01407) 720437 / 07836 573294
BobParry@anglesey.gov.uk

Eric Roberts (*Ind: Trearddur Bay*), Greenacres, Porth y Post, Trearddur Bay, Holyhead LL65 2UP ☎ (01407) 860601
EricRoberts@anglesey.gov.uk

Gareth Winston Roberts OBE (*Ind: Amlwch Rural*), Erwau'r Gwynt, Burwen, Amlwch, LL68 9RR ☎ (01407) 832273
GarethWinstonRoberts@anglesey.gov.uk

J Arwel Roberts (*Lab: Morawelon*), 2 New Street, Four Mile Bridge, Holyhead, LL65 2PZ ☎ (01407) 742498
JArwelRoberts@anglesey.gov.uk

Peter S Rogers (*Unaffil: Rhosyr*), Bodrida, Brynsiencyn, LL61 6NZ ☎ (01248) 430241
PeterRogers@anglesey.gov.uk

Hefin Wyn Thomas (*Ind: Pentraeth*), Parc yr Odyn, Pentraeth, LL75 8UL ☎ (01248) 450566
HefinWynThomas@anglesey.gov.uk

Elwyn Schofield (*Ind: Llanerch-y-Medd*), Olgra, Marianglas, LL73 8PL ☎ (01248) 853306

Ieuan Williams (*Ind: Brynteg*), Bryn Arfon, Lôn Pant y Cydun, Tynygongl, LL74 8UF ☎ (01248) 851070
IeuanWilliams@anglesey.gov.uk

Selwyn Williams (*Lib D: Tysilio*), 45 Penlon, Menai Bridge, Anglesey, LL59 5NE ☎ (01248) 714429 / 07757 011843
SelwynWilliams@anglesey.gov.uk

Clerks to the Community Councils

Aberffraw Community Council, *Menna Evans*, Cwyrtai, Aberffraw, Tŷ Croes, LL63 5SX ☎ (01407) 840272
cwyrtai@btconnect.com

Amlwch Town Council, *Mrs M Hughes*, Council Office, Lôn Goch, Amlwch, LL68 9EN ☎ (01407) 832228 / 710007
marilynhughes@amlwchcf.org

Beaumaris Town Council, *Professor TW Ashenden*, Town Hall, Beaumaris, LL58 8AP ☎ (01248) 810317
beaumaristowncouncil@tiscali.co.uk

Bodedern Community Council, *Iona Jones*, 15 Llys yr Engan, London Road, Bodedern, Holyhead, LL65 3SX ☎ (01407) 749107 / 07701 038988
ijxcs@btinternet.com

Bodffordd Community Council, *Derek Owen*, Penant, 18 The Links, Amlwch, LL68 9EG ☎ 07766 552583

Bodorgan Community Council, *Deborah Evans*, Cerrig Iago, Llangadwaladr, Bethel, Bodorgan, LL62 5HP ☎ (01407) 840915

Bryngwran Community Council, *Graham Owen*, Parc Uchaf, Rhosmeirch, Llangefni, LL77 7NQ ☎ (01248) 750974
council@gowen97.freeserve.co.uk

Cwm Cadnant Community Council, *Alun Foulkes*, 9 Brynteg, Llandegfan, Menai Bridge, LL59 5TY ☎ (01248) 713501

Cylch-y-Garn Community Council, *Mr O Arfon Owen*, Post Office, Llanrhuddlad, Holyhead, LL65 4HP ☎ (01407) 730704

Holyhead Town Council, *Mr C L Everett*, Town Hall, Newry Street, Holyhead, LL65 1HN ☎ (01407) 764608
townclerk@holyheadcouncil.co.uk / deputyclerk@holyheadcouncil.co.uk

Llanbadrig Community Council, *Llio Johnson, Skerries*, Llanfechell, Amlwch, LL68 0SD ☎ (01407) 711 610
lliojohnson@btinternet.com

Llanddaniel Fab Community Council, *Lynwen Jones*, Bryn Efrog, Dwyran, Ynys Môn, LL61 6YD ☎ (01248) 430958

Llanddona Community Council, *Geraint Parry*, 4 Gorddinog Terrace, Llangoed, Beaumaris, LL58 8NG ☎ (01248) 490326

Llanddyfnan Community Council, *Graham Owen*, Parc Uchaf, Rhosmeirch, Llangefni, LL77 7NQ ☎ (01248) 750974
llanddyfnan@gowen97.freeserve.co.uk

Llaneilian Community Council, *Gwyn Roberts*, 1 Ty'n Rhos, Penysarn, LL69 9BZ ☎ (01407) 831107

Llanerchymedd Community Council, *Sydna Roberts*, Brynodol, 4 Bryncir, Llannerchymedd, LL71 8EG
cyngorllannerchymedd@fsmail.net

Llaneugrad Community Council, *John Parry*, Y Dalar Arian, Marianglas, LL73 8PA

Llanfachraeth Community Council, *Derek Owen*, Penant, 18 The Links, Amlwch, LL68 9EG
☎ 07766 552583

Llanfaelog Community Council, *Mr R A Dew*, Glangors, Llanfaelog, Ty Croes, LL63 5SR
☎ (01407) 810825

Llanfaethlu Community Council, *John Arfon Jones*, Bryngwyn, Llanfaethlu, Caergybi, Ynys Môn, LL65 4NW ☎ (01407) 730674
johnarf@live.co.uk

Llanfair Mathafarn Eithaf Community Council, *Griff E Pritchard*, Llys Newydd, Dwyran, Llanfairpwll, LL61 6UU
☎ (01248) 430402 / 07717350557
llanfair.m.e@talktalk.net

Llanfairpwll Community Council, *Anwen Le Cras*, Community Council Office, Memorial Hall, Llanfairpwll, LL61 5JB ☎ (01248) 715240 / 07795 250440
anwenlecras@hotmail.co.uk

Llanfair yn Neubwll Community Council, *Mai Owen*, Bodawen, Four Mile Bridge, Holyhead, LL65 2PJ ☎ (01407) 740739

Llanfihangelesceifiog Community Council, *Myra Evans*, Heddfan, Newborough, LL61 6TN
☎ (01248) 440611

Llangefni Town Council, *Arnold Milburn*, Room 109, Shire Hall, Llangefni, LL77 7TW
☎ (01248) 723332
llangefnitc@supanet.com

Llangoed & Penmon Community Council, *Geraint Parry*, 4 Gorddinog Terrace, Llangoed, Beaumaris, LL58 8NG
☎ (01248) 490326

Llangristiolus Community Council, *Rhian Khardani*, Rhosyr, Lôn Rhostrehwfa, Llangefni, LL77 7YP
rhianpig@yahoo.co.uk

Llanidan Community Council, *Mr M E Jones*, 5 Plas Hen, Llanddaniel Fab, LL60 6EG, (01248) 421867

Mechell Community Council, *Helen Mai Beck*, 20 Wesley Street, Amlwch, LL68 9EY
☎ 07810 803249

Menai Bridge Town Council, *Linda Fraser-Williams*, Canolfan Tysilio, Wood Street, Menai Bridge, LL59 5AS ☎ (01248) 716959
cyngordref@hotmail.com

Moelfre Community Council, *Gwenda Parry*, Rhuo'r Gwynt, Ffordd Seiriol, Moelfre, LL72 8LP
☎ (01248) 410686

Penmynydd & Star Community Council, *Graham Owen*, Parc Uchaf, Rhosmeirch, LL77 7NQ
☎ (01248) 750974
cyngor.cymuned@btinternet.com

Pentraeth Community Council, *Eifion H Jones*, Felin, Bryn Hyrddin, Pentraeth, LL75 8HJ
☎ (01248) 450360

Rhoscolyn Community Council, *Mr W M Roberts*, Pengwern, 12 Morawelon, Four Mile Bridge, Holyhead, LL65 2PQ
☎ (01407) 740163

Rhosybol Community Council, *Gwenda Pritchard*, Hafan Deg, Rhosybol, LL68 9TS
☎ (01407) 832205
cc.rhosybol@yahoo.co.uk

Rhosyr Community Council, *Myra Evans*, Heddfan, Newborough, LL61 6TN
☎ (01248) 440611

Trearddur Community Council, *Mr G D Evans*, Heddfan, Newborough, LL61 6TN
☎ (01248) 440611

Tref Alaw Community Council, *Anna M Jones*, Porfa Las, Llanddeusant, Holyhead, LL65 4AD ☎ (01407) 730172

Trewalchmai Community Council, *Margaret Price*, Groeslon, Gwalchmai, Holyhead, LL65 4SP
☎ (01407) 721295

Valley Community Council, *Gwenda Owen*, Trigfa, Four Mile Bridge, Holyhead, LL65 2EZ
☎ (01407) 740046 / 07971 880101
gwenda.owen1@ntlworld.com

COUNTY BOROUGH COUNCIL OF MERTHYR TYDFIL
CYNGOR BWRDEISTREF SIROL MERTHYR TUDFUL

Civic Centre, Castle Street,
Merthyr Tydfil CF47 8AN
Tel: (01685) 725000
Fax: (01685) 722146

Website: www.merthyr.gov.uk

Leader
Cllr Brendan Toomey

Chief Executive
Gareth Chapman

LABOUR CONTROL	Lab **23** Ind **7** Merthyr Independents **2** UKIP **1**	TOTAL 33

ELECTION RESULT 2012

	Seats	Change	Votes	Share
Labour	23	15	23,317	53.2%
Independent	7	-9	14,118	32.2%
Merthyr Ind	2	-1	2,212	5.0%
UKIP	1	1	588	1.3%
Lib Dem	0	-6	2,130	4.9%
Plaid Cymru	0	-	1,059	2.4%
Welsh Communist Party	0	-	383	0.9%

Socio-economic Profile

		Rank 1<22
Area (sq km)	111	21
Population ('000s)	55.6	22
% able to speak Welsh	17.7	15
% born in Wales	92.0	2
% non-white ethnic groups	2.9	12
Gross rev expenditure (2011-12)	£141.6m	22
Forecast capital expenditure (2011-12)	£21.5m	22
% dwellings in Band D (2012-13)	7.7	21
Band D council tax (2011-12)	£1,343.02	3
% over retirement age	17.3	18
% pupils 5+ GCSEs A*-C (2010-11)	60.6	21
Unemployment (% claimant count 2011)	6.1	2
Index of Deprivation (2011)	61	2
(% of Authority in most deprived 30%)		

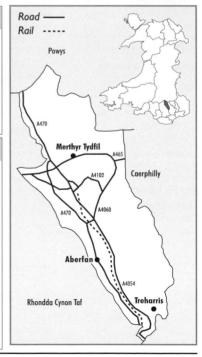

Road ——
Rail -----

Powys

A470

Merthyr Tydfil
A465

A4102
Caerphilly

A470
A4060

Aberfan

A4054

Rhondda Cynon Taf
Treharris

Principal Officers

Chief Executive:	**Gareth Chapman**
Director of Customer Services:	**Gary Thomas**
Director of Community Services:	**Gio Isingrini**

Cabinet Members 2012-2013

Leader:	**Brendan Twoomey** (Lab)
Deputy Leader & Chief Executive' Services:	**Phil Williams** (Lab)
Technical & Environmental Services:	**David Jones** (Lab)
Business & Regulatory Services:	**Chris Barry** (Lab)
Social Services & Social Regeneration:	**Brent Carter** (Lab)
Schools:	**Harvey Jones** (Lab)

Committee Chairs 2012-2013

Audit Committee:	**Richard Thomas** (Ind)
Planning, Regulatory & Licensing Committee:	**Clive Jones** (Lab)
Chief Executive's Scrutiny Committee:	**Tom Lewis** (Lab)
Customer Services Scrutiny Committee:	**Darren Roberts** (Lab)
Social Services & Social Regeneration Scrutiny Committee:	**Bill Smith** (Lab)
Schools Scrutiny Committee:	**Paul Brown** (Merthyr Ind)

Salaries

Basic Salary: £13,175
Senior Salaries: Leader: £42,300; Deputy Leader: £29,820
Cabinet Members: £25,660; Chairs of Scrutiny Committees: £21,910
Chairs of Other Committees: £21,910; Civic Head £19,035; Deputy Civic Head: £14,805

Councillors ♂ 29 ♀ 4

Mayor: Cllr Lisa Mytton

Howard Barrett (Ind: Vaynor), 25 Bryntaf, Cefn Coed, Merthyr Tydfil, CF48 2PU ☎ (01685) 389515 Howard.Barrett@merthyr.gov.uk

Chris Barry (Lab: Park), 9 Old School Close, Georgetown, Merthyr Tydfil, CF48 1DA ☎ (01685) 370078 chris.barry@merthyr.gov.uk

Rhonda Braithwaite (Lab: Gurnos), 47 Bramble Close, Gurnos, Merthyr Tydfil, CF47 9DF ☎ (01685) 375593 democratic@merthyr.gov.uk

Paul Brown (Ind: Cyfarthfa), 11 Salisbury Close, Heolgerrig, Merthyr Tydfil, CF48 1SD ☎ (01685) 371752 paul.brown@merthyr.gov.uk

Brent Carter (Lab: Plymouth), 8 Anthony Grove, Abercanaid, Merthyr Tydfil, CF48 1YX ☎ (01685) 388058 Brent.Carter@merthyr.gov.uk

Tony Chaplin (Lab: Cyfarthfa), 10 Andrews Close, Heolgerrig, Merthyr Tydfil, CF48 1SS ☎ (01685) 370081 democratic@merthyr.gov.uk

David Davies (Lab: Town), 44 Primrose Hill, Twynyrodyn, Merthyr Tydfil, CF47 0TF ☎ (01685) 383244 democratic@merthyr.gov.uk

Graham Davies (Lab: Town), Llys Penydarren, Penydarren Park, Merthyr Tydfil, CF47 8YW ☎ (01685) 722511 democratic@merthyr.gov.uk

Les Elliott (Ind: Cyfarthfa), 40 Heol Tai Mawr, Gellideg Estate, Merthyr Tydfil, CF48 1NF (01685) 359670 les.elliott@merthyr.gov.uk

Ernie Galsworthy *(Lab: Treharris)*, 17 Railway Terrace, Treharris, CF46 5HD ☎ (01443) 412961 democratic@merthyr.gov.uk

Neil Greer *(UKIP: Penydarren)*, 3 Hodges Street, Penydarren, Merthyr Tydfil, CF47 9NX ☎ (01685) 387530 Neil.Greer@Merthyr.gov.uk

David Isaac *(Lab: Penydarren)*, 73 Brynhyfryd Street, Penydarren, Merthyr Tydfil, CF47 9YW ☎ 07538 830 903 david.isaac@merthyr.gov.uk

David Jarrett *(Lab: Gurnos)*, 19 Alder Grove, Gurnos, Merthyr Tydfil, CF47 9SF ☎ (01685) 375949 democratic@merthyr.gov.uk

Allan Jones *(Ind: Penydarren)*, 28 Brynheulog Street, Penydarren, Merthyr Tydfil, CF47 9UY ☎ (01685) 388352 allan.jones@merthyr.gov.uk

Clive Jones *(Lab: Park)*, 88 Lakeside Gardens, Merthyr Tydfil, CF48 1EW ☎ (01685) 371538 clive.jones@merthyr.gov.uk

David Jones *(Lab: Town)*, Farmers Arms, 25 Penheolferthyr, Mountain Hare, Merthyr Tydfil, CF47 0LF ☎ 07811 686 328 David.Jones2@merthyr.gov.uk

Gareth Jones *(Ind: Bedlinog)*, Witbank House, 1 Muriel Terrace, Bedlinog, Treharris, CF46 6TP ☎ (01443) 710807 Gareth.Jones1@Merthyr.gov.uk

Harvey Jones *(Lab: Plymouth)*, Ty Graig, Canal Bank, Abercanaid, Merthyr Tydfil, CF48 1YS ☎ (01685) 389092 democratic@merthyr.gov.uk

Gareth Lewis *(Lab: Plymouth)*, 43 Anthony Grove, Abercanaid, Merthyr Tydfil, CF48 1YX ☎ (01685) 725284 democratic@merthyr.gov.uk

Tom Lewis *(Lab: Dowlais)*, 25 Ivor Street, Dowlais, Merthyr Tydfil, CF48 3LP ☎ (01685) 373337 democratic@merthyr.gov.uk

Brian Mansbridge *(Lab: Merthyr Vale)*, 32 Taff Vale Estate, Edwardsville, Treharris, CF46 5NJ ☎ (01443) 410770 brian.mansbridge@merthyr.gov.uk

Linda Matthews *(Lab: Town)*, 13 Llwyn Yr Eos Grove, Bradley Gardens, Penyard, Merthyr Tydfil, CF47 0GD ☎ (01685) 371053 democratic@merthyr.gov.uk

Kate Moran *(Lab: Treharris)*, 4 Wingfield Rise, Quakers Yard, Treharris, CF46 5EN ☎ (01685) 725284 democratic@merthyr.gov.uk

Lisa Mytton *(Ind: Vaynor)*, 32 Cyfarthfa Gardens, Cefn Coed, Merthyr Tydfil, CF48 2SE ☎ (01685) 383126 Lisa.Mytton@merthyr.gov.uk

Darren Roberts *(Lab: Merthyr Vale)*, 16 Coronation Place, Aberfan, Merthyr Tydfil, CF48 4QW ☎ (01685) 725284 councillordarrenroberts@yahoo.co.uk

Leighton Smart *(Ind: Bedlinog)*, 33 Nant Gwyn, Trelewis, Merthyr Tydfil, CF46 6DB ☎ (01443) 410644 leighton.smart@merthyr.gov.uk

Bill Smith *(Lab: Gurnos)*, 101 Gurnos Road, Gurnos, Merthyr Tydfil, CF47 9PU ☎ (01685) 373863 bill.smith@merthyr.gov.uk

Ray Thomas MBE *(Lab: Downlais)*, Crud Yr Awel, Station Terrace, Dowlais Top, Merthyr Tydfil, CF48 3PU ☎ (01685) 374252 ray.thomas@merthyr.gov.uk

Richard Thomas JP *(Ind: Treharris)*, 83 Tŷ Llwyd Parc, Quakers Yard, Treharris, CF46 5LB ☎ (01443) 413584, richard.thomas@merthyr.gov.uk

Brendan Toomey *(Lab: Park)*, 16 Chapel Banks, Georgetown, Merthyr Tydfil, CF48 1BP ☎ (01685) 377755 brendan.toomey@merthyr.gov.uk

Clive Tovey *(Ind: Gurnos)*, Autumn Leaves, Grawen Lane, Cefn Coed, Merthyr Tydfil, CF48 2NP ☎ (01685) 722729 clive.tovey@merthyr.gov.uk

Phil Williams *(Lab: Dowlais)*, 13 Caeracca Villas, Pant, Dowlais, Merthyr Tydfil, CF48 2AS ☎ (01685) 376555 phil.williams@merthyr.gov.uk

Simon Williams *(Lab: Dowlais)*, 61 The Hawthorns, Pant, Merthyr Tydfil, CF48 3EJ ☎ (01685) 721225 democratic@merthyr.gov.uk

Clerks to the Community Councils

Bedlinog Community Council, *Evan Thomas,* 38 Gellideg Road, Maes-y-Coed, Pontypridd CF37 1EJ ☎ (01443) 409392

MONMOUTHSHIRE COUNTY COUNCIL
CYNGOR SIR FYNWY

County Hall, Cwmbran NP44 2XH
Tel: (01633) 644644
Fax: (01633) 644666
Email:
feedback@monmouthshire.gov.uk
Website:
www.monmouthshire.gov.uk

Leader
Cllr Peter Fox

CYNGOR
monmouthshire
COUNTY COUNCIL
sir fynwy

Chief Executive
Paul Matthews

NO OVERALL CONTROL	Con **19** Lab **11** Ind **10** Lib D **3**	TOTAL 43

ELECTION RESULT 2012

	Seats	Change	Votes	Share
Conservative	19	-10	8,572	35.2%
Labour	11	4	7,241	29.7%
Independent	10	9	5,971	24.5%
Lib Dem	3	-2	1,785	7.3%
Plaid Cymru	0	-1	567	2.3%
Others	0	-	221	0.9%

Socio-economic Profile

		Rank 1<22
Area (sq km)	851	7
Population ('000s)	88.0	18
% able to speak Welsh	16.7	18
% born in Wales	61.3	17
% non-white ethnic groups	3.3	8
Gross rev expenditure (2011-12)	£175.3m	18
Forecast capital expenditure (2011-12)	£21.8m	20
% dwellings in Band D (2012-13)	20.8	5
Band D council tax (2011-12)	£1,224.52	8
% over retirement age	21.0	7
% pupils 5+ GCSEs A*-C (2010-11)	71.2	7
Unemployment (% claimant count 2011)	2.2	21
Index of Deprivation (2011)	9	19
(% of Authority in most deprived 30%)		

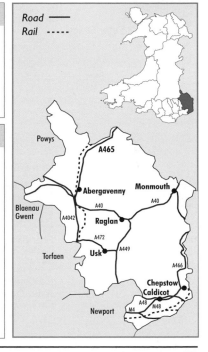

Road ——
Rail -----

LOCAL GOVERNMENT

MONMOUTHSHIRE

Principal Officers

Chief Executive:	**Paul Matthews**
Deputy Chief Executive:	**Moyna Wilkinson**
Chief Officer: Children & Young People:	**Andrew Keep**
Chief Officer: Social Care Health & Housing:	**Simon Burch**
Chief Officer: Regeneration & Culture:	**Kellie Beirne**
Head of Finance/Section 151 Officer:	**Joy Robson**
Monitoring Officer:	**Murray Andrews**

Cabinet Members 2012-2013

Leader; Corporate Services & Organizational Development:	**Peter A Fox** (Con)
Deputy Leader; Modernisation & Enterprise:	**Robert J W Greenland** (Con)
Deputy Leader; Community Development & Communications:	**Phylip Hobson** (Lib D)
Children, Young People & Learning:	**Elizabeth Hacket Pain** (Con)
Culture & Environment:	**Giles Howard** (Con)
Social Care, Health & Housing:	**Geoffrey Burrows** (Con)
Finance & Performance Improvement:	**Phillip Murphy** (Con)
County Operations:	**Bryan Jones** (Con)

Select & Scrutiny Committee Chairs 2012-2013

Audit Select:	**Tba**	Children & Young People Select:	**Paul Jordan** (Con)
Licensing:	**Tba**	Strong Communities Select:	**Simon Howarth** (Ind)
Planning:	**Tba**	Economy & Development Select:	**John Prosser** (Con)
Adults Select: **Peter Farley** (Lab)			

Salaries

Basic Salary: £13,175; Senior Salaries: Leader: £29,125
Deputy Leader: £14,565; Cabinet Members: £12,485
Chairs of Scrutiny Committees: £8,735; Chairs of Other Committees: £8,735
Leader of the Main Opposition Group: £8,735

Councillors   ♂30 ♀13

Chair: Cllr Maureen Powell   Vice-Chair: Cllr David Dovey

Dimitri Batrouni *(Lab: St Christopher's)*, 2 Laurel Close, Undy, Monmouthshire, NP26 3NP
☎ 07585 344967
dimitribatrouni@monmouthshire.gov.uk

Debby Blakebrough *(Ind: Trellech United)*, Redwood Studio, Llanishen, Monmouthshire NP16 6QH ☎ (01600) 860186
debbyblakebrough@monmouthshire.gov.uk

Geoff C Burrows *(Con: Mitchel Troy)*, Agincourt House, Llanddewi Rhydderch, Abergavenny, NP7 9TS
☎ (01873) 840589 / 07860 379767
geoffburrows@monmouthshire.gov.uk

Ralph F Chapman *(Ind: Mardy)*, 6 Midway Lane, Mardy, Abergavenny, NP7 6ND
☎ 07754 771094
ralphchapman@monmouthshire.gov.uk

Peter Clarke *(Con: Llangybi Fawr)*, Beeches, Pontypool Road, Llanbadoc, Usk, NP5 1SY
☎ (01291) 671220
peterclarke@monmouthshire.gov.uk

Jessica Crook *(Lab: The Elms)*, Crooklands, Church Road, Undy, Monmouthshire, NP26 3EN
☎ 07542 720055
jessicacrook@monmouthshire.gov.uk

David Dovey *(Con: St Kingsmark)*, Apartment 3, Mounton Chambers, Mounton Close, Chepstow, NP16 5EG ☎ (01291) 621464
daviddovey@monmouthshire.gov.uk

Graham Down *(Ind: Shirenewton)*, 7 Wyelands View, Mathern, Chepstow, NP16 6HN
☎ (01291) 621846 / 07790 993654
grahamdown@monmouthshire.gov.uk

Tony Easson *(Lab: Dewstow)*, 60 Castle Lodge Crescent, Caldicot, Monmouthshire, NP26 4JS
☎ (01291) 421250
anthonyeasson@monmouthshire.gov.uk

Douglas Edwards *(Lib D: Grofield)*, Stanhope Lodge, Chapel Lane, Abergavenny, NP7 7BT
☎ 07954 292398
douglasedwards@monmouthshire.gov.uk

Ruth Edwards *(Con: Llantilio Crossenny)*, Whitehall Farm, Rockfield Village, Monmouth, NP25 5NH ☎ (01600) 714941
ruthedwards@monmouthshire.gov.uk

David Evans *(Lab: West End)*, 32 Denny View, Caldicot, NP26 5LS ☎ (01291) 420354
davidevans2@monmouthshire.gov.uk

Peter Farley *(Lab: Chepstow, St Mary's)*, Cobweb Cottage, Belle Vue Place, Steep Street, Chepstow, Monmouthshire, NP16 5PL
☎ (01291) 627125
peterfarley@monmouthshire.gov.uk

Peter Fox *(Con: Portskewett)*, 25 Leechpool Holdings, Portskewett, Caldicot, NP26 5UB
☎ (01633) 644020
peterfox@monmouthshire.gov.uk

James George *(Lab: Lansdown)*, 2 Bishop Crescent, Abergavenny, NP7 6BT ☎ 07432 106135
jamesgeorge@monmouthshire.gov.uk

Robert Greenland *(Con: Devauden)*, Tŷ Croes, Model Farm, Wolvesnewton, Chepstow, NP16 6NZ ☎ (01291) 650231
robertgreenland@monmouthshire.gov.uk

Linda Guppy *(Lib D: Rogiet)*, 9 Starling Close, Rogiet, Caldicot, NP26 3UU ☎ (01291) 422460
lindaguppy@monmouthshire.gov.uk

Elizabeth Hacket Pain *(Con: Wyesham)*, c/o Members Secretary, @Innovation House, PO Box 106, Caldicot, NP26 9AN
☎ (01600) 712006 / 07968 147984
lizhacketpain@monmouthshire.gov.uk

Roger Harris *(Lab: Croesonen)*, The Hamlet, Llwyndu, Abergavenny, NP7 7HY
☎ (01873) 858143/07552 6
rogerharris@monmouthshire.gov.uk

Robert Hayward *(Ind: Dixton with Osbaston)*, Chalfont House, 12 Duchess Road, Monmouth, NP25 3HT ☎ (01600) 716529
bobhayward@monmouthshire.gov.uk

Martin Hickman *(Con: Llanfoist Fawr)*, Blorenge View, 26 Station Road, Abergavenny, Monmouthshire, NP7 5HS ☎ (01873) 859543
martinhickman@monmouthshire.gov.uk

Jim Higginson *(Lab: Severn)*, 31 Eagle Close, Caldicot, NP26 5FA
☎ (01291) 420663
ronhigginson@monmouthshire.gov.uk

Phil Hobson *(Lib D: Chepstow, Larkfield)*, Yr Hen Archdy, 8 Church Road, Chepstow, Monmouthshire, NP16 5HD
☎ 07966 343978
philhobson@monmouthshire.gov.uk

Giles Howard *(Con: Llanelly Hill)*, 28 Malford Grove, Gilwern, Monmouthshire, NP7 0RN
☎ 07930 544668
gileshoward@monmouthshire.gov.uk

Simon Howarth *(Ind: Llanelly Hill)*, Dyffryn Clydach Farm, Gilwern, Abergavenny, NP7 0EG
☎ (01873) 831003
simonhowarth@monmouthshire.gov.uk

Bryan Jones *(Con: Goytre Fawr)*, Ford Cottage, Llanfair Cilgedyn, Abergavenny, NP7 9DS
☎ (01873) 880688
bryanjones@monmouthshire.gov.uk

David Jones *(Ind: Crucorney)*, Cartref, Llanvetherine, Abergavenny, Monmouthshire, NP7 8RD ☎ (01873) 821497
davidhughesjones@monmouthshire.gov.uk

Penny Jones *(Con: Raglan)*, Llanusk Cottage, Llanbadoc, Nr Usk, Monmouthshire, NP15 1TA
☎ (01291) 673674
pennyjones@monmouthshire.gov.uk

Sara Jones *(Con: Llanover)*, Dwr Gul Bungalow, Tump Farm, Llantrisant, Usk, Monmouthshire, NP15 1UL ☎ (01291) 672573
sarajones2@monmouthshire.gov.uk

Paul Jordan *(Con: Cantref)*, 3 Chapel Orchard, Abergavenny, Monmouthshire, NP7 7BQ
☎ (01873) 855763
pauljordan@monmouthshire.gov.uk

John Marshall *(Ind: Green Lane)*, 115 Newport Road, Caldicot, Monmouthshire, NP26 4BS
☎ (01291) 422470
johnmarshall@monmouthshire.gov.uk

Phil Murphy *(Con: Caerwent)*, Swn Aderyn, Llanfair Discoed, Chepstow, NP16 6LX
☎ (01633) 400387
philmurphy@monmouthshire.gov.uk

Maureen Powell *(Con: Castle)*, 1 De Cantelupe Close, Ysbyty Fields, Abergavenny, NP7 9JB
☎ (01873) 851761
maureenpowell@monmouthshire.gov.uk

John Prosser *(Con: Priory)*, Elephant House, Clifton Road, Abergavenny, NP7 6AG
☎ (01873) 850534
johnprosser@monmouthshire.gov.uk

Val Smith *(Ind: Llanbadoc)*, Prospect, Glascoed, NP4 0TZ
☎ (01495) 785338
valsmith@monmouthshire.gov.uk

Brian Strong *(Con: Usk)*, Oakdene, Monmouth Road, Usk, NP15 1SE, (01291) 673404
brianstrong@monmouthshire.gov.uk

Frances Taylor *(Ind: Mill)*, Merevale House, West End, Magor, Monmouthshire, NP26 3HT
francestaylor@monmouthshire.gov.uk

Armand Watts *(Lab: Thornwell)*, 11 Middle Street, Chepstow, NP16 5ET ☎ 07980 962669
armandwatts@monmouthshire.gov.uk

Pauline Watts *(Lab: Caldicot Castle)*, Manor Farm House, Portskewett, Caldicot, Monmouthshire, NP26 5UL
☎ (01291) 422104
wattspauline@monmouthshire.gov.uk

Ann Webb *(Con: St Arvans)*, Home Farm, Trellech Grange, Chepstow, NP16 6QW
☎ (01291) 689559
annwebb@monmouthshire.gov.uk

Susan White *(Con: Overmonnow)*, Portfield Farm, Wonastow Road, Monmouth, NP25 4DQ ☎ (01600) 712611
susanwhite@monmouthshire.gov.uk

Kevin Williams *(Lab: Llanwenarth Ultra)*, 13 De Braose Close, Ysbytty Fields, Abergavenny, Monmouthshire,NP7 9JJ
☎ 07920 225417
kevinwilliams@monmouthshire.gov.uk

Alan Wintle *(Ind: Drybridge)*, 4 Tower View, Field House Farm, Monmouth, NP25 5FD
☎ (01600) 772155
alanwintle@monmouthshire.gov.uk

Clerks to the Community Councils

Abergavenny Town Council, *Mr P C Johns*, 6 Chapel Orchard, Abergavenny, NP7 7BQ
☎ (01873) 853817
abertownclerk@btinternet.com

Caerwent Community Council, *Mrs L McKeon*, Mayfield, Pill Road, Caldicot, NP26 4JD ☎ (01291) 424802
caerwentcouncil@aol.com

Caldicot Town Council, *Gail McIntyre*, Council Offices, Sandy Lane, Caldicot, Newport, NP26 4NA ☎ (01291) 420441
towncouncil@caldicottc.org.uk

Chepstow Town Council, *Sandra Bushell*, The Gate House, Chepstow, NP26 5LH ☎ (01291) 626370
towncouncil@chepstow.co.uk

Crucorney Community Council, *Mr S G Cooper*, Llwynon, Pandy, Abergavenny, NP7 8DN
☎ (01873) 890754
gerald@geraldcooper.wanadoo.uk

Goetre Fawr Community Council, *Dawn Hallmark James*, Ty Draw Barn, Tŷ Draw, Little Mill, Pontypool, NP4 0HR
☎ (01495) 785520
dhallmarkjames@btinternet.com

Grosmont Community Council, *Mr R J B Wilcox*, Annwylfa, Grosmont, Abergavenny, NP7 8EP
☎ (01981) 240297
bobandjenwilcox@btinternet.com

Gwehelog Fawr Community Council, *Alun Window*, 8 Blackbarn Lane, Usk, Monmouthshire, NP15 1BP ☎ (01291) 671190
alun.window@tiscali.co.uk

Llanarth Community Council, *Mrs M Mercer*, Post Office, Llanarth, Nr. Raglan, Usk, NP15 2AU ☎ (01873) 840104
melaniemercer_@hotmail.com

Llanbadoc Community Council, *Alun Window*, 8 Blackbarn Lane, Usk, Monmouthshire, NP15 1BP
☎ (01291) 671190
alun.window@tiscali.co.uk

Llanelly Community Council, *Adrian Edwards*, Council Chamber, School Lane, Gilwern, NP7 0AT
☎ (01873) 832550
clerk@llanellycc.org.uk

Llanfoist Fawr Community Council, *Mrs M Mercer*, Post Office, Llanarth, Nr. Raglan, Usk, NP15 2AU ☎ (01873) 840104
melaniemercer_@hotmail.com

Llangattock-Vibon-Avel Community Council, *Mr R G Nicholas*, 16 Rushey Meadow, Monmouth, NP25 5BT
☎ (01600) 714181

Llangwm Community Council, *Carleen Martin*, 32 Kingswood Road, Monmouth, NP25 5BX
☎ (01600) 713126
carleenmartin@imica.co.uk

Llangybi Community Council, *Jem Quemper*, Llan Orchard, 12b Black Barn Lane, Usk, Monmouthshire, NP15 1BP
☎ (01291) 675548 / 07953 223963
jemquemper@aol.com

Llanhennock Community Council, *Jem Quemper*, Llan Orchard, 12b Black Barn Lane, Usk, Monmouthshire, NP15 1BP
☎ (01291) 675548 / 07953 223963
jemquemper@aol.com

Llanover Community Council, *Mr A H B Candler*, 32 Monk Street, Abergavenny, NP7 5NP
☎ (01873) 852432
Sam.elliott@gabb.co.uk

Llantilio Crossenny Community Council, *Ms K Jordan*, 3 Chapel Orchard, Abergavenny, NP7 7BQ
☎ (01873) 855763
katherinejordan1@hotmail.com

Llantilio Pertholey Community Council, *Mr Neil Chambers*, 201 Malpas Road, Newport, NP20 5PP
☎ (01633) 855021 / 07860 839765

Llantrisant Fawr Community Council, *Mr J Turner*, 45 Laburnum Drive, New Inn, Pontypool, NP4 0EY ☎ (01495) 756845

Magor with Undy Community Council, *Miss B Reed*, c/o Hilltop Cottage, Vinegar Hill, Undy, Caldicot, Mon, NP26 3EJ
☎ (01633) 880646 / 07785 747762
admin@magorundy.co.uk

Mathern Community Council, *Jane Kelley*, 3 Parklands, Mathern, Chepstow, NP16 6JL
☎ (01291) 621031
matherncc@googlemail.com

Mitchel Troy Community Council, *Mr M J Woods*, 20 Auden Close, Osbaston, Monmouth, NP25 3NW ☎ (01600) 714165

Monmouth Town Council, *Sue James*, Shire Hall, Agincourt Square, Monmouth, NP25 3DY
☎ (01600) 715662
townclerk@monmouth.gov.uk

Portskewett Community Council, *Beverley Young*, 54 Main Road, Portskewett, Monmouthshire
☎ (01291) 430818
t0paz30@02.co.uk

Raglan Community Council, *Mr P C Johns*, 6 Chapel Orchard, Abergavenny, NP7 7BQ
☎ (01873) 853817
peter.johns1@btinternet.com

Rogiet Community Council, *Maureen Williams*, Blackthorn House, Green Lane, Caerwent, Caldicot, Monmouthshire, NP26 5AR ☎ (01291) 422089
Rogiet.cc@talktalk.net

Shirenewton Community Council, *Hilary Counsell*, Five Lanes House, Caerwent, Caldicot, Monmouthshire, NP26 5PQ
☎ (01291) 421307
briancounsell@tiscali.co.uk

St. Arvans Community Council, *Ms J Bolton*, 14 Grange Park, St. Arvans, Chepstow, Monmouthshire, NP16 6EA
☎ (01291) 626318
judith.bolton@talktalk.net

Tintern Community Council, *Elizabeth Greatorex Davies*, The Poplars, Whitelye, Catbrook, Chepstow, NP16 6NP
☎ (01291) 689861
tinternccclerk@aol.co.uk

Trellech United Community Council, *Ann Davison*, Wyeholme, Llandogo, Monmouth, Monmouthshire, NP25 4TW
☎ (01594) 530295
ann.davison1@btinternet.com

Usk Town Council, *Jenny Mee*, Sessions House, 43 Maryport Street, Usk, NP15 1AD
☎ (01291) 673011
clerk.usk@btconnect.com

NEATH PORT TALBOT COUNTY BOROUGH COUNCIL
CYNGOR BWRDEISTREF SIROL
CASTELL-NEDD PORT TALBOT

Civic Centre, Port Talbot SA13 1PJ
Tel: (01639) 686868
Fax: (01639) 763444
Email: contactus@npt.gov.uk
Website: www.npt.gov.uk

Leader
Cllr Ali Thomas

Neath Port Talbot
Castell-nedd Port Talbot
County Borough Council Cyngor Bwrdeistref Sirol

Chief Executive
Steven Phillips

LABOUR CONTROL	Lab **52** PC **8** Ind **3** Others **1**	TOTAL 64

ELECTION RESULT 2012

	Seats	Change	Votes	Share
Labour	52	15	38,596	57.1%
Plaid Cymru	8	-3	11,575	17.1%
Independent	3	-3	4,628	6.9%
Others	1	-5	11,035	16.3%
Lib Dem	0	-4	1,057	1.6%
Con	0	-	669	1.0%

Socio-economic Profile

		Rank 1<22
Area (sq km)	442	11
Population ('000s)	137.3	8
% able to speak Welsh	18.8	10
% born in Wales	89.5	5
% non-white ethnic groups	2.6	15
Gross rev expenditure (2011-12)	£343.0m	6
Forecast capital expenditure (2011-12)	£71.8m	2
% dwellings in Band D (2012-13)	10.8	18
Band D council tax (2011-12)	£1,3483.73	2
% over retirement age	18.9	10
% pupils 5+ GCSEs A*-C (2010-12)	74.6	2
Unemployment (% claimant count 2011)	3.8	12
Index of Deprivation (2011)	44	4
(% of Authority in most deprived 30%)		

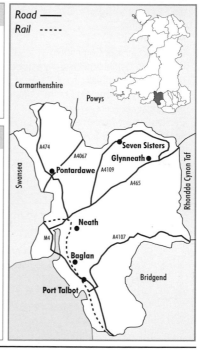

Road ——
Rail -----

Carmarthenshire

Powys

Swansea

A474

A4067

Pontardawe

A4109

Seven Sisters

Glynneath

A465

Rhondda Cynon Taf

Neath

M4

A4107

Baglan

Bridgend

Port Talbot

LOCAL GOVERNMENT

NEATH PORT TALBOT

Corporate Directors

Chief Executive:	**Steven Phillips**
Director of Education, Leisure & Lifelong Learning:	**Karl Napieralla**
Director of Social Services, Health & Housing:	**Tony Clements**
Director of Finance & Corporate Services:	**Derek Davies**
Director of Environment:	**John Flower**

Cabinet Members 2012-2013

Leader & Community & Strategic Leadership:	**Alun H Thomas** (Lab)
Deputy Leader & Finance, Transformation & Corporate Services:	**Peter A Rees** (Lab)
Social Care, Health & Housing:	**John Rogers** (Lab)
Children & Young People:	**Peter Richards** (Lab)
Education & Lifelong Learning:	**David Lewis** (Lab)
Community & Leisure Services:	**Michael L James** (Lab)
Economic Development & Property Services:	**Colin Morgan** (Lab)
Environment:	**Ted Latham** (Lab)
Streetcare & Highway Services:	**Sandra Miller** (Lab)

Committee Chairs 2012-2013

Appeals Panel:	**Lynda Williams** (Lab)
Audit Committee:	**Lella James** (Ind)
Demcratic Services Committee:	**Lella James** (Ind)
Licensing & Gambling Acts Committee:	**Collin Crowley** (Lab)
Personnel Committee:	**Peter Rees** (Lab)
Planning & Development Control Committee:	**Arwyn Woolcock** (Lab)
Registration & Licensing Committee	**Collin Crowley** (Lab)
Cabinet / Policy Resources Scrutiny Committee	**Des Davies** (Lab)
Social Care, Health & Housing Scrutiny Committee	**Sheila Penry** (Lab)
Children, Young People & Education Scrutiny Committee	**Glyn Rawlings** (Lab)
Economic & Community Regeneration Scrutiny Committee	**Alun Llewelyn** (PC)
Environment & Highways Scrutiny Committee:	**David Williams** (Lab)
Standards Committee:	**Godfrey Pullen**

Salaries

Basic Salary: £13,175 per annum; Senior Salaries: Leader: £47,500
Deputy Leader: £33,460; Other Executive Members: £28,780
Chairs of Scrutiny Committees: £21,910, Chairs of Other Committees £21,910
Leader of Main Opposition Group: £21,910
Mayor: £21,375; Deputy Mayor: £16,625

Councillors   ♂ 47   ♀ 17

Mayor: Cllr Martyn Peters   Deputy Mayor: Cllr Marion Lewis

Lynda Williams *(Lab: Gwaun-Cae-Gurwe)*, 3 Neuadd Road, Gwaun-Cae-Gurwen, Ammanford, SA18 1UG ☎ (01269) 825242 / 07779 231602
cllr.l.g.williams@npt.gov.uk

Arwyn Woolcock *(Lab: Lower Brynamman)*, 8 Barry Road, Lower Brynamman, Ammanford, SA18 1TU ☎ (01269) 825767 / 07977 588282
cllr.a.n.woolcock@npt.gov.uk

Eirion Richards *(Lab: Cwmllynfell)*, 57 Bryn Road, Cwmllynfell, Swansea, SA9 2FR
☎ (01639) 830703 / 07785 590768
cllr.c.e.richards@npt.gov.uk

Mike James *(Lab: Pontardawe)*, 24 Heol Las, Pontardawe, Swansea, SA8 4PR
☎ (01792) 869626 / 07831 227404
cllr.m.l.james@npt.gov.uk

Linet Purcell *(PC: Pontardawe)*, 39 New Road, Ynysmeudwy, Swansea, SA8 4PJ ☎ 08451 567381
cllr.l.purcell@npt.gov.uk

Alun Llewelyn *(PC: Ystalyfera)*, 5 Twyn yr Ysgol, Ystalyfera, Abertawe, SA9 2AN
☎ (01639) 849729 / 07528137093
cllr.a.llewelyn@npt.gov.uk

Rosalyn Davies *(PC: Godre'r Graig)*, 102 Heol Cilmaengwyn, Cilmaengwyn, Pontardawe, Swansea, SA8 4QN
☎ (01792) 862447 / 07989 661280
cllr.r.davies@npt.gov.uk

Rebeca Lewis *(PC: Trebanos)*, Brookway, 73A Swansea Road, Trebanos,SA8 4BL
☎ 07875 239140
cllr.r.lewis@npt.gov.uk

David Lewis *(Lab: Allt-wen)*, 45 Derwen Road, Alltwen, Pontardawe, SA8 3AU
☎ (01792) 864006 / 07973189238
cllr.d.lewis@npt.gov.uk

Alex Thomas *(Lab: Rhos)*, 22 Pen-y-Wern Road, Neath SA10 7AR ☎ 07773 377520
cllr.a.l.thomas@npt.gov.uk

Karen Pearson *(Lab: Crynant)*, 21 Maes Mawr Road, Crynant, Neath, SA10 8SY
☎ (01639) 750426
cllr.k.pearson@npt.gov.uk

Martyn Peters *(PC: Dyffryn)*, 140 The Highlands, Neath Abbey, Neath, SA10 6PE ☎ (01792) 813174
cllr.d.m.peters@npt.gov.uk

John Bryant *(PC: Bryncoch North)*, Woodland Gardens, Dyffryn, Bryncoch, Neath, SA10 7BQ ☎ (01792) 321637
cllr.j.r.bryant@npt.gov.uk

Janice Dudley *(PC: Bryncoch South)*, Hanley Cottage, 27 The Sinnatts, Court Herbert, Neath, SA10 7BY ☎ (01639) 635908 / 07969771417
cllr.j.dudley@npt.gov.uk

Rob James *(Lab: Bryncoch South)*, 11 Talbot Road, Westernmoor, Neath, SA11 1UT
☎ (01639) 768660 / 07760667102
cllr.r.james@npt.gov.uk

Annette Wingrave *(Lab: Cadoxton)*, 9 Pretyman Drive, Llandarcy, Neath, SA10 6HZ
☎ (01792) 321423
cllr.a.wingrave@npt.gov.uk

Alan Richard Lockyer *(Lab: Neath North)*, 37 Harle Street, Neath, SA11 3DN ☎ (01639) 770718
cllr.a.r.lockyer@npt.gov.uk

Mark Protheroe *(Lab: Neath North)*, 64 Harle Street, Neath, SA11 3DL ☎ (01639) 769231
cllr.m.protheroe@npt.gov.uk

Peter Rees *(Lab: Neath South)*, 9 Kenway Avenue, Cimla, Neath, SA11 3TU ☎ (01639) 636204 / 07811326568
cllr.p.a.rees@npt.gov.uk

Mal Gunter *(Lab: Neath South)*, 31 Dalton Road, Hillside, Neath, SA11 1UG
☎ (01639) 638227
cllr.m.b.gunter@npt.gov.uk

Sandra Miller *(Lab: Neath East)*, 39 Pantyrheol, Penrhiwtyn, Neath, SA11 2HN
☎ (01639) 631897 / 07530970796
cllr.s.miller@npt.gov.uk

John Miller *(Lab: Neath East)*, 39 Pantyrheol, Penrhiwtyn, Neath, SA11 2HN ☎ (01639) 631897 / 07969675964
cllr.j.miller@npt.gov.uk

Sheila Penry *(Lab: Neath East)*, 32 Walters Road Flats, Melyn, Neath, SA11 2DP
☎ (01639) 793881 / 07939 007209
cllr.s.m.penry@npt.gov.uk

Doreen Jones *(Lab: Aberdulais)*, Gwalia House, 1B New Road, Cilfrew, Neath, SA10 8LL
☎ (01639) 642499
cllr.d.jones@npt.gov.uk

Cari Morgans *(Lab: Tonna)*, 77 Henfaes Road, Tonna, Neath, SA11 3EX ☎ (01639) 630426 / 07982246744
cllr.c.morgans@npt.gov.uk

Mike Harvey *(Lab: Coedffranc North)*, 28 Hill Road, Neath Abbey, Neath, SA10 7NR
☎ (01792) 812628 / 07536096615
cllr.m.harvey@npt.gov.uk

Paula Bebell *(Lab: Coedffranc Central)*, 38 Elba Crescent, Crymlyn Burrows, Swansea, SA1 8QQ ☎ (01792) 641604
cllr.p.bebell@npt.gov.uk

Arthur Davies *(Lab: Coedffranc Central)*, 65 Cardonnel Road, Skewen, Neath, SA10 6BS
☎ (01792) 814910 / 07964800162
cllr.a.p.h.davies@npt.gov.uk

LOCAL GOVERNMENT

Harry Bebell *(Lab: Coedffranc West)*, 38 Elba Crescent, Crymlyn Burrows, Swansea, SA1 8QQ
☎ (01792) 641604
cllr.h.m.bebell@npt.gov.uk

Hugh James *(Lab: Briton Ferry West)*, 65 Shelone Road, Briton Ferry, Neath, SA11 2PT
☎ (01639) 820955 / 07791389073
cllr.h.n.james@npt.gov.uk

Colin Morgan *(Lab:Briton Ferry East)*, 14 Regent Street East, Briton Ferry, Neath, SA11 2RR
☎ (01639) 812940 / 07711108629
cllr.c.morgan@npt.gov.uk

Alan Carter *(Lab: Cimla)*, 2 Y Berllan, Cimla, Neath, SA11 3YH
☎ (01639) 632442 / 07432018534
cllr.a.carter@npt.gov.uk

John Warman *(Lab: Cimla)*, 66 Glannant Way, Cimla, Neath, SA11 3YN ☎ (01639) 778933 / 07843255446
cllr.j.warman@npt.gov.uk

Martin Ellis *(Ind: Pelenna)*, 22 Heol Bedwas, Birchgrove, Swansea, SA7 9LF
☎ (01792) 865171 / 07837883542
cllr.m.ellis@npt.gov.uk

Steve Hunt *(Ind: Seven Sisters)*, 153 Dulais Road, Seven Sisters, Neath, SA10 9EY
☎ (01639) 700063 / 07850429957
cllr.s.k.hunt@npt.gov.uk

Alun Thomas *(Lab: Onllwyn)*, 2 Nidum Close, Barrons Court, Neath, SA10 7JE ☎ (01639) 642740
leader@npt.gov.uk

Eddie Jones *(Lab: Glynneath)*, 31 Min-y-Coed, Glynneath, Neath, SA11 5RY ☎ (01639) 720938 / 07791674095
cllr.e.e.jones@npt.gov.uk

Del Morgan *(PC: Glynneath)*, 11 Lon-y-Nant, Glynneath, Neath, SA11 5BD ☎ (01639) 722300
cllr.j.d.morgan@npt.gov.uk

Alf Siddley *(Lab: Blaengwrach)*, 1 School Street, Cwmgwrach, Neath, SA11 5PP ☎ (01639) 721536
cllr.a.j.siddley@npt.gov.uk

Des Davies *(Lab: Resolven)*, Hazeldene, 12 Lletty Dafydd, Clyne, Neath, SA11 4BG
☎ (01639) 711300 / 07957884407
cllr.d.w.davies@npt.gov.uk

Glyn Rawlings *(Lab: Glyncorrwg)*, 4 Sunny Bank, Glyncorrwg, Port Talbot, SA13 3BU ☎ (01639) 850525 / 07811853094
cllr.h.g.rawlings@npt.gov.uk

Scott Jones *(Lab: Cymmer)*, 43 Brynheulog Road, Croeserw, Cymmer, Port Talbot, SA13 3RR
☎ (01639) 852203 / 07879202747
cllr.s.jones@npt.gov.uk

Ralph Thomas *(Lab: Gwynfi)*, 131 Jersey Road, Blaengwynfi, Port Talbot, SA13 3TE
☎ (01639) 851356,
cllr.r.thomas@npt.gov.uk

Carol Clement *(Lab: Baglan)*, 44 Thorney Road, Baglan, Port Talbot, SA12 8LW
☎ (01639) 795759 / 07815128023
cllr.c.clement@npt.gov.uk

Paul Greenaway *(Lab: Baglan)*, 7 Rowantree Avenue, Baglan, Port Talbot, SA12 8EZ
☎ (01639) 821074
cllr.p.greenaway@npt.gov.uk

Peter Richards *(Lab: Baglan)*, 159 Tyn Y Twr, Baglan, Port Talbot, SA12 8YE
☎ (01639) 821869 / 07792264113
cllr.p.d.richards@npt.gov.uk

Marian Lewis *(Lab: Bryn & Cwmavon)*, Tyler-Fedwen Farm, Cwmafan, Port Talbot, SA12 9YA
☎ (01639) 632324 / 07974656124
cllr.m.a.lewis@npt.gov.uk

Dave Whitelock *(Lab: Bryn & Cwmavon)*, 13 Brynglas Avenue, Cwmafan, Port Talbot, SA12 9LE
☎ (01639) 792534 / 07866783888
cllr.d.whitelock@npt.gov.uk

David Williams *(Lab: Bryn & Cwmavon)*, 10 Church Square, Cwmafan, Port Talbot, SA12 9AP
☎ (01639) 896999 / 07967 489151
cllr.i.d.williams@npt.gov.uk

Audrey Chaves *(Lab: Sandfields West)*, 50 Scarlet Avenue, Sandfields, Port Talbot, SA12 7PH
☎ (01639) 772983 / 07896326659
cllr.a.chaves@npt.gov.uk

James Evans *(Lab: Sandfields West)*, 44 Pier Way, Sandfields, Port Talbot, SA12 7NS
☎ (01639) 793657 / 07581005452
cllr.j.s.evans@npt.gov.uk

Suzanne Paddison *(Lab: Sandfields West)*, 249 Western Avenue, Sandfields, Port Talbot, SA12 7NF ☎ (01639) 770422
cllr.s.paddison@npt.gov.uk

Collin Crowley *(Lab: Sandfields East)*, The Annex, Mattrock House, 61 Sitwell Way, Little Warren, Port Talbot, SA12 6BH
☎ (01639) 775103
cllr.c.crowley@npt.gov.uk

Lella James *(Ind: Sandfields East)*, 20 Lingfield Avenue, Port Talbot, SA12 6NX ☎ (01639) 888252
cllr.l.h.james@npt.gov.uk

Ted Latham *(Lab: Sandfields East)*, 17 Darwin Road, Port Talbot, SA12 6BR ☎ (01639) 891365 / 07811888998
cllr.e.v.latham@npt.gov.uk

Ceri Golding *(Lab: Aberavon)*, 17 Castle Street, Aberavon, Port Talbot, SA12 6DR
☎ (01639) 884389 / 07791 853963
cllr.c.p.golding@npt.gov.uk

Mark Jones *(Lab: Aberavon)*, 1 Castle Street, Aberavon, Port Talbot, SA12 6DR
☎ 07904 499087
cllr.m.jones@npt.gov.uk

Tony Taylor *(Soc D: Aberavon)*, 9 Castle Street, Aberavon, Port Talbot, SA12 6DR
☎ (01639) 892541 / 07989231952
cllr.a.taylor@npt.gov.uk

Ian James *(Lab: Port Talbot)*, 33 Mansel Street, Port Talbot, SA13 1BL ☎ (01639) 899979 / 07918110645
cllr.i.b.james@npt.gov.uk

Dennis Keogh (*Lab: Port Talbot*),
10 Broad Street, Port Talbot,
SA13 1EW ☎ (01639) 882926 /
07967897072
cllr.d.keogh@npt.gov.uk

Saifur Rahaman (*Lab: Port Talbot*), 12 Mansel Street, Port Talbot, SA13 1BH ☎ 07824445991
cllr.s.rahaman@npt.gov.uk

John Rogers (*Lab:Tai-Bach*),
6 Prince Street, Margam, Port
Talbot, SA13 1NB
☎ (01639) 887589 / 07791900885
cllr.j.rogers@npt.gov.uk

Anthony Taylor (*Lab: Tai-Bach*),
79 Margam Road, Margam,
Port Talbot, SA13 2LB
☎ (01639) 687435 / 07920111869
cllr.a.j.taylor@npt.gov.uk

Rob Jones (*Lab: Margam*),
Richmond House, Richmond Place,
Taibach, Port Talbot, SA13 1TR
☎ (01639) 681253 / 07885649064
cllr.r.g.jones@npt.gov.uk

Clerks to the Community Councils

Blaengwrach Community Council, *Mrs D Roberts*, 12 Heol Wenalt, Cwmgwrach, Neath, SA11 5PT ☎ (01639) 722083
Clerk@blaengwrachcommunitycouncil.co.uk

Blaenhonddan Community Council, *Mrs M Hewitt*, 11 Maes Llwynonn, Cadoxton, Neath, SA10 8AQ ☎ (01639) 632436
blaenhonddancc.clerk@btconnect.com

Briton Ferry Town Council, *Mr D M Isaac*, 12 Ffrwd Vale, Neath, SA10 7BA
☎ (01639) 772618
townclerk@britonferrycouncil.org.uk

Cilybebyll Community Council, *Mr R Lanchbury*, 13 Heol Y Parc, Alltwen, Pontardawe, Swansea, SA8 3BN ☎ (01792) 864061
cilybebyll@sky.com

Clyne & Melincourt Community Council, *Mr K Thomas*, 17 Ynys-yr-Afon, Clyne, Neath, SA11 4BP
☎ 07968661295

Coedffranc Community Council, *Mrs W Thomas*, Memorial Hall, Skewen Park, Off Wern Road, Skewen, Neath, SA10 6DP
☎ (01792) 817754
wendy-thomas@btconnect.com

Crynant Community Council, *Mr H Thomas*, 26 Leiros Parc Drive, The Rhyddings, Neath, SA10 7EW
☎ (01639) 632231
hywelthomas1@aol.com

Cwmllynfell Community Council, *Mr P Lloyd-Jones*, Brynderwen, Coronation Road, Brynamman, Ammanford, SA18 1BB ☎ (01269) 825308
cwmllynfellcc@aol.com

Dyffryn Clydach Community Council, *Mr D R Shopland*, Hafan Deg, 6 Dulais Close, Aberdulais, Neath, SA10 8HA
☎ (01639) 635787
mail@ranshop.wanadoo.co.uk

Glynneath Town Council, *Mr C Baker*, Bethania Chapel, High Street, Glynneath, SA11 5DA
☎ 07519 278651
clive8377@btinternet.com

Gwaun Cae Gurwen Community Council, *Mr D M Key*, 3 Upper Coelbren Road, Gwaun Cae Gurwen, Ammanford, SA18 1HR ☎ (01269) 824953
mikekeygcg@hotmail.com

Neath Town Council, *Mrs A Ellis*, 10 Orchard Street, Neath, SA11 1DU ☎ (01639) 642126
clerk@neathtowncouncil.gov.uk

Onllwyn Community Council, *Mr B L Parfitt*, 22 Dulais Road, Seven Sisters, Neath, SA10 9EL
☎ (01639) 700814

Pelenna Community Council, *Mr D S Mackerras*, 2 Burnham Drive, Newton, Swansea, SA3 4TW ☎ (01792) 361526
davidmackerras@btopenworld.com

Pontardawe Town Council, *Ms D Phillips*, Pontardawe Town Council, PO Box 556, Swansea, SA8 4WL ☎ (01792) 863422
pontardawetc@aol.co.uk

Resolven Community Council, *Mr N Williams*, 9 Coronation Avenue, Resolven, Neath, SA11 4AF ☎ (01639) 711318
williamsmargaret649@hotmail.com

Seven Sisters Community Council, *Mr B L Parfitt*, 22 Dulais Road, Seven Sisters, Neath, SA10 9EL ☎ (01639) 700814

Tonna Community Council, *Mr P L White*, 32 Heol Caredig, Tonna, Neath, SA11 3LQ
☎ (01639) 644886
peterwhite111@aol.com

Ystalyfera Community Council, *Mr G Morgan*, 2 St. David's Road, Ystalyfera, Swansea, SA9 2JQ
☎ (01639) 842448
ystalyfera.council@btinternet.com

NEWPORT CITY COUNCIL
CYNGOR DINAS CASNEWYDD

Civic Centre, Newport NP20 4UR
Tel: (01633) 656656
Fax: (01633) 244721
Email: Website: www.newport.gov.uk

Leader
Cllr Robert Bright

Managing Director
Tracey Lee

LABOUR CONTROL

Lab **37**   Con **10**   Ind **2**   Lib D **1**

TOTAL 50

ELECTION RESULT 2012

	Seats	Change	Votes	Share
Lab	37	15	47,083	53.7%
Con	10	-7	25,116	28.7%
Ind	2	1	3,245	3.7%
Lib D	1	-8	9,569	10.9%
PC	0	-1	1,749	2.0%
Others	0	-	844	1.0%

Socio-economic Profile

		Rank 1<22
Area (sq km)	190	18
Population ('000s)	141.3	7
% able to speak Welsh	18.9	9
% born in Wales	81.1	9
% non-white ethnic groups	6.2	2
Gross rev expenditure (2011-12)	£314.9m	7
Forecast capital expenditure (2011-12)	£35.5m	13
% dwellings in Band D (2012-13)	17.8	9
Band D council tax (2011-12)	£994.64	21
% over retirement age	16.7	21
% pupils 5+ GCSEs A*-C (2010-11)	69.8	9
Unemployment (% claimant count 2011)	5.3	3
Index of Deprivation (2011)	43	5
(% of Authority in most deprived 30%)		

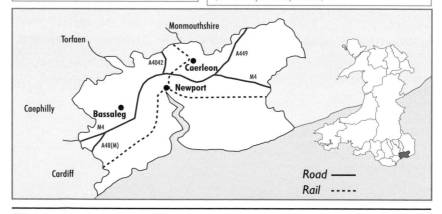

LOCAL GOVERNMENT

NEWPORT

Corporate Directors

Managing Director:	**Tracey Lee**
Corporate Director of Regeneration & Environment:	**Sheila Davies**
Corporate Director of Care & Customers:	**Stewart Greenwell**
(Interim) Director for Corporate Services	**Debra Wood-Lawson**

Cabinet 2012-2013

Leader:	**Robert Bright** (Lab)
Deputy Leader:	**Ray Truman** (Lab)
Licensing & Statutory Functions:	**Gail Giles** (Lab)
Regeneration & Development:	**John Richards** (Lab)
Infrastructure:	**Ken Critchley** (Lab)
Human Resources & Assets:	**Mark Whitcutt** (Lab)
Leisure & Culture:	**Debbie Wilcox** (Lab)
Social Care & Well-being:	**Paul Cockeram** (Lab)
Skills & Work	**Deborah Davies** (Lab)
Education & Young People:	**Robert Poole** (Lab)

Committee Chairs 2012-2013

Planning Committee:	**Ron Jones** (Lab)
Licensing Committee:	**Allan Morris** (Lab)
Street Scene, Regeneration & Safety Scrutiny Committee:	**Roger Jeavons** (Lab)
Learning, Caring & Leisure Scrutiny Committee:	**David Mayer** (Lab)
Community Planning & Development Committee:	**David Atwell** (Con)
Audit Committee:	**Tba**
Democratic Services Committee:	**Charles Ferrris** (Con)

Salaries

Basic Salary: £13,175 per annum
Senior Salaries:
Leader: £34,325; Deputy Leader: £20,285
Cabinet Member: £15,605; Chairs of Scrutiny Committees: £8,735
Chairs of Other Committees: £8,735; Leader of Main Opposition Party: £8,735

Councillors ♂ 37 ♀ 13

Mayor: Cllr John Guy

Miqdad Al-Nuaimi *(Lab: Stow Hill)*, 106 Cae Perllan Road, Newport, NP20 3FT
☎ (01633) 668973
miqdad.al-nuaimi@newport.gov.uk

David Atwell *(Con: Langstone)*, The Chantry, Old Roman Road, Langstone, Newport, NP18 2JW
☎ (01633) 416078
david.atwell@newport.gov.uk

Tom Bond *(Lab: Rogerstone)*, 73 Jones Street, Newport, NP20 4GL ☎ 07880 742886
tom.bond@newport.gov.uk

Robert Bright *(Lab: Ringland)*, 80 Allt-yr-yn Road, Newport, NP20 5EF ☎ (01633) 254315
bob.bright@newport.gov.uk

Paul Cockeram *(Lab: Shaftesbury)*, 117 Brynglas Avenue, Newport, NP20 5LQ ☎ (01633) 858568
paul.cockeram@newport.gov.uk

Margaret Cornelious *(Con: Graig)*, 34 Caerphilly Close, Rhiwderin, Newport, NP10 8RF
☎ (01633) 894198
margaret.cornelious@newport.gov.uk

Emma Corten *(Lab: Ringland)*, 12 Bishpool View, Ringland, Newport, NP19 9BG ☎ 07730 771048
emma.corten@newport.gov.uk

Ken Critchley *(Lab: Liswerry)*, 38 Traston Road, Newport, NP19 4RQ ☎ (01633) 275000
ken.critchley@newport.gov.uk

Deb Davies *(Lab: Beechwood)*, 30 Brynderwen Road, Newport, NP19 8LQ ☎ (01633) 779795
deborah.davies@newport.gov.uk

Val Delahaye *(Lab: Bettws)*, 12 Selskar Court, Usk Way, Newport, NP20 2FW ☎ (01633) 214975
valerie.delahaye@newport.gov.uk

Chris Evans *(Lab: Rogerstone)*, 99 Tregwillym Road, Rogerstone, Newport, NP10 9EQ
☎ 07778 279235
chris.evans@newport.gov.uk

Matthew Evans *(Con: Allt-yr-Yn)*, 100 Allt-yr-yn Avenue, Newport, NP20 5DE ☎ (01633) 211271
matthew.evans@newport.gov.uk

Charles Ferris *(Con: Caerleon)*, 7 Fields Park Avenue, Newport, NP20 5BG ☎ (01633) 250148
charles.ferris@newport.gov.uk

David Fouweather *(Con: Allt-yr-Yn)*, 31 Allt-yr-yn Road, Newport, NP20 5EA ☎ (01633) 252923
david.fouweather@newport.gov.uk

Emma Garland *(Lab: St Julians)*, 118 Conway Road, Newport, NP19 8NT ☎ (01633) 281567
emma.garland@newport.gov.uk

Gail Giles *(Lab: Caerleon)*, 13 Hazel Walk, Caerleon, Newport, NP18 3SE ☎ (01633) 421947
gail.giles@newport.gov.uk

John Guy *(Lab: Alway)*, 72 The Nurseries, Old Chepstow Road, Langstone, Newport, NP18 2NT
☎ (01633) 411917
john.guy@newport.gov.uk

Paul Hannon *(Lab: Beechwood)*, 37 Gibbs Road, Newport, NP19 8AR ☎ (01633) 669859
paul.hannon@newport.gov.uk

Debbie Harvey *(Lab: Alway)*, 9 Mount Bax, Newport, NP19 9SQ
☎ 07714 577014
debbie.harvey@newport.gov.uk

Ibrahim Hayat *(Lab: Pillgwenlly)*, 12 Carlisle Street, Newport, NP20 2JD ☎ (01633) 244720
ibrahim.hayat@newport.gov.uk

Paul Huntley *(Lab: Caerleon)*, 18 Augustan Close, Caerleon, Newport, NP18 3DJ
☎ (01633) 421449
paul.huntley@newport.gov.uk

Rhys Hutchings *(Lab: St Julians)*, c/o Newport City Council, Civic Centre, Newport NP20 4UR
☎ 07534 559727
rhys.hutchings@newport.gov.uk

Roger Jeavons *(Lab: Liswerry)*, 13 Cromwell Road, Somerton, Newport, NP19 0FY
☎ (01633) 677750
roger.jeavons@newport.gov.uk

Christine Jenkins *(Lab: Victoria)*, 32 London Street, Newport, NP19 8DG ☎ (01633) 668016
christine.jenkins@newport.gov.uk

Ron Jones *(Lab: Pillgwenlly)*, 33 Alice Street, Pillgwenlly, Newport, NP20 2HT ☎ (01633) 214597
ron.jones@newport.gov.uk

Martyn Kellaway *(Con: Llanwern)*, Damson Tree, Landevaud, Newport, NP18 2AF
☎ (01633) 401069
martyn.kellaway@newport.gov.uk

Malcolm Linton *(Lab: Ringland)*, 20 Nelson Drive, Royal Oak, Newport, NP19 9FU ☎ (01633) 673791
malcolm.linton@newport.gov.uk

Christine Maxfield *(Lab: Malpas)*, 32 Graig Park Road, Newport, NP20 6HD ☎ (01633) 771913
christine.maxfield@newport.gov.uk

David Mayer *(Lab: Malpas)*, 13 Hollybush Close, Malpas, Newport, NP20 6EU
☎ (01633) 770525
david.mayer@newport.gov.uk

Sally Mlewa *(Lab: Rogerstone)*, 8 Cefn Court, Rogerstone, Newport, NP10 9AH
☎ (01633) 452602
sally.mlewa@newport.gov.uk

Ray Mogford *(Con: Langstone)*, 'Kanebri' Tabernacle Road, Caldicot, Newport, NP26 3BL
☎ (01633) 401045
ray.mogford@newport.gov.uk

Allan Morris *(Lab: Liswerry)*, 11 Jamaica Walk, Coedkernew, Newport, NP10 8AG
☎ 07747 693429
allan.morris@newport.gov.uk

Jane Mudd *(Lab: Malpas)*, 85 Robertson Way, Malpas, Newport, NP20 6QQ
☎ (01633) 672545
jane.mudd@newport.gov.uk

Bob Poole *(Lab: Shaftesbury)*, 286 Malpas Road, Newport, NP20 6GQ ☎ (01633) 821102
bob.poole@newport.gov.uk

Majid Rahman *(Lab: Victoria)*, 45 Corporation Road, Newport, NP19 0AY ☎ 07761 550078
majid.rahman@newport.gov.uk

NEWPORT

John Richards (Lab: Liswerry), 43 Balmoral Road, Lliswerry, Newport, NP19 8LF ☎ (01633) 556422
john.richards@newport.gov.uk

Mark Spencer (Lab: Beechwood), 9 Goya Close, Beechwood, Newport, NP19 7RG ☎ (01633) 667904
mark.spencer@newport.gov.uk

Cliff Suller (Lab: Caerleon), 564A Caerleon Road, Newport, NP18 1QA ☎ (01633) 221922
cliff.suller@newport.gov.uk

Tom Suller (Con: Marshfield), 104 Woodside, Duffryn, Newport, NP10 8XE ☎ (01633) 300114
tom.suller@newport.gov.uk

Herbie Thomas (Lab: Gaer), 46 Walford Street, Newport, NP20 5PG ☎ (01633) 852146
herbert.thomas@newport.gov.uk

Kate Thomas (Lab: Stow Hill), 164 Stow Hill, Newport, NP20 4FZ ☎ (01633) 782774
kate.thomas@newport.gov.uk

Ed Townsend (Lib D: St Julians), 43 St Julians Road, Newport, NP19 7GN ☎ (01633) 211809
ed.townsend@newport.gov.uk

Noel Trigg (Ind: Bettws), Waterford, The Bridge, Bettws Lane, Newport, NP20 7AB
☎ (01633) 855934
noel.trigg@newport.gov.uk

Ray Truman (Lab: Alway), 154 Ringland Circle, Newport, NP19 9PL ☎ (01633) 671991
ray.truman@newport.gov.uk

Trevor Watkins (Lab: Tredegar Park), 68 Kestrel Way, Duffryn, Newport, NP10 8WG
☎ (01633) 817270
trevor.watkins@newport.gov.uk

Mark Whitcutt (Lab: Gaer), 59 Lansdowne Road, Newport, NP20 3GA ☎ (01633) 669125,
mark.whitcutt@newport.gov.uk

Richard White (Con: Marshfield), 4 Nellive Park, St Brides, Wentloog, Newport, NP10 8SE
☎ (01633) 680116
richard.white@newport.gov.uk

Kevin Whitehead (Ind: Bettws), 4 Ribble Walk, Bettws, Newport, NP20 7EB ☎ (01633) 859757
kevin.whitehead@newport.gov.uk

Debbie Wilcox (Lab: Gaer), 25 Delphinium Road, Rogerstone, Newport, NP10 9JF
☎ (01633) 891857
debbie.wilcox@newport.gov.uk

David Williams (Con: Graig), The Wagon House, Croescarneinion Farm, Holly Lane, Newport, NP10 8RR ☎ (01633) 892134
david.williams@newport.gov.uk

Clerks to the Community Councils

Bishton Community Council, Beverley Cousins, 5 Holybush Close, Malpas, Newport, NP20 6EU
bishtoncc@live.co.uk

Coedkernew Community Council, Mrs H Boswell, 4 Smithfield Cottages, Coedkernew, Newport, NP10 8TR
☎ (01633) 682834
heather.boswell@btinternet.com

Goldcliff Community Council, Miss A Harris, Chy-an-dour, Goldcliff, Newport, NP18 2PH
☎ 07710 773296
Goldcliffcc@gmail.com

Graig Community Council, Mrs S Davies, 6 Vale View, Gelli Park, Risca, Newport, NP11 6HS
☎ (01633) 614119 / 07971 094382
clerk@graigcc.co.uk

Langstone Community Council, Mrs S Hancock, 5 Miller Close, Langstone, Newport, NP18 2LE
☎ (01633) 411023
langstoneclerk@btinternet.com

Llanvaches Community Council, Mrs L Johnson, Willow Lodge, Llanvaches, Caldicot, NP26 3AY
☎ (01633) 400983
JhnsLyn@aol.com

Llanwern Community Council, Mr A Whiting, 3 Dockwell Terrace, Llanwern, Newport, NP18 2DX
☎ 07547 681998,
awhiting60@yahoo.co.uk

Marshfield Community Council, Mr G C Thomas, 4 Kenilworth Road, Newport, NP20 8QJ
☎ (01633) 664285
marshfieldcommunitycouncil@googlemail.com

Michaelstone-y-Fedw Community Council, Ms C Sainsbury, Graig View, Michaelstone-y-Fedw, CF3 6XT
☎ (01633) 680921
catherine@graigview.co.uk

Nash Community Council, Mrs P Bartlett, Bay Cottage, Straits Lane, Nash, Newport, NP18 2BY
☎ (01633) 272136
patbartlett@onetel.com

Penhow Community Council, Mrs B Morgan, Ferndale, Market Road, Penhow, Newport, NP26 3AB ☎ (01633) 400624
morgan1485@tiscali.co.uk

Redwick Community Council, Mrs G Williams, Green Court, South Row, Redwick, NP26 3DU
☎ (01633) 882631
grncourt@btinternet.com

Rogerstone Community Council, Mr C Atyeo, c/o Tydu Community Hall, Welfare Grounds, Tregwilym Road, Rogerstone, Newport, NP10 9EQ
☎ (01633) 893350
tpc.rcc@virgin.net

Wentloog Community Council, Mrs C Turner, Church Farm, St Brides, Wentloog, Newport, NP10 8SQ ☎ (01633) 689030
wentloogecc@live.co.uk

LOCAL GOVERNMENT

CYNGOR SIR BENFRO
PEMBROKESHIRE COUNTY COUNCIL

County Hall, Haverfordwest,
Pembrokeshire SA61 1TP
Tel: (01437) 764551
Fax: (01437) 775303
Email:
enquiries@pembrokeshire.gov.uk
Website: www.pembrokeshire.gov.uk

Leader
Cllr Jamie Adams

Chief Executive
D Bryn Parry-Jones

INDEPENDENT CONTROL	Ind **32** Others **12** Lab **8** PC **5** Con **2** Lib D **1**	TOTAL 60

ELECTION RESULT 2012

	Seats	Change	Votes	Share
Independent	32	-6	13,351	40.6%
Others	12	8	7,434	22.6%
Labour	8	3	3,780	11.5%
Plaid Cymru	5	-	2,621	8.0%
Conservative	2	-3	5,499	16.7%
Lib Dem	1	-2	238	0.7%

Socio-economic Profile

		Rank 1<22
Area (sq km)	1,619	5
Population ('000s)	117.0	14
% able to speak Welsh	16.2	19
% born in Wales	68.7	15
% non-white ethnic groups	3.5	7
Gross rev expenditure (2011-12)	£263.1m	14
Forecast capital expenditure (2011-12)	£46.1m	10
% dwellings in Band D (2012-13)	17.9	8
Band D council tax (2011-12)	£922.83	22
% over retirement age	21.8	4
% pupils 5+ GCSEs A*-C (2010-11)	68.3	11
Unemployment (% claimant count 2011)	3.4	16
Index of Deprivation (2011)	14	18
(% of Authority in most deprived 30%)		

Road ——
Rail -----

PEMBROKESHIRE

Principal Officers

Chief Executive:	**Bryn Parry-Jones**
Director of Development:	**Steven Jones**
Director of Education & Children's Services:	**Graham Longster**
Director of Finance & Leisure:	**Mark Lewis**
Director of Social Services:	**Jake Morgan**
Director of Transportation & Environment:	**Ian Westley**

Cabinet / Board Members 2012-2013

Leader / Corporate Matters & Finance:	**Jamie Adams** (Ind)
Deputy Leader / Education & Welsh Language:	**Huw George** (Ind)
Deputy Leader / Highways & Planning:	**Robert Lewis** (Ind)
Adult Services & Equalities:	**Simon Hancock** (Ind)
Culture, Sport & Leisure:	**Elwyn Morse** (Ind)
Safeguarding & Children's Services:	**Susan Perkins** (Lab)
Economy, Tourism & Communities:	**David Pugh** (Ind)
Environmental & Regulatory Services:	**Kenneth Rowlands** (Ind)
Housing & Sustinability:	**David Simpson** (Ind)
Health, Well-being & Voluntary Sector:	**David Wildman** (Ind)

Committee Chairs 2012-2013

Planning & Rights of Way Committee:	**Myles Pepper** (Ind)
Licensing Committee:	**Pearl Llewellyn** (Ind)
Children & Families Overview & Scrutiny Committee:	**Thomas Tudor** (Lab)
Safeguarding Overview & Scrutiny Committee:	**Rhys Sinnett** (PC)
Older Persons, Health & Well-being Overview & Scrutiny Committee:	**David Howlett** (Con)
Economy Overview & Scrutiny Committee:	**Keith Lewis** (Ind)
Environment Overview & Scrutiny Committee:	**Brian Hall** (Ind)
Senior Staff Committee	**Jamie Adams** (Ind)
Democratic Services Committee:	**Rhys Sinnett** (PC)
Coporate Governance Committee:	**Tba**
Audit Committee:	**Tba**
Standards Committee:	**Tba**
Urgency Committee:	**Tba**

Salaries

Basic Salary: £13,175 + £500 Supplement
(IT/Communications & Office Support) per annum
Senior Salary: Leader: £47,500; Deputy Leader: £31,120
Cabinet Members: £28,780; Chairs of Scrutiny Committees: £21,910
Chairs of Other Committees: £21,910; Leader of Main Opposition Group: £21,910

Councillors ♂51 ♀9

Chair: Cllr Peter Morgan

James Llewellyn Adams *(Ind: Camrose)*, Keyston Hill Farm, Keyston, Haverfordwest, SA62 6EJ
☎ (01437) 710416
cllr.jamie.adams@pembrokeshire.gov.uk

John Seymour Allen-Mirehouse *(Ind: Hundleton)*, The Hall, Angle, Pembroke, SA71 5AN
☎ (01646) 641260
cllr.john.allen-mirehouse@pembrokeshire.gov.uk

Philip Raymond Baker *(Unaffil: Saundersfoot)*, Northover, Rushy Lake, Saundersfoot, Pembrokeshire, SA69 9PA ☎ (01834) 811298
cllr.phil.baker@pembrokeshire.gov.uk

Roderick Gwilym Bowen *(PC: Clydau)*, Tŷ Preseli, Tegryn, Llanfyrnach, Pembrokeshire, SA35 0BE ☎ (01239) 698449
cllr.rod.bowen@pembrokeshire.gov.uk

John Anthony Brinsden *(Unaffil: Amroth)*, Norton Lodge, Llanteg, Narberth, Pembrokeshire, SA67 8PS
☎ (01834) 831775 / 07970 460424
brinsden-2@supanet.com

David Michael Bryan *(Unaffil: Haverfordwest Priory)*, 60 Clover Park, Haverfordwest, Pembrokeshire, SA61 1UE
☎ (01437) 765785
cllr.david.bryan@pembrokeshire.gov.uk

Daphne Bush *(Ind: Pembroke St Mary South)*, Hollybush Cottage, 7 Golden Brake, Pembroke, Pembrokeshire, SA71 4BU
☎ (01646) 681437 / 07790310830
cllr.daphne.bush@pembrokeshire.gov.uk

John Thomas Davies *(Ind: Cilgerran)*, Cwmbetws, Eglwyswrw, Crymych, Pembrokeshire, SA41 3PL
☎ (01239) 891566
john.cwmbetws@virgin.net

Pat Davies *(Lab: Fishguard North West)*, 6 Feidr Dylan, Fishguard, Pembrokeshire, SA65 9EG
☎ (01348) 874253
cllr.pat.davies@pembrokeshire.gov.uk

David Mark Edwards *(Ind: Haverfordwest Prendergast)*, Withybrook, Withybush Road, Haverfordwest, Pembrokeshire, SA61 4BN ☎ 07838 390572
cllr.mark.edwards@pembrokeshire.gov.uk

Michael Llewellyn Evans *(Unaffil: Tenby South)*, Trem-Byr, Fourwinds Lane, Penally, Tenby, SA70 7PB
☎ (01834) 842546
cllr.mike.evans@pembrokeshire.gov.uk

Wynne Edwin Evans *(Ind: Narberth)*, Shay-Dove Cottage, 37 Old Mart Ground, Narberth, Pembrokeshire, SA67 7BR
☎ (01834) 861022 / 07867 748631
cllr.wynne.evans@pembrokeshire.gov.uk

Lyndon Leslie Frayling *(Ind: Haverfordwest Garth)*, 25 Fleming Crescent, Haverfordwest, Pembrokeshire, SA61 2SQ
☎ 07528 727581
cllr.lyndon.frayling@pembrokeshire.gov.uk

Huw Meredydd George *(Ind: Maenclochog)*, Parson's Lodge, Clunderwen, Pembrokeshire, SA66 7NQ ☎ (01437) 563065 / 07967 807908
cllr.huw.george@pembrokeshire.gov.uk

Brian John Hall *(Ind: Pembroke Dock Market)*, 2 Presely View, Pennar, Pembroke Dock, Pembrokeshire, SA72 6NP
☎ (01646) 685171
cllr.brian.hall@pembrokeshire.gov.uk

Simon Leslie Hancock *(Ind: Neyland East)*, 5 Scurlock Drive, Honeyborough, Neyland, Milford Haven, SA73 1PJ ☎ (01646) 601081
simon615@btinternet.com

Paul Harries *(Ind: Newport)*, Gwalia, East Street, Newport, Pembrokeshire, SA42 0SY
☎ (01239) 820809
cllr.paul.harries@pembrokeshire.gov.uk

Mary Umelda Havard *(Ind: Merlins Bridge)*, 10 Walters Avenue, Merlins Bridge, Haverfordwest, Pembrokeshire, SA61 1LL
☎ (01437) 765854
cllr.umelda.havard@pembrokeshire.gov.uk

Tessa Hodgson *(Unaffil: Lamphey)*, North Down, Sixth Lane, Lamphey, Pembroke, SA71 5PL
☎ (01646) 672116 / 07815582618
cllr.tessa.hodgson@pembrokeshire.gov.uk

David Kenneth Howlett *(Con: Wiston)*, Porth-y- Llyn, Llys-y-Fran, Clarbeston Road, Pembrokeshire, SA63 4RR ☎ (01437) 532523 / 07974 109329
cllr.david.howlett@pembrokeshire.gov.uk

Stanley Thomas Hudson *(Con: Milford North)*, The White House, 13 Mount Pleasant Way, Milford Haven, Pembrokeshire, SA73 1AA
☎ (01646) 693286
cllr.stanley.hudson@pembrokeshire.gov.uk

David Griffith Michael James *(Ind: St Dogmaels)*, Bronllwyn, 7 Grove Terrace, St Dogmaels, SA43 3ER ☎ (01239) 614020

Owen Watkin James *(Unaffil: Scleddau)*, Ffynnon Druidion, Goodwick, Pembrokeshire, SA64 0LD ☎ (01348) 891664
cllr.owen.james@pembrokeshire.gov.uk

Lyn Jenkins *(Ind: Solva)*, 31 Bryn Seion, Solva, Haverfordwest, Pembrokeshire, SA62 6TP
☎ (01437) 721697 / 07875 156902
cllr.lyn.jenkins@pembrokeshire.gov.uk

Michael James John *(Ind: Llangwm)*, Millbrook House, 23 Main Street, Llangwm, Haverfordwest, SA62 4HP
☎ (01437) 890175
cllr.michael.john@pembrokeshire.gov.uk

Stephen Joseph *(PC: Milford Central)*, 105 Charles Street, Milford Haven, Pembrokeshire, SA73 2HW
cllr.stephen.joseph@pembrokeshire.gov.uk

Phillip Kidney *(Unaffil: Manorbier)*, Kidbraesons, Jameston, Manorbier, Tenby, SA70 8QE
☎ (01834) 871923
cllr.phillip.kidney@pembrokeshire.gov.uk

Bob Kilmister *(Lib D: Dinas Cross)*, Fagwyr Einon, Llanychaer, Fishguard, Pembrokeshire, SA65 9SP ☎ (01348) 875566
cllr.bob.kilmister@pembrokeshire.gov.uk

Alison Lee *(Lab: Pembroke Dock Central)*, 2 Meyrick Street, Pembroke Dock, Pembrokeshire, SA72 6UT ☎ (01646) 681564
cllr.alison.lee@pembrokeshire.gov.uk

Keith Lewis *(Ind: Crymych)*, Bro-Dyfed, Crymych, Pembrokeshire, SA41 3QF ☎ (01239) 831293
cllr.keith.lewis@pembrokeshire.gov.uk

Robert Mark Lewis *(Ind: Martletwy)*, Stanley Villa, Landshipping, Narberth, Pembrokeshire, SA67 8BE
☎ (01834) 891214
cllr.rob.lewis@pembrokeshire.gov.uk

Pearl Llewellyn *(Ind: Pembroke Monkton)*, 6 School Terrace, Monkton, Pembroke, Pembrokeshire, SA71 4LH
☎ (01646) 621572
cllr.pearl.llewellyn@pembrokeshire.gov.uk

David Lloyd *(Unaffil: St Davids)*, Felin Isaf, St Davids, Pembrokeshire, SA62 6QB ☎ (01437) 720853
cllr.david.lloyd@pembrokeshire.gov.uk

Paul Miller *(Lab: Neyland West)*, 19 Westfield Drive, Honeyborough, Neyland, Pembrokeshire, SA73 1SB
cllr.paul.miller@pembrokeshire.gov.uk

Peter John Morgan *(Ind: The Havens)*, Rock House, Little Haven, Haverfordwest, SA62 3UE
☎ (01437) 781010
cllr.peter.morgan@pembrokeshire.gov.uk

Elwyn Albert Morse *(Ind: Narberth Rural)*, Ogmore House, Templeton, Narberth, Pembrokeshire, SA67 8RZ
☎ (01834) 860401
cllr.elwyn.morse@pembrokeshire.gov.uk

David James Neale *(Ind: Carew)*, The Willows, White Hill, Cresselly, Kilgetty, Pembrokeshire, SA68 0TX
☎ (01646) 651754
cllr.david.neale@pembrokeshire.gov.uk

Jonathan Nutting *(Unaffil: Pembroke St Michael)*, The Royal Oak, 138-140 Main Street, Pembroke, Pembrokeshire, SA71 4HN ☎ (01646) 682537
cllr.jonathan.nutting@pembrokeshire.gov.uk

Reg Owens *(Ind: St Ishmaels)*, Herbrandston Post Office, Herbrandston, Milford Haven, Pembrokeshire, SA73 3SJ
☎ (01646) 692203
cllr.reg.owens@pembrokeshire.gov.uk

Myles Pepper *(Ind: Fishguard North East)*, West Wales Arts Centre, 16 West Street, Fishguard, Pembrokeshire, SA65 9AE
☎ 07779 049971
cllr.myles.pepper@pembrokeshire.gov.uk

Susan Margaret Dorothy Perkins *(Lab: Pembroke Dock Llanion)*, The Powder House, Richmond Road, Llanion Park, Pembroke Dock, Pembrokeshire, SA72 6TG
☎ (01646) 681459
cllr.susan.perkins@pembrokeshire.gov.uk

Jonathan Preston *(PC: Penally)*, 5 Holloway Court, Penally, Tenby, Pembrokeshire, SA70 7NX
☎ 07792 289021
cllr.jonathan.preston@pembrokeshire.gov.uk

Gwilym Price *(Lab: Goodwick)*, Min-Yr-Ochr, Maesgwyn Road, Fishguard, Pembrokeshire SA65 9BE ☎ (01348) 875673 / 07833251139
cllr.gwilym.price@pembrokeshire.gov.uk

David John Pugh *(Ind: Kilgetty/Begelly)*, Westwinds, Carmarthen Road, Kilgetty, Pembrokeshire, SA68 0YA
☎ 0845 419 2920,
cllr.david.pugh@pembrokeshire.gov.uk

David William Mansel Rees *(Ind: Llanrhian)*, Trefochlyd Farm, Solva, Haverfordwest, Pembrokeshire, SA62 6XY ☎ (01348) 831293
cllr.david.rees@pembrokeshire.gov.uk

Thomas James Richards *(Ind: Letterston)*, St Lawrence House, St Lawrence, Wolfscastle, Haverfordwest, Pembrokeshire, SA62 5NR ☎ (01348) 840623

Kenneth Rowlands *(Ind: Johnston)*, Woodlands, Church Road, Johnston, Haverfordwest, Pembrokeshire, SA62 3HE
☎ (01437) 891069
cllr.ken.rowlands@pembrokeshire.gov.uk

David Simpson *(Ind: Lampeter Velfrey)*, County Hall, Haverfordwest, Pembrokeshire, SA61 1TP ☎ (01437) 775600
cllr.david.simpson@pembrokeshire.gov.uk

David Rhys Sinnett *(PC: Milford West)*, 126 Priory Road, Milford Haven, Pembrokeshire, SA73 2ED
☎ (01646) 698310
cllr.rhys.sinnett@pembrokeshire.gov.uk

Peter Alan Stock *(Ind: Haverfordwest Portfield)*, Plumstone Cottage, 126A Haven Road, Haverfordwest, Pembrokeshire, SA61 1DP ☎ (01437) 764039
cllr.peter.stock@pembrokeshire.gov.uk

Robert Michael Stoddart *(Unaffil: Milford Hakin)*, Court Farm, Liddeston, Milford Haven, Pembrokeshire, SA73 3QA
☎ (01646) 692758
cllr.mike.stoddart@pembrokeshire.gov.uk

Vivien Mary Stoddart *(Unaffil: Milford Hubberston)*, Court Farm, Liddeston, Milford Haven, Pembrokeshire, SA73 3QA
☎ (01646) 692758
cllr.vivien.stoddart@pembrokeshire.gov.uk

LOCAL GOVERNMENT

Clerks to the Community Councils

Ambleston Community Council,
Mrs M A Griffiths, The Garn,
Ambleston, Haverfordwest,
SA62 5RA ☎ (01437) 731339
amblestoncc@btinternet.com

Amroth Community Council,
Mrs P Davies, c/o The Barn, Amroth,
Narberth, SA67 8NP
☎ (01834) 810360
paulinetdavies@gmail.com

Angle Community Council,
Mrs S Goldsworthy, 79 Ashdale
Lane, Pembroke, SA71 4PF
☎ (01646) 687794 / 07940046762
shirlandden@btinternet.com

Boncath Community Council,
Mrs H Edwards, 23 Maes-y-Frenni,
Crymych, SA41 3QJ
☎ (01239) 831521
HilaryEdwards58@aol.com

Brawdy Community Council,
Mr S O'Connor, 10 Heol Emrys,
Fishguard, SA65 9EE
☎ (01348) 873081
sjoc57@aol.com

Burton Community Council,
Mr P Horton, Greenland,
Cucumber Hill, Clarbeston Road,
Haverfordwest, SA63 4QP
☎ (01646) 602818
burtoncommunitycouncil@tesco.net

Camrose Community Council,
Miss C Codd, Upper North Hill
Farm, Treffgarne, Haverfordwest,
SA62 5YL ☎ (01437) 741218
cherylcodd@mypostoffice.co.uk

Carew Community Council, *Mrs S
Edwards*, 43 Bartletts Well Road,
Carew Park, Sageston, Nr Tenby,
SA70 8SW ☎ (01646) 651830
edwards956@btinternet.com

Cilgerran Community Council,
Mrs V Varmey, Plas Y Wennol,
Rhoshill, Cardigan, Pembrokeshire,
SA43 2TR ☎ (01239) 841822 /
07527450496
valeria.varney@gmail.com

Clydau Community Council,
Mrs R Chambers, Brynawel, Clydey,
Llanfyrnach, SA35 0AH
☎ (01239) 698658

Clynderwen Community Council,
Mrs W Rowland, Derwen Las,
Llandissilio, Clunderwen, Pembs,
SA66 7SU ☎ (01437) 563504
derland@tiscali.co.uk

Cosheston Community Council,
Miss K Donoghue, Southlands
Farm, Cosheston, Pembroke Dock,
SA72 4TZ ☎ (01646) 682904
coshestoncc@yahoo.co.uk

Crymych Community Council,
Mrs H Edwards, 23 Maes-y-Frenni,
Crymych, SA41 3QJ
☎ (01239) 831521
HilaryEdwards58@aol.com

**Cwm Gwaun Community
Council,** *Miss G Eynon*, Glan
Gwaun, Pontfaen, Fishguard,
SA65 9SG ☎ (01348) 881366/873263
gwenno@accountants-pritchard.co.uk

Dale Community Council, *Mr H
Bishop*, Headland House, St Annís
Head, Dale, Haverfordwest,
SA62 3RT ☎ (01646) 636668
bishophc@btinternet.com

Dinas Cross Community Council,
Mr N O Thomas, Y Bont, Cwm-yr-
Eglwys, Dinas Cross, Newport,
SA42 0SN ☎ (01348) 811258
norman.thomas7@btinternet.com

**East Williamston Community
Council,** *Ms C Payne*, Ty'r
Arglwydd, Lyndhurst Avenue,
Broadmoor, Kilgetty, SA68 0RZ,
(01834) 811590 / 07791 644528,
eastwilliamstoncc@googlemail.com

Eglwyswrw Community Council,
Miss P M Griffiths, Maes-yr-Awel,
Eglwyswrw, Crymych, SA41 3PT
☎ (01239) 891466 / 841645
pam.maesyrawel@virgin.net

**Fishguard & Goodwick Town
Council,** Ms V Tyrwhitt-Walker,
Town Hall, Market Square,
Fishguard, SA65 9HE
☎ (01348) 874406
clerk@fgtc.demon.co.uk

Freystrop Community Council,
Mrs K L Roach, Bal Ami, Targate
Road, Freystrop, Haverfordwest,
SA62 4EV ☎ (01437) 890022

Haverfordwest Town Council,
Mrs J Clark, Picton House, 2 Picton
Place, Haverfordwest, SA61 2LU
☎ (01437) 763771
jane.clark@haverfordwest-town-council.co.uk

Hayscastle Community Council,
Mr W R Griffiths, Brodawel,
Hayscastle Cross, Haverfordwest,
SA62 5NY ☎ (01348) 840696

**Herbrandston Community
Council,** *Clive Griffith*, 17 Little
Castle Grove, Herbrandston,
Milford Haven, SA73 3SP
☎ (01646) 697295
herbrandstoncc@yahoo.co.uk

Hook Community Council,
Mr G Lloyd, 7 Greenhill Park Drive,
Pembroke Road, Haverfordwest,
SA61 1LS ☎ (01437) 783682
rgrahamlloyd@fsmail.net

Hundleton Community Council,
Mrs B Rapley, 2 River View,
Hundleton, Pembroke, SA71 5RH
☎ (01646) 685399
barrap1@btinternet.com

Jeffreyston Community Council,
Mrs W A Vincent, Willow Glen,
Templeton, Narberth, SA67 8RS
☎ (01834) 861940
anne.vincent@hotmail.co.uk

Johnston Community Council,
Mr G W O Nicholls, 2 Addison
Road, Haverfordwest, SA61 1UB
☎ (01437) 764316
gwonicholls@yahoo.com

Kilgetty/Begelly Community Council, *Ms L Curran*, Awel-y-Mor, Pendine, Carmarthen, Carmarthenshire, SA33 4PA
☎ (01994) 453516 / 07919 837745
kilgetty-begellycc@live.co.uk

Lampeter Velfrey Community Council, *Mrs L Thomas*, Red Hill Cottage, Mill Pond Road, Narberth, SA67 8QZ ☎ (01834) 860147
lizat1@hotmail.com

Lamphey Community Council, *Mr P T Lewis*, Malvern, The Beacon, Rosemarket, Milford Haven, SA73 1JX ☎ (01646) 600819

Letterston Community Council, *Ms P Messer*, 26 Church Road, Roch, Haverfordwest, SA62 6BG
☎ (01437) 710540
barchington@msn.com

Llanddewi Velfrey Community Council, *Mrs L Hill*, Cartrefle, Llanddewi Velfrey, Narberth, SA67 8UR ☎ (01834) 860554
lghill500@btinternet.com

Llandissilio West Community Council, *Nia Davies*, Caeglas, Llandissilio, Clunderwen, SA66 7TF
☎ (01437) 563220
niajane1@yahoo.co.uk

Llangwm Community Council, *Mrs K Codd*, Tumblewood, 70 Port Lion, Llangwm, Haverfordwest, SA62 4JT ☎ (01646) 601655
codd1946@btinternet.com

Llanrhian Community Council, *Ms V Tyrwhitt-Walker*, Plas y Mabws, Mabws Fawr, Mathry, Haverfordwest, SA62 5LL
☎ (01348) 837411
vanessa@mabws.net

Llanstadwell Community Council, *Mrs R Johnson*, Jordanston Cottage, St Maryís Park, Jordanston, Milford Haven, SA73 1HS
☎ (01646) 602818
llanstadwell@tiscali.co.uk

Llawhaden Community Council, *Mrs M Bradley*, Debros End, Llawhaden, Narberth, SA67 8DU
☎ (01437) 541448

Maenclochog Community Council, *Mr D Williams*, Ddolwen, Rosebush, Clynderwen, SA66 7QY
☎ (01437) 532465 / 07805774167
david.williams@pembrokeshire.gov.uk

Manorbier Community Council, *Mr I Morris*, 8 Mayfield Acres, Kilgetty, SA68 0UW
☎ (01834) 450064
manorbiercc@btinternet.com

Manordeifi Community Council, *Ms B Picton-Davies*, Cwmbetws, Eglwyswrw, Crymych, SA41 3PL
☎ (01239) 891285
john.cwmbetws@virgin.net

Marloes & St Brides Community Council, *Mrs Y C Evans*, Lower Mullock Farm, Marloes, Haverfordwest, SA62 3AR
☎ (01646) 636251
ycevans@hotmail.com

Martletwy Community Council, *Mrs C Clemson*, Parsonage Bungalow, Amroth, Narberth, SA67 8PR ☎ (01834) 831600
clemscr@aol.com

Mathry Community Council, *Ms V Tyrwhitt-Walker*, Plas y Mabws, Mabws Fawr, Mathry, Haverfordwest, SA62 5LL
☎ (01348) 837411
vanessa@mabws.net

Merlins Bridge Community Council, *Mrs R Johnson*, Jordanston Cottage, Jordanston, Milford Haven, SA73 1HS ☎ (01646) 602818
merlinsbridgecc@live.co.uk

Milford Haven Town Council, *Mrs M Galliford*, Town Hall, Hamilton Terrace, Milford Haven, SA73 3JW ☎ (01646) 692505
mhtownclerk@btconnect.com

Mynachlogddu Community Council, *Mr H Parri-Roberts*, Bryn Glandy, Efailwen, Clynderwen, SA66 7RS ☎ (01994) 419376
hefinroberts@tesco.net

Narberth Town Council, *Mrs C A Coaker*, Sunnyhill, Woodford Lane, Robeston Wathen, Nr Narberth, SA67 8EN ☎ (01834) 861924
caroline.coaker@btopenworld.com

Nevern Community Council, *Mrs J Weston*, Morfa Isaf, Newport, Pembs, SA42 0NT
☎ (01239) 820920

New Moat Community Council, *Mrs M Thomas*, Erwlas, New Moat, Clarbeston Road, SA63 4SA
☎ (01437) 532415

Newport Town Council, *Mrs J Weston*, Morfa Isaf, Newport, SA42 0NT ☎ (01239) 820920

Neyland Town Council, *Mrs N Caplen*, Council Offices, High Street, Neyland, Milford Haven, SA73 1TF
☎ (01646) 602873
townclerk@neyland.org.uk

Nolton & Roch Community Council, *Ms P Messer*, 26 Church Road, Roch, Haverfordwest, SA62 6BG ☎ (01437) 710540
Barchington@msn.com

Pembroke Town Council, *Mr W H Colley*, Town Hall, Main Street, Pembroke, SA71 4JS
☎ (01646) 683092
hughcolley@pembstowncouncil.plus.com

Pembroke Dock Town Council, *Ms M Saunders*, Pater Hall, Lewis Street, Pembroke Dock, SA72 6DD
☎ (01646) 684410
townclerk@thedock.org.uk

Penally Community Council, *Mr J F Everett*, Stoney Bridge, Moreton, Saundersfoot, SA69 9DX
☎ (01834) 811470
johnathan.everett@sky.com

LOCAL GOVERNMENT

Pencaer Community Council,
Ms V Tyrwhtt-Walker, Plas y
Mabws, Mabws Fawr, Mathry,
Haverfordwest, SA62 5LL
☎ (01348) 837411
vanessa@mabws.net

Puncheston Community Council,
Mr J M Griffiths, Y Garn, Ambleston,
Haverfordwest, SA62 5RA
☎ (01437) 731339

Rosemarket Community Council,
Mr P Horton, Greenland,
Cucumber Hill, Clarbeston Road,
Haverfordwest, SA63 4QP
☎ (01646) 602818
rosemarketcommunitycouncil@tesco.net

Rudbaxton Community Council,
Mr G S Elcock, Kay-Gee, 12 Elm
Park, Crundale, Haverfordwest,
SA62 4DN ☎ (01437) 763739
gselcock@yahoo.co.uk

St Davids City Town Council,
Ms H Gray, City Hall, High Street,
St. Davids, Haverfordwest,
SA62 6SD ☎ (01437) 721137
clerk@stdavids.co.uk

St Dogmaels Community Council,
Mrs S Houghton, Gwynfryn, Sarnau,
Llandysul, SA44 6QS
☎ (01239) 654408 / 07580909467
sue_houghton@hotmail.co.uk

St Florence Community Council,
Mrs S Morgan, 5 Hop Gardens
Road, Sageston, Tenby, SA70 8SF
☎ (01646) 651420 / 07795692084
samjedimorgan@hotmail.co.uk

St Ishmaels Community Council,
Mrs L Thomas, Cartref, Lindsway
Road, St Ishmaels, Haverfordwest,
SA62 3TD ☎ (01646) 636298
kenothomas@btinternet.com

**St Mary-Out-Liberty Community
Council,** *Mr B Waters,* Kai Tor,
Ragged Staff, Saundersfoot,
SA69 9HT ☎ (01834) 813665,
brianwaters74@bt.internet.com

**Saundersfoot Community
Council,** *Mr J C Griffiths,* Sunnyside,
Pentlepoir, Saundersfoot, SA69 9BN
☎ (01834) 813209
johngriffiths5316@yahoo.co.uk

Scleddau Community Council,
Mr G Stickler, Cefn-y-Dre, Fishguard,
SA65 9QS ☎ (01348) 875663
clerk@scleddaucc.org.uk

Solva Community Council,
Mr B Payne, Simpson Hill Farm,
Old Nolton Road, Simpson Cross,
Haverfordwest, SA62 6ET
☎ (01437) 711308
brucepayne241@gmail.com

Spittal Community Council,
Mrs C Williams, Daneleigh,
20 Castle Rise, Spittal, Haverfordwest,
SA62 5QW ☎ (01437) 741637
cwills1807@aol.com

Stackpole & Castlemartin,
Mrs D A James, Sampson Farm,
Stackpole, Pembroke, SA71 5DL
☎ (01646) 661395
sampsonfarm@btinternet.com

Templeton Community Council,
Mrs C Payne, Ty'r Arglwydd,
14 Lyndhurst Avenue, Broadmoor,
Kilgetty, SA68 0RZ
☎ (01834) 811590 / 07791 644528
cheryl.payne@btinternet.com

Tenby Town Council, *Andrew
Davies,* De Valence Pavilion, Upper
Frog Street, Tenby, SA70 7JD
☎ (01834) 842730
tenbytownclerk@btconnect.com

The Havens Community Council,
Mr A Sage, 10 Puffin Way,
Broadhaven, Haverfordwest,
SA62 3HP ☎ (01437) 781014
antonysage@sky.com

Tiers Cross Community Council,
Mr G W O Nicholls, 2 Addison Road,
Haverfordwest, SA61 1UB
☎ (01437) 764316
gwonicholls@yahoo.com

Trecwn Community Council,
Ms E Clark, 12 Morfa Las, Fishguard,
Pembrokeshire, SA65 9JT
☎ (01348) 872 955
elenor.clark@talktalk.net

**Uzmaston, Boulston & Slebech
Community Council,** *Mrs J Lloyd,*
18 Byron Road, Priory Park,
Haverfordwest, SA61 1RQ
☎ (01437) 779077
uzmastonboulstonslebech@gmail.com

**Walwyns Castle Community
Council,** *Mrs A Evans,* Little Fenton,
Little Haven, Haverfordwest,
SA62 3TU ☎ (01437) 781452
angela.herbie@btconnect.com

Wiston Community Council, *Mr D
L Davies,* Benlyn, Clarbeston Road,
SA63 4XA ☎ (01437) 731481
dylanldavies@hotmail.co.uk

Wolfscastle Community Council,
Rev G Eynon, The Manse,
Wolfscastle, Haverfordwest,
SA62 5NB ☎ (01437) 741335
Geoffrey@ymans.freeserve.co.uk

POWYS COUNTY COUNCIL
CYNGOR SIR POWYS

Leader
Cllr David Jones

County Hall, Llandrindod Wells,
Powys LD1 5LG
Tel: 08456 027030
Tel: (01597) 827460
Fax: (01597) 826230
Email: customer@powys.gov.uk
Website: www.powys.gov.uk

Chief Executive
Jeremy Patterson

Powys

INDEPENDENT CONTROL	Ind **48** Con **10** Lib D **8** Lab **7**	**TOTAL 73**

ELECTION RESULT 2012

	Seats	Change	Votes	Share
Independent	48	3	14,770	46.3%
Conservative	10	1	5,866	18.4%
Lib Dem	8	-7	6,244	19.6%
Labour	7	3	2,956	9.3%
Others	0	-	1,998	6.3%
Plaid Cymru	0	-	87	0.3%

Socio-economic Profile

		Rank 1<22
Area (sq km)	**5,196**	**1**
Population ('000s)	**131.3**	**11**
% able to speak Welsh	**23.9**	**8**
% born in Wales	**55.6**	**20**
% non-white ethnic groups	**2.7**	**14**
Gross rev expenditure (2011-12)	**£293.9m**	**10**
Forecast capital expenditure (2011-12)	**£51.7m**	**8**
% dwellings in Band D (2012-13)	**15.7**	**14**
Band D council tax (2011-12)	**£1,137.58**	**13**
% over retirement age	**23.1**	**2**
% pupils 5+ GCSEs A*-C (2010-11)	**74.0**	**3**
Unemployment (% claimant count 2011)	**2.4**	**20**
Index of Deprivation (2011)	**8**	**20**
(% of Authority in most deprived 30%)		

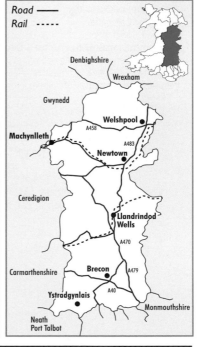

Road ——
Rail - - - - -

LOCAL GOVERNMENT

POWYS

Principal Officers

Chief Executive:	**Jeremy Patterson**
Finance & Infrastructure:	**Geoff Petty**
Law & Governance:	**Clarence Meredith**
Communities, Skills & Learning:	**Paul Griffiths**
Care & Well-being (Interim):	**Parry Davies**

Council Cabinet 2012-2013

Leader:	**David Jones** (Ind)
Property & Assets:	**Garry Banks** (Ind)
Planning:	**Graham Brown** (Ind)
Finance:	**Dai Davies** (Ind)
Children & Partnerships:	**Melanie Davies** (Unaligned)
Social Services, Care, Health & Housing:	**Rosemarie Harris** (Unaligned)
Corporate Governance:	**Gary Price** (Ind)
Human Resources:	**Gareth Ratcliffe** (Unaligned)
Highways:	**Barry Thomas** (Ind)
Learning & Leisure:	**Myfanwy Alexander** (Ind)

Committee Chairs 2012-2013

People Scrutiny Committee:	**Wynne Jones** (Ind)
Regulatory Committee:	**David Price** (Ind)
Licensing Committee:	**David Price** (Ind)
Environment, Infrastructure, Crime & Disorder Scrutiny Committee:	**Kathryn Silk** (Lib D)
Democratic Services Committee:	**Sandra Davies** (Lab)
Employment & Appeals Committee:	**John Morris** (Lib D)
Pensions & Investments Committee:	**Tony Thomas** (Ind)

Salaries

Basic Salary: £13,175 per annum
Senior Salaries Allowances:
Leader: £34,500
Cabinet Members: £24,500; Chairs of Scrutiny Committees: £21,910
Chairs of Other Committees: £21,910; Leader of Main Opposition Group: £21,910
Chair of Council: £21,375; Vice Chair of Council: £16,625

LOCAL GOVERNMENT

POWYS

Councillors   ♂ 53 ♀ 20

Chair: Cllr Susan McNicholas   Vice-Chair: Cllr John Brunt

BRECKNOCKSHIRE

Paul J Ashton *(Lib D: Brecon St Mary)*, 16 Camden Crescent, Brecon, Powys, LD3 7BY
☎ (01874) 623507
cllr.paul.ashton@powys.gov.uk

Melanie J B Davies *(Unaligned: Llangors)*, Castle House, Llangorse, Brecon, Powys, LD3 7UD
☎ (01874) 658179
cllr.melanie.davies@powys.gov.uk

Sandra C Davies *(Lab: Cwmtwrch)*, 26 Heol Maes Pica, Lower Cwmtwrch, Swansea, SA9 2PP ☎ (01639) 830835
cllr.sandra.davies@powys.gov.uk

Steve Davies *(Ind: Bronllys)*, Penyworlod, Erwood, Builth Wells, Powys, LD2 3AJ
☎ (01982) 560217
cllr.steve.davies@powys.gov.uk

Matthew J Dorrance *(Lab: Brecon St John)*, 11 Priory Hill, Brecon, Powys, LD3 9DH
☎ 07507 597503
cllr.matthew.dorrance@powys.gov.uk

Liam Fitzpatrick *(Ind: Talybont-on-Usk)*, 6 School Row, Llanfrynach, Brecon, LD3 7AZ
☎ (01874) 665519
cllr.liam.fitzpatrick@powys.gov.uk

M Rosemarie Harris *(Ind: Llangynidr)*, Berth-Y-Beili Farm, Libanus, Brecon, Powys, LD3 8ND, (01874) 623614,
cllr.rosemarie.harris@powys.gov.uk

Jeff C Holmes *(Ind: Llangattock)*, 1 Park Dive, Llangattock, Crickhowell, Powys, NP8 1PP
☎ (01873) 812053
cllr.jeff.holmes@powys.gov.uk

Geraint G Hopkins *(Ind: Gwernyfed)*, Beacons Edge, Pontithel, Brecon, Powys, LD3 0SA
☎ (01874) 712179
cllr.geraint.hopkins@powys.gov.uk

Susan McNicholas *(Lab: Ynyscedwyn)*, 6 Maesydderwen Gardens, Ystradgynlais, Swansea, SA9 1EL ☎ (01639) 849912
cllr.susan.mcnicholas@powys.gov.uk

David W Meredith *(Lab: Brecon St David Within)*, Cilmery, The Avenue, Brecon, Powys, LD3 9BG
☎ (01874) 623373
cllr.david.meredith@powys.gov.uk

Evan T Morgan *(Ind: Maescar / Llywel)*, Bailea, Maescar, Sennybridge, Brecon, Powys, LD3 3TB ☎ (01874) 636373
cllr.evan.morgan@powys.gov.uk

John G Morris *(Lib D: Crickhowell)*, Craig Barn Farm, Llangenny Lane, Crickhowell, NP8 1HB ☎ (01873) 810275
cllr.john.morris@powys.gov.uk

William D Powell *(Lib D: Talgarth)*, Middle Genffordd, Penbont Road, Talgarth, Brecon, Powys, LD3 0EH
☎ 07703 112113
cllr.william.powell@powys.gov.uk

David R Price *(Ind: Llanafanfawr)*, Noyadd, Llanddewi'r Cwm, Builth Wells, Powys, LD2 3RX
☎ (01982) 553229
cllr.david.price@powys.gov.uk

Gareth W Ratcliffe *(Unaligned: Hay)*, 14 Warren Close, Hay-On-Wye, Hereford, HR3 5EL
☎ 07974 353121
cllr.gareth.ratcliffe@powys.gov.uk

Kathryn S Silk *(Lib D: Bwlch)*, Mill Cottage, Felindre, Cwmdu, Crickhowell, Powys, NP8 1SA
☎ (01874) 730759
cllr.kathryn.silk@powys.gov.uk

D Gillian Thomas *(Ind: Yscir)*, 45 Beacons Park, Brecon, Powys, LD3 9BR ☎ (01874) 625302
cllr.gillian.thomas@powys.gov.uk

David A Thomas *(Lab: Tawe Uchaf)*, 16 Ynyswen, Penycae, Swansea, SA9 1YS
☎ (01639) 730033
cllr.david.thomas@powys.gov.uk

Tony Thomas *(Ind: Felinfach)*, Ysgubor, 1 Penmaes Barns, Llanfilo, Brecon, Powys, LD3 0RE
☎ (01874) 711607
cllr.tony.thomas@powys.gov.uk

Tim J Van-Rees *(Ind: Llanwrtyd)*, Abernant House, Llanwrtyd Wells, Powys, LD5 4RR
☎ (01591) 610552
cllr.tim.van-rees@powys.gov.uk

D Huw Williams *(Unaligned: Ystradgynlais)*, 4 Brynawel Road, Ystradgynlais, Swansea, SA9 1JT
☎ (01639) 845868
cllr.huw.williams@powys.gov.uk

Sarah L Williams *(Lab: Aber-craf)*, Oakland HouseE, Maes-Y-Fron Terrace, Abercrave, Swansea, SA9 1XE
cllr.sarah.williams@powys.gov.uk

Avril York *(Ind: Builth)*, 6 Church Street, Builth Wells, Powys, LD2 3BS ☎ (01982) 553765
cllr.avril.york@powys.gov.uk

LOCAL GOVERNMENT

MONTGOMERYSHIRE

Myfanwy Catherine Alexander *(Ind: Banwy)*, Tyn Y Gerddi, Llanfair Caereinion, Welshpool, SY21 0EF
☎ (01938) 811180
cllr.myfanwy.alexander@powys.gov.uk

Dawn Bailey *(Ind: Trewern)*, Tyn Wald, Middletown, Welshpool, SY21 8EJ ☎ (01938) 570632
cllr.dawn.bailey@powys.gov.uk

Gemma-Jane Bowker *(Lib D: Newtown Llanllwchaiarn North)*, 14 Bryn Close, Newtown, SY16 2DT ☎ (01686) 951104
cllr.gemma.bowker@powys.gov.uk

R Graham Brown *(Ind: Llandrinio)*, Preswylfa, Haughton, Llandrinio, Llanymynech, Powys, SY22 6SH ☎ (01691) 830570
cllr.graham.brown@powys.gov.uk

L V Corfield *(Ind: Forden)*, Ashbury House, Forden, Welshpool, Powys, SY21 8JJ ☎ (01938) 580725
cllr.linda.corfield@powys.gov.uk

Aled W Davies *(Con: Llanrhaeadr-ym-Mochnant / Llansilin)*, Glanogeu, Rhiwlas, Oswestry, Shropshire, SY10 7JJ ☎ (01691) 600235
cllr.aled.davies@powys.gov.uk

Dai E Davies *(Ind: Berriew)*, Maes-y-Nant, Berriew, Welshpool, Powys, SY21 8BG ☎ (01686) 640885
cllr.dai.davies@powys.gov.uk

E Rachel Davies *(Ind: Caersws)*, Red House, Caersws, Powys, SY17 5SF ☎ (01686) 688247
cllr.rachel.davies@powys.gov.uk

L Roche E Davies *(Ind: Llandinam)*, Trewythen, Llandinam, Powys, SY17 5BG ☎ (01686) 688444
cllr.roche.davies@powys.gov.uk

Viola E Evans *(Ind: Llanfair Caereinion)*, Elkhorn, Llanfair Caereinion, Welshpool, Powys, SY21 0BU ☎ (01938) 810481
cllr.viola.evans@powys.gov.uk

Russell I George *(Con: Newtown Central)*, 13 Parkers Lane, Newtown, Powys, SY16 2LT ☎ (01686) 688592
cllr.russell.george@powys.gov.uk

Peter Harris *(Con: Newtown Llanllwchaiarn West)*, Arlington, Tregynon, Newtown, Powys, SY16 3PG ☎ 07928 036749
cllr.peter.harris@powys.gov.uk

Stephen M Hayes *(Ind: Montgomery)*, Weston Hill, Montgomery, Powys, SY15 6HP ☎ (01686) 668545
cllr.stephen.hayes@powys.gov.uk

Ann Holloway *(Ind: Welshpool Llanerchyddol)*, 13 Lledan Terrace, Welshpool, Powys, SY21 7NP
cllr.ann.holloway@powys.gov.uk

Dai C Jones *(Ind: Llanbrynmair)*, 1 Tawelfan, Llan, Llanbrynmair, SY19 7DP
cllr.dai.jones@powys.gov.uk

David R Jones *(Ind: Guilsfield)*, The Bridge, Guilsfield, Welshpool, Powys, SY21 9LP ☎ (01938) 590312
cllr.david.jones@powys.gov.uk

E Arwel Jones *(Ind: Llandysilio)*, Gwynfa, Four Crosses, Llanymynech, Powys, SY22 6RJ ☎ (01691) 830248
cllr.arwel.jones@powys.gov.uk

Eldrydd M Jones *(Ind: Meifod)*, Tanyforl, Lower Hall, Meifod, Powys, SY22 6HR ☎ (01938) 501123
cllr.eldrydd.jones@powys.gov.uk

Graham M Jones *(Con: Blaen Hafren)*, Oak View, Glan-Y-Nant, Llanidloes, SY18 6PQ
cllr.graham.jones@powys.gov.uk

Joy R Jones *(Lib D: Newtown East)*, 399 Heol Pengwern, Newtown, SY16 1RG ☎ (01686) 623201
cllr.joy.jones@powys.gov.uk

Michael J Jones *(Ind: Churchstoke)*, Whym Abermule, Mongomery, Powys, SY15 6JJ ☎ (01588) 620339
cllr.michael.john.jones@powys.gov.uk

Wynne T Jones *(Ind: Dolforwyn)*, Whym Abermule, Mongomery, Powys, SY15 6JJ ☎ (01686) 630655
cllr.wynne.jones@powys.gov.uk

Francesca H Jump *(Lib D: Welshpool Gungrog)*, Glan Camas, Powis Arms, Yard, Salop Road, Welshpool, Powys, SY21 7EE ☎ (01938) 555767
cllr.francesca.jump@powys.gov.uk

Peter E Lewis *(Con: Llanfyllin)*, Caeau, Llanfyllin, Powys, SY22 5LF ☎ (01691) 648025
cllr.peter.lewis@powys.gov.uk

Darren J Mayor *(Unaligned: Llanwddyn)*, Penarth, Cregrina, Llandrindod Wells, Powys, LD1 5SF ☎ (01691) 648214
cllr.darren.mayor@powys.gov.uk

Bob Mills *(Ind: Newtown South)*, Flat 1, 16 Market Street, Newtown, SY16 2PQ ☎ (01686) 621637
cllr.bob.mills@powys.gov.uk

Gareth Morgan *(Ind: Llanidloes)*, Severn View, China Street, LLANIDLOES, Powys, SY18 6AB ☎ (01686) 413031
cllr.gareth.morgan@powys.gov.uk

Phil C Pritchard *(Ind: Welshpool Castle)*, 15 Oldford Close, Welshpool, Powys, SY21 7SX ☎ (01938) 553092
cllr.phil.pritchard@powys.gov.uk

Kath M Roberts-Jones *(Ind: Kerry)*, 56 Dolforgan View, Kerry, Newtown, Powys, SY16 4DZ ☎ (01686) 670502
cllr.kath.roberts-jones@powys.gov.uk

Joy G Shearer *(Ind: Rhiwcynon)*, Cochsidan, Tregynon, Newtown, Powys, SY16 3PU ☎ (01686) 650254
cllr.joy.shearer@powys.gov.uk

R Gwynfor Thomas *(Con: Llansanffraid)*, Pontypentre, Llansanffraid, SY22 6XP ☎ (01691) 828103
cllr.gwynfor.thomas@powys.gov.uk

W Barry Thomas *(Ind: Llanfihangel)*, Glanverniew (The Smithy), Llangyniew, Welshpool, Powys, SY21 9EH ☎ (01938) 810435
cllr.barry.thomas@powys.gov.uk

Gwilym P Vaughan *(Ind: Glantwymyn)*, Pandy, Abercegir, Machynlleth, Powys, SY20 8NR ☎ (01650) 511212
cllr.gwilym.vaughan@powys.gov.uk

J Michael Williams *(Ind: Machynlleth)*, 5 Bryn-y-Gog, Machynlleth, Powys, SY20 8HL ☎ (01654) 702517
cllr.michael.williams@powys.gov.uk

RADNORSHIRE

Garry R Banks *(Lib D: Presteigne)*, Harford House, Hereford Street, Presteigne, Powys, LD8 2AT ☎ (01544) 267212 cllr.garry.banks@powys.gov.uk

John H Brunt *(Ind: Beguildy)*, Upper Tyn-y-Cefn Barn, Lloyney, Knighton, Powys, LD7 1RH ☎ (01547) 510399 cllr.john.brunt@powys.gov.uk

Kelvyn W Curry *(Lib D: Rhayader)*, Pen-Y-Lan, Nantmel, Llandrindod Wells, Powys, LD1 6EF ☎ (01597) 822231 cllr.kelvyn.curry@powys.gov.uk

Chris Davies *(Con: Glasbury)*, Ty Gwyn, 4 Brookside, Glasbury-on-Wye, HR3 5NF cllr.chris.davies@powys.gov.uk

David O Evans *(Ind: Nantmel)*, Hafan Gymreig, Bryntirion Lane, Rhayader, Powys, LD6 5LT ☎ (01597) 810298 cllr.david.evans@powys.gov.uk

W John Evans *(Ind: Llanyre)*, Lower Trawscoed, Newbridge-On-Wye, Llandrindod Wells, Powys, LD1 6HR ☎ (01597) 860227 cllr.john.evans@powys.gov.uk

E Michael Jones *(Ind: Old Radnor)*, Weythel Farm, Old Radnor, Presteigne, Powys, LD8 2RR ☎ (01544) 370259 cllr.michael.jones@powys.gov.uk

Hywel Lewis *(Ind: Llangunllo)*, The Neuadd, Bleddfa, Knighton, LD7 1PB ☎ (01547) 550668 cllr.hywel.lewis@powys.gov.uk

Maureen C Mackenzie *(Lib D: Llanelwedd)*, Penarth, Cregrina, Llandrindod Wells, Powys, LD1 5SF ☎ (01982) 570212 cllr.maureen.mackenzie@powys.gov.uk

Peter J Medlicott *(Ind: Knighton)*, The Chestnuts, Station Road, Knighton, LD7 1DU ☎ 07972 579152 cllr.peter.medlicott@powys.gov.uk

W John T Powell *(Ind: Llanbadarnfawr)*, Rhydllyn Hydllyn, Dolau, Llandrindod Wells, LD1 6UR ☎ (01597) 851694 cllr.john.powell@powys.gov.uk

Gary D Price *(Ind: Llandrindod North)*, Tad-Cu, Almond Avenue, Llandrindod Wells, Powys, LD1 6DH ☎ (01597) 829171 cllr.gary.price@powys.gov.uk

Keith F Tampin *(Ind: Llandrindod East West)*, 56 Holcolmbe Drive, Llandrindod Wells, Powys, LD1 6DN ☎ (01597) 823263 cllr.keith.tampin@powys.gov.uk

Tom Turner *(Con: Llandrindod South)*, The Old Mill, Llanwrthwl, Llandrindod Wells, LD1 6NT ☎ (01597) 810147 cllr.tom.turner@powys.gov.uk

Gwilym Williams *(Con: Disserth & Trecoed)*, Blaenglynolwyn, Newbridge-On-Wye, Llandrindod Wells, LD1 6ND cllr.gwilym.williams@powys.gov.uk

Clerks to the Community Councils

BRECKNOCKSHIRE

Brecon Community Council, *Mrs G Rofe*, Town Clerk, Brecon Town Council, The Guildhall, Brecon, Powys, LD3 7AL ☎ (01874) 622884 brecon.guildhall@btinternet.com

Bronllys Community Council, *Denise Abberley-Williams*, The View, 1 Dolfach, Bronllys, Brecon, Powys, LD3 0BR ☎ (01874) 711835 / 07870 159777

Builth Wells Community Council, *Gareth Williams*, The Streand Hall, Strand Street, Builth Wells, LD2 3AA ☎ (01597) 860865 builthwellstowncouncil@ymail.com

Cilmery Community Council, *Mrs N Williams*, 2 Cae Llewelyn, Cilmery, Builth Wells, LD2 3FA ☎ (01982) 552580, cilmericommunitycouncil@gmail.com

Cray Community Council, *Mrs B Price*, Pantymaes, Defynnog, Brecon, Powys, LD3 8YH ☎ (01874) 636271

Crickhowell Community Council, *Mrs J Pritchard*, Wenllan Farm, Hillside, Llangattock, Crickhowell, NP8 1LH ☎ (01873) 811648 crickhowell.tc@btinternet.com

Cwmdu & District Community Council, *Major (Ret'd) R A B Doak*, 15 Danygraig, Crickhowell, NP8 1DD ☎ (01873) 811016 bob.doak1@btinternet.com

Duhonw Community Council, *Mrs E Price*, Noyadd, Llandewi'r Cwm, Builth Wells, Powys, LD2 3RX ☎ (01982) 553229

Erwood Community Council, *Mrs E G Davies*, Lower Gletwen, Gwenddwr, Builth Wells, Powys, LD2 3HJ ☎ (01982) 560648

Felinfach Community Council, *Mr R J Williams*, Y Derw, Talachddu, Brecon, LD3 0UG ☎ (01874) 625140

Glyn Tarrell Community Council, *Mr A Griffiths*, 4 Mountain View Close, Libanus, Brecon, LD3 8FB ☎ (01874) 610730 andrewgtcc@gmail.com

Gwernyfed Community Council, *Michael Hutchings*, The Tardis, Harold's Field, Boughrood, Brecon, Powys, LD3 0YQ ☎ (01874) 754654 michael@creativeorganics.co.uk

Hay-on-Wye Town Council, *Nigel Lewis*, Council Offices, Broad Street, Hay-on-Wye, Via Hereford, HR3 5BX ☎ (01497) 820296 haytownclerk@hotmail.co.uk

Honddu Isaf Community Council, *Mrs G P Williams*, Castell Fechan, Lower Chapel, Brecon, LD3 9RF

Llanafan-fawr Community Council, *Miss M Price*, Brongarth, Llanafanfawr, Builth Wells, LD2 3PH ☎ (01591) 620640

POWYS

Llanddew Community Council, *Michael Hutchings*, The Tardis, Harold's Field, Boughrood, Brecon, Powys, LD3 0YQ ☎ (01874) 754654 michael@creativeorganics.co.uk

Llanfrynach Community Council, *Barbara Smith*, Twyn Cottage, Cantref, Brecon, LD3 8LN ☎ (01874) 623947 barbara.smith777@btinternet.com

Llangammarch Community Council, *Becky Webb*, 12 Irfon Bridge Road, Builth Wells, LD2 3HF ☎ (01982) 551618 beckyhwebb@hotmail.com

Llangattock Community Council, *Mr A Morgan*, Hen Tŷ Ysgol, 1 St Cadwg's Close, Llangattock, Crickhowell, NP8 1PJ ☎ (01873) 811922 / 07919 334956 alanmorganlcc@btinternet.com

Llangors Community Council, *Mrs J Phillips*, Tysiriol, Llanfihangel Talyllyn, Brecon, LD3 7TG ☎ (01874) 658348 clerk@llangorse.org.uk

Llangynidr Community Council, *Ms S Dale*, Boathouse, Coed-yr-Ynys Road, Llangynidr, Powys, NP8 1NA ☎ (01874) 730202 sedale@btinternet.com

Llanigon Community Council, *Rosemary Vaughan*, Lower Maesterglwydd, Llanigon, Hereford, HR3 5QH ☎ (01497) 847239 blackmountains@hotmail.co.uk

Llanwrthwl Community Council, *Miss M Price*, Brongarth, Llanafanfawr, Builth Wells, LD2 3PH ☎ (01591) 620640

Llanwrtyd Wells Community Council, *Pat Dryden*, 4 Post Office Terrace, Garth, Llangammarch Wells, Powys, LD5 4AR ☎ (01591) 620287 llanwrtydtc@googlemail.com

Llywel Community Council, *Joanne Davies*, Tainewydd, Llywel, Brecon, LD3 8RF ☎ (01874) 636789

Maescar Community Council, *Sharon Pritchard*, Tycanol, Senni, Brecon, LD3 8SU ☎ (01874) 636251 clerktomaescar@gmail.com

Merthyr Cynog Community Council, *Mrs A Thomas MBE*, 66 Pendre Gardens, Brecon, Powys, LD3 9EQ ☎ (01874) 622892

Talgarth Community Council, *Mrs J M E Rumsey*, Tŷ Carrig, Bronllys Road, Talgarth, Brecon, LD3 0HH ☎ (01874) 711565 josephine@kite35.freeserve.co.uk

Talybont-on-Usk Community Council, *Katy Tutt*, 20 Dan y Gollen, Cwrt y Gollen, Crickhowell, NP8 1TN ☎ (01873) 810733 katy@katyandsteve.co.uk

Tawe Uchaf Community Council, *Mr J E Gwilym*, 8 Maes y Gorof, Ystradgynlais, Swansea, SA9 1DA ☎ (01639) 843003 elwyn@gwilym.fsworld.co.uk

Trallong Community Council, *Ruth Jefferies*, Brynteg, Trallong, Brecon, LD3 8HP ☎ (01874) 638024 ruthjefferies@hotmail.co.uk

Treflys Community Council, *Mr M R Thomas*, Maendu, Beulah, Llanwrtyd Wells, LD5 4UF ☎ (01591) 620579

Vale of Grwyney Community Council, *Maria James*, Pleasant View, Forest Coal Pit, Abergavenny, NP7 7LH ☎ (01873) 890777

Ysgir Community Council, *Mike Westhorpe*, Far Cottage, Penoyre, Brecon, LD3 9LP ☎ (01874) 623774 m.westhorpe@gmail.com

Ystradfellte Community Council, *Mrs S Harvey-Powell*, Hepste, Penderyn, Aberdare, CF44 9QA ☎ (01685) 813201 s.harvey.powell.farm@lineone.net

Ystradgynlais Community Council, *Mr D B Rees*, 14 Alder Avenue, Ystradgynlais, Swansea, SA9 1AQ, (01639) 845269, ystradtowncouncil@btinternet.com

MONTGOMERYSHIRE

Aberhafesb Community Council, *Mrs J Morgan*, Maes Hydref, Llanwnog, Powys, SY17 5PD ☎ (01686) 688638

Abermule with Llandyssil Community Council, *Mr G J Rippon*, 12 Agincourt Drive, Guilsfield, Welshpool, Powys, SY21 9NA ☎ (01938) 554065 llandyssilcommunitycouncil@yahoo.co.uk

Banwy Community Council, *Llinos Jones*, Pen Isa'r Cyffin, Dolanog, Trallwng, Powys, SY21 0NA ☎ (01938) 810750 ccBanwy@hotmail.co.uk

Bausley with Criggion Community Council, *Ms J Shaw*, 13A Maes Hafren, Crew Green, Shrewsbury, Powys, SY5 9BT ☎ (01743) 884971 jane@jsbusinessadmin.co.uk

Berriew Community Council, *Mrs K A Jones*, Dol-Hafren, Caerhowell Meadows, Caerhowell, Montgomery, Powys, SY15 6JF ☎ (01686) 668182 berriewcommunitycouncil@hotmail.co.uk

Cadfarch Community Council, *Glyn Jones*, Caerffynnon, Forge Road, Machynlleth, Powys, SY20 8EG ☎ (01654) 700122 cadfrachcc@hotmail.co.uk

Caersws Community Council, *Miss L Yapp*, Old Hall, Pontdolgoch, Caersws, Powys, SY17 5NJ ☎ (01686) 688403 clerk@caerswscommunitycouncil.co.uk

Carno Community Council, *Mr A Humphreys*, 3 Tanllyn, Carno, Caersws, Powys, SY17 5LH ☎ (01686) 420329 carnocouncil@btinternet.com

Carreghofa Community Council, *Mrs J Stanistreet*, Chapel View, Wern, Llanymynech, Powys, SY22 6PD ☎ (01691) 831413

Castle Caereinion Community Council, *Gill Wood*, Henfaes Lane, Welshpool, Powys, SY21 7BE ☎ (0800) 7831489 gilly@walesmr.com

Churchstoke Community Council,
Mr E J Humphreys, 2 Rowes Terrace,
Pool Road, Montgomery, Powys,
SY15 6QD ☎ (01686) 668790

Dwyriw Community Council,
Mrs S J Yeomans, Llwyn y Brain,
Adfa, Newtown, Powys, SY16 3DA
☎ (01938) 810394
yeomans.ranch@btinternet.com

Forden Community Council,
M Hewitt Edderton, Lodge, Forden,
Welshpool, Powys, SY21 8RZ
☎ (01938) 580121

**Glantwymyn Community
Council**, *Mr S Tudor*, Llwyn,
Cemmaes, Machynlleth, Powys,
SY20 9AA ☎ (01650) 511238

Guilsfield Community Council,
Dorothy Williams, Llwyn Derw,
Arddleen Road, Guilsfield, Welshpool,
Powys, SY21 9PR ☎ (01938) 552323
dotllwynderw@btinternet.com

Kerry Community Council, *Angela
Feltham*, Bryn Gethin, Tregynon,
Newtown, SY16 3PJ ☎ (01686) 650747
clerkkcc@gmail.com

**Llanbrynmair Community
Council**, *Undeg Griffiths*, Tynywern,
Cwmlline, Machynlleth, Powys,
SY20 9PF ☎ (01650) 511995
cwmlline@btinternet.com

Llandinam Community Council,
Irena Selwyn-Smith, Glendare,
Glan-y-Nant, Llanidloes, SY18 6PQ
☎ (01686) 413589
llandinamcc@hotmail.co.uk

**Llandrinio & Arddleen
Community Council**, *Mrs C E
Davies*, The Crest, Four Crosses,
Llanymynech, Powys, SY22 6RB
☎ (01691) 831008
davies.thecrest@virgin.net

Llandysilio Community Council,
Carol Davies, The Crest, Four
Crosses, Llanymynech, Powys,
SY22 6RB ☎ (01691) 831008
davies.thecrest@virgin.net

Llanerfyl Community Council,
Mrs L W Rees, Caerfynnon, Llanerfyl,
Welshpool, Powys, SY21 0EG
☎ (01938) 820223

**Llanfair Caereinion Town
Council**, *Mrs I Watkin*, The Coach
House, Bryn Penarth, Llanfair
Caereinion, Welshpool, Powys,
SY21 0BZ ☎ (01938) 810019
llanfairtowncouncil@gmail.com

Llanfechain Community Council,
Mrs D Crecraft, 23 Maes Dinas,
Llanfechain, Oswestry, SY22 6YR
☎ (01691) 828542

Llanfihangel Community Council,
J Gareth Thomas, Y Berth, Brynfa
Avenue, Welshpool, Powys,
SY21 7TS ☎ (01938) 554080
jgareth@tiscali.co.uk

Llanfyllin Community Council,
Mrs A Vause, Wernddu Farm,
Penybontfawr, Oswestry, Shropshire,
SY10 0HW ☎ (01691) 860748
ericvause@onetel.com

Llangedwyn Community Council,
Mrs F Holland, Tanybwlch,
Bwlchydda, Llangedwyn, Shropshire,
SY21 1HU ☎ (01743) 248899

Llangurig Community Council,
Mrs S George, Nantllemysten,
Llangurig, Llanidloes, Powys,
SY18 6RZ ☎ (01686) 440381
nantllemysten@hotmail.co.uk

Llangyniew Community Council,
J Gareth Thomas, Y Berth, Brynfa
Avenue, Welshpool, Powys,
SY21 7TS ☎ (01938) 554080
jgareth@tiscali.co.uk

Llangynog Community Council,
Mrs E Jones, 11 Dolhendre, Llangynog,
Oswestry, Shropshire, SY10 0EU

Llanidloes Town Council, *Ms S
Pritchard*, Town Hall, Great Oak
Street, Llanidloes, Powys, SY18 6BN
☎ (01686) 412353
townclerkllani@pc-q.net

**Llanidloes Without Community
Council**, *Shirley Lewis*, Tan-y Graig,
Old Hall, Llanidloes, Powys, SY18 6PW
llanidloeswithoutcc@hotmail.co.uk

**Llanrhaeadr-ym-Mochnant
Community Council**, *Mrs P M
Jones*, Cefnhir-Fawr, Llanrhaeadr ym
Mochnant, Oswestry, Shropshire,
SY10 0DZ ☎ (01691) 780344

**Llansantffraid Community
Council**, *Mrs A Davies*, Arosfa,
Llansantffraid, Powys, SY22 6AU
☎ (01691) 829060

Llansilin Community Council,
Mrs L Quance, Tyn Llan, Llansilin,
Oswestry, Powys, SY10 7QB
☎ (01691) 791692

Llanwddyn Community Council,
Graham Bradley, Blaen Hirnant,
Hirnant, Penybontfawr, Oswestry,
SY10 0HR ☎ (0845) 2935755
grahambradley@woodlandtrust.org.uk

Machynlleth Community Council,
Melanie Biffin, Y Plas, Machynlleth,
Powys, SY20 8ER ☎ (01654) 702571
mach.council@plasmachynlleth.co.uk

Manafon Community Council,
Mrs R Davies, Old Hall, Manafon,
Welshpool, Powys, SY21 8BW
☎ (01686) 650274
jrdavies@xln.co.uk

Meifod Community Council,
Mrs H Owen, Tanycoed, Meifod,
Powys, SY22 6HP ☎ (01938) 500514

Mochdre Community Council,
Kathryn Wigley, Ashford, The Bank,
Newtown, Powys, SY16 2AB
☎ (01686) 626446
kath.wigley@hotmail.co.uk

Montgomery Town Council,
Mrs G Smith, 2 Siop Fach, Kerry,
Newtown, Powys, SY16 4LD
☎ (01686) 670819
townclerk.monty@btinternet.com

**Newtown & Llanllwchaiarn Town
Council**, *Mr S Geary*, Town Clerk,
The Council Offices, The Cross,
Broad Street, Newtown, Powys,
SY16 2LS ☎ (01686) 625544
townclerk@newtown.org.uk

**Pen-y-bont-fawr Community
Council**, *Mr G D Bradley*, Blaen
Hirnant, Hirnant, Penybontfawr,
Oswestry, Powys, SY10 0HR
☎ (0845) 2935755
grahambradley@woodlandtrust.org.uk

Trefeglwys Community Council,
Ms M Shergold, Coed y Gardden,
Trefeglwys, Caersws, Powys,
SY17 5QQ ☎ (01686) 430316
trefeglwyscc@hotmail.co.uk

Tregynon Community Council,
Rachael S Jones, Cae Gwyl, 4
Minhafren, Aberhafesp, Newtown,
Powys, SY16 3HW ☎ (01686) 689128

Trewern Community Council,
Jane Shaw, 13A Maes Hafren, Crew
Green, Shrewsbury, Powys, SY5 9BT
☎ (01743) 884971
jane@jsbusinessadmin.co.uk

Welshpool Community Council,
Mr R Robinson, Triangle House,
Union Street, Welshpool, Powys,
SY21 7PG ☎ (01938) 553142
wtcouncil@btinternet.com

LOCAL GOVERNMENT

RADNORSHIRE

Abbey Cwm-hir Community Council, *Mr P Kirk*, Sunnydale, Abbeycwmhir, Llandrindod Wells, Powys, LD1 6PG ☎ (01597) 850093 abbeycwmhircc@gmail.com

Aberedw Community Council, *Mr P Batten*, The Bowling Green, Aberedw, Builth Wells, Powys, LD2 3UW ☎ (01982) 560328 clerk.aberedwcc@hotmail.co.uk

Beguildy Community Council, *Neil King*, 9 Grove Close, Knighton, LD7 1LJ ☎ (01547) 520536 neil@neilking.wanadoo.co.uk

Clyro Community Council, *Joy Thompson*, 35 Westfields, Talgarth, Brecon, Powys, LD3 0HG ☎ (01874) 711866 councilclerk@clyro.org

Disserth & Trecoed Community Council, *Mrs J Johnston*, 10 Ddole Road, Llandrindod Wells, Powys, LD1 6RF ☎ (01597) 824479 jane.johnst@btinternet.com

Gladestry Community Council, *Mrs S Croose*, Grove Farm, Huntington, Kington, Herefordshire, HR5 3PJ ☎ (01544) 370285 clerk@gladestry.org.uk

Glasbury Community Council, *Michael Hutchings*, The Tardis, Harold's Field, Boughrood, Brecon, Powys, LD3 0YQ ☎ (01874) 754654 michael@creativeorganics.co.uk

Glasgwm Community Council, *Mrs J Hammonds*, Tygwyn, Glascwm, Llandrindod Wells, Powys, LD1 5SE ☎ (01982) 570289 Jo.hammonds@powys.gov.uk

Knighton Community Council, *Neil King*, 9 Grove Close, Knighton, LD7 1LJ ☎ (01547) 520536 neil@neilking.wanadoo.co.uk

Llanbadarn Fawr Community Council, *Sheila Simpson*, Cabalfa, Crossgates, Llandrindod Wells, LD1 6RS ☎ (01597) 851361 s.simpson51@btinternet.com

Llanbadarn Fynydd Community Council, *David Jones*, The Ddol, Llanbadarn Fynydd, Llandrindod Wells, Powys, LD1 6YF ☎ (01597) 840307

Llanbister Community Council, *Mrs J Thomas*, The Lion, Llanbister, Llandrindod Wells, Powys, LD1 6TN ☎ (01597) 840224

Llanddewi Ystradenni Community Council, *Mrs S Morgan*, Dolidre, Llanddewi, Llandrindod Wells, Powys, LD1 6SE ☎ (01597) 851378

Llandrindod Wells Town Councill, *Mrs J Johnston*, Town Hall, Temple Street, Llandrindod Wells, Powys, LD1 5DL ☎ (01597) 823116 llandrindodcouncil@btconnect.com

Llanelwedd Community Council, *Mrs M Cox*, 2 Oaklands Crescent, Builth Wells, Powys, LD2 3EP ☎ (01982) 553657 megan.cox@powys.gov.uk

Llanfihangel Rhydeithion Community Council, *Mr R K J Trend*, The Crossing House, Dolau, Llandrindod Wells, LD1 5TG ☎ (01597) 851503 rtrend@btinternet.com

Llangunllo Community Council, *Mrs Y Charker*, 5 Village Close, Crossgates, Llandrindod Wells, Powys, LD1 6TB ☎ (01597) 851860

Llanyre Community Council, *Mrs L Brown*, Dingle View, Franksbridge, Llandrindod Wells, Powys, LD1 5SA ☎ (01982) 570317 rbrown212@btinternet.com

Nantmel Community Council, *Ms J Johnston*, 10 Ddole Road, Llandrindod Wells, Powys, LD1 6PF ☎ (01597) 824479 jane.johnst@btinternet.com

New Radnor Community Council, *Mrs P Everett*, Pyecorner, Llandegley, Llandrindod Wells, Powys, LD1 5UE ☎ (01597) 851594 pyecorner@tiscali.co.uk

Old Radnor Community Council, *Mrs A Jauncey*, Burlingjobb Farm, Burlingjobb, Presteigne, Powys, LD8 2PW ☎ (01544) 230247

Painscastle Community Council, *Mr R E Price*, Trewyrlod, Painscastle, Builth Wells, Powys, LD2 3JQ ☎ (01497) 851244 reprice@hotmail.co.uk

Pen-y-bont & Llandegley Community Council, *Mrs M Powell*, Trawsty Newydd, Penybont, Llandrindod Wells, Powys, LD1 5SR ☎ (01597) 851896 monica.powell@powys.gov.uk

Presteigne & Norton Community Council, *Mrs T Price*, Garn Farm, Chapel Lawn, Bucknall, SY7 0BT ☎ (01547) 528575 pntc@hotmail.com

Rhayader Community Council, *Mr C Baker*, Glennydd, South Street, Rhayader, Powys, LD6 5BH ☎ (01597) 810405

St Harmon Community Council, *Mark Thompson*, Hirfon, Pant-y-Dwr, Rhayader, LD6 5LR ☎ (01597) 870694

Whitton Community Council, *Helen Carter*, 2 Lords Land, Whitton, Presteigne, LD7 1NJ ☎ 07813 718714 helencarter@tesco.net

RHONDDA CYNON TAF COUNTY BOROUGH COUNCIL
CYNGOR BWRDEISTREF SIROL RHONDDA CYNON TAF

The Pavillions, Cambrian Park,
Clydach Vale, Tonypandy CF40 2XX
Tel: (01443) 424000
Fax: (01443) 424027
Website:
www.rhondda-cynon-taf.gov.uk

Leader
Cllr Anthony Christopher

RHONDDA·CYNON·TAF

Chief Executive
Mr Keith Griffiths

LABOUR CONTROL	Lab **60** PC **9** Ind **4** Con **1** Lib D **1**	**TOTAL 75**

ELECTION RESULT 2012

	Seats	Change	Votes	Share
Labour	60	14	54,126	56.5%
Plaid Cymru	9	-10	27,318	28.5%
Independent	4	-2	8,246	8.6%
Lib Dem	1	-2	2,350	2.5%
Conservative	1	-	2,296	2.4%
Others	0	-	1,427	1.5%

Socio-economic Profile

		Rank 1<22
Area (sq km)	424	13
Population ('000s)	234.3	2
% able to speak Welsh	18.0	13
% born in Wales	89.9	4
% non-white ethnic groups	2.6	16
Gross rev expenditure (2011-12)	£566.4m	2
Forecast capital expenditure (2011-12)	£55.2m	6
% dwellings in Band D (2012-13)	8.2	20
Band D council tax (2011-12)	£1,303.18	4
% over retirement age	17.1	19
% pupils 5+ GCSEs A*-C (2010-11)	64.4	15
Unemployment (% claimant count 2011)	4.5	6
Index of Deprivation (2011)	51	3
(% of Authority in most deprived 30%)		

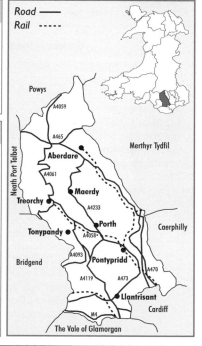

Road ———
Rail - - - - -

LOCAL GOVERNMENT

Principal Officers

Chief Executive: **Keith Griffiths**
Group Director Corporate Services: **Steve Merritt**
Group Director of Community & Children's Services: **Ellis Williams**
Group Director of Environmental Services: **George Jones**
Director of Education & Lifelong Learning: **Chris Bradshaw**
Director of Finance: **Chris Lee**
Director of Human Resources: **Tony Wilkins**
Director of Legal & Democratic Services: **Paul Lucas**

Cabinet Members 2012-2013

Leader & Chair of Cabinet: **Anthony Christopher** (Lab)
Deputy Leader & Economic Development & Community Safety: **Paul Cannon** (Lab)
Frontline Services: **Andrew Morgan** (Lab)
Council Business & Public Relations: **Maureen Webber** (Lab)
Human Resources & Service Improvement: **Clayton Willis** (Lab)
Education, Skills & Lifelong Learning: **Eudine Hanagan** (Lab)
Partnerships & Adults' Social Services: **Mike Forey** (Lab)
Social Justice & Customer Care: **Craig Middle** (Lab)
Sustainable Development, Leisure & Tourism: **Robert Bevan** (Lab)
Children's Social Services: **Annette Davies** (Lab)

Committees & Chairs 2012-2013

Development Control Committee: **Robert McDonald** (Lab)
Licensing Committee: **Adam Fox** (Lab)
Overview & Scrutiny Committee: **Roger Turner** (Lab)
Audit Committee: **Tba**
Education & Lifelong Learning Scrutiny Committee: **Joyce Cass** (Lab)
Environmental Services Scrutiny Committee: **Geraint Davies** (PC)
Corporate Services Scrutiny Committee: **Graham Stacey** (Lab)
Community & Children's Services Scrutiny Committee: **Margaret Davies** (Lab)
Democratic Services Committee: **Pauline Jarman** (PC)

Salaries

Basic Salary: £13,175 per annum
Senior Salaries: Leader: £39,925; Deputy Leader: £23,925
Cabinet Members: £18,725; Chairs of Scrutiny Committees: £8,735
Chairs of Other Committes: £8,735
Chair of Democratic Services Committee: No remuneration
Leader of Main Opposition Group: £8,735

Councillors ♂ 47 ♀ 28

Chair: Cllr Doug Williams Vice-Chair: Cllr Ann Crimmings

Mark Adams *(Lab: Tylorstown)*, 22 Mackintosh Road, The Common, Pontypridd, CF37 4AG
☎ (01443) 491453
Lewis.M.Adams@rhondda-cynon-taff.gov.uk

Paul Baccara *(Ind: Talbot Green)*, Lanelay House, Lanelay Road, Talbot Green, Pontyclun, CF72 8HY
☎ (01443) 662079
Paul.Baccara@Rhondda-Cynon-Taff.gov.uk

Teressa Bates *(Lab: Hawthorn)*, Pitlochry, Oakfield, r/o Spencer Place, Hawthorn, Pontypridd, CF37 5AF ☎ (01443) 662079
Teressa.Bates@rhondda-cynon-taff.gov.uk

Robert Bevan *(Lab: Tylorstown)*, 7 Church Terrace, Tylorstown, Ferndale, CF43 3AB
☎ (01443) 756746
Robert.Bevan@rhondda-cynon-taff.gov.uk

Helen Boggis *(Lab: Penywaun)*, 16 Haulfryn, Penywaun, Aberdare, CF44 9DG ☎ 07780435989
Helen.Boggis@rhondda-cynon-taff.gov.uk

Jill Bonetto *(Lab: Taffs Well)*, 12 West View, Tŷ Rhiw, Taffs Well, Cardiff, CF15 7SF ☎ 07806506018
Jill.Bonetto@rhondda-cynon-taff.gov.uk

Steven Bradwick *(Lab: Aberdare East)*, 69 Monk Street, Aberdare, CF44 7PA ☎ (01685) 877156
Steven.A.Bradwick@rhondda-cynon-taff.gov.uk

Jacqui Bunnage *(Lab: Llantwit Fardre)*, 3 St Andrew's Close, Llantwit Fardre, Pontypridd, CF38 2NN ☎ (01443) 205004
Jacqui.Bunnage@rhondda-cynon-taff.gov.uk

Anita Calvert *(Lab: Aberaman South)*, 156 Brynmair Road, Godreaman, Aberdare, CF44 6LT
☎ (01685) 877488
Anita.Calvert@rhondda-cynon-taff.gov.uk

Paul Cannon *(Lab: Ystrad)*, Maindy Farm House, The Parade, Ton Pentre, Pentre, CF41 7EX
☎ 07795 391706
Paul.Cannon@rhondda-cynon-taff.gov.uk

Steve Carter *(Lab: Pontypridd Town)*, Tŷ Pen, Darren Ddu, 16 Pen-Y-Darren Close, Graigwen, Pontypridd, CF37 2ES
☎ (01443) 406355
Stephen.Carter@rhondda-cynon-taff.gov.uk

Joyce Cass *(Lab: Graig)*, Woodland House, Llantrisant Road, Pontypridd, CF37 1PG ☎ (01443) 403458
Joyce.Cass@rhondda-cynon-taff.gov.uk

Anthony Christopher *(Lab: Aberaman North)*, 14 Curre Street, Aberaman, Aberdare, CF44 6UF
☎ (01685) 875894
Anthony.Christopher@rhondda-cynon-taff.gov.uk

Ann Crimmings *(Lab: Aberdare West / Llwydcoed)*, 8 Maesycoed, Cwmdare, Aberdare, CF44 8RG
☎ (01685) 876456
Ann.Crimmings@rhondda-cynon-taff.gov.uk

John David *(Lab: Tonteg)*, 21 Monmouth Close, Tonteg, Pontypridd, CF38 1HU
☎ (01443) 203670
John.David@rhondda-cynon-taff.gov.uk

Albert Davies *(Lab: Abercynon)*, 7a Elizabeth Street, Mountain Ash, CF45 4NS ☎ (01443) 740655 / 07780466151
Alby.Davies@rhondda-cynon-taff.gov.uk

Annette Davies *(Lab: Ferndale)*, 34 North Road, Ferndale, CF43 4PS
☎ (01443) 731357
Annette.Davies@rhondda-cynon-taff.gov.uk

Cennard Davies *(PC: Treorchy)*, Myrtle Hill, Treorchy, CF42 6PF
☎ (01443) 435563
Cennard.Davies@rhondda-cynon-taff.gov.uk

John Davies *(Lab: Aberdare West / Llwydcoed)*, 3 Gadlys Street, Aberdare, CF44 8BG
☎ (01685) 551365
John.Davies2@rhondda-cynon.taff.gov.uk

Geraint Davies *(PC: Treherbert)*, 6 St. Maryís Close, Treherbert, Treorchy, CF42 5RL
☎ (01443) 771850
Geraint.R.Davies@rhondda-cynon-taff.gov.uk

Margaret Davies *(Lab: Porth)*, 28 Caemawr Gardens, Porth, CF39 9DB ☎ (01443) 684114
Margaret.Davies2@rhondda-cynon-taff.go.uk

Linda De Vet *(Lab: Aberaman North)*, 36 Gwawr Street, Aberaman, Aberdare, CF44 6YP
☎ (01685) 872127
Linda.DeVet@rhondda-cynon-taff.gov.uk

Jeffrey Elliott *(Lab: Cwmbach)*, 5 Greenfield Terrace, Cwmbach, Aberdare, CF44 0BG
☎ 07415 269985
Jeffrey.Elliott@rhondda-cynon-taff.gov.uk

Sêra Evans-Fear *(PC: Treorchy)*, 32 Dinam Park, Ton Pentre, RCT, CF41 7DX ☎ (01443) 442614
treorci@yahoo.com

Michael Forey *(Lab: Aberdare East)*, 10 The Walk, Abernant, Aberdare, CF44 0RQ
☎ (01685) 882629
Mike.Forey@rhondda-cynon-taff.gov.uk

Adam Fox *(Lab: Penrhiwceiber)*, 12 Monmouth Street, Penrhiwceiber, Mountain Ash, CF45 3NJ ☎ (01443) 475556
Adam.S.Fox@rhondda-cynon-taff.gov.uk

Margaret Griffiths *(Lab: Pontyclun)*, 6 Llantrisant Road, Pontyclun, CF72 9DQ
☎ (01443) 229301
Margaret.Griffiths@rhondda-cynon-taff.gov.uk

Paul Griffiths *(Lab: Pontyclun)*, 6 Llantrisant Road, Pontyclun, CF72 9DQ ☎ (01443) 229301
Paul.Griffiths@rhondda-cynon-taff.gov.uk

Eudine Hanagan *(Lab: Tonyrefail West)*, 67 Tylcha Ganol, Tonyrefail, Porth, CF39 8BY
☎ (01443) 670862/(01443) 424199
Eudine.Hanagan@rhondda-cynon-taff.gov.uk

Glynne Holmes *(Lab: Llantrisant Town)*, Castle Lodge, Yr Allt, Llantrisant, CF72 8EF
☎ (01443) 225678
Glynne.Holmes@rhondda-cynon-taff.gov.uk

LOCAL GOVERNMENT

Geraint Hopkins *(Lab: Llanharan)*,
20 Coed Bychan Crescent,
Llanharan, Pontyclun, CF72 9PQ
☎ 07813 814257
Geraint.E.Hopkins@rhondda-cynon-taff.gov.uk

Philip Howe *(Ind: Ferndale)*,
25 Frederick Street, Ferndale,
CF43 4HR ☎ 07779 278437
Philip.Howe@rhondda-cynon-taff.gov.uk

Joel James *(Dem A: Llantwit
Fardre)*, 9 Queenís Drive, Crown Hill
Estate, Llantwit Fardre, Pontypridd,
CF38 2NT ☎ (01443) 204009
Joel.S.James@rhondda-cynon-taff.gov.uk

Pauline Jarman *(PC: Mountain Ash
East)*, 3 Middle Row, Cwmpennar,
Mountain Ash, CF45 4DN
☎ (01443) 473241

Sylvia Jones *(Lab: Llwynypia)*,
62 Eleanor Street, Tonypandy,
CF40 1DP ☎ (01443) 422927
Sylvia.J.Jones@rhondda-cynon-taff.gov.uk

Lionel Langford *(Lab: Ynyshir)*,
1 Heol-y-Twyn, Wattstown,
CF39 0PS ☎ (01443) 730649
Lionel.Langford@rhondda-cynon-taff.gov.uk

Rhys Lewis *(Lab: Abercynon)*,
34 North Street, Abercynon,
CF45 4ST ☎ (01443) 742160 /
07725953327
Rhys.Lewis@rhondda-cynon-taff.gov.uk

Christina Leyshon *(Lab: Rhondda)*,
Tŷ Berw, Hafod Lane, Hopkinstown,
Pontypridd, CF37 2PF
☎ (01443) 402140
Christina.Leyshon@rhondda-cynon-taff.gov.uk

Simon Lloyd *(Lab: Mountain Ash
West)*, 5 Gwernifor Street,
Mountain Ash, CF45 3NA
☎ (01443) 478221
Simon.Lloyd@rhondda-cynon-taff.gov.uk

Robert McDonald *(Lab: Tonyrefail
East)*, 42 Winslade Avenue,
Tonyrefail, Porth, CF39 8NW
☎ (01443) 676551
Robert.McDonald@rhondda-cynon-taff.gov.uk

Craig Middle *(Lab: Tonypandy)*,
Ty Gwyn, Wyndham Street,
Penygraig, Tonypandy, CF40 1EP
☎ 07720 038283
Craig.J.Middle@rhondda-cynon-taff.gov.uk

Keiron Montague *(Lab: Maerdy)*,
29 Blake Street, Maerdy, CF43 4AH
☎ (01443)-265944
Keiron.Montague@rhondda-cynon-taff.gov.uk

Andrew Morgan *(Lab: Mountain
Ash West)*, 13 Rock Street,
Mountain Ash, CF45 3LP
☎ (01443) 479545
Andrew.Morgan2@rhondda-cynon-taff.gov.uk

Barrie Morgan *(Lab: Cilfynydd)*,
2 Heol Gronfa, Cilfynydd,
Pontypridd, CF37 4HE
☎ (01443) 263950
Barrie.J.Morgan@rhondda-cynon-taff.gov.uk

Karen Morgan *(PC: Hirwaun)*,
11 Lisburn Rise, Hirwaun, Aberdare,
CF44 9TR ☎ (01685) 812344
Karen.Morgan2@rhondda-cynon-taff.gov.uk

Mark Norris *(Lab: Cwm Clydach)*,
26 Wern Street, Clydach Vale,
Tonypandy, CF40 2BQ
☎ (01443) 435322
Mark.A.Norris@rhondda-cynon-taff.gov.uk

Irene Elizabeth Pearce *(PC:
Treherbert)*, 137 Dumfries Street,
Treherbert, CF42 5PY
☎ 07876054424
Irene.E.Pearce@rhondda-cynon-taff.gov.uk

Sue Pickering *(Lab: Ynysybwl)*,
1 Windsor Cottages, Ynysybwl,
Pontypridd, CF37 3HS
☎ (01443) 799264 / 07813 534395
Sue.Pickering@rhondda-cynon-taff.gov.uk

Steve Powderhill *(Lab: Treforest)*,
124 Broadway, Treforest, CF37 1BE
☎ (01443) 719184
Steve.Powderhill@rhondda-cynon-taff.gov.uk

Michael Powell *(Dem A: Trallwng)*,
8 The Parade, Pontypridd, CF37 4PU
☎ 07779 337839
Michael.J.Powell@rhondda-cynon-taff.gov.uk

Kenneth Privett *(Lab: Penygraig)*,
56 Hendrecafn Road, Penygraig,
Tonypandy, CF40 1LW
☎ (01443) 435037

Sharon Rees *(Lab: Aberdare West /
Llwydcoed)*, 27 Birchgrove, Landare,
Aberdare, CF44 8DP
☎ (01685) 882990
Sharon.Rees2@rhondda-cynon-taff.gov.uk

Shelley Rees-Owen *(PC: Pentre)*,
9 Crawshay Street, Ton-Pentre,
Rhondda, CF41 7EP
☎ (01443) 440788 / 07855 490582
Shelley.Rees-Owen@rhondda-cynon-taff.gov.uk

Aurfron Roberts *(Lab: Gilfach
Goch)*, 44 Oak Street, Gilfach Goch,
Porth, CF39 8UG
☎ (01443) 674032
Aurfron.Roberts@rhondda-cynon-taff.gov.uk

Joy Rosser *(Lab: Trealaw)*, 136 Rhys
Street, Trealaw, CF40 2QQ
☎ (01443) 434810 / 07977 012784
Joy.Rosser@rhondda-cynon-taff.gov.uk

Graham Smith *(Lab: Porth)*,
98 Birchgrove Street, Porth,
CF39 9UT ☎ (01443) 684993
Graham.Smith@rhondda-cynon.taff.gov.uk

Robert Smith *(Lab: Rhondda)*,
17 Penylan Road, Maesycoed,
Pontypridd, CF37 1EG
☎ (01443) 409925
Robert.W.Smith@rhondda-cynon-taff.gov.uk

Graham Stacey *(Lab: Church
Village)*, 6 Llys Coed Derw, Llantwit
Fardre, CF38 2JB ☎ (01443) 203152
Graham.Stacey@rhondda-cynon-taff.gov.uk

Barry Stephens *(Lab: Lanharry)*,
Hazeldene, Brynna Road, Pencoed,
Bridgend, CF35 6PG
☎ (01656) 864944 / 07768 100210
Barry.Stephens2@rhondda-cynon-taff.gov.uk

Margaret Tegg *(Lab: Cymmer)*,
70 Rhiwgarn Road, Trebanog,
Porth, CF39 9HJ ☎ (01443) 687265
Margaret.Tegg@rhondda-cynon-taff.gov.uk

Graham Thomas *(Lab: Rhigos)*,
10 Greenwood Drive, Hirwaun,
Aberdare, CF44 9QZ
☎ 07805 037406
Graham.P.Thomas@rhondda-cynon-taff.gov.uk

Roger Turner *(Lab: Brynna)*,
10 Red Roofs Close, Brynna Road,
Pencoed, CF35 6PH
Roger.K.Turner@rhondda-cynon-taff.gov.uk

Lyndon Walker *(Ind: Tonteg)*,
15 Carmarthen Drive, Tonteg,
Pontypridd, CF38 1HY
☎ 07747 392428
Lyndon.Walker@rhondda-cynon-taff.gov.uk

Jane Ward *(Lab: Penrhiwceiber)*, Eirianfa, Woodfield Terrace, Penrhiwceiber, Mountain Ash, CF45 3UT ☎ (01443) 476000
Jane.Ward@rhondda-cynon-taff.gov.uk

Paul Wasley *(Dem A: Tonyrefail East)*, Linsdale, Gwern Heulog, Coedely, Tonyrefail, CF39 8BJ ☎ 07971 683338
Paul.Wasley@rhondda-cynon-taff.gov.uk

Malcolm Watts *(Lab: Ystrad)*, 5 Bodringallt Terrace, Ystrad, Pentre, CF41 7QD ☎ (01443) 438045
Malcolm.J.Watts@rhondda-cynon-taff.gov.uk

Maureen Weaver *(PC: Pentre)*, 8 Parry Street, Ton-Pentre, Rhondda, CF41 7AG ☎ (01443) 434558
Maureen.Weaver@rhondda-cynon-taff.gov.uk

Maureen Webber *(Lab: Rhydfelin Central)*, 7 Gellidawel Road, Rhydyfelin, Pontypridd, CF37 5PR ☎ (01443) 409008
Maureen.Webber@rhondda-cynon-taff.gov.uk

Emyr Webster *(PC: Treorchy)*, 129 High Street, Treorchy, CF42 6PA ☎ 07828 019431
Emyr.J.Webster@rhondda-cynon-taff.gov.uk

Dennis Weeks *(Lab: Penygraig)*, 24 Bank Street, Penygraig, Tonypandy, CF40 1PJ ☎ (01443) 439581
William.D.Weeks@rhondda-cynon-taff.gov.uk

Christopher Williams *(Lab: Cymmer)*, 190 High Street, Cymmer, Porth, CF39 9AW ☎ (01443) 687386
Christopher.J.Williams3@rhondda-cynon-taff.gov.uk

Doug Williams *(Lab: Glyncoch)*, Hafen-y-Graig, 13 Westfield Road, Glyncoch, Pontypridd, CF37 3AG ☎ (01443) 403512
Doug.Williams@rhondda-cynon-taff.gov.uk

Tina Williams *(Lab: Aberaman South)*, 101 Fforchaman Road, Cwmaman, Aberdare, CF44 6NF ☎ 07972 367569
Tina.Williams@rhondda-cynon-taff.gov.uk

Clayton Willis *(Lab: Tyn-y-Nant)*, 64 Moorland Crescent, Tynant, Beddau, Pontypridd, CF38 2DW ☎ (01443) 206805
Clayton.Willis@rhondda-cynon-taff.gov.uk

Richard Yeo *(Lab: Beddau)*, 6 Castleford Close, Gwaun Miskin, Beddau, Pontypridd, CF38 2RW ☎ (01443) 201972
Richard.Yeo@rhondda-cynon-taff.gov.uk

Clerks to the Community Councils

Gilfach Goch Community Council, *Mrs E Jones*, 19 Wood Street, Gilfach Goch, Rhondda Cynon Taf, CF39 8UF ☎ (01443) 673415

Hirwaun & Penderyn Community Council, *Mr M Burke*, Village Hall, Hirwaun, Aberdare, CF44 9SL ☎ (01685) 811566

Llanharan Community Council, *P Davies*, 71 The Dell, Tonteg, Pontypridd, CF38 1TG ☎ (01443) 218154

Lanharry Community Council, *Mrs G Lewis*, Groes Sannor, Degar Road, Llanharry, Pontyclun, CF72 9JX ☎ (01443) 223007

Llantrisant Town Council, *Mrs A Jenkins*, New Parish Offices, Caerlan Hall, Newbridge Road, Llantrisant, CF72 8EX ☎ (01443) 223796

Llantwit Fardre Community Council, *Ms L Handley*, Parish Hall, Main Road, Church Village, Pontypridd, CF38 1PY ☎ (01443) 209779

Pontyclun Community Council, *Mr G Lewis*, Mandalay, Cowbridge Road, Talygarn, Pontyclun, CF7 9BZ ☎ (01443) 227094

Pontypridd Town Council, *Mr G Williams*, Civic Offices, 133 Berw Road, Pontypridd, CF37 2AA ☎ (01443) 490740

Rhigos Community Council, *Mrs S H Powell*, Llwynfedwen Farm, Hpeste, Penderyn, Aberdare, CF44 9QA ☎ (01685) 813201

Taffs Well Community Council, *Mr D Allinson*, 28 Mill Close, Llanishen, Cardiff, CF14 0XQ ☎ (07815) 913417

Tonyrefail Community Council, *Mrs P Williams*, Trane Cemetery Office, Gilfach road, Tonyrefail, CF39 8HL ☎ (01443) 673991

Ynysybwl Coedycwm Community Council, *Mrs P Williams*, 2 Heol Pen y Parc, Coedycwm, Pontypridd, CF37 3JL ☎ (01443) 790673

LOCAL GOVERNMENT

CITY AND COUNTY OF SWANSEA
DINAS A SIR ABERTAWE

Civic Centre, Oystermouth
Road, Swansea SA1 3SN
Tel: (01792) 636000
Fax: (01792) 636340
Website: www.swansea.gov.uk

Leader
Cllr David Phillips

CITY AND COUNTY OF SWANSEA
DINAS A SIR ABERTAWE

Chief Executive
Jack Straw

LABOUR CONTROL

Lab **49** Lib D **12** Oth **5** Con **4** Ind **2**

TOTAL 72

ELECTION RESULT 2012

	Seats	Change	Votes	Share
Lab	49	19	79,341	53.4%
Lib D	12	-11	25,967	17.5%
Others	5	4	10,394	7.0%
Con	4	-	15,961	10.7%
Ind	2	-11	9,455	6.4%
PC	0	-1	7,363	5.0%

Socio-economic Profile

		Rank 1<22
Area (sq km)	378	14
Population ('000s)	232.5	3
% able to speak Welsh	16.2	19
% born in Wales	82.1	8
% non-white ethnic groups	4.8	4
Gross rev expenditure (2011-12)	£514.5m	3
Forecast capital expenditure (2011-12)	£64.4m	4
% dwellings in Band D (2012-13)	14.4	16
Band D council tax (2011-12)	£1,161.65	11
% over retirement age	18.3	14
% pupils 5+ GCSEs A*-C (2010-11)	65.8	13
Unemployment (% claimant count 2011)	3.5	15
Index of Deprivation (2011)	32	10
(% of Authority in most deprived 30%)		

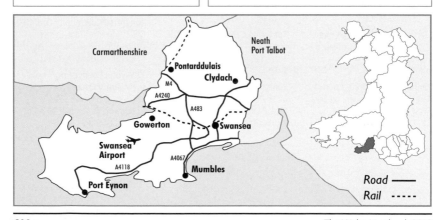

LOCAL GOVERNMENT

SWANSEA

Principal Officers

Chief Executive:	**Jack Straw**
Corporate Director - Social Services:	**Phil Hodgson**
Corporate Director - Education:	**Richard Parry**
Corporate Director - Environment:	**Reena Owen**
Corporate Director - Regeneration & Housing:	**Phil Roberts**

Cabinet Members 2012-2013

Leader / Anti-Poverty:	**David Phillips** (Lab)
Deputy Leader / Citizen & Community Engagement & Democracy:	**Christine Richards** (Lab)
Place:	**June Burtonshaw** (Lab)
Finance & Resources:	**Rob Stewart** (Lab)
Opportunities for Children & Young People:	**Mitchell Theaker** (Lab)
Learning Skills:	**William Evans** (Lab)
Regeneration:	**Nick Bradley** (Lab)
Sustainability:	**Sybil Crouch** (Lab)
Well-being:	**Mark Child** (Lab)
Target Areas:	**Ryland Doyle** (Lab)

Committee Chairs 2012-2013

Cabinet Committee:	**David Phillips** (Lab)
Council Committee:	**Des Thomas** (Lab)
Licensing Committee & Licensing Sub Committee:	**Penny Matthews** (Lab)
Democratic Services Committee:	**Mary Jones** (Lib D)
Development Management & Control Committee:	**Robert Francis-Davies** (Lab)
Equalities Committee:	**Fiona Gordon** (Lab)
Performance & Delivery Committee:	**Des Thomas** (Lab)
People Scrutiny Board:	**Mike Day** (Lib D)
Place Scrutiny Board:	**John Newbury** (Lib D)
Stronger & Safer Communities Scrutiny Board:	**Uta Clay** (Lab)

Salaries

Basic Salary: £13,175; Senior Salaries: Leader: £52,700; Deputy Leader: £37,100
Cabinet Member: £31,900; Chairs of Scrutiny Committees: £21,910
Chairs of Other Committees: £21,910
Leader of Main Opposition Group: £21,910; Leaders of all other Groups: £16,920
Civic Head: £23,715; Deputy Civic Head: £18,445

Councillors ♂ 44 ♀ 28

Lord Mayor: Cllr Dennis James Deputy Lord Mayor: Cllr June Stanton

John Bayliss (Lab: Uplands),
160 King Edward Road, Basement
Flat, Uplands, Swansea, SA1 4LW
☎ 07936 349314
John.Bayliss@swansea.gov.uk

Peter Black (Lib D: Cwmbwrla),
115 Cecil Street, Manselton,
Swansea, SA5 8QL
☎ (01792) 473743
peter.black@swansea.gov.uk

Nick Bradley (Lab: Townhill),
257 Carmarthen Road, Cwmbwrla,
Swansea, SA5 8NJ
☎ (01792) 474715
nicholas.bradley@swansea.gov.uk

LOCAL GOVERNMENT

June Burtonshaw *(Lab: Penderry)*, 20 Church Gardens, Cockett, Swansea, SA2 0FE ☎ (01792) 581407 june.burtonshaw@swansea.gov.uk

Mark Child *(Lab: West Cross)*, 35 Riversdale Road, West Cross, Swansea, SA3 5PX ☎ (01792) 518473 mark.child@swansea.gov.uk

Ann Cook *(Lab: Cockett)*, 1216 Carmarthen Road, Fforestfach, Swansea, SA5 4BN ☎ (01792) 539791 Ann.Cook@swansea.gov.uk

Anthony Colburn *(Con: Oystermouth)*, 14 St Peters Road, Newton, Swansea, SA3 4SB ☎ (01792) 362457 tony.colburn@swansea.gov.uk

David Cole *(Lab: Penyrheol)*, 209 Frampton Road, Gorseinon, Swansea, SA4 4FX ☎ (01792) 895602 David.Cole@swansea.gov.uk

Uta Clay *(Lab: Llansamlet)*, 2 Greys Terrace, Birchgrove, Swansea, SA7 9QB ☎ 07970 052389 Uta.Clay@swansea.gov.uk

Sybil Crouch *(Lab: Castle)*, 13 Oaklands Terrace, Swansea, SA1 6JJ ☎ (01792) 646004 / 07929 053858 Sybil.Crouch@swansea.gov.uk

Jan Curtice *(Lab: Penyrheol)*, Bidna, 22 Dyffryn Road, Gorseinon, Swansea, SA4 6BB ☎ (01792) 417563 / 07841 580604 Jan.Curtice@swansea.gov.uk

John Davies *(Lab: Morriston)*, 9 Elizabeth Close, Ynysforgan, Swansea, SA6 6RW ☎ (01792) 773362 john.davies@swansea.gov.uk

Nick Davies *(Lab: Uplands)*, 60 Glanbrydan Avenue, Uplands, Swansea, SA2 0HY ☎ 07951 342740 Nick.Davies2@swansea.gov.uk

Mike Day *(Lib D: Sketty)*, 120 Rhyd-y-Defaid Drive, Sketty, Swansea, SA2 8AW ☎ (01792) 297792 mike.day@swansea.gov.uk

Phillip Downing *(Lab: Pontarddulais)*, 33 Heol-Y-Cae, Pontarddulais, Swansea, SA4 8PP ☎ (01792) 884351 / 07929377157 Philip.Downing@swansea.gov.uk

Ryland Doyle *(Lab: Llansamlet)*, 32 Golwg y Coed, Birchgrove, Swansea, SA7 0HY ☎ (01792) 794500 ryland.doyle@swansea.gov.uk

Mandy Evans *(Lab: Bonymaen)*, 127 Brokesby Road, Bonymaen, Swansea, SA1 7BX ☎ (01792) 642387 Mandy.Evans2@swansea.gov.uk

William Evans *(Lab: Kingsbridge)*, The Willows, 10 Clos Bryngwyn, Garden Village, Gorseinon, Swansea, SA4 4BJ ☎ (01792) 895058 william.evans@swansea.gov.uk

Wendy Fitzgerald *(Ind: Penllergaer)*, 10 Clos Cilfwnwr, Penllergaer, Swansea, SA4 9BU ☎ (01792) 895330 wendy.fitzgerald@swansea.gov.uk

Robert Francis-Davies *(Lab: Morriston)*, 25 Lon Cadog, Sketty, Swansea, SA2 0TN ☎ (01792) 427189 / 07812635401 robert.davies@swansea.gov.uk

Fiona Gordon *(Lab: Castle)*, 5 St. Christopher's Court, Marina, Swansea, SA1 1UA ☎ 07859 090707 Fiona.Gordon2@swansea.gov.uk

Joe Hale *(Lab: St Thomas)*, 1 Gwynne Terrace, St Thomas, Swansea, SA1 8HP ☎ (01792) 428866 Joe.Hale@swansea.gov.uk

Andrea Harrington *(Lab: Morriston)*, 60 Gelli Aur, Treboeth, Swansea, SA5 9DG ☎ 07584 670061 Andrea.Harrington2@swansea.gov.uk

Jane Harris *(Lab: Pontarddulais)*, 109/109a Bolgoed Road, Pontarddulais, Swansea, SA4 8JP ☎ (01792) 884339 / 07775561909 Jane.Harris@swansea.gov.uk

Terry Hennegan *(Lab: Penderry)*, 168 Woodford Road, Blaen-Y-Maes, Swansea, SA5 5PU ☎ (01792) 546554 Terry.Hennegan@swansea.gov.uk

Christopher Holley *(Lib D: Cwmbwrla)*, 446 Middle Road, Gendros, Swansea, SA5 8EH ☎ (01792) 419957 chris.holley@swansea.gov.uk

Paxton Hood-Williams *(Con: Fairwood)*, 50 Pant-y-Dwr, Three Crosses, Swansea, SA4 3PG ☎ (01792) 872038 / 07939467566 paxton.hood-williams@swansea.gov.uk

Beverley Hopkins *(Lab: Landore)*, 4 Morgan Street, Hafod, Swansea, SA1 2LU ☎ (01792) 655956 Beverley.Hopkins@swansea.gov.uk

David Hopkins *(Lab: Townhill)*, 4 Morgan Street, Hafod, Swansea, SA1 2LU ☎ (01792) 655956 david.hopkins@swansea.gov.uk

Yvonne Jardine *(Lab: Morriston)*, 111 Frederick Place, Llansamlet, Swansea, SA7 9TS ☎ (01792) 814894 Yvonne.Jardine@swansea.gov.uk

Dennis Henry James *(Lab: Llansamlet)*, 123 Pontardawe Road, Clydach, Swansea, SA6 5PB ☎ (01792) 844362 dennis.james@swansea.gov.uk

Lynda James *(Ind: Pennard)*, 39 Pennard Road, Kittle, Swansea, SA3 3JY ☎ (01792) 234316 / 07789 816374 Lynda.James@swansea.gov.uk

Andrew Jones *(Lab: Cockett)*, 7 Venables Close, Fforestfach, Swansea, SA5 5BY ☎ (01792) 511694 Andrew.Jones@swansea.gov.uk

Jeff Jones *(Lib D: Killay South)*, 366 Gower Road, Killay, Swansea, SA2 7AH ☎ (01792) 204136 jeff.w.jones@swansea.gov.uk

Mary Jones *(Lib D: Killay North)*, 366 Gower Road, Killay, Swansea, SA2 7AH ☎ (01792) 204136 / 07814 698469 mary.jones@swansea.gov.uk

Susan Mary Jones *(Ind: Gowerton)*, 52 Park Road, Gowerton, Swansea, SA4 3DG ☎ (01792) 872561 susan.m.jones@swansea.gov.uk

Erika Kirchner *(Lab: Castle)*, 23 Portia Terrace, Swansea, SA1 6XW ☎ (01792) 551970 / 07974145304 erika.kirchner@swansea.gov.uk

David Lewis *(Lab: Gorseinon)*, 46 Cecil Road, Gorseinon, Swansea, SA4 4BY ☎ 07917 724805 David.Lewis2@swansea.gov.uk

Richard Lewis *(Lib D: Gower)*, Northwood, Horton, Swansea, SA3 1LQ ☎ (01792) 390368 richard.lewis@swansea.gov.uk

Clive Lloyd *(Lab: St Thomas)*, 32 Milton Terrace, Swansea, SA1 6XP ☎ (01792) 468317 / 07862 702755 Clive.Lloyd@swansea.gov.uk

Paul Lloyd *(Lab: Bonymaen)*, 2 Hafnant, Winch Wen, Swansea, SA1 7LG ☎ (01792) 774482 / 07789167128 Paul.Lloyd@swansea.gov.uk

Keith Marsh *(Ind: Bishopston)*, 16 Brandy Cove Road, Bishopston, Swansea, SA3 3HB ☎ (01792) 233735 keith.marsh@swansea.gov.uk

Penny Matthews *(Lab: Llansamlet)*, 17 Eileen Road, Llansamlet, Swansea, SA7 9TR ☎ (01792) 795666 penny.matthews@swansea.gov.uk

Paul Michael Meara *(Lib D: Sketty)*, 23 Kimberley Road, Sketty, Swansea, SA2 9DP ☎ (01792) 202578 paul.meara@swansea.gov.uk

Hazel Morris *(Lab: Penderry)*, 22 Penmynydd Road, Penlan, Swansea, SA5 7EH ☎ (01792) 416520 hazel.morris@swansea.gov.uk

John Newbury *(Lib D: Dunvant)*, 40 Priors Way, Dunvant, Swansea, SA2 7UJ ☎ (01792) 201220 john.newbury@swansea.gov.uk

Byron Owen *(Lab: Mynyddbach)*, 20 Glasbury Road, Morriston, Swansea, SA6 7PA ☎ (01792) 774370 / 07977682733 byron.g.owen@swansea.gov.uk

Geraint Owens *(Lab: Cockett)*, 15 Eastfield Close, Townhill, Swansea, SA1 6SG Geraint.Owens@swansea.gov.uk

David Phillips *(Lab: Castle)*, 13 Oaklands Terrace, Swansea, SA1 6JJ ☎ (01792) 646004 david.phillips@swansea.gov.uk

Cheryl Philpott *(Lib D: Sketty)*, 21 Brynmead Close, Tycoch, Swansea, SA2 9EY ☎ (01792) 296481

cheryl.philpott@swansea.gov.uk

Jennifer Raynor *(Lab: Dunvant)*, 35 Brynaeron, Dunvant, Swansea, SA2 7UX ☎ (01792) 207807, Jennifer.Raynor@swansea.gov.uk

Huw Rees *(Lib D: Sketty)*, 24 Sketty Park Drive, Sketty, Swansea, SA2 8LN ☎ (01792) 201726 huw.rees2@swansea.gov.uk

Julie Christine Richards *(Lab: Loughor Lower)*, 76 Castle Street, Loughor, Swansea, SA4 6TS ☎ (01792) 896069 christine.richards@swansea.gov.uk

Neil Ronconi-Woollard *(Lab: Uplands)*, 4 Richmond Road, Uplands, Swansea, SA2 0RB ☎ 07730 784232 Neil.Ronconi-Woollard@swansea.gov.uk

Paulette B Smith *(Lab: Clydach)*, The Coppins, 1 Heol-y-Ffin, Clydach, Swansea, SA8 4DA (01792) 843423 / 07977412780 paulette.smith@swansea.gov.uk

Robert Charles Stewart *(Lab: Morriston)*, 52 Denbigh Crescent, Morriston, Swansea, SA6 6TH ☎ (01792) 549417 rob.stewart@swansea.gov.uk

Ioan Richard *(Ind: Mawr)*, Bron-y-Mynydd, 23 Heol-y-Mynydd, Craig Cefn Parc, Swansea, SA6 5RH ☎ (01792) 843861 ioan.richard@swansea.gov.uk

Pearleen Sangha *(Lab: Uplands)*, Flat B, 9 Uplands Crescent, Swansea, SA2 0PA ☎ (01792) 651184 / 07598946422 Pearleen.Sangha@swansea.gov.uk

Gareth Sullivan *(Ind: Llangyfelach)*, 34 Pengors Road, Llangyfelach, Swansea, SA5 7JE ☎ (01792) 773441 gareth.sullivan@swansea.gov.uk

Gloria Tanner *(Lab: Mynyddbach)*, 88 Hill View Crescent, Clase, Swansea, SA6 7HW ☎ (01792) 421119 / 07986515038 Gloria.Tanner@swansea.gov.uk

Mitchell Theaker *(Lab: Cockett)*, 33 Bryn Road, Brynmill, Swansea, SA2 0AP ☎ 07933 111009 Mitchell.Theaker@swansea.gov.uk

Ceinwen Thomas *(Lab: Mynyddbach)*, 11 Bryngelli Drive, Trebeoth, Swansea, SA5 9BW ☎ (01792) 702451 / 07828640422 ceinwen.thomas@swansea.gov.uk

Des Thomas *(Lab: West Cross)*, 64 Southlands Drive, West Cross, Swansea, SA3 5RJ ☎ (01792) 404288 des.thomas@swansea.gov.uk

Graham Thomas *(Lib D: Cwmbwrla)*, 126 Manor Road, Manselton, Swansea, SA5 9PW ☎ (01792) 416467 graham.thomas@swansea.gov.uk

Mark Thomas *(Lab: Penclawdd)*, Swn-y-Don, West End, Penclawdd, Swansea, SA4 3YX ☎ (01792) 851397 / 07794017704 Mark.Thomas2@swansea.gov.uk

Miles Thomas *(Con: Newton)*, 27 Langland Bay Road, Langland Bay, Swansea, SA3 4QP ☎ (01792) 367241 / 07778596973 miles.thomas2@swansea.gov.uk

Linda Tyler-Lloyd *(Con: Mayals)*, 11 Emmanuel Gardens, Sketty, Swansea, SA2 8EF ☎ (01792) 204662 Linda.Tyler-Lloyd@swansea.gov.uk

Robert Smith *(Lab: Loughor Upper)*, 20 Swansea Road, Gorseinon, Swansea, SA4 4HE ☎ (01792) 898323 Robert.Smith@swansea.gov.uk

June Stanton *(Lib D: Sketty)*, 143 Derwen Fawr Road, Sketty, Swansea, SA2 8ED ☎ (01792) 207935 june.stanton@swansea.gov.uk

Gordon Walker *(Ind: Clydach)*, Bryn Ar Afon, Lon Eithrym, Clydach, Swansea, SA6 5ER ☎ (01792) 842255 / 07794534563 Gordon.Walker@swansea.gov.uk

Lesley Walton *(Lab: Townhill)*, 34 Carlton Terrace, Mount Pleasant, Swansea, SA1 6AD ☎ 07503 702327 Lesley.Walton@swansea.gov.uk

Mike White *(Lab: Landore)*, 24 Saddler Street, Landore, Swansea, SA1 2PP ☎ (01792) 643354 Mike.White@swansea.gov.uk

Clerks to the Community Councils

Bishopston Community Council, *Nigel Richards*, 9 Copley Close, Bishopston, Swansea, SA3 3JL
☎ (01792) 233058
bishopstoncc@yahoo.co.uk

Clydach Community Council, *Stewart McCulloch*, 22 Royal Sovereign Apartments, Phoebe Road, Copper Quarter, Swansea, SA1 7FH ☎ (01792) 463949
clydachcommunitycouncil@gmail.com

Gorseinon Town Council, *John Millard*, 39 Gorseinon Road, Penllergaer, Swansea, SA4 9AE
☎ (01792) 895690
john.millard@gorseinontowncouncil.gov.uk

Gowerton Community Council, *Serena Thomas*, 2 Castle Street, Loughor, Swansea, SA4 6TU
☎ (01792) 415987
s.thomasclerkgcc@ntlworld.com

Grovesend & Waungron Community Council, *John Burge*, 8 Brodawel, Cimla, Neath, SA11 3YB ☎ (01639) 630683
johnburge2000@hotmail.com

Ilston Community Council, *John Jacobs*, 20 Linkside Drive, Southgate, Swansea, SA3 2BP
☎ (01792) 234563

Killay, North & South Community Council, *Susan Bagley*, 90 Summerland Park, Upper Killay, Swansea, SA2 7AJ
☎ (01792) 208281
sue.bagley.killay@gmail.com

Llangennith, Llanmadoc & Cheriton Community Council, *Margaret Waymark*, 23 Anderson Lane, Southgate, Swansea, SA3 2BX ☎ (01792) 233607
margaret.waymark@googlemail.com

Llangyfelach Community Council, *David Jenkins*, 88 Saunders Way, Derwen Fawr, Swansea, SA2 8BH
☎ (01792) 201934
d.jenkins511@btinternet.com

Llanrhidian Higher Community Council, *Anthony John*, Cross 5 Blodwen Terrace, Penclawdd, Swansea, SA4 3XU
☎ (01792) 851345
lanrhidianhcc@aol.com

Llanrhidian Lower Community Council, *Sue Evans*, Courtlands, Llanrhidian, Swansea, SA3 1 EE
☎ (01792) 391157

Llwchwr Town Council, *Anthony Davies*, 4 Lady Margaret Villas, Sketty, Swansea, SA2 0RX
☎ (01792) 428460
a.davies73@ntlworld.com

Mawr Community Council, *Robert King*, 1 Lewis Terrace, Abergarwed, Resolven, Neath, SA11 4DL ☎ (01639) 711480
joy.king32@btinternet.com

Mumbles Community Council, *Steve Heydon*, Council Offices, Walters Crescent, Mumbles, Swansea, SA3 4BB
☎ (01792) 363598
clerk@mumbles.gov.uk

Pennard Community Council, *Chris James*, 39 Pennard Road, Kittle, Swansea, SA3 3JY
☎ (01792) 448399
pennardcommunitycouncil@gmail.com

Penrice Community Council, *Sam Caswell*, 762 Gower Road, Upper Killay, Swansea, SA2 7HQ
☎ (01792) 449802
sam.cas@tiscali.co.uk

Penllergaer Community Council, *David Hoskins*, Tan y Bryn, 1 Bryntawe Road, Ynystawe, Swansea, SA5 5AD
☎ (01792) 842228
davidllew@aol.com

Pontarddulais Community Council, *Aneurin John*, 45 St Teilo Street, Pontarddulais, Swansea, SA4 8SY ☎ (01792) 885890
pontarddulaistowncouncil@yahoo.co.uk

Pontlliw & Tircoed Community Council, *Mr P Newman*, Pontlliw and Tircoed Community Council, P.O. Box 639, Pontarddulais, Swansea, SA4 8WT
officers@pontlliw-tircoed.org.uk

Port Eynon Community Council, *Mr B J Stubbings*, 5 Cadwgan Road, Craig Cefn Parc, Swansea, SA6 5TD ☎ (01792) 843452
howardcefnparc1@btinternet.com

Rhossili Community Council, *Caroline Johnson*, Rhossili Community Council, Hampstead, Rhossili, Swansea, SA3 1PL
☎ (01792) 391775
rhossilicc@gmail.com

Three Crosses Community Council, *Temporary Clerk*
warren.smart5@btinternet.com

Upper Killay Community Council, *Robert Kelvin Evans*, 12 Beaufort Gardens, Kittle, Swansea, SA3 3LE
☎ (01792) 232958 / (01792) 529657
kelvin.evans@jcpsolicitors.co.uk

TORFAEN COUNTY BOROUGH COUNCIL
CYNGOR BWRDEISTREF SIROL TORFAEN

Civic Centre, Pontypool,
Torfaen NP4 6YB
Tel: (01495) 762200
Fax: (01495) 755513
Email: your.call@torfaen.gov.uk
Website: www.torfaen.gov.uk

Leader
Cllr Bob Wellington

TORFAEN COUNTY BOROUGH | *BWRDEISTREF SIROL TORFAEN*

Chief Executive
Alison Ward

LABOUR CONTROL	Lab **30** Ind **8** Con **4** PC **2**	TOTAL 44

ELECTION RESULT 2012

	Seats	Change	Votes	Share
Labour	30	12	23,471	47.1%
Independent	8	-5	15,516	31.1%
Conservative	4	-1	5,781	11.6%
Plaid Cymru	2	-1	3,608	7.2%
Others	0	-3	909	1.8%
Lib Dem	0	-2	533	1.1%

Socio-economic Profile

		Rank 1<22
Area (sq km)	126	20
Population ('000s)	90.5	17
% able to speak Welsh	18.2	12
% born in Wales	85.5	6
% non-white ethnic groups	2.2	19
Gross rev expenditure (2011-12)	£214.8m	17
Forecast capital expenditure (2011-12)	£28.2m	18
% dwellings in Band D (2012-13)	9.9	19
Band D council tax (2011-12)	£1,180.03	10
% over retirement age	18.7	11
% pupils 5+ GCSEs A*-C (2010-11)	61.4	19
Unemployment (% claimant count 2011)	4.8	5
Index of Deprivation (2011)	35	8
(% of Authority in most deprived 30%)		

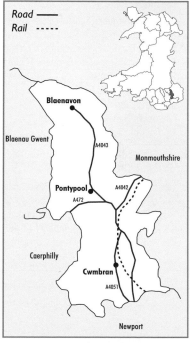

Road ——
Rail - - - - -

Blaenavon

Blaenau Gwent

A4043

Monmouthshire

Pontypool

A4042

A472

Caerphilly

Cwmbran

A4051

Newport

LOCAL GOVERNMENT

TORFAEN

Principal Officers

Chief Executive:	**Alison Ward**
Deputy Chief Executive:	**Peter Durkin**
Assistant Chief Executive, Communities:	**Dave Congreve**
Assistant Chief Executive, Resources:	**Nigel Aurelius**
Chief Legal Officer & Monitoring Officer:	**Lynda Willis**

Cabinet Members 2012-2013

Leader:	**Bob Wellington** (Lab)
Deputy Leader:	**Lewis Jones** (Lab)
Children & Young People:	**Mary Barnett** (Lab)
Health, Social Care, Well-being & Equalities:	**Cynthia Beynon** (Lab)
Housing, Planning & Public Protection:	**Gwyneira Clark** (Lab)
Corporate Governance & Community Safety:	**Richard Clark** (Lab)
Neighbourhood Services:	**B John Cunningham** (Lab)
Resources:	**Anthony Hunt** (Lab)

Committee Chairs 2012-2013

Healthier Communities Scrutiny Committee:	**Raymond Mills** (Con)
Safer Communities Scrutiny Committee:	**Stuart Evans** (Ind)
Cleaner Communities Scrutiny Committee:	**Alan Jones** (Lab)
Learning Communities Scrutiny Committee:	**Glyn Caron** (Lab)
Resources & Corporate Business Scrutiny Committee:	**David Yeowell** (Lab)
Planning Committee:	**Brian Mawby** (Lab)
Licensing Committee:	**Norma Parrish** (Lab)
Pensions Committee:	**John Marshall** (Lab)
Members' Services Committee:	**Colette Thomas** (Lab)
Democratic Services Committee:	**Elizabeth Haynes** (Ind)

Salaries

Basic Salary: £13,175 per annum
Senior Salaries:
Leader of the Council: £29,125; Deputy Leader: £16,645
Executive Member: £12,485; Chairs of Scrutiny Committes: £8,735
Chairs of Other Committes: £8,735; Mayor's Allowance: £5,860
Deputy Mayor's Allowance: £1,630; Care Allowance: £403 per month

TORFAEN

Councillors ♂ 32 ♀ 12

Mayor: Cllr Wayne Tomlinson

Stuart W J Ashley *(Lab: Pontnewydd)*, 16 Paddock Close, Pontnewydd, Cwmbran, NP44 1LL
☎ (01633) 868413
stuart.ashley@torfaen.gov.uk

Mary Barnett *(Lab: Upper Cwmbran)*, Tŷ Canol, Upper Cwmbran Road, Upper Cwmbran, Cwmbran, NP44 5SL ☎ (01633) 484002
mary.barnett@torfaen.gov.uk

Huw L Bevan *(Con: Llanyrafon South)*, 15 Moyle Grove, Ponthir, Newport, NP18 1GP
☎ (01633) 421983
huw.bevan@torfaen.gov.uk

Cynthia Beynon MBE *(Lab: Croesyceiliog North)*, 15 St Augustine Road, Griffithstown, Pontypool, NP4 5EX
☎ (01495) 751740
cynthia.beynon@torfaen.gov.uk

Stephen J Brooks JP *(Lab: St Dials)*, 12b Cefn Milwr, Hollybush, Cwmbran, NP44 7PH
☎ (01633) 868283
Stephen.brooks@torfaen.gov.uk

Ronald A Burnett *(Ind: Two Locks & Henllys)*, 5 Sunny Bank, Henllys, Cwmbran, NP44 6HB
☎ (01633) 874157
ronald.burnett@torfaen.gov.uk

Pamela A Cameron *(Lab: Two Locks & Henllys)*, 8 Garth Road, Ty Coch, Cwmbran, NP44 7AB
☎ (01633) 873793
pamela.cameron@torfaen.gov.uk

Glyn Caron *(Lab: Llanyrafon North)*, 16 Llanyrafon Way, Llanyrafon, Cwmbran, NP44 8HN
☎ (01633) 871047
glyn.caron@torfaen.gov.uk

Gwyneira R Clark *(Lab: Abersychan)*, 1 Stanley Road, Garndiffaith, Pontypool, NP4 7LZ
☎ (01495) 773737
gwyneira.clark@torfaen.gov.uk

Richard G Clark *(Lab: Croesyceiliog North)*, 29 Glaslyn Court, Croesyceiliog, Cwmbran, NP44 2JF
☎ (01633) 480083
richard.clark@torfaen.gov.uk

Leonard Constance *(Lab: Brynwern)*, 15 Bryngwyn Road, Pontypool, NP4 6ET
☎ 07576 772064
leonard.constance@torfaen.gov.uk

Veronica A Crick JP *(Lab: Croesyceiliog South)*, 49 The Highway, Croesyceiliog, Cwmbran, NP44 2BQ ☎ (01633) 860668
veronica.crick@torfaen.gov.uk

Fiona C Cross *(PC: Coed Eva)*, 130 Oaksford, Coed Eva, Cwmbran, NP44 6UN
☎ 07881 855553
fiona.cross@torfaen.gov.uk

Bernard John Cunningham MBE *(Lab: Upper Cwmbran)*, 6 Tŷ Pwca Road, Upper Cwmbran, Cwmbran, NP44 1SZ ☎ (01633) 862050
john.cunningham@torfaen.gov.uk

David R Daniels *(Lab: Llantarnam)*, 37 Five Locks Close, Pontnewydd, Cwmbran, NP44 1DB
☎ 07809 869440
david.daniels@torfaen.gov.uk

Giles D Davies *(Lab: Abersychan)*, 37 Waterloo Road, Talywain, Pontypool, NP4 7HW
☎ 07429 185409
giles.davies@torfaen.gov.uk

Stuart H Evans *(Ind: Blaenavon)*, 2 Charles Street, Blaenavon, NP4 9JT ☎ (01495) 792335
stuart.evans@torfaen.gov.uk

Alun W Furzer *(Lab: Blaenavon)*, 25 Queen Street, Blaenavon, NP4 9PN ☎ (01495) 792497
alun.furzer@torfaen.gov.uk

Maria D Graham *(Ind: Llantarnam)*, 2 Cwrt Dowlais, Ty Coch Way, Cwmbran, NP44 7AP
☎ 07817 609419
maria.graham@torfaen.gov.uk

Kelvin Harnett JP *(Ind: Pontnewynydd)*, 58 Hanbury Road, Pontnewynydd, Pontypool, NP4 6PF
☎ (01495) 760295
kelvin.harnett@torfaen.gov.uk

Mike Harris *(Ind: Pontypool)*, 37 Heol Bueno, New Inn, Pontypool, NP4 0QU
☎ 07725 982550
mike.harris@torfaen.gov.uk

Elizabeth Haynes *(Ind: St Dials)*, 46 Brunel Road, Fairwater, Cwmbran, NP44 4QT
☎ (01633) 870119
elizabeth.haynes@torfaen.gov.uk

Anthony J Hunt *(Lab: Panteg)*, 24 Greenhill Road, Griffithstown, Pontypool, NP4 5BE
☎ 07870 116463
anthony.hunt@torfaen.gov.uk

David K James *(Con: New Inn)*, 121 Chester Close, New Inn, Pontypool, NP4 0LW
☎ (01495) 758559
keith.james@torfaen.gov.uk

Mike Jeremiah *(Ind: Wainfelin)*, 83 Wainfelin Avenue, Wainfelin, Pontypool, NP4 6DP
☎ (01495) 755830
mike.jeremiah@torfaen.gov.uk

Alan S Jones *(Lab: Blaenavon)*, 22 Llanover Road, Blaenavon, NP4 9HR ☎ (01495) 790477
alan.s.jones@torfaen.gov.uk

Lewis W Jones *(Lab: Trevethin)*, 44 Glenview Close, Trevethin, Pontypool, NP4 8ED
☎ (01495) 756950
deputyleader@torfaen.gov.uk

LOCAL GOVERNMENT

TORFAEN

Robert D Kemp *(Ind: Upper Cwmbran)*, 6 Crown Close, Pontnewydd, Cwmbran, NP44 1BW
☎ (01633) 793009
robert.kemp@torfaen.gov.uk

John A Marshall *(Lab: Trevethin)*, Kelsha Bungalow, Pentwyn, Pontypool, NP4 7TA
☎ (01495) 755812
john.marshall@torfaen.gov.uk

Neil Mason *(Lab: St Cadocs & Penygarn)*, 42 Folly View, Penygarn, Pontypool, NP4 8BU
☎ (01495) 750019
neil.mason@torfaen.gov.uk

Brian Mawby *(Lab: Pontnewydd)*, 55 Station Road, Pontnewydd, Cwmbran, NP44 1NZ
☎ (01633) 484948
brian.mawby@torfaen.gov.uk

Raymond F B Mills *(Con: New Inn)*, 11 Hillcrest, New Inn, Pontypool, NP4 0NG
☎ (01495) 750327
raymond.mills@torfaen.gov.uk

Mandy Owen *(Lab: Greenmeadow)*, 94 Beddick, Greenmeadow, Cwmbran, NP44 4UX ☎ (01633) 872665
amanda.owen@torfaen.gov.uk

Norma Parrish *(Lab: Panteg)*, 26 Lansdowne Road, Sebastopol, Pontypool, NP4 5EF
☎ (01495) 763067
norma.parrish@torfaen.gov.uk

Jessica C Powell *(Lab: Pontnewydd)*, 44 Wayfield Crescent, Northville, Cwmbran, NP44 1NH ☎ 07773 880380
jessica.powell@torfaen.gov.uk

Jeff Rees *(PC: Fairwater)*, 6 Crown Close, Pontnewydd, Cwmbran, NP44 1BW ☎ 07517 467262
jeff.rees@torfaen.gov.uk

Philip J Seabourne *(Lab: Fairwater)*, 15 Dale Path, Fairwater, Cwmbran, NP44 4QR
☎ (01633) 863744
phil.seabourne@torfaen.gov.uk

Graham S Smith *(Con: New Inn)*, 105a The Highway, New Inn, Pontypool, NP4 0PJ
☎ 07527 963774
graham.smith@torfaen.gov.uk

Barry M Taylor JP *(Lab: Snatchwood)*, Glen View, North Road, Snatchwood, Pontypool, NP4 7BN ☎ (01495) 774281
barry.taylor@torfaen.gov.uk

Colette A Thomas *(Lab: Two Locks & Henllys)*, 2 Sandybrook Close, Off Ton Road, Cwmbran, NP44 7JA ☎ (01633) 482104
colette.thomas@torfaen.gov.uk

Wayne Tomlinson *(Lab: Abersychan)*, 3 Elizabeth Row, Talywain, Pontypool, NP4 7US
☎ (01495) 774953
wayne.tomlinson@torfaen.gov.uk

Neil C Waite *(Lab: Cwmynyscoy)*, 73 Blaendare Road, Pontypool, NP4 5RU ☎ (01495) 759468
neil.waite@torfaen.gov.uk

Robert G Wellington *(Lab: Greenmeadow)*, The Rowans, Craig Road, Greenmeadow, Cwmbran, NP44 5YY
☎ (01633) 868402
leader@torfaen.gov.uk

David A Yeowell *(Lab: Panteg)*, 21 Sunnybank Road, Griffithstown, Pontypool, NP4 5LT
☎ (01495) 762095
david.yeowell@torfaen.gov.uk

Clerks to the Community Councils

Blaenavon Town Council, *Susan Price*, Office 1, Church View, Church Road, Blaenavon, NP4 9NA
☎ (01495) 790643
blaenavontc@btconnect.com

Croesyceiliog & Llanyrafon Community Council, *Robert Deakin*, C/o Woodland Road Social Centre, Croesyceiliog, Cwmbran, NP44 2DZ ☎ (01633) 869933
croesy.llanycc@yahoo.co.uk

Cwmbran Community Council, *David Collins*, The Council House, Ventnor Road, Cwmbran, NP44 3JY
☎ (01633) 624152
david@cwmbran.gov.uk

Henllys Community Council, *Laura Grey*, Henllys Village Hall, Henllys Village Road, Henllys, Cwmbran, NP44 6JZ
☎ 07703 194263
lauragrey1@hotmail.com

Ponthir Community Council, *Karen Price*, Ponthir Village Hall, Caerleon Road, Ponthir, NP18 1GX
☎ (01633) 420968
ponthircc@hotmail.co.uk

Pontypool Community Council, *Ruth Tucker*, 35a Commercial Street, Pontypool, NP4 6JQ
☎ (01495) 756736
rtucker@pontypoolcc.gov.uk

THE VALE OF GLAMORGAN COUNCIL
CYNGOR BRO MORGANNWG

Leader
Cllr Neil Moore

Civic Offices, Holton Road,
Barry CF63 4RU
Tel: (01446) 700111
Fax: (01446) 746837
Email: contactonevale@valeofglamorgan.gov.uk
Website: www.valeofglamorgan.gov.uk

VALE of GLAMORGAN

BRO MORGANNWG

Managing Director
Sian Davies

NO OVERALL CONTROL
Lab **22** Con **11** PC **6** LLFI **4**
Ind **3** UKIP **1**
TOTAL 47

ELECTION RESULT 2012

	Seats	Change	Votes	Share
Lab	22	9	27,792	34.5%
Con	11	-14	26,501	32.9%
PC	6	-	13,451	16.7%
LLFI	4	4	6,488	8.1%
Ind	3	-	4,862	6.0%
UKIP	1	1	633	0.8%
Others	0	-	669	0.9%

Socio-economic Profile

		Rank 1<22
Area (sq km)	331	15
Population ('000s)	124.9	12
% able to speak Welsh	17.0	16
% born in Wales	75.7	11
% non-white ethnic groups	4.8	3
Gross rev expenditure (2011-12)	£273.0m	12
Forecast capital expenditure (2011-12)	£21.6m	21
% dwellings in Band D (2012-13)	19.3	6
Band D council tax (2011-12)	£1,123.35	16
% over retirement age	18.4	13
% pupils 5+ GCSEs A*-C (2010-11)	75.3	1
Unemployment (% claimant count 2011)	3.9	10
Index of Deprivation (2011)	18	16
(% of Authority in most deprived 30%)		

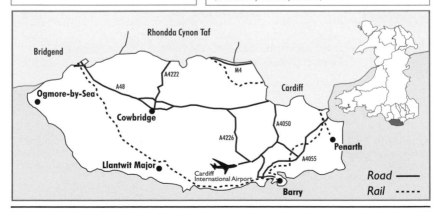

LOCAL GOVERNMENT

Principal Officers

Managing Director:	**Sian Davies**
Director of Development Services:	**Rob Thomas**
Director of Visible Services:	**Miles Punter**
Director of Social Services:	**Phil Evans**
Director of Learning & Skills:	**Tba**

Cabinet Members 2012-2013

Leader / Policy, Corporate Management & Services, Equalities & Public Protection:	**Neil Moore** (Lab)
Deputy Leader / Social Care & Health (Adults), Lifelong Learning & Libraries:	**Stuart Egan** (Lab)
Housing, Building Maintenance and Community Safety:	**Bronwen Brooks** (Lab)
Business Innovation, Regeneration, Economic Development, Planning & Transportation:	**Lis Burnett** (Lab)
Environment & Visible Services:	**Rob Curtis** (Lab)
Social Care, Health (Children) & Schools:	**Christopher Elmore** (Lab)
Leisure, Parks, Culture & Sports Development:	**Gwyn John** (LLFI)

Committee Chairs 2012-2013

Corporate Resources Scrutiny Committee:	**Mark Wilson** (Lab)
Economy & Environment Scrutiny Committee:	**Rhodri Traherne** (Con)
Housing & Public Protection Scrutiny Committee:	**Margaret Wilkinson** (Lab)
Lifelong Learning Scrutiny Committee:	**Nic Hodges** (PC)
Social Care & Health Scrutiny Committee:	**Richard Bertin** (Ind)
Planning Committee	**Fred Johnson** (Lab)
Appeals Committee	**Gwyn Roberts** (Lab)
Audit Committee	**Tba**
Early Retirement / Redundancy Committee	**Stuart Egan** (Lab)
Standards Committee	**Tba**

Salaries

Basic Salary: £13,175; Senior Salaries: Leader: £47,500
Deputy Leader: £33,460; Cabinet Members: £28,780; Chairs of Scrutiny Commitees: £21,910
Chairs of Other Committees: £21,910; Mayor: £21,375
Deputy Mayor: £16,625

Councillors ♂ 35 ♀ 12

Mayor: Cllr Eric Hacker

Richard Bertin *(Ind: Court)*,
33 Maes-y-Cwm Street, Barry,
CF63 4EJ ☎ (01446) 736227
rjbertin@valeofglamorgan.gov.uk

M E Janice Birch *(Lab: Stanwell)*,
10 Victoria Square, Penarth,
CF64 3EJ ☎ (029) 2070 2443
jbirch@valeofglamorgan.gov.uk

Rhiannon Birch *(Lab: Cornerswell)*,
9 Grove Place, Penarth, CF64 2LB
RBirch@valeofglamorgan.gov.uk

Jonathan C Bird *(Con: Wenvoe)*, Beili-Mawr, Dyffryn, Cardiff, CF5 6SU ☎ (029) 2059 9488 / 07917 142523
jbird@valeofglamorgan.gov.uk

Bronwen Brooks *(Lab: Court)*, 149 Gladstone Road, Barry, CF62 8NB ☎ (01446) 742387 / 07525 158391
bbrooks@valeofglamorgan.gov.uk

Lis Burnett *(Lab: St Augustines)*, 71 Redlands Road, Penarth, CF64 2WE ☎ (029) 2025 6295 / 07736 771017
lburnett@valeofglamorgan.gov.uk

Philip J Clarke *(Ind: Rhoose)*, Deg Erw, Cwm Ciddy Lane, Barry, CF62 3NA ☎ (01446) 746729 / 07946 643898
PJClarke@valeofglamorgan.gov.uk

Geoff Cox *(Con: Cowbridge)*, 27 St Johns Close, Llanblethian, Cowbridge, CF71 7HN
☎ (01446) 773637 / 07866 525711
gacox@valeofglamorgan.gov.uk

Claire Curtis *(Lab: Dyfan)*, 118 Merthyr Dyfan Road, Barry, CF62 9TJ ☎ (01446) 736287
CCurtis@valeofglamorgan.gov.uk

Robert F Curtis *(Lab: Gibbonsdown)*, 118 Merthyr Dyfan Road, Barry, CF62 9TJ
☎ (01446) 736287 / 07855 329942
rfcurtis@valeofglamorgan.gov.uk

Pamela Drake *(Lab: Castleland)*, 44 Pyke Street, Barry, CF63 4PF
☎ (01446) 742657 / 07867 538979
pdrake@valeofglamorgan.gov.uk

John Drysdale *(Lab: Illtyd)*, 28 Le Sor Hill, Peterston-Super-Ely, CF5 6LW ☎ 07879 815478
jdrysdale@valeofglamorgan.gov.uk

Kate Edmunds *(Lab: Llandough)*, 2 Millbrook Road, Dinas Powys, CF64 4DA ☎ (029) 2140 7725
KEdmunds@valeofglamorgan.gov.uk

Stuart Egan *(Lab: Buttrills)*, 26 Montgomery Road, Barry, CF62 7DB ☎ (01446) 418221 / 07976 978795
scegan@valeofglamorgan.gov.uk

Christopher P J Elmore *(Lab: Castleland)*, 7 Tŷ Camlas, Y Rhodfa, The Waterfront, Barry, CF63 4BF
☎ (01446) 402220 / 07867 506116
celmore@valeofglamorgan.gov.uk

Christopher Franks *(PC: Dinas Powys)*, Tŷ Isaf, 41 Highwalls Avenue, Dinas Powys, CF64 4AQ
☎ 07725 497423
CFranks@valeofglamorgan.gov.uk

Keith J Geary *(PC: Llantwit Major)*, 29 Cwrt Syr Dafydd, Llantwit Major, CF61 2SR ☎ (01446) 792087
KJGeary@valeofglamorgan.gov.uk

Eric Hacker *(Ind: Llantwit Major)*, 24 Llanmaes Road, Llantwit Major, CF61 2XF ☎ (01446) 792037 / 07837 275225
ehacker@valeofglamorgan.gov.uk

Howard C Hamilton *(Lab: Illtyd)*, 54 Brookfield Avenue, Barry, CF63 1EQ ☎ (01446) 730100 / 07977 792416
HHamilton@valeofglamorgan.gov.uk

Valerie M Hartrey *(PC: Dinas Powys)*, 159 Cardiff Road, Dinas Powys, CF64 4JW
☎ (029) 2051 3274 / 07725 826316
vmhartrey@valeofglamorgan.gov.uk

Keith Hatton *(PC: Dinas Powys)*, 9 Millbrook Heights, Dinas Powys, CF64 4JJ ☎ (029) 2051 4173 / 07749 825751
khatton@valeofglamorgan.gov.uk

Nic Hodges *(PC: Baruc)*, 19 Romilly Road, Barry, CF62 6AZ ☎ (01446) 736906 / 07504 489594
nphodges@valeofglamorgan.gov.uk

H. Jeffrey W James *(Con: Rhoose)*, 1 Lon Cefn Mably, Rhoose, CF62 3DY ☎ (01446) 710690 / 07885 236959
hjwjames@valeofglamorgan.gov.uk

Hunter Jarvie *(Con: Cowbridge)*, The Armoury, 46 Eastgate, Cowbridge, CF71 7AB
☎ (01446) 773841 / 07710 969653
hjarvie@valeofglamorgan.gov.uk

Gwyn John *(Ind: Llantwit Major)*, Ashgrove House, High Street, Llantwit Major, CF61 1SS
☎ (01446) 793669 / 07731 652380
gjohn@valeofglamorgan.go.uk

Fred Johnson *(Lab: Cadoc)*, 11 Glan-y-Mor, Y Rhodfa, Barry, CF63 4BB ☎ (01446) 734534 / 07917 885957
ftjohnson@valeofglamorgan.gov.uk

Maureen Kelly Owen *(Con: Plymouth)*, Sea Roads, 5 Cliff Parade, Penarth, CF64 5BP
☎ (029) 2070 7776 / 07939 206604
mkellyowen@valeofglamorgan.gov.uk

Peter G King *(Lab: Cornerswell)*, 7 Corbett Road, Llandough, CF64 2QX ☎ (029) 2070 1094 / 07973 966632
PKing@valeofglamorgan.gov.uk

Kevin P Mahoney *(UKIP: Sully)*, 40 Bendrick Road, Barry, CF63 3RE
☎ (01446) 746671 / 07753 987209
KPMahoney@valeofglamorgan.gov.uk

Anne Moore *(Lab: Cadoc)*, 6 Cardiff Road, Barry, CF63 2QY
☎ (01446) 721525
ajmoore@valeofglamorgan.gov.uk

Neil Moore *(Lab: Cadoc)*, 6 Cardiff Road, Barry, CF63 2QY
☎ (01446) 721525 / 07812 357876
nmoore@valeofglamorgan.gov.uk

Andrew Parker *(Con: Cowbridge)*, The Great Barn, Lilly Pot, Bonvilston, CF5 6TR ☎ (01446) 781010 / 781185 / 07702 262516
AParker@valeofglamorgan.gov.uk

Bob Penrose *(Ind: Sully)*, Mor Hafren, 7 Oyster Bend, Sully, CF64 5LW ☎ (029) 2053 0368 / 07831 349856
BPenrose@valeofglamorgan.gov.uk

Anthony G Powell *(Lab: Dyfan)*, 5 Coleridge Crescent, Barry, CF62 9TT ☎ (01446) 412144
AGPowell@valeofglamorgan.gov.uk

Audrey J Preston *(Con: St Brides Major)*, Kings Hall Court, Wick Road, St Brides Major, CF32 0SE
☎ (01656) 880965 / 07878 057515
ajpreston@valeofglamorgan.gov.uk

Rhona F Probert *(Lab: Illtyd)*, 28 Le Sor Hill, Peterston Super Ely, CF5 6LW ☎ 07799 136215
RProbert@valeofglamorgan.gov.uk

Gwyn H Roberts *(Lab: St Augustines)*, 7 Plas Glen Rosa, Portway Marina, Penarth, CF64 1TS
☎ (029) 2070 5855 / 07866 276709
GRoberts@valeofglamorgan.gov.uk

John W Thomas *(Con: St Athan)*, Flemingston Court, Flemingston, Nr Barry, CF62 4QJ
☎ (01446) 750216 / 07725 828625
jwthomas@valeofglamorgan.gov.uk

Ray P Thomas *(Con: Llandow/Ewenny)*, Sutton Newydd Farm, Llandow, CF71 7PY
☎ (01656) 890661 / 07976 676895
rathomas@valeofglamorgan.gov.uk

LOCAL GOVERNMENT

Rhodri Traherne (Con: Peterston-Super-Ely), Coedarhydyglyn, St Nicholas, Nr Cardiff, CF5 6SF
☎ (01446) 760321 / 760889 / 07710 680764
rtraherne@valeofglamorgan.gov.uk

Steffan T Wiliam (PC: Baruc), 14 Friars Road, Barry, CF62 5TR
☎ (01446) 730797/07779 236439
stwiliam@valeofglamorgan.gov.uk

Margaret R Wilkinson (Lab: Gibbonsdown), 26 Aberaeron Close, Barry, CF62 9BT
☎ (01446) 742950 / 07758 147629
mrwilkinson@valeofglamorgan.gov.uk

A Clive Williams (Con: Plymouth), 2 Cherwell Road, Penarth, CF64 3PE ☎ (029) 2070 5206 / 07766 172364
cwilliams@valeofglamorgan.gov.uk

Christopher J Williams (PC: Dinas Powys), 40 Longmeadow Drive, Dinas Powys, CF64 4TB
☎ (029) 2051 4166 / 07834 254968
cjwiliams@valeofglamorgan.gov.uk

Edward Williams (Ind: Llantwit Major), 3 Grange Gardens, Llantwit Major, CF61 2XB
☎ (01446) 793021 / 07979 096787
EdWilliams@valeofglamorgan.gov.uk

Mark R Wilson (Lab: Stanwell), 9 Grove Place, Penarth, CF64 2LB
☎ (029) 2070 8728 / 07796 976349
mrwilson@valeofglamorgan.gov.uk

Clerks to the Community Councils

Barry Town Council, Mr C Lewis, Council Offices, 7 Gladstone Road, Barry, CF62 8NA ☎ (01446) 704920
clifflewis@barrytowncouncil.gov.uk

Cowbridge with Llanblethian Town Council, Mr A Davies, Town Hall, Cowbridge, CF71 7AD
☎ (01446) 773385
enquiries@cowbridge-tc.gov.uk

Llantwit Major Town Council, Ms R Quinn, Town Hall, Llantwit Major, CF61 1SD ☎ (01446) 793707
lm.tc@btconnect.com

Penarth Town Council, Mrs S Bowden, Penarth Town Council, West House, Stanwell Road, Penarth, CF61 1SD ☎ (029) 2070 0721
sbowden@penarthtowncouncil.gov.uk

Colwinston Community Council, Mr B J Graham-Wollard, Yew Tree Farmhouse, Colwinston, Cowbridge, CF71 7ND ☎ (01656) 645721 / 07885 772907
clerk.colcommcoun@yahoo.co.uk

Dinas Powys Community Council, Mrs F A Butler, Council Office, Parish Hall, Britway Road, Dinas Powys, CF64 4AF, (029) 2051 3114,
theclerk@dinaspowys.org

Ewenny Community Council, Mrs M K Long, Cartref, Wick Road, Ewenny, Bridgend, CF35 5BL
☎ (01656) 654250
ewennycc@talktalk.net

Llancarfan Community Council, Mrs M L Sleeth, Grovelands House, Moulton, Nr Barry, CF62 3AB
☎ (01446) 746979

Llandough Community Council, Mr P R Egan, 63 Woodham Park, Barry, CF62 8FJ ☎ (01446) 409294
p.egan67@ntlworld.com

Llandow Community Council, Mr D L Jones, Overt House, 47 Cefn Road, Cefn Cribwr, Bridgend, CF32 0BA ☎ (01656) 741354
davidlloyd.jones@btinternet.com

Llanfair Community Council, Mrs J Griffin, 41 The Verlands, Cowbridge, CF71 7BY
☎ (01446) 773385
jackie.griffin1@btopenworld.com

Llangan Community Council, Mrs M Major, 49 Priory Avenue, Bridend, CF31 3LP ☎ (01656) 664105
mari-major@supanet.com

Llanmaes Community Council, Mrs J Griffin, 41 The Verlands, Cowbridge, CF71 7BY
☎ (01446) 773385
jackie.griffin1@btopenworld.com

Michaelston le Pit with Leckwith Community Council, Mr P Akers, 3 Archer Road, Penarth, CF64 3HW
☎ (029) 2070 5554
peterakers@btinternet.com

Pendoylan Community Council, Mrs J Roberts, 44, Heol St. Cattwg, Pendoylan, Cowbridge, CF71 7UG
☎ (01446) 760685
judith123roberts@btinternet.com

Penllyn Community Council, Mr C Farrant, 24 St John's Close, Cowbridge, CF71 7HN
☎ 07525 443913
Penllyn.community.council@talktalk.net

Peterston-Super-Ely Community Council, Alex Davies, Trecefn, St Brides-Super-Ely ☎ (01446) 460662
kim.davies2@btopenworld.com

St. Athan Community Council, Mr J Haswell, 8 Tathan Crescent, St Athan, CF62 4PE ☎ (01446) 750050
st.athan@btconnect.com

St. Brides Major Community Council, Mrs D Brunsdon, 31 Tŷ Gwyn Drive, Brackla, Bridgend, CF31 2QF ☎ (01656) 650004
clerk.sbmcc@gmail.com

St Donats Community Council, Mrs R P Smith, 66 Monmouth Way, Boverton, Llantwit Major, CF61 2GU ☎ (01446) 678619
clerkstdonatscc@talktalk.net

St. Georges and St.Brides-Super-Ely Community Council, Ms L Perna, 6 Cornwood Close, Fairwater, Cardiff, CF5 3QY
☎ (029) 2033 9930
clerk494@gmail.com

St. Nicholas & Bonvilston Community Council, Mr D Meirion Evans, Glan-y-Nant, Peterston-Super-Ely, Cardiff, CF5 6LG
☎ (01446) 760568
glanynant6@gmail.com

Sully Community Council, Mr D Roberts, c/o Jubilee Hall, Smithies Avenue, Sully, CF64 5SS
☎ (029) 2053 0006
sullycouncil@btconnect.com

Welsh St. Donats Community Council, Mrs V Pearce, Maendy House, Maendy, Cowbridge, CF71 7TG ☎ (01446) 774833
pearce.va@virgin.net

Wenvoe Community Council, Mr R Hulin, 24 Vennwood Close, Wenvoe, CF5 6BZ
☎ (029) 2059 7931 / 07742 922980
wenvoecc@googlemail.com

Wick Community Council, Ms K Whittington, Arosfa, Ewenny Road, Wick, CF71 7QA ☎ (01656) 890313
karoline.whittington@btinternet.com

WREXHAM COUNTY BOROUGH COUNCIL
CYNGOR BWRDEISTREF SIROL WRECSAM

Leader
Cllr Neil Rogers

Guildhall,
Wrexham LL11 1AY
Tel: (01978) 292000
Fax: (01978) 292106
Website: www.wrexham.gov.uk

wrexham
COUNTY BOROUGH COUNCIL
CYNGOR BWRDEISTREF SIROL
wrecsam

Chief Executive
Helen Paterson

NO OVERALL CONTROL

Lab **23** Ind **19** Con **5**
Lib D **4** PC **1**

TOTAL 52

ELECTION RESULT 2012

	Seats	Change	Votes	Share
Lab	23	12	15,245	41.4%
Ind	19	-1	9,717	26.4%
Con	5	-	4,557	12.4%
Lib Dem	4	-8	4,204	11.4%
PC	1	-3	2,567	7.0%
Others	-	-	490	1.3%

Socio-economic Profile

		Rank 1<22
Area (sq km)	504	10
Population ('000s)	133.5	10
% able to speak Welsh	17.0	16
% born in Wales	71.9	13
% non-white ethnic groups	2.6	17
Gross rev expenditure (2011-12)	£264.0m	13
Forecast capital expenditure (2011-12)	£60.5m	5
% dwellings in Band D (2012-13)	16.7	12
Band D council tax (2011-12)	£1,135.42	14
% over retirement age	17.3	17
% pupils 5+ GCSEs A*-C (2010-11)	61.2	20
Unemployment (% claimant count 2011)	3.7	14
Index of Deprivation (2011)	29	11
(% of Authority in most deprived 30%)		

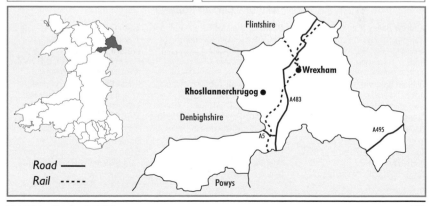

Road ——
Rail - - - - -

LOCAL GOVERNMENT

WREXHAM

Principal Officers

Chief Executive: **Helen Paterson**
Strategic & Performance Director: **Clare Field**
Strategic & Performance Director: **Lee Robinson**
Strategic & Performance Director: **Phil Walton**

Executive Board 2012-2013

Leader / Economic Development & Regeneration:	**Neil Rogers** (Lab)
Deputy Leader / Housing & Planning:	**Mark Pritchard** (Ind)
Children's Services & Education:	**Michael Williams** (Lab)
Environment:	**Bob Dutton OBE** (Ind)
Policy, Finance, Performance & Governance:	**Malcolm King OBE** (Lab)
Health & Adult Social Care:	**David Griffiths** (Lab)
Communities, Partnership & Collaboration:	**Hugh Jones** (Con)
Without Portfolio:	**David Bithell** (Ind); **Joan Lowe** (Ind); **Carol O'Toole** (Lib D)

Committee Chairs 2010-2011

Planning Committee:	**Michael Morris** (Con)
Licensing Committee:	**Alan Edwards** (Ind)
Democratic Services Committee:	**Arfon Jones** (PC)
Audit Committee:	**Paul Blackwell** (Lab)
Employment, Business & Investment Scrutiny Committee:	**Rodney Skelland** (Con)
Education, Safeguarding & Well-being Scrutiny Committee:	**Andrew Bailey** (Lab)
Homes, Environment & Communities (Place) Scrutiny Committee:	**David Kelly** (Ind)
Customers, Performance & Resources (Organization) Scrutiny Committee:	**Steve Wilson** (Lab)
Partnerships & Collaboration (Partnership) Scrutiny Committee:	**Ronnie Prince** (Ind)

Salaries

Basic Salary: £13,175 per annum; Senior Salaries: Leader: £47,500
Deputy Leader: £33,460; Cabinet Members: £28,780; Chairs of Scrutiny Committees: £21,910
Chairs of Other Committes: £21,910; Mayor: £21,375; Deputy Mayor: £16,625

Councillors   ♂ 45 ♀ 7

Mayor – Cllr Ian Roberts

Andrew Bailey (Lab: Gresford East & West), Woodvale, Pant Lane, Gresford, Wrexham, LL12 8EU
☎ (01978) 855144
andrew.bailey@wrexham.gov.uk

William Baldwin (Wre Ind: Little Acton), 24 Frances Avenue, Wrexham, LL12 8BN ☎ (01978) 361327
william.baldwin@wrexham.gov.uk

David A Bithell (Wre Ind: Johnstown), The Hollies, Bangor Road, Eyton, Wrexham, LL13 0SW
☎ (01978) 781422
davida.bithell@wrexham.gov.uk

David I Bithell MBE (Lab: Stansty), 27 Clarence Road, Rhosddu, Wrexham, LL11 2EU
☎ (01978) 355009
idavid.bithell@wrexham.gov.uk

Paul Blackwell (Lab: Plas Madoc), The Croft, Abernant, Acrefair, Wrexham, LL14 3SN
☎ (01490) 430873 / 07855620891
paul.blackwell@wrexham.gov.uk

Terry Boland (Lab: Llay), 166 Bryn Place, Llay, Wrexham, LL12 0LT
☎ 07946 789714
terry.boland@wrexham.gov.uk

Brian Cameron (Lab: Whitegate), 17 Clifton Close, Kings Mill, Wrexham, LL13 0YJ
☎ (01978) 264795 / 07933152723
brian.cameron@wrexham.gov.uk

Krista Childs (Lab: Coedpoeth), Yr Hen Garreg, 10 Penygelli Road, Coedpoeth, Wrexham, LL11 3RN
☎ (01978) 759175 / 07875090490
krista.childs@wrexham.gov.uk

Dana Davies (Lab: Ruabon), 6 Bedwell Close, Ruabon, Wrexham, LL14 6BW ☎ (01978) 824433 / 07516069760
dana.davies@wrexham.gov.uk

WREXHAM

Bob Dutton *(Dem Ind: Erddig)*, 28 Drws y Coed, Sontley Road, Wrexham, LL13 7QB ☎ (01978) 357112 bob.dutton@wrexham.gov.uk

Mike Edwards *(Lib D: Marford & Hoseley)*, 13 Sandrock Road, Marford, Wrexham, LL12 8LT ☎ (01978) 854992 michael.edwards@wrexham.gov.uk

T Alan Edwards *(Dem Ind: New Broughton)*, Gwynfa Stores, Gatewen Road, New Broughton, Wrexham, LL11 6UY ☎ (01978) 755501 talan.edwards@wrexham.gov.uk

Anne Evans *(Lab: Rhosnesni)*, 23 Hilltop View Road, Borras Park, Wrexham, LL12 7SF ☎ (01978) 291452 anne.evans@wrexham.gov.uk

Terry Evans *(Dem Ind: Chirk South)*, Hazelgrove, Church View, Chirk, Wrexham, LL14 5PE ☎ (01691) 772015 terry.evans@wrexham.gov.uk

Pat Jeffares *(Wre Ind: Llangollen Rural)*, Wexford, 16 Wenfryn Close, Trevor, Llangollen, LL20 7TU ☎ (01978) 820570 pat.jeffares@wrexham.gov.uk

Alun Jenkins *(Lib D: Offa)*, 1 Maes Glas, Court Road, Wrexham, LL13 7SN ☎ (01978) 352879 alun.jenkins@wrexham.gov.uk

Arfon Jones *(Wre Ind: Gwersyllt West)*, 12 Fairways Gardens, Gwersyllt, Wrexham, LL11 4XB ☎ (01978) 755048 arfon.jones@wrexham.gov.uk

Hugh Jones *(Con: Rossett)*, 5 Stonewalls, Burton, Rossett, Wrexham, LL12 0LG ☎ (01244) 571747 hugh.jones@wrexham.gov.uk

David Kelly *(Dem Ind: Minera)*, Min-Y-Mynydd, Old Road, Minera, Wrexham, LL11 3YR ☎ (01978) 752317 david.kelly@wrexham.gov.uk

James Kelly *(Lib D: Borras Park)*, 21 Stratford Close, Acton Park, Wrexham, LL12 7UR ☎ (01978) 354271 james.kelly@wrexham.gov.uk

Lloyd Kenyon *(Con: Overton)*, Gredington, Whitchurch, Shropshire, SY13 3DH ☎ (01948) 830305 lloyd.kenyon@wrexham.gov.uk

Keith Gregory *(Wre Ind: Smithfield)*, 13 Colwyn Road, Smithfield, Caia Park, Wrexham, LL13 8ET ☎ (01978) 263552 / 07776312744 keith.gregory@wrexham.gov.uk

David Griffiths *(Lab: Gwersyllt East & South)*, Tŷ Newydd, Glan Llyn Road, Bradley, Wrexham, LL11 4BB ☎ (01978) 759491 david.griffiths@wrexham.gov.uk

Gareth Wyn Griffiths *(Lab: Coedpoeth)*, 9 Maes Tyddyn, off Talwrn Road, Coedpoeth, Wrexham, LL11 3LA ☎ (01978) 754338 gareth.wyngriffiths@wrexham.gov.uk

Kevin Hughes *(Lab: Ponciau)*, Penrhos, Erw Gerrig, Rhosllanerchrugog, Wrexham, LL14 2BS ☎ (01978) 840884 kevin1.hughes@wrexham.gov.uk

Malcolm Christopher King OBE, *(Lab: Wynnstay)*, Tyddyn Draw, Llanelidan, Denbighshire, LL15 2TA ☎ (01978) 355761 / (01824) 750710 malcolm.king@wrexham.gov.uk

Geoff Lowe *(Lab: Acton)*, 117 Herbert Jennings Avenue, Wrexham, LL12 7YA ☎ (01978) 359493 geoff.lowe@wrexham.gov.uk

Joan Lowe *(Wre Ind: Penycae & Ruabon South)*, Plas Issa, Penycae, Wrexham, LL14 1TT ☎ (01978) 840156 joan.lowe@wrexham.gov.uk

Bernie McCann *(Lab: Gwersyllt East & South)*, 4 Sherbourne Avenue, Bradley, Wrexham, LL11 4AZ ☎ (01978) 756085 / 07931 720210 bernard.mccann@wrexham.gov.uk

Michael Morris *(Con: Holt)*, Denverra, Sun Lane, Bowling Bank, Wrexham, LL13 9RW ☎ (01978) 661815 michael.morris@wrexham.gov.uk

Carole O'Toole *(Lib D: Maesydre)*, 24 Park Avenue, Wrexham, LL12 7AH ☎ (01978) 291250 carole.otoole@wrexham.gov.uk

Mark Owens *(Dem Ind: Pant)*, 14 Maes Glan, Rhos, Wrexham, LL14 2DT ☎ (01978) 841083 marka.owens@wrexham.gov.uk

John Phillips *(Wre Ind: Pen y Cae)*, 57 Ffordd Llanerch, Penycae, Wrexham, LL14 2ND ☎ 07707 209603 johnc.phillips@wrexham.gov.uk

Paul Howard Pemberton *(Dem Ind: Ponciau)*, Gilfach Goch, Queen Street, Rhosllanerchrugog, Wrexham, LL14 1PY ☎ (01978) 842579 paul.pemberton@wrexham.gov.uk

Colin Powell *(Lab: Queensway)*, 26 Ashbourne Avenue, Gwersyllt, Wrexham, LL11 4RR ☎ (01978) 269003 colin.powell@wrexham.gov.uk

Ronnie Prince *(Wre Ind: Cartrefle)*, 1 Harvard Way, Wrexham, LL13 9LP ☎ (01978) 362749 ron.prince@wrexham.gov.uk

John Pritchard *(Wre Ind: Marchwiel)*, 21 Elwyn Drive, Marchwiel, Wrexham, LL13 0RD ☎ (01978) 358153 / 07746857511 john.pritchard@wrexham.gov.uk

Mark Pritchard *(Dem Ind: Esclusham)*, Adaley, Henry Street, Rhostyllen, Wrexham, LL14 4BY ☎ (01978) 356856 / 07740637591 mark.pritchard@wrexham.gov.uk

Ian Roberts *(Dem Ind: Chirk North)*, 62 Church View, Shepherds Lane, Chirk, LL14 5PF ☎ (01691) 773758 ian1.roberts@wrexham.gov.uk

Barbara Roberts *(Dem Ind: Ceiriog Valley)*, The Gables, High Street, Glyn Ceiriog, Llangollen, LL20 7EH ☎ (01691) 718387 barbara.roberts@wrexham.gov.uk

Graham Rogers *(Lab: Hermitage)*, 7 Bell Court, Hightown, Wrexham, LL13 8QP ☎ (01978) 351107 / 07968214189 graham1.rogers@wrexham.gov.uk

Neil Rogers *(Lab: Gwenfro)*, 1 Cripps Avenue, Southsea, Wrexham, LL11 6RA ☎ (01978) 750237 neil.rogers@wrexham.gov.uk

Paul Rogers *(Con: Brymbo)*, 19 Ffordd Owain, Brymbo, Wrexham, LL11 5AY ☎ (01978) 753304 paul2.rogers@wrexham.gov.uk

Barbara Roxburgh *(Lab: Bryn Cefn)*, Tanpant Teg, Pendwll Road, Moss Valley, Wrexham, LL11 6EU ☎ (01978) 756426 / 07729 680333 barbara.roxburgh@wrexham.gov.uk

David Taylor *(Wre Ind: Cefn)*, Cefn Mawr P.O, Crane Street, Cefn Mawr, Wrexham, LL14 3LN ☎ (01978) 823090 / 07875 204981 david.taylor@wrexham.gov.uk

Malcolm Taylor *(Lab: Llay)*, 11 Second Avenue, Llay, Wrexham, LL12 0TB ☎ (01978) 853098 malcolm.taylor@wrexham.gov.uk

Rodney Skelland *(Con: Bronington)*, Willington Cross Farm, Willington, Malpas, Cheshire, SY14 7NA ☎ (01948) 830361 rodney.skelland@wrexham.gov.uk

LOCAL GOVERNMENT

Andy Williams (*Lab: Garden Village*), 11 Haytor Road, Garden Village, Wrexham, LL11 2PT ☎ (01978) 351153 andy.williams@wrexham.gov.uk

Michael Williams (*Lab: Gwersyllt North*), 3 Summerhill Park, Wrexham, LL11 4SY ☎ (01978) 758295 michael.williams@wrexham.gov.uk

Steve Wilson (*Lab: Grosvenor*), 15 Spring Road, Rhosddu, Wrexham, LL11 2LU ☎ (01978) 355879 steve.wilson@wrexham.gov.uk

Derek Wright (*Lab: Cefn*), Fern Villa, Church Street, Rhosymedre, Wrexham, LL14 3EA ☎ (01978) 822497 derek.wright@wrexham.gov.uk

Phil Wynn (*NA: Brynyffynnon*), 6 Court Road, Wrexham, LL13 7RH ☎ (01978) 291208 / (01829) 773939 / 07792542679 phil.wynn@wrexham.gov.uk

Clerks to the Community Councils

Abenbury Community Council, *Stephen Nott*, Woodbank Cottage, Pontcysyllte, Llangollen, LL20 7YR ☎ (01978) 820999

Acton Community Council, *Carole Roberts*, 40 Mile Barn Road, Wrexham, LL13 9JY ☎ 07913071470 carole.roberts@micro-plus-web.net

Bangor Isycoed Community Council, *Mrs D Ford*, The Barn, Dawsonís Farm Church Road, Worthenbury, LL13 0AW

Bronington Community Council, *Ruth Jacks Broselake*, Cottage, Greenway Lane, Malpas, Cheshire, SY14 8DE ☎ (01948) 861353 broningtoncommunitycouncil@hotmail.co.uk

Broughton Community Council, *Steve Wilson*, 15 Spring Road, Rhosddu, Wrexham, LL11 2LU ☎ (01978) 355879

Brymbo Community Council, *Bethan Hughes*, 15 Chestnut Avenue, Acton, Wrexham, LL12 7HS ☎ (01978) 361006

Caia Park Community Council, *M G Morris*, Caia Park Council Rooms, Cartrefle, Cefn Road, Wrexham, LL13 9NH ☎ (01978) 354825

Ceiriog Uchaf Community Council, *Sheila Crawshaw*, Glan-y-Geifr, Llanarmon DC, Llangollen, LL20 7LH ☎ (01691) 600613

Chirk Town Council, *S A Hughes*, 4 Castle Crescent, Chirk, Wrexham, LL14 5LY ☎ (01691) 772596

Cefn Community Council, *Rhona Roberts*, Council Offices, George Edwards Hall, Well Street, Cefn Mawr, Wrexham, LL14 3AE ☎ (01978) 821298 (01978) 820658

Coedpoeth Community Council, *The Clerk to the Council*, The Old Carnegie Library, Park Road, Coedpoeth, Wrexham LL11 3TD ☎ (01978) 756890 clerk@coedpoeth.com

Erbistock Community Council, *James Wild*, Haddon Bank, Erbistock, Wrexham, LL13 0DW ☎ (01978) 780116

Esclusham Community Council, *Alan Vaughan Thomas*, Parish Hall, Vicarage Hill, Rhosyllen, Wrexham, LL14 4AR ☎ (01978) 366491

Glyn-Traian Community Council, *David R E Lloyd*, 5 Afonwen, Pontfadog, Llangollen, LL20 7AP ☎ (01691) 718080

Gresford Community Council, *M Paddock*, 23 Richmond Road, Wrexham, LL12 8AA ☎ (01978) 355519

Gwersyllt Community Council, *Keith Bryan*, 12 Ffordd Mailyn, Wrexham, LL13 7JB ☎ (01978) 359691

Hanmer Community Council, *Mrs P Edwards*, Chadwell, Hanmer, Whitchurch, Shropshire, SY13 3DE ☎ (01948) 830043

Holt Community Council, *Mrs J Pierce*, 142 Borras Road, Wrexham, LL13 9ER ☎ (01978) 359791

Isycoed Community Council, Steve Wilson, 15 Spring Road, Rhosddu, Wrexham, LL11 2LU ☎ (01978) 355879

Llangollen Rural Community Council, *Sue Jones*, 1 Ael Y Bryn, Llangollen Road, Trevor, Llangollen, Wrexham, LL20 7TF ☎ (01978) 810466

Llansantfraid Glyn Ceiriog Community Council, *Jean Davies*, Maes y Coed, Glyn Ceiriog, Llangollen, LL20 7NL ☎ (01691) 718419

Llay Community Council, *Sheila Woolrich*, 5 Forest Road, Off Gresford Road, Llay, Wrexham, LL12 0UB ☎ (01978) 852602

Maelor South Community Council, *Rachel Coathupe-Fox*, 28 Winston Way, Penley, Wrexham, LL13 0JT ☎ (01948) 830119 / 07523730674 maelorsouth@gmail.com

Marchwell Community Council, *Mrs V M Jones*, Sandhurst, Croeshowell Hill, Rossett, Wrexham, LL12 0AA ☎ (01244) 570629

Minera Community Council, *Rebecca Sparey-Taylor*, PO Box 2305, Wrexham, LL11 0FS ☎ (01978) 753641 mineracc@gmail.com

Offa Community Council, *Karen Benfield*, Upper Floor, Parciau Community Centre, Bellevue Road, Wrexham, LL13 7NH ☎ (01978) 291562

Overton Community Council, *Katrina Chalk*, c/o Overton Village Hall, 5 Penyllan, Street, Overton, LL13 0EE ☎ (01978) 710055

Pen-y-Cae Community Council, *Mrs S Hallard*, Bryn Offa, Heol y Felin, off Jones Street, Rhos, Wrexham, LL14 1AT ☎ (01978) 841584

Rhosddu Community Council, *E N Hodges*, 12 Miller Road, Brymbo Heights, Brymbo, Wrexham, LL11 5FH ☎ (01978) 449230

Rhosllannerchrugog Community Council, *Wendy Owens*, Bryn Maelor, Peter Street, Rhosllanerchrugog, Wrexham, LL14 1RG ☎ (01978) 840007

Rossett Community Council, *Mr F B Doyle*, 9 Caernarvon Road, Rhosnesni, Wrexham, LL12 7TT ☎ (01978) 290380 clerktothecouncil@rossett.net

Ruabon Community Council, *Claire Klimaszewski*, 1 Woodwards Cottages, New Brighton, Minera, Wrexham, LL11 3ED ☎ (01978) 759114 / 07720344196 ruaboncommunitycouncil@gmail.com

Sesswick Community Council, *John Hurst, Acting Clerk*, Oaklea, Kiln Lane, Cross Lanes, Wrexham, LL13 0TH

Willington / Worthenbury Community Council, *Michael Arnold*, Willow Cottage, Tallarn Green, Malpas, Cheshire, SY14 7LJ ☎ (01948) 770697

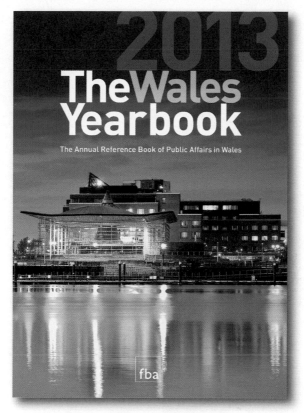

DIRECTORY
OF WELSH
ORGANIZATIONS

Sponsored by

Royal Mail

The postal service of choice
www.royalmail.com

Mae Heledd yn siarad Cymraeg.
Mae newydd ffonio'r Post Brenhinol yn Saesneg.

Ffonia 08457 468 469 er mwyn trafod gwasanaethau'r Post Brenhinol,
Swyddfa'r Post a Parcelforce Worldwide yn Gymraeg.

mae gen ti ddewis...

This is an advert drawing attention to our Welsh language services

CLASSIFIED ENTRIES

Agriculture

ADAS Cymru Wales
Henstaff Court Business Centre, Groesfaen,
Cardiff CF72 8NG
☎ (029) 2089 9674
Email: enys.young@adas.co.uk
www.adas.co.uk/wales
Managing Director: Colin Speller

Also at:

Unit 10D Cefn Llan Science Park,
Aberystwyth, Ceredigion SY23 3AH
☎ (01970) 617309
Group Manager: Cate Barrow

Agriculture Land Tribunal (Wales)
Unit 32 Ddole Road Enterprise Park,
Llandrindod Wells, Powys LD1 6DF
☎ (01597) 829809 ▯ (01597) 829801
Email: altwales@wales.gsi.gov.uk
www.wales.gov.uk/environmentandcountryside
Secretary: Sarah Smith

Cambrian Training Company
Centre of Excellence
Cambrian House, Unit 14, Severn Farm
Enterprise Park, Severn Rd, Welshpool,
Powys SY21 7DF
☎ (01938) 556890 ▯ (01938) 556624
Email: tammy@cambriantraining.com
www.cambriantraining.com
Managing Director: Arwyn Watkins

Coed Cymru
The Old Sawmill, Tregynon,
Newtown, Powys SY16 3PL
☎ (01686) 650777 ▯ (01686) 650696
Email: coedcymru@coedcymru.org.uk
www.coedcymru.org.uk
Director: David Jenkins

Country Land & Business Association (CLA)
Cymdeithas Tir & Busnes Cefngwlad
Unit 8, Broadaxe Business Park,
Presteigne, Powys LD8 2LA
☎ (01547) 317085 ▯ (01544) 260023
Email: info.wales@cla.org.uk info@cla.org.uk
www.cla.org.uk
Director Policy Wales: Sue Evans
Regional Surveyor Wales: Charles De Winton

Countryside Council for Wales
Cyngor Cefn Gwlad Cymru
Headquarters: Maes-y-Ffynnon, Penrhosgarnedd,
Bangor, Gwynedd LL57 2DW
☎ (0845) 1306229 ▯ (01248) 385505
Email: Enquiries@ccw.gov.uk
www.ccw.gov.uk
Chair: Morgan Parry
Chief Executive: Roger Thomas
Director Evidence & Advice: Dr David Parker
Director, Planning & Resources: Adrian Williams

Also at:

Rivers House, St Mellons Business Park,
Fortran Road, St Mellon's, Cardiff CF3 0EY
☎ (0845) 1306229 ▯ (01248) 355782
Email: southernteam@ccw.gov.uk

First Floor, Ladywell House, Park St,
Newtown, Powys SY16 1RD
☎ (0845) 1306229 ▯ (01248) 385505
Email: southernteam@ccw.gov.uk

Welsh Government Building, Rhodfa Padarn,
Llanbadarn Fawr, Aberystwyth SY23 3UR
☎ (01970) 631160 ▯ (01970) 631161
Email: Enquiries@ccw.gov.uk
www.ccw.gov.uk
Director West Region: David Worrall

Beechwood Office, Beechwood Industrial
Estate, Talley Rd, Llandeilo, Carms SA19 7HR
☎ (0845) 1306229 ▯ (01248) 385505
Email: westernteam@ccw.gov.uk

Llanion House , Llanion Park, Pembroke
Dock, Pembrokeshire SA72 6DY
☎ (0845) 1306229 ▯ (01248) 385505
Email: westernteam@ccw.gov.uk

Maes Newydd, Britannic Way West,
Llandarcy, Neath Port Talbot SA10 6JQ
☎ (01792) 326450 ▯ (01792) 326451
Email: westernteam@ccw.gov.uk

Plas Tan y Bwlch, Maentwrog,
Gwynedd LL41 3YU
☎ (01766) 772600 ▯ (01766) 772609
Email: twm.elias@eryri-npa.gov.uk
www.plastanybwlch.co.uk
Secretary: Twm Elias

Sponsored by: www.royalmail.com

Royal Mail

Environment Agency Wales
Asiantaeth yr Amgylchedd Cymru
Head Office, Tŷ Cambria, 29 Newport Rd,
Cardiff CF24 0TP
☎ (0370) 850 6506
Email: enquiries@environment-
agency.wales.gov.uk
www.environment-agency.wales.gov.uk
Director, Wales: Chris Mills

Also at:

South West Area Office, Maes Newydd,
Llandarcy, Neath SA10 6JQ
☎ (0370) 850 6506
Area Manager: Steve Brown

South East Area Office, Rivers House,
St Mellons Business Park, St Mellons,
Cardiff CF3 0EY
☎ (0370) 850 6506
Area Manager: Gareth O'Shea

North Area Office, Ffordd Penlan,
Parc Menai, Bangor LL57 4DE
☎ (0370) 850 6506
Area Manager: David Edwell

Farmers' Union of Wales (FUW)
Undeb Amaethwyr Cymru
Llys Amaeth, Plas Gogerddan,
Bow Street, Aberystwyth SY23 3BT
☎ (01970) 820820
▣ (01970) 820821
Email: Head.Office@fuw.org.uk
www.fuw.org.uk
President: Emyr Jones
Director, Business Development: Emyr James
Director, Agricultural Policy: Nick Fenwick
Director, Operations: Mark Roberts
Director, Administration: Peter Davies
Director, Public Relations: Peter Roberts

Food & Farming Sector Panel
Welsh Government, Rhodfa Padarn,
Llanbadarn Fawr, Aberystwyth SY23 3UR
☎ (0300) 062 2384
Email: foodpolicy@wales.gsi.gov.uk

Forestry Commission Wales
Comisiwn Coedwigaeth Cymru
Welsh Government, Rhodfa Padarn,
Llanbadarn Fawr, Aberystwyth SY23 3UR
☎ (0300) 068 0300 ▣ (0300) 068 0301
Email: fcwenquiries@forestry.gsi.gov.uk
www.forestry.gov.uk
Director: Trefor Owen
Chair, Woodland Strategy Advisory Panel: Roger Cooper

Hybu Cig Cymru
Meat Promotion Wales
Tŷ Rheidol, Parc Merlin, Aberystwyth,
Ceredigion SY23 3FF
☎ (01970) 625050
▣ (01970) 615148
Email: info@hccmpw.org.uk
www.hccmpw.org.uk
Chair: Dai Davies
Chief Executive: Gwyn Howells

i2LResearch Limited
Capital Business Park, Wentloog,
Cardiff CF3 2PX
☎ (029) 2077 6220
▣ (029) 2077 6221
Email: peter@i2lresearch.com
www.i2lresearch.com
Managing Director: Dr Peter McEwen

Institute of Biological, Environmental
& Rural Science (IBERS)
Aberystwyth University, Penglais,
Aberystwyth SY23 3DA
☎ (01970) 622316
▣ (01970) 621981
Email: ibers@aber.ac.uk
www.aber.ac.uk/en/ibers
Director: Professor Wayne Powell

International Bee Research Association
16 North Rd, Cardiff CF10 3DY
☎ (029) 2037 2409
▣ (029) 05601 135640
Email: mail@ibra.org.uk
www.ibra.org.uk
Publications Manager: Sarah Jones

LANTRA
Royal Welsh Showground, Llanelwedd,
Builth Wells, Powys LD2 3WY
☎ (01982) 552646
Email: wales@lantra.co.uk
www.lantra.co.uk
National Director Wales: Kevin Thomas

NFU Cymru
Tŷ Amaeth, Agriculture House, Royal Welsh
Showground, Builth Wells, Powys LD2 3TU
☎ (01982) 554200
▣ (01982) 554201
Email: nfu.cymru@nfu.org.uk
www.nfu-cymru.org.uk
Director NFU Cymru: Mary James
President: Ed Bailey

AGRICULTURE

Organic Centre Wales
Institute of Biological, Environmental & Rural Sciences, Gogerddan Campus, Aberystwyth University, Ceredigion SY23 3EE
☎ (01970) 622248 🖷 (01970) 622238
Email: organic@aber.ac.uk
www.organic.aber.ac.uk
Director: Sue Fowler
Manager: Neil Pearson

Royal Welsh Agricultural Society
Llanelwedd, Builth Wells, Powys LD2 3SY
☎ (01982) 553683 🖷 (01982) 553563
Email: requests@rwas.co.uk
www.rwas.co.uk
Chief Executive: David B Walters

Welsh Agricultural Organisation Society
PO Box 8, Brynawel, Great Darkgate Street, Aberystwyth SY23 1DR
☎ (01970) 636688 🖷 (01970) 624049
Email: dont@wfsagri.net
Chief Executive: Don Thomas

Welsh Black Cattle Society
13 Bangor St, Caernarfon, Gwynedd LL55 1AP
☎ (01286) 672391 🖷 (01286) 672022
Email: welshblack@btclick.com
www.welshblackcattlesociety.com
Society Council Chairman: Robert Jones

Welsh Lamb & Beef Producers Ltd
Gorseland, North Rd, Aberystwyth, Ceredigion SY23 2WB
☎ (01970) 636688 🖷 (01970) 624049
Email: info@wlbp.co.uk
www.wlbp.co.uk
Chair: Richard Howells
Managing Director: Don Thomas

The Welsh Pony & Cob Society
Bronaeron, Felinfach, Lampeter, Ceredigion SA48 8AG
☎ (01570) 471754 🖷 (01570) 470435
Email: secretary@wpcs.uk.com
www.wpcs.uk.com
President: Mr E.T.E Davies, Maesmynach Stud

Wales Young Farmers' Clubs (YFC) Cffi Cymru
YFC Centre, Llanelwedd, Builth Wells, Powys LD2 3NJ
☎ (01982) 553502 🖷 (01982) 552979
Email: information@yfc-wales.org.uk
www.yfc-wales.org.uk
Chief Executive: Nia Lloyd

Wales Young Farmers' Clubs (YFC) Cffi Cymru
Also at:

YFC Brecknock Office
Room 15, Neuadd Brycheiniog, Cambrian Way, Brecon, Powys LD3 7HR
☎ (01874) 612207/386 🖷 (01874) 612389
Email: brecknock@yfc-wales.org.uk
www.brecknockyfc.co.uk
County Chair: Vicky Hope
Organizer: Claire Price

YFC Carmarthen Office
Agriculture House, Cambrian Place, Carmarthen, Carms SA31 1QG
☎ (01267) 237693 🖷 (01267) 237693
Email: sir.gar@yfc-wales.org.uk
www.carmsyfc.org.uk
County Chair: Rhian Howells Jones;
County Organizer: Eirios Thomas

CFfI Ceredigion YFC
Canolfan Addysg Felinfach, Dyffryn Aeron, Llanbedr Pont Steffan, Ceredigion SA48 8AF
☎ (01545) 571333 🖷 (01545) 571444
Email: ceredigion@yfc-wales.org.uk
www.yfc-ceredigion.org.uk
County Chair: Manon Richards
Development Officer: Mared Jones

YFC Clwyd Office
Pentrecelyn, Ruthin, Denbighshire LL15 2LB
☎ (01978) 790403 🖷 (01978) 790403
Email: yfc@deeside.ac.uk / yfc@llysfasi.ac.uk
www.yfc-clwyd.org.uk
County Chair: Caroline Dawson
County Organizer: Eleri Roberts

YFC Eryri Office
Uned 12, Parc Glynllifon, Ffordd Clynnog, Caernarfon, Gwynedd LL54 5DU
☎ (01286) 831214
Email: eryri@yfc-wales.org.uk
County Chair: Arwel Thomas
Organizer: Eleri Evans

Post Brenhinol

Royal Mail

Wales Young Farmers' Clubs (YFC)
Cffi Cymru

Also at:

YFC Glamorgan Office
Bridgend College, Pencoed Campus,
Pencoed, Bridgend CF35 5LG
☎ (01656) 864488 ☐ (01656) 862398
Email: glamorgan@yfc-wales.org.uk
County Chair: Martyn John
County Organizer: Gwyneth Thomas

YFC Gwent Office
Coleg Gwent, Usk Campus, Usk,
Monmouthshire NP5 1XJ
☎ (01291) 672602 ☐ (01291) 671261
Email: gwent@yfc-wales.org.uk
www.gwent-yfc.btik.com
County Chair: Tim Jenkins
County Organizer: Sarah Davies

YFC Meironnydd Office
Cae Penarlâg, Dolgellau, Gwynedd LL40 2YB
☎ (01341) 423846
Email: cffimeirionnydd@gwynedd.org.uk
www.yfc-meirionnydd.org.uk
County Chair: Telor Edwards

YFC Montgomery Office
Old College, Station Rd,
Newtown, Powys SY16 1BE
☎ (01686) 614028 ☐ (01686) 614079
Email: maldwyn@powys.org.uk
www.yfc-montgomery.org.uk
County Organizer: Lorraine Stokes

YFC Pembrokeshire Office
Agriculture House, Winch Lane,
Haverfordwest, Pembrokeshire SA61 1RW
☎ (01437) 762639
☐ (01437) 768996
Email: sir.benfro@yfc-wales.org.uk
www.pembrokeshireyfc.org.uk
County Chair: Ros Bushell
County Organizer: Dill Williams

YFC Radnor
Rhoslyn, High St, Llandrindod Wells,
Powys LD1 6AG
☎ (01597) 829008 ☐ (01597) 824096
Email: gaynor.james@powys.gov.uk
www.radnoryfc.org.uk
County Chair: Avril Hardwick
County Organizer: Gaynor James

YFC Ynys Môn
Anglesey Showground, Gwalchmai,
Holyhead, Ynys Môn LL65 4RW
☎ (01407) 720256 ☐ (01407) 720262
Email: ynys.mon@yfc-wales.org.uk
www.cffi-ynysmon.org.uk
County Chair: Dafydd Foulkes
County Organizer: Elen Jones

Arts

Canolfan y Celfyddydau
Aberystwyth Arts Centre
Prifysgol Aberystwyth University,
Aberystwyth, Ceredigion SY23 3DE
☎ (01970) 622882 ☐ (01970) 622883
Email: aeh@aber.ac.uk
www.aber.ac.uk/artscentre
Director: Alan Hewson
Deputy Director: Louise Amery

The Albany Gallery
74b Albany Road, Cardiff CF24 3RS
☎ (029) 2048 7158
Email: info@albanygallery.com
www.albanygallery.com

Amgueddfa Cymru
National Museum Wales
Cathays Park, Cardiff CF10 3NP
☎ (029) 2039 7951 ☐ (029) 2057 3321
Email: post@museumwales.ac.uk /
post@amgueddfacymru.ac.uk
www.museumwales.ac.uk /
www.amgueddfacymru.ac.uk
President: Elizabeth Elias
Director General: David Anderson

Andrew Logan Museum of Sculpture
Berriew, Nr Welshpool, Powys SY21 8PJ
☎ (01686) 640689
www.andrewlogan.com

ARTS

Archives & Records Council Wales
Cyngor Archifau a Chofnodion Cymru
The National Library of Wales, Aberystwyth,
Ceredigion SY23 3BU
☎ (01970) 632803 ☎ (01970) 632882
Email: avril.jones@llgc.org.uk
www.llgc.org.uk/cac
Director of Collection Services: Avril Jones

Artes Mundi
Wales International Visual Arts Prize, St John's
Chambers, High Street Arcade, Cardiff CF10 1BD
☎ (029) 2055 5300 ☎ (029) 2055 5800
Email: info@artesmundi.org
www.artesmundi.org
Chair: William Wilkins CBE DL
Artistic Director: Ben Borthwick
Head of Finance & Operations: Carl Grainger
Head of Development: Caron Thomas

Arts & Business Cymru
South Wales Office,16 Museum Place,
Cardiff CF10 3BH
☎ (029) 2030 3023 ☎ (029) 2030 3024
Email: contactus@aandbcymru.org.uk
www.aandbcymru.org.uk
Chair: Huw Roberts
Chief Executiver: Rachel Jones

Also at:

North Wales Office, Room 40,
The Town Hall, Llandudno LL30 2UP
☎ (01492) 574003 ☎ (01492) 877045
Email: contactus@aandbcymru.org.uk
www.aandbcymru.org.uk
Chair: Huw Roberts
Chief Executiver: Rachel Jones

Arts Council of Wales
Bute Place, Cardiff CF10 5AL
☎ (0845) 8734 900 ☎ (0845) 029 2044 1400
Email: info@artswales.org.uk
www.artswales.org.uk / www.celfcymru.org.uk
Chair: Prof Dai Smith
Chief Executive: Nick Capaldi

Also at:

6 Gardd Llydaw, Jackson's Lane,
Carmarthen SA31 1QD
☎ (01267) 234248 ☎ (01267) 233084
Email: midandwest@artswales.org.uk
www.artswales.org.uk
www.celfcymru.org.uk

Arts Council of Wales
Also at:

36 Prince's Drive, Colwyn Bay LL29 8LA
☎ (01492) 533440 ☎ (01492) 533677
Minicom: 01492 532288
Email: north@artswales.org.uk
www.artswales.org.uk/www.celfcymru.org.uk

Bute Place, Cardiff CF10 5AL
☎ (029) 8734 900 ☎ (029) 029 2044 1400

Attic Gallery
37 Pocketts Wharf, Maritime Quarter,
Swansea SA1 3XL
☎ (01792) 653387
Email: roe@atticgallery.co.uk
www.atticgallery.co.uk

Audiences Wales Ltd
Chapter Arts Centre, Market Rd,
Cardiff CF5 1QE
☎ (029) 2037 3736 ☎ (029) 2034 2272
Email: contact@audienceswales.co.uk
www.audienceswales.co.uk
Chair: Dorothy James
Chief Executive: Nick Beasley

BBC National Orchestra of Wales
BBC Hoddinott Hall, Bute Place,
Cardiff Bay, Cardiff CF10 5AL
☎ (0800) 052 1812 ☎ (0800) 029 2055 9721
Email: now@bbc.co.uk www.bbc.co.uk/now
Director: David Murray
Orchestra Manager: Byron Jenkins
Senior Producer: Tim Thorne

Bodelwyddan Castle Trust
Bodelwyddan, Rhyl, Denbighshire LL18 5YA
☎ (01745) 584060 ☎ (01745) 584563
Email: enquiries@bodelwyddan-castle.co.uk
www.bodelwyddan-castle.co.uk
Director: Dr Kevin Mason

Brecknock Museum & Art Gallery
Captain's Walk, Brecon, Powys LD3 7DS
☎ (01874) 624121 ☎ (01874) 614046
Email: brecknock.museum@powys.gov.uk
www.powys.gov.uk/brecknockmuseum
Curator: Nigel Blackamore

Brecon Jazz
The Drill Hall, 25 Lion Street,
Hay-on-Wye HR3 5AD
☎ (01470) 822 620
Email: jazz@hayfestival.com
www.breconjazz.org

Royal Mail

Canolfan Cymry Llundain
The London Welsh Centre
157-163 Grays Inn Road, London WC1X 8UE
☎ (020) 7837 3722
Email: rhian@lwcentre.demon.co.uk
www.londonwelsh.org
Chief Executive Officer: Rhian Jones

Carmarthenshire Theatres - Theatr Elli
Theatr Elli, Station Rd, Llanelli,
Carmarthenshire SA15 1AH
☎ (0845) 2263510
Email: theatres@carmarthenshire.gov.uk
www.carmarthenshiretheatres.co.uk

Carmarthenshire Theatres - Lyric Theatre
King St, Carmarthen SA31 1BD
☎ (0845) 2263510
Email: theatres@carmarthenshire.gov.uk
www.carmarthenshiretheatres.co.uk

Carmarthenshire Theatres - Miners' Theatre
Wind Street, Ammanford SA18 3DN
☎ (0845) 2263510
Email: theatres@carmarthenshire.gov.uk
www.carmarthenshiretheatres.co.uk

Centre for Performance Research
The Foundry, Parry Williams Building,
Penglais Campus, Aberystwyth SY23 3AJ
☎ (01970) 622133 ☐ (01970) 622132
Email: info@thecpr.org.uk
www.thecpr.org.uk
Artistic Director: Richard Gough
Executive Director: Judie Christie

Chapter Arts Centre
Market Rd, Canton, Cardiff CF5 1QE
☎ (029) 2031 1050
Email: enquiry@chapter.org
www.chapter.org
Chief Executive: Andy Eagle

CLERA Cymdeithas Offerynnau
Traddodiadol Cymru
Bronant, Llansadwrn, Ynys Môn
☎ (01286) 450508
Email: post@clera.org   www.clera.org
Cadeirydd: John Idris Jones

Clwyd Theatr Cymru
Mold, Flintshire CH7 1YA
☎ (01352) 756331 ☐ (01352) 701558
Email: admin@clwyd-theatr-cymru.co.uk
www.clwyd-theatr-cymru.co.uk
Director: Terry Hands
General Manager: Julia Grime

Community Music Wales
Unit 8, 24 Norbury Rd, Fairwater,
Cardiff CF5 3AU
☎ (029) 2083 8060 ☐ (029) 2056 6573
Email: admin@communitymusicwales.org.uk
www.communitymusicwales.org.uk
Director: Hannah Jenkins

CREU CYMRU
Development Agency for Theatres
& Art Centres in Wales
PO Box 242, Bow Street, Aberystwyth SY23 9AX
☎ (01970) 822 222
Email: post@creucymru.com
www.creucymru.com
Programme Manager: Deborah Keyser
Administrator: Yvonne O'Donovan

Cwmni Mega Cyf
Tinopolis Centre, Park Street, Llanelli,
Carmarthenshire SA15 3YE
☎ (01554) 880923
Email: cwmnimega@hotmail.com
www.cwmnimega.com
Chief Executive: Dafydd Hywel

Cwmni Theatr Cydweithredol Troed-y-rhiw
Swyddfa Troed-y-Rhiw, Campws Felin-Fach,
Dyffryn Aeron, Ceredigion SA48 8AF
☎ (01570) 471328 / 07813 173155
☐ (01570) 471030
Email: swyddfa@theatrtroedyrhiw.com
www.theatrtroedyrhiw.com
Cyswllt: Euros Lewis

Cyfansoddwyr Cymru
Composers of Wales
11 Rhododendron Close, Cyncoed, Cardiff CF23 7HS
☎ (029) 2021 9857
www.composersofwales.org /
www.cyfansoddwyrcymru.org
Chair: Andrew Powell
Secretary/Administrator: Audrey Morgan
Treasurer: Fiona Lawson

Cyfarthfa Castle Museum & Art Gallery
Brecon Rd, Merthyr Tydfil CF47 8RE
☎ (01685) 727371 ☐ (01685) 723112
Email: museum@merthyr.gov.uk
www.merthyr.gov.uk/museum
Museums Officer: Scott Reid

ARTS

Cyfnewidfa Lên Cymru (CLC)
Wales Literature Exchange (WLE)
Mercator Centre, Prifysgol Aberystwyth
University, Aberystwyth SY23 3AS
☎ (01970) 622544 ☎ (01970) 621524
Email:post@walesliterature.org / post@cyfnewidfalen.org
www.walesliterature.org / www.cyfnewidfalen.org
Director/Cyfarwyddwr: Sioned Puw Rowlands
Projects Officer/Swyddog Prosiectau: Catrin Ashton
Gwefan & Chysylltiadau Cyhoeddus/Public
Relations & Web content: Manon Edwards Ahir
Ffeiriau Llyfrau/Book Fairs: Robin Grossmann

Y Cylch/The Circuit
PO Box 123, Montgomery, Powys SY15 6WL
Email: circuit@tym.eclipse.co.uk
Co-ordinator: Lydia Bassett

Cymdeithas Genedlaethol
Dawns Werin Cymru
The Welsh National Folk Dance Society
10 River View Court, Llandâf, Caerdydd CF5 2QJ
Email: chair@dawnsio.com
www.dawnsio.com
Chair: Eiry Hunter

Cyngor Crefft Cymru Cyf
Wales Craft Council Ltd
London House, The Square,
Corwen, Denbighshire LL21 0DE
☎ 07435754825 ☎ 01490 412911
Email: info@walescraftcouncil.co.uk
www.walescraftcouncil.co.uk
Chair: Philomena Hearn

The Dylan Thomas Centre
Somerset Place, Swansea SA1 1RR
☎ (01792) 463980 (Literature & General Enq);
463892 (Box Office) ☎ (01792) 463993
Email: dylanthomas.lit@swansea.gov.uk
www.dylanthomas.com
Literature Officer: Jo Furber
Cultural Development Officer: Nick McDonald

Eisteddfod Genedlaethol Cymru
National Eisteddfod of Wales
40 Parc Tŷ Glas, Llanisien, Caerdydd CF14 5DU
☎ (0845) 4090 300 ☎ (0845) 2076 3737
Email: gwyb@eisteddfod.org.uk
www.eisteddfod.org.uk
President: Prydwen Elfed-Owens
Chief Executive: Elfed Roberts

Ffotogallery
c/o Chapter Arts Centre, Market Rd,
Canton, Cardiff CF5 1QE
☎ (029) 2034 1667 ☎ (029) 2034 1672
Email: info@ffotogallery.org
www.ffotogallery.org
Director: David Drake

Galeri Betws-y Coed
Ffordd Caergybi, Betws Y Coed,
Conwy LL24 0BW
☎ (01690) 710432
Email: info@galeribetwsycoed.co.uk
www.galeribetwsycoed.co.uk

Glynn Vivian Art Gallery
Alexandra Rd, Swansea SA1 5DZ
☎ (01792) 516900 ☎ (01792) 516903
Email: glynn.vivian.gallery@swansea.gov.uk
www.glynnviviangallery.org
Curator: Jenni Spencer-Davies

The Grand Pavilion
The Esplanade, Porthcawl CF36 3YW
☎ (01656) 815995 ☎ (01656) 815990
Email: pavilion@bridgend.gov.uk
www.grandpavilion.co.uk
Manager: Mark Phillips

Grand Theatre & Arts Wing
Singleton St, Swansea SA1 3QJ
☎ (01792) Admin: 475242
Box office: 475715 ☎ (01792) 475379
Email:swansea.grandmarketing@swansea.gov.uk
www.swanseagrand.co.uk
Strategic, Finance & Operations Manager:
Gerald Morris
Programming, Marketing & Development
Manager: Paul Hopkins
Marketing Manager: Helen Dalling

The Hay Festival
Hay Festival of Literature & the Arts,
The Drill Hall, 25 Lion St, Hay-on-Wye Powys
☎ (0870) 9901299 (Box Office); 01497 822 620
☎ (0870) 01497 821066
Email: admin@hayfestival.com
www.hayfestival.com
Director: Peter Florence
Artists Managers: Jesse Ingham & Rhodri Jones
General Manager: Lyndy Cooke

Royal Mail

Hijnx Theatre
Wales Millennium Centre, Bute Place,
Cardiff Bay CF10 5AL
☎ (029) 2030 0331
Email: info@hijinx.org.uk
www.hijinx.org.uk
Executive Director: Val Hill
Artistic Director: Gaynor Loughor

Literature Wales (formerly Academi)
Llenyddiaeth Cymru
includes Yr Academi Gymreig/The Welsh
Academy & Tŷ Newydd Writers' Centre,
Mount Stuart House, Mount Stuart Square,
Cardiff CF10 5FQ
☎ (029) 2047 2266 ☐ (029) 2049 2930
Email: post@literaturewales.org
www.literaturewales.org
Chief Executive: Lleucu Siencyn

Also at:

The Glyn Jones Centre,
Wales Millennium Centre, Cardiff
☎ (029) 2047 2266 ☐ (029) 2047 0691
Email: post@literaturewales.org
www.literaturewales.org
Chief Executive: Lleucu Siencyn

Tŷ Newydd, Llanystumdwy, Cricieth,
Gwynedd LL52 0LW
☎ (01766) 522811 ☐ (01766) 523095
Email: tynewydd@literaturewales.org
www.literaturewales.org
Chief Executive: Lleucu Siencyn

Llangollen International Musical Eisteddfod
Royal International Pavilion,
Abbey Rd, Llangollen LL20 8SW
☎ (01978) 862000 ☐ (01978) 862002
Email: info@international-eisteddfod.co.uk
www.international-eisteddfod.co.uk
President: Terry Waite CBE

Llantrisant Model House & Gallery
Model House, Bull Ring, Llantrisant,
Rhondda Cynon Taf CF72 8EB
☎ (01443) 238884
Email: becky@llantrisantgallery.com
www.llantrisantgallery.com

Martin Tinney Gallery
18 St. Andrew's Crescent, Cardiff CF10 3DD
☎ (029) 20641411
Email: mtg@artwales.com
www.artwales.com

Mission Gallery
Gloucester Place, Maritime Quarter,
Swansea SA1 1TY
☎ (01792) 652016
Email: info@missiongallery.co.uk
www.missiongallery.co.uk
Director: Amanda Roderick
Gallery Development Officer: Hannah Kelly

MOMA WALES
MOMA CYMRU
Y Tabernacl, Heol Penrallt, Machynlleth,
Powys SY20 8AJ
☎ (01654) 703355 ☐ (01654) 702160
Email: info@momawales.org.uk
www.momawales.org.uk
Administrator: Raymond Jones

The National Library of Wales
Llyfrgell Genedlaethol Cymru
Penglais, Aberystwyth, Ceredigion SY23 3BU
☎ (01970) 632800 ☐ (01970) 615709
Email: holi@llgc.org.uk
www.llgc.org.uk
Librarian: Andrew Green
President: Sir Deian Hopkin

National Waterfront Museum
Oystermouth Rd, Maritime Quarter,
Swansea SA1 3RD
☎ (029) 2057 3600
Email: waterfront@museumwales.ac.uk
www.museumwales.ac.uk/en/swansea
Head of Museum: Stephanos Mastoris

National Wool Museum
Amgueddfa Wlân Cymru
Dre-fach Felindre, Llandysul, Castell Newydd
Emlyn, Sir Gaerfyrddin SA44 5UP
☎ (01559) 370929 ☐ (01559) 371592
Email: wool@museumwales.ac.uk /
gwlan@amgueddfacymru.ac.uk
www.museumwales.ac.uk
www.amgueddfacymru.ac.uk
Manager: Ann Whittall

New Theatre
Park Place, Cardiff CF10 3LN
☎ (029) 2087 8787 (Admin);
(029) 2087 8889 (Box Office)
☐ (029) 2087 8788
Email: ntmailings@cardiff.gov.uk
www.newtheatrecardiff.co.uk
Operations Manager: Grant McFarlane

ARTS

Newport Museum & Art Gallery
John Frost Square, Newport,
South Wales NP20 1PA
☎ (01633) 414701
Email: museum@newport.gov.uk

Oriel Cymru Gallery
Glanrafon, Pentrefelin, Criccieth,
Gwynedd LL52 0PT
☎ (01766) 522530 ◲ (01766) 523282
Email: gwybodaeth@oriel-cymru.com
www.oriel-cymru.com
Director: Valerie Wynne-Williams

Oriel Davies Gallery
The Park, Newtown, Powys SY16 2NZ
☎ (01686) 625041 ◲ (01686) 623633
Email: desk@orieldavies.org
www.orieldavies.org
Director: Amanda Farr. Curator: Ruth Gooding

Oriel Mostyn Gallery
12 Vaughan St, Llandudno LL30 1AB
☎ (01492) 879201 ◲ (01492) 878869
Email: post@mostyn.org
www.mostyn.org
Director: Alfredo Cramerotti
Operations & Facilities Manager: Mark Hughes

Oriel Myrddin Gallery
Church Lane, Carmarthen,
Carmarthenshire SA31 1LH
☎ (01267) 222775 ◲ (01267) 220599
Email: orielmyrddin@carmarthenshire.gov.uk
www.orielmyrddingallery.co.uk
Gallery Manager & Administrator: Meg Anthony

Oriel Pen y Fan Gallery
35 Stryd Fawr, Brecon, Powys LD3 7AN
☎ (01874) 611102
Email: ann@orielpenyfangallery.co.uk
www.orielpenyfangallery.co.uk
Proprietor: Ann Mathias

Oriel Plas Glyn-y-Weddw
Llanbedrog, Pwllheli, Gwynedd LL53 7TT
☎ (01758) 740763
Email: enquiry@oriel.org.uk
www.oriel.org.uk
Director: Gwyn Jones

Oriel Rob Piercy
Porthmadog, Gwynedd LL49 9BT
☎ (01766) 513833
Email: gallery@robpiercy.com
www.robpiercy.com

Oriel Wrecsam
Rhosddu Rd, Wrexham LL11 1AU
☎ (01978) 292093 ◲ (01978) 292611
Email: oriel.wrecsam@wrexham.gov.uk

Oriel Ynys Môn
Rhosmeirch, Llangefni, Anglesey LL77 7TQ
☎ (01248) 724444
Email: pwxed@anglesey.gov.uk
Principal Officer, Museums Culture & Archives:
Pat West

Pafiliwn Bont
Pontrhydfendigaid, Ystrad Meurig,
Ceredigion SY25 6BB
☎ (01974) 831635
Email: post@pafiliwnbont.co.uk
www.pafiliwnbont.co.uk

The Pavilion Theatre
The Promenade, Rhyl, Denbighshire LL18 3AQ
☎ (01745) 330000 ◲ (01745) 339819
Email: rhyl.pavilion@denbighshire.gov.uk
www.rhylpavilion.co.uk
General Manager: Gareth Owen
Operations Manager: Val Simmons
Marketing Officer: Sian Williams
Technical Manager: Andy Hughes

RCT Theatres:
The Coliseum Theatre , Mount Pleasant St,
Trecynon, Aberdare CF44 8NG
☎ (01685) 882380 Box Office: 08000 147 111
Email: Andrea.morgan2@rhondda-cynon-taff.gov.uk
www.coliseum.rct-arts.org
Manager: Andrea Morgan
Assistant Manager: Andrew Warren

Also at:

The Park and Dare Theatre, Station Rd,
Treorci CF42 6NL
☎ (01443) 775654; Box Office: 08000 147 111
www.parkdare.rct-arts.org
Manager: Simon Davey

The Muni Arts Centre, Gelliwastad Rd,
Pontypridd CF37 2DP
☎ (01443) 485934
www.muni.rct-arts.org
Manager: Leon Kruger

Real Institute/Rêl Institiwt
Ciafaic, 25 Heol Watling, Llanrwst LL26 0LS
☎ 07765 147 680
Email: media@realinstitute.org
www.realinstitute.org

Post Brenhinol

Royal Mail

Royal Cambrian Academy
Academi Frenhinol Gymreig
Crown Lane, Conwy LL32 8AN
☎ (01492) 593413
Email: rca@rcaconwy.org
www.rcaconwy.org
President: Ivor Davies
Gallery Asst: Gwawr Dafydd

Ruthin Craft Centre
Park Rd, Ruthin, Denbighshire LL15 1BB
☎ (01824) 704774
Email: thegallery@rccentre.org.uk
www.ruthincraftcentre.org.uk
Gallery Director: Philip Hughes
Deputy Director: Jane Gerrard

Sherman Cymru
Senghennydd Rd, Cardiff CF24 4YE
☎ (029) 2064 6900
Email: elin.partridge@shermancymru.co.uk
www.shermancymru.co.uk
Chair: Emyr Jenkins
Director: Chris Ricketts

Skillset Media Academy Wales
Academi Cyfryngau Cymru
Suite 2, 33-35 West Bute Street,
Cardiff Bay, Cardiff CF10 5LH
☎ (029) 2048 0141
Email: hannah@mediaacademywales.org
www.mediaacademywales.org
Project Manager: Hannah Raybould
Marketing Coordinator: Kathryn Latham

Also at:

c/o University of Wales Newport,
City Campus, Usk Way,
Newport NP20 2BP
☎ (01633) 432679
Email: hannah@mediaacademywales.org
www.mediaacademywales.org

St Donats Arts Centre
St Donats Castle, Vale of Glamorgan CF61 1WF
☎ (01446) 799099 ☐ (01446) 799101
Email: sharonstone@stdonats.com
www.stdonats.com
General Manager: Sharon Stone

Taliesin Arts Centre
Swansea University, Singleton Park,
Swansea SA2 8PZ
☎ (01792) 602060
Email: office@taliesinartscentre.co.uk
www.taliesinartscentre.co.uk
Manager: Sybil Crouch
Technical Management: Dave Palmer/Andrew Knight
Marketing: Nia Mills

Theatr Bara Caws
Uned A1, Stad Ddiwydiannol, Cibyn,
Caernarfon, Gwynedd LL55 2BD
☎ (01286) 676335
Email: tbaracaws@btconnect.com
www.baracaws.com
Artistic Director: Betsan Llwyd
Admin: Linda Brown

Theatr Brycheiniog
Canal Wharf, Brecon, Powys LD3 7EW
☎ (01874) 622838; Box Office: 611622
☐ (01874) 622583
Email: paula@brycheiniog.co.uk
www.brycheiniog.co.uk
Director: Paula Redway

Theatr Colwyn
Abergele Rd, Colwyn Bay, Clwyd LL29 7RU
☎ (01492) 577888
Email: phil.batty@conwy.gov.uk
www.theatrcolwyn.co.uk
Theatre Manager: Phil Batty

Theatr Fforwm Cymru
Milford House, Quay Rd, Goodwick,
Pembs SA64 0BS
☎ (1348) 873805
Email: info@theatrfforwmcymru.org.uk
www.theatrfforwmcymru.org.uk
Director: Gill Dowsett

Theatr Genedlaethol Cymru
Y Llwyfan, Heol y Coleg, Carmarthen SA31 3EQ
☎ (01267) 233 882 ☐ (01267) 243 840
Email: thgc@theatr.com
www.theatr.com
Artistic Director: Arwel Gruffydd

Hafren: The Entertainment Venue
Llanidloes Rd, Newtown, Powys SY16 4HU
☎ (01686) 614555 (Box Office) ☐ (01686) 622246
Email: admin@theatrhafren.co.uk
www.thehafren.co.uk
Administrator: Sara Clutton
Marketing Manager: Del Thomas
Technical Manager: Pete Whitehead

ARTS

Theatr Harlech
Harlech, Gwynedd LL46 2PU
☎ (01766) 780667
Email: post@theatrharlech.com
www.theatrharlech.com
Director: Clare Williams

Theatr Iolo
Chapter Arts Centre, Market Road,
Canton, Cardiff CF5 1QE
☎ (029) 2061 3782 ⓕ (029) 2002 2805
Email: info@theatriolo.com
www.theatriolo.com
Artistic Director: Kevin Lewis
Producer: John Carey Williams

Theatr Mwldan
Bath House Road, Cardigan SA43 1JY
☎ (01239) 621200
Email: boxoffice@mwldan.co.uk
www.mwldan.co.uk
Theatr Director: Dilwyn Davies

Theatr Na n'Og
Unit 3, Millands Road Industrial Estate,
Neath SA11 1NJ
☎ (01639) 641771 ⓕ (01639) 647941
Email: drama@theatr-nanog.co.uk
www.theatr-nanog.co.uk
Artistic Director: Geinor Styles
Associate Director: Phylip Harries
Administrator: Janet Huxtable

Theatr Stiwt
Broad St, Rhosllannerchrugog,
Wrexham LL141RB
☎ (01978) 844053 (Admin) 841300 (Box office)
Email: admin@stiwt.co.uk
www.stiwt.co.uk
Manager: Rebecca Griffiths

trac: folk development for Wales
trac: datblygu traddodiadau gwerin
PO Box 428, Cardiff CF11 1DP
☎ (029) 2031 8863
Email: trac@trac-cymru.org
www.trac-cymru.org
Director: Danny Kilbride

Turner House Gallery
Plymouth Rd, Penarth,
Vale of Glamorgan CF64 3DM
☎ (029) 2070 8870
www.turner-house-gallery-penarth.wales.info/

Tŷ Cerdd - Music Centre Wales
Wales Millennium Centre, Bute Place,
Cardiff CF10 5AL
☎ (029) 2063 5640 ⓕ (029) 2063 5641
Email: enquiries@tycerdd.org
www.tycerdd.org
Director/Cyfarwyddwr: Robert Nicholls

Tŷ Newydd National Writers' Centre for Wales
Llanystumdwy, Cricieth, Gwynedd LL52 0LW
☎ (01766) 522811
Email: tynewydd@literaturewales.org
www.tynewydd.org
Director: Sally Baker

Venue Cymru
The Promenade, Llandudno, Conwy LL30 1BB
☎ (01492) 872000 (box Office)
Email: info@venuecymru.co.uk
www.venuecymru.co.uk
General Manager: Sarah Ecob

Voluntary Arts Wales
121 Cathedral Rd, Pontcanna, Cardiff CF11 9PH
☎ (029) 2039 5395
Email: info@voluntaryarts.org
www.vaw.org.uk
Chief Executive Officer: Robin Simpson;
Voluntary Arts Wales Projects Development
Officer: Sioned Best

Wales Arts International
Celfyddydau Rhyngwladol Cymru
Bute Place, Cardiff CF10 5AL
☎ (029) 2044 1320 ⓕ (029) 2044 1400
Email: info@wai.org.uk
www.wai.org.uk
Head of Wales: Eluned Haf

Wales Millennium Centre
Canolfan Mileniwm Cymru
Bute Place, Cardiff CF10 5AL
☎ (029) 2063 6400 ⓕ (029) 2063 6401
Email: info@wmc.org.uk
www.wmc.org.uk
Chair: Sir Emyr Jones Parry
General Manager: Mathew Milsom

Wales Theatre Company
21 Dogo St, Pontcanna, Cardiff CF11 9JJ
☎ (029) 2064 0069 ⓕ (029) 2064 0069
Email: info@walestheatrecompany.com
www.walestheatrecompany.com
Artistic Director/Cyfarwyddwr Creadigol:
Michael Bogdanov

Welsh Books Council
Cyngor Llyfrau Cymru
Castell Brychan, Aberystwyth,
Ceredigion SY23 2JB
☎ (01970) 624151 ▣ (01970) 625385
Email: castellbrychan@cllc.org.uk
www.cllc.org.uk
Chair: Prof M Wynn Thomas OBE
Chief Executive: Elwyn Jones

Welsh Music Guild
71 Broad St, Barry, Vale of Glamorgan CF62 7AG
Email: chris@christopherpainter.co.uk
www.welshmusic.org.uk
Chair: Richard Thomas
Secretary: Christopher Painter

Welsh National Opera
Wales Millennium Centre,
Bute Place, Cardiff Bay CF10 5AL
☎ (029) 2063 5000 ▣ (029) 2063 5099
Email: enquiry@wno.org.uk;
firstname.surname@wno.org.uk
www.wno.org.uk
Chair: Geraint Talfan Davies
Managing Director: Peter Bellingham

Wyeside Arts Centre
13 Castle St, Builth Wells, Powys LD2 3BN
☎ (01982) 553668 ▣ (01982) 553995
www.wyeside.co.uk
Operations Manager: Jill Mustafa

Business Groups

Alliance Sector Skills Councils
LANTRA, Royal Welsh Showground,
Llanelwedd, Builth Wells, Powys LD2 3WY
Email: info@sscalliance.org
www.sscalliance.org
Vice Chair: Kevin Thomas

Antur Conwy Enterprise
Conwy Business Centre, Junction Way,
Llandudno Junction, Conwy LL31 9XX
☎ (01492) 574555
Email: anturconwyenterprise@conwy.gov.uk
www.conwy.gov.uk

Antur Nantlle
Antur Nantlle Technology Centre, 20 Water
Street, Penygroes, Caernarfon LL54 6LR
☎ (01286) 882688
Email: enquiries@anturnantlle.com
Principal Officer: Robat Jones

Antur Penllyn
Gweithdai Penllyn, Stryd y Plase,
Y Bala, Gwynedd LL23 7SP
☎ (01678) 520920

Antur Teifi
Business Park, Aberarad, Newcastle Emlyn,
Carmarthenshire SA38 9DB
☎ (01239) 710238 ▣ (01239) 710358
Email: info@anturteifi.org.uk
www.anturteifi.org.uk
Chair: Owain Davies
Managing Director: Dewi Williams

Antur Teifi - Business Services
Cardigan Office, 36-38 Pendre,
Cardigan SA43 1JS
☎ (01239) 621828 ▣ (01239) 621987
Email: info@anturteifi.org.uk
www.anturteifi.org.uk

Also at:

Lampeter Office, 23 High Street,
Lampeter SA48 7BH
☎ (01570) 422624 ▣ (01570) 422624
Email: info@anturteifi.org.uk
www.anturteifi.org.uk

Brecon Office, Unit 6 Cartrefi Cymru,
Brecon Enterprise Park, Brecon LD3 8BT
☎ (01874) 622632
Email: info@anturteifi.org.uk
www.anturteifi.org.uk

Cardiff Office, 54A Bute Street,
Cardiff CF10 5AF
☎ (029) 2048 0880
Email: info@anturteifi.org.uk
www.anturteifi.org.uk

Newcastle Emlyn Office, Antur Teifi Business
Park, Aberarad, Newcastle Emlyn SA38 9DB
☎ (01239) 710238
Email: info@anturteifi.org.uk
www.anturteifi.org.uk

Llandrindod Wells Office, 1 & 2 High Street,
Llandrindod Wells LD1 6AG
☎ (01597) 825714
Email: info@anturteifi.org.uk
www.anturteifi.org.uk

Welshpool Office, 15 Severn Farm Enterprise Park, Welshpool, Powys SY21 7DF
☎ (01938) 556060
Email: info@anturteifi.org.uk
www.anturteifi.org.uk

Ystradgynlais Office, Unit 300, Ystradgynlais Workshops, Trawsffordd, Swansea SA9 1BS
☎ (01639) 845416
Email: info@anturteifi.org.uk
www.anturteifi.org.uk

Aberystwyth Office, Office 3, Unit 2, Parc Merlin, Llanbadarn Fawr, Aberystwyth SY23 3JQ
☎ (01970) 627787
Email: info@anturteifi.org.uk
www.anturteifi.org.uk

Newtown Office, Office 203/204, Tŷ Ladywell, Newtown, Powys SY16 1JB
☎ (01686) 617184
Email: info@anturteifi.org.uk
www.anturteifi.org.uk

Llanelli Office, 12-14 John Street, Llanelli, Carmarthenshire SA15 1UH
☎ (01554) 772122
Email: info@anturteifi.org.uk
www.anturteifi.org.uk

Ammanford Office, Betws Park Workshop, Park Street, Ammanford SA18 2ET
☎ (01269) 591583
Email: info@anturteifi.org.uk
www.anturteifi.org.uk

Carmarthen Office, Suit C Darkgate Building, 3 Red Street, Carmarthen SA31 1BN
☎ (01267) 235777 ☐ (01267) 235779
Email: info@anturteifi.org.uk
www.anturteifi.org.uk

Machynlleth Office, Room 33 Machynlleth & District Care Centre, Forge Road, Machynlleth SY20 8EQ
☎ (01654) 702252
Email: info@anturteifi.org.uk
www.anturteifi.org.uk

Antur Waunfawr Cyf.
Bryn Pistyll, Waunfawr, Caernarfon, Gwynedd LL55 4BJ
☎ (01286) 650721
www.anturwaunfawr.org
Chief Executive: Menna Jones

Arts & Business Cymru
South Wales Office,16 Museum Place, Cardiff CF10 3BH
☎ (029) 2030 3023 ☐ (029) 2030 3024
Email: contactus@aandbcymru.org.uk
www.aandbcymru.org.uk
Chair: Huw Roberts
Chief Executiver: Rachel Jones

Arts & Business Cymru
North Wales Office, Room 40, The Town Hall, Llandudno LL30 2UP
☎ (01492) 574003 ☐ (01492) 877045
Email: contactus@aandbcymru.org.uk
www.aandbcymru.org.uk
Chair: Huw Roberts
Chief Executive: Rachel Jones

Asset Skills Cymru
☎ (01685) 387914
Email: wales@assetskills.org
www.assetskills.org/Wales/
Welsh Contact: Jan Holdaway

ACCA Cymru/Wales
PO Box 2520, Cardiff CF23 0GN
☎ (029) 2026 3657 ☐ (029) 2026 3700
Email: wales@accaglobal.com
www.wales.accaglobal.com
Head of ACCA Wales: Ben Cottam

BIC Innovation Ltd
1b Llys Onnen, Ffordd y Llyn, Parc Menai, Bangor LL57 4DF
☎ (01248) 671101 ☐ (01248) 671102
Email: info@bic-innovation.com
www.bic-innovation.com
Chief Executive: Dafydd Glyn Davies
Also at:
Pencoed Technology Centre, Pencoed, Bridgend CF35 5HZ
☎ (01656) 861536

Post Brenhinol
Royal Mail

Business in Focus Ltd

Business Development Centre, Main Ave,
Treforest Industrial Estate, Pontypridd CF37 5UR
☎ (01443) 841842 ◨ (01443) 842925
Email: enquiries@businessinfocus.co.uk
www.businessinfocus.co.uk
Chief Executive: Gareth Bray

Also at:

Enterprise House, 127 Bute St,
Cardiff Bay CF10 5LE
☎ (029) 2049 4411 ◨ (029) 2048 1623
Email: enquiries@businessinfocus.co.uk
www.businessinfocus.co.uk
Chief Executive: Gareth Bray

8 St Andrew's Place, Cardiff CF10 3BE
☎ (0870) 950 90 90
Email: enquiries@businessinfocus.co.uk
www.businessinfocus.co.uk
Chief Executive: Gareth Bray

Maesteg Business Centre, Tyle Teg,
Heol Tŷ Gwyn Industrial Estate,
Maesteg CF34 0BQ
☎ (01656) 812750
Email: alisong@businessinfocus.co.uk
www.businessinfocus.co.uk
Chief Executive: Gareth Bray

BSC, Barry, Innovation Quarter,
Hood Rd, The Waterfront, Barry,
Vale of Glamorgan CF62 5QN
☎ (0870) 950 90 90
Email: enquiries@businessinfocus.co.uk
www.businessinfocus.co.uk
Chief Executive: Gareth Bray

Tondu Enterprise Centre, Bryn Rd,
Tondu, Bridgend CF32 9BS
☎ (01656) 724414 ◨ (01656) 721163
Email: enquiries@businessinfocus.co.uk
www.businessinfocus.co.uk
Chief Executive: Gareth Bray

Henley House, Queensway, Swansea West
Business Park, Fforestfach, Swansea SA5 4DJ
☎ (0870) 950 90 90
Email: enquiries@businessinfocus.co.uk
www.businessinfocus.co.uk
Chief Executive: Gareth Bray

Business in Focus Ltd

Also at:

Pyle Enterprise Centre, Village Farm Road,
Village Farm Insustrial Estate, Pyle,
Bridgend CF33 6BL
☎ (01656) 812750
Email: alisong@businessinfocus.co.uk
www.businessinfocus.co.uk
Chief Executive: Gareth Bray

Business in the Community Cymru Wales

2nd Floor, Riverside House,
31 Cathedral Road, Cardiff CF11 9HB
☎ (029) 2078 0050 ◨ (029) 2023 5116
Email: wales@bitc.org.uk
www.bitc.org.uk/wales
Chair: John Union
Director Wales: Simon Harris

Also at:

St Andrews Park, Queens Lane, Mold CH7 1XB
☎ (01352) 706213 ◨ (01352) 706212
Email: wales@bitc.org.uk
www.bitc.org.uk/wales

Business Wales

Mid Wales Regional Office

Welsh Government, Welshpool Enterprise
Centre, Salop Road, Welshpool SY21 7SW
☎ (01938) 559259 ◨ (01938) 559260
Email: ibwmid@wales.gsi.gov.uk
www.ibwales.com
International Trade Counsellor: Paul Fuga

Also at:

North Wales Regional Office

Welsh Government, Government Buildings,
Dinerth Road, Colwyn Bay LL28 4UL
☎ (01492) 549719 ◨ (01492) 548799
Email: ibwnorth@wales.gsi.gov.uk
www.ibwales.com
International Trade Counsellor: John Farrell
International Trade Administrator:
Moira Chapman

South East Region & Head Office

Welsh Government, Trafalgar House,
5 Fitzalan Place, Cardiff CF24 0ED
☎ (029) 2082 8951 ◨ (029) 2044 2696
Email: ibwsoutheast@wales.gsi.gov.uk
www.ibwales.com
International Trade Counsellor:
Elaine Choules

BUSINESS GROUPS

Business Wales

Also at:

South West Wales Regional Office

Welsh Government,
Penllergaer Business Park, Swansea SA4 9NX
☎ (01792) 229350 ☒ (01792) 892592
Email: ibwsouthwest@wales.gsi.gov.uk
www.ibwales.com
International Trade Counsellor: Kevin Davies
International Business Administrator:
Helen Proctor

Cadwyn Clwyd

Llys Clwyd, Lôn Parcwr Business Park,
Ruthin, Denbighshire LL15 1NJ
☎ (01824) 705802 ☒ (01824) 709853
Email: admin@cadwynclwyd.co.uk
www.cadwynclwyd.co.uk
Manager: Allan Forrest

Canolfan Cymry Llundain
The London Welsh Centre

157-163 Grays Inn Road, London WC1X 8UE
☎ (020) 7837 3722
Email: rhian@lwcentre.demon.co.uk
www.londonwelsh.org
Chief Executive Officer: Rhian Jones

Capital Law LLP

Capital Building, Tyndall Street, Cardiff CF10 4AZ
☎ (0333) 2400 489 ☒ (0333) 2400 487
Email: info@capitallaw.co.uk
www.capitallaw.co.uk
Managing Partner: Christopher Nott
Partner: Duncan Macintosh
Partner: Elin Pinnell

Cardiff Business Club

PO Box 1073, Cardiff CF11 1SD
☎ (029) 2066 6555
Email: office@cardiffbusinessclub.org
www.cardiffbusinessclub.org
President: Lord Rowe-Beddoe DL
Chair: Gerald Davies CBE DL
Secretary: Alun Davies

CBI Cymru Wales, Confederation
of British Industry

2 Caspian Point, Caspian Way, Cardiff Bay,
Cardiff CF10 4DQ
☎ (029) 2097 7600 ☒ (029) 2097 7619
Email: emmageorgiades@cbi.org.uk
www.cbi.org.uk/wales
Chair: Graham Edwards
Director for Wales: Emma Watkins
Assistant Director-Policy: Leighton Jenkins

Central Wales Economic Forum

Rhodfa Padarn, Llanbadarn Fawr,
Aberystwyth SY23 3UR
☎ (0300) 062 2387 ☒ (0300) 01686 622499
Email: bethan.evans@wales.gsi.gov.uk
www.cwef.org.uk
Chair: James Harrison

Centre for Business

Head Office, Orion Suite,
Enterprise Way, Newport NP20 2AQ
☎ (01633) 254041 ☒ (01633) 215774
Email: info@centreforbusiness.co.uk
www.centreforbusiness.co.uk
Managing Director: David Russ

Chartered Institute of Public Relations
Cymru Wales

Wharton Place, Wharton St, Cardiff CF10 1GS
☎ (029) 2038 8621 ☒ (029) 20228 554
Email: val.bodden@royalmail.com
mappleby@golleyslater.co.uk
www.cipr.co.uk/wales
Chair: Val Bodden
Vice-chair: Matt Appleby

Cogent SSC Ltd (Wales)

☎ (029) 2061 3630
Email: andrew.evans@cogent-ssc.com
www.cogent-ssc.com
Wales Manager: Andrew Evans

Community Enterprise Wales
Menter Gymunedol Cymru

The Innovation Centre, Festival Drive,
Victoria Business Park, Ebbw Vale NP23 8XA
☎ (01495) 356734
Email: admin@cewales.co.uk
www.cewales.org
Chief Executive: Shannon Robinson

Constructing Excellence in Wales

2nd Flr East, Longcross Court,
47 Newport Rd, Cardiff CF24 0AD
☎ (029) 2049 3322 ☒ (029) 2049 3233
Email: info@cewales.org.uk
www.cewales.org.uk
Chief Executive: Milica Kitson

Construction Skills

Units 4 & 5 Bridgend Business Centre, David St,
Bridgend Ind Estate, Bridgend CF31 3SH
☎ (0344) 994 7000 ☒ (0344) 01656 655232
Email: wales.office@cskills.org
www.constructionskills.net
Director Wales: Wyn Prichard

Consult Capital
Capital Building, Tyndall Street, Cardiff CF10 4AZ
☎ (0333) 2409 778 🖷 (0333) 2400 487
Email: info@consultcapital.co.uk
www.consultcapital.co.uk
Directors: Christopher Nott & Elin Pinnell

Co-operatives & Mutuals Wales
15 Samuels Crescent, Whitchurch,
Cardiff CF14 2TH
☎ (07914) 762 546
Email: alex@cooperatives-wales.coop
www.cooperatives-wales.coop
Executive Chair: Alex Bird
Treasurer: Paul Mallett

Creative & Cultural Skills
1 Caspian Point, Pierhead St,
Cardiff Bay, Cardiff CF10 4DQ
☎ (029) 2044 4195 🖷 (029) 2044 4196
Email: simon.dancey@ccskills.org.uk
www.ccskills.org.uk
Nations & International Director, Wales:
Simon Dancey

Denbighshire Enterprise Agency
Clwydfro Business Centre, Lôn Parcwr,
Ruthin, Denbighshire LL15 1NJ
☎ (01824) 705782 🖷 (01824) 705541
Email: enquiries@denbighbiz.co.uk
www.denbighbiz.co.uk
Chief Executive: Eirlys Evans

Also at:

Morfa Clwyd Business Centre,
84 Marsh Rd, Rhyl, Denbighshire LL18 2AT
☎ (01745) 330777 🖷 (01745) 331331

Design Wales
PDR, Cardiff Metropolitan University,
200 Western Ave, Cardiff CF5 2YB
☎ (029) 2041 7043
www.designwales.org.uk
Director: Gavin Cawood

EEF
Waterton Technology Centre,
Waterton, Bridgend CF31 3WT
☎ (01656) 641790 🖷 (01656) 641799
Email: enquiries@eef-cymruwales.org.uk
www.eef.org.uk
External Affairs Adviser: Paul Byard

ESTnet
☎ (029) 2002 9700
Email: enquiries@estnet.uk.net
www.estnet.uk.net

Federation of Master Builders
96 Cardiff Rd, Llandaff, Cardiff CF5 2DT
☎ (029) 2057 7711 🖷 (029) 2057 7722
Email: richardjenkins@fmb.org.uk
www.fmb.org.uk
Director: Richard Jenkins
Wales Business Development Executive:
Joanne Ellis

Federation of Small Businesses in Wales
1 Cleeve House, Lambourne Crescent,
Cardiff CF14 5GP
☎ (029) 2074 7406 🖷 (029) 2074 7595
Email: wales.policy@fsb.org.uk
www.fsb.org.uk/wales
Chair: Janet Jones
Head of External Affairs: Iestyn Davies

Food & Farming Sector Panel
Welsh Government, Rhodfa Padarn,
Llanbadarn Fawr, Aberystwyth SY23 3UR
☎ (0300) 062 2384
Email: foodpolicy@wales.gsi.gov.uk

Freight Transport Association
Regus House, Falcon Drive, Cardiff Bay,
Cardiff CF10 4RU
☎ (029) 2050 4070 🖷 (029) 2050 4224
Email: igallagher@fta.co.uk
www.fta.co.uk
Chair: Bill Simons
Secretary: Ian Gallagher

Glasu
Antur Gwy, Park Rd, Builth Wells,
Powys LD2 3BA
☎ (01982) 552224/553305 🖷 (01982) 552872
Email: glasu@powys.gov.uk
www.glasu.org.uk

GO Wales (Graduate Opportunities Wales)
Swansea University, Careers Centre, Singleton
Park, Swansea SA2 8PP
☎ (0845) 225 60 50
Email: info@gowales.co.uk
www.gowales.co.uk

Hybu Cig Cymru
Meat Promotion Wales
Tŷ Rheidol, Parc Merlin, Aberystwyth,
Ceredigion SY23 3FF
☎ (01970) 625050 ☐ (01970) 615148
Email: info@hccmpw.org.uk
www.hccmpw.org.uk
Chair: Dai Davies
Chief Executive: Gwyn Howells

Home Builders Federation
PO Box 2512, Cardiff CF23 0GB
☎ (029) 2075 1076
Email: richard.price@hbf.co.uk
www.hbf.co.uk
Planning and Policy Manager: Richard Price

ICAEW (Institute of Chartered Accountants in England & Wales)
PO Box 4274, Cardiff CF14 8GA
☎ (029) 2002 1481
Email: wales@icaew.com
www.icaew.com/wales
Director for Wales: David Lermon
Media & Public Affairs Consultant: Phil Nifield

Institute of Directors Wales
Park House Club, 20 Park Place, Cardiff CF10 3DQ
☎ (029) 2038 9990 ☐ (029) 2038 9989
Email: iod.wales@iod.com
www.iod.com/wales
Chair: Huw Roberts
Director Wales: Robert Lloyd Griffiths

Institution of Civil Engineers (ICE Wales Cymru)
Suite 2, Bay Chambers, West Bute St,
Cardiff CF10 5BB
☎ (029) 2063 0561 ☐ (029) 2063 0666
Email: wales.cymru@ice.org.uk
www.ice.org.uk/wales
Director for Wales: Keith Jones

London Stock Exchange plc
10 Paternoster Square, London EC4M 7LS
☎ (020) 7797 1000 Mobile: 07766 421 679
Email: mrusson@londonstockexchange.com
www.londonstockexchange.com
Business Development Manager: Mark Russon

MediWales
5 Schooner Way, Atlantic Wharf,
Cardiff CF10 4DZ
☎ (029) 2047 3456
Email: ruth.campbell@mediwales.com
www.mediwales.com
Project Co-ordinator: Ruth Campbell

Menter a Busnes
The Science Park, Aberystwyth,
Ceredigion SY23 3AH
☎ (01970) 636565 ☐ (01970) 611366
Email: aber@menterabusnes.co.uk
www.menterabusnes.com
Chief Executive: Alun Jones

Menter Môn
Llys Goferydd, Stad Ddiwydiannol Bryn Cefni,
Bryn Cefni Ind Est, Llangefni,
Ynys Môn LL77 7XA
☎ (01248) 725700 ☐ (01248) 725735
www.mentermon.com

Mid Wales Manufacturing Group (MWMG)
Unit 7, St Giles Technology Park,
Newtown, Powys SY16 3AJ
☎ (01686) 628778 ☐ (01686) 621880
Email: info@mwmg.org
www.mwmg.org
Group Manager Ceri Stephens

North Wales Chamber of Commerce
Chester Office, Riverside Innovation Centre,
1 Castle Drive, Chester CH1 1SL
☎ (01244) 669988 ☐ (01244) 669989
Email: info@cepnwchamber.org.uk
www.wcnwchamber.org.uk
General Manager: Colin Brew

North Wales Economic Forum
Business Point, Coleg Llandrillo Cymru,
Unit 6 St Asaph Business Park, St Asaph,
Denbighshire LL17 0LJ
☎ (0845) 4505960 ☐ (01745) 536372
www.nwef.org.uk
Co-ordinator: Henry Roberts
Administrator: Janice Johnson

Pera Cymru
Pencoed Technology Park,
Pencoed, Bridgend CF35 5HZ
☎ (01656) 861536
Email: rod.howells@pera.com
www.peracymru.com
Contact: Will Campion 07913 482207

Also at:

1b, Llys Onnen, Ffordd Y Llyn,
Parc Menai, Bangor LL57 4DF
☎ (01248) 67110
Email: rod.howells@pera.com
www.peracymru.com

Post Brenhinol
Royal Mail

PLANED (Pembrokeshire Local Action Network for Enterprise & Development)
The Old School, Station Rd,
Narberth, Pembs SA67 7DU
☎ (01834) 860965   ☎ (01834) 861547
Email: information@planed.org.uk
www.planed.org.uk
Chief Executive: Helen Murry

Prime Cymru
Mile End, 9 Broad Street, Llandovery,
Carmarthenshire SA20 0AR
☎ (01550) 721813 or (0800) 587 4085
☎ (01550) 721291
Email: enquiries@prime-cymru.co.uk
www.prime-cymru.co.uk
Chair: Stephen Pegge
Chief Executive: David Pugh

The Prince's Trust Cymru
Head Office, Baltic House,
Mount Stuart Square, Cardiff CF10 5FH
☎ (029) 2043 7000   ☎ (029) 2043 7001
Email: webinfowa@princes-trust.org.uk
www.princes-trust.org.uk
Chair: Steve Thomas CBE
Director: Rick Libbey

The Royal Institution of Chartered Surveyors Wales (RICS)
7 St Andrews Place, Cardiff CF10 3BE
☎ (029) 2022 4414   ☎ (029) 2022 4416
Email: wales@rics.org
www.rics.org/wales
Chair: Neil Brierley. Director: Ben Collins

RPS Planning & Development
Park House, Greyfriars Rd, Cardiff CF10 3AF
☎ (029) 2066 8662   ☎ (029) 2066 8622
Email: rpsca@rpsgroup.com
www.rpsgroup.com
Operational Director: Darren Parker

South East Wales Economic Forum
QED Centre, Main Ave, Treforest Estate,
Treforest, Pontypridd CF37 5YR
☎ (0300) 061 5807/5581
Email: swewf@wales.gsi.gov.uk
www.sewales-econforum.co.uk
Director: Dr Elizabeth Haywood

South Wales Chamber of Commerce
Orion Suite, Enterprise Way, Newport,
South Wales NP20 2AQ
☎ (01633) 222664
Email: info@southwaleschamber.co.uk
www.southwaleschamber.co.uk
Chamber Director: Graham Morgan

Also at:

The Maltings, East Tyndall St,
Cardiff CF24 5EZ
☎ (029) 2048 1532
Email: info@southwaleschamber.co.uk
www.southwaleschamber.co.uk

1st Floor, Suite 2, Vivian Court,
Enterprise Park, Swansea SA7 9FG
☎ (01792) 793686
Email: info@southwaleschamber.co.uk
www.southwaleschamber.co.uk

Llys Y Ddraig, Penllergaer Business Park,
Swansea SA4 9NX
☎ (01792) 222427   ☎ (01792) 222464
Email: swwef@wales.gsi.gov.uk
Co-ordinator: Richard Crawshaw

The Finance Wales Group
Oakleigh House, Park Place, Cardiff CF10 3DQ
☎ (0800) 587 4140   ☎ (029) 2033 8101
Email: info@financewales.co.uk
www.financewales.co.uk
Chair: Ian Johnson
Chief Executive: Siân Lloyd Jones

Venture Wales Head Office
Tŷ Menter, Navigation Park,
Abercynon CF45 4SN
☎ (01443) 742888   ☎ (01443) 742444
Email: abercynon@venturewales.com
www.venturewales.com
Managing Director: Philip Cooper

Also at:

Unit F2 Intec, Ffordd-y-Parc,
Parc Menai, Bangor LL57 4FG
☎ (01248) 672640   ☎ (01248) 672641
Email: bangor@venturewales.com
Regional Manager Bangor: Maldwyn Jones

Lakeside Business Centre, Pond Rd,
Nantyglo, Brynmawr NP23 4BL
☎ (01495) 313999
Email: brynmawr@venturewales.com
Regional Manager Tredegar: Chris Jarvis

Post Brenhinol
Royal Mail

Venture Wales

Also at:

23 Park Place, Cardiff CF10 3BA
☎ (029) 2037 5940 ☎ (029) 2037 5949
Email: cardiff@venturewales.com
Regional Manager Cardiff: Phil Watkins

Merthyr Industrial Park, Pentrebach,
Merthyr Tydfil CF48 4DR
☎ (01443) 692233 ☎ (01443) 692912
Email: pentrebach@venturewales.com
Regional Manager Pentrebach: Mark Adams

Beechwood House, Christchurch Rd,
Newport NP19 8AJ
☎ (01633) 273502 ☎ (01633) 282136
Email: newport@venturewales.com
Regional Manager South East Wales:
David Bolton

Acorn House, Office Suite 1, Block A,
Phoenix Business Park, Lion Way Enterprise
Park, Swansea SA7 9FZ
☎ (01792) 701199 ☎ (01792) 701120
Email: swansea@venturewales.com
Regional Manager Swansea: Carwyn
Richards

Tredomen Business & Technology Centre,
Tredomen Business Park, Ystrad Mynach,
Hengoed CF82 7FN
☎ (01443) 866250 ☎ (01443) 866254
Email: tredomen@venturewales.com
Regional Manager Tredomen: Phil Watkins

Unit 14, Wilkinson Business Park,
Clywedog Road South,
Wrexham Industrial Estate, Wrexham LL13 9AE
☎ (01978) 669050 ☎ (01978) 661949
Email: wrexham@venturewales.com
Head of North Wales Division: Brian Colley

Wales Co-operative Centre Ltd

Llandaff Court, Fairwater Road, Cardiff CF5 2XP
☎ (0300) 111 5050 ☎ (0300) 111 5051
Email: info@walescooperative.org
www.walescooperative.org
Chief Executive: Derek Walker
Director of Operations: Nia Wright-Morgan
Director of Corporate Services: Mair Gwynant

Wales in London

15 Richmond Crescent,
Islington, London N1 0LZ
Email: Robert.john@rllj.com
www.walesinlondon.com
Chair: Robert Ll John

Wales International Business Council (WIBC)

Kiln Suite, The Maltings,
East Tyndall Street, Cardiff CF24 5EA
☎ (029) 2009 0041
Email: enquiries@walesibc.com
www.walesibc.com
Chair: Byron Davies

Wales Management Council

PO Box 4284, Cardiff CF14 8GP
☎ (0845) 371 0691
Email: gwyneth@walesmanagementcouncil.org.uk
www.walesmanagementcouncil.org.uk
Contact: Gwyneth Stroud

The Wales Social Partners Unit Ltd

Room 208 Titan House, Cardiff Bay Business
Centre, Titan Road, Cardiff CF24 5BS
☎ (029) 2048 2328
Email: admin@wspu.co.uk
www.wspu.co.uk
Chair: Julie Cook
Senior Policy Adviser: Nigel Keane

Welsh Centre for Printing & Coating (WCPC)

School of Engineering, Swansea University,
Singleton Park, Swansea SA2 8PP
☎ (01792) 295634/295091 ☎ (01792) 295814
Email: c.a.hammett@swansea.ac.uk
www.swansea.ac.uk/printing
Centre Directors:
Dr Tim C Claypole, Prof David T Gethin
Secretary: Christine Hammett

Welsh Government Business Information

Welsh Government, Enterprise House,
127 Bute St, Cardiff CF10 5LE
☎ 0300 060 3000
Email: businesssupport@wales.gsi.gov.uk
www.business.wales.gov.uk

Welsh Opto-Electronics Forum

OpTIC Technium, Ffordd William Morgan,
St Asaph Business Park, Denbighshire LL17 0JD
☎ (01745) 535235 ☎ (01745) 535101
Email: susan.sheridan@wof.org.uk
www.wof.org.uk
WOF Administrator: Susan Sheridan

Welsh Timber Forum

Unit 7, Dyfi Eco Park,
Machynlleth, Powys SY20 8AX
☎ (0845) 456 0342 ☎ (0845) 700 051
Email: welsh.timber@welshtimberforum.co.uk
www.welshtimberforum.co.uk
Chair: Richard Withers

West Wales Chamber of Commerce
Cresswell Buildings,
1 Burrows Place,
Swansea SA1 1SW
☎ (01792) 648345

WestBridge Capital
The Gatehouse, Melrose Hall,
Cypress Drive, Cardiff CF3 0EG
☎ (029) 2054 6250
🖷 (029) 2054 6251
Email: info@westbridgecapital.co.uk
www.westbridgecapital.co.uk
Managing Partner: Guy Davies

xenos -The Wales Business Angel Network
Oakleigh House, Park Place, Cardiff CF10 3DQ
☎ (029) 2033 8144
🖷 (029) 2080 1760
Email: info@xenos.co.uk
www.xenos.co.uk
Chief Executive Finance Wales: Siân Lloyd Jones
Network & Regional Manager South East Wales:
David Maas
North & Mid Wales Regional Manager: Nick Bradley
South, West & Mid Wales Regional Manager:
Colin Lucas

Charitable Trusts

BBC Children in Need (Wales)
Broadcasting House, Llandaff, Cardiff CF5 2YQ
☎ (029) 2032 2383
Email: marc.phillips@bbc.co.uk
www.bbc.co.uk/pudsey
National Head: Marc Phillips

Bernard Piggott Charitable Trust
4 Streetsbrook Rd, Shirley, Solihull B90 3PL
☎ (0121) 744 1695 🖷 (0121) 744 1695
Contact: Jenny Whitworth

The Brecon Beacons Trust
The Orchids, Blaenavon Rd,
Govilon, Abergavenny NP7 9NY
☎ (01873) 832490
Email: alan@breconbeaconstrust.org
www.breconbeaconstrust.org
Trust Secretary: Alan Underwood

The Gaynor Cemlyn-Jones Trust
Park Cottage, Gannock Park,
Deganwy, Conwy LL31 9PZ
☎ (01492) 596360

Charity Commission
Comisiwn Elusennau
8th Floor, Clarence House,
Clarence Place, Newport NP19 7AA
☎ (0845) 3000218
www.charity-commission.gov.uk

The Charles Lloyd Foundation
8-10 Grosvenor Road, Wrexham LL11 1BU
☎ (01978) 291000
Email: susanelder@allingtonhughes.co.uk

Clwyd Voluntary Initiative Community Chest
Denbighshire Voluntary Services Council,
Naylor Leyland Centre, Well St, Ruthin LL15 1AF
☎ (01824) 702441 / 703805 🖷 (01824) 705412
Email: office@dvsc.co.uk

The Community Foundation in Wales
9 Coopers Yard, Curran Rd, Cardiff CF10 5NB
☎ (029) 2053 6590 🖷 (029) 2034 2118
Email: mail@cfiw.org.uk
www.cfiw.org.uk
Chair: Antony Lewis
Chief Executive: Liza Kellett

The CLA Charitable Trust
Hophine Farmhouse, Ossington,
Newark NG23 6LJ
☎ (01636) 823835
Email: petergeldart@btinternet.com
www.cla.org.uk
Director: Peter Geldart

Cronfa Goffa Saunders Lewis
Saunders Lewis Memorial Trust
Tŷ'r Ysgol, Ffordd y Gogledd,
Aberystwyth, Ceredigion SY23 2EL
☎ (01970) 624534
Email: elwynjones@ymail.com
www.cronfagoffasaunderslewis.org
Ysg/Sec: Elwyn Jones

The Cwmbran Trust
c/o Arvinmeritor Ltd, Grange Rd,
Cwmbran NP44 3XU
☎ (01633) 834040
Email: cwmbrantrust@arvinmeritor.com
Kenneth L Maddox

The Eric & Dorothy Leach Charitable Trust
c/o Swayne Johnson Ltd, 17 Trinity Square,
Llandudno, Conwy LL30 2RN
☎ (01492) 876271
Email: richardc@swaynejohnson.com

Family Fund
4 Alpha Court, Monks Cross Drive,
York YO32 9WN
☎ (08449) 744 099   ☎ (01904) 652625
Email: info@familyfund.org.uk
www.familyfund.org.uk

Ford Britain Trust
Room 1/445, c/o Ford Motor Company Ltd,
Eagle Way, Brentwood, Essex CM13 3BW
☎ (01277) 252551
Email: fbtrust@ford.com
www.ford.co.uk/fbtrust
Director: Andy Taylor

The G C Gibson Charitable Trust
Deloitte PCS LLP, 5 Callaghan Square,
Cardiff CF10 5BT
☎ (029) 2026 4391
Trustee: Martin Gibson

The Gane Charitable Trust
Bristol Guild of Applied Art Ltd,
68-70 Park Street, Bristol BS1 5JY
☎ (0117) 9265548
Trustee: Kenneth Stradling

Garthgwynion Charities
13 Osborne Close, Feltham TW13 6SR
☎ (020) 8890 0469
Contact: June Barker

The Goodman & Ruthin Charity
Llys Goodman, Church Walks,
Ruthin, Clwyd LL15 lBW
☎ (01824) 705241
Contact: M Baines

The Gwendoline & Margaret Davies Charity
Plas Dolerw, Milford Road
Newtown, Powys SY16 2EH
☎ (01686) 625228
Email: susan@daviescharities.freeserve.co.uk
Secretary: Susan Hamer

The Hoover Foundation
Pentrebach, Merthyr Tydfil CF48 4TU
☎ (01685) 721222   ☎ (01685) 725538
Email: susan.whetter@hoovercandy.com
Correspondent: Susan Whetter

The Isle of Anglesey Charitable Trust
Isle of Anglesey County Council,
Council Offices, Llangefni LL77 7TW
☎ (01248) 752610
www.anglesey.gov.uk

The James Pantyfedwen Foundation
Pantyfedwen, 9 Market St,
Aberystwyth, Ceredigion SY23 1DL
☎ (01970) 612806   ☎ (01970) 612806
Email: pantyfedwen@btinternet.com
www.jamespantyfedwenfoundation.org.uk
Executive Secretary: Richard H Morgan

The Jane Hodge Foundation
Tŷ Gwyn, Lisvane Road, Cardiff CF14 0SG
☎ (029) 2076 6521
Email: dianne.lydiard@janehodgefoundation.co.uk
Trustee: Derrek Jones

The Jenour Foundation
Deloitte PCS LLP, 5 Callaghan Square,
Cardiff CF10 5BT
☎ (029) 2026 4391
Contact: Karen griffin

Joseph Strong Frazer Trust
Floor A, Milburn House, Dean St,
Newcastle Upon Tyne, Tyne and Wear NE1 1LE
☎ (0191) 232 8065   ☎ (0191) 222 1554
Email: uj@joseph-miller.co.uk
Contact: Correspondent

Laspen Trust
The Estate Office, Port Penrhyn,
Bangor, Gwynedd LL57 4HN
Trustee: E H Douglas Pennant

The Ashley Family Foundation
Ladywell House, Park St, Newtown,
Powys SY16 1JB
☎ (01686) 610648
Email: lafwales@tiscali.co.uk
www.ashleyfamilyfoundation.org.uk
Grants Manager: Wendy Abel

Lloyds TSB Foundation for England and Wales
Pentagon House, 52-54 Southwark St,
London SE1 1UN
☎ (0870) 4111223
Email: enquiries@lloydstsbfoundations.org.uk
www.lloydstsbfoundation.org.uk
Mrs Linda Kelly

Post Brenhinol

Royal Mail

The Llysdinam Trust
Rees Richards & Partners Managing Agents,
Druslyn House, De La Beche St,
Swansea SA1 3HH
☎ (01792) 650705

The Millennium Stadium Charitable Trust
c/o Fusion, Sophia House,
28 Cathedral Road, Cardiff CF11 9LJ
☎ (029) 2066 0297
Email: MSCT@fusionuk.org.uk
www.millenniumstadiumtrust.co.uk
Chair: Russell Goodway

The Mr & Mrs J T Morgan Foundation
Calvert House, Calvert Terrace,
Swansea SA1 6AP
☎ (01792) 655178

The Newstead Charity
Port of Liverpool Building,
Pier Head, Liverpool L3 1NW
☎ (0151) 236 6666
The Secretary

The Owen Family Trust
Mill Dam House, Mill Lane Aldridge,
Walsall WS9 0NB
☎ (0121) 526 3131

The Payne Charitable Trust
(specific to christian activities), Copthorne House,
The Broadway, Abergele, Conwy LL22 7DD
☎ (01745) 825779
Email: Paynecharitable@aol.com
Contact: J Payne

The Rainford Trust
c/o Pilkington Group Ltd, Prescot Rd,
St Helens, Merseyside WA10 3TT
☎ (01744) 20574
Email: rainfordtrust@btconnect.com
Secretary: William Hadfield Simm

The Rhymney Trust
11 Forge Crescent, Rhymney, Tredegar NP22 5PR
☎ (01685) 843094
Secretary: David Brennan MBE

The Rhys Davies Trust
10 Heol Don, Whitchurch, Cardiff CF14 2AU
☎ (029) 2062 3359
Email: hwncomanco@hotmail.co.uk
Chair: Prof Dai Smith
Secretary: Dr Meic Stephens

The Severn Trent Water Charitable Trust Fund
12-14 Mill Street, Sutton Coldfield,
Birmingham B72 1TP
☎ (0121) 355 7766
Email: office@sttf.org.uk
www.sttf.org.uk
Derek William Harris

The Simon Gibson Charitable Trust
Wild Rose House, Llancarfan,
Vale of Glamorgan CF62 3AD
☎ (01446) 781459
Email: marsh575@btinternet.com
Trustee: Bryan Marsh

The Sir Julian Hodge Charitable Trust
Tŷ-Gwyn, Lisvane, Cardiff CF14 0SG
☎ (029) 2076 6521
Secretary: Margaret Cason

St Teilo's Trust
Stradey Estate Office, 53 New Road,
Llanelli, Carms SA15 3DP
☎ (01554) 773059
www.saintteilostrust.org.uk
Chair: Patrick Mansel Lewis

Synthite Charities Fund
Denbigh Rd, Mold, Flintshire CH7 1BT
☎ (01352) 752521
Email: davidkelso@synthite.co.uk
Trustee: David J Kelso

The Waterloo Foundation
46-48 Cardiff Rd, Llandaff, Cardiff CF5 2DT
☎ (029) 2083 8980   ▤ (029) 2056 0620
Email: info@waterloofoundation.org.uk
www.waterloofoundation.org.uk
Trustees: David G Stevens CBE,
Heather Stevens CBE, Ms J Alexander,
Mrs C Oakes

The Wrexham Concern Trust
39 Pritchard Court, 40 Cardiff Road,
Llandaff, Cardiff CF5 2DE
☎ (029) 2056 0271

CONSUMER GROUPS

Consumer Groups

Bus Users UK Cymru
PO Box 1045, Cardiff CF11 1JE
☎ (029) 2022 1370
Email: wales@bususers.org
www.bususers.org
Senior Officer for Wales: Margaret Everson
Officer for Wales: Barclay Davies

Community Housing Cymru
2 Ocean Way, Cardiff CF24 5TG
☎ (029) 2067 4800 🖷 (029) 2067 4081
Email: enquiries@chcymru.org.uk
www.chcymru.org.uk
Chair: Peter Cahill
Group Chief Executive: Nick Bennett
Director, Policy & Social Enterprise: Sioned Hughes

Consumer Council for Water Wales
Room 140, Tŷ Caradog,
1-6 St Andrew's Place, Cardiff CF10 3BE
☎ (029) 2023 9852 🖷 (029) 2023 9847
Email: wales@ccwater.org.uk
www.ccwater.org.uk
Chair: Diane McCrea
Regional Manager of CCWater Wales: Gaynor Nelson

Consumer Focus Wales
Llais Defnyddwyr Cymru
Ground Floor, Portcullis House,
21 Cowbridge Road East, Cardiff CF11 9AD
☎ (029) 2078 7100 🖷 (029) 2078 7101
Email: contactwales@consumerfocus.org.uk
www.consumerfocus.org.uk/wales
Chair: Vivienne Sugar
Senior Director: Rhys Evans

Food Standards Agency Wales
11th Floor, Southgate House, Wood St,
Cardiff CF10 1EW
☎ (029) 2067 8999
Email: wales@foodstandards.gsi.gov.uk
www.food.gov.uk
Director Wales: Steve Wearne

National Lottery Commission
4th Floor, Victoria Square House,
Victoria Square, Birmingham B2 4BP
☎ (0121) 2306750 🖷 (0121) 2306720
Email: info@natlotcomm.gov.uk
www.natlotcomm.gov.uk
Chief Executive: Mark Harris

Passenger Focus
PO Box 114, Chepstow NP16 6WR
☎ (0300) 123 2350 🖷 (0845) 850 1392
Email: info@passengerfocus.org.uk
www.passengerfocus.org
Rail Passenger Manager Wales: Simon Pickering
Member for Wales/Chair: Stella Mair Thomas

Education: Universities & Colleges

Bangor University
Bangor, Gwynedd LL57 2DG
☎ (01248) 351151
Email: d.m.roberts@bangor.ac.uk
www.bangor.ac.uk
Chair of Council: Lord Davies of Abersoch
President: Rt Hon Lord Elis-Thomas
Vice-Chancellor: Prof John Hughes

Cardiff Metropolitan University
Western Ave, Cardiff CF5 2YB
☎ (029) 2041 6070 🖷 (029) 2041 6286
Email: info@cardiffmet.ac.uk
www.cardiffmet.ac.uk
Chair: Barbara Wilding CBE
Vice-Chancellor: Prof Antony J Chapman

Cardiff University
Museum Ave, Cardiff CF10 3XQ
☎ (029) 2087 4000 🖷 (029) 2087 4000
www.cardiff.ac.uk
President: Prof Sir Martin Evans FRS
Vice-Chancellor: Prof Colin Riordan

Coleg Cymraeg Cenedlaethol
Y Llwyfan, College Rd, Carmarthen SA31 3EQ
☎ (0844) 800 7375
Email: gwybodaeth@colegcymraeg.ac.uk
www.colegcymraeg.ac.uk
Chair: Prof R Merfyn Jones
Chief Executive: Dr Ioan Matthews

Sponsored by: www.royalmail.com

Post Brenhinol

Royal Mail

Gregynog Hall - University of Wales
Tregynon, Newtown, Powys SY16 3PW
☎ (01686) 650224 ☐ (01686) 650656
Email: gregynog@wales.ac.uk
www.gregynog.wales.ac.uk
Director: Karen Armstrong

The Open University in Wales
18 Custom House St, Cardiff CF10 1AP
☎ (029) 2047 1019 ☐ (029) 2038 8132
Email: wales@open.ac.uk
www.open.ac.uk/wales
Vice Chancellor: Martin Bean
Director for Wales: Rob Humphreys

Prifysgol Aberystwyth University
Old College, King St, Aberystwyth SY23 2AX
☎ (01970) 623111 ☐ (01970) 628548
Email: vice-chancellor@aber.ac.uk
www.aber.ac.uk
President: Sir Emyr Jones Parry
Vice-Chancellor: Prof April McMahon

Prifysgol Glyndŵr University
Plas Coch, Mold Rd, Wrexham LL11 2AW
☎ (01978) 290666 ☐ (01978) 290008
Email: g.beer@glyndwr.ac.uk
www.glyndwr.ac.uk
Chancellor: Sir Jon Shortridge
Vice-Chancellor & Chief Executive: Prof Michael Scott DL

Royal Welsh College of Music & Drama
Castle Grounds, Cathays Park, Cardiff CF10 3ER
☎ (029) 2034 2854 ☐ (029) 2039 1304
Email: info@rwcmd.ac.uk www.rwcmd.ac.uk
Interim Chair: Vincent McNabb
Principal: Hilary Boulding

Swansea Metropolitan University
Mount Pleasant, Swansea SA1 6ED
☎ (01792) 481000 ☐ (01792) 481085
Email: enquiry@smu.ac.uk www.smu.ac.uk
Chair: Dr Gerald Lewis
Vice-Chancellor: Prof David Warner CBE

Swansea University
Singleton Park, Swansea SA2 8PP
☎ (01792) 205678 ☐ (01792) 295157
Email: info@swansea.ac.uk
www.swansea.ac.uk
Chair of Council: Sir Roger Jones OBE
Vice-Chancellor: Prof Richard B Davies

University of Wales Trinity Saint David
Prifysgol Cymru Y Drindod Dewi Sant
Carmarthen Campus, Carmarthen SA31 3EP
☎ (01267) 676767 ☐ (01267) 676766
www.trinitysaintdavid.uk
Chair of Council: Dr Geoffrey P Thomas
Vice-Chancellor: Prof Medwin Hughes DL

Also at:
Lampeter Campus, Lampeter,
Ceredigion SA48 7ED
☎ (01570) 422351 ☐ (01570) 423423
www.trinitysaintdavid.ac.uk
Chair of Council: Dr Geoffrey P Thomas
Vice-Chancellor: Dr Medwin Hughes

learndirect Cymru
Priory House, Beignon Close,
Ocean Way, Cardiff CF24 5PB
☎ (029) 2049 4540 ☐ (029) 2049 4262
Email: cymru@ufi.com
www.learndirect.co.uk
Head of Wales: Jeff Greenidge

Universities Heads of the Valleys Institute (UHOVI)
Crownford House, Swan Street,
Merthyr Tydfil CF47 8ES
☎ (0800) 1223 220 or (01685) 726156
☐ (01685) 726190
Email: enquiries@uhovi.ac.uk www.uhovi.ac.uk

University of Glamorgan
Pontypridd CF37 1DL
☎ (01443) 480480 ☐ (01443) 654050
Email: press@glam.ac.uk www.glam.ac.uk
Chancellor: Rt Hon Lord Morris of Aberavon KG QC
Vice-Chancellor: Julie Lydon

University of Wales
University Registry, King Edward VII Ave,
Cathays Park, Cardiff CF10 3NS
☎ (029) 2037 6999 ☐ (029) 2037 6980
Email: uniwales@wales.ac.uk
www.wales.ac.uk
Chair of Council: Alun Thomas
Vice-Chancellor: Prof Medwin Hughes DL

University of Wales Centre for Advanced Welsh & Celtic Studies
Canolfan Uwchefnydiau Cymreig a Cheltaidd Prifysgol Cymru
The National Library of Wales, Penglais,
Aberystwyth, Ceredigion SY23 3HH
☎ (01970) 636543 ☐ (01970) 639090
Email: canolfan@cymru.ac.uk
www.wales.ac.uk/cawcs
Director: Prof Dafydd Johnston

University of Wales, Newport
Caerleon Campus, Lodge Rd,
Caerleon, Newport NP18 3QT
☎ (01633) 432432 ☐ (01633) 432046
Email: uic@newport.ac.uk www.newport.ac.uk
Chair: Andrew Wilkinson
Vice-Chancellor: Prof Stephen Hagen

FURTHER EDUCATION

Education: Further Education & Tertiary Colleges

Bridgend College
Bridgend Campus, Cowbridge Road,
Bridgend CF31 3DF
☎ (01656) 302302
Email: enquiries@bridgend.ac.uk
www.bridgend.ac.uk
Principal: Mark Jones

Also at:

Maesteg Campus,
Bridgend College,
Castle Street, Maesteg CF34 9UN
☎ (01656) 730569
Email: maesteg@bridgend.ac.uk
www.bridgend.ac.uk
Principal: Mark Jones

Cardiff & Vale College
Cardiff Construction Training Centre (CCTC),
Dumballs Rd, Cardiff CF10 5TX
☎ (030) 30 30 10 10
Email: info@cavc.ac.uk
www.cavc.ac.uk
Principal: Mike James

Also at:

International Centre for
Aerospace Training (ICAT),
Cardiff Airport Business Park,
Rhoose, Vale of Glamorgan CF62 3DP
☎ (01446) 711447

Barry Waterfront,
Hood Rd,
Barry CF62 5QL
☎ (01446) 725074

Colcot Rd, Barry,
Vale of Glamorgan CF62 8YJ
☎ (01446) 725000

Gladstone Road Centre, Barry,
Vale of Glamorgan CF62 6NA
☎ (01446) 747273

Coleg Ceredigion
Cardigan Campus, Park Place,
Cardigan/Aberteifi, Ceredigion SA43 1AB
☎ (01239) 612032 📠 (01239) 622339
Email: enquiries@ceredigion.ac.uk
www.ceredigion.ac.uk
Principal: Jacqui Weatherburn

Coleg Ceredigion
Also at:

Llanbadarn Campus,
Llanbadarn Fawr,
Aberystwyth, Ceredigion SY23 3BP
☎ (01970) 639700
📠 (01970) 623206
Email: enquiries@ceredigion.ac.uk
www.ceredigion.ac.uk
Principal: Jacqui Weatherburn

Coleg Gwent
City of Newport Campus,
Nash Rd, Newport NP19 4TS
☎ (01633) 466000
📠 (01633) 466100
Email: info@coleggwent.ac.uk
www.coleggwent.ac.uk
Principal: Jim Bennett
Chair: Angela Lloyd

Also at:

Crosskeys Campus, Risca Rd,
Crosskeys NP11 7ZA
☎ (01495) 333456
📠 (01495) 333386
Email: info@coleggwent.ac.uk
www.coleggwent.ac.uk
Principal: Jim Bennett
Chair: Angela Lloyd

Ebbw Vale Campus,
College Rd,
Ebbw Vale NP23 6GT
☎ (01495) 333000
📠 (01495) 333099
Email: info@coleggwent.ac.uk
www.coleggwent.ac.uk
Principal: Jim Bennett
Chair: Angela Lloyd

Business Development Unit,
The Rhadyr, Usk NP15 1XJ
☎ (01495) 333526
📠 (01495) 333526
Email: info@coleggwent.ac.uk
bdu@coleggwent.ac.uk
www.coleggwent.ac.uk
Principal: Jim Bennett
Chair: Angela Lloyd

Post Brenhinol

Royal Mail

Coleg Gwent

Also at:

Pontypool Campus, Blaendare Rd,
Pontypool NP4 5YE
☎ (01495) 333100
🖷 (01495) 333130
Email: info@coleggwent.ac.uk
www.coleggwent.ac.uk
Principal: Jim Bennett
Chair: Angela Lloyd

Usk Campus, The Rhadyr, Usk NP15 1XJ
☎ (01495) 333639
🖷 (01495) 333629
Email: info@coleggwent.ac.uk
www.coleggwent.ac.uk
Principal: Jim Bennett
Chair: Angela Lloyd

Coleg Harlech WEA(N)

Harlech, Gwynedd LL46 2PU
☎ (01766) 780363
🖷 (01766) 781919
Email: info@harlech.ac.uk
www.harlech.ac.uk
Principal: Trefor Fôn Owen

Coleg Llysfasi (part of Deeside College)

Ruthin LL15 2LB
☎ (01978) 790263
Email: enquiries@deeside.ac.uk
www.deeside.ac.uk/llysfasi

Grŵp Llandrillo Menai

(including Coleg Llandrillo, Coleg Menai and
Coleg Meirion Dwyfor)

Llandudno Road, Rhos-on-Sea, Colwyn Bay,
Conwy LL28 4HZ
☎ (01492) 546666
www.gllm.ac.uk

Coleg Morgannwg

Ynys Terrace, Rhydyfelin, Pontypridd CF37 5RN
☎ (01443) 662800
🖷 (01443) 663028
Email: college@morgannwg.ac.uk
www.morgannwg.ac.uk
Principal: Judith Evans

Coleg Morgannwg

Also at:

Aberdare Campus
Cwmdare Rd, Aberdare CF44 8ST
☎ (01685) 887500
🖷 (01685) 876635
Email: college@morgannwg.ac.uk
www.morgannwg.ac.uk
Principal: Judith Evans

Nantgarw Campus & Art Centre
Heol yr Odyn, Parc Nantgarw, Cardiff CF15 7QX
☎ (01443) 663379
🖷 (01443) 663358
Email: college@morgannwg.ac.uk
www.morgannwg.ac.uk
Principal: Judith Evans

Rhonnda Campus
Llwynypia, Tonypandy CF40 2TQ
☎ (01443) 663202
🖷 (01443) 663358
Email: college@morgannwg.ac.uk
www.morgannwg.ac.uk
Principal: Judith Evans

Coleg Powys

3 Brecon Rd, Ystradgynlais, Powys SA9 1HE
☎ (0845) 4086 500 🖷 (01639) 849234
Email: enquiries@coleg-powys.ac.uk
www.coleg-powys.ac.uk
Principal: Simon Pirotte

Also at:

Llanidloes Rd, Newtown, Powys SY16 4HU
☎ (0845) 4086 200
Email: enquiries@coleg-powys.ac.uk
www.coleg-powys.ac.uk
Principal: Simon Pirotte

Spa Rd, Llandrindod Wells, Powys LD1 5ES
☎ (0845) 4086 300 🖷 (01597) 825122
Email: enquiries@coleg-powys.ac.uk
www.coleg-powys.ac.uk
Principal: Simon Pirotte

Coleg Sir Gâr

Graig Campus, Sandy Rd, Pwll,
Llanelli SA15 4DN
☎ (01554) 748000 🖷 (01554) 748170
Email: admissions@colegsirgar.ac.uk
www.colegsirgar.ac.uk
Principal: Barry Liles

FURTHER EDUCATION

Coleg Sir Gâr

Also at:

Construction Technology and Development Support Centre, Ammanford Campus, Dyffryn Rd, Ammanford SA18 3TA
☎ (01554) 748318 / 748505
Email: construction.centre@colegsirgar.ac.uk
www.constructioncentre.sirgar.com
Ammanford Campus Manager: Gaynor Davies

The College Ystrad Mynach

Twyn Rd, Ystrad Mynach,
Hengoed CF82 7XR
☎ (01443) 816888
Email: enquiries@ystrad-mynach.ac.uk
www.ystrad-mynach.ac.uk
Principal: Brynley Davies

Deeside College
Coleg Glannau Dyfrdwy

Kelsterton Rd, Connah's Quay,
Deeside CH5 4BR
☎ (01244) 831531
🖷 (01244) 814305
Email: enquiries@deeside.ac.uk
www.deeside.ac.uk
Principal: David Jones

Gower College Swansea

Belgrave Rd, Gorseinon, Swansea SA4 6RD
☎ (01792) 890700
Email: admin@gowercollegeswansea.ac.uk
www.gowercollegeswansea.ac.uk
Principal: Nick Bennett

Also at:

Tycoch Rd, Swansea SA2 9EB
☎ (01792) 284000
Email: info@gowercollegeswansea.ac.uk
www.gowercollegeswansea.ac.uk
Principal: Nick Bennett

Merthyr Tydfil College - University of Glamorgan

Ynysfach, Merthyr Tydfil CF48 1AR
☎ (01685) 726000 🖷 (01685) 726100
Email: Enquiries@merthyr.ac.uk
www.merthyr.ac.uk
Principal: John O'Shea

Neath Port Talbot College
Coleg Castell Nedd Port Talbot

Afan Campus, Margam, Port Talbot SA13 2AL
☎ (01639) 648200
Email: admissions@nptc.ac.uk
www.nptc.ac.uk
Principal: Mark Dacey

Neath Port Talbot College
Coleg Castell Nedd Port Talbot

Also at:

Building Crafts Training Centre,
St Davids Close, Llansamlet,
Swansea SA6 8QL
☎ (01639) 648120
Email: admissions@nptc.ac.uk
www.nptc.ac.uk
Principal: Mark Dacey

Queen St, Neath SA11 1DL
☎ (01639) 648110
Email: admissions@nptc.ac.uk
www.nptc.ac.uk
Principal: Mark Dacey

Neath Campus, Dŵr-y-Felin Rd,
Neath SA10 7RF
☎ (01639) 648000
🖷 (01639) 648009
Email: admissions@nptc.ac.uk
www.nptc.ac.uk
Principal: Mark Dacey

Northop College (part of Deeside College)

Holywell Rd, Northop, Mold CH7 6AA
☎ (01352) 841000
🖷 (01352) 841031
Email: enquiries@deeside.ac.uk
www.deeside.ac.uk

Pembrokeshire College
Coleg Sir Benfro

Merlins Bridge, Haverfordwest SA61 1SZ
☎ (01437) 753000
Email: admissions@pembrokeshire.ac.uk
www.pembrokeshire.ac.uk
Acting Principal: Sharron Lusher

St David's Catholic Sixth Form College

Tŷ Gwyn Rd , Penylan, Cardiff CF2 5YD
☎ (029) 2049 8555
Email: enquiries@st-davids-coll.ac.uk
www.st-davids-coll.ac.uk/
Principal: Mark Leighfield

Post Brenhinol

Royal Mail

Wrexham Training (part of Deeside College)
Felin Puleston, Ruabon Rd, Wrexham LL13 7RF
☎ (01978) 363033
Email: enquiries@deeside.ac.uk
www.deeside.ac.uk/wrexhamtraining

Yale College, Wrexham
Grove Park Rd, Wrexham LL12 7AA
☎ (01978) 311794 🖷 (01978) 291569
Email: college@yale-wrexham.ac.uk
www.yale-wrexham.ac.uk
Principal: Mr J.S Dhesi

Also at:

Bersham Road Campus, Bersham Rd,
Wrexham LL13 7UH
☎ (01978) 311794 🖷 (01978) 291569

YMCA Wales Community College
Unit 6, Cleeve House, Lambourne Crescent,
Cardiff Business Park, Llanishen,
Cardiff CF14 5GP
☎ (029) 2075 5444
🖷 (029) 2075 5445
Email: info@ymca-wales.ac.uk
www.ymca-wales.ac.uk
Head of College: Mark Isherwood

Education: Secondary Schools

Blaenau Gwent

Abertillery Comprehensive School
Alma St, Abertillery NP13 1YL
☎ (01495) 217121
Email: abertillery.comprehensive@blaenau-gwent.gov.uk
www.abertilleryschool.net
Headteacher: Paul A Stock

Brynmawr Foundation School
Intermediate Rd, Rhydw,
Brynmawr NP23 4XT
☎ (01495) 310527 🖷 (01495) 311944
Email: brynmawr.school@blaenau-gwent.gov.uk
www.brynmawrschool.co.uk
Headteacher: James Retallick

Ebbw Vale Comprehensive School
Waun-Y-Pound Rd, Ebbw Vale NP23 6LE
☎ (01495) 303409 🖷 (01495) 304857
Email: evcs@blaenau-gwent.gov.uk
Headteacher: Mick M Fahy

Glyncoed Comprehensive School
Badminton Grove, Ebbw Vale NP23 5UW
☎ (01495) 303216 🖷 (01495) 307829
Email: glyncoedcompschool@blaenau-gwent.gov.uk
Headteacher: Colin James

Tredegar Comprehensive School
Stable Lane, Tredegar NP22 4BH
☎ (01495) 723551 🖷 (01495) 725686
Email: tredegar.comprehensive@blaenau-gwent.gov.uk

Bridgend

**Archbishop McGrath Catholic High School
Ysgol Uwchradd Gatholig Archesgob
McGrath**
Bramble Close, Brackla, Bridgend CF31 2PQ
☎ (01656) 815500 🖷 (01656) 669952
Email: archmcgrathrc@bridgend.gov.uk
www.archbishopmg.co.uk
Headteacher: Rev Dr Philip Manghan

**Brynteg School
Ysgol Brynteg**
Ewenny Rd, Bridgend CF31 3ER
☎ (01656) 641800 🖷 (01656) 641802
Email: admin@bryntegcs.bridgend.sch.uk
www.bryntegschool.co.uk
Headteacher: D H Jenkins

Bryntirion Comprehensive School
Merlin Crescent, Cefn Glas,
Bridgend CF31 4QR
☎ (01656) 641100 🖷 (01656) 641106
Email: bryntirioncomp@bridgend.gov.uk
www.bryntirionschool.bridgend.gov.uk
Headteacher: A J Thomas

Cynffig Comprehensive School
East Ave, Kenfig Hill, Bridgend CF33 6NP
☎ (01656) 740294
🖷 (01656) 747940
Email: headteacher.cynffig@bridgend.gov.uk
www.cynffig.net
Headteacher: Sue Davies

Ogmore Comprehensive School
Bryncethin, Bridgend CF32 9NA
☎ (01656) 815920
🖷 (01656) 815924
Email: ogmoreschool@bridgend.gov.uk
www.ogmore.org
Acting Headteacher: Mr G Davies

Porthcawl Comprehensive School
52 Park Ave, Porthcawl CF36 3ES
☎ (01656) 774100
🖷 (01656) 774101
Email: info@porthcawlschool.co.uk
www.porthcawlschool.co.uk
Headteacher: K E Dykes

Ynysawdre Comprehensive School
Heol yr Ysgol, Tondu, Bridgend CF32 9EL
☎ (01656) 720643
🖷 (01656) 722571
Email: contact.ynysawdre@bridgend.gov.uk
www.ynysawdrecs.bridgend.gov.uk
Headteacher: Trevis Woodward

Ysgol Gyfun Gymraeg Llangynwyd
Llangyndwyd, Maesteg,
Bridgend CF34 9RW
☎ (01656) 815700
Email: post.yggllangynwyd@bridgend.gov.uk
www.yggllangynwyd.org.uk
Headteacher: Mark Jones

Ysgol Maesteg School
Ffordd Dysgu, Maesteg, Bridgend CF34 0LQ
☎ (01656) 815950
🖷 (01656) 815954
Email: maestegschool.maesteg@bridgend.gov.uk
www.maestegcs.bridgend.sch.uk
Headteacher: Ms A Carhart

Ysgol Pencoed Comprehensive School
Coychurch Rd, Pencoed, Bridgend CF35 5LZ
☎ (01656) 867100
🖷 (01656) 867107
Email: admin.pencoedcomp@bridgend.gov.uk
www.pencoedcs.bridgend.sch.uk
Headteacher: David George

Caerphilly

Bedwas High School
Newport Rd, Bedwas, Caerphilly CF83 8BJ
☎ (029) 2085 9800
🖷 (029) 2085 9818
Email: bwaca@caerphilly.gov.uk
www.bedwashighschool.co.uk
Headteacher: Peter Ward

Blackwood Comprehensive School
Tŷ-Isha Terrace, Blackwood,
Gwent NP12 1ER
☎ (01495) 225566/223326
🖷 (01495) 225625
Email: blkca@caerphilly.gov.uk
www.blackwood.caerphilly.sch.uk
Headteacher: Mr Ravi Pawar

Cwmcarn High School (Foundation)
Chapel Farm, Cwmcarn,
Crosskeys NP11 7NG
☎ (01495) 270982
Email: cmcca@caerphilly.gov.uk
www.cwmcarnhigh.co.uk
Headmaster: Mrs J Peplinski

Heolddu Comprehensive School
Mountain Rd, Bargoed CF81 8XL
☎ (01443) 875531
Email: heoca@caerphilly.gov.uk
www.heolddu.org.uk
Headteacher: Mr P M Jones

Lewis Girls' Comprehensive School
Oakfield St, Ystrad Mynach,
Hengoed CF82 7WW
☎ (01443) 813168
🖷 (01443) 862538
Email: lgsca@caerphilly.gov.uk
Headteacher: Ms Heather Duncan

Lewis School Pengam
Gilfach, Bargoed CF81 8LJ
☎ (01443) 873873
🖷 (01443) 873860
Email: lbuca@caerphilly.gov.uk
Headteacher: Dr Christopher Howard

Newbridge School
Bridge St, Newbridge,
Newport NP11 5FE
☎ (01495) 243243
Email: NEWCA@caerphilly.gov.uk
Headteacher: Mrs L Perry

Sponsored by: www.royalmail.com

Post Brenhinol
Royal Mail

Oakdale Comprehensive School
Penmaen Rd, Oakdale,
Blackwood NP12 0DT
☎ (01495) 233600
🖷 (01495) 233655
Email: oakca@caerphilly.gov.uk
Headteacher: Mr C David

Pontllanfraith Comprehensive School
Coed Cau Ddu Rd, Pontllanfraith,
Blackwood NP12 2YB
☎ (01495) 224929
🖷 (01495) 232815
Email: plfca@caerphilly.gov.uk
www.pontllanfraith.org.uk
Headteacher: Robert Davies

Rhymney Comprehensive School
Abertysswg Rd, Rhymney NP22 5XF
☎ (01685) 846900
🖷 (01685) 846905
Email: Rhyca@caerphilly.gov.uk
Headteacher: Mr R P Davies
Administrator: M England

St Cenydd School
Trecenydd, Caerphilly CF83 2RP
☎ (029) 2085 2504
🖷 (029) 2088 9526
Email: stcca@caerphilly.gov.uk
learn.caerphilly.ork.uk/stcenyddcomprehensive
Headteacher: Ian Kilcoyne

St Martin's Comprehensive School
Hillside, Caerphilly CF83 1UW
☎ (029) 2085 8050
🖷 (029) 2085 8051
Email: stmca@caerphilly.gov.uk
www.learn.caerphilly.org.uk/stmartinscomprehensive
Headteacher: Mrs K Davies

Ysgol Gyfun Cwm Rhymni
Heol Gelli Haf, Fleur de Lys,
Blackwood, Caerffili NP12 3JQ
☎ (01443) 875227
🖷 (01443) 829777
Email: ycuca@caerphilly.gov.uk
www.cwmrhymni.com
Headteacher: Owain ap Dafydd

Cardiff

Bishop of Llandaff Church in Wales High School
Rookwood Close, Llandaff,
Cardiff CF5 2NR
☎ (029) 2056 2485
🖷 (029) 2057 8862
Email: bishopofllandaffhigh@cardiff.gov.uk
www.bishopofllandaff.org
Headteacher: The Revd C G Hollowood

Cantonian High School
Fairwater Rd, Fairwater,
Cardiff CF5 3JR
☎ (029) 2041 5250
🖷 (029) 2041 5273
Email: cawest@cardiff.gov.uk
www.cantonian.cardiff.sch.uk
Headteacher: Lois A Spargo

Cardiff High School
Llandennis Rd, Cyncoed,
Cardiff CF23 6WG
☎ (029) 2075 7741
🖷 (029) 2068 0850
Email: Hrichards@cardiff.gov.uk
www.cardiffhigh.cardiff.sch.uk
Headteacher: Michael Griffiths

Ysgol Uwchradd Cathays High School
Crown Way, Gabalfa,
Cardiff CF14 3XG
☎ (029) 2054 4400
🖷 (029) 2054 4401
Email: schooladmin@cathays.cardiff.sch.uk
www.web.cathays.cardiff.sch.uk
Headteacher: Rodney Phillips

Corpus Christi High School
Tŷ-Draw Rd, Lisvane,
Cardiff CF23 6XL
☎ (029) 2076 1893
🖷 (029) 2076 1970
Email: bmullins@cardiff.gov.uk
www.corpuschristi.cardiff.sch.uk
Headteacher: David Stone

Glyn Derw High School
Penally Rd, Caerau,
Cardiff CF5 5XD
☎ (029) 2059 0920
🖷 (029) 2059 0922
Email: glynderwhigh@cardiff.gov.uk
www.glynderw.cardiff.sch.uk
Headteacher: Mr P Davies

Llanedeyrn High School
Roundwood, Llanedeyrn,
Cardiff CF23 9US
☎ (029) 2073 4718
🖷 (029) 2054 0688
Email: Llanedeyrnhighschool@cardiff.gov.uk
www.llanedeyrn.cardiff.sch.uk
Headteacher: Julian Doroszczuk

Llanishen High School
Heol Hir, Llanishen,
Cardiff CF14 5YL
☎ (029) 2068 0800
🖷 (029) 2068 0830
Email: RSmyth@cardiff.gov.uk
www.llanishen.cardiff.sch.uk
Headteacher: R A Smyth

Llanrumney High School
Ball Rd, Llanrumney,
Cardiff CF3 4YW
☎ (029) 2036 5500
🖷 (029) 2036 5501
Email: LlanrumneyHigh@cardiff.gov.uk
www.llanrumney.cardiff.sch.uk
Headteacher: Mr D Neil

Mary Immaculate High School
Caerau Lane, Wenvoe,
Cardiff CF5 5QZ
☎ (029) 2059 3465
🖷 (029) 2067 2750
Email: admin@maryimmaculate.org.uk
www.maryimmaculate.cardiff.sch.uk
Headteacher: Marc Belli

Michaelston Community College
Michaelston Rd, Ely,
Cardiff CF5 4SX
☎ (029) 2067 2700
🖷 (029) 2067 2701
Email: michaelstoncommunitycollege@cardiff.gov.uk
www.michaelstoncollege.cardiff.sch.uk
Principal: Mary Campbell

Radyr Comprehensive School
Heol Isaf, Radyr,
Cardiff CF15 8XG
☎ (029) 2084 5100
🖷 (029) 2084 5101
Email: Radyrhigh@cardiff.gov.uk
www.radyr.cardiff.sch.uk
Headteacher: Steven M Fowler

Rumney High School
Newport Rd, Rumney, Cardiff CF3 3XG
☎ (029) 2079 2751 🖷 (029) 2079 0938
Email: J.M.Evans@cardiff.gov.uk
www.rumney.cardiff.sch.uk
Headteacher: Gareth Cooke

St Illtyd's Catholic High School
Newport Rd, Rumney, Cardiff CF3 1XQ
☎ (029) 2077 8174 🖷 (029) 2036 1641
Email: stilltydshigh@cardiff.gov.uk
www.stilltyds.cardiff.sch.uk
Headteacher: Elizabeth York

St Teilo's C W High School
Llanedeyrn Rd, Penylan, Cardiff CF23 9DT
☎ (029) 2043 4700 🖷 (029) 2049 9232
Email: CGrimwood@cardiff.gov.uk
www.stteilos.cardiff.sch.uk
Headteacher: Mrs Beverley Walker

Whitchurch High School
Penlline Rd, Whitchurch, Cardiff CF14 2XJ
☎ (029) 2062 9700 🖷 (029) 2062 9701
Email: WHS@whitchurch.cardiff.sch.uk
www.whitchurchhs.com
Headteacher: Huw Jones-Williams

Willows High School
Willows Ave, Tremorfa, Cardiff CF24 2YE
☎ (029) 2041 4243
Email: jsheehan@cardiff.gov.uk
www.willows.cardiff.sch.uk
Headteacher: Joy Ballard

Ysgol Gyfun Gymraeg Glantaf
Bridge Rd, Llandaff North, Cardiff CF14 2JL
☎ (029) 2033 3090 🖷 (029) 2033 3091
Email: hysbys@glantaf.cardiff.sch.uk
www.glantaf.cardiff.sch.uk
Headteacher: Alun Davies

Ysgol Gyfun Gymraeg Plasmawr
Prentrebaen Rd, Fairwater, Cardiff CF5 3PZ
☎ (029) 2040 5499 🖷 (029) 2040 5496
Email: ysgol@plasmawr.cardiff.sch.uk
www.plasmawr.cardiff.sch.uk
Headteacher: John Hayes

Ysgol Uwchradd Fitzalan
Fitzalan High School
Lawrenny Avenue, Leckwith, Cardiff CF11 8XB
☎ (029) 2023 2850 🖷 (029) 2087 7800
Email: fitzalanhigh@cardiff.gov.uk
www.fitzalan.cardiff.sch.uk
Headteacher: Cath Bradshaw

Carmarthenshire

Bryngwyn School
Dafen, Llanelli, Carmarthenshire SA14 8RP
☎ (01554) 750661 🖷 (01554) 758255
Email: enq@bryngwyn.carmarthen.sch.uk
www.bryngwynschool.co.uk
Headteacher: Paul Jones

Coedcae School
Trostre Rd, Llanelli SA15 1LJ
☎ (01554) 750574 🖷 (01554) 755158
Email: info@coedcae..org
Headteacher: P A Spencer
www.coedcae.com

Dyffryn Tâf School
North Rd, Whitland SA34 0BD
☎ (01994) 242100 🖷 (01994) 240929
Email: head@dyffryntaf.org.uk
office@dyffryntaf.org.uk
www.dyffryntaf.co.uk
Headmaster: D R Newsome

Queen Elizabeth High School
Llansteffan Rd, Johnstown,
Carmarthen SA31 3NL
☎ (01267) 245300 🖷 (01267) 238224
Email: office@qehs.carms.sch.uk
www.qehs.carms.sch.uk
Headteacher: Pete Spencer

St John Lloyd Catholic Comprehensive School
Havard Rd, Llanelli SA14 8SD
☎ (01554) 772589 🖷 (01554) 773954
Email: office@stjlloyd.carms.sch.uk
www.stjohnlloyd.co.uk
Headteacher: P R White

Ysgol Glan-y-Môr School
Heol Elfed, Burry Port,
Carmarthenshire SA16 0AL
☎ (01554) 832507 🖷 (01554) 836110
Email: ysgol@glanymor.carms.sch.uk
www.glanymor.carms.sch.uk
Headteacher: Stephen Jones

Ysgol Dyffryn Aman
Margaret St, Ammanford SA18 2NW
☎ (01269) 592441 🖷 (01269) 597247
Email: admin@ammanvalley.carms.sch.uk
www.ammanvalley.amdro.org.uk
Headteacher: D Stephen Perks

Ysgol Gyfun Emlyn
Newcastle Emlyn,
Carmarthenshire SA38 9LN
☎ (01239) 710447 🖷 (01239) 710962
Email: admin@emlyn.carms.sch.uk
www.ysgolgyfunemlyn.org.uk
Headteacher: Ian A McCloy

Ysgol Gyfun Gymraeg Bro Myrddin
Croes- y-Ceiliog,
Caerfyrddin SA32 8DN
☎ (01267) 234829 🖷 (01267) 232218
Email: swyddfa@bromyrddin.sirgar.sch.uk
www.bromyrddin.sirgar.sch.uk
Headteacher: Dorian Williams

Ysgol Gyfun Maes Yr Yrfa
Heol y Parc, Cefneithin,
Llanelli SA14 7DT
☎ (01269) 833900 🖷 (01269) 833906
Email: swyddfa@maesyryrfa.carms.sch.uk
www.maesyryrfa.amdro.org.uk
Headteacher: Iwan M Rees

Ysgol Gyfun Pantycelyn
Heol Cilycwm,
Llanymddyfri SA20 0DY
☎ (01550) 720395 🖷 (01550) 720067
Email: admin@pantycelyn.org
Headteacher: Mrs J D Griffiths

Ysgol Gyfun Y Strade
Heol Sandy, Llanelli,
Carmarthenshire SA15 4DL
☎ (01554) 745100 🖷 (01554) 745106
Email: swyddfa@strade.sirgar.sch.uk
www.ysgolystrade.org
Headteacher: Heather Lewis

Ysgol Tre-Gib
Ffairfach, Llandeilo SA19 6TB
☎ (01558) 823477 🖷 (01558) 823116
Email: se@tregib.org.uk
frontdesk@tregib.org.uk
www.amdro.org.uk/eng/School_Websites/Secon
dary/Tre-Gib
Headteacher: J D Griffiths

Ysgol Y Gwendraeth
Drefach, Llanelli,
Carmarthenshire SA14 7AB
☎ (01269) 841322 🖷 (01269) 845645
Email: admin@gwendraeth.carms.sch.uk
www.ysgolygwendraeth.co.uk
Headteacher: Mrs Anna Williams

Ceredigion

Penglais Comprehensive School
Waunfawr, Aberystwyth SY23 3AW
☎ (01970) 624811 ᴆ (01970) 625830
Email: melanieg.penglais@ceredigion.gov.uk
www.penglais.org.uk
Headmaster: Mr H J Davey

Ysgol Dyffryn Teifi
Ffordd Llynyfran,
Llandysul SA44 4HP
☎ (01559) 362310 ᴆ (01559) 362856
Email: admin.dyffrynt@ceredigion.co.uk
www.dyffrynteifi.org
Headteacher: J Aeron Rees

Ysgol Gyfun Aberaeron
Stryd y Fro,
Aberaeron SA46 0DT
☎ (01545) 570217 ᴆ (01545) 570183
Email: adaeron@ceredigion.gov.uk
www.ysgol-gyfun-aberaeron.co.uk
Headteacher: Wyn Evans

Ysgol Gyfun Gymunedol Penweddig
Ffordd Llanbadarn, Llangawsai,
Aberystwyth SY23 3QN
☎ (01970) 639499 ᴆ (01970) 626641
Email: ymholiadau.penweddig@ceredigion.gov.uk
www.penweddig.ceredigion.sch.uk
Headteacher: Gwenallt Llwyd Ifan

Ysgol Gyfun Llanbedr Pont Steffan
Peterwell Terrace, Lampeter,
Ceredigion SA48 7BX
☎ (01570) 422214 ᴆ (01570) 423664
Email: admin.llanbedrps@ceredigion.gov.uk
www.ysgol-llambed.org.uk
Headteacher: Dylan Wyn

Ysgol Uwchradd Aberteifi
Park Place, Cardigan/Aberteifi SA43 1AD
☎ (01239) 612670 ᴆ (01239) 621108
Email: swyddfa.aberteifi@ceredigion.gov.uk
www.ysgol-uwchradd-aberteifi.co.uk
Headteacher: Nicola James

Ysgol Uwchradd Tregaron
Lampeter Rd,
Tregaron SY25 6HG
☎ (01974) 298231 ᴆ (01974) 298515
Email: admin.tregaron@ceredigion.gov.uk
Headteacher: Eirwen James

Conwy

Ysgol Aberconwy
Morfa Drive, Conwy LL32 8ED
☎ (01492) 593243 ᴆ (01492) 592537
Email: pennaeth@aberconwy.conwy.sch.uk
www.aberconwy.conwy.sch.uk
Headteacher: David K Wylde

Ysgol Bryn Elian
Windsor Drive, Old Colwyn,
Colwyn Bay LL29 8HU
☎ (01492) 518215 ᴆ (01492) 518570
Email: head@brynelian.conwy.sch.uk
www.brynelian.conwy.sch.uk
Head/Pennaeth: Eithne Hughes

Ysgol Dyffryn Conwy
Nebo Rd, Llanrwst LL26 0SD
☎ (01492) 642800 ᴆ (01492) 642801
Email: cyff@dyffrynconwy.conwy.sch.uk
www.ysgoldyffrynconwy.org
Headteacher: Paul Matthews-Jones

Ysgol Eirias
Eirias Rd, Colwyn Bay LL29 7SP
☎ (01492) 532025 ᴆ (01492) 531684
Email: general@eirias.conwy.sch.uk
www.eirias.conwy.sch.uk
Headteacher: Philip McTague

Ysgol Emrys ap Iwan
Faenol Ave, Abergele,
Conwy LL22 7HE
☎ (01745) 832287 ᴆ (01745) 826268
Email: info@emrysapiwan.conwy.sch.uk
www.emrysapiwan.conwy.sch.uk
Headteacher: Nayland Southorn

Ysgol John Bright
Maesdu Road, Llandudno,
Conwy LL30 1LF
☎ (01492) 864200 ᴆ (01492) 864299
Email: general@johnbright.conwy.sch.uk
www.johnbright.conwy.sch.uk
Headteacher: Graham Davies

Ysgol y Creuddyn
Ffordd Derwen, Bae Penrhyn,
Llandudno, Conwy LL30 3LB
☎ (01492) 544344 ᴆ (01492) 547594
Email: pennaeth@creuddyn.conwy.sch.uk
www.creuddyn.co.uk
Headteacher: Dr Meirion Davies

Sponsored by: www.royalmail.com

Post Brenhinol
Royal Mail

Denbighshire

Blessed Edward Jones Catholic High School
Cefndy Rd, Rhyl LL18 2EU
☎ (01745) 343433 ▣ (01745) 344723
Email: blessed.edwards@denbighshire.gov.uk
www.bej.d-wdl.net
Headteacher: J P Westaway-Green

Denbigh High School
Ruthin Rd, Denbigh LL16 3EX
☎ (01745) 812485 ▣ (01745) 815052
Email: ourschool@denbighhighschool.co.uk
www.denbighhighschool.co.uk
Headteacher: Mr S Molloy

Prestatyn High School
2 Prince's Ave,
Prestatyn LL19 8RS
☎ (01745) 852312 ▣ (01745) 855204
Email: prestatyn.high@denbighshire.gov.uk
www.prestatynhighschool.net
Headteacher: Phillip J Pierce

Rhyl High School
86 Grange Rd,
Rhyl LL18 4BY
☎ (01745) 343533 ▣ (01745) 342169
Email: rhyl.high@denbighshire.gov.uk
www.rhylhigh.denbighshire.sch.uk
Headteacher: Claire Armitstead

Ysgol Brynhyfryd
Ffordd yr Wyddgrug, Rhuthun,
Denbighshire LL15 1EG
☎ (01824) 703933 ▣ (01824) 705345
Email: ysgol.brynhyfryd@denbighshire.gov.uk
www.ysgolbrynhyfryd.org.uk
Headteacher: Eleri E Jones

Ysgol Dinas Brân
Dinbren Rd, Llangollen LL20 8TG
☎ (01978) 860669 ▣ (01978) 860491
Email: dinas.bran@denbighshire.gov.uk
www.dinasbran.co.uk
Headteacher: Mrs A Duffy

Ysgol Glan Clwyd
Ffordd Uchaf Dinbych,
Llanelwy/St Asaph,
Sir Ddinbych LL17 0RP
☎ (01745) 582611 ▣ (01745) 583130
Email: ysgol.glanclwyd@sirddinbych.gov.uk
www.ysgolglanclwyd.co.uk
Headteacher: Meurig Rees

Flintshire

Alun School
Wrexham Rd, Mold, Flintshire CH7 1EP
☎ (01352) 750755 ▣ (01352) 707131
Email: alun.school@flintshire.gov.uk
www.alunschool.co.uk
Headteacher: Ashley Jones

Argoed High School
Bryn Road, Bryn-y-Baal, Mold, Flintshire CH7 6RY
☎ (01352) 756414 ▣ (01352) 750798
Email: argoed_high_school@flintshire.gov.uk
www.argoed-hs.flintshire.sch.uk
Headteacher: Mrs D Spence

Castell Alun High School
Fagl Lane, Hope, Flintshire LL12 9PY
☎ (01978) 760238 ▣ (01978) 760935
Email: Castell_Alun_High_School@flintshire.gov.uk
www.castellalun.flintshire.sch.uk
Headteacher: David Mountfort

Connah's Quay High School
Golftyn Lane, Connah's Quay, Deeside CH5 4BH
☎ (01244) 813491 ▣ (01244) 823000
Headteacher: G Dixon
www.connahsquayhs.org.uk

Elfed High School
Ysgol Uwchradd Elfed
Mill Lane, Buckley CH7 3HQ
☎ (01244) 550217 ▣ (01244) 550524
Email: beadmin@elfed-hs.flintshire.sch.uk
www.elfed-hs.flintshire.sch.uk
Headteacher: Rosemary A Jones

Flint High School
Maes Hyfryd, Flint, Flintshire CH6 5LL
☎ (01352) 732268 ▣ (01352) 731066
Email: fhmail@flint.flintshire.sch.uk
www.flinthighschool.co.uk
Headteacher: Mrs P McClean

Hawarden High School
The Highway, Hawarden, Flintshire CH5 3DJ
☎ (01244) 526400 ▣ (01244) 534699
Email: hhmail@hawardenhigh.flintshire.sch.uk
www.hawardenhigh.org.uk
Headteacher: Roger Davies

Holywell High School
The Strand, Holywell CH8 7AW
☎ (01352) 710011 ▣ (01352) 714662
Email: info@holywell-hs.flintshire.sch.uk
www.holywellhighschool.co.uk
Headteacher: W J Putt

SECONDARY SCHOOLS

John Summers High School
Queensferry Campus, Queensferry,
Deeside CH5 1SE
☎ (01244) 831575 ◧ (01244) 831559
Headteacher: Mr M A Rashud

St David's High School
St David's Terrace, Saltney CH4 0AE
☎ (01244) 671583 ◧ (01244) 680309
Email: st_davids_high_school@flintshire.gov.uk
Headteacher: Tony Davidson

St Richard Gwyn Catholic High School
Albert Ave, Flint CH6 5JZ
☎ (01352) 736900 ◧ (01352) 731895
Email: srgadmin@flintshire.gov.uk
www.strichardgwyn.com
Headteacher: Mr Derek Doran

Ysgol Maes Garmon
Stryd Conwy, Mold/Yr Wyddgrug CH7 1JB
☎ (01352) 750678 ◧ (01352) 707107
Email: mgmail@ysgolmaesgarmon.siryfflint.sch.uk
www.ysgolmaesgarmon.siryfflint.sch.uk
Headteacher: Bronwen Hughes

Gwynedd

Ysgol Ardudwy
Ffordd Glan y Mor, Harlech LL46 2UH
☎ (01766) 780331 ◧ (01766) 780900
Email: pennaeth@ardudwy.gwynedd.sch.uk
www.ardudwy.gwynedd.sch.uk
Headteacher: Tudur O Williams

Ysgol Botwnnog
Botwnnog, Pwllheli,
Gwynedd LL53 8PY
☎ (01758) 730220 ◧ (01758) 730439
Email: pennaeth@botwnnog.gwynedd.sch.uk
Headmaster: Gareth T Morris Jones

Ysgol Brynrefail
Ffordd Crawia, Llanrug LL55 4AD
☎ (01286) 672381 ◧ (01286) 672066
Email: swyddfa@brynrefail.gwynedd.sch.uk
www.brynrefail.gwynedd.sch.uk
Headteacher: Eifion Jones

Ysgol Dyffryn Nantlle
Ffordd y Brenin, Penygroes,
Gwynedd LL54 6AA
☎ (01286) 880345 ◧ (01286) 881953
Email: pennaeth@ydn.gwynedd.sch.uk
www.moodle.ydn.gwynedd.sch.uk
Headteacher: Richard Emyr Hughes

Ysgol Dyffryn Ogwen
Ffordd Coetmor, Bethesda,
Gwynedd LL57 3NN
☎ (01248) 600291 ◧ (01248) 600082
Email: ydo@dyffrynogwen.gwynedd.sch.uk
www.dyffrynogwen.gwynedd.sch.uk
Headmaster: Alun Llwyd

Ysgol Eifionydd
High St, Porthmadog LL49 9HS
☎ (01766) 512114 ◧ (01766) 514785
Email: pennaeth@eifionydd.gwynedd.sch.uk
www.eifionydd.gwynedd.sch.uk
Headteacher: Alwen P Watkin

Ysgol Friars
Lôn-y-Bryn, Bangor LL57 2LN
☎ (01248) 364905 ◧ (01248) 352235
Email: pennaeth@friars.gwynedd.sch.uk
www.friars.gwynedd.sch.uk
Headteacher: Neil Foden

Ysgol Glan y Môr
Cardiff Rd, Pwllheli,
Gwynedd LL53 5NU
☎ (01758) 701244 ◧ (01758) 701310
Email: post@ysgolglanymor.org
www.ysgolglanymor.org
Headteacher: Menai Jones

Ysgol Syr Hugh Owen
Bethel Rd, Caernarfon LL55 1HW
☎ (01286) 673076 ◧ (01286) 674521
Email: pennaeth@syrhughowen.gwynedd.sch.uk
www.ysgolsyrhughowen.org
Headteacher: Elwyn Vaughan Williams

Ysgol Tryfan
Lôn Powys, Bangor, Gwynedd LL57 2TU
☎ (01248) 352633 ◧ (01248) 361264
Email: pennaeth@tryfan.gwynedd.sch.uk
www.tryfan.gwynedd.sch.uk
Headteacher: Gwyn Tudur

Ysgol Uwchradd Tywyn
Ffordd yr Orsaf, Tywyn, Gwynedd LL36 9EU
☎ (01654) 710256 ◧ (01654) 711815
Email: pennaeth@tywyn.gwynedd.sch.uk
www.tywyn.gwynedd.sch.uk
Headteacher: Helen M Lewis

Ysgol y Berwyn
Ffrydan Rd, Y Bala LL23 7RU
☎ (01678) 520259 ◧ (01678) 520547
Email: pennaeth@berwyn.gwynedd.sch.uk
Headteacher: Andrew Roberts

Post Brenhinol

Royal Mail

Ysgol y Gader
Wern Las, Dolgellau LL40 1HY
☎ (01341) 422578 📠 (01341) 424064
Email: pennaeth@gader.gwynedd.sch.uk
www.gader.gwynedd.sch.uk
Headteacher: Peter Maddocks

Ysgol y Moelwyn
Wynne Rd, Blaenau Ffestiniog LL41 3DW
☎ (01766) 830435 📠 (01766) 831629
Email: swyddfa@moelwyn.gwynedd.sch.uk
Headteacher: Dewi M Lake

Isle of Anglesey

Ysgol David Hughes
Ffordd Pentraeth, Menai Bridge, Anglesey LL59 5SS
☎ (01248) 712287 📠 (01248) 713919
Email: ydhpen@anglesey.gov.uk
www.ysgoldavidhughes.org
Headteacher: Dr Brian Jones

Ysgol Gyfun Llangefni
Llangefni, Anglesey LL77 7NG
☎ (01248) 723441 📠 (01248) 750884
Email: ygllpen@ynysmon.gov.uk
www.llangefni.anglesey.sch.uk
Headteacher/Prifathro: L Haydn Davies

Ysgol Syr Thomas Jones
Pentrefelin, Amlwch, Ynys Môn LL68 9TH
☎ (01407) 830287 📠 (01407) 830967
Email: ystjpen@ynysmon.gov.uk
www.ystj.co.uk
Headteacher: H Emyr Williams

Ysgol Uwchradd Bodedern
Bodedern, Bro Alaw LL65 3TL
☎ (01407) 741000 📠 (01407) 742343
Email: yubpen@anglesey.gov.uk
Headteacher: Anwen Morgan

Ysgol Uwchradd Caergybi
Alderley Terrace, Holyhead LL65 1NP
☎ (01407) 762219 📠 (01407) 769958
Email: yucpen@anglesey.gov.uk
Headteacher: M Wise

Merthyr Tydfil

Afon Tâf High School
Yew St, Troedyrhiw, Merthyr Tydfil CF48 4ED
☎ (01685) 351830 📠 (01685) 01443 690459
Email: office@afontaf.merthyr.sch.uk
www.afontaf.merthyr.sch.uk
Headteacher: C B Smith

Bishop Hedley Catholic High School
Gwaunfarren Road, Penydarren,
Merthyr Tydfil CF47 9AN
☎ (01685) 721747 📠 (01685) 385292
Email: office@bishophedleyhigh.merthyr.sch.uk
www.bishophedleyhigh.merthyr.sch.uk
Headteacher: Mrs M Harris

Cyfarthfa High School
(Lower School) Cyfarthfa Castle,
Cyfarthfa Park, Merthyr Tydfil CF47 8RA
☎ (01685) 721725
Email: office@cyfarthfahigh.merthyr.sch.uk
www.cyfarthfahigh.merthyr.sch.uk
Headteacher: Alan Pritchard

Cyfarthfa High School
(Upper School) Cae Mari Dwn,
Queen's Rd, Merthyr Tydfil CF47 0LS
☎ (01685) 721725
Email: office@cyfarthfahigh.merthyr.sch.uk
www.cyfarthfahigh.merthyr.sch.uk
Headteacher: Alan Pritchard

Pen-y-dre High School
Gurnos, Merthyr Tydfil CF47 9BY
☎ (01685) 721726 📠 (01685) 721986
Email: office@penydre.biblio.net
www.penydre.merthyr.sch.uk
Headteacher: Mr K J O'Shea

Monmouthshire

Caldicot Comprehensive School
Mill Lane, Caldicot, Monmouthshire NP26 5XA
☎ (01291) 426436 📠 (01291) 426430
Email: contactus@caldicotschool.com
www.caldicotschool.com
Headteacher: Mrs S Gwyer-Roberts

Chepstow Comprehensive School
Welsh St, Chepstow NP16 5LR
☎ (01291) 635777
Email: enquiries@chepstow.monmouthshire.sch.uk
www.chepstowschool.com
Headteacher: Ms Claire Price

King Henry VIII School
Old Hereford Rd, Abergavenny NP7 6EP
☎ (01873) 735373
Email: info@kinghenry.monm.sch.uk
www.kinghenry.monm.sch.uk
Headteacher: Mr N Oaten

Monmouth Comprehensive School
Old Dixton Rd, Monmouth,
Monmouthshire NP25 3YT
☎ (01600) 775177 ☒ (01600) 775151
Email:monmouthcomprehensive@monmouthshire.gov.uk
www.monmouth.monmoodle.co.uk
Headteacher: Mr R Vaughan Davies

Neath Port Talbot

Cefn Saeson Comprehensive School
Afan Valley Rd, Cimla,
Neath SA11 3TA
☎ (01639) 791300 ☒ (01639) 791339
Email: cefnsaesoncomprehensiveschool@npted.org
www.cefnsaeson.baglanit.org.uk
Headteacher: Mel Lewis

**Cwmtawe Community School
Ysgol Gymunedol Cwmtawe**
Parc Ynysderw, Pontardawe,
Swansea SA8 4EG
☎ (01792) 863200 ☒ (01792) 864773
Email: cwmtaweschool@npted.org
www.cwmtawe.org
Headteacher: Alan Tudor Jones

Cwrt Sart Community Comprehensive
Old Rd, Briton Ferry, Neath SA11 2ET
☎ (01639) 777890 ☒ (01639) 770099
Email: cwrtsartcommunitycomprehensive@npted.org
www.cwrtsartcomp.co.uk
Headteacher: A L Rowlands

Cymer Afan Comprehensive School
Cymer, Port Talbot SA13 3EL
☎ (01639) 850237 ☒ (01639) 850334
Email: cymerafancomprehensiveschool@npted.org
www.npted.org/schools/cymerafan
Headteacher: Mike Tate

Dwr-y-Felin Comprehensive School
Dwr-y-Felin Rd, Neath SA10 7LD
☎ (01639) 635161 ☒ (01639) 632142
Email: dwryfelin@neath-porttalbot.gov.uk
www.dyf.org.uk
Headteacher: N E Stacey

Dyffryn School
Bertha Rd, Margam,
Port Talbot SA13 2AN
☎ (01639) 760110 ☒ (01639) 760111
Email: dyffrynschool@npted.org
www.npted.org/schools/dyffryn
Headmaster: Martin Grimes

Glanafan Comprehensive School
Station Rd, Port Talbot SA13 1LZ
☎ (01639) 883964 ☒ (01639) 898887
Email: glanafancomprehensiveschool@npted.org
Headteacher: Susan Handley

Llangatwg Community School
Main Rd, Cadoxton, Neath SA10 8DB
☎ (01639) 634700 ☒ (01639) 634708
Email: llangatwgschool@npted.org
www.llangatwg.org.uk
Headteacher: R W Skilton

Sandfields Comprehensive School
Southdown View, Port Talbot SA12 7AH
☎ (01639) 884246 ☒ (01639) 894951
Email: sandfieldscomprhensiveschool@npted.org
www.npted.org/schools/sandfieldscomp
Headmaster: Mr Michael Gibbon

St Joseph's Catholic School and Sixth Form Centre
Newton Ave, Port Talbot SA12 6EY
☎ (01639) 884305 ☒ (01639) 898070
Email: stjosephscomprehensive@npted.org
www.npted.org/schools/stjosephs
Headteacher: Michael Callas

Ysgol Gyfun Ystalyfera
Glan-yr-afon, Ystalyfera, Swansea SA9 2JJ
☎ (01639) 842129 ☒ (01639) 845681
Email: ygystalyfera@npted.org
www.ysgolgyfunystalyfera.co.uk
Headteacher: Matthew H.T Evans

Newport

Bassaleg School
Forge Lane, Bassaleg, Newport NP10 8NF
☎ (01633) 892191 ☒ (01633) 894699
Email: bassaleg.school@newport.gov.uk
www.bassaleg.newport.sch.uk
Headteacher: Mrs E J Thomas

Caerleon Comprehensive School
Cold Bath Rd, Caerleon, Newport NP18 1NF
☎ (01633) 420106 ☒ (01633) 430048
Email: caerleon.comprehensive@newport.gov.uk
www.caerleoncomprehensiveschool.co.uk
Headteacher: Mr T Pratt

Duffryn High School
Lighthouse Rd, Duffryn, Newport NP10 8YD
☎ (01633) 654100 ☒ (01633) 654110
Email: post@duffryn.org
www.duffryn.net
Headteacher: Jonathan M Wilson

Post Brenhinol

Royal Mail

Hartridge High School
Hartridge Farm Rd,
Newport NP18 2YE
☎ (01633) 412487 ▯ (01633) 412880
Email: hartridge.high@newport.gov.uk
www.newportlearn.net/hartridge
Headteacher: Peter Jenkins

Lliswerry High School
Nash Rd, Newport NP19 4RP
☎ (01633) 277867
▯ (01633) 290464
Email: lliswerry.high@newport.gov.uk
www.newportlearn.net/lliswerry
Headteacher: Mrs Alyson Mills

Newport High School
Bettws Lane, Bettws NP20 7YB
☎ (01633) 820100 ▯ (01633) 820101
Email: info@newporthigh.co.uk
www.newporthigh.co.uk
Headteacher: Mrs K Keane

St Joseph's RC High School
Pencarn Way, Tredegar Park,
Newport NP10 8XH
☎ (01633) 653110
▯ (01633) 653128
Email: sjhs@newport.gov.uk
www.sjhs.org.uk
Headteacher: Miss S M Jenkins

St Julian's Comprehensive School
Heather Rd, Newport NP19 7JZ
☎ (01633) 224490
▯ (01633) 216500
Email: stjulians.school@newport.gov.uk
www.stjulians.org.uk
Headteacher: Denise Richards

Pembrokeshire

Milford Haven Comprehensive School
Steynton Rd, Milford Haven SA73 1AE
☎ (01646) 690021 ▯ (01646) 696600
Email: admin@milfordhavenschool.co.uk
www.milfordhavenschool.co.uk
Headteacher: Mr I Morgan

Sir Thomas Picton School
Queensway,
Haverfordwest SA61 2NX
☎ (01437) 765394
Email: maria@stp.pembrokeshire.sch.uk
Headteacher: Mrs S J Bessant

Tasker Milward VC School
Portfield Ave, Haverfordwest,
Pembrokeshire SA61 1EQ
☎ (01437) 764147 ▯ (01437) 768764
Email: enquiries@taskermilward.org.uk
www.pgfl.org.uk/schools/tmf/TaskerMilward
Headteacher: M A Haines

Ysgol Bro Gwaun
Heol Dyfed, Fishguard,
Pembrokeshire SA65 9DT
☎ (01348) 872268 ▯ (01348) 872716
Email: admin@yuabergwaun.co.uk
www.ysgolbrogwaun.co.uk
Headteacher: Mr A Andrews

Ysgol Dewi Sant
St Davids, Pembrokeshire SA62 6QH
☎ (01437) 725000 ▯ (01437) 721935
Email: general@dewisant.pembroke.sch.uk
www.dewisant.pembroke.sch.uk
Headteacher: Ray Bevan

Ysgol Greenhill School
Heywood Lane, Tenby,
Pembrokeshire SA70 8BN
☎ (01834) 840100 ▯ (01834) 843288
Email: admin@greenhill.pembrokeshire.sch.uk
www.greenhill.pembrokeshire.sch.uk
Headteacher: Mrs J Kingston

Ysgol Y Preseli
Crymych, Pembrokeshire SA41 3QH
☎ (01239) 831406 ▯ (01239) 831416
Email: swyddfa@ysgolypreseli.com
www.ysgolypreseli.com
Headteacher: Michael Davies

Powys

Brecon High School
Penlan, Brecon, Powys LD3 9SR
☎ (01874) 622361 ▯ (01874) 624855
Email: bhs@brecon-hs.powys.sch.uk
www.brecon-hs.powys.sch.uk
Headteacher: Mr M Morris (as from 1 Sept 2012)

Builth Wells High School
Ysgol Uwchradd Llanfair-ym-Muallt
College Rd, Builth Wells LD2 3BW
☎ (01982) 553292 ▯ (01982) 553825
Email: office@builth-hs.powys.sch.uk
www.builth-hs.powys.sch.uk
Acting Head: Mr Colin Rees

Caereinion High School
Llanfair Caereinion,
Welshpool SY21 0HW
☎ (01938) 810888
Email: office@caer-hs.powys.sch.uk
www.caer-hs.powys.sch.uk
Headteacher: David Evans

Crickhowell High School
New Rd, Crickhowell NP8 1AW
☎ (01873) 813500
Email: office@crickhowell-hs.powys.sch.uk
www.crickhowell-hs.powys.sch.uk
Headteacher: Jackie Parker

Gwernyfed High School
Three Cocks, Brecon LD3 0SG
☎ (01497) 847445
Email: office@gwernyfed-hs.powys.sch.uk
www.gwernyfed-hs.powys.sch.uk
Headteacher: John Hopkins

John Beddoes School
Broadaxe Lane, Presteigne LD8 2YT
☎ (01544) 267259 ☐ (01544) 267173
Email: office@johnbeddoes.org
www.johnbeddoes.org
Headteacher: Glyn Richards

Llandrindod High School
Dyffryn Rd, Llandrindod Wells LD1 6AW
☎ (01597) 822992 ☐ (01597) 822452
Email: office@llandod-hs.powys.sch.uk
www.llandod-hs.powys.sch.uk
Headteacher: Mrs C Morgans

Llanfyllin High School
Llanfyllin SY22 5BJ
☎ (01691) 648391 ☐ (01691) 648898
Email: office@llanfyllin-hs.powys.sch.uk
www.llanfyllin-hs.powys.sch.uk
Headteacher: Mr C Mincher

Llanidloes High School
Llangurig Road, Llanidloes,
Powys SY18 6EX
☎ (01686) 412289 ☐ (01686) 413812
Email: office@llanidloes-hs.powys.sch.uk
www.llanidloeshighschool.co.uk
Headteacher: Darren Davies

Newtown High School
Dolfor Rd, Newtown SY16 1JE
☎ (01686) 626304 ☐ (01686) 629956
Email: office@newtown-hs.powys.sch.uk
www.newtown-hs.powys.sch.uk
Headteacher: Mrs J Pryce

Welshpool High School
Salop Rd, Welshpool, Powys SY21 7RE
☎ (01938) 552014 ☐ (01938) 555711
Email: dw@welshpool-hs.powys.sch.uk
www.welshpool-hs.powys.sch.uk
Headteacher: Mr J Toal

Ysgol Bro Ddyfi
Greenfields, Machynlleth, Powys SY20 8DR
☎ (01654) 702012 ☐ (01654) 702994
Email: office@broddyfi-hs.powys.sch.uk
www.broddyfo.co.uk
Headteacher: Dafydd M B Jones

Ysgol Maesydderwen
Tudor St, Ystradgynlais SA9 1AP
☎ (01639) 842115
Email: office@maesydderwen.co.uk
www.ysgolmaesydderwen.co.uk
Headteacher: Mrs S Speedy

Rhondda Cynon Taf

Aberdare Boys Comprehensive School
Cwmdare Rd, Aberdare CF44 8SS
☎ (01685) 872642 ☐ (01685) 873689
Headteacher: K I Machin

Aberdare Girls' Comprehensive School
Ysgol Y Merched, Aberdar
Heol Cwmbach, Aberdar CF44 0NF
☎ (01685) 872460 ☐ (01685) 887438
Email: info@aberdaregirls.com
www.aberdaregirls.com
Headteacher: Jane Rosser

Blaengwawr Comprehensive School
Club St, Aberaman, Aberdare,
Rhondda Cynon Taf CF44 6TN
☎ (01685) 874341 ☐ (01685) 883834
Email: office@blaengwawr.co.uk
www.blaengwawr.co.uk
Headmaster: David S Evans

Bryn Celynnog Comprehensive School
Penycoedcae Rd, Beddau, Pontypridd CF38 2AE
☎ (01443) 203411 ☐ (01443) 219619
Email: school@bryncelynnog.co.uk
www.bryncelynnog.org.uk
Headteacher: Ms Debbie Baldock

Cardinal Newman RC School
Dynea Rd, Rhydyfelin, Pontypridd CF37 5DP
☎ (01443) 494110 ☐ (01443) 494112
Email: admin.newmanrc@rctednet.net
www.rctednet.net/newmanrc
Headteacher: Mr Justin O'Sullivan

Royal Mail

Ferndale Community School
Ferndale, Rhondda CF43 4AR
☎ (01443) 755337 ▣ (01443) 756810
Email:
Admin.Ferndalecommunitysch@rctednet.net
Headteacher: Mrs H Nicholas

Hawthorn High School
School Lane, Hawthorn,
Pontypridd CF37 5AL
☎ (01443) 841228 ▣ (01443) 846464
Email: AdminHawthornHigh@rctednet.net
Headteacher: Mr J Hicks

Mountain Ash Comprehensive School
New Rd, Mountain Ash CF45 4DG
☎ (01443) 479199 ▣ (01443) 473412
Email: Admin.Mountainashcomp@rctednet.net
www.macs.rhondda.sch.uk
Headteacher: Huw Lloyd

Y Pant Comprehensive School
Cowbridge Rd, Talbot Green,
Pontyclun CF72 8YQ
☎ (01443) 237701 ▣ (01443) 229248
Email: Admin@ypantcomp@rctednet.net
www.ypant.co.uk
Headteacher: Stuart Tucker

Pontypridd High School
Albion Community Campus,
Cilfynydd, Pontypridd CF37 4SF
☎ (01443) 486133 ▣ (01443) 480512
www.pontypriddhighschool.co.uk
Headteacher: Huw Cripps

Porth County Community School
Cemetery Rd, Porth CF39 0BS
☎ (01443) 682137 ▣ (01443) 682076
Email: Admin.Porthcomp@rctednet.net
www.porthcommunityschool.com
Headteacher: Mrs A Francis

St John Baptist (Church in Wales: Voluntary Aided) High School
Glan Rd, Aberdare CF44 8BW
☎ (01685) 875414 ▣ (01685) 881582
Email: office@stjohnbaptist.co.uk
Headteacher: Dr S M Mitchell

Tonypandy Community College
Llewellyn St, Penygraig, Rhondda CF40 1HQ
☎ (01443) 436171 ▣ (01443) 430918
Email: head@tonypandycollege.co.uk
www.tonypandycollege.co.uk
Headteacher: Mrs H O'Sullivan

Tonyrefail Comprehensive
Gilfach Rd, Tonyrefail, Porth CF39 8HG
☎ (01443) 670647 ▣ (01443) 671780
Email: admin.tonyrefail.comp@rctedent.net
Headteacher: E Keeble

Treorchy Comprehensive School
Pengelli, Treorchy CF42 6UL
☎ (01443) 773128 ▣ (01443) 776658
Email: school@treorchycomp.org.uk
www.treorchycomp.org.uk
Headteacher: Mr R Jones

Ysgol Gyfun Cymer Rhondda
Heol Graigwen, Cymer, Porth,
Rhondda Cynon Taff CF39 9HA
☎ (01443) 680800 ▣ (01443) 680810
Email: hjm@ysgolcymer.co.uk
www.cymer.org.uk
Headteacher: Mr A.H. Davies

Ysgol Gyfun Garth Olwg
Y Brif Ffordd, Pentre'r Eglwys, Pontypridd CF38 1DX
☎ (01443) 219580/81 ▣ (01443) 219596
Email: gweinyddol@campwsgartholwg.org.uk
www.gartholwg.co.uk
Headteacher: T Anne Morris

Ysgol Gyfun Llanhari
Llanhari, Pontyclun CF72 9XE
☎ (01443) 237824 ▣ (01443) 227365
Email: post@llanhari.com
www.llanhari.com
Headteacher: Meirion Stephens

Ysgol Gyfun Rhydywaun
Lawrence Ave, Penywaun, Hirwaun CF44 9ES
☎ (01685) 813500 ▣ (01685) 812208
Email: ysgol@rhydywaun.org
www.rhydywaun.org
Headteacher: Hywel Price

Swansea

Birchgrove Comprehensive School
Birchgrove Road, Birchgrove, Swansea SA7 9NB
☎ (01792) 535400 ▣ (01792) 535444
www.swansea-edunet.gov.uk/en/schools/birchgrove
Headteacher: Karen Holland

Bishop Gore School
De-la-Beche Road, Sketty, Swansea SA2 9AP
☎ (01792) 411400 ▣ (01792) 411800
Email: contactus@bishopgore.net
www.bishopgore.swansea.sch.uk
Headteacher: Ryan Davies

Bishop Vaughan Catholic Comprehensive School
Mynydd Garnllwyd Road,
Morriston, Swansea SA6 7QG
☎ (01792) 772006
🖷 (01792) 790565
Email: bishop.vaughan.school@swansea-edunet.gov.uk
www.bishopvaughan.swansea.sch.uk
Headteacher: Joseph Blackburn

Bishopston Comprehensive School
The Glebe, Bishopston,
Swansea SA3 3JP
☎ (01792) 234121
🖷 (01792) 234808
Email: bishopston.comprehensive.school@swansea-edunet.gov.uk
www.bishopston.swansea.sch.uk
Headteacher: Ian P Thompson

Cefn Hengoed Community School
Caldicot Rd, Winch Wen,
Swansea SA1 7HX
☎ (01792) 773464
🖷 (01792) 701649
Email: cefn.hengoed.community.school@swansea-edunet.gov.uk
www.cefnhengoed.swansea.sch.uk
Headteacher: S Hollister

Dylan Thomas Community School
John St, Cockett,
Swansea SA2 0FR
☎ (01792) 610300
🖷 (01792) 610320
Email: dylan.thomas.community.school@swansea-edunet.gov.uk
Headteacher: Mr R Phillips

Gowerton Comprehensive School
Cecil Rd, Gowerton SA4 3DL
☎ (01792) 873461
🖷 (01792) 873986
Headteacher: Peter B Harrison

Morriston Comprehensive School
Cwmrhydyceirw,
Swansea SA6 6NH
☎ (01792) 797745
🖷 (01792) 795883
Email: mcs@swansea-edunet.gov.uk
www.morriston.swansea.sch.uk
Headteacher: Mr K W Newton

Olchfa Comprehensive School
Gower Rd, Sketty, Swansea SA2 7AB
☎ (01792) 534300 🖷 (01792) 534307
Email: Olchfa.school@swansea-edunet.gov.uk /
olchfa@olchfa.org.uk
www.olchfa.org.uk
Headteacher: H Davies
Deputy Headteacher: Mrs J Cowley

Pentrehafod School
Pentremawr Rd, Hafod, Swansea SA1 2NN
☎ (01792) 410400 🖷 (01792) 410401
Email: Pentrehafod.School@swansea-edunet.gov.uk
www.pentrehafod.swansea.sch.uk

Penyrheol Comprehensive School
Pontarddulais Rd, Gorseinon SA4 4FG
☎ (01792) 533066 🖷 (01792) 533366
Email: penyrheol.comprehensive.School@swansea-edunet.gov.uk
www.penyrheol-comp.net
Headteacher: A J Tootill

Pontardulais Comprehensive School
Caecerrig Rd, Pontarddulais SA4 8PD
☎ (01792) 884556 🖷 (01792) 884658
Email: pontarddulais.comprehensive.school@swansea.gov.uk
Headteacher: Miss J Waldron

Ysgol Gyfun Gwyr
Stryd Talbot, Tre-gwyr, Abertawe SA4 3DB
☎ (01792) 872403 🖷 (01792) 874197
Email: ysgol.gyfun.gwyr@swansea-edunet.gov.uk
www.yggwyr.swansea.sch.uk
Headteacher: Katherine Davies

Torfaen

Abersychan School
Incline Road, Abersychan, Pontypool,
Torfaen NP4 7DF
☎ (01495) 773068
Email: jodi.jones@torfaen.gov.uk;
jodijones@live.co.uk (out of school hours)
www.abersychan.torfaen.sch.uk
Headteacher: Michael J Conway

Croesyceiliog Comprehensive School
Woodland Rd, Croesyceiliog, Cwmbran NP44 2YB
☎ (01633) 645900 🖷 (01633) 645901
www.croesyceiliog.org.uk
Headteacher: H Mansfield

Fairwater High School
Tŷ Gwyn Way, Fairwater,
Cwmbran, Torfaen NP44 4YZ
☎ (01633) 643950 📠 (01633) 643951
Email: head.fairwatercomp@torfaen.gov.uk
www.fairwater.torfaen.sch.uk
Headteacher: Mr D Marshall

Llantarnam School
Llantarnam, Cwmbran NP44 3XB
☎ (01633) 866711 📠 (01633) 876652
Email: head.llantarnamcomp@torfaen.gov.uk
www.llantarnamschool.com
Headteacher: David Bright

St Alban's R C High School
The Park, Pontypool NP4 6XG
☎ (01495) 765800 📠 (01495) 765802
Email: enquiries@stalbans-pontypool.org.uk
www.stalbans-pontypool.org.uk
Headteacher: M Coady

West Monmouth School
Blaendare Rd, Pontypool NP4 5YG
☎ (01495) 762080/764817 📠 (01495) 762201
Email: head.westmonmouthschool@torfaen.gov.uk
www.westmonmouthschool.com
Headteacher: Clive Jackson

Ysgol Gyfun Gwynllyw
Folly Rd, Trevethin, Pontypool,
Torfaen NP4 8JD
☎ (01495) 750405 📠 (01495) 757414
Email: hgriffiths@gwynllyw.org
www.gwynllyw.org
Headteacher: Hywel Ellis Griffiths

Vale of Glamorgan

Barry Comprehensive School
Port Rd West, Barry CF62 8ZJ
☎ (01446) 411411 📠 (01446) 411422
Email: barrycs@valeofglamorgan.gov.uk
www.barrycomp.com
Headteacher: Jennifer Ford

Bryn Hafren Comprehensive School
Merthyr Dyfan Rd, Barry CF62 9YQ
☎ (01446) 403500 📠 (01446) 403504
Email: brynhafrencs@valeofglamorgan.gov.uk
www.brynhafren.webeden.co.uk
Headteacher: P D Whitcombe

Cowbridge Comprehensive School
Aberthin Rd, Cowbridge,
Vale of Glamorgan CF71 7EN
☎ (01446) 772311 📠 (01446) 775357
Email: cowbridgehs@valeofglamorgan.gov.uk
www.cowbridgehs.lea.valeofglamorgan.sch.uk
Headteacher: Mrs Debra Thomas

Llantwit Major School
Ham Lane East, Llantwit Major CF61 1TQ
☎ (01446) 793301 📠 (01446) 793760
Email: llantwitmajorhs@valeofglamorgan.gov.uk
www.llantwitschool.org.uk
Acting Headteacher: Mrs D Thomas

St Cyres School
Murch Lane, Dinas Powys CF64 4RF
☎ (029) 2051 2113 📠 (029) 2051 5930
Email: contact@stcyres.valeofglamorgan.sch.uk
www.stcyres.glamorgan.sch.uk
Headteacher: Dr J P Hicks

St Cyres School
St Cyres Rd, Penarth,
Vale of Glamorgan CF64 2XP
☎ (029) 2070 8708
📠 (029) 2070 0851
Email: contact@stcyres.org
www.stcyres.org
Headteacher: Dr J P Hicks

St Richard Gwyn Catholic High School
Argae Lane, Barry CF63 1BL
☎ (01446) 729250
📠 (01446) 720898
Email: info@strichardgwyn.co.uk
www.strichardgwyn.co.uk
Headteacher: M J Clinch

Stanwell School
Archer Rd, Penarth CF64 2XL
☎ (029) 2070 7633 📠 (029) 2071 1792
Email: school@stanwell.org
www.stanwell.org
Headteacher: Mr D Jones

Ysgol Gyfun Bro Morgannwg
Colcot Rd, Barry CF62 8YU
☎ (01446) 450280
📠 (01446) 450281
Email: post@bromorgannwg.org.uk
www.bromorgannwg.org.uk
Headteacher: Dr Dylan E Jones

INDEPENDENT SCHOOLS

Wrexham

Darland High School
Chester Rd, Rossett,
Wrexham LL12 0DL
☎ (01244) 570588 ☐ (01244) 571053
Email: headteacher@darland.wrexham.sch.uk
www.darlandschool.co.uk
Headteacher: Mr Peter Agnew

The Maelor School
Penley, nr Wrexham LL13 0LU
☎ (01948) 830291 ☐ (01948) 830616
Email: mailbox@maelor-high.wrexham.sch.uk
www.maelorschool.org.uk
Headteacher: Mr Eiddwyn Hall

St Joseph's Catholic & Anglican High School
Sontley Rd,
Wrexham LL13 7EN
☎ (01978) 360310 ☐ (01978) 360311
Email: mailbox@st-joseph.wrexham.sch.uk
www.st-joseph.wrexham.sch.uk
Headteacher: Maria B Rimmer

Ysgol Bryn Alyn
Church Street, Gwersyllt,
Wrexham LL11 4HB
☎ (01978) 720700 ☐ (01978) 752889
Email: mailbox@ysgolbrynalyn.wrexham.sch.uk
www.ysgol-brynalyn.co.uk
Headteacher: Brian Whiteley

Ysgol Clywedog
Ffordd Rhuthun, Wrecsam LL13 7UB
☎ (01978) 346800 ☐ (01978) 346814
Email: mailbox@clywedog.wrexham.sch.uk
www.clywedog.wrexham14to19.net
Headteacher: Dr David Kirby

Ysgol Morgan Llwyd
Ffordd Cefn, Wrecsam LL13 9NG
☎ (01978) 315050 ☐ (01978) 315051
Email: bocspost@ysgolmorganllwyd.wrexham.sch.uk
www.morganllwyd.wrexham14to19.net
Headteacher: Huw Foster Evans

Ysgol Rhiwabon
Pont Adam, Ruabon, Wrexham LL14 6BT
☎ (01978) 822392 ☐ (01978) 814918
Email: mailbox@rhiwabon-high.wrexham.sch.uk
www.ysgolrhiwabon.co.uk
Headteacher: Angela Williams

Ysgol Rhosnesni High School
Rhosnesni Lane, Wrexham LL13 9ET
☎ (01978) 340840 ☐ (01978) 340841
Email: mailbox@rhosnesni-high.wrexham.sch.uk
www.rhosnesni-high.wrexham.sch.uk
Headteacher: Mr G Hughes

Ysgol Y Grango
Allt Tŷ Gwyn, Rhosllanerchrugog, Wrecsam LL14 1EL
☎ (01978) 833010 ☐ (01978) 833011
Email: mailbox@grango-high.wrexham.sch.uk
www.ysgolygrango.co.uk
Headteacher: Stephen Garthwaite

Education: Independent Secondary Schools

United World College of the Atlantic
St Donats Castle, Llantwit Major, Vale of
Glamorgan CF61 1WF
☎ (01446) 799000 ☐ (01446) 799013
Email: principal@atlanticcollege.org
www.atlanticcollege.org
Principal: John Walmsley
Bursar: Paul Motte

Cardiff Academy
40-41 The Parade, Roath, Cardiff CF24 3AB
☎ (029) 2040 9630 ☐ (029) 2045 5273
Email: 40-41@theparade.fsbusiness.co.uk
www.cardiffacademy.org.uk
Principal: Dr Stephen R Wilson
Vice Principal: Jennifer A Davies

The Cathedral School
Cardiff Rd, Llandaff, Cardiff CF5 2YH
☎ (029) 2056 3179
Email: enquiries@cathedral-school.co.uk
www.cathedral-school.co.uk
Headmaster: Stephen Morris

Christ College
Brecon, Powys LD3 8AF
☎ (01874) 615440 ☐ (01874) 615475
Email: enquiries@christcollegebrecon.com
www.christcollegebrecon.com
Head: Emma Taylor

Ffynone House School
36 St James' Crescent, Swansea SA1 6DR
☎ (01792) 464967 📠 (01792) 455202
Email: info@ffynonehouseschool.co.uk
www.ffynonehouseschool.co.uk
Headmistress: Mrs N Walker

Haberdashers' Monmouth School for Girls
Hereford Rd, Monmouth NP25 5XT
☎ (01600) 711100 📠 (01600) 711233
Email: enquiries@hmsg.co.uk
www.habs-monmouth.org
Headmistress: Ms H Davy

Hillgrove School
Ffriddoedd Rd, Bangor, Gwynedd LL57 2TW
☎ (01248) 353568 📠 (01248) 353971
Email: headmaster@hillgrove.gwynedd.sch.uk
www.hillgrove.gwynedd.sch.uk
Headteacher: James G Porter

Howell's School
Park Street, Denbigh LL16 3EN
☎ (01745) 813631 📠 (01745) 814443
Email: enquiries@howells.org
www.howells.org
Principal: Miss Emma Jones

Howell's School Llandaff
Cardiff Rd, Cardiff CF5 2YD
☎ (029) 2056 2019 📠 (029) 2057 8879
Email: mail@how.gdst.net
www.howells-cardiff.gdst.net
Principal: Sally Davis

Kings Monkton School
6 West Grove, Cardiff CF24 3XL
☎ (029) 2048 2854 📠 (029) 2049 0484
Email: mail@kingsmonkton.org.uk
www.kingsmonkton.org.uk
Principal: Nick Dorey

Llandovery College
Llandovery, Carmarthenshire SA20 0EE
☎ (01550) 723000 📠 (01550) 723002
Email: mail@llandoverycollege.com
www.llandoverycollege.com
Warden: Mr Ian M Hunt

Monmouth School
Almshouse St, Monmouth, Monmouthshire NP25 3XP
☎ (01600) 713143 📠 (01600) 772701
Email: enquiries@monmouthschool.org
www.habs-monmouth.org
Headmaster: Dr Steven Connors

Rougemont School
Llantarnam Hall, Malpas Rd,
Newport NP20 6QB
☎ (01633) 820800 📠 (01633) 855598
Email: registrar@rsch.co.uk
www.rougemontschool.co.uk
Headteacher: Dr Jonathan Tribbick

Ruthin School
Mold Rd, Ruthin, Denbighshire LL15 1EE
☎ (01824) 702543 📠 (01824) 707141
Email: office@ruthinschool.co.uk
www.ruthinschool.co.uk
Principal: Toby J Belfield

Rydal Penrhos School
Pwllycrochan Ave, Colwyn Bay, Conwy,
North Wales LL29 7BT
☎ (01492) 530155
Email: info@rydal-penrhos.com
www.rydal-penrhos.com
Headmaster: Patrick Lee-Browne

St Brigid's School
Plas-yn-Green, Mold Rd, Denbigh,
Denbighshire LL16 4BH
☎ (01745) 815228 📠 (01745) 816928
Email: stbrigidsadmin@denbighshire.gov.uk
www.stb.d-wdl.net

St Clare's School
Newton, Porthcawl CF36 5NR
☎ (01656) 782509 📠 (01656) 789960
Email: info@stclares-school.co.uk
www.stclares-school.co.uk
Headmistress: John Aguilar

St David's College
Llandudno LL30 1RD
☎ (01492) 875974 📠 (01492) 870383
Email: hmsec@stdavidscollege.co.uk
www.stdavidscollege.co.uk
Headmaster: Stuart Hay

St Gerard's School Trust
Ffriddoedd Rd, Bangor, Gwynedd LL57 2EL
☎ (01248) 351656 📠 (01248) 351204
www.st-gerards.org
Headteacher: Anne Parkinson

St John's College
Old St Mellons, Cardiff CF3 5YX
☎ (029) 2077 8936
Email: admin@stjohnscollegecardiff.co.uk
www.stjohnscollegecardiff.com
Headteacher: Dr David Neville

EDUCATION AUTHORITIES

St John's School
Church St, Newton, Porthcawl CF36 5NP
☎ (01656) 783404 🖷 (01656) 787535
Email: office@stjohnsschool-porthcawl.com
www.stjohnsschool-porthcawl.com
Headteacher: Carol Clint

St Michael's School
Bryn, Llanelli, Carmarthenshire SA14 9TU
☎ (01554) 820325 🖷 (01554) 821716
Email: office@stmikes.co.uk
www.stmikes.co.uk
Headmaster: D T Sheehan

Westbourne School
4 Hickman Rd, Penarth,
Vale of Glamorgan CF64 2AJ
☎ (029) 2070 5705 🖷 (029) 2070 9988
Email: enquiries@westbourneschool.com
www.westbourneschool.com
Senior School Headteacher: Mr Kenneth
Underhill

Wyclif Independent Christian School
Wyndham St, Machen, Caerphilly CF83 8PU
☎ (01633) 441582
Email: info@wyclifchristianschool.org
www.wics.org.uk
Headteacher: Andrew Tamplin

Education: Authorities

**Blaenau Gwent Directorate of Education
and Leisure Services**
County Borough of Blaenau Gwent,
Central Depot, Barleyfields Industrial Estate,
Barleyfields Way, Brynmawr NP23 4YF
☎ (01495) 355658 🖷 (01495) 355330
Email: education.department@blaenau-
gwent.gov.uk
www.blaenau-gwent.gov.uk
Corporate Director of Education & Leisure
Services: Sylvia Lindoe

Bridgend Children's Services Department
Bridgend County Borough Council, Sunnyside,
Bridgend CF31 4AR
☎ (01656) 642615 🖷 (01656) 642646
Email: hilary.anthony@bridgend.gov.uk
www.bridgend.gov.uk
Corporate Director - Children: Hilary Anthony

Caerphilly Directorate of Education & Leisure
Tredomen Park, Ystrad Mynach, Hengoed CF82 7PG
☎ (01443) 864948 🖷 (01443) 864869
Email: evanslg@caerphilly.gov.uk
www.caerphilly.gov.uk
Director, Education & Leisure: Sandra Aspinall

Cardiff Council Education
Cardiff County Council,
County Hall,
Atlantic Wharf, Cardiff CF10 4UW
☎ (029) 2087 2700 🖷 (029) 2087 2705
Email: ChJones@cardiff.gov.uk
www.cardiff.gov.uk/schools
Chief Education Officer: Chris Jones

**Carmarthenshire Department for Education
& Children**
Carmarthenshire County Council,
Building 2 St David's Park, Jobs Well Road,
Carmarthen SA31 3HB
☎ (01267) 246649 🖷 (01267) 246497
Email: Wwilliams@carmarthenshire.gov.uk
www.carmarthenshire.gov.uk
Head, Education Services: Wyn Williams

**Ceredigion Education and Community
Services Department
Adran Addysg a Gwasanaethau
Cymunedol Ceredigion**
Canolfan Rheidol,
Rhodfa Padarn,
Llanbadarn Fawr,
Aberystwyth SY23 3UR
☎ (01970) 617911 🖷 (01970) 633663
Email: education@ceredigion.gov.uk
www.ceredigion.gov.uk
Director, Education & Community Services: Eifion Evans

Conwy Education Services
Conwy County Borough Council,
Government Buildings,
Dinerth Rd,
Colwyn Bay LL28 4UL
☎ (01492) 575031 🖷 (01492) 541311
Email: education@conwy.gov.uk
www.conwy.gov.uk
Statutory Head of Education Services: R Geraint James

Denbigshire Directorate of Lifelong Learning
Denbighshire County Council,
Council Offices, Wynnstay Rd,
Ruthin LL15 1YN
☎ (01824) 706016 ▣ (01824) 707446
Email: hywyn.williams@denbighshire.gov.uk
www.denbighshire.gov.uk
Corporate Director Lifelong Learning: Hywyn Williams

Flintshire County Council Lifelong Learning Directorate
Flintshire County Council,
County Hall, Mold, Flintshire CH7 6ND
☎ (01352) 704010 ▣ (01352) 754202
www.flintshire.gov.uk
Director: Ian Budd

Gwynedd Council - Education
Council Offices, Caernarfon,
Gwynedd LL55 1SH
☎ (01766) 771000 ▣ (01286) 677347
Email: DewiRJones@gwynedd.gov.uk
www.gwynedd.gov.uk
Head of Education: Dewi R. Jones

Isle of Anglesey Education Department Adran Addysg Cyngor Sir Ynys Môn
Isle of Anglesey County Council, Glanhwfa Rd,
Llangefni, Anglesey LL77 7EY
☎ (01248) 752900 ▣ (01248) 752999
Email: rpjed@anglesey.gov.uk
www.anglesey.gov.uk
Corporate Director Education & Leisure:
Richard Parry Jones

Merthyr Tydfil Schools Department
Merthyr Tydfil County Borough Council, Tŷ Keir
Hardie, Riverside Court, Merthyr Tydfil CF47 8XD
☎ (01685) 724600 ▣ (01685) 721965
Email: mike.southcoat@merthyr.gov.uk
www.merthyr.gov.uk
Chief Education Officer: Mike Southcoat

Monmouthshire Education Department
Monmouthshire County Council, Lifelong
Learning & Leisure, Floor 5 County Hall,
Cwmbran NP44 2XH
☎ (01633) 644644 ▣ (01633) 644488
Email: andrewkeep@monmouthshire.gov.uk
www.monmouthshire.gov.uk
Corporate Director, Lifelong Learning: Andrew Keep

Neath Port Talbot Education, Leisure & Lifelong Learning Services
Neath Port Talbot County Borough Council,
Civic Centre, Port Talbot SA13 1PJ
☎ (01639) 763298 ▣ (01639) 763150
Email: k.napieralla@neath-porttalbot.gov.uk
www.npt.gov.uk
Director, Education, Leisure & Lifelong Learning:
Karl Napieralla

Newport City Council, Lifelong Learning & Leisure Department
Newport City Council, Civic Centre,
Newport, South Wales NP20 4UR
☎ (01633) 656656 ▣ (01633) 232808
Email: info@newport.gov.uk
www.newport.gov.uk
Chief Education Officer: Dr Brett Pugh

Pembrokeshire Department of Education & Children's Services Adran Addysg a Gwasanaethau i Blant
Pembrokeshire County Council, County Hall,
Haverfordwest, Pembrokeshire SA61 1TP
☎ (01437) 764551 ▣ (01437) 775838
Email: graham.longster@pembrokeshire.gov.uk
www.pembrokeshire.gov.uk
Director: Graham Longster

Powys Schools Service - Communities, Skills and Learning
Powys County Council, County Hall,
Llandrindod Wells, Powys LD1 5LG
☎ (01597) 826422 ▣ (01597) 826475
Email: education@powys.gov.uk
www.powys.gov.uk

Also at:

Powys County Council, Brecon Area Office,
Neuadd Brycheiniog, Cambrian Way,
Brecon LD3 7BB
☎ (01874) 624141 ▣ (01874) 615781

Powys County Council, Newtown Area Office,
Old College, Off Station Rd, Newtown SY16 1BE
☎ (01686) 626395 ▣ (01686) 629626

Rhondda Cynon Taf Education & Lifelong Learning
Rhondda Cynon Taf County Borough Council,
Tŷ Trevithick, Abercynon, Mountain Ash CF45 4UQ
☎ (01443) 744000 ▣ (01443) 744023
Email: mike.keating@rhondda-cynon-taff.gov.uk
www.rhondda-cynon-taff.gov.uk
Director of Education & Lifelong Learning:
Mike Keating

Swansea Education Department
City & County of Swansea, Civic Centre,
Oystermouth Rd, Swansea SA1 3SN
☎ (01792) 637515 🖻 (01792) 636700
Email: richard.parry@swansea.gov.uk
www.swansea.gov.uk
Corporate Director, Education: Richard J Parry

Torfaen Education Service
Torfaen County Borough Council, Civic Centre,
Pontypool NP4 6YB
☎ (01633) 647637 🖻 (01633) 647778
Email: education@torfaen.gov.uk
www.torfaen.gov.uk
Director: Mark Provis

Vale of Glamorgan Learning Development Directorate
Civic Offices, Provincial House,
Kendrick Rd, Barry CF62 8BF
☎ (01446) 709517 🖻 (01446) 701642
Email: BJJeffreys@valeofglamorgan.gov.uk
www.valeofglamorgan.gov.uk
Director: Bryan Jeffreys

Wrexham Children & Young People's Services
Wrexham County Borough Council,
16 Lord St, Wrexham LL11 1LG
☎ (01978) 298818
www.wrexham.gov.uk
Head of Children & Young People: Susan Evans

Education: Associations & Organizations

Agored Cymru
3-4 Ash Court, Parc Menai, Bangor,
Gwynedd LL57 4DF
☎ (01248) 670011 🖻 (01248) 673469
www.agored.org.uk
Chief Executive: Janet Barlow

Agored Cymru
1-2 Purbeck House, Lambourne Crescent,
Llanishen, Cardiff CF14 5GJ
☎ (029) 2074 7866 🖻 (029) 2074 1079
www.agored.org.uk
Chief Executive: Janet Barlow

Association of Directors of Education in Wales (ADEW)
c/o Welsh Local Government Association,
Local Government House, Drake Walk,
Cardiff CF10 4LG
☎ (029) 2046 8672 Mob: 07799 763251
Email: pierre.bernhard-grout@wlga.gov.uk
www.adew.org.uk
Chair: Brett Pugh
Policy Officer: Pierre Bernhard-Grout

British Council Wales
2nd Flr, 1 Kingsway, Cardiff CF10 3AQ
☎ (029) 2092 4300 🖻 (029) 2092 4301
Email: wales.enquiries@britishcouncil.org
www.britishcouncil.org/wales
Director Wales: Rebecca Matthews
Chair: Aled Eirug

Cambrian Training Company
The Offices @ Coed y Dinas, Welshpool,
Powys SY21 8RP
☎ (01938) 555893 🖻 (01938) 555205
Email: info@cambriantraining.com
www.cambriantraining.com
Managing Director: Arwyn Watkins

Cambrian Training Company Centre of Excellence
Cambrian House, Unit 14, Severn Farm
Enterprise Park, Severn Rd, Welshpool,
Powys SY21 7DF
☎ (01938) 556890 🖻 (01938) 556624
Email: tammy@cambriantraining.com
www.cambriantraining.com
Managing Director: Arwyn Watkins

Careers Wales
Ty Glyn, Unit 1, Brecon Court, William Browne Close,
Llantarnam Park, Cwmbran NP44 3AB
☎ (01633) 487600
CWO helpline: 0845 434 8334
Email: enquiries@careerswalesassociation.co.uk
www.careerswales.com / www.gyrfacymru.com
Chief Executive: Trina Neilson

Post Brenhinol

Royal Mail

Careers Wales Cardiff and Vale Ltd
Careers Centre, 53 Charles St, Cardiff CF10 2GD
☎ (029) 2090 6700 Freephone: 0800 100 900
🖷 (029) 2090 6799
Email: ica@careerswalesgyrfacymru.com
www.careerswales.com

Careers Wales Mid Glamorgan & Powys
Head Office,10/11 Centre Court,
Treforest Industrial Estate, Pontypridd CF37 5YR
☎ (01443) 842207 Freephone: 0800 183 0283
www.careerswales.com

Careers Wales North East
Head Office, St David's Buildings,
Daniel Owen Square, Earl Rd , Mold CH7 1DD
☎ (01352) 750456 Freephone: 0800 919 520
Email: enquiries@cwne.org
www.careerswales.com

Careers Wales North West
Head Office, 5 Llys Castan,
Parc Menai, Bangor LL57 4FH
☎ (01248) 672800; Freephone: 0800 100 900
🖷 (01248) 672801
www.careerswales.com

Careers Wales West
Heol Nantyreos, Cross Hands, Carmarthen SA14 6RJ
☎ (01269) 846000 Freephone: 0800 100 900
www.careerswales.com

CEWC-Cymru (Council for Education in World Citizenship-Cymru)
Temple of Peace, Cathays Park, Cardiff CF10 3AP
☎ (029) 2022 8549 🖷 (029) 2064 0333
Email: cewc@wcia.org.uk
www.cewc-cymru.org.uk
Chief Executive: Martin Pollard

Cilt Cymru
245 Western Avenue, Cardiff CF5 2YX
☎ (029) 2026 5400 🖷 (029) 2026 5411
Email: info@ciltcymru.org.uk
www.ciltcymru.org.uk
Director: Ceri James

City & Guilds Cymru/Wales
Cardiff Business Park, 12 Lambourne Crescent,
Llanishen, Cardiff CF14 5GF
☎ (029) 2074 8600 🖷 (029) 2074 8625
Email: wales@cityandguilds.com
www.cityandguilds.com/wales.html
National Manager Wales: Mandy James

Colegau Cymru/Colleges Wales
Unit 7 Cae Gwyrdd, Green Meadow Springs
Business Park, Tongwynlais, Cardiff CF15 7AB
☎ (029) 2052 2500 🖷 (029) 2052 8372
Email: hello@collegeswales.ac.uk
helo@colegaucymru.ac.uk
www.colegaucymru.ac.uk www.collegeswales.ac.uk
Chair: David Jones
Chief Executive: Dr John Graystone

ContinYou Cymru
Unit 1 Forest Studios, Ceinws, Machynlleth,
Powys SY20 9HA
☎ (01654) 761568
Email: info.cardiff@continyou.org.uk
www.continyou.org.uk/wales_cymru/
Executive Director: Pam Boyd

Cyfanfyd
The Development Education Association for Wales,
Temple of Peace, Cathays Park, Cardiff CF10 3AP
☎ (029) 2066 8999 🖷 (029) 2064 0333
Email: info@cyfanfyd.org.uk
www.cyfanfyd.org.uk
Co-ordinator: Dominic Miles

Cymraeg i Oedolion
Welsh for Adults
CBAC/WJEC , 245 Rhodfa'r Gorllewin,
Caerdydd/Cardiff CF5 2YX
☎ (029) 2026 5007
Email: emyr.davies@cbac.co.uk www.cbac.co.uk
Examinations Officer: Emyr Davies

Engineering Education Scheme - Wales
Waterton Centre, Waterton, Bridgend CF31 3WT
☎ (01656) 669381 🖷 (01656) 662402
Email: info@stemcymru.org.uk
www.eesw.org.uk
National Director: Bob Cater

Estyn (Her Majesty's Inspectorate for Education and Training in Wales) Arolygiaeth Ei Mawrhydi Dros Addysg a Hyfforddiant yng Nghymru
Anchor Court, Keen Rd, Cardiff CF24 5JW
☎ (029) 2044 6446 🖷 (029) 2044 6448
Email: enquiries@estyn.gov.uk
www.estyn.gov.uk
Her Majesty's Chief Inspector of Education
& Training in Wales: Ann Keane

EDUCATION ASSOCIATIONS

General Teaching Council for Wales
9th Floor, Eastgate House, 35-43 Newport Road,
Cardiff CF24 0AB
☎ (029) 2046 0099 ◈ (029) 2047 5850
Email: information@gtcw.org.uk
www.gtcw.org.uk
Chair: Angela Jardine
Chief Executive: Gary Brace

Governors Wales
Ground Floor, 3 Oaktree Court, Mulberry Drive,
Cardiff Gate Business Park, Cardiff CF23 8RS
☎ (029) 20731546; Helpline: (0845) 6020100
◈ (029) 2073 2448
Email: contact@governorswales.org.uk
www.governorswales.org.uk
Chair: Terry O'Marah
Director: Jane Morris

Higher Education Funding Council For Wales (HEFCW)
Linden Court, The Orchards, Ilex Close,
Llanishen, Cardiff CF14 5DZ
☎ (029) 2076 1861 ◈ (029) 2076 3163
Email: info@hefcw.ac.uk
www.hefcw.ac.uk
Chair: Roger Thomas OBE
Chief Executive: Dr David Blaney

Higher Education Wales (HEW)
2 Caspian Point, Caspian Way, Cardiff CF10 4DQ
☎ (029) 2044 8020 ◈ (029) 2048 9531
Email: hew@hew.ac.uk
www.hew.ac.uk
Director: Amanda Wilkinson

The Learned Society of Wales Cymdeithas Ddysgedig Cymru
PO Box 586, Cardiff CF11 1NU
☎ (029) 2037 6951
Email: lsw@wales.ac.uk
www.learnedsocietywales.ac.uk
President and Chair of Council: Sir John
Cadogan CBE, DSc, FRSE, FRSC, PLSW, FRS
Chief Executive and Secretary: Dr Lynn Williams

Mid Wales Food and Land Trust
Frolic House, Frolic St, Newtown,
Powys SY16 1AP
☎ (01686) 622388
Email: cath@midwalesfoodandlandtrust.org.uk
www.midwalesfoodandlandtrust.org.uk
Executive Director: Cath Smith

Mudiad Meithrin Association of Welsh Medium Nursery Schools and Playgroups
Boulevard De St Brieuc, Aberystwyth,
Ceredigion SY23 1PD
☎ (01970) 639639 ◈ (01970) 639638
Email: post@mym.co.uk
www.mym.co.uk
Chief Executive: Hywel Jones

National Foundation for Educational Research Welsh Unit (NFER/SCYA) Sefydliad Cenedlaethol er Ymchwil i Addysg (SCYA/NFER)
Room TK128 Swansea Metropolitan University,
Townhill Campus, Townhill Rd, Swansea SA2 0UT
☎ (0300) 1231363 ◈ (0300) 1231365
Email: scya@nfer.ac.uk
www.nfer.ac.uk
Head of Research and Evaluation (Wales) Robert Smith

National Training Federation for Wales Federasiwn Hyfforddiant Cenedlaethol Cymru
Unit 7, Greenmeadow Springs, Cardiff CF15 7AB
☎ (029) 2061 8228 ◈ (029) 2061 9838
Email: arwyn@cambriantraining.com
www.ntfw.org
National Chair: Mr Arwyn Watkins
Mob: 07831697494

NIACE Dysgu Cymru
3rd Floor, 35 Cathedral Road, Cardiff CF11 9HB
☎ (029) 2037 0900 ◈ (029) 2037 0909
Email: enquiries@niacedc.org.uk
www.niacedc.org.uk
Director for Wales: Richard Spear

NUS Wales
2nd Floor Cambrain Buildings,
Mount Stuart Square, Cardiff CF10 5FL
☎ (029) 2043 5390
Email: office@nus-wales.org.uk
www.nus.org.uk/wales
President: Luke Young
Deputy President: Raechel Mattey
Women's Officer: Stephanie Lloyd

Plas Menai National Watersports Centre
Caernarfon, Gwynedd LL55 1UE
☎ (01248) 670964 ◈ (01248) 673939
Email: info@plasmenai.co.uk
www.plasmenai.co.uk
Rheolwr/Manager: Alan Williams

Plas y Brenin National Mountain Centre
Capel Curig, Conwy LL24 0ET
☎ (01690) 720214 ☒ (01690) 720394
Email: info@pyb.co.uk
www.pyb.co.uk
Chief Executive: Martin Doyle

Rhieni Dros Addysg Gymraeg (RhAG)
Tŷ Cymru, Greenwood Close, Parc Busnes
Porth Caerdydd, Caerdydd CF23 8RD
☎ (029) 20 739207 Mob: 07912175403
☒ (029) 2073 9201
Email: ceri@rhag.net
www.rhag.net
Swyddog Datblygu: Ceri Owen

Skillset Cymru
33-35 West Bute St, Cardiff CF10 5LH
☎ (029) 2045 2828 ☒ (029) 2048 9539
Email: cymru@skillset.org
www.skillset.org
Director: Gwawr Hughes

Techniquest
Stuart St, Cardiff Bay, Cardiff CF10 5BW
☎ (029) 2047 5475 ☒ (029) 2048 2517
Email: info@techniquest.org
www.techniquest.org
Chief Executive: Peter Trevitt
Development Director: Dr Anita Shaw

Theatr Felinfach
Dyffryn Aeron, Ceredigion SA48 8AF
☎ (01570) 470697 ☒ (01570) 471030
Email: theatrfelinfach@ceredigion.gov.uk
www.theatrfelinfach.com
Pennaeth: Dwynwen Lloyd Evans

Theatr Fforwm Cymru
Milford House, Quay Rd,
Goodwick, Pembs SA64 0BS
☎ (01348) 873805
Email: info@theatrfforwmcymru.org.uk
www.theatrfforwmcymru.org.uk
Director: Gill Dowsett

UK Statistics Authority
Statistics House, Tredegar Park,
Newport, S Wales NP10 8XG
☎ (0845) 604 1857
Email: authority.enquiries@statistics.gsi.gov.uk
www.statisticsauthority.gov.uk
Chair: Andrew Dilnot CBE
Deputy Chair (ONS): Lord David Rowe-Beddoe
National Statistcian: Jil Matheson

Wales Pre-school Providers Association (Wales PPA)
Unit 1 The Lofts, 9 Hunter St,
Cardiff Bay, Cardiff CF10 5GX
Email: info@walesppa.org
www.walesppa.org
Chief Executive Officer: Sian C M Davies

WISC
Welsh Independent Schools Council
☎ Mob: 0779 189 1593
Email: info@welshisc.co.uk
www.welshisc.co.uk
General Secretary: Emma Verrier

WJEC
CBAC
245 Western Ave, Llandaff, Cardiff CF5 2YX
☎ (029) 2026 5000
Email: info@wjec.co.uk
www.wjec.co.uk
Chief Executive: Gareth Pierce
Director of Examinations: Derec Stockley
Marketing & Communications Manager: Ceri Thomas

XLWales
4 Highpool Lane, Newton, Swansea SA3 4TT
☎ (01792) 324060
Email: info@xlwales.org.uk
www.xlwales.org.uk

The Year in Industry in Wales
Electronic, Electrical & Computing Engineering,
The University of Birmingham, Birmingham B15 2TT
☎ (0121) 414 8116 ☒ (0121) 414 4136
Email: wales@yini.org.uk
www.yini.org.uk

Environment

Brecknock Wildlife Trust
Lion House, Bethel Square, Brecon LD3 7AY
☎ (01874) 625708
Email: enquiries@brecknockwildlifetrust.org.uk
www.brecknockwildlifetrust.org.uk
Trust Leader: Jackie Symmons
Office Manager: Clare Morgan
Reserves Manager: Phil Sutton
Conservation Manager: Bev Lewis
Education Officer: Alexa Farley
Wildlife Sites Officer: Steph Coates
UTV Project Officer: Ben Mullen

Brecon Beacons National Park Authority
Plas y Ffynnon, Cambrian Way,
Brecon, Powys LD3 7HP
☎ (01874) 624437 ☐ (01874) 622574
Email: enquiries@breconbeacons.org
www.breconbeacons.org
Chair: Julie James
Chief Executive: John Cook

British Waterways North Wales & Borders
Navigation House, Navigation Rd,
Northwich CW8 1BH
☎ (01606) 723800
Email:
enquiries.northwalesborders@britishwaterways.co.uk
www.britishwaterways.co.uk
www.waterscape.com
Waterway Manager: Wendy Capelle

BTCV Cymru
The Conservation Centre, Forest Farm Rd,
Whitchurch, Cardiff CF14 7JJ
☎ (029) 2052 0990 ☐ (029) 2052 2181
Email: wales@btcv.org.uk
www.btcvcymru.org
Director: Ioan Jenkins

Canal & River Trust South Wales & Severn
The Dock Office, Commercial Road,
Gloucester GL1 2EB
☎ (0303) 040 4040 ☐ (01452) 831788
Email:
enquiries.southwalessevern@canalrivertrust.org.uk
www.canalrivertrust.org.uk
www.waterscape.com
Waterway Manager: Nick Worthington

Campaign for the Protection of Rural Wales
Ymgyrch Diogelu Cymru Wledig
Tŷ Gwyn, 31 High St, Welshpool SY21 7YD
☎ (01938) 552525/556212 ☐ (01938) 871552
Email: info@cprwmail.org.uk
www.cprw.org.uk
Director: Peter Ogden
Office Manager: Carys Matthews

The Carbon Trust in Wales
Tredomen Gateway, Tredomen Park,
Ystrad Mynach CF82 7EH
☎ (01443) 845944 ☐ (01443) 845940
Email: contactwales@carbontrust.com
www.carbontrust.co.uk/wales
Manager: Mike Batt

Centre for Alternative Technology
Machynlleth, Powys SY20 9AZ
☎ (01654) 705950 ☐ (01654) 703409
Email: info@cat.org.uk
www.cat.org.uk
Development Director: Paul Allen

The Civic Trust for Wales
East Wing, Windsor House,
Windsor Lane, Cardiff CF10 3DE
☎ (029) 2034 3336
Email: post@civictrustwales.org
www.civictrustwales.org;
www.opendoorsdays.org.uk
Director: Dr Matthew Griffiths
Development Officer: Jo Coles
Open Doors Manager: Derw Thomas
Characterisation Officer: Anna Lermon

The Clwyd-Powys Archaeological Trust
41 Broad Street, Welshpool, Powys SY21 7RR
☎ (01938) 553670 ☐ (01938) 552179
Email: trust@cpat.org.uk
www.cpat.org.uk
Director: Bill Britnell

Sponsored by: www.royalmail.com

Post Brenhinol

Royal Mail

CND Cymru (Campaign for Nuclear Disarmament Wales)
Llysgwyn, Glynarthen, Llandysul,
Ceredigion SA44 6PS
☎ (01239) 851188
Email: heddwch@cndcymru.org
www.cndcymru.org
National Secretary: Jill Gough Chair: Stephen Thomas

Coed Cadw (The Woodland Trust)
3 Iard y Cowper/3 Cooper's Yard, Ffordd
Curran/Curran Rd, Caerdydd/Cardiff CF10 5NB
☎ (08452) 935 860
Email: info@coedcadw.org.uk
www.woodlandtrust.org.uk/wales or
www.coedcadw.org.uk/cymru
Director, Wales: Jerry Langford
Public Affairs & Press Officer: Rory Francis

Coed Cymru
The Old Sawmill, Tregynon,
Newtown, Powys SY16 3PL
☎ (01686) 650777 🖷 (01686) 650696
Email: coedcymru@coedcymru.org.uk
www.coedcymru.org.uk
Director: David Jenkins

Countryside Council for Wales
Cyngor Cefn Gwlad Cymru
Headquarters: Maes-y-Ffynnon,
Penrhosgarnedd, Bangor, Gwynedd LL57 2DW
☎ (0845) 1306229 🖷 (01248) 385505
Email: Enquiries@ccw.gov.uk
www.ccw.gov.uk
Chair: Morgan Parry
Chief Executive: Roger Thomas
Director Evidence & Advice: Dr David Parker
Director, Planning & Resources: Adrian Williams

Also at:

Plas Penrhos, Ffordd Penrhos,
Bangor, Gwynedd LL57 2BX
☎ (0845) 1306229 🖷 (01248) 385505
Email: northernteam@ccw.gov.uk
www.ccw.gov.uk
Director, North Region: Tim Jones

Government Buildings, Arran Rd,
Dolgellau, Gwynedd LL40 1LW
☎ (0845) 1306229 🖷 (01248) 385505
Email: northernteam@ccw.gov.uk

Glan y Nant, Unit 19, Mold Business Park,
Wrexham Rd, Mold, Flintshire CH7 1XP
☎ (0845) 1306229 🖷 (01248) 385505
Email: northernteam@ccw.gov.uk

Countryside Council for Wales
Cyngor Cefn Gwlad Cymru
Also at:

Cantref Court, Brecon Rd, Abergavenny,
Monmouthshire NP7 7AX
☎ (0845) 1306229 🖷 (01248) 385505
Email: southernteam@ccw.gov.uk
www.ccw.gov.uk
Director, South & East Region: Dr Maggie Hill

Unit 13, Drake Walk, Waterfront 2000,
Atlantic Wharf, Cardiff CF10 4AN
☎ (0845) 1306229 🖷 (01248) 385505
Email: southernteam@ccw.gov.uk

Rivers House, St Mellons Business Park,
Fortran Road, St Mellon's, Cardiff CF3 0EY
☎ (0845) 1306229 🖷 (01248) 355782
Email: southernteam@ccw.gov.uk

First Floor, Ladywell House, Park St,
Newtown, Powys SY16 1RD
☎ (0845) 1306229 🖷 (01248) 385505
Email: southernteam@ccw.gov.uk

Welsh Government Building, Rhodfa Padarn,
Llanbadarn Fawr, Aberystwyth SY23 3UR
☎ (01970) 631160 🖷 (01970) 631161
Email: Enquiries@ccw.gov.uk
www.ccw.gov.uk
Director West Region: David Worrall

Beechwood Office, Beechwood Industrial
Estate, Talley Rd, Llandeilo, Carms SA19 7HR
☎ (0845) 1306229 🖷 (01248) 385505
Email: westernteam@ccw.gov.uk

Llanion House , Llanion Park, Pembroke
Dock, Pembrokeshire SA72 6DY
☎ (0845) 1306229 🖷 (01248) 385505
Email: westernteam@ccw.gov.uk

Maes Newydd, Britannic Way West,
Llandarcy, Neath Port Talbot SA10 6JQ
☎ (01792) 326450 🖷 (01792) 326451
Email: westernteam@ccw.gov.uk

Cylch - Wales Community Recycling Network
196 Whitchurch Road, Cardiff CF14 3NB
☎ (029) 2051 9000
Email: mail@cylch.org.uk
www.cylch.org
CEO: Mal Williams

Cymdeithas Edward Llwyd
☎ (01286) 677319
www.cymdeithasedwardllwyd.org.uk
Cadeirydd: Tom Jones

ENVIRONMENT

Cynnal Cymru - Sustain Wales
Cambrian Buildings, Mount Stuart Square,
Cardiff Bay, Cardiff CF10 5FL
☎ (029) 2019 2021
Email: info@cynnalcymru.com
www.cynnalcymru.com www.sustainwales.com
Executive Director: Helen Nelson
Head of Communications: Roz Robinson

Dyfed Archaeological Trust
The Shire Hall, 8 Carmarthen St, Llandeilo SA19 6AF
☎ (01558) 823121/131 ☐ (01558) 823133
Email: info@dyfedarchaeology.org.uk
www.cambria.org.uk
Trust Director: Ken Murphy
Office Manager: Judith Holland

ECO Centre Wales (Newport Office)
Old School Business Centre,
Lower St Mary St, Newport, Pembs SA42 0TS
☎ (01239) 820235 ☐ (01239) 820801
Email: westwales@ecocentre.org.uk
www.ecocentre.org.uk
Chairman: Dr Clive Morgan

ECO Centre Wales (Mold Office)
Ground Floor, Cambrian Chambers,
Earl Road, Mold, Flintshire CH7 1AJ
☎ (01352) 753902 ☐ (01352) 756319
www.ecocentre.org.uk

Energy Saving Trust Wales
1 Caspian Point, Caspian Way,
Cardiff Bay, Cardiff CF10 4DQ
☎ (029) 2046 8340 Advice Line: 0300 123 1234
☐ (029) 2046 8341
www.est.org.uk/wales
Head, Energy Saving Trust Wales: Helen Northmore

Environment Agency Wales
Asiantaeth yr Amgylchedd Cymru
Head Office, Tŷ Cambria,
29 Newport Rd, Cardiff CF24 0TP
☎ (0870) 850 6506
Email: enquiries@environment-
agency.wales.gov.uk
www.environment-agency.wales.gov.uk
Director, Wales: Chris Mills

> *Also at:*
>
> South West Area Office, Maes Newydd,
> Llandarcy, Neath SA10 6jq
> ☎ (0870) 850 6506
> Area Manager: Steve Brown

South East Area Office,
Rivers House, St Mellons Business Park,
St Mellons, Cardiff CF3 0EY
☎ (0870) 850 6506
Area Manager: Gareth O'Shea

North Area Office, Ffordd Penlan,
Parc Menai, Bangor LL57 4DE
☎ (0870) 850 6506
Area Manager: David Edwell

Environment Wales
Baltic House, Cardiff Bay, Cardiff CF10 5FH
☎ (029) 2043 1746
☐ (029) 2043 1701
Email: info@environment-wales.org
www.environment-wales.org
Administrator: Kate Fletcher

Field Studies Council
Rhyd-y-creuau, The Drapers' Field Centre,
Betws-y-coed, Conwy LL24 0HB
☎ (01690) 710494
☐ (01690) 710458
Email: enquiries.rc@field-studies-council.org
www.field-studies-council.org
Centre Director: Daniel Moncrieff

Fields In Trust Cymru (FIT Cymru)
Sport Wales National Centre,
Sophia Gardens, Cardiff CF11 9SW
☎ (029) 2033 4935
Email: cymru@fieldsintrust.org
www.fieldsintrust.org
Manager Wales: Rhodri Edwards

Forestry Commission Wales
Comisiwn Coedwigaeth Cymru
Welsh Government, Rhodfa Padarn,
Llanbadarn Fawr, Aberystwyth SY23 3UR
☎ (0300) 068 0300
☐ (0300) 068 0301
Email: fcwenquiries@forestry.gsi.gov.uk
www.forestry.gov.uk
Director: Trefor Owen
Chair, Woodland Strategy Advisory Panel: Roger Cooper

Friends of the Earth Cymru
33 Castle Arcade Balcony, Cardiff CF10 1BY
☎ (029) 2022 9577
☐ (029) 2022 8775
Email: cymru@foe.co.uk
www.foecymru.co.uk (English)
www.cyddcymru.co.uk (Cymraeg)
Director: Gareth Clubb

Royal Mail

The Glamorgan-Gwent Archaeological Trust Ltd
Heathfield House, Heathfield, Swansea SA1 6EL
☎ (01792) 655208 ☒ (01792) 474469
Email: enquiries@ggat.org.uk
www.ggat.org.uk
Chief Executive: Andrew Marvell

The Gower Society
c/o Swansea Museum, Victoria Rd, Swansea SA1 1SN
☎ (01792) 371665
Email: ridgegower@btinternet.com
www.gowersociety.org.uk
Chair: Malcolm Ridge. Secretary: Ruth Ridge

Groundwork Wales
Unit G5, Main Ave, Treforest Industrial Estate,
Pontypridd CF37 5YL
☎ (01443) 844866 ☒ (01443) 844822
Email: info@groundworkwales.org.uk
www.groundworkwales.org.uk
Chair: Gareth John
Executive Director: Ian McIntosh

Gwent Wildlife Trust
Seddon House, Dingestow, Monmouth NP25 4DY
☎ (01600) 740358 ☒ (01600) 740299
Email: info@gwentwildlife.org
www.gwentwildlife.org
Chief Executive: Tom Clarke

Gwynedd Archaeological Trust
Ymddiriedolaeth Archaeolegol Gwynedd
Craig Beuno, Garth Rd, Bangor, Gwynedd LL57 2RT
☎ (01248) 352535 ☒ (01248) 370925
Email: gat@heneb.co.uk
www.heneb.co.uk
Chief Archaeologist: Andrew Davidson

Hafod Trust
Ymddiriedolaeth yr Hafod
c/o Estate Office, Hafod Old Mansion,
Pontrhydygroes, Ceredigion SY25 6DX
☎ (01974) 282568 ☒ (01974) 282579
Email: trust@hafod.org
www.hafod.org
Chair: Richard Broyd
Company Secretary: Mrs J Macve

Institute of Biological, Environmental
& Rural Science (IBERS)
Aberystwyth University, Penglais,
Aberystwyth SY23 3DA
☎ (01970) 622316 ☒ (01970) 621981
Email: ibers@aber.ac.uk
www.aber.ac.uk/en/ibers
Director: Professor Wayne Powell

International Centre for
Protected Landscapes
Frondeg, Llandre, Bow Street, Ceredigion SY24 5BZ
☎ (01970) 622620 ☒ (01970) 622619
Executive Director: Dr Elizabeth Hughes

Keep Wales Tidy
Cadwch Gymru'n Daclus
33-35 Cathedral Rd, Cardiff CF11 9HB
☎ (029) 2025 6767 ☒ (029) 2025 6768
Email: south@keepwalestidy.org
www.keepwalestidy.org
Chief Executive: Lesley Jones

Llanelli Millennium Coastal Park
Discovery Centre, North Dock, Llanelli SA15 2LF
☎ (01554) 777744 ☒ (01554) 757825
Email: redickinson@carmarthenshire.gov.uk /
pjreed@carmarthenshire.gov.uk
www.millenniumcoastalpark.com
Manager: Rory Dickinson
Administrator: Pam Reed

Merthyr Tydfil Central Library
High St, Merthyr Tydfil CF47 8AF
☎ (01685) 370690 ☒ (01685) 722146
Email: library.services@merthyr.gov.uk
Principal Librarian: Jane Sellwood

Mid & South West Wales Energy
Efficiency Advice Center
West Wales Eco Centre, Old School Business Centre,
Lower St Mary St, Newport, Pembs SA42 0TS
☎ (01239) 820156 ☒ (01239) 820801
Centre Manager: Becci Johnson

Montgomeryshire Wildlife Trust
42 Broad St, Welshpool, Powys SY21 7RR
☎ (01938) 555654
Email: info@montwt.co.uk
www.montwt.co.uk
Chief Executive: Estelle Bailey
Operations Manager: Eley Hart

National Botanic Garden of Wales
Gardd Fotaneg Genedlaethol Cymru
Llanarthne, Carmarthenshire SA32 8HG
☎ (01558) 668768 ☒ (01558) 668933
Email: info@gardenofwales.org.uk
www.gardenofwales.org.uk
Chair: Robert Jolliffe
Director: Dr Rosetta Plummer

National Parks Wales
Parciau Cenedlaethol Cymru
126 Bute St, Cardiff Bay, Cardiff CF10 5LE
☎ (029) 2049 9966 ⓕ (029) 2049 9980
Email: nationalparkswales@anpa.gov.uk
www.nationalparkswales.gov.uk
www.parciaucenedlaetholcymru.gov.uk
Policy Officer: Greg Pycroft

National Trust Wales
Ymddiriedolaeth Genedlaethol Cymru
Office for Wales, Trinity Square/Sgwâr y Drindod,
Llandudno, Conwy LL30 2DE
☎ (01492) 860123 ⓕ (01492) 860233
Email: wa.customerenquiries@nationaltrust.org.uk
www.nationaltrust.org.uk/wales
Chair Wales Advisory Board: Keith James OBE
Director for Wales: Justin Albert

North Wales Wildlife Trust
376 High St, Bangor, Gwynedd LL57 1YE
☎ (01248) 351541 ⓕ (01248) 353192
Email: nwwt@wildlifetrustswales.org
www.wildlifetrust.org.uk/northwales
Trust Director: Frances Cattanach

Pembrokeshire Coast National Park Authority
Llanion Park, Pembroke Dock,
Pembrokeshire SA72 6DY
☎ (0845) 345 7275 ⓕ (01646) 689076
Email: info@pembrokeshirecoast.org.uk
www.pembrokeshirecoast.org.uk
Chair: Cllr Tony Brinsden
Chief Executive: Tegryn Jones

The Penllergare Trust
Ymddiriedolaeth Penllergare
Coed Glantawe, Esgairdawe, Llandeilo SA19 7RT
☎ (01558) 650735
Email: contact@penllergare.org
www.penllergare.org
Secretary: Michael Norman

Planning Aid Wales
1st Flr, 174 Whitchurch Rd, Heath,
Cardiff CF14 3NB
☎ (029) 2062 5009
Email: info@planningaidwales.org.uk
www.planningaidwales.org.uk
Chair: Lucie Taylor
Chief Executive: Elwyn Thomas

Primrose Earth Awareness Trust
Felindre, nr Talgarth, Powys LD3 0ST
☎ (01497) 847636
Email: paul.benham33@gmail.com
www.primrosetrust.org.uk

Radnorshire Wildlife Trust
Warwick House, High St, Llandrindod Wells,
Powys LD1 6AG
☎ (01597) 823298 ⓕ (01597) 823274
Email: info@rwtwales.org
www.rwtwales.org
Trust Director: Julian Jones
Admin Officer: Emma Morgan
Reserves Officer: Jonathan Stone
Consultancy Manager: Chris Ledbury
Estates Worker: Rob Podmore
People & Wildlife Officer: Suzie Fraser

Ramblers' Association/Cymdeithas
y Cerddwyr
3 Coopers Yard, Curran Rd, Cardiff CF10 5NB
☎ (029) 2064 4308 ⓕ (029) 2064 5187
Email: cerddwyr@ramblers.org.uk
www.ramblers.org.uk/wales
Director: Angela Charlton

Royal Society of Architects in Wales
(RIBA Wales Region)
Cymdeithas Frenhinol Penseiri yng Nghymru
4 Cathedral Road, Cardiff CF11 9LJ
☎ (029) 2022 8987 ⓕ (029) 2023 0030
Email: rsaw@riba.org
www.architecture.com/wales
Director: Liz Walder

RSPB Cymru
North Wales Office, Unit 14, Llys Castan, Ffordd
y Parc, Parc Menai, Bangor, Gwynedd LL57 4FW
☎ (01248) 672850
www.rspb.org.uk
Office Manager: Natalie Thomas

Also at:

Wales Headquarters, Sutherland House,
Castlebridge, Cowbridge Rd East,
Cardiff CF11 9AB
☎ (029) 2035 3000
Email: cymru@rspb.org.uk
www.rspb.org.uk
Director, Wales: Katie-Jo Luxton

North Wales Office, Uned 14, Llys Castan,
Ffordd y Parc, Parc Menai, Bangor,
Gwynedd LL57 4FD
☎ (01248) 672850
Email: cymru@rspb.org.uk
www.rspb.org.uk

Sponsored by: www.royalmail.com

Royal Mail

RTPI Cymru
Royal Town Planning Institute
PO Box 2465, Cardiff CF23 0DS
☎ (029) 2049 8215
Email: wales@rtpi.org.uk
www.rtpi.org.uk
National Director: Roisin Willmott

Snowdonia National Park Authority
National Park Office, Penrhyndeudraeth,
Gwynedd LL48 6LF
☎ (01766) 770274 ☎ (01766) 771211
Email: [first name].[surname]@eryri-npa.gov.uk
www.eryri-npa.gov.uk
Chair: Cllr E C Roberts OBE JP
Chief Executive (National Park Officer): Aneurin Phillips

Snowdonia National Park Study Centre
Canolfan Astudiaeth Parc Cenedlaethol Eryri
Plas Tan-y-Bwlch, Maentwrog, Blaenau
Ffestiniog, Gwynedd LL41 3YU
☎ (01766) 772600 ☎ (01766) 772609
Email: plas@eryri-npa.gov.uk
www.plastanybwlch.com
Head of Education Alun Gruffydd
Head of Business: Andrew Oughton

Snowdonia Society
Cymdeithas Eryri
Caban, Brynrefail, Caernarfon, Gwynedd LL55 3NR
☎ (01286) 685498
Email: sarah@snowdonia-society.org.uk
www.snowdonia-society.org.uk
www.cymdeithas-eryri.org.uk
Chair: David Lewis
Director: Gareth Clubb
Acting Director: Sarah Medcalf

South East Wales Energy Advice Centre
Floor 6, Clarence House, Clarence Place,
Newport NP19 7AA
☎ (0800) 622 6110 / (01633) 223 111
Email: advice@sewenergy.org.uk
www.sewenergy.org.uk
Director: Andrew David

Sustainable Energy Ltd
2 Alexandra Gate, Ffordd Pengam, Cardiff CF24 2SA
☎ (029) 2089 4940 ☎ (029) 2089 4941
Email: info@sustainable-energy.co.uk
www.sustainable-energy.co.uk
Director: Chrissy Woodman
Managing Director: Dr Gabriel Gallagher

Sustainable Gwynedd Gynaladwy
Adeilad Galw Cyf, Penrhyndeudraeth, Gwynedd
☎ (01766) 543033 ☎ (01766) 512608
Email: cynthia@gwyneddgynaladwy.org.uk
www.gwyneddgynaladwy.org.uk
Sustainable Development Co-ordinator: Seran Dolma

Sustainable Wales
Cymru Gynhaliol
41 John St, Porthcawl CF36 3AP
☎ (01656) 783405
Email: info@sustainablewales.org.uk
www.sustainablewales.org.uk
Director: Margaret Minhinnick

Tir Coed (North Wales Office)
Lisburne House, Pontrhydygroes,
Ystrad Meurig, Ceredigion SY25 6DQ
☎ (01974) 282476
Email: gwyneth@tircoed.org.uk
www.tircoed.org.uk
Project Officer: Gwyneth Davies

Tir Coed
Denmark Farm, Betws Bledrws,
Lampeter, Ceredigion SA48 8PB
☎ (01570) 493224
Email: becky@tircoed.org.uk
www.tircoed.org.uk
Project Officer: Becky Hulme & Angie Martin

Tŷ-Mawr Ltd Ecological Building Products
Unit 12 Brecon Enterprise Park,
Brecon, Powys LD3 8BT
☎ (01874) 611350 ☎ (01874) 658502
Email: tymawr@lime.org.uk
www.lime.org.uk
Directors: Nigel Gervis
Joyce Morgan-Gervis

Wales Environment Link
27 Pier St, Aberystwyth, Ceredigion SY23 2LN
☎ (01970) 611621
Email: enquiry@waleslink.org
www.waleslink.org
Director: Susan Evans
Advocacy Officer: Raoul Bhambral

The Wales Environment Trust
Ymddiriedolaeth Yr Amgylchedd Cymru
2 Alexandra Gate, Ffordd Pengam, Cardiff CF24 2SA
☎ (029) 2089 4868
Email: info@walesenvtrust.org.uk
www.walesenvtrust.org.uk
Directors: Gerald Morris & Dr Stephen Bentley
Business Development Manager: Graham Bishop

Welsh Historic Gardens Trust
Ymddiriedolaeth Gerddi Hanesyddol Cymru
The Bothy, Aberglasney Gardens,
Llangathen, Carmarthen SA32 8QH
☎ (01558) 668485
Email: admin@whgt.org.uk;
welshhistoric@btconnect.com
www.whgt.org.uk

The Wildfowl & Wetlands Trust
National Wetland Centre Wales,
Llwynhendy, Llanelli,
Carms SA14 9SH
☎ (01554) 741087
🖷 (01554) 744101
Email: info.llanelli@wwt.org.uk
www.wwt.org.uk
Centre Manager: Mr Nigel Williams

The Wildlife Trust
of South & West Wales
Nature Centre, Fountain Rd,
Tondu, Bridgend CF32 0EH
☎ (01656) 724100
🖷 (01656) 726980
Email: info@welshwildlife.org
www.welshwildlife.org
Chief Executive: Sarah Kessell

The Wildlife Trust
of South & West Wales
Welsh Wildlife Centre,
Cilgerran, Cardigan,
Pembrokeshire SA43 2TB
☎ (01239) 621600
Email: wwc@welshwildlife.org
www.welshwildlife.org
Chief Executive: Sarah Kessell

WWF Cymru
Baltic House,
Mount Stuart Sq,
Cardiff CF10 5FH
☎ (029) 2045 4970
🖷 (029) 2045 1306
Email: cymru@wwf.org.uk
www.wwf.org.uk/cymru
Head WWF Cymru: Anne Meikle

Waste Awareness Wales
Local Government House,
Drake Walk, Cardiff CF10 4LG
☎ (029) 2046 8613
www.wasteawarenesswales.org.uk

Government, Police & other Official Agencies

ACAS, Advisory Conciliation
& Arbitration Service
3rd Floor, Fusion Point 2,
Dumballs Rd, Cardiff CF10 5BF
☎ (029) 2076 2636;
Helpline: 08457 474747
🖷 (029) 2075 1334
Email: gpetty@acas.org.uk
www.acas.org.uk
Director Acas Wales: Gareth Petty

ADAS Cymru Wales
Henstaff Court Business Centre, Groesfan,
Cardiff CF72 8NG
☎ (029) 2089 9674
Email: enys.young@adas.co.uk
www.adas.co.uk/wales
Managing Director: Colin Speller

ADAS Cymru Wales
Unit 10D Cefn Llan Science Park,
Aberystwyth, Ceredigion SY23 3AH
☎ (01974) 847000
www.adas.co.uk/wales
Group Manager: Cate Barrow

The Army
Headquarters 160 (Wales) Brigade,
The Barracks, Brecon, Powys LD3 7EA
☎ (01874) 613280
🖷 (01874) 613903
Email: 160bdecomd@land.army.mod.uk
www.army.mod.uk
Commander Wales: Brigadier R Wardle OBE
Late R Welsh

Sponsored by: www.royalmail.com

Royal Mail

The Arts Council of Wales
Bute Place, Cardiff CF10 5AL
☎ (0845) 8734 900 🖷 (029) 2044 1400
Email: info@artswales.org.uk
www.artswales.org.uk / www.celfcymru.org.uk
Chair: Prof Dai Smith
Chief Executive: Nick Capaldi

Also at:

6 Gardd Llydaw, Jackson's Lane,
Carmarthen SA31 1QD
☎ (01267) 234248 🖷 (01267) 233084
Email: midandwest@artswales.org.uk
www.artswales.org.uk /
www.celfcymru.org.uk

36 Prince's Drive, Colwyn Bay LL29 8LA
☎ (01492) 533440 🖷 (01492) 533677
Minicom: (01492) 532288
Email: north@artswales.org.uk
www.artswales.org.uk/www.celfcymru.org.uk

Bute Place, Cardiff CF10 5AL
☎ (029) 8734 900 🖷 (029) 2044 1400
www.artswales.org.uk/www.celfcymru.org.uk

Bank of England Agency for Wales
4 Village Way, Greenmeadow Springs,
Tongwynlais, Cardiff CF15 7NE
☎ (029) 2061 4678 🖷 (029) 2061 3043
Email: wales@bankofengland.co.uk
www.bankofengland.co.uk
Agent for Wales: Neil Ashbridge
Deputy Agent: Ian Derrick

Boundary Commission for Wales
1st Floor, Caradog House,
1-6 St Andrews Place, Cardiff CF10 3BE
☎ (029) 2039 5031 🖷 (029) 2039 5250
Email: bcomm.wales@wales.gsi.gov.uk
www.bcomm-wales.gov.uk
Chair: The Speaker of House of Commons
Deputy Chair: The Hon Mr Justice Lloyd Jones
Commission Members: Paul E Loveluck CBE,
Professor Robert McNabb

British Council Wales
2nd Flr, 1 Kingsway, Cardiff CF10 3AQ
☎ (029) 2092 4300 🖷 (029) 2092 4301
Email: wales.enquiries@britishcouncil.org
www.britishcouncil.org/wales
Director Wales: Simon Dancey
Chair: Aled Eirug

Cadw Welsh Historic Monuments
Welsh Government, Plas Carew, Unit 5-7 Cefn
Coed, Parc Nantgarw, Cardiff CF15 7QQ
☎ (01443) 336000
🖷 (01443) 336001
Email: cadw@wales.gsi.gov.uk
www.cadw.wales.gsi.gov.uk
Director: Marilyn Lewis

CAFCASS Cymru
Welsh Government, Sarn Mynach,
Llandudno Junction LL31 9RZ
☎ (0300) 062 5500
🖷 (0300) 062 5049
Email: Cafcasscymru@Wales.gsi.gov.uk
www.wales.gov.uk/cafcasscymru
Chief Executive: Gillian Baranski

CAFCASS Cymru
Llys y Delyn, 107-111 Cowbridge Rd East,
Cardiff CF11 9AG
☎ (029) 2064 7979
🖷 (029) 2039 8540
Chief Executive: Gillian Baranski

Cardiff Harbour Authority
Queen Alexandra House, Cargo Road,
Cardiff Bay CF10 4LY
☎ (029) 2087 7900
www.cardiffharbour.com

Care Council for Wales
Cyngor Gofal Cymru
Southgate House, Wood St, Cardiff CF10 1EW
☎ (029) 2022 6257 🖷 (029) 2038 4764
Email: info@ccwales.org.uk
www.ccwales.org.uk
Chair: Arwel Ellis Owen
Chief Executive: Rhian Huws Williams

Charity Commission
Comisiwn Elusennau
8th Floor, Clarence House,
Clarence Place, Newport NP19 7AA
☎ (0845) 3000218
www.charity-commission.gov.uk

Children's Commissioner for Wales
North Wales Office, Penrhos Manor,
Oak Drive, Colwyn Bay LL29 7YW
☎ (01492) 523333 🖷 (01492) 523336
Email: post@childcomwales.org.uk
www.childcomwales.org.uk
Children's Commissioner: Keith Towler

OFFICIAL AGENCIES

Children's Commissioner for Wales
Also at:

South Wales Office, Oystermouth House,
Phoenix Way, Llansamlet, Swansea SA7 9FS
☎ (01792) 765600 🖷 (01792) 765601
Email: post@childcomwales.org.uk
www.childcomwales.org.uk
Children's Commissioner: Keith Towler

Community Development Foundation Wales (CDF)
Williams House, 11-15 Columbus Walk,
Cardiff CF10 4BZ
☎ (029) 2002 0632 🖷 (029) 2049 5985
Email: wales@cdf.org.uk
www.cdf.org.uk
Head of Operations, Wales: Liz Court

Community Housing Cymru
2 Ocean Way, Cardiff CF24 5TG
☎ (029) 2067 4800 🖷 (029) 2067 4801
Email: enquiries@chcymru.org.uk
www.chcymru.org.uk
Chair: Peter Cahill
Group Chief Executive: Nick Bennett
Director, Policy & Social Enterprise: Sioned Hughes

Companies House
Crown Way, Maindy, Cardiff CF14 3UZ
☎ (0303) 123 4500
Email: enquiries@companieshouse.gov.uk
www.companieshouse.gov.uk
Acting Chief Executive: Tim Moss

Consumer Focus Wales
Llais Defnyddwyr Cymru
Ground Floor, Portcullis House,
21 Cowbridge Road East, Cardiff CF11 9AD
☎ (029) 2078 7100 🖷 (029) 2078 7101
Email: contactwales@consumerfocus.org.uk
www.consumerfocus.org.uk/wales
Chair: Vivienne Sugar
Senior Director: Rhys Evans

Cronfa Loteri Fawr
Big Lottery Fund
2nd Floor, Ladywell House,
Newtown, Powys SY16 1JB
☎ (01686) 611700 🖷 (01686) 622458
Email: enquiries.wales@biglotteryfund.org.uk
www.biglotteryfund.org.uk
Chair: Sir Adrian Webb
Director for Wales:John Rose
Also at:

10th Flr, Helmont House,
Churchill Way,
Cardiff CF10 2NB
☎ (029) 2067 8200
🖷 (029) 2066 7275
Email: enquiries.wales@biglotteryfund.org.uk
www.biglotteryfund.org.uk
Chair: Sir Adrian Webb
Director: John Rose

Care & Social Services Inspectorate Wales (CSSIW) National Office
Welsh Government,
Rhydycar Business Park,
Merthyr Tydfil CF48 1UZ
☎ (0300) 062 8800
Email: cssiw@wales.gsi.gov.uk
www.cssiw.org.uk
Chief Inspector: Imelda Richardson

Also at:

North Wales Region
Government Buildings,
Sarn Mynach,
Llandudno Junction LL31 9RZ
☎ (0300) 062 5609
Email: CSSIW.North@wales.gsi.gov.uk

South East Wales Region
Welsh Government,
Rhydycar Business Park,
Merthyr Tydfil CF48 1UZ
☎ (0300) 062 8888
Email: cssiw.southeast@wales.gsi.gov.uk

South West Region
Government Buildings,
Picton Terrace, Carmarthen SA31 3BT
☎ (01267) 245160
🖷 (01267) 245140
Email: cssiw.southwest@wales.gsi.gov.uk

Cynnal Cymru - Sustain Wales
Cambrian Buildings,
Mount Stuart Square,
Cardiff Bay, Cardiff CF10 5FL
☎ (029) 2019 2021
Email: info@cynnalcymru.com
www.cynnalcymru.com www.sustainwales.com
Executive Director: Helen Nelson
Head of Communications: Roz Robinson

Sponsored by: www.royalmail.com

Post Brenhinol

Royal Mail

Design Commission for Wales
Comisiwn Dylunio Cymru
4th Floor, Building Two, Caspian Point,
Caspian Way, Cardiff Bay CF10 4DQ
☎ (029) 2045 1964
🖷 (029) 2045 1958
Email: info@dcfw.org
www.dcfw.org
Chair: Alan Francis
Chief Executive: Carole-Anne Davies

Development Trusts Association Wales
35b Albert Rd, Penarth,
Vale of Glamorgan CF64 1BY
☎ (029) 2019 0260
🖷 (029) 2019 0258
Email: info@dtawales.org.uk
www.dtawales.org.uk
Chair: Elwyn James
Director: Peter Williams

DVLA, Driver and Vehicle Licensing Agency
Longview Rd, Morriston, Swansea SA6 7JL
☎ (0300) 123 0791
Email: press.office@dvla.gsi.gov.uk
www.dft.gov.uk/dvla

Dyfed-Powys Police Authority
Police Headquarters, PO Box 99,
Llangunnor, Carmarthen SA31 2PF
☎ (01267) 226440
🖷 (01267) 226448
Email: police.authority@dyfed-
powys.pnn.police.uk
www.dyfedpowyspoliceauthority.co.uk
Chair: Delyth Humfryes
Chief Constable: Jackie Roberts

The Electoral Commission Wales
Y Comisiwn Etholiadol Cymru
Caradog House, 1-6 St Andrews Place,
Cardiff CF10 3BE
☎ (029) 2034 6800
🖷 (029) 2034 6805
Email: infowales@electoralcommission.org.uk
www.comisiwnetholiadol.org.uk
www.electoralcommission.org.uk
Commissioner Wales: Ian Kelsall OBE
Head of Office: Kay Jenkins

Environment Agency Wales
Asiantaeth yr Amgylchedd Cymru
Head Office, Tŷ Cambria,
29 Newport Rd, Cardiff CF24 0TP
☎ (0870) 850 6506
Email: enquiries@environment-
agency.wales.gov.uk
www.environment-agency.wales.gov.uk
Director, Wales: Chris Mills

Also at:

South West Area Office, Maes Newydd,
Llandarcy, Neath SA10 6jq
☎ (0870) 850 6506
Area Manager: Steve Brown

South East Area Office,
Rivers House, St Mellons Business Park,
St Mellons, Cardiff CF3 0EY
☎ (0870) 850 6506
Area Manager: Gareth O'Shea

North Area Office, Ffordd Penlan,
Parc Menai, Bangor LL57 4DE
☎ (0870) 850 6506
Area Manager: David Edwell

Equality & Human Rights Commission
3rd Floor, 3 Callaghan Square, Cardiff CF10 5BT
☎ (029) 2044 7710
🖷 (029) 2044 7712
Minicon: (029) 2044 7713
Helpline: (0845) 604 8810
Email: wales@equalityhumanrights.com
www.equalityhumanrights.com
Commissioner for Wales: Ann Beynon OBE
National Director, Wales: Kate Bennett

Estyn (Her Majesty's Inspectorate
for Education and Training in Wales)
Arolygiaeth Ei Mawrhydi Dros Addysg
a Hyfforddiant yng Nghymru
Anchor Court, Keen Rd,
Cardiff CF24 5JW
☎ (029) 2044 6446
🖷 (029) 2044 6448
Email: enquiries@estyn.gov.uk
www.estyn.gov.uk
Her Majesty's Chief Inspector of Education
& Training in Wales: Ann Keane

European Parliament
Bât.Winston Churchill
M02101
1, Avenue du Président Robert Schuman
CS 91024
F-67070-Strasbourg Cedex France
☎ (00 33 03 88) 17 40 01
🖷 (00 33 03 88) 17 92 01
www.europarl.europa.eu

European Parliament, UK Office
Europe House, 32 Smith Square, London SW1P 3EU
☎ (020) 7227 4300
🖷 (020) 7227 4302
Email: eplondon@europarl.europa.eu
www.europarl.org.uk
Head of Office: Björn Kjellström

Food Standards Agency Wales
11th Floor, Southgate House,
Wood St, Cardiff CF10 1EW
☎ (029) 2067 8999
Email: wales@foodstandards.gsi.gov.uk
www.food.gov.uk/wales/
Director Wales: Steve Wearne

General Teaching Council for Wales
9th Floor, Eastgate House,
35-43 Newport Road, Cardiff CF24 0AB
☎ (029) 2046 0099
🖷 (029) 2047 5850
Email: information@gtcw.org.uk
www.gtcw.org.uk
Chair: Angela Jardine
Chief Executive: Gary Brace

Gwent Police Authority
Police Headquarters, Croesyceiliog,
Cwmbran NP44 2XJ
☎ (01633) 642200
🖷 (01633) 643095
Email: policeauthority@gwent.pnn.police.uk
www.gwentpa.police.uk
Chair: Cilla Davies OBE JP
Chief Constable: Carmel Napier

Health & Safety Executive
Awdurdod Gweithredol Iechyd a Diogelwch
Cardiff Office, Government Buildings,
Tŷ Glas, Llanishen, Cardiff CF14 5SH
☎ (029) 2026 3000
🖷 (029) 2026 3120
Email: jane.lassey@hse.gsi.gov.uk
www.hse.gov.uk
Head of Operations Wales: Jane Lassey

Also at:
Clwyd Office,
Unit 7 & 8 Edison Court, Ellice Way,
Wrexham Technology Park, Wrexham LL13 7YT
🖷 01978 355669

Dyfed Office,
TyMyrddin, Old Station Rd, Carmarthen SA31 1LP
🖷 01267 223267

Health Commission Wales
Unit 3a, Caerphilly Business Park,
Caerphilly CF83 3ED
☎ (029) 2080 7575   🖷 (029) 2080 7599
Email: hcw.enquiries@wales.gsi.gov.uk

Heritage Lottery Fund Committee for Wales
Suite 5a, Hodge House,
Guildhall Place, Cardiff CF10 1DY
☎ (029) 2034 3413
🖷 (029) 2034 3427
Email: wales@hlf.org.uk
www.hlf.org.uk
Chair: Dr Manon Williams
Head of HLF, Wales: Jennifer Stewart

Intellectual Property Office
Concept House, Cardiff Rd, Newport,
South Wales NP10 8QQ
☎ (01633) 814000
🖷 (01633) 817777
Email: information@ipo.gov.uk
www.ipo.gov.uk

Jobcentre Plus
Access to Work Operational Support Unit,
Alexandra House, 377 Cowbridge Road East,
Cardiff CF5 1WU
☎ (029) 2042 3291
🖷 (029) 2042 3342
Email: atwosu.cardiff@jobcentreplus.gsi.gov.uk
www.dwp.gov.uk/jobcentreplus
Customer Services Director, Wales: Linda Badman

Land Registry - Wales Office
Cofrestrfa Tir - Swyddfa Cymru
Tŷ Cwm Tawe, Phoenix Way,
Llansamlet, Swansea SA7 9FQ
☎ (01792) 355000
🖷 (01792) 355055
Email: mike.harris@landregistry.gsi.gov.uk
terry.lewis@landregistry.gsi.gov.uk
www.landregistry.gov.uk
Land Registrar: Terry Lewis
Area Manager: Mike Harris

Sponsored by: www.royalmail.com

Royal Mail

Legal Services Commission Wales
2nd Floor, Churchill House,
17 Churchill Way, Cardiff CF10 2HH
☎ (0300) 200 2020; Welsh Language Service:
0845 609 9989 ☐ (01264) 341 920
Email: cardiff@legalservices.gsi.gov.uk
www.legalservices.gov.uk
Wales Director: Paul Davies

Local Government Boundary Commission for Wales
1st Floor, Caradog House,
1-6 St Andrews Place, Cardiff CF10 3BE
☎ (029) 2039 5031 ☐ (029) 2039 5250
Email: lgbc.wales@wales.gsi.gov.uk
www.lgbc-wales.gov.uk
Acting Chair: Max Caller CBE
Acting Secretary: Steve Halsall

Local Government Data Unit Wales
3-7 Columbus Walk, Cardiff CF10 4SD
☎ (029) 2090 9500 ☐ (029) 2090 9510
Email: enquiries@dataunitwales.gov.uk
www.dataunitwales.gov.uk
Executive Director: Andrew Stephens

Maritime & Coastguard Agency
Milford Haven Marine Office, Gorsewood Drive,
Hakin, Milford Haven SA73 3HB
☎ (01646) 699604 ☐ (01646) 699606
www.mcga.gov.uk

Maritime & Coastguard Agency
Cardiff Marine Office, Anchor Court,
Keen Rd, Cardiff CF24 5JW
☎ (029) 2044 8822 ☐ (029) 2044 8811
Email: cardiff_mo@mcga.gov.uk
www.dft.gov.uk/mca

Mid & West Wales Fire & Rescue Authority
Headquarters, Lime Grove Avenue,
Carmarthen SA31 1SP
☎ (0370) 6060699 ☐ (01267) 220562
Email: mail@mawwfire.gov.uk
www.mawwfire.gov.uk
Chair: Tba (24 Sept 2012)
Chief Fire Officer: Richard Smith

Milford Haven Port Authority
Gorsewood Drive, Milford Haven,
Pembrokeshire SA73 3ER
☎ (01646) 696100 ☐ (01646) 696125
Email: enquiries@mhpa.co.uk
www.mhpa.co.uk
Chief Executive: Alec Don

The National Assembly for Wales
Cardiff Bay, Cardiff CF99 1NA
☎ (0845) 010 5500
Textphone: 0845 010 5678
Email: assembly.info@wales.gov.uk
www.assemblywales.org
www.cynulliadcymru.org
Chief Executive: Claire Clancy

North Wales Fire & Rescue Authority
Fire & Rescue Service HQ,
Ffordd Salesbury,
St Asaph Business Park,
St Asaph LL17 0JJ
☎ (01745) 535250
☐ (01745) 535296
www.nwales-fireservice.org.uk
Chair: Cllr Sharon Frobisher
Chief Fire Officer: Simon A Smith

North Wales Police Authority
Police Headquarters, Glan y Don,
Colwyn Bay LL29 8AW
☎ (01492) 805486
☐ (01492) 805489
Email: NWPA@north-wales.police.uk
www.nwalespa.org
Chair: Alun Lewis
Chief Constable: Mark Polin

North Wales Traffic Management Centre
Ffordd Sam Pari, Morfa, Conwy LL32 8HH
☎ (0845) 602 6020
☐ (01492) 572395
Email: contact@traffic-wales.com
www.traffic-wales.com

Office for National Statistics
Government Buildings,
Cardiff Rd, Newport NP10 8XG
☎ (0845) 6013034
☐ (01633) 652747
Email: info@statistics.gov.uk
www.ons.gov.uk
National Statistician: Karen Dunnell

Ofgem
1 Caspian Point, Caspian Way,
Cardiff Bay CF10 4DQ
☎ (029) 2044 4042
Email: nick.speed@ofgem.gov.uk
www.ofgem.gov.uk
External Relations Manager: Nick Speed

Older People's Commissioner for Wales
Cambrian Buildings,
Mount Stuart Square,
Cardiff CF10 5FL
☎ (08442) 640670
🖷 (08442) 640680
Email: ask@olderpeoplewales.com /
gofyn@olderpeoplewales.com
www.olderpeoplewales.com
Commissioner for Older People: Sarah Rachira

Ombudsman, Public Services Ombudsman for Wales
1 Ffordd yr Hen Gae,
Pencoed, Bridgend CF35 5LJ
☎ (01656) 641150
🖷 (01656) 641199
Email: ask@ombudsman-wales.org.uk
www.ombudsman-wales.org
Ombudsman for Wales: Peter Tyndall

One Voice Wales Un Llais Cymru
24c College St,
Ammanford, Carms SA18 3AF
☎ (01269) 595400
🖷 (01269) 598510
Email: admin@onevoicewales.org.uk
www.onevoicewales.org.uk
Chief Executive: Lyn Cadwallader

The Planning Inspectorate for England and Wales
Crown Buildings, Cathays Park,
Cardiff CF10 3NQ
☎ (029) 2082 3866
🖷 (029) 2082 5150
Email: wales@pins.gsi.gov.uk
www.planningportal.gov.uk
Director for Wales: Richard Poppleton

Public Service Management Wales (PSMW) Academi Wales
Welsh Government,
Second Floor, Cathays Park,
Cardiff CF10 3NQ
☎ (029) 2082 6687
Email: psmw@wales.gsi.gov.uk
www.wales.gov.uk/psmw
Director: Neil Wooding

Reserve Forces & Cadets Association for Wales
Centre Block, Maindy Barracks,
Cardiff CF14 3YE
☎ (029) 2037 5746 🖷 (029) 2022 4828
Email: wa-cadets@wa.rfca.mod.uk
www.rfca-wales.org.uk
Chief Executive: Col Nick Beard TD DL

Residential Property Tribunal
Southgate House, Wood St , Cardiff CF10 1EW
☎ (029) 2092 2777 🖷 (029) 2023 6146
Email: rpt@wales.gsi.gov.uk
President: Andrew Morris
Vice President: Rhys Davies

H M Revenue & Customs
Government Buildings, Tŷ Glas,
Llanishen, Cardiff CF14 5YA
☎ (029) 2032 5363 🖷 (029) 2032 5957
www.hmrc.gov.uk

Royal Air Force
No 4 School of Technical Training, MoD St
Athan, Barry, Vale of Glamorgan CF62 4WA
Email: co@4stt.mod.uk
www.raf.mod.uk
Commanding Officer: Wing Commander P Regan

Royal Commission on the Ancient and Historical Monuments of Wales (including the National Monuments Record of Wales)
Plas Crug, Aberystwyth, Ceredigion SY23 1NJ
☎ (01970) 621200 🖷 (01970) 627701
Email: nmr.wales@rcahmw.gov.uk
www.rcahmw.gov.uk
Commission Chair: Eurwyn Wiliam
Secretary: Peter Wakelin

Royal Mint
Freepost NAT23496, PO Box 500,
Llantrisant, Pontyclun CF72 8YT
☎ (01443) 222111 🖷 (01443) 623326
www.royalmint.com
Chair: Mike Davies
Chief Executive: Adam Lawrence

Royal Navy HQ
(Wales & Western England), HMS Flying Fox,
Bristol BS3 2NS
☎ (0117) 786010
Email: nrcwwe@a.dii.mod.uk
Naval Regional Commander:
Commodore JamieMiller CBE RN

Royal Society of Architects in Wales (RIBA Wales Region)
Cymdeithas Frenhinol Penseiri yng Nghymru
4 Cathedral Road, Cardiff CF11 9LJ
☎ (029) 2022 8987 ⓕ (029) 2023 0030
Email: rsaw@riba.org
www.architecture.com/wales
Director: Liz Walder

SaBRE Wales
Maindy Barracks, Cardiff CF14 3YE
☎ (029) 2037 5734
ⓕ (029) 2022 4828
Email: wa-empsp@wa.rfca.mod.uk
www.sabre.mod.uk
Campaign Director: David Hammond

South Wales Fire & Rescue Service
Fire Service HQ, Forest View Business Park,
Llantrisant, Pontyclun CF72 9XA
☎ (01443) 232000
ⓕ (01443) 232180
Email: swfs@southwales-fire.gov.uk
www.southwales-fire.gov.uk
Chair: Cllr D T Davies
Acting ACFO: Huw Jakeway

South Wales Police Authority
Tŷ Morgannwg, Police Headquarters,
Bridgend CF31 3SU
☎ (01656) 869366
ⓕ (01656) 869407
Email: police.authority@south-wales.pnn.police.uk
www.southwalespoliceauthority.org.uk
Interim Chair: John Littlechild MBE JP
Chief Constable: Peter Vaughan

South Wales Traffic Management Centre
M4, Junction 32, Coryton, Cardiff CF14 7EF
☎ (0845) 6026020/ 029 20629424
ⓕ (029) 2062 9424
Email: info@traffic-wales.com
www.traffic-wales.com

Valuation Tribunal Service for Wales
East Wales Valuation Tribunal,
22 Gold Tops, Newport NP20 4PG
☎ (01633) 266367
ⓕ (01633) 253270
Email: eastwales.vt@vto.gsx.gov.uk
www.valuation-tribunals-wales.org.uk
Chief Executive & Clerk of the Tribunal: Simon Hill; Regional Representative: E C Beaumont

Also at:

North Wales Region, Government Buildings
Block A(L1), Sam Mynach,
Llandudno Junction LL31 9RZ
☎ (03000) 625350 ⓕ (03000) 625368
Email: northwales.vt@vto.gsx.gov.uk
www.valuation-tribunals-wales.org.uk
Clerk of the Tribunal: Mr J C Owen
Regional Representative - Mr H M McEvoy MBE

South Wales Valuation Tribunal,
22 Gold Tops, Newport NP20 4PG
☎ (01633) 255003 ⓕ (01633) 255004
Email: southwales.vt@vto.gsx.gov.uk
www.valuation-tribunals-wales.org.uk
Clerk of the Tribunal: Wendy Bowen Beynon
Regional Representative: Miss C Cobert JP

West Wales Region, 1st Floor,
14 King St, Carmarthen SA31 1BH
☎ (01267) 235071 ⓕ (01267) 221579
Email: westwales.vt@vto.gsx.gov.uk
www.valuation-tribunals-wales.org.uk
Clerk of the Tribunal: Mrs Ann Smith;
Regional Representative: Mr N K L Thomas

Wales & South West, UK Border Agency
3rd Flr, General Building,
31-33 Newport Rd, Cardiff CF24 0AB
☎ (029) 2092 4620 Press Office: 029 2092 4665
www.ukba.homeoffice.gov.uk
Regional Director, Wales and South West: Jane Farleigh
Press Officer: Chris Herdman Mob: 07795 044181

Wales Audit Office
Swyddfa Archwilio Cymru
24 Cathedral Rd, Cardiff CF11 9LJ
☎ (029) 2032 0500 ⓕ (029) 2032 0600
Email: info@wao.gov.uk
www.wao.gov.uk
Auditor General for Wales: Huw Vaughan Thomas

Wales Coastal & Maritime Partnership
Welsh Government, Cathays Park, Cardiff CF10 3NQ
☎ (029) 2082 5579 ⓕ (029) 2082 3327
Email: wcmp@wales.gsi.gov.uk
www.walescoastalpartnership.org.uk
Chair: Professor Lynda Warren

The Wales Office Y Swyddfa Gymreig
Wales Office/Y Swyddfa Gymreig,
Gwydyr House, Whitehall, London SW1A 2ER
☎ (020) 7270 0534
Email: wales.office@walesoffice.gsi.gov.uk
www.walesoffice.gov.uk
Director: Fiona Adams-Jones

HEALTH

Wales Office
1 Caspian Point, Caspian Way
Cardiff CF10 4DQ

Wales Migration Partnership (Asylum Seekers, Refugees and Migrants)
3-7 Columbus Walk,
Brigantine Place, Cardiff CF10 4SD
☎ (029) 2090 9550
🖷 (029) 2090 9510
Email: anne.hubbard@wmp.org.uk
www.wmp.org.uk
Chair: Reverend Aled Edwards
Partnership Director: Anne Hubbard

Welsh Industrial Development Advisory Board
Invest Wales, Dept,
Economy & Transport,
Welsh Government,
QED Centre, Main Ave,
Treforest, Pontypridd CF37 5YR
☎ (01443) 845729
🖷 (01443) 845869
www.wales.gsi.gov.uk
Secretary: Ian G Shuttleworth

Welsh Language Commissioner Comisiynydd y Gymraeg
Market Chambers/Siambrau'r Farchnad,
5-7 St Mary St/Heol Eglwys Fair,
Cardiff/Caerdydd CF10 1AT
☎ (0845) 603 3221
🖷 (029) 2087 7551
Email: post@comisynyddygymraeg.org
www.welshlanguagecommissioner.org /
www.comisiynyddygymraeg.org
Comissioner/Comisiynydd: Meri Huws

Welsh Local Government Association Cymdeithas Llywodraeth Leol Cymru
Local Government House,
Drake Walk, Cardiff CF10 4LG
☎ (029) 2046 8600
🖷 (029) 2046 8601
Email: wlga@wlga.gov.uk
www.wlga.gov.uk
Chief Executive: Steve Thomas CBE
Chair: Cllr John Davies

Health

Alcoholics Anonymous - Wales and Borders Region
☎ (0845) 769 7555
Email: walesandborders-reclo@aa-email.org.uk
www.alcoholics-anonymous.co.uk
www.aa-gb.org.uk/walesborders/region/index.html

Wales Drug and Alcohol Helpline Dan 24/7 Cyffuriau ac Alcohol Cymru
☎ 0808 808 2234 (Helpline)
01978 366 206 (Office)
www.dan247.org.uk
Service Manager: Janet Roberts

Alzheimer's Society
South Wales Office, 16 Columbus Walk,
Atlantic Wharf, Cardiff CF10 4BY
☎ (029) 2048 0593
Email: SDAreaOffice-
SouthWales@alzheimers.org.uk
www.alzheimers.org.uk
Director Wales: Ian Thomas

Alzheimer's Society
North & West Wales Office,
6a Llys Onnen, Parc Menai,
Bangor LL57 4DF
☎ (01248) 671137
Email: nwa@alzheimers.org.uk
www.alzheimers.org.uk
Director Wales: Ian Thomas

Anheddau Cyf
6 Llys Britannia, Parc Menai,
Bangor LL57 4BN
☎ (01248) 675910
🖷 (01248) 676280
Email: post@anheddau.co.uk
www.anheddau.co.uk
Chief Executive Officer: Janetta Toleman Jones
Company Secretary: Nia Prendergast

Sponsored by: www.royalmail.com

Post Brenhinol
Royal Mail

ASH Cymru Wales
2nd Floor, 8 Museum Place, Cardiff CF10 3BG
☎ (029) 2064 1101 ☐ (029) 2064 1045
Email: sue@ashwales.org.uk
www.ashwales.org.uk
Chief Executive: Elen de Lacy
Press & Campaigns Manager: Felicity Waters

Association of the British Pharmaceutical Industry Cymru Wales
Fourth Floor, 2 Caspian Point,
Pierhead St, Cardiff Bay CF10 4DQ
☎ (0870) 890 4333 Extn: 1312
☐ (029) 2045 4298
Email: wales@abpi.org.uk
www.abpi.org.uk
Director: Dr Richard Greville
Policy & Projects Executive: Joanne Ferris
Executive Assistant: Hayley Morton

Board of Community Health Councils in Wales
2nd Floor, 33-35 Cathedral Rd, Cardiff CF11 9HB
☎ (0845) 644 7814 ☐ (029) 2023 5574
Email: enquiries@waleschc.org.uk
www.communityhealthcouncils.org.uk
Chair: Gillian Davies
Director: Carol Lamyman-Jones

British Dental Association
Fourth Floor, 2 Caspian Point,
Cardiff Bay, Cardiff CF10 4DQ
☎ (029) 2049 6174 ☐ (029) 2049 6984
Email: bda.wales@bda.org
www.bda-dentistry.org.uk
Director: Stuart Geddes

British Heart Foundation Cymru
Admail 4065, Cardiff CF1 1ZA
☎ (029) 2038 2368 ; Media: (029) 2038 2406
Email: wales@bhf.org.uk
www.bhf.org.uk
Volunteering & Fundraising: Luke Mallett
Media & Public Affairs: Delyth Lloyd
Prevention & Care Development: Elaine Tanner

British Medical Association
5th Floor, 2 Caspian Point,
Caspian Way, Cardiff Bay, Cardiff CF10 4DQ
☎ (029) 2047 4646 ☐ (029) 2047 4600
Email: bmawales@bma.org.uk
www.bma.org.uk
Welsh Secretary: Dr Richard J P Lewis
Senior Public Affairs Officer: John Jenkins
(email: jjenkins@bma.org.uk)

Cancer Research UK
Rowan House, Hazel Drive,
Newport, South Wales NP10 8FY
☎ (01633) 654764
Email: james.hunt@cancer.org.uk /
linda.strange@cancer.org.uk
www.cancerresearchuk.org
Contact: James Hunt, Linda Strange

Centre for Health Informatics
Institute of Life Science, Swansea University,
Singleton Park, Swansea SA2 8PP
☎ (01792) 602351 ☐ (01792) 513430
Email: chiral@swansea.ac.uk
www.swan.ac.uk/ils/research/chiral
Marketing Development Manager: Stephanie Lee

Changing Faces Cymru
PO Box 562, Swansea SA8 9AD
☎ (0845) 4500240 ☐ (0845) 4500240
Email: cymru@changingfaces.org.uk
www.changingfaces.org.uk
Welsh Officer/Swyddog Cymru: Simon Boex

The Chartered Society of Physiotherapy
3rd Flr, 1 Cathedral Rd, Cardiff CF11 9SD
☎ (029) 2038 2428 or 2429 ☐ (029) 2022 7383
Email: wales@csp.org.uk
www.csp.org.uk
Employment Relations: Peter Finch
Policy Officer for Wales: Philippa Ford

Community Pharmacy Wales
3rd Floor, Caspian Point 2,
Caspian Way, Cardiff CF10 4DQ
☎ (029) 2044 2070 ☐ (029) 2044 2071
Email: info@cpwales.org.uk
www.cpwales.org.uk
Chief Executive: Russell Goodway

Care & Social Services Inspectorate Wales (CSSIW) National Office
Welsh Government, Rhydycar Business Park,
Merthyr Tydfil CF48 1UZ
☎ (0300) 062 8800
Email: cssiw@wales.gsi.gov.uk
www.cssiw.org.uk
Chief Inspector: Imelda Richardson

Also at:

North Wales Region
Government Buildings, Sarn Mynach,
Llandudno Junction LL31 9RZ
☎ (0300) 062 5609
Email: CSSIW.North@wales.gsi.gov.uk

HEALTH

South East Wales Region
Welsh Government,
Rhydycar Business Park,
Merthyr Tydfil CF48 1UZ
☎ (0300) 062 8888
Email: cssiw.southeast@wales.gsi.gov.uk

South West Region
Government Buildings, Picton Terrace,
Carmarthen SA31 3BT
☎ (01267) 245160
⊡ (01267) 245140
Email: cssiw.southwest@wales.gsi.gov.uk

Drugaid Wales
1st Floor, St Fagan's House,
St Fagan's St, Caerphilly CF83 1FZ
☎ (029) 2088 1000
⊡ (029) 2088 1008
Email: office@drugaidcymru.com
www.drugaidcymru.com
Executive Director: Caroline Phipps

Fitness Wales
1b Clarke St, Cardiff CF5 5AL
☎ (029) 2057 5155
⊡ (029) 2056 8886
Email: enquiries@fitnesswales.co.uk
www.fitnesswales.co.uk
Administrative Manager: Ceri Dunn

General Medical Council
Wales Office, Regus House,
Falcon Drive, Cardiff Bay CF10 4RU
☎ (029) 2050 4060
Email: gmcwales@gmc-uk.org
www.gmc-uk.org
Head of Welsh Affairs: Rachel Podolak

Gofal Cymru
26 Dunraven Place, Bridgend CF31 1JD
☎ (01656) 647722
⊡ (01656) 2045 3845
Email: enquiries@gofal.org.uk
www.gofal.org.uk
Executive Director: Ewan Hamilton
Public Affairs Manager: Alexandra McMillan

HAFAL
Suite C2, William Knox House, Britannic Way,
Llandarcy, Neath SA10 6EL
☎ (01792) 816600 ⊡ (01792) 813056
Email: hafal@hafal.org
www.hafal.org www.mentalhealthwales.net
Chief Executive: Bill Walden-Jones

Health Communication Research Centre
School of English, Communication & Philosophy,
Cardiff University, Humanities Building, Colum
Drive, Cardiff CF10 3EU
☎ (029) 2087 6154
Email: healthcom@cf.ac.uk
www.cardiff.ac.uk/encap/hcrc
Director: Professor Srikant Sarangi

Health Solutions Wales
12th Floor, Brunel House,
2 Fitzalan Rd, Cardiff CF24 0HA
☎ (029) 2050 0500 ⊡ (029) 2050 2330
Email: reception@hsw.wales.nhs.uk
www.hsw.wales.nhs.uk
Director: Hugh Morgan

Institute of Rural Health
St David's House, New Road,
Newtown, Powys SY16 1RB
☎ (01686) 629480 ⊡ (01686) 626291
Email: info@irh.ac.uk
www.rural-health.ac.uk
Chief Executive: Jane Randall-Smith
Information Officer: Helen Porter

Mind Cymru
3rd Floor, Quebec House, Castlebridge,
Cowbridge Road East, Cardiff CF11 9AB
☎ (029) 2039 5123
Mind infoline: (0845) 766 0163
⊡ (029) 2034 6585
Email: contactwales@mind.org.uk
www.mind.org.uk
Director: Lindsay Foyster

Motor Neurone Disease (MND) Association
David Niven House, 10-15 Notre Dame Mews,
Northampton NN1 2BG
☎ (01604) 250505 ⊡ (01604) 624726
Email: enquiries@mndassociation.org
www.mndassociation.org
Chief Executive: Dr Kirstine Knox
Regional Care Development Adviser
(North Wales): Kevin Thomas 01248 853428
Regional Care Development Adviser
(South Wales): Jenny James 01454 414176

Multiple Sclerosis Society Cymru
Temple Court, Cathedral Rd, Cardiff CF11 9HA
☎ (029) 2078 6676 ⊡ (029) 2078 6677
Email: mscymru@mssociety.org.uk
www.mssociety.org.uk/wales
Director: Judi Rhys

NAS Cymru - National Autistic Society
6-7 Village Way, Greenmeadow Springs Business Park, Tongwynlais, Cardiff CF15 7NE
☎ (029) 2062 9310
Email: karen.shore@nas.org.uk
www.nascymru.org.uk
Regional Officer South Wales: Karen Shore

The National Autistic Society Cymru
6-7 Village Way, Greenmeadow Springs Business Park, Tongwynlais, Cardiff CF15 7NE
☎ (029) 2062 9312
🖷 (029) 2062 9317
Email: cymru@nas.org.uk
www.autism.org.uk/wales

The Optometry Wales
One Caspian Point, Cardiff Bay,
Cardiff CF10 4DQ
☎ (029) 2044 4072
🖷 (029) 2044 4073
Email: salidavis@optometrywales.com
www.optometrywales.org.uk
Chief Executive: Sali Davis

Royal College of Nursing Wales
Tŷ Maeth, King George V Drive East, Cardiff CF14 4XZ
☎ (029) 2068 0738
Email: welsh.board@rcn.org.uk
www.rcn.org.uk
Director: Tina Donnelly

St John Cymru-Wales
National Headquarters, Priory House, Beignon Close, Ocean Way, Cardiff CF24 5PB
☎ (029) 2044 9644
🖷 (029) 2044 9645
Email: keith@stjohnwales.org.uk
www.stjohnwales.org.uk
Chief Executive: Keith M Dunn OBE

The Stroke Association
Y Gymdeithas Strôc
Wales Office, Greenmedow Springs Business Park, Unit 8, Cae Gwyrdd, Tongwynlais, Cardiff CF15 7AB
☎ (029) 20524400
Email: info.cymru@stroke.org.uk
www.stroke.org.uk
Director Cymru: Ana Palazon
Deputy Director Paul Underwood
Assistant Regional Managers:
Terri Williams, Helyn Salt
Head of Communications & External Affairs:
Lowri Griffiths

Also at:
Suite 2, Block 5, 56 Carlton Court,
St Asaph Business park,
St Asaph LL17 0JG
☎ (01745) 586902
www.stroke.org.uk
Assistant Regional Manager:
Lyn Siebenmann

Tenovus The Cancer Charity
9th Floor, Gleider House,
Cardiff CF14 5BD
☎ (029) 2076 8850
🖷 (029) 2076 8888
Email: post@tenovus.org.uk
www.tenovus.org.uk
Chief Executive: Claudia McVie
Freephone Cancer Help: (0808) 808 1010

Welsh Council on Alcohol and other Drugs
Cyngor Cymru ar Alcohol a Chyffuriau Eraill
58 Richmond Rd,
Cardiff CF24 3AT
☎ (029) 2049 3895
Email: info@welshcouncil.org.uk
www.welshcouncil.org.uk
Chief Executive: Wynford Ellis Owen

Welsh Hospitals & Health Services Association
60 Newport Rd, Cardiff CF24 0YG
☎ (029) 2048 5461
🖷 (029) 2048 8859
Email: mail@whahealthcare.co.uk
www.whahealthcare.co.uk
Chief Executive: Huw L Cooke

West Wales Action for Mental Health
Llys Steffan, Temple Terrace,
Lampeter, Ceredigion SA48 7BJ
☎ (01570) 422559
🖷 (01570) 422698
Email: wwamh_ceredigion@yahoo.co.uk
wwamh.org.uk
Co-Director: Lynette Morgan

HOUSING ASSOCIATIONS

Housing Associations

Aelwyd Housing Association Ltd
58 Richmond Rd, Roath, Cardiff CF24 3ET
☎ (029) 2048 1203
🖷 (029) 2043 5370
Email: enquiries@aelwyd.co.uk
www.aelwyd.co.uk
Chair: Jonathan Morris
Director: Chris Woodward

Baneswell Housing Association Ltd
19c West St, Newport NP20 4DD
☎ (01633) 265528
🖷 (01633) 265528
Email: baneswell@shaw.co.uk
Chair: Mrs Linda Williams
Secretary: Annette Palmer

Bro Myrddin Housing Association Ltd
Cillefwr Industrial Estate, Johnstown,
Carmarthen SA31 3RB
☎ (01267) 232714 🖷 (01267) 238107
Email: info@bromyrddin.co.uk
www.bromyrddin.co.uk
Chair: Gethin Davies
Chief Executive: Hilary Jones

Bron Afon Community Housing
Tŷ Bron Afon, William Brown Close,
Llantarnam Industrial Park, Cwmbran NP44 3AB
☎ (01633) 620111
Email: enquiries@bronafon.org.uk
www.bronafon.org.uk
Chair: Tamsin Stirling
Chief Executive: Duncan Forbes

The Cadarn Housing Group Ltd
Tŷ Cadarn, 5 Village Way, Tongwynlais,
Cardiff CF15 7NE
☎ (0870) 2420673 🖷 (0870) 2420674
Email: enquiries@cadarn.co.uk
www.cadarn.co.uk
Chair: Chris Koehli
Chief Executive: Paul Roberts

Cadwyn Housing Association Ltd
197 Newport Rd, Roath, Cardiff CF24 1AJ
☎ (029) 2049 8898 🖷 (029) 2046 4222
Email: mail@cadwyn.co.uk
www.cadwyn.co.uk
Chair: John Bevan
Chief Executive: Christine O'Meara

Cardiff Community Housing Association Ltd
Tolven Court, Dowlais Road, Cardiff CF24 5LQ
☎ (029) 2046 8490
Email: info@ccha.org.uk
www.ccha.org.uk
Chief Executive: Kevin Protheroe

Cardiff YMCA Housing Association
The Walk, Roath, Cardiff CF24 3AG
☎ (029) 2046 5250 🖷 (029) 2047 1826
Email: enquiries@cardiffymcaha.co.uk
www.cardiffymcaha.co.uk
Chair: Robin Wynne-Hughes
Chief Executive: Andrew Jenkins

Cartrefi Conwy
Head Office: Bryn Eirias, Heritage Gate,
Abergele Rd, Colwyn Bay LL29 8BY
☎ (01492) 805500 🖷 (01492) 805555
Email: enquiries@cartreficonwy.org
www.cartreficonwy.org
Chair: Pam Lonie
Chief Executive: Andrew Bowden

Charter Housing Association
Exchange House, High St,
Newport NP20 1AA
☎ (01633) 212375
🖷 (01633) 256271
Email: sue.tidley@charterhousing.co.uk
www.charterhousing.co.uk
Chair: John Evans

Coastal Housing Group
3rd Floor, 220 High Street,
Swansea SA1 1NW
☎ (01792) 479200
🖷 (0845) 680 8888 (out of hours number)
Email: ask@coastalhousing.co.uk
www.coastalhousing.co.uk
Chair: Francis Jones
Vice Chair: Kay Howell

Cymdeithas Tai Cantref Cyf
Llys Cantref, Church Lane,
Newcastle Emlyn SA38 9AB
☎ (01239) 712000 🖷 (01239) 712001
Email: post@cantref.co.uk
www.cantref.co.uk
Chair: David Willcox
Chief Executive: Lynne Sacale

Post Brenhinol

Royal Mail

Cymdeithas Tai Clwyd Cyf
54 Stryd y Dyffryn, Dinbych,
Sir Ddinbych LL16 3BW
☎ (0345) 2303140 ◫ (0345) 2303145
Email: taiclwyd@taiclwyd.com
www.taiclwyd.com
Chair: Merfyn Roberts
Chief Executive: Alwyn Llwyd

Cymdeithas Tai Eryri Cyf
Tŷ Silyn, Y Sgwâr, Penygroes,
Gwynedd LL54 6LY
☎ (01286) 881588
◫ (01286) 881141
Email: taieryri@taieryri.co.uk
www.taieryri.co.uk
Chair: Melfyn Parry
Director: Walis George

Cynon Taf Community Housing Group
Unit 4, Navigation Park, Abercynon,
Mountain Ash CF45 4SN
☎ (0345) 2602633 ◫ (0345) 2602634
Email: ctha@cynon-taf.org.uk
www.cynon-taf.org.uk
Chair: Julie Haigh
Chief Executive: Antonia Forte

Family Housing Association (Wales) Ltd
43 Walter Rd, Swansea SA1 5PN
☎ (01792) 460192 ◫ (01792) 473726
Email: info@fha-wales.com
www.fha-wales.com
Chair: Alan Lloyd
Chief Executive: Jeffrey Evans

First Choice Housing Association Ltd
Cymdeithas Tai Dewis Cyntaf Cyf
19 Stanwell Rd, Penarth,
Vale of Glamorgan CF64 2EZ
☎ (029) 2071 1382 ◫ (029) 2071 1382
Email: admin@fcha.org.uk†
www.fcha.org.uk
Chair: Andrew Jones
Chief Executive: Hilary Ryan†

Grŵp Gwalia Cyf
7-13 The Kingsway,
Swansea SA1 5JN
☎ (01792) 460609 ◫ (01792) 466198
Email: enquiries@gwalia.com
www.gwalia.com
Chair: Rt Rev Anthony Pierce
Chief Executive: Prof Michael Williams

Hafan Cymru
5-6 Queen Street, Carmarthen SA31 1JR
☎ (01267) 225558 ◫ (01267) 221592
Email: enquiries@hafancymru.co.uk
www.hafancymru.co.uk
Chair: Kathryn Williams
Chief Executive: Cathy Davies

Hafod Housing Association
1st Floor, St Hilary Court, Copthorne Way,
Culverhouse Cross, Cardiff CF5 6ES
☎ (029) 2067 5800 ◫ (029) 2067 2499
Email: enquiries@hafod.org.uk
www.hafod.org.uk
Chair: Elgar Lewis
Managing Director: Alan Morgan

Hendre Group
St Hilary Court, Copthorne Way, Cardiff CF5 6ES
☎ (029) 2067 5888 ◫ (029) 2067 5898
Email: enquiries@hendre.org.uk
www.hendre.org.uk
Chair: John Wreford:
Group Chief Executive: Ian Williams

Linc Cymru Housing Association
387 Newport Rd, Cardiff CF24 1GG
☎ (029) 2047 3767 ◫ (029) 2048 2474
Email: info@linc-cymru.co.uk
www.linc-cymru.co.uk
Chair: David Clarke
Chief Executive: Robert Smith

Melin Homes Ltd
Ty'r Efail, Lower Mill Field,
Pontypool, Torfaen NP4 0XJ
☎ (0845) 310 1102
Email: enquiries@melinhomes.co.uk
www.melinhomes.co.uk
Chair: Dorian Jones
Chief Executive: Mark Gardner

Merthyr Tydfil Housing Association Ltd
11-12 Lower High St, Merthyr Tydfil CF47 8EB
☎ (01685) 352800 ◫ (01685) 352801
Email: mtha@mtha.org.uk
www.mtha.org.uk
Chair: Keith Fletcher
Chief Executive: Karen Dusgate

Merthyr Valleys Homes Ltd
Martin Evans House, Riverside Court,
Avenue De Clichy, Merthyr Tydfil CF47 8LD
☎ (01685) 727878 or freephone 0800 085 7843
Email: info@mvhomes.org.uk
mvhomes.org.uk
Chief Executive: Mike Owen

Mid Wales Housing Association Ltd
Tŷ Canol House, Ffordd Croesawdy,
Newtown, Powys SY16 1AL
☎ (0300) 111 3030
🖷 (0300) 111 3031
Email: info@mid-walesha.co.uk
www.mid-walesha.co.uk
Chair: Nick Hoskins
Chief Executive: Shane Perkins

Monmouthshire Housing Association Ltd
Nant-Y-Pia House, Mamhilad Technology Park,
Mamhilad, Monmouthshire NP4 0JJ
☎ (0845) 677 2277 or (01495) 761100
www.monmouthshirehousing.co.uk
Chair: Judith Langmead
Chief Executive: John Keegan

Newydd Housing Association
Tŷ Cadarn, 5 Village Way,
Tongwynlais, Cardiff CF15 7NE
☎ (0303) 040 1998
🖷 (0870) 242 0674
Email: enquiries@newydd.co.uk
www.newydd.co.uk
Chair: Gail Lancaster
Chief Executive: Paul Roberts

North Wales Housing Association Ltd
Plas Blodwel, Broad St,
Llandudno Junction, Conwy LL31 9HL
☎ (01492) 572727
🖷 (01492) 572202
Email: customerservices@nwha.org.uk
www.nwha.org.uk
Chair: Peter Gibson
Chief Executive: Paul Diggory

Pembrokeshire Housing Association Ltd
Meyler House, St Thomas' Green,
Haverfordwest, Pembrokeshire SA61 1QP
☎ (01437) 763688 🖷 (01437) 763997
Email: pembshousing@pembs-ha.co.uk
www.pembs-ha.co.uk
Chair: Brian Charles
Chief Executive: Peter Maggs

Pennaf Housing Group
72 Ffordd William Morgan, St Asaph
Business Park, St Asaph, Denbighshire LL17 0JD
☎ (01745) 538393 🖷 (01745) 538392
Email: enquiries@pennaf.co.uk
www.pennaf.co.uk
Chair: Roger M Waters
Chief Executive: Graham Worthington

Polish Housing Society Ltd
Penrhos Home, Pwllheli, Gwynedd LL53 7HN
☎ (01758) 612731
🖷 (01758) 701418
Email: phs@btconnect.com
www.phsltd.org
Chair: Czeslaw Maryszczak
Director: Edward Hryniewiecki

RCT Homes Ltd
Cartrefi RCT
Tŷ Pennant, Mill St,
Pontypridd CF37 2SW
☎ (08453) 14141
Email: enquiries@rcthomes.co.uk
www.rcthomes.co.uk
Chair: Stella Wheeler
Chief Executive: Andrew Lycett

Reach (Supported Living) Ltd
11 Devon Place, Newport NP20 4NP
☎ (01633) 679899
Email: wendy.wilmott@reach-support.co.uk
www.reach-support.co.uk
Chair: Haydn Jones
Corporate Director: Judith North

Rhondda Housing Association Ltd
9 Compton Rd, Tonypandy,
Rhondda Cynon Taf CF40 1BE
☎ (01443) 424200
Email: enquiries@rhondda.org
www.rhondda.org
Chair: John Andrews
Chief Executive: Lesley Davies

Seren Group Ltd
Exchange House, The Old Post Office,
High St, Newport NP20 1AA
☎ (01633) 233863
Email: contact@seren-group.co.uk
www.seren-group.co.uk
Chair: Jonathon Davies
Group Chief Executive: Amanda Davies

Taff Housing Association Ltd
Alexandra House, 307-315 Cowbridge Rd East,
Canton, Cardiff CF5 1JD
☎ (029) 2025 9100
0800 121 6064 (Freephone)
🖷 (029) 2025 9199
www.taffhousing.co.uk
Chair: Jane Pagler
Chief Executive: Elaine Ballard

Tai Ceredigion Cyf
Unit 4, Pont Steffan Business Park,
Station Terrace, Lampeter,
Ceredigion SA48 7HH
☎ (0345) 606 7654
Email: post@taiceredigion.org.uk
www.taiceredigion.org.uk
Chief Executive: Steve Jones

United Welsh Housing Association Ltd
Y Borth, 13 Beddau Way,
Caerphilly CF83 2AX
☎ (029) 2085 8100
Freephone: 0800 294 0195
▣ (029) 2085 8110
Email: tellmemore@uwha.co.uk
www.uwha.co.uk
Chair: Ian Gilbert
Chief Executive: Anthony Whittaker

United Welsh Housing Association Ltd
Walters Buildings,
Clarence Road,
Butetown, Cardiff CF10 5UU
☎ (029) 2085 8100
Freephone: (0800) 294 0195
▣ (029) 2089 5500
Email: tellmemore@uwha.co.uk
www.uwha.co.uk
Chair: Ian Gilbert
Chief Executive: Anthony Whittaker

Valleys to Coast Housing
No 1 Court Rd, Nolton Court
Bridgend CF31 1BE
☎ (0300) 123 2100
Email: info@v2c.org.uk
www.v2c.org.uk
Chair: Roger Thomas
Chief Executive: Stephen Cook

Wales & West Housing Association Ltd
3 Alexandra Gate, Ffordd Pengam,
Tremorfa, Cardiff CF24 2UD
☎ (0800) 052 2526
Minicom: (0800) 052 5205
▣ (029) 2041 5380
Email: contact@wwha.co.uk
www.wwha.net
Chair: Ivor Gittens
Chief Executive: Anne Hinchey

Media: Film & Television

BAFTA Cymru
Chapter Arts Centre, Market Rd,
Canton, Cardiff CF5 1QE
☎ (029) 2022 3898
▣ (029) 2066 4189
Email: fional@bafta.org
www.bafta-cymru.org.uk
Director: Allison Dowzell
Events Co-ordinator: Fiona Lynch

BBC Cymru Wales
Broadcasting House, Llandaff,
Cardiff CF5 2YQ
☎ (029) 2032 2000
▣ (029) 2032 2280
Email: feedback.wales@bbc.co.uk
www.bbc.co.uk/wales
Director: Rhodri Talfan Davies
National Trustee for Wales: Elan Closs Stephens CBE

BBC Wales Aberystwyth
Parry Williams Building,
Prifysgol Aberystwyth University,
Penglais Campus,
Aberystwyth SY23 3AJ
☎ (01970) 833972
▣ (01970) 833963
Email: newsgathering.wales@bbc.co.uk
Regional Reporter (Welsh lang) John Meredith
Regional Reporter (English lang): Carl Yapp

BBC Cymru Wales
Bryn Meirion, Bangor, Gwynedd LL57 2BY
☎ (01248) 370880
Email: w.rees@bbc.co.uk
northnews@bbc.co.uk irfon.jones@bbc.co.uk
bbc.co.uk/cymru
bbc.co.uk/walesnews
bbc.co.uk/radiocymru
Head of Centre: Wendy Rees
News Editor: Bethan Williams
Assistant Editor Radio Cymru: Irfon Jones

BBC Wales Carmarthen
Old School House, Priory Rd,
Carmarthen SA31 1NE
☎ (01267) 225722 ☒ (01267) 223060
Contact: Aled Scourfield

BBC Wales Swansea
Broadcasting House,
32 Alexandra Rd, Swansea SA1 5DT
☎ (01792) 463722/468819 ☒ (01792) 468194

BBC Cymru Wales Wrexham
Creative Industries Building,
Glyndwr University, Mold Road,
Wrexham LL11 2AW
☎ (01978) 221100
Email: cath.steward@bbc.co.uk
www.bbc.co.uk/wales/radiowales
Contact: Cath Steward

Boom Talent
218 Penarth Rd, Cardiff CF11 8NN
☎ (029) 2067 1523 ☒ (029) 2055 0551
Email: sioned.james@boomerang.co.uk
www.boomtalent.co.uk
Sioned James

Cyfle Cyf.
33-35 West Bute Street,
Cardiff Bay, Cardiff CF10 5LH
☎ (029) 2046 5533 ☒ (029) 2046 3344
Email: caerdydd@cyfle.co.uk
www.cyfle.co.uk
Training & Marketing Officer: Rhian Iolo Brewster

Also at:

Galeri 13, Victoria Dock, Caernarfon,
Gwynedd LL55 1SQ
☎ (01286) 668003
Email: caernarfon@cyfle.co.uk
www.cyfle.co.uk
Chief Executive: Iona Williams
Finance Manager: Ian Wyn Roberts

Cwmni Pawb
W0007 Tŷ Oldfield, Llantrisant Rd,
Llandaff, Cardiff CF5 2YQ
☎ (029) 2032 2582
Email: sian.gale@pawb.org
Cyfarwyddwraig: Siân Gale

The Film Agency for Wales
Suite 7, 33-35 West Bute St, Cardiff CF10 5LH
☎ (029) 2046 7480 ☒ (029) 2046 7481
Email: enquiries@filmagencywales.com
www.filmagencywales.com
Chair: Peter Edwards
Chief Executive: Pauline Burt

Gwifren Gwylwyr S4C Viewers' Hotline
Parc Tŷ Glas, Llanishen,
Caerdydd/Cardiff CF14 5DU
☎ (0870) 6004141
Minicom: 01766 514410
Email: gwifren@s4c.co.uk/hotline@s4c.co.uk
www.s4c.co.uk

International Film School Wales
Ysgol Ffilm Ryngwladol Cymru
Newport School of Art,
Media & Design, University of Wales,
Newport, Caerleon Campus,
PO Box 179, Newport NP18 3YG
☎ (01633) 432210
☒ (01633) 432610
Email: post@ifsw.newport.ac.uk
www.amd.newport.ac.uk
Head of IFSW: Humphry Trevelyan

ITN
The Wales and West of England Bureau, Media Centre,
Culverhouse Cross, Cardiff CF5 6XJ
☎ ITV Newsdesk: (029) 2059 0764
London Newsdesk: (020) 74304551
Mobile: 07753 775 797
☒ (029) 2059 0118
Email: emily.morgan@itn.co.uk
Wales & West Correspondents: Emily Morgan

ITV Wales
The Television Centre,
Culverhouse Cross, Cardiff CF5 6XJ
☎ (0844) 8810 100 ☒ (029) 2059 7183
Email: phil.henfrey@itvwales.com
huw.rossiter@itvwales.com
www.itv.com/wales
Head of News & Programmes, ITV Wales: Phil Henfrey
Public Affairs Manager: Huw Rossiter

Royal Mail

ITV Wales News
Celtic Business Centres, Plas Eirias, Heritage Gate,
Abergele Rd, Colwyn Bay LL29 8BW
☎ (01492) 513888
🖷 (01492) 513388
Email: news@itvwales.com
ian.lang@itvwales.com
carole.green@itvwales.com
www.itvwales.com
North Wales Reporters: Ian Lang, Carole Green

ITV Wales News
Ground Floor, St David's House,
New Church St, Newtown, Powys SY16 1RB
☎ (01686) 623381
🖷 (01686) 624816
Email: news@itvwales.com
rob.shelley@itvwales.com
www.itvwales.com
Mid Wales Reporter: Rob Shelley

ITV Wales News
Top Floor, 19-20 Lammas St,
Carmarthen SA31 3AL
☎ (01267) 236806 🖷 (01267) 238228
Email: news@itvwales.com
www.itvwales.com

National Screen & Sound Archive of Wales
Archif Genedlaethol Sgrin a Sain Cymru
The National Library of Wales, Penglais,
Aberystwyth SY23 3BU
☎ (01970) 632828
🖷 (01970) 632544
Email: English: nssaw@llgc.org.uk
Welsh: agssc@llgc.org.uk
www.archif.com
Manager: Dafydd Pritchard
Access and Events: Anwen Jones
Administration: Catrin Jenkins, Elen Jones

S4C Sianel Pedwar Cymru
Parc Tŷ Glas, Llanishen, Cardiff CF14 5DU
☎ (029) 2074 7444
🖷 (029) 2075 4444
Email: s4c@s4c.co.uk
www.s4c.co.uk
Chair: Huw Jones
Chief Executive: Ian Jones

S4C Sianel Pedwar Cymru
Unit 1, Victoria Dock, Caernarfon LL55 1TH
Email: s4c@s4c.co.uk
www.s4c.co.uk

Skillset Cymru
33-35 West Bute St, Cardiff CF10 5LH
☎ (029) 2045 2828
🖷 (029) 2048 9539
Email: cymru@skillset.org
www.skillset.org
Director: Gwawr Hughes

TAC - Welsh Independent Producers
Suite 17 Bay Chambers,
West Bute Street,
Caerdydd CF10 5BB
☎ (029) 2049 0051
www.teledwyr.com
Chair: Iestyn Garlick

Wales Screen Commission
Comisiwn Sgrîn Cymru
Mid Wales Office, Welsh Government,
Rhodfa Padarn, Llanbadarn Fawr,
Aberyswyth SY23 3UR
☎ (0300) 062 2414
Email: mike.wallwork@wales.gsi.gov.uk
www.walesscreencommission.co.uk
Mike Wallwork

Also at:

North Wales Office, Room 223,
Welsh Government Building,
Penrallt, Caernarfon LL55 1EP
☎ (01286) 662 341
Email: arwyn.williams31@wales.gsi.gov.uk
www.walesscreencommission.co.uk
Arwyn Williams

South Wales Office,
Welsh Government,
Creative Sector,
1st Floor North,
QED Treforest Ind. Est.
Pontypridd CF37 5YR
☎ (0300) 061 5634
Email: penny@walesscreencommission.co.uk
www.walesscreencommission.com
Penny Skuse

Video Wales
2 Bro Nant, Church Road,
Pentyrch, Cardiff CF15 9QG
☎ (029) 2089 0311
Email: info@videowales.com
www.videowales.com
Director: Steve Benbow

Welsh Independent TV & Film Producers

MEDIA: WELSH IND TV & FILM

Aden
6 Raleigh Walk, Brigantine Place, Cardiff CF10 4LN
☎ (029) 2046 5600 📠 (029) 2046 5601
Email: ymhol@cynyrchiadauaden.com
www.aden.co
John Gwyn, Emma Ford

Al Fresco
218 Penarth Rd, Caerdydd CF11 8NN
☎ (029) 2055 0620
Email: alfresco@alfrescotv.co.uk
www.boomerang.co.uk
Ronw Protheroe, Liz Lloyd Griffiths

Antena
Cardiff Office: Media Centre,
Culverhouse Cross, Cardiff CF5 6XJ
☎ (029) 2059 0363
Email: caerdydd@antena.co.uk
www.antena.co.uk
Iestyn Garlick

Also at:

Caernarfon Office: Uned 2,
Stad Ddiwidianol Cibyn,
Caernarfon, Gwynedd LL55 2BD
☎ (01286) 662200
Email: swyddfa@antena.co.uk
www.antena.co.uk
Iestyn Garlick

Atsain
26-28 Dalcross St, Roath, Cardiff CF24 4SD
☎ (029) 2065 8089 📠 (029) 2045 1151
Email: patsain@hotmail.com

Bang Post Production Ltd
Unit M105, Cardiff Bay Business Park,
Titan Rd, Ocean Park, Cardiff CF24 5EJ
☎ (029) 2045 3344 📠 (029) 2049 2622
Email: doug@bangpostproduction.com
www.bangpostproduction.com
Paul McFadden / Doug Sinclair

Beca TV
Glasfryn, Pwlllheli, Gwynedd LL53 6RD
☎ (01766) 819155 Mobile: 07702 876754
Email: helen@beca-tv.com
www.beca-tv.com
Helen Williams-Ellis

Blue Egg Productions Ltd
Pen y Wyrlod, Llanvetherine,
Abergavenny, Monmouthshire NP7 8RG
☎ (01873) 851885
Mobile: 07720 039936
Email: info@blueeggproductions.co.uk
www.blueeggproductions.co.uk
Director: Sarah Dickins

Boomerang
218 Penarth Rd, Cardiff CF11 8NN
☎ (029) 2055 0550 📠 (029) 2055 0551
Email: enquiries@boomerang.co.uk
www.boomerang.co.uk
Huw Eurig Davies, Dafydd Felix Richards,
Nia Thomas

Bwcibo Cyf
Caeredin Villa, Heol Gorrig,
Llandysul, Ceredigion SA44 4LD
☎ 07968501260
Email: owain@bwcibo.com
www.bwcibo.com
Owain Llŷr

Calon Ltd
Phoenix Buildings, 3 Mount Stuart Sq,
Butetown, Cardiff CF10 5EE
☎ (029) 2048 8400 📠 (029) 2048 5962
Email: enquiries@calon.tv

Cartwn Cymru
12 Queen's Rd, Mumbles, Swansea SA3 4AN
☎ 07771 640 400
Email: production@cartwn-cymru.com
Naomi Jones

Cynhyrchiadau Ceidiog Creations
92 Kings Rd, Cardiff CF11 9DD
Email: nia@ceidiog.com
Nia Ceidiog, Ceidiog Hughes

Cinetig
Chapter Arts Centre, Market Rd,
Treganna, Cardiff CF5 1QE
☎ (029) 2038 4802
Email: info@cinetig.co.uk
www.cinetig.co.uk
Gerald Conn

Cwmni Da
Cae Llenor, Lôn Parc,
Caernarfon, Gwynedd LL55 2HH
☎ (01286) 685300 ☐ (01286) 685301
Email: post@cwmnida.tv
www.cwmnida.tv/
Dylan Huws, Ifor ap Glyn, Neville Hughes

Also at:

Hen Ysgol Aberpwll, Ffordd Bangor,
Y Felinheli, Gwynedd LL56 4JS
☎ (01248) 671167 ☐ (01248) 671172
Email: post@cwmnida.tv
www.cwmnida.tv/

Dinamo Productions Ltd
Uned A3 Rizla House, Severn Rd, Treforest
Industrial Estate, Pontypridd CF37 5SP
☎ (029) 2047 0480
Email: info@dinamo.co.uk
www.dinamo.co.uk
Aron Rhys Evans

Dream Team Television
Bron y Garth, Harlech LL46 2SS
☎ (01766) 780944
Email: ron@dreamteamtv.co.uk
www.dreamteamtv.co.uk
Ron Isles

Element Productions
5th Floor, 11-12 Mount Stuart Square,
Cardiff Bay CF10 5EE
☎ (029) 2047 2122 ☐ (029) 2047 2230
Email: office@elementproductions.co.uk
www.elementproductions.co.uk
Managing Director/Executive Producer:
Richard Edwards

Fflic
59 Sgwâr Mount Stuart, Cardiff CF10 5LR
☎ (029) 2040 9000 ☐ (029) 2040 9001
Email: gwenda-griffith@fflic.com
Gwenda Griffith

Fiction Factory
1-2 Mount Stuart Square, Cardiff Bay CF10 5EE
☎ (029) 2030 0320 ☐ (029) 2030 0321
Email: post@fictionfactoryfilms.com
www.fictionfactoryfilms.com
Creative Director: Ed Thomas

Fresh Catch Films
33 Syr David's Ave, Cardiff CF5 1GH
☎ (029) 2037 8795 ☐ (029) 2037 8795
Email: sian.roderick@virgin.net
Sian Roderick

Genesis Media
114 Whitchurch Rd, Cardiff CF14 3LY
☎ (029) 2066 6007
Email: info@genesis-media.co.uk
www.genesis-media.co.uk
Alan Torjussen

Gorilla TV
20 Cathedral Rd, Cardiff CF11 9LJ
☎ (029) 2039 9800 ☐ (029) 2039 9700
Email: bookings@gorillagroup.tv
www.gorillagroup.tv
Facilities Manager: Eve Moss

Green Bay Media
Talbot Studios, 1 Talbot St, Cardiff CF11 9BW
☎ (029) 2064 2370 ☐ (029) 2023 2210
Email: post@green-bay.tv
www.green-bay.tv
Creative Directors: John Geraint, Phil George

Griffilms
Unit 5, Doc Fictoria, Caernarfon, Gwynedd LL55 1TH
☎ (01286) 676678 ☐ (01286) 676577
Email: mail@griffilms.com
www.griffilms.com
Hywel Griffith, Dylan Jones

Gwylan
62a High Street, Cowbridge,
Bro Morgannwg CF71 7AH
☎ (01446) 771345
Email: emyr@gwylan.com
Emyr Morgan Evans

Hiraethog
Blwch / PO Box 36, Rhuthun LL15 1ZH
☎ (01824) 707040; 07887 990210 (mobile)
Email: medwen@hiraethog.tv
Medwen Roberts

Indus Films
20 Cathedral Rd, Cardiff CF11 9LJ
☎ (029) 2039 9555 ☐ (029) 2039 9777
Email: info@indusfilms.com
www.indusfilms.com
Steve Robinson

ITV Wales
The Television Centre,
Culverhouse Cross, Cardiff CF5 6XJ
☎ (0844) 8810 100 🖷 (029) 2059 7183
Email: phil.henfrey@itvwales.com
huw.rossiter@itvwales.com
www.itv.com/wales
Head of News & Programmes, ITV Wales: Phil Henfrey
Public Affairs Manager: Huw Rossiter

K2 Television Production
22 Meadow Hill, Church Village,
Pontypridd, RCT CF38 1RX
☎ (01443) 218181
Email: info@k2television.co.uk
www.k2television.co.uk

Orchard Media and Events Group Ltd
Television Centre, Culverhouse Cross,
Cardiff CF5 6XJ
☎ (029) 2059 0334
🖷 (029) 2059 0335
Email: matt@thinkorchard.com /
tim@thinkorchard.com
www.thinkorchard.com
Matt Wordley, Tim Powell

P.A.N.
7 Tanygraig Road, Llwynhendy,
Llanelli SA14 9LF
☎ (01554) 753638 🖷 (01554) 753638
Email: eirwenhopkins@aol.com
Eirwen Hopkins

P.O.P. 1
Canolfan Agenda, Stryd y Parc,
Llanelli SA15 3YE
☎ (01554) 880880
Email: dafydd.rhys@tinopolis.com

Pixel Foundry & Culture Colony
Creative Unit 08, Aberystwyth Arts Centre,
Aberystwyth University, Aberystwyth SY23 3DE
☎ (01654) 761461; Mobile 07713 604341
Email: pete@pixelfoundry.co.uk
www.pixelfoundry.co.uk
Managing Director: Pete Telfer

Presentable Ltd
46 Cardiff Rd, Llandaff, Cardiff CF5 2DT
☎ (029) 2057 5729 🖷 (029) 2057 5605
Email: rebecca.candy@presentable.co.uk
www.presentable.co.uk
Managing Director: Jamie Hall
Head of Production: Chris Cadenne

Rondo Media
60 Severn Grove, Pontcanna, Cardiff CF11 9EP
☎ (029) 2022 3456 🖷 (029) 2037 7746
Email: rondo@rondomedia.co.uk
www.rondomedia.co.uk
Gareth Williams, Robin Evans, Susan Waters,
Dudley Newbery, Hefin Owen, Emyr Davies,
Eryl Huw Phillips

Also at:

Lôn Cae Ffynnon, Cibyn,
Caernarfon LL55 2BD
☎ (01286) 675722
Email: rondo@rondomedia.co.uk
www.rondomedia.co.uk
Gareth Williams, Robin Evans, Susan Waters,
Dudley Newbery, Hefin Owen, Emyr Davies,
Eryl Huw Phillips

Satellite Production Ltd
17 Cawnpore St, Penarth,
Vale of Glamorgan CF64 2JU
☎ Mob: 07720 836616
Email: humphj@hotmail.com
Humphrey James

Sianco
Pen-y-graig, Llanfaglan,
Caernarfon, Gwynedd LL54 5RF
☎ (01286) 676100
Email: sian@sianco.tv
Sian Teifi

Sports Media Services
Pencoed Technology Centre, Sony Digital
Technium, Pencoed Technology Park,
Pencoed CF35 5HZ
☎ (01656) 776030 / (0845) 4679600
Email: enquiries@livecastwales.co.uk
www.livecastwales.co.uk
Russell Isaac, Keith Williams

Stiwdio Capel Mawr
Melin Crawia, Llanrug,
Caernarfon, Gwynedd LL55 2BB
☎ (01286) 671509

Teledu Apollo
21 Allensbank Rd, Cardiff CF14 3PN
☎ (029) 2025 1811 🖷 (029) 2025 1821
Email: info@teleduapollo.tv

Teledu Avanti
36 Cardiff Rd, Llandaff, Cardiff CF5 2DR
☎ (029) 2056 6729
Email: info@avantimedia.tv

Teledu Solo
Media Centre, Culverhouse Cross, Cardiff CF5 6XJ
☎ (029) 2059 0568 🖷 (029) 2059 7183
Email: solotv1@aol.com
Will Davies

Teledu Telesgôp
Ethos, Kings Rd, Swansea SA1 8AS
☎ (01792) 824567 🖷 (01792) 641006
Email: info@telesgop.co.uk
www.telesgop.co.uk
Managing Director: Elin Rhys

Tinopolis Television
Park St, Llanelli,
Carmarthenshire SA15 3YE
☎ (01554) 880880 🖷 (01554) 880881
Email: info@tinopolis.com
www.tinopolis.com
Executive Director: Angharad Mair

Tracrecord Cyf
10 River View Court, Llandaff, Cardiff CF5 2QJ
☎ (029) 2055 5055 Mob: 07720009902
Email: eiry@tracrecord.co.uk
www.tracrecord.com
Eiry Palfrey

Truth Department Ltd
Y Gyfnewidfa Lo, Sgwâr Mount Stuart, Caerdydd CF10 5EB
☎ (029) 2049 6862
Email: dewi@truthdepartment.com
www.truthdepartment.com
Dewi Gregory

Unigryw
PO Box 183, Aberystwyth, Ceredigion SY23 1AS
☎ (01970) 627000
Email: post@unigryw.com
www.unigryw.com

Zip TV
109 Heol Isaf, Radyr, Cardiff CF15 8DW
☎ (029) 2021 0889
Email: mary.ziptv@ntlworld.com
richard.ziptv@ntlworld.com
www.ziptvmedia.com
Contact: Mary Simmonds or Richard Pawelko

Greenfield Media
Y Ganolfan Ddarlledu, Croes Cwrlwys,
Caerdydd CF5 6XJ
☎ (029) 2059 0334 🖷 (029) 2059 0335
Email: bethan@greenfieldmedia.com
www.greenfieldmedia.com
Bethan Mair Tame

Media: Radio

106.3 Bridge FM
PO Box 1063 , Bridgend CF35 6WY
☎ (029) 2141 4100
Email: Studio@bridge.fm
www.bridge.fm
Programme Director: Andy Griffiths

Bay Radio
20 Llan Coed House, Llandarcy SA10 6FG
☎ (01792) 716200 Newsroom (029) 2141 4120
Studio: (01792) 716 100
Email: studio@baywales.com
www.baywales.com
News Editor: Mathew Williams

BBC Radio Cymru (Cardiff)
Broadcasting House, Llandaff, Cardiff CF5 2YQ
☎ (029) 2032 2787 🖷 (029) 2055 5960
Email: radio.cymru@bbc.co.uk
www.bbc.co.uk/cymru/radio

BBC Radio Wales
Broadcasting House, Llandaff, Cardiff CF5 2YQ
☎ (03700) 100 110
Email: radio.wales@bbc.co.uk
www.bbc.co.uk/radiowales

Calon FM 105
Glyndwr University,
Plas Coch Campus,
Mold Rd, Wrexham LL11 2AW
☎ (01978) 293393
Email: info@calonfm.com
www.calonfm.com
General Manager: Mike Wright
Station Editors: Katherine Wade, Amy Wright

Gold (South Wales)
Red Dragon Centre,
Hemingway Rd,
Cardiff CF10 4DJ
☎ (029) 2094 2940
Email: news@reddragonfm.com
www.mygoldmusic.co.uk
News Editor: Vicky Etchells

Gold North Wales & Chester
The Studios, Mold Rd,
Gwersyllt, Wrexham LL11 4AF
☎ (01978) 722230 🖷 (01978) 722239
www.mygoldmusic.co.uk
News Editor: Philip Topham

MEDIA: RADIO

GTFM
Pinewood Studios, Pinewood Ave,
Rhydyfelin, Pontypridd CF37 5EA
☎ (01443) 406111 📠 (01443) 492744
Email: news@gtfm.co.uk mail@gtfm.co.uk
www.gtfm.co.uk
Station Manager: Terry Mann

Heart 103 Cymru
Llys y Dderwen, Parc Menai, Bangor LL57 4BN
☎ (01248) 673400
Email: paul.holmes@heart.co.uk
www.heartcymru.co.uk
Programme Controller: Paul Holmes

Heart 103.4 North West and Wales
The Studios, Mold Rd, Gwersyllt, Wrexham LL11 4AF
☎ (01978) 722200
Email: paul.holmes@heart.co.uk
www.heart.co.uk/wrexham
Programme Controller: Paul Holmes
Senior Broadcast Journalists:
Philip Topham, Mair Thomas

Heart 96.3
The Studios, Mold Rd, Gwersyllt,
Wrexham LL11 4AF
☎ (01978) 722200
Email: paul.holmes@heart.co.uk
www.heartwalescoast.co.uk/
Programme Controller: Paul Holmes

Nation Radio
The Media Centre, Culverhouse Cross,
Cardiff CF5 6XJ
☎ (029) 2141 4100 📠 (029) 2141 4101
Email: enquiries@nationwales.com
www.nationwales.com
Head of News: Mathew Williams

Cwmni Pawb
W0007 Tŷ Oldfield, Llantrisant Rd,
Llandaff, Cardiff CF5 2YQ
☎ (029) 2032 2582
Email: sian.gale@pawb.org
Cyfarwyddwraig: Siân Gale

Radio Cardiff 98.7 FM
Unit 5, Hayes Building, Curran Rd,
Butetown, Cardiff CF10 5DF
☎ (029) 2023 5664 📠 (029) 2022 2302
Email: shouts@radiocardiff.org
Office Administrator: Linda Bryan

Radio Carmarthenshire & Scarlet 97.1 FM
PO Box 971, Llanelli, Carms SA15 1YH
☎ (01834) 862021
Email: news@radiocarmarthenshire.com
www.radiocarmarthenshire.com
Group Managing Director: Martin Mumford

Radio Ceredigion
Merlin House, Parc Merlin, Glan Yr Afon
Industrial Estate, Aberystwyth SY23 3FF
☎ (01970) 626991 (Office) 229113 (Studio)
(0845) 890 2000 (Newsroom)
📠 (01970) 626992
Email: news@radioceredigion.co.uk
www.radioceredigion.co.uk
Senior Broadcast Journalist: Matthew Williams

Radio Hafren
The Studios, The Park, Newtown, Powys SY16 2NZ
☎ (01686) 623555 📠 (01686) 623666
Email: studio@radiohafren.co.uk
www.radiohafren.co.uk

Radio Pembrokeshire 102.5 FM
14 Old School Estate, Station Rd,
Narberth SA67 7DU
☎ (01834) 861071 📠 (01834) 861524
Email: news@radiopembrokeshire.com
www.radiopembrokeshire.com
News: Ceri Coleman

Real Radio Wales
Unit 1, Tŷ-Nant Court,
Morganstown, Cardiff CF15 8LW
☎ (029) 2031 5100 📠 (029) 2031 5150
Email: news@realradio.co.uk
www.realradiowales.co.uk
Station Director: Tony Dowling
Programme Director: Gareth Setter

Swansea Sound/ The Wave 96.4 FM
Victoria Rd, Gowerton, Swansea SA4 3AB
☎ (01792) 511964 📠 (01792) 511171
Email: news@swanseasound.co.uk
reception@thewave.co.uk
www.swanseasound.co.uk www.thewave.co.uk
News Editor: Emma Grant

XS FM 97.4 & 107.9
Aquadrome Afan Lido, Hollywood Park,
Princess Margaret Way, Port Talbot SA12 6QW
☎ (01639) 896292
www.xswales.com
Station Manager: Hannah Lewis

Post Brenhinol

Royal Mail

Media: National & Regional Newspapers

Y Cymro
9 Bank Place, Porthmadog, Gwynedd LL49 9AA
☎ (01766) 515514
Email: y-cymro@cambrian-news.co.uk
Editor: Dylan Halliday

Daily Post (Wales)
PO Box 202, Vale Rd, Llandudno Junction LL31 9ZD
☎ (01492) 574452 📠 (01492) 574433
Email: welshnews@dailypost.co.uk
www.dailypost.co.uk
Editor: Allison Gow

Financial Times
Regional Bureau, Somerville House, 20-22
Harborne Rd, Edgbaston, Birmingham B15 3AA
☎ (0121) 454 0922
Email: john.murraybrown@ft.com
John Murray Brown

Metro (Cardiff, Swansea & Newport)
Bristol United Press Ltd, Temple Way, Bristol BS99 7HD
☎ (0117) 934 3728 📠 (0117) 934 3729
Email: news.cardiff@ukmetro.co.uk
clare.ogden@ukmetro.co.uk
www.metro.co.uk
Regional Arts Editor: Clare Ogden

**Ninnau - The North American Welsh
Newspaper Incorporating Y Drych**
Ninnau Publications Inc, 11 Post Terrace,
Basking Ridge, NJ 07920 USA
☎ (1) 908 766 4151 📠 (1) 908 221 0744
Email: ninnaupubl@cs.com
www.ninnau.com
Publisher & Executive Editor: Arturo Roberts
Managing Editor: Olga Williams
Design & Production: Mair Roberts

Shropshire Star
Ketley, Telford TF1 5HU
☎ (01952) 242424 📠 (01952) 254605
Email: newsroom@shropshirestar.co.uk
www.shropshirestar.com
Chief Reporter: Anwen Evans

South Wales Echo
6 Park St, Cardiff CF10 1XR
☎ (029) 2022 3333 📠 (029) 2024 3640
Email: newsdesk@mediawales.co.uk
www.walesonline.co.uk
Editor: Tim Gordon

Wales On Sunday
6 Park St, Cardiff CF10 1XR
☎ (029) 2022 3333 📠 (029) 2024 3640
Email: newsdesk@mediawales.co.uk
www.walesonline.co.uk
Editor: Alison Gow

Western Mail
6 Park St, Cardiff CF10 1XR
☎ (029) 2022 3333 📠 (029) 2024 3640
Email: newsdesk@mediawales.co.uk
www.walesonline.co.uk
Editor: Alan Edmunds

Media: Local Newspapers - North Wales

**Bangor & Anglesey Mail, Holyhead
Anglesey Mail**
14 Eastgate Street, Caernarfon, Gwynedd LL55 1AG
☎ (01286) 671111 📠 (01286) 676937
Email: caernarfon.herald@northwalesnews.co.uk
www.theonlinemail.co.uk
Editor: Linda Roberts

Caernarfon & Denbigh Herald
14 Eastgate St, Caernarfon LL55 1AG
☎ (01286) 671111 📠 (01286) 676937
Email: caernarfon.herald@northwalesnews.co.uk
www.caernarfonherald.co.uk
Editor: Linda Roberts

Denbighshire Free Press
Mold Business Park, Wrexham Road, Mold CH7 1XY
☎ (01352) 707707
Email: nic.outterside@nwn.co.uk
www.denbighshirefreepress.co.uk
Editor: Nic Outterside

Y Dydd
9 Bank Place, Porthmadog LL49 9AA
☎ (01766) 515514 📠 (01766) 514738
Email: ydydd@cambrian-news.co.uk
Editor: Iwan Jones

Flintshire Chronicle
Chronicle House, Commonhall St, Chester CH1 2AA
☎ (01244) 821911 ☒ (01244) 830786
Email: chroniclenews@cheshirenews.co.uk
www.flintshirechronicle.co.uk
Editor: Mike Green

Yr Herald Cymraeg
PO Box 202, Vale Rd , Llandudno Junction,
Conwy LL31 9ZD
☎ (01492) 574455 ☒ (01492) 574433
Email: tudur.jones@northwalesnews.co.uk
www.yrherald.co.uk
Editor: Tudur Huws Jones

North Wales Chronicle
302 High St, Bangor LL57 1UL
☎ (01248) 387400 ☒ (01248) 354793
Email: news@northwaleschronicle.co.uk
www.northwaleschronicle.co.uk
Editor: Matt Warner

The North Wales Pioneer
21 Penrhyn Rd, Colwyn Bay LL29 8HY
☎ (01492) 531188 ☒ (01492) 533564
Email: terry.canty@nwn.co.uk
www.northwalespioneer.co.uk
Editorial Manager: Andrew Martin

North Wales Weekly News Series
Vale Rd, Llandudno Junction, Conwy LL31 9SL
☎ (01492) 584321 ☒ (01492) 596498
Email: news.desk@northwalesnews.co.uk
www.northwalesweeklynews.co.uk
Executive Editor: Dan Owen

Rhyl, Prestatyn & Abergele Journal
Accent House, 23 Kinmel St,
Rhyl, Denbighshire LL18 1AH
☎ (01745) 357500 ☒ (01745) 343510
Email: editor@rhyljournal.co.uk
www.rhyljournal.co.uk
Deputy Editor: Terry Canty

The Leader (Flintshire & Wrexham editions)
Mold Business Park, Wrexham Rd, Mold CH7 1XY
☎ (01352) 707707 ☒ (01352) 752180
Email: editor@leaderlive.co.uk
www.leaderlive.co.uk
Editor-in-chief: Barrie Jones

Media: Local Newspapers - Mid & West Wales

Brecon & Radnor Express
11 The Bulwark, Brecon, Powys LD3 7AE
☎ (01874) 610111 ☒ (01874) 624097
Email: theeditor@brecon-radnor.co.uk
www.brecon-radnor-today.co.uk
Editor: Julie Chappell

Cambrian News
7 Science Park, Aberystwyth SY23 3AH
☎ (01970) 615000 ☒ (01970) 611925
Email: edit@cambrian-news.co.uk
www.cambrian-news.co.uk
Editor: Beverly Thomas

Carmarthen Journal
18 King St, Carmarthen SA31 1BN
☎ (01267) 227222 ☒ (01267) 227229
Email: cathryn.ings@swwmedia.co.uk
www.thisissouthwales.co.uk
Editor: Cathryn Ings

County Echo & St Davids City Chronicle
Parc Y Shwt, Fishguard SA65 9AP
☎ (01348) 874445 ☒ (01348) 873651
Email: edit@countyecho.co.uk
www.fishguard-today.co.uk
Editor: Beverly Thomas

Llanelli Star Series
11 Cowell St, Llanelli SA15 1UU
☎ (01554) 745320 ☒ (01554) 745335
Email: bede.macgowan@swwmedia.co.uk
www.thisissouthwales.co.uk
Editor: Bede MacGowan

Mid Wales Journal
Marina Gallery, Middleton St,
Llandrindod Wells, Powys LD1 5ET
☎ (01597) 828060 ☒ (01597) 828069
Email: mary.queally@Shropshirestar.co.uk
Editor: Mary Queally

Milford & West Wales Mercury
Press Buildings, Old Hakin Rd,
Merlins Bridge, Haverfordwest SA61 1XF
☎ (01437) 763133 🖷 (01437) 760482
Email: holly.robinson@westerntelegraph.co.uk
Editor: Holly Robinson

Oswestry & Border Chronicle
14 Salop Rd, Oswestry SY11 7NU
☎ (01691) 668094
Email: news@oswestrychronicle.co.uk
www.oswestrychronicle.com
Associate Editor: Graham Breeze

Powys County Times and Express
11c Broad St, Welshpool, Powys SY21 7LE
☎ (01938) 553354 🖷 (01938) 554667
Email: news@countytimes.co.uk
www.countytimes.co.uk
Editor: Nick Knight
Chief Reporter: Richard Jones
Chief Photographer: Phil Blagg
Sports Editor: Gavin Grosvenor

South Wales Guardian Series
37 Quay St, Ammanford, Carmarthenshire SA18 3BS
☎ (01269) 592781 🖷 (01269) 591020
Email: mike.lewis@southwalesguardian.co.uk
www.southwalesguardian.co.uk
Editor: Mike Lewis

Tenby Observer Series
Tindle House, Warren St, Tenby, Pembs SA70 7JY
☎ (01834) 843262 🖷 (01834) 844774
Email: editor@thetenbyobserver.co.uk
www.tenby-today.co.uk
Editor: Neil Dickinson

Tivy-Side Advertiser
39 St Mary St, Cardigan SA43 1EU
☎ (01239) 614343 🖷 (01239) 615386
Email: sue.lewis@gwent-wales.co.uk
www.tivysideadvertiser.co.uk
Editor: Sue Lewis

Western Telegraph Series
Merlins Bridge, Old Hakin Rd,
Haverfordwest SA61 1XF
☎ (01437) 763133 🖷 (01437) 760482
Email: holly.robinson@westerntelegraph.co.uk
www.westerntelegraph.co.uk
Editor: Holly Robinson

Media: Local Newspapers - South Wales

Abergavenny Chronicle
Tindle House, 13 Nevill St, Abergavenny NP7 5AA
☎ (01873) 852187 🖷 (01873) 857677
Email: liz@tindlenews.co.uk
www.abergavenny-chronicle-today.co.uk
Editorial Manager: Liz Davies

Barry & District News
156 Holton Rd, Barry CF63 4TY
☎ (01446) 733456 🖷 (01446) 732719
Email: barrynews@barryanddistrictnews.co.uk
www.barryanddistrictnews.co.uk
Editor: Shira Valek

Caerphilly Campaign Series
Cardiff Rd, Maesglas, Newport NP20 3QN
☎ (01633) 810000 🖷 (01633) 777202
Email: charles.booth@gwent-wales.co.uk
www.campaignseries.co.uk
Campaign Series Editor: Charles Booth

Cardiff & South Wales Advertiser
Mackintosh House, 136 Newport Rd, Cardiff CF24 1DJ
☎ (029) 2030 3900 🖷 (029) 2040 2744
Email: info@cardiffandsouthwalesadvertiser.com
www.cardiffandsouthwalesadvertiser.com
General Manager/Editor: David Hynes
Sales Director: Miss Cheryl Willis

The Courier Series (Neath & Port Talbot)
PO Box 14, Adelaide St, Swansea SA1 1QT
☎ (01792) 510000 🖷 (01792) 469665
www.thisissouthwales.com
News Editor: Chris Davies

Cynon Valley Leader
52-53 Glebland Street, Merthyr Tydfil CF14 8AT
☎ (01685) 789230 🖷 (01685) 789232
Email: cynon.valley.leader@walesonline.co.uk
www.walesonline.co.uk
Editor: Gary Marsh

The Free Press Newspaper Series
3 Portland Buildings,
Commercial St, Pontypool NP4 6JS
☎ (01495) 751751 ☐ (01495) 751911
Email: pontypoolnews@gwent-wales.co.uk
Managing Editor: Nicole Garnon
Reporter: Leanne Fender

Glamorgan Gazette Series
2 Brackla St , Bridgend CF31 1DD
☎ (01656) 349300 ☐ (029) 2024 3919
Email: glamorgan.gazette@walesonline.co.uk
www.walesonline.co.uk
Editor: Sandra Loy

Gwent Gazette
52Glebeland Street, Merthyr Tydfil CF47 8AT
☎ (01685) 789230 ☐ (01685) 789232
Email: gwent.gazette@mediawales.co.uk
www.walesonline.co.uk
Editor: Sandra Loy

Merthyr Express Series
52-53 Glebeland St, Merthyr Tydfil CF47 8AT
☎ (01685) 789230 ☐ (01685) 789232
Email: merthyr.express@mediawales.co.uk
www.walesonline.co.uk
Editor: Sandra Loy

Monmouthshire Beacon
56 Monnow St, Monmouth NP25 3XJ
☎ (01600) 712142 ☐ (01600) 715531
Email: beaconnews@tindlenews.co.uk
www.monmouth-today.co.uk
General Manager: Lyn Vokes

Penarth Times
156 Holton Rd, Barry CF63 4TY
☎ (01446) 733456 ☐ (01446) 732719
Email: penarthtimes@penarthtimes.co.uk
www.penarthtimes.co.uk
Editor: Shira Valek

Pontypridd & Llantrisant Observer
10 Market St, Pontypridd CF37 2ST
☎ (01443) 629200 ☐ (01443) 629203
Email: pontypridd.observer@mediawales.co.uk
www.walesonline.co.uk
Executive Editor: Sandra Loy

Rhondda Leader
10 Market St, Pontypridd CF37 2ST
☎ (01443) 629200 ☐ (01443) 629203
Email: rhondda.leader@mediawales.co.uk
www.walesonline.co.uk
Executive Editor: Sandra Loy

Rhymney Valley Express
52-53 Glebeland St, Merthyr Tydfil CF47 8AT
☎ (01685) 789230 ☐ (01685) 789232
Email: rhymney.valley.express@mediawales.co.uk
www.walesonline.co.uk
Executive Editor: Sandra Loy

South Wales Argus
Cardiff Rd, Maesglas, Newport NP20 3QN
☎ (01633) 810000 ☐ (01633) 777202
Email: newsdesk@southwalesargus.co.uk
www.southwalesargus.co.uk
Editor: Nicole Garnon

South Wales Evening Post
PO Box 14, Adelaide St, Swansea SA1 1QT
☎ (01792) 510000 ☐ (01792) 469665
Email: postnews@swwmedia.co.uk
www.thisissouthwales.co.uk
News Editor: Rebecca Davies

South Wales Guardian Series
37 Quay St, Ammanford SA18 3BS
☎ (01269) 592781 ☐ (01269) 591020
Email: mike.lewis@southwalesguardian.co.uk
www.southwalesguardian.co.uk
Editor: Mike Lewis

Weekly Argus - Newport, Cwmbran & Risca
Cardiff Rd, Maesglas, Newport NP20 3QN
☎ (01633) 810000 ☐ (01633) 777160
Email: newsdesk@gwent-wales.co.uk
www.thisisgwent.co.uk
Editor: Kevin Ward

Media: Magazines, Periodicals & Journals

Agenda
Journal of the Institute of Welsh Affairs,
4 Cathedral Rd, Cardiff CF11 9LJ
☎ (029) 2066 0820 ☎ (029) 2023 3741
Email: wales@iwa.org.uk
www.iwa.org.uk
Editor: John Osmond

Yr Athro
UCAC, Ffordd Penglais, Aberystwyth,
Ceredigion SY23 2EU
☎ (01970) 639950 ☎ (01970) 626765
Email: ucac@athrawon.com
www.athrawon.com

Barddas
Teifi, 106 Heol Llancayo, Bargoed,
Caerffilli CF81 8TP
☎ (01443) 830994
www.barddas.com
Ysgrifennydd/Secretary: Dafydd Islwyn

Barn
Swyddfa Barn, Y Llwyfan, College Rd,
Carmarthen SA31 3EQ
☎ (01267) 245676
Email: swyddfa@cylchgrawnbarn.com
www.cylchgrawnbarn.com
Editors: Menna Baines & Vaughan Hughes

Blown Ltd
Canolfan Chapter Arts Centre,
Market Rd, Canton, Cardiff CF5 1QE
☎ (01446) 776950
Email: info@blownmag.com
www.blownmag.com
Executive Editor: Ed Pereira
Editor: Ric Bower

Blue Tattoo
PO Box 221, Aberystwyth SY23 2XZ
Email: dafydd.prys@yahoo.co.uk
Editor: Dafydd Prys

Business in Wales
Six Park St, Cardiff CF10 1XR
☎ (029) 2022 3333
Email: biw@mediawales.co.uk
www.mediawales.co.uk

Cambria Magazine
Blwch Post 22, Caerfyrddin SA32 7YH
☎ (01267) 290188
Email: editor@cambriamagazine.com
www.cambriamagazine.com
Editor: Frances Jones-Davies

Carmarthenshire Life
21-25 West End, Llanelli,
Carmarthenshire SA15 3DN
☎ (01554) 752935
www.carmarthenshirelife.org.uk
Editor: Jenna Fulford

Y Casglwr
Tanycastell, Llanuwchlyn,
Bala, Gwynedd LL23 7TA
☎ (01678) 540652
Email: tanycastell@yahoo.com
www.casglwr.org
Editor: Mel Williams

Contemporary Wales
Gwasg Prifysgol Cymru/University of Wales Press,
10 Columbus Walk, Brigantine Place,
Cardiff CF10 4UP
☎ (029) 2049 6899 ☎ (029) 2049 6108
Email: journals@press.wales.ac.uk
Editors: Paul Chaney, Elin Royles

**Cylchgrawn Cymry Llundain
The London Welsh Magazine**
157-163 Grays Inn Rd, London WC1X 8UE
☎ (020) 7837 3722
Email: administrator@lwcentre.demon.co.uk
www.londonwelsh.org
Editor: David Daniels

Fferm a Thyddyn
Plas Tan y Bwlch, Maentwrog, Gwynedd LL41 3YU
☎ (01766) 772610 ☎ (01766) 772609
Email: twm.elias@eryri-npa.gov.uk
www.plastanybwlch.com
Editor: Twm Elias

Golwg
PO Box 4, Lampeter, Ceredigion SA48 7LX
☎ (01570) 423529 ☎ (01570) 423538
Email: ymholiadau@golwg.com
www.golwg360.com
Managing Editor: Dylan Iorwerth
Editor: Sian Sutton

MEDIA: MAGAZINES, JOURNALS

Lingo Newydd
PO Box 4, Lampeter, Ceredigion SA48 7LX
☎ (01570) 423529 ᐧ (01570) 423538
Email: lingonewydd@golwg.com
www.golwg.com
Managing Editor: Dylan Iorwerth
Business Director: Enid Jones

Llafar Gwlad
Gwasg Carreg Gwalch, 12 Iard yr Orsaf,
Llanrwst, Gwynedd LL26 0EH
☎ (01492) 642031 ᐧ (01492) 641502
Email: llanrwst@carreg-gwalch.com
www.carreg-gwalch.com
Editor: Myrddin ap Dafydd

Llên Cymru
University of Wales Press, 10 Columbus Walk,
Brigantine Place, Cardiff CF10 4UP
☎ (029) 2049 6899 ᐧ (029) 2049 6108
Email: press@press.wales.ac.uk
www.uwp.co.uk
Editor: Professor Gruffydd Aled Williams

Monmouthshire County Life
Newsquest Wales & Gloucestershire, Cardiff
Road, Maesglas, Newport NP20 3QN
☎ (01633) 777 240
Email: jo.barnes@southwalesargus.co.uk
www.monmouthshirecountylife.co.uk
Editor: Jo Barnes

Natur Cymru - Nature of Wales
Maes y Ffynnon, Penrhosgarnedd, Bangor,
Gwynedd LL57 2DW
☎ (01248) 387373 ᐧ (01248) 385427
Email: info@naturcymru.org.uk
www.naturcymru.org.uk
Editor: James Robertson
Manager: Mandy Marsh
Marketing: Huw Jenkins

New Welsh Review
PO Box 170, Aberystwyth, Ceredigion SY23 1WZ
☎ (01970) 628410
Email: editor@newwelshreview.com
admin@newwelshreview.com
www.newwelshreview.com
Editor: Gwen Davies

Pembrokeshire Life
Swan House Publishing, Bridge Street,
Newcastle Emlyn SA38 9DX
☎ (01559) 371126
Email: eleanorswanhouse@btinternet.com
Editor: David Fielding

Planet - The Welsh Internationalist
PO Box 44, Aberystwyth, Ceredigion SY23 3ZZ
☎ (01970) 611255 ᐧ (01970) 611197
Email: planet.enquries@planetmagazine.org.uk
www.planetmagazine.org.uk
Editor: Emily Trahair

Poetry Wales
57 Nolton St, Bridgend CF31 3AE
☎ (01656) 663018
Email: info@poetrywales.co.uk
www.poetrywales.co.uk
Editor: Dr Zoë Skoulding

Prole
15 Maes-y-Dre, Abergele, Conwy LL22 7HW
☎ (01745) 823180
Email: admin@prolebooks.co.uk
www.prolebooks.co.uk
Editors: Brett Evans and Phil Robertson

Pure Poetry
Flat 2, 53 Richmond Rd, Cardiff CF24 3AR
Email: mail@pure-poetry.co.uk
www.pure-poetry.co.uk

Rural Wales
Tŷ Gwyn, 31 High St, Welshpool SY21 7YD
☎ (01938) 552525 ᐧ (01938) 552741
Email: info@cprwmail.org.uk
www.cprw.org.uk
Editor: Peter Ogden

Taliesin
Yr Academi Gymreig, 3rd Floor, Mount Stuart
House, Mount Stuart Square, Cardiff CF10 5FQ
☎ (029) 2047 2266 ᐧ (029) 2049 2930
Email: taliesin@llenyddiaethcymru.org
www.llenyddiaethcymru.org
Editors: Sian Melangell Dafydd, Angharad Elen

Tu Chwith
d/o Elin Angharad Owen, Pen-y-Berth,
Ffordd Gwenllian, Nefyn, Pwllheli LL53 6ND
Email: tuchwith@googlemail.com†
www.tuchwith.com
Gol: Elin Angharad Owen a Rhiannon Marks

The Wales Yearbook
4 The Science Park, Aberystwyth,
Ceredigion SY23 3DU
☎ (01970) 636400 ᐧ (01970) 636414
Email: info@walesyearbook.co.uk
www.walesyearbook.co.uk

Sponsored by: www.royalmail.com

Post Brenhinol

Royal Mail

Welsh Country
Aberbanc, Penrhiwllan, Llandysul SA44 5NP
☎ (01559) 372010 ☒ (01559) 371995
Email: kath@welshcountry.co.uk
www.welshcountry.co.uk
Editor: Kath Rhodes

Welsh Football Magazine
57 Thornhill Rd, Rhiwbina, Cardiff CF14 6PE
☎ (029) 2075 3179
Email: welshfootball@lineone.net
www.welsh-football.net
Editor: David Collins

WM Magazine
Six Park St, Cardiff CF10 1XR
☎ (029) 2022 3333
Email: Claire.rees@walesonline.co.uk
www.walesonline.co.uk
Editor: Claire Rees

Media: Papurau Bro

Yr Angor
32 Garth Drive, Liverpool L18 6HW
☎ (0151) 7241989 ☒ (0151) 7245691
Email: ben@garthdrive.fsnet.co.uk
www.liverpool-welsh.co.uk
Editor: Dr D Ben Rees

Yr Angor
24 Penrheidol, Penparcau,
Aberystwyth, Ceredigion SY23 1QW
Email: yrangor@hotmail.co.uk
Cad: Megan Jones

Yr Arwydd
Wenllys, Ffordd Porthllechog,
Amlwch, Ynys Môn LL68 9EA
☎ (01407) 830552
Email: geraintthomas123@btinternet.com
Ysg: R Geraint Thomas

Y Barcud
Pant-y-dail, Pont-rhyd-y-groes,
Ceredigion SY23 6DP
☎ (01974) 282294
Golygyddol: Celia Bailey Jones

Y Bedol
Clywedog, Ty'n Parc, Rhuthun LL15 1LH
☎ (01824) 704350
Email: morfuddmenna@boyns.net
Secretary: Menna E Jones

Y Bigwn
18 Llys Marchell, Parc Myddleton,
Dinbych LL16 4AR
☎ (01745) 817485
Email: ybigwn@hotmail.co.uk
Ysg: Nia Angharad Jones

Y Blewyn Glas
85 Tregarth, Machynlleth, Powys SY20 8HY
☎ (01654) 702881
Email: maesterran@btopenworld.com
Secretary: Eirian Jones

Y Cardi Bach
Bro Gronw, Cwmfelinmynach,
Hendygwyn-ar-Daf, Sir Gâr SA34 0DH
☎ (01994) 448283
Email: ycardibach@btopenworld.com
Editor: Rhoswen Llewellyn

Y Clawdd
Sycharth, 6 Heol Llawhaden, Wrecsam LL12 8JU
☎ (01978) 359846
Editor: Alun J Emanuel

Clochdar
11 Belmont Terrace, Aberaman, Aberdare,
Rhondda Cynon Taf CF44 6UW
☎ (01685) 882165
Email: clochdar@googlemail.com
Editor: Susan Jenkins

Clonc
Maesglas, Dre-fach, Llanybydder SA40 9YB
☎ (01570) 480015
Email: ysgrifennydd@clonc.co.uk
www.clonc.co.uk
Contact: Mary Davies

Cwlwm
13 Parcmaen, Caerfyrddin SA31 3DP
☎ (07968) 379119
Email: cwlwm@btinternet.com
Uwch Olygydd: Iwan Evans

Dail Dysynni
Llain y Grug, Bryncrug, Tywyn, Gwynedd LL36 9RB
☎ (01654) 711470
Ysg: Arwel Pierce

Dan Y Landsker
66 Fleming Way, Neyland, Sir Benfro SA73 1RZ
☎ (07819) 421615
Email: frizbybarker@hotmail.com
Ysg: Louvain Jones

Y Ddolen
Brynawel, Trefenter, Aberystwyth,
Ceredigion SY23 4HJ
☎ (01974) 272131
Email: y.ddolen@googlemail.com
Secretary: Rina Tandy

Y Dinesydd
www.dinesydd.com

Eco'r Wyddfa
Cilgerran, Bethel, Caernarfon, Gwynedd
Email: geraintelis@tesco.net
Geraint Elis

Y Fan a'r Lle
Bryn Hyfryd, Peppercorn Lane,
Aberhonddu, Powys LD3 9EG
☎ (01874) 624015
Secretary: Gwenno Hutchinson

Y Ffynnon
Fferm Trefan, Llanstumdwy, Cricieth,
Gwynedd LL52 0LP
☎ (01766) 523310
Secretary: Siân Parry

Y Gadlas
Tan y Fron, Bylchau, Dinbych LL16 5LY
☎ (01745) 860280
Email: ygadlas@btinternet.com
Secretary: Ilyd Davies

Y Gambo
Y Graig, Aberporth, Aberteifi, Ceredigion SA43 2DU
☎ (01239) 810555
Email: johnygraig@tiscali.co.uk
Secretary: John Davies

Y Garthen
Heddfryn, New Inn, Pencader,
Carmarthenshire SA39 9AY
☎ (01559) 384252
Email: ygarthen@yahoo.com
Editor: Marina Davies

Y Glannau
12 Ffordd Lâs, Prestatyn, Sir Ddinbych LL19 9SG
☎ (01745) 856599
Email: marilyn.davies1@virgin.net
Ysgrifennydd/Secretary: Marilyn Davies

Glo-mân
37 Heol Waterloo, Capel Hendre, Rhydaman,
Sir Gaerfyrddin SA18 3SF
☎ (01269) 845435
Email: edwyn@edwyn.wanadoo.co.uk
www.gloman.blogspot.com
Secretary: Edwyn Williams

Y Gloran
Brynmyrtwydd, Treorci, Rhondda Cynon Taf CF42 6PF
☎ (01443) 435563
Email: ygloran@hotmail.com
Editor: Cennard Davies

Y Glorian
Blaen y Wawr, Rhosmeirch, Llangefni,
Ynys Môn LL77 7TQ
☎ (01248) 724489
Dewi Williams

Goriad
26 Penyffridd, Penrhosgarnedd, Bangor,
Gwynedd LL57 2LZ
Email: papurbrogoriad@yahoo.co.uk
Secretary: Howard Huws

Yr Hogwr
45 Heol Maendy, Corneli,
Pen-y-Bont ar Ogwr CF33 4DK
Email: rtprice@supanet.com
Golygydd: Tom Price

Llafar Bro
Rhiwbach, 7 Trem y Fron,
Blaenau Ffestiniog, Gwynedd LL41 3DP
☎ (01766) 831814
Secretary: Vivian Parry Williams

Llais
Afallon, 23 Kingrosia Park,
Clydach, Swansea SA6 5PN
☎ (01792) 842853
Email: llais@tiscali.co.uk
Editor: John Evans

Llais Aeron
Sychpant, Talsarn, Dyffryn Aeron, Ceredigion
☎ (01570) 470350
Secretary: Beti Davies

Llais Ardudwy
Bellaport, Dyffryn Ardudwy, Tal-y-Bont, Gwynedd
☎ (01341) 247338
Editor: Ken Roberts

Llanw Llŷn
Towyn, Llangïan, Pwllheli, Gwynedd LL53 7LS
☎ (01758) 712302
www.penllyn.com-llanw
Ysg: Janet Roberts

Lleu
Hafod y Gân, Ffordd Clynnog,
Penygroes, Gwynedd LL54 6NS
☎ (01286) 880521
Email: papurbro.lleu@googlemail.com
Ysg: Carys Vaughan Jones

Y Llien Gwyn
Penlanwynt, Cwm Gwaun, Trefdraeth,
Sir Benfro SA65 9TU
☎ (01239) 820333
Email: lliengwyn@papurbro.org
Editor: Bonni Davies

Y Lloffwr
Sarn Gelli, Llanegwad, Nantgaredig,
Carmarthenshire SA32 7NL
☎ (01558) 668823
Email: ylloffwr@papurbro.org
www.ylloffwr.org
Editor: Mansel Charles

Nene
Cil y Ri, Pentrebychan,
Rhosllannerchrugog, Wrexham LL14 4EN
☎ (01978) 841386
Email: papurbronene@btinternet.com
Editor: Gwynne Williams & Gareth P Hughes

Newyddion Mynwy
Bronllys, Clements End, Coleford,
Swydd Gaerloyw GL16 8LL
☎ (01594) 563172
Email: robinbronllys@aol.com
Editor: Robin Davies

Yr Odyn
Cefn Rhydd, Capel Garmon,
Llanrwst, Gwynedd LL26 0RP
☎ (01690) 710688
Ysg: Meri Williams

Papur Bro Llais Ogwan
Talgarnedd, 3 Sgwâr Buddug,
Bethesda, Gwynedd LL57 3AH
☎ (01248) 601415
Email: post@llaisogwan.com
garethllwyd197@btinternet.com
www.llaisogwan.com
Ysgrifennydd: Gareth Llwyd

Papur Dre
Borthwen, Ael y Garth, Caernarfon LL55 1HA
☎ (01286) 674980
Email: tomos882@btinternet.com
Chair: Glyn Tomos

Papur Fama
10 Hillside Crescent, Yr Wyddgrug, Sir Fflint CH7 1RL
☎ (01352) 756557
Email: papurfama@hotmail.co.uk
Golygydd: Iwan Jones

Papur Menai
Caerberllan, Lôn Las, Porthaethwy,
Ynys Môn LL59 5BT
☎ (01248) 712615
Email: caerberllan@gmail.com
Golygydd: John Meirion Davies

Papur Pawb
Maesgwyn, Tal-y-bont, Ceredigion SY24 5DY
☎ (01970) 832560
Email: golygydd@papurpawb.com
www.papurpawb.com
General Editor: Gwyn Jenkins

Papur y Cwm
Bryn Teg, Meol Maesybont, Castell-y-Rhingyll,
Llanelli SA14 7NA
☎ (01269) 842151   ₤ (01269) 832170
Email: dafyddguard-papurycwm@yahoo.co.uk
Secretary: Dafydd Thomas

Y Pentan
Rhiwen, 351 Ffordd Conwy, Mochdre,
Colwyn Bay LL28 5AL
☎ (01492) 540367
Email: eluneddelwynjones351@talktalk.net
Secretary: Eluned Jones

Pethe Penllyn
Trefan, 11 Tai'n Rhôs, Parc, Y Bala LL23 7YR
☎ (01678) 540384
Email: beryl@nantyllyn.fsnet.co.uk
Secretary: Mrs Jean Roberts

Plu'r Gweunydd
Eirianfa, Llanfair Caereinion, Y Trallwng SY21 0SB
☎ (01938) 810048
Email: clicied@btconnect.com
Golygydd: Mary Steele
Ysgrifenydd: Gwyndaf ac Eirlys Richards

Y Rhwyd
Llifon, Ffordd Trearddur, Y Fali,
Ynys Môn LL65 3EY
☎ (01407) 740072
Secretary: Owena Wyn Jones

Seren Hafren
Ger y Parc, Dolerw Park Drive,
Y Drenewydd, Powys SY16 2BA
☎ (01686) 627410
Email: nelian@geraint-jones-solicitors.co.uk
Secretary: Nelian Richards

Sosbanelli
Uned 6 a 7,
Canolfan Fenter Llynnoedd Delta,
Y Rhodfa, Llanelli SA15 2DS
☎ (01554) 755994 ✆ (01554) 758355

Tafod-Elai
Hendre, 4 Pantbach,
Pentyrch,
Cardiff CF15 9TG
☎ (029) 2089 0040
Email: pentyrch@tafelai.net
www.tafelai.net
Editor: Penri Williams

Tafod Tafwys
Heol yr Orsaf,
Llanishen,
Caerdydd CF14 5LU
☎ (029) 2075 3587
Lynne Davies

Y Tincer
Rhos Helyg,
23 Maes yr Efail,
Penrhyn-coch, Aberystwyth,
Ceredigion SY23 3HE
☎ (01970) 828017
Email: rhoshelyg@btinternet.com
Editor: Ceris Gruffudd

Tua'r Goleuni
58 Bryn Siriol, Tŷ Isaf,
Caerffili CF83 2AJ
☎ (029) 2086 7769
Email: denzil.john@btinternet.com
Editor: Denzil Ieuan John

Wilia
Hafan, 2 Lôn Rhianfa,
Ffynhonne, Abertawe SA1 6DJ
☎ (01792) 455410
Email: wilia@hotmail.co.uk
www.menterabertawe.org/cymraeg/wilia.php
Editor: Heini Gruffudd

Yr Wylan
3 Teras Meirion,
Beddgelert, Gwynedd LL55 4NB
☎ (01766) 890483
Email: yrwylan@hotmail.com
Chairman: Glyn E Roberts

Yr Ysgub
Y Dderwen, Llanfyllin,
Powys SY22 5HZ
☎ (01691) 648787
Email: alwennaevans@yahoo.co.uk
Secretary: Alwenna Evans

Publishers & News Agencies

Accent Press Ltd
The Old School, Upper High St,
Bedlinog CF46 6RY
☎ (01443) 710930
✆ (01443) 710940
Email: info@accentpress.co.uk
www.accentpress.co.uk
Managing Director: Hazel Cushion

Alun Books
3 Crown St,
Port Talbot SA13 1BG
☎ (01639) 886186
Email: enquiries@alunbooks.co.uk
www.alunbooks.co.uk
Sally Roberts Jones

APECS Press
Ashtree Studios, Ash Cottage,
Pillmawr Rd, Caerleon,
Newport NP18 3QZ
☎ (01633) 852944
✆ (01633) 858161
Email: margaretisaac@welshstories.com
www.apecspress.co.uk
Dr Alun Isaac

Welsh Academic Press
PO Box 733,
Caerdydd - Cardiff CF14 7ZY
☎ (029) 2021 8187
Email: post@welsh-academic-press.com
www.welsh-academic-press.com
Rheolwr Gyfarwyddwr/Managing Director:
Mr Ashley Drake

atebol
Fagwyr Buildings , Llandre,
Aberystwyth SY24 5AQ
☎ (01970) 832172 ◨ (01970) 832259
Email: info@atebol.com
www.atebol.com

Blorenge Books
Church Lane, Llanfoist,
Abergavenny NP7 9NG
☎ (01873) 856114
Email: cbarber@aol.com
www.blorenge-books.co.uk
Chris Barber

Bridge Books
61 Park Ave, Wrexham LL12 7AW
☎ (0845) 166 2851or (01978) 358661
Email: enquiries@bridgebooks.co.uk
www.bridgebooks.co.uk
W Alister Williams

Ceiniog
7 Teilo St, Cardiff CF11 9JN
☎ (029) 2022 9095
Email: penny.fishlock@penandinc.demon.co.uk
Managing Director: Penny Symon

Cinnamon Press
Meirion House, Glan yr afon, Tanygrisiau,
Blaenau Ffestiniog LL41 3SU
☎ (01766) 832112
Email: jan@cinnamonpress.com
www.cinnamonpress.com
Jan Fortune, Rowan Fortune

The Collective
Fferm Penlanlas, Llantilio Pertholey,
Abergavenny NP7 7HN
Email: jj@jojowales.co.uk
www.welshwriters.com
Editor: Frank Olding
Events Manager: Ric Hool
Co-ordinator: John Jones

Crown House Publishing Limited
Crown Buildings, Bancyfelin,
Carmarthen SA33 5ND
☎ (01267) 211345
◨ (01267) 211882
Email: books@crownhouse.co.uk
www.crownhouse.co.uk
Managing Director: David Bowman

Cwmni CURIAD Cyf
Capel Salem, Talysarn, Caernarfon,
Gwynedd LL54 6AB
☎ (01286) 882166
Email: curiad@curiad.co.uk
www.curiad.co.uk
Ruth Edwards

Cwm Nedd Press
1 Rhes Lewis, Abergarwed, Neath SA11 4DL
☎ (01639) 711480
Contact: J J Morgan, Robert King

Cyhoeddiadau Barddas
Pen-rhiw, 71 Ffordd Pentrepoeth, Morriston,
Swansea SA6 6AE
☎ (01792) 792829
Email: alan.llwyd@googlemail.com
www.barddas.com
Administrative Officer: Alan Llwyd

Dee News Service, Mold
c/o 4 Stryd y Brython, Brynhyfryd Park,
Ruthin, Denbighshire LL15 1JA
☎ (07813) 182363
Email: elwyn@deenews.co.uk
Elwyn Roberts

Derek Bellis
Seabreezes, 14b Kenelm Rd,
Rhos on Sea, Colwyn Bay LL28 4ED
☎ (01492) 543226

Dinefwr Press
Heol Rawlings, Llandybïe, Carms SA18 3YD
☎ (01269) 850576
www.dinefwr-press-publishers-printers.co.uk

Dragon News and Picture Agency
14 Brynymor Rd, Swansea SA1 4JQ
☎ (01792) 464800 ◨ (01792) 475264
www.dragon-pictures.com

Draisey Publishing
73 Conway Rd, Penlan, Swansea SA5 7AU
☎ (01792) 429968
Contact: Derek Draisey/Ann Hughes

Dref Wen
28 Heol yr Eglwys, Yr Eglwys Newydd,
Caerdydd CF14 2EA
☎ (029) 2061 7860
Email: gwilym@drefwen.com
www.drefwen.com
Contact: Gwilym Boore

MEDIA: PUBLISHERS, AGENCIES

FBA Publications
Cyhoeddiadau FBA
4 The Science Park, Cefn Llan,
Aberystwyth, Ceredigion SY23 3AH
☎ (01970) 636400 🖷 (01970) 636414
Email: info@fbagroup.co.uk
www.fbalearning.co.uk
www.walesyearbook.co.uk
Managing Director: Sue Balsom
Chair: Denis Balsom

Fflach
Llys-y-Coed, Tenby, Cardigan SA43 3AH
☎ (01239) 614691
Email: info@fflach.co.uk
www.fflach.co.uk

GLMP Ltd comprising of Mr Education Teaching & Learning Solutions Aber Publishing
Studymates Publishing, Lamorna House,
Abergele LL22 8DD
☎ (01745) 832863 🖷 (01745) 826606
Email: info@aber-publishing.co.uk
info@studymates.co.uk
graham@studymates.co.uk
www.aber-publishing.co.uk
www.studymates.co.uk www.mr-educator.com
Managing Director: Dr Graham Lawler

Greencroft Books
Trefelin, Cilgwyn, Newport,
Pembs SA42 0QN
☎ (01239) 820470
Email: brianjohn4@mac.com
www.books-wales.co.uk
Proprietor: Brian John

Gwasg Carreg Gwalch
12 Iard yr Orsaf, Llanrwst, Conwy LL26 0EH
☎ (01492) 642031 🖷 (01492) 641502
Email: llanrwst@carreg-gwalch.com
www.carreg-gwalch.com
Director: Myrddin ap Dafydd

Gwasg Gee
Uned 7, Bethesda, Gwynedd LL57 4YY
☎ (01248) 800135 🖷 (01248) 602692
Email: archebion@gwasggee.com or/neu
orders@gwasggee.com
www.gwasggee.com

Gwasg Gomer
Gomer Press
Parc Menter Llandysul, Ceredigion SA44 4JL
☎ (01559) 362371 🖷 (01559) 363758
Email: gwasg@gomer.co.uk
www.gomer.co.uk
Managing Director: Jonathan Lewis

Gwasg Gwynedd
Hafryn, Llwyn Hudol, Pwllheli, Gwynedd LL53 5YE
☎ (01758) 612483
Email: cyhoeddi@gwasggwynedd.com
Cyfarwyddwr: Alwyn Elis

Gwasg Pantycelyn Gwasg y Bwthyn
Lôn Ddewi, Caernarfon, Gwynedd LL55 1ER
☎ (01286) 672018
🖷 (01286) 677823
Email: gwasgybwythyn@btconnect.com
Manager: June Jones

Gwynn Publishing Company
Cwmni Cyhoeddi Gwynn
Uned 7, Hen Gapel Salem, Ffordd Bryncelyn,
Talysarn LL54 6AB
☎ (01286) 881797
Email: gwybodaeth@gwynn.co.uk
www.gwynn.co.uk
Arfon Gwilym

Hall Press Agency
Fox Hollow Cottage, Heol Penyfelin,
Coedpoeth, Wrexham LL11 3TU
☎ (01970) 752233

Honno Welsh Women's Press
Unit 14, Creative Units, Aberystwyth Arts Centre,
Aberystwyth SY23 3GL
☎ (01970) 623150
🖷 (01970) 623150
Email: post@honno.co.uk
www.honno.co.uk
Editor: Caroline Oakley
Office Administrator: Lesley Rice

Houdmont
14 Lôn y Dail, Rhiwbina, Caerdydd/Cardiff CF14 6DZ
☎ 077 9156 3079
Email: holi@houdmont.co.uk
www.houdmont.co.uk
Richard Houdmont

Joseph Biddulph
32 Stryd Ebeneser, Pontypridd CF37 5PB
☎ (01443) 662559
Email: Joseph.Biddulph@gmail.com
Proprietor: Joseph Biddulph

Royal Mail

Llanerch Press
48 Rectory Rd, Burnham on Sea TA8 2BZ
☎ (01278) 781278
🖷 (01278) 795309
www.llanerchpress.com
Contact: Debbie Sprugg

Y Lolfa
Tal-y-bont, Ceredigion SY24 5HE
☎ (01970) 832304
🖷 (01970) 832782
Email: ylolfa@ylolfa.com
www.ylolfa.com

Media Wales Ltd
Six Park St, Cardiff CF10 1XR
☎ (029) 2022 3333
www.walesonline.co.uk

Mid Glamorgan Press Agency
21 Mary Street,
Porthcawl CF36 3YL
☎ (01656) 782915
🖷 (01656) 744773
Email: midglam@aol.com
Chris Smart

North Wales Press Agency
157 High St, Prestatyn LL19 9AY
☎ (01745) 852262 🖷 (01745) 855534
Michael McEvoy

Parthian
The Old Surgery, Napier St, Cardigan,
Ceredigion SA43 1ED
☎ (01239) 615888
Email: parthianbooks@yahoo.co.uk
www. parthianbooks.com /
www.thelibraryofwales.com
Publishing Director: Richard Davies
Editor: Kathryn Gray
Publisher: Gillian Griffiths

The Photolibrary Wales
2 Bro-nant, Church Rd, Pentyrch, Cardiff CF15 9QG
☎ (029) 2089 0311
Email: info@photolibrarywales.com
www.photolibrarywales.com
Director: Steve Benbow

Planet Books
PO Box 44, Aberystwyth, Ceredigion SY23 3ZZ
☎ (01970) 611255 🖷 (01970) 611197
Email: planet.enquiries@planetmagazine.org.uk
www.planetmagazine.org.uk

The Press Association (PA News)
☎ Mobile 07803229760
Email: antony.stone@pressassociation.com
www.pressassociation.com
Regional Reporter - Cardiff: Antony Stone

Rack Press
The Rack, Kinnerton, Presteigne,
Powys LD8 2PF
☎ (01547) 560 411
Email: rackpress@nicholasmurray.co.uk
www.rackpress.blogspot.com
Nicholas Murray

Seren Books
57 Nolton St, Bridgend CF31 3AE
☎ (01656) 663018
🖷 (01656) 649226
Email: seren@serenbooks.com
www.serenbooks.com
Mick Felton

Starborn Books
Glanrhydwilym, Llandisilio,
Clunderwen SA66 7QH
Email: sales@starbornbooks.co.uk
www.starbornbooks.co.uk
Contact: Peter Oram

University of Wales Press
10 Columbus Walk,
Brigantine Place, Cardiff CF10 4UP
☎ (029) 2049 6899
Email: press@press.wales.ac.uk
www.wales.ac.uk/press
Head: Helgard Krause
Sales & Marketing Manager: Bethan James

**Wales News and Picture Service -
Press Agency**
Cardiff Arms Park Club Office,
Westgate St, Cardiff CF10 1JA
☎ (029) 2066 6366
🖷 (029) 2066 4181
Email: news@walesnews.com
www.walesnews.com
Paul Horton, Tom Bedford

Museums, Libraries & Archives

Amgueddfa ac Oriel Gwynedd
Ffordd Gwynedd, Bangor, Gwynedd LL57 1DT
☎ (01248) 353368 ☐ (01248) 370149
Email: AmgueddfaGwynedd@gwynedd.gov.uk

Amgueddfa Ceredigion Museum
Terrace Rd, Aberystwyth, Ceredigion SY23 2AQ
☎ (01970) 633088
Email: museum@ceredigion.gov.uk
www.amgueddfa.ceredigion.gov.uk
Curator: Carrie Canham

Amgueddfa Cymru
National Museum Wales
Cathays Park, Cardiff CF10 3NP
☎ (029) 2039 7951 ☐ (029) 2057 3321
Email: post@museumwales.ac.uk /
post@amgueddfacymru.ac.uk
www.museumwales.ac.uk /
www.amgueddfacymru.ac.uk
President: Elizabeth Elias
Director General: David Anderson

Amgueddfa Howell Harris
Trefeca, Aberhonddu/Brecon, Powys LD3 0PP
☎ (01874) 711423 ☐ (01874) 712212
Email: colegtrefeca@ebcpcw.org.uk
www.trefeca.org.uk
Trefeca Centre Manager /
Rheolydd Canolfan Trefeca: Mair Jones

Amgueddfa Lloyd George Museum
Llanystumdwy, Criccieth, Gwynedd LL52 0SH
☎ (01766) 522071 ☐ (01766) 522071
Email: amgueddfalloydgeorge@gwynedd.gov.uk
www.gwynedd.gov.uk/museums
Museums & Galleries Officer: Nêst Thomas

Anglesey Antiquarian Society & Field Club
Cymdeithas Hynafiaethwyr a Naturiaethwyr Môn
1 Fronheulog, Sling, Tregarth, Gwynedd LL57 4RD
☎ (01248) 600083
Email: mail@hanesmon.org.uk
www.hanesmon.org.uk
Honorary General Secretary: Siôn Caffell

Archives & Records Council Wales
Cyngor Archifau a Chofnodion Cymru
The National Library of Wales, Aberystwyth,
Ceredigion SY23 3BU
☎ (01970) 632803 ☐ (01970) 632882
Email: avril.jones@llgc.org.uk
www.llgc.org.uk/cac
Director of Collection Services: Avril Jones

Big Pit National Coal Museum
Amgueddfa Lofaol Cymru
Blaenafon, Torfaen NP4 9XP
☎ (01495) 790311 ☐ (01495) 792618
Email: bigpit@amgueddfacymru.ac.uk
www.museumwales.ac.uk/en/bigpit
Keeper: Peter Walker

Blaenau Gwent Libraries
Anvil Court, Church St, Abertillery NP13 1DB
☎ (01495) 355950 ☐ (01495) 355900
Email: info@blaenau-gwent.gov.uk
www.blaenau-gwent.gov.uk
Learning Services Manager: Byron Jones
Principal Librarian: Sue White

Brecknock Museum & Art Gallery
Captain's Walk, Brecon, Powys LD3 7DS
☎ (01874) 624121 ☐ (01874) 614046
Email: brecknock.museum@powys.gov.uk
www.powys.gov.uk/brecknockmuseum
Curator: Nigel Blackamore

Brecknock Society & Museum Friends
Cymdeithas Brycheiniog a Chyfeillion
yr Amgueddfa
Captain's Walk, Brecon, Powys LD3 7DS
☎ (01874) 730747
Email: gibbs@keme.co.uk
www.brecknocksociety.co.uk
Chairman: Dr John Gibbs

Bridgend County Borough Library
& Information Service
Wing 1, Raven's Court, Brewery Lane,
Bridgend CF31 4AP
☎ (01656) 754800 ☐ (01656) 642431
Email: blis@bridgend.gov.uk
www.bridgend.gov.uk/libraries
County Borough Librarian: John C Woods

Caerphilly County Borough Libraries
Penallta House, Tredomen Park,
Ystrad Mynach, Hengoed CF82 7PG
☎ (01443) 864068
Email: libraries@caerphilly.gov.uk
www.caerphilly.gov.uk
Principal Education Officer - Community
Education & Libraries: Steve Mason

Cardiff Central Library
The Hayes, Cardiff CF10 1FL
☎ (029) 2038 2116 ▣ (029) 2078 0989
Email: centrallibrary@cardiff.gov.uk
www.cardiff.gov.uk/libraries
Central Library Manager: Nicola Richards

The Cardiff Story
Stori Caerdydd
The Old Library, The Hayes, Cardiff CF10 1BH
☎ (029) 2078 8334
Email: cardiffstory@cardiff.gov.uk
www.cardiffstory.com www.storicaerdydd.com

Carmarthenshire County Council - Education & Children's Services
Building 2, St David's Park, Jobs Well Rd, Carmarthen
☎ (01267) 246649
Director of Education & Children's Services: Robert Sully
Head of Education Services: Wyn Williams
Head of Governance and Inclusion: Gareth Morgans
Head of Children's Services: Jake Morgan

Carmarthenshire County Council - Library Services
Building 2, St David's Park, Jobs Well Rd, Carmarthen
☎ (01267) 228337 ▣ (01267) 238584
Email: mjewell@carmarthenshire.gov.uk
Head of Business and Specialist Services
Elin Cullen; Library Service Manager: Mark Jewell

Ceredigion County Council Public Library
Town Hall, Queen's Square, Aberystwyth, Ceredigion SY23 2EB
☎ (01970) 633717
▣ (01970) 625059
Email: ystwythllb@ceredigion.gov.uk
www.ceredigion.gov.uk/libraries
Swyddog Llyfrgelloedd y Sir /
County Libraries Officer: W H Howells

CILIP Cymru Wales (Chartered Institute of Library & Information Professionals Wales)
Bute Library, Cardiff University,
PO Box 430, Cardiff CF24 0DE
☎ (020) 7255 0500
Email: mandy.powell@cilip.org.uk
www.cilipwales.blogspot.com
CILIP Policy Officer, Wales: Mandy Powell
Mob: 07837 032 536

Conwy Library
Library Building, Mostyn Street, Llandudno LL30 2RP
☎ (01492) 576139 ▣ (01492) 577552
Email: library@conwy.gov.uk
www.conwy.gov.uk/library
Service Head: Rhian Williams

Cyfarthfa Castle Museum & Art Gallery
Brecon Rd, Merthyr Tydfil CF47 8RE
☎ (01685) 727371 ▣ (01685) 723112
Email: museum@merthyr.gov.uk
www.merthyr.gov.uk/museum
Museums Officer: Scott Reid

CyMAL: Museums Archives & Libraries Wales
Welsh Government, Rhodfa Padarn,
Llanbadarn Fawr, Aberystwyth SY23 3UR
☎ (0300) 062 2112 ▣ (0300) 062 2052
Email: cymal@wales.gsi.gov.uk
www.cymal.wales.gov.uk
Director: Linda Tomos

Cymdeithas Hanes Ceredigion
Ceredigion Historical Society
Penygeulan, Abermagwr, Aberystwyth,
Ceredigion SY23 4AR
☎ (01974) 261222
Email: ymholiadau@cymdeithashanesceredigion.org
www.ceredigionhistoricalsociety.org
Honorary Secretary: Eirionedd A Baskerville

Denbighshire Historical Society
Cymdeithas Hanes Sir Ddinbych
c/o Bridge Books, 61 Park Avenue,
Wrexham LL12 7AW
Email: geraint@gowain.freeserve.co.uk
www.glyndwr.ac.uk/dhs
Chairman: Dr David Jones
Secretary: Geraint Owen

Denbighshire Library Service
Yr Hen Garchar, Clwyd St,
Ruthin, Denbighshire LL15 1HP
☎ (01824) 708204 ▣ (01824) 708202
Email: library.services@denbighshire.gov.uk
www.denbighshire.gov.uk
Lead Officer, Libraries, Archives & Arts: R Arwyn Jones

The Dylan Thomas Centre
Somerset Place, Swansea SA1 1RR
☎ (01792) 463980 (Literature & General Enq);
463892 (Box Office) ▣ (01792) 463993
Email: dylanthomas.lit@swansea.gov.uk
www.dylanthomas.com
Literature Officer: Jo Furber; Cultural
Development Officer: Nick McDonald

Firing Line: The Cardiff Castle Museum of the Welsh Soldier
The Interpretation Centre,
Cardiff Castle, Cardiff CF10 2RB
☎ (029) 2022 9367
www.cardiffcastlemuseum.org.uk
Curator: Rachel Silverson

Flintshire Historical Society
69 Pen y Maes Ave, Rhyl LL18 4ED
☎ (01745) 332220
www.flintshirehistory.org.uk/
Honorary Secretary: Mrs N P Parker

Flintshire Culture and Leisure
Library Headquarters, County Hall,
Mold, Flintshire CH7 6NW
☎ (01352) 704400   ▣ (01352) 753662
Email: libraries@flintshire.gov.uk
www.flintshire.gov.uk
Head of Culture and Leisure:
Lawrence Rawsthorne

Glamorgan History Society
87 Gabalfa Rd, Sketty, Swansea SA2 8ND
☎ (01792) 205888
Email: paulreynolds44@googlemail.com
www.glamorganhistory.org
Honorary Secretary: Paul Reynolds

Gwent County History Association
c/o Mrs Kathleen Norton, Hon Secretary, 2,
Brunel Avenue, Rogerstone, Newport NP10 0DN
Email: kathleen.norton@ntlworld.com

Gwynedd Library & Information Service
Caernarfon Library, Pavilion Hill,
Caernarfon LL55 1AS
☎ (01286) 679463/679465
▣ (01286) 671137
Email: LLCaernarfon@gwynedd.gov.uk
www.gwynedd.gov.uk/library or
www.gwynedd.gov.uk/llyfrgell
Principal Librarian: Hywel James

Isle of Anglesey Lifelong Learning & Information Service
Llangefni Library, Lôn y Felin,
Llangefni, Ynys Môn LL77 7RT
☎ (01248) 752095
Email: libraries@anglesey.gov.uk
www.ynysmon.gov.uk
Corporate Director, Education & Leisure:
Richard Parry Jones
Heads of Service, Education: Gwyn Parri
Leisure & Community: Aled Roberts
Lifelong Learning & Information: John Rees Thomas

Llancaiach Fawr Manor
Living History Museum, Nelson, Caerphilly CF46 6ER
☎ (01443) 412248
▣ (01443) 412688
Email: llancaiachfawr@caerphilly.gov.uk
www.llancaiachfawr.co.uk
General Manager: Diane Walker

Llanrwst Almshouse Museum
1-12 Church St, Ancaster Square,
Llanrwst, Conwy LL26 0LE
☎ (01492) 642550
Email: info@llanrwstalmshouses.wanadoo.co.uk
www.llanrwstalmshouses.org.uk
Chair: Wyn Owen

Merioneth Historical and Record Society Cymdeithas Hanes a Chofnodion Sir Feirionnydd
c/o Archifdy Meirionnydd, Ffordd y Bala,
Dolgellau, Gwynedd LL40 2YF
☎ (01341) 424680
▣ (01341) 424683
Email: merfynwyntomos@gwynedd.gov.uk
Secretary: Merfyn Wyn Tomos

MOMA WALES MOMA CYMRU
Y Tabernacl, Heol Penrallt,
Machynlleth, Powys SY20 8AJ
☎ (01654) 703355   ▣ (01654) 702160
Email: info@momawales.org.uk
www.momawales.org.uk
Administrator: Raymond Jones

Monmouthshire Antiquarian Association
1 Fields Park Ave, Newport NP20 5BG
Email: monmouthshireantiquarian@googlemail.com
www.monmouthshireantiquarianassociation.org
Secretary: G V Jones

Monmouthshire Libraries and Information Service
Chepstow Library, Manor Way, Chepstow,
Monmouthshire NP16 5HZ
☎ (01291) 635730   ▣ (01291) 635736
Email: infocentre@monmouthshire.gov.uk
www.libraries.monmouthshire.gov.uk
Libraries, Museums & Arts Manager: Ann Jones

Nantgarw Chinaworks Museum
Tyla Gwyn, Nantgarw, Rhondda Cynon Taff CF15 7TB
☎ (01656) 862908
Email: alanpugh@hotmail.co.uk
natgarwchinaworksmuseum.co.uk

The National Library of Wales
Llyfrgell Genedlaethol Cymru
Penglais, Aberystwyth, Ceredigion SY23 3BU
☎ (01970) 632800 ᐁ (01970) 615709
Email: holi@llgc.org.uk
www.llgc.org.uk
Librarian: Andrew Green
President: Sir Deian Hopkin

National Roman Legion Museum
High St, Caerleon, Gwent NP18 1AE
☎ (01633) 423134 ᐁ (01633) 422869
www.museumwales.ac.uk/en/roman
Manager: Dai Price

National Slate Museum
Amgueddfa Lechi Cymru
Gilfach Ddu, Parc Padarn,
Llanberis, Gwynedd LL55 4TY
☎ (01286) 870630 ᐁ (01286) 871906
Email: slate@museumwales.ac.uk
llechi@amgueddfacymru.ac.uk
www.museumwales.ac.uk/en/slate
www.amgueddfacymru.ac.uk
Keeper: Dr Dafydd Roberts
Education Officer: Elen Wyn Roberts

National Waterfront Museum
Oystermouth Rd, Maritime Quarter,
Swansea SA1 3RD
☎ (029) 2057 3600
Email: waterfront@museumwales.ac.uk
www.museumwales.ac.uk/en/swansea
Head of Museum: Stephanos Mastoris

Neath Port Talbot County Borough Library
Library and Information Services,
Reginald St, Velindre, Port Talbot SA13 1YY
☎ (01639) 899829 ᐁ (01639) 899152
Email: npt.libhq@neath-porttalbot.gov.uk
www.neath-porttalbot.gov.uk/libraries
County Librarian: Wayne John

Newport Community Learning and Libraries Service
John Frost Sq, Newport NP20 1PA
☎ (01633) 656656
Email: central.library@newport.gov.uk
www.newport.gov.uk

Newport Museum & Art Gallery
John Frost Square, Newport, South Wales NP20 1PA
☎ (01633) 414701
Email: museum@newport.gov.uk

Old Bell Museum
Arthur St, Montgomery, Powys SY15 6RA
☎ (01686) 668313
Email: curator@oldbellmuseum.org.uk
www.oldbellmuseum.org.uk

Pembrokeshire County Library
Dew St, Haverfordwest, Pembrokeshire SA61 1SU
☎ (01437) 775244 ᐁ (01437) 767092
Email: anita.thomas@pembrokeshire.gov.uk
www.pembrokeshire.gov.uk/libraries
Principal Officer: Anita Thomas

Pembrokeshire Historical Society
Headlands, Broad Haven, Haverfordwest SA62 3JP
☎ (01437) 781339
Email: dfgpusey@aol.com
Secretary: Dr David Pusey

Powys Library Service
Library Headquarters, Cefnllys Lane,
Llandrindod Wells, Powys LD1 5LD
☎ (01597) 826860 ᐁ (01597) 826872
Email: library@powys.gov.uk
www.powys.gov.uk/libraries
Principal Librarian: Mark Jones

Radnorshire Society
49 Holcombe Drive, Llandrindod Wells,
Powys LD1 6DN
☎ (01597) 823142
Email: c.p.f.hughes@btinternet.com
www.radnorshiresociety.org.uk
Dr Colin Hughes

Rhondda Cynon Taf County Borough Library Service
Education & Lifelong Learning Directorate,
Tŷ Trevithick, Abercynon, Mountain Ash CF45 4UQ
☎ (01443) 744000
ᐁ (01443) 744023
www.rhondda-cynon-taf.gov.uk/libraries
Head of Libraries, Museums, Heritage & Welsh Language Services: Gillian Evans

Rhondda Heritage Park
Lewis Merthyr Colliery, Coed Cae Rd,
Trehafod, Rhondda Cynon Taf CF37 2NP
☎ (01443) 682036
ᐁ (01443) 687420
Email: info@rhonddaheritagepark.com
www.rhonddaheritagepark.com
Director: Chris Wilson; Business Development/Events Manager: Nicola Newhams

MUSEUMS & LIBRARIES

Robert Owen Museum
The Cross, Broad St, Newtown, Powys SY16 2BB
☎ (0798) 696 1819
Email: info@robert-owen-museum.org.uk
www.robert-owen-museum.org.uk
Curator: Pat Brandwood

Royal Commission on the Ancient and Historical Monuments of Wales (including the National Monuments Record of Wales)
Plas Crug, Aberystwyth, Ceredigion SY23 1NJ
☎ (01970) 621200
🖷 (01970) 627701
Email: nmr.wales@rcahmw.gov.uk
www.rcahmw.gov.uk
Commission Chair: Eurwyn Wiliam
Secretary: Peter Wakelin

The Royal Welch Fusiliers Museum
The Queen's Tower, Caernarfon Castle,
Caernarfon LL55 2AY
☎ (01286) 673362
🖷 (01286) 677042
Email: rwfusiliers@callnetuk.com
www.rwfmuseum.org.uk
Curator: Brian Owen

South Wales Borderers Museum
The Barracks, Brecon, Powys LD3 7EB
☎ (01874) 613310
🖷 (01874) 613275
Email: swb@rrw.org.uk
www.rrw.org.uk

South Wales Miners' Library
Swansea University, Hendrefoelan Campus,
Gower Rd, Swansea SA2 7NB
☎ (01792) 518603/518693
🖷 (01792) 518694
Email: miners@swansea.ac.uk
www.swansea.ac.uk/iss/swml
Librarian: Siân Williams

**St Fagans: National History Museum
Sain Ffagan: Amgueddfa Werin Cymru**
Sain Ffagan/St Fagans, Caerdydd/Cardiff CF5 6XB
☎ (029) 2057 3500
🖷 (029) 2057 3490
Email: post@museumwales.ac.uk
www.museumwales.ac.uk
www.amgueddfacymru.ac.uk
Head of Museum: Bethan Lewis

Swansea City & County Library and Information Service
Library Headquarters, Civic Centre,
Oystermouth Rd, Swansea SA1 3SN
☎ (01792) 636464
🖷 (01792) 636235
Email: swansea.libraries@swansea.gov.uk
www.swansea.gov.uk/libraries
Library Services Manager: Steve Hardman

Torfaen County Borough Libraries
Library HQ, County Hall, Cwmbran NP44 2WN
☎ (01633) 647676
🖷 (01633) 648088
Email: christine.george@torfaen.gov.uk
www.torfaen.gov.uk/en/LeisureCulture/Libraries/
Libraries.aspx
Torfaen Library & Information Manager:
Christine George

Vale of Glamorgan Library & Information Service
Provincial House, Kendrick Rd, Barry CF62 8UF
☎ (01446) 709381 🖷 (01446) 709448
Email: sjones@valeofglamorgan.gov.uk
www.valeofglamorgan.gov.uk/working/libraries.aspx
Chief Librarian: Siân Jones

The Welsh Political Archive
The National Library of Wales, Aberystwyth SY23 3BU
☎ (01970) 632866 🖷 (01970) 632883
Email: graham.jones@llgc.org.uk
www.llgc.org.uk
Director: Dr J Graham Jones

Wrexham Museum and Archives
County Buildings, Regent St, Wrexham LL11 1RB
☎ (01978) 297460 🖷 (01978) 297461
Email: museum@wrexham.gov.uk

Wrexham Library and Information Service
Lord Street Offices, 16 Lord Street, Wrexham LL11 1LG
☎ (01978) 298855
Email: dylan.hughes@wrexham.gov.uk
www.wrexham.gov.uk
Libraries Officer: Dylan Hughes

Sponsored by: www.royalmail.com

Post Brenhinol
Royal Mail

Political Parties

The Co-operative Party
Transport House, 1 Cathedral Rd, Cardiff CF11 9HA
☎ (020) 7367 4178
Email: k.wilkie@party.coop
www.party.coop
Deputy General Secretary: Karen Wilkie

Plaid Cymru - The Party of Wales
Tŷ Gwynfor, Marine Chambers, Anson Court,
Atlantic Wharf, Cardiff CF10 4AL
☎ (029) 2047 2272
Email: post@plaidcymru.org
www.plaidcymru.org
Chief Executive: Rhuanedd Richards

Plaid Gomwnyddol Cymru / Communist Party of Wales (PGC/CPW)
PO Box 21, Corwen LL21 9WZ
☎ (0845) 330 6754
National Secretary: Dr Alun Hughes

Socialist Labour Party Wales
44 Madeline Street, Pontygwaith,
Rhondda, Rhondda Cynon Taf CF43 3NA
🖪 Mobile: 07939 600305
Email: slpcymru@gmail.com
www.slpcymru.com
Wales Regional President: Craig Jones
Wales Regional Vice-President: Bob English
Wales Regional Secretary: Liz Screen

UK Independence Party (UKIP Wales) Plaid Annibyniaeth y Deyrnas Unedig (UKIP Cymru)
Celyn, Coed-y-Caerau, Kemeys Inferior,
Newport, S Wales NP18 1JR
☎ (01633) 400626 🖪 (01633) 400626
Email: office@ukipwales.org
www.ukipwales.org
Chairman: Warwick Nicholson
Secretary: Hugh Moelwyn-Hughes
Treasurer: David Bevan

Wales Green Party
400 Elstob Way,
Monmouth NP25 5ET
☎ (07799) 351017
Email: info@walesgreenparty.org.uk
www.walesgreenparty.org.uk
General Secretary: Ann Were

Welsh Conservatives Ceidwadwyr Cymreig
Ground Floor, Rhymney House,
1-2 Copse Walk, Cardiff Gate Business Park,
Pontprennau, Cardiff CF23 8RB
☎ (029) 2073 6562
Email: info@welshconservatives.com
www.welshconservatives.com
Chair: Catrin Edwards; Director: Matthew Lane

Welsh Labour Party Llafur Cymru
1 Cathedral Rd,
Cardiff CF11 9HA
☎ (029) 2087 7700
🖪 (029) 2022 1153
Email: wales@new.labour.org.uk
www.welshlabour.org.uk
General Secretary: David Hagendyk

Welsh Liberal Democrats Democratiaid Rhyddfrydol Cymru
Freedom Central, Blake Court,
Schooner Way, Cardiff CF10 4DW
☎ (029) 2031 3400
🖪 (029) 2031 3401
Email: enquiries@welshlibdems.org.uk
www.welshlibdems.org.uk
Chief Executive: Richard Thomas

Religion

The Apostolic Church
National Administration Office,
PO Box 51298, London SE27 9PZ
☎ (020) 7587 1802
Email: admin@apostolic-church.org
www.apostolic-church.org
National Leader: Emmanuel Mbakwe
National Administrator: Helen Moore

The Arabic Church in Wales
109 Llanishen St, Heath, Cardiff CF14 3QD
☎ (029) 2073 4818
Email: johnbenham@ntlworld.com
Revd John Benham

RELIGION

Associating Evangelical Churches of Wales (AECW)
Pennant, 110 Coed Onn Road,
Flint, Flintshire CH6 5QE
☎ (01352) 732308
Email: secretary@aecw.org.uk
www.aecw.org.uk
Acting Secretary: Chris Thomas

The Baptist Union of Wales Undeb Bedyddwyr Cymru
Y Llwyfan, Coleg Prifysgol y Drindod Dewi Sant /
Trinity Saint David University College,
Heol y Coleg / College Road,
Caerfyrddin/Carmarthen SA31 3EQ
☎ (01267) 245660 ▣ (01267) 245680
Email: peter@bedyddwyrcymru.co.uk
www.buw.org.uk
Ysgrifennydd Cyffredinol/General Secretary:
Y Parchg / TheRevd Peter M Thomas

Cardiff Buddhist Centre
12 St Peter's Street, Roath, Cardiff CF24 3BA
☎ (029) 2046 2492
Email: connect@cardiffbuddhistcentre.com
www.cardiffbuddhistcentre.com
Contact: Padmasimha

Cardiff Chinese Christian Church
65 Llandaff Rd, Canton, Cardiff CF11 9NG
☎ (029) 2038 8724
Email: sam23wong@yahoo.com
www.cardiffccc.org
Revd Sam Wong

The Catholic Agency for Overseas Development (CAFOD) - Wales
South Wales Office,
11 Richmond Rd, Cardiff CF24 3AQ
☎ (029) 2045 3360
Email: southwales@cafod.org.uk
www.cafod.org.uk
Head CAFOD Wales: Richard Laydon

The Catholic Agency for Overseas Development (CAFOD) - Wales
North Wales Office, 37 Kingsmills Rd,
Wrexham LL13 8NH
☎ (01978) 355084
Email: northwales@cafod.org.uk
www.cafod.org.uk
North Wales Diocesan Manager: Katja Jewell

Centre for Christian Unity & Renewal in Wales
(Non-denominational), Ymddiriedolaeth Hen
Gapel John Hughes Trust, Pont Robert, Meifod,
Powys SY22 6JA
☎ (01938) 500631
www.gtj.org.uk
Custodian: Nia Rhosier

Christian Aid Cymorth Cristnogol
5 Station Rd, Radyr, Cardiff CF15 8AA
☎ (029) 2084 4646
Email: jwilliams@christian-aid.org
www.christianaid.org.uk
National Secretary: Revd Jeff Williams

Church in Wales Yr Eglwys yng Nghymru
39 Cathedral Rd, Cardiff CF11 9XF
☎ (029) 2034 8200 ▣ (029) 2038 7835
Email: information@churchinwales.org.uk
www.churchinwales.org.uk
Provincial Secretary: John Shirley

The Church of Jesus Christ of Latter Day Saints
LDS Chapel, Heol y Deri, Rhiwbina, Cardiff CF14 6UH
☎ (029) 20620205 Mobile: 0771 1950689
Email: adearden.cardiff@virgin.net
Public Affairs: Andrew Dearden

Churches Tourism Network Wales
Head Office, 4 Church View Close,
Llandough, Penarth CF64 2NN
☎ (029) 2071 0014 Mobile: 07815 062040
Email: john@ctnw.co.uk
www.ctnw.co.uk
National Director: John Winton

Coleg Trefeca
Trefeca, Aberhonddu/Brecon, Powys LD3 0PP
☎ (01874) 711423 ▣ (01874) 712212
Email: colegtrefeca@ebcpcw.org.uk
www.trefeca.org.uk
Centre Manager: Mair Jones

Congregational Federation in Wales
Crosslyn House, Spittal, Haverfordwest SA62 5QT
☎ (01437) 741260 ▣ (01437) 741566
Email: tabernacle@haverfordwest.freeserve.co.uk
www.cfwales.org.uk
Secretary: Revd C L Gillham

Post Brenhinol
Royal Mail

Cyngor Ysgolion Sul ac Addysg Gristnogol Cymru
Council for Sunday Schools and Christian Education in Wales
Ael y Bryn, Chwilog, Pwllheli, Gwynedd LL53 6SH
☎ (01766) 810092 ▣ (01766) 819120
Email: aled@ysgolsul.com
www.ysgolsul.com
Ysgrifennydd Cyffredinol/General Secretary:
D Aled Davies

Cytûn
Churches Together in Wales Eglwysi ynghyd yng Nghymru
58 Richmond Rd, Cardiff CF24 3UR
☎ (029) 2046 4204
Email: post@cytun.org.uk
www.cytun.org.uk
Chief Executive: Revd Aled Edwards OBE
Office Administrator: Sasha Perriam
Policy Officer: Geraint Hopkins
Faith Order and Witness Officer: Rhian Linecar

Diocese of Llandaff Board for Social Responsibility
The Court, Coychurch, Bridgend CF35 5EH
☎ (01656) 868868/868853 ▣ (01656) 868869
Email: jondurley@churchinwales.org.uk
Community Development Officer: Revd Jon Durley

Evangelical Alliance - Wales
Cynghrair Efengylaidd - Cymru
20 High St/Heol Fawr, Cardiff/Caerdydd CF10 1PT
☎ (029) 2022 9822
Email: cymru@eauk.org
www.eauk.org/wales
National Director: Revd. Elfed Godding

Evangelical Movement of Wales
Mudiad Efengylaidd Cymru
Bryntirion, Bridgend CF31 4DX
☎ (01656) 655886
Email: office@emw.org.uk
www.emw.org.uk
www.mudiad-efengylaidd.org

Fellowship of Reconciliation in Wales
Cymdeithas y Cymod yng Nghymru
3 Tai Minffordd, Rhostryfan,
Caernarfon, Gwynedd LL54 7NF
☎ (01286) 830913
Email: cymdeithasycymod@btinternet.com
www.cymdeithasycymod.org.uk

The Free Church Council of Wales
Cyngor Eglwysi Rhyddion Cymru
c/o CYTUN, 58 Richmond Rd, Cardiff CF24 3UR
☎ (029) 2046 4204
Email: garethmorganjones@btinternet.com
President: Revd Gareth Morgan Jones

Hindu Cultural Association of Wales
The India Centre, Saquhar St,
Splott, Cardiff CF24 2AA
☎ (029) 2045 1707
Email: info@indiacentre.co.uk
www.indiacentre.co.uk
Chairman: Dr Chandrahas Roy

International Gospel Outreach Network of Churches & Christian Organisations (Churches, Wales)
(incorporating IGO Fellowship of Ministers)
Head Office: The Oasis, Ysguborwen Rd,
Dwygyfylchi, Conwy LL34 6PS
☎ (01492) 623229
Email: mail@igo.org.uk
www.igo.org.uk
Revd Bob Searle, Revd Kingsley Armstrong

Meeting of Friends in Wales (Quakers)
Cyfarfod y Cyfeillion yng Nghymru
1 Clôs Leland, Penygawsi,
Llantrisant, Pontyclun CF72 8QN
☎ (01443) 225732
Email: trevettc@lineone.net
www.quakersinwales.org.uk
Christine Trevett

The Methodist Church in Wales
Wales Synod
Cyncoed Methodist Church,
Westminster Crescent, Cardiff CF23 6SE
☎ (029) 2076 1515
Email: office@methodistwales.org.uk
www.methodistwales.org.uk
Secretary: Judy Lister

Presbyterian Church of Wales
Eglwys Bresbyteraidd Cymru
Tabernacle Chapel, 81 Merthyr Rd,
Whitchurch, Cardiff CF14 1DD
☎ (029) 2062 7465 ▣ (029) 2061 6188
Email: swyddfa.office@ebcpcw.org.uk
www.ebcpcw.org.uk

Roman Catholic Archdiocese of Cardiff
Archbishop's House, 41-43 Cathedral Rd,
Cardiff CF11 9HD
☎ (029) 2022 0411 ▯ (029) 2037 9036
Email: p.a@rcadc.org
www.rcadc.org

The Salvation Army
South & Mid Wales Division, East Moors Rd,
Ocean Park, Cardiff CF24 5SA
☎ (029) 2044 0600 ▯ (029) 2044 0611
Email: southmidwales@salvationarmy.org.uk
www2.salvationarmy.org.uk/southandmidwales
Divisional Leaders: Majors Peter Moran OBE
& Sandra Moran
Secretary Valerie Wornham

Shree Swaminarayan Temple Cardiff
4 Merches Place, Grangetown, Cardiff CF11 6RD
☎ (029) 2037 1128 ▯ (029) 2037 1128
Email: info@swaminarayanwales.org.uk
www.swaminarayanwales.org.uk

South Wales Jewish Representative Council
141 Carisbrooke Way, Cardiff CF23 9HU
☎ (029) 2048 8198
Email: ruthandpaullevene@tiscali.co.uk
Chairman: Alan Schwartz MBE

Sri Damis Sikh Sabha Gurdwara
Bhatra Sikh Temple & Community Centre,
97-103 Tudor St, Riverside, Cardiff CF11 6AE
☎ (029) 2022 4806
Secretary: Rajinder Sing Lakhampal

Union of Welsh Independents
Undeb Yr Annibynwyr Cymraeg
Tŷ John Penri, 5 Axis Court, Riverside Business
Park, Swansea Vale, Swansea SA7 0AJ
☎ (01792) 795888 ▯ (01792) 795376
Email: undeb@annibynwyr.org
www.annibynwyr.org
General Secretary: Y Parchg (Revd) Dr Geraint Tudur

United Reformed Church (Wales) Trust
Synod Office, Minster Rd, Roath, Cardiff CF23 5AS
☎ (029) 2019 5728
Email: trustsec@urcwales.org.uk
www.urcwales.org.uk
Trust Secretary: Chris Atherton

United Reformed Church National Synod of Wales
Synod Office, Minster Rd, Roath, Cardiff CF23 5AS
☎ (029) 2019 5729
Email: synodclerk@urcwales.org.uk
www.urcwales.org.uk
Synod Clerk

The Wales Orthodox Mission
11 Heol y Manod, Blaenau Ffestiniog,
Gwynedd LL41 4DE
☎ (01766) 831272 ▯ (01766) 831272
Email: deiniol@copticmail.com
The Very Revd Archimandrite Father Deiniol

Special Interest Groups

Age Cymru
Tŷ John Pathy, 13/14 Neptune Court,
Vanguard Way, Cardiff CF24 5PJ
☎ (029) 2043 1555
Email: enquiries@agecymru.org.uk
www.agecymru.org.uk
Chair, Board of Trustees: Dr Bernadette Fuge
Chief Executive: Robert Taylor OBE
Campaigns Coordinator: Rhea Stevens

The Bevan Foundation
The Innovation Centre, Festival Drive,
Victoria Business Park, Ebbw Vale NP23 8XA
☎ (01495) 356702 ▯ (01495) 356703
Email: info@bevanfoundation.org
www.bevanfoundation.org
Chair: Paul O'Shea
Director: Victoria Winckler

Campaign for the Protection of Rural Wales
Ymgyrch Diogelu Cymru Wledig
Tŷ Gwyn, 31 High St, Welshpool SY21 7YD
☎ (01938) 552525/556212 ▯ (01938) 871552
Email: info@cprwmail.org.uk
www.cprw.org.uk
Director: Peter Ogden
Office Manager: Carys Matthews

CND Cymru (Campaign for Nuclear Disarmament Wales)
Llysgwyn, Glynarthen,
Llandysul, Ceredigion SA44 6PS
☎ (01239) 851188
Email: heddwch@cndcymru.org
www.cndcymru.org
National Secretary: Jill Gough
Chair: Stephen Thomas

Council for Wales of Voluntary Youth Services (CWVYS)
Baltic House/Tŷ'r Baltic, Mount Stuart Square, Cardiff/Caerdydd CF10 5FH
☎ (029) 2047 3498 ☈ (029) 2045 1245
Email: admin@cwvys.org.uk
www.cwvys.org.uk
Chief Executive: Paul Glaze

Cymdeithas Hanes Plaid Cymru
History Society
47 Wingfield Rd, Cardiff CF14 1NJ
☎ (029) 2062 3275
Email: history@hanesplaidcymru.org
www.hanesplaidcymru.org
Chair: Dafydd Williams
General Secretary: Alan Jobbins
Treasurer: Yvonne Balankrishnan

Cymuned
Tŷ Iorwerth, Ffordd y Sir, Penygroes, Gwynedd LL54 6ES
☎ (01286) 881696
Email: cymuned@cymuned.org
www.cymuned.org
Prif Weithredwr/Chief Executive: Aran Jones
Cadeirydd/Chair: Richard Evans

Electorol Reform Society Wales
Temple Court, 13a Cathedral Road, Cardiff CF11 9HA
☎ (029) 2078 6522
Email: wales@electoral-reform.org.uk
www.electoral-reform.org.uk/wales
Director: Stephen Brooks
Campaign & Research Officer Wales: Owain Llyr ap Gareth

Fair Trade Wales
Masnach Deg Cymru
5th Floor, 5-7 Market Buildings, St Marys Street, Cardiff CF10 1AT
☎ (029) 2080 3293
Email: info@fairtradewales.org.uk
www.fairtradewales.com
National Co-ordinator: Elen Jones

Federation of Small Businesses in Wales
1 Cleeve House, Lambourne Crescent, Cardiff CF14 5GP
☎ (029) 2074 7406 ☈ (029) 2074 7595
Email: wales.policy@fsb.org.uk
www.fsb.org.uk/wales
Chair: Janet Jones
Head of External Affairs: Iestyn Davies

Fellowship of Reconciliation in Wales
Cymdeithas y Cymod yng Nghymru
3 Tai Minffordd, Rhostryfan, Caernarfon, Gwynedd LL54 7NF
☎ (01286) 830913
Email: cymdeithasycymod@btinternet.com
www.cymdeithasycymod.org.uk

Friends of the Earth Cymru
33 Castle Arcade Balcony, Cardiff CF10 1BY
☎ (029) 2022 9577 ☈ (029) 2022 8775
Email: cymru@foe.co.uk
www.foecymru.co.uk (English)
www.cyddcymru.co.uk (Cymraeg)
Director: Gareth Clubb

Heart of Wales Line Travellers' Association
Llandovery Station, Llandovery, Carms SA20 0BG
Email: gillwright.glandwr@gmail.com
www.howlta.org.uk
Chair: Gill Wright
Publicity Co-ordinator: David Edwards

Institute of Directors Wales
Park House Club, 20 Park Place, Cardiff CF10 3DQ
☎ (029) 2038 9990 ☈ (029) 2038 9989
Email: iod.wales@iod.com
www.iod.com/wales
Chair: Huw Roberts
Director Wales: Robert Lloyd Griffiths

Institute of Welsh Affairs
2nd Flr, 4 Cathedral Rd, Cardiff CF11 9LJ
☎ (029) 2066 0820 ☈ (029) 2023 3741
Email: wales@iwa.org.uk
www.iwa.org.uk
Chair: Geraint Talfan Davies
Director: John Osmond
Deputy Director: Kirsty Davies

Also at:

Cardiff & The Valleys Secretariat
3 De Clare Drive, Radyr, Cardiff CF15 8FY
☎ (07971) 246116

Gwent Secretariat
Pear Tree Cottage, Bettws Newydd, Usk NP15 1JW
☎ (01873) 880061
Email: gethinw@ptc.waitrose.com
Chair: Chris O'Malley
Secretary: Dr Gethin Williams

North Wales Secretariat
6 Maes yr Haul, Mold CH7 1NS
☎ (01352) 758311
Email: huwml@btinternet.com
Chair: Professor R Merfyn Jones
Secretary: Huw M Lewis

Swansea Bay Secretariat
c/o Beti Williams, Dept Computer Science,
Swansea University, Swansea SA2 8PP
☎ (01792) 295625
Chair: Prof John Tucker
Secretary: Beti Williams

West Wales Branch
c/o Sustainable Commission for Wales,
Room 1, University of Wales,University Registry,
King Edward VII Avenue, Cardiff CF10 3NS
☎ (029) 2037 6956
Chair: Peter Davies

The Joseph Rowntree Foundation
The Homestead, 40 Water End, York YO30 6WP
☎ (01904) 629241
Email: info@jrf.org.uk
www.jrf.org.uk
Adviser, Welsh Affairs: Michael Trickey

MEWN Cymru
Basement Suite, Crichton House,
11-12 Mount Stuart Square, Cardiff CF10 5EE
☎ (029) 2046 4445
Email: administration@mewn-cymru.org.uk
www.mewn-cymru.org.uk

Rails4Wales / Yn Ein Blaenau
11 Heol y Manod, Blaenau Ffestiniog,
Gwynedd LL41 4DE
☎ (01766) 831272
Email: admin@rails4wales.org.uk
The Very Reverend Father Archimandrite Deiniol

Shelter Cymru
25 Walter Rd, Swansea SA1 5NN
☎ (01792) 469400 ᐃ (01792) 460050
Email: mail@sheltercymru.org.uk
www.sheltercymru.org.uk
Director: John Puzey

Tomorrow's Wales
Cymru Yfory
Tŷ Meandros, 54a Bute Street, Cardiff CF10 5AF
☎ (029) 2048 0880 ᐃ (029) 2043 1275
Email: ymholiadau@cymru-yfory.co.uk
www.cymru-yfory.org

True Wales
Y Gwir Cymru
Email: info@truewales.org.uk
www.truewales.org.uk

United Nations Association Wales
Temple of Peace, Cathays Park, Cardiff CF10 3AP
☎ (029) 2022 8549 ᐃ (029) 2064 0333
Email: una@wcia.org.uk
www.wcia.org.uk/una_wales/756
Chief Executive: Martin Pollard

Wales Council for Voluntary Action (WCVA)
Cyngor Gweithredu Gwirfoddol Cymru (CGGC)
Head Office: Baltic House, Mount Stuart Square,
Cardiff Bay, Cardiff CF10 5FH
☎ (0800) 2888 329 Minicom: (0800) 032 8012
WCVA Helpdesk: ᐃ (029) 2043 1701
Email: help@wcva.org.uk
www.wcva.org.uk
Chair: Win Griffiths
Chief Executive: Graham Benfield OBE

Also at:

Mid Wales Office, 2 Science Park,
Aberystwyth, Ceredigion SY23 3AH
☎ (0800) 2888 329 ᐃ (01970) 631121
Minicom: 0808 1804 080
Email: help@wcva.org.uk
www.wcva.org.uk

North Wales Office, Morfa Hall,
Bath St, Rhyl LL18 3EB
☎ (0800) 2888 329 ᐃ (01745) 357541
Minicom: 0808 1804 080
Email: help@wcva.org.uk
www.wcva.org.uk

The Wales Council of the European Movement
ᐃ Mobile: 07703 112113
Email: williampowell300@btinternet.com
www.euromove.org.uk
President: Wayne David MP
Chair: Cllr William Powell
Secretary: David Peter
Treasurer: Peter Sain Ley Berry

Wales Nicaragua Solidarity Campaign
Ymgyrch Gefnogi Cymru Nicaragua
7 Tŷ Iorwerth, Ffordd y Sir,
Penygroes, Gwynedd LL54 6ES
☎ (01286) 882134
Email: benica@gn.apc.org

Welsh Council on Alcohol and other Drugs
Cyngor Cymru ar Alcohol a Chyffuriau Eraill
58 Richmond Rd, Cardiff CF24 3AT
☎ (029) 2049 3895
Email: info@welshcouncil.org.uk
www.welshcouncil.org.uk
Chief Executive: Wynford Ellis Owen

WWF Cymru
Baltic House, Mount Stuart Sq, Cardiff CF10 5FH
☎ (029) 2045 4970 🖷 (029) 2045 1306
Email: cymru@wwf.org.uk
www.wwf.org.uk/cymru
Head WWF Cymru: Anne Meikle

Sport

Badminton Wales
Sport Wales National Centre,
Sophia Gardens, Cardiff CF11 9SW
☎ (0845) 045 4301 / 07794 676781
🖷 (029) 2013 28011
Email: Laura.Cairns@badmintonwales.net
www.badmintonwales.net
General Enquiries: Laura Cairns

Basketball Wales
c/o Rhondda Fach Sports Centre, East Street,
Tylorstown, Ferndale CF43 3HR
☎ (0845) 450902
www.basketballwales.com
Chair: Phil John

Canoe Wales
The National White Water Centre,
Frongoch, Bala, Gwynedd LL23 7NU
☎ (01678) 521199 🖷 (01678) 521158
Email: admin@canoewales.com
www.canoewales.com

Commonwealth Games Council for Wales (CGCW)
Welsh Institute of Sport,
Sophia Gardens, Cardiff CF11 9SW
☎ (07738) 516734
Email: cjenkins@teamwales.net
www.teamwales.net
Chair: Gareth John
President: Anne Ellis OBE

Cricket Wales
c/o Glamorgan Cricket, SWALEC Stadium,
Cardiff CF11 9XR
☎ (029) 2041 9328
Email: peterhybart@cricketwales.org.uk
www.cricketwales.org.uk
Chair: Roger Morris
Chief Executive Officer: Peter Hybart

CTC (Cyclists Touring Club) Cymru
Email: info@welshcycling.co.uk
www.ctc-wales.org.uk
Chair: Claudine Conway

Disability Sport Wales
Sport Wales National Centre,
Sophia Gardens, Cardiff CF11 9SW
☎ (0845) 8460021 🖷 (029) 2066 5781
Email: office@fdsw.org.uk
www.disabilitysportwales.com
Support Services Manager: Claire Venn

FAW Football in the Community (trading as Welsh Football Trust)
3 Charnwood Court, Heol Billingsley, Nantgarw,
Rhondda Cynon Taff CF15 7QZ
☎ (01443) 844113 🖷 (01443) 841441
Email: info@welshfootballtrust.org.uk
www.welshfootballtrust.org.uk
Chief Executive: Neil Ward

Fields In Trust Cymru (FIT Cymru)
Sport Wales National Centre,
Sophia Gardens, Cardiff CF11 9SW
☎ (029) 2033 4935
Email: cymru@fieldsintrust.org
www.fieldsintrust.org
Manager Wales: Rhodri Edwards

Fitness Wales
1b Clarke St, Cardiff CF5 5AL
☎ (029) 2057 5155 🖷 (029) 2056 8886
Email: enquiries@fitnesswales.co.uk
www.fitnesswales.co.uk
Administrative Manager: Ceri Dunn

The Football Association of Wales
11/12 Neptune Court,
Vanguard Way, Cardiff CF24 5PJ
☎ (029) 2043 5830 🖷 (029) 2049 6953
Email: Info@faw.co.uk
www.faw.org.uk
President: Philip C Pritchard
Chief Executive: Jonathan Ford

Glamorgan Cricket Club
SWALEC Stadium, Cardiff CF11 9XR
☎ (029) 2040 9380
Email: info@glamorgancricket.co.uk
www.glamorgancricket.com
Chair:Barry O'Brien
Chief Executive: Alan Hamer

Golf Union of Wales
Catsash, Newport NP18 1JQ
☎ (01633) 436040 🖷 (01633) 430843
Email: office@golfunionwales.org
www.golfunionwales.org
Chief Executive: Richard Dixon

Hockey Wales
Sport Wales National Centre,
Sophia Gardens, Cardiff CF11 9SW
☎ (0845) 045 4303 🖷 (029) 2033 4997
Email: info@hockeywales.org.uk
www.hockeywales.org.uk
President: Anne Ellis OBE
Chair: Karen Evans; CEO: Helen Bushell
Head of Development: Caroline Spanton;
Operations Manager: Chris Brewer

Plas Menai National Watersports Centre
Caernarfon, Gwynedd LL55 1UE
☎ (01248) 670964 or (0845) 8460 029
Email: info@plasmenai.co.uk
www.plasmenai.co.uk
Rheolwr/Manager: Alan Williams

Plas y Brenin National Mountain Centre
Capel Curig, Conwy LL24 0ET
☎ (01690) 720214 🖷 (01690) 720394
Email: info@pyb.co.uk
www.pyb.co.uk
Chief Executive: Martin Doyle

Ramblers' Association / Cymdeithas y Cerddwyr
3 Coopers Yard, Curran Rd, Cardiff CF10 5NB
☎ (029) 2064 4308 🖷 (029) 2064 5187
Email: cerddwyr@ramblers.org.uk
www.ramblers.org.uk/wales
Director: Angela Charlton

Snowsport Cymru Wales
Cardiff Ski & Snowboard Centre,
198 Fairwater Park, Fairwater, Cardiff CF5 3JR
☎ (029) 2056 1904
Email: admin@snowsportwales.net
www.snowsportwales.net
Manager: Robin Kellen
Administrator: Wendy Petschenyk

Sport Wales
Sophia Gardens, Cardiff CF11 9SW
☎ (0845) 045 0904 🖷 (0845) 846 0014
Email: info@sportwales.co.uk
www.sportwales.org.uk
Chair: Prof Laura McAllister
Chief Executive: Dr Huw G Jones

Squash Wales Ltd
Sport Wales National Centre,
Sophia Gardens, Cardiff CF11 9SW
☎ (029) 2033 4911
Email: squashwales@squashwales.co.uk
www.squashwales.co.uk
Finance & Office Manager: Sue Evans

Surf Life Saving Wales
Kinsale, Princess Margaret Way, Port Talbot SA12 6QW
Email: chair@slsawales.org.uk
www.slsawales.org.uk
President: Peter Lake, MBE
Chair: Patrick Thomas

Swim Wales
Wales National Pool, Sketty Lane, Swansea SA2 8QG
☎ (01792) 513636 🖷 (01792) 513637
Email: secretary@welshasa.co.uk
www.welshasa.co.uk
Chief Executive: Robert James
Head of Administration: Zita Cameron

Table Tennis Association of Wales
Email: admin@ttaw.co.uk
www.ttaw.co.uk

Volleyball Wales
13 Beckgrove Close,
Pengam Green, Cardiff CF24 2SE
☎ (029) 2041 6537 📠 (029) 2041 6768
Email: mail@volleyballwales.org
www.volleyballwales.org
Chair: Yvonne Saker

Welsh Athletics
Cardiff International Sport Stadium,
Leckwith Rd, Cardiff CF11 8AZ
☎ (029) 2064 4870 📠 (029) 2034 2687
Email: office@welshathletics.org
www.welshathletics.org
CEO: Matt Newman
Director of Athletics: Steve Brace

Welsh Billiards & Snooker Association
www.welshsnooker.com

Welsh Bowling Association
5 Grove Cottages, Bagleys Lane,
Four Crosses, Powys SY22 6RP
☎ (029) 2019 1129
Email: secretary@welshbowlingassociation.co.uk
www.welshbowlingassociation.co.uk
Secretary: Brian Rogers

Welsh Clay Target Shooting Association Ltd
Gellifiog, Gwynfe, Llangadog, Carms SA19 9PG
☎ (01550) 740159
Email: wctsa@hotmail.co.uk
www.wctsa.co.uk
Mrs A E Snelgrove

Welsh Cycling/Beicio Cymru
Wales National Velodrome, Newport
International Sports Village, Newport,
South Wales NP19 4PS
☎ (01633) 670540 📠 (01633) 277116
Email: info@welshcycling.co.uk
www.welshcycling.co.uk
Chair: Caroline Oay

Welsh Federation of Sea Anglers
23 Park Rd, Bargoed CF81 8SQ
☎ (01443) 831684
Email: cdoyle0361@aol.com
www.wfsa.org.uk
Secretary: Colin Doyle

Welsh Gymnastics Ltd
Sport Wales National Centre,
Sophia Gardens, Cardiff CF11 9SW
☎ (0845) 045 4304 📠 (029) 2021 328033
Email: office@welshgymnastics.org
www.welshgymnastics.org
CEO: Rhian Gibson

Welsh Judo Association
Sport Wales National Centre,
Sophia Gardens, Cardiff CF11 9SW
☎ (029) 2033 4945
Email: office@welshjudo.com
www.welshjudo.com
National Coach: Craig Ewers
Office Manager: Emily Brown

Welsh Karate Governing Body Ltd
105 Queen's Drive, Llantwit Fardre,
Pontypridd CF38 2NY
☎ (01443) 203733
Email: wkgb@sky.com
www.welshkarate.org.uk
Admin Officer

Welsh Netball Association
Sport Wales National Centre,
Sophia Gardens, Cardiff CF11 9SW
☎ (0845) 045 4302
Email: welshnetball@welshnetball.com
www.welshnetball.co.uk
Chief Executive: Mike Fatkin
WNA Office Manager: Louise Carter

Welsh Orienteering Association
Newlands, Penallt, Monmouth NP25 4SE
Email: secretary@woa.org.uk
www.woa.org.uk
Chair: Vacant
Secretary: Anne May

Welsh Quoiting Board
Noddfa, Oakford, Llanarth, Ceredigion SA47 0RW
☎ (01545) 580756
Email: linhome@btinternet.com
Joint Secretaries: Parry Evans, Linda Evans

Welsh Rugby Union
Millennium Stadium,
Westgate Street, Cardiff CF10 1NS
☎ (0870) 013 8600
Email: info@wru.co.uk
www.wru.co.uk
Chair: David Pickering
Group Chief Executive: Roger Lewis

Welsh Salmon & Trout Angling Association
☎ (01974) 298177
www.wstaa.org
Chair: Euros Jones
Hon Secretary: Cheryl Bulman

Post Brenhinol
Royal Mail

TOURISM

Welsh Sports Associaton
Sport Wales National Centre,
Sophia Gardens, Cardiff CF11 9SW
☎ (029) 2033 8237
Email: wendy.yardley@sportwales.org.uk
www.welshsports.org.uk
Chair: Anne Ellis

The Welsh Surfing Federation
17 Southerndown Ave, Mayals, Swansea SA3 5EL
☎ (01792) 536032 ☒ (01792) 413408
Email: welshsurfing@gmail.com
www.welshsurfingfederation.org.uk
Secretary: Eryl Mason

The Welsh Target Shooting Federation Ltd
PO Box 749, Cardiff CF14 6YY
Email: morganaj@cf.ac.uk
Secretary: Anthony Morgan

Welsh Yachting Association
8 Llys y Môr, Plas Menai, Caernarfon LL55 1UE
☎ (01248) 670738 ☒ (01248) 671320
Email: admin@welshsailing.org
www.welshsailing.org
Chief Executive: Steven Morgan
Office Manager: Cari Yeomans

Tourism

Amgueddfa ac Oriel Gwynedd
Ffordd Gwynedd, Bangor, Gwynedd LL57 1DT
☎ (01248) 353368 ☒ (01248) 370149
Email: AmgueddfaGwynedd@gwynedd.gov.uk

Amgueddfa Ceredigion Museum
Terrace Rd, Aberystwyth, Ceredigion SY23 2AQ
☎ (01970) 633088
Email: museum@ceredigion.gov.uk
www.amgueddfa.ceredigion.gov.uk
Curator: Carrie Canham

Amgueddfa Cymru
National Museum Wales
Cathays Park, Cardiff CF10 3NP
☎ (029) 2039 7951 ☒ (029) 2057 3321
Email: post@museumwales.ac.uk /
post@amgueddfacymru.ac.uk
www.museumwales.ac.uk /
www.amgueddfacymru.ac.uk
President: Elizabeth Elias
Director General: David Anderson

Amgueddfa Lloyd George Museum
Llanystumdwy, Criccieth, Gwynedd LL52 0SH
☎ (01766) 522071 ☒ (01766) 522071
Email: amgueddfalloydgeorge@gwynedd.gov.uk
www.gwynedd.gov.uk/museums
Museums & Galleries Officer: Nêst Thomas

Big Pit National Coal Museum
Amgueddfa Lofaol Cymru
Blaenafon, Torfaen NP4 9XP
☎ (01495) 790311 ☒ (01495) 792618
Email: bigpit@amgueddfacymru.ac.uk
www.museumwales.ac.uk/en/bigpit
Keeper: Peter Walker

Bodelwyddan Castle Trust
Bodelwyddan, Rhyl, Denbighshire LL18 5YA
☎ (01745) 584060 ☒ (01745) 584563
Email: enquiries@bodelwyddan-castle.co.uk
www.bodelwyddan-castle.co.uk
Director: Dr Kevin Mason

Brecon Beacons National Park Authority
Plas y Ffynnon, Cambrian Way,
Brecon, Powys LD3 7HP
☎ (01874) 624437 ☒ (01874) 622574
Email: enquiries@breconbeacons.org
www.breconbeacons.org
Chair: Julie James
Chief Executive: John Cook

Cadw Welsh Historic Monuments
Welsh Government, Plas Carew, Unit 5-7 Cefn Coed,
Parc Nantgarw, Cardiff CF15 7QQ
☎ (01443) 336000 ☒ (01443) 336001
Email: cadw@wales.gsi.gov.uk
www.cadw.wales.gsi.gov.uk
Director: Marilyn Lewis

Capital Region Tourism
Uwch Ranbarth Twristiaeth
North Lodge, Dyffryn Gardens, St Nicholas,
Vale of Glamorgan CF5 6SU
☎ (029) 2059 9221 ▯ (029) 2059 2083
Email: crt@capitalregiontourism.org
www.capitalregiontourism.org
Regional Strategy Director: Peter Cole

Cardiff Castle
Castle St, Cardiff CF10 3RB
☎ (029) 2087 8100 ▯ (029) 2023 1417
Email: cardiffcastle@cardiff.gov.uk
www.cardiffcastle.com
Castle Manager: Kevin Burt

Care Council for Wales
Cyngor Gofal Cymru
Southgate House, Wood St, Cardiff CF10 1EW
☎ (029) 2022 6257 ▯ (029) 2038 4764
Email: info@ccwales.org.uk
www.ccwales.org.uk
Chair: Arwel Ellis Owen
Chief Executive: Rhian Huws Williams

Centre for Alternative Technology
Machynlleth, Powys SY20 9AZ
☎ (01654) 705950 ▯ (01654) 703409
Email: info@cat.org.uk
www.cat.org.uk
Development Director: Paul Allen

Countryside Council for Wales
Cyngor Cefn Gwlad Cymru
Headquarters: Maes-y-Ffynnon,
Penrhosgarnedd, Bangor, Gwynedd LL57 2DW
☎ (0845) 1306229 ▯ (01248) 385505
Email: Enquiries@ccw.gov.uk
www.ccw.gov.uk
Chair: Morgan Parry
Chief Executive: Roger Thomas
Director Evidence & Advice: Dr David Parker;
Director, Planning & Resources: Adrian Williams

Also at:

Plas Penrhos, Ffordd Penrhos,
Bangor, Gwynedd LL57 2BX
☎ (0845) 1306229 ▯ (01248) 385505
Email: northernteam@ccw.gov.uk
www.ccw.gov.uk
Director, North Region: Tim Jones

Countryside Council for Wales
Also at:

Government Buildings, Arran Rd,
Dolgellau, Gwynedd LL40 1LW
☎ (0845) 1306229 ▯ (01248) 385505
Email: northernteam@ccw.gov.uk

Glan y Nant, Unit 19, Mold Business Park,
Wrexham Rd, Mold, Flintshire CH7 1XP
☎ (0845) 1306229 ▯ (01248) 385505
Email: northernteam@ccw.gov.uk

Cantref Court, Brecon Rd,
Abergavenny, Monmouthshire NP7 7AX
☎ (0845) 1306229 ▯ (01248) 385505
Email: southernteam@ccw.gov.uk
www.ccw.gov.uk
Director, South & East Region: Dr Maggie Hill

Unit 13, Drake Walk, Waterfront 2000,
Atlantic Wharf, Cardiff CF10 4AN
☎ (0845) 1306229 ▯ (01248) 385505
Email: southernteam@ccw.gov.uk

Rivers House, St Mellons Business Park,
Fortran Road, St Mellon's, Cardiff CF3 0EY
☎ (0845) 1306229 ▯ (01248) 355782
Email: southernteam@ccw.gov.uk

First Floor, Ladywell House, Park St,
Newtown, Powys SY16 1RD
☎ (0845) 1306229 ▯ (01248) 385505
Email: southernteam@ccw.gov.uk

Welsh Government Building, Rhodfa Padarn,
Llanbadarn Fawr, Aberystwyth SY23 3UR
☎ (01970) 631160 ▯ (01970) 631161
Email: Enquiries@ccw.gov.uk
www.ccw.gov.uk
Director West Region: David Worrall

Beechwood Office, Beechwood Industrial
Estate, Talley Rd, Llandeilo, Carms SA19 7HR
☎ (0845) 1306229 ▯ (01248) 385505
Email: westernteam@ccw.gov.uk

Llanion House, Llanion Park, Pembroke
Dock, Pembrokeshire SA72 6DY
☎ (0845) 1306229 ▯ (01248) 385505
Email: westernteam@ccw.gov.uk

Maes Newydd, Britannic Way West,
Llandarcy, Neath Port Talbot SA10 6JQ
☎ (01792) 326450 ▯ (01792) 326451
Email: westernteam@ccw.gov.uk

Electric Mountain Visitor Centre
International Power - First Hydro Company ,
Dinorwig Power Station, Electric Mountain,
Llanberis LL55 4UR
☎ (01286) 870636
Email: info@electricmountain.co.uk
www.fhc.co.uk
Manager: Diane Rowlands

Forestry Commission Wales
Comisiwn Coedwigaeth Cymru
Welsh Government, Rhodfa Padarn,
Llanbadarn Fawr, Aberystwyth SY23 3UR
☎ (0300) 068 0300 ⅄ (0300) 068 0301
Email: fcwenquiries@forestry.gsi.gov.uk
www.forestry.gov.uk
Director: Trefor Owen
Chair, Woodland Strategy Advisory Panel:
Roger Cooper

Glasu
Antur Gwy, Park Rd, Builth Wells, Powys LD2 3BA
☎ (01982) 552224/553305 ⅄ (01982) 552872
Email: glasu@powys.gov.uk
www.glasu.org.uk

Glynn Vivian Art Gallery
Alexandra Rd, Swansea SA1 5DZ
☎ (01792) 516900 ⅄ (01792) 516903
Email: glynn.vivian.gallery@swansea.gov.uk
www.glynnviviangallery.org
Curator: Jenni Spencer-Davies

Llancaiach Fawr Manor
Living History Museum, Nelson, Caerphilly CF46 6ER
☎ (01443) 412248 ⅄ (01443) 412688
Email: llancaiachfawr@caerphilly.gov.uk
www.llancaiachfawr.co.uk
General Manager: Diane Walker

Mid Wales Tourism
The Station, Machynlleth, Powys SY20 8TG
☎ (01654) 702653 ⅄ (01654) 703235
Email: mwt@midwalestourism.co.uk
www.midwalestourism.co.uk
Chief Executive: Valerie Hawkins

MOMA WALES
MOMA CYMRU
Y Tabernacl, Heol Penrallt,
Machynlleth, Powys SY20 8AJ
☎ (01654) 703355 ⅄ (01654) 702160
Email: info@momawales.org.uk
www.momawales.org.uk
Administrator: Raymond Jones

The National Botanic Garden of Wales
Gardd Fotaneg Genedlaethol Cymru
Llanarthne, Carmarthenshire SA32 8HG
☎ (01558) 668768 ⅄ (01558) 668933
Email: info@gardenofwales.org.uk
www.gardenofwales.org.uk
Chair: Robert Jolliffe
Director: Dr Rosetta Plummer

National Roman Legion Museum
High St, Caerleon, Gwent NP18 1AE
☎ (01633) 423134 ⅄ (01633) 422869
www.museumwales.ac.uk/en/roman
Manager: Dai Price

The National Showcaves Centre for Wales
Abercrave, Swansea SA9 1GJ
☎ (01639) 730284
Email: info@showcaves.co.uk
www.showcaves.co.uk
Manager: Carl Shaw

National Slate Museum
Amgueddfa Lechi Cymru
Gilfach Ddu, Parc Padarn,
Llanberis, Gwynedd LL55 4TY
☎ (01286) 870630 ⅄ (01286) 871906
Email: slate@museumwales.ac.uk /
llechi@amgueddfacymru.ac.uk
www.museumwales.ac.uk/en/slate /
www.amgueddfacymru.ac.uk
Keeper: Dr Dafydd Roberts
Education Officer: Elen Wyn Roberts

North Wales Tourism
77 Conway Rd, Colwyn Bay LL29 7LN
☎ (01492) 531731 ⅄ (01492) 530059
Email: croeso@nwt.co.uk
www.gonorthwales.co.uk
Managing Director: Esther Roberts

Plantasia
Parc Tawe, Swansea SA1 2AL
☎ (01792) 474555 ⅄ (01792) 464743
Email: swansea.plantasia@swansea.gov.uk
www.plantasia.org
Manager: Claire Riordan

Portmeirion Limited
Gwynedd LL48 6ER
☎ (01766) 770000 ⅄ (01766) 770300
Email: enquiries@portmeirion-village.com
www.portmeirion-village.com
Managing Director: Robin Llywelyn

TOURISM

Rhondda Heritage Park
Lewis Merthyr Colliery, Coed Cae Rd,
Trehafod, Rhondda Cynon Taf CF37 2NP
☎ (01443) 682036 ☎ (01443) 687420
Email: info@rhonddaheritagepark.com
www.rhonddaheritagepark.com
Director: Chris Wilson; Business
Development/Events Manager: Nicola Newhams

RSPB Cymru
Wales Headquarters, Sutherland House,
Castlebridge, Cowbridge Rd East, Cardiff CF11 9AB
☎ (029) 2035 3000
Email: cymru@rspb.org.uk
www.rspb.org.uk
Director, Wales: Katie-Jo Luxton

RSPB Cymru
North Wales Office, Uned 14, Llys Castan, Ffordd
y Parc, Parc Menai, Bangor, Gwynedd LL57 4FD
☎ (01248) 672850
Email: cymru@rspb.org.uk
www.rspb.org.uk

Snowdonia National Park Authority
National Park Office, Penrhyndeudraeth,
Gwynedd LL48 6LF
☎ (01766) 770274 ☎ (01766) 771211
Email: [first name].[surname]@eryri-npa.gov.uk
www.eryri-npa.gov.uk
Chair: Cllr E C Roberts OBE JP
Chief Executive (National Park Officer):
Aneurin Phillips

South West Wales Tourism Partnership
Partneriaeth Twristiaeth De Orllewin Cymru
The Coach House, Aberglasney,
Llangathen, Carms SA32 8QH
☎ (01558) 669091 ☎ (01558) 669019
Email: karine.thomas@swwtp.co.uk
www.swwtp.co.uk
Regional Strategy Director: Gary Davies

St Fagans: National History Museum
Sain Ffagan: Amgueddfa Werin Cymru
Sain Ffagan/St Fagans, Caerdydd/Cardiff CF5 6XB
☎ (029) 2057 3500 ☎ (029) 2057 3490
Email: post@museumwales.ac.uk
www.museumwales.ac.uk /
www.amgueddfacymru.ac.uk
Head of Museum: Bethan Lewis

Techniquest
Stuart St, Cardiff Bay, Cardiff CF10 5BW
☎ (029) 2047 5475 ☎ (029) 2048 2517
Email: info@techniquest.org
www.techniquest.org
Chief Executive: Peter Trevitt
Development Director: Dr Anita Shaw

Theatr Felinfach
Felinfach, Dyffryn Aeron, Ceredigion SA48 8AF
☎ (01570) 470697 ☎ (01570) 471030
Email: theatrfelinfach@ceredigion.gov.uk
www.theatrfelinfach.com
Pennaeth: Dwynwen Lloyd Evans

Tourism Partnership Mid Wales
Partneriaeth Twristiaeth Canolbarth Cymru
Y Plas, Machynlleth, Powys SY20 8ER
☎ (01654) 705940 ☎ (01654) 705949
Email: dee.reynolds@tpmw.co.uk
www.tpmw.co.uk
Regional Strategy Director: Dee Reynolds

Tourism Partnership North Wales
Partneriaeth Twrisiaeth Gogledd Cymru
Suite 6, Carlton Court, 56 Ffordd William
Morgan, St Asaph Business Park LL19 9LW
☎ (01745) 585440
Email: dewi.davies@tpnw.org
www.tpnw.org
Regional Strategy Director: Dewi Davies

Visit Wales
(see Welsh Government)

Wales Tourism Alliance
Cynghrair Twristiaeth Cymru
77 Conway Rd, Colwyn Bay, Clwyd LL29 7LN
☎ (07749) 785147
Email: adrian@wta.org.uk
www.wta.org.uk
Chair: Chris Osborne
Executive Director: Adrian D Greason-Walker

TRADE UNIONS

Trade Unions

ATL Cymru, Association of Teachers & Lecturers
Cymdeithas Athrawon a Darlithwyr
1st Floor, 64b Newport Rd, Cardiff CF24 0DF
☎ (029) 2046 5000
Email: cymru@atl.org.uk
www.atl.org.uk
Director: Dr Philip Dixon
Research and Information Officer: Zoe Brewis

BECTU
Unite House, 1 Cathedral Rd, Cardiff CF11 9SD
☎ (029) 2066 6557   ᐩ (029) 2066 6447
Email: ddonovan@bectu.org.uk
www.bectu.org.uk
National Officer: David Donovan

BFAWU, Bakers Food & Allied Workers Union
19a West Bute St, The Courtyard,
The Docks, Cardiff CF10 5EP
☎ (029) 2048 1518   ᐩ (029) 2046 0296
Email: dave.dash@bfawu.org
www.bfawu.org
Regional Officer: Dave Dash

British Medical Association
5th Floor, 2 Caspian Point,
Caspian Way, Cardiff Bay, Cardiff CF10 4DQ
☎ (029) 2047 4646   ᐩ (029) 2047 4600
Email: bmawales@bma.org.uk
www.bma.org.uk
Welsh Secretary: Dr Richard J P Lewis
Senior Public Affairs Officer: John Jenkins
(email: jjenkins@bma.org.uk)

Communication Workers Union
CWU Offices, Moss Building,
Mill St, Newport NP20 5HA
☎ (01633) 250040
Email: walesandthemarchesregion@cwu.org
www.cwu.org
Regional Secretary (Wales): Gary Watkins

Community - The Union for Life
South Wales & South West Division, Pembroke
House, 20 Cathedral Rd, Cardiff CF11 9LJ
☎ (029) 2066 8800   ᐩ (029) 2066 8811
Email: redwards@community-tu.org
www.community-tu.org
Campaign Manager: Rob Edwards

Equity
Transport House, 1 Cathedral Rd, Cardiff CF11 9SD
☎ (029) 2039 7971   ᐩ (029) 2023 0754
Email: wales@equity.org.uk
cymru@equity.org.uk
www.equity.org.uk
Mair James

Farmers' Union of Wales (FUW)
Undeb Amaethwyr Cymru
Llys Amaeth, Plas Gogerddan,
Bow Street, Aberystwyth SY23 3BT
☎ (01970) 820820   ᐩ (01970) 820821
Email: Head.Office@fuw.org.uk
www.fuw.org.uk
President: Emyr Jones
Director, Business Development: Emyr James
Director, Agricultural Policy: Nick Fenwick
Director, Operations: Mark Roberts
Director, Administration: Peter Davies
Director, Public Relations: Peter Roberts

Fire Brigades Union - Wales
4 Ffordd yr Hen Gae, Pencoed, Bridgend CF35 5LJ
☎ (01656) 867910
Email: chris.howells@fbu.org.uk
www.fbu.org.uk
Chair: Cerith Griffiiths
EC Member: Grant Mayos
Secretary: Chris Howells

GMB - Britain's General Union
Williamson House, 17 Newport Rd, Cardiff CF24 0TB
☎ (029) 2049 1260   ᐩ (029) 2046 2056
Email: allan.garley@gmb.org.uk
www.gmb.org.uk
Regional Secretary: John E Phillips

Musicians' Union
199 Newport Rd, Cardiff CF24 1AJ
☎ (029) 2045 6585   ᐩ (029) 2045 1980
Email: cardiff@themu.org
www.theMU.org
Regional Organizer: Paul Westwell

NACODS, National Association of Colliery Overmen, Deputies & Shotfirers (S Wales area)
2nd Floor, 8 Drake Walk, Brigantine Place,
Cardiff Bay CF10 4AN
☎ (029) 2047 0992   ᐩ (029) 2047 0993

Post Brenhinol

Royal Mail

NAHT Cymru/National Association of School Leaders in Wales
Cymdeithas Genedlaethol Arweinyddion Ysgol yng Nghymru
9 Columbus Walk, Brigantine Place, Cardiff CF10 4BY
☎ (029) 2048 4546
Email: cymru@naht.org.uk
www.naht.org.uk
Director, Wales: Anna Brychan
Regional Officers: Anne Hovey, Caroline Bennett
Specialist Assistant: Manon Humphreys

NASUWT Cymru The Teachers' Union
Greenwood Close, Cardiff Gate Business Park, Cardiff CF23 8RD
☎ (029) 2054 6080 ▣ (029) 2054 6089
Email: rc-wales-cymru@mail.nasuwt.org.uk
www.nasuwt.org.uk
Wales Organizer: Rex Phillips
Wales Policy Official: Geraint Davies
Senior Wales Official: David Browne
Wales Official: Colin Adkins; Professional Assistants: Rufus Waddington/Menai Jones

> *Also at:*
>
> 89 Bowen Court, Ffordd William Morgan, St Asaph Business Park, St Asaph LL17 0JE
> ☎ (029) 2054 6080
> ▣ (029) 01745 585723

National Union of Mineworkers
South Wales Area Office,
Woodland Terrace, Maesycoed,
Pontypridd, Rhondda Cynon Taf CF37 1DZ
☎ (01443) 404092
Email: numsouthwales@fut.net
www.num.org.uk
Area Secretary: Wayne Thomas

> *Also at:*
>
> North Wales Area Office,
> 4 Grosvenor Rd, Wrexham,
> Clwyd LL11 1BU
> ☎ (01978) 265638
> www.num.org.uk
> Area Secretary: Mr L Kelly
>
> Cokemen's Area, Cartref,
> Pamela St, Mountain Ash CF45 3LH
> ☎ (01443) 478829
> www.num.org.uk
> Area Secretary: Mr I Morgan

NFU Cymru
Tŷ Amaeth, Agriculture House, Royal Welsh Showground, Builth Wells, Powys LD2 3TU
☎ (01982) 554200 ▣ (01982) 554201
Email: nfu.cymru@nfu.org.uk
www.nfu-cymru.org.uk
Director NFU Cymru: Mary James
President: Ed Bailey

NUS Wales
2nd Floor Cambrain Buildings,
Mount Stuart Square, Cardiff CF10 5FL
☎ (029) 2043 5390
Email: office@nus-wales.org.uk
www.nus.org.uk/wales
President: Luke Young
Deputy President: Raechel Mattey
Women's Officer: Stephanie Lloyd

NUT Cymru, National Union of Teachers
Tŷ Sinnott, 18 Neptune Court, Vanguard Way, Cardiff CF24 5PJ
☎ (029) 2049 1818 ▣ (029) 2049 2491
Email: cymru.wales@nut.org.uk
www.teachers.org.uk
Wales Secretary: David Evans

Prospect Cymru
Landore Court, 51 Charles St, Cardiff CF10 2GD
☎ (029) 2066 7770 ▣ (029) 2066 7692
Email: wales@prospect.org.uk
www.prospect.org.uk
Negotiations Officer for Wales: Gareth Howells

Royal College of Nursing Wales
Tŷ Maeth, King George V Drive East, Cardiff CF14 4XZ
☎ (029) 2068 0738
Email: welsh.board@rcn.org.uk
www.rcn.org.uk
Director: Tina Donnelly

UCAC, Undeb Cenedlaethol Athrawon Cymru National Union of the Teachers of Wales (UCAC)
Ffordd Penglais, Aberystwyth, Ceredigion SY23 2EU
☎ (01970) 639950 ▣ (01970) 626765
Email: ucac@athrawon.com
www.athrawon.com
Ysgrifennydd Cyffredinol/General Secretary: Elaine Edwards

UCATT, Union of Construction Allied Trades & Technicians
Wales & South West, 199 Newport Rd,
Cardiff CF24 1AJ
☎ (029) 2049 8664 ⓕ (029) 2048 1166
Email: nblundell@ucatt.org.uk
www.ucatt.org.uk
Regional Secretary: Nick Blundell

UCU, University & College Union
Wales Regional Office, Unit 33, The Enterprise
Centre, Bryn Rd, Tondu, Bridgend CF32 9BS
☎ (01656) 721 951 ⓕ (01656) 723 834
Email: bridgend@ucu.org.uk
www.ucu.org.uk/wales
Regional Official, Wales: Margaret Phelan
Political Officer: Lleu Williams

Unions Together Wales
Transport House, 1 Cathedral Rd, Cardiff CF11 9SD
☎ (029) 2039 4521
Email: graham.smith@unitetheunion.com
www.unionstogether.org.uk
Chair: Andy Richards
Secretary: Graham Smith

UNISON - Cymru/Wales
UNISON House, Custom House St, Cardiff CF10 1AP
☎ (029) 2072 9413 ⓕ (029) 2038 7531
Email: cymruwales@unison.co.uk
www.unison.org.uk/Cymruwales
Regional Secretary: Margaret Thomas

Unite, The Union
Regional Office, 1 Cathedral Rd, Cardiff CF11 9SD
☎ (029) 2039 4521 ⓕ (029) 2039 0684
www.unitetheunion.org.uk
Regional Secretary: Andy Richards

USDAW, Union of Shop, Distributive & Allied Workers
Unit 10, Oak Tree Court, Mulberry Drive, Cardiff
Gate Business Park, Pontprennau, Cardiff CF23 8RS
☎ (029) 2073 1131 ⓕ (029) 2073 9700
Email: cardiff@usdaw.org.uk
www.usdaw.org.uk

Voice Cymru, Union for Educational Professionals
☎ (01332) 378029
Email: nickgriffin@voicetheunion.org.uk
www.voicetheunion.org.uk
Director for Wales: Nick Griffin

Transport

Anglesey Airport Maes Awyr Mon
RAF Valley
☎ (01407) 762241
Email: info@europa-services.co.uk
www.angleseyairport.com

ARRIVA Buses Wales
Head Office, Llandegai Industrial Estate,
Bangor LL57 4YH
☎ (01492) 564022
www.arrivabus.co.uk
Managing Director Arriva Buses Wales: Michael Morton

ARRIVA Trains Wales Ltd Trenau ARRIVA Cymru
St Mary's House, 47 Penarth Rd, Cardiff CF10 5DJ
☎ (0845) 6061660
Email: customer.services@arrivatrainswales.co.uk
www.arrivatrainswales.co.uk
Managing Director: Tim Bell
Customer Services Director: Ian Bullock

Bws Caerdydd - Cardiff Bus
Leckwith Depot & Offices, Sloper Rd,
Leckwith, Cardiff CF11 8TB
☎ (029) 2066 6444
Email: talktous@cardiffbus.com
www.cardiffbus.com
Managing Director: David Brown
Finance Director: Cynthia Ogbonna
Engineering Director: Andrew Hoseason

Cardiff Airport
Vale of Glamorgan CF62 3BD
☎ (01446) 711111 ⓕ (01446) 712555
Email: info@cwl.aero
www.tbicardiffairport.com
Director of Operations: Mrs Kerry Quinn

Community Transport Association
South Wales Office, Room 10, Forge Fach Centre,
Hebron Rd, Clydach, Swansea SA6 5EJ
☎ (0870) 130 6195 (Advice)
South Wales Office (01792) 844 290
North Wales Office: (01745) 356 751
Email: ctawales@ctauk.org
www.ctauk.org
Director for Wales:
Betsan Caldwell & Tomi Jones (job share)
Senior Support & Development Officer: Kerry Lane
Wales Projects Officer: Alice Tolley; Wales
Administrator: Lindsay Adams-Jones

Community Transport Association
North Wales Office, Unit 11,
Morfa Hall, Bath Street, Rhyl LL18 3EB
☎ (01745) 356 751
www.ctauk.org

First Cymru Buses Ltd
Heol Gwyrosydd, Penlan, Swansea SA5 7BN
☎ (01792) 572255
www.firstgroup.com/ukbus/wales/swwales
General Manager, Wales: Kevin Hart

First Great Western Trains
Freepost SWB40576, Plymouth PL4 6ZZ
☎ (08457) 000 125 (Customer Services)
General Manager for Wales: John Pockett

Heart of Wales Line Forum
c/o 32 Hendre Rd, Llangennech, Llanelli SA14 8TG
☎ (01554) 820586
Email: david.edwards5@which.net
www.heart-of-wales.co.uk
Line Development Officer: David Edwards

Manx2
Cardiff - Anglesey Flights, Hanger 9, Isle of Man
Airport, Ballasallla, Isle of Man IM9 2AY
☎ (0871) 200 0440 (Reservations)
Email: customer.services@manx2.com
reservations@manx2.com
www.manx2.com
Chair: Noel Hayes

National Express
4 Vicarage Rd, Edgbaston, Birmingham B15 3ES
☎ (08705) 808080 ☐ (0121) 456 1397
www.nationalexpress.com
Marketing Development Manager: Susanna Cobham

Network Rail - Wales & West
Western House, 1 Holbrook Way, Swindon SN1 1BD
☎ (01793) 389 749
Email: mavis.choong@networkrail.co.uk
www.networkrail.co.uk
Route Managing Director Wales: Mark Langman
Media Relations Manager: Mavis Choong

North Wales Traffic Management Centre
Ffordd Sam Pari, Morfa, Conwy LL32 8HH
☎ (0845) 602 6020 ☐ (01492) 572395
Email: contact@traffic-wales.com
www.traffic-wales.com

Railfuture Wales/Cymru
Cambrian Lines, 1 Maesmaelor,
Penparcau, Aberystwyth SY23 1SZ
☎ (01970) 624582
Email: dylan.lewis@railfuturewales.org.uk
www.railfuture.org.uk
Secretary: Dylan Lewis

Also at:

North Wales Office, 11 Banc y Chwarel,
Bodfari, Dinbych LL16 4DJ
☎ (01745) 710464
Email:david.mawdsley@railfuturewales.org.uk
Secretary: David Mawdsley

South Wales Office, 2 Llewellyn Street,
Natymoel, Bridgend CF32 7RF
☎ (01656) 840111
Email: john.rogers@railfuturewales.org.uk
Chairman: John Rogers

SEWTA (South East Wales Transport Alliance)
Tŷ Gwent, Lake View, Llantarnam Park,
Cwmbran NP44 3HR
☎ (01633) 876345
Email: mail@sewta.gsi.gov.uk
www.sewta.gov.uk
Chair of Board: Andrew Morgan

South Wales Traffic Management Centre
M4, Junction 32, Coryton, Cardiff CF14 7EF
☎ (0845) 6026020/ (029) 20629424
☐ (029) 2062 9424
Email: info@traffic-wales.com
www.traffic-wales.com

Stagecoach in South Wales
1 St David's Rd, Cwmbran, Torfaen NP44 1PD
☎ (01633) 838856 ☐ (01633) 865299
Email: southwales.enquiries@stagecoachbus.com
www.stagecoachbus.com
Managing Director: John Gould

UTILITIES

Stena Line Ltd
Fishguard Stena Line, Fishguard Harbour,
Goodwick, Pembs SA64 0BU
☎ (01348) 404404 📠 (01348) 404446
Email: info@stenaline.com
www.stenaline.com

Stena Line Ltd
Holyhead Stena Line, Stena House, Station
Approach, Holyhead, Anglesey LL65 1DQ
☎ (01407) 606666 📠 (01407) 606604
Email: info@stenaline.com
www.stenaline.com

Sustrans Cymru
123 Bute St, Cardiff CF10 5AE
☎ (029) 2065 0602
Information Service: (0845) 113 00 65
📠 (029) 2065 0603
Email: sustranscymru@sustrans.org.uk
www.sustrans.org.uk/wales
Chair: Lawrence Conway
Director: Lee Waters

South Wales Trunk Road Agency (SWTRA)
12a Llandarcy House,
The Courtyard, Llandarcy, Neath SA10 6EJ
☎ (0845) 602 6020
Email: enquiries@southwales-tra.gov.uk
www.southwales-tra.gov.uk
Head of SWTRA: Richard Jones

SWWITCH (South West Wales Integrated Transport Consortium)
c/o Penllergaer Offices, City & County of
Swansea, Penllergaer, Swansea SA4 9GJ
☎ (01792) 637760 📠 (01792) 637761
Email: jayne.cornelius@swansea.gov.uk
www.swwitch.net
Travel Plan Co-ordinator: Jayne Cornelius

TAITH
Flint Station, Market Square, Flint CH6 5NW
☎ (01352) 704561 📠 (01352) 704560
Email: iwan.prys-jones@taith.gov.uk
www.taith.gov.uk
Interim Executive Officer: Iwan Prys-Jones

TraCC
Canolfan Rheidol, Rhodfa Padarn, Llanbadarn
Fawr, Aberystwyth SY23 3UE
☎ (01970) 633431
Email: enquiries@tracc.gov.uk
www.tracc.gov.uk
Chair: Cllr Trevor Roberts
Co-ordinator: Chris Wilson

Traffic Wales
North Wales Traffic Management Centre,
Ffordd Sam Pari, Morfa, Conwy LL32 8HH
☎ (0845) 602 6020 (Information Line)
Email: contact@traffic-wales.com
www.traffic-wales.com

Virgin Trains (North Wales Line)
PO Box 713, Birmingham B5 4HH
☎ (0870) 789 1234 📠 (0121) 654 7500
Email: retail.support@virgintrains.co.uk
Chief Operating Officer: Chris Gibb

Wales Transport Research Centre
Canolfan Ymchwil Trafnidiaeth Cymru
Glamorgan Business School, University of
Glamorgan, Pontypridd CF37 1DL
☎ (01443) 654047
www.transport.research.glam.ac.uk
Emeritus Professor of Transport: Prof Stuart Cole
Senior Research Fellow: Owen Clark

Utilities

ACAS, Advisory Conciliation & Arbitration Service
3rd Floor, Fusion Point 2,
Dumballs Rd, Cardiff CF10 5BF
☎ (029) 2076 2636
Helpline: 08457 474747 📠 (029) 2075 1334
Email: gpetty@acas.org.uk
www.acas.org.uk
Director Acas Wales: Gareth Petty

British Gas
Penarth Road, Bute Town, Cardiff CF10 5NB
☎ (0845) 955 5820
www.britishgas.co.uk

BT Wales
Tŷ Cynnal, Watkiss Way, Ely Fields, Cardiff CF11 0SW
☎ (029) 2036 7100
Email: ann.beynon@bt.com
www.bt.com/wales
BT Director Wales: Ann Beynon

Sponsored by: www.royalmail.com
Royal Mail

Charity Commission
Comisiwn Elusennau
8th Floor, Clarence House,
Clarence Place, Newport NP19 7AA
☎ (0845) 3000218
www.charity-commission.gov.uk

Dŵr Cymru
Welsh Water
Pentwyn Rd, Nelson, Treharris CF46 6LY
☎ (01443) 452300 ☐ (01443) 452323
www.dwrcymru.com
Managing Director: Nigel Annett

e.on UK
Suite 5G, Building 1, Eastern Business Park,
Wernfawr Lane, St Mellons, Cardiff CF3 5EA
☎ (029) 2036 1899
www.eon-uk.com

First Hydro Company
Dinorwig Power Station, Llanberis,
Caernarfon, Gwynedd LL55 4TY
☎ (01286) 870166
Email: info@fhc.co.uk
www.fhc.co.uk
Stations Manager: Mike Hickey

First Hydro Company
Ffestiniog Power Station, Tan y Grisiau,
Blaenau Ffestiniog, Gwynedd LL41 3TP
☎ (01766) 830465
Email: info@fhc.co.uk
www.fhc.co.uk
Stations Manager: Mike Hickey

Glas Cymru
Dŵr Cymru Welsh Water, PO Box 690,
Cardiff CF3 5WL
☎ (0800) 052 0145
www.dwrcymru.com
Chair: Bob Ayling
Managing Director: Nigel Annette

Royal Mail Group External Relations Wales
Grŵp y Post Brenhinol, Cysylltiadau Allanol Cymru
Cardiff Mail Centre, 3rd Floor,
220 Penarth Rd, Cardiff CF11 8TA
☎ (029) 2039 2500 ☐ (029) 2039 2505
Email: external.relations.wales@royalmail.com
pressofficewales@postoffice.co.uk
www.royalmailgroup.com
Head of External Relations, Royal Mail:
Heulyn Gwyn Davies
Head of External Relations, Post Office Ltd:
Stuart Taylor

SP MANWEB plc
3 Prenton Way, Prenton,
Birkenhead CH43 3ET
☎ (0845) 270 6543
Email:gwasanaeth.cwsmeiriaid@scottishpower.co.uk /
customer.services@scottishpower.co.uk
www.scottishpower.co.uk

SWALEC
Tŷ Meridian, Malthouse Ave, Cardiff Gate
Business Park, Cardiff CF23 8AU
☎ (0800) 052 5252 (Customer Services)
www.swalec.com

Western Power Distribution
Lamby Way Industrial Estate,
Rumney, Cardiff CF3 2EQ
☎ (0800) 052 0400
Email: info@westernpower.co.uk
www.westernpower.co.uk
Network Services Manager Wales: Phil Davies
Logistics Manager: Phil Allen

Voluntary Organizations

Action for Children Wales
Gweithredu dros Blant
St David's Court, 68a Cowbridge Rd East,
Cardiff CF11 9DN
☎ (029) 2022 2127
Email: sasha.mansworth@actionforchildren.org.uk
www.actionforchildren.org.uk
News and Media Relations Officer:
Sasha Mansworth

Action on Hearing Loss Cymru
Tudor House, 16 Cathedral Rd, Cardiff CF11 9LJ
☎ (029) 2033 3034; Minicom: (029) 2033 3036
☐ (029) 2033 3035
Email: wales@hearingloss.org.uk
www.actiononhearingloss.org.uk
Chair: Gerald Corbett
Chief Executive: Jackie Ballard
Director-Wales: Richard Williams

Post Brenhinol
Royal Mail

The Adolescent and Children's Trust (TACT)
20 Victoria Gardens, Neath SA11 3BH
☎ (01639) 622320
Email: cymru@tactcare.org.uk
d.jones@tactcare.org.uk
www.tactcare.org.uk
Director Children's Services, Wales: Dot Jones

Age Cymru
Tŷ John Pathy, 13/14 Neptune Court,
Vanguard Way, Cardiff CF24 5PJ
☎ (029) 2043 1555
Email: enquiries@agecymru.org.uk
www.agecymru.org.uk
Chair, Board of Trustees Dr Bernadette Fuge;
Chief Executive: Robert Taylor OBE; Campaigns
Coordinator: Rhea Stevens

Alcoholics Anonymous - Wales and Borders Region
☎ (0845) 769 7555
Email: walesandborders-reclo@aa-email.org.uk
www.alcoholics-anonymous.co.uk
www.aa-gb.org.uk/walesborders/region/index.html

Alzheimer's Society
South Wales Office, 16 Columbus Walk,
Atlantic Wharf, Cardiff CF10 4BY
☎ (029) 2048 0593
Email: SDAreaOffice-
SouthWales@alzheimers.org.uk
www.alzheimers.org.uk
Director Wales: Ian Thomas

Also at:

North & West Wales Office, 6a Llys Onnen,
Parc Menai, Bangor LL57 4DF
☎ (01248) 671137
Email: nwa@alzheimers.org.uk
www.alzheimers.org.uk
Director Wales: Ian Thomas

Amnesty International Wales Amnest Rhyngwladol Cymru
Temple Court, Cathedral Rd, Cardiff CF11 9HA
☎ (029) 2078 6415 ☐ (029) 2078 6416
Email: wales@amnesty.org.uk
www.amnesty.org.uk/wales
Programme Director: Cathy Owens

Anheddau Cyf
6 Llys Britannia, Parc Menai, Bangor LL57 4BN
☎ (01248) 675910 ☐ (01248) 676280
Email: post@anheddau.co.uk
www.anheddau.co.uk
Chief Executive Officer: Janetta Toleman Jones
Company Secretary: Nia Prendergast

Arthritis Care Wales Gofal Arthritis
1 Caspian Point, Cardiff Waterside,
Pierhead Street, Cardiff CF10 4DQ
☎ (029) 2044 4155
Email: Wales@arthritiscare.org.uk
www.arthritiscare.org.uk
Wales Administrator: Lorraine Fletcher
Local Development Manager, South Wales:
Mary Cowern
Local Development Manager, North Wales:
Stuart Chadbourne
Information Services Manager: Victoria Kalmaru

ASH Cymru Wales
2nd Floor, 8 Museum Place, Cardiff CF10 3BG
☎ (029) 2064 1101 ☐ (029) 2064 1045
Email: sue@ashwales.org.uk
www.ashwales.org.uk
Chief Executive: Elen de Lacy
Press & Campaigns Manager: Felicity Waters

Association of Voluntary Organisations in Wrexham
21 Egerton St, Wrexham LL11 1ND
☎ (01978) 312556
Email: chief@avow.org
www.avow.org
Chief Officer: John Gallanders

Autism Cymru
c/o Thomas Simon Solicitors,
62 Newport Rd, Cardiff CF24 0DF
☎ (029) 2046 3263 ☐ (029) 2046 3263
Email: maaggie@autismcymru.org
www.awares.org
Chief Executive: Hugh Morgan

BAAF Cymru
7 Cleeve House, Lambourne Crescent,
Llanishen, Cardiff CF14 5GP
☎ (029) 2076 1155 ☐ (029) 2074 7934
Email: cardiff@baaf.org.uk
www.baaf.org.uk
Director: Wendy Keidan
Regional Administrators: Val Leung/Fiona Probert

BAAF Cymru Rhyl (British Association for Adoption & Fostering)
W2 Morfa Clwyd Business Centre,
84 Marsh Rd, Rhyl LL18 2AF
☎ (01745) 336336
Email: rhyl@baaf.org.uk
www.baaf.org.uk
Regional Administrator: Erina Roberts

Barnardo's Cymru
Trident Court, Eastmoors Rd, Cardiff CF24 5TD
☎ (029) 2049 3387 🖷 (029) 2048 9802
Email: cym.national@barnardos.org.uk
www.barnardos.org.uk
Director, Barnardo's Cymru: Yvonne Rodgers

Black Voluntary Sector Network Wales (BVSN Wales)
Second Floor - East, Chamber of Commerce
Building, 113/116 Bute Street, Cardiff Bay CF10 5EQ
☎ (029) 2045 0068 🖷 (029) 2044 0186
Email: info@bvsnw.org.uk
www.bvsnw.org.uk
Project Director: Michael Flynn

Bridgend Association of Voluntary Organisations
112-113 Commercial St,
Maesteg, Bridgend CF34 9DL
☎ (01656) 810400
Email: bavo@bavo.org.uk
www.bavo.org.uk
Director: Heidi Bennett

BTCV Cymru
The Conservation Centre, Forest Farm Rd,
Whitchurch, Cardiff CF14 7JJ
☎ (029) 2052 0990 🖷 (029) 2052 2181
Email: wales@btcv.org.uk
www.btcvcymru.org
Director: Ioan Jenkins

C3SC
Ground Floor, Brunel House,
2 Fitzalan Road, Cardiff CF24 0EB
☎ (029) 2048 5722
www.c3sc.org.uk

Cardiff & the Vale Parents Federation
Canton House, 435 Cowbridge Rd East,
Cardiff CF5 1JH
☎ (029) 2022 7800 🖷 (029) 2022 7878
Email: admin@parentsfed.org
www.parentsfed.org
Director: John Cushen
Development Officer: Hasina Kaderbhai

Care & Repair Cymru
National Office, 2 Ocean Way, Cardiff CF24 5TG
☎ (029) 2067 4830 🖷 (029) 2067 4801
Email: enquiries@careandrepair.org.uk
www.careandrepair.org.uk
Managing Director: Chris Jones

Care & Repair Cymru
North Wales Office, 6b Llys Onnen,
Parc Menai, Bangor LL57 4DF
☎ (01248) 671880
Email: enquiries@careandrepair.org.uk
www.careandrepair.org.uk
Managing Director: Chris Jones

Carers Wales
River House, Ynysbridge Court,
Gwaelod y Garth, Cardiff CF15 9SS
☎ (029) 2081 1370 🖷 (029) 2081 1575
Email: info@carerswales.org
www.carerswales.org
Director: Roz Williamson

Carmarthenshire Association of Voluntary Services (CAVS)
18 Queen St, Carmarthen SA31 1JT
☎ (01267) 245 555 🖷 (01267) 245550
Email: info@cavs.org.uk
www.cavs.org.uk
Executive Director: Mandy Jones

Cartrefi Cymru
5-6 Cooper's Yard, Curran Rd, Cardiff CF10 5NB
☎ (029) 2064 2250 🖷 (029) 2064 2264
Email: enquiries@cartrefi.org
www.cartreficymru.org
Chief Executive: Adrian Roper

The Catholic Agency for Overseas Development (CAFOD) - Wales
South Wales Office,
11 Richmond Rd, Cardiff CF24 3AQ
☎ (029) 2045 3360
Email: southwales@cafod.org.uk
www.cafod.org.uk
Head CAFOD Wales: Richard Laydon

The Catholic Agency for Overseas Development (CAFOD) - Wales
North Wales Office, 37 Kingsmills Rd,
Wrexham LL13 8NH
☎ (01978) 355084
Email: northwales@cafod.org.uk
www.cafod.org.uk
North Wales Diocesan Manager: Katja Jewell

CCN Cymru
Care Co-ordination Network Cymru, Ebenezer Business Centre, Crane Street, Cefn Mawr, Wrexham LL14 3AB
☎ (01978) 821324
Email: wales@ccnuk.org.uk
sally.rees@ccnuk.org.uk
www.ccnuk.org.uk
Wales Manager: Sally Rees
Wales Development: Ann Davies
Wales Administrator: Jacqui Williams
Wales Finance: Deb Jones

Ceredigion Association of Voluntary Organisations
Bryndulais, 67 Bridge St, Lampeter SA48 7AB
☎ (01570) 423232
Email: gen@cavo.org.uk
www.cavo.org.uk
Chief Executive: Hazel Lloyd Lubran

CFBT Education Trust trading as include
ITV Wales, The Television Centre,
Culverhouse Cross, Cardiff CF5 6XJ
☎ (029) 2059 5923 ⓑ (029) 2059 8462
Email: pshort@cfbt.com
www.cfbt.com / include.org.uk
Senior Manager: Pam Short

Changing Faces Cymru
PO Box 562, Swansea SA8 9AD
☎ (0845) 4500240 ⓑ (0845) 4500240
Email: cymru@changingfaces.org.uk
www.changingfaces.org.uk
Welsh Officer/Swyddog Cymru: Simon Boex

ChildLine Cymru/Wales
Warren House, Warren Drive,
Prestatyn, Clwyd LL19 7HT
☎ (0844) 8920230
Email: childlineprestatyn@nspcc.org.uk
www.childline.org.uk

Children in Wales
Plant yng Nghymru
Victoria Dock, Caernarfon, Gwynedd LL55 1TH
☎ (01286) 677570
Email: info@childreninwales.org.uk
www.childreninwales.org.uk
Chair: Dr Mike Shooter CBE
Chief Executive: Catriona Williams

Children in Wales
Plant yng Nghymru
25 Windsor Place, Cardiff CF10 3BZ
☎ (029) 2034 2434 ⓑ (029) 2034 3134
Email: info@childreninwales.org.uk
www.childreninwales.org.uk
Chair: Dr Mike Shooter CBE
Chief Executive: Catriona Williams

Christian Aid
Cymorth Cristnogol
5 Station Rd, Radyr, Cardiff CF15 8AA
☎ (029) 2084 4646
Email: jwilliams@christian-aid.org
www.christianaid.org.uk
National Secretary: Revd Jeff Williams

Christian Rebuild
Crosslyn House, Spittal, Haverfordwest SA62 5QT
☎ (01437) 741260 ⓑ (01437) 741566
Email: info@christianrebuild.com
www.christianrebuild.com
Secretary: Revd C L Gillham

Chwarae Teg
Fairplay (Workforce) Ltd
Anchor Court, Keen Rd, Cardiff CF24 5JW
☎ (029) 2047 8900 ⓑ (029) 2047 8901
Email: post@chwaraeteg.com
www.chwaraeteg.com
Chief Executive: Katy Chamberlain

Citizens Advice Cymru
(Admin Office only)
Morfa Hall, Bath Street, Rhyl, Denbighshire LL18 3EB
☎ (01745) 354198
Email: cymru@citizensadvice.org.uk;
adviceguide@citizensadvice.org.uk
www.citizensadvice.org.uk
Director Citizens Advice Cymru: Fran Targett OBE

Citizens Advice Cymru
(Admin Office only)
Quebec House, Castlebridge,
5-19 Cowbridge Rd East, Cardiff CF11 9AB
☎ (029) 2037 6750 ⓑ (029) 2034 1541
Email: cymru@citizensadvice.org.uk
adviceguide@citizensadvice.org.uk
www.citizensadvice.org.uk
Director Citizens Advice Cymru: Fran Targett OBE

Post Brenhinol
Royal Mail

The Civic Trust for Wales
East Wing, Windsor House,
Windsor Lane, Cardiff CF10 3DE
☎ (029) 2034 3336
Email: post@civictrustwales.org
www.civictrustwales.org;
www.opendoorsdays.org.uk
Director: Dr Matthew Griffiths
Development Officer: Jo Coles
Open Doors Manager: Derw Thomas
Characterisation Officer: Anna Lermon

Clubs for Young People Wales
Western Business Centre, Riverside Terrace,
Ely Bridge, Cardiff CF5 5AS
☎ (029) 2057 5705 ◻ (029) 2057 5715
Email: office@cypwales.org.uk
www.cypwales.org.uk
Chief Executive: Joff Carroll

Coalfields Regeneration Trust
Welsh Office, Part Unit 3, Maritime Office,
Woodland Terrace, Maes-y-Coed,
Pontypridd CF37 1DZ
☎ (01443) 404455
◻ (01443) 408804
Email: info@coalfields-regen.org.uk
www.coalfields-regen.org.uk
Operations Manager: Siân Sykes
Programme Manager: Alun Taylor
Development Officer: Hayley Doorhof
Programme Officer: Michelle Rowson-Woods

Community Development Cymru
Plas Dolerw, Milford Rd,
Newtown, Powys SY16 2EH
☎ (01686) 627377 ◻ (01686) 627377
Email: emma@cdcymru.org
www.cdcymru.org
Chief Executive: Derith Powell

Community Music Wales
Unit 8, 24 Norbury Rd, Fairwater, Cardiff CF5 3AU
☎ (029) 2083 8060 ◻ (029) 2056 6573
Email: admin@communitymusicwales.org.uk
www.communitymusicwales.org.uk
Director: Hannah Jenkins

Community Transport Association
South Wales Office, Room 10, Forge Fach
Centre, Hebron Rd, Clydach, Swansea SA6 5EJ
☎ (0870) 130 6195 (Advice)
South Wales Office (01792) 844 290
North Wales Office: (01745) 356 751
Email: ctawales@ctauk.org
www.ctauk.org
Director for Wales:
Betsan Caldwell & Tomi Jones (job share)
Senior Support & Development Officer:
Kerry Lane
Wales Projects Officer: Alice Tolley
Wales Administrator: Lindsay Adams-Jones

Community Transport Association
North Wales Office, Unit 11,
Morfa Hall, Bath Street, Rhyl LL18 3EB
☎ (01745) 356 751
www.ctauk.org

Connect Disability Rights Advice
Unit 2 Goodwick Industrial Estate,
Main St, Goodwick, Pembs SA64 0BD
☎ (01348) 875220
Email: connect_dra@hotmail.com

Conwy Voluntary Services Council
8 Riviere's Ave, Colwyn Bay LL29 7DP
☎ (01492) 534091 ◻ (01492) 535397
Email: mail@cvsc.org.uk
www.cvsc.org.uk
Chief Officer: Wendy Jones

Council for Wales of Voluntary Youth Services (CWVYS)
Baltic House/Tŷ'r Baltic, Mount Stuart Square,
Cardiff/Caerdydd CF10 5FH
☎ (029) 2047 3498 ◻ (029) 2045 1245
Email: admin@cwvys.org.uk
www.cwvys.org.uk
Chief Executive: Paul Glaze

Carers Trust
3rd Flr, 33-35 Cathedral Rd, Cardiff CF11 9HB
☎ (029) 2009 0087 ◻ (029) 2022 8859
Email: wales.office@crossroads.org.uk
www.carers.org
Director Carers Trust Wales: Angela Roberts

Cynnydd - Wales Youth Justice Forum
Email: mike.mccarthy@cynnydd.net
www.cynnydd.net
Treasurer: Mike McCarthy

Denbighshire Voluntary Services Council
Naylor Leyland Centre, Well St, Ruthin,
Denbighshire LL15 1AF
☎ (01824) 702441 ⓕ (01824) 705412
Email: info@dvsc.co.uk
www.dvsc.co.uk
Chief Executive Officer: John Watkin

Diabetes UK Cymru
Argyle House, Castlebridge,
Cowbridge Road East, Cardiff CF11 9AB
☎ (029) 2066 8276 ⓕ (029) 2066 8329
Email: wales@diabetes.org.uk
www.diabetes.org/wales
National Director: Dai Williams

Disability Arts Wales
Sbectrwm, Bwlch Rd, Fairwater, Cardiff CF5 3EF
☎ (& Text 029) 2055 1040
ⓕ (& Text 029) 2055 1036
Email: post@dacymru.com
www.dacymru.com
Director: Maggie Hampton

Disability Wales
Anabledd Cymru
Bridge House, Caerphilly Business Park,
Van Road, Caerphilly CF83 3GW
☎ (029) 2088 7325 ⓕ (029) 2088 8702
Email: info@disabilitywales.org
www.disabilitywales.org
Chair: Wendy Ashton
Chief Executive: Rhian Davies

Dolen Cymru/Wales Lesotho Link
Enterprise House, 127 Bute St, Cardiff CF10 5LE
☎ (029) 2049 7390
Email: swyddfa@dolencymru.org
www.dolencymru.org
Executive Director: Veronica German

Drugaid Wales
1st Floor, St Fagan's House,
St Fagan's St, Caerphilly CF83 1FZ
☎ (029) 2088 1000 ⓕ (029) 2088 1008
Email: office@drugaidcymru.com
www.drugaidcymru.com
Executive Director: Caroline Phipps

Duke of Edinburgh's Award (Wales)
Market House, Market Approach,
Brecon, Powys LD3 7DA
☎ (01874) 623086
Email: wales@DofE.org
www.DofE.org
DofE Director Wales: Stephanie Price
DofE Operations Manager Wales: Ian Gwilym

Firebrake Wales
Atal Tân Cymru
Ground Floor, Willow House,
6 Hazell Drive, Newport NP10 8FY
☎ (01633) 654000 ⓕ (01633) 654001
Email: info@firebrake.org
www.firebrake.org
Chief Executive: Helen Prior

Flintshire Local Voluntary Council
Corlan, Unit 3, Mold Business Park,
Wrexham Rd, Mold CH7 1XP
☎ (01352) 744000
Email: info@flvc.org.uk
www.flvc.org.uk
Chief Officer: Kieran Duff

Friends of the Earth Cymru
33 Castle Arcade Balcony, Cardiff CF10 1BY
☎ (029) 2022 9577 ⓕ (029) 2022 8775
Email: cymru@foe.co.uk
www.foecymru.co.uk (English)
www.cyddcymru.co.uk (Cymraeg)
Director: Gareth Clubb

Gingerbread Wales (South Wales)
4th Floor, Baltic House,
Mount Stuart Square, Cardiff CF10 5FH
☎ (029) 2048 8225 / 2047 1900
ⓕ (029) 2047 1900
Email: wales@gingerbread.org.uk
www.gingerbread.org.uk

GWEINI - The Council of the Christian Voluntary Sector in Wales
20 High Street, Cardiff CF10 1YR
☎ (029) 2022 9822
Email: info@gweini.org.uk
www.gweini.org.uk
President: To be appointed

Gwent Association of Voluntary Organisations
Head Office, Tŷ Derwen,
Church Rd, Newport, Gwent NP19 7EJ
☎ (01633) 241550 ⓕ (01633) 241583
www.gavowales.org.uk
Director: Jennifer Render

Gwent Association of Voluntary Organisations
Blaenau Gwent Office, 16a Market Sq,
Brynmawr, Blaenau Gwent NP23 4AJ
☎ (01495) 315626/315534

Gwent Association of Voluntary Organisations
Caerphilly Office, Unit 1A, First Floor,
Withey Duffryn Court, Duffryn Business Park,
Ystrad Mynach CF82 7TT
☎ (01443) 863540

Gwent Association of Voluntary Organisations
Monmouthshire Office, Holly House,
Llancayo Court, Llancayo, Usk NP15 1HY
☎ (01291) 672352

HAFAL
Suite C2, William Knox House,
Britannic Way, Llandarcy, Neath SA10 6EL
☎ (01792) 816600 ☐ (01792) 813056
Email: hafal@hafal.org
www.hafal.org www.mentalhealthwales.net
Chief Executive: Bill Walden-Jones

Hafan Cymru
5-6 Queen Street, Carmarthen SA31 1JR
☎ (01267) 225558 ☐ (01267) 221592
Email: enquiries@hafancymru.co.uk
www.hafancymru.co.uk
Chair: Kathryn Williams
Chief Executive: Cathy Davies

HUGGARD
Huggard , Tresillian Terrace,
Bute Town, Cardiff CF10 5JZ
☎ (029) 2034 9980 ☐ (029) 2023 0283
Email: info@huggard.org.uk
www.huggard.org.uk
Chief Executive: Richard Edwards
Deputy Chief Executive - Facilities: Layton Percy Jones
Deputy Chief Executive - Support &
Development: Tim Paddock

Institute of Fundraising Cymru
1st Flr, 21 Cathedral Rd, Cardiff CF11 9HA
☎ (029) 2034 0062
Email: cymru@institute-of-fundraising.org.uk
www.institute-of-fundraising.org.uk
Wales Manager: Pam Dodd

Interlink
6 Melin Corrwg, Cardiff Road,
Upper Boat, Pontypridd CF37 5BE
☎ (01443) 846200 ☐ (01443) 844843
Email: info@interlinkrct.org.uk
www.interlinkrct.org.uk
Chief Executive Officer: Simon James

Leonard Cheshire Disability Wales
Regional Office (Wales & West), Llanhennock
Lodge, Llanhennock, Nr Caerleon,
Newport NP18 1LT
☎ (01633) 431309
www.lcdisability.org

Llamau Ltd
23 Cathedral Rd, Cardiff CF11 9HA
☎ (029) 2023 9585 ☐ (029) 2038 8740
Email: enquiries@llamau.org.uk
www.llamau.org.uk
Chair: Angela Gascoigne
Chief Executive: Frances J Beecher

Macmillan Cancer Support
Cymorth Canser Macmillan
Wales Office, 1st Floor, 1 Oldfield Rd,
Bocam Park, Bridgend CF35 5LJ
☎ (01656) 867960
www.macmillan.org.uk/wales
Director for Wales, Scotland & N Ireland:
Elspeth Atkinson
General Manager for Wales: Susan Morris
External Affairs Manager: Gwenllian Griffiths

Mantell Gwynedd
23-25 Y Bont Bridd, Caernarfon, Gwynedd LL55 1AB
☎ (01286) 672626 ☐ (01286) 678430
Email: enquiries@mantellgwynedd.com
www.mantellgwynedd.com
Chief Officer: Bethan Russell Williams

Medrwn Môn
Unit 5c, Bryn Cefni Industrial Park,
Llangefni, Ynys Môn LL77 7XA
☎ (01248) 724944 ☐ (01248) 750149
Email: post@medrwnmon.org
www.medrwnmon.org
Chief Officer: John R Jones

Mencap Cymru
31 Lambourne Crescent, Cardiff Business Park,
Llanishen, Cardiff CF14 5GF
☎ (029) 2074 7588;
Freephone: (0808) 808 1111
☐ (029) 2074 7550
Email: helpline.wales@mencap.org.uk
www.mencap.org.uk/cymru
Director: Wayne Crocker

Merched y Wawr
Canolfan Genedlaethol Merched y Wawr,
Stryd yr Efail, Aberystwyth, Ceredigion SY23 1JH
☎ (01970) 611661 🖷 (01970) 626620
Email: swyddfa@merchedywawr.com
www.merchedywawr.co.uk
Cyfarwyddwr Genedlaethol/National Director:
Tegwen Morris

MEWN Cymru
Basement Suite, Crichton House,
11-12 Mount Stuart Square, Cardiff CF10 5EE
☎ (029) 2046 4445
Email: administration@mewn-cymru.org.uk
www.mewn-cymru.org.uk

Mid Wales Food and Land Trust
Frolic House, Frolic St, Newtown, Powys SY16 1AP
☎ (01686) 622388
Email: cath@midwalesfoodandlandtrust.org.uk
www.midwalesfoodandlandtrust.org.uk
Executive Director: Cath Smith

Mind Cymru
3rd Floor, Quebec House, Castlebridge,
Cowbridge Road East, Cardiff CF11 9AB
☎ (029) 2039 5123
Mind infoline: (0845) 766 0163
🖷 (029) 2034 6585
Email: contactwales@mind.org.uk
www.mind.org.uk
Director: Lindsay Foyster

Mudiad Meithrin
Association of Welsh Medium Nursery Schools and Playgroups
Boulevard De St Brieuc,
Aberystwyth, Ceredigion SY23 1PD
☎ (01970) 639639 🖷 (01970) 639638
Email: post@mym.co.uk
www.mym.co.uk
Chief Executive: Hywel Jones

Multiple Sclerosis Society Cymru
Temple Court, Cathedral Rd, Cardiff CF11 9HA
☎ (029) 2078 6676 🖷 (029) 2078 6677
Email: mscymru@mssociety.org.uk
www.mssociety.org.uk/wales
Director: Judi Rhys

Nacro Cymru
c/o Neath Port Talbot Youth Offending Team,
Cramic Way, Port Talbot SA13 1RU
☎ (07968) 315072
Email: suethomas@btinternet.com
www.nacro.org.uk/cymru
Contact: Sue Thomas

NAS Cymru - National Autistic Society
6-7 Village Way, Greenmeadow Springs Business Park,
Tongwynlais, Cardiff CF15 7NE
☎ (029) 2062 9310
Email: karen.shore@nas.org.uk
www.nascymru.org.uk
Regional Officer South Wales: Karen Shore

The National Autistic Society Cymru
6-7 Village Way, Greenmeadow Springs Business Park, Tongwynlais, Cardiff CF15 7NE
☎ (029) 2062 9312 🖷 (029) 2062 9317
Email: cymru@nas.org.uk
www.autism.org.uk/wales

National Federation of Womenís Institutes - Wales
19 Cathedral Rd, Cardiff CF11 9HA
☎ (029) 2022 1712
Email: walesoffice@nfwi-wales.org.uk
www.theWI.org.uk
Head of Wales Office: Rhian Connick

Neath Port Talbot Council for Voluntary Service
Tŷ Margaret Thorne,
17-19 Alfred St, Neath SA11 1EF
☎ (01639) 631246 🖷 (01639) 643368
Email: info@nptcvs.org.uk
www.nptcvs.co.uk
Director: Gaynor Richards

NSPCC Cymru Wales
Wales Headquarters, Diane Engelhardt House,
Treglown Court, Dowlais Road, Cardiff CF24 5LQ
☎ (0844) 892 0290
Email: angela.stokes@nspcc.org.uk
www.nspcc.org.uk
Head of Policy & Public Affairs: Vivienne Laing

Oxfam Cymru
5th Floor, Market Buildings,
5-7 St Mary St, Cardiff CF10 1AT
☎ (0300) 2001269 🖷 (029) 2080 3290
Email: oxfamcymru@oxfam.org.uk
www.oxfam.org.uk/cymru
Head of Oxfam Cymru: Stephen Doughty
Media & Communications Officer: Luned Jones

Parkinson's UK Cymru
Maritime Offices, Woodland Terrace,
Maesycoed, Pontypridd CF37 1DZ
☎ (0844) 225 3784 🖷 (01443) 408970
Email: wales@parkinsons.org.uk
www.parkinsons.org.uk

Pen Yr Enfys
273 Cowbridge Road East,
Canton, Cardiff CF5 1JB
☎ (029) 2038 8715   ✆ (029) 2038 8717
Email: admin@penyrenfys.org
www.penyrenfys.org
Chair: Jeff Champney-Smith

PLANED (Pembrokeshire Local Action Network for Enterprise & Development)
The Old School, Station Rd,
Narberth, Pembs SA67 7DU
☎ (01834) 860965   ✆ (01834) 861547
Email: information@planed.org.uk
www.planed.org.uk
Chief Executive: Jane Howells

Planning Aid Wales
1st Flr, 174 Whitchurch Rd, Heath, Cardiff CF14 3NB
☎ (029) 2062 5009
Email: info@planningaidwales.org.uk
www.planningaidwales.org.uk
Chair: Lucie Taylor
Chief Executive: Elwyn Thomas

Play Wales
Chwarae Cymru
Baltic House, Mount Stuart Square, Cardiff CF10 5FH
☎ (029) 2048 6050   ✆ (029) 2048 9359
Email: mail@playwales.org.uk
www.playwales.org.uk
www.chwarae.cymru.org.uk
Director: Mike Greenaway

Powys Association of Voluntary Organisations
Marlow, South Crescent, Llandrindod Wells,
Powys LD1 5DH
☎ (01597) 822191   ✆ (01597) 828675
Email: info@pavo.org.uk
www.pavo.org.uk
Chief Executive: Carl Cooper

Prince's Trust Cymru
Head Office, Baltic House,
Mount Stuart Square, Cardiff CF10 5FH
☎ (029) 2043 7000   ✆ (029) 2043 7001
Email: webinfowa@princes-trust.org.uk
www.princes-trust.org.uk
Chair: Steve Thomas CBE
Director: Rick Libbey

The Prince's Trust Pembrokeshire Adventure Centre
Cleddau Reach, Pembroke Dock SA72 6UJ
☎ (01646) 622013
Email: adventure@princes-trust.org.uk
www.princes-trust.org.uk/adventure

Race Equality First
The Friary Centre, The Friary, Cardiff CF10 3FA
☎ (029) 2022 4097   ✆ (029) 2022 9339
Email: info@raceequalityfirst.org.uk
www.refweb.org.uk
Chair: Jaswant Singh

Ramblers' Association
Cymdeithas y Cerddwyr
3 Coopers Yard, Curran Rd, Cardiff CF10 5NB
☎ (029) 2064 4308   ✆ (029) 2064 5187
Email: cerddwyr@ramblers.org.uk
www.ramblers.org.uk/wales
Director: Angela Charlton

Relate Cymru
47 Walter Rd, Swansea SA31 1ER
☎ (01792) 480088
www.relatecymru.org.uk

Relate Cymru
8 Rivieres Ave, Colwyn Bay, Conwy LL29 7DP
☎ (01492) 533920   ✆ (01492) 535140
Email: administratornorthwales@relatecymru.org.uk
www.relatecymru.org.uk

RNIB Cymru
Trident Court, East Moors Rd, Cardiff CF24 5TD
☎ (029) 2045 0440   ✆ (029) 2044 9550
Email: CymruEvents@rnib.org.uk
www.rnib.org.uk/cymru
Director: Sarah Rochira
Public Affairs Manager: Alexandra McMillan

RNLI Lifeboats
9 Drake Walk, Brigantine Place, Cardiff CF10 4AN
☎ (0845) 045 6999
Email: wales@rnli.org.uk
www.rnli.org.uk

RSPCA Cymru (Royal Society for the Prevention of Cruelty to Animals)
10 Tŷ Nant Court, Morganstown, Cardiff CF15 8LW
☎ (0300) 123 8910
(0300) 123 4999 (Cruelty Hotline)
Email: externalaffairscymru@rspca.org.uk
www.rspca.org.uk/wales
External Affairs Manager for Wales:
Claire Lawson; Public Affairs & Campaigns
Officer: Tina Reece
Projects Officer: Karen Browne
National Press Officers for Wales:
Gethin Russell-Jones & Lowri Jones

VOLUNTARY ORGANIZATIONS

Safer Wales Ltd
4th Floor, 113-116 Bute St,
Butetown, Cardiff CF10 5EQ
☎ (029) 2046 1564 ▯ (029) 2046 1225
Email: admin@saferwales.com
www.saferwales.com
Chief Executive: Barbara Natasegara

Samaritans
75 Cowbridge Rd East, Canton, Cardiff CF11 9AF
☎ (029) 2034 4022 (24 hours)
Email: jo@samaritans.org (or anonymously:
samaritans@anon.tuwells.com)
www.samaritans.org.uk

Save the Children UK
Achub y Plant DU
Wales Programme/Rhaglen Cymru, 3rd Floor,
Phoenix House / Trydydd Llawr, Tŷ Ffenics,
8 Cathedral Rd / 8 Ffordd yr Eglwys Gadeiriol,
Cardiff/Caerdydd CF11 9LJ
☎ (029) 2039 6838 ▯ (029) 2022 7797
Email: walesinfo@savethechildren.org.uk
www.savethechildren.org.uk
Head of Save the Children in Wales / Pennaeth
Achub y Plant yng Nghymru: James Pritchard
Head of Programmes (Wales)/Rheolwr Rhaglen:
Mary Powell-Chandler

Scope Cymru
4 Tŷ Nant Court, Morganstown, Cardiff CF15 8LW
☎ (029) 2081 5450
www.scope.org.uk

Shelter Cymru
25 Walter Rd, Swansea SA1 5NN
☎ (01792) 469400 ▯ (01792) 460050
Email: mail@sheltercymru.org.uk
www.sheltercymru.org.uk
Director: John Puzey

SNAP Cymru
10 Coopers Yard, Curran Rd, Cardiff CF10 5NB
☎ (029) 2034 8990 ▯ (029) 2034 8998
Email: headoffice@snapcymru.org
www.snapcymru.org
Chief Executive Director: Denise Inger

Solas Cymru
11 Devon Place, Newport, Gwent NP20 4NP
☎ (01633) 664045
Email: admin@solas-cymru.co.uk
www.solas-cymru.co.uk
Chair: Brian Adcock

SOVA Cymru/Wales
Marine House, 23 Mount Stuart Square,
Cardiff CF10 5DP
☎ (029) 2049 5281 ▯ (029) 2049 2148
Email: wales@sova.org.uk
www.sova.org.uk

Spina Bifida - Hydrocephalus - Information - Networking - Equality - SHINE Cymru
PO Box 325, Bridgend CF31 9LD
☎ (01656) 864102
Email: kate.thomas@shinecharity.org.uk
www.shinecharity.org.uk
Director for Wales: Kate Thomas

St John Cymru-Wales
National Headquarters, Priory House,
Beignon Close, Ocean Way, Cardiff CF24 5PB
☎ (029) 2044 9644 ▯ (029) 2044 9645
Email: keith@stjohnwales.org.uk
www.stjohnwales.org.uk
Chief Executive: Keith M Dunn OBE

Stonewall Cymru (Cardiff Office)
Transport House, 1 Cathedral Rd, Cardiff CF11 9SB
☎ (029) 2023 7744 ▯ (029) 2023 7749
Email: cymru@stonewallcymru.org.uk
www.stonewallcymru.org.uk
Director: Andrew White

Stonewall Cymru (North Wales Office)
The Equality Centre, Bangor Rd,
Penmaenmawr, Conwy LL34 6LF
☎ (01492) 622202 ▯ (07092) 333962
Email: cymru@stonewallcymru.org.uk
www.stonewallcymru.org.uk
Community Liaison Officer: Jenny Porter

Swansea Council for Voluntary Service
Voluntary Action Centre,
7 Walter Rd, Swansea SA1 5NF
☎ (01792) 544000 ▯ (01792) 544037
Email: scvs@scvs.org.uk
www.scvs.org.uk
Director: Carol Green

Tearfund Wales
Tŷ Catherine, Capel Cildwrn, Llangefni,
Ynys Môn LL77 7NN
☎ (07799) 76695
Email: hywel.meredydd@tearfund.org
www.tearfund.org
Director: Hywel Meredydd
Regional Manager - Volunteers: Fiona Michael

Sponsored by: www.royalmail.com

Post Brenhinol

Royal Mail

Tenovus The Cancer Charity
9th Floor, Gleider House, Cardiff CF14 5BD
☎ (029) 2076 8850 🖷 (029) 2076 8888
Email: post@tenovus.org.uk
www.tenovus.org.uk
Chief Executive: Claudia McVie
Freephone Cancer Help: (0808) 808 1010

Time Banking Wales
10, The Circle, Tredegar, Blaenau Gwent NP22 3PS
☎ (01495) 722799
Email: geoff@timebankingwales.org.uk
www.timebankingwales.co.uk
Co-ordinator: Geoff Thomas

Torfaen Voluntary Alliance
Portland Buildings, Commercial St,
Pontypool, Torfaen NP4 6JS
☎ (01495) 742420
Email: Marie@tvawales.org.uk
www.torfaenvoluntaryalliance.org.uk

TPAS Cymru
(Tenant Participation Advisory Service)
The Unite Building, 1 Cathedral Rd, Cardiff CF11 9SD
☎ (029) 2023 7303 🖷 (029) 2034 5597
Email: enquiries@tpascymru.org.uk
www.tpascymru.org.uk
Director: John Drysdale
Project Officer: Judith Bateson

Also at:

Tŷ Blodwel, Broad St,
Llandudno Junction, Conwy LL31 9HL
☎ (01492) 593046 🖷 (01492) 593182
Email: iona@tpascymru.org.uk
www.tpascymru.org.uk
Project Manager: Helen Cook
Office Manager: Iona Robertson

Tros Gynnal Plant
12 North Rd, Cardiff CF10 3DY
☎ (029) 2039 6974 🖷 (029) 2066 8202
Email: admin@trosgynnal.org.uk
www.trosgynnal.org.uk
Executive Director: Roger Bishop

UNA Exchange
Temple of Peace, Cathays Park, Cardiff CF10 3AP
☎ (029) 2022 3088 🖷 (029) 2022 2540
Email: info@unaexchange.org
www.unaexchange.org
Director: Sheila Smith

United Nations Association Wales
Temple of Peace, Cathays Park, Cardiff CF10 3AP
☎ (029) 2022 8549 🖷 (029) 2064 0333
Email: una@wcia.org.uk
www.wcia.org.uk/una_wales/756
Chief Executive: Martin Pollard

UnLtd
4th Floor, Baltic House,
Mount Stuart Square, Cardiff CF10 5FH
☎ (029) 2048 4811 🖷 (029) 2048 4833
Email: garethbickerton@unltd.org.uk
melissawilliams@unltd.org.uk
www.unltd.org.uk
Director: Gareth Bickerton
Awards Administrator: Melissa Williams
Network Development Manager: Samantha Minas

Vale Centre for Voluntary Services
Barry Community Enterprise Centre,
Skomer Rd, Barry CF62 9DA
☎ (01446) 741706 🖷 (01446) 421442
Email: vcvs@valecvs.org.uk
www.valecvs.org.uk
Executive Director: Rachel Connor

Valleys Race Equality Council
Tŷ Menter, Navigation Park, Abercynon CF45 4SN
☎ (01443) 742704 🖷 (01443) 742704
Email: info@valrec.org
www.valrec.org/
Director: Rt Hon Ron Davies
Deputy Director: Elaine Clayton

Victim Support Wales
Wales Regional Office, First Floor, 1 Alexandra
Gate, Ffordd Pengam, Tremorfa, Cardiff CF24 2SA
☎ (029) 2046 4585
Email: yvonne.murray@victimsupport.org.uk
www.victimsupport.org.uk
Regional HR Manager: Yvonne Murray

Voluntary Action Centre Merthyr Tydfil
89-90 High St, Pontmorlais, Merthyr Tydfil CF47 8UH
☎ (01685) 353900 🖷 (01685) 353909
Email: enquiries@vamt.net
www.vamt.net
Chief Officer: Ian Davy

Wales Air Ambulance Charitable Trust
Tŷ Elusen, Tawe Business Park, Phoenix Way,
Swansea Enterprise Park, Swansea SA7 9LA
☎ (0844) 8584999
www.walesairambulance.com

Wales Air Ambulance Charitable Trust
Clwyd House, 57 Regent Street, Wrexham LL11 1PF
☎ (0844) 8584999
www.walesairambulance.com

Wales Council for Deaf People
Glenview House, Courthouse St,
Pontypridd CF37 1JY
☎ (01443) 485687 (Voice)
(01443) 485686 (Text) 🖷 (01443) 408555
Email: mail@wcdeaf.org.uk
www.wcdeaf.org.uk
Director: Norman B Moore

Wales Council for the Blind (WCB) Cyngor Cymru i'r Deillion (CCD)
2nd Flr, Hallinans House,
22 Newport Rd, Cardiff CF24 0TD
☎ (029) 2047 3954
Email: staff@wcb-ccd.org.uk
www.wcb-ccd.org.uk
Director: Phil Stevens

Wales Council for Voluntary Action (WCVA) Cyngor Gweithredu Gwirfoddol Cymru (CGGC)
Head Office: Baltic House, Mount Stuart Square,
Cardiff Bay, Cardiff CF10 5FH
☎ (0800) 2888 329; Minicom: (0800) 032 8012
WCVA Helpdesk: 🖷 (029) 2043 1701
Email: help@wcva.org.uk www.wcva.org.uk
Chair: Win Griffiths
Chief Executive: Graham Benfield OBE

Also at:

Mid Wales Office, 2 Science Park,
Aberystwyth, Ceredigion SY23 3AH
☎ (0800) 2888 329 🖷 (01970) 631121
Minicom: 0808 1804 080

North Wales Office, Morfa Hall,
Bath St, Rhyl LL18 3EB
☎ (0800) 2888 329 🖷 (01745) 357541
Minicom: 0808 1804 080

Wales Pre-school Providers Association (Wales PPA)
Unit 1 The Lofts, 9 Hunter St,
Cardiff Bay, Cardiff CF10 5GX
Email: info@walesppa.org
www.walesppa.org
Chief Executive Officer: Sian C M Davies

Wales Rural Forum Fforwm Gwledig Cymru
8B Y Parc Gwyddoniaeth / The Science Park,
Cefn Llan, Aberystwyth SY23 3AH
☎ (01970) 625616
Email: post@cefngwlad.org.uk
Chair: Arfon Hughes
Hon Secretary: Joan Asby

Wales Young Farmers' Clubs (YFC) Cffi Cymru
YFC Centre, Llanelwedd, Builth Wells, Powys LD2 3NJ
☎ (01982) 553502
🖷 (01982) 552979
Email: information@yfc-wales.org.uk
www.yfc-wales.org.uk
Chief Executive: Nia Lloyd

Welsh Asian Council
4 Eton Rd, Newport, Gwent NP19 0BL
☎ (01633) 255727
🖷 (01633) 255727

Welsh Centre for International Affairs
Temple of Peace, Cathays Park, Cardiff CF10 3AP
☎ (029) 2022 8549
🖷 (029) 2064 0333
Email: centre@wcia.org.uk
www.wcia.org.uk
Chief Executive: Martin Pollard

Welsh Livery Guild
c/o Village House, Peterston-Super-Ely,
Cardiff CF5 6LH
☎ (01446) 760695
Email: cspse@tiscali.co.uk
www.welshliveryguild.org
Master: Mr Stuart Fletcher OBE
Clerk: Sqn Ldr Charles Slatter

Welsh Philatelic Society Cymdeithas Ffilatelig Cymru
14 Victoria Park, Bangor, Gwynedd LL57 2EW
☎ (01248) 352682
Email: peter@wps.wales.org
www.wps.wales.org
President: Peter Brindley

Welsh Refugee Council
Phoenix House, 389 Newport Rd, Cardiff CF24 1TP
☎ (029) 2048 9800 🖷 (029) 2043 2980
Email: info@welshrefugeecouncil.org
www.welshrefugeecouncil.org
Chief Executive: Mike Lewis

Welsh Scout Council
The Old School, Wine St, Llantwit Major CF61 1RZ
☎ (01446) 795277 🖷 (01446) 795272
Email: admin@scoutswales.org.uk
www.scoutswales.org.uk

Welsh Women's Aid (WWA)
38-48 Crwys Rd, Cardiff CF24 4NN
☎ (029) 2039 0874 🖷 (029) 2039 0878
Email: admin@welshwomensaid.org.uk
www.welshwomensaid.org
Chief Executive: Paula Hardy

Sponsored by: www.royalmail.com

Post Brenhinol

Royal Mail

WRVS
WRVS Cardiff Gate, Beck Court, Cardiff Gate
Business Park, Cardiff CF23 8RP
☎ (0845) 600 5885
Email: enquiries@wrvs.org.uk
www.wrvs.org.uk
Chief Executive: Lynne Berry

YFC Brecknock Office
Room 15, Neuadd Brycheiniog,
Cambrian Way, Brecon, Powys LD3 7HR
☎ (01874) 612207/386 ▤ (01874) 612389
Email: brecknock@yfc-wales.org.uk
www.brecknockyfc.co.uk
County Chair: Vicky Hope
Organizer: Claire Price

YFC Carmarthen Office
Agriculture House, Cambrian Place,
Carmarthen, Carms SA31 1QG
☎ (01267) 237693 ▤ (01267) 237693
Email: sir.gar@yfc-wales.org.uk
www.carmsyfc.org.uk
County Chair: Rhian Howells Jones
County Organizer: Eirios Thomas

CFfI Ceredigion YFC
Canolfan Addysg Felinfach, Dyffryn Aeron,
Llanbedr Pont Steffan, Ceredigion SA48 8AF
☎ (01545) 571333 ▤ (01545) 571444
Email: ceredigion@yfc-wales.org.uk
www.yfc-ceredigion.org.uk
County Chair: Manon Richards
Development Officer: Mared Jones

YFC Clwyd Office
Pentrecelyn, Ruthin, Denbighshire LL15 2LB
☎ (01978) 790403 ▤ (01978) 790403
Email: yfc@deeside.ac.uk / yfc@llysfasi.ac.uk
www.yfc-clwyd.org.uk
County Chair: Caroline Dawson
County Organizer: Eleri Roberts

YFC Eryri Office
Uned 12, Parc Glynllifon, Ffordd Clynnog,
Caernarfon, Gwynedd LL54 5DU
☎ (01286) 831214
Email: eryri@yfc-wales.org.uk
County Chair: Arwel Thomas
Organizer: Eleri Evans

YFC Glamorgan Office
Bridgend College, Pencoed Campus,
Pencoed, Bridgend CF35 5LG
☎ (01656) 864488 ▤ (01656) 862398
Email: glamorgan@yfc-wales.org.uk
County Chair: Martyn John
County Organizer: Gwyneth Thomas

YFC Gwent Office
Coleg Gwent, Usk Campus, Usk,
Monmouthshire NP5 1XJ
☎ (01291) 672602 ▤ (01291) 671261
Email: gwent@yfc-wales.org.uk
www.gwent-yfc.btik.com
County Chair: Tim Jenkins
County Organizer: Sarah Davies

YFC Meironnydd Office
Cae Penarl,g, Dolgellau, Gwynedd LL40 2YB
☎ (01341) 423846
Email: cffimeirionnydd@gwynedd.org.uk
www.yfc-meirionnydd.org.uk
County Chair: Telor Edwards

YFC Montgomery Office
Old College, Station Rd, Newtown, Powys SY16 1BE
☎ (01686) 614028 ▤ (01686) 614079
Email: maldwyn@powys.org.uk
www.yfc-montgomery.org.uk
County Organizer: Lorraine Stokes

YFC Pembrokeshire Office
Agriculture House, Winch Lane, Haverfordwest,
Pembrokeshire SA61 1RW
☎ (01437) 762639 ▤ (01437) 768996
Email: sir.benfro@yfc-wales.org.uk
www.pembrokeshireyfc.org.uk
County Chair: Ros Bushell
County Organizer: Dill Williams

YFC Radnor
Rhoslyn, High St, Llandrindod Wells, Powys LD1 6AG
☎ (01597) 829008 ▤ (01597) 824096
Email: gaynor.james@powys.gov.uk
www.radnoryfc.org.uk
County Chair: Avril Hardwick
County Organizer: Gaynor James

YFC Ynys Môn
Anglesey Showground, Gwalchmai, Holyhead,
Ynys Môn LL65 4RW
☎ (01407) 720256 ▤ (01407) 720262
Email: ynys.mon@yfc-wales.org.uk
www.cffi-ynysmon.org.uk
County Chair: Dafydd Foulkes
County Organizer: Elen Jones

Y Groes Coch Brydeinig
S E Wales Locality Office, Bradbury House,
Misson Court, Newport NP20 2DW
☎ (01633) 245750 ▤ (01633) 216337
Email: newport@redcross.org.uk
www.redcross.org.uk
Operation Director: Jeff Collins
Senior Service Manager: Lisa Kenny

YMCA Wales
Room 2, 1 The Kingsway, Swansea SA1 5QJ
☎ (01792) 480141
Email: info@ymcawales.co.uk
www.ymcawales.co.uk
Chief Executive: Mo Sykes
Development Officer: Lyndsey Holmes

Youth Cymru
Unit D, Upper Boat Business Centre, Treforest,
Rhondda Cynon Taff CF37 5BP
☎ (01443) 827840 ☐ (01443) 843461
Email: mailbox@youthcymru.org.uk
www.youthcymru.org.uk
Chief Executive: Helen Mary Jones
Training and Accreditation Manager: Julia Griffiths

Wales Abroad

Council of the European Union
Rue de la Loi, 175, B-1048 Brussels, Belgium
☎ (00 322) 281 6111 ☐ (00 322) 281 4977
www.consilium.europa.eu

Enterprise Europe Network Wales
WEIC Ltd, c/o Cardiff University, 1st Flr, McKenzie
House, 30-36 Newport Rd, Cardiff CF24 0DE
☎ (029) 2087 9192
Email: info@enterpriseeuropewales.org.uk
www.enterpriseeuropewales.org.uk
Head of WEIC: Nigel Tidy

Enterprise Europe Network Wales
Flintshire Library & Information Service,
County Hall, Mold CH7 6NW
☎ (01352) 704748 ☐ (01352) 753662
Email: Eirian.Harrison@flintshire.gov.uk
Information Officer: Eirian Harrison

**European Centre for Training & Regional
Co-operation (ECTARC)**
Parade St, Llangollen, Denbighshire LL20 8RB
☎ (01978) 861514 ☐ (01978) 861804
Email: sharon.thomas@denbighshire.gov.uk
www.ectarc.com
Executive Director: Sharon Thomas

The European Commission Office in Wales
2 Caspian Point, Caspian Way, Cardiff CF10 4QQ
☎ (029) 2089 5020 ☐ (029) 2089 5035
Email: david.hughes@ec.europa.eu
www.ec.europa.eu/wales
Head of Office: David Hughes

European Documentation Centre
Information Services, Cardiff University,
PO Box 430, Cardiff CF24 0DE
☎ (029) 2087 4262
Email: edc@cardiff.ac.uk
www.cardiff.ac.uk/insrv/edc
Director: Ian Thomson

European Economic & Social Committee
99, Rue Belliard, B-1040 Brussels, Belgium
☎ (+32(0)2) 546 90 11
☐ (+32(0)2) 513 48 93
www.eesc.europa.eu

European Parliament
Rue Wiertz, Wiertzstraat, B-1047 Brussels, Belgium
☎ (00 32 02) 2842111 ☐ (00 32 02) 284 9201
www.europarl.europa.eu

European Parliament
MO2101, 1, Avenue du Président Robert
Schuman, F-67070, Strasbourg Cedex, France
☎ (00 33 03 88) 17 40 01 ☐ (00 33 03 88) 179201
www.europarl.europa.eu

European Parliament Information Office, UK Office
Europe House, 32 Smith Square, London SW1P 3EU
☎ (020) 7227 4300
☐ (020) 7227 4302
Email: eplondon@europarl.europa.eu
www.europarl.org.uk
Head of Office: Björn Kjellström

German-British Chamber in Wales
c/o International Business Wales, Trafalgar
House, 5 Fitzalan Place, Cardiff CF24 0ED
Email: steve.holt@ibwales.com
grossbritannien.ahk.de/en/
Wales Chair: Steve Holt

International Business Centre
Welsh Government, Trafalgar House,
5 Fitzalan Place, Cardiff CF24 0ED
☎ (03000) 603 000
Email: ibwales@wales.gsi.gov.uk
www.ibwales.com

Post Brenhinol

Royal Mail

International Business Centre
Also at:

Australia - Sydney
Level 33, Australia Square, 264 George St,
Sydney, NSW Australia 2000
☎ (61) 2 9258 1100 🖷 (61) 2 9258 1111
Email: ibwales@wales.gsi.gov.uk
www.ibwales.com

International Business Centre

Also at:

Benelux & Nordics
Welsh Government, Lomanstraat 81hs, 1075
PX Amsterdam, The Netherlands
☎ (00 31) 20 775 1367
Mel Crisp

China - Beijing
Room 1201-21, China Resources Building,
8 Jiangguomenbei Ave, Beijing 100005 China
☎ (8610) 58111811 🖷 (8610) 58111999
www.ibwales.com
Susan Jiang

Also at:

China - Shanghai
35F Citic Square, 1168 Nanjing Road West
Rd, Shanghai 200041
☎ (8621) 5111 9080 🖷 (8621) 5252 4616
www.ibwales.com
Karen Sun

Germany
Regus Centre Maximilianstrasse,
Maximilianstrasse 35a, D-80539 Munich,
Germany
☎ (00 44) (0) 7967 357 163
www.ibwales.com
Malcom Davies

Hong Kong
16/F Cheung Kong Centre,
2 Queen's Rd Central, Hong Kong
☎ (852) 2297 2888 🖷 (852) 2297 0066
www.ibwales.com

India - Bangalore
Evoma, Office 166, (Hash Key)
14 Bhattarahalli, Old Madras Rd, Nr Garden
City College, KR Puram, Bangalore ñ 560049 India
☎ (00 91) 80 4190 3030 🖷 (00 91) 80 4190 3005
www.ibwales.com
Divyashree Hegde

India - Mumbai
The Executive Center, Level 2, Kalpataru
Synergy, Opposite the Grand Hyatt,
Santacruz (East), Mumbai, India 400 055
☎ (91) 22 3953 7255 🖷 (91) 22 3953 7200
www.ibwales.com
Dr Kant Singh, Fiona Rodrigues

Ireland
Welsh Government, 65-66 The Pavilion,
Marine Rd, Dun Laoghaire,
South Co Dublin Ireland
☎ (00 353) 8765 999 06
www.ibwales.com
Nick Naysmith

Japan - Tokyo
Akasaka Tokyu Bldg, 10F 2-14-3,, Nagata-
cho, Chinyoda-ku, Tokyo, 100-0014 Japan
☎ (81) 3 3595 7051
🖷 (81) 3 3595 7502
www.ibwales.com
Takeharu Nakajima (Tiger),
Yoko Kobori, Goro Okada

New York
Wales International Center, British Consulate
General, 845 3rd Avenue, New York NY 10174
☎ (+001 212) 745 0392
🖷 (+001 212) 745 0428
www.ibwales.com
Dan Cecchin, David Parker, Chris Gardiner,
Chris Williams, Neil Welch, Efe Izilein,
Janine Murphy

United Arab Emirates - Dubai
British Embassy, PO Box 65, Dubai,
United Arab Emirates
☎ (00 971) 4309 4344
🖷 (00 971) 4309 4302
www.ibwales.com
Lee Jennings, Chitra Chainani

MEDIA Antenna Cymru Wales
c/o Creative Industries, Welsh Government,
QED Centre, Main Ave, Treforest Ind. Est.
Pontypridd CF37 5YR
☎ (0300) 061 5637
Email: judy.wasdell@wales-uk.com
www.mediadeskuk.eu
Media Antenna Co-ordinator: Judy Wasdell

Mercator Institute for Media, Languages and Culture
Adran Astudiaethau Theatr, Ffilm a Theledu,
Prifysgol Cymru Aberystwyth, Aberystwyth SY23 3AS
☎ (01970) 622533
🖷 (01970) 621524
Email: mercator@aber.ac.uk
www.aber.ac.uk/mercator/
Cyfarwyddwr/Director: Elin Haf Gruffydd Jones
Cyfarwyddwr Academaidd/Academic Director:
Ned Thomas

National Assembly for Wales EU Office
Tŷ Cymru House, Rond-Point Schuman 11,
B-1040 Brussels, Belgium
☎ (00 32 (0)2 226 6692) 00 32 (0)2 226 6694
Email: gregg.jones@wales.gov.uk
www.assemblywales.org
Head of Office: Gregg Jones

National Welsh American Foundation
Sefydliad Cenedlaethol Cymru-America
9 St. David's Avenue, Carmarthen SA31 3DW
☎ (01267) 232338
Email: post@nwaf-cymru.org
www.wales-usa.org
Chair: Paul Loveluck
The Honorary Secretary: Dr. Dulais Rhys

UK Permanent Representation to the European Union
10 Ave d'Auderghem, 1040 Brussels, Belgium
☎ (003 22) 2878211 🖷 (003 22) 2878398
Email: susan.sills@fco.gov.uk
www.ukeu.fco.gov.uk
John Cunliffe

WEFO Welsh European Funding Office
Spatial Support & Regeneration Branch,
Government Buildings, Picton Terrace,
Carmarthen SA31 3BT
☎ (01267) 225479
Email: enquiries-wefo@wales.gsi.gov.uk
www.wefo.wales.gov.uk
Project Development Manager: David Thomas

WEFO Welsh European Funding Office
Welsh Goverment, Rhodfa Padarn,
Llanbadarn Fawr, Aberystwyth SY23 3UR
Email: enquiries-wefo@wales.gsi.gov.uk
www.wefo.wales.gov.uk
Director: Damien O'Brian
Director of Finance and Corporate Services: Rob Hunter
Head of Programme Management Division: Rob Halford
Acting Head of Planning and Strategy Division:
Sue Price/Jane McMillan

WEFO Welsh European Funding Office
Merthyr Tydfil Office, Rhydycar Business Park,
Merthyr Tydfil CF48 1UZ
☎ (0845) 010 3355
Email: enquiries-wefo@wales.gsi.gov.uk
www.wefo.wales.gov.uk

Welsh Centre for International Affairs
Temple of Peace,
Cathays Park, Cardiff CF10 3AP
☎ (029) 2022 8549 🖷 (029) 2064 0333
Email: centre@wcia.org.uk
www.wcia.org.uk
Chief Executive: Martin Pollard

Welsh Government European Union Office
Tŷ Cymru/Wales House, 6th Flr,
Rond-Point Schuman 11,
B-1040 Brussels
☎ (00 32) (0)2 506 4470
Email: euofficebrussels@wales.gsi.gov.uk

Welsh Higher Education Brussels
Tŷ Cymru/Wales House,
6th Flr, Rond-Point Schuman 11,
B-1040 Brussels, Belgium
☎ (00 32) (0)2 226 6698
🖷 (00 32) (0)2 502 8360
Email: info@wheb.ac.uk
www.wheb.ac.uk
Head of Office: Berwyn Davies

Welsh Local Government Association European Office
Tŷ Cymru/Wales House,
6th Flr, Rond-Point Schuman 11,
B-1040 Brussels, Belgium
☎ (00 32) (0)2 506 4488
Email: brussels.office@wlga-brussels.org.uk
www.wlga.gov.uk/europe
Euro Affairs Manager: Katie Cavell
European Policy & Communications Officer:
Iwan Williams

West Wales European Centre
2nd Floor, Dewi Building,
University of Wales: Trinity Saint David,
Carmarthen SA31 3EP
☎ (01267) 242359
Email: wwec@carmarthenshire.gov.uk
www.wwec.org.uk
Head of European Policy and External Funding:
Neville Davies

Post Brenhinol

Royal Mail

Welsh Government

Welsh Government, Crown Buildings,
Cathays Park, Cardiff CF10 3NQ
English: ☎ (0300) 060 3300 or (0845) 010 3300
Welsh: ☎ (0300) 060 4400 or (0845) 010 4400
🖷 (029) 2082 5390
Email: wag.en@mail.uk.custhelp.com
www.wales.gov.uk

Also at:

Government Buildings, Rhodfa Padarn,
Llanbadarn Fawr, Aberystwyth SY23 3UR

25 Victoria Street, City of Westminster,
London SW1H 0EX
☎ (020) 7799 5880

Government Buildings, Rhydycar,
Merthyr Tydfil CF48 1UZ

Government Buildings, Sarn Mynach,
Llandudno Junction, Conwy, LL31 9RZ

Statistical Directorate, Welsh Government,
Crown Buildings, Cathays Park,
Cardiff CF10 3NQ
☎ (029) 2082 5050 Information Desk
(English) 2080 1440 Information Desk
(Welsh) Email: stats.info.desk@wales.gsi.gov.uk

Children, Education, Lifelong Learning & Skills

Dept Children, Education, Lifelong Learning
& Skills (DCELLS), Welsh Government,
Cathays Park, Cardiff CF10 3NQ
English: ☎ (0300) 060 3300 or (0845) 010 3300
Welsh: ☎ (0300) 060 4400 or (0845) 010 4400
Email: DCELLS.Enquiries@wales.gsi.gov.uk
www.new.wales.gov.uk/topics/educationandskills

Also at:

Tŷ Afon, Bedwas Rd, Bedwas,
Caerphilly CF83 8WT
🖷 (01443) 663906

Tŷ'r Llyn, Clos Llyn Cwm, Swansea
Enterprise Park, Llansamlet,
Swansea SA6 8AH

Ffynnon-las, The Orchards, Ilex Close,
Llanishen, Cardiff CF14 5DZ

Government Buildings, Sarn Mynach,
Llandudno Junction, Conwy, LL31 9RZ

Ladywell House, Newtown SY16 1RB
☎ (01686) 613109

Economy & Transport

Dept for Economy & Transport (DE&T)
Welsh Government, Cathays Park,
Cardiff CF10 3NQ
English: ☎ (0300) 060 3300 or (0845) 010 3300
Welsh: ☎ (0300) 060 4400 or (0845) 010 4400
Email: DEandT@wales.gsi.gov.uk

Also at:

St Line House, Mount Stuart Square,
Cardiff Bay, Cardiff CF10 5LR

Brunel House, 2 Fitzalan Rd,
Cardiff CF24 0UY

CardiffEIN(CreativeIndustries)
33-35 West Bute Street,
Cardiff Bay, Cardiff CF10 5LH

Waterton Technology Centre,
Waterton Ind Est,
Bridgend CF31 3WT
☎ (01656) 646400

Suite 2, Floor 3,
Clarence House,
Clarence Place,
Newport NP19 7AA
☎ (01633) 264265

Unit 3A Fairway Court,
Tonteg Rd,
Treforest CF37 5UA
☎ (01443) 846700

QED Centre, Main Ave,
Treforest Estate,
Pontypridd CF37 5YR

Ebbw Vale Works,
Steelworks Rd,
Ebbw Vale NP23 6YL

Llys-y-Ddraig,
Penllergaer Business Park,
Penllergaer, Swansea SA4 1HL
☎ (01792) 222 422

Ladywell House, Newtown SY16 1JB

Sarn Mynach,
Llandudno Junction,
Conwy, LL31 9RZ
☎ (0300) 062 5034

WELSH GOVERNMENT

Environment, Sustainability & Housing

Dept, Environment, Sustainability & Planning;
Regeneration, Welsh Government,
Cathays Park, Cardiff CF10 3NQ
English: ☎ (0300) 060 3300 or (0845) 010 3300
Welsh: ☎ (0300) 060 4400 or (0845) 010 4400
Email:
DeshWebCorrespondence@wales.gsi.gov.uk

Dept, Housing: Welsh Government,
Merthyr Tydfil Offices, Rhydycar,
Merthyr Tydfil CF48 1UZ

Sustainable Futures: Ffynnon Las, The Orchards,
Ilex Close, Tŷ Glas Avenue, Llanishen,
Cardiff CF14 5EZ

Sustainable Futures: Rhodfa Padarn,
Llanbadarn Fawr, Aberystwyth SY23 3UR

Sarn Mynach, Llandudno Junction,
Conwy, LL31 9RZ
☎ (0300) 062 5034

Health & Social Services

Dept for Health & Social Services,
Welsh Government, Cathays Park,
Cardiff CF10 3NQ
☎ (029) 2037 0011
Email: health.enquiries@wales.gsi.gov.uk

Also at:

Hill House, Picton Terrace, Carmarthen,
Carmarthenshire SA31 3BS
☎ (01267) 225250

Winchway House, Winch Lane,
Haverfordwest SA61 1RS

Heritage

Welsh Government, Cathays Park,
Cardiff CF10 3NQ
English: ☎ (0300) 060 3300 or (0845) 010 3300
Welsh: ☎ (0300) 060 4400 or (0845) 010 4400
Also at:

Historic environment: cadw@wales.gsi.gov.uk

Museums, archives & libraries:
CyMAL@wales.gsi.gov.uk

Culture, Welsh language & sport:
cwls@wales.gsi.gov.uk

Visit Wales: info@visitwales.co.uk

Legal Services

Welsh Government,
Cathays Park, Cardiff CF10 3NQ
Director of Legal Services: Jeff Godfrey
Jeffrey.godfrey@wales.gsi.gov.uk

Public Health & Health Professions

Welsh Government, Cathays Park,
Cardiff CF10 3NQ
Chief Medical Officer Wales: Dr Tony Jewell
English: ☎ (0845) 010 3300
Welsh: ☎ (0845) 010 4400

Public Service Improvement

Operations Team 2nd Floor Welsh Government,
Cathays Park, Cardiff CF10 3NQ
English: ☎ (0300) 060 3300 or (0845) 010 3300
Welsh: ☎ (0300) 060 4400 or (0845) 010 4400

Winchway House, Winch Lane,
Haverfordwest SA6 11RS
☎ (01437) 762441

Rural Affairs

Welsh Government, Cathays Park,
Cardiff CF10 3NQ
English: ☎ (0300) 060 3300 or (0845) 010 3300
Welsh: ☎ (0300) 060 4400 or (0845) 010 4400
Email: rural-affairs@wales.gsi.gov.uk

Also at:

Penrallt, Caernarfon, Gwynedd LL55 1EP

Hill House Picton Terrace,
Carmarthen SA31 3BS
☎ (01267) 225250

Winchway House, Winch Lane,
Haverfordwest, SA6 11RS

Government Buildings, Spa Road East,
Llandrindod Wells LD1 5HA
☎ (01597) 823777

Plas y Ffynnon, Cambrian Way,
Brecon LD3 7HP
☎ (01874) 625123

Sponsored by: www.royalmail.com

Royal Mail

Fisheries

Suite 3, Cedar Court, Havens Head Business Park, Milford Haven SA73 3LS
☎ (01646) 693412

The Old Vicarage, Newry Street, Holyhead, Anglesey LL65 1DB
☎ (01407) 765757

Tir Gofal

Llys Tawe, Kings Road, Swansea SA1 8PG
☎ (01792) 675700

Ladywell House, Newtown SY16 1JB
☎ (01686) 613109

Llys y Bont, Ffordd y Parc, Parc Menai, Bangor, LL57 4BN
☎ (01248) 694000

CCW Mold, Unit 19, Mold Business Park, Mold CH7 1XP
☎ (01352) 706600

ARAD, Government Buildings, Arran Road, Dolgellau LL40 1LW
☎ (01341) 422199

Social Justice & Local Government

Operations Team, 2nd Floor,
Welsh Government, Cathays Park,
Cardiff CF10 3NQ
English: ☎ (0300) 060 3300 or (0845) 010 3300
Welsh: ☎ (0300) 060 4400 or (0845) 010 4400
Email: sjlg.enquiries@wales.gsi.gov.uk

Also at:

Dept for Social Justice & Local Government,
Welsh Government,
Rhydycar, Merthyr Tydfil CF48 1UZ

Strategic Planning, Finance & Performance

The Welsh Government, Crown Buildings,
Cathays Park, Cardiff CF10 3NQ
🖷 (029) 2082 3359
finance.enquiries@wales.gsi.gov.uk
valuewales@wales.gsi.gov.uk

Welsh Language & Cultural Groups

Archives & Records Council Wales
Cyngor Archifau a Chofnodion Cymru
The National Library of Wales,
Aberystwyth, Ceredigion SY23 3BU
☎ (01970) 632803
🖷 (01970) 632882
Email: avril.jones@llgc.org.uk
www.llgc.org.uk/cac
Director of Collection Services: Avril Jones

Association of Welsh Medium Nursery
Schools and Playgroups
Mudiad Meithrin
Boulevard De St Brieuc,
Aberystwyth, Ceredigion SY23 1PD
☎ (01970) 639639
🖷 (01970) 639638
Email: post@mym.co.uk
www.mym.co.uk
Chief Executive: Hywel Jones

The Celtic Congress, Welsh Branch
Arwel, 8 Maes y Drindod,
Aberystwyth, Ceredigion SY23 1LT
☎ (01970) 615057
www.celtic-congress.org
Secretary of the Welsh Branch: Gwyneth Roberts

CERED Menter Iaith Ceredigion
Y Ganolfan Addysg, Campws Felin-fach,
Dyffryn Aeron, Ceredigion SA48 8AF
☎ (01545) 572350
Email: cered@ceredigion.gov.uk
www.cered.org
Rheolwr: Gwenno Hywel

Cwmni Acen
Ivor House, Bridge St, Cardiff CF10 2EE
☎ (029) 2030 0800
Email: post@acen.co.uk
www.acen.co.uk
Chief Executive Officer: Elen Rhys
Financial Controller: John Bisset

Post Brenhinol
Royal Mail

Cylch yr Iaith
Talgarreg, Ffordd Carneddi, Bethesda,
Gwynedd LL57 3SG
☎ (01248) 600297
Email: cylch@tiscali.co.uk
Cadeirydd: Elfed Roberts
Ysgrifennydd: Ieuan Wyn

Cymdeithas Carnhuanawc
47 Wingfield Rd, Eglwys Newydd,
Caerdydd CF14 1NJ
☎ (029) 2062 3275
Email: asjobbins@btinternet.com
www.carhuanawc.org
Cadeirydd: Keith Bush
Ysgrifennydd Cyffredinol: Alan Jobbins

Cymdeithas Cerdd Dant Cymru
14 Ffordd Ffrydlas, Carneddi, Bethesda,
Gwynedd LL57 3BL
☎ (01248) 602323
Email: delythfon@hotmail.com
www.cerdd-dant.org
Swyddog Gweinyddol: Delyth Vaughan

Cymdeithas Cyfieithwyr Cymru
(The Association of Welsh Translators and Interpreters)
Bryn Menai, Ffordd Caergybi, Bangor, Gwynedd LL57 2JA
☎ (01248) 371839 ▣ (01248) 371850
Email: swyddfa@cyfieithwyrcymru.org.uk
www.cyfieithwyrcymru.org.uk
Cadeirydd: Berwyn Prys Jones
Prif Weithredwr: Geraint Wyn Parry

Cymdeithas Cymru-Ariannin
(Wales-Argentina Society)
Rhos Helyg, 23 Maesyrefail, Penrhyn-coch,
Aberystwyth, Ceredigion SY23 3HE
☎ (01970) 828017
Email: rhoshelyg@btinternet.com
www.cymru-ariannin.org
Ysgrifennydd/Secretary: Ceris Gruffudd

Cymdeithas Edward Llwyd
☎ (01286) 677319
www.cymdeithasedwardllwyd.org.uk
Cadeirydd: Tom Jones

Cymdeithas yr Iaith Gymraeg
Welsh Language Society
Y Cambria, Rhodfa'r Môr, Aberystwyth SY23 2AZ
☎ (01970) 624501 ▣ (01970) 627122
Email: swyddfa@cymdeithas.org
www.cymdeithas.org
Cadeirydd: Bethan Williams
Swyddog Gweinyddol: Dafydd Morgan Lewis

Cymraeg i Oedolion
Welsh for Adults
CBAC/WJEC, 245 Rhodfa'r Gorllewin,
Caerdydd/Cardiff CF5 2YX
☎ (029) 2026 5007
Email: emyr.davies@cbac.co.uk
www.cbac.co.uk
Examinations Officer: Emyr Davies

Cymuned
Tŷ Iorwerth, Ffordd y Sir, Penygroes,
Gwynedd LL54 6ES
☎ (01286) 881696
Email: cymuned@cymuned.org
www.cymuned.org
Prif Weithredwr/Chief Executive: Aran Jones
Cadeirydd/Chair: Richard Evans

Dyfodol i'r Iaith
c/o Y Lolfa, Talybont, Ceredigion SY24 5HE
Email: post@dyfodol.net
www.dyfodol.net

Eisteddfod Genedlaethol Cymru
National Eisteddfod of Wales
40 Parc Tŷ Glas, Llanisien, Caerdydd CF14 5DU
☎ (0845) 4090 300
▣ (0845) 2076 3737
Email: gwyb@eisteddfod.org.uk
www.eisteddfod.org.uk
President: Prydwen Elfed-Owens
Chief Executive: Elfed Roberts

Fforwm Hanes Cymru
History Forum for Wales
Y Gelli, Stryd Fawr, Llandysul,
Ceredigion SA44 4DP
☎ (01559) 362429
www.fforwmhanescymru.org.uk
Swyddog Cysylltiadau/Communications Officer:
Dr. John H. Davies

The Honourable Society of Cymmrodorion
PO Box 55178, London N12 2AY
☎ (01582) 832971 Mob: 07739 179120
Email: secretary@cymmrodorion.org
membership@cymmrodorion.org
www.cymmrodorion.org
Hon Secretary: Peter Jeffreys
Membership Secretary: Adrian Morgan
(Mob: 07811 787 536)

Royal Mail

Literature Wales (formerly Academi) Llenyddiaeth Cymru
includes Yr Academi Gymreig/
The Welsh Academy & Tŷ Newydd Writers'
Centre, Mount Stuart House,
Mount Stuart Square, Cardiff CF10 5FQ
☎ (029) 2047 2266
🖷 (029) 2049 2930
Email: post@literaturewales.org
www.literaturewales.org
Chief Executive: Lleucu Siencyn

Also at:

The Glyn Jones Centre, Cardiff
☎ (029) 2047 2266
🖷 (029) 2047 0691
Email: post@literaturewales.org
www.literaturewales.org
Chief Executive: Lleucu Siencyn

Tŷ Newydd, Llanystumdwy, Cricieth,
Gwynedd LL52 0LW
☎ (01766) 522817
🖷 (01766) 523095
Email: post@literaturewales.org
www.literaturewales.org
Chief Executive: Lleucu Siencyn

Llysgenhadaeth Glyndwr Embassy
34 Bethesda Court, Prince of Wales Rd,
Abertawe/Swansea SA1 2EY
☎ (01792) 533 806
Email: s.ifan@ntlworld.com
Siân Ifan

Menter Aberystwyth
Penbryn, Aberystwyth University, Penglais
Campus, Aberystwyth SY23 3BY
☎ (01970) 628725
Email: enquiries@menter-aberystwyth.org.uk
www.visitaberystwyth.com

Menter Bro Dinefwr
Swyddfeydd y Cyngor, Heol Cilgant,
Llandeilo, Sir Gaerfyrddin SA19 6HW
☎ (01558) 825336
🖷 (01558) 825339
Email: post@menterbrodinefwr.org
www.menterbrodinefwr.org
Prif Weithredwr: Owain Siôn Gruffydd

Menter Bro Ogwr
Tŷ'r Ysgol, Pen yr Ysgol,
Maesteg CF34 9YE
☎ (01656) 732200
Email: menter@broogwr.org
www.menterbroogwr.org
Prif Swyddog Iaith: Amanda Jaine Evans

Menter Brycheiniog & Maesyfed
Yr Uned Gymraeg, Cyngor Sir Powys,
Neuadd y Sir, Llandrindod Wells LD1 5LG
☎ (08708) 510583
Email: menterb@powys.gov.uk
www.mbam.org.uk

Menter Caerdydd
42 Lambourne Crescent, Parc Busnes Caerdydd,
Llanishen, Caerdydd CF14 5GG
☎ (029) 2068 9888
Email: menter@caerdydd.org
www.mentercaerdydd.org
Prif Swyddog: Sian Lewis

Menter Castell Nedd Port Talbot
Ystafell 14, Canolfan Gymunedol y Groes,
Pontardawe SA8 4HU
☎ (01792) 864949
Email: menter@micnpt.org
www.micnpt.org
Prif Swyddog: Alun Pugh

Menter Cwm Gwendraeth
11-15 Heol Coalbrook, Pontyberem,
Llanelli SA15 5HU
☎ (01269) 871600
Email: ymholiadau@mentercwmgwendraeth.org.uk
www.mentercwmgwendraeth.org
Rheolwr Gyfarwyddwr: Deris Williams

Menter Gorllewin Sir Gâr
Llawr 1af CCF Cyf, Stryd y Bont, Castell Newydd
Emlyn, Sir Gaerfyrddin SA38 9DX
☎ (01239) 712934 🖷 (01239) 712934
Email: ymholiad@mentergorllewinsirgar.org.uk
www.mentergorllewinsirgar.org.uk

Menter Iaith Abertawe
Tŷ Tawe, 9 Stryd Christina, Abertawe SA1 4EW
☎ (01792) 460906 🖷 (01792) 460906
Email: menter@menterabertawe.org
www.menterabertawe.org
Rheolwr: Elgan Davies-Jones

WELSH LANG & CULTURAL GROUPS

Menter Iaith Conwy
Tŷ Apothecary, Y Sgwâr, Llanrwst,
Sir Conwy LL26 0LG
☎ (01492) 642357
www.mentrauiaith-gogledd.com
Cyfarwyddwr Datblygu: Meirion Ll Davies

Menter Iaith Gwynedd
Pencadlys Cyngor Gwynedd, Stryd y Jel,
Caernarfon, Gwynedd LL54 5LL
☎ (01286) 679452
Email: hunaniaith@gwynedd.gov.uk
www.mentrauiaith-gogledd.com
Swyddog Hyrwyddo Iaith/Welsh Language
Officer: Debbie Anne Williams Jones

Menter Iaith Maelor
Tŷ AVOW, 21 Stryd Egerton,
Wrecsam LL11 1ND
☎ (01978) 363791
Email: busnes@menteriaithmaelor.org
www.mentrauiaith-gogledd.com
Rheolwr: Gwawr Cordiner

Menter Iaith Maldwyn
Yr Hen Goleg, Ffordd yr Orsaf,
Y Drenewydd, Powys SY16 1BE
☎ (01686) 614020
Email: menterm@powys.gov.uk
www.mentrauiaith-gogledd.com
Prif Swyddog: Lowri Davies

Menter Iaith Môn
Llys Goferydd, Stâd Ddiwydiannol Bryn Cefni,
Llangefni LL77 7XA
☎ (01248) 725700
Email: iaith@mentermon.com
www.mentrauiaith-gogledd.com
Prif Swyddog Iaith: Helen Thomas

Menter Iaith Rhondda Cynon Taf
Llawr Cyntaf, 9 Stryd Fawr,
Pontypridd CF73 1QJ
☎ (01443) 407570 🖷 (01443) 493715
Email: menter@menteriaith.org
www.menteriaith.org
Prif Weithredwr: Kevin Davies
Gweinyddol & Ariannol: Eurig Jenkins

Menter Iaith Sir Benfro
Community Learning Centre, Ysgol Bro Gwaun,
Heol Dyfed, Fishguard, Pembs SA65 9DT
☎ (01348) 873700 🖷 (01348) 873700
Email: ymholiad@mentersirbenfro.com
www.mentersirbenfro.com
Prif Swyddog: Rhidian Evans

Menter Iaith Sir Benfro
Tŷ'r Ysgol, Ysgol y Preseli, Heol Hermon,
Crymych, Sir Benfro SA41 3QH
☎ (01239) 831129
Email: ymholiad@mentersirbenfro.com
www.mentersirbenfro.com
Prif Swyddog: Rhidian Evans

Menter Iaith Sir Caerffili
YMCA, Aeron Place, Gilfach, Bargoed,
Caerffili CF81 8JA
☎ (01443) 820913
Email: menter@caerffili.org
www.mentercaerffili.org
Swyddog Datblygu: Lowri Catrin Jones

Menter Iaith Sir Ddinbych
Adeilad Deiamwnt, 6 Heigad, Dinbych LL16 3LE
☎ (01745) 812822
Email: ymholiadau@menteriaithdinbych.co.uk
Prif Swyddog/Chief Officer: Gill Stephen

Menter Iaith Sir y Flint
Uned 3, Parc Busnes Yr Wyddgrug,
Ffordd Wrecsam, Yr Wyddgrug/Mold,
Sir y Fflint CH1 1XP
☎ (01352) 744040
Email: gwybod@menteriaithsiryfflint.co.uk
www.mentrauiaith-gogledd.com
Prif Swyddog: Gwawr Cordiner

Menter Merthyr Tudful
Canolfan Soar, Pontmorlais, Merthyr Tudful CF47 8UB
☎ (01686) 722176
Email: lis@merthyrtudful.com
www.merthyrtudful.com
Swyddog Datblygu: Lis McLean
Swyddog Maes: Greg Snelgrove

Menter y Fro (Vale of Glamorgan)
Uned 12, Canolfan Fenter Gymunedol,
Skomer Road, Y Barri CF62 9DA
☎ (01446) 720600
Email: swyddfa@menteryfro.com
Swyddog Datblygu: Elen Elias

Merched y Wawr
Canolfan Genedlaethol Merched y Wawr,
Stryd yr Efail, Aberystwyth, Ceredigion SY23 1JH
☎ (01970) 611661 🖷 (01970) 626620
Email: swyddfa@merchedywawr.com
www.merchedywawr.co.uk
Cyfarwyddwr Genedlaethol/National Director:
Tegwen Morris

Sponsored by: www.royalmail.com

Post Brenhinol
Royal Mail

The Montgomeryshire Society
Cymdeithas Maldwyn
9 Walpole Ave, Kew, Surrey TW9 2DJ
☎ (020) 8255 3960
Email: contact@montsoc.org.uk
www.montsoc.org.uk
Hon Secretary: Margaret Tudor-Jones

Nant Gwrtheyrn
The Welsh Language and Heritage Centre
Llithfaen, Pwllheli, Gwynedd LL53 6NL
☎ (01758) 750334 ☐ (01758) 750335
Email: post@nantgwrtheyrn.org
www.nantgwrtheyrn.org
General Manager: Mair Saunders
Consultant: Jim O'Rourke

The National Library of Wales
Llyfrgell Genedlaethol Cymru
Penglais, Aberystwyth, Ceredigion SY23 3BU
☎ (01970) 632800 ☐ (01970) 615709
Email: holi@llgc.org.uk www.llgc.org.uk
Librarian: Andrew Green
President: Sir Deian Hopkin

National Welsh American Foundation
Sefydliad Cenedlaethol Cymru-America
9 St Davids Avenue, Carmarthen SA31 3DW
☎ (01267) 232338
Email: post@nwaf-cymru.org
www.wales-usa.org
Chair: Paul Loveluck
The Honorary Secretary: Dr. Dulais Rhys

Popeth Cymraeg
Welsh Unlimited
Canolfan Iaith Clwyd, Pwll Y Grawys /
Lenten Pool, Dinbych/Denbigh,
Sir Ddinbych/Denbighshire LL16 3LF
☎ (01745) 812287 ☐ (01745) 813783
Email: gwybod@popethcymraeg.com
www.popethcymraeg.com
Rheolwr/Manager: Verona Pritchard-Jones
Prif Weithredwr/Chief Executive: Ioan Talfryn

Undeb Cymru a'r Byd
Wales International
Heulfryn, 7 Lôn Victoria/Victoria Rd, Hen
Golwyn/Old Colwyn, Conwy LL29 9SN
☎ (01492) 515558
Email: bryan.jones8@btinternet.com
www.wales-international.org
Hon Secretary: J Bryan Jones

Urdd Gobaith Cymru
Canolfan Mileniwm Cymru,
Plas Bute, Caerdydd CF10 5AL
☎ (029) 2063 5670 ☐ (029) 2063 5679
Email: efa@urdd.org
www.urdd.org
Chief Executive: Efa Gruffudd Jones

Wales Millennium Centre
Canolfan Mileniwm Cymru
Bute Place, Cardiff CF10 5AL
☎ (029) 2063 6400 ☐ (029) 2063 6401
Email: info@wmc.org.uk
www.wmc.org.uk
Chair: Sir Emyr Jones Parry
General Manager: Mathew Milsom

Welsh Books Council
Cyngor Llyfrau Cymru
Castell Brychan, Aberystwyth, Ceredigion SY23 2JB
☎ (01970) 624151 ☐ (01970) 625385
Email: castellbrychan@cllc.org.uk
www.cllc.org.uk
Chair: Prof M Wynn Thomas OBE
Chief Executive: Elwyn Jones

Welsh Language Commissioner
Comisiynydd y Gymraeg
Market Chambers/Siambrau'r Farchnad, 5-7 St
Mary St/Heol Eglwys Fair, Cardiff/Caerdydd CF10 1AT
☎ (0845) 603 3221 ☐ (0845) 029 2087 7551
Email: post@comisynyddygymraeg.org
www.welshlanguagecommissioner.org /
www.comisiynyddygymraeg.org
Comissioner/Comisiynydd: Meri Huws

The Welsh Centre for Language Planning
Y Ganolfan Cynllunio Iaith
Uned 2-4, Parc Busnes Aberarad,
Castell Newydd Emlyn,
Sir Gaerfyrddin SA38 9DB
☎ (01239) 711668
☐ (01239) 711698
Email: post@iaith.eu
www.iaith.eu
Prif Weithredwr: Gareth Ioan

The Welsh Centre for Language Planning
Y Ganolfan Cynllunio Iaith
Uned 95a, Llys Bowen,
Parc Busnes Llanelwy, Llanelwy,
Sir Ddinbych LL17 0JE
☎ (01745) 585120
www.iaith.eu

Combined index to
The Wales Yearbook 2013

Sponsored by

Royal Mail®

The postal service of choice
www.royalmail.com

*Page numbers in **Bold** refer to the main text, those in Plain type to the Directory of Welsh Organizations*

Post Brenhinol

Royal Mail

Sponsored by: www.royalmail.com

Royal Mail

C

Sponsored by: www.royalmail.com

Post Brenhinol

Royal Mail

Sponsored by: www.royalmail.com

Royal Mail

Sponsored by: www.royalmail.com

Post Brenhinol

Royal Mail

Sponsored by: www.royalmail.com

Royal Mail

Sponsored by: www.royalmail.com

Royal Mail

Sponsored by: www.royalmail.com

Post Brenhinol
Royal Mail

Sponsored by: www.royalmail.com

Royal Mail

Post Brenhinol

Royal Mail

Sponsored by: www.royalmail.com

Royal Mail

Index of Advertisers

BRANCH: CN DATE: 9/12